Mathematical Analysis for
Machine Learning
and Data Mining

Mathematical Analysis for
Machine Learning
and Data Mining

Dan Simovici
University of Massachusetts, Boston, USA

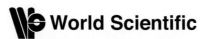

NEW JERSEY · LONDON · SINGAPORE · BEIJING · SHANGHAI · HONG KONG · TAIPEI · CHENNAI · TOKYO

Published by

World Scientific Publishing Co. Pte. Ltd.

5 Toh Tuck Link, Singapore 596224

USA office: 27 Warren Street, Suite 401-402, Hackensack, NJ 07601

UK office: 57 Shelton Street, Covent Garden, London WC2H 9HE

Library of Congress Cataloging-in-Publication Data
Names: Simovici, Dan A., author.
Title: Mathematical analysis for machine learning and data mining / by Dan Simovici
 (University of Massachusetts, Boston, USA).
Description: [Hackensack?] New Jersey : World Scientific, [2018] |
 Includes bibliographical references and index.
Identifiers: LCCN 2018008584 | ISBN 9789813229686 (hc : alk. paper)
Subjects: LCSH: Machine learning--Mathematics. | Data mining--Mathematics.
Classification: LCC Q325.5 .S57 2018 | DDC 006.3/101515--dc23
LC record available at https://lccn.loc.gov/2018008584

British Library Cataloguing-in-Publication Data
A catalogue record for this book is available from the British Library.

For any available supplementary material, please visit
http://www.worldscientific.com/worldscibooks/10.1142/10702#t=suppl

Desk Editors: V. Vishnu Mohan/Steven Patt

Typeset by Stallion Press
Email: enquiries@stallionpress.com

Printed in Singapore

Making mathematics accessible to the educated layman, while keeping high scientific standards, has always been considered a treacherous navigation between the Scylla of professional contempt and the Charybdis of public misunderstanding.

Gian-Carlo Rota

Preface

Mathematical Analysis can be loosely described as is the area of mathematics whose main object is the study of function and of their behaviour with respect to limits. The term "function" refers to a broad collection of generalizations of real functions of real arguments, to functionals, operators, measures, etc.

There are several well-developed areas in mathematical analysis that present a special interest for machine learning: topology (with various flavors: point-set topology, combinatorial and algebraic topology), functional analysis on normed and inner product spaces (including Banach and Hilbert spaces), convex analysis, optimization, etc. Moreover, disciplines like measure and integration theory which play a vital role in statistics, the other pillar of machine learning are absent from the education of a computer scientists. We aim to contribute to closing this gap, which is a serious handicap for people interested in research.

The machine learning and data mining literature is vast and embraces a diversity of approaches, from informal to sophisticated mathematical presentations. However, the necessary mathematical background needed for approaching research topics is usually presented in a terse and unmotivated manner, or is simply absent. This volume contains knowledge that complements the usual presentations in machine learning and provides motivations (through its application chapters that discuss optimization, iterative algorithms, neural networks, regression, and support vector machines) for the study of mathematical aspects.

Each chapter ends with suggestions for further reading. Over 600 exercises and supplements are included; they form an integral part of the material. Some of the exercises are in reality supplemental material. For these, we include solutions. The mathematical background required for making the best use of this volume consists in the typical sequence calculus — linear algebra — discrete mathematics, as it is taught to Computer Science students in US universities.

Special thanks are due to the librarians of the *Joseph Healy Library* at the University of Massachusetts Boston whose diligence was essential in completing this project. I also wish to acknowledge the helpfulness and competent assistance of Steve Patt and D. Rajesh Babu of World Scientific.

Lastly, I wish to thank my wife, Doina, a steady source of strength and loving support.

Dan A. Simovici
Boston and Brookline
January 2018

Contents

PART I

Set-Theoretical and Algebraic
Preliminaries

Chapter 1

Preliminaries

1.1 Introduction

This introductory chapter contains a mix of preliminary results and notations that we use in further chapters, ranging from set theory, and combinatorics to metric spaces.

The membership of x in a set S is denoted by $x \in S$; if x is not a member of the set S, we write $x \notin S$.

Throughout this book, we use standardized notations for certain important sets of numbers:

$\mathbb{C}$	the set of complex numbers	$\mathbb{R}$	the set of real numbers
$\mathbb{R}_{\geqslant 0}$	the set of non-negative real numbers	$\mathbb{R}_{>0}$	the set of positive real numbers
$\mathbb{R}_{\leqslant 0}$	the set of non-positive real numbers	$\mathbb{R}_{<0}$	the set of negative real numbers
$\hat{\mathbb{C}}$	the set $\mathbb{C} \cup \{\infty\}$		
$\hat{\mathbb{R}}$	the set $\mathbb{R} \cup \{-\infty, +\infty\}$	$\hat{\mathbb{R}}_{\geqslant 0}$	the set $\mathbb{R}_{\geqslant 0} \cup \{+\infty\}$
$\hat{\mathbb{R}}_{\leqslant 0}$	the set $\mathbb{R}_{\leqslant 0} \cup \{-\infty\}$	$\hat{\mathbb{R}}_{>0}$	the set $\mathbb{R}_{<>0} \cup \{+\infty\}$
$\mathbb{Q}$	the set of rational numbers	$\mathbb{I}$	the set of irrational numbers
$\mathbb{Z}$	the set of integers	$\mathbb{N}$	the set of natural numbers

The usual order of real numbers is extended to the set $\hat{\mathbb{R}}$ by $-\infty < x < +\infty$ for every $x \in \mathbb{R}$. Addition and multiplication are extended by

$$x + \infty = \infty + x = +\infty, \text{ and }, x - \infty = -\infty + x = -\infty,$$

for every $x \in \mathbb{R}$. Also, if $x \neq 0$ we assume that

$$x \cdot \infty = \infty \cdot x = \begin{cases} +\infty & \text{if } x > 0, \\ -\infty & \text{if } x < 0, \end{cases}$$

and

$$x \cdot (-\infty) = (-\infty) \cdot x = \begin{cases} -\infty & \text{if } x > 0, \\ \infty & \text{if } x < 0. \end{cases}$$

Additionally, we assume that $0 \cdot \infty = \infty \cdot 0 = 0$ and $0 \cdot (-\infty) = (-\infty) \cdot 0 = 0$. Note that $\infty - \infty$, $-\infty + \infty$ are undefined.

Division is extended by $x/\infty = x/-\infty = 0$ for every $x \in \mathbb{R}$.

The set of complex numbers $\mathbb{C}$ is extended by adding a single "infinity" element ∞. The sum $\infty + \infty$ is *not defined* in the complex case.

If S is a finite set, we denote by $|S|$ the number of elements of S.

1.2   Sets and Collections

We assume that the reader is familiar with elementary set operations: union, intersection, difference, etc., and with their properties. The empty set is denoted by $\emptyset$.

We give, without proof, several properties of union and intersection of sets:

(1) $S \cup (T \cup U) = (S \cup T) \cup U$ (*associativity of union*),
(2) $S \cup T = T \cup S$ (*commutativity of union*),
(3) $S \cup S = S$ (*idempotency of union*),
(4) $S \cup \emptyset = S$,
(5) $S \cap (T \cap U) = (S \cap T) \cap U$ (*associativity of intersection*),
(6) $S \cap T = T \cap S$ (*commutativity of intersection*),
(7) $S \cap S = S$ (*idempotency of intersection*),
(8) $S \cap \emptyset = \emptyset$,

for all sets S, T, U.

The associativity of union and intersection allows us to denote unambiguously the union of three sets S, T, U by $S \cup T \cup U$ and the intersection of three sets S, T, U by $S \cap T \cap U$.

Definition 1.1. The sets S and T are *disjoint* if $S \cap T = \emptyset$.

Sets may contain other sets as elements. For example, the set

$$\mathcal{C} = \{\emptyset, \{0\}, \{0, 1\}, \{0, 2\}, \{1, 2, 3\}\}$$

contains the empty set $\emptyset$ and $\{0\}, \{0, 1\}, \{0, 2\}, \{1, 2, 3\}$ as its elements. We refer to such sets as *collections of sets* or simply *collections*. In general, we use calligraphic letters $\mathcal{C}, \mathcal{D}, \ldots$ to denote collections of sets.

If $\mathcal{C}$ and $\mathcal{D}$ are two collections, we say that $\mathcal{C}$ is *included* in $\mathcal{D}$, or that $\mathcal{C}$ is a *subcollection* of $\mathcal{D}$, if every member of $\mathcal{C}$ is a member of $\mathcal{D}$. This is denoted by $\mathcal{C} \subseteq \mathcal{D}$.

Two collections $\mathcal{C}$ and $\mathcal{D}$ are equal if we have both $\mathcal{C} \subseteq \mathcal{D}$ and $\mathcal{D} \subseteq \mathcal{C}$. This is denoted by $\mathcal{C} = \mathcal{D}$.

Definition 1.2. Let $\mathcal{C}$ be a collection of sets. The *union of* $\mathcal{C}$, denoted by $\bigcup \mathcal{C}$, is the set defined by

$$\bigcup \mathcal{C} = \{x \mid x \in S \text{ for some } S \in \mathcal{C}\}.$$

If $\mathcal{C}$ is a *non-empty* collection, its *intersection* is the set $\bigcap \mathcal{C}$ given by

$$\bigcap \mathcal{C} = \{x \mid x \in S \text{ for every } S \in \mathcal{C}\}.$$

If $\mathcal{C} = \{S, T\}$, we have $x \in \bigcup \mathcal{C}$ if and only if $x \in S$ or $x \in T$ and $x \in \bigcup \mathcal{C}$ if and only if $x \in S$ and $y \in T$. The union and the intersection of this two-set collection are denoted by $S \cup T$ and $S \cap T$ and are referred to as the union and the intersection of S and T, respectively.

The difference of two sets S, T is denoted by $S - T$. When T is a subset of S we write $\overline{T}$ for $S - T$, and we refer to the set $\overline{T}$ as the *complement* of T with respect to S or simply the *complement of* T.

The relationship between set difference and set union and intersection is well-known: for every set S and non-empty collection $\mathcal{C}$ of sets, we have

$$S - \bigcup \mathcal{C} = \bigcap \{S - C \mid C \in \mathcal{C}\} \text{ and } S - \bigcap \mathcal{C} = \bigcup \{S - C \mid C \in \mathcal{C}\}.$$

For any sets S, T, U, we have

$$S - (T \cup U) = (S - T) \cap (S - U) \text{ and } S - (T \cap U) = (S - T) \cup (S - U).$$

With the notation previously introduced for the complement of a set, the above equalities become:

$$\overline{T \cup U} = \overline{T} \cap \overline{U} \text{ and } \overline{T \cap U} = \overline{T} \cup \overline{U}.$$

For any sets T, U, V, we have

$$(U \cup V) \cap T = (U \cap T) \cup (V \cap T) \text{ and } (U \cap V) \cup T = (U \cup T) \cap (V \cup T).$$

Note that if $\mathcal{C}$ and $\mathcal{D}$ are two collections such that $\mathcal{C} \subseteq \mathcal{D}$, then

$$\bigcup \mathcal{C} \subseteq \bigcup \mathcal{D} \text{ and } \bigcap \mathcal{D} \subseteq \bigcap \mathcal{C}.$$

We initially excluded the empty collection from the definition of the intersection of a collection. However, within the framework of collections of subsets of a given set S, we extend the previous definition by taking

$\bigcap \emptyset = S$ for the empty collection of subsets of S. This is consistent with the fact that $\emptyset \subseteq \mathcal{C}$ implies $\bigcap \mathcal{C} \subseteq S$.

The *symmetric difference* of sets denoted by $\oplus$ is defined by $U \oplus V = (U - V) \cup (V - U)$ for all sets U, V.

We leave to the reader to verify that for all sets U, V, T we have

(i) $U \oplus U = \emptyset$;

(ii) $U \oplus V = V \oplus T$;

(iii) $(U \oplus V) \oplus T = U \oplus (V \oplus T)$.

The next theorem allows us to introduce a type of set collection of fundamental importance.

Theorem 1.1. *Let $\{\{x, y\}, \{x\}\}$ and $\{\{u, v\}, \{u\}\}$ be two collections such that $\{\{x, y\}, \{x\}\} = \{\{u, v\}, \{u\}\}$. Then, we have $x = u$ and $y = v$.*

Proof. Suppose that $\{\{x, y\}, \{x\}\} = \{\{u, v\}, \{u\}\}$.

If $x = y$, the collection $\{\{x, y\}, \{x\}\}$ consists of a single set, $\{x\}$, so the collection $\{\{u, v\}, \{u\}\}$ also consists of a single set. This means that $\{u, v\} = \{u\}$, which implies $u = v$. Therefore, $x = u$, which gives the desired conclusion because we also have $y = v$.

If $x \neq y$, then neither (x, y) nor (u, v) are singletons. However, they both contain exactly one singleton, namely $\{x\}$ and $\{u\}$, respectively, so $x = u$. They also contain the equal sets $\{x, y\}$ and $\{u, v\}$, which must be equal. Since $v \in \{x, y\}$ and $v \neq u = x$, we conclude that $v = y$. $\qquad \square$

Definition 1.3. An *ordered pair* is a collection of sets $\{\{x, y\}, \{x\}\}$.

Theorem 1.1 implies that for an ordered pair $\{\{x, y\}, \{x\}\}$, x and y are uniquely determined. This justifies the following definition.

Definition 1.4. Let $\{\{x, y\}, \{x\}\}$ be an ordered pair. Then x is *the first component of p* and y is *the second component of p*.

From now on, an ordered pair $\{\{x, y\}, \{x\}\}$ is denoted by (x, y). If both $x, y \in S$, we refer to (x, y) as an *ordered pair on the set S*.

Definition 1.5. Let X, Y be two sets. Their *product* is the set $X \times Y$ that consists of all pairs of the form (x, y), where $x \in X$ and $y \in Y$.

The set product is often referred to as the *Cartesian product of sets*.

Example 1.1. Let $X = \{a, b, c\}$ and let $Y = \{1, 2\}$. The Cartesian product $X \times Y$ is given by

$$X \times Y = \{(a, 1), (b, 1), (c, 1), (a, 2), (b, 2), (c, 2)\}.$$

Definition 1.6. Let $\mathcal{C}$ and $\mathcal{D}$ be two collections of sets such that $\bigcup \mathcal{C} = \bigcup \mathcal{D}$. $\mathcal{D}$ is a *refinement* of $\mathcal{C}$ if, for every $D \in \mathcal{D}$, there exists $C \in \mathcal{C}$ such that $D \subseteq C$.

This is denoted by $\mathcal{C} \sqsubseteq \mathcal{D}$.

Example 1.2. Consider the collection $\mathcal{C} = \{(a, \infty) \mid a \in \mathbb{R}\}$ and $\mathcal{D} = \{(a, b) \mid a, b \in \mathbb{R}, a < b\}$. It is clear that $\bigcup \mathcal{C} = \bigcup \mathcal{D} = \mathbb{R}$.

Since we have $(a, b) \subseteq (a, \infty)$ for every $a, b \in \mathbb{R}$ such that $a < b$, it follows that $\mathcal{D}$ is a refinement of $\mathcal{C}$.

Definition 1.7. A collection of sets $\mathcal{C}$ is *hereditary* if $U \in \mathcal{C}$ and $W \subseteq U$ implies $W \in \mathcal{C}$.

Example 1.3. Let S be a set. The collection of subsets of S, denoted by $\mathcal{P}(S)$, is a hereditary collection of sets since a subset of a subset T of S is itself a subset of S.

The set of subsets of S that contain k elements is denoted by $\mathcal{P}_k(S)$. Clearly, for every set S, we have $\mathcal{P}_0(S) = \{\emptyset\}$ because there is only one subset of S that contains 0 elements, namely the empty set. The set of all finite subsets of a set S is denoted by $\mathcal{P}_{\text{fin}}(S)$. It is clear that $\mathcal{P}_{\text{fin}}(S) = \bigcup_{k \in \mathbb{N}} \mathcal{P}_k(S)$.

Example 1.4. If $S = \{a, b, c\}$, then $\mathcal{P}(S)$ consists of the following eight sets: $\emptyset, \{a\}, \{b\}, \{c\}, \{a, b\}, \{a, c\}, \{b, c\}, \{a, b, c\}$. For the empty set, we have $\mathcal{P}(\emptyset) = \{\emptyset\}$.

Definition 1.8. Let $\mathcal{C}$ be a collection of sets and let U be a set. The *trace of the collection* $\mathcal{C}$ *on the set* U is the collection $\mathcal{C}_U = \{U \cap C \mid C \in \mathcal{C}\}$.

We conclude this presentation of collections of sets with two more operations on collections of sets.

Definition 1.9. Let $\mathcal{C}$ and $\mathcal{D}$ be two collections of sets. The collections $\mathcal{C} \vee \mathcal{D}$, $\mathcal{C} \wedge \mathcal{D}$, and $\mathcal{C} - \mathcal{D}$ are given by

$$\mathcal{C} \vee \mathcal{D} = \{C \cup D \mid C \in \mathcal{C} \text{ and } D \in \mathcal{D}\},$$
$$\mathcal{C} \wedge \mathcal{D} = \{C \cap D \mid C \in \mathcal{C} \text{ and } D \in \mathcal{D}\},$$
$$\mathcal{C} - \mathcal{D} = \{C - D \mid C \in \mathcal{C} \text{ and } D \in \mathcal{D}\}.$$

Example 1.5. Let $\mathcal{C}$ and $\mathcal{D}$ be the collections of sets defined by

$$\mathcal{C} = \{\{x\}, \{y, z\}, \{x, y\}, \{x, y, z\}\},$$
$$\mathcal{D} = \{\{y\}, \{x, y\}, \{u, y, z\}\}.$$

We have

$$\mathcal{C} \vee \mathcal{D} = \{\{x, y\}, \{y, z\}, \{x, y, z\}, \{u, y, z\}, \{u, x, y, z\}\},$$
$$\mathcal{C} \wedge \mathcal{D} = \{\emptyset, \{x\}, \{y\}, \{x, y\}, \{y, z\}\},$$
$$\mathcal{C} - \mathcal{D} = \{\emptyset, \{x\}, \{z\}, \{x, z\}\},$$
$$\mathcal{D} - \mathcal{C} = \{\emptyset, \{u\}, \{x\}, \{y\}, \{u, z\}, \{u, y, z\}\}.$$

Unlike "$\cup$" and "$\cap$", the operations "$\vee$" and "$\wedge$" between collections of sets are not idempotent. Indeed, we have, for example,

$$\mathcal{D} \vee \mathcal{D} = \{\{y\}, \{x, y\}, \{u, y, z\}, \{u, x, y, z\}\} \neq \mathcal{D}.$$

The trace $\mathcal{C}_K$ of a collection $\mathcal{C}$ on K can be written as $\mathcal{C}_K = \mathcal{C} \wedge \{K\}$.

We conclude this section by introducing a special type of collection of subsets of a set.

Definition 1.10. A *partition* of a non-empty set S is a collection π of non-empty subsets of S that are pairwise disjoint and whose union equals S.

The members of π are referred to as the *blocks* of the partition π.

The collection of partitions of a set S is denoted by $PART(S)$. A partition is finite if it has a finite number of blocks. The set of finite partitions of S is denoted by $PART_{\text{fin}}(S)$.

If $\pi \in PART(S)$ then a subset T of S is π-*saturated* if it is a union of blocks of π.

Example 1.6. Let $\pi = \{\{1, 3\}, \{4\}, \{2, 5, 6\}\}$ be a partition of $S = \{1, 2, 3, 4, 5, 6\}$. The set $\{1, 3, 4\}$ is π-saturated because it is the union of blocks $\{1, 3\}$ and 4.

1.3   Relations and Functions

Definition 1.11. Let X, Y be two sets. A *relation* on X, Y is a subset ρ of the set product $X \times Y$.

If $X = Y = S$ we refer to ρ as a *relation on S*.

The relation ρ on S is:
- *reflexive* if $(x, x) \in \rho$ for every $x \in S$;
- *irreflexive* if $(x, x) \notin \rho$ for every $x \in S$;
- *symmetric* if $(x, y) \in \rho$ implies $(y, x) \in \rho$ for all $x, y \in S$;

- *antisymmetric* if $(x, y) \in \rho$ and $(y, x) \in \rho$ imply $x = y$ for all $x, y \in S$;
- *transitive* if $(x, y) \in \rho$ and $(y, z) \in \rho$ imply $(x, z) \in \rho$ for all $x, y, z \in S$.

Denote by $REFL(S), SYMM(S), ANTISYMM(S)$ and $TRAN(S)$ the sets of reflexive relations, the set of symmetric relations, the set of antisymmetric, and the set of transitive relations on S, respectively.

A *partial order on S* is a relation ρ that belongs to $REFL(S) \cap ANTISYMM(S) \cap TRAN(S)$, that is, a relation that is reflexive, symmetric and transitive.

Example 1.7. Let δ be the relation that consists of those pairs (p, q) of natural numbers such that $q = pk$ for some natural number k. We have $(p, q) \in \delta$ if p evenly divides q. Since $(p, p) \in \delta$ for every p it is clear that δ is symmetric.

Suppose that we have both $(p, q) \in \delta$ and $(q, p) \in \delta$. Then $q = pk$ and $p = qh$. If either p or q is 0, then the other number is clearly 0. Assume that neither p nor q is 0. Then $1 = hk$, which implies $h = k = 1$, so $p = q$, which proves that δ is antisymmetric.

Finally, if $(p, q), (q, r) \in \delta$, we have $q = pk$ and $r = qh$ for some $k, h \in \mathbb{N}$, which implies $r = p(hk)$, so $(p, r) \in \delta$, which shows that δ is transitive.

Example 1.8. Define the relation λ on $\mathbb{R}$ as the set of all ordered pairs (x, y) such that $y = x + t$, where t is a non-negative number. We have $(x, x) \in \lambda$ because $x = x + 0$ for every $x \in \mathbb{R}$. If $(x, y) \in \lambda$ and $(y, x) \in \lambda$ we have $y = x + t$ and $x = y + s$ for two non-negative numbers t, s, which implies $0 = t + s$, so $t = s = 0$. This means that $x = y$, so λ is antisymmetric. Finally, if $(x, y), (y, z) \in \lambda$, we have $y = x + u$ and $z = y + v$ for two non-negative numbers u, v, which implies $z = x + u + v$, so $(x, z) \in \lambda$.

In current mathematical practice, we often write $x\rho y$ instead on $(x, y) \in \rho$, where ρ is a relation of S and $x, y \in S$. Thus, we write $p\delta q$ and $x\lambda y$ instead on $(p, q) \in \delta$ and $(x, y) \in \lambda$. Furthermore, we shall use the standard notations "$|$" and "$\leqslant$" for δ and λ, that is, we shall write $p \mid q$ and $x \leqslant y$ if p divides q and x is less or equal to y. This alternative way to denote the fact that (x, y) belongs to ρ is known as the *infix notation*.

Example 1.9. Let $\mathcal{P}(S)$ be the set of subsets of S. It is easy to verify that the inclusion between subsets "$\subseteq$" is a partial order relation on $\mathcal{P}(S)$. If $U, V \in \mathcal{P}(S)$, we denote the inclusion of U in V by $U \subseteq V$ using the infix notation.

Functions are special relation that enjoy the property described in the next definition.

Definition 1.12. Let X, Y be two sets. A *function (or a mapping) from X to Y* is a relation f on X, Y such that $(x, y), (x, y') \in f$ implies $y = y'$.

In other words, the first component of a pair $(x, y) \in f$ determines uniquely the second component of the pair. We denote the second component of a pair $(x, y) \in f$ by $f(x)$ and say, occasionally, that f *maps* x to y.

If f is a function from X to Y we write $f : X \longrightarrow Y$.

Definition 1.13. Let X, Y be two sets and let $f : X \longrightarrow Y$.
The *domain* of f is the set

$$\mathrm{Dom}(f) = \{x \in X \mid y = f(x) \text{ for some } y \in Y\}.$$

The *range* of f is the set

$$\mathsf{Ran}(f) = \{y \in Y \mid y = f(x) \text{ for some } x \in X\}.$$

Definition 1.14. Let X be a set, $Y = \{0, 1\}$ and let L be a subset of S. The *characteristic function* is the function $1_L : S \longrightarrow \{0, 1\}$ defined by:

$$1_L(x) = \begin{cases} 1 & \text{if } x \in L, \\ 0 & \text{otherwise} \end{cases}$$

for $x \in S$.

The *indicator function* of L is the function $I_L : S \longrightarrow \hat{r}r$ defined by

$$I_L(x) = \begin{cases} 0 & \text{if } x \in L, \\ \infty & \text{otherwise} \end{cases}$$

for $x \in S$.

It is easy to see that:

$$1_{P \cap Q}(x) = 1_P(x) \cdot 1_Q(x),$$
$$1_{P \cup Q}(x) = 1_P(x) + 1_Q(x) - 1_P(x) \cdot 1_Q(x),$$
$$1_{\bar{P}}(x) = 1 - 1_P(x),$$

for every $P, Q \subseteq S$ and $x \in S$.

Theorem 1.2. Let X, Y, Z be three sets and let $f : X \longrightarrow Y$ and $g : Y \longrightarrow Z$ be two functions. The relation $gf : X \longrightarrow Z$ that consists of all pairs (x, z) such that $y = f(x)$ and $g(y) = z$ for some $y \in Y$ is a function.

Proof. Let $(x, z_1), (x, z_2) \in gf$. There exist $y_1, y_2 \in Y$ such that

$$y_1 = f(x), y_2 = f(x), g(y_1) = z_1, \text{ and } g(y_2) = z_2.$$

The first two equalities imply $y_1 = y_2$; the last two yield $z_1 = z_2$, so gf is indeed a function. □

Note that the composition of the function f and g has been denoted in Theorem 1.2 by gf rather than the relation product fg. This manner of denoting the function composition is applied throughout this book.

Definition 1.15. Let X, Y be two sets and let $f : X \longrightarrow Y$. If U is a subset of X, the *restriction* of f to U is the function $g : U \longrightarrow Y$ defined by $g(u) = f(u)$ for $u \in U$.

The restriction of f to U is denoted by $f \restriction_U$.

Example 1.10. Let f be the function defined by $f(x) = |x|$ for $x \in \mathbb{R}$. Its restriction to $\mathbb{R}_{<0}$ is given by $f \restriction_{\mathbb{R}_{<0}} (x) = -x$.

Definition 1.16. A function $f : X \longrightarrow Y$ is:
- (i) *injective* or *one-to-one* if $f(x_1) = f(x_2)$ implies $x_1 = x_2$ for $x_1, x_2 \in$ $\mathrm{Dom}(f)$;
- (ii) *surjective* or *onto* if $\mathsf{Ran}(f) = Y$;
- (iii) *total* if $\mathrm{Dom}(f) = X$.

If f is both injective and surjective, then it is a *bijective function*.

Theorem 1.3. *A function $f : X \longrightarrow Y$ is injective if and only if there exists a function $g : Y \longrightarrow X$ such that $g(f(x)) = x$ for every $x \in \mathrm{Dom}(f)$.*

Proof. Suppose that f is an injective function. For $x \in \mathrm{Dom}(f)$ and $y = f(x)$ define $g(y) = x$. Note that g is well defined for if $y = f(x_1) = f(x_2)$ then $x_1 = x_2$ due to the injectivity of f. It follows immediately that $g(f(x)) = x$ for $x \in \mathrm{Dom}(f)$.

Conversely, suppose that there exists a function $g : Y \longrightarrow X$ such that $g(f(x)) = x$ for every $x \in \mathrm{Dom}(f)$. If $f(x_1) = f(x_2)$, then $x_1 = g(f(x_1)) = g(f(x_2)) = x_2$, which proves that f is indeed injective. □

The function g whose existence is established by Theorem 1.3 is said to be the *left inverse* of f. Thus, a function $f : X \longrightarrow Y$ is injective if and only if it has a left inverse.

To prove a similar result concerning surjective functions we need to state a basic axiom of set theory.

The Axiom of Choice: Let $\mathcal{C} = \{C_i \mid i \in I\}$ be a collection of non-empty sets indexed by a set I. There exists a function $\phi : I \longrightarrow \bigcup \mathcal{C}$ (known as a *choice function*) such that $\phi(i) \in C_i$ for each $i \in I$.

Theorem 1.4. *A function $f : X \longrightarrow Y$ is surjective if and only if there exists a function $h : X \longrightarrow Y$ such that $f(h(y)) = y$ for every $y \in Y$.*

Proof. Suppose that f is a surjective function. The collection $\{f^{-1}(y) \mid y \in Y\}$ indexed by Y consists of non-empty sets. By the Axiom of Choice there exists a choice function for this collection, that is a function $h : Y \longrightarrow \bigcup_{y \in Y} f^{-1}(y)$ such that $h(y) \in f^{-1}(y)$, or $f(h(y)) = y$ for $y \in Y$.

Conversely, suppose that there exists a function $h : X \longrightarrow Y$ such that $f(h(y)) = y$ for every $y \in Y$. Then, $f(x) = y$ for $y = h(y)$, which shows that f is surjective. □

The function h whose existence is established by Theorem 1.4 is said to be the *right inverse* of f. Thus, a function has a right inverse if and only if it is surjective.

Corollary 1.1. *A function $f : X \longrightarrow X$ is a bijection if and only if there exists a function $k : X \longrightarrow X$ that is both a left inverse and a right inverse of f.*

Proof. This statement follows from Theorems 1.3 and 1.4.

Indeed, if f is a bijection, there exists a left inverse $g : X \longrightarrow X$ such that $g(f(x)) = x$ and a right inverse $h : X \longrightarrow X$ such that $f(h(x)) = x$ for every $x \in Y$. Since $h(x) \in X$ we have $g(f(h(x))) = h(x)$, which implies $g(x) = h(x)$ because $f(h(x)) = x$ for $x \in X$. This yields $g = h$. □

The relationship between the subsets of a set and characteristic functions defined on that set is discussed next.

Theorem 1.5. *There is a bijection $\Psi : \mathcal{P}(S) \longrightarrow (S \longrightarrow \{0,1\})$ between the set of subsets of S and the set of characteristic functions defined on S.*

Proof. For $P \in \mathcal{P}(S)$ define $\Psi(P) = 1_P$. The mapping Ψ is one-to-one. Indeed, assume that $1_P = 1_Q$, where $P, Q \in \mathcal{P}(S)$. We have $x \in P$ if and only if $1_P(x) = 1$, which is equivalent to $1_Q(x) = 1$. This happens if and only if $x \in Q$; hence, $P = Q$ so Ψ is one-to-one.

Let $f : S \longrightarrow \{0,1\}$ be an arbitrary function. Define the set $T_f = \{x \in S \mid f(x) = 1\}$. It is easy to see that f is the characteristic function of the set T_f; hence, $\Psi(T_f) = f$ which shows that the mapping Ψ is also onto; hence, it is a bijection. $\qquad\square$

Definition 1.17. A set S is *indexed* be a set I if there exists a surjection $f : I \longrightarrow S$. In this case we refer to I as an index set.

If S is indexed by the function $f : I \longrightarrow S$ we write the element $f(i)$ just as s_i, if there is no risk of confusion.

Definition 1.18. A *sequence of length* n on a set X is a function $\mathbf{x} : \{0, 1, \ldots, n - 1\} \longrightarrow X$.

At times we will use the same term to designate a function $\mathbf{x} : \{1, \ldots, n\} \longrightarrow X$.

Sequences are denoted by bold letters. If $\mathbf{x}$ is a sequence of length n we refer to $\mathbf{x}(i)$ as the ith of $\mathbf{x}$; this element of X is denoted usually by x_i. We specify a sequence $\mathbf{x}$ of length n by writing

$$\mathbf{x} = (x_0, x_1, \ldots, x_{n-1}).$$

The set of sequence of length n on a set X is denoted by $\mathbf{Seq}_n(X)$.

Note that an ordered pair $(x, y) \in X \times Y$ can be regarded as a sequence $\mathbf{p}$ of length 2 on $X \cup Y$ such that $p_0 = x$ and $p_1 = y$. This point of view allows an immediate generalization of set products.

Definition 1.19. An *infinite sequence*, or, simply a *sequence* on a set X is a function $\mathbf{x} : \mathbb{N} \longrightarrow X$. The set of infinite sequences on X is denoted by $\mathbf{Seq}(X)$.

Definition 1.20. Let $S_0, \ldots, S_{n-1}$ be n sets. An n-*tuple* on $S_0, \ldots, S_{n-1}$ is a function $t : \{0, \ldots, n - 1\} \longrightarrow S_0 \cup \cdots S_{n-1}$ such that $t(i) \in S_i$ for $0 \leqslant i \leqslant n - 1$. The n-tuple t is denoted by $(t(0), \ldots, t(n - 1))$.

The set of all n-tuples on $S_0, \ldots, S_{n-1}$ is referred to as the *Cartesian product* of $S_0, \ldots, S_{n-1}$ and is denoted by $S_0 \times \cdots \times S_{n-1}$.

The Cartesian product of a finite number of sets can be generalized for arbitrary families of sets. Let $\mathcal{S} = \{S_i \mid i \in I\}$ be a collection of sets indexed by the set I. The Cartesian product of $\mathcal{S}$ is the set of all functions of the form $s : I \longrightarrow \bigcup \mathcal{S}$ such that $s(i) \in S_i$ for every $i \in I$. This set is denoted by $\prod_{i \in I} S_i$.[1]

The notion of *projection* is closely associated to Cartesian products.

---

[1] This constructions is implicitly using the axiom of choice that implies the existence of functions $s : I \longrightarrow \bigcup_{i \in I}$ such that $s(i) \in S_i$ for every $i \in I$.

Definition 1.21. Let $\mathcal{S} = \{S_i \mid i \in I\}$ be a collection of sets indexed by the set I. The jth *projection* (for $j \in I$) is the mapping $p_j : \prod_{i \in I} S_i \longrightarrow S_j$ defined by $p_j(s) = s(j)$ for $j \in I$.

Definition 1.22. Let X, Y be two sets and let $f : X \longrightarrow Y$ be a function. If $U \subseteq \mathrm{Dom}(f)$, the *image* of U under f is the set

$$f(U) = \{y \in Y \mid y = f(u) \text{ for some } u \in X\}.$$

If $T \subseteq Y$, the *pre-image* of T under f is the set $f^{-1}(T) = \{x \in X \mid f(x) \in Y\}$.

Theorem 1.6. *Let X, Y be two sets and let $f : X \longrightarrow Y$ be a function. If $V \subseteq Y$, then $X - f^{-1}(V) = f^{-1}(Y - V)$.*

Proof.   If $x \in X - f^{-1}(V)$, we have $f(x) \notin V$, so $f(x) \in Y - V$, which means that $x \in f^{-1}(Y - V)$. Therefore, $X - f^{-1}(V) \subseteq f^{-1}(Y - V)$.

Conversely, suppose that $x \in f^{-1}(Y - V)$, so $f(x) \notin V$, hence $x \notin f^{-1}(V)$, which means that $x \in X - f^{-1}(V)$, which completes the proof. $\square$

Theorem 1.7. *Let $f : X \longrightarrow Y$ be a function. If $U, V \subseteq \mathrm{Dom}(f)$ we have $f(U \cup V) = f(U) \cup f(V)$ and $f(U \cap V) \subseteq f(U) \cap f(V)$.*

If $S, T \subseteq \mathsf{Ran}(f)$, then $f^{-1}(S \cup T) = f^{-1}(S) \cup f^{-1}(T)$ and $f^{-1}(S \cap T) = f^{-1}(S) \cap f^{-1}(T)$.

Proof.   This statement is a direct consequence of Definition 1.22. $\square$

Theorem 1.8. *Let $f : X \longrightarrow Y$ be a function. We have $U \subseteq f^{-1}(f(U))$ for every subset U of X and $f(f^{-1}(V)) \subseteq V$ for every subset V of Y.*

Proof.   Let $x \in u$. Since $f(x) \in f(U)$, it follows that $u \in f^{-1}(f(U))$, so $U \subseteq f^{-1}(f(U))$.

If $y \in f(f^{-1}(V))$ there exists $x \in f^{-1}(V)$ such that $y = f(x)$. Since $f(x) \in V$, it follows that $y \in V$, so $f(f^{-1}(V)) \subseteq V$. $\square$

Theorem 1.9. *Let X, Y be two sets and let $f : X \longrightarrow Y$ be a function. If $U \subseteq X$, then $\mathsf{Ran}(f) - f(U) \subseteq f(\mathrm{Dom}(f) - U)$. If f is injective, then $\mathsf{Ran}(f) - f(U) = f(\mathrm{Dom}(f) - U)$.*

Proof.   Let $y \in \mathsf{Ran}(f) - f(U)$. Then, there exists $x \in \mathrm{Dom}(f)$ such that $y = f(x)$; however, since $y \notin f(U)$, there is no $x_1 \in U$ such that $y = f(x_1)$. Thus, $x \in \mathrm{Dom}(f) - U$ and we have the desired inclusion.

Suppose now that f is injective and let $y \in f(\mathrm{Dom}(f) - U)$. Then, $y = f(x)$ for some x such that $x \notin U$. Clearly, $y \in \mathsf{Ran}(f)$. Furthermore,

$y \notin f(U)$ for otherwise, we would have $y = f(x_1)$ for some $x_1 \in U$, $x \neq x_1$ (because $x \notin U$ and $x_1 \in U$), and this would contradict the injectivity of f. Thus, $y \in \mathsf{Ran}(f) - f(U)$ and we obtain the desired equality. □

Corollary 1.2. *Let* $f : X \longrightarrow X$ *be a injection. We have* $f(\overline{U}) = \overline{f(U)}$ *for every subset U of X.*

Proof. Since f is a bijection, we have $\mathsf{Ran}(f) = X$, so $X - f(U) = f(X - U)$ by Theorem 1.9, which amounts to $\overline{f(U)} = f(\overline{U})$. □

Theorem 1.10. *Let* $f : X \longrightarrow Y$ *be a function. If* $V, W \subseteq Y$, *then* $f^{-1}(V - W) = f^{-1}(V) - f^{-1}(W)$. *Furthermore, if* $\mathcal{C} = \{Y_i \mid i \in I\}$ *is a collection of subsets of Y we have* $f^{-1}\left(\bigcap_{i \in I} C_i\right) = \bigcap_{i \in I} f^{-1}(C_i)$ *and* $f^{-1}\left(\bigcup_{i \in I} C_i\right) = \bigcup_{i \in I} f^{-1}(C_i)$.

Proof. Let $x \in f^{-1}(V - W)$. We have $f(x) \in V$ and $f(x) \notin W$. Therefore, $x \in f^{-1}(V)$ and $x \notin f^{-1}(W)$, so $x \in f^{-1}(V) - f^{-1}(W)$. Conversely, suppose that $x \in f^{-1}(V) - f^{-1}(U)$, that is, $x \in f^{-1}(V)$ and $x \notin f^{-1}(U)$. This means that $f(x) \in V$ and $f(x) \notin U$, so $f(x) \in V - U$, which yields $f(x) \in V - U$. Thus, $x \in f^{-1}(V - U)$, which concludes the proof of the first equality.

Let now $x \in f^{-1}\left(\bigcap_{i \in I} C_i\right)$. This implies $f(x) \in C_i$ for every $i \in I$, so $x \in f^{-1}(C_i)$ for each $i \in I$. Therefore, $x \in \bigcap_{i \in I} f^{-1}(C_i)$, so $f^{-1}\left(\bigcap_{i \in I} C_i\right) \subseteq \bigcap_{i \in I} f^{-1}(C_i)$.

Conversely, let $x \in \bigcap_{i \in I} f^{-1}(C_i)$. We have $x \in f^{-1}(C_i)$ for every $i \in I$, so $f(x) \in C_i$ for $i \in I$. Therefore, $f(x) \in \bigcap_{i \in I} C_i$, hence $x \in f^{-1}\left(\bigcap_{i \in I} C_i\right)$.

We leave to the reader to prove the third equality of the theorem. □

Definition 1.23. Let X, Y be two finite non-empty and disjoint sets and let ρ be a relation, $\rho \subseteq X \times Y$. A *perfect matching* for ρ is an injective mapping $f : X \longrightarrow Y$ such that if $y = f(x)$, then $(x, y) \in \rho$.

Note that a perfect matching of ρ is an injective mapping f such that $f \subseteq \rho$.

For a subset A of X define the set $\rho[A]$ as

$$\rho[A] = \{y \in Y \mid (x, y) \in \rho \text{ for some } x \in A\}.$$

Theorem 1.11. (Hall's Perfect Matching Theorem) *Let* X, Y *be two finite non-empty and disjoint sets and let ρ be a relation, $\rho \subseteq X \times Y$. There exists a perfect matching for ρ if and only if for every $A \in \mathcal{P}(X)$ we have* $|\rho[A]| \geqslant |A|$.

Proof.   The proof is by induction on $|X|$. If $|X| = 1$, the statement is immediate.

Suppose that the statement holds for $|X| \leqslant n$ and consider a set X with $|X| = n + 1$. We need to consider two cases: either $|\rho[A]| > |A|$ for every subset A of X, or there exists a subset A of X such that $|\rho[A]| = |A|$.

In the first case, since $|\rho[\{x\}]| > 1$ there exists $y \in Y$ such that $(x, y) \in \rho$. Let $X' = X - \{x\}$, $Y' = Y - \{y\}$, and let $\rho' = \rho \cap (X' \times Y')$. Note that for every $B \subseteq X'$ we have $|\rho'[B]| \geqslant |B| + 1$ because for every subset A of X we have $|\rho[A] \geqslant |A| + 1$ and deleting a single element y from $\rho[A]$ still leaves at least $|A|$ elements in this set. By the inductive hypothesis, there exists a perfect matching f' for ρ'. This matching extends to a matching f for ρ by defining $f(x) = y$.

In the second case, let A be a proper subset of X such that $|\rho[A]| = |A|$. Define the sets X', Y', X'', Y'' as

$$X' = A, \quad X'' = X - A,$$
$$Y' = \rho[A], \ Y'' = Y - \rho[A]$$

and consider the relations $\rho' = \rho \cap (X' \times Y')$, and $\rho'' = \rho \cap (X'' \times Y'')$. We shall prove that there are perfect matchings f' and f'' for the relations ρ' and ρ''. A perfect matching for ρ will be given by $f' \cup f''$.

Since A is a proper subset of X we have both $|A| \leqslant n$ and $|X - A| \leqslant n$.

For any subset B of A we have $\rho'[B] = \rho[B]$, so ρ' satisfies the condition of the theorem and a perfect matching f' for ρ' exists.

Suppose that there exists $C \subseteq X''$ such that $|\rho''[C]| < |C|$. This would imply $|\rho[C \cup A]| < |C \cup A|$ because $\rho[C \cup A] = \rho''[C] \cup \rho[A]$, which is impossible. Thus, ρ'' also satisfies the condition of the theorem and a perfect matching exists for ρ''. $\square$

1.4   Sequences and Collections of Sets

Definition 1.24. A sequence of sets $\mathbf{S} = (S_0, S_1, \ldots, S_n, \ldots)$ is *expanding* if $i < j$ implies $S_i \subseteq S_j$ for every $i, j \in \mathbb{N}$.

If $i < j$ implies $S_j \subseteq S_i$ for every $i, j \in \mathbb{N}$, then we say that $\mathbf{S}$ is a *contracting* sequence of sets.

A sequence of sets is *monotone* if it is expanding or contracting.

Definition 1.25. Let $\mathbf{S}$ be an infinite sequence of subsets of a set S, where $\mathbf{S}(i) = S_i$ for $i \in \mathbb{N}$.

The set $\bigcup_{i=0}^{\infty} \bigcap_{j=i}^{\infty} S_j$ is referred to as the *lower limit* of $\mathbf{S}$; the set $\bigcap_{i=0}^{\infty} \bigcup_{j=i}^{\infty} S_j$ is the *upper limit* of $\mathbf{S}$. These two sets are denoted by $\liminf \mathbf{S}$ and $\limsup \mathbf{S}$, respectively.

If $x \in \liminf \mathbf{S}$, then there exists i such that $x \in \bigcap_{j=i}^{\infty} S_j$; in other words, x belongs to all but finitely many sets S_i.

If $x \in \limsup \mathbf{S}$, then, for every i there exists $j \geqslant i$ such that such that $x \in S_j$; in this case x belongs to infinitely many sets of the sequence.

Clearly, we have $\liminf \mathbf{S} \subseteq \limsup \mathbf{S}$.

Definition 1.26. A sequence of sets $\mathbf{S}$ is *convergent* if $\liminf \mathbf{S} = \limsup \mathbf{S}$. In this case the set $L = \liminf \mathbf{S} = \limsup \mathbf{S}$ is said to be the *limit* of the sequence $\mathbf{S}$ and is denoted by $\lim \mathbf{S}$.

Example 1.11. Every expanding sequence of sets is convergent. Indeed, since $\mathbf{S}$ is expanding we have $\bigcap_{j=i}^{\infty} S_j = S_i$. Therefore, $\liminf \mathbf{S} = \bigcup_{i=0}^{\infty} S_i$. On the other hand, $\bigcup_{j=i}^{\infty} S_j \subseteq \bigcup_{i=0}^{\infty} S_i$ and, therefore, $\limsup \mathbf{S} \subseteq \liminf \mathbf{S}$. This shows that $\liminf \mathbf{S} = \limsup \mathbf{S}$, that is, $\mathbf{S}$ is convergent.

A similar argument can be used to show that $\mathbf{S}$ is convergent when $\mathbf{S}$ is contracting.

In this chapter we will use the notion of set countability discussed, for example, in [56].

Definition 1.27. Let $\mathcal{C}$ be a collection of subsets of a set S. The collection $\mathcal{C}_\sigma$ consists of all countable unions of members of $\mathcal{C}$.

The collection $\mathcal{C}_\delta$ consists of all countable intersections of members of $\mathcal{C}$,

$$\mathcal{C}_\sigma = \left\{ \bigcup_{n \geqslant 0} C_n \mid C_n \in \mathcal{C} \right\} \text{ and } \mathcal{C}_\delta = \left\{ \bigcap_{n \geqslant 0} C_n \mid C_n \in \mathcal{C} \right\}.$$

Observe that by taking $C_n = C \in \mathcal{C}$ for $n \geqslant 0$ it follows that $\mathcal{C} \subseteq \mathcal{C}_\sigma$ and $\mathcal{C} \subseteq \mathcal{C}_\delta$. Furthermore, if $\mathcal{C}, \mathcal{C}'$ are two collections of sets such that $\mathcal{C} \subseteq \mathcal{C}'$, then $\mathcal{C}_\sigma \subseteq \mathcal{C}'_\sigma$ and $\mathcal{C}'_\delta \subseteq \mathcal{C}_\delta$.

Theorem 1.12. *For any collection of subsets $\mathcal{C}$ of a set S we have $(\mathcal{C}_\sigma)_\sigma = \mathcal{C}_\sigma$ and $(\mathcal{C}_\delta)_\delta = \mathcal{C}_\delta$.*

Proof. The argument is left to the reader. $\square$

The operations σ and δ can be applied iteratively. We denote sequences of applications of these operations by subscripts adorning the affected collection. The order of application coincides with the order of these symbols in the subscript. For example $(\mathcal{C})_{\sigma\delta\sigma}$ means $((\mathcal{C}_\sigma)_\delta)_\sigma$. Thus, Theorem 1.12 can be restated as the equalities $\mathcal{C}_{\sigma\sigma} = \mathcal{C}_\sigma$ and $\mathcal{C}_{\delta\delta} = \mathcal{C}_\delta$.

Observe that if $\mathbf{C} = (C_0, C_1, \ldots)$ is a sequence of sets, then $\limsup \mathbf{C} = \bigcap_{i=0}^\infty \bigcup_{j=i}^\infty C_j \in \mathcal{C}_{\sigma\delta}$ and $\liminf \mathbf{C} = \bigcup_{i=0}^\infty \bigcap_{j=i}^\infty C_j$ belongs to $\mathcal{C}_{\delta\sigma}$, where $\mathcal{C} = \{C_n \mid n \in \mathbb{N}\}$.

1.5   Partially Ordered Sets

If ρ is a partial order on S, we refer to the pair (S, ρ) as a *partially ordered set* or as a *poset*.

A *strict partial order*, or *a strict order* on S, is a relation $\rho \subseteq S \times S$ that is irreflexive and transitive.

Note that if ρ is a partial order on S, the relation

$$\rho_1 = \rho - \{(x, x) \mid x \in S\}$$

is a strict partial order on S.

From now on we shall denote by "$\leqslant$" a generic partial order on a set S; thus, a generic partially ordered set is denoted by $(S, \leqslant)$.

Example 1.12. Let $\delta = \{(m, n) \mid m, n \in \mathbb{N}, n = km \text{ for some } k \in \mathbb{N}\}$. Since $n = 1 \, n$ it follows that $(n, n) \in \delta$ for every $n \in \mathbb{N}$, so δ is a reflexive relation. Suppose that $(m, n) \in \delta$ and $(n, m) \in \delta$, so $n = mk$ and $m = nh$ for some $k, h \in \mathbb{N}$. This implies $n(1 - kh) = 0$. If $n = 0$, it follows that $m = 0$. If $n \neq 0$ we have $kh = 1$, which means that $k = h = 1$ because $k, h \in \mathbb{N}$, so again, $m = n$. Thus, δ is antisymmetric. Finally, if $(m, n), (n, p) \in \delta$ we have $n = rm$ and $p = sn$ for some $r, s \in \mathbb{N}$, so $p = srm$, which implies $(m, p) \in \delta$. This shows that δ is also transitive and, therefore, it is a partial order relation on $\mathbb{N}$.

Example 1.13. Let π, σ be two partitions in $PART(S)$. We define $\pi \leqslant \sigma$ if each block C of σ is a π-saturated set.

It is clear that "$\leqslant$" is a reflexive relation. Suppose that $\pi \leqslant \sigma$ and $\sigma \leqslant \tau$, where $\pi, \sigma, \tau \in PART_{\text{fin}}(S)$. Then each block D of τ is a union of blocks of σ, and each block of σ is a union of blocks of π. Thus, D is a union of blocks of π and, therefore, $\pi \leqslant \tau$.

Suppose now that $\pi \leqslant \sigma$ and $\sigma \leqslant \pi$. Then, each block C of σ is a union of π-blocks, $C = \bigcup_{i \in I} B_i$, and every π-block is a union of σ-blocks.

Since no block of a partition can be a subset of another block of the same partition, it follows that each block of σ coincides with a block of π, that is $\sigma = \pi$.

Definition 1.28. Let $(S, \leqslant)$ be a poset and let $K \subseteq S$. The *set of upper bounds* of the set K is the set $K^s = \{y \in S \mid x \leqslant y \text{ for every } x \in K\}$.

The *set of lower bounds* of the set K is the set $K^i = \{y \in S \mid y \leqslant x \text{ for every } x \in K\}$.

If $K^s \neq \emptyset$, we say that the set K is *bounded above*. Similarly, if $K^i \neq \emptyset$, we say that K is *bounded below*. If K is both bounded above and bounded below we will refer to K as a *bounded set*.

If $K^s = \emptyset$ ($K^i = \emptyset$), then K is said to be *unbounded above (below)*.

Theorem 1.13. *Let $(S, \leqslant)$ be a poset and let U and V be two subsets of S. If $U \subseteq V$, then we have $V^i \subseteq U^i$ and $V^s \subseteq U^s$.*

Also, for every subset T of S, we have $T \subseteq (T^s)^i$ and $T \subseteq (T^i)^s$.

Proof. The argument for both statements of the theorem amounts to a direct application of Definition 1.28. □

Note that for every subset T of a poset S, we have both

$$T^i = ((T^i)^s)^i \tag{1.1}$$

and

$$T^s = ((T^s)^i)^s. \tag{1.2}$$

Indeed, since $T \subseteq (T^i)^s$, by the first part of Theorem 1.13, we have $((T^s)^i)^s \subseteq T^s$. By the second part of the same theorem applied to T^s, we have the reverse inclusion $T^s \subseteq ((T^s)^i)^s$, which yields $T^s = ((T^s)^i)^s$.

Theorem 1.14. *For any subset K of a poset (S, ρ), the sets $K \cap K^s$ and $K \cap K^i$ contain at most one element.*

Proof. Suppose that $y_1, y_2 \in K \cap K^s$. Since $y_1 \in K$ and $y_2 \in K^s$, we have $(y_1, y_2) \in \rho$. Reversing the roles of y_1 and y_2 (that is, considering now that $y_2 \in K$ and $y_1 \in K^s$), we obtain $(y_2, y_1) \in \rho$. Therefore, we may conclude that $y_1 = y_2$ because of the antisymmetry of the relation ρ, which shows that $K \cap K^s$ contains at most one element.

A similar argument can be used for the second part of the proposition; we leave it to the reader. □

Definition 1.29. Let $(S, \leqslant)$ be a poset. The *least (greatest) element* of the subset K of S is the unique element of the set $K \cap K^i$ ($K \cap K^s$, respectively) if such an element exists.

If K is unbounded above, then it is clear that K has no greatest element. Similarly, if K is unbounded below, then K has no least element.

Applying Definition 1.29 to the set S, the *least (greatest) element* of the poset $(S, \leqslant)$ is an element a of S such that $a \leqslant x$ ($x \leqslant a$, respectively) for all $x \in S$.

It is clear that if a poset has a least element u, then u is the unique minimal element of that poset. A similar statement holds for the greatest and the maximal elements.

Definition 1.30. The subset K of the poset $(S, \leqslant)$ has a *least upper bound* u if $K^s \cap (K^s)^i = \{u\}$.

K has the *greatest lower bound* v if $K^i \cap (K^i)^s = \{v\}$.

We note that a set can have at most one least upper bound and at most one greatest lower bound. Indeed, we have seen above that for any set U the set $U \cap U^i$ may contain an element or be empty. Applying this remark to the set K^s, it follows that the set $K^s \cap (K^s)^i$ may contain at most one element, which shows that K may have at most one least upper bound. A similar argument can be made for the greatest lower bound.

If the set K has a least upper bound, we denote it by $\sup K$. The greatest lower bound of a set will be denoted by $\inf K$. These notations come from the Latin terms *supremum* and *infimum* used alternatively for the least upper bound and the greatest lower bound, respectively.

Lemma 1.1. *Let U, V be two subsets of a poset $(S, \leqslant)$. If $U \subseteq V$ then $V^s \subseteq U^s$ and $V^i \subseteq U^i$.*

Proof.   This statement follows immediately from the definitions of the sets of upper bounds and lower bounds, respectively. $\square$

Theorem 1.15. *Let $(S, \leqslant)$ be a poset and let K, L be two subsets of S such that $K \subseteq L$.*

If $\sup K$ and $\sup L$ exist, then $\sup K \leqslant \sup L$; if $\inf K$ and $\inf L$ exist, then $\inf L \leqslant \inf K$.

Proof.   By Lemma 1.1 we have $L^s \subseteq K^s$ and $L^i \subseteq K_i$. By the same Lemma, we have: $(K^s)^i \subseteq (L^s)^i$ and $(K^i)^s \subseteq (L^i)^s$.

Let $a = \sup K$ and $b = \sup L$. Since $\{a\} = K^s \cap (K^s)^i$ and $(K^s)^i \subseteq (L^s)^i$, it follows that $a \in (L^s)^i$. Since $b \in L^s$, this implies $a \leqslant b$.

If $c = \inf K$ and $d = \inf L$, taking into account that $\{c\} = K^i \cap (K^i)^s$, we have $c \in (L^i)^s$ because $K^i \cap (K^i)^s \subseteq (L^i)^s$. Since $d \in L^i$ we have $d \leqslant c$. $\square$

Example 1.14. A two-element subset $\{m, n\}$ of the poset $(\mathbb{N}, \delta)$ introduced in Example 1.12 has both an infimum and a supremum. Indeed, let p be the least common multiple of m and n. Since $(n, p), (m, p) \in \delta$, it is clear that p is an upper bound of the set $\{m, n\}$. On the other hand, if k is an upper bound of $\{m, n\}$, then k is a multiple of both m and n. In this case, k must also be a multiple of p because otherwise we could write $k = pq + r$ with $0 < r < p$ by dividing k by p. This would imply $r = k - pq$; hence, r would be a multiple of both m and n because both k and p have this property. However, this would contradict the fact that p is the least multiple that m and n share! This shows that the least common multiple of m and n coincides with the supremum of the set $\{m, n\}$. Similarly, $\inf\{m, n\}$ equals the greatest common divisor m and n.

Example 1.15. Let π, σ be two partitions in $PART(S)$. It is easy to see that the collection $\theta = \{B \cap C \mid B \in \pi, C \in \sigma, B \cap C \neq \emptyset\}$ is a partition of S; furthermore, if τ is a partition of S such that $\pi \leqslant \tau$ and $\sigma \leqslant \tau$, then each block E of τ is both a π-saturated set and a σ-saturated set, and, therefore a θ-saturated set. This shows that $\tau = \inf\{\pi, \sigma\}$.

The partition will be denoted by $\pi \wedge \sigma$.

Definition 1.31. A *minimal element* of a poset $(S, \leqslant)$ is an element $x \in S$ such that $\{x\}^i = \{x\}$. A *maximal element* of $(S, \leqslant)$ is an element $y \in S$ such that $\{y\}^s = \{y\}$.

In other words, x is a minimal element of the poset $(S, \leqslant)$ if there is no element less than or equal to x other than itself; similarly, x is maximal if there is no element greater than or equal to x other than itself.

For the poset $(\mathbb{R}, \leqslant)$, it is possible to give more specific descriptions of the supremum and infimum of a subset when they exist.

Theorem 1.16. *If $T \subseteq \mathbb{R}$, then $u = \sup T$ if and only if u is an upper bound of T and, for every $\epsilon > 0$, there is $t \in T$ such that $u - \epsilon < t \leqslant u$.*

The number v is $\inf T$ if and only if v is a lower bound of T and, for every $\epsilon > 0$, there is $t \in T$ such that $v \leqslant t < v + \epsilon$.

Proof. We prove only the first part of the theorem; the argument for the second part is similar and is left to the reader.

Suppose that $u = \sup T$; that is, $\{u\} = T^s \cup (T^s)^i$. Since $u \in T^s$, it is clear that u is an upper bound for T. Suppose that there is $\epsilon > 0$ such that no $t \in T$ exists such that $u - \epsilon < t \leqslant u$. This means that $u - \epsilon$ is also an upper bound for T, and in this case u cannot be a lower bound for the set of upper bounds of T. Therefore, no such ϵ may exist.

Conversely, suppose that u is an upper bound of T and for every $\epsilon > 0$, there is $t \in T$ such that $u - \epsilon < t \leqslant u$. Suppose that u does not belong to $(K^s)^i$. This means that there is another upper bound u' of T such that $u' < u$. Choosing $\epsilon = u - u'$, we would have no $t \in T$ such that $u - \epsilon = u' < t \leqslant u$ because this would prevent u' from being an upper bound of T. This implies $u \in (K^s)^i$, so $u = \sup T$. $\square$

Theorem 1.17. *In the extended poset of real numbers* $(\hat{\mathbb{R}}, \leqslant)$ *every subset has a supremum and an infimum.*

Proof. If a set is bounded then the existence of the supremum and infimum is established by the Completeness Axiom. Suppose that a subset S of $\hat{\mathbb{R}}$ has no upper bound in $\mathbb{R}$. Then $x \leqslant \infty$, so ∞ is an upper bound of S in $\hat{\mathbb{R}}$. Moreover ∞ is the unique upper bound of S, so $\sup S = \infty$. Similarly, if S has no lower bound in $\mathbb{R}$, then $\inf S = -\infty$ in $\hat{\mathbb{R}}$. $\square$

The definitions of infimum and supremum of the empty set in $(\hat{\mathbb{R}}, \leqslant)$ are

$$\sup \emptyset = -\infty \text{ and } \inf \emptyset = \infty,$$

in order to remain consistent with Theorem 1.15.

A very important axiom for the set $\mathbb{R}$ is given next.

> **The Completeness Axiom for** $\mathbb{R}$**:** If T is a non-empty subset of $\mathbb{R}$ that is bounded above, then T has a supremum.

A statement equivalent to the Completeness Axiom for $\mathbb{R}$ follows.

Theorem 1.18. *If T is a non-empty subset of $\mathbb{R}$ that is bounded below, then T has an infimum.*

Proof. Note that the set T^i is not empty. If $s \in T^i$ and $t \in T$, we have $s \leqslant t$, so the set T^i is bounded above. By the Completeness Axiom $v = \sup T^i$ exists and $\{v\} = (T^i)^s \cap ((T^i)^s)^i = (T^i)^s \cap T^i$ by equality (1.1). Thus, $v = \inf T$. $\square$

We leave to the reader to prove that Theorem 1.18 implies the Completeness Axiom for $\mathbb{R}$.

Another statement equivalent to the Completeness Axiom is the following.

Theorem 1.19. (Dedekind's Theorem) *Let U and V be non-empty subsets of $\mathbb{R}$ such that $U \cup V = \mathbb{R}$ and $x \in U, y \in V$ imply $x < y$. Then, there exists $a \in \mathbb{R}$ such that if $x > a$, then $x \in V$, and if $x < a$, then $x \in U$.*

Proof. Observe that $U \neq \emptyset$ and $V \subseteq U^s$. Since $V \neq \emptyset$, it means that U is bounded above, so by the Completeness Axiom $\sup U$ exists. Let $a = \sup U$. Clearly, $u \leq a$ for every $u \in U$. Since $V \subseteq U^s$, it also follows that $a \leqslant v$ for every $v \in V$.

If $x > a$, then $x \in V$ because otherwise we would have $x \in U$ since $U \cup V = \mathbb{R}$ and this would imply $x \leqslant a$. Similarly, if $x < a$, then $x \in U$. $\square$

Using the previously introduced notations, Dedekind's theorem can be stated as follows: if U and V are non-empty subsets of $\mathbb{R}$ such that $U \cup V = \mathbb{R}$, $U^s \subseteq V$, $V^i \subseteq U$, then there exists a such that $\{a\}^s \subseteq V$ and $\{a\}^i \subseteq U$.

One can prove that Dedekind's theorem implies the Completeness Axiom. Indeed, let T be a non-empty subset of $\mathbb{R}$ that is bounded above. Therefore $V = T^s \neq \emptyset$. Note that $U = (T^s)^i \neq \emptyset$ and $U \cup V = \mathbb{R}$. Moreover, $U^s = ((T^s)^i)^s = T^s = V$ and $V^i = (T^s)^i = U$. Therefore, by Dedekind's theorem, there is $a \in \mathbb{R}$ such that $\{a\}^s \subseteq V = T^s$ and $\{a\}^i \subseteq U = (T^s)^i$. Note that $a \in \{a\}^s \cap \{a\}^i \subseteq T^s \cap (T^s)^i$, which proves that $a = \sup T$.

By adding the symbols $+\infty$ and $-\infty$ to the set $\mathbb{R}$, one obtains the set $\hat{\mathbb{R}}$. The partial order $\leqslant$ defined on $\mathbb{R}$ can now be extended to $\hat{\mathbb{R}}$ by $-\infty \leqslant x$ and $x \leqslant +\infty$ for every $x \in \mathbb{R}$.

Note that, in the poset $(\hat{\mathbb{R}}, \leqslant)$, the sets T^i and T^s are non-empty for every $T \in \mathcal{P}(\hat{\mathbb{R}})$ because $-\infty \in T^i$ and $+\infty \in T^s$ for any subset T of $\hat{\mathbb{R}}$.

Theorem 1.20. *For every set $T \subseteq \hat{\mathbb{R}}$, both $\sup T$ and $\inf T$ exist in the poset $(\hat{\mathbb{R}}, \leqslant)$.*

Proof. We present the argument for $\sup T$. If $\sup T$ exists in $(\mathbb{R}, \leqslant)$, then it is clear that the same number is $\sup T$ in $(\hat{\mathbb{R}}, \leqslant)$.

Assume now that $\sup T$ does not exist in $(\mathbb{R}, \leqslant)$. By the Completeness Axiom for $\mathbb{R}$, this means that the set T does not have an upper bound in $(\mathbb{R}, \leqslant)$. Therefore, the set of upper bounds of T in $(\hat{T}, \leqslant)$ is $T^{\hat{s}} = \{+\infty\}$. It follows immediately that in this case $\sup T = +\infty$ in $(\hat{\mathbb{R}}, \leqslant)$. $\square$

Theorem 1.21. *Let I be a partially ordered set and let $\{x_i \mid i \in I\}$ be a subset of $\hat{\mathbb{R}}$ indexed by I. For $i \in I$ let $S_i = \{x_j \mid j \in I$ and $i \leqslant j\}$. We have*

$$\sup \inf S_i \leqslant \inf \sup S_i. \tag{1.3}$$

Proof. Note that if $i \leqslant h$, then $S_h \subseteq S_i$ for $i, h \in I$. As we saw earlier, each set S_i has both an infimum y_i and a supremum z_i in the poset $(\hat{\mathbb{R}}, \leqslant)$. It is clear that if $i \leqslant h$, then $y_i \leqslant y_h \leqslant z_h \leqslant z_i$. We claim that

$$\sup\{y_i \mid i \in I\} \leqslant \inf\{z_h \mid h \in I\}.$$

Indeed, since then $y_i \leqslant z_h$ for all i, h such that $i \leqslant h$, we have $y_i \leqslant \inf\{z_h \mid h \in I\}$ for all $i \in I$. Therefore,

$$\sup\{y_i \mid i \in I\} \leqslant \inf\{z_h \mid h \in I\},$$

which can be written as

$$\sup \inf S_i \leqslant \inf \sup S_i.$$

$\square$

Let S be a set and let $f : S \longrightarrow \hat{\mathbb{R}}$. The image of S under f is the set $f(S) = \{f(x) \mid x \in S\}$. Since $f(S) \subseteq \hat{\mathbb{R}}$, $\sup f(S)$ exists. Furthermore, if there exists $u \in S$ such that $f(u) = \sup f(S)$, then we say that f *attains its supremum* at u. This is not always the case as the next example shows.

Example 1.16. Let $f : (0, 1) \longrightarrow \hat{\mathbb{R}}$ be defined by $f(x) = \frac{1}{1-x}$. It is clear that $\sup f((0, 1)) = \infty$. However, there is no $u \in (0, 1)$ such that $f(u) = \infty$, so f does not attain its supremum on $(0, 1)$.

Let X, Y be two sets and let $f : X \times Y \longrightarrow \hat{\mathbb{R}}$ be a function. We have

$$\sup_{x \in X} \inf_{y \in Y} f(x, y) \leqslant \inf_{y \in Y} \sup_{x \in X} f(x, y). \tag{1.4}$$

Indeed, note that $\inf_{y \in Y} f(x, y) \leqslant f(x, y)$ for every $x \in X$ and $y \in Y$ by the definition of the infimum. Note that the left member of the inequality depends only on x. The last inequality implies $\sup_{x \in X} \inf_{y \in Y} f(x, y) \leqslant \sup_{x \in X} f(x, y)$, by the monotonicity of sup and now the current left member is a lower bound of the set $\{z = \sup_{x \in X} f(x, y) \mid y \in Y\}$. This implies immediately the inequality (1.4).

If instead of inequality (1.4) the function f satisfies the equality:

$$\sup_{x \in X} \inf_{y \in Y} f(x, y) = \inf_{y \in Y} \sup_{x \in X} f(x, y), \tag{1.5}$$

then the common value of both sides is a *saddle value* for f.

Since $\inf_{y \in Y} f(x, y)$ is a function $h(x)$ of x and $\sup_{x \in X} f(x, y)$ is a function $g(y)$ of y, the existence of a saddle value for f implies that $\sup_{x \in X} h(x) = \inf_{y \in Y} g(y) = v$.

If both $\sup_{x \in X} h(x)$ and $\inf_{y \in Y} g(y)$ are attained, that is, there are $x_0 \in X$ and $y_0 \in Y$ such that

$$h(x_0) = \sup_{x \in X} h(x) = \sup_{x \in X} \inf_{y \in Y} f(x, y),$$

$$g(y_0) = \inf_{y \in Y} g(y) = \inf_{y \in Y} \sup_{x \in X} f(x, y),$$

we have

$$h(x_0) = \sup_{x \in X} \inf_{y \in Y} f(x, y)$$

$$= \inf_{y \in Y} \sup_{x \in X} f(x, y)$$

(because of the existence of the saddle value)

$$= \inf_{y \in Y} g(y) = g(y_0).$$

Therefore,

$$g(y_0) = \sup_{x \in X} f(x, y_0) = f(x_0, y_0) = \inf_{y \in Y} f(x_0, y) = h(x_0),$$

and

$$f(x, y_0) \leqslant f(x_0, y_0) \leqslant f(x_0, y).$$

The pair (x_0, y_0) that satisfies the inequalities

$$f(x, y_0) \leqslant f(x_0, y_0) \leqslant f(x_0, y)$$

is referred to as a *saddle point* for f.

Conversely, if there exists a saddle point (x_0, y_0) such that $f(x, y_0) \leqslant f(x_0, y_0) \leqslant f(x_0, y)$, then $f : X \times Y \longrightarrow \mathbb{R}$ has a saddle value. Indeed, in this case we

$$\sup_{x \in X} f(x, y_0) \leqslant f(x_0, y_0) \leqslant \inf_{y \in Y} f(x_0, y),$$

hence

$$\inf_{y \in Y} \sup_{x \in X} f(x, y) \leqslant \sup_{x \in X} f(x, y_0) \leqslant f(x_0, y_0) \leqslant \inf_{y \in Y} f(x_0, y) \leqslant \sup_{x \in X} \inf_{y \in Y} f(x, y).$$

Since a saddle value exists, these inequalities become equalities and we have a saddle value.

Definition 1.32. Let $(S, \leqslant)$ be a poset. A *chain* of $(S, \leqslant)$ is a subset T of S such that for every $x, y \in T$ such that $x \neq y$ we have either $x < y$ or $y < x$. If the set S is a chain, we say that $(S, \leqslant)$ is a *totally ordered set* and the relation $\leqslant$ is a *total order*.

Example 1.17. The set of real numbers equipped with the usual partial order $(\mathbb{R}, \leqslant)$ is a chain since, for every $x, y \in \mathbb{R}$, we have either $x \leqslant y$ or $y \leqslant x$.

Theorem 1.22. *If $\{U_i \mid i \in I\}$ is a chain of the poset $(CHAINS(S), \subseteq)$ (that is, a chain of chains of $(S, \leqslant)$), then $\bigcup \{U_i \mid i \in I\}$ is itself a chain of $(S, \leqslant)$ (that is, a member of $(CHAINS(S), \subseteq)$).*

Proof. Let $x, y \in \bigcup \{U_i \mid i \in I\}$. There are $i, j \in I$ such that $x \in U_i$ and $y \in U_j$ and we have either $U_i \subseteq U_j$ or $U_j \subseteq U_i$. In the first case, we have either $x_i \leqslant x_j$ or $x_j \leqslant x_i$ because both x and y belong to the chain U_j. The same conclusion can be reached in the second case when both x and y belong to the chain U_i. So, in any case, x and y are comparable, which proves that $\bigcup \{U_i \mid i \in I\}$ is a chain of $(S, \leqslant)$. $\square$

A statement equivalent to a fundamental principle of set theory known as the Axiom of Choice is Zorn's lemma stated below.

> **Zorn's Lemma:** If every chain of a poset $(S, \leqslant)$ has an upper bound, then S has a maximal element.

Theorem 1.23. *The following three statements are equivalent for a poset $(S, \leqslant)$:*

   (i) *If every chain of $(S, \leqslant)$ has an upper bound, then S has a maximal element (Zorn's Lemma).*

  (ii) *If every chain of $(S, \leqslant)$ has a least upper bound, then S has a maximal element.*

 (iii) *S contains a chain that is maximal with respect to set inclusion (Hausdorff[2] maximality principle).*

Proof. (i) implies (ii) is immediate.

(ii) implies (iii): Let $(CHAINS(S), \subseteq)$ be the poset of chains of S ordered by set inclusion. Every chain $\{U_i \mid i \in I\}$ of the poset $(CHAINS(S), \subseteq)$ has a least upper bound $\bigcup \{U_i \mid i \in I\}$ in the poset $(CHAINS(S), \subseteq)$.

---

[2]Felix Hausdorff was born on November 8th, 1868 in Breslau in Prussia, (now Germany) and died on January 26th, 1942 in Bonn, Germany. Hausdorff is one of the founders of modern topology and set theory, and has major contributions in measure theory, and functional analysis.

Hausdorff studied in Leipzig, where he obtained his doctorate in 1891. He taught at the Universities of Bonn, Greifswald, and Leipzig. Life became very difficult for German Jews under the National Socialist regime and on 26 January 1942, Felix Hausdorff, along with his wife and his sister-in-law, committed suicide to avoid being deported.

Therefore, by (ii), $(CHAINS(S), \subseteq)$ has a maximal element that is a chain of $(S, \leqslant)$ that is maximal with respect to set inclusion.

(iii) implies (i): Suppose that S contains a chain W that is maximal with respect to set inclusion and that every chain of $(S, \leqslant)$ has an upper bound. Let w be an upper bound of W.

If $w \in W$, then w is a maximal element of S. Indeed, if this were not the case, then S would contain an element t such that $w < t$ and $W \cup \{t\}$ would be a chain that would strictly include W.

If $w \notin W$, then $W \cup \{w\}$ would be a chain strictly including W, which, again, would contradict the maximality of W. Thus, w is a maximal element of $(S, \leqslant)$. □

Let $(S, \leqslant)$ and $(T, \leqslant)$ be two posets.

Definition 1.33. A *morphism* between $(S, \leqslant)$ and $(T, \leqslant)$ or a *monotonic mapping* (or an *increasing mapping*) between $(S, \leqslant)$ and $(T, \leqslant)$ is a mapping $f : S \longrightarrow T$ such that $u, v \in S$ and $u > v$ imply $f(u) \leqslant f(v)$.

A mapping $g : S \longrightarrow T$ is *antimonotonic* or a *decreasing mapping* if $u, v \in S$ and $u > v$ imply $g(u) \geqslant g(v)$.

The mapping f is *strictly monotonic* (or *strictly increasing*) if $u < v$ implies $f(u) < f(v)$; f is *strictly antimonotonic* (or *strictly decreasing*) if $u < v$ implies $f(u) < f(v)$.

Note that $g : S \longrightarrow T$ is antimonotonic if and only if g is a monotonic mapping between the poset $(S, \leqslant)$ and the dual $(T, \geqslant)$ of the poset $(T, \leqslant)$.

Example 1.18. Consider a set M, the poset $(\mathcal{P}(M), \subseteq)$, and the functions $f, g : (\mathcal{P}(M))^2 \longrightarrow \mathcal{P}$, defined by $f(K, H) = K \cup H$ and $g(K, H) = K \cap H$, for $K, H \in \mathcal{P}(M)$. If the Cartesian product is equipped with the product partial order, then both f and g are monotonic. Indeed, if $(K_1, H_1) \subseteq (K_2, H_2)$, we have $K_1 \subseteq K_2$ and $H_1 \subseteq H_2$, which implies that

$$f(K_1, H_1) = K_1 \cup H_1 \subseteq K_2 \cup H_2 = f(K_2, H_2).$$

The argument for g is similar, and it is left to the reader.

Theorem 1.24. *Let $(P, \leqslant), (R, \leqslant), (S, \leqslant)$ be three posets and let $f : P \longrightarrow R$, $g : R \longrightarrow S$ be two monotonic mappings. The mapping $gf : P \longrightarrow S$ is also monotonic.*

Proof. Let $x, y \in P$ be such that $x \leqslant y$. In view of the monotonicity of f, we have $f(x) \leqslant f(y)$, and this implies $(g(f(x)) \leqslant g(f(y))$ because of the monotonicity of g. Therefore, gf is monotonic. □

Monotonic functions map chains to chains, as we show next.

Theorem 1.25. *Let $(P, \leqslant)$ and $(R, \leqslant)$ be two posets and $f : P \longrightarrow R$ be a monotonic function. If $L \subseteq P$ is a chain in $(P, \leqslant)$, then $f(L)$ is a chain in $(R, \leqslant)$.*

Proof. Let $u, v \in f(L)$ be two elements of $f(L)$. There exist $x, y \in L$ such that $f(x) = u$ and $f(y) = v$. Since L is a chain, we have either $x \leqslant y$ or $y \leqslant x$. In the former case, the monotonicity of f implies $u \leqslant v$; in the latter situation, we have $v \leqslant u$. $\square$

Let $\mathbf{x} \in \mathbf{Seq}(X)$. A sequence $\mathbf{y} \in \mathbf{Seq}(S)$ is a *subsequence* of $\mathbf{x}$ if there exists a strictly increasing function $h : \mathbb{N} \longrightarrow \mathbb{N}$ such that $y_n = x_{h(n)}$ for $n \in \mathbb{N}$.

Example 1.19. The sequence $\mathbf{y} = (x_0, x_1, x_4, x_9, \ldots)$ is a subsequence of the sequence $\mathbf{x}$ because we can write $y_k = x_{k^2}$ for $k \in \mathbb{N}$.

If $\mathbf{x} \in \mathbf{Seq}(X)$ we will denote the subsequence $(x_p, x_{p+1}, \ldots, x_q)$ of $\mathbf{x}$ by $\mathbf{x}_{p:q}$.

1.6   Closure and Interior Systems

Closure and interior systems introduced in this section are significant in algebra, measure theory, and topology.

Definition 1.34. Let S be a set. A *closure system on S* is a collection $\mathcal{C}$ of subsets of S that satisfies the following conditions:
   (i) $S \in \mathcal{C}$, and
   (ii) for every collection $\mathcal{D} \subseteq \mathcal{C}$, we have $\bigcap \mathcal{D} \in \mathcal{C}$.

Example 1.20. Let $\mathcal{C}$ be the collection of all intervals $[a, b] = \{x \in \mathbb{R} \mid a \leqslant x \leqslant b\}$ with $a, b \in \mathbb{R}$ and $a \leqslant b$ together with the empty set and the set $\mathbb{R}$. Note that $\bigcup \mathcal{C} = \mathbb{R} \in \mathcal{C}$, so the first condition of Definition 1.34 is satisfied.

Let $\mathcal{D}$ be a non-empty subcollection of $\mathcal{C}$. If $\emptyset \in \mathcal{D}$, then $\bigcap \mathcal{D} = \emptyset \in \mathcal{C}$. If $\mathcal{D} = \{\mathbb{R}\}$, then $\bigcap \mathcal{D} = \mathbb{R} \in \mathcal{C}$. Therefore, we need to consider only the case when $\mathcal{D} = \{[a_i, b_i] \mid i \in I\}$. Then, $\bigcap \mathcal{D} = \emptyset$ unless $a = \sup\{a_i \mid i \in I\}$ and $b = \inf\{b_i \mid i \in I\}$ both exist and $a \leqslant b$, in which case $\bigcap \mathcal{D} = [a, b]$. Thus, $\mathcal{C}$ is a closure system.

Many classes of relations define useful closure systems.

Theorem 1.26. *The sets* $REFL(S), SYMM(S)$ *and* $TRAN(S)$ *are closure systems on* S.

Proof. Note that $S \times S$ is a reflexive, symmetric, and transitive relation on S. Therefore, $\bigcup REFL(S) = S \times S \in REFL(S)$, $\bigcup SYMM(S) = S \times S \in SYMM(S)$, and $\bigcup TRAN(S) = S \times S \in TRAN(S)$.

Now let $\mathcal{C} = \{\rho_i \mid i \in I\}$ be a collection of transitive relations and let $\rho = \bigcap\{\rho_i \mid i \in I\}$. Suppose that $(x, y), (y, z) \in \rho$. Then $(x, y), (y, z) \in \rho_i$ for every $i \in I$, so $(x, z) \in \rho_i$ for $i \in I$ because each of the relations ρ_i is transitive. Thus, $(x, z) \in \rho$, which shows that $\bigcap \mathcal{C} \in TRAN(S)$. This allows us to conclude that $TRAN(S)$ is indeed a closure system. We leave it to the reader to prove that $REFL(S)$ and $SYMM(S)$ are also closure systems. $\square$

Theorem 1.27. *The set of equivalences on* S, $\mathsf{EQUIV}(S)$, *is a closure system.*

Proof. The relation $\theta_S = S \times S$, is clearly an equivalence relation. Thus, $\bigcup \mathsf{EQUIV}(S) = \theta_S \in \mathsf{EQUIV}(S)$.

Now let $\mathcal{C} = \{\rho_i \mid i \in I\}$ be a collection of transitive relations and let $\rho = \bigcap\{\rho_i \mid i \in I\}$. It is immediate that ρ is an equivalence on S, so $\mathsf{EQUIV}(S)$ is a closure system. $\square$

Definition 1.35. A mapping $\mathbf{K} : \mathcal{P}(S) \longrightarrow \mathcal{P}(S)$ is a *closure operator* on a set S if it satisfies the conditions
   (i) $U \subseteq \mathbf{K}(U)$ *(expansiveness)*,
   (ii) $U \subseteq V$ implies $\mathbf{K}(U) \subseteq \mathbf{K}(V)$ *(monotonicity)*, and
   (iii) $\mathbf{K}(\mathbf{K}(U)) = \mathbf{K}(U)$ *(idempotency)*
for $U, V \in \mathcal{P}(S)$.

Example 1.21. Let X, Y be two sets and let $f : X \longrightarrow Y$ be a function. Define the mapping $\mathbf{K}_f : \mathcal{P}(X) \longrightarrow \mathcal{P}(X)$ as $\mathbf{K}_f(S) = f^{-1}(f(S))$ for $S \in \mathcal{P}(X)$. We claim that $\mathbf{K}_f$ is a closure operator.

Indeed, if $x \in S$, then $f(x) \in f(S)$, which implies that $x \in f^{-1}(f(S))$. Thus, $S \subseteq \mathbf{K}_f(S)$.

The monotonicity of $\mathbf{K}_f$ is immediate. Taking into account the expansiveness and the monotonicity of $\mathbf{K}_f$ we have $\mathbf{K}_f(S) \subseteq \mathbf{K}_f(\mathbf{K}_f(S))$ for $S \in \mathcal{P}(X)$. To prove the converse inclusion, let $x \in \mathbf{K}_f(\mathbf{K}_f(S)) = f^{-1}f(\mathbf{K}_f(S))$. We have $f(x) \in f(\mathbf{K}_f(S))$, so there exists $z \in \mathbf{K}_f(S)$

such that $f(x) = f(z)$. Since $z \in \mathbf{K}_f(S)$, there exists $s \in S$ such that $f(z) = f(s)$, so $f(x) = f(s)$. Therefore, $x \in f^{-1}(f(s)) \subseteq \mathbf{K}_f(S)$ and we obtain the equality $\mathbf{K}_f(S) = \mathbf{K}_f(\mathbf{K}_f(S))$.

Example 1.22. Let $\mathbf{K} : \mathcal{P}(\mathbb{R}) \longrightarrow \mathcal{P}(\mathbb{R})$ be defined by

$$\mathbf{K}(U) = \begin{cases} \emptyset & \text{if } U = \emptyset, \\ [a, b] & \text{if both } a = \inf U \text{ and } b = \sup U \text{ exist}, \\ \mathbb{R} & \text{otherwise}, \end{cases}$$

for $U \in \mathcal{P}(\mathbb{R})$. We leave to the reader the verification that $\mathbf{K}$ is a closure operator.

Definition 1.36. Let S be a set. A collection $\mathcal{M}$ of subsets of S is a *monotone* if the following conditions are satisfied:

(i) if $\mathbf{C} = (C_n)$ is an increasing sequence of sets in $\mathcal{M}$, then $\bigcup_{n \in \mathbb{N}} C_n \in \mathcal{M}$;

(ii) if $\mathbf{D} = (D_n)$ is a decreasing sequence of sets in $\mathcal{M}$, then $\bigcap_{n \in \mathbb{N}} D_n \in \mathcal{M}$.

Note that $\mathcal{P}(S)$ is a monotone collection. If $\{\mathcal{M}_i \mid i \in I\}$ is a set of monotone collections of subsets of S, then $\bigcap_{i \in I} \mathcal{M}_i$ is a monotone collection. This, the family of monotone collections is a closure system. The corresponding closure operator is denoted by $\mathbf{K}_{\mathrm{mon}}$.

Closure operators induce closure systems, as shown by the next lemma.

Lemma 1.2. Let $\mathbf{K} : \mathcal{P}(S) \longrightarrow \mathcal{P}(S)$ be a closure operator. Define the family of sets $\mathcal{C}_{\mathbf{K}} = \{H \in \mathcal{P}(S) \mid H = \mathbf{K}(H)\}$. Then, $\mathcal{C}_{\mathbf{K}}$ is a closure system on S.

Proof. Since $S \subseteq \mathbf{K}(S) \subseteq S$, we have $S \in \mathcal{C}_{\mathbf{K}}$, so $\bigcup \mathcal{C}_{\mathbf{K}} = S \in \mathcal{C}_{\mathbf{K}}$.

Let $\mathcal{D} = \{D_i \mid i \in I\}$ be a collection of subsets of S such that $D_i = \mathbf{K}(D_i)$ for $i \in I$. Since $\bigcap \mathcal{D} \subseteq D_i$, we have $\mathbf{K}(\bigcap \mathcal{D}) \subseteq \mathbf{K}(D_i) = D_i$ for every $i \in I$. Therefore, $\mathbf{K}(\bigcap \mathcal{D}) \subseteq \bigcap \mathcal{D}$, which implies $\mathbf{K}(\bigcap \mathcal{D}) = \bigcap \mathcal{D}$. This proves our claim. $\square$

Note that $\mathcal{C}_{\mathbf{K}}$, as defined in Lemma 1.2, equals the range of $\mathbf{K}$. Indeed, if $L \in \mathrm{Ran}(\mathbf{K})$, then $L = \mathbf{K}(H)$ for some $H \in \mathcal{P}(S)$, so $\mathbf{K}(L) = \mathbf{K}(\mathbf{K}(H)) = \mathbf{K}(H) = L$, which shows that $L \in \mathcal{C}_{\mathbf{K}}$. The reverse inclusion is obvious.

We refer to the sets in $\mathcal{C}_{\mathbf{K}}$ as the *$\mathbf{K}$-closed subsets* of S.

In the reverse direction from Lemma 1.2, we show that every closure system generates a closure operator.

Lemma 1.3. *Let* $\mathcal{C}$ *be a closure system on the set* S. *Define the mapping* $\mathbf{K}_{\mathcal{C}} : \mathcal{P}(S) \longrightarrow \mathcal{P}(S)$ *by* $\mathbf{K}_{\mathcal{C}}(H) = \bigcap \{L \in \mathcal{C} \mid H \subseteq L\}$. *Then,* $\mathbf{K}_{\mathcal{C}}$ *is a closure operator on the set* S.

Proof. Note that the collection $\{L \in \mathcal{C} \mid H \subseteq L\}$ is not empty since it contains at least S, so $\mathbf{K}_{\mathcal{C}}(H)$ is defined and is clearly the smallest element of $\mathcal{C}$ that contains H. Also, by the definition of $\mathbf{K}_{\mathcal{C}}(H)$, it follows immediately that $H \subseteq \mathbf{K}_{\mathcal{C}}(H)$ for every $H \in \mathcal{P}(S)$.

Suppose that $H_1, H_2 \in \mathcal{P}(S)$ are such that $H_1 \subseteq H_2$. Since

$$\{L \in \mathcal{C} \mid H_2 \subseteq L\} \subseteq \{L \in \mathcal{C} \mid H_1 \subseteq L\},$$

we have

$$\bigcap \{L \in \mathcal{C} \mid H_1 \subseteq L\} \subseteq \bigcap \{L \in \mathcal{C} \mid H_2 \subseteq L\},$$

so $\mathbf{K}_{\mathcal{C}}(H_1) \subseteq \mathbf{K}_{\mathcal{C}}(H_2)$.

We have $\mathbf{K}_{\mathcal{C}}(H) \in \mathcal{C}$ for every $H \in \mathcal{P}(S)$ because $\mathcal{C}$ is a closure system. Therefore, $\mathbf{K}_{\mathcal{C}}(H) \in \{L \in \mathcal{C} \mid \mathbf{K}_{\mathcal{C}}(H) \subseteq L\}$, so $\mathbf{K}_{\mathcal{C}}(\mathbf{K}_{\mathcal{C}}(H)) \subseteq \mathbf{K}_{\mathcal{C}}(H)$. Since the reverse inclusion clearly holds, we obtain $\mathbf{K}_{\mathcal{C}}(\mathbf{K}_{\mathcal{C}}(H)) = \mathbf{K}_{\mathcal{C}}(H)$. $\square$

Definition 1.37. Let $\mathcal{C}$ be a closure system on a set S and let T be a subset of S. The $\mathcal{C}$-*set generated by* T is the set $\mathbf{K}_{\mathcal{C}}(T)$.

Note that $\mathbf{K}_{\mathcal{C}}(T)$ is the least set in $\mathcal{C}$ that includes T.

Theorem 1.28. *Let* S *be a set. For every closure system* $\mathcal{C}$ *on* S, *we have* $\mathcal{C} = \mathcal{C}_{\mathbf{K}_{\mathcal{C}}}$. *For every closure operator* $\mathbf{K}$ *on* S, *we have* $\mathbf{K} = \mathbf{K}_{\mathcal{C}_{\mathbf{K}}}$.

Proof. Let $\mathcal{C}$ be a closure system on S and let $H \subseteq M$. Then, we have the following equivalent statements:

(1) $H \in \mathcal{C}_{\mathbf{K}_{\mathcal{C}}}$.
(2) $\mathbf{K}_{\mathcal{C}}(H) = H$.
(3) $H \in \mathcal{C}$.

The equivalence between (2) and (3) follows from the fact that $\mathbf{K}_{\mathcal{C}}(H)$ is the smallest element of $\mathcal{C}$ that contains H.

Conversely, let $\mathbf{K}$ be a closure operator on S. To prove the equality of $\mathbf{K}$ and $\mathbf{K}_{\mathcal{C}_{\mathbf{K}}}$, consider the following list of equal sets, where $H \subseteq S$:

(1) $\mathbf{K}_{\mathcal{C}_{\mathbf{K}}}(H)$.
(2) $\bigcap \{L \in \mathcal{C}_{\mathbf{K}} \mid H \subseteq L\}$.
(3) $\bigcap \{L \in \mathcal{P}(S) \mid H \subseteq L = \mathbf{K}(L)\}$.
(4) $\mathbf{K}(H)$.

We need to justify only the equality of the last two members of the list. Since $H \subseteq \mathbf{K}(H) = \mathbf{K}(\mathbf{K}(H))$, we have $\mathbf{K}(H) \in \{L \in \mathcal{P}(S) \mid H \subseteq L = \mathbf{K}(L)\}$. Thus, $\bigcap\{L \in \mathcal{P}(S) \mid H \subseteq L = \mathbf{K}(L)\} \subseteq \mathbf{K}(H)$. To prove the reverse inclusion, note that for every $L \in \{L \in \mathcal{P}(S) \mid H \subseteq L = \mathbf{K}(L)\}$, we have $H \subseteq L$, so $\mathbf{K}(H) \subseteq \mathbf{K}(L) = L$. Therefore, $\mathbf{K}(H) \subseteq \bigcap\{L \in \mathcal{P}(S) \mid H \subseteq L = \mathbf{K}(L)\}$. $\square$

Theorem 1.28 shows the existence of a natural bijection between the set of closure operators on a set S and the set of closure systems on S.

Definition 1.38. Let $\mathcal{C}$ be a closure system on a set S and let T be a subset of S. The $\mathcal{C}$-closure of the set T is the set $\mathbf{K}_{\mathcal{C}}(T)$.

As we observed before, $\mathbf{K}_{\mathcal{C}}(T)$ is the smallest element of $\mathcal{C}$ that contains T.

Example 1.23. Let $\mathbf{K}$ be the closure operator given in Example 1.22. Since the closure system $\mathcal{C}_{\mathbf{K}}$ equals the range of $\mathbf{K}$, it follows that the members of $\mathcal{C}_{\mathbf{K}}$, the $\mathbf{K}$-closed sets, are $\emptyset$, $\mathbb{R}$, and all closed intervals $[a, b]$ with $a \leqslant b$. Thus, $\mathcal{C}_{\mathbf{K}}$ is the closure system $\mathcal{C}$ introduced in Example 1.20. Therefore, $\mathbf{K}$ and $\mathcal{C}$ correspond to each other under the bijection of Theorem 1.28.

For a relation ρ, on S define ρ^{+} as $\mathbf{K}_{TRAN(S)}(\rho)$. The relation ρ^{+} is called the *transitive closure* of ρ and is the least transitive relation containing ρ.

Theorem 1.29. *Let ρ be a relation on a set S. We have*

$$\rho^{+} = \bigcup\{\rho^{n} \mid n \in \mathbb{N} \text{ and } n \geqslant 1\}.$$

Proof. Let τ be the relation $\bigcup\{\rho^{n} \mid n \in \mathbb{N} \text{ and } n \geqslant 1\}$. We claim that τ is transitive. Indeed, let $(x, z), (z, y) \in \tau$. There exist $p, q \in \mathbb{N}$, $p, q \geqslant 1$ such that $(x, z) \in \rho^{p}$ and $(z, y) \in \rho^{q}$. Therefore, $(x, y) \in \rho^{p}\rho^{q} = \rho^{p+q} \subseteq \rho^{+}$, which shows that ρ^{+} is transitive. The definition of ρ^{+} implies that if σ is a transitive relation such that $\rho \subseteq \sigma$, then $\rho^{+} \subseteq \sigma$. Therefore, $\rho^{+} \subseteq \tau$.

Conversely, since $\rho \subseteq \rho^{+}$ we have $\rho^{n} \subseteq (\rho^{+})^{n}$ for every $n \in \mathbb{N}$. The transitivity of ρ^{+} implies that $(\rho^{+})^{n} \subseteq \rho^{+}$, which implies $\rho^{n} \subseteq \rho^{+}$ for every $n \geqslant 1$. Consequently, $\tau = \bigcup\{\rho^{n} \mid n \in \mathbb{N} \text{ and } n \geqslant 1\} \subseteq \rho^{+}$. This proves the equality of the theorem. $\square$

It is easy to see that the set of all reflexive and transitive relations on a set S, $REFTRAN(S)$, is also a closure system on the set of relations on S.

For a relation ρ on S, define ρ^* as $\mathbf{K}_{REFTRAN(S)}(\rho)$. The relation ρ^* is called the *transitive-reflexive closure* of ρ and is *the least transitive and reflexive relation* containing ρ. We have the following analog of Theorem 1.29.

Theorem 1.30. *Let ρ be a relation on a set S. We have*

$$\rho^* = \bigcup \{\rho^n \mid n \in \mathbb{N}\}.$$

Proof. The argument is very similar to the proof of Theorem 1.29; we leave it to the reader. $\qquad\square$

Definition 1.39. Let S be a set and let F be a set of operations on S. A subset P of S is *closed under F*, or *F-closed*, if P is closed under f for every $f \in F$; that is, for every operation $f \in F$, if f is n-ary and $p_0, \ldots, p_{n-1} \in P$, then $f(p_0, \ldots, p_{n-1}) \in P$.

Note that S itself is closed under F. Further, if $\mathcal{C}$ is a non-empty collection of F-closed subsets of S, then $\bigcap \mathcal{C}$ is also F-closed.

Example 1.24. Let F be a set of operations on a set S. The collection of all F-closed subsets of a set S is a closure system.

Definition 1.40. An *interior operator* on a set S is a mapping $\mathbf{I} : \mathcal{P}(S) \longrightarrow \mathcal{P}(S)$ that satisfies the following conditions:
   (i) $U \supseteq \mathbf{I}(U)$ *(contraction)*,
   (ii) $U \supseteq V$ implies $\mathbf{I}(U) \supseteq \mathbf{I}(V)$ *(monotonicity)*, and
   (iii) $\mathbf{I}(\mathbf{I}(U)) = \mathbf{I}(U)$ *(idempotency)*,
for $U, V \in \mathcal{P}(S)$. Such a mapping is known as an *interior operator on the set S*.

Interior operators define certain collections of sets.

Definition 1.41. An *interior system on a set S* is a collection $\mathcal{I}$ of subsets of S such that
   (i) $\emptyset \in \mathcal{I}$ and,
   (ii) for every subcollection $\mathcal{D}$ of $\mathcal{I}$ we have $\bigcup \mathcal{D} \in \mathcal{I}$.

Theorem 1.31. *Let $\mathbf{I} : \mathcal{P}(S) \longrightarrow \mathcal{P}(S)$ be an interior operator. Define the family of sets $\mathcal{I}_{\mathbf{I}} = \{U \in \mathcal{P}(S) \mid U = \mathbf{I}(U)\}$. Then, $\mathcal{I}_{\mathbf{I}}$ is an interior system on S.*

Conversely, if $\mathcal{I}$ is an interior system on the set S, define the mapping $\mathbf{I}_{\mathcal{I}} : \mathcal{P}(S) \longrightarrow \mathcal{P}(S)$ by $\mathbf{I}_{\mathcal{I}}(U) = \bigcup \{V \in \mathcal{I} \mid V \subseteq U\}$. Then, $\mathbf{I}_{\mathcal{I}}$ is an interior operator on the set S.

Moreover, for every interior system $\mathfrak{I}$ on S, we have $\mathfrak{I} = \mathfrak{I}_{I_\mathfrak{I}}$. For every interior operator $\boldsymbol{I}$ on S, we have $\boldsymbol{I} = \boldsymbol{I}_{\mathfrak{I}_I}$.

Proof.   This statement follows by duality from Lemmas 1.2 and 1.3 and from Theorem 1.28.   □

We refer to the sets in $\mathfrak{I}_\mathbf{I}$ as the *$\boldsymbol{I}$-open subsets* of S.

Theorem 1.32. *Let $\boldsymbol{K} : \mathcal{P}(S) \longrightarrow \mathcal{P}(S)$ be a closure operator on the set S. Then, the mapping $\boldsymbol{I} : \mathcal{P}(S) \longrightarrow \mathcal{P}(S)$ given by $\boldsymbol{I}(U) = S - \boldsymbol{K}(S - U)$ for $U \in \mathcal{P}(S)$ is an interior operator on S.*

Proof.   Since $S - U \subseteq \boldsymbol{K}(S-U)$, it follows that $\boldsymbol{I}(U) \subseteq S - (S-U) = U$, which proves property (i) of Definition 1.41.

Suppose that $U \subseteq V$, where $U, V \in \mathcal{P}(S)$. Then, we have $S - V \subseteq S - U$, so $\boldsymbol{K}(S - V) \subseteq \boldsymbol{K}(S - U)$ by the monotonicity of closure operators. Therefore,

$$\boldsymbol{I}(U) = S - \boldsymbol{K}(S - U) \subseteq S - \boldsymbol{K}(S - V) = \boldsymbol{I}(V),$$

which proves the monotonicity of $\boldsymbol{I}$.

Finally, observe that we have $\boldsymbol{I}(\boldsymbol{I}(U)) \subseteq \boldsymbol{I}(U)$ because of the contraction property already proven for $\boldsymbol{I}$. Thus, we need only show that $\boldsymbol{I}(U) \subseteq \boldsymbol{I}(\boldsymbol{I}(U))$ to prove the idempotency of $\boldsymbol{I}$. This inclusion follows immediately from

$$\boldsymbol{I}(\boldsymbol{I}(U)) = \boldsymbol{I}(S - \boldsymbol{K}(S - U)) \supseteq \boldsymbol{I}(S - (S - U)) = \boldsymbol{I}(U).$$ □

We can prove that if $\boldsymbol{I}$ is an interior operator on a set S, then $\boldsymbol{K} : \mathcal{P}(S) \longrightarrow \mathcal{P}(S)$ defined as $\boldsymbol{K}(U) = S - \boldsymbol{I}(S - U)$ for $U \in \mathcal{P}(S)$ is a closure operator on the same set.

1.7   Algebras and σ-Algebras of Sets

Definition 1.42. Let S be a non-empty set. An *algebra of sets* on S is a non-empty collection $\mathcal{E}$ of subsets of S such that:

(i) if $U \in \mathcal{E}$, then its complement $\overline{U} = S - U$ belongs to $\mathcal{E}$;
(ii) if $U_1, \ldots, U_n$ belong to $\mathcal{E}$, then $\bigcup_{i=1}^n U_i \in \mathcal{E}$.

In other words, a non-empty family of subsets of S, $\mathcal{E}$, is an algebra of sets on S, it is closed with respect to complement and to finite unions.

Every algebra of sets $\mathcal{E}$ on a set S contains both S and $\emptyset$. Indeed, since $\mathcal{E}$ is non-empty, there exists $T \in \mathcal{E}$. Therefore, $\overline{T} \in \mathcal{E}$ and this implies $S = T \cup \overline{T} \in \mathcal{E}$. Therefore, $\emptyset = \overline{S} \in \mathcal{E}$.

Example 1.25. The collection $\mathcal{E}_0 = \{\emptyset, S\}$ is an algebra on S; moreover, as we saw, every algebra $\mathcal{E}$ on S contains $\mathcal{E}_0$.

The set $\mathcal{P}(S)$ of all subsets of a set S is an algebra on S.

If T is a subset of S, then the collection $\mathcal{E}(T) = \{\emptyset, T, S - T, S\}$ is a algebra on S referred to as the *algebra generated by T*.

An algebra of sets $\mathcal{E}$ on S is closed with respect to finite intersections because

$$\bigcap_{i=1}^{n} A_i = S - \left(\bigcup_{i=1}^{n} (S - A_i) \right).$$

The difference $A - B$ of two sets in $\mathcal{E}$ belongs to $\mathcal{E}$ because $A - B = A \cap \overline{B}$.

A very important type of algebras of sets that play a central role in measure theory is introduced next.

Definition 1.43. A *σ-algebra of sets* on S is a non-empty family of subsets $\mathcal{E}$ of S such that

    (i) if $A \in \mathcal{E}$, then its complement $\overline{A} = S - A$ belongs to $\mathcal{E}$;

    (ii) if $\{A_n \mid n \in \mathbb{N}\}$ is a countable collection of subsets of S that belong to $\mathcal{E}$, then $\bigcup_{n \in \mathbb{N}} A_n \in \mathcal{E}$.

It is clear that every σ-algebra is also an algebra on S.

Example 1.26. Let S be an arbitrary set and let $\mathcal{C}$ be the family of sets that consist of sets that either countable or are complements of countable sets. We claim that $(S, \mathcal{C})$ is a measurable space.

Note that $S \in \mathcal{C}$ because S is the complement of $\emptyset$, which is countable. Next, if $A \in \mathcal{C}$ is countable, $\overline{A}$ is a complement of a countable set, so $\overline{A} \in \mathcal{C}$; otherwise, if A is not countable, then it is the complement of a countable set, which means that $\overline{A}$ is countable, so $\overline{A} \in \mathcal{C}$.

Let A, B be two sets of $\mathcal{C}$. If both are countable, then $A \cup B \in \mathcal{C}$. If $\overline{A}$ and $\overline{B}$ are countable, then $\overline{A \cup B} = \overline{A} \cap \overline{B}$, so $A \cup B \in \mathcal{C}$, because it has a countable complement. If A is countable and $\overline{B}$ is countable, then $\overline{A} \cap \overline{B}$ is countable because is a subset of $\overline{B}$. Therefore, $A \cup B \in \mathcal{C}$ as a complement of a countable sets. The case when $\overline{A}$ and B are countable is treated similarly. Thus, in any case, the union of two sets of $\mathcal{C}$ belongs to $\mathcal{C}$.

Finally, we have to prove that if $\{A_i \mid i \in \mathbb{N}\}$ is a family of sets included in $\mathcal{C}$, then the set $A = \bigcup_{i \in \mathbb{N}} A_i$ belongs to $\mathcal{C}$. Indeed, let us split the set I into I' and I'', where $i \in I'$ if the set A_i is countable and $i \in I''$ if the complement $\overline{A_i} = S - A_i$ is countable. Note that both $A' = \bigcup_{i \in I'} A_i$ and

$A'' = \bigcap_{i \in I''} \overline{A_i}$ are countable sets, and that $A = A' \cup \overline{A''}$. Since both A' and $\overline{A''}$ belong to $\mathcal{C}$, it follows that $A \in \mathcal{C}$.

We give now a technical result that concerns σ-algebras.

Theorem 1.33. *Let $(S, \mathcal{E})$ be a measurable space and let $\{U_i \in \mathcal{E} \mid i \in \mathbb{N}\}$ a family of sets from $\mathcal{E}$. There exists a family of sets $\{V_i \in \mathcal{E} \mid i \in \mathbb{N}\} \subseteq \mathcal{E}$ that satisfies the following conditions:*

  (i) *the sets V_i are pairwise disjoint, that is, if $i, j \in \mathbb{N}$ and $i \neq j$, then $V_i \cap V_j = \emptyset$;*
  (ii) *$V_i \subseteq U_i$ for $i \in \mathbb{N}$;*
  (iii) *$\bigcup\{V_i \mid i \in \mathbb{N}\} = \bigcup\{U_i \mid i \in \mathbb{N}\}$.*

Proof.   The sets V_n are defined inductively by:

$$V_0 = U_0,$$
$$V_i = U_i - \bigcup\{U_j \mid 0 \leqslant j \leqslant i - 1\}.$$

It is immediate that $V_i \in \mathcal{E}$ for $i \in \mathbb{N}$ and that the first two conditions of the theorem are satisfied; we prove the last part of the theorem.

For $x \in \bigcup\{U_i \mid i \in \mathbb{N}\}$ let i_x be the least i such that $x \in U_i$; clearly, $x \notin U_j$ for $j < i$, so $x \in V_i$. Thus, $\bigcup\{U_i \mid i \in \mathbb{N}\} \subseteq \bigcup\{V_i \mid i \in \mathbb{N}\}$. The reverse inclusion follows from the fact that $V_i \subseteq U_i$ for every $i \in \mathbb{N}$. $\square$

Next, we describe the σ-algebra generated by a countable partition of a set.

Theorem 1.34. *Let $\pi = \{B_i \mid i \in I\}$ be a countable partition of a set S. In other words we assume that the set of indices I of the blocks of π is countable.*

The σ-algebra generated by π is the collection of sets:

$$\mathcal{E}_\pi = \left\{ \bigcup_{i \in J} B_i \mid J \subseteq I \right\}.$$

Proof.   We have:

$$\pi \subseteq \{\bigcup_{i \in J} B_i \mid J \subseteq I\} \subseteq \mathcal{E}_\pi.$$

We claim that the collection $\mathcal{E} = \{\bigcup_{i \in J} B_i \mid J \subseteq I\}$ is a σ-algebra. Indeed, we have $S = \bigcup\{B \mid B \in \pi\}$, so $S \in \{\bigcup_{i \in J} B_i \mid J \subseteq I\}$. If $A = \bigcup\{B_i \mid i \in J\}$, then $\bar{A} = \{B_i \mid i \in I - J\}$, which shows that $\bar{A} \in \{\bigcup_{i \in J} B_i \mid J \subseteq I\}$.

Finally, suppose that $A_0, \ldots, A_n, \ldots$ belong to $\mathcal{E}$, so $A_k = \bigcup\{B_i \mid i \in J_k\}$, where $J_k \subseteq I$ for $k \in \mathbb{N}$. Then, $\bigcup_{k \geqslant 0} A_k = \bigcup\{B_i \mid i \in \bigcup_{k \geqslant 0} J_k\}$, which implies that $\bigcup_{k \geqslant 0} A_k \in \{\bigcup_{i \in J} B_i \mid J \subseteq I\}$. Thus, $\mathcal{E}$ is a σ-algebra, so $\mathcal{E}_\pi \subseteq \mathcal{E}$. The converse inclusion is immediate, so $\mathcal{E} = \mathcal{E}_\pi$, which completes the argument. $\square$

Theorem 1.35. *Every σ-algebra $\mathcal{E}$ is a monotone collection.*

Proof. Let (C_n) be an increasing sequence of sets in $\mathcal{E}$. We have $\bigcup_{n \in \mathbb{N}} C_n \in \mathcal{E}$ by the definition of σ-algebras.

If (D_n) is a decreasing sequence of sets in $\mathcal{E}$, then $(S - D_n)$ is an increasing sequence in $\mathcal{E}$, so by the first part, $\bigcup_{n \in \mathbb{N}}(S - D_n) \in \mathcal{E}$. This implies

$$\bigcap_{n \in \mathbb{N}} D_n = \overline{\bigcup_{n \in \mathbb{N}}(S - D_n)} \in \mathcal{E},$$

hence $\mathcal{E}$ is indeed a monotone collection. $\square$

Theorem 1.36. *An algebra of sets on a set S that is a monotone collection is a σ-algebra on S.*

Proof. Let $\mathcal{E}$ be an algebra of sets on a set S and let $\{U_j \mid j \in \mathbb{N}\}$ be a countable family of sets included in $\mathcal{E}$. Define the sequence $\mathbf{W} = (W_0, W_1, \ldots)$ by $W_n = \bigcup_{j=0}^{n} U_j$. It is immediate that $\mathbf{W}$ is a monotone sequence and that $\bigcup_{j \in \mathbb{N}} U_j = \bigcup_{j \in \mathbb{N}} W_j$. Since $\mathcal{E}$ is a monotone collection it follows that $\bigcup_{j \in \mathbb{N}} W_j \in \mathcal{E}$, so $\bigcup_{j \in \mathbb{N}} U_j$ belongs to $\mathcal{E}$, so $\mathcal{E}$ is a σ-algebra. $\square$

Theorem 1.37. *Let $\mathfrak{E}$ be a collection of algebras (σ-algebras) of sets on a set S. Then, the collection $\bigcap \mathfrak{E}$ is a an algebra (a σ-algebra) on the set S.*

Proof. We give the argument for a collection of algebras of sets $\mathfrak{E} = \{\mathcal{E}_i \mid i \in I\}$ on S. Since $S \in \mathcal{E}_i$ for every $i \in I$ it follows that $S \in \bigcap\{\mathcal{E}_i \mid i \in I\}$.

Suppose that $A \in \bigcap \mathfrak{E}$. Since $A \in \mathcal{E}_i$ for every $i \in I$ it follows that $\bar{A} \in \mathcal{E}_i$ for every $i \in I$, which implies that $\bar{A} \in \bigcap\{\mathcal{E}_i \mid i \in I\}$.

Finally, if $\{A_i \mid 1 \leqslant i \leqslant n\} \in \bigcap\{\mathcal{E}_i \mid i \in I\}$, it is easy to see that $\bigcup_{i=1}^{n} A_i \in \bigcap\{\mathcal{E}_i \mid i \in I\}$.

A similar argument can be applied to σ-algebras. $\square$

Thus, the class of algebras and the class of σ-algebras define closure systems on $\mathcal{P}(\mathcal{P}(S))$. We denote by $\mathbf{K}_{\text{alg}}$ and $\mathbf{K}_{\sigma\text{-alg}}$ the closure operators generated by these two classes, respectively.

By the properties of closure operators, if $\mathcal{C}$ is a collection of subsets of S, $\mathbf{K}_{\text{alg}}(\mathcal{C})$ and $\mathbf{K}_{\sigma\text{-alg}}(\mathcal{C})$ are the algebra and the σ-algebra generated by $\mathcal{C}$, respectively. Consequently, if $\mathcal{C} \subseteq \mathbf{K}_{\sigma\text{-alg}}(\mathcal{C}')$, we have $\mathbf{K}_{\sigma\text{-alg}}(\mathcal{C}) \subseteq \mathbf{K}_{\sigma\text{-alg}}(\mathcal{C}')$.

Example 1.27. Let A be a subset of the set S. The σ-algebra generated by the collection $\{A\}$ is $\{\emptyset, A, \bar{A}, S\}$.

Example 1.28. Let $\pi = \{B_i \mid i \in I\}$ be a countable partition of a set S. The σ-algebra generated by π is:

$$\mathcal{E}_\pi = \left\{ \bigcup_{i \in J} B_i \,\middle|\, J \subseteq I \right\}.$$

In other words, the σ-algebra generated by π consists of sets that are countable unions of blocks of π. Such sets are referred to as π-*saturated* sets.

Every block B_i belongs to $\mathcal{E}_\pi$, so $\pi \subseteq \mathcal{E}_\pi$.

To verify that $\mathcal{E}_\pi$ is a σ-algebra note first that we have $S \in \mathcal{E}_\pi$ since $S = \bigcup_{i \in I} B_i$. If $A \in \mathcal{E}_{pi}$, then $A = \bigcup_{i \in J} B_i$ for some subset J of I, so $\bar{A} = \bigcup_{i \in I - J} B_i$, which shows that $\bar{A} \in \mathcal{E}_\pi$. Let $\{A_\ell \mid \ell \in L\}$ be a family of sets included in $\mathcal{E}_\pi$. For each set A_ℓ there exists a set J_ℓ such that $A_\ell = \bigcup \{B_i \mid i \in J_\ell\}$. Therefore,

$$\bigcup_{\ell \in L} A_\ell = \bigcup \left\{ B_i \,\middle|\, i \in \bigcup_{\ell \in L} J_\ell \right\},$$

which shows that $\bigcup_{\ell \in L} A_\ell \in \mathcal{E}_\pi$. This proves that $\mathcal{E}_\pi$ is a σ-algebra. Moreover, any σ-algebra on S that includes π also includes $\mathcal{E}_\pi$, which concludes the argument.

If π is a finite partition of S, then the algebra generated by π consists of unions of blocks of π.

For a subset U of a set S and $a \in \{0, 1\}$ denote by U^a the set:

$$U^a = \begin{cases} U & \text{if } a = 1, \\ S - U & \text{if } a = 0. \end{cases}$$

This notation allows us to generalize Example 1.28.

Theorem 1.38. *Let S be a set and let $\mathcal{U} = \{U_1, \ldots, U_n\}$ be a finite collection of subsets of S. For $(a_1, \ldots, a_n) \in \{0, 1\}^n$ denote by $U^{a_1 \cdots a_n}$ the set*

$$U^{a_1 \cdots a_n} = U_1^{a_1} \cap \cdots \cap U_n^{a_n}.$$

If $\mathcal{E}$ is the algebra of sets generated by $\mathcal{U}$, then the collection

$$\mathcal{A} = \{U^{a_1 \cdots a_n} \mid U_{a_1 \cdots a_n} \neq \emptyset\},$$

is the set of minimal non-empty elements of $\mathcal{E}$ and every element of $\mathcal{E}$ is a union of a subcollection of $\mathcal{A}$.

Proof. Observe that any two distinct sets in $\mathcal{A}$ are disjoint and that $\bigcup \mathcal{A} = S$. In other words, $\mathcal{A}$ is a partition of S. Therefore, the set of all unions of subcollections of $\mathcal{A}$ is a algebra of sets $\mathcal{E}'$ that contains each of the sets B_i. Therefore, $\mathcal{E} \subseteq \mathcal{E}'$. On the other hand, we have $\mathcal{E}' \subseteq \mathcal{E}$, so $\mathcal{E} = \mathcal{E}'$. $\qquad\square$

Theorem 1.39. (Monotone Collection Theorem) *If $\mathcal{A}$ is an algebra of subsets of a set S, then $\boldsymbol{K}_{\mathrm{mon}}(\mathcal{A}) = \boldsymbol{K}_{\sigma\text{-alg}}(\mathcal{A})$.*

Proof. Since every σ-algebra is a monotone class we need to prove that $\mathcal{C} = \boldsymbol{K}_{\mathrm{mon}}(\mathcal{A})$ is a σ-algebra.

For $C \in \mathcal{C}$ define

$$\mathcal{M}(C) = \{B \in \mathcal{C} \mid C \cap B, C - B, B - C \in \mathcal{C}\}.$$

If (B_n) is an ascending sequence in $\mathcal{M}(C)$ and $B = \bigcup_{n \in \mathbb{N}} B_n$ we have

$$\bigcup_{n \in \mathbb{N}} (C \cap B_n) = C \cap B,$$

$$\bigcup_{n \in \mathbb{N}} (B_n - C) = B - C,$$

$$\bigcap_{n \in \mathbb{N}} (C - B_n) = C - B,$$

which show that $\mathcal{M}(C)$ is a monotone collection. Since $\mathcal{C}$ is a monotone collection, it follows that $C \cap B, C - B, B - C \in \mathcal{C}$, so $B \in \mathcal{M}(C)$, which means $\mathcal{M}(C)$ is a monotone class for all $C \in \mathcal{C}$.

If $A \in \mathcal{A} \subseteq \mathcal{C}$, we have $A \cap B, A - B, B - A \in \mathcal{A} \subseteq \mathcal{C}$ for all $B \in \mathcal{A}$, hence $\mathcal{A} \subseteq \mathcal{M}(A) \subseteq \mathcal{C}$. Since $\mathcal{C} = \boldsymbol{K}_{\mathrm{mon}}(\mathcal{A})$, we have $\mathcal{M}(A) = \mathcal{C}$ for every $A \in \mathcal{A}$.

Let $B \in \mathcal{C}$. Note that $A \in \mathcal{M}(B)$ if and only of $B \in \mathcal{M}(A)$. Therefore, since $\mathcal{M}(A) = \mathcal{C}$ for all $A \in \mathcal{A}$ implies $\mathcal{A} \subseteq \mathcal{M}(B) \subseteq \mathcal{C}$ for all $B \in \mathcal{C}$. Since $\mathcal{C} = \boldsymbol{K}_{\mathrm{mon}}(\mathcal{A})$ and $\mathcal{M}(B)$ is a monotone class, we conclude that $\mathcal{M}(B) = \mathcal{C}$ for all $B \in \mathcal{C}$. Therefore, $\mathcal{C}$ is closed under complements (since $S \in \mathcal{A} \subseteq \mathcal{C}$), finite intersections and countable unions, which implies that $\mathcal{C}$ is a σ-algebra. $\qquad\square$

Definition 1.44. Let $\mathcal{C}$ be a collection of sets and let T be a set. The *restriction* of $\mathcal{C}$ to T is the collection $\mathcal{C}\restriction_T$ defined by:

$$\mathcal{C}\restriction_T = \{C \cap T \mid C \in \mathcal{C}\}.$$

Theorem 1.40. *Let $\mathcal{E}$ be a σ-algebra of subsets of a set S and let T be a non-empty subset of S. The collection*

$$\mathcal{E}\restriction_T = \{U \cap T \mid U \in \mathcal{E}\}$$

is a σ-algebra of subsets of T.

Proof. Let $A \in \mathcal{E}\restriction_T$. There exists $E \in \mathcal{E}$ such that $A = E \cap T$, hence

$$T - A = T \cap \overline{A} = T \cap (\overline{E} \cup T) = T \cap \overline{E} \in \mathcal{E}\restriction_T$$

because $\overline{E} \in \mathcal{E}$.

Suppose now that $\{A_n \mid n \in \mathbb{N}\}$ is a countable collection of sets in $\mathcal{E}\restriction_T$. There exists a countable collection of sets $\{E_n \mid n \in \mathbb{N}\} \subseteq \mathcal{E}$ such that $A_n = E_n \cap T$. Therefore,

$$\bigcup_{n \in \mathbb{N}} A_n = \bigcup_{n \in \mathbb{N}} (E_n \cap T) = \left(\bigcup_{n \in \mathbb{N}} E_n\right) \cap T \in \mathcal{E}\restriction_T$$

because $\bigcup_{n \in \mathbb{N}} E_n \in \mathcal{E}$. $\qquad\square$

Corollary 1.3. *Let $\mathcal{C}$ be a collection of subsets of a set S and let T be a non-empty subset of S. We have $\mathbf{K}_{\sigma\text{-alg}}(\mathcal{C}\restriction_T) = \mathbf{K}_{\sigma\text{-alg}}(\mathcal{C})\restriction_T$.*

Proof. It is immediate that $\mathcal{C}\restriction_T \subseteq \mathbf{K}_{\sigma\text{-alg}}(\mathcal{C})\restriction_T$. This implies

$$\mathbf{K}_{\sigma\text{-alg}}(\mathcal{C}\restriction_T) \subseteq \mathbf{K}_{\sigma\text{-alg}}(\mathcal{C})\restriction_T.$$

Let $\mathcal{S} = \{U \subseteq S \mid U \cap T \in \mathbf{K}_{\sigma\text{-alg}}(\mathcal{C}\restriction_T)\}$. We claim that $\mathcal{S}$ is a σ-algebra of subsets of S.

Suppose that $U \in \mathcal{S}$, so $U \cap T \in \mathbf{K}_{\sigma\text{-alg}}(\mathcal{C}\restriction_T)$. Since $(S - U) \cap T = T - (U \cap T) \in \mathbf{K}_{\sigma\text{-alg}}(\mathcal{C}\restriction_T)$, it follows that $S - U \in \mathbf{K}_{\sigma\text{-alg}}(\mathcal{C}\restriction_T)$.

Suppose now that $U_1, U_2, \ldots$ is a sequence of sets in $\mathcal{S}$, hence $U_1 \cap T, U_2 \cap T, \ldots$ is a sequence of sets in $\mathbf{K}_{\sigma\text{-alg}}(\mathcal{C}\restriction_T)$. Therefore,

$$\left(\bigcup_{n \geqslant 1} U_n\right) \cap T = \bigcup_{n \geqslant 1} (U_n \cap T) \in \mathbf{K}_{\sigma\text{-alg}}(\mathcal{C}\restriction_T),$$

hence $\bigcup_{n \geqslant 1} U_n \in \mathcal{S}$, so $\mathcal{S}$ is indeed a σ-algebra.

If $U \in \mathcal{C}$, then $U \cap T \in \mathcal{C}\restriction_T \subseteq \mathbf{K}_{\sigma\text{-alg}}(\mathcal{C}\restriction_T)$, hence $U \in \mathcal{S}$. Therefore, $\mathcal{C} \subseteq \mathcal{S}$, hence $\mathbf{K}_{\sigma\text{-alg}}(\mathcal{C}) \subseteq \mathcal{S}$.

If $B \in \mathbf{K}_{\sigma\text{-alg}}(\mathcal{C})\restriction_T$ we have $B = A \cap T$ for some $A \in \mathbf{K}_{\sigma\text{-alg}}(\mathcal{C}) \subseteq \mathcal{S}$ and, therefore, $B \in \mathbf{K}_{\sigma\text{-alg}}(\mathcal{C}\restriction_T)$. This yields

$$\mathbf{K}_{\sigma\text{-alg}}(\mathcal{C})\restriction_T \subseteq \mathbf{K}_{\sigma\text{-alg}}(\mathcal{C}\restriction_T). \qquad\square$$

Definition 1.45. Let S be a set. A π-*system on* S is a collection of sets $\mathcal{C}$ such that $U, V \in \mathcal{C}$ implies $U \cap V \in \mathcal{C}$.

A *Dynkin system* on a set S is a collection $\mathcal{D}$ of subsets of S that satisfies the following conditions:

(i) $S \in \mathcal{D}$,

(ii) $U, V \in \mathcal{D}$ and $U \subseteq V$ implies $V - U \in \mathcal{D}$;

(iii) if $\mathbf{T} = (T_0, T_1, \ldots)$ is an increasing sequence of subsets of S that belong to $\mathcal{D}$, then $\bigcup_{i \in \mathbb{N}} T_i$ belongs to $\mathcal{D}$.

Example 1.29. The collections of subsets of $\hat{\mathbb{R}}$:

$$\mathcal{I} = \{(a, b) \mid a, b \in \hat{\mathbb{R}}, -\infty \leqslant a \leqslant b \leqslant \infty\},$$
$$\mathcal{G} = \{(a, b] \mid a, b \in \hat{\mathbb{R}}, -\infty \leqslant a \leqslant b < \infty\},$$
$$\mathcal{H} = \{[a, b) \mid a, b \in \hat{\mathbb{R}}, -\infty < a \leqslant b \leqslant \infty\},$$
$$\mathcal{K} = \{[a, b] \mid a, b \in \hat{\mathbb{R}}, -\infty < a \leqslant b < \infty\},$$

are π-systems. Indeed, if $(a, b), (c, d) \in \mathcal{I}$, then $(a, b) \cap (c, d) = (\min\{a, c\}, \max\{b, d\}) \in \mathcal{I}$. Similar observations can be made about the other collections.

Theorem 1.41. *A collection $\mathcal{D}$ of subsets of a set S is a Dynkin system if and only if the following conditions are satisfied:*

(i) $S \in \mathcal{D}$;

(ii) *if $U \in \mathcal{D}$, then $\overline{U} = S - U$ belongs to $\mathcal{D}$;*

(iii) *if $\mathbf{U} = (U_0, U_1, \ldots)$ is a sequence of pairwise disjoint subsets of S that belong to $\mathcal{D}$, then $\bigcup_{n \in \mathbb{N}} U_n$ belongs to $\mathcal{D}$.*

Proof. Let $\mathcal{D}$ be a Dynkin system on S. Since $S \in \mathcal{D}$ and $U \subseteq S$ for each $U \in \mathcal{D}$, it follows that $S - U = \overline{U} \in \mathcal{D}$. Let $\mathbf{U} = (U_0, U_1, \ldots)$ is a sequence of pairwise disjoint subsets of S that belong to $\mathcal{D}$, and let $V_n = \bigcup_{k \leqslant n}$ for $n \in \mathbb{N}$. It is clear that $\bigcup_{n \in \mathbb{N}} U_n = \bigcup_{n \in \mathbb{N}} V_n$ and, since (V_n) is an increasing sequence of sets in $\mathcal{D}$, it follows that $\bigcup_{n \in \mathbb{N}} U_n \in \mathcal{D}$.

Conversely, suppose now that $\mathcal{D}$ satisfies the conditions of the theorem. If $U, V \in \mathcal{D}$ and $U \subseteq V$, then U and $\overline{V}$ are two disjoint sets, so $U \cup \overline{V} \in \mathcal{D}$ by the third condition of the theorem. Therefore, $\overline{U \cup \overline{V}} = V - U$ belongs to S. Finally, suppose that $(T_0, T_1, \ldots)$ is an increasing sequence of subsets of S that belong to $\mathcal{D}$. Then, the sequence $(T_0, T_1 - T_2, T_2 - T_3, \ldots)$ is a sequence of disjoint sets that belong to $\mathcal{D}$, hence the set $T_0 \cup \bigcup_{n \geqslant 0}(T_{n+1} - T_n) = \bigcup_{n \geqslant 0} T_n$ belongs to $\mathcal{D}$. Thus, $\mathcal{D}$ is indeed a Dynkin system. $\square$

It is easy to verify that the collection of π-systems and the collection of Dynkin systems on a set S are both closure systems. Their corresponding closure operators are denoted by $\mathbf{K}_\pi$ and $\mathbf{K}_{\mathrm{Dyn}}$, respectively.

Theorem 1.42. *If $\mathcal{C}$ is a π-system on a set S, then $\mathbf{K}_{\sigma\text{-alg}}(\mathcal{C}) = \mathbf{K}_{\mathrm{Dyn}}(\mathcal{C})$.*

Proof.   Let $\mathcal{D} = \mathbf{K}_{\mathrm{Dyn}}(\mathcal{C})$ and let $\mathcal{E} = \mathbf{K}_{\sigma\text{-alg}}(\mathcal{C})$. Since a σ-algebra is a Dynkin system, it follows that $\mathcal{D} \subseteq \mathcal{E}$.

To prove the reverse inclusion, we begin by showing that $\mathcal{D} = \mathbf{K}_{\mathrm{Dyn}}(\mathcal{C})$ is closed with respect to finite intersections.

Consider the collections of sets defined by

$$\mathcal{D}_1 = \{A \in \mathcal{D} \mid A \cap C \in \mathcal{D} \text{ for each } C \in \mathcal{C}\}, \text{ and}$$
$$\mathcal{D}_2 = \{B \in \mathcal{D} \mid B \cap A \in \mathcal{D} \text{ for each } A \in \mathcal{D}\}.$$

We have $\mathcal{D} \subset \mathcal{D}_1$ and $\mathcal{D} \subset \mathcal{D}_2$ and both $\mathcal{D}_1$ and $\mathcal{D}_2$ are Dynkin systems.

Since $\mathcal{C} \subseteq \mathcal{D}$, $S \in \mathcal{D}_1$. Taking into account that

$$(A - B) \cap C = (A \cap C) - (B \cap C)$$

$$\left(\bigcup_{n \in \mathbb{N}} A_n \right) \cap C = \bigcup_{n \in \mathbb{N}} (A_n \cap C),$$

it follows that $\mathcal{D}_1$ is closed with respect to set difference and to unions of increasing sequences of sets, so it is a Dynkin system.

Since $\mathcal{C} \subseteq \mathcal{D}_1$, it follows that $\mathcal{D} = \mathbf{K}_{\mathrm{Dyn}}(\mathcal{C}) \subseteq \mathcal{D}_1$, which implies $\mathcal{D} = \mathcal{D}_1$ because $\mathcal{D}_1$ consists of sets that belong to $\mathcal{D}$. Thus, $\mathcal{D}_1$ is a Dynkin system. The equality $\mathcal{D}_1 = \mathcal{D}$ implies that $\mathcal{C} \subseteq \mathcal{D}_2$.

By an argument similar to the one used for $\mathcal{D}_1$, it follows that $\mathcal{D}_2$ is a Dynkin system, and then, $\mathcal{D}_2 = \mathcal{D}$. Thus, $\mathcal{D}$ is closed under finite intersections and, therefore, it is an algebra of sets. Since $\mathcal{D}$ is also a monotone collection it is also a σ-algebra that includes $\mathcal{C}$. Therefore, $\mathbf{K}_{\sigma\text{-alg}}(\mathcal{C}) \subseteq \mathcal{D}$, hence $\mathbf{K}_{\sigma\text{-alg}}(\mathcal{C}) = \mathcal{D}$. $\square$

Theorem 1.43. *A collection $\mathcal{C}$ of subsets of a set S is a σ-algebra of sets if and only if it is both a π-system and a Dynkin system.*

Proof.   If $\mathcal{C}$ is a σ-algebra, then it is clearly both a Dynkin system and a π-system.

Conversely, suppose that $\mathcal{C}$ is both a Dynkin system and a π-system, so $\mathbf{K}_{\mathrm{Dyn}}(\mathcal{C}) = \mathcal{C}$. By Theorem 1.42, we have $\mathcal{C} = \mathbf{K}_{\sigma\text{-alg}}(\mathcal{C})$, which means that $\mathcal{C}$ is a σ-algebra. $\square$

1.8 Dissimilarity and Metrics

The notion of a metric was introduced in mathematics by the French mathematician Maurice René Fréchet[3] in [58] as an abstraction of the notion of distance between two points. In this chapter, we explore the notion of metric and the related notion of metric space, as well as a number of generalizations and specializations of these notions.

Dissimilarities are functions that allow us to evaluate the extent to which data objects are different.

Definition 1.46. A *dissimilarity on a set S* is a function $d : S^2 \longrightarrow \mathbb{R}_{\geqslant 0}$ satisfying the following conditions:

  (i) $d(x, x) = 0$ for all $x \in S$;
  (ii) $d(x, y) = d(y, x)$ for all $x, y \in S$.

The pair (S, d) is a *dissimilarity space*.

The set of dissimilarities defined on a set S is denoted by $\mathcal{D}_S$.

Let (S, d) be a dissimilarity space and let $S(x, y)$ be the set of all non-null sequences $\mathbf{s} = (s_1, \ldots, s_n) \in \mathbf{Seq}(S)$ such that $s_1 = x$ and $s_n = y$. The *d-amplitude of $\mathbf{s}$* is the number $amp_d(\mathbf{s}) = \max\{d(s_i, s_{i+1}) \mid 1 \leqslant i \leqslant n-1\}$.

Next we introduce the notion of extended dissimilarity by allowing ∞ as a value of a dissimilarity.

Definition 1.47. Let S be a set. An *extended dissimilarity on S* is a function $d : S^2 \longrightarrow \hat{\mathbb{R}}_{\geqslant 0}$ that satisfies the conditions of Definition 1.46.

The pair (S, d) is an *extended dissimilarity space*.

Additional properties may be satisfied by dissimilarities. A non-exhaustive list is given next.

  (1) $d(x, y) = 0$ implies $d(x, z) = d(y, z)$ for every $x, y, z \in S$ (*evenness*);
  (2) $d(x, y) = 0$ implies $x = y$ for every x, y (*definiteness*);
  (3) $d(x, y) \leqslant d(x, z) + d(z, y)$ for every x, y, z (*triangular inequality*);
  (4) $d(x, y) \leqslant \max\{d(x, z), d(z, y)\}$ for every x, y, z (*the ultrametric inequality*);
  (5) $d(x, y) + d(u, v) \leqslant \max\{d(x, u) + d(y, v), d(x, v) + d(y, u)\}$ for every x, y, u, v (*Buneman's inequality*, also known as the *four-point condition*).

---

[3]Fréchet was born on September 2nd 1878 in Maligny, France and died on June 4th 1973 in Paris. He made major contributions in topology, introduced metric spaces, and is considered as one of the founders of modern analysis. Fréchet studied at the École Normale Supérieure and taught at the Universities of Poitieres, Strassbourg, and at Sorbonne.

If $d : S^2 \longrightarrow \mathbb{R}$ is a function that satisfies the properties of dissimilarities and the triangular inequality, then the values of d are non-negative numbers. Indeed, by taking $x = y$ in the triangular inequality, we have

$$0 = d(x, x) \leqslant d(x, z) + d(z, x) = 2d(x, z),$$

for every $z \in S$.

Various connections exist among these properties. As an example, we can show the following statement.

Theorem 1.44. *Both the triangular inequality and definiteness imply evenness.*

Proof.   Suppose that d is a dissimilarity that satisfies the triangular inequality, and let $x, y \in S$ be such that $d(x, y) = 0$. By the triangular inequality, we have both $d(x, z) \leqslant d(x, y) + d(y, z) = d(y, z)$ and $d(y, z) \leqslant d(y, x) + d(x, z) = d(x, z)$ because $d(y, x) = d(x, y) = 0$. Thus, $d(x, z) = d(y, z)$ for every $z \in S$.

We leave it to the reader to prove the second part of the statement. $\square$

We denote the set of definite dissimilarities on a set S by $\mathcal{D}'_S$. Further notations are introduced shortly for other types of dissimilarities.

Definition 1.48. A dissimilarity $d \in \mathcal{D}_S$ is
   (i) a *pseudo-metric* if it satisfies the triangular inequality;
   (ii) a *metric* if it satisfies the definiteness property and the triangular inequality;
   (iii) a *tree metric* if it satisfies the definiteness property and Buneman's inequality;
   (iv) an *ultrametric* if it satisfies the definiteness property and the ultrametric inequality.

The set of metrics on a set S is denoted by $\mathcal{M}_S$. The sets of tree metrics and ultrametrics on a set S are denoted by $\mathcal{T}_S$ and $\mathcal{U}_S$, respectively.

If d is a metric or an ultrametric on a set S, then (S, d) is a *metric space* or an *ultrametric space*, respectively.

If d is a metric defined on a set S and $x, y \in S$, we refer to the number $d(x, y)$ as the *d-distance* between x and y or simply the *distance* between x and y whenever d is clearly understood from context.

Thus, a function $d : S^2 \longrightarrow \mathbb{R}_{\geqslant 0}$ is a metric if it has the following properties:
   (i) $d(x, y) = 0$ if and only if $x = y$ for $x, y \in S$;

(ii) $d(x, y) = d(y, x)$ for $x, y \in S$;

(iii) $d(x, y) \leqslant d(x, z) + d(z, y)$ for $x, y, z \in S$.

If the first property is replaced by the weaker requirement that $d(x, x) = 0$ for $x \in S$, then we refer to d as a *semimetric* on S. Thus, if d is a semimetric $d(x, y) = 0$ does not necessarily imply $x = y$ and we can have for two distinct elements x, y of S, $d(x, y) = 0$.

The notions of extended metric and extended ultrametric are defined starting from the notion of extended dissimilarity using the same process as in the definitions of metrics and ultrametrics.

A collection of semimetrics on a set S is said to be a *gauge* on S.

Example 1.30. Let S be a non-empty set. Define the mapping $d : S^2 \longrightarrow \mathbb{R}_{\geqslant 0}$ by

$$d(u, v) = \begin{cases} 1 & \text{if } u \neq v, \\ 0 & \text{otherwise,} \end{cases}$$

for $x, y \in S$. It is clear that d satisfies the definiteness property. The triangular inequality, $d(x, y) \leqslant d(x, z) + d(z, y)$ is satisfied if $x = y$. Therefore, suppose that $x \neq y$, so $d(x, y) = 1$. Then, for every $z \in S$, we have at least one of the inequalities $x \neq z$ or $z \neq y$, so at least one of the numbers $d(x, z)$ or $d(z, y)$ equals 1. Thus d satisfies the triangular inequality. The metric d introduced here is the *discrete metric* on S.

Example 1.31. Consider the mapping $d_h : (\mathbf{Seq}_n(S))^2 \longrightarrow \mathbb{R}_{\geqslant 0}$ defined by

$$d_h(\mathbf{p}, \mathbf{q}) = |\{i \mid 0 \leqslant i \leqslant n - 1 \text{ and } \mathbf{p}(i) \neq \mathbf{q}(i)\}|$$

for all sequences $\mathbf{p}, \mathbf{q}$ of length n on the set S.

Clearly, d_h is a dissimilarity that is both even and definite. Moreover, it satisfies the triangular inequality. Indeed, let $\mathbf{p}, \mathbf{q}, \mathbf{r}$ be three sequences of length n on the set S. If $\mathbf{p}(i) \neq \mathbf{q}(i)$, then $\mathbf{r}(i)$ must be distinct from at least one of $\mathbf{p}(i)$ and $\mathbf{q}(i)$. Therefore,

$$\{i \mid 0 \leqslant i \leqslant n - 1 \text{ and } \mathbf{p}(i) \neq \mathbf{q}(i)\}$$
$$\subseteq \{i \mid 0 \leqslant i \leqslant n - 1 \text{ and } \mathbf{p}(i) \neq \mathbf{r}(i)\} \cup \{i \mid 0 \leqslant i \leqslant n - 1 \text{ and } \mathbf{r}(i) \neq \mathbf{q}(i)\},$$

which implies the triangular inequality. This is a rather rudimentary distance known as the *Hamming distance* on $\mathbf{Seq}_n(S)$. If we need to compare sequences of unequal length, we can use an extended metric d'_h defined by

$$d'_h(\mathbf{x}, \mathbf{y}) = \begin{cases} |\{i \mid 0 \leqslant i \leqslant |\mathbf{x}| - 1, x_i \neq y_i\} & \text{if } |\mathbf{x}| = |\mathbf{y}|, \\ \infty & \text{if } |\mathbf{x}| \neq |\mathbf{y}|. \end{cases}$$

Example 1.32. Define the mapping $d : \mathbb{R} \times \mathbb{R} \longrightarrow \mathbb{R}_{\geqslant 0}$ as $d(x, y) = |x - y|$ for $x, y \in \mathbb{R}$. It is clear that $d(x, y) = 0$ if and only if $x = y$ and that $d(x, y) = d(y, x)$ for $x, y \in S$;

To prove the triangular inequality suppose that $x \leqslant y \leqslant z$. Then, $d(x, z) + d(z, y) = z - x + z - y = 2z - x - y$ and we have $2z - x - y > y - x = d(x, y)$ because $z > y$. The triangular inequality is similarly satisfied no matter what the relative order of x, y, z is.

We use frequently use the notions of closed sphere and open sphere.

Definition 1.49. Let (S, d) be a metric space. The *closed sphere* centered in $x \in S$ of radius r is the set

$$B_d[x, r] = \{y \in S | d(x, y) \leqslant r\}.$$

The *open sphere* centered in $x \in S$ of radius r is the set

$$B_d(x, r) = \{y \in S | d(x, y) < r\}.$$

The *spherical surface* centered in $x \in S$ of radius r is the set

$$S_d(x, r) = \{y \in S \mid d(x, y) = r\}.$$

If the metric d is clear from context we drop the subscript d and replace $B_d[x, r]$, $B_d(x, r)$, and $S_d(x, r)$ by $B[x, r]$, $B(x, r)$, and $S_d(x, r)$, respectively.

Definition 1.50. Let (S, d) be a metric space. The *diameter* of a subset U of S is the number $diam_{S,d}(U) = \sup\{d(x, y) \mid x, y \in U\}$. The set U is *bounded* if $diam_{S,d}(U)$ is finite.

The *diameter* of the metric space (S, d) is the number

$$diam_{S,d} = \sup\{d(x, y) \mid x, y \in S\}.$$

If the metric space is clear from the context, then we denote the diameter of a subset U just by $diam(U)$.

If (S, d) is a finite metric space, then $diam_{S,d} = \max\{d(x, y) \mid x, y \in S\}$.

A notion close to the notion of dissimilarity is given next.

Definition 1.51. A *similarity on a set S* is a function $s : S^2 \longrightarrow [0, 1]$ satisfying the following conditions:

   (i) $s(x, x) = 1$ for all $x \in S$;
   (ii) $s(x, y) = s(y, x)$ for all $x, y \in S$.

If $s(x, y) = 1$ implies $x = y$, then s is a *definite similarity*.

The pair (S, s) is referred to a *similarity space*.

In other words, the similarity between an object x and itself is the largest; also, the similarity is symmetric.

Example 1.33. Let $d : S^2 \longrightarrow \mathbb{R}_{\geqslant 0}$ be a dissimilarity on S. The function $s : S^2 \longrightarrow [0,1]$ defined by $s(x,y) = e^{-\frac{d^2(x,y)}{2\sigma^2}}$ for $x, y \in S$ and $\sigma \in \mathbb{R}$ is easily seen to be a similarity. Note that s is definite if and only if d is definite.

Definition 1.52. Let (S, d) and (T, d') be two metric spaces. An *isometry* between these spaces is a function $f : S \longrightarrow T$ such that $d'(f(x), f(y)) = d(x, y)$ for every $x, y \in S$.

If an isometry exists between (S, d) and (T, d') we say that these metric spaces are *isometric*.

Note that if $f : S \longrightarrow T$ is an isometry, then $f(x) = f(y)$ implies $d(f(x), f(y)) = d(x, y) = 0$, which yields $x = y$ for $x, y \in S$. Therefore, every isometry is injective and a surjective isometry is a bijection.

1.9 Elementary Combinatorics

Definition 1.53. A *permutation* of a set S is a bijection $f : S \longrightarrow S$.

A permutation f of a finite set $S = \{s_0, \ldots, s_{n-1}\}$ is completely described by the sequence $(f(s_0), \ldots, f(s_{n-1}))$. No two distinct components of such a sequence may be equal because of the injectivity of f, and all elements of the set S appear in this sequence because f is surjective. Therefore, the number of permutations equals the number of such sequences, which allows us to conclude that there are $n(n-1) \cdots 2 \cdot 1$ permutations of a finite set S with $|S| = n$.

The number $n(n-1) \cdots 2 \cdot 1$ is denoted by $n!$. This notation is extended by defining $0! = 1$ to capture the fact that there exists exactly one bijection of $\emptyset$, namely the empty mapping.

The *set of permutations* of the set $S = \{1, \ldots, n\}$ is denoted by $PERM_n$. If $f \in PERM_n$ is such a permutation, we write

$$f : \begin{pmatrix} 1 & \cdots & i & \cdots & n \\ a_1 & \cdots & a_i & \cdots & a_n \end{pmatrix},$$

where $a_i = f(i)$ for $1 \leqslant i \leqslant n$. To simplify the notation, we specify f just by the sequence $(a_1, \ldots, a_i, \ldots, a_n)$.

Another way to describe a permutation f of a finite set $S = \{a_1, \ldots, a_n\}$ is by using a $\{0, 1\}$-matrix $P_f \in \{0, 1\}^{n \times n}$ defined by

$$(P_f)_{ij} = \begin{cases} 1 & \text{if } f(a_i) = a_j, \\ 0 & \text{otherwise}, \end{cases}$$

for $1 \leqslant i, j \leqslant n$.

Example 1.34. The matrix P_f of permutation $f \in PERM_5$ defined as

$$f : \begin{pmatrix} 1\ 2\ 3\ 4\ 5 \\ 2\ 4\ 5\ 3\ 1 \end{pmatrix},$$

is

$$P_f = \begin{pmatrix} 0\ 1\ 0\ 0\ 0 \\ 0\ 0\ 0\ 1\ 0 \\ 0\ 0\ 0\ 0\ 1 \\ 0\ 0\ 1\ 0\ 0 \\ 1\ 0\ 0\ 0\ 0 \end{pmatrix}.$$

Note that for every row and every column of P_f contains exactly one 1.

Conversely, if P is a $\{0, 1\}^{n \times n}$-matrix such that every row and every column of P_f contains exactly one 1, there exists a permutation $f \in PERM_n$ such that $P = P_f$. Indeed, in this case, f can be defined as $f(i) = j$ if $P_{ij} = 1$.

We refer to matrices $P \in \{0, 1\}^{n \times n}$ having exactly one 1 entry in each row and each column as *permutation matrices*.

Theorem 1.45. *Let $f, g \in PERM_n$. We have $P_{fg} = P_g P_f$.*

Proof. We have $(P_g P_f)_{ij} = \sum_{h=1}^{n} (P_g)_{ih} (P_f)_{hj}$. Since $(P_g)_{ih} = 1$ if and only if $g(i) = h$, it follows that $(P_g P_f)_{ij} = (P_f)_{g(i)j}$. Therefore, $(P_g P_f)_{ij} = 1$ if and only if $f(g(i)) = j$, that is, if and only if $(P_{fg})_{ij} = 1$, which shows that $P_{fg} = P_g P_f$. $\qquad \square$

Definition 1.54. A *stochastic matrix* is a matrix $A \in \mathbb{R}^{n \times n}$ that satisfies the conditions:

(i) $a_{ij} \in [0, 1]$ for $1 \leqslant i \leqslant n$ and $1 \leqslant j \leqslant n$;
(ii) $\sum_{j=1}^{n} a_{ij} = 1$ for each i, $1 \leqslant i \leqslant n$.

A matrix $A \in \mathbb{R}^{n \times n}$ is *doubly stochastic* if both A and its transpose A' are stochastic matrices.

It is clear that every permutation matrix P_f is a doubly stochastic matrix.

Let $S = \{1, \ldots, n\}$ be a finite set. For every $x \in \{1, \ldots, n\}$ and $f \in PERM_n$ there exists $k \in \mathbb{N}$ such that $x = f^k(x)$. If k is the least number with this property, the set $\{x, f(x), \ldots, f^{k-1}(x)\}$ is the *cycle* of x and is denoted by $C_{f,x}$. The number $|C_{f,x}|$ is the *length of the cycle*.

Cycles of length 1 are said to be *trivial*.

Note that each pair of elements $f^i(x)$ and $f^j(x)$ of $C_{f,x}$ are distinct for $0 \leqslant i, j \leqslant |C_{f,x}| - 1$.

If $z \in C_{f,x}$ and $|C_{f,x}| = k$, then $z = f^j(x)$ for some j, $0 \leqslant j \leqslant k - 1$. Since $x = f^k(x)$, it follows that $x = f^{k-j}(z)$, which shows that $x \in C_{f,z}$. Consequently, $C_{f,x} = C_{f,z}$.

Thus, the cycles of a permutation $f \in PERM_n$ form a partition π_f of $\{1, \ldots, n\}$.

Definition 1.55. A *k-cyclic permutation* of $\{1, \ldots, n\}$ is a permutation such that π_f consists of a cycle of length k, $(j_1, \ldots, j_k)$ and a number of $n - k$ cycles of length 1.

A *transposition* of $\{1, \ldots, n\}$ is a 2-cyclic permutation.

Note that if f is a transposition of $\{1, \ldots, n\}$, then $f^2 = 1_S$.

Theorem 1.46. *Let f be a permutation in $PERM_n$, and $\pi_f = \{C_{f,x_1}, \ldots, C_{f,x_m}\}$ be the cycle partition associated to f. Define the cyclic permutations $g_1, \ldots, g_m$ of $\{1, \ldots, n\}$ as*

$$g_p(t) = \begin{cases} f(t) & \text{if } t \in C_{f,x_p}, \\ t & \text{otherwise}. \end{cases}$$

Then, $g_p g_q = g_q g_p$ for every p, q such that $1 \leqslant p, q \leqslant m$.

Proof. Observe first that $u \in C_{f,x}$ if and only if $f(u) \in C_{f,x}$ for any cycle $C_{f,x}$.

We can assume that $p \neq q$. Then, the cycles C_{f,x_p} and C_{f,x_q} are disjoint. If $u \notin C_{f,x_p} \cup C_{f,x_q}$, then we can write $g_p(g_q(u)) = g_p(u) = u$ and $g_q(g_p(u)) = g_q(u) = u$.

Suppose now that $u \in C_{f,x_p} - C_{f,x_q}$. We have $g_p(g_q(u)) = g_p(u) = f(u)$. On the other hand, $g_q(g_p(u)) = g_q(f(u)) = f(u)$ because $f(u) \notin C_{f,x_q}$. Thus, $g_p(g_q(u)) = g_q(g_p(u))$. The case where $u \in C_{f,x_q} - C_{f,x_p}$ is treated similarly. Also, note that $C_{f,x_p} \cap C_{f,x_q} = \emptyset$, so, in all cases, we have $g_p(g_q(x)) = g_q(g_p(u))$. $\square$

The set of cycles $\{g_1, \ldots, g_m\}$ is the *cyclic decomposition of the permutation* f.

Definition 1.56. A *standard transposition* is a transposition that changes the places of two adjacent elements.

Example 1.35. The permutation $f \in PERM_5$ given by

$$f : \begin{pmatrix} 1\ 2\ 3\ 4\ 5 \\ 1\ 3\ 2\ 4\ 5 \end{pmatrix}$$

is a standard transposition of the set $\{1, 2, 3, 4, 5\}$.

On the other hand, the permutation

$$g : \begin{pmatrix} 1\ 2\ 3\ 4\ 5 \\ 1\ 5\ 3\ 4\ 2 \end{pmatrix}$$

is a transposition but not a standard transposition of the same set because the pair of elements involved is not consecutive.

If $f \in PERM_n$ is specified by the sequence $(a_1, \ldots, a_n)$, we refer to each pair (a_i, a_j) such that $i < j$ and $a_i > a_j$ as an *inversion* of the permutation f. The set of all such inversions is denoted by $INV(f)$. The number of elements of $INV(f)$ is denoted by $inv(f)$.

A *descent* of a permutation $f \in PERM_n$ is a number j such that $1 \leqslant j \leqslant n - 1$ and $a_j > a_{j+1}$. The set of descents of f is denoted by $D(f)$.

Example 1.36. Let $f \in PERM_6$ be:

$$f : \begin{pmatrix} 1\ 2\ 3\ 4\ 5\ 6 \\ 4\ 2\ 5\ 1\ 6\ 3 \end{pmatrix}.$$

We have $INV(f) = \{(4,2), (4,1), (4,3), (2,1), (5,1), (5,3), (6,3)\}$ and $inv(f) = 7$. Furthermore, $D(f) = \{1, 3, 5\}$.

It is easy to see that the following conditions are equivalent for a permutation $f \in PERM_n$:

    (i) $f = 1_S$;
    (ii) $inv(f) = 0$;
    (iii) $D(f) = \emptyset$.

Theorem 1.47. *Every permutation* $f \in PERM_n$ *can be written as a composition of transpositions.*

Proof. If $D(f) = \emptyset$, then $f = 1_S$ and the statement is vacuous. Suppose therefore that $D(f) \neq \emptyset$, and let $j \in D(f)$, which means that (a_j, a_{j+1}) is an inversion f. Let g be the standard transposition that exchanges a_j and a_{j+1}. It is clear that $inv(gf) = inv(f) - 1$. Thus, if g_i are the transpositions that correspond to all standard inversions of f for $1 \leqslant i \leqslant p = inv(f)$, it follows that $g_p \cdots g_1 f$ has 0 inversions and, as observed above, $g_p \cdots g_1 f = 1_S$. Since $g^2 = 1_S$ for every transposition g, we have $f = g_p \cdots g_1$, which gives the desired conclusion. □

Theorem 1.48. *If $f \in PERM_n$, then $inv(f)$ equals the least number of standard transpositions, and the number of standard transpositions involved in any other factorization of f as a product of standard transposition differs from $inv(f)$ by an even number.*

Proof. Let $f = h_q \cdots h_1$ be a factorization of f as a product of standard transpositions. Then, $h_1 \cdots h_q f = 1_S$ and we can define the sequence of permutations $f_l = h_l \cdots h_1 f$ for $1 \leqslant l \leqslant q$. Since each h_i is a standard transposition, we have $inv(f_{l+1}) - inv(f_l) = 1$ or $inv(f_{l+1}) - inv(f_l) = -1$. If

$$|\{l \mid 1 \leqslant l \leqslant q - 1 \text{ and } inv(f_{l+1}) - inv(f_l) = 1\}| = r,$$

then $|\{l \mid 1 \leqslant l \leqslant q - 1 \text{ and } inv(f_{l+1}) - inv(f_l) = -1\}| = q - r$, so $inv(f) + r - (q - r) = 0$, which means that $q = inv(f) + 2r$. This implies the desired conclusion. □

An important characteristic of permutations is their *parity*. Namely, the permutation parity is defined as the parity of the number of their inversions: a permutation $f \in PERM_n$ is *even (odd)* if $inv(f)$ is an even (odd) number.

Theorem 1.48 implies that any factorization of a permutation as a product m standard transpositions determines whether the permutation is odd or even.

Note that any transposition is an odd permutation. Indeed, if $f \in PERM_n$ is a transposition of i and j, where $i < j$ we have

$$f = (1, 2, \ldots, i - 1, j, i + 1, \ldots, j - 1, i, j + 1, \ldots, n).$$

The number j generates $j - i$ inversions, and each of the numbers $i + 1, \ldots, j - 1$ generates one inversion because they are followed by i. Thus, the total number of inversions is $j - i + (j - i - 1) = 2(j - i) - 1$, which is obviously an odd number.

Theorem 1.49. *A cyclic permutation f of length k is the composition of $k - 1$ transpositions.*

Proof. Let $(j_1, \ldots, j_k)$ be the cycle of length k of f. It is immediate that f is the product of the $k-1$ transpositions $(j_1, j_2), (j_2, j_3), \ldots,$ (j_{k-1}, j_1). □

Thus, the parity of a cyclic permutation of even length is odd.

Corollary 1.4. *Let $f \in PERM_n$ be a permutation that has c_ℓ cycles of length ℓ for $\ell \geqslant 1$. The parity of f is the parity of the number $c_2 + c_4 + \cdots$; in other words, the parity of a permutation is given by the parity of the number of its even cycles.*

Proof. By Theorem 1.49 a cyclic transposition of length ℓ is the composition of $\ell - 1$ transpositions. Thus, if f has c_ℓ cycles of length ℓ, then f is a product of $\sum_{\ell \geqslant 1} c_\ell(\ell - 1)$ transpositions. It is clear that the parity of this sum is determined by those terms where $\ell - 1$ is impair. Thus the parity of f is given by the parity of $c_2 + 3c_4 + 5c_6 + \cdots$ and this equals the parity of $c_2 + c_4 + c_6 + \cdots$. □

Let S be a non-empty finite set, $S = \{s_1, \ldots, s_n\}$. We need to evaluate the number of injective functions of the form $f : \{1, \ldots, m\} \longrightarrow S$. To this end we will define such an injection by examining the number of choices we have when f is specified in increasing order of its values $f(1), \ldots, f(m)$.

Note that $f(1)$ can be chosen as any of the elements of S, so we have n choices; for $f(2)$ we have $n-1$ choices since $f(2)$ must be distinct from $f(1)$ and so on. Assuming that we defined $f(1), \ldots, f(k)$ there are $n-k$ choices left for $f(k+1)$ among the elements of $S - \{f(1), \ldots, f(k)\}$. Thus, there exist $n(n-1) \cdots (n-m+1)$ injections of the form $f : \{1, \ldots, m\} \longrightarrow S$ and this number can be written as $\frac{n!}{(n-m)!}$.

Let T be a subset of S such that $|T| = m$, so $m \leqslant n$ Note that there are exactly $m!$ injections of the form $f : \{1, \ldots, m\} \longrightarrow S$ such that $f(\{1, \ldots, m\}) = T$. Therefore, there exist $\frac{n!}{(n-m)!m!}$ subsets T of S having m elements. The number $\frac{n!}{(n-m)!m!}$ is denoted by $\binom{n}{m}$ and it is known as a *binomial coefficient* for reasons that will become apparent later.

The value of $\binom{n}{m}$ is extended to $m = 0$ by taking $\binom{n}{0} = 1$ for every $n \in \mathbb{N}$. This corresponds to the fact that there is exactly one empty subset of a set S.

Multinomial coefficients generalize binomial coefficients. If $n, p_1, \ldots, p_k$ are natural numbers such that $n = p_1 + \cdots + p_k$ we have the following definition of a multinomial coefficient:

$$\binom{n}{p_1 \; p_2 \; \cdots \; p_k} = \frac{n!}{p_1! \, p_2! \, \cdots \, p_k!}.$$

It is immediate that each multinomial coefficient can be written as a product of binomial coefficients:

$$\binom{p_1 + p_2 + \cdots + p_k}{p_1 \ p_2 \ \cdots \ p_k}$$
$$= \binom{p_1 + \cdots + p_k}{p_1} \cdots \binom{p_{k-2} + p_{k-1} + p_k}{p_{k-2}} \binom{p_{k-1} + p_k}{p_{k-1}} \binom{p_k}{p_k}. \quad (1.6)$$

Let $p(x) = (x + b_1)(x + b_2) \cdots (x + b_n)$ be a polynomial of degree n. The coefficient of x^{n-m} in p is the sum of all products of the form $b_{i_1} b_{i_2} \cdots b_{i_m}$, where $\{i_1, i_2, \ldots, i_m\}$ is an m-element subset of the set $\{1, \ldots, n\}$. Recall that there exist $\binom{n}{m}$ such subsets.

For $1 \leqslant m \leqslant n$ the function $f_m : \mathbb{R}^n \longrightarrow \mathbb{R}$ defined by

$$f_m(b_1, \ldots, b_n) = \sum \{b_{i_1} b_{i_2} \cdots b_{i_m} \mid \{i_1, \ldots, i_m\} \in \mathcal{P}_m(\{1, \ldots, n\})\}$$

is the mth *symmetric function* in $b_1, \ldots, b_n$.

If the roots of a polynomial p of degree n,

$$p(x) = x^n + a_1 x^{n-1} + \cdots + a_k x^{n-k} + \cdots + a_n$$

are the complex numbers $\lambda_1, \ldots, \lambda_n$, then

$$p(x) = (x - \lambda_1) \cdots (x - \lambda_n),$$

and by the previous argument, $f_m(\lambda_1, \ldots, \lambda_n) = (-1)^m a_m$.

If we have $b_1 = b_2 = \cdots = b_n = y$ in the polynomial $p(x) = (x + b_1)(x + b_2) \cdots (x + b_n)$, we have $p(x) = (x + y)^n$ and the coefficient of x^{n-m} is $\binom{n}{m} y^m$ and we can write:

$$(x + y)^n = \sum_{m=0}^{n} \binom{n}{m} x^{n-m} y^m.$$

This is the well-known *Newton's binomial formula*.

Newton's binomial formula can be extended to the *multinomial formula*:

$$(x_1 + \cdots + x_k)^n$$
$$= \sum \left\{ \binom{n}{p_1 \ p_2 \ \cdots \ p_k} x_1^{p_1} x_2^{p_2} \cdots x_k^{p_k} \ \middle| \ p_1, p_2, \ldots, p_k \in \mathbb{N}, \sum_{i=1}^{k} p_i = n \right\}.$$

The proof of the multinomial formula can be made by induction on k, where $k \geqslant 1$.

For the base step, $k = 1$, the equality is immediate. For the induction step suppose that the equality holds for k. This allows us to write

$$(x_1 + \cdots + x_k + x_{k+1})^n = (x_1 + \cdots + (x_k + x_{k+1}))^n$$

$$= \sum \left\{ \binom{n}{p_1 \ p_2 \ \cdots \ p_k} x_1^{p_1} x_2^{p_2} \cdots x_{k-1}^{p_{k-1}} (x_k + x_{k+1})^p \right) \; \middle| \; p_1, p_2, \ldots, p_{k-1}, p \in \mathbb{N}, \sum_{i=1}^{k-1} p_i + p = n \right\}$$

$$= \sum \left\{ \binom{n}{p_1 \ p_2 \ \cdots \ p_k} x_1^{p_1} x_2^{p_2} \cdots x_{k-1}^{p_{k-1}} \left(\sum \binom{p}{p_k \ p_{k+1}} x_k^{p_k} x_{k+1}^{p_{k+1}} \; \middle| \; p_k + p_{k+1} = p \right) \right. $$
$$\left. \middle| \; p_1, p_2, \ldots, p_{k-1}, p \in \mathbb{N}, \sum_{i=1}^{k-1} p_i + p = n \right\}.$$

Note that for $p_k, p_{k+1}, p \in \mathbb{N}$ and $p_k + p_{k+1} = p$ we have

$$\binom{n}{p_1 \ p_2 \ \cdots \ p_{k-1} \ p} \binom{p}{p_k \ p_{k+1}} = \binom{n}{p_1 \ p_2 \ \cdots \ p_{k-1} \ p_k \ p_{k+1}},$$

due to the definition of multinomial coefficients. This allows us to write

$$(x_1 + \cdots + x_k + x_{k+1})^n = \sum \left\{ \binom{n}{p_1 \ p_2 \ \cdots \ p_k \ p_{k+1}} x_1^{p_1} x_2^{p_2} \cdots x_k^{p_k} x_{k+1}^{p_{k+1}} \right. $$
$$\left. \middle| \; p_1, p_2, \ldots, p_k, p_{k+1} \in \mathbb{N}, \sum_{i=1}^{k+1} p_i = n \right\},$$

which concludes the argument.

If we take $x_1 = \cdots = x_k$ in the multinomial formula we obtain the sum of multinomial coefficients:

$$\sum \left\{ \binom{n}{p_1 \ p_2 \ \cdots \ p_k} \; \middle| \; p_1, p_2, \ldots, p_k \in \mathbb{N}, \sum_{i=1}^{k} p_i = n \right\} = k^n.$$

For binomial coefficients this amounts to taking $k = 2$, $p_1 = p$ and $p_2 = n - p$ for $0 \leqslant p \leqslant n$ and we have

$$\sum_{p=0}^{n} \binom{n}{p} = 2^n.$$

Exercises and Supplements

(1) Let $\mathcal{C}, \mathcal{D}$ be two collections of sets. Prove that:

    (a)

$$\bigcup \mathcal{C} \cup \bigcup \mathcal{D} = \bigcup (\mathcal{C} \cup \mathcal{D}),$$
$$\bigcup \mathcal{C} \cap \bigcup \mathcal{D} = \bigcup \{ C \cap D \mid C \in \mathcal{C} \text{ and } D \in \mathcal{D} \};$$

(b) if $\mathcal{D}$ is non-empty, then for each $D \in \mathcal{D}$, define $F_D = \bigcup\{C - D \mid C \in \mathcal{C}\}$. Prove that

$$\bigcup \mathcal{C} - \bigcup \mathcal{D} = \bigcap\{F_D \mid D \in \mathcal{D}\};$$

if $\mathcal{C}$ and $\mathcal{D}$ are both non-empty, then

$$\bigcup \mathcal{C} \cup \bigcup \mathcal{D} = \bigcup\{C \cup D \mid C \in \mathcal{C} \text{ and } D \in \mathcal{D}\}.$$

(2) Let A, B be two sets. Prove that $A \times B \subseteq \mathcal{P}(\mathcal{P}(A \cup B))$.

(3) Let U be a set and let A and B be subsets of U. Prove that
   (a) The equation $A \cap X = B$ has a solution $X \in \mathcal{P}(U)$ if and only if $B \subseteq A$. Show that, in this case, X is a solution if and only if there is a $P \subseteq U - A$ with $X = B \cup P$.
   (b) Prove that the equation $A \cup X = B$ has a solution in X if and only if $A \subseteq B$. In this case, show that X is a solution if and only if $B - A \subseteq X \subseteq B$.

(4) For each inequality, give examples of sets A, B, and C that satisfy the inequality (and thereby show that various possible distributive laws do not hold).

$$A \cup (B - C) \neq (A \cup B) - (A \cup C),$$
$$A \cup (B \times C) \neq (A \cup B) \times (A \cup C),$$
$$A \cap (B \times C) \neq (A \cap B) \times (A \cap C),$$
$$A - (B \cup C) \neq (A - B) \cup (A - C),$$
$$A - (B \cap C) \neq (A - B) \cap (A - C),$$
$$A - (B - C) \neq (A - B) - (A - C),$$
$$A - (B \times C) \neq (A - B) \times (A - C),$$
$$(B \times C) - A \neq (B - A) \times (C - A),$$
$$A \times (B \times C) \neq (A \times B) \times (A \times C),$$
$$(B \times C) \times A \neq (B \times A) \times (C \times A).$$

(5) Prove the following equalities for all sets A, B, C:
   (a) $A \oplus B = (A \cup B) - (A \cap B)$.
   (b) If $B \subseteq A$, then $A \oplus B = A - B$.
   (c) If A and B are disjoint, then $A \oplus B = A \cup B$.
   (d) $A \oplus \emptyset = \emptyset \oplus A = A$.
   (e) $A \oplus B = \emptyset$ if and only if $A = B$.
   (f) $A \oplus B = B \oplus A$.
   (g) $A \oplus (B \oplus C) = (A \oplus B) \oplus C$.
   (h) $A \cap (B \oplus C) = (A \cap B) \oplus (A \cap C)$.
   (i) $(B \oplus C) - A = (B - A) \oplus (C - A)$.

(j) $A \times (B \oplus C) = (A \times B) \oplus (A \times C)$.
(k) $(B \oplus C) \times A = (B \times A) \oplus (C \times A)$.
(l) $A \cup B = A \oplus (B \oplus (A \cap B))$.
(m) If $A - C = B - C$, then $A \oplus B \subseteq C$.
(n) If $A \oplus B = A \oplus C$, then $B = C$.

(6) For a subset U of a set S denote by U^a the set

$$U^a = \begin{cases} U & \text{if } a = 1, \\ S - U & \text{if } a = 0. \end{cases}$$

Let $\mathcal{C} = \{C_1, \ldots, C_n\}$ be a finite collection of subsets of a non-empty set S such that $\bigcup_{j=1}^{n} C_j = S$. Define the collection π as containing the non-empty subsets of the form $C_1^{a_1} \cap C_2^{a_2} \cap \cdots \cap C_n^{a_n}$, where $(a_1, \ldots, a_n) \in \{0,1\}^n$. Prove that:

(a) π is a partition of S;
(b) every set $C_i \in \mathcal{C}$ is π-saturated.

Solution: For $x \in S$ let $\mathcal{C}_x = \{C_{i_1}, \ldots, C_{i_p}\}$ be the subcollection of $\mathcal{C}$ that consists of those sets in $\mathcal{C}$ that contain x. Since $\mathcal{C}$ is a cover for S it is clear that $\mathcal{C}_x \neq \emptyset$ for every $x \in S$.

Let $K_x = \bigcap_{k=1}^{p} C_{i_k}$. Since $x \in K_x$ it follows that $\bigcup_{x \in S} K_x = S$. We have $K_x = \bigcap_{j=1}^{n} C_j^{a_j}$, where

$$a_j = \begin{cases} 1 & \text{if } x \in C_j, \\ 0 & \text{if } x \notin C_j, \end{cases}$$

for $1 \leqslant j \leqslant n$. This shows that if $K_x \neq K_y$ we have $K_x \cap K_y = \emptyset$, which proves the first part of this supplement.

The fact that each set $C_i \in \mathcal{C}$ is π follows from the fact that $C_i = \bigcup \{K_x \mid x \in C_i\}$.

(7) Let S be a set and let $U_1, \ldots, U_n$ be n subsets of S. Prove that

$$S^n - (U_1 \times U_2 \times \cdots \times U_n)$$
$$= \bigcup_{j=1}^{n} S^{j-1} \times (S - U_j) \times S^{n-j}$$
$$= ((S - U_1) \times S^{n-1}) \cup (U_1 \times (S - U_2) \times S^{n-2})$$
$$\cup (U_1 \times \cdots \times U_{k-1} \times (S - U_k) \times S^{n-k})$$
$$\cup (U_1 \times U_2 \times \cdots \times U_{n-1} \times (S - U_n)).$$

Solution: Note that $(x_1, \ldots, x_n) \in S^n - (U_1 \times U_2 \times \cdots \times U_n)$ amounts to the existence of j, $1 \leqslant j \leqslant n$ such that $x_j \notin U_j$. This implies the first equality.

To prove the second equality, for $(x_1, \ldots, x_n) \in S^n - (U_1 \times U_2 \times \cdots \times U_n)$ let k be the least number such that $x_k \notin U_k$ (hence $x_k \in S - U_k$)). Then, $(x_1, \ldots, x_n) \in U_1 \times \cdots \times U_{k-1} \times (S - U_k) \times S^{n-k}$ and the second equality follows.

(8) Let U, V be two subsets of a set S. Prove that:

(a) $1_U(x) \leqslant 1_V(x)$ for $x \in S$ if and only if $U \subseteq V$;

(b) if $f : S \longrightarrow [0, 1]$, then $1_U(x) \leqslant f(x) \leqslant 1_V(x)$ for $x \in S$, if and only if $f(x) = 1$ for $x \in U$ and $f(x) = 0$ if $x \in S - V$;

(c) if U, W are disjoint subsets of S and $g : S \longrightarrow [0, 1]$ is a function, then $1_U(x) \leqslant g(x) \leqslant 1_{S-W}(x)$ if and only if $g(x) = 1$ for $x \in U$ and $g(x) = 0$ for $x \in W$.

(9) Let $\rho \subseteq X \times Y$ be a relation on the finite sets X, Y. Prove that ρ is a function defined on X if and only if $|X| = |\rho|$.

(10) Let U, V be two subsets of a set S. Prove that $1_{U \oplus V}(x) = 1_U(x) + 1_V(x) - 2 \cdot 1_U(x)1_V(x)$ for $x \in S$.

An interval of $\mathbb{R}$ is a subset J of $\mathbb{R}$ that is either an open interval (a, b), a closed interval $[a, b]$, or one of the semi-open intervals $(a, b]$ or $[a, b)$. Let $\ell(J) = b - a$ for any of these cases.

(11) Let $[a, b]$ be a closed interval in $\mathbb{R}$ and set $\{J_k \mid 1 \leqslant k \leqslant n\}$ be n intervals of $\mathbb{R}$ such that $[a, b] \subseteq \bigcup_{k=1}^n J_k$. Prove that:

$$1_{[a,b]}(x) \leqslant \sum_{k=1}^n 1_{J_k}(x)$$

for $x \in \mathbb{R}$.

(12) Prove that if $\mathcal{J} = \{J_k \mid 1 \leqslant k \leqslant n\}$ is a collection of n open intervals of $\mathbb{R}$ such that $[a, b] \subseteq \bigcup_{k=1}^n J_k$, then $b - a \leqslant \sum_{k=1}^n \ell(J_k)$.

Solution: Without loss of generality we may assume that every open intervals in $\mathcal{J}$ has a non-empty intersection with $[a, b]$. Let $J_k = (a_k, b_k)$ for $1 \leqslant k \leqslant n$.

If $n = 1$ we have $[a, b] \subseteq (a_1, b_1)$, which implies immediately the inequality.

Suppose that the inequality holds for collection of fewer than n open intervals and let $\mathcal{J}$ be a collection of n open intervals that covers $[a, b]$.

Since $[a, b] \subseteq \bigcup_{k=1}^n J_k$, there exists an open interval in $\mathcal{J}$ that is not included in $[a, b]$. Without loss of generality we may assume that this interval is (a_n, b_n). Since each of the intervals of $\mathcal{J}$ has a non-empty intersection with $[a, b]$, we have either $[a, b] \subseteq [a, a_n] \cup (a_n, b_n)$ or $[a, b] \subseteq [a, b_n] \cup (a_n, b_n)$ depending whether $a_n \in [a, b]$ or $b_n \in [a, b]$, respectively.

In the first case, $b-a \leqslant a_n - a + \ell((a_n, b_n))$ and $[a, a_n] \subseteq \bigcup_{k=1}^{n-1}(a_k, b_k)$. By the inductive hypothesis we have $a_n - a \leqslant \sum_{k=1}^{n-1} \ell((a_k, b_k))$, which implies $b - a \leqslant \sum_{k=1}^{n} \ell((a_k, b_k))$. The second case can be dealt with in a similar manner.

(13) Let $\{\mathbf{s}_n \mid n \in \mathbb{N}, n \geqslant 1\}$ be a family of sequences, where $\mathbf{s}_n = (x_{n1}, \ldots, x_{nm}, \ldots)$. Arrange the elements of the set $\{x_{nm} \mid n \geqslant 1, m \geqslant 1\}$ in a rectangular infinite array

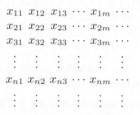

$$
\begin{array}{cccccc}
x_{11} & x_{12} & x_{13} & \cdots & x_{1m} & \cdots \\
x_{21} & x_{22} & x_{23} & \cdots & x_{2m} & \cdots \\
x_{31} & x_{32} & x_{33} & \cdots & x_{3m} & \cdots \\
\vdots & \vdots & \vdots & \vdots & \vdots & \vdots \\
x_{n1} & x_{n2} & x_{n3} & \cdots & x_{nm} & \cdots \\
\vdots & \vdots & \vdots & \vdots & \vdots & \vdots
\end{array}
$$

The kth diagonal D_k of this array contains the elements x_{mn} such that $m + n = k + 1$. If the elements of the array are listed diagonally and from top to bottom, prove that there exists a bijection $\ell : \mathbb{P} \times \mathbb{P} \longrightarrow \mathbb{P}$ such that x_{mn} is placed at position $\ell(n, m) = \frac{1}{2}(n + m - 2)(n + m - 1) + n$ for $m, n \in \mathbb{P}$. We will refer to the sequence obtained in this manner as the *amalgam* of the sequences $\mathbf{s}_n$.

Solution: Note that x_{nm} belongs to the diagonal D_{n+m-1}. This diagonal is preceded by $D_1, \ldots, D_{n+m-2}$ which contain a total number of $1 + 2 + \cdots + (n + m - 2) = \frac{1}{2}(n + m - 2)(n + m - 1)$ elements. Since x_{nm} occupies the nth place on the diagonal D_{n+m-1}, it follows that $\ell(n, m) = \frac{1}{2}(n + m - 2)(n + m - 1) + n$. Since the place of x_{nm} is uniquely determined by n, m, ℓ is indeed a bijection.

(14) Let K, L be two subsets of $\mathbb{R}$. Prove that if $K^s = L^s$, then $\sup K = \sup L$ and that $K^i = L^i$ implies $\inf K = \inf L$.

Solution: This follows immediately from

$$\{\sup K\} = K^s \cap (K^s)^i = L^s \cap (L^s)^i = \{\sup L\}.$$

A similar argument can be used for the second part.

(15) Let K, L be two subsets of $\mathbb{R}$. Prove that if $K^s = L^i$, then $\sup K \leqslant \inf L$.

(16) Let U be a subset of $\mathbb{R}$, and let $b \in \mathbb{R}$ be such that $\sup U \leqslant b$. Prove that if $a < b$ implies $a \leqslant \sup U$, then $b = \sup U$.

Solution: Suppose that $\sup U < b$. Then, there exists $c \in \mathbb{R}$ such that $\sup U < c < b$, which implies $c \leqslant \sup U$. This contradiction means that so such c exists, so $\sup U = b$.

(17) Let T be a subset of $\mathbb{R}$. For $a \in \mathbb{R}$ define $aT = \{at \mid t \in T\}$. Prove that

   (a) if $a \geqslant 0$, $\sup aT = a \sup T$ and $\inf aT = a \inf T$;

(b) if $a \leqslant 0$, $\sup aT = a \inf T$ and $\inf aT = a \sup T$.

(18) Let U, V be two subsets of $\mathbb{R}$ such that $U \subseteq V$. Prove that:

    (a) if $\sup U$, $\sup V$ exist, then $\sup U \leqslant \sup V$;

    (b) if $\inf U$, $\inf V$ exist, then $\inf U \geqslant \inf V$.

(19) For $U, V \subseteq \mathbb{R}$ define $U + V = \{u + v \mid u \in U, v \in V\}$. Prove that if U and V are non-empty then

$$\sup(U + V) = \sup U + \sup V,$$
$$\inf(U + V) = \inf U + \inf V.$$

Solution: Note that $(U + V)^s \neq \emptyset$ if and only if $U^s \neq \emptyset$ and $V^s \neq \emptyset$. Therefore, $\sup(U + V)$ exists if and only if both $\sup U$ and $\sup V$ exist.

If $u \in U$ and $v \in V$, then $u + v \leqslant \sup U + \sup V$, hence $\sup U + \sup V$ is an upper bound of $U + V$. Therefore, $\sup(U + V) \leqslant \sup U + \sup V$.

Let $\epsilon > 0$. There exist $u \in U$ and $v \in V$ such that $\sup U - \frac{\epsilon}{2} < u$ and $\sup V - \frac{\epsilon}{2} < v$, hence $\sup U + \sup V - \epsilon \leqslant u + v$ for every $\epsilon > 0$, which implies $\sup(U + V) \geqslant \sup U + \sup V$. Thus, $\sup(U + V) = \sup U + \sup V$.

The second equality has a similar argument.

(20) Let C be a subset of $\mathbb{R}$ and let $f, g : C \longrightarrow \mathbb{R}$ be two real-valued functions. Prove that

$$\inf_{x \in C} f(x) + \inf_{x \in C} g(x) \leqslant \inf_{x \in C} (f + g)(x),$$
$$\sup_{x \in C} f(x) + \sup_{x \in C} g(x) \geqslant \sup_{x \in C} (f + g)(x).$$

Solution: Let $p = \inf_{x \in C} f(x)$ and $q = \inf_{x \in C} g(x)$. We have $p \leqslant f(x)$ and $q \leqslant g(x)$ for every $x \in C$. Therefore, $p + q \leqslant f(x) + g(x) = (f + g)(x)$ for every $x \in C$, hence $p + q \leqslant \inf_{x \in C} f + g$. The second inequality has a similar argument based on the definition of sup.

Let C be a set and let $f : C \longrightarrow \mathbb{R}$ be a function. Define

$$\sup_C f = \sup\{f(x) \mid x \in C\} \text{ and } \inf_C f = \inf\{f(x) \mid x \in C\}.$$

Also, if $f, g : C \longrightarrow \mathbb{R}$ we write $f \leqslant g$ if $f(x) \leqslant g(x)$ for every $x \in C$.

(21) Let C be a set and let $f : C \longrightarrow \mathbb{R}$ and $g : C \longrightarrow \mathbb{R}$ be two functions. Prove that if $f \leqslant g$ and $\sup_C$ is finite, then $\sup_C f \leqslant \sup_C g$. Also, prove that if $\inf_C f$ is finite, then $\inf_C f \leqslant \inf_C g$.

(22) Give an example of two functions $f, g : C \longrightarrow \mathbb{R}$ such that $f \leqslant g$ but $\sup_C f \not\leqslant \inf_C g$.

(23) Let $f : C \longrightarrow \mathbb{R}$ be a function such that $\sup_C f$ is finite and let $a \in \mathbb{R}$. Prove that $\sup_C(af) = a \sup_C f$ and $\inf_C(af) = a \inf_C f$.

(24) Let C be a set and let $f, g : C \longrightarrow \mathbb{R}$ be two real-valued functions. Prove that

$$\inf_{x \in C} f(x) + \inf_{x \in C} g(x) \leqslant \inf_{x \in C} (f+g)(x),$$
$$\sup_{x \in C} f(x) + \sup_{x \in C} g(x) \geqslant \sup_{x \in C} (f+g)(x).$$

Solution: Let $p = \inf_{x \in C} f(x)$ and $q = \inf_{x \in C} g(x)$. We have $p \leqslant f(x)$ and $q \leqslant g(x)$ for every $x \in C$. Therefore, $p + q \leqslant f(x) + g(x) = (f+g)(x)$ for every $x \in C$, hence $p + q \leqslant \inf_{x \in C} f + g$. The second inequality has a similar argument based on the definition of sup.

(25) Let C be a set and let $f, g : C \longrightarrow \mathbb{R}$ be two real-valued bounded functions. Prove that $|\sup_C f - \sup_C g| \leqslant \sup_C |f - g|$.

(26) Let $\mathbf{K}_1, \mathbf{K}_2$ be two closure operators on a set S and let $\mathcal{C}$ be a collection of subsets of S such that

$$\mathbf{K}_1(\mathbf{K}_2(\mathcal{C})) = \mathbf{K}_2(\mathcal{C}) \text{ and } \mathbf{K}_2(\mathbf{K}_1(\mathcal{C})) = \mathbf{K}_1(\mathcal{C}).$$

Prove that $\mathbf{K}_1(\mathcal{C}) = \mathbf{K}_2(\mathcal{C})$.
Solution: Since $\mathbf{K}_1(\mathbf{K}_2(\mathcal{C})) = \mathbf{K}_2(\mathcal{C})$.

(27) Let $\mathcal{A}$ be an algebra of subsets of a set S. Prove that if $\mathcal{A}$ is closed under formation of unions of ascending sequences of sets or under the formation of intersections of descending sequences of sets, then $\mathcal{A}$ is a σ-algebra.

(28) Prove that if (U_n) is a sequence of sets in a σ-algebra of subsets of a set S, then $\limsup U_n$ and $\liminf U_n$ belong to S.

(29) Prove that if $\mathcal{A}$ is an algebra of subsets of a set S, then the collection $\mathcal{A}_\sigma$ is closed with respect to intersection.

(30) Let $\mathcal{E}$ be a σ-algebra of subsets of a set S and let $T = \{t_1, \ldots, t_n\}$ be a finite set. Prove that the collection $\mathcal{E} \sqcup T = \{E \cup U \mid E \in \mathcal{E} \text{ and } U \subseteq T\}$ is a σ-algebra of sets on the $S \cup T$.
Solution: If $E \cup U$, $\overline{E \cup U} = (S - E) \cup (T - U)$, so $E \cup U \in \mathcal{E} \sqcup T$.

Suppose now that $\{E_n \cup U_n \mid n \in \mathbb{N}\}$ is a countable collection of subsets of $\mathcal{E} \sqcup T$. Then $\bigcup_{n \in \mathbb{N}}(E_n \cup U_n) = \bigcup_{n \in \mathbb{N}} E_n \cup \bigcup_{n \in \mathbb{N}} U_n \in \mathcal{E} \sqcup T$, because $\bigcup_{n \in \mathbb{N}} E_n \in \mathcal{E}$ and $\bigcup_{n \in \mathbb{N}} U_n \in T$ since $\mathcal{E}$ is a σ-algebra and T is a finite set.

(31) Let $\mathcal{E}$ be an algebra of sets. Prove that if $\mathcal{E}$ is closed under countable increasing unions, then $\mathcal{E}$ is a σ-algebra.

(32) Let $\mathcal{C}$ be a collection of subsets of a set S. Prove that $\mathbf{K}_{\mathrm{alg}}(\mathcal{C}) \subseteq \mathbf{K}_{\sigma\text{-alg}}(\mathcal{C})$.

(33) Let S be a set and let $\mathcal{C}$ be a collection of subsets of S. Define the collections of sets:

$$\mathcal{C}' = \mathcal{C} \cup \{S - T \mid T \in \mathcal{C}\},$$

$$\mathcal{C}'' = \left\{ \bigcap \mathcal{D} \,\middle|\, \mathcal{D} \subseteq \mathcal{C}' \right\},$$

$$\mathcal{C}''' = \left\{ \bigcup \mathcal{D} \,\middle|\, \mathcal{D} \subseteq \mathcal{C}'' \right\}.$$

Prove that $\mathcal{C}'''$ equals the σ-algebra generated by $\mathcal{C}$.

(34) Let S, T be two sets and let $f : S \longrightarrow T$ be a function. Prove that if $\mathcal{E}'$ is a σ-algebra on T, then $\{f^{-1}(V) \mid V \in \mathcal{E}'\}$ is a σ-algebra on A.

A *semi-ring* of sets is a collection $\mathcal{S}$ of sets that satisfies the following conditions:

(i) $\emptyset \in \mathcal{S}$;

(ii) if $U, V \in \mathcal{S}$, then $U \cap V \in \mathcal{S}$;

(iii) if $U, V \in \mathcal{S}$ and $V \subseteq U$, then there exists a finite collection $\mathcal{U}$ of pairwise disjoint sets in $\mathcal{S}$ such that $U - V = \bigcup \mathcal{U}$.

(35) An *open-closed interval* in $\mathbb{R}^n$ is a set of the form $G = (a_1, b_1] \times \cdots \times (a_n, b_n]$.

Prove that the collection $\{\emptyset\} \cup \{G \mid G$ is an open-closed interval in $\mathbb{R}^n\}$ is a semi-ring on $\mathbb{R}$.

Solution: Let $G' = (a_1', b_1'] \times \cdots \times (a_n', b_n']$ be an open-closed interval such that $G' \subseteq G$. We have $(a_j', b_j'] \subseteq (a_j, b_j]$, hence

$$(a_j, b_j] = (a_j, a_j'] \cup (a_j', b_j'] \cup (b_j', b_j],$$

where $(a_j, a_j'], (a_j', b_j'], (b_j', b_j]$ are disjoint. Consider the open-closed intervals $R_1 \times \cdots \times R_n$, where R_j is one of $(a_j, a_j'], (a_j', b_j'], (b_j', b_j]$. One of these intervals equals G'; the union of the rest of them equals $G - G'$, so the class of open-closed intervals (together with $\emptyset$) is indeed a semi-ring.

(36) Prove that if $\mathcal{S}$ and $\mathcal{T}$ are semi-rings on the sets S and T, respectively, then the collection $\mathcal{Y} = \{U \times V \mid U \in \mathcal{S}, V \in \mathcal{T}\}$ is a semi-ring on $S \times T$.

Let S be a set. A *ring* of sets on S is a non-empty family of subsets $\mathcal{E}$ of S that satisfies the following conditions:

(i) if $U, V \in \mathcal{E}$, then $U \cap V \in \mathcal{E}$;

(ii) if $U, V \in \mathcal{E}$, then $U - V \in \mathcal{E}$.

If $S \in \mathcal{E}$, then $\mathcal{E}$ is an *algebra of sets* on S.

(37) Let $\mathcal{R}$ be the collection of subsets of $\mathbb{R}^2$ that can be written as a finite union of disjoint intervals. Prove that $\mathcal{R}$ is a ring.

(38) Let $\mathcal{B}$ the collection of all bounded subsets of $\mathbb{R}$. Prove that $\mathcal{B}$ is a ring but not an algebra. Also, show that the collection $\mathcal{I} = \{[x, y] \mid x, y \in [a, b]\}$ is a semi-ring but not a ring.

(39) Prove that the collection of rings of subsets of a set S is a closure system.

(40) Prove that if $\mathcal{S}$ is a semi-ring of sets, then the collection $\mathcal{R}$ of all finite unions of sets in $\mathcal{S}$ is a ring of sets.

(41) Let $\mathcal{S}$ be a semi-ring of sets. Prove that if $U, U_1, \ldots, U_n \in \mathcal{S}$, then there are pairwise disjoint sets $V_1, \ldots, V_m$ in $\mathcal{S}$ such that $U \cap \overline{U_1} \cap \cdots \cap \overline{U_n} = V_1 \cup \cdots \cup V_m$.

Solution: The argument is by induction on $n \geqslant 1$. The base case, $n = 1$ is immediate from the definition of semi-rings. Suppose that the statement holds to n. Then, $U \cap \overline{U_1} \cap \cdots \cap \overline{U_n} \cap \overline{U_{n+1}} = (V_1 \cap \overline{U_{n+1}}) \cup \cdots \cup (V_m \cap \overline{U_{m+1}})$. By applying the case $n = 1$ to each of the sets $V_j \cap \overline{U_{m+1}}$, the desired conclusion follows.

(42) Prove that if $\mathcal{E}$ is an infinite σ-algebra on a set S, then $\mathcal{E}$ is not countable.

Solution: Suppose that $\mathcal{E}$ is an infinite σ-algebra of subsets of S. Clearly, this implies that S is infinite.

Suppose that $\mathcal{E}$ is countable. Let $f : S \longrightarrow \mathcal{E}$ be a function such that $f(x) = \bigcap \{U \in \mathcal{E} \mid x \in U\}$. Note that $x \in f(x)$. Since σ-algebras are closed with respect to countable intersections the function f is well-defined.

Suppose that $f(x) \cap f(y) \neq \emptyset$. If $x \notin f(y)$, then $x \in f(x) - f(y) \subset f(x)$, which is a contradiction because $f(x) - f(y) \in \mathcal{E}$. Therefore, $x \in f(y)$ and, similarly, $y \in f(x)$. Since f maps a point to the least element of $\mathcal{E}$ containing that element, it follows that $x \in f(x) \subseteq f(y)$ and $y \in f(y) \subseteq f(x)$, so $f(x) = f(y)$. Thus, the collection $\{f(x) \mid x \in S\}$ is a partition π_f of S.

Each set $U \in \mathcal{E}$ can be written as $U = \bigcup \{f(u) \mid u \in U\}$. Therefore, π_f cannot be finite because otherwise S would be finite. Since π_f is infinite, the set $\mathcal{P}(\{f(x) \mid x \in S\})$ is not countable.

The function $\phi : \mathcal{E} \longrightarrow \mathcal{P}(\{f(x) \mid x \in S\})$ given by $\phi(E) = \{f(x) \mid x \in E\}$ for every $E \in \mathcal{E}$ is surjective, which implies that $\mathcal{E}$ is not countable.

(43) Let (S, d) be a metric space and let $f : S \longrightarrow \mathbb{R}$ be a function. Define the relation $\preceq$ on S as $x \preceq y$ if $f(x) + d(x, y) \leqslant f(y)$. Define $M(x) = \{t \in S \mid t \leqslant x\}$. Prove that:

    (a) $\preceq$ is a partial order on S;
    (b) $y \preceq x$ if and only if $M(y) \subseteq M(x)$;
    (c) y is a minimal element of the poset $(S, \preceq)$ if and only if $M(y) = \{y\}$.

(44) Let (S, d) be a metric space and let k be a positive number. Prove that the mapping $d_k : S \times S \longrightarrow \mathbb{R}$ defined by $d_k(x, y) = \min\{d(x, y), k\}$ is a metric on S.

Solution: It is immediate to verify that $d_k(x, y) = 0$ if and only if $x = y$ and that $d_k(x, y) = d_k(y, x)$ for $x, y \in S$. We need to prove only the triangular inequality.

Note that $d_k(x, y) \leqslant d(x, y)$ for $x, y \in S$.

If at least one of the numbers $d_k(x, z), d_k(z, y)$ equals k, then the triangular inequality $d_k(x, y) \leqslant d_k(x, z) + d(z, y)$ is satisfied. Otherwise, we have $d_k(x, z) = d(x, z)$ and $d_k(z, y) = d(z, y)$ and, since $d_k(x, y) \leqslant d(x, y) \leqslant d(x, z) + d(z, y)$, the triangular inequality is satisfied.

(45) The arctan function is usually defined on $\mathbb{R}$ and ranges in the interval $(-\pi/2, \pi/2)$. Extend arctan to $\hat{\mathbb{R}}$ by defining $\arctan +\infty = \pi/2$ and $\arctan -\infty = -\pi/2$. Prove that the function d defined on $\hat{\mathbb{R}} \times \hat{\mathbb{R}}$ by $d(x, y) = |\arctan x - \arctan y|$ for $x, y \in \hat{\mathbb{R}}$ is a metric on $\hat{\mathbb{R}}$.

(46) Let p be a prime number. For $n \in \mathbb{N}$, $n \geqslant 1$ define $\ell_p(n)$ as the exponent of the prime p in the factorization on n as a product of prime numbers. Prove that

  (a) $\ell_p(mn) = \ell_p(m) + \ell_p(n)$ for $m, n \in \mathbb{N}$ and $m, n \geqslant 1$.
  (b) If $q = s\frac{m}{n}$ is a rational number, where $s \in \{-1, 1\}$ and $m, n \in \mathbb{N}$, $m, n \geqslant 1$, define $\ell_p(q) = \ell_p(m) - \ell_p(n)$. Prove that $\ell_p(qr) = \ell_p(q) + \ell_p(r)$ for any rational numbers q, r.
  (c) Define the mapping $d_p : \mathbb{Q}^2 \longrightarrow \mathbb{R}$ as

$$
d_p(q, r) = \begin{cases} p^{-\ell_p(q, r)} & \text{if } q \neq r, \\ 0 & \text{if } q = r \end{cases}
$$

for $q, r \in \mathbb{Q}$. Prove that $d_p(q, r) \leqslant \max\{d_p(q, s), d_p(s, r)\}$ for $q, r, s \in \mathbb{Q}$.

(47) Let (S, d) be a metric space and let $\{B(x_i, r) \mid 1 \leqslant i \leqslant n\}$ be a collection of spheres in S. Prove that the set $C = \bigcup_{i=1}^{n} B(x_i, r)$ is a bounded set and

$$
diam_{S,d}(C) \leqslant \max\{d(x_i, x_j) \mid 1 \leqslant i, j \leqslant n\} + 2r.
$$

(48) Let (S, d) be a metric space. Prove that if $h : \mathbb{R} \longrightarrow \mathbb{R}$ is a differentiable function such that $h(0) = 0$, $h'(x) > 0$ for $x > 0$, and $h'(x)$ is decreasing on $[0, \infty)$, then hd is a metric on S.

(49) Prove that for $h \in \mathbb{R}$ and $h > -1$ we have $(1 + h)^n \geqslant 1 + nh$ for $n \in \mathbb{N}$. This inequality is known as the *Bernoulli inequality*.

(50) Let $\phi \in PERM_n$ be

$$
\phi : \begin{pmatrix} 1 & \cdots & i & \cdots & n \\ a_1 & \cdots & a_i & \cdots & a_n \end{pmatrix},
$$

and let $v_p(\phi) = |\{(i_k, i_l) \mid i_l = p, k < l, i_k > i_l\}|$ be the number of inversions of ϕ that have p as their second component, for $1 \leqslant p \leqslant n$. Prove that

(a) $v_p \leqslant n - p$ for $1 \leqslant p \leqslant n$;

(b) for every sequence of numbers $(v_1, \ldots, v_n) \in \mathbb{N}^n$ such that $v_p \leqslant n - p$ for $1 \leqslant p \leqslant n$ there exists a unique permutation ϕ that has $(v_1, \ldots, v_n) \in \mathbb{N}^n$ as its sequence of inversions.

(51) Let p be the polynomial $p(x_1, \ldots, x_n) = \prod_{i < j}(x_i - x_j)$. For a permutation $\phi \in PERM_n$,

$$\phi : \begin{pmatrix} 1 & \cdots & i & \cdots & n \\ a_1 & \cdots & a_i & \cdots & a_n \end{pmatrix},$$

define the number p_ϕ as $p_\phi = p(a_1, \ldots, a_n)$. Prove that

(a) $(-1)^{inv(\phi)} = \frac{p_\phi}{p_{\iota_n}}$ for any permutation ϕ;

(b) $(-1)^{inv(\psi\phi)} = (-1)^{inv(\psi)}(-1)^{inv(\phi)}$.

Bibliographical Comments

Several reference books provide useful continuations of the topics presented here. For the sections that deal with set-theoretical concepts (sets and collections, relations and functions, sequences of sets, and partially ordered sets) we recommend [56].

Closure and interior systems are presented in a broad algebraic sense (see, for example [33]). Fundamental structures for measure theory (set algebras and σ-algebras) are also a part of this chapter; basic references are [16, 113, 32, 130].

Chapter 2

Linear Spaces

2.1 Introduction

This chapter includes topics of linear algebra that we deem to be essential for the presentation of mathematical analysis aspects. After introducing linear spaces and the notion of linearly independent set, we discuss normed linear spaces and linear spaces equipped with inner products as a prelude to the study of Banach and Hilbert spaces in subsequent chapters. The chapter concludes with sections dedicated to linear functionals and to hyperplanes.

2.2 Linear Spaces and Linear Independence

The symbol $\mathbb{F}$ stands for $\mathbb{R}$ or $\mathbb{C}$. In the context of linear spaces the elements of $\mathbb{F}$ are referred to as *scalars*.

Definition 2.1. An $\mathbb{F}$-*linear space* is a non-empty set L whose elements are referred to as *vectors*. The set L is equipped with a binary operation "+" called *vector addition* and with a multiplication between elements of F and vectors called *multiplication by scalars*. If u, v are vectors and a is a scalar, the result of adding $u, v \in L$ is denoted by $u + v$; the result of multiplying a scalar a and a vector v is denoted by av. Vector addition satisfies the following conditions:

   (i) $u + (v + w) = (u + v) + w$;
   (ii) there exists 0_L in L such that $u + 0_L = 0_L + u = u$ for every $u \in L$;
   (iii) $u + v = v + u$;
   (iv) for each $u \in L$ there exists $-u \in L$ such that $u + (-u) = 0_L$.

Multiplication by scalars satisfies the following conditions:
   (i) $a \cdot (b \cdot u) = (a \cdot b) \cdot u$;
   (ii) $1 \cdot u = u$;

(iii) $a \cdot (u + v) = a \cdot u + a \cdot v$;

(iv) $(a + b) \cdot u = a \cdot u + b \cdot v$,

for every $a, b \in F$ and $u, v \in L$.

If $\mathbb{F} = \mathbb{R}$, then we refer to L as a *real linear space*; for $\mathbb{F} = \mathbb{C}$ we say that L is a *complex linear space*.

If $L \neq 0_L$ we say that L is *non-trivial*.

The commutative binary operation of L is denoted by the same symbol "+" as the corresponding operation of the field $\mathbb{F}$.

The elements of the set L are denoted using letters from the end of the alphabet. Members of $\mathbb{F}$ are denoted by small letters from the beginning of the alphabet.

The neutral additive element 0_L of L is referred to as the *zero element* of L; every linear space must contain at least this element. If there is no risk of confusion we shall omit the subscript L.

A *vector of length n over* $\mathbb{F}$ is a function $\mathbf{v} : \{1, \ldots, n\} \longrightarrow \mathbb{F}$, that is a sequence of length n of elements of $\mathbb{F}$. We denote $\mathbf{v}$ by

$$\mathbf{v} = \begin{pmatrix} v_1 \\ \vdots \\ v_n \end{pmatrix},$$

where $v_i = v(i)$ is the ith *component* of v for $1 \leqslant i \leqslant n$. The set of vectors of length n over $\mathbb{F}$ is denoted by $\mathbb{F}^n$.

An $m \times n$-*matrix* over $\mathbb{F}$ is a function $A : \{1, \ldots, m\} \times \{1, \ldots, n\} \longrightarrow \mathbb{F}$. A matrix is usually denoted as a table

$$A = \begin{pmatrix} A(1,1) & A(1,2) & \cdots & A(1,n), \\ A(2,1) & A(2,2) & \cdots & A(2,n), \\ \vdots & \vdots & \cdots & \vdots \\ A(m,1) & A(m,2) & \cdots & A(m,n) \end{pmatrix}.$$

The entry $A(p, q)$ of A is usually denoted as a_{pq}.

The *Hermitian conjugate* of a matrix $A \in \mathbb{C}^{m \times n}$ is the matrix $A^{\mathsf{H}} \in \mathbb{C}^{n \times m}$ defined by

$$A^{\mathsf{H}} = \begin{pmatrix} \overline{a_{11}} & \overline{a_{21}} & \cdots & \overline{a_{m1}} \\ \overline{a_{12}} & \overline{a_{22}} & \cdots & \overline{a_{m2}} \\ \vdots & \vdots & \cdots & \vdots \\ \overline{a_{1n}} & \overline{a_{2n}} & \cdots & \overline{a_{mn}} \end{pmatrix}.$$

If $A \in \mathbb{R}^{m \times n}$ the Hermitian conjugate is the *transposed matrix* A' of A:

$$A' = \begin{pmatrix} a_{11} & a_{21} & \cdots & a_{m1} \\ a_{12} & a_{22} & \cdots & a_{m2} \\ \vdots & \vdots & \cdots & \vdots \\ a_{1n} & a_{2n} & \cdots & a_{mn} \end{pmatrix}.$$

Clearly, we have $(A^{\mathsf{H}})^{\mathsf{H}} = A$ for every $A \in \mathbb{C}^{m \times n}$ and $(A')' = A$ for every $A \in \mathbb{R}^{m \times n}$.

Example 2.1. The set $\mathbb{R}^n$ of vectors of length n over $\mathbb{R}$ is a real linear space under the definition of vector addition:

$$\mathbf{x} + \mathbf{y} = \begin{pmatrix} x_1 + y_1 \\ \vdots \\ x_n + y_n \end{pmatrix}$$

and of multiplication of vectors by scalars:

$$a \cdot \mathbf{x} = \begin{pmatrix} a \cdot x_1 \\ \vdots \\ a \cdot x_n \end{pmatrix}.$$

In this linear space we use the notation

$$\mathbf{0}_n = \begin{pmatrix} 0 \\ \vdots \\ 0 \end{pmatrix}.$$

Similarly, the set $\mathbb{C}^n$ of n-tuples of complex numbers is a real linear space under the same formal definitions of vector sum and scalar multiplication as $\mathbb{R}^n$.

Example 2.2. The set of infinite sequences of real numbers $\mathbf{Seq}_\infty(\mathbb{R})$ can be organized as a real linear space by defining the addition of two sequences

$$\mathbf{x} = (x_0, x_1, \ldots) \text{ and } \mathbf{y} = (y_0, y_1, \ldots)$$

as $\mathbf{x} + \mathbf{y} = (x_0 + y_0, x_1 + y_1, \ldots)$, and the multiplication by $c\mathbf{x}$ as $c\mathbf{x} = (cx_0, cx_1, \ldots)$ for $c \in \mathbb{R}$.

Example 2.3. Let L be an $\mathbb{F}$-linear space and let S be a non-empty set. The set of functions $f : S \longrightarrow L$ is a linear space denoted by L^S.

The addition of functions is given by $(f + g)(s) = f(s) + g(s)$, and the multiplication of a function with by $a \in \mathbb{F}$ is defined by $(af)(s) = af(s)$ for $s \in S$.

In particular, the set $\mathbb{C}^S$ is a complex linear space and the set $\mathbb{R}^S$ is a real linear space.

For $\mathbf{x}, \mathbf{y} \in \mathbb{R}^n$ we write

  (i) $\mathbf{x} \geqslant \mathbf{y}$ if $x_i \geqslant y_i$ for $1 \leqslant i \leqslant n$;

  (ii) $\mathbf{x} \geq \mathbf{y}$ if $\mathbf{x} \geqslant \mathbf{y}$ and $\mathbf{x} \neq \mathbf{y}$;

  (iii) $\mathbf{x} > \mathbf{y}$ if $x_i > y_i$ for $1 \leqslant i \leqslant n$.

If $\mathbf{x} \geqslant \mathbf{0}_n$, we say that $\mathbf{x}$ is *non-negative*; if $\mathbf{x} \geq \mathbf{0}_n$, $\mathbf{x}$ is said to be *semi-positive*, and if $\mathbf{x} > \mathbf{0}_n$, then $\mathbf{x}$ is *positive*. The relation "$\geqslant$" is a partial order on $\mathbb{R}^n$; the other two relations, "$\geq$" and "$>$" are strict partial orders on the same set because they lack reflexivity.

In some cases, when $\mathbf{x}, \mathbf{y} \in \mathbb{R}^n$ and ξ is one of the relations $\{\geqslant, \geq, >\}$ we write $\mathbf{x}\xi_n\mathbf{y}$ in order to stress that the relation involves vectors in $\mathbb{R}^n$.

Further, if $\mathbf{x}, \mathbf{y} \in \mathbb{R}^n$, $\mathbf{u}, \mathbf{v} \in \mathbb{R}^p$, and ξ, ζ are symbols in the set $\{\geqslant, \geq, >\}$ we write

$$\begin{pmatrix} \mathbf{x} \\ \mathbf{y} \end{pmatrix} \begin{bmatrix} \xi \\ \zeta \end{bmatrix} \begin{pmatrix} \mathbf{u} \\ \mathbf{v} \end{pmatrix}$$

if and only if $\mathbf{x} \, \xi \, \mathbf{u}$ and $\mathbf{y} \, \zeta \, \mathbf{v}$.

Definition 2.2. Let L be an $\mathbb{F}$-linear space and let K be a subset of L. A *linear combination of K* is a *finite* sum of the form $c_1 x_1 + \cdots + c_m x_m$, where $c_1, \ldots, c_m \in \mathbb{F}$.

The *empty linear combination* corresponds to $m = 0$ and is defined to be the zero vector 0_L of L.

The notion of linear combination is used for defining linearly independent sets in linear spaces.

Definition 2.3. A subset K of L is *linearly independent* if for every linear combination $c_1 x_1 + \cdots + c_m x_m$ of elements of K, the equality $c_1 x_1 + \cdots + c_m x_m = 0_L$ implies $c_1 = \cdots = c_m = 0$.

If K is not linearly independent, we refer to K as a *linearly dependent* set.

If $x \neq 0_L$, then the set $\{x\}$ is linearly independent. Of course, the set $\{0_L\}$ is not linearly independent because $1 \, 0_L = 0_L$. If K is a linearly independent subset of a linear space, then any subset of K is linearly independent.

Example 2.4. Let

$$\mathbf{e}_i = \begin{pmatrix} 0 \\ \vdots \\ 1 \\ \vdots \\ 0 \end{pmatrix}$$

be a vector in $\mathbb{R}^n$ that has a unique non-zero component equal to 1 in place i, where $1 \leqslant i \leqslant n$.

The set $E = \{\mathbf{e}_1, \ldots, \mathbf{e}_n\}$ is linearly independent. Indeed, suppose that $c_1 \mathbf{e}_1 + \cdots + c_n \mathbf{e}_n = \mathbf{0}_n$. This is equivalent to

$$\begin{pmatrix} c_1 \\ \vdots \\ c_n \end{pmatrix} = \begin{pmatrix} 0 \\ \vdots \\ 0 \end{pmatrix}$$

that is, with $c_1 = \cdots = c_n = 0$. Thus, E is linearly independent.

Theorem 2.1. *Let L be an $\mathbb{F}$-linear space. A subset K of L is linearly independent if and only if for every linear combination $x = \sum_{i=1}^{m} c_i x_i$ (where $x_i \in K$ for $1 \leqslant i \leqslant m$) the coefficients c_i are uniquely determined.*

Proof. Let K be linearly independent subset of L, and suppose that $x = c_1 x_1 + \cdots + c_m x_m = c_1' x_1 + \cdots + c_m' x_m$, where $x_1, \ldots, x_m \in K$. If there exists i such that $c_i \neq c_i'$, then $\sum_{i=1}^{m}(c_i - c_i')x_i = 0_L$ and $c_i - c_i' \neq 0$, which contradicts the linear independence of K.

Conversely, suppose that K is not linearly independent, that is, there exists a linear combination $d_1 x_1 + \cdots + d_m x_m = 0_L$ such that at least one d_i is not 0. Then, if $x = \sum_{i=1}^{m} c_i x_i$ we also have $x = \sum_{i=1}^{m}(c_i + d_i)x_i$ and at there exists i such that $c_i \neq c_i + d_i$, which contradicts the uniqueness of the coefficients of x. $\qquad\square$

Definition 2.4. A subset S of an $\mathbb{F}$-linear space L *spans* the space L (or S *generates* the linear space) if every $x \in L$ is a linear combination of S.

A *Hamel basis* (or, simply a *basis*) of the linear space L is a linearly independent subset that spans the linear space.

In view of Theorem 2.1, a set B is a Hamel basis if every $x \in L$ can be written uniquely as a linear combination of elements of B.

Definition 2.5. A *subspace* of an $\mathbb{F}$-linear space L is a non-empty subset U of L such that $x, y \in U$ implies $x + y \in U$ and $a \cdot x \in U$ for every $a \in \mathbb{F}$.

If U is a subspace of an $\mathbb{F}$-linear space, then U itself can be regarded as a real linear space and various notions introduced for real linear spaces are applicable to U.

The set $\{0_L\}$ is a subspace of any $\mathbb{F}$-linear space L referred to as the *trivial subspace* of L. Note that $\{0_L\}$ is included in every subspace of L.

If $\{U_i \mid i \in I\}$ is a non-empty collection of subspaces of an $\mathbb{F}$-linear space L, then $\bigcap\{U_i \mid i \in I\}$ is also a subspace of L. Also, L itself is a subspace, so the collection of subspaces of an $\mathbb{F}$-linear space is a closure system.

If U is a subset of L and $\mathbf{K}_{\mathrm{subs}}$ is the corresponding closure operator for the closure system of linear subspaces, then we say that U is *spanning* the subspace $\mathbf{K}_{\mathrm{subs}}(U)$ of L. The subspace $\mathbf{K}_{\mathrm{subs}}(U)$ is said to be *spanned* or *generated* by U. Frequently, we denote this subspace by $\langle U \rangle$.

Theorem 2.2. *If U is a subset of a linear space L, then $\langle U \rangle$ consists of all linear combinations of elements of U.*

Proof. The set T of linear combinations of elements of U is clearly a subspace of L such that $U \subseteq T \subseteq \langle U \rangle$. Since $\langle U \rangle$ is the minimal subspace that contains U, it follows that $\langle U \rangle = T$. $\qquad\qquad\square$

Theorem 2.3. *Let P, Q be two subspaces of an $\mathbb{F}$-linear space L. Then, the set*

$$P + Q = \{u + v \mid u \in P, v \in Q\}$$

is a subspace of L and $\langle P \cup Q \rangle = P + Q$.

Proof. Suppose that $x, y \in P + Q$, where $x = u_1 + v_1$, $y = u_2 + v_2$, where $u_1, u_2 \in P$ and $v_1, v_2 \in Q$. Since P and Q are subspaces of L, we have $u_1 + u_2 \in P$ and $v_1 + v_2 \in Q$. This, in turn, implies

$$x + y = u_1 + v_1 + u_2 + v_2 = (u_1 + u_2) + (v_1 + v_2) \in P + Q.$$

If $a \in \mathbb{F}$ is a scalar, then $au_1 \in P$ and $av_1 \in Q$, so

$$ax = au_1 + av_1 \in Q + P,$$

which shows that $P + Q$ is indeed a subspace of L.

Note that $P \cup Q \subseteq P + Q$, so $\langle P \cup Q \rangle \subseteq P + Q$. The converse inclusion follows from the fact that every element of $P + Q$ is a linear combination of the elements of $P \cup Q$. $\qquad\qquad\square$

Theorem 2.4. *The following statements that concern an $\mathbb{F}$-linear space L are equivalent:*

(i) *the finite set $B = \{x_1, \ldots, x_n\}$ is spanning L and B is minimal with this property;*

(ii) *B is a finite basis for L;*

(iii) *the finite set B is linearly independent, and B is maximal with this property.*

Proof. (i) implies (ii): We need to prove that B is linearly independent. Suppose that this is not the case. Then, there exist $c_1, \ldots, c_n \in \mathbb{F}$ such that $c_1 x_1 + \cdots + c_n x_n = 0$ and at least one of $c_1, \ldots, c_n$, say c_i, is non-zero. Then, $x_i = -\frac{c_1}{c_i} x_1 - \cdots - \frac{c_n}{c_i} x_n$, and this implies that $B - \{x_i\}$ also spans the linear space, thus contradicting the minimality of B.

(ii) implies (i): Let B be a finite basis. Suppose that B' is a proper subset of S that spans L. Then, if $z \in B - B'$, z is a linear combination of elements of B', which contradicts the fact that B is a basis.

We leave to the reader the proof of the equivalence between (ii) and (iii). □

Corollary 2.1. *Every $\mathbb{F}$-linear space L that is spanned by a finite subset has a finite basis. Further, if B is a finite basis for an $\mathbb{F}$-linear space L, then each finite subset U of L such that $|U| = |B| + 1$ is linearly dependent.*

Proof. This statement follows directly from Theorem 2.4. □

Corollary 2.2. *If B and B' are two finite bases for an $\mathbb{F}$-linear space L, then $|B| = |B'|$.*

Proof. If B is a finite basis, then $|B|$ is the maximum number of linearly independent elements in L. Thus, $|B'| \leqslant |B|$. Reversing the roles of B and B', we obtain $|B| \leqslant |B'|$, so $|B| = |B'|$. □

Thus, the number of elements of a finite basis of L is a characteristic of L and does not depend on any particular basis.

Definition 2.6. An $\mathbb{F}$-linear space L is *n-dimensional* if there exists a basis of L such that $|B| = n$. The number n is the *dimension* of L and is denoted by $\dim(L)$.

An $\mathbb{F}$-linear space L is *finite-dimensional* if there exists $n \in \mathbb{N}$ such that $\dim(L) = n$.

If a linear space V is not finite-dimensional than we say that $\dim(V)$ is infinite.

Example 2.5. Let S be a non-empty, finite set. The linear space of functions $\mathbb{C}^S$ has dimension $|S|$. Indeed, for each $t \in S$ consider the function $f_t : S \longrightarrow \mathbb{C}$ defined by

$$f_t(s) = \begin{cases} 1 & \text{if } s = t, \\ 0 & \text{otherwise} \end{cases}$$

for $t \in S$. If $S = \{t_1, \ldots, t_n\}$, then the set of functions $\{f_{t_1}, \ldots, f_{t_n}\}$ is linearly independent, for if $c_1 f_{t_1}(s) + \cdots + c_n f_{t_n}(s) = 0$, then by taking $s = t_k$ we obtain $c_k = 0$ for any k, $1 \leqslant k \leqslant n$. Furthermore, if $f : S \longrightarrow \mathbb{C}$ is a function and $f(t_i) = c_i$, then $f = \sum_{i=1}^n c_i f_{t_i}$, so $\{f_{t_1}, \ldots, f_{t_n}\}$ is a basis for $\mathbb{C}^S$.

Theorem 2.5. *Let L be a finite-dimensional $\mathbb{F}$-linear space and let $U = \{u_1, \ldots, u_k\}$ be a linearly independent subset of L. There exists an extension of U that is a basis of L.*

Proof. If $\langle U \rangle = L$, then U is a basis of L. If this is not the case, let $w_1 \in L - \langle U \rangle$. The set $U \cup \{w_1\}$ is linearly independent and we have the strict inclusion $\langle U \rangle \subset \langle U \cup \{w_1\} \rangle$. The subspace $\langle U \cup \{w\} \rangle$ is $(k+1)$-dimensional. This argument can be repeated no more than $n - k$ times, where $n = \dim(L)$. Thus, $U \cup \{w_1, \ldots, w_{n-k}\}$ is a basis for L that extends U. $\qquad \square$

Definition 2.7. Let L be an F-linear space and let U, V be subspaces of L. The *sum* of the subspaces U and V is the set $U + V$ defined by:

$$U + V = \{\mathbf{u} + \mathbf{v} \mid \mathbf{u} \in U \text{ and } \mathbf{v} \in V\}.$$

It is easy to verify that $U + V$ is also a subspace of L.

Theorem 2.6. *Let U, V be two subspaces of a finite-dimensional $\mathbb{F}$-linear space L. We have*

$$\dim(U + V) + \dim(U \cap V) = \dim(U) + \dim(V).$$

Proof. Let $\{w_1, \ldots, w_k\}$ be a basis for $U \cap V$, where $k = \dim(U \cap V)$ which can be extended to a basis $\{w_1, \ldots, w_k, u_{k+1}, \ldots, u_p\}$ for U and to a basis $\{w_1, \ldots, w_k, v_{k+1}, \ldots, v_q\}$ for V.

Define $B = \{w_1, \ldots, w_k, u_{k+1}, \ldots, u_p, v_{k+1}, \ldots, v_q\}$. It is clear that $\langle B \rangle = U + V$. Suppose that there exist $c_1, \ldots, c_{p+q-k}$ such that

$$c_1 w_1 + \cdots + c_k w_k + c_{k+1} u_{k+1} + \cdots + c_p u_p + c_{p+1} v_{k+1} + \cdots + c_{p+q-k} v_q = \mathbf{0}.$$

The last equality implies

$$c_1 w_1 + \cdots + c_k w_k + c_{k+1} u_{k+1} + \cdots + c_p u_p = -c_{p+1} v_{k+1} - \cdots - c_{p+q-k} v_q.$$

Therefore, $c_1 \mathbf{w}_1 + \cdots + c_k \mathbf{w}_k + c_{k+1} u_{k+1} + \cdots + c_p u_p$ belongs to $U \cap V$, which implies $c_{k+1} = \cdots = c_p = 0$. Since

$$c_1 w_1 + \cdots + c_k w_k + c_{p+1} v_{k+1} + \cdots + c_{p+q-k} v_q = \mathbf{0},$$

and $\{w_1, \ldots, w_k, v_{k+1}, \ldots, v_q\}$ is a basis for V, it follows that $c_1 = \cdots = c_k = c_{p+1} = \cdots = c_{p+q-k} = 0$.

This allows to conclude that $\dim(U + V) = p + q - k$ and this implies the equality of the theorem. □

Example 2.6. Let $\mathsf{Pol}(\mathbb{R})$ be the set of one-argument polynomials with real coefficients. This set is a real linear space under the addition of polynomials and multiplication by a real number. Every polynomial in $\mathsf{Pol}(\mathbb{R})$, $p(x) = a_n x^n + a_{n-1} x^{n-1} + \cdots + a_1 x + a_0$ is a finite linear combination of the set of polynomials $B = \{1, x, \ldots, x_m, \ldots\}$. Also if $z(x)$ is the zero polynomial (that is, p is a polynomial that equals 0 for every $x \in \mathbb{R}$), then all coefficients of z are 0, which implies that the set B is linearly independent and therefore it is a basis for $\mathsf{Pol}(\mathbb{R})$. This shows that $\dim(\mathsf{Pol}(\mathbb{R}))$ is infinite.

Using Zorn' Lemma it is possible to show that every linear space has a basis. However, this is an existence statement and, in many cases, such a basis cannot be effectively specified.

Theorem 2.7. *Every non-trivial linear space has a basis.*

Proof. Let L be a non-trivial linear space. Consider the collection $\mathcal{L}$ of linearly independent sets ordered by inclusion. Let $\mathcal{C}$ be a chain of linearly independent sets and let $\hat{C} = \bigcup \mathcal{C}$.

We claim that $\hat{C}$ is itself linearly independent. Suppose that $\sum_{i \in I} a_i x_i = 0$, where at least one of a_i is not 0, $x_i \in C_i$ for $i \in I$ and I is a finite set. Since $\mathcal{C}$ is a chain one of the sets C_i, say C_{i_*} contains x_i for each $i \in I$. This contradicts the linear independence of C_{i_*}, which implies that $\hat{C}$ is linearly independent. Thus shows that every chain of linearly independent sets has an upper bound. By Zorn's Lemma, the set of linearly independent sets has a maximal element M.

Let $x \in L$. The set $M \cup \{x\}$ is either linearly independent or $x \in M$. In either case, x is a linear combination of M. Moreover, x can be represented uniquely as a linear combination of M for, otherwise, we would have 0 as a non-trivial linear combination of elements of M, contradicting the linear independence of M. □

Corollary 2.3. *Let L be a linear space. Every linearly independent subset of L can be extended to a base of L.*

Proof. This statement follows immediately from the proof of Theorem 2.7. □

2.3 Linear Operators and Functionals

Linear operators between linear spaces are functions that are compatible with the algebraic operations of linear spaces.

Definition 2.8. Let L and K be two $\mathbb{F}$-linear spaces. A *linear operator* is a function $h : L \longrightarrow K$ such that $h(ax + by) = ah(x) + bh(y)$ for every $a, b \in \mathbb{F}$ and $x, y \in L$.

An *isomorphism* between the $\mathbb{F}$-linear spaces L and K is a linear operator between these spaces which is a bijection.

In the special case, when K is the field $\mathbb{F}$, linear operators are referred to as *linear functionals*.

The set of linear operators between two linear spaces L and K is denoted by $\mathfrak{L}(L, K)$.

We denote by 1_L the identity linear operator, $1_L : L \longrightarrow L$ defined by $1_L(x) = x$ for $x \in L$. The operator $0_L : L \longrightarrow L$ maps every $x \in L$ into 0_L.

Theorem 2.8. *Let L, K be two $\mathbb{F}$-linear spaces and let $h : L \longrightarrow K$ be a linear operator. The sets*
$$\text{Null}(h) = \{x \in L \mid h(x) = 0_K\},$$
$$\text{Img}(h) = \{y \in K \mid y = h(x) \text{ for some } x \in L\}$$
are subspaces of L and K, respectively.

Proof. Let $u, v \in \text{Null}(h)$. Since $h(u) = h(v) = 0_K$ it follows that $h(au + bv) = ah(u) + bh(v) = 0_K$, for $a, b \in \mathbb{F}$, so $au + bv \in \text{Null}(h)$. This shows that $\text{Null}(h)$ is indeed a subspace of L.

Let now $s, t \in \text{Img}(h)$. There exist $x, y \in L$ such that $s = h(x)$ and $t = h(y)$. Therefore, $as + bt = ah(x) + bh(y) = h(ax + by)$, hence $as + bt \in \text{Img}(h)$. This implies that $\text{Img}(h)$ is a subspace of K. □

$\text{Null}(h)$ and $\text{Img}(h)$ are referred to as the *null subspace* and the *image subspace* of h, respectively.

Theorem 2.9. *Let L, K be two $\mathbb{F}$-linear spaces and let $h : L \longrightarrow K$ be a linear operator. The operator h is injective if and only if $\text{Null}(h) = \{0_L\}$.*

Proof. Let h be an injective linear operator. If $x \neq 0_L$ and $x \in \mathsf{Null}(h)$, then $h(x) = h(0_L) = 0_K$, so h is not injective. Thus, $\mathsf{Null}(h) = \{0_L\}$.

Conversely, suppose that $\mathsf{Null}(h) = \{0_L\}$. If $h(u) = h(v)$ for $u, v \in L$, then $h(u - v) = 0_K$, so $u - v \in \mathsf{Null}(h)$, which implies $u - v = 0_L$, that is, $u = v$. □

In other words, h is injective if and only if $h(x) = 0_K$ implies $x = 0_L$.

Corollary 2.4. *Let L and K be two linear spaces having 0_L and 0_K as their zero elements, respectively. A linear operator $h \in \mathfrak{L}(L, K)$ is an isomorphism if and only if $h(x) = 0_K$ implies $x = 0_L$ and $h(L) = K$.*

Proof. This is an immediate consequence of Theorem 2.9. □

An *endomorphism* of an $\mathbb{F}$-linear space L is a linear operator $h : L \longrightarrow L$. The set of endomorphisms of L is denoted by $\mathfrak{L}(L)$. Often, we refer to endomorphisms of L as *linear operators* on L.

Theorem 2.10. *Let L and K be two finite-dimensional linear spaces. The linear operator $h \in \mathfrak{L}(L, K)$ is injective if and only if its surjective.*

Proof. Suppose that h is an injective linear operator and that $\{u_1, \ldots, u_n\}$ is a basis in L. The injectivity of h means that we have n distinct vectors $h(u_1), \ldots, h(u_n)$ in K and the set $\{h(u_1), \ldots, h(u_n)\}$ is linearly independent. Indeed, suppose that $c_1 h(u_1) + \cdots + c_n h(u_n) = 0_K$. Then $h(c_1 u_1 + \cdots + c_n u_n) = 0_K$, hence $c_1 u_1 + \cdots + c_n u_n = \mathbf{0}_L$. This, in turn, implies $c_1 = \cdots = c_n = 0$. Thus, $\{h(u_1), \ldots, h(u_n)\}$ is a basis in K and every element $y \in K$ can be written as

$$y = b_1 h(u_1) + \cdots + b_n h(u_n) = h(b_1 u_1 + \cdots + h_n u_n) \in h(L),$$

which allows us to conclude that h is surjective.

Conversely, suppose that h is surjective. If $v_1, \ldots, v_n$ is a basis in K, there exist $u_1, \ldots, u_n$ in L such that $h(u_i) = v_i$ for $1 \leqslant i \leqslant n$. Note that the set $\{u_1, \ldots, u_n\}$ is a basis for L.

Let $x \in L$ and assume that $h(x) = 0_K$. If $x = \sum_{i=1}^{n} a_i u_i$, then $h(x) = \sum_{i=1}^{n} a_i h(u_i) = \sum_{i=1}^{n} a_i v_i = 0_K$, which implies $a_1 = \cdots = a_i = 0$. This, in turn, means that $x = 0_L$, so h is an injective function by Theorem 2.9. □

Corollary 2.5. *Let L and K be two finite-dimensional linear spaces and let $h \in \mathfrak{L}(L, K)$. The following statements are equivalent:*

   (i) *h is an isomorphism;*

   (ii) *h is injective;*

   (iii) *h is surjective.*

Proof. The equivalence of the three statements follows immediately from Theorem 2.10. □

Definition 2.9. A linear operator $h : L \longrightarrow K$ between the linear spaces L and K is *invertible* if there exists a linear operator $g : K \longrightarrow L$ such that $gh = 1_L$ and $hg = 1_K$. In this case, we say that g is the *inverse* of h and we denote this operator by h^{-1}.

Theorem 2.11. *Let L be a finite-dimensional space and let h, g be two linear operators such that $gh = 1_L$. We have $hg = 1_L$, so g is the inverse of h.*

Proof. Suppose that $gh = 1_L$. Then, for every $x \in L$ we have $x = g(h(x))$, so g is surjective operator and, therefore, by Corollary 2.5, g is isomorphism. If $h(u) = h(v)$ then $u = g(h(u)) = g(h(v)) = v$, so h is injective and, therefore, an isomorphism. This shows that h and g are inverse isomorphisms. □

For an $\mathbb{F}$-linear space, the function $\ell_0 : L \longrightarrow \mathbb{F}$ given by $\ell_0(x) = 0$ is a linear functional referred to as the *trivial functional* or the *zero functional*.

Theorem 2.12. *Let L be an $\mathbb{F}$-linear space. Any non-trivial linear functional on L is a surjective function.*

Proof. Let $\ell : L \longrightarrow \mathbb{F}$ be a non-trivial functional on L. There exists $x_0 \in L$ such that $\ell(x_0) \neq 0$. Note that $\ell(\frac{x_0}{\ell(x_0)}) = 1$. Therefore, for each $a \in \mathbb{F}$ we have

$$\ell\left(a \frac{x_0}{\ell(x_0)}\right) = a,$$

which shows that ℓ is surjective. □

Theorem 2.13. *Let L be an $\mathbb{F}$-linear space. If $x \in L$ is such that $\ell(x) = 0$ for every linear functional ℓ, then $x = 0_L$.*

Proof. Suppose that $\ell(x) = 0$ for every linear functional ℓ and $x \neq 0_L$. Since $x \neq 0_L$, there exists a basis B of L that includes x.

Every $y \in L$ can be expressed as a linear combination of elements of B, so there exists $c \in \mathbb{F}$ such that $y = \cdots + cx + \cdots$. It is easy to see that the function $g : L \longrightarrow \mathbb{F}$ defined by $g(y) = c$ is a linear functional on L. Since $g(x) = 1$, this contradicts the hypothesis. Thus, $x = 0_L$. □

Example 2.7. Let L be an $\mathbb{F}$-linear space and let B be a basis of L. For $x \in B$ define $e_x : L \longrightarrow \mathbb{F}$ as $e_x(y) = a$ if $y = \cdots + ax + \cdots$. The function e_x is a linear functional on L.

Example 2.8. Let L be an $\mathbb{F}$-linear space. The *translation* generated by $z \in L$ is the mapping $\mathsf{t}_z : L \longrightarrow L$ defined by $\mathsf{t}_z(x) = x + z$. Any such mapping is a bijection on L but not a linear operator unless $z = 0_L$. Its inverse is t_{-z}.

Example 2.9. Let L be an $\mathbb{F}$-linear space. The *homothety* generated by $a \in F$ is the mapping $\mathsf{h}_a : L \longrightarrow L$ defined by $\mathsf{h}_a(x) = ax$. Any homothety is a linear operator; if $a \neq 0$, the inverse of h_a is $\mathsf{h}_{\frac{1}{a}}$.

Example 2.10. Let L be an $\mathbb{F}$-linear space. The *reflection* is the mapping $\mathsf{r} : L \longrightarrow L$ defined by $\mathsf{r}(x) = -x$. Any reflection is a linear operator. The inverse of r is r itself.

If L, K are two $\mathbb{F}$-linear spaces, then the set $\mathfrak{L}(L, K)$ is never empty because the zero linear operator $0_L : L \longrightarrow K$ given by $0_L(x) = 0_K$ for $x \in L$ is always an element of $\mathfrak{L}(L, K)$.

Definition 2.10. Let L and K be two F-linear spaces. If $f, g \in \mathfrak{L}(L, K)$, the *sum* $f + g$ is defined by $(f + g)(x) = f(x) + g(x)$ for $x \in L$.

The sum of two linear operators is also a linear operator because

$$
\begin{aligned}
(f + g)(ax + by) &= f(ax + by) + g(ax + by) \\
&= af(x) + bf(y) + ag(x) + bg(y) \\
&= f(ax + by) + g(ax + by),
\end{aligned}
$$

for all $a, b \in F$ and $x, y \in L$.

Theorem 2.14. *Let M, P, Q be three real linear spaces. The following properties of compositions of linear operators hold:*
   (i) *If $f \in \mathfrak{L}(M, P)$ and $g \in \mathfrak{L}(P, Q)$, then $gf \in \mathfrak{L}(M, Q)$.*
   (ii) *If $f \in \mathfrak{L}(M, P)$ and $g_0, g_1 \in \mathfrak{L}(P, Q)$, then*

$$f(g_0 + g_1) = fg_0 + fg_1.$$

  (iii) *If $f_0, f_1 \in \mathfrak{L}(M, P)$ and $g \in \mathfrak{L}(P, Q)$, then*

$$(f_0 + f_1)g = f_0 g + f_1 g.$$

Proof. We prove only the second part of the theorem and leave the proofs of the remaining parts to the reader.

Let $x \in M$. Then, $f(g_0 + g_1)(x) = f((g_0 + g_1)(x)) = f(g_0(x) + g_1(x)) = f(g_0(x)) + f(g_1(x))$ for $x \in M$, which yields the desired equality. $\qquad\square$

We leave to the reader to verify that for any linear spaces M and P the algebra $(\mathfrak{L}(M, P), \{h_0, +, -\})$ is an Abelian group that has the zero linear operator h_0 as its zero-ary operations and the addition of linear operators as its binary operation; the opposite of a linear operator h is the operator $-h$.

Moreover, $(\mathfrak{L}(M), \{h_0, i_M, +, -, \cdot\})$ is a unitary ring, where the multiplication is defined as the composition of linear operators.

If M and P are linear spaces, $\mathfrak{L}(M, P)$ is itself an linear space, where the multiplication of a linear operator h by a scalar c is the linear operator ch defined by $(ch)(x) = c \cdot h(x)$. Indeed, the operator ch is linear because

$$(ch)(ax + by) = c(ah(x) + bh(y)) = cah(x) + cbh(y)$$
$$= ach(x) + bch(y) = a(ch)(x) + b(ch)(y),$$

for every $a, b, c \in F$ and $x, y \in M$.

Definition 2.11. Let h be an endomorphism of a linear space M. The mth *iteration* of h (for $m \in \mathbb{N}$) is defined as
  (i) $h^0 = i_M$;
  (ii) $h^{m+1}(x) = h(h^m(x))$ for $m \in \mathbb{N}$.

For every $m \geqslant 1$, h^m is an endomorphism of M; this can be shown by a straightforward proof by induction on m.

Definition 2.12. A linear operator $h : L \longrightarrow L$ on a linear space L is *idempotent* if $h(h(x)) = h(x)$ for every $x \in L$.

Theorem 2.15. *Let $h : L \longrightarrow L$ be an idempotent linear operator on a linear space L. The linear operator $g = 1_L - h$ is also idempotent. Furthermore, we have* $\mathsf{Img}(h) = \mathsf{Null}(1_L - h)$ *and* $\mathsf{Img}(1_L - h) = \mathsf{Null}(h)$.

Proof. Note that $g(x) = (1_L - h)(x) = x - h(x)$. Therefore,

$$g(g(x)) = g(x) - h(g(x)) = g(x) - h(x) + h(h(x)) = g(x),$$

because $h(h(x)) = h(x)$.

If $y \in \mathsf{Img}(h)$, then $y = h(x)$. This is equivalent to $h(y) = h(h(x)) = h(x) = y$, which means that $(1_L - h)(y) = 0_L$. Therefore, $\mathsf{Img}(h) = \mathsf{Null}(1_L - h)$. Replacing h by $1_K - h$ we obtain $\mathsf{Img}(1_L - h) = \mathsf{Null}(h)$. $\quad\square$

In general, we shall refer to an idempotent linear operator on a linear space as a *projection*.

Theorem 2.16. *Let L be an $\mathbb{F}$-linear space and let $p : L \longrightarrow L$ be a projection. If $\mathsf{Img}(p)$ is a finite-dimensional subspace of L having the basis $\{v_1, \ldots, v_n\}$, then there exist n linear functionals $\ell_1, \ldots, \ell_n$ such that*

$$\ell_i(v_j) = \begin{cases} 1 & \text{if } i = j, \\ 0 & \text{otherwise} \end{cases} \qquad (2.1)$$

for $1 \leqslant i, j \leqslant n$ and $p(x) = \sum_{j=1}^{n} \ell_j(x) v_j$.

Proof. Let $v \in \mathsf{Img}(h)$. If $v = \sum_{j=1}^{n} a_j v_j$, define $f_j(v) = a_j$ for $1 \leqslant j \leqslant n$. It is immediate that the mappings $f_j : \mathsf{Img}(h) \longrightarrow \mathbb{R}$ are linear functionals. Since $p(x) \in \mathsf{Img}(p)$ for every $x \in L$, it follows that $p(x) = \sum_{j=1}^{n} f_j(p(x)) v_j$. Let $\ell_j : L \longrightarrow \mathbb{F}$ be defined as $\ell_j(x) = f_j(p(x))$ for $1 \leqslant j \leqslant n$.

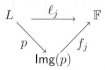

Clearly, ℓ_j is a linear functional. Since $p(v_j) = v_j$ for $1 \leqslant j \leqslant n$, equalities (2.1) follow. $\qquad \square$

Definition 2.13. Let L be an $\mathbb{F}$-linear space and let U be a subspace of L. A pair $(x, y) \in L^2$ is *U-congruent* if $x - y \in U$. This is denoted by $x \sim_U y$.

For a subspace U of an $\mathbb{F}$-linear space the relation $\sim_U$ that consists of all pairs of U-congruent elements is an equivalence relation on L. Indeed, $x \sim_U x$ because $x - x = 0 \in U$. Since $x - y \in U$ is equivalent to $y - x \in U$, it follows that $\sim_U$ is symmetric. Finally, suppose that $x \sim_U y$ and $y \sim_U z$. Since

$$x - z = (x - y) + (y - z) \in U,$$

it follows that $\sim_U$ is symmetric, so $\sim_U$ is an equivalence.

The equivalence class of $x \in L$ relative to $\sim_U$ is denoted by $[x]_U$ and the set of such equivalence classes is denoted by $L/ \sim_U$. This set can be organized, in turn, as an $\mathbb{F}$-linear space by defining $a[x]_U = [ax]_U$ for $a \in \mathbb{F}$ and $[x]_U + [y]_U = [x + y]_U$ for $x, y \in L$. Indeed, it is easy to verify that the definition of these operations is independent of the choice of class representative.

Let $h \in \mathfrak{L}(L, K)$ be a linear operator between the two finite-dimensional linear spaces L and K having the Hamel bases $R = \{r_1, \ldots, r_m\}$, and $S = \{s_1, \ldots, s_n\}$, respectively.

Since $h(r_j) \in K$ we can write:

$$h(r_j) = a_{1j}s_1 + a_{2j}s_2 + \cdots + a_{nj}s_n.$$

In a more compact form, the last equality can be written using matrices as

$$h(r_j) = (s_1, \ldots, s_n) \begin{pmatrix} a_{1j} \\ \vdots \\ a_{nj} \end{pmatrix}.$$

The *matrix $A_h \in \mathbb{C}^{n \times m}$ associated to the linear operator $h : L \longrightarrow K$ is the* matrix that has

$$h(r_j) = \begin{pmatrix} a_{1j} \\ a_{2j} \\ \vdots \\ a_{nj} \end{pmatrix}$$

as its jth column for $1 \leqslant j \leqslant m$, where $h(r_j) = a_{1j}s_1 + a_{2j}s_2 + \cdots + a_{nj}s_n$ for $1 \leqslant j \leqslant m$. In other words, the image of r_j under h is represented by the jth column of the matrix A_h.

Let $v \in L$ be a vector such that $v = v_1 r_1 + \cdots + v_m r_m$. The image of v under h is

$$h(v) = h\left(\sum_{j=1}^{m} v_j r_j\right) = \sum_{j=1}^{m} v_j h(r_j)$$

$$= \sum_{j=1}^{m} v_j \begin{pmatrix} a_{1j} \\ a_{2j} \\ \vdots \\ a_{nj} \end{pmatrix} = \begin{pmatrix} \sum_{j=1}^{m} a_{1j}v_j \\ \sum_{j=1}^{m} a_{2j}v_j \\ \vdots \\ \sum_{j=1}^{m} a_{nj}v_j \end{pmatrix},$$

which is easily seen to equal $A_h v$.

The matrix A_h attached to $h : L \longrightarrow K$ depends on the bases chosen for the linear spaces L and K. The previous discussion also shows that a linear operator between two finite-dimensional spaces is completely determined by the values of the operator on the elements of the basis in the definition space.

Matrix multiplication corresponds to the composition of linear operators, as we show next.

Theorem 2.17. *Let L, K, H be three finite-dimensional linear spaces. Let $h \in \mathfrak{L}(L, K)$ and $g \in \mathfrak{L}(K, H)$. Then,*

$$A_{gh} = A_g A_h.$$

Proof. If $p_1, \ldots, p_m$ is a basis for L, then $A_{gh}(p_i) = gh(p_i) = g(h(p_i)) = g(A_h p_i) = A_g(A_h(p_i))$ for every i, where $1 \leqslant i \leq n$. This proves that $A_{gh} = A_g A_h$. $\square$

Starting from a matrix $A \in \mathbb{C}^{m \times n}$ we can define a *linear operator associated to* A, $h_A : \mathbb{C}^n \longrightarrow \mathbb{C}^m$ as $h_A(\mathbf{x}) = A\mathbf{x}$ for $\mathbf{x} \in \mathbb{C}^n$. If $\mathbf{e}_1, \ldots, \mathbf{e}_n$ is a basis for $\mathbb{C}^n$, then $h_A(\mathbf{e}_i)$ is the ith column of the matrix A.

It is immediate that $A_{h_A} = A$ and $h_{A_h} = h$.

Definition 2.14. A matrix $A \in \mathbb{C}^{n \times n}$ is:

   (i) *upper triangular* if $a_{kj} = 0$ when $j > k$;
   (ii) *lower triangular* if $a_{kj} = 0$ when $j < k$;
   (iii) *diagonal* if $a_{kj} = 0$ when $j \neq k$.

If $A \in \mathbb{C}^{n \times n}$ is a diagonal matrix whose diagonal elements are $d_1, \ldots, d_n$ we shall use the notation $A = \mathsf{diag}(d_1, \ldots, d_n)$.

Definition 2.15. Let L be a finite-dimensional space with $\dim(L) = n$ and let $h : L \longrightarrow L$ be a linear operator. The *determinant* of h, $\det(h)$ is the determinant $\det(A)$ of the matrix $A_h \in \mathbb{C}^{n \times n}$.

Example 2.11. The matrix of the operator 1_L (where $\dim(L) = n$) is $A_{1_L} = \mathsf{diag}(1, 1, \ldots, 1)$. Also, $\det(1_L) = 1$.

We have $\det(A_{gh}) = \det(A_g) \det(A_h)$. If $h : L \longrightarrow L$ is invertible, then $hh^{-1} 1_L$, so $\det(h) \det(h^{-1}) = \det(1_L) = 1$, hence

$$\det(h^{-1}) = \frac{1}{\det(h)}.$$

Let L be an n-dimensional $\mathbb{C}$-linear space. The sum $f + g$ of two linear functionals $f, g : L \longrightarrow \mathbb{C}$ is defined by $(f+g)(x) = f(x) + g(x)$; the *product of a linear functional* f with a scalar a is defined by $(af)(x) = af(x)$ for $x \in L$.

Definition 2.16. The *dual* of an $\mathbb{F}$-linear space L is the set L^* of $\mathbb{F}$-valued linear functionals equipped with the sum and the product with scalars defined above.

Theorem 2.18. *The dual L^* of an n-dimensional linear space L is an n-dimensional linear space.*

Proof. Let $b_1, \ldots, b_n$ be a basis in L. Define n linear functionals $g_i : L \longrightarrow \mathbb{C}$ by $g_i(x) = x_i$, where $x = x_1 b_1 + \cdots + x_n b_n$. Note that

$$g_i(b_j) = \begin{cases} 1 & \text{if } i = j, \\ 0 & \text{otherwise,} \end{cases}$$

for $1 \leqslant i, j \leqslant n$.

Let $f \in L^*$. The linearity of f allows us to write

$$f(x) = f(x_1 b_1 + \cdots + x_n b_n) = x_1 f(b_1) + \cdots + x_n f(b_n)$$
$$= f(b_1) g_1(x) + \cdots f(b_n) g_n(x),$$

for every $x \in P$ which shows that $f = f(b_1) g_1 + \cdots + f(b_n) g_n$. Thus, f is a linear combination of $g_1, \ldots, g_n$.

Next, we need to show that the set $\{g_1, \ldots, g_n\}$ is linearly independent. Suppose that $a_1 g_1 + a_n g_n = 0$. This implies $a_1 g_1(x) + a_n g_n(x) = 0_L$ for every $x \in L$. Choosing $x = b_j$ we have $a_j = 0$ for $1 \leqslant j \leqslant n$, which proves that the set $\{g_1, \ldots, g_n\}$ is linearly independent and, therefore, is a basis of L^*. Thus, $\dim(L^*) = \dim(L) = n$. $\square$

Theorem 2.19. (Real Hahn-Banach Theorem) *Let L be a real linear space and let $f : K \longrightarrow \mathbb{R}$ be a linear functional defined on a subspace K of L. If $p : L \longrightarrow \mathbb{R}$ is a function such that $p(x + y) \leqslant p(x) + p(y)$, $p(ax) = ap(x)$ if $a \geqslant 0$ for all $x, y \in L$, and $f(x) \leqslant p(x)$ for $x \in K$, then f has an extension to F to L such that $F(x) \leqslant p(x)$ for $x \in L$ and $F(x) = p(x)$ for $x \in K$.*

Proof. Suppose that $K \subset L$ and let $z \in L - K$. Consider the set $H_z = \{y + az \mid y \in K \text{ and } a \in \mathbb{R}\}$. To extend f from K to a linear functional defined on H_z we seek to have

$$f(y + az) = f(y) + af(z) \leqslant p(y + az) \qquad (2.2)$$

for $a \in \mathbb{R}$. To this end we need to specify a choice for $f(z)$.

If inequality (2.2) holds for $a \in \mathbb{R}$, then we have

$$f(y_1 + z) = f(y_1) + f(z) \leqslant p(y_1 + z)$$
$$f(y_2 - z) = f(y_2) - f(z) \leqslant p(y_2 - z)$$

for all $y_1, y_2 \in K$ (by taking $a = 1$ and $a = -1$, respectively). Inequalities (2.3) and (2.3) imply

$$f(y_2) - p(y_2 - z) \leqslant f(z) \leqslant p(y_1 + z) - f(y_1).$$

Thus, to be able to define $f(z)$ it suffices to have $f(y_2) - p(y_2 - z) \leqslant p(y_1 + z) - f(y_1)$, or $f(y_1) + f(y_2) \leqslant p(y_1 + z) + p(y_2 - z)$ for all $y_1, y_2 \in K$. This is indeed the case because

$$f(y_1) + f(y_2) = f(y_1 + y_2)$$

(because of the linearity of f)

$$\leqslant p(y_1 + y_2)$$

(because $y_1 + y_2 \in K$)

$$= p(y_1 + z + y_2 - z)$$

$$\leqslant p(y_1 + z) + p(y_2 - z)$$

(because p is subadditive).

Denote an extension of f to a subspace G that contains K by (G, f_G). We introduce a partial order on these extensions by writing $(G, f_G) \leqslant (G', f_{G'})$ if $G \subseteq G'$ and $f_{G'}$ is the extension of f_G to G'.

Let $\{(G_i, f_i) \mid i \in I\}$ be a chain of extensions of f. Define the function f_* on $G_* = \bigcup_{i \in I} G_i$ to coincide with f_i on G_i. It is clear that $f_*(x) \leqslant p(x)$ and $(G, f_G) \leqslant (G_*, f_*)$. By Zorn's Lemma there exists a maximal extension F of f to the entire space L. $\qquad \square$

Let now L be a complex linear space and let $f : L \longrightarrow \mathbb{C}$ be a linear functional defined on L. If g, h are the real and imaginary parts of f, that is, $g(x) = \Re(f(x))$ and $h(x) = \Im(f(x))$, then $f(x) = g(x) + ih(x)$ for $x \in L$. Since $g(x) = \frac{1}{2}(f(x) + \overline{f(x)})$ and $h(x) = \frac{1}{2i}(f(x) - \overline{f(x)})$, it follows immediately that both g and h are linear functionals on L. Therefore,

$$g(ix) = \frac{1}{2}(if(x) - i\overline{f(x)})$$

$$= \frac{i}{2}(f(x) - \overline{f(x)}) = -h(x),$$

which shows that

$$f(x) = g(x) - ig(ix) \tag{2.3}$$

for $x \in L$.

Theorem 2.20. (Complex Hahn-Banach Theorem) *Let L be a complex linear space and let $f : K \longrightarrow \mathbb{R}$ be a linear functional defined on a subspace K of L. If $p : L \longrightarrow \mathbb{R}_{\geqslant 0}$ is a real valued function such that $p(x+y) \leqslant p(x) + p(y)$ for all $x, y \in L$ and $p(ax) = |a|p(x)$, and $|f(x)| \leqslant p(x)$ for $x \in K$, then f has an extension F to L such that $|F(x)| \leqslant p(x)$ for $x \in L$ and $F(x) = p(x)$ for all $x \in K$.*

Proof. Let $g = \Re(f)$. Since $p(x + y) \leqslant p(x) + p(y)$ for $x, y \in L$, $p(ax) = |a|p(x)$, and $|f(x)| \leqslant p(x)$ for $x \in K$, g has a real linear extension G to the entire space L such that $G(x) \leqslant p(x)$ by the real Hahn-Banach theorem.

Define $F : L \longrightarrow \mathbb{C}$ as $F(x) = G(x) - iG(ix)$. F clearly extends f, $F(x_1 + x_2) = F(x_1) + F(x_2)$ for $x_1, x_2 \in L$, and $F(ax) = aF(x)$ for $a \in \mathbb{R}$. Moreover, $F(ix) = iG(ix) - iG(x) = iF(x)$, so F is also linear in the complex field.

Note that $p(ax) = p(x)$ if $|a| = 1$. If $F(x) = |F(x)|e^{i\theta}$, then

$$|F(x)| = e^{-i\theta}F(x) = F(e^{-i\theta}x).$$

Since $F(e^{-i\theta}x) = |F(x)|$ is a real number, so

$$|F(x)| = G(e^{-\theta}x) \leqslant p(e^{-i\theta}x) = p(x). \qquad \square$$

Definition 2.17. Let L be a linear space and let $h : L \longrightarrow L$ be a linear operator. A subspace U is an *invariant subspace* of h if $x \in U$ implies $h(x) \in U$.

Example 2.12. Let $P_n(\mathbb{R})$ be the linear space of polynomials of degree not larger than n. Note that if $m \leqslant n$, then $P_m(\mathbb{R})$ is a subspace of $P_n(\mathbb{R})$. The differentiation operator $D : P_n(\mathbb{R}) \longrightarrow P_n(\mathbb{R})$ defined as $D(p) = p'$ has $P_m(\mathbb{R})$ as an invariant subspace because the derivative of a polynomial of degree at most m is a polynomial of degree at most m.

Definition 2.18. Let L be a $\mathbb{C}$-linear space. An *eigenvalue* of a linear operator $h : L \longrightarrow L$ is a number $\lambda \in \mathbb{C}$ such that there exists $x \in L - \{0_L\}$ for which $h(x) = \lambda x$. The vector $\mathbf{x}$ is referred to as an *eigenvector* of λ.

Note that if $h(x) = \lambda x$, then $(h - \lambda 1_L)x = 0_L$, hence $h - \lambda 1_L$ is not injective, and therefore, it is not invertible.

Definition 2.19. The λ-*resolvent* of the linear operator $h : L \longrightarrow L$ is the linear operator $\mathsf{R}_{h,\lambda} = (h - \lambda 1_L)^{-1}$.

Note that the set of eigenvectors that correspond to λ constitute the null space of the operator $h - \lambda 1_L = \mathsf{R}_{h,\lambda}^{-1}$.

Example 2.13. Let $h : \mathbb{C} \longrightarrow \mathbb{C}$ be the linear operator defined by $h(x + iy) = -y + ix$ for $x, y \in \mathbb{R}$. It is immediate that h is a linear operator. Then, λ is an eigenvalue if $h(x + iy) = \lambda(x + iy)$ for some $x + iy \neq 0_{\mathbb{C}}$. This amounts to $-y + ix = \lambda(x + iy)$, which implies $-y = \lambda x$ and $x = \lambda y$. Note that $y \neq 0$ because this would entail $x = 0$, and $x + iy = 0$. Consequently, we have $\lambda^2 y = -y$, so $\lambda^2 = -1$, which imply $\lambda = i$, or $\lambda = -i$. Eigenvectors that correspond to $\lambda = i$ have the form $a - ia$ and those that correspond to $\lambda = -i$ have the form $a + ia$.

Theorem 2.21. *Let L be a linear space and let $h : L \longrightarrow L$ be a linear operator. If $\lambda_1, \ldots, \lambda_m$ are distinct eigenvalues of h and $x_1, \ldots, x_m$ are corresponding eigenvectors, then $\{x_1, \ldots, x_m\}$ is a linearly independent set.*

Proof. Suppose that $\{x_1, \ldots, x_m\}$ is a linearly dependent set. Let k be the least number such that $x_k \in \langle x_1, \ldots, x_{k-1}$. There exist $k - 1$ scalars $a_1, \ldots, a_{k-1}$ such that $x_k = a_1 x_1 + \cdots + a_{k-1} x_{k-1}$. By applying h to both sides we obtain $\lambda_k x_k = a_1 \lambda_1 x_1 + \cdots + a_{k-1} \lambda_{k-1} x_{k-1}$. Therefore, $0 = a_1(\lambda_k - \lambda_1)x_1 + \cdots + a_{k-1}(\lambda_k - \lambda_{k-1} x_{k-1}$. The definition of k implies that the set $\{x_1, \ldots, x_{k-1}\}$ is linearly independent. Therefore, $a_1 = \cdots = a_{k-1} = 0$, which implies $x_k = 0$. This contradiction yields the desired conclusion. $\square$

Theorem 2.22. *Let L be a linear space and let $h : L \longrightarrow L$ be a linear operator. Then h has at most $\dim(L)$ distinct eigenvalues.*

Proof. Suppose that $\lambda_1, \ldots, \lambda_m$ are m distinct eigenvalues of h. Let $x_1, \ldots, x_m$ be the corresponding eigenvectors. Theorem 2.21 implies that the set $\{x_1, \ldots, x_m\}$ is linearly independent. Thus, $m \leqslant \dim(L)$. $\square$

2.4 Linear Spaces with Inner Products

Definition 2.20. Let L be a complex linear space. An *inner product* on L is a two-argument function $(\cdot, \cdot) : L \times L \longrightarrow \mathbb{C}$ with the following properties:

   (i) $(ax + by, z) = a(x, z) + b(y, z)$,
   (ii) $(x, y) = \overline{(y, x)}$ (the skew-symmetry property),
   (iii) (x, x) is a non-negative real number, and
   (iv) $(x, x) = 0$ implies $x = 0_L$

for all $a, b \in \mathbb{C}$ and $x, y, z \in L$.

The pair $(L, (\cdot, \cdot))$ is called an *inner product space*.

Observe that for $a \in \mathbb{C}$ we have
$$(x, ay) = \overline{a}(x, y)$$
for $a \in \mathbb{C}$ and $x, y \in L$. Therefore, for a complex inner product we have the *skew-linearity*skew-linearity property, namely
$$(x, ay + bz) = \overline{a}(x, y) + \overline{b}(x, z)$$
for $x, y, z \in L$ and $a, b \in \mathbb{C}$.

In general, a function $f : L \times L \longrightarrow \mathbb{C}$ that is linear in the first argument and skew-linear in the second is said to be *sesquilinear*. Thus, an inner product on a complex linear space is sesquilinear.

If L is a real linear space we assume that $(x, y) \in \mathbb{R}$ for $x, y \in L$. Thus, for an inner product on a real linear space we have the symmetry property $(x, y) = (y, x)$ for $x, y \in L$.

Example 2.14. If $\mathbf{a}, \mathbf{b} \in \mathbb{C}^n$ the function $(\cdot, \cdot) : \mathbb{C}^n \times \mathbb{C}^n \longrightarrow \mathbb{R}$ defined by $(\mathbf{a}, \mathbf{b}) = \mathbf{b}^{\mathsf{H}} \mathbf{a} = a_1 \overline{b_1} + \cdots + a_n \overline{b_n}$ is an inner product on $\mathbb{C}^n$.

Example 2.15. Let $\mathbb{C}^{n \times n}$ be the set of square complex matrices. We remind the reader that the *trace* of a matrix $A \in \mathbb{C}^{n \times n}$ is the complex number $trace(A) = \sum_{i=j}^{n} a_{jj}$.

The function $(A, B) = trace(AB^{\mathsf{H}}) = \sum_{j=1}^{n} (AB^{\mathsf{H}})_{jj} = \sum j = 1^n$ $\sum_{k=1}^{n} a_{jk} \overline{b_{jk}}$ is an inner product on $\mathbb{C}^{n \times n}$.

The linearity in the first argument is immediate.

We have

$$\overline{(B, A)} = \overline{\sum_{j=1}^{n} \sum_{k=1}^{n} b_{kj} \overline{a_{kj}}}$$

$$= \sum_{j=1}^{n} \sum_{k=1}^{n} \overline{b_{kj}} a_{kj}$$

$$= \sum_{j=1}^{n} \sum_{k=1}^{n} a_{kj} \overline{b_{kj}} = (A, B),$$

which shows that this function satisfies the second property of Definition 2.20.

Also, $(A, A) = \sum_{j=1}^{n} \sum_{k=1}^{n} a_{jk} \overline{a_{jk}} = \sum_{j=1}^{n} \sum_{k=1}^{n} |a_{jk}|^2$, which is a real non-negative number. Finally, it is clear that $(A, A) = 0$ implies $A = O_{n,n}$, where $O_{n,n}$ is the $n \times n$ square matrix whose entries are 0.

Note that for a fixed y_0 the function $f : L \longrightarrow \mathbb{C}$ given by $f(x) = (x, y_0)$ is linear.

A fundamental property of the inner product defined on $\mathbb{R}^n$ is the equality

$$(A\mathbf{x}, \mathbf{y}) = (\mathbf{x}, A'\mathbf{y}), \tag{2.4}$$

which holds for every matrix $A \in \mathbb{R}^{n \times n}$ and $\mathbf{x}, \mathbf{y} \in \mathbb{R}^n$. Indeed, we have

$$(A\mathbf{x}, \mathbf{y}) = \sum_{i=1}^{n} (A\mathbf{x})_i y_i = \sum_{i=1}^{n} \sum_{j=1}^{n} a_{ij} x_j y_i = \sum_{j=1}^{n} x_j \sum_{i=1}^{n} a_{ij} y_i$$

$$= \sum_{j=1}^{n} x_j \sum_{i=1}^{n} a_{ij} y_i = (\mathbf{x}, A'\mathbf{y}).$$

For the complex linear space $\mathbb{C}^n$ and a matrix $A \in \mathbb{C}^{n \times n}$ we have

$$(A\mathbf{x}, \mathbf{y}) = (\mathbf{x}, A^{\mathsf{H}}\mathbf{y}), \tag{2.5}$$

where A^{H} is obtained is the transposed conjugate matrix of A. Indeed, we have

$$(A\mathbf{x}, \mathbf{y}) = \sum_{i=1}^{n} (A\mathbf{x})_i \overline{y_i} = \sum_{i=1}^{n} \sum_{j=1}^{n} a_{ij} x_j \overline{y_i} = \sum_{j=1}^{n} x_j \sum_{i=1}^{n} a_{ij} \overline{y_i}$$

$$= \sum_{j=1}^{n} x_j \sum_{i=1}^{n} \overline{a_{ij}} y_i = (\mathbf{x}, A^{\mathsf{H}}\mathbf{y})$$

for $\mathbf{x}, \mathbf{y} \in \mathbb{C}^n$.

A very important inequality is presented next.

Theorem 2.23. (Cauchy[1]-Schwarz[2] Inequality) *Let $(L, (\cdot, \cdot))$ be an inner product $\mathbb{F}$-linear space. For $x, y \in L$ we have*

$$|(x, y)|^2 \leqslant (x, x)(y, y).$$

Proof. We discuss the complex case. If $a, b \in \mathbb{C}$ we have

$$(ax + by, ax + by) = a\overline{a}(x, x) + a\overline{b}(x, y) + b\overline{a}(y, x) + b\overline{b}(y, y)$$

$$= |a|^2 (x, x) + 2\Re(a\overline{b}(x, y)) + |b|^2 (y, y) \geqslant 0.$$

Let $a = (y, y)$ and $b = -(x, y)$. We have

$$(y, y)^2 (x, x) - 2(y, y)|(x, y)|^2 + |(x, y)|^2 (y, y) \geqslant 0,$$

---

[1] Augustin-Louis Cauchy was born on 21 August 21st 1789 and died on May 23rd 1857 in Sceaux (Seine), France. He was a French mathematician who made pioneering contributions to analysis. He was one of the first to state and prove theorems of calculus rigorously. He founded complex analysis and the study of permutation groups in abstract algebra. Cauchy taught at École Polytechnique starting in 1815 where he became a full professor in 1816, at the University of Turin, at the Faculté des sciences of Paris and at Collège de France.

[2] Karl Hermann Amandus Schwarz was born on January 23rd 1843 in Hermsdorf, Prussia (now in Poland) and died on November 30th 1921, in Berlin. Schwarz has major contribution in complex analysis and calculus of variations. He received his doctorate from the University of Berlin, and taught at the Universities of Halle, at ETH in Zürch and at the University of Berlin.

hence

$$(y, y)|(x, y)|^2 \leqslant (y, y)^2 (x, x).$$

If $y = 0$ the inequality obviously holds. If $y \neq 0$, the inequality follows. □

2.5   Seminorms and Norms

Definition 2.21. Let L be an $\mathbb{F}$-linear space. A *seminorm* on L is a mapping $\nu : L \longrightarrow \mathbb{R}_{\geqslant 0}$ that satisfies the following conditions:

(i) $\nu(x + y) \leqslant \nu(x) + \nu(y)$ (subadditivity), and

(ii) $\nu(ax) = |a|\nu(x)$ (positive homogeneity),

for $x, y \in L$ and every scalar a.

By taking $a = 0$ in the second condition of the definition we have $\nu(0_L) = 0$ for every seminorm on a real or complex space.

Theorem 2.24. *If L is a real linear space and $\nu : L \longrightarrow \mathbb{R}$ is a seminorm on L, then $\nu(x - y) \geqslant |\nu(x) - \nu(y)|$ for $x, y \in L$.*

Proof.   We have $\nu(x) \leqslant \nu(x - y) + \nu(y)$, so $\nu(x) - \nu(y) \leqslant \nu(x - y)$. Since $\nu(y - x) + \nu(x) \leqslant \nu(y)$ and $\nu(y - x) = \nu(x - y)$, we have the inequalities

$$\nu(x) - \nu(y) \leqslant \nu(x - y) \leqslant \nu(y) - \nu(x),$$

which imply the inequality of the theorem.   □

Definition 2.22. Let L be a real or complex linear space. A *norm* on L is a seminorm $\nu : L \longrightarrow \mathbb{R}$ such that $\nu(x) = 0$ implies $x = 0$ for $x \in L$.

The pair (L, ν) is referred to as a *normed linear space*.

Inner products on linear spaces induce norms.

Theorem 2.25. *Let $(L, (\cdot, \cdot))$ be an inner product $\mathbb{F}$-linear space. The function $\| \cdot \| : L \longrightarrow \mathbb{R}_{\geqslant 0}$ defined by $\|x\| = \sqrt{(x, x)}$ is a norm on L.*

Proof.   We present the argument for inner product complex linear spaces.

It is immediate from the properties of the inner product listed in Definition 2.20 that $\|x\|$ is a real non-negative number and that $\|ax\| = |a|\|x\|$ for $a \in \mathbb{C}$.

Note that

$$\begin{aligned}
\|x + y\|^2 &= (x + y, x + y) \\
&= (x, x) + (x, y) + (y, x) + (y, y) \\
&= (x, x) + 2\Re(x, y) + (y, y) \\
&\quad \text{(because } (y, x) = \overline{(x, y)}) \\
&\leqslant (x, x) + 2|(x, y)| + (y, y) \\
&\quad \text{(because } \Re(y, x) \leqslant |(x, y)|) \\
&\leqslant \|x\|^2 + 2\|x\|\|y\| + \|y\|^2 \\
&\quad \text{(be the Cauchy-Schwarz Inequality)} \\
&= (\|x\| + \|y\|)^2,
\end{aligned}$$

which produces the desired inequality. $\qquad\square$

The Cauchy-Schwarz Inequality shown in Theorem 2.23 can now be formulated using norms as

$$|(x, y)| \leqslant \|x\| \cdot \|y\|.$$

for any vectors of an inner product linear space.

Theorem 2.26. (Complex Polarization Identity) *Let $\| \cdot \|$ be a norm on a complex linear space L that is generated by the inner product $(\cdot, \cdot)$. We have the* complex polarization identity:

$$(x, y) = \frac{1}{4}\left(\|x + y\|^2 - \|x - y\|^2 - i\|x - iy\|^2 + i\|x + iy\|^2\right)$$

for $x, y \in L$.

Proof. We have

$$\begin{aligned}
\|x + y\|^2 &= (x + y, x + y) = \|x\|^2 + \|y\|^2 + (x, y) + (y, x) \\
&= (x + y, x + y) = \|x\|^2 + \|y\|^2 + (x, y) + \overline{(x, y)} \\
&= \|x\|^2 + \|y\|^2 + 2\Re(x, y).
\end{aligned}$$

Replacing y by $-y$ we have

$$\|x - y\|^2 = \|x\|^2 + \|y\|^2 - 2\Re(x, y),$$

hence

$$\|x + y\|^2 - \|x - y\|^2 = 4\Re(x, y). \tag{2.6}$$

Replacing now y by iy we obtain

$$\|x + iy\|^2 - \|x - iy\|^2 = 4\Re(x, iy).$$

Note that

$$(x, iy) = -i(x, y) = -i(\Re(x, y) + i\Im(x, y)) = \Im(x, y) - i\Re(x, y),$$

so $\Re(x, iy) = \Im(x, y)$, which implies

$$\|x + iy\|^2 - \|x - iy\|^2 = 4\Im(x, iy).$$

Taking into account the previous equalities we can write

$$\|x+y\|^2 - \|x-y\|^2 + i\|x+iy\|^2 - i\|x-iy\|^2 = 4\Re(x, y) + 4i\Im(x, y) = 4(x, y),$$

which is the desired identity. □

Corollary 2.6. (Real Polarization Identity) *Let* $\| \cdot \|$ *be a norm on a real linear space* L *that is generated by the inner product* $(\cdot, \cdot)$. *We have the polarization identity*

$$(x, y) = \frac{1}{4} \left(\|x + y\|^2 - \|x - y\|^2 \right)$$

for $x, y \in L$.

Proof. The proof of this identity follows directly from equality (2.6). □

Theorem 2.27. (Parallelogram Equality) *Let* $\| \cdot \|$ *be a norm on a linear space* L *that is generated by the inner product* $(\cdot, \cdot)$. *We have the parallelogram equality:*

$$\|x\|^2 + \|y\|^2 = \frac{1}{2} \left(\|x + y\|^2 + \|x - y\|^2 \right)$$

for $x, y \in L$.

Proof. By applying the definition of $\| \cdot \|$ and the properties of the inner product we can write:

$$\frac{1}{2} \left(\|x + y\|^2 + \|x - y\|^2 \right)$$
$$= \frac{1}{2} \left((x + y, x + y) + (x - y, x - y) \right)$$
$$= \frac{1}{2} \left((x, x) + 2(x, y) + (y, y) + (x, x) - 2(x, y) + (y, y) \right)$$
$$= \|x\|^2 + \|y\|^2,$$

which concludes the proof. □

Lemma 2.1. *For* $a, b \in \mathbb{R}_{\geqslant 0}$ *and* $t \in (0, 1)$ *we have*

$$a^t b^{1-t} \leqslant ta + (1 - t)b.$$

Equality takes place when $a = b$.

Proof. Let $f : \mathbb{R}_{\geqslant 0} \longrightarrow \mathbb{R}$ be the function defined as

$$f(x) = x^t - xt + x - 1.$$

We have $f'(x) = tx^{t-1} - t = t(x^{t-1} - 1)$. Since $t \in (0, 1)$, we have $f'(x) > 0$ when $x \in (0, 1)$ and $f'(x) < 0$ for $x > 1$. It follows that $f(x) \leqslant f(1) = 0$ with equality for $x = 1$. Hence, $x^t \leqslant tx + 1 - t$. If $b = 0$ the inequality holds trivially. Suppose that $b \neq 0$. Substituting $x = \frac{a}{b}$ we have:

$$\frac{a^t}{b^t} \leqslant \frac{ta}{b} + 1 - t.$$

A final multiplication by b delivers the result. The equality holds when $x = 1$, that is, when $a = b$. $\qquad\square$

Theorem 2.28. (Discrete Hölder's Inequality) *Let $a_1, \ldots, a_n$ and $b_1, \ldots, b_n$ be $2n$ positive numbers, and let p and q be two numbers such that $\frac{1}{p} + \frac{1}{q} = 1$ and $p > 1$. We have:*

$$\sum_{i=1}^{n} a_i b_i \leqslant \left(\sum_{i=1}^{n} a_i^p \right)^{\frac{1}{p}} \cdot \left(\sum_{i=1}^{n} b_i^q \right)^{\frac{1}{q}}.$$

Equality holds when

$$\frac{a_i^p}{\sum_{k=1}^{n} a_k^p} = \frac{b_i^q}{\sum_{k=1}^{n} b_k^q}$$

for $1 \leqslant i \leqslant n$.

Proof. Define the numbers

$$x_i = \frac{a_i^p}{\sum_{k=1}^{n} a_k^p} \text{ and } y_i = \frac{b_i^q}{\sum_{k=1}^{n} b_k^q}$$

for $1 \leqslant i \leqslant n$. Lemma 2.1 applied to x_i, y_i with $t = \frac{1}{p}$ and $1 - t = \frac{1}{q}$ implies

$$x_i^{\frac{1}{p}} y_i^{\frac{1}{q}} \leqslant \frac{1}{p} x_i + \frac{1}{q} y_i,$$

or

$$\frac{a_i b_i}{(\sum_{k=1}^{n} a_k^p)^{\frac{1}{p}} (\sum_{k=1}^{n} b_k^q)^{\frac{1}{q}}} \leqslant \frac{1}{p} \frac{a_i^p}{\sum_{k=1}^{n} a_k^p} + \frac{1}{q} \frac{b_i^q}{\sum_{k=1}^{n} b_k^q}$$

Adding these inequalities, we obtain

$$\sum_{i=1}^{n} a_i b_i \leqslant \left(\sum_{i=1}^{n} a_i^p \right)^{\frac{1}{p}} \left(\sum_{i=1}^{n} b_i^q \right)^{\frac{1}{q}}.$$

Note that to obtain an equality we must have $x_i = y_i$ for $1 \leqslant i \leqslant n$. This justifies the last claim of the theorem. $\qquad\square$

Theorem 2.29. *Let $a_1, \ldots, a_n$ and $b_1, \ldots, b_n$ be 2n real numbers and let p and q be two numbers such that $\frac{1}{p} + \frac{1}{q} = 1$ and $p > 1$. We have*

$$\left| \sum_{i=1}^{n} a_i b_i \right| \leqslant \left(\sum_{i=1}^{n} |a_i|^p \right)^{\frac{1}{p}} \cdot \left(\sum_{i=1}^{n} |b_i|^q \right)^{\frac{1}{q}}.$$

Proof. By Theorem 2.28, we have

$$\sum_{i=1}^{n} |a_i| |b_i| \leqslant \left(\sum_{i=1}^{n} |a_i|^p \right)^{\frac{1}{p}} \cdot \left(\sum_{i=1}^{n} |b_i|^q \right)^{\frac{1}{q}}.$$

The inequality follows from the fact that

$$\left| \sum_{i=1}^{n} a_i b_i \right| \leqslant \sum_{i=1}^{n} |a_i| |b_i|.$$

$\square$

Theorem 2.30. (Minkowski's Inequality) *Let $a_1, \ldots, a_n$ and $b_1, \ldots, b_n$ be 2n non-negative numbers. If $p \geqslant 1$, we have*

$$\left(\sum_{i=1}^{n} (a_i + b_i)^p \right)^{\frac{1}{p}} \leqslant \left(\sum_{i=1}^{n} a_i^p \right)^{\frac{1}{p}} + \left(\sum_{i=1}^{n} b_i^p \right)^{\frac{1}{p}}.$$

For $1 < p < \infty$ the equality holds if and only if $c \begin{pmatrix} a_1 \\ \vdots \\ a_n \end{pmatrix} = d \begin{pmatrix} b_1 \\ \vdots \\ b_n \end{pmatrix}$ for some positive numbers c, d.

Proof. For $p = 1$, the inequality is immediate. Therefore, we can assume that $p > 1$. Note that

$$\sum_{i=1}^{n} (a_i + b_i)^p = \sum_{i=1}^{n} a_i (a_i + b_i)^{p-1} + \sum_{i=1}^{n} b_i (a_i + b_i)^{p-1}.$$

By Hölder's inequality for p, q such that $p > 1$ and $\frac{1}{p} + \frac{1}{q} = 1$, we have

$$\sum_{i=1}^{n} a_i (a_i + b_i)^{p-1} \leqslant \left(\sum_{i=1}^{n} a_i^p \right)^{\frac{1}{p}} \left(\sum_{i=1}^{n} (a_i + b_i)^{(p-1)q} \right)^{\frac{1}{q}}$$

$$= \left(\sum_{i=1}^{n} a_i^p \right)^{\frac{1}{p}} \left(\sum_{i=1}^{n} (a_i + b_i)^p \right)^{\frac{1}{q}}. \tag{2.7}$$

Similarly, we can write

$$\sum_{i=1}^{n} b_i(a_i + b_i)^{p-1} \leqslant \left(\sum_{i=1}^{n} b_i^p\right)^{\frac{1}{p}} \left(\sum_{i=1}^{n} (a_i + b_i)^p\right)^{\frac{1}{q}}. \tag{2.8}$$

Adding the last two inequalities yields

$$\sum_{i=1}^{n} (a_i + b_i)^p \leqslant \left(\left(\sum_{i=1}^{n} a_i^p\right)^{\frac{1}{p}} + \left(\sum_{i=1}^{n} b_i^p\right)^{\frac{1}{p}}\right) \left(\sum_{i=1}^{n} (a_i + b_i)^p\right)^{\frac{1}{q}},$$

which is equivalent to the desired inequality

$$\left(\sum_{i=1}^{n} (a_i + b_i)^p\right)^{\frac{1}{p}} \leqslant \left(\sum_{i=1}^{n} a_i^p\right)^{\frac{1}{p}} + \left(\sum_{i=1}^{n} b_i^p\right)^{\frac{1}{p}}.$$

To have the equality we must have equalities in each of inequalities (2.7) and (2.8). An elementary computation yields the condition mentioned above. $\square$

Note that if $p < 1$, the inequality sign in Minkowski's inequality is reversed.

Theorem 2.31. *For $p \geqslant 1$, the function $\nu_p : \mathbb{R}^n \longrightarrow \mathbb{R}_{\geqslant 0}$ defined by*

$$\nu_p(\boldsymbol{x}) = \left(\sum_{i=1}^{n} |x_i|^p\right)^{\frac{1}{p}},$$

is a norm on the linear space $(\mathbb{R}^n, +, \cdot)$.

Proof. Let $\mathbf{x}, \mathbf{y} \in \mathbb{R}^n$. Minkowski's inequality (Theorem 2.30) applied to the non-negative numbers $a_i = |x_i|$ and $b_i = |y_i|$ amounts to

$$\left(\sum_{i=1}^{n} (|x_i| + |y_i|)^p\right)^{\frac{1}{p}} \leqslant \left(\sum_{i=1}^{n} |x_i|^p\right)^{\frac{1}{p}} + \left(\sum_{i=1}^{n} |y_i|^p\right)^{\frac{1}{p}}.$$

Since $|x_i + y_i| \leqslant |x_i| + |y_i|$ for every i, $1 \leqslant i \leqslant n$, we have

$$\left(\sum_{i=1}^{n} (|x_i + y_i|)^p\right)^{\frac{1}{p}} \leqslant \left(\sum_{i=1}^{n} |x_i|^p\right)^{\frac{1}{p}} + \left(\sum_{i=1}^{n} |y_i|^p\right)^{\frac{1}{p}},$$

that is, $\nu_p(\mathbf{x} + \mathbf{y}) \leqslant \nu_p(\mathbf{x}) + \nu_p(\mathbf{y})$. Thus, ν_p is a norm on $\mathbb{R}^n$. $\square$

We refer to ν_p as a *Minkowski norm* on $\mathbb{R}^n$.

Example 2.16. Consider the mappings $\nu_1, \nu_\infty : \mathbb{R}^n \longrightarrow \mathbb{R}$ given by

$$\nu_1(\mathbf{x}) = |x_1| + |x_2| + \cdots + |x_n| \text{ and } \nu_\infty(\mathbf{x}) = \max\{|x_1|, |x_2|, \ldots, |x_n|\},$$

for every $\mathbf{x} \in \mathbb{R}^n$. Both ν_1 and ν_∞ are norms on $\mathbb{R}^n$.

To verify that ν_∞ is a norm we start from the inequality $|x_i + y_i| \leqslant |x_i| + |y_i| \leqslant \nu_\infty(\mathbf{x}) + \nu_\infty(\mathbf{y})$ for $1 \leqslant i \leqslant n$. This in turn implies

$$\nu_\infty(\mathbf{x} + \mathbf{y}) = \max\{|x_i + y_i| \mid 1 \leqslant i \leqslant n\} \leqslant \nu_\infty(\mathbf{x}) + \nu_\infty(\mathbf{y}),$$

which gives the desired inequality.

This norm can be regarded as a limit case of the norms ν_p. Indeed, let $\mathbf{x} \in \mathbb{R}^n$ and let $M = \max\{|x_i| \mid 1 \leqslant i \leqslant n\} = |x_{l_1}| = \cdots = |x_{l_k}|$ for some $l_1, \ldots, l_k$, where $1 \leqslant l_1, \ldots, l_k \leqslant n$. Here $x_{l_1}, \ldots, x_{l_k}$ are the components of $\mathbf{x}$ that have the maximal absolute value and $k \geqslant 1$. We can write:

$$\lim_{p \to \infty} \nu_p(\mathbf{x}) = \lim_{p \to \infty} M \left(\sum_{i=1}^n \left(\frac{|x_i|}{M} \right)^p \right)^{\frac{1}{p}} = \lim_{p \to \infty} M(k)^{\frac{1}{p}} = M,$$

which justifies the notation ν_∞.

We frequently use the alternative notation $\|\mathbf{x}\|_p$ for $\nu_p(\mathbf{x})$. We refer to the norm ν_2 as the *Euclidean norm*.

Example 2.17. Let $\mathbf{x} = \begin{pmatrix} x_1 \\ x_2 \end{pmatrix} \in \mathbb{R}^2$ be a unit vector in the sense of the Euclidean norm. We have $|x_1|^2 + |x_2|^2 = 1$. Since x_1 and x_2 are real numbers we can write $x_1 = \cos\alpha$ and $x_2 = \sin\alpha$. This allows us to write

$$\mathbf{x} = \begin{pmatrix} \cos\alpha \\ \sin\alpha \end{pmatrix}.$$

Theorem 2.32. *Each norm* $\nu : L \longrightarrow \mathbb{R}_{\geqslant 0}$ *on a linear space* L *generates a metric on the set* L *defined by* $d_\nu(x, y) = \nu(x - y)$ *for* $x, y \in L$.

Proof. Note that if $d_\nu(x, y) = \nu(x - y) = 0$, it follows that $x - y = 0_L$, so $x = y$.

The symmetry of d_ν is obvious and so we need to verify only the triangular axiom. Let $x, y, z \in L$. We have:

$$\nu(x - z) = \nu(x - y + y - z) \leqslant \nu(x - y) + \nu(y - z)$$

or, equivalently, $d_\nu(x, z) \leqslant d_\nu(x, y) + d_\nu(y, z)$, for every $x, y, z \in L$, which concludes the argument. $\square$

We refer to d_ν as the *metric induced by the norm ν on the linear space L*.

Note that the metric d_ν on L induced by a norm is translation invariant, that is, $d_\nu(x + z, y + z) = d_\nu(x, y)$ for every $z \in L$. Also, for every $a \in \mathbb{R}$ and $x, y \in L$ we have the homogeneity property $d_\nu(ax, ay) = |a| d_\nu(x, y)$ for $x, y \in L$.

Theorem 2.33. *Let L be a real linear space and let $d : L \times L \longrightarrow \mathbb{R}_{\geqslant 0}$ be a metric on L. If d is translation invariant and homogeneous, then there exists a norm ν of L such that $d = d_\nu$.*

Proof. Let d be a metric on L that is translation invariant and homogeneous. Define $\nu(x) = d(x, 0_L)$. It follows immediately that ν is a norm on L. □

For $p \geqslant 1$, then d_p denotes the metric d_{ν_p} induced by the norm ν_p on the linear space $(\mathbb{R}^n, +, \cdot)$ known as the *Minkowski metric* on $\mathbb{R}^n$.

The metrics d_1, d_2 and d_∞ defined on $\mathbb{R}^n$ are given by

$$d_1(\mathbf{x}, \mathbf{y}) = \sum_{i=1}^n |x_i - y_i|, \tag{2.9}$$

$$d_2(\mathbf{x}, \mathbf{y}) = \sqrt{\sum_{i=1}^n |x_i - y_i|^2}, \tag{2.10}$$

$$d_\infty(\mathbf{x}, \mathbf{y}) = \max\{|x_i - y_i| \mid 1 \leqslant i \leqslant n\}, \tag{2.11}$$

for $\mathbf{x}, \mathbf{y} \in \mathbb{R}^n$.

These metrics are visualized in Figure 2.1 for the special case of $\mathbb{R}^2$. If

$$\mathbf{x} = \begin{pmatrix} x_0 \\ x_1 \end{pmatrix} \text{ and } \mathbf{y} = \begin{pmatrix} y_0 \\ y_1 \end{pmatrix},$$

then $d_1(\mathbf{x}, \mathbf{y})$ is the sum of the lengths of the two legs of the triangle, $d_2(\mathbf{x}, \mathbf{y})$ is the length of the hypotenuse of the right triangle and $d_\infty(\mathbf{x}, \mathbf{y})$ is the largest of the lengths of the legs.

Theorem 2.34 to follow allows us to compare the norms ν_p (and the metrics of the form d_p) that were introduced on $\mathbb{R}^n$. We begin with a preliminary result.

Lemma 2.2. *Let $a_1, \ldots, a_n$ be n positive numbers. If p and q are two positive numbers such that $p \leqslant q$, then $(a_1^p + \cdots + a_n^p)^{\frac{1}{p}} \geqslant (a_1^q + \cdots + a_n^q)^{\frac{1}{q}}$.*

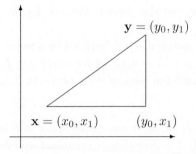

Fig. 2.1   The distances $d_1(\mathbf{x}, \mathbf{y})$, $d_2(\mathbf{x}, \mathbf{y})$, and $d_\infty(\mathbf{x}, \mathbf{y})$.

Proof. Let $f : \mathbb{R}_{>0} \longrightarrow \mathbb{R}$ be the function defined by $f(r) = (a_1^r + \cdots + a_n^r)^{\frac{1}{r}}$. Since

$$\ln f(r) = \frac{\ln (a_1^r + \cdots + a_n^r)}{r},$$

it follows that

$$\frac{f'(r)}{f(r)} = -\frac{1}{r^2} (a_1^r + \cdots + a_n^r) + \frac{1}{r} \cdot \frac{a_1^r \ln a_1 + \cdots + a_n^r \ln a_r}{a_1^r + \cdots + a_n^r}.$$

To prove that $f'(r) < 0$, it suffices to show that

$$\frac{a_1^r \ln a_1 + \cdots + a_n^r \ln a_r}{a_1^r + \cdots + a_n^r} \leqslant \frac{\ln (a_1^r + \cdots + a_n^r)}{r}.$$

This last inequality is easily seen to be equivalent to

$$\sum_{i=1}^n \frac{a_i^r}{a_1^r + \cdots + a_n^r} \ln \frac{a_i^r}{a_1^r + \cdots + a_n^r} \leqslant 0,$$

which holds because

$$\frac{a_i^r}{a_1^r + \cdots + a_n^r} \leqslant 1$$

for $1 \leqslant i \leqslant n$. $\square$

Theorem 2.34. *Let p and q be two positive numbers such that $p \leqslant q$. We have $\|\boldsymbol{u}\|_p \geqslant \|\boldsymbol{u}\|_q$ for $\boldsymbol{u} \in \mathbb{R}^n$.*

Proof.   This statement follows immediately from Lemma 2.2. $\square$

Corollary 2.7. *Let p, q be two positive numbers such that $p \leqslant q$. For every $\boldsymbol{x}, \boldsymbol{y} \in \mathbb{R}^n$, we have $d_p(\boldsymbol{x}, \boldsymbol{y}) \geqslant d_q(\boldsymbol{x}, \boldsymbol{y})$.*

Proof. This statement follows immediately from Theorem 2.34. □

Theorem 2.35. *Let $p \geqslant 1$. We have*

$$\|\boldsymbol{x}\|_\infty \leqslant \|\boldsymbol{x}\|_p \leqslant n\|\boldsymbol{x}\|_\infty$$

for $\boldsymbol{x} \in \mathbb{R}^n$.

Proof. The first inequality is an immediate consequence of Theorem 2.34. The second inequality follows by observing that

$$\|\mathbf{x}\|_p = \left(\sum_{i=1}^n |x_i|^p \right)^{\frac{1}{p}} \leqslant n \max_{1\leqslant i\leqslant n} |x_i| = n\|\mathbf{x}\|_\infty.$$

□

Corollary 2.8. *Let p and q be two numbers such that $p, q \geqslant 1$. For $\boldsymbol{x} \in \mathbb{R}^n$ we have:*

$$\frac{1}{n}\|\boldsymbol{x}\|_q \leqslant \|\boldsymbol{x}\|_p \leqslant n\|\boldsymbol{x}\|_q.$$

Proof. Since $\|\mathbf{x}\|_\infty \leqslant \|\mathbf{x}\|_p$ and $\|x\|_q \leqslant n\|\mathbf{x}\|_\infty$, it follows that $\|x\|_q \leqslant n\|\mathbf{x}\|_p$. Exchanging the roles of p and q, we have $\|x\|_p \leqslant n\|\mathbf{x}\|_q$, so

$$\frac{1}{n}\|\mathbf{x}\|_q \leqslant \|\mathbf{x}\|_p \leqslant n\|\mathbf{x}\|_q$$

for every $\mathbf{x} \in \mathbb{R}^n$. □

For $p = 1$ and $q = 2$ and $\mathbf{x} \in \mathbb{R}^n$ we have the inequalities

$$\frac{1}{n}\sqrt{\sum_{i=1}^n x_i^2} \leqslant \sum_{i=1}^n |x_i| \leqslant n\sqrt{\sum_{i=1}^n x_i^2}. \tag{2.12}$$

Corollary 2.9. *For every $\boldsymbol{x}, \boldsymbol{y} \in \mathbb{R}^n$ and $p \geqslant 1$, we have $d_\infty(\boldsymbol{x}, \boldsymbol{y}) \leqslant d_p(\boldsymbol{x}, \boldsymbol{y}) \leqslant nd_\infty(\boldsymbol{x}, \boldsymbol{y})$. Further, for $p, q > 1$, there exist $c, c' \in \mathbb{R}_{>0}$ such that*

$$c\, d_q(\boldsymbol{x}, \boldsymbol{y}) \leqslant d_p(\boldsymbol{x}, \boldsymbol{y}) \leqslant c'\, d_q(\boldsymbol{x}, \boldsymbol{y})$$

for $\boldsymbol{x}, \boldsymbol{y} \in \mathbb{R}^n$.

Proof. This follows from Theorem 2.35 and from Corollary 2.9. □

Corollary 2.7 implies that if $p \leqslant q$, then the closed sphere $B_{d_p}[\mathbf{x}, r]$ is included in the closed sphere $B_{d_q}[\mathbf{x}, r]$. For example, we have

$$B_{d_1}[\mathbf{0}, 1] \subseteq B_{d_2}[\mathbf{0}, 1] \subseteq B_{d_\infty}[\mathbf{0}, 1].$$

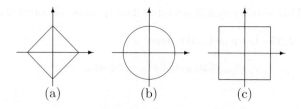

Fig. 2.2   Spheres $B_{d_p}[\mathbf{0}, 1]$ for $p = 1, 2, \infty$.

In Figures 2.2(a)–(c) we represent the closed spheres $B_{d_1}[\mathbf{0}, 1]$, $B_{d_2}[\mathbf{0}, 1]$, and $B_{d_\infty}[\mathbf{0}, 1]$.

An useful consequence of Theorem 2.28 is the following statement.

Theorem 2.36. *Let* $x_1, \ldots, x_m$ *and* $y_1, \ldots, y_m$ *be* $2m$ *non-negative numbers such that* $\sum_{i=1}^{m} x_i = \sum_{i=1}^{m} y_i = 1$ *and let* p *and* q *be two positive numbers such that* $\frac{1}{p} + \frac{1}{q} = 1$. *We have*

$$\sum_{j=1}^{m} x_j^{\frac{1}{p}} y_j^{\frac{1}{q}} \leqslant 1.$$

Proof.   The Hölder inequality applied to $x_1^{\frac{1}{p}}, \ldots, x_m^{\frac{1}{p}}$ and $y_1^{\frac{1}{q}}, \ldots, y_m^{\frac{1}{q}}$ yields the inequality of the theorem:

$$\sum_{j=1}^{m} x_j^{\frac{1}{p}} y_j^{\frac{1}{q}} \leqslant \sum_{j=1}^{m} x_j \sum_{j=1}^{m} y_j = 1.$$

$\square$

The set of real number sequences $\mathbf{Seq}(\mathbb{R})$ is a real linear space where the sum of the sequences $\mathbf{x} = (x_n)$ and $\mathbf{y} = (y_n)$ is defined as $\mathbf{x} + \mathbf{y} = (x_n + y_n)$ and the product of a real with $\mathbf{x}$ is $a\mathbf{x} = (ax_n)$.

The subspace $\ell^1(\mathbb{R})$ of $\mathbf{Seq}(\mathbb{R})$ consists of all sequences $\mathbf{x} = (x_n)$ such that $\sum_{n \in \mathbb{N}} |x_n|$ is convergent. Note that a norm exists on ℓ^1 defined by $\|\mathbf{x}\| = \sum_{n \in \mathbb{N}} |x_n|$.

The set of sequences $\mathbf{x} \in \mathbf{Seq}_\infty(\mathbb{R})$ such that $\|\mathbf{x}\|_p$ is finite is a real normed linear space.

In Example 2.2 we saw that $\mathbf{Seq}_\infty(\mathbb{R})$ can be organized as a linear space. Let $\mathbf{x}, \mathbf{y} \in \mathbf{Seq}_\infty(\mathbb{R})$ be two sequences such that $\|\mathbf{x}\|_p$ and $\|\mathbf{y}\|_p$ are finite.

By Minkowski's inequality, if $p \geqslant 1$ we have

$$\left(\sum_{i=1}^{n} |x_i + y_i|^p \right)^{\frac{1}{p}} \leqslant \left(\sum_{i=1}^{n} (|x_i| + |y_i|)^p \right)^{\frac{1}{p}} \leqslant \left(\sum_{i=1}^{n} |x_i|^p \right)^{\frac{1}{p}} + \left(\sum_{i=1}^{n} |y_i|^p \right)^{\frac{1}{p}}.$$

When n tends to ∞ we have $\|\mathbf{x} + \mathbf{y}\|_p \leqslant \|\mathbf{x}\|_p + \|\mathbf{y}\|_p$, so the function $\| \cdot \|_p$ is indeed a norm.

If $S_p(\mathbb{R})$ is the set of all sequences $\mathbf{x}$ in $\mathbf{Seq}_\infty(\mathbb{R})$ such that $\|\mathbf{x}\|_p < \infty$, then $(S_p(\mathbb{R}), \| \cdot \|_p)$ is a normed space denoted by $\ell^p(\mathbb{R})$.

The space $\ell^\infty(\mathbb{R})$ consists of bounded sequences in $\mathbf{Seq}_\infty(\mathbb{R})$.

The Cauchy-Schwarz Inequality implies that $|(\mathbf{x}, \mathbf{y})| \leqslant \|\mathbf{x}\|_2 \|\mathbf{y}\|_2$. Equivalently, this means that

$$-1 \leqslant \frac{(\mathbf{x}, \mathbf{y})}{\|\mathbf{x}\|_2 \|\mathbf{y}\|_2} \leqslant 1.$$

This double inequality allows us to introduce the notion of angle between two vectors $\mathbf{x}, \mathbf{y}$ of a real linear space L.

Definition 2.23. The *angle* between the vectors $\mathbf{x}$ and $\mathbf{y}$ is the number $\alpha \in [0, \pi]$ defined by

$$\cos \alpha = \frac{(\mathbf{x}, \mathbf{y})}{\|\mathbf{x}\|_2 \|\mathbf{y}\|_2}.$$

This angle is denoted by $\angle(\mathbf{x}, \mathbf{y})$.

Example 2.18. Let $\mathbf{u} = \begin{pmatrix} u_1 \\ u_2 \end{pmatrix} \in \mathbb{R}^2$ be a unit vector. Since $u_1^2 + u_2^2 = 1$, there exists $\alpha \in [0, 2\pi]$ such that $u_1 = \cos \alpha$ and $u_2 = \sin \alpha$. Thus, for any two unit vectors in $\mathbb{R}^2$,

$$\mathbf{u} = \begin{pmatrix} \cos \alpha \\ \sin \alpha \end{pmatrix} \quad \text{and} \quad \mathbf{v} = \begin{pmatrix} \cos \beta \\ \sin \beta \end{pmatrix}$$

we have $(\mathbf{u}, \mathbf{v}) = \cos \alpha \cos \beta + \sin \alpha \sin \beta = \cos(\alpha - \beta)$, where $\alpha, \beta \in [0, 2\pi]$. Consequently, $\angle(\mathbf{u}, \mathbf{v})$ is the angle in the interval $[0, \pi]$ that has the same cosine as $\alpha - \beta$.

Theorem 2.37. (The Cosine Theorem) *Let $\boldsymbol{x}$ and $\boldsymbol{y}$ be two vectors in $\mathbb{R}^n$ equipped with the Euclidean inner product. We have:*

$$\|\boldsymbol{x} - \boldsymbol{y}\|^2 = \|\boldsymbol{x}\|^2 + \|\boldsymbol{y}\|^2 - 2\|\boldsymbol{x}\| \|\boldsymbol{y}\| \cos \alpha,$$

where $\alpha = \angle(\boldsymbol{x}, \boldsymbol{y})$.

Proof.   Since the norm is induced by the inner product we have

$$\|\mathbf{x} - \mathbf{y}\|^2 = (\mathbf{x} - \mathbf{y}, \mathbf{x} - \mathbf{y})$$
$$= (\mathbf{x}, \mathbf{x}) - 2(\mathbf{x}, \mathbf{y}) + (\mathbf{y}, \mathbf{y})$$
$$= \|\mathbf{x}\|^2 - 2\|\mathbf{x}\|\|\mathbf{y}\| \cos \alpha + \|\mathbf{y}\|^2,$$

which is the desired equality. $\square$

Definition 2.24. Let L be an inner product space. Two vectors x and y of L are *orthogonal* if $(x, y) = 0$.

A pair of orthogonal vectors (x, y) is denoted by $x \perp y$.

Definition 2.25. An *orthogonal set of vectors* in an inner product space L is a subset W of L such that for every distinct $u, v \in W$ we have $u \perp v$.

If, in addition, $\|u\| = 1$ for every $u \in W$, then we say that W is *orthonormal*.

Theorem 2.38. *If W is a set of non-zero orthogonal vectors in an inner product space $(V, (\cdot, \cdot))$, then W is linearly independent.*

Proof.   Let $a_1 \mathbf{w}_1 + \cdots + a_n \mathbf{w}_n = \mathbf{0}$ for a linear combination of elements of W. This implies $a_i \|\mathbf{w}_i\|^2 = 0$, so $a_i = 0$ because $\|\mathbf{w}_i\|^2 \neq 0$, and this holds for every i, where $1 \leqslant i \leqslant n$. Thus, W is linearly independent. $\square$

Corollary 2.10. *Let L be an n-dimensional linear space. If W is an orthonormal set and $|W| = n$, then W is an orthonormal basis of L.*

Proof.   This statement is an immediate consequence of Theorem 2.38.

$\square$

Corollary 2.11. *Let L be an n-dimensional linear space. If $V = \{v_1, \ldots, v_n\}$ is an orthonormal basis in V, then*

$$x = (x, v_1)v_1 + \cdots + (x, v_n)v_n$$

for all $x \in L$.

Proof.   Since V is a basis, there exist $a_1, \ldots, a_n$ such that $x = a_1 v_1 + \ldots + a_n v_n$. This implies $(x, v_j) = a_j(v_j, v_j) = a_j$ for $1 \leqslant j \leqslant n$. $\square$

The *Gram-Schmidt algorithm* constructs an orthonormal basis for a finitely dimensional linear space L starting from an arbitrary basis of L.

Suppose that $\{u_1, \ldots, u_m\}$ is a basis of L. The orthonormal basis $\{w_1, \ldots, w_m\}$ is constructed sequentially such that $\langle w_1, \ldots, w_k \rangle = \langle u_1, \ldots, u_k \rangle$ for $1 \leqslant k \leqslant m$.

Let $W_k = \langle w_1, \ldots, w_k \rangle$. Note that $W_1 = \langle w_1 \rangle = \langle u_1 \rangle$, which allows us to define w_1 as the unit vector $w_1 = \frac{1}{\|u_1\|} u_1$.

Suppose that we have constructed an orthonormal basis for $W_k = \langle u_1, \ldots, u_k \rangle$ and we seek to construct w_{k+1} such that $\{w_1, \ldots, w_k, w_{k+1}\}$ is an orthonormal basis for $W_{k+1} = \langle u_1, \ldots, u_k, u_{k+1} \rangle$.

The expansion of u_{k+1} relative to the orthonormal basis $\{w_1, \ldots, w_k, w_{k+1}\}$ is

$$u_{k+1} = \sum_{i=1}^{k+1} (u_{k+1}, w_i) w_i,$$

which implies that

$$w_{k+1} = \frac{u_{k+1} - \sum_{i=1}^{k} (u_{k+1}, w_i) w_i}{(u_{k+1}, w_{k+1})}.$$

Note that by Fourier expansion of u_{k+1} with respect to the orthonormal set $\{w_1, \ldots, w_k, w_{k+1}\}$ we have

$$\|u_{k+1}\|^2 = \sum_{i=1}^{k} (u_{k+1}, w_i)^2 + (u_{k+1}, w_{k+1})^2.$$

Therefore,

$$\left\| u_{k+1} - \sum_{i=1}^{k} (u_{k+1}, w_i) w_i \right\|^2$$

$$= \left(u_{k+1} - \sum_{i=1}^{k} (u_{k+1}, w_i) w_i, u_{k+1} - \sum_{i=1}^{k} (u_{k+1}, w_i) w_i \right)$$

$$= \|u_{k+1}\|^2 - 2 \sum_{i=1}^{k} (u_{k+1}, w_i)^2 + \sum_{i=1}^{k} (u_{k+1}, w_i)^2$$

$$= \|u_{k+1}\|^2 - \sum_{i=1}^{k} (u_{k+1}, w_i)^2 = (u_{k+1}, w_{k+1})^2.$$

The last equalities imply

$$\left\| u_{k+1} - \sum_{i=1}^{k} (u_{k+1}, w_i) w_i \right\| = |(u_{k+1}, w_{k+1})|.$$

It follows that we can define

$$w_{k+1} = \frac{u_{k+1} - \sum_{i=1}^{k} (u_{k+1}, w_i) w_i}{\left\| u_{k+1} - \sum_{i=1}^{k} (u_{k+1}, w_i) w_i \right\|},$$

or as

$$w_{k+1} = -\frac{u_{k+1} - \sum_{i=1}^{k}(u_{k+1}, w_i)w_i}{\|u_{k+1} - \sum_{i=1}^{k}(u_{k+1}, w_i)w_i\|}.$$

Theorem 2.39. *Let $(w_1, \ldots, w_m)$ be the sequence of vectors constructed by the Gram-Schmidt algorithm starting from the basis $\{u_1, \ldots, u_m\}$ of an m-dimensional linear space L. The set $\{w_1, \ldots, w_m\}$ is an orthogonal basis of U and $\langle w_1, \ldots, w_k \rangle = \langle u_1, \ldots u_k \rangle$ for $1 \leqslant k \leqslant m$.*

Proof. We begin by proving that $\{w_1, \ldots, w_k\}$ is an orthonormal set. The argument is by induction on $k \geqslant 1$.

The base case, $k = 1$, is immediate. Suppose that the statement of the theorem holds for k, that is, the set $\{w_1, \ldots, w_k\}$ is an orthonormal basis for $U_k = \langle u_1, \ldots, u_k \rangle$. It is clear that $\|w_{k+1}\| = 1$, so it remains to show that $w_{k+1} \perp w_j$ for $1 \leqslant j \leqslant k$. We have

$$
\begin{aligned}
(w_{k+1}, w_j) &= \frac{1}{(u_{k+1}, w_{k+1})} \left(u_{k+1} - \sum_{i=1}^{k}(u_{k+1}, w_i)w_i, w_j \right) \\
&= \frac{1}{(u_{k+1}, w_{k+1})} \left((u_{k+1}, w_j) - (u_{k+1}, w_j)(w_j, w_j) \right) = 0,
\end{aligned}
$$

because $(w_j, w_j) = 1$.

The equality $\langle u_1, \ldots, u_k \rangle = \langle w_1, \ldots, w_k \rangle$ clearly holds for $k = 1$. Suppose that it holds for k. Since $w_1, \ldots, w_k$ belong to the subspace $\langle u_1, \ldots, u_k \rangle$ (by inductive hypothesis) it follows that $w_{k+1} \in \langle u_1, \ldots, u_k, u_{k+1} \rangle$, so $\langle w_1, \ldots, w_{k+1} \rangle \subseteq \langle u_1, \ldots, u_k \rangle$.

For the converse inclusion, note that w_{k+1} was defined such that $u_{k+1} \in \langle w_1, \ldots, w_k, w_{k+1} \rangle$. Thus, $\langle u_1, \ldots, u_k, u_{k+1} \rangle \subseteq \langle w_1, \ldots, w_k, w_{k+1} \rangle$. $\qquad\square$

Corollary 2.12. *Every finite-dimensional inner-product linear space L has an orthonormal basis.*

Proof. This follows by applying the Gram-Schmidt algorithm to a basis of the space L. $\qquad\square$

Theorem 2.40. *Let V be a finite-dimensional linear space. If U is an orthonormal set of vectors, then there exists a basis T of V that consists of orthonormal vectors such that $U \subseteq T$.*

Proof. Let $U = \{\mathbf{u}_1, \ldots, \mathbf{u}_m\}$ be an orthonormal set of vectors in V. There is an extension of U, $Z = \{\mathbf{u}_1, \ldots, \mathbf{u}_m, \mathbf{u}_{m+1}, \ldots, \mathbf{u}_n\}$ to a basis of V, where $n = \dim(V)$, by the Extension Corollary. Now, apply the Gram-Schmidt algorithm to the set U to produce an orthonormal basis $W = \{\mathbf{w}_1, \ldots, \mathbf{w}_n\}$ for the entire space V. It is easy to see that $\mathbf{w}_i = \mathbf{u}_i$ for $1 \leqslant i \leqslant m$, so $U \subseteq W$ and W is the orthonormal basis of V that extends the set U. $\square$

Corollary 2.13. *Let U be a subspace of an n-dimensional linear space V such that $\dim(U) = m$, where $m < n$. Then $\dim(U^\perp) = n - m$.*

Proof. Let $\mathbf{u}_1, \ldots, \mathbf{u}_m$ be an orthonormal basis of U, and let

$$\mathbf{u}_1, \ldots, \mathbf{u}_m, \mathbf{u}_{m+1}, \ldots, \mathbf{u}_n$$

be its completion to an orthonormal basis for V, which exists by Theorem 2.40. Then, $\mathbf{u}_{m+1}, \ldots, \mathbf{u}_n$ is a basis of the orthogonal complement $U^\perp$, so $\dim(U^\perp) = n - m$. $\square$

Let L be an n-dimensional inner product linear space and let $\{e_1, \ldots, e_n)\}$ be an orthonormal basis in L. Then any $v \in L$ can be written as

$$v = a_1 e_1 + \cdots + a_n e_n.$$

Note that $(e_i, v) = \sum_{k=1}^n a_k (e_i, e_k) = a_k$, which shows that any $v \in L$ can be written as

$$v = (e_1, v) e_1 + \cdots + (e_n, v) e_n.$$

For an arbitrary subset T of an inner product space L the set $T^\perp$ is defined by:

$$T^\perp = \{\mathbf{v} \in L \mid \mathbf{v} \perp \mathbf{t} \text{ for every } \mathbf{t} \in T\}.$$

Note that $T \subseteq U$ implies $U^\perp \subseteq T^\perp$.

If S, T are two subspaces of an inner product space L, then S and T are *orthogonal* if $s \perp t$ for every $s \in S$ and every $t \in T$. This is denoted as $S \perp T$.

Theorem 2.41. *Let L be an inner product space and let T be a subset of an inner product $\mathbb{F}$-linear space L. The set $T^\perp$ is a subspace of L.*

Proof. Let x and y be two members of T. We have $(x, t) = (y, t) = 0$ for every $t \in T$. Therefore, for every $a, b \in \mathbb{F}$, by the linearity of the inner product we have $(ax + by, t) = a(x, t) + b(y, t) = 0$, for $t \in T$, so $ax + by \in T^\perp$. Thus, $T^\perp$ is a subspace of L. $\square$

Theorem 2.42. *Let L be a finite-dimensional inner product $\mathbb{F}$-linear space and let T be a subset of L. We have $\langle T \rangle^{\perp} = T^{\perp}$.*

Proof. By a previous observation, since $T \subseteq \langle T \rangle$, we have $\langle T \rangle^{\perp} \subseteq T^{\perp}$. To prove the converse inclusion, let $\mathbf{z} \in T^{\perp}$.

If $y \in \langle T \rangle$, y is a linear combination of vectors of T, $y = a_1 t_1 + \cdots + a_m t_m$, so $(y, z) = a_1(t_1, z) + \cdots + a_m(t_m, z) = 0$. Therefore, $z \perp y$, which implies $z \in \langle T \rangle^{\perp}$. This allows us to conclude that $\langle T \rangle^{\perp} = T^{\perp}$. $\qquad\square$

We refer to $T^{\perp}$ as the *orthogonal complement* of T.

Note that $T \cap T^{\perp} \subseteq \{0\}$. If T is a subspace, then this inclusion becomes an equality, that is, $T \cap T^{\perp} = \{0\}$.

Theorem 2.43. *Let T be a subspace of the finite-dimensional linear space L. We have $L = T \oplus T^{\perp}$.*

Proof. We observed that $T \cap T^{\perp} = 0_L$. Suppose that B and B' are two orthonormal bases in T and $T^{\perp}$, respectively. The set $B \cup B'$ is a basis for $S = T \oplus T^{\perp}$.

Suppose that $S \subset L$. The set $B \cup B'$ can be extended to a orthonormal basis $B \cup B' \cup B''$ for L. Note that $B'' \perp B$, so $B'' \perp T$, which implies $B'' \subseteq T^{\perp}$. This is impossible because $B \cup B' \cup B''$ is linearly independent. Therefore, $B \cup B'$ is a basis for L, so $L = T \oplus T^{\perp}$. $\qquad\square$

Theorem 2.44. *Let $(L, (\cdot, \cdot))$ be an inner product linear space, $Y = \{y_1, \ldots, y_k\}$ be a linearly independent set in L and let $T = \langle Y \rangle$.*

For $\mathbf{c} = \begin{pmatrix} c_1 \\ \vdots \\ c_k \end{pmatrix} \in \mathbb{R}^k$ let $U_\mathbf{c} = \{x \in L \mid (x, y_i) = c_i \text{ for } 1 \leqslant i \leqslant k\}$.

There exists a translation t_z of L such that $U_\mathbf{c} = t_z(T^{\perp})$.

Proof. Let $u, z \in U_\mathbf{c}$. We have $(u, y_i) = (z, y_i) = c_i$ for $1 \leqslant i \leqslant k$, hence $(u - z, y_i) = 0$, that is, $u - z \in T^{\perp}$. For a fixed z, $u \in t_z(T^{\perp})$, hence $U_\mathbf{c} \subseteq t_z(T^{\perp})$. Conversely, if $u \in t_z(T^{\perp})$, where $(z, y_i) = c_i$ for $1 \leqslant i \leqslant k$, then $u = z + w$, where $w \in T^{\perp}$, which implies $(u, y_i) = c_i$ for $1 \leqslant i \leqslant k$, hence $u \in U_\mathbf{c}$. $\qquad\square$

Theorem 2.45. (Pythagora's Theorem) *Let $x_1, \ldots, x_n$ be a finite orthogonal set on n distinct elements in an inner product space L. We have*

$$\left\| \sum_{i=1}^{n} x_i \right\|^2 = \sum_{i=1}^{n} \|x_i\|^2.$$

Proof. By applying the definition of the norm induced by the inner product we have

$$\left\| \sum_{i=1}^{n} x_i \right\|^2 = \left(\sum_{i=1}^{n} x_i, \sum_{j=1}^{n} x_j \right)$$

$$= \sum_{i=1}^{n} \sum_{j=1}^{n} (x_i, x_j) = \sum_{i=1}^{n} (x_i, x_i)$$

$$(\text{because } (x_i, x_j) = 0 \text{ for } i \neq j)$$

$$= \sum_{i=1}^{n} \|x_i\|^2.$$

$\square$

Definition 2.26. A subspace T of a inner product linear space is an *approximating subspace* if for every $x \in L$ there is a unique element in T that is closest to x.

Theorem 2.46. *Let T be a subspace in the inner product space L. If $x \in L$ and $t \in T$, then $x - t \in T^{\perp}$ if and only if t is the unique element of T closest to x.*

Proof. Suppose that $x - t \in T^{\perp}$. Then, for any $u \in T$ we have

$$\|x - u\|^2 = \|(x - t) + (t - u)\|^2 = \|x - t\|^2 + \|t - u\|^2,$$

by observing that $x - t \in T^{\perp}$ and $t - u \in T$ and applying Pythagora's Theorem to $x - t$ and $t - u$. Therefore, we have $\|x - u\|^2 \geqslant \|x - t\|^2$, so t is the unique element of T closest to x.

Conversely, suppose that t is the unique element of T closest to x and $x - t \notin T^{\perp}$, that is, there exists $u \in T$ such that $(x - t, u) \neq 0$. This implies, of course, that $u \neq 0_L$. We have

$$\|x - (t + au)\|^2 = \|x - t - au\|^2 = \|x - t\|^2 - 2(x - t, au) + |a|^2 \|u\|^2.$$

Since $\|x - (t + au)\|^2 \geqslant \|x - t\|^2$ (by the definition of t), we have

$$-2(x - t, au) + |a|^2 \|u\|^2 \geqslant 0$$

for every $a \in \mathbb{F}$.

For $a = \frac{1}{\|u\|^2}(x - t, u)$ we have

$$-2(x - t, \frac{1}{\|u\|^2}(x - t, u)u) + |\frac{1}{\|u\|^2}(x - t, u)|^2\|u\|^2$$
$$= -2(x - t, \frac{1}{\|u\|^2}(x - t, u)u) + |\frac{1}{\|u\|^2}(x - t, u)|^2\|u\|^2$$
$$= -2\frac{|(x - t, u)|^2}{\|u\|^2} + \frac{|(x - t, u)|^2}{\|u\|^2}$$
$$= -\frac{|(x - t, u)|^2}{\|u\|^2} \geqslant 0,$$

which is a contradiction. $\square$

Theorem 2.47. *A subspace T of an inner product linear space L is an approximating subspace of L if and only if $L = T \oplus T^\perp$.*

Proof. Let T be an approximating subspace of L and let $x \in L$. By Theorem 2.46, we have $x - t \in T^\perp$, where t is the element of T that best approximates x. If $y = x - t$, we can write x uniquely as $x = t + y$, where $t \in T$ and $y \in T^\perp$, so $L = T \oplus T^\perp$.

Conversely, suppose that $L = T \oplus T^\perp$, where T is a subspace of L. Every $x \in L$ can be uniquely written as $x = t + y$, where $t \in T$ and $y \in T^\perp$, so $x - t \in T^\perp$. By Theorem 2.46, t is the element in T that is closest to x, so T is an approximating subspace of L. $\square$

Theorem 2.48. *Any subspace T of a finite-dimensional inner product linear space L is an approximating subspace of L.*

Proof. Let T be a subspace of L. By Theorem 2.47 it suffices to show that $L = T \oplus T^\perp$.

If $T = \{\mathbf{0}_L\}$, then $T^\perp = L$ and the statement is immediate. Therefore, we can assume that $T \neq \{\mathbf{0}_L\}$. We need to verify only that every $x \in L$ can be uniquely written as a sum $x = t + v$, where $t \in T$ and $v \in T^\perp$.

Let $t_1, \ldots, t_m$ be an orthonormal basis of T, that is, a basis such that

$$(t_i, t_j) = \begin{cases} 1 & \text{if } i = j, \\ 0 & \text{otherwise,} \end{cases}$$

for $1 \leqslant i, j \geqslant m$. Define $t = (x, t_1)t_1 + \cdots + (x, t_m)t_m$ and $v = x - t$.

The vector v is orthogonal to every vector t_i because

$$(v, t_i) = (x - t, t_i) = (x, t_i) - (t, t_i) = 0.$$

Therefore $v \in T^\perp$ and x has the necessary decomposition. To prove that the decomposition is unique suppose that $x = s + w$, where $s \in T$ and $w \in T_\perp$. Since $s + w = t + v$ we have $s - t = v - w \in T \cap T^\perp = \{\mathbf{0}_L\}$, which implies $s = t$ and $w = v$. $\qquad\square$

Theorem 2.49. *Let T be a subspace of an inner product space L of finite dimension. We have $(T^\perp)^\perp = T$.*

Proof. Observe that $T \subseteq (T^\perp)^\perp$. Indeed, if $t \in T$, then $(t, z) = 0$ for every $z \in T^\perp$, so $t \in (T^\perp)^\perp$.

To prove the reverse inclusion, let $x \in (T^\perp)^\perp$. Theorem 2.48 implies that we can write $x = u + v$, where $u \in T$ and $v \in T^\perp$, so $x - u = v \in T^\perp$.

Since $T \subseteq (T^\perp)^\perp$, we have $u \in (T^\perp)^\perp$, so $x - u \in (T^\perp)^\perp$. Consequently, $x - u \in T^\perp \cap (T^\perp)^\perp = \{\mathbf{0}\}$, so $x = u \in T$. Thus, $(T^\perp)^\perp \subseteq T$, which concludes the argument. $\qquad\square$

Definition 2.27. Let $W = \{\mathbf{w}_1, \dots, \mathbf{w}_n\}$ be an orthonormal set and let $\mathbf{x} \in \langle W \rangle$. The equality

$$\mathbf{x} = (\mathbf{x}, \mathbf{w}_1)\mathbf{w}_1 + \cdots + (\mathbf{x}, \mathbf{w}_n)\mathbf{w}_n \qquad (2.13)$$

is the *Fourier expansion of* $\mathbf{x}$ with respect to the orthonormal set W.

2.6 Linear Functionals in Inner Product Spaces

A linear functional on a finite-dimensional space can be represented using an inner product, as we prove next.

Theorem 2.50. *Let L be an n-dimensional inner product linear space and let $f : L \longrightarrow \mathbb{C}$ be a linear functional on L. There exists a unique $w \in L$ such that $f(x) = (x, w)$ for $x \in L$.*

Proof. We have shown in Theorem 2.18 that the dual L^* of an n-dimensional space L is also n-dimensional.

Starting from a basis $B = \{b_1, \dots, b_n\}$ in L it is possible to construct a basis $\tilde{B} = \{g_1, \dots, g_n\}$ in L^* that consists of the linear functionals such that $g_i(x) = x_i$ for every $x \in L$ such that $x = x_1 b_1 + \cdots + x_n b_n$.

Let $f : L \longrightarrow \mathbb{C}$ be a linear functional on L. Since $g_1, \dots, g_n$ is a basis in L^*, we have $f = w_1 g_1 + \cdots + w_n g_n$, where $w_1, \dots, w_n \in \mathbb{C}$. This allows us to write:

$$f(x) = w_1 g_1(x) + \cdots + w_n g_n(x)$$
$$= w_1 x_1 + \cdots + w_n x_n = (x, w),$$

where $\mathbf{w} = \begin{pmatrix} w_1 \\ \vdots \\ w_n \end{pmatrix}$.

Suppose that we also have $f(x) = (x, u)$ for $x \in L$. Then $(x, u) = (x, w)$, or $(x, u - w) = 0$. Taking $x = u - w$ we obtain $\|u - w\| = 0$ and, therefore, $u = w$, which shows the uniqueness of w. $\square$

The extension of Theorem 2.50 to infinite-dimensional spaces, known as the Riesz Theorem is a very important result of functional analysis. We present this result in Chapter 11.

Theorem 2.51. *Let L be a $\mathbb{F}$-normed space, where $\mathbb{F}$ is $\mathbb{R}$ or $\mathbb{C}$. For every $u_0 \in L - \{0_L\}$, there exists a non-trivial linear functional $f : L \longrightarrow \mathbb{C}$ such that $f(u_0) = \|u_0\|$ and $\|f\| = 1$.*

Proof. Let S be the subspace of L generated by u_0, that is, $S = \langle u_0 \rangle$ and let $f_0 : S \longrightarrow \mathbb{C}$ be given by $f_0(u) = a\|u_0\|$, for $u = au_0$.

It is clear that $f_0(u_0) = \|u_0\|$ and that $|f_0(u)| = \|u\|$ for all $u \in \langle u_0 \rangle$. By the Hahn-Banach Theorem (see Theorem 2.19) there exists an extension f of f_0 to L such that $|f(u)| \leqslant \|u\|$ for all $u \in L$, so $\|f\| = 1$. $\square$

Corollary 2.14. *Let L be a $\mathbb{F}$-normed space, where $\mathbb{F}$ is $\mathbb{R}$ or $\mathbb{C}$. For every $u_0 \in L$ we have $\|u_0\| = \max\{|f(u_0)| \mid f \in L^*, \|f\| \leqslant 1\}$.*

Proof. Since $|f(u_0)| \leqslant \|f\|\|u_0\|$, the equality follows from Theorem 2.51. $\square$

Corollary 2.15. *Let L be a $\mathbb{F}$-normed space, where $\mathbb{F}$ is $\mathbb{R}$ or $\mathbb{C}$. If $f(u) = 0$ for every $f \in L^*$, then $u = 0_L$.*

Proof. This is an immediate consequence of Theorem 2.51. $\square$

Definition 2.28. Let $\mathbb{F}$ be $\mathbb{R}$ or $\mathbb{C}$. The *bidual* of the $\mathbb{F}$-linear space L is the linear space L^{**} that consists of all linear functionals $F : L^* \longrightarrow \mathbb{F}$.

The linear space L is said to be *reflexive* if for every $F \in L^{**}$ there exists $u \in L$ such that $F(f) = f(u)$ for every $f \in L^*$.

Theorem 2.52. *Let L be an $\mathbb{F}$-normed linear space. Define $\phi : L \longrightarrow L^{**}$ as $\phi(u) = F$ if $F(f) = f(u)$ for $f \in L^*$. The mapping ϕ is linear and $\|\phi(u)\| = \|u\|$ for all $u \in L$. Furthermore, L is reflexive if and only if ϕ is bijective.*

Proof. By Definition 2.28, L is reflexive if and only if the mapping ϕ is surjective. Suppose that $\phi(u) = F$ and $\phi(v) = G$ for $u, v \in L$, that is, $F(f) = f(u)$ and $G(f) = f(v)$ for every $f \in L^*$. We have

$$(a\phi(u) + b\phi(v))(f) = a\phi(u)(f) + b\phi(v)(f)$$
$$= af(u) + bf(v) = f(au + bv)$$
$$\text{(because } f \text{ is a linear functional)}$$
$$= \phi(au + bv)(f),$$

hence ϕ is a linear mapping. Furthermore, we have

$$\|\phi(u)\| = \sup\{f(u) \mid f \in L^*, \|f\| \leqslant 1\} = \|u\|$$

by Corollary 2.14. If $\phi(u) = 0$ it follows that $u = 0$, so ϕ is injective. Therefore, L is reflexive if and only if ϕ is a bijection. $\qquad\square$

Theorem 2.53. *Let* $(L, (\cdot, \cdot))$ *be a real inner product linear space, S be a subspace of L, and let $x \in L$. There exists at most one vector $y_0 \in S$ such that $\|x - y_0\| \leqslant \|x - y\|$ for every $y \in S$. Furthermore, y_0 is a unique vector in S that minimizes $\|x - y\|$ if and only if $x - y_0$ is orthogonal on S.*

Proof. Let that $y_0 \in S$ is such that $\|x - y_0\| \leqslant \|x - y\|$ for every $y \in S$. We claim that $x - y_0$ is orthogonal on S, that is, $x - y_0$ is orthogonal on every $y \in S$.

Suppose that $x - y_0$ is not orthogonal on $y \in S$, that is, $(x - y_0, y) = a$, where $a \neq 0$. Without loss of generality, we may assume that $\|y\| = 1$. If $y_1 = y_0 + ay$, we have

$$\|x - y_1\|^2 = \|x - y_0 - ay\|^2$$
$$= \|x - y_0\|^2 - 2a(x - y_0, y) + a^2$$
$$= \|x - y_0\|^2 - a^2 < \|x - y_0\|^2,$$

which contradicts the minimality of $\|x - y_0\|$, Therefore, $x - y_0$ is orthogonal on S.

Conversely, suppose that $x - y_0$ is orthogonal on S. Then, $\|x - y_0\|$ is minimal and y_0 is unique.

For $y \in S$ we have

$$\|x - y\|^2 = \|x - y_0\|^2 + \|y_0 - y\|^2,$$

so $\|x - y\| > \|x - y_0\|$ for $y \neq y_0$, which means that $\|x - y_0\|$ is minimal and that y_0 is unique. $\qquad\square$

2.7   Hyperplanes

Affine subspaces of a linear space L are obtained by translating subspaces of L.

Definition 2.29. An *affine subspace* of a linear space L is a set of the form $t_w(U)$, where U is a subspace of L and $w \in L$.

A *hyperplane* in a non-trivial linear space L is a maximal proper affine subspace.

It is clear that in a non-trivial linear space every maximal linear space is a hyperplane.

If H is a hyperplane in L, we have $H \neq L$, and if U is any other affine subspace such that $H \subseteq U$, then $U = H$ or $U = L$. Note that if H is a hyperplane obtained as a translation $H = t_z(S)$ where S is a subspace of L, then S is a maximal subspace of L.

Theorem 2.54. *If H is a hyperplane in the real, non-trivial linear space L, then there exists a non-trivial linear functional f on L and a number $a \in \mathbb{R}$ such that $H = \{x \in L \mid f(x) = a\}$. Conversely, if f is a non-trivial linear functional on L, then $\{x \in L \mid f(x) = a\}$ is a hyperplane in L.*

Proof.   Let H be a hyperplane in L. There exists a maximal subspace S of L such that $H = w + S$. If $w \notin S$, then $\langle \{w\} \cup S \rangle = L$. Thus, every $x \in L$ can be written as $x = aw + y$ such that $a \in \mathbb{R}$ and $y \in S$.

Define f as $f(x) = a$ for $x \in L$. This is a linear functional. Indeed, suppose that for $u, v \in L$ we have $u = a_1 w + y_1$ and $v = a_2 w + y_2$. We have $f(u) = a_1$ and $f(v) = a_2$. Also, for $c, d \in \mathbb{R}$ we can write $cu + dv = (ca_1 + da_2) + cy_1 + d_2$, which yields

$$f(cu + dv) = ca_1 + da_2 = cf(u) + df(v),$$

which proves that f is a linear functional. It is clear that $H = \{x \in L \mid f(x) = 1\}$.

If $w \in S$, then $H = S$ and we can take $w_1 \notin S$. We have $L = \langle \{w_1\} \cup S \rangle$ and, for $x = aw_1 + y$, we define $f(x) = a$. Then $H = \{x \in L \mid f(x) = 0\}$. Since $H \neq L$, the functional f is non-trivial.

Conversely, let f be a non-trivial linear functional. Define the subspace $S = \{x \in L \mid f(x) = 0\}$. Let $x_0 \in L$ be such that $f(x_0) = 1$. For every $x \in L$ we have

$$f(x - f(x)x_0) = 0,$$

hence $x - f(x)x_0 \in S$. Therefore, $L = \langle \{x_0\} \cup S \rangle$, which means that S is a proper maximal subspace of L. If $a \in \mathbb{R}$ let $x_1 \in L$ be such that $f(x_1) = a$. Then

$$\{x \in L \mid f(x) = a\} = \{x \in L \mid f(x - x_0) = 0\} = x_1 + S,$$

so $\{x \in L \mid f(x) = a\}$ is a hyperplane in L. $\qquad\square$

Theorem 2.55. *If H is a hyperplane in the real linear space L such that $0_L \notin H$. There exists a unique non-trivial linear functional f on L such that $H = \{x \in L \mid f(x) = 1\}$.*

Proof. By Theorem 2.54 there exists a functional f that satisfies the condition of the theorem. If g is another functional such that $H = \{x \in L \mid g(x) = 1\}$ then $H \subseteq \{x \in L \mid f(x) - g(x) = 0\}$ and $\{x \in L \mid f(x) - g(x) = 0\}$ is a subspace of L. Since the smallest subspace that contains H is L, it follows that $f = g$. $\qquad\square$

A hyperplane H in a linear space L, defined by $H = \{x \in L \mid f(x) = a\}$, where f is a linear functional generates four subsets known as *half-spaces* shown in Table 2.1.

Table 2.1   Half spaces defined by a hyperplane.

Designation	Definition
negative closed half space	$\{x \in L \mid f(x) \leqslant a\}$
negative open half space	$\{x \in L \mid f(x) < a\}$
positive closed half space	$\{x \in L \mid f(x) \geqslant a\}$
positive open half space	$\{x \in L \mid f(x) > a\}$

By Theorem 2.54 for every hyperplane H in $\mathbb{R}^n$ there exists a linear functional f on L and a number $a \in \mathbb{R}$ such that $H = \{x \in L \mid f(\mathbf{x}) = a\}$. Applying Theorem 2.50, there exists $\mathbf{w} \in \mathbb{R}^n$ such that $f(\mathbf{x}) = (\mathbf{w}, \mathbf{x})$. Thus, each hyperplane H in $\mathbb{R}^n$ can be written as

$$H = \{\mathbf{x} \in \mathbb{R}^n \mid x_1 w_1 + \cdots + x_n w_n = a\},$$

where $w_1, \ldots, w_n, a \in \mathbb{R}^n$. This allows us to use the alternative notation $H_{\mathbf{w},a}$ for H. Note that it is impossible to have both $\mathbf{a} = \mathbf{0}_n$ and $a = 0$ because, in this case, we would have $H = \mathbb{R}^n$.

If $\mathbf{x}_0 \in H_{\mathbf{w},a}$, then $\mathbf{w}'\mathbf{x}_0 = a$, so $H_{\mathbf{w},a}$ is also described by the equality:

$$H_{\mathbf{w},a} = \{\mathbf{x} \in \mathbb{R}^n \mid \mathbf{w}'(\mathbf{x} - \mathbf{x}_0) = 0\}.$$

The negative closed half-space and the positive closed half-space introduced in Table 2.1 are denoted as

$$H_{\mathbf{w},a}^{\geqslant} = \{\mathbf{x} \in \mathbb{R}^n \mid \mathbf{w}'\mathbf{x} \geqslant a\},$$
$$H_{\mathbf{w},a}^{\leqslant} = \{\mathbf{x} \in \mathbb{R}^n \mid \mathbf{w}'\mathbf{x} \leqslant a\},$$

respectively. Similarly, the *positive* and *negative open* half-spaces are

$$H_{\mathbf{w},a}^{>} = \{\mathbf{x} \in \mathbb{R}^n \mid \mathbf{w}'\mathbf{x} > a\},$$
$$H_{\mathbf{w},a}^{<} = \{\mathbf{x} \in \mathbb{R}^n \mid \mathbf{w}'\mathbf{x} < a\}.$$

respectively.

If $\mathbf{x}_1, \mathbf{x}_2 \in H_{\mathbf{w},a}$, then $\mathbf{w} \perp \mathbf{x}_1 - \mathbf{x}_2$. Since $\mathbf{x}_1 - \mathbf{x}_2$ is located in $H_{\mathbf{w},a}$, it follows that $\mathbf{w}$ is orthogonal on any vector in $H_{\mathbf{w},a}$. This justifies referring to $\mathbf{w}$ as the *normal to the hyperplane* $H_{w,a}$. Observe that a hyperplane is fully determined by a vector $\mathbf{x}_0 \in H_{\mathbf{w},a}$ and by $\mathbf{w}$.

Let $\mathbf{x}_0 \in \mathbb{R}^n - H_{\mathbf{w},a}$, then the line ℓ passing through $\mathbf{x}_0$ and is orthogonal on $H_{\mathbf{w},a}$ is described by $\mathbf{x} - \mathbf{x}_0 = \lambda\mathbf{w}$, where $\lambda \in \mathbb{R}$. Therefore, the intersection of this line with $H_{\mathbf{w},a}$ is given by

$$\mathbf{w}'(\mathbf{x}_0 - \lambda\mathbf{w}) = a,$$

which means that $\lambda = \frac{\mathbf{w}'\mathbf{x}_0 - a}{\|\mathbf{w}\|^2}$. Thus, the intersection of ℓ with $H_{\mathbf{w},a}$ is $\mathbf{x} = \mathbf{x}_0 + \frac{\mathbf{w}'\mathbf{x}_0 - a}{\|\mathbf{w}\|^2}\mathbf{w}$. Thus, the closest point in $H_{\mathbf{w},a}$ to $\mathbf{x}_0$ is

$$\mathbf{x} = \mathbf{x}_0 - \frac{\mathbf{w}'\mathbf{x}_0 - a}{\|\mathbf{w}\|^2}\mathbf{w}.$$

The smallest distance between $\mathbf{x}_0$ and a point in the hyperplane $H_{\mathbf{w},a}$ is given by

$$\|\mathbf{x}_0 - \mathbf{x}\| = \frac{|\mathbf{w}'\mathbf{x}_0 - a|}{\|\mathbf{w}\|}.$$

If we define the distance $d(H_{\mathbf{w},a}, \mathbf{x}_0)$ between $\mathbf{x}_0$ and $H_{\mathbf{w},a}$ as this smallest distance we have:

$$d(H_{\mathbf{w},a}, \mathbf{x}_0) = \frac{|\mathbf{w}'\mathbf{x}_0 - a|}{\|\mathbf{w}\|}. \tag{2.14}$$

A hyperplane $H_{\mathbf{w},a}$ in $\mathbb{R}^{n+1}$ is said to be *vertical* if $w_{n+1} = 0$; otherwise, $H_{\mathbf{w},a}$ is said to be *non-vertical*.

Exercises and Supplements

(1) Let $\{x_1, \ldots, x_n\}$ be a linearly independent set in the linear space L. Prove that if the set $\{x_1 + x, \ldots, x_n + x\}$ is linearly dependent, then $x \in \langle x_1, \ldots, x_n \rangle$.

(2) Let L be a linear space. Prove that L is infinite-dimensional if and only if there exists a sequence of vectors (x_n) in L such that $\{x_1, \ldots, x_n\}$ is linearly independent for each $n \in \mathbb{N}$.

(3) Let L be a finite-dimensional linear space and let K be a subspace of L. Prove that if $\dim(K) = \dim(L)$, then $K = L$.

(4) Let L be an $\mathbb{F}$-linear space and let $f, g_1, \ldots, g_n$ be linear functionals. Prove that $f = \sum_{i=1}^{n} a_i g_i$ for some $a_1, \ldots, a_n$ if and only if $\bigcap_{i=1}^{n} \mathsf{Null}(g_i) \subseteq \mathsf{Null}(f)$.

Solution: It is clear that if $f = \sum_{i=1}^{n} a_i g_i$, then $\bigcap_{i=1}^{n} \mathsf{Null}(g_i) \subseteq \mathsf{Null}(f)$. Conversely, assume that $\bigcap_{i=1}^{n} \mathsf{Null}(g_i) \subseteq \mathsf{Null}(f)$. Define the operator $h : L \longrightarrow \mathbb{F}^n$ as $h(x) = (g_1(x), \ldots, g_n(x))$. If $h(x) = h(y)$, then $g_i(x) = g_i(y)$, or $g_i(x - y) = 0$ for $1 \leqslant i \leqslant n$, hence $x - y \in \bigcap_{i=1}^{n} \mathsf{Null}(g_i) \subseteq \mathsf{Null}(f)$. Thus, the linear functional $k : h(L) \longrightarrow \mathbb{F}$ given by $k(g_1(x), \ldots, g_n(x)) = f(x)$ for $x \in L$ is well-defined. By extending k to the entire $\mathbb{F}^n$, we obtain the existence of the scalars $a_1, \ldots, a_n$ such that $k(x_1, \ldots, x_n) = \sum_{i=1}^{n} a_i x_i$. Thus, $f(x) = \sum_{i=1}^{n} a_i g_i(x)$.

(5) Let L, K be two $\mathbb{F}$-linear spaces and let $h : L \longrightarrow K$ be a linear operator. Prove that if h is injective and $\{x_1, \ldots, x_n\}$ is a linearly independent set in L, then $\{h(x_1), \ldots, h(x_n)\}$ is linearly independent in K.

(6) Let L be a linear space. Prove that if $h : L \longrightarrow L$ is a linear mapping such that both $\mathsf{Null}(h)$ and $\mathsf{Img}(h)$, then L is finite-dimensional.

(7) Let h_1, h_2 be two linear operators on a finite-dimensional linear space L. Prove that $h_1 h_2$ is invertible if and only if both h_1 and h_2 are invertible.

(8) Let L be a finite-dimensional $\mathbb{F}$-space and let $h : L \longrightarrow L$ be a linear operator. Prove that h is invertible is equivalent to h being injective, and also, with h being surjective.

Let L_1, L_2 and L be real linear spaces. A mapping $\phi : L_1 \times L_2 \longrightarrow L$ is *bilinear* if the following conditions are satisfied:

(i) the mapping $\phi_{x_1} : L_2 \longrightarrow L$ defined by $\phi_{x_1}(x_2) = \phi(x_1, x_2)$ is linear for every $x_1 \in L_1$;

(ii) the mapping $\phi_{x_2} : L_1 \longrightarrow L$ defined by $\phi_{x_2}(x_1) = \phi(x_1, x_2)$ is linear for every $x_2 \in L_2$.

A *duality* is a quadruple (L_1, L_2, L, ϕ), where and $\phi : L_1 \times L_2 \longrightarrow L$ is a bilinear mapping such that the following supplementary conditions are satisfied:

(i) if $\phi(x_1, x_2) = 0_L$ for every $x_2 \in L_2$, then $x_1 = 0_{L_1}$;

(ii) if $\phi(x_1, x_2) = 0_L$ for every $x_1 \in L_1$, then $x_2 = 0_{L_2}$.

(9) Prove that:

    (a) $(\mathbb{R}^n, \mathbb{R}^n, \mathbb{R}, \phi)$ is a duality, where $\phi(x, y) = \sum_{i=1}^n x_i y_i$;

    (b) if L is a real linear space and L' is its algebraic dual (that consists of all linear functionals defined on L), then $(L, L', \mathbb{R}, \phi)$ is a duality, where $\phi(x, f) = f(x)$ for $x \in L$ and $f \in L'$.

(10) Prove that if (L_1, L_2, L, ϕ) is a duality, than L_1 is isomorphic to a subspace of the linear space L^{L_2}.

    Solution: Let $F : L_1 \longrightarrow L^{L_2}$ be defined by $F(x_1) = \phi_{x_1}$ for $x_1 \in L_1$. It is immediate that F is a linear mapping. Suppose that $F(x) = F(y)$ for $x, y \in L_1$, that is, $\phi_x(u) = \phi_y(u)$ for $u \in L_2$, or $\phi(x - y, u) = 0$ for $u \in L_1$. Thus, $x - y = 0_L$, or $x = y$, so F is injective. This proves that L is isomorphic to $F(L)$, a subspace of L^{L_2}.

(11) Let L_1, L_2, L be inner product real linear spaces. Prove that if $\phi : L_1 \times L_2 \longrightarrow L$ is a bilinear mapping such that $\|\phi(x_1, x_2)\| \leqslant \|\mathbf{x}_1\| \|x_2\|$, then ϕ is a duality.

(12) Consider the linear operator $h : \mathbb{R}^2 \longrightarrow \mathbb{R}^2$ over the linear space $\mathbb{R}^2$ defined as

$$h \begin{pmatrix} x_1 \\ x_2 \end{pmatrix} = \begin{pmatrix} -x_2 \\ x_1 \end{pmatrix}$$

for $x_1, x_2 \in \mathbb{R}$. Prove that h has no eigenvalue.

    Solution: Suppose that λ were an eigenvalue and that $\mathbf{x} = \begin{pmatrix} x_1 \\ x_2 \end{pmatrix} \neq 0_2$ were an eigenvector of h, that is:

$$\begin{pmatrix} -x_2 \\ x_1 \end{pmatrix} = \lambda \begin{pmatrix} x_1 \\ x_2 \end{pmatrix}.$$

This implies $-x_2 = \lambda x_1$ and $x_1 = \lambda x_2$. At least one of x_1, x_2 is not equal to 0. If $x_1 \neq 0$, we have $x_1(1 + \lambda^2) = 0$, which is contradictory, etc.

(13) Let L be a linear space and let $h_1, h_2 : L \longrightarrow L$ be two linear operators. Prove that $h_1 h_2$ and $h_2 h_1$ has the same set of eigenvalues.

(14) Let $h : L \longrightarrow L$ be an invertible linear operator. Prove that $\lambda \neq 0$ is an eigenvalue of h if and only if $\frac{1}{\lambda}$ is an eigenvalue of h^{-1}.

(15) Let $h : L \longrightarrow L$ be a linear operator such that every $x \in L$ is an eigenvector of h. Prove that there exists a constant $a \in \mathbb{F}$ such that $h = a 1_L$.

(16) Determine the eigenvalues and eigenvectors of the linear operator $h : \mathbb{R}^2 \longrightarrow \mathbb{R}^2$ defined by $h(\mathbf{x}) = (x_1 + x_2, x_1 + x_2)$ for $\mathbf{x} \in \mathbb{R}^2$.

(17) Let $h : L \longrightarrow L$ be a linear operator. Prove the following equality involving the resolvents of h:

$$\mathsf{R}_{h,\lambda} - \mathsf{R}_{h,\mu} = (\lambda - mu)\mathsf{R}_{h,\lambda}\mathsf{R}_{h,\mu}.$$

Solution: We have

$$(h - \lambda 1_L)(\mathsf{R}_{h,\lambda} - \mathsf{R}_{h,\mu})(h - \mu 1_L)$$
$$= (1_L - (h - \lambda 1_L)\mathsf{R}_{h,\mu})(h - \mu 1_L)$$
$$= ((h - \mu 1_L) - (h - \lambda 1_L))$$
$$= (\lambda - \mu)1_L,$$

which implies desired equality.

(18) Let $\{u_1, \ldots, u_n, \ldots\}$ and $\{v_1, \ldots, v_n, \ldots\}$ be two orthonormal sets in an inner product space L. Prove that $(u_j - v_j, u_i) = (u_i - v_i, v_j)$ for $i, j \geqslant 1$.

The subsets $B = \{\mathbf{b}_1, \ldots, \mathbf{b}_n\}$ and $C = \{\mathbf{c}_1, \ldots, \mathbf{c}_n\}$ of $\mathbb{R}^n$ are *reciprocal* if $(\mathbf{b}_i, \mathbf{c}_j) = 1$ if $i = j$ and $(\mathbf{b}_i, \mathbf{c}_j) = 0$ if $i \neq j$, for $1 \leqslant i, j \leqslant n$.

(19) Let $B = \{\mathbf{b}_1, \ldots, \mathbf{b}_n\}$ be a basis of $\mathbb{R}^n$. Prove that there exists a unique reciprocal set of B.

Solution: Let U_i be the subspace of $\mathbb{R}^n$ generated by the set $B - \{\mathbf{b}_i\}$ and let $U_i^\perp$ be its orthogonal complement. We have $\dim(U_i^\perp) = 1$ because $\dim(U_i) = n - 1$. Thus, there exists a vector $\mathbf{t} \neq \mathbf{0}$ in $U_i^\perp$. Note that $(\mathbf{t}, \mathbf{b}_i) \neq 0$ because $\mathbf{b}_i \notin U_i$. Define

$$\mathbf{c}_i = \frac{1}{(\mathbf{t}, \mathbf{b}_i)}\mathbf{b}_i.$$

Then, $(\mathbf{b}_i, \mathbf{c}_i) = 1$ and $(\mathbf{b}_i, \mathbf{c}_j) = 0$ if $j \neq i$. This construction can be applied to all i, where $1 \leqslant i \leqslant n$ and this yields a set $C = \{\mathbf{c}_1, \ldots, \mathbf{c}_n\}$, which is reciprocal to B.

To prove the uniqueness of the set C, assume that $D = \{\mathbf{d}_1, \ldots, \mathbf{d}_n\}$ is another reciprocal set of the basis B. Then, since $(\mathbf{b}_i, \mathbf{c}_j) = (\mathbf{b}_i, \mathbf{d}_j)$, it follows that $(\mathbf{b}_i, \mathbf{c}_j - \mathbf{d}_j) = 0$ for every i, j. Since $\mathbf{c}_j - \mathbf{d}_j$ is orthogonal on all vectors of B it follows that $\mathbf{c}_j - \mathbf{d}_j = \mathbf{0}$, so $\mathbf{c}_j = \mathbf{d}_j$. Thus $D = C$.

(20) If $B = \{\mathbf{b}_1, \ldots, \mathbf{b}_n\}$ is a basis of $\mathbb{R}^n$ then the reciprocal set C of B is also a basis of $\mathbb{R}^n$.

(21) Let ν be a norm on $\mathbb{C}^n$. Prove that there exists a number $k \in \mathbb{R}$ such that for any vector $\mathbf{x} \in \mathbb{C}^n$ we have $\nu(\mathbf{x}) \leqslant k \sum_{i=1}^n |x_i|$.

(22) Prove that if $\mathbf{x}, \mathbf{y}, \mathbf{z}$ are three vectors in $\mathbb{R}^n$ and ν is a norm on $\mathbb{R}^n$, then $\nu(\mathbf{x} - \mathbf{y}) \leqslant \nu(\mathbf{x} - \mathbf{z}) + \nu(\mathbf{z} - \mathbf{y})$.

(23) Prove that for any vector norm ν on $\mathbb{R}^n$ we have

$$\nu(\mathbf{x} + \mathbf{y})^2 + \nu(\mathbf{x} - \mathbf{y})^2 \leqslant 4(\nu(\mathbf{x})^2 + \nu(\mathbf{y})^2)$$

for every $\mathbf{x}, \mathbf{y} \in \mathbb{R}^n$.

(24) Let $\mathbf{x} \in \mathbb{R}^n$. Prove that for every $\epsilon > 0$ there exists $\mathbf{y} \in \mathbb{R}^n$ such that the components of the vector $\mathbf{x} + \mathbf{y}$ are distinct and $\|\mathbf{y}\|_2 < \epsilon$.

(25) Prove that if $\mathbf{x} \in \mathbb{R}^n$, then $\|\mathbf{x}\|_1 = \max\{\mathbf{a}'\mathbf{x} \mid \mathbf{a} \in \{-1, 1\}^n\}$.

(26) Let $\nu_0 : \mathbb{R}^n \longrightarrow \mathbb{R}$ be the function defined by $\nu_0(\mathbf{x}) = \{i \mid 1 \leqslant i \leqslant n, x_i \neq 0\}$. Prove that ν_0 is not a norm, although $\nu_0(\mathbf{x} + \mathbf{y}) \leqslant \nu_0(\mathbf{x}) + \nu_0(\mathbf{y})$.

(27) Let $p : L \longrightarrow V$ be a projection of a linear normed space on a subspace V and let h be a linear operator on L. If $v \in V$,

$$u - h(u) - b = v - h(v) - b = 0_L,$$

and $1_L - ph$ is invertible, prove that

$$\|u - v\| \leqslant \|(1_L - ph)^{-1}\| \, \|u - p(u)\|.$$

Solution: Since $v \in V$ we have $p(v) = v$. Therefore, from $v - h(v) - b = 0_L$ it follows that $p(v - h(v) - b) = 0_L$, or $v - ph(v) = p(b)$.

Taking into account that $u - h(u) = b$ we obtain $p(u) - ph(u) = p(b)$, hence $v - ph(v) = p(u) - ph(u)$, or $u - v - ph(u - v) = u - p(u)$, which amounts to $(1_L - ph)(u - v) = u - p(u)$, hence $u - v = (1_L - ph)^{-1}(u - p(u))$. This implies the desired inequality.

(28) Let $\{x_1, \ldots, x_n\}$ be a linearly independent space in a normed linear space L. Prove that there exists $\delta > 0$ such that if $\|y_i - x_i\| < \delta$ for $1 \leqslant i \leqslant n$, then the set $\{y_1, \ldots, y_n\}$ is linearly independent.

Bibliographical Comments

Among the many useful references we mention [98, 67, 132, 116, 93] and [121], a volume dedicated to applications of linear algebra in data mining. An novel, interesting approach to linear algebra that emphasizes linear operators is provided in [5, 4].

Chapter 3

Algebra of Convex Sets

3.1 Introduction

The notion of convex set that we study in this chapter is a pillar of optimization theory and is essential for the study of convex functions.

After introducing convex sets in linear spaces and presenting several examples of such sets we discuss techniques for generating new convex sets starting from existing such sets. Cones are another type of subsets of linear spaces that we present in this chapter.

Extreme points of convex sets are important in optimization problem and we treat then in Section 3.5. Finally, we present balanced and absorbing sets that are useful in the study of certain topological spaces. Special types of convex sets (polytopes and polyhedra) are studied in the last section.

3.2 Convex Sets and Affine Subspaces

Let L be a real linear space and let $x, y \in L$. The *closed segment* determined by x and y is the set

$$[x, y] = \{(1 - a)x + ay \mid 0 \leqslant a \leqslant 1\}.$$

The *closed-open segment* determined by x and y is the set:

$$[x, y) = \{(1 - a)x + ay \mid 0 \leqslant a < 1\}.$$

The *open-closed segment* determined by x and y is the set:

$$(x, y] = \{(1 - a)x + ay \mid 0 < a \leqslant 1\}.$$

The *open segment* determined by x and y is

$$(x, y) = \{(1 - a)x + ay \mid 0 < a < 1\}.$$

A *line* passing through x_0 and having direction u is a set of the form $\ell = \{z \in L \mid z = x_0 + tu, t \in \mathbb{R}\}$, where $x_0 \in L$ and $u \neq 0_L$.

Suppose that x and y are two points located on the line ℓ. If $z \in L$, then the vectors $z - y$ and $y - z$ are collinear, so there exists t such that $y - z = t(z - x)$, or $z = \frac{t}{1+t}x + \frac{1}{1+t}y$. If we denote $a = \frac{1}{1+t}$, z has the form $z = (1-a)x + ay$ for $t \in \mathbb{R}$. Thus, the line determined by x and y has the form

$$\ell_{x,y} = \{(1-a)x + ay \mid a \in \mathbb{R}\}.$$

It is clear that for any $x, y \in L$ we have

$$(x, y) \subseteq [x, y), (x, y] \subseteq [x, y] \subseteq \ell_{x,y}.$$

Definition 3.1. A subset C of L is *convex* if we have $[x, y] \subseteq C$ for all $x, y \in C$.

Note that the empty subset and every singleton $\{x\}$ of L are convex.

In Figure 3.1(a) we show a convex set in $\mathbb{R}^2$; the quadrilateral in Figure 3.1(b) is not convex for both $\mathbf{x}, \mathbf{y}$ are inside the quadrilateral, while the segment $[\mathbf{x}, \mathbf{y}]$ is not included in the quadrilateral.

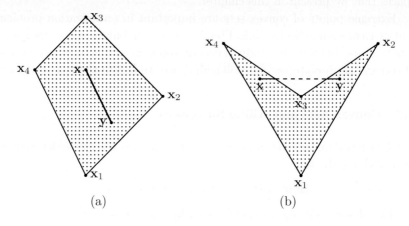

(a)   (b)

Fig. 3.1   Convex set (a) vs. a non-convex set (b).

Example 3.1. The set $\mathbb{R}^n_{\geqslant 0}$ of all vectors of $\mathbb{R}^n$ having non-negative components is a convex set called the *non-negative orthant* of $\mathbb{R}^n$.

Example 3.2. The convex subsets of $(\mathbb{R}, +, \cdot)$ are the intervals of $\mathbb{R}$. Regular polygons are convex subsets of $\mathbb{R}^2$.

Example 3.3. Every linear subspace T of a real linear space L is convex.

Example 3.4. Let $(L, \|\cdot\|)$ be a normed linear space. An open sphere $B(x_0, r) \subseteq L$ is convex.

Indeed, suppose that $x, y \in B(x_0, r)$, that is, $\|x - x_0\| < r$ and $\|x_0 - y\| < r$.

Let $a \in [0, 1]$ and let $z = (1 - a)x + ay$. We have

$$\|x_0 - z\| = \|x_0 - (1 - a)x - ay\|$$
$$= \|a(x_0 - y) + (1 - a)(x_0 - x)\|$$
$$\leqslant a\|x_0 - y\| + (1 - a)\|x_0 - x\| < r,$$

so $z \in B(x_0, r)$.

Similarly, a closed sphere $B[x_0, r]$ is a convex set.

Next we introduce a local variant of convexity.

Definition 3.2. A non-empty subset S of a linear space L and let $x \in S$. The set S is *locally convex* set or *star-shaped* at x if for every $y \in S$ we have $(1 - a)x + ay \in S$ for all $a \in [0, 1]$.

Every non-empty convex subset S of L is locally convex at every $x \in S$; conversely, every non-empty subset S of L that is locally convex at every $x \in S$ is convex.

Theorem 3.1. *Let x, y, z be three distinct points in the real linear space L such that $z \in \ell_{x,y}$. Then, one of these points belongs to the open segment determined by the remaining two points.*

Proof. Since $z \in \ell_{x,y}$, we have $z = (1 - a)x + ay$ for some $a \in \mathbb{R}$ (see Figure 3.2).

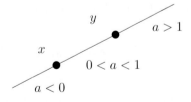

Fig. 3.2 Relative position of three collinear points in a real linear space.

We have $a \notin \{0, 1\}$ because the points x, y, z are distinct.

If $a > 1$ we have $y = \frac{a-1}{a}x + \frac{1}{a}z$, so $y \in (x, z)$ because $\frac{a-1}{a}, \frac{1}{a} \in (0, 1)$.

If $0 < a < 1$ we have $z \in (x, y)$. Finally, if $a < 0$, since $x = (1 + \frac{a}{1-a})z + \frac{-a}{1-a}y$, we have $x \in (z, y)$.   □

We introduce next several sets of vectors that can be defined starting from a subset of a real linear space L.

Definition 3.3. Let U be a subset of a real linear space L and let $x_1, \ldots, x_k \in U$. A linear combination of U, $a_1 x_1 + \cdots + a_k x_k$, where $a_1, \ldots, a_k \in \mathbb{R}$ and $k \geqslant 1$ is:

   (i) an *affine combination* of U if $\sum_{i=1}^{k} a_i = 1$;
   (ii) a *non-negative combination of U* if $a_i \geqslant 0$ for $1 \leqslant i \leqslant k$;
   (iii) a *positive combination of U* if $a_i > 0$ for $1 \leqslant i \leqslant k$;
   (iv) a *convex combination of U* if it is both a non-negative and an affine combination of U.

Note that the empty linear combination is neither an affine nor a convex combination.

Theorem 3.2. *Let L be a real linear space. A subset C of L is convex if and only if any convex combination of elements of C belongs to C.*

Proof.   The sufficiency of this condition is immediate. To prove its necessity consider $x_1, \ldots, x_k \in C$ and the convex combination

$$y = a_1 x_1 + \cdots + a_k x_k.$$

We prove by induction on $k \geqslant 1$ that $y \in C$. The base case, $m = 1$ is immediate since in this case $y = a_1 x_1$ and $a_1 = 1$.

For the inductive step, suppose that the statement holds for k and let y be given by $y = a_1 x_1 + \cdots + a_k x_k + a_{k+1} x_{k+1}$, where $a_1 + \cdots + a_k + a_{k+1} = 1$, $a_i \geqslant 0$ and $x_i \in C$ for $1 \leqslant i \leqslant k + 1$. We have

$$y = (1 - a_{k+1}) \sum_{i=1}^{k} \frac{a_i}{1 - a_{k+1}} x_i + a_{k+1} x_{k+1}.$$

Since $z = \sum_{i=1}^{k} \frac{a_i}{1 - a_{k+1}} x_i$ is a convex combination of k vectors, we have $z \in C$ by the inductive hypothesis, and the equality $y = (1 - a_{k+1})z + a_{k+1} x_{k+1}$ implies $y \in C$.   □

Definition 3.4. Let L, K be two linear spaces. A mapping $f : L \longrightarrow K$ is *affine* when there exists a linear mapping $h : L \longrightarrow K$ and some $b \in K$ such that $f(x) = h(x) + b$ for every $x \in L$.

Theorem 3.3. *Let L, K be two linear spaces and let $f : L \longrightarrow K$ be an affine mapping.*

If C be a convex subset of L, then $f(C)$ is a convex subset of K. If D is a convex subset of K, then $f^{-1}(D) = \{x \in L \mid f(x) \in D\}$ is a convex subset of L.

Proof. Since f is an affine mapping, we have $f(x) = h(x) + b$, where $h : L \longrightarrow K$ is a linear mapping and $b \in K$ for $x \in L$. Therefore, if $y_1, y_2 \in f(C)$ we can write $y_1 = h(x_1) + b$ and $y_2 = h(x_2) + b$. This, in turn, allows us to write for $a \in [0, 1]$:

$$(1 - a)y_1 + ay_2 = (1 - a)h(x_1) + (1 - a)b + ah(x_2) + ab$$
$$= h((1 - a)x_1 + ax_2) + b = f((1 - a)x_1 + ax_2).$$

The convexity of C implies $(1 - a)x_1 + ax_2 \in C$, so $(1 - a)y_1 + ay_2 \in f(C)$, which shows that $f(C)$ is convex.

The proof of the second part is left to the reader. □

Definition 3.5. A subset C of a linear space L is *affine subspace* if $\ell_{x,y} \subseteq C$ for all $x, y \in C$.

Other terms used to designate an affine subspace are *flat*, or *variety*.

In other words, C is a non-empty affine subspace if every point on the line determined by two members of C, x and y belongs to C. Note that C is a subspace of L if and only if $0_L \in C$ and C is an affine subspace.

Example 3.5. The empty set $\emptyset$, every singleton $\{x\}$, and the entire space L are affine subspaces of L. Also, every hyperplane H is an affine subspace of L.

Theorem 3.4. *A non-empty subset C of a linear space L is an affine subspace if and only if any affine combination of elements of C belongs to C.*

Proof. The argument is similar to the proof of Theorem 3.2. □

It is immediate to verify that any translation of a linear space K is an affine subspace. The converse is also true as we show next.

Theorem 3.5. *Let D be a non-empty affine subspace in a linear space L. There exists a translation t_u and a unique subspace K of L such that $D = t_u(K)$.*

Proof. Let $K = \{x - y \mid x, y \in D\}$ and let $x_0 \in D$. We have $0_L = x_0 - x_0 \in K$ and it is immediate that K is subspace of L.

Let u be an element of D. We claim that $D = \mathsf{t}_u(K)$. Indeed, if $z \in D$, $z - u \in K$, so $z \in \mathsf{t}_u(K)$, which implies $D \subseteq \mathsf{t}_u(K)$. Conversely, if $x \in \mathsf{t}_u(K)$ we have $x = u + v$ for some $v \in K$ and, therefore, $x = u + s - t$ for some $s, t \in D$, where $v = s - t$. This implies $x \in D$ because $u + s - t$ is an affine combination of D.

To prove the uniqueness of the subspace K suppose that $D = \mathsf{t}_u(K_1) = \mathsf{t}_\mathbf{v}(K_2)$, where both K_1 and K_2 are subspaces of L.

Since $0_L \in K_2$, it follows that there exists $w \in K_1$ such that $u + w = v$. Similarly, since $0_L \in K_1$, it follows that there exists $t \in K_1$ such that $u = v + t$, which implies $w + t = 0_L$. Thus, both w and t belong to both subspaces K_1 and K_2.

If $s \in K_1$, it follows that $u + s = v + z$ for some $z \in K_2$. Therefore, $s = (v - u) + z \in K_2$ because $w = v - u \in K_2$. This implies $K_1 \subseteq K_2$. The reverse inclusion can be shown similarly. $\square$

Definition 3.6. Let D be a non-empty affine subspace in a linear space L. The *dimension* of D (denoted by $\dim(D)$) is the dimension of the unique subspace K of L such that $D = \mathsf{t}_u(K)$ for some translation t_u of L.

The *dimension of a convex set* C is the dimension of the affine space $\mathbf{K}_{\mathrm{aff}}(C)$.

Since $\emptyset$ is an affine subspace of L and there is no subspace of L that can be translated into $\emptyset$, the dimension of $\emptyset$ is set through the special definition $\dim(\emptyset) = -1$.

Let D, E be two affine subspaces in a linear space L. The sets D, E are *parallel* if $E = \mathsf{t}_a(D)$, for some translation t_u of L. In this case we write $D \parallel E$.

It is easy to see that "$\parallel$" is an equivalence relation on the set of affine subspaces of a linear space L. Furthermore, each equivalence class contains exactly one subspace of L.

Affine subspaces in spaces of the form $\mathbb{R}^n$ arise in conjunction with solving linear systems.

Theorem 3.6. *Let $A \in \mathbb{R}^{m \times n}$ and let $\boldsymbol{b} \in \mathbb{R}^m$. The set $S = \{\boldsymbol{x} \in \mathbb{R}^n \mid A\boldsymbol{x} = \boldsymbol{b}\}$ is an affine subset of $\mathbb{R}^n$. Conversely, every affine subset of $\mathbb{R}^n$ is the set of solutions of a system of the form $A\boldsymbol{x} = \boldsymbol{b}$.*

Proof. It is immediate that the set of solutions of a linear system is affine. Conversely, let S be an affine subspace of $\mathbb{R}^n$ and let L be the linear subspace such that $S = \mathbf{u} + L$. Let $\{\mathbf{a}_1, \ldots, \mathbf{a}_m\}$ be a basis of $L^\perp$. We have

$$L = \{\mathbf{x} \in \mathbb{R}^n \mid \mathbf{a}'_i \mathbf{x} = 0 \text{ for } 1 \leqslant i \leqslant m\} = \{\mathbf{x} \in \mathbb{R}^n \mid A\mathbf{x} = \mathbf{0}\},$$

where A is a matrix whose rows are $\mathbf{a}'_1, \ldots, \mathbf{a}'_m$. By defining $\mathbf{b} = A\mathbf{u}$ we have

$$S = \{\mathbf{u} + \mathbf{x} \mid A\mathbf{x} = \mathbf{0}\} = \{\mathbf{y} \in \mathbb{R}^n \mid A\mathbf{y} = \mathbf{b}\}. \qquad \square$$

Definition 3.7. A subset $U = \{x_1, \ldots, x_n\}$ of a real linear space L is *affinely dependent* if any of the vectors of U is an affine combination of the remaining vectors. If none of the vectors can be expressed as such an affine combination, then U is *affinely independent*.

Suppose that $U = \{x_1, \ldots, x_n\}$ is an affinely dependent set and $x_n = \sum_{i=1}^{n-1} a_i x_i$, where $\sum_{i=1}^{n-1} a_i = 1$. Then, we have

$$x_n = \left(\sum_{i=1}^{n-1} a_i\right) x_n = \sum_{i=1}^{n-1} a_i x_i,$$

hence $\sum_{i=1}^{n-1} a_i(x_i - x_n) = 0$. Note that not all coefficients a_i can be 0, so the set $\{x_1 - x_n, \ldots, x_{n-1} - x_n\}$ is linearly dependent.

Theorem 3.7. *Let $U = \{x_1, \ldots, x_n\}$ be a finite subset of a real linear space L. The set U is affinely independent if and only if the set $V = \{x_1 - x_n, \ldots, x_{n-1} - x_n\}$ is linearly independent.*

Proof. We have seen above that linear independence of $\{x_1 - x_n, \ldots, x_{n-1} - x_n\}$ implies affine independence of $\{x_1, \ldots, x_n\}$.

To prove the reverse implication, suppose that the set $\{x_1, \ldots, x_n\}$ is affinely independent but the set $\{x_1 - x_n, \ldots, x_{n-1} - x_n\}$ is linearly dependent. There exists a linear combination of the vectors $x_1 - x_n, \ldots, x_{n-1} - x_n$ such that

$$a_1(x_1 - x_n) + \cdots + a_{n-1}(x_{n-1} - x_n) = 0_L$$

such that not all coefficients equal 0. Equivalently, we have

$$a_1 x_1 + \cdots + a_{n-1} x_{n-1} - \left(\sum_{i=1}^{n-1} a_i\right) x_n = 0.$$

Suppose that $a_i \neq 0$. Then, we have

$$x_i = \frac{1}{a_i}\left(-a_1 x_1 - \cdots - a_{i-1} x_{i-1} - a_{i+1} x_{i+1} + \left(\sum_{i=1}^{n-1} a_i\right) x_n\right).$$

Note that the sum of the coefficients in the parentheses is a_i, so x_i is an affine combination of the remaining vectors, which contradicts the affine independence of $\{x_1, \ldots, x_n\}$. $\qquad \square$

Corollary 3.1. *The maximal size of an affinely independent set of vectors in $\mathbb{R}^n$ is $n + 1$.*

Proof. Since the maximal size of a linearly independent set in $\mathbb{R}^n$ is n, it follows that the maximal size of an affinely independent set in $\mathbb{R}^n$ is $n + 1$. $\square$

Definition 3.8. The subset $U = \{\mathbf{x}_1, \ldots, \mathbf{x}_n\}$ is in *general position* if its points are affinely independent, or equivalently, if the set $V = \{x_1 - x_n, \ldots, x_{n-1} - x_n\}$ is linearly independent.

Example 3.6. Let $\mathbf{x}_1, \mathbf{x}_2$ be vectors in $\mathbb{R}^2$. The line that passes through $\mathbf{x}_1$ and $\mathbf{x}_2$ consists of all vectors $\mathbf{x}$ such that $\mathbf{x} - \mathbf{x}_1$ and $\mathbf{x} - \mathbf{x}_2$ are collinear; that is, $a(\mathbf{x} - \mathbf{x}_1) + b(\mathbf{x} - \mathbf{x}_2) = 0$ for some $a, b \in \mathbb{R}$ such that $a + b \neq 0$. Thus, we have $\mathbf{x} = a_1 \mathbf{x}_1 + a_2 \mathbf{x}_2$, where $a_1 = \frac{a}{a+b}$, $a_2 = \frac{b}{a+b}$ and $a_1 + a_2 = 1$, so $\mathbf{x}$ is an affine combination of $\mathbf{x}_1$ and $\mathbf{x}_2$. On other hand, the segment of line contained between $\mathbf{x}_1$ and $\mathbf{x}_2$ is consists of convex combinations of $\mathbf{x}_1$ and $\mathbf{x}_2$.

Theorem 3.8. *The intersection of any collection of convex sets in a real linear space is a convex set.*

The intersection of any collection of affine subspaces in a real linear space is an affine subspace.

Proof. Let $\mathcal{C} = \{C_i \mid i \in I\}$ be a collection of convex sets and let $C = \bigcap \mathcal{C}$. Suppose that $x_1, \ldots, x_k \in C$, $a_i \geqslant 0$ for $1 \leqslant i \leqslant k$, and $a_1 + \cdots + a_k = 1$. Since $x_1, \ldots, x_k \in C_i$, it follows that $a_1 x_1 + \cdots + a_k x_k \in C_i$ for every $i \in I$. Thus, $a_1 x_1 + \cdots + a_k x_k \in C$, which proves the convexity of C.

The argument for the affine subspaces is similar. $\square$

Corollary 3.2. *The families of convex sets and non-empty affine subspaces in a real linear space L are closure systems.*

Proof. This statement follows immediately from Theorem 3.8 by observing that L itself is both a convex set and an affine subspace. $\square$

Corollary 3.2 allows us to define the *convex hull* (or the *convex closure*) of a subset U of L as the closure $\mathbf{K}_{\mathrm{conv}}(U)$ of U relative to the closure system of the convex subsets of L.

Similarly, the affine hull of U is the closure $\mathbf{K}_{\mathrm{aff}}(U)$ of U relative to the collection of non-empty affine subspaces of L.

It is immediate that $\mathbf{K}_{\mathrm{conv}}(U)$ consists of all convex combinations of elements of U, $\mathbf{K}_{\mathrm{aff}}(U)$ consists of all affine combinations of the same elements, and

$$\mathbf{K}_{\mathrm{conv}}(U) \subseteq \mathbf{K}_{\mathrm{aff}}(U) \subseteq \langle U \rangle$$

because each convex combination is also an affine combination and each affine combination is a linear combination.

Recall that the dimension $\dim(D)$ of an affine subspace D was introduced in Definition 3.6 as the dimension of the unique subspace K of L such that $D = \mathbf{t}_u(K)$ for some translation $\mathbf{t}_u$.

Theorem 3.9. *For an affine subspace D of $\mathbb{R}^n$ we have $\dim(D) = m - 1$ if and only if m is the largest non-negative integer such that there exists an affinely independent set of m elements of D.*

Proof. Suppose that $\dim(D) = m - 1$ and $D = \mathbf{t}_{\mathbf{u}}(K)$, where K is a subspace of $\mathbb{R}^n$ of dimension $m - 1$ and $\mathbf{u} \notin K$. Let $Y = \{\mathbf{y}_1, \ldots, \mathbf{y}_{m-1}\}$ be a basis of K.

The set that consists of m vectors of D

$$\mathbf{x}_1 = \mathbf{u} + \mathbf{y}_1, \ldots, \mathbf{x}_{m-1} = \mathbf{u} + \mathbf{y}_{m-1}, \mathbf{x}_m = \mathbf{u}$$

is affinely independent because the set $\{\mathbf{x}_1 - \mathbf{x}_m, \ldots, \mathbf{x}_{m-1} - \mathbf{x}_m\}$ is linearly independent.

There is no affinely independent set in D that consists of more than m point because this would entail the existence in K of a basis that consists of more than $m - 1$ vectors. $\qquad\square$

By analogy with the notion of basis for a subspace we introduce the notion of affine basis for an affine subspace of $\mathbb{R}^n$.

Definition 3.9. An *affine basis* of an affine subspace D of $\mathbb{R}^n$ is an affinely independent subset B of S such that $\mathbf{K}_{\mathrm{aff}}(B) = S$.

Let S be a non-empty subset of $\mathbb{R}^n$. If $\mathbf{0}_n \in \mathbf{K}_{\mathrm{aff}}(S)$, it follows that $\mathbf{K}_{\mathrm{aff}}(S)$ is a subspace of $\mathbb{R}^n$ that coincides with the subspace $\langle S \rangle$ generated by S, and $\dim(\mathbf{K}_{\mathrm{aff}}(S)) = \dim(\langle S \rangle)$.

Example 3.7. Let $\mathbf{u} \in \mathbb{R}^n$ and let δ be a positive number. The set

$$K_{n,\mathbf{u},\delta} = \{\mathbf{x} \in \mathbb{R}^n \mid |x_i - u_i| \leq \delta\}$$

is an n-dimensional cube centered in $\mathbf{u}$ having sides length 2δ. The set of vertices of this cube is the set of points

$$V_{n,\mathbf{u},\delta} = \{\mathbf{u} + (b_1, \ldots, b_n)\delta \mid b_i \in \{-1, 1\}^n\}.$$

Let $\mathbf{v_b} = \mathbf{u} + \mathbf{b}\delta$, where $\mathbf{b} = (b_1, \ldots, b_n) \in \{-1, 1\}^n$.

We claim that $K_{n,\mathbf{u},\delta} = \mathbf{K}_{\mathrm{conv}}(V_{n,\mathbf{u},\delta})$. The argument is by induction on n. For the base case, $n = 1$, $K_1 = \{x \in \mathbb{R} \mid |x - u| \leq \delta\}$ and $V_1 = \{u - \delta, u + \delta\}$. Clearly, $K_{1,\delta}$ consists of all convex combinations of $u - \delta$ and $u + \delta$, so the statement holds.

Suppose that the statement holds for n and let $\mathbf{x} \in K_{n+1,\mathbf{u},\delta}$, where $\mathbf{u} \in \mathbb{R}^{n+1}$. Then,

$$
\mathbf{x} = \begin{pmatrix} x_1 \\ \vdots \\ x_n \\ x_{n+1} \end{pmatrix},
$$

where $|x_i - u_i| < \delta$ for $1 \leq i \leq n+1$.

Let $\mathbf{w} \in \mathbb{R}^n$ be the vector that consists of the first n components of $\mathbf{u}$ and let $\mathbf{z} \in \mathbb{R}^n$ be

$$
\mathbf{z} = \begin{pmatrix} x_1 \\ \vdots \\ x_n \end{pmatrix}.
$$

Clearly $\mathbf{z} \in K_{n,\mathbf{w},\delta}$, so by the inductive hypothesis $\mathbf{z}$ is a convex combination of the elements of $V_{n,\mathbf{w},\delta}$. In other words, for every $\mathbf{z} \in K_{n,\mathbf{w},\delta}$ there exist 2^n non-negative numbers $a_\mathbf{b}$, where $\mathbf{b} \in \{-1, 1\}^n$ such that

$$
\mathbf{z} = \sum \{a_\mathbf{b}(\mathbf{w} + \delta\mathbf{b}) \mid \mathbf{b} \in \{-1, 1\}^n\},
$$

and $\sum\{a_\mathbf{b} \mid \mathbf{b} \in \{-1, 1\}^n\} = 1$. Define $\mathbf{r}$ and $\mathbf{s}$ in $\mathbb{R}^{n+1}$ as

$$
\mathbf{r} = \begin{pmatrix} \mathbf{w} \\ u_{n+1} - \delta \end{pmatrix} \text{ and } \mathbf{s} = \begin{pmatrix} \mathbf{w} \\ u_{n+1} + \delta \end{pmatrix}.
$$

It is easy to see that the vector

$$
\mathbf{r} = \begin{pmatrix} \mathbf{z} \\ u_{n+1} - \delta \end{pmatrix}
$$

can be written as

$$
\begin{pmatrix} \mathbf{z} \\ u_{n+1} - \delta \end{pmatrix} = \sum \left\{ a_\mathbf{b} \left(\begin{pmatrix} \mathbf{w} \\ u_{n+1} \end{pmatrix} + \delta \begin{pmatrix} \mathbf{b} \\ -1 \end{pmatrix} \right) \,\middle|\, \mathbf{b} \in \{-1, 1\}^n \right\}.
$$

Similarly, we can write:

$$
\mathbf{s} = \begin{pmatrix} \mathbf{z} \\ u_{n+1} + \delta \end{pmatrix} = \sum \left\{ a_\mathbf{b} \left(\begin{pmatrix} \mathbf{w} \\ u_{n+1} \end{pmatrix} + \delta \begin{pmatrix} \mathbf{b} \\ 1 \end{pmatrix} \right) \,\middle|\, \mathbf{b} \in \{-1, 1\}^n \right\}.
$$

Since $u_{n+1} - \delta \leq x_{n+1} \leq u_{n+1} + \delta$, it is clear that x_{n+1} is a convex combination of $u_{n+1} - \delta$ and $u_{n+1} + \delta$,

$$x_{n+1} = c(u_{n+1} - \delta) + (1 - c)(u_{n+1} + \delta),$$

where

$$c = \frac{u_{n+1} + \delta - x_{n+1}}{2\delta}.$$

Thus, $\mathbf{x}$ can be written as

$$\mathbf{x} = c \begin{pmatrix} \mathbf{z} \\ u_{n+1} - \delta \end{pmatrix} + (1 - c) \begin{pmatrix} \mathbf{z} \\ u_{n+1} - \delta \end{pmatrix}$$

$$= \sum \left\{ c a_{\mathbf{b}} \left(\begin{pmatrix} \mathbf{w} \\ u_{n+1} \end{pmatrix} + \delta \begin{pmatrix} \mathbf{b} \\ -1 \end{pmatrix} \right) \right.$$

$$\left. + (1 - c) a_{\mathbf{b}} \left(\begin{pmatrix} \mathbf{w} \\ u_{n+1} \end{pmatrix} + \delta \begin{pmatrix} \mathbf{b} \\ 1 \end{pmatrix} \right) \middle| \mathbf{b} \in \{-1, 1\}^n \right\}$$

$$= \sum \left\{ a_b \begin{pmatrix} \mathbf{w} \\ u_{n+1} \end{pmatrix} + c a_b \delta \begin{pmatrix} \mathbf{b} \\ -1 \end{pmatrix} + (1 - c) \delta a_{\mathbf{b}} \begin{pmatrix} \mathbf{b} \\ 1 \end{pmatrix} \middle| \mathbf{b} \in \{-1, 1\}^n \right\}$$

$$= \sum \left(a_b c \mathbf{u} + c a_b \delta \begin{pmatrix} \mathbf{b} \\ -1 \end{pmatrix} \middle| \mathbf{b} \in \{-1, 1\}^n \right)$$

$$+ \sum \left(a_b (1 - c) \mathbf{u} + (1 - c) \delta a_{\mathbf{b}} \begin{pmatrix} \mathbf{b} \\ 1 \end{pmatrix} \middle| \mathbf{b} \in \{-1, 1\}^n \right),$$

which proves that $\mathbf{x}$ is a convex combination of the set $V_{n+1, \mathbf{u}, \delta}$.

Theorem 3.10. (Stone's[1] Theorem) *Let L be a real linear space and let A, B be two disjoint convex subsets of L. There exists a partition $\pi = \{C, D\}$ of L such that C and D are convex, $A \subseteq C$ and $B \subseteq D$.*

Proof. Let $\mathcal{E} = \{E \in \mathcal{P}(L) \mid E \text{ is convex}, A \subseteq E, B \cap E = \emptyset\}$. Clearly, $\mathcal{E} \neq \emptyset$ because $A \in \mathcal{E}$. The collection $\mathcal{E}$ is partially ordered by set inclusion, so by Zorn's Lemma, it contains a maximal element C, which is clearly convex and disjoint from B. We need to show only that $D = L - C$ is convex.

If $D = B$, D is convex and the argument is complete. Therefore, we assume that $B \subset D$, so the set $D - B$ is non-empty.

---

[1] Marshall H. Stone was born on April 8th 1903 in New York and died on January 9th 1989 in Madras, India. He studied at Harvard from 1919 to 1922 and taught at Yale and Harvard. Stone has important contributions in functional analysis, and Boolean algebra. In 1946 he was appointed Chair of the mathematics department at the University of Chicago. He retired from this institution in 1968.

If D were not convex, then we would have x, z in D such that $[x, z] \cap C \neq \emptyset$, so we would have $y \in (x, z) \cap C$, that is $y = (1-c)x + cz$ for some $c \in (0, 1)$.

Note that we cannot have both $x \in B$ and $z \in B$ because this would imply that $C \cap B \neq \emptyset$. Thus, at least one of x and z must not belong to B. Suppose for now that neither x nor z belong to B.

We claim that there is a point $p \in C$ such that $(p, x) \cap B \neq \emptyset$ and a point $q \in C$ such that $(q, z) \cap B \neq \emptyset$. Equivalently, if for all $p \in C$, $(p, x) \cap B = \emptyset$, or for all $q \in C$, $(q, z) \cap B = \emptyset$, then C is not a maximal convex set that contains A and is disjoint from B. Assume that for all $p \in C$, $(p, x) \cap B = \emptyset$. Then, $C \subseteq \mathbf{K}_{\text{conv}}(\{x\} \cup C)$. Since $x \notin B$, $\mathbf{K}_{\text{conv}}(\{x\} \cup C)$ is disjoint from B, which contradicts the maximality of C. Therefore, there exists $p \in C$ such that $(p, x) \cap B \neq \emptyset$. Similarly, there exists $q \in C$ such that $(q, z) \cap B \neq \emptyset$.

Let $u \in (p, x) \cap B$ and let $v \in (q, z) \cap B$. We have

$$u = (1 - a)p + ax \text{ and } v = (1 - b)q + bz$$

for some $a, b \in (0, 1)$. Since

$$x = \frac{1}{a}u - \frac{1 - a}{a}p,$$

$$z = \frac{1}{b}v - \frac{1 - b}{b}q,$$

we have

$$y = \frac{1 - c}{a}u - \frac{(1 - c)(1 - a)}{a}p + \frac{c}{b}v - \frac{c(1 - b)}{b}q,$$

or, equivalently

$$\frac{1 - c}{a}u + \frac{c}{b}v = y + \frac{(1 - c)(1 - a)}{a}p + \frac{c(1 - b)}{b}q. \tag{3.1}$$

Observe that

$$\frac{1 - c}{a} + \frac{c}{b} = 1 + \frac{(1 - c)(1 - a)}{a} + \frac{c(1 - b)}{b}. \tag{3.2}$$

Let k be the value of either side of equality (3.2). Since the coefficients that occur in both sides of equality (3.1) are non-negative, by dividing both sides of this equality by k we obtain a convex combination of u and v equal to a convex combination of y, p and q. This contradicts that C and B are disjoint. Therefore, D is convex.

Suppose now that $x \in B$ and $z \notin B$. The role played previously by u will be played by x and the previous argument is applicable with $x = u$.

$\square$

Theorem 3.11. *Every affine subspace S of $\mathbb{R}^n$ is the intersection of a finite collections of hyperplanes.*

Proof. By Theorem 3.6, S can be written as $S = \{\mathbf{x} \in \mathbb{R}^n \mid A\mathbf{x} = \mathbf{b}\}$, where $A \in \mathbb{R}^{m \times n}$ and $\mathbf{b} \in \mathbb{R}^m$. Therefore, $\mathbf{x} \in S$ if and only if $\mathbf{a}_i'\mathbf{x} = b_i$, where $\mathbf{a}_i$ is the ith row of A. Thus, $S = \bigcap_{i=1}^{m} H_{\mathbf{a}_i, b_i}$. $\square$

3.3 Operations on Convex Sets

The class of convex set is closed with respect to scalar multiplications and translations. In other words, if C is a subset of a real linear space, then $h_r(C) = rC = \{rx \mid x \in C\}$ is a convex set for $r \in \mathbb{R}$; also, for $b \in L$ the set $t_b(C) = C + b = \{x + b \mid x \in C\}$ is convex.

Theorem 3.12. *If C_1, C_2 are convex subsets of a real linear space L, their Minkowski sum $C_1 + C_2$ is a convex subset of L.*

Proof. Let $x, y \in C_1 + C_2$. We have $x = x_1 + x_2$ and $y = y_1 + y_2$, where $x_1, y_1 \in C_1$ and $x_2, y_2 \in C_2$. Therefore, for $c \in [0, 1]$ we have

$$(1 - a)x + ay = (1 - a)(x_1 + x_2) + a(y_1 + y_2)$$
$$= (1 - a)x_1 + ay_1 + (1 - a)x_2 + ay_2 \in C_1 + C_2,$$

because $(1 - a)x_1 + ay_1 \in C_1$ and $(1 - a)x_2 + ay_2 \in C_2$ because of the convexity of C_1 and C_2. $\square$

Corollary 3.3. *If $C_1, \ldots, C_m$ are convex subsets of a real linear space L, then the set $r_1 C_1 + \cdots + r_m C_m$ is convex.*

Proof. Theorem 3.12 implies immediately the current statement. $\square$

Note that if C_1, C_2 are convex sets, the set $C_1 - C_2 = \{x - y x \in C_1, y \in C_2\}$ is convex.

Theorem 3.13. *Let C be a convex subset of a real linear space L. If $r_1, r_2 \in \mathbb{R}_{\geqslant 0}$, then we have*

$$(r_1 + r_2)C = r_1 C + r_2 C.$$

Proof. If at least one of r_1, r_2 is 0 the equality obviously holds; therefore, assume that both r_1 and r_2 are positive.

Let $z \in r_1 C + r_2 C$. There exists $x, y \in C$ such that $z = r_1 x + r_2 y$, and therefore,

$$z = (r_1 + r_2)\left(\frac{r_1}{r_1 + r_2}x + \frac{r_1}{r_1 + r_2}y\right).$$

Since C is convex, $\frac{r_1}{r_1+r_2}x + \frac{r_1}{r_1+r_2}y \in C$, which implies $z \in (r_1 + r_2)C$, so $r_1 C + r_2 C \subseteq (r_1 + r_2)C$. The reverse inclusion is immediate and makes no use of the convexity of C. $\square$

3.4   Cones

Definition 3.10. Let L be a real linear space. A *cone* in L is a non-empty set $C \subseteq L$ such that $x \in C$ and $a \in \mathbb{R}_{\geqslant 0}$ imply $ax \in C$.

   A *pointed cone* is a cone C that does not contain a line.

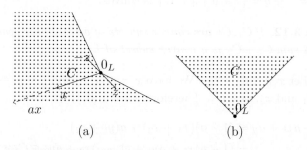

Fig. 3.3   Non-pointed (a) vs. pointed cone (b).

   Note that for a cone C in L we have $0_L \in C$.

Example 3.8. Let L be a real linear space and let S be a non-empty subset of L. The set

$$C_S = \{ax \mid a \geqslant 0 \text{ and } x \in S\}$$

is cone contained by every other cone that contains S.

Example 3.9. The set $(\mathbb{R}_{\geqslant 0})^n$ is a pointed cone in $\mathbb{R}^n$. Indeed, suppose that there exists a line ℓ passing through $\mathbf{x}$ and having direction u such that $\ell \subseteq \mathbb{R}_{\geqslant}^n$. If $\mathbf{x} \in \ell$ we have $\mathbf{x} = \mathbf{x}_0 + t\mathbf{u}$. Since $\mathbf{u} \neq \mathbf{0}_n$, there exists one non-zero component of $\mathbf{u}$. Suppose, for example that $u_1 > 0$. Then, if $t < 0$ and $|t|$ is sufficiently large, we would have $\mathbf{x} + t\mathbf{u} \notin (\mathbb{R}_{\geqslant 0})^n$. Thus, no line is included in $(\mathbb{R}_{\geqslant 0})^n$.

Theorem 3.14. *Let L be a real linear space and let $C \in L$ be a cone. C is convex if and only if $x + y \in C$ for $x, y \in \mathbb{R}$.*

Proof.   Let C be a convex cone. If $x, y \in C$ and $a \in (0, 1)$, then $\frac{1}{a}x \in C$ and $\frac{1}{1-a}y \in C$. Therefore, by convexity we have

$$x + y = a\frac{1}{a}x + (1 - a)\frac{1}{1 - a}y \in C.$$

   Conversely, let C be a cone such that $x, y \in C$ imply $x + y \in C$. For $u, v \in C$ and $a \in [0, 1]$ let $z_a = au + (1 - a)v$. Since C is a cone, $au \in C$ and $(1 - a)v \in C$, hence $z_a = au + (1 - a)v \in C$. Therefore, C is convex.

$\square$

Example 3.10. Let U be a non-empty subset of a real linear space L. The set of all non-negative combinations of U is a convex cone that is included in every convex cone that contains U.

Theorem 3.15. *The intersection of any collection of cones (convex cones) in a real liner space L is a cone (a convex cone).*

Proof. The proof is similar to the argument of Theorem 3.8 and is omitted. □

Corollary 3.4. *The families of cones (convex cones) in a real linear space L is a closure system.*

Proof. This statement follows immediately from Theorem 3.15 by observing that $\mathbb{R}^n$ itself is cone (a convex cone). □

We will denote the closure operator corresponding to the family of cones by $\mathbf{K}_{\text{cone}}$; the similar operator for convex cones will be denoted by $\mathbf{K}_{\text{ccone}}$.

Theorem 3.16. *Let S be a non-empty subset of a real linear space L. We have $\mathbf{K}_{\text{cone}}(S) = \{ax \mid a \geqslant 0 \text{ and } x \in S\}$.*

Proof. We saw in Example 3.8 that $\{ax \mid a \geqslant 0 \text{ and } x \in S\}$ is a cone that contains S, so $\mathbf{K}_{\text{cone}}(S) \subseteq \{ax \mid a \geqslant 0 \text{ and } x \in S\}$.

Conversely, since $S \subseteq \mathbf{K}_{\text{cone}}(S)$, if $x \in S$ it follows that $ax \in \mathbf{K}_{\text{cone}}(S)$ for every $a \geqslant 0$, so $\{ax \mid a \geqslant 0 \text{ and } x \in S\} \subseteq \mathbf{K}_{\text{cone}}(S)$. □

Theorem 3.17. (Carathéodory's Theorem for Cones) *Let S be a subset of $\mathbb{R}^n$ and let $\boldsymbol{x} \in \boldsymbol{K}_{\text{cone}}(S)$, $\boldsymbol{x} \neq \boldsymbol{0}_n$. Then, $\boldsymbol{x}$ is a positive linear combination of no more than n linearly independent vectors of S.*

Proof. Let $\mathbf{x}$ be a non-null vector of $\mathbf{K}_{\text{cone}}(S)$ and let m be the smallest integer such that $\mathbf{x}$ can be written as a positive linear combination of vectors of S, $\mathbf{x} = \sum_{i=1}^{m} a_i \mathbf{x}_i$.

If $\mathbf{x}_1, \ldots, \mathbf{x}_m$ were linearly dependent we would have the non-zero numbers $b_1, \ldots, b_m \in \mathbb{R}$ such that at least one of theses numbers is positive and $\sum_{i=1}^{m} b_i \mathbf{x}_i = 0$, which allows us to write

$$\mathbf{x} = \sum_{i=1}^{m} (a_i - cb_i)\mathbf{x}_i$$

for $c \in \mathbb{R}$. Let $c_0 = \max\{c \in \mathbb{R} \mid a_i - cb_i \geqslant 0 \text{ for } 1 \leqslant i \leqslant m\}$. At least one of the numbers $a_i - c_0 b_i$ is zero because, if this were not the case, the definition of c_0 would be contradicted. This contradicts the minimality of m. Therefore, $\mathbf{x}_1, \ldots, \mathbf{x}_m$ are linearly independent. □

Cones define partial order relations on linear spaces.

Definition 3.11. A *partially ordered linear space* is a pair $(L, \leqslant)$, where L is a linear space and $\leqslant$ is a partial order on L such that $x \leqslant y$ and $u \leqslant v$ imply $x + u \leqslant y + v$ and $ax \leqslant ay$ for every $a \in \mathbb{R}_{\geqslant 0}$.

Theorem 3.18. *Let* $(L, \leqslant)$ *be a partially ordered linear space. The set* $C = \{x \in L \mid 0_L \leqslant x\}$ *is a pointed convex cone.*

Conversely, if C is a pointed convex cone in L, the relation "$\leqslant$" defined by $x \leqslant y$ if $y - x \in C$ is a partial order.

Proof. If is immediate that C is a convex cone (by Theorem 3.14). Suppose that both x and $-x$ belong to C, that is, $0_L \leqslant x$ and $0_L \leqslant -x$. This implies $x = 0_L$, so C is indeed a pointed cone.

For the converse implication let C be a pointed convex cone. Since $0_L \in C$ it follows that $x \leqslant x$. Further, suppose that $x \leqslant y$ and $y \leqslant x$, that is, $y - x \in C$ and $x - y = -(y - x) \in C$. This implies $y - x = 0_L$, so $x = y$, which shows that "$\leqslant$" is anti-symmetric. Finally, if $x \leqslant y$ and $y \leqslant z$, that is, if $y - x, z - y \in C$ we have $y - z = (y - x) + (x - z) \in C$ because C is a convex cone. $\qquad\square$

The pointed convex cone that generates a partial order $\leqslant$ is referred in this context as an *ordering cone*.

3.5　Extreme Points

Definition 3.12. Let C be a non-empty convex subset of a real linear space L. An *extreme point* of C is a point $x \in C$ such that if $x \in [u, v]$ and $u, v \in C$, then $u = v = x$.

Theorem 3.19. *Let C be a non-empty convex subset of a real linear space L. A point $x \in C$ is an extreme point of C if the set $C - \{x\}$ is convex.*

Proof. Suppose that $C - \{x\}$ is a convex set for $x \in C$ and that $x \in [u, v]$, where $u, v \in C$.

If x is distinct from both u and v, then u, v belong to the convex set $C - \{x\}$, which yields the contradiction $x \in C - \{x\}$. Thus, x is an extreme point of C.

Conversely, suppose that x is an extreme point of C. Let $u, v \in C - \{x\}$, so $u \neq x$ and $y \neq x$. If $x \in [u, v]$, we obtain a contradiction since this implies $u = v = x$. Therefore $[u, v] \subseteq C - \{x\}$, so $C - \{x\}$ is convex. $\qquad\square$

The set of extreme points of a convex set C is denoted by $\mathsf{extr}(C)$.

Example 3.11. Let $B[\mathbf{x}_0, r]$ be a closed sphere of radius r in $\mathbb{R}^n$. Each point $\mathbf{x}$ located on the circumference of this sphere, that is, each point $\mathbf{x}$ such that $\|\mathbf{x}_0 - \mathbf{x}\| = r$ is an extreme point of $B[\mathbf{x}_0, r]$.

Indeed, suppose that $a\mathbf{u} + (1-a)\mathbf{v} = \mathbf{x}$ for some $a \in (0, 1)$ and $\|\mathbf{x}_0 - \mathbf{u}\| = \|\mathbf{x}_0 - \mathbf{v}\| = r$. Then, by Supplement 6, we have $\mathbf{u} = \mathbf{v} = \mathbf{x}$.

Example 3.12. An open sphere $B(\mathbf{x}_0, r)$ in $\mathbb{R}^n$ has no extreme points for if $\mathbf{x} \in B(\mathbf{x}_0, r)$. Indeed, let $\mathbf{u}$ be a vector such that $\mathbf{u} \neq \mathbf{0}_n$ and let $\mathbf{x}_1 = \mathbf{x} + a\mathbf{u}$ and $\mathbf{x}_2 = \mathbf{x} - a\mathbf{u}$, where $a > 0$. Observe that if $a < \frac{r - \|\mathbf{x} - \mathbf{x}_0\|}{\|\mathbf{u}\|}$, we have

$$\|\mathbf{x}_1 - \mathbf{x}_0\| = \|\mathbf{x} + a\mathbf{u} - \mathbf{x}_0\| \leqslant \|\mathbf{x} - \mathbf{x}_0\| + a\|\mathbf{u}\| < r$$

and

$$\|\mathbf{x}_2 - \mathbf{x}_0\| = \|\mathbf{x} - a\mathbf{u} - \mathbf{x}_0\| \leqslant \|\mathbf{x} - \mathbf{x}_0\| + a\|\mathbf{u}\| < r,$$

and we have both $\mathbf{x}_1 \in B(\mathbf{x}_0, r)$ and $\mathbf{x}_2 \in B(\mathbf{x}_0, r)$. Since $\mathbf{x} = \frac{1}{2}\mathbf{x}_1 + \frac{1}{2}\mathbf{x}_2$, $\mathbf{x}$ is not an extreme point.

Example 3.13. The extreme points of the cube $[0, 1]^n$ are all its 2^n "corners" $(a_1, \ldots, a_n) \in \{0, 1\}^n$.

Definition 3.13. Let C be a convex set in a real linear space L. A convex subset F of C is a *face* of C if for every open segment $(u, v) \subseteq C$ such that at least one of u, v is not in F we have $(u, v) \cap F = \emptyset$.

If $F \neq C$, we say that F is a *proper face* of C.

A k-*face* of C is a face F of C such that $\dim(F) = k$.

In other words, a convex subset F is a face of C if $u, v \in C$ and $(u, v) \cap F \neq \emptyset$ implies $u \in F$ and $v \in F$, which is equivalent to $[u, v] \subseteq F$.

Note that if $F = \{x\}$ is a face of C if and only if $x \in \mathsf{extr}(C)$. An convex subset C is a face of itself.

Example 3.14. Let C be a convex subset of $\mathbb{R}^n$ and let $\mathbf{a} \in \mathbb{R}^n$. The set $F_{\mathbf{a}} = \{\mathbf{z} \in C \mid \mathbf{a}'\mathbf{z} \leqslant \mathbf{a}'\mathbf{x} \text{ for every } \mathbf{x} \in C\}$ is a face of C.

Indeed, suppose that there exists $\mathbf{z} \in (\mathbf{u}, \mathbf{v})$ such that $\mathbf{z} \in F_{\mathbf{a}}$, that is, $\mathbf{a}'\mathbf{z} \leqslant \mathbf{a}'\mathbf{x}$ for every $\mathbf{x} \in C$. Since $\mathbf{z} \in (\mathbf{u}, \mathbf{v})$, $\mathbf{z} = (1 - t)\mathbf{u} + t\mathbf{v}$ for some $t \in (0, 1)$, so $\mathbf{a}'\mathbf{z} = (1 - t)\mathbf{a}'\mathbf{u} + t\mathbf{a}'\mathbf{v} \leq \mathbf{a}'\mathbf{x}$ for every $\mathbf{x} \in C$. In particular, for $\mathbf{x} = \mathbf{u}$ and $\mathbf{x} = \mathbf{v}$ we obtain $\mathbf{a}'(\mathbf{v} - \mathbf{u}) \leqslant 0$ and $\mathbf{a}'(\mathbf{v} - \mathbf{u}) \geqslant 0$, so $\mathbf{a}'(\mathbf{v} - \mathbf{u}) = 0$, which implies $\mathbf{a}'\mathbf{u} = \mathbf{a}'\mathbf{v} = \mathbf{a}\mathbf{z}$. Therefore, $\mathbf{u}, \mathbf{v} \in F_{\mathbf{a}}$, so $F_{\mathbf{a}}$ is indeed a face of C. Any face of C of the form $F_{\mathbf{a}}$ is called an *exposed face* of C.

Theorem 3.20. *If F is a face of a convex set C, then $F = \mathbf{K}_{aff}(F) \cap C$.*

Proof. If $z \in \mathbf{K}_{aff}(F) \cap C$, we have $x = a_1 y_1 + \cdots + a_k y_k$, where $\sum_{i=1}^{k} a_i = 1$ and $y_1, \ldots, y_k \in F$. If all a_i are non-negative, then it is immediate that $x \in F$. Otherwise, let $b = -\sum \{a_i \mid a_i < 0\}$ and let

$$u = \frac{1}{1+b} \sum \{a_i y_i \mid a_i \geqslant 0\},$$

$$v = -\frac{1}{b} \sum \{a_i y_i \mid a_i < 0\}.$$

We have $x \in C, v \in C$, and

$$u = \frac{1}{1+b} x + \frac{b}{1+b} \in [x, v] \cap F.$$

Since F is a face, we have $u \in F$. Thus, $\mathbf{K}_{aff}(F) \cap C \subseteq F$. The reverse inclusion is immediate. $\qquad\square$

A *functional* on an $\mathbb{F}$-linear space L is a function $f : L \longrightarrow \mathbb{F}$. A *linear functional* on L is a functional f on L that satisfies the condition $f(ax + by) = af(x) + bf(y)$ for $a, b \in \mathbb{F}$ and $x, y \in L$.

If $\mathcal{F}(C)$ is the collection of faces of a convex set C, then $C \in \mathcal{F}(C)$ and $\bigcap \mathcal{F}$ is a face of C. Thus, $\mathcal{F}(C)$ is a closure system.

Example 3.14 that includes the definition of a face of a convex set in $\mathbb{R}^n$ is generalized in the next statement.

Theorem 3.21. *Let C be a convex subset of a real linear space L and let $f : L \longrightarrow \mathbb{R}$ be a linear functional that is not a constant on C and $k = \sup\{f(x) \mid x \in C\}$ is finite. If the set $F = \{x \mid f(x) = k\}$ is non-empty, then it is a proper face of C.*

Proof. It is immediate that the set F is convex. If $y, z \in F$ and $a \in (0, 1)$ is such that $ay + (1 - a)z \in F$, it follows that $af(y) + (1 - a)f(z) = k$. Since $f(y) \leqslant k$ and $f(z) \leqslant k$, it follows that $f(y) = f(z) = k$, so $y, z \in F$. This shows that F is a face of C. $\qquad\square$

As it was the case in Example 3.14, faces of a convex set that can be defined using linear functionals as shown in Theorem 3.21 are referred to as *exposed faces*. The hyperplane $\{x \mid f(x) = k\}$ is called a *support hyperplane* of C.

Theorem 3.22. *Let S be a subset of $\mathbb{R}^n$. The set $Q(S)$ defined by*

$$Q(S) = \bigcup \{\boldsymbol{x} \in \mathbb{R}^n \mid [\boldsymbol{x}, \boldsymbol{y}] \subseteq S \text{ for every } \boldsymbol{y} \in S\}$$

is a convex set.

Proof. Suppose that $\mathbf{u}, \mathbf{v} \in Q(S)$. We need to prove that $\mathbf{w} = b\mathbf{u} + (1 - b)\mathbf{v} \in Q(S)$ for every $b \in [0, 1]$. This means that for every $\mathbf{y} \in S$ and $c \in [0, 1]$ we need to show that $\mathbf{t} = c\mathbf{w} + (1 - c)\mathbf{y} \in S$.

Suppose initially that $bc < 1$ and let $d = \frac{c(1-b)}{1-bc}$. Clearly, d is defined if $bc < 1$ and that $d \in [0, 1]$. Let $\mathbf{z} = d\mathbf{v} + (1 - d)\mathbf{y}$. Clearly, $\mathbf{z} \in \overline{\mathbf{vy}}$, so $\mathbf{z} \in S$. Note that we can write $\mathbf{t} = bc\mathbf{u} + (1 - bc)\mathbf{z}$, which means that $\mathbf{t} \in \overline{\mathbf{uz}}$, so $\mathbf{t} \in S$.

If $bc = 1$ we have both $b = 1$ and $c = 1$, so $\mathbf{w} = \mathbf{u}$ and $\mathbf{t} = \mathbf{w}$, when the statement holds trivially. $\qquad\square$

Example 3.15. Let $R^{n \times n}$ be the linear space of square matrices of format $n \times n$. The set of $(n \times n)$-stochastic matrices is a convex set in $\mathbb{R}^{n \times n}$.

Let $A, B \in \mathbb{R}^{n \times n}$ be two stochastic matrices, let $a \in [0, 1]$, and let $C = (1 - a)A + aB$. We have

$$\sum_{j=1}^{n} c_{ij} = (1 - a)\sum_{j=1}^{n} a_{ij} + a\sum_{j=1}^{n} b_{ij} = 1,$$

because

$$\sum_{j=1}^{n} a_{ij} = \sum_{j=1}^{n} b_{ij} = 1,$$

so C is a stochastic matrix. Similarly, the set of doubly-stochastic matrices is convex in $R^{n \times n}$.

Theorem 3.23. *If C is a convex subset of a real linear space L, then for any translation t_z, the set $t_z(C)$ is convex.*

Proof. Let x and y be two elements of $t_z(C)$. There exist u and v in C such that $x = u + z$ and $y = v + z$. If w is a convex combination of x and y, then there exists $a \in [0, 1]$ such that

$$w = ax + (1 - a)y = a(u + z) + (1 - a)(v + z)$$
$$= au + (1 - a)v + z = t_z(au + (1 - a)v) \in t_z(C),$$

which proves that $t_z(C)$ is convex. $\qquad\square$

We observed that permutation matrices are doubly-stochastic matrices. Therefore, any convex combination of permutation matrices is a doubly-stochastic matrix. An important converse statement is discussed next.

Theorem 3.24. (Birkhoff-von Neumann Theorem) *If $A \in \mathbb{R}^{n \times n}$ is a doubly-stochastic matrix, then A is a convex combination of permutation matrices.*

Proof. Let $A \in \mathbb{R}^{n \times n}$ be a doubly-stochastic matrix and let $R = \{r_1, \ldots, r_m\}$ be the set of its rows, and $C = \{c_1, \ldots, c_m\}$ be the set of its columns, respectively.

Define the relation $\rho \subseteq R \times C$ as

$$\rho = \{(r_i, c_j) \mid r_i \in R, c_j \in C, a_{ij} > 0\}.$$

Since A is a doubly-stochastic matrix we have $\sum_{j=1}^{n} a_{ij} = 1$ for every i, $1 \leqslant i \leqslant m$ and $\sum_{i=1}^{m} a_{ij} = 1$ for every j, $1 \leqslant j \leqslant n$.

For a set of rows T we have

$$\sum \{a_{ij} \mid r_i \in T, c_j \in \rho[\{r_i\}]\} = |T|,$$

because for each row r_i the sum of the elements a_{ij} equals 1. Also, for each set of columns Z, we have

$$\sum \{a_{ij} \mid c_j \in Z, r_i \in \rho^{-1}[\{c_j\}]\} = |Z|.$$

Therefore,

$$|\rho[T]| = \sum \{a_{ij} \mid r_i \in T, c_j \in C\}$$

$$\geqslant \sum \{a_{ij} \mid r_i \in T, c_j \in \rho[\{r_i\}]\} = |T|,$$

which shows that we can apply Hall's Matching Theorem to R, C and ρ. By this theorem there exists a matching f for ρ. Define the matrix P by

$$p_{ij} = \begin{cases} 1 & \text{if } f(r_i) = c_j, \\ 0 & \text{otherwise.} \end{cases}$$

We claim that P is a permutation matrix.

For every row i of P there exists a column c_j such that $p_{ij} = 1$. There exists only one 1 in the jth column of P for, if $p_{i_1 j} = p_{i_2 j} = 1$ for $i_1 \neq i_2$, it would follow that we have both $f(i_1) = j$ and $f(i_2) = j$ contradicting the fact that f is a matching.

Let $a = \min\{a_{ij} \mid p_{ij} \neq 0\}$. Clearly, $a > 0$ and $a = a_{pq}$ for some p and q. Let $B = A - aP$. If $B = O_{n,n}$, then A is a permutation matrix. Otherwise, note that

(i) $\sum_{j=1}^{n} c_{ij} = 1 - a$ and $\sum_{i=1}^{n} c_{ij} = 1 - a$;
(ii) $0 \leq c_{ij} \leq 1 - a$ for $1 \leq i \leq n$ and $1 \leq j \leq n$;
(iii) $c_{pq} = 0$.

Therefore, the matrix $D = \frac{1}{1-a} C$ is doubly-stochastic and we have $A = aP + (1-a)D$, where D has at least one more zero element than A.

The equality $A = aP + (1-a)D$ shows that A is a convex combination of a permutation matrix and a doubly-stochastic matrix with strictly more zero components than A. The statement follows by repeatedly applying this procedure. $\qquad\square$

Theorem 3.25. (Carathéodory's Theorem) *If U is a subset of $\mathbb{R}^n$, then for every $\boldsymbol{x} \in \boldsymbol{K}_{\mathrm{conv}}(U)$ we have $\boldsymbol{x} = \sum_{i=1}^{n+1} a_i \boldsymbol{x}_i$, where $\boldsymbol{x}_i \in U$, $a_i \geqslant 0$ for $1 \leqslant i \leqslant n+1$, and $\sum_{i=1}^{n+1} a_i = 1$.*

Proof. Consider $\mathbf{x} \in \mathbf{K}_{\mathrm{conv}}(U)$. We can write $\mathbf{x} = \sum_{i=1}^{p+1} a_i \mathbf{x}_i$, where $\mathbf{x}_i \in U$, $a_i \geqslant 0$ for $1 \leqslant i \leqslant p+1$, and $\sum_{i=1}^{p+1} a_i = 1$. Let p be the smallest number which allows this kind of expression for $\mathbf{x}$. We prove the theorem by showing that $p \leqslant n$.

Suppose that $p \geqslant n+1$. Then, the set $\{\mathbf{x}_1, \ldots, \mathbf{x}_{p+1}\}$ is affinely dependent, so there exist $b_1, \ldots, b_{p+1}$ not all zero such that $\mathbf{0}_n = \sum_{i=1}^{p+1} b_i \mathbf{x}_i$ and $\sum_{i=1}^{p+1} b_i = 0$. Without loss of generality, we can assume $b_{p+1} > 0$ and $\frac{a_{p+1}}{b_{p+1}} \leqslant \frac{a_i}{b_i}$ for all i such that $1 \leqslant i \leqslant p$ and $b_i > 0$. Define

$$c_i = b_i \left(\frac{a_i}{b_i} - \frac{a_{p+1}}{b_{p+1}} \right)$$

for $1 \leqslant i \leqslant p$. We have

$$\sum_{i=1}^{p} c_i = \sum_{i=1}^{p} a_i - \frac{a_{p+1}}{b_{p+1}} \sum_{i=1}^{p} b_i = 1.$$

Furthermore, $c_i \geqslant 0$ for $1 \leqslant i \leqslant p$. Indeed, if $b_i \leqslant 0$, then $c_i \geqslant a_i \geqslant 0$; if $b_i > 0$, then $c_i \geqslant 0$ because $\frac{a_{p+1}}{b_{p+1}} \leqslant \frac{a_i}{b_i}$ for all i such that $1 \leqslant i \leqslant p$ and $b_i > 0$. Thus, we have:

$$\sum_{i=1}^{p} c_i \mathbf{x}_i = \sum_{i=1}^{p} \left(a_i - \frac{a_p}{b_p} b_i \right) \mathbf{x}_i = \sum_{i=1}^{p} a_i \mathbf{x}_i = \mathbf{x},$$

which contradicts the choice of p. $\qquad\square$

Theorem 3.26 (Radon's Theorem). Let $P = \{\boldsymbol{x}_i \in \mathbb{R}^n \mid 1 \leqslant i \leqslant n+2\}$ be a set of $n+2$ points in $\mathbb{R}^n$. Then, there are two disjoint subsets R and Q of P such that $\boldsymbol{K}_{\mathrm{conv}}(R) \cap \boldsymbol{K}_{\mathrm{conv}}(Q) \neq \emptyset$.

Proof. Since $n+2$ points in $\mathbb{R}^n$ are affinely dependent, there exist $a_1, \ldots, a_{n+2}$ not all equal to 0 such that

$$\sum_{i=1}^{n+2} a_i \mathbf{x}_i = \mathbf{0} \tag{3.3}$$

and $\sum_{i=1}^{n+2} a_i = 0$. Without loss of generality, we can assume that the first k numbers are positive and the last $n+2-k$ are not. Let $a = \sum_{i=1}^{k} a_i > 0$ and let $b_j = \frac{a_j}{a}$ for $1 \leqslant j \leqslant k$. Similarly, let $c_l = -\frac{a_l}{a}$ for $k+1 \leqslant l \leqslant n+2$. Equality (3.3) can now be written as

$$\sum_{j=1}^{k} b_j \mathbf{x}_j = \sum_{l=k+1}^{n+2} c_l \mathbf{x}_l.$$

Since the numbers b_j and c_l are non-negative and $\sum_{j=1}^{k} b_j = \sum_{l=k+1}^{n+2} c_l = 1$, it follows that $\mathbf{K}_{\text{conv}}\left(\{\mathbf{x}_1, \ldots, \mathbf{x}_k\}\right) \cap \mathbf{K}_{\text{conv}}\left(\{\mathbf{x}_{k+1}, \ldots, \mathbf{x}_{n+2}\}\right) \neq \emptyset.$ $\qquad\square$

Theorem 3.27. (Shapley-Folkman Theorem) *Let $X_1, \ldots, X_m$ be non-empty subsets of $\mathbb{R}^n$ and let $X = X_1 + \cdots + X_m$ be their Minkowski sum. Every $\mathbf{x} \in \mathbf{K}_{\text{conv}}(X)$ can be represented as a sum $\mathbf{x} = \mathbf{x}_1 + \ldots + \mathbf{x}_m$ such that*

(i) $\mathbf{x}_i \in \mathbf{K}_{\text{conv}}(X_i)$, *and*

(ii) $|\{i \mid 1 \leqslant i \leqslant m, \mathbf{x}_i \in X_i\}| \geqslant m - n.$

Proof. Let $\mathbf{x} = \sum_{i=1}^{m} \mathbf{y}_i$, where $\mathbf{y}_i \in \mathbf{K}_{\text{conv}}(X_i)$ and let $\mathbf{y}_i = \sum_{j=1}^{m_i} a_{ij} \mathbf{y}_{ij}$, where $a_{ij} > 0$, $\sum_{j=1}^{m_j} a_{ij} = 1$ and $\mathbf{y}_{ij} \in X_i$ for $1 \leqslant j \leqslant m_i$.

Consider the vectors in $\mathbb{R}^{n+m}$:

$$\mathbf{z} = \begin{pmatrix} \mathbf{x} \\ \mathbf{1}_m \end{pmatrix}, \mathbf{z}_{1j} = \begin{pmatrix} \mathbf{y}_{1j} \\ \mathbf{e}_1 \end{pmatrix}, \ldots, \mathbf{z}_{mj} = \begin{pmatrix} \mathbf{y}_{mj} \\ \mathbf{e}_m \end{pmatrix},$$

so that $\mathbf{z} = \sum_{i=1}^{m} \sum_{j=1}^{m_i} a_{ij} \mathbf{z}_{ij}$. By Carathéodory's Theorem for Cones (Theorem 3.17) we can write

$$\mathbf{z} = \sum_{i=1}^{m} \sum_{j=1}^{m_i} b_{ij} \mathbf{z}_{ij},$$

where $b_{ij} \geqslant 0$ and at most $n + m$ of them are positive. In particular,

$$\mathbf{x} = \sum_{i=1}^{m} \sum_{i=1}^{m_i} b_{ij} \mathbf{x}_{ij} \text{ and } \sum_{j=1}^{m_i} b_{ij} = 1 \text{ for } 1 \leqslant i \leqslant m.$$

If $\mathbf{x}_i = \sum_{j=1}^{m_i} b_{ij} \mathbf{y}_{ij}$ for $1 \leqslant i \leqslant m$, then $\mathbf{x} = \mathbf{x}_1 + \cdots + \mathbf{x}_m$. Since for each i at least one of $b_{i1}, \ldots, b_{im_i}$ is positive and at most $n + m$ of b_{ij} are positive, it follows that for at least $m - n$ indices i we have $b_{ik} = 1$ for some k and $b_{ij} = 0$ for all $j \neq k$. $\qquad\square$

3.6   Balanced and Absorbing Sets

Definition 3.14. Let L be a real linear space. A subset W of L is

(i) *balanced* if $|r| \leqslant 1$ implies $rW \subseteq W$;

(ii) *symmetric* if $w \in W$ implies $-w \in W$;

(iii) *absolutely convex* if it is both convex and balanced.

The subset W is balanced if for each $w \in W$ we have the segment $[-w, w] \subseteq W$. Clearly, every balanced set is symmetric.

Example 3.16. The closed sphere $B[0, 1]$ of a real normed linear space $(L, \| \cdot \|)$ is balanced and, therefore, is absolutely convex. Also, it is clear that the empty subset of L is balanced.

Theorem 3.28. *Let L be a real linear space and let U be a balanced set. The following statements hold:*

    (i) $0_L \in U$;

    (ii) *U is symmetric, that is, $-U = U$;*

    (iii) *aU is balanced for every $a \in \mathbb{R}$;*

    (iv) *for $x \in L$ and $a \in \mathbb{R}$ we have $ax \in U$ if and only if $|a|x \in U$;*

    (v) *if $|a| \leqslant |b|$ for some $a, b \in \mathbb{R}$, then $aU \subseteq bU$.*

Proof. The arguments for the first four parts are straightforward. We prove only part (v).

If $b = 0$, then $a = 0$ and both aU and bU equal $\{0\}$, so we obtain the inclusion. Suppose now that $b \neq 0$. We have $aU = b\left(\frac{a}{b}U\right) \subseteq bU$ because $\frac{|a|}{|b|} \leqslant 1$ and U is balanced. $\qquad\square$

It is easy to see that the collection of balanced sets of a real linear space is closed with respect to arbitrary union and intersection.

Definition 3.15. Let L be a real linear space. A subset U of L is *absorbing* if for every $x \in L$ there exists $\delta > 0$ such that $|a| \leqslant \delta$ implies $ax \in U$.

Note that if U is an absorbing subset of L we have $0_L \in U$. Also, any set W that includes an absorbing set is itself absorbing.

Example 3.17. The closed sphere $B[0_L, 1]$ of a real normed linear space $(L, \| \cdot \|)$ is an absorbing set because for $x \in L$, $a \leqslant \|x\|$ implies $x \in aB[0, 1]$.

For a seminorm ν defined on a real linear space L we consider the sets

$$B_\nu(x_0, r) = \{x \in K \mid \nu(x - x_0) < r\},$$
$$B_\nu[x_0, r] = \{x \in K \mid \nu(x - x_0) \leqslant r\}.$$

These sets represent generalizations of the sets $B_d(x_0, r)$ and $B_d[x_0, r]$ previously introduced for metric spaces in Definition 1.49 and will be referred to as the *open sphere* and the *closed sphere* determined by ν, respectively.

Example 3.18. Let ν be a seminorm on the linear space L. The set $B_\nu(0, r) = \{x \in L \mid \nu(x) < r\}$ is absorbing. Indeed, if $\nu(x) = 0$, then $ax \in B_\nu(0, r)$ for every a because $\nu(ax) = |a|\nu(x) = 0$.

If $\nu(x) > 0$ and $|a| < \frac{r}{\nu(x)}$, then $\nu(ax) = |a|\nu(x) < r$, that is $ax \in B_\nu(0, r)$, which shows that $B_\nu(0, r)$ is indeed, absorbing.

A subset W of L is said to be *absorbing in x_0* if $W - x_0$ is absorbing.

By taking $a = 0$ it is clear that every absorbing set contains 0_L. Furthermore, if W is absorbing in x_0 then $x_0 \in W$.

Theorem 3.29. *The collections of absorbing sets of a real linear space L is closed with respect to arbitrary union and finite intersection.*

Proof. Let $\{W_i \mid i \in I\}$ be a collection of absorbing sets and let $W = \bigcup_{i \in I} W_i$. Let $x \in L$ and let W_i be one of the sets of the collection. Since W_i is absorbing there exists a positive number δ such that $|a| \leqslant \delta$ implies $ax \in W_i$. Since $W_i \subseteq W$, it follows that $ax \in W$, so W is absorbing.

Let now $\{Z_i \mid 1 \leqslant i \leqslant n\}$ be a finite collection of absorbing subsets and let $Z = \bigcap_{i=1}^n Z_i$. Since each of the sets Z_i is absorbing, there exist n positive numbers $\delta_1, \ldots, \delta_n$ such that $|a| < \delta_i$ implies $ax_i \in Z_i$ for $1 \leqslant i \leqslant n$. Let δ be the least of the numbers $\delta_1, \ldots, \delta_n$. Then $|a| < \delta$ implies $ax \in Z_i$ for $1 \leqslant i \leqslant n$, that is, $ax \in Z$. Thus, Z is an absorbing set. $\qquad\square$

Definition 3.16. Let L be a real linear space and let C be a convex set such that $0_L \in L$. The *Minkowski functional* of C is the functional $\mathsf{m}_C : L \longrightarrow \hat{\mathbb{R}}_{\geqslant 0}$ given by:

$$\mathsf{m}_C(x) = \inf\{r \in \hat{\mathbb{R}}_{>0} \mid x \in rC\}.$$

If C is clear from context the subscript C may be omitted.

Theorem 3.30. *Let L be a real linear space and let C be a convex subset of L. For $k \in \mathbb{R}_{>0}$ we have:*
(i) *$\mathsf{m}_C(x) < k$ implies $x \in kC$ and $\mathsf{m}_C(x) > k$ implies $x \notin kC$;*
(ii) *if $x \in kC$, then $\mathsf{m}_C(x) \leqslant k$.*

Proof. If $\mathsf{m}_C(x) < k$, taking into account the definition of $\mathsf{m}_C(x)$ as an infimum, there exists $r > 0$ such that $\mathsf{m}_C(x) \leqslant r < k$ and $x \in rC \subseteq kC$, which gives the first implication of part (i).

The second implication of part (i), as well as part (ii) follow from the same definition. $\qquad\square$

If C is an absorbing set, the set $\{r \in \mathbb{R}_{>0} \mid x \in rC\}$ is non-empty for every x. Therefore, if C is convex and absorbing, $m_C(x)$ is defined and is non-negative for every $x \in L$.

Example 3.19. Let $C = B[0,1]$ be the unit sphere centered in 0 in a real normed linear space $(L, \|\cdot\|)$. It is clear that C is convex, balanced and absorbing. The Minkowski functional of C is given by

$$m_C(x) = \inf\{r \in \mathbb{R}_{>0} \mid x \in B[0,r]\}.$$

Thus, in this case we have $m_C(x) = \|x\|$.

Theorem 3.31. *Let L be a real linear space and let C be a convex subset of L such that $0_L \in C$. We have:*
  (i) $m_C(kx) = k m_C(x)$ *for $k \geqslant 0$;*
  (ii) $m_C(x+y) \leqslant m_C(x) + m_C(y)$.

Proof. Note that for $k > 0$ we have:

$$m_C(kx) = \inf\{r \in \mathbb{R}_{>0} \mid kx \in h_r(B(0,1))\}$$
$$= \inf\{r \in \mathbb{R}_{>0} \mid kx \in B(0,r)\}$$
$$= k m_C(x).$$

For $k = 0$ the equality is immediate.

To prove part (ii) consider a positive number ϵ and let s, t be two numbers such that $m_C(x) < s < m_C(x) + \epsilon$ and $m_C(y) < t < m_C(y) + \epsilon$. Since $m_C\left(\frac{x}{s}\right) < 1$, hence $\frac{x}{s} \in C$. Similarly, we have $\frac{y}{t} \in C$. Since C is convex, we have

$$\frac{s}{s+t}\frac{x}{s} + \frac{t}{s+t}\frac{y}{t} = \frac{x+y}{s+t} \in C.$$

Thus, $\frac{1}{s+t} m_C(x+y) < 1$. We saw that $m_C(x+y) \leqslant s+t \leqslant m_C(x) + m_C(y) + 2\epsilon$. Since ϵ is arbitrary we obtain the subadditivity of m_C. $\square$

Theorem 3.32. *Let L be a real linear space and let C be a convex subset of L such that $0_L \in C$. Then m_C is a seminorm on L and*

$$B_{m_C}(0,1) \subseteq C \subseteq B_{m_C}[0,1].$$

Moreover, m_C is the unique seminorm on L that satisfies this double inclusion.

Proof.　The subadditivity of m_C was shown in Theorem 3.31. Let $k \in \mathbb{R}$. If $k \neq 0$ we have

$$\mathsf{m}_C(kx) = \mathsf{m}_C\left(|k|\frac{k}{|k|}C\right)$$

(by the first part of Theorem 3.31)

$$= |k|\mathsf{m}_C\left(\frac{k}{|k|}x\right)$$

$$= |k|\mathsf{m}_C(x),$$

(because C is a balanced set),

which implies the positive homogeneity of m_C.

The double inclusion can be obtained by taking $k = 1$ in Theorem 3.30.

Suppose now that there exists another seminorm ν on L such that $B_\nu(0,1) \subseteq C \subseteq B_\nu[0,1]$. This implies $B_{\mathsf{m}_C}(0,1) \subseteq B_\nu[0,1]$ and $B_\nu(0,1) \subseteq B_{\mathsf{m}_C}[0,1]$ due to the transitivity of inclusion. Therefore, $\mathsf{m}_C(x) < 1$ implies $\nu(x) \leqslant 1$ and $\nu(x) < 1$ implies $\mathsf{m}_C(x) \leqslant 1$.

If $z = \frac{1}{\mathsf{m}_C(x)+\epsilon}x$ for $\epsilon > 0$, then $\mathsf{m}_C(z) = \frac{1}{\mathsf{m}_C(x)+\epsilon}\mathsf{m}_C(x) < 1$ so $\nu(z) = \frac{1}{\mathsf{m}_C(x)+\epsilon}\nu(x) \leqslant 1$. Thus, $\nu(x) \leqslant \mathsf{m}_C(x) + \epsilon$ for every positive ϵ, which implies $\nu(x) \leqslant \mathsf{m}_C(x)$.

Similarly, from the fact that $\nu(x) < 1$ implies $\mathsf{m}_C(x) \leqslant 1$ we can show that $\mathsf{m}_C(x) \leqslant \nu(x)$ for $x \in L$, which shows the uniqueness of m_C. $\qquad\square$

3.7　Polytopes and Polyhedra

Definition 3.17. A *polytope* is the convex closure of a finite set of points in $\mathbb{R}^n$.

A polytope P that is the convex closure of a set V of $k + 1$ affinely independent points is called a *k-simplex* or a *simplex of dimension k*.

Definition 3.18. A *polyhedron* in $\mathbb{R}^n$ is a non-empty subset P of $\mathbb{R}^n$ that can be written as

$$P = \{\mathbf{x} \in \mathbb{R}^n \mid W'\mathbf{x} \leqslant \mathbf{b}\},$$

where $W = (\mathbf{w}_1\ \mathbf{w}_2\ \cdots\ \mathbf{w}_m) \in \mathbb{R}^{n \times m}$ and $\mathbf{b} \in \mathbb{R}^m$.

The *boundary hyperplanes* of the polyhedron P are the hyperplanes $\mathbf{w}_i'\mathbf{x} = b_i$ for $1 \leqslant i \leqslant m$.

The polyhedron P defined above is the intersection on m half-spaces $\mathbf{w}_i'\mathbf{x} \leqslant b_i$ for $1 \leqslant i \leqslant m$. If a boundary hyperplane $H_{\mathbf{w}_j,b_j}$ of P contains P itself, we say that $H_{\mathbf{w}_j,b_j}$ is a *singular boundary hyperplane*.

A polyhedron P is a convex set. Indeed, suppose that $P = \{\mathbf{x} \in \mathbb{R}^n \mid W'\mathbf{x} \leqslant \mathbf{b}\}$, and let $\mathbf{x}, \mathbf{y}$, that is, $W'\mathbf{x} \leqslant \mathbf{b}$ and $W'\mathbf{y} \leqslant \mathbf{b}$. For $a \in [0,1]$ we have

$$W'(a\mathbf{x} + (1-a)\mathbf{y}) = aW'\mathbf{x} + (1-a)W'\mathbf{y} \leqslant a\mathbf{b} + (1-a)\mathbf{b} = \mathbf{b},$$

so $a\mathbf{x} + (1-a)\mathbf{y} \in P$. Also, it is clear that every polyhedron is a closed set.

Theorem 3.33. *Let P be a polyhedron in $\mathbb{R}^n$ defined by*

$$P = \{\boldsymbol{x} \in \mathbb{R}^n \mid W'\boldsymbol{x} \leqslant \boldsymbol{b}\},$$

where $W = (\boldsymbol{w}_1 \ \boldsymbol{w}_2 \ \cdots \ \boldsymbol{w}_m) \in \mathbb{R}^{n \times m}$ and $\boldsymbol{b} \in \mathbb{R}^m$. Let I be the set of active indices,

$$I = \{i \mid 1 \leqslant i \leqslant m, w_i'\boldsymbol{x} = b_i\}.$$

For $\boldsymbol{x} \in P$ we have $\boldsymbol{x} \in \mathsf{extr}(P)$ if and only if there exist n linearly independent vectors $\boldsymbol{w}_{i_1}, \ldots, \boldsymbol{w}_{i_n}$ such that $\boldsymbol{w}_{i_j}'\boldsymbol{x} = b_{i_j}$ for $1 \leqslant j \leqslant n$.

Proof. Without loss of generality we may assume that the first n vectors $\mathbf{w}_1, \ldots, \mathbf{w}_n$ are linearly independent and $\mathbf{w}_i'\mathbf{x} = b_i$ for $1 \leqslant i \leqslant n$. Suppose that $\mathbf{x}$ is not an extreme point. There exists a vector $\mathbf{h} \neq \mathbf{0}_n$ such that $\mathbf{x} + \mathbf{h} \in P$ and $\mathbf{x} - \mathbf{h} \in P$. In other words, we would have $\mathbf{w}_i'(\mathbf{x} + \mathbf{h}) = b_i$ and $\mathbf{w}_i'(\mathbf{x} - \mathbf{h}) = b_i$ for $1 \leqslant i \leqslant n$, which implies $\mathbf{w}_i'\mathbf{h} = 0$. The linear independence of $\mathbf{w}_1, \ldots, \mathbf{w}_n$ implies $\mathbf{h} = \mathbf{0}_n$, which contradicts the initial assumption about $\mathbf{h}$. This implies that $\mathbf{x}$ is an extreme point.

Conversely, let $\mathbf{x}$ be an extreme point of P and let I be the set of active indices

$$I = \{i \mid \mathbf{w}_i'\mathbf{x} = b_i\}.$$

We prove that the set $\{\mathbf{w}_i \mid i \in I\}$ is a linearly independent set of n vectors or, equivalently that $\langle\{\mathbf{w}_i \mid i \in I\}\rangle = \mathbb{R}^n$ (see Theorem 2.4).

Suppose that this is not the case. Then $\langle\{\mathbf{w}_i \mid i \in I\}\rangle^{\perp}$ contains a vector $\mathbf{h} \neq \mathbf{0}_n$. Consider the segment $A_\epsilon = [\mathbf{x} - \epsilon\mathbf{h}, \mathbf{x} + \epsilon\mathbf{h}]$. If $\mathbf{y} \in A_\epsilon$, we have $\mathbf{y} = \mathbf{x} + a\mathbf{h}$, where $|a| \leqslant \epsilon$. Since $\mathbf{w}_i \perp \mathbf{h}$, $\mathbf{y} \in A_\epsilon$ implies $\mathbf{w}_i'\mathbf{y} = b_i$ for $i \in I$. If $j \notin I$, then $\mathbf{w}_j'\mathbf{y} = \mathbf{w}_j'\mathbf{x} + a\mathbf{w}_j'\mathbf{h} = \mathbf{w}_j'\mathbf{x} \leqslant b_j$ if ϵ is sufficiently small because $|a| \leqslant \epsilon$. With this choice of ϵ we get $A_\epsilon \subseteq P$, which contradicts the assumption that $\mathbf{x}$ is an extreme point. Thus, $\{\mathbf{w}_i \mid i \in I\}$ is linearly independent. $\square$

Since every extreme point of the polyhedron P defined by
$$P = \{\mathbf{x} \in \mathbb{R}^n \mid W'\mathbf{x} \leqslant \mathbf{b}\},$$
where $W = (\mathbf{w}_1 \ \mathbf{w}_2 \ \cdots \ \mathbf{w}_m) \in \mathbb{R}^{n \times m}$ corresponds to a set of n independent columns of W, it follows that the maximum number of extreme points of P is $\binom{m}{n}$.

If $\mathbf{x}_1, \ldots, \mathbf{x}_k, \mathbf{x}_{k+1}$ are affinely independent points in $\mathbb{R}^m$, where $m \geqslant k$, we denote the simplex $\mathbf{K}_{\text{conv}}(\{\mathbf{x}_1, \ldots, \mathbf{x}_k, \mathbf{x}_{k+1}\})$ by $S[\mathbf{x}_1, \ldots, \mathbf{x}_k, \mathbf{x}_{k+1}]$. The vectors $\mathbf{x}_1, \ldots, \mathbf{x}_k, \mathbf{x}_{k+1}$ are the *vertices* of this simplex. In Figure 3.4 we show three simplexes, $S[\mathbf{x}_1, \mathbf{x}_2]$, $S[\mathbf{x}_1, \mathbf{x}_2, \mathbf{x}_3]$, and $S[\mathbf{x}_1, \mathbf{x}_2, \mathbf{x}_3, \mathbf{x}_4]$ in $\mathbb{R}^3$.

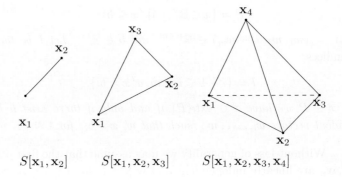

$$S[\mathbf{x}_1, \mathbf{x}_2] \qquad S[\mathbf{x}_1, \mathbf{x}_2, \mathbf{x}_3] \qquad S[\mathbf{x}_1, \mathbf{x}_2, \mathbf{x}_3, \mathbf{x}_4]$$

Fig. 3.4   Simplexes in $\mathbb{R}^3$.

Let $S[\mathbf{x}_1, \ldots, \mathbf{x}_{k+1}]$ be the k-dimensional simplex generated by set of affinely independent points $\{\mathbf{x}_1, \ldots, \mathbf{x}_k, \mathbf{x}_{k+1}\}$ in $\mathbb{R}^m$ (where $m \geqslant k$) and let $\mathbf{x} \in S$, which is a convex combination of $\mathbf{x}_1, \ldots, \mathbf{x}_k, \mathbf{x}_{k+1}$. In other words, there exist $a_1(\mathbf{x}), \ldots, a_k(\mathbf{x}), a_{k+1}(\mathbf{x})$ such that $a_1(\mathbf{x}), \ldots, a_k(\mathbf{x}), a_{k+1}(\mathbf{x}) \in [0, 1]$, $\sum_{i=1}^{k+1} a_i(\mathbf{x}) = 1$, and $\mathbf{x} = a_1(\mathbf{x})\mathbf{x}_1 + \cdots + a_k(\mathbf{x})\mathbf{x}_k + a_{k+1}(\mathbf{x})\mathbf{x}_{k+1}$.

The numbers $a_1(\mathbf{x}), \ldots, a_k(\mathbf{x}), a_{k+1}(\mathbf{x})$ are the *barycentric coordinates* of $\mathbf{x}$ relative to the simplex S.

Theorem 3.34. *The barycentric coordinates of $\boldsymbol{x} \in S[\boldsymbol{x}_1, \ldots, \boldsymbol{x}_k, \boldsymbol{x}_{k+1}]$ are uniquely determined.*

Proof.   If we have
$$\mathbf{x} = a_1(\mathbf{x})\mathbf{x}_1 + \cdots + a_k(\mathbf{x})\mathbf{x}_k + a_{k+1}(\mathbf{x})\mathbf{x}_{k+1} = b_1\mathbf{x}_1 + \cdots + b_k\mathbf{x}_k + b_{k+1}\mathbf{x}_{k+1},$$
and $a_i(\mathbf{x}) \neq b_i$ for some i, this implies
$$(a_1(\mathbf{x}) - b_1)\mathbf{x}_1 + \cdots + (a_k(\mathbf{x}) - b_k)\mathbf{x}_k + (a_{k+1}(\mathbf{x}) - b_{k+1})\mathbf{x}_{k+1} = \mathbf{0}_n,$$
which contradicts the affine independence of $\mathbf{x}_1, \ldots, \mathbf{x}_{k+1}$. $\qquad\square$

Definition 3.19. The *barycenter* of the simplex $S[\mathbf{x}_1, \ldots, \mathbf{x}_k, \mathbf{x}_{k+1}] \subseteq \mathbb{R}^n$ is the point

$$\mathbf{z} = \frac{1}{k+1}(\mathbf{x}_1 + \cdots + \mathbf{x}_k + \mathbf{x}_{k+1}).$$

Definition 3.20. If $\mathbf{x} \in S[\mathbf{x}_1, \ldots, \mathbf{x}_{k+1}]$, the *carrier* of $\mathbf{x}$ is the set $L(\mathbf{x}) = \{j \mid 1 \leqslant j \leqslant k+1 \text{ and } a_j(\mathbf{x}) > 0\}$.

The *standard simplex* in $\mathbb{R}^n$ is the simplex $S[\mathbf{e}_1, \ldots, \mathbf{e}_n]$.

Definition 3.21. Let $X = \{\mathbf{x}_1, \ldots, \mathbf{x}_k, \mathbf{x}_{k+1}\}$. A *subsimplex* of the simplex $S[X]$ is a simplex of the form $S[Y]$, where $Y \subseteq X$.

If S' is a subsimplex of a simplex S we write $S' \prec S$.

Theorem 3.35. *Let $X = \{\boldsymbol{x}_1, \ldots, \boldsymbol{x}_k, \boldsymbol{x}_{k+1}\}$ be a set of affinely independent points in $\mathbb{R}^n$. Each subsimplex of the form $S[Y]$, where Y is a non-empty subset of $\{\boldsymbol{x}_1, \ldots, \boldsymbol{x}_k, \boldsymbol{x}_{k+1}\}$ is a face of $S[X]$.*

Proof. For $x \in S[X]$ let $a_1(\mathbf{x}), \ldots, a_k(\mathbf{x}), a_{k+1}(\mathbf{x})$ be the barycentric coordinates of $\mathbf{x}$. Let $Y = \{\mathbf{x}_j \mid j \in J\}$, where $J \subseteq \{1, \ldots, k, k+1\}$.

Suppose that for $\mathbf{u}, \mathbf{v} \in S[X]$ we have $(\mathbf{u}, \mathbf{v}) \cap S[Y] \neq \emptyset$. If $\mathbf{u} = \sum_{i=1}^{k+1} a_i(\mathbf{u})\mathbf{x}_i$ and $\mathbf{v} = \sum_{i=1}^{k+1} a_i(\mathbf{v})\mathbf{x}_i$, there exists $c \in (0, 1)$ such that

$$c\mathbf{u} + (1-c)\mathbf{v} = \sum_{i=1}^{k+1}(ca_i(\mathbf{u}) + (1-c)a_i(\mathbf{v}))\mathbf{x}_i \in S[Y],$$

which means that $ca_i(\mathbf{u}) + (1-c)a_i(\mathbf{v}) = 0$ for $i \notin J$. Since $c \in (0, 1)$ and $a_i(\mathbf{u}), a_i(\mathbf{v}) \geqslant 0$, it follows that we have $a_i(\mathbf{u}) = a_i(\mathbf{v}) = 0$ for $i \in J$, so both $\mathbf{u}$ and $\mathbf{v}$ belong to $S[Y]$. Thus, $S[Y]$ is a face of $S[X]$. $\square$

If $X = \{\mathbf{x}_1, \ldots, \mathbf{x}_k, \mathbf{x}_{k+1}\}$ the *face opposite to a vertex* $\boldsymbol{x}_i$ is the subsimplex $S[X - \{\mathbf{x}_i\}]$. This simplex is denoted $\mathsf{opp}_i(S[X])$.

A finite set of points P in $\mathbb{R}^2$ is a *convex polygon* if no member p of P lies in the convex closure of $P - \{p\}$.

Theorem 3.36. *A finite set of points P in $\mathbb{R}^2$ is a convex polygon if and only if no member p of P lies in a two-dimensional simplex formed by three other members of P.*

Proof. The argument is straightforward and is left to the reader as an exercise. $\square$

Definition 3.22. Let S be a k-simplex. A *triangulation* of S is a collection $\mathcal{T}$ of distinct k-simplexes whose union is S such that any two simplexes of the collection are either disjoint or their intersection is a common face.

The *mesh* of the triangulation $\mathcal{T}$ is the largest diameter of a simplex of $\mathcal{T}$.

Given a k-simplex S any face spanned by k of the $k+1$ vertices of S is called a *facet* of S.

Example 3.20. Figure 3.5(a) shows a triangulation of $S[\mathbf{x}_1, \mathbf{x}_2, \mathbf{x}_3]$ that consists of the simplexes

$$S[\mathbf{x}_1, \mathbf{x}_3, \mathbf{x}_4], S[\mathbf{x}_2, \mathbf{x}_3, \mathbf{x}_4], S[\mathbf{x}_1, \mathbf{x}_2, \mathbf{x}_4].$$

The simplexes shown in Figure 3.5(b) do not constitute a triangulation of $S[\mathbf{x}_1, \mathbf{x}_2, \mathbf{x}_3]$ because the intersection of the simplexes $S[\mathbf{x}_1, \mathbf{x}_4, \mathbf{x}_5]$ and $S[\mathbf{x}_2, \mathbf{x}_3, \mathbf{x}_5]$ is $S[\mathbf{x}_4, \mathbf{x}_5]$, which is a face of $S[\mathbf{x}_1, \mathbf{x}_4, \mathbf{x}_5]$ but not of $S[\mathbf{x}_2, \mathbf{x}_3, \mathbf{x}_5]$.

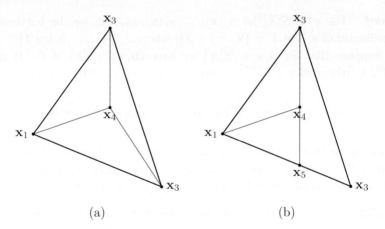

Fig. 3.5 (a) A triangulation of the simplex $S[\mathbf{x}_1, \mathbf{x}_2, \mathbf{x}_3]$; (b) a non-triangulation of $S[\mathbf{x}_1, \mathbf{x}_2, \mathbf{x}_3]$.

Definition 3.23. Let L be a real linear space and let T, S be two subsets of L. The *core of T relative to S* is the set

$$\mathsf{core}_S(T) = \{t \in T \mid \text{ for each } s \in S \text{ there is } x \in (t, s) \text{ such that } [t, x] \subseteq T\}.$$

The set $\mathsf{core}_L(T)$ is referred to as the core of T and is denoted by $\mathsf{core}(T)$.

If $S_1 \subseteq S_2$ then $\mathsf{core}_{S_2}(T) \subseteq \mathsf{core}_{S_1}(T)$ for every $S_1, S_2 \subseteq L$.

Theorem 3.37. *If C is a convex subset of a real linear space L, then* core(C) *is a convex set.*

Proof. Let $u, v \in$ core(C). Then, for each $z \in L$ there is $x \in (u, z)$ and there is $y \in (v, z)$ such that $[u, x] \subseteq C$ and $[v, y] \subseteq C$.

Let $c \in (0, 1)$ and let $w = cu + (1 - c)v$. There exist $a, b \in (0, 1)$ such that $x = au + (1 - a)z$, $y = bv + (1 - b)z$, $[u, x] \subseteq C$ and $[c, y] \subseteq C$. We have

$$w = c \left(\frac{1}{a}x - \frac{1 - a}{a}z \right) + (1 - c) \left(\frac{1}{b}y - \frac{1 - b}{b}z \right)$$
$$= \frac{c}{a}x - \frac{c(1 - a)}{a}z + \frac{1 - c}{b}y - \frac{(1 - c)(1 - b)}{b}z$$
$$= \frac{c}{a}x + \frac{1 - c}{b}y - \left(\frac{c(1 - a)}{a} + \frac{(1 - c)(1 - b)}{b} \right)z.$$

This implies

$$w + \left(\frac{c(1 - a)}{a} + \frac{(1 - c)(1 - b)}{b} \right)z = \frac{c}{a}x + \frac{1 - c}{b}y.$$

Note that the sums of coefficients in both sides of the equality is the same number S, so by dividing both members by S we obtain

$$t = \frac{1}{S} \left(w + \left(\frac{c(1 - a)}{a} + \frac{(1 - c)(1 - b)}{b} \right)z \right) = \frac{1}{S} \left(\frac{c}{a}x + \frac{1 - c}{b}y \right).$$

Thus, t is a convex combination of w and z and, also, a convex combination of x and y. Consequently, $t \in C$ and $[w, t] \subseteq C$, which proves that $w \in$ core(C). Therefore, C is a convex set. $\qquad\square$

Definition 3.24. Let L be a real linear space and let T be a subset of L. The *intrinsic core of T* is the set core$_{\mathbf{K}_{\mathrm{aff}}(T)}(T)$, that is, the core of T relative to the affine space generated by T.

The intrinsic core of T is denoted by icr(T).

Theorem 3.38. *Let L be a real linear space and let T be a convex subset of L. We have $t \in$ icr(T) if and only if for each $x \in T - \{t\}$ there exists $y \in T$ such that $t \in (x, y)$.*

Proof. Let t be such that for each $x \in T - \{t\}$ there is an $y \in T$ such that $t \in (x, y)$.

Let $z \in \mathbf{K}_{\mathrm{aff}}(T)$ and consider the line $\ell_{t,z}$ and a point $x \in \ell_{t,z} \cap T$ such that $x \neq t$. We have

$$x = (1 - a)t + az$$

for some $a \neq 0$.

By hypothesis, there exists $y \in T$ such that $t = (1 - c)x + cy$, where $c \in (0, 1)$. Thus,

$$
\begin{aligned}
y &= \frac{1}{c}t - \frac{1-c}{c}x \\
&= \frac{1}{c}t - \frac{1-c}{c}((1-a)t + az) \\
&= \left(1 - \frac{ac-a}{c}\right)t - \frac{a-ac}{c}z.
\end{aligned}
$$

If $a > 0$ we have $x \in (t, z)$ and $[t, x] \subseteq T$. Otherwise, that is, if $a < 0$, we have $\frac{ac-a}{c} > 0$ because $c \in (0, 1)$. In this case, $y \in (t, z)$ and $[t, y] \subseteq T$. Thus, in either case, $t \in \mathsf{icr}(T)$.

Suppose now that $t \in \mathsf{icr}(T)$ and let $u \in T$. We have

$$
\ell_{t,u} = at + (1-a)u \mid a \in \mathbb{R} = \{u + a(t-u) \mid a \in \mathbb{R}\} \subseteq \mathbf{K}_{\mathrm{aff}}(T).
$$

Let $z = u + b(t - u) \in \ell_{t,u}$ with $b > 1$. Since $t \in \mathsf{icr}(T)$, there exists $y \in [t, z]$ such that we have $[t, y] \subseteq T$, so $y = u + c(t - u)$, where $1 < c < b$. Since $t \in \ell_{t,u}$ (for $a = 1$), $u \in \ell_{t,u}$ (for $a = 0$) and $y \in \ell_{t,u}$, it follows that $t \in (u, y)$. $\square$

Example 3.21. Let $S = S[\mathbf{x}_1, \ldots, \mathbf{x}_k, \mathbf{x}_{k+1}]$ be a k-simplex. Its intrinsic interior $\mathsf{icr}(S)$ consists of all points of S that have positive barycentric coordinates.

In Definition 3.20 we introduced the carrier $L(\mathbf{x})$ of a point $\mathbf{x}$ of a k-simplex $S[\mathbf{x}_1, \ldots, \mathbf{x}_{k+1}]$ in $\mathbb{R}^n$.

Definition 3.25. Let $S[\mathbf{x}_1, \ldots, \mathbf{x}_{k+1}]$ be a simplex in $\mathbb{R}^n$ and let $\mathcal{T}$ be a triangulation of this simplex having the set of vertices $V_{\mathcal{T}}$. A *labeling* of $\mathcal{T}$ is a mapping $\ell : V_{\mathcal{T}} \longrightarrow \{1, \ldots, k+1\}$ such that $\ell(\mathbf{x}) \in L(\mathbf{x})$ for every $\mathbf{x} \in V_{\mathcal{T}}$.

A simplex Z of $\mathcal{T}$ is *complete* if $\ell(Z) = \{1, \ldots, k, k+1\}$.

Example 3.22. An 1-simplex $S[\mathbf{x}_1, \mathbf{x}_2]$ in $\mathbb{R}^n$ is simply a closed segment in this space. A triangulation of this simplex is a sequence of closed intervals $[\mathbf{z}_j, \mathbf{z}_{j+1}]$ for $1 \leqslant j \leqslant p$, where $\mathbf{z}_1 = \mathbf{x}_1$, $\mathbf{z}_{j+1} = \mathbf{x}_2$ and a labeling of this triangulation is a function $f : \{\mathbf{z}_1, \ldots, \mathbf{z}_{p+1}\} \longrightarrow \{1, 2\}$, since $L(\mathbf{z}_j)\{1, 2\}$.

Since the label of $\mathbf{z}_1$ is 1 and the label of $\mathbf{z}_{k+1}$ is 2, when we scan the labels of the vertices of the triangulation from left to right, the label must change an odd number of times. Therefore, the triangulation $\mathcal{T}$ contains an odd number of complete simplexes, which ensures that there exists at least one complete simplex in the triangulation $\mathcal{T}$. As we shall see, a general statement that extends this result to k-simplexes is known as Sperner's Lemma.

Example 3.23. Let $S[\mathbf{x}_1, \mathbf{x}_2, \mathbf{x}_3]$ be a 2-simplex, which is a triangle In Figure 3.6 we show a triangulation of this simplex. It is apparent that this triangulation contains seven complete simplexes.

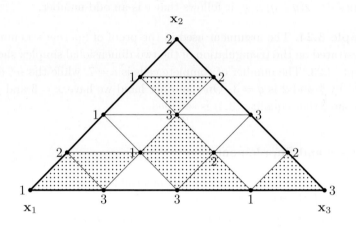

Fig. 3.6   Triangulation of a 2-simplex $S[\mathbf{x}_1, \mathbf{x}_2, \mathbf{x}_3]$.

Theorem 3.39. (Sperner's Lemma) *Let $\mathcal{T}$ be a triangulation of a k-simplex S. If the vertices of S have a labeling, then there exists an odd number of complete simplexes in $\mathcal{T}$.*

Proof. The proof is by induction on k. The argument for $k = 1$ was given in Example 3.22.

Suppose that the statement holds for simplexes of dimension less than k. Let C be the set of complete cells of $\mathcal{T}$, $c = |C|$, and let Q be the set of cells labeled by all numbers in $\{1, \ldots, k\}$ such that *exactly one* of this color is used twice and the remainder of the colors are used once, and let $q = |Q|$.

Let X be the set of $(k-1)$-dimensional faces on the boundary of S that are labeled by $\{1, \ldots, k\}$, and let Y the set of such faces inside S. Denote $|X| = x$ and $|Y| = y$.

Each cell in C contributes exactly one $(k-1)$-dimensional face labeled by $\{1, \ldots, k\}$. Each cell in Q contributes two faces labeled by $\{1, \ldots, k\}$.

Inside faces appear in two cells while boundary cells appear in one cell, so

$$c + 2q = x + 2y. \tag{3.4}$$

On the boundary of S, the only $(k-1)$-dimensional face labeled $\{1, \ldots, k\}$ can be on the face F whose vertices are labeled $\{1, \ldots, k\}$. By the inductive hypothesis, F contains an odd number of complete $(k-1)$-dimensional cells, so x is odd.

Since $c = 2(y - q) + x$, it follows that c is an odd number.   □

Example 3.24. The argument used in the proof of Sperner's Lemma can be illustrated on the triangulation of the two-dimensional simplex shown in Example 3.23. The number of complete cells is $c = 7$, while the set of cells labeled by 1 and 2 is $q = 3$. On the other hand we have $x = 3$ and $y = 5$, which show that equality (3.4) is satisfied.

Exercises and Supplements

(1) Prove that if C is a convex subset of a real linear space L, then for every $u \in L$ the set $\mathbf{t}_u(C)$ is convex.

(2) Prove that a subset C of a real linear space L is convex if and only if $aC + bC = (a + b)C$ for all $a, b \in \mathbb{R}_{>0}$.

(3) Prove that D is an affine subspace in $\mathbb{R}^n$ if and only if $\mathbf{u} + D = \{\mathbf{u} + \mathbf{x} \mid \mathbf{x} \in D\}$ is an affine subspace for every $\mathbf{u} \in \mathbb{R}^n$.

(4) Let S a subset of $\mathbb{R}^n$ such that $\mathbf{0}_n \notin \mathbf{K}_{\mathrm{aff}}(S)$. Prove that $\dim(\mathbf{K}_{\mathrm{aff}}(S)) = \dim(\langle S \rangle) - 1$.

(5) Let S be a convex set in $\mathbb{R}^n$ such that $|S| \geqslant n$ and let $\mathbf{x} \in S$. If $r \in \mathbb{N}$ such that $n + 1 \leqslant r \leqslant |S|$ prove that there exist $\binom{|S|-n}{r-n}$ set of points Y, $Y \subseteq S$, such that $\mathbf{x} \in \mathbf{K}_{\mathrm{conv}}(Y)$.

    Hint: Use induction on $k = |S| - n$ and Carathéodory's Theorem.

(6) Let $\mathbf{x}_0, \mathbf{u}, \mathbf{v}, \mathbf{x} \in \mathbb{R}^n$ such that $\mathbf{x} = (1 - a)\mathbf{u} + a\mathbf{v}$ for some $a \in (0, 1)$ and $d(\mathbf{x}_0, \mathbf{u}) = d(\mathbf{x}_0, \mathbf{v}) = d(\mathbf{x}_0, \mathbf{x})$. Prove that $\mathbf{u} = \mathbf{v} = \mathbf{x}$.

    Solution: Since $d(\mathbf{x}_0, \mathbf{u}) = d(\mathbf{x}_0, \mathbf{x}) = r$, by the cosine theorem we have

$$\|\mathbf{x} - \mathbf{u}\|^2 = \|\mathbf{x}_0 - \mathbf{u}\|^2 + \|\mathbf{x}_0 - \mathbf{x}\|^2 - 2\|\mathbf{x}_0 - \mathbf{u}\|\|\mathbf{x}_0 - \mathbf{x}\| \cos \alpha,$$

where $\alpha = \angle(\mathbf{x}_0 - \mathbf{u}, \mathbf{x}_0 - \mathbf{x})$. This implies $\|\mathbf{x} - \mathbf{u}\| = 2r \sin \frac{\alpha}{2}$.

    Similarly, if $\beta = \angle(\mathbf{x}_0 - \mathbf{x}, \mathbf{x}_0 - \mathbf{v})$, we have $\|\mathbf{x} - \mathbf{v}\| = 2r \sin \frac{\beta}{2}$. Note that $\angle(\mathbf{x}_0 - \mathbf{u}, \mathbf{x}_0 - \mathbf{v}) = \alpha + \beta$, so $\|\mathbf{u} - \mathbf{v}\| = 2r \sin \frac{\alpha+\beta}{2}$.

Since $\mathbf{x} = (1-a)\mathbf{u} + a\mathbf{v}$ we have

$$\mathbf{x} - \mathbf{v} = (1-a)(\mathbf{u} - \mathbf{v}), \text{ and}$$
$$\mathbf{u} - \mathbf{x} = a(\mathbf{u} - \mathbf{v}),$$

so

$$\|\mathbf{x} - \mathbf{v}\| = (1-a)\|\mathbf{u} - \mathbf{v}\|, \text{ and}$$
$$\|\mathbf{u} - \mathbf{x}\| = a\|\mathbf{u} - \mathbf{v}\|.$$

Therefore, we have

$$\sin\frac{\beta}{2} = (1-a)\sin\frac{\alpha+\beta}{2}. \sin\frac{\alpha}{2} = a\sin\frac{\alpha+\beta}{2},$$

which yields

$$\sin\frac{\alpha}{2} + \sin\frac{\alpha}{2} = \sin\frac{\alpha+\beta}{2}.$$

This, in turn implies $\alpha = 0$ or $\beta = 0$. In the first case, $\mathbf{x} = \mathbf{v}$, which implies $\mathbf{x} = \mathbf{u} = \mathbf{v}$ because $\mathbf{x} = (1-a)\mathbf{u} + a\mathbf{v}$. In the second case, $\mathbf{x} = \mathbf{u}$, which has the same consequence.

(7) Prove that for every set $S \subseteq \mathbb{R}^n$ we have $S + \{\mathbf{0}\} = S$ and $S + \emptyset = \emptyset$.

(8) If $P \subseteq \mathbb{R}^2$ is a set of five points such that no three of them are collinear, prove that P contains four points that form a convex quadrilateral. This result is known as *Klein's Theorem*.

Solution: Let $P = \{\mathbf{x}_i \mid 1 \leqslant i \leqslant 5\}$. If these five points form a convex polygon, then any four of them form a convex quadrilateral. If exactly one point is in the interior of a convex quadrilateral formed by the remaining four points, then the desired conclusion is reached.

Suppose that none of the previous cases occur. Then, two of the points, say $\mathbf{x}_p, \mathbf{x}_q$, are located inside the triangle formed by the remaining points $\mathbf{x}_i, \mathbf{x}_j, \mathbf{x}_k$. Note that the line $\mathbf{x}_p\mathbf{x}_q$ intersects two sides of the triangle $\mathbf{x}_i\mathbf{x}_j\mathbf{x}_k$, say $\mathbf{x}_i\mathbf{x}_j$ and $\mathbf{x}_i\mathbf{x}_k$ (see Figure 3.7). Then $\mathbf{x}_p\mathbf{x}_q\mathbf{x}_k\mathbf{x}_j$ is a convex quadrilateral.

(9) Let S be a subset of $\mathbb{R}^n$. The *polar* of S is the set

$$S^\star = \{\mathbf{y} \in \mathbb{R}^n \mid \mathbf{y}'\mathbf{x} \leqslant 1 \text{ for every } \mathbf{x} \in S\}.$$

Prove that for every subset S of $\mathbb{R}^n$, $S^\star$ is a convex subset of $\mathbb{R}^*$ and $\mathbf{0}_n \in S^\star$.

(10) Let $Y = \{\mathbf{y}_1, \ldots, \mathbf{y}_k, \mathbf{y}_{k+1}\}$ be an affinely independent subset of $\mathbb{R}^n$. Prove that the set $W_\epsilon = \{\mathbf{w}_1, \ldots, \mathbf{w}_k, \mathbf{w}_{k+1}\}$ defined as

$$\mathbf{w}_1 = \mathbf{y}_1, \mathbf{w}_2 = \mathbf{y}_1 + \epsilon(\mathbf{y}_2 - \mathbf{y}_1), \ldots, \mathbf{w}_{k+1} = \mathbf{y}_k + \epsilon(\mathbf{y}_{k+1} - \mathbf{y}_k),$$

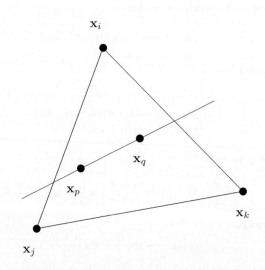

Fig. 3.7 A five-point configuration in $\mathbb{R}^2$.

is affinely independent and generates the same affine subspace as the set Y.

Solution: We claim that the set $\{\mathbf{w}_1, \ldots, \mathbf{w}_k, \mathbf{w}_{k+1}\}$ is affinely independent. Indeed suppose that one of its members, say $\mathbf{w}_{k+1}$ is an affine combination of the remaining vectors, that is,

$$\mathbf{w}_{k+1} = a_1 \mathbf{w}_1 + \cdots + a_k \mathbf{w}_k,$$

where $\sum_{i=1}^{k} a_i = 1$. Since

$$\mathbf{w}_p = \epsilon \mathbf{y}_p + (1 - \epsilon)\mathbf{y}_{p-1}$$

for $2 \leqslant p \leqslant k + 1$, we have

$$
\begin{aligned}
&\epsilon \mathbf{y}_{k+1} + (1 - \epsilon)\mathbf{y}_k \\
&= a_1 \mathbf{y}_1 + a_2(\epsilon \mathbf{y}_2 + (1 - \epsilon)\mathbf{y}_1) + \cdots + a_k(\epsilon \mathbf{y}_k + (1 - \epsilon)\mathbf{y}_{k-1}) \\
&= (a_1 + a_2(1 - \epsilon))\mathbf{y}_1 + (a_2 \epsilon + a_3 - a_3 \epsilon)\mathbf{y}_2 \\
&\quad + \cdots + (a_{k-1}\epsilon + a_k - a_k \epsilon)\mathbf{y}_{k-1} + a_k \epsilon \mathbf{y}_k.
\end{aligned}
$$

This implies

$$
\begin{aligned}
\mathbf{y}_{k+1} = {} & \frac{a_1 + a_2(1 - \epsilon)}{\epsilon}\mathbf{y}_1 + \frac{a_2 \epsilon + a_3(1 - \epsilon)}{\epsilon}\mathbf{y}_2 \\
& + \cdots + \frac{a_{k-1}\epsilon + a_k(1 - \epsilon)}{\epsilon}\mathbf{y}_{k-1} + + \frac{a_k \epsilon - 1 + \epsilon}{\epsilon}\mathbf{y}_k,
\end{aligned}
$$

which means that $\mathbf{y}_{k+1}$ is an affine combination of $\mathbf{y}_1, \ldots, \mathbf{y}_k$, which is impossible because the set Y is affinely independent.

Note that each vector $\mathbf{w}_p$ is an affine combination of y_{p-1} and y_p for $2 \leqslant p \leqslant k+1$. Thus, the affine subspace generated by $\{\mathbf{w}_1, \ldots, \mathbf{w}_k, \mathbf{w}_{k+1}\}$ is included in the affine subspace generated by $\{\mathbf{y}_1, \ldots, \mathbf{y}_k, \mathbf{y}_{k+1}\}$.

Conversely, since $y_p = \frac{1}{\epsilon} z_p + \frac{\epsilon-1}{\epsilon} z_{p-1}$ for $2 \leqslant p \leqslant k+1$ it follows that the affine subspace generated by $\{\mathbf{y}_1, \ldots, \mathbf{y}_k, \mathbf{y}_{k+1}\}$ is included in the affine subspace generated by $\{\mathbf{w}_1, \ldots, \mathbf{w}_k, \mathbf{w}_{k+1}\}$.

(11) Let $Y = \{\mathbf{y}_1, \ldots, \mathbf{y}_k, \mathbf{y}_{k+1}\}$ be an affinely independent subset of $\mathbb{R}^n$. Prove that the set $Z_\epsilon = \{\mathbf{z}_1, \ldots, \mathbf{z}_k, \mathbf{z}_{k+1}\}$ defined as

$$\mathbf{z}_1 = \mathbf{y}_1, \mathbf{z}_2 = \mathbf{y}_1 + \epsilon(\mathbf{y}_2 - \mathbf{y}_1), \ldots, \mathbf{z}_{k+1} = \mathbf{y}_1 + \epsilon(\mathbf{y}_{k+1} - \mathbf{y}_1),$$

is affinely independent and generates the same affine subspace as the set $Y = \{\mathbf{y}_1, \ldots, \mathbf{y}_k, \mathbf{y}_{k+1}\}$. Furthermore, prove that for every $r > 0$, there exists $\epsilon > 0$ such that $Z_\epsilon \subseteq B(\mathbf{y}_1, r)$.

Hint: It suffices to choose $\epsilon < \frac{r}{\max_{2 \leqslant j \leqslant k+1} \|y_j - y_1\|}$.

(12) Let C be a convex subset of $\mathbb{R}^n$ and let $B(\mathbf{z}_0, r)$ be a open sphere included in C. Prove that there exists a simplex $S[\mathbf{z}_1, \ldots, \mathbf{z}_k, \mathbf{z}_{k+1}]$ included in $B(\mathbf{z}_0, r)$ such that $k = \dim(\mathbf{K}_{\text{aff}}(C))$ and $\mathbf{z}_0$ is the barycenter of the set $\{\mathbf{x}_1, \ldots, \mathbf{x}_{k+1}\}$.

Solution: Let $\mathbf{y}_1, \ldots, \mathbf{y}_k, \mathbf{y}_{k+1}$ be an affinely independent set in $\mathbf{K}_{\text{aff}}(C)$, where $\mathbf{y}_1 = \mathbf{z}_0$. For $\epsilon > 0$ consider the set Z_ϵ as defined in Exercise 11. It is clear that Z_ϵ is affinely independent and $Z_\epsilon \subseteq \mathbf{K}_{\text{aff}}(C)$. Therefore, if ϵ is sufficiently small the simplex $S[Z_\epsilon]$ is included in $B(\mathbf{y}_1, r)$ and so is its barycenter.

(13) Prove that the union of two convex sets is not necessarily convex.

(14) Let C, D be two convex subsets of $\mathbb{R}^n$. Prove that the set $C + D$ defined by

$$C + D = \{\mathbf{x} + \mathbf{y} \mid \mathbf{x} \in C, \mathbf{y} \in D\}$$

is a convex subset of $\mathbb{R}^n$.

(15) Let $h : \mathbb{R}^n \longrightarrow \mathbb{R}^m$ be a linear operator. Prove that

    (a) if C is a convex subset of $\mathbb{R}^n$, then $h(C)$ is a convex subset of $\mathbb{R}^m$;
    (b) if D is a convex subset of $\mathbb{R}^m$, then $h^{-1}(D)$ is a convex subset of $\mathbb{R}^n$.

(16) Prove that if C is a convex subset of $\mathbb{R}^n$ and L is a subspace of $\mathbb{R}^n$, then the projection of C on L is a convex set.

(17) Prove that if C is a convex subset of $\mathbb{R}^n$ and D is a convex subset of $\mathbb{R}^m$, then $C \oplus D = \left\{ \begin{pmatrix} \mathbf{x} \\ \mathbf{y} \end{pmatrix} \mid \mathbf{x} \in C, \mathbf{y} \in D \right\}$ is a convex subset of $\mathbb{R}^{n+m}$.

(18) Prove that if C is a convex subset of $\mathbb{R}^n$ and $a, b \in \mathbb{R}_{\geqslant 0}$, then $(a+b)C = aC + bC$.

(19) Let S, T be two subsets of $\mathbb{R}^n$. Prove that $\mathbf{K}_{\text{conv}}(S+T) = \mathbf{K}_{\text{conv}}(S) + \mathbf{K}_{\text{conv}}(T)$.

(20) Prove that if S is a convex set, then $aS + bS$ is a convex set; furthermore, prove that $aS + bS = (a+b)S$ for every $a, b \geqslant 0$.

(21) Let A, B be two subsets of $\mathbb{R}^n$ such that there exists a hyperplane $H_{\mathbf{w},a}$ such that $A \subseteq H_{\mathbf{w},a}^{\geqslant}$ and $B \subseteq H_{\mathbf{w},a}^{\leqslant}$. Prove that:

    (a) $\mathbf{K}_{\text{conv}}(A) \cap \mathbf{K}_{\text{conv}}(B) = \emptyset$;

    (b) for

$$A - B = \{\mathbf{x} - \mathbf{y} \mid \mathbf{x} \in A, \mathbf{y} \in B\}$$

    we have $A - B \subseteq H_{\mathbf{w},0}^{\geqslant}$ and $\mathbf{0}_n \in H_{\mathbf{w},0}^{\leqslant}$.

Solution: Since $A \subseteq H_{\mathbf{w},a}^{\geqslant}$ for each $\mathbf{x} \in A$, we have $\mathbf{w}'\mathbf{x} > a$; similarly, for every $\mathbf{y} \in B$ we have $\mathbf{w}'\mathbf{y} < a$.

If $\mathbf{u} \in \mathbf{K}_{\text{conv}}(A)$ we can write $\mathbf{u} = \sum_{i=1}^{n} a_i \mathbf{x}_i$, where $\sum_{i=1}^{n} a_i = 1$, $0 \leqslant a_i \leqslant 1$ and $\mathbf{x}_i \in A$ for $1 \leqslant i \leqslant n$. Therefore,

$$\mathbf{w}'\mathbf{u} = \mathbf{w}' \left(\sum_{i=1}^{n} a_i \mathbf{x}_i \right) = \sum_{i=1}^{n} a_i \mathbf{w}'\mathbf{x}_i > a \sum_{i=1}^{n} a_i = a.$$

Similarly, if $\mathbf{v} \in B$ we obtain $\mathbf{w}'\mathbf{v} < a$. Therefore, if $\mathbf{t}$ would belong to $\mathbf{K}_{\text{conv}}(A) \cap \mathbf{K}_{\text{conv}}(B)$ we would have the contradictory inequalities $\mathbf{w}'\mathbf{t} > a$ and $\mathbf{w}'\mathbf{t} < a$.

For the second part, let $\mathbf{x} \in A$ and $\mathbf{y} \in B$, so $\mathbf{w}'\mathbf{x} > a$ and $\mathbf{w}'\mathbf{y} < a$ (that is, $-\mathbf{w}'\mathbf{y} > -a$). This implies $\mathbf{w}'(\mathbf{x} - \mathbf{y}) > 0$, so $A - B \in H_{\mathbf{w},0}^{\geqslant}$; clearly, $\mathbf{0}_n \in H_{\mathbf{w},0}^{\leqslant 0}$.

(22) Prove that the intersection of two convex polygons in $\mathbb{R}^2$ having a total of n edges is either empty or is a convex polygon with at most n edges.

(23) Let $\mathcal{C} = \{C_1, \ldots, C_m\}$ be a collection of m convex sets in $\mathbb{R}^n$, where $m \geq n+1$ such that if every subcollection $\mathcal{C}'$ of $\mathcal{C}$ that contains $n+1$ sets has a non-empty intersection. Prove that $\bigcap \mathcal{C} \neq \emptyset$.

    Hint: Proceed by induction on $k = m - (n+1)$. Apply Radon's theorem in the inductive step of the proof.

(24) Prove that the border of a polytope is the union of its proper faces.

(25) Let $S[\mathbf{x}_1, \ldots, \mathbf{x}_k, \mathbf{x}_{k+1}]$ be a k-simplex in $\mathbb{R}^n$. Prove that there exists a triangulation of this simplex whose mesh is less that a positive number ϵ.

(26) Let $C_1, \ldots, C_k$ be k convex subsets of $\mathbb{R}^n$, where $k \geqslant n+2$. Prove that if any $n+1$ of these sets have a common point, then all the sets have a common point. This fact is known as Helly's Theorem.

Solution: For $i \in \{1, \dots, k\}$ there exists $\mathbf{x}_i \in C_1 \cap \dots \cap C_{i-1} \cap C_{i+1} \cap \dots \cap C_k$. This results in a set $\{\mathbf{x}_1, \dots, \mathbf{x}_k\}$ of more than $n+2$ vectors that are affinely dependent. By Radon's Theorem we obtain that after a suitable renumbering we have

$$\mathbf{x} \in \mathbf{K}_{\text{conv}}(\{\mathbf{x}_1, \dots, \mathbf{x}_j\}) \cap \mathbf{K}_{\text{conv}}(\{\mathbf{x}_{j+1}, \dots, \mathbf{x}_k\})$$

for some j, where $1 \leqslant j \leqslant k-1$. Since each of the points $\mathbf{x}_1, \dots, \mathbf{x}_j$ belong to $C_{j+1} \cap \dots \cap C_k$ we have

$$\mathbf{x} \in \mathbf{K}_{\text{conv}}(\{\mathbf{x}_1, \dots, \mathbf{x}_j\}) \subseteq C_{j+1} \cap \dots \cap C_k.$$

Similarly, $x \in \mathbf{K}_{\text{conv}}(\{\mathbf{x}_{j+1}, \dots, \mathbf{x}_k\}) \subseteq C_1 \cap \dots \cap C_j$.

(27) Let $\mathcal{C}$ be a finite collection of convex subsets in $\mathbb{R}^n$ and let C be a convex subset of $\mathbb{R}^n$. Prove that if any $n+1$ subsets of $\mathcal{C}$ are intersected by some translate of C, then all sets of $\mathcal{C}$ are intersected by some translate of C.

(28) The following result is known as the *Motzkin's Theorem*.

Let $\wp : \mathbb{R}^n \longrightarrow \mathbb{R}^{n-1}$ be the projection defined by $\wp(\mathbf{x}) = \begin{pmatrix} x_2 \\ \vdots \\ x_n \end{pmatrix}$, where $\mathbf{x} \in \mathbb{R}^n$. Prove that if P is a polyhedron in $\mathbb{R}^n$, then $\wp(P)$ is a polyhedron in $\mathbb{R}^{n-1}$.

Solution: Suppose that $P = \{\mathbf{x} \in \mathbb{R}^n \mid W'\mathbf{x} \leqslant \mathbf{b}\}$, where $W = (\mathbf{w}_1 \ \mathbf{w}_2 \ \cdots \ \mathbf{w}_m) \in \mathbb{R}^{n \times m}$ and $\mathbf{b} \in \mathbb{R}^m$. In other words, P is defined by the inequalities

$$\mathbf{w}_1'\mathbf{x} \leqslant b_1, \dots, \mathbf{w}_m'\mathbf{x} \leqslant b_m.$$

If $w_{1j} > 0$ the inequality

$$w_{1j}x_1 + \dots + w_{nj}x_n \leqslant b_j$$

implies $x_1 \leqslant \tilde{w}_{2j}x_2 + \dots + \tilde{w}_{nj}x_n + \tilde{b}_j$, where $\tilde{w}_{kj} = -\frac{w_{kj}}{w_{1j}}$ for $2 \leqslant k \leqslant n$ and $\tilde{b}_j = \frac{b_j}{w_{1j}}$. Similarly, if $w_{1j} < 0$, the above inequality is equivalent to $x_1 \geqslant \tilde{w}_{2j}x_2 + \dots + \tilde{w}_{nj}x_n + \tilde{b}_j$. Therefore, the inequalities $\mathbf{w}_j'\mathbf{x} \leqslant \mathbf{b}$ where $w_{1j} \neq 0$ are equivalent to

$$\max\{\tilde{w}_{2j}x_2 + \dots + \tilde{w}_{nj}x_n + \tilde{b}_j \mid w_{1j} < 0\} \leqslant x_1$$
$$\leqslant \min\{\tilde{w}_{2j}x_2 + \dots + \tilde{w}_{nj}x_n + \tilde{b}_j \mid w_{1j} > 0\}.$$

Note that $\begin{pmatrix} x_2 \\ \vdots \\ x_n \end{pmatrix} \in \wp(P)$ only if $w_{ij} = 0$ implies $w_{2j}x_2 + \dots + w_{nj}x_n < b_j$

and if for $w_{1j} > 0$ and $w_{1k} < 0$ we have

$$\tilde{w}_{2j}x_2 + \cdots + \tilde{w}_{nj}x_n + \tilde{b}_j \leqslant \tilde{w}_{2k}x_2 + \cdots + \tilde{w}_{nk}x_n + \tilde{b}_k,$$

or, equivalently,

$$(\tilde{w}_{2j} - \tilde{w}_{2k})x_2 + \cdots + (\tilde{w}_{nj} - \tilde{w}_{nk})x_n \leqslant \tilde{b}_k - \tilde{b}_j.$$

Thus, the set $\wp(P)$ is defined by a collection of inequalities involving $x_2, \ldots, x_n$, so $\wp(P)$ is indeed a polyhedron.

(29) Prove that a cone in a linear space L is pointed if and only if $x \in C$ and $-x \in C$ imply $x = 0_L$.

(30) Prove that the set of cones in $\mathbb{R}^n$ is closed under intersection, union, and complement.

(31) Prove that if C is a cone in $\mathbb{R}^n$, then $-C$ is a cone in the same space; prove that if C, D are cones in $\mathbb{R}^n$, then $C + D$ is a cone in $\mathbb{R}^n$.

(32) Prove that the set $C \subseteq \mathbb{R}^3$ defined by

$$C = \{(x, y, z) \mid z \geqslant 0, x^2 + y^2 \leqslant z^2\}$$

is a cone.

(33) Let C be a convex set in $\mathbb{R}^n$. Define the set

$$R(C) = \{\mathbf{d} \in \mathbb{R}^n \mid \mathbf{x} + \mathbf{d} \in C \text{ for every } \mathbf{x} \in C\}.$$

Prove that $R(C)$ is a cone (it is known as the *recession cone* for C). Furthermore, prove that if C is a convex cone, then $R(C) = C$.

(34) Let L be a linear space and let C be a cone in L such that $0_L \in C$. Define the relation $\rho_C \subseteq L \times L$ as

$$\rho_C = \{(x, y) \in L \times L \mid y - x \in C\}.$$

Prove that:
   (a) ρ_C is reflexive and $(x, y) \in \rho_C$ imply $(ax, ay) \in \rho_C$ for $a > 0$ and $(x + z, y + z) \in \rho_C$;
   (b) ρ_C is transitive if and only if C is convex;
   (c) ρ_C is antisymmetric if and only if $C \cap (-C) = \{0_L\}$.

(35) Let ρ be a reflexive relation on a linear space L such that $(x, y) \in \rho$ imply $(ax, ay) \in \rho$ for $a > 0$ and $(x + z, y + z) \in \rho$. Prove that the set $C = \{x \in L \mid (x, 0_L) \in \rho\}$ is a cone and $\rho = \rho_C$.

(36) Let $A \in \mathbb{R}^{m \times n}$. Prove that the set

$$C_A = \{\mathbf{x} \in \mathbb{R}^n \mid A\mathbf{x} \geqslant \mathbf{0}_m\}$$

is a convex cone. C_A is the *polyhedral cone determined by A*.

(37) Let $A \in \mathbb{R}^{m \times n}$ and $\mathbf{b} \in \mathbb{R}^m$. Prove that the non-empty polyhedron $P_{A,\mathbf{b}} = \{\mathbf{x} \in \mathbb{R}^n \mid A\mathbf{x} \leqslant \mathbf{b}\}$ is a polyhedral cone if and only if $\mathbf{b} = \mathbf{0}_m$. Further, prove that $P_{A,\mathbf{0}_m}$ is a pointed cone if $rank(A) = n$.

Solution: It is immediate that if $\mathbf{b} = \mathbf{0}_m$, $P_{A,\mathbf{0}}$ is a cone. Conversely, suppose that $P_{A,\mathbf{b}}$ is a cone and let $\mathbf{x}_0 \in P_{A,\mathbf{b}}$. Since $\mathbf{0}_n \in P_{A,\mathbf{b}}$ we have $\mathbf{0}_m \leqslant \mathbf{b}$, hence $\{\mathbf{x} \mid A\mathbf{x} \leqslant \mathbf{0}_m\} \subseteq P_{A,\mathbf{b}}$. If $\mathbf{x} \in P_{A,\mathbf{b}}$ and $A\mathbf{x} \not\leqslant \mathbf{0}_m$, then there is a row $\mathbf{a}_j$ of A such that $\mathbf{a}_j\mathbf{x} > 0$ and $\mathbf{a}_j(t\mathbf{x}) \leqslant b_j$ for every $t \geqslant 0$ because $P_{A,\mathbf{b}}$ is a cone. This leads to a contradiction. Therefore, $\mathbf{b} = \mathbf{0}_m$.

If $rank(A) < n$ there exists a non-zero vector $\mathbf{u} \in \mathbb{R}^n$ such that $A\mathbf{u} = \mathbf{0}_m$, so the line $\{t\mathbf{u} \mid t \geqslant 0\}$ is included in $P_{A,\mathbf{0}_m}$, which implies that $P_{A,\mathbf{0}}$ is not a pointed cone.

Conversely, suppose that $P_{A,\mathbf{0}_m}$ is not a pointed cone, that is, it contains the line $\{\mathbf{x} \mid \mathbf{x} = \mathbf{x}_0 + t\mathbf{u}\}$ with $\mathbf{u} \neq \mathbf{0}_n$. If $\mathbf{a}'_j\mathbf{u} \neq 0$ for some j, there exists t such that $\mathbf{a}'_j\mathbf{x}_0 + t\mathbf{a}_j\mathbf{u} > 0$, which contradicts the inclusion $\ell \subseteq P_{A,\mathbf{0}_m}$. Thus, $A\mathbf{u} = 0$, hence $rank(A) < n$.

(38) A *Weyl pair of matrices* is a pair (A, B), where $A \in \mathbb{R}^{m \times n}$ and $B \in \mathbb{R}^{n \times p}$ such that:

$$\{x \in \mathbb{R}^n \mid Ax \leqslant \mathbf{0}_m\} = \{B\mathbf{y} \mid \mathbf{y} \in \mathbb{R}^p \text{ and } \mathbf{y} \geqslant \mathbf{0}_p\}.$$

Prove that for every matrix $B \in \mathbb{R}^{n \times p}$ there exists a matrix $A \in \mathbb{R}^{m \times n}$ such that (A, B) is a Weyl pair.

Solution: Let P be the polyhedral cone $P \subseteq \mathbb{R}^{p+n}$ defined as

$$P = \left\{ \begin{pmatrix} \mathbf{x} \\ \mathbf{y} \end{pmatrix} \in \mathbb{R}^{p+n} \middle| \mathbf{y} = B\mathbf{x}, \mathbf{x} \geqslant 0 \right\}$$

$$= \left\{ \begin{pmatrix} \mathbf{x} \\ \mathbf{y} \end{pmatrix} \in \mathbb{R}^{p+n} \middle| \mathbf{y} - B\mathbf{x} \leqslant 0, B\mathbf{x} - \mathbf{y} \leqslant 0, -\mathbf{x} \leqslant 0 \right\}.$$

If $\wp : \mathbb{R}^{p+n} \longrightarrow \mathbb{R}^n$ is the function defined as $\wp \begin{pmatrix} \mathbf{x} \\ \mathbf{y} \end{pmatrix} = \mathbf{y}$, then $\wp(P) = C$. Since $\wp(t\mathbf{x}) = t\wp(\mathbf{x})$ for $t \geqslant 0$ and $\mathbf{x} \in P$, C is a cone and the existence of the matrix A follows from Supplements 28 and 37.

(39) Prove that a subset B of $\mathbb{R}^n$ is a convex cone if and only if it is closed under addition and non-negative scalar multiplication.

(40) Prove that the smallest subspace of a linear space L that contains a convex cone C is $C - C$ and the largest subspace contained in C is $(-C) \cap C$.

(41) Prove that if $T \subseteq L$ then the sets $\tilde{T} = T \cup h_{-1}(T)$ and $\hat{T} = T \cap h_{-1}(T)$ are symmetric.

(42) Let C be a convex subset of a real linear space L. Prove that C is a balanced set if and only if $x \in C$ implies $-x \in C$.

Solution: The condition is clearly necessary.

To prove that it is sufficient let C be a convex set. If C is empty then C is balanced. Therefore, let C be a non-empty set and let $x \in C$. We have $-x \in C$. If $r \in \mathbb{R}$ is such that $|r| \leqslant 1$, then $0 \leqslant t = \frac{1+r}{2} \leqslant 1$. The convexity of C implies:

$$rx = tx + (1-t)(-x) \in C,$$

which shows that C is balanced.

Bibliographical Comments

The books [111, 23, 15, 18, 99] contain a vast amount of results in convexity theory. References that focus on geometric aspects are [69, 115].

PART II
Topology

Chapter 4

Topology

4.1 Introduction

Topology is an area of mathematics that investigates the local and the global structure of space. We present in this chapter an introduction to point-set topology. After introducing the notion of topology and topological space, we present several of the most important topological space. Then, we study closure and interior operators as they are defined by topologies, as well as some alternative techniques for defining topologies such as systems of neighborhoods and bases.

The notion of compact set in a topological space is the object of a dedicated section in view of its importance as a generalization of closed and bounded sets in Euclidean spaces.

We discuss the separation hierarchy of topological spaces, a device that allows topologists to impose restrictions on these spaces in order to obtain certain desired results. Locally compact spaces are topological spaces that satisfy a certain separation requirement such that every point has a local basis consisting of compact sets.

A series of sections that follow concentrate on the all important notion of limit and on function continuity.

We continue with connected topological space, that is, with spaces that cannot be represented as the union of two or more disjoint topological spaces. After discussing products of topological spaces we end the chapter with a study of semicontinuous functions and with epigraphs and hypographs of functions, two subjects of importance in optimization theory.

4.2 Topologies

The term "topology" is used both to designate a mathematical discipline and to name the fundamental notion of this discipline, which is introduced next.

Definition 4.1. A *topology* on a set S is a family $\mathcal{O}$ of subsets of S that satisfies the following conditions:
  (i) for every collection $\mathcal{C}$ such that $\mathcal{C} \subseteq \mathcal{O}$, $\bigcup \mathcal{C} \in \mathcal{O}$;
  (ii) if $\mathcal{D}$ is a finite collection and $\mathcal{D} \subseteq \mathcal{O}$, then $\bigcap \mathcal{D} \in \mathcal{O}$.
  The sets that belong to $\mathcal{O}$ are referred to as the *open sets* of the topology $\mathcal{O}$. The pair $(S, \mathcal{O})$ is referred to as a *topological space*. The elements of S are commonly referred to as *points*.

The intersection of the empty collection of subsets of S belongs to $\mathcal{O}$, and this intersection is S. On the other hand, the union of the empty collection (which is the empty set) belongs to $\mathcal{O}$, which allows us to conclude that the empty set and the set S belong to every topology defined on the set S.

Example 4.1. The pair $(S, \mathcal{P}(S))$ is a topological space. The topology $\mathcal{P}(S)$ is known as the *discrete topology*.
  The collection $\{\emptyset, S\}$ is the *indiscrete topology*.

Example 4.2. The pair $(\emptyset, \{\emptyset\})$ is a topological space as the reader can easily verify. We refer to $(\emptyset, \{\emptyset\})$ as the *empty topological space*.

Example 4.3. Let $\mathcal{O}$ be the collection of subsets of $\mathbb{R}$ defined by $L \in \mathcal{O}$ if for every $x \in L$ there exists $\epsilon \in \mathbb{R}_{>0}$ such that $|u - x| < \epsilon$ implies $u \in L$. The pair $(\mathbb{R}, \mathcal{O})$ is a topological space. In other words, for every $x \in L$, there exists ϵ such that $B(x, \epsilon) \subseteq L$.
  Indeed, it is immediate that $\emptyset$ and $\mathbb{R}$ belong to $\mathcal{O}$.
  Let $\mathcal{C}$ be such that $\mathcal{C} \subseteq \mathcal{O}$ and let $x \in \bigcup \mathcal{C}$. There exists $L \in \mathcal{C}$ such that $x \in L$ and, therefore, by the definition of $\mathcal{O}$, there is $\epsilon > 0$ such that $|u - x| < \epsilon$ implies $u \in L$. Thus, $u \in \bigcup \mathcal{C}$, so $\bigcup \mathcal{C} \in \mathcal{O}$.
  Suppose now that $\mathcal{D}$ is a finite subcollection of $\mathcal{O}$, $\mathcal{D} = \{D_1, \ldots, D_n\}$, and let $x \in \bigcap \mathcal{D}$. Since $x \in D_i$ for $1 \leqslant i \leqslant n$, there exists $\epsilon_1, \ldots, \epsilon_n$ such that $|u - x| < \epsilon_i$ implies $u \in D_i$ for every i, $1 \leqslant i \leqslant n$. Therefore, by defining $\epsilon = \min\{\epsilon_i \mid 1 \leqslant i \leqslant n\}$, it follows that $|x - u| \leqslant \epsilon$ implies $u \in \bigcap \mathcal{D}$, which proves that $\bigcap \mathcal{D} \in \mathcal{O}$. We conclude that $\mathcal{O}$ is a topology on $\mathbb{R}$. This topology is called the *usual topology* on $\mathbb{R}$. Unless stated otherwise, we assume that the set of real numbers is equipped with the usual topology.

In the topological space $(\mathbb{R}, \mathcal{O})$, every open interval (a, b) with $a < b$ is an open set. Indeed, if $x \in (a, b)$ and $|x - u| < \epsilon$, where $\epsilon = \frac{1}{2} \min\{|x - a|, |x - b|\}$, then $u \in (a, b)$. A similar argument shows that the half-lines $(b, +\infty)$ and $(-\infty, a)$ are open sets for $a, b \in \mathbb{R}$. Thus, every set (a, b) with $-\infty \leqslant a < b \leqslant \infty$ is open.

Example 4.4. Let S be an infinite set. The family of sets

$$\mathcal{O} = \{\emptyset\} \cup \{L \in \mathcal{P}(S) \mid S - L \text{ is finite}\}$$

is a topology on S. We refer to $\mathcal{O}$ as the *cofinite topology* on S.

Note that both $\emptyset$ and S belong to $\mathcal{O}$. Further, if $\mathcal{C}$ is a subcollection of $\mathcal{O}$, then $S - \bigcup \mathcal{C} = \bigcap\{(S - L) \mid L \in \mathcal{C}\}$, which is a finite set because it is a subset of every finite set $S - L$, where $L \in \mathcal{C}$.

Also, if $U, V \in \mathcal{O}$, then $S - (U \cap V) = (S - U) \cup (S - V)$, which shows that $S - (U \cap V)$ is a finite set. Thus, $U \cap V \in \mathcal{O}$.

Example 4.5. Let $(S, \leqslant)$ be a partially ordered set. A subset T of S is *upward closed* if $x \in T$ and $x \leqslant y$ implies $y \in T$. The collection of upwards closed sets $\mathcal{O}^\uparrow$ is a topology on S.

It is clear that both $\emptyset$ and S belong to $\mathcal{O}^\uparrow$. Further, if $\{L_i \mid i \in I\}$ is a family of upwards closed sets, then $\bigcup\{L_i \mid i \in I\}$ is also an upwards closed set. Indeed, suppose that $x \in \bigcup\{L_i \mid i \in I\}$ and $x \leqslant y$. There exists L_i such that $x \in L_i$ and therefore $y \in L_i$, which implies $y \in \bigcup\{L_i \mid i \in I\}$. Moreover, it is easy to see that any intersection of sets from $\mathcal{O}^\uparrow$ belongs to $\mathcal{O}^\uparrow$, not just a finite intersection (which would suffice for $\mathcal{O}^\uparrow$ to be a topology). This topology is known as the *Alexandrov topology* on the poset $(S, \leqslant)$.

Open sets of the topological space $(\mathbb{R}, \mathcal{O})$, where $\mathcal{O}$ is the usual topology on the set of real numbers have the following useful characterization.

Theorem 4.1. *A subset U of $\mathbb{R}$ is open in the topological space $(\mathbb{R}, \mathcal{O})$ if and only if it equals the union of a countable collection of disjoint open intervals.*

Proof. Since every open interval (finite or not) is an open set, it follows that the union of a countable collection of disjoint open intervals is open.

To prove the converse, let U be an open set. Note that U can be written as a union of open intervals since for each $x \in U$ there exists $\epsilon > 0$ such that $x \in (x - \epsilon, x + \epsilon) \subseteq U$.

Define the relation θ_U on the set U by $x \theta_U y$ if there exist $a, b \in \mathbb{R}$ such that $\{x, y\} \subseteq (a, b) \subseteq U$. We claim that θ_U is an equivalence relation on U.

Since U is open, $x \in U$ implies the existence of a positive number ϵ such that $\{x\} \subseteq (x - \epsilon, x + \epsilon) \subseteq U$ for every $x \in U$, so θ_U is reflexive. The symmetry of θ_U is immediate. To prove its transitivity, let $x, y, z \in U$ be such that $x\theta_U z$ and $z\theta_U y$. There are $a, b, c, d \in \mathbb{R}$ such that $\{x, z\} \subseteq (a, b) \subseteq U$ and $\{z, y\} \subseteq (c, d) \subseteq U$. Since $z \in (a, b) \cap (c, d)$, it follows that $(a, b) \cup (c, d)$ is an interval (e, e') such that $\{x, y\} \subseteq (e, e') \subseteq U$, which shows that $x\theta_U y$. Thus, θ_U is an equivalence on U.

We claim that each equivalence class $[x]_{\theta_U}$ is an open interval, or a set of the form $(a, +\infty)$, or a set of the form $(-\infty, b)$. Indeed, suppose that $u, v \in [x]_{\theta_U}$ (that is, $u\theta_U x$ and $v\theta_U x$) and that $t \in (u, v)$. We now prove that $t\theta_U x$.

There are two open intervals (a, b) and (c, d) such that $\{u, x\} \subseteq (a, b) \subseteq U$ and $\{x, v\} \subseteq (c, d) \subseteq U$. Again, $(a, b) \cup (c, d)$ is an open interval (e, e') and we have $(u, v) \subseteq (e, e') \subseteq U$. Thus, if $[x]_{\theta_U}$ contains two numbers u and v, it also contains the interval (u, v) determined by these numbers.

To prove that $[x]_{\theta_U}$ has the desired form, we shall prove that this set has no least element and no greatest element. Suppose that $[x]_{\theta_U}$ has a least element y. Then, there exist a and b such that $a < y < x < b$ and $(a, b) \subseteq U$. Since y is supposed to be the least element of $[x]_{\theta_U}$, if $a < z < y$, we have $z \notin [x]_{\theta_U}$. This contradicts $y\theta_U z$ and $y\theta_U x$. In a similar manner, it is possible to show that $[x]_{\theta_U}$ has no largest element.

Finally, we prove that the partition that corresponds to θ_U is countable. Select a rational number $r_x \in [x]_{\theta_U} \cap \mathbb{Q}$. Since the equivalence classes $[x]_{\theta_U}$ are pairwise disjoint, it follows that $[x]_{\theta_U} \neq [y]_{\theta_U}$ implies $r_x \neq r_y$. Thus, we have an injection $r : U/\theta_U \longrightarrow \mathbb{Q}$ given by $r([x]_{\theta_U}) = r_x$ for $x \in U$. Therefore, the set U/θ_U is countable. $\qquad\square$

Example 4.6. The *lower topology* $\mathcal{O}_l$ of $\mathbb{R}$ consists of the sets $\emptyset, \mathbb{R}$ and all sets of the form (a, ∞) for $a \in \mathbb{R}$. Note that $(a, \infty) \cap (b, \infty) = (\min\{a, b\}, \infty)\}$ and for any set $\{a_i \mid i \in I\}$, $\bigcup_{i \in I}(a_i, \infty) = (\inf\{a_i \mid i \in I\}, \infty)$, which shows that $\mathcal{O}_l$ is indeed a topology.

Similarly, the *upper topology* $\mathcal{O}_u$ of $\mathbb{R}$ consists of the sets $\emptyset, \mathbb{R}$ and all sets of the form $(-\infty, a)$ for $a \in \mathbb{R}$.

The upper and lower topologies can be defined on the extended set of reals as follows. The *lower topology* $\mathcal{O}_l$ on $\hat{r}r$ consists of $\emptyset, \hat{\mathbb{R}}$, and sets of the form $U_a = (a, \infty]$, where $a \in \mathbb{R}$ or $a = -\infty$. Similarly, the *upper topology* $\mathcal{O}_u$ on the set $\hat{\mathbb{R}}$ consists of $\emptyset, \hat{\mathbb{R}}$, and sets of the form $W_a = [-\infty, a)$, where $a \in \mathbb{R}$ or $a = \infty$.

Definition 4.2. Let $(S, \mathcal{O})$ be a topological space. A subset T of S is *closed* if its complement $S - T$ is open.

The collection of closed sets of $(S, \mathcal{O})$ is denoted by *closed*$(\mathcal{O})$.

Theorem 4.2. *The following statements hold for any topological space* $(S, \mathcal{O})$:

   (i) *$\emptyset$ and S are closed sets;*

   (ii) *for every collection $\mathcal{C}$ of closed sets, $\bigcap \mathcal{C}$ is a closed set;*

   (iii) *for every finite collection $\mathcal{D}$ of closed sets, $\bigcup \mathcal{D}$ is a closed set.*

Proof. This is an immediate consequence of Definition 4.1. □

Example 4.7. Observe that $(-\infty, a) \cup (b, +\infty)$ is an open set in $\mathbb{R}$ which implies that its complement, the interval $[a, b]$, is closed. Also, $(-\infty, b]$ and $[a, \infty)$ are closed sets (as complements of the open sets (b, ∞) and (a, ∞), respectively).

Every subset X of $\mathbb{R}$ of the form $X = \{x_0, x_1, \ldots, x_n, \ldots\}$ is closed. Indeed, since

$$\mathbb{R} - X = (-\infty, x_0) \cup \bigcup_{i \in \mathbb{N}} (x_i, x_{i+1})$$

is open (as a countable union of open sets), it follows that X is closed.

Definition 4.3. A topology $\mathcal{O}$ is *finer* (or *stronger*) than a topology $\mathcal{O}'$ or, equivalently, $\mathcal{O}'$ is a *coarser* (or *weaker*) than $\mathcal{O}$, if $\mathcal{O}' \subseteq \mathcal{O}$.

Every topology on a set S is finer than the indiscrete topology on S; the discrete topology $\mathcal{P}(S)$ (which has the largest collection of open sets) is finer than any topology on S.

Theorem 4.3. *Let $(S, \mathcal{O})$ be a topological space and let T be a subset of S. The collection $\mathcal{O} \restriction_T$ defined by $\mathcal{O} \restriction_T = \{L \cap T \mid L \in \mathcal{O}\}$ is a topology on the set T.*

Proof. We leave the proof of this theorem to the reader as an exercise. □

Definition 4.4. If U is a subset of S, where $(S, \mathcal{O})$ is a topological space, then we refer to the topological space $(U, \mathcal{O} \restriction_U)$ as a *subspace* of the topological space $(S, \mathcal{O})$.

To simplify notation, we refer to the subspace $(U, \mathcal{O} \restriction_U)$ as $(U, \mathcal{O})$, or even as U.

Theorem 4.4. *Let $(S, \mathcal{O})$ be a topological space and let $(T, \mathcal{O} \restriction_T)$ be a subspace of this space. Then, a set H is closed in $(T, \mathcal{O} \restriction_T)$ if and only if there exists a closed set H_0 in $(S, \mathcal{O})$ such that $H = T \cap H_0$.*

Proof.   Suppose that H is closed in $(T, \mathcal{O} \restriction_T)$. Then, the set $T - H$ is open in this space and therefore there exists an open set L_0 in $(S, \mathcal{O})$ such that $T - H = T \cap L_0$. This is equivalent to $H = T - (T \cap L_0) = T \cap (S - L_0)$. We define H_0 as the closed set $S - L_0$.

Conversely, suppose that $H = T \cap H_0$, where H_0 is a closed set in S. Since $T - H = T \cap (S - H_0)$ and $S - H_0$ is an open set in $(S, \mathcal{O})$, it follows that $T - H$ is open in the subspace and therefore H is closed.   □

4.3   Closure and Interior Operators in Topological Spaces

Theorem 4.2 implies that for every topological space $(S, \mathcal{O})$ the collection *closed*$(\mathcal{O})$ of closed sets is a closure system on S. In addition to the properties listed in Definition 1.35:

  (i) $U \subseteq \mathbf{K}(U)$ *(expansiveness)*,
  (ii) $U \subseteq V$ implies $\mathbf{K}(U) \subseteq \mathbf{K}(V)$ *(monotonicity)*, and
  (iii) $\mathbf{K}(\mathbf{K}(U)) = \mathbf{K}(U)$ *(idempotency)*

for $U, V \in \mathcal{P}(S)$. the closure operator attached to a topological space satisfies the following supplementary property:

$$\mathbf{K}(H \cup L) = \mathbf{K}(H) \cup \mathbf{K}(L) \tag{4.1}$$

for all subsets H, L of S. Since $H, L \subseteq H \cup L$, we have $\mathbf{K}(H) \subseteq \mathbf{K}(H \cup L)$ and $\mathbf{K}(L) \subseteq \mathbf{K}(H \cup L)$ due to the monotonicity of $\mathbf{K}$. Therefore,

$$\mathbf{K}(H) \cup \mathbf{K}(L) \subseteq \mathbf{K}(H \cup L).$$

To prove the reverse inclusion, note that the set $\mathbf{K}(H) \cup \mathbf{K}(L)$ is a closed set by the third part of Theorem 4.2 and $H \cup L \subseteq \mathbf{K}(H) \cup \mathbf{K}(L)$. Therefore, the closure of $H \cup L$ is a subset of $\mathbf{K}(H) \cup \mathbf{K}(L)$, so $\mathbf{K}(H \cup L) \subseteq \mathbf{K}(H) \cup \mathbf{K}(L)$, which implies equality (4.1).

Also, note that $\mathbf{K}(\emptyset) = \emptyset$ because the empty set itself is closed.

Note that equality (4.1) is satisfied for every $H, L \in \mathcal{P}(S)$ if and only if the union of two $\mathbf{K}$-closed sets is $\mathbf{K}$-closed. Indeed, suppose that equality (4.1) is satisfied, and let U and V be two $\mathbf{K}$-closed sets. Since $U = \mathbf{K}(U)$ and $V = \mathbf{K}(V)$, it follows that $U \cup V = \mathbf{K}(U) \cup \mathbf{K}(V) = \mathbf{K}(U \cup V)$, which shows that $U \cup V$ is $\mathbf{K}$-closed. Conversely, suppose that the union of two $\mathbf{K}$-closed sets is $\mathbf{K}$-closed. Then, $\mathbf{K}(U) \cup \mathbf{K}(V)$ is $\mathbf{K}$-closed and contains

$U \cup V$. Therefore, $\mathbf{K}(U \cup V) \subseteq \mathbf{K}(U) \cup \mathbf{K}(V)$. The reverse equality follows from the monotonicity of $\mathbf{K}$.

Theorem 4.5. *Let S be a set and let $\mathbf{K} : \mathcal{P}(S) \longrightarrow \mathcal{P}(S)$ be a closure operator that satisfies equality (4.1) for every $H, L \in \mathcal{P}(S)$ and $\mathbf{K}(\emptyset) = \emptyset$. The collection $\mathcal{O}_{\mathbf{K}} = \{S - U \mid U \in \mathcal{C}_{\mathbf{K}}\}$ is a topology on S.*

Proof. We have $\mathbf{K}(S) = S$, so both $\emptyset$ and S are $\mathbf{K}$-closed sets, which implies $\emptyset, S \in \mathcal{O}_{\mathbf{K}}$.

Suppose that $\mathcal{C} = \{L_i \mid i \in I\} \subseteq \mathcal{O}_{\mathbf{K}}$. Since $S - L_i \in \mathcal{C}_{\mathbf{K}}$, it follows that $\bigcap\{S - L_i \mid i \in I\} = S - \bigcup_{i \in I} L_i \in \mathcal{C}_{\mathbf{K}}$. Thus, $\bigcup_{i \in I} L_i \in \mathcal{O}_{\mathbf{K}}$.

Finally, suppose that $\mathcal{D} = \{D_1, \ldots, D_n\}$ is a finite collection of subsets such that $\mathcal{D} \subseteq \mathcal{O}_{\mathbf{K}}$. Since $S - D_i \in \mathcal{C}_{\mathbf{K}}$ we have $S - \bigcup_{i=1}^{n} D_i = \bigcap_{i=1}^{n}(S - D_i) \in \mathcal{C}_{\mathbf{K}}$, hence $\bigcup_{i=1}^{n} D_i \in \mathcal{O}_{\mathbf{K}}$. This proves that $\mathcal{O}_{\mathbf{K}}$ is indeed a topology. $\qquad\square$

Definition 4.5. Let $(S, \mathcal{O})$ be a topological space, U be a subset of S and let $x \in S$; x is an *adherent* point of a set to U if $x \in \mathbf{K}(U)$.

Clearly, every member of U is adherent to U; the converse is false.

Theorem 4.6. *Let $(S, \mathcal{O})$ be a topological space and let U and W be two subsets of S. If U is open and $U \cap W = \emptyset$, then $U \cap \mathbf{K}(W) = \emptyset$.*

Proof. $U \cap W = \emptyset$ implies $W \subseteq S - U$. Since U is open, the set $S - U$ is closed, so $\mathbf{K}(W) \subseteq \mathbf{K}(S - U) = S - U$. Therefore, $U \cap \mathbf{K}(W) = \emptyset$. $\quad\square$

Often, we use the contrapositive of this statement: if U is an open set such that $U \cap \mathbf{K}(W) \neq \emptyset$ for some set W, then $U \cap W \neq \emptyset$.

Corollary 4.1. *Let $(S, \mathcal{O})$ be a topological space and let $T \subseteq S$. Denote by $\mathbf{K}_S$ and $\mathbf{K}_T$ the closure operators of $(S, \mathcal{O})$ and $(T, \mathcal{O} \upharpoonright_T)$, respectively. For every subset W of T, we have $\mathbf{K}_T(W) = \mathbf{K}_S(W) \cap T$.*

Proof. The set $\mathbf{K}_S(W)$ is closed in S, so $\mathbf{K}_S(W) \cap T$ is closed in T by Theorem 4.4. Since $W \subseteq \mathbf{K}_S(W) \cap T$, it follows that $\mathbf{K}_T(W) \subseteq \mathbf{K}_S(W) \cap T$.

To prove the converse inclusion, observe that we can write $\mathbf{K}_T(W) = T \cap H$, where H is a closed set in S because $\mathbf{K}_T(W)$ is a closed set in T. Since $W \subseteq H$, it follows that $\mathbf{K}_S(W) \subseteq H$, so $\mathbf{K}_S(W) \cap T \subseteq H \cap T = \mathbf{K}_T(W)$. $\qquad\square$

Corollary 4.2. *Let $(S, \mathcal{O})$ be a topological space and let $T \subseteq S$. If $U \subseteq S$, then $\mathbf{K}_T(U \cap T) \subseteq \mathbf{K}_S(U) \cap T$.*

Proof. By applying Corollary 4.1 to the subset $U \cap T$ of T we have $\mathbf{K}_T(U \cap T) = \mathbf{K}_S(U \cap T) \cap T$. The needed inclusion follows from the monotonicity of $\mathbf{K}_S$. $\square$

Definition 4.6. A set U is *dense* in a topological space $(S, \mathcal{O})$ if $\mathbf{K}(U) = S$.

A topological space is *separable* if there exists a countable set U that is dense in $(S, \mathcal{O})$.

Theorem 4.7. *If T is a subspace of a separable topological space $(S, \mathcal{O})$, then T itself is separable.*

Proof. Since S is separable, there exists a countable set U such that $\mathbf{K}_S(U) = S$. On the other hand, $\mathbf{K}_T(U \cap T) = \mathbf{K}_S(U \cap T) \cap T \subseteq \mathbf{K}_S(U) \cap T = S \cap T = T$, which implies that the countable set $U \cap T$ is dense in T. Thus, T is separable. $\square$

Theorem 4.8. *If T is a separable subspace of a topological space $(S, \mathcal{O})$, then so is $\mathbf{K}(T)$.*

Proof. Let U be a countable subset of T that is dense in T, that is, $\mathbf{K}_T(U) = T$. We need to prove that $\mathbf{K}_{\mathbf{K}_S(T)}(U) = \mathbf{K}_S(T)$ to prove that U is dense in $\mathbf{K}_S(T)$ also.

By Corollary 4.1, we have

$$\mathbf{K}_{\mathbf{K}_S(T)}(U) = \mathbf{K}_S(U) \cap \mathbf{K}_S(T) = \mathbf{K}_S(U)$$

due to the monotonicity of $\mathbf{K}_S$.

Note that $T = \mathbf{K}_T(U) = \mathbf{K}_S(U) \cap T$, so $T \subseteq \mathbf{K}_S(U)$, which implies $\mathbf{K}_S(T) \subseteq \mathbf{K}_S(U)$. Since $\mathbf{K}_S$ is monotonic, we have the reverse inclusion $\mathbf{K}_S(U) \subseteq \mathbf{K}_S(T)$, so $\mathbf{K}_S(U) = \mathbf{K}_S(T)$. This allows us to conclude that $\mathbf{K}_{\mathbf{K}_S(T)}(U) = \mathbf{K}_S(T)$, so U is dense in $\mathbf{K}_S(T)$. $\square$

Theorem 4.9. *Let $(S, \mathcal{O})$ be a topological space. The set U is dense in $(S, \mathcal{O})$ if and only if $U \cap L \neq \emptyset$ for every non-empty open set L.*

Proof. Suppose that U is dense, so $\mathbf{K}(U) = S$. Since $\mathbf{K}(U \cap L) = \mathbf{K}(U) \cap \mathbf{K}(L) = S \cap \mathbf{K}(L) = \mathbf{K}(L)$, $U \cap L = \emptyset$ would imply $\mathbf{K}(L) = \mathbf{K}(\emptyset) = \emptyset$, which is a contradiction because $\emptyset \neq L \subseteq \mathbf{K}(L)$.

Conversely, suppose that U has a non-empty intersection with every non-empty open set L. Since $\mathbf{K}(U)$ is closed, $S - \mathbf{K}(U)$ is open. Observe that $U \cap (S - \mathbf{K}(U)) = \emptyset$, so the open set $S - \mathbf{K}(U)$ must be empty. Therefore, we have $\mathbf{K}(U) = S$. $\square$

Since $\emptyset$ is an open set in any topological space $(S, \mathcal{O})$ and any union of open sets is an open set, it follows that the topology itself is an interior system on S. In addition, an interior system of open sets is closed to finite intersection. Definition 4.7 which follows is a restatement of the definition of the interior operator associated to an interior system contained by Theorem 1.31.

Definition 4.7. Let $(S, \mathcal{O})$ be a topological space. The *interior* of a set U, $U \subseteq S$, is the set $\mathbf{I}(U) = \bigcup \{L \in \mathcal{O} \mid L \subseteq U\}$.

The interior $\mathbf{I}(U)$ of a set U is the largest open set included in U, because the union of any collection of open sets is an open set. Furthermore, a set is open in a topological space if and only if it equals its interior.

Theorem 4.10. *Let $(S, \mathcal{O})$ be a topological space and let U be a subset of S. We have*
$$\mathbf{K}(\overline{U}) = \overline{\mathbf{I}(U)} \text{ and } \overline{\mathbf{K}(U)} = \mathbf{I}(\overline{U}).$$

Proof. Since $\mathbf{I}(U)$ is an open set, the set $\overline{\mathbf{I}(U)}$ is closed. Note that $\overline{U} \subseteq \overline{\mathbf{I}(U)}$. Therefore, $\mathbf{K}(\overline{U}) \subseteq \overline{\mathbf{I}(U)}$.

Conversely, the inclusion $\overline{U} \subseteq \mathbf{K}(\overline{U})$ implies $\overline{\mathbf{K}(\overline{U})} \subseteq U$. Since $S - \mathbf{K}(\overline{U})$ is an open set included in U and $\mathbf{I}(U)$ is the largest such set, it follows that $S - \mathbf{K}(\overline{U}) \subseteq \mathbf{I}(U)$, which implies $\overline{\mathbf{I}(U)} \subseteq \mathbf{K}(\overline{U})$.

The second equality follows from the first equality by replacing U by its complement $\overline{U}$. $\square$

Corollary 4.3. *For every subset U of a topological space $(S, \mathcal{O})$, we have*
$$\mathbf{I}(U) = \overline{\mathbf{K}(\overline{U})} \text{ and } \mathbf{K}(U) = \overline{\mathbf{I}(\overline{U})}.$$

Proof. Both equalities follow immediately from Theorem 4.10. $\square$

An interior operator generated by a topological space $(S, \mathcal{O})$ can be defined axiomatically, as a mapping $\mathbf{I} : \mathcal{P}(S) \longrightarrow \mathcal{P}(S)$ that satisfies the conditions of Definition 1.40 and the additional condition:
$$\mathbf{I}(U \cap V) = \mathbf{I}(U) \cap \mathbf{I}(V)$$
for $U, V \in \mathcal{P}(S)$.

Theorem 4.11. *The following statements are equivalent for a topological space $(S, \mathcal{O})$:*

(i) *every countable intersection of dense open sets is a dense set;*

(ii) *every countable union of closed sets that have an empty interior has an empty interior.*

Proof. (i) implies (ii): Suppose that $(S, \mathcal{O})$ is a topological space such that every countable intersection of dense open sets is a dense set.

Let $H_1, \ldots, H_n, \ldots$ be a sequence of closed sets with $\mathbf{I}(H_i) = \emptyset$ for $n \geqslant 1$. Then, for the open sets $L_i = S - H_i$, we have

$$\mathbf{K}(L_i) = \mathbf{K}(S - H_i) = S - \mathbf{I}(H_i) = S,$$

so every set L_i is dense. By (i), we have $\mathbf{K}(\bigcap_{i \geqslant 1} L_i) = S$, so

$$\mathbf{I}\left(\bigcup_{i \geqslant 1} H_i\right) = S - \mathbf{K}\left(S - \bigcup_{i \geqslant 1} H_i\right)$$

$$= S - \mathbf{K}\left(\bigcap_{i \geqslant 1}(S - H_i)\right) = S - \mathbf{K}\left(\bigcap_{i \geqslant 1} L_i\right) = \emptyset,$$

which shows that (ii) holds.

(ii) implies (i): Conversely, suppose that in $(S, \mathcal{O})$ every countable union of closed sets that have an empty interior has an empty interior.

Let $L_1, \ldots, L_n, \ldots$ be a countable collection of dense open sets. Since each of the sets L_i is dense we have $\mathbf{K}(L_i) = S$. Therefore, for the closed sets $H_i = S - L_i$ we have $\mathbf{I}(H_i) = S - \mathbf{K}(L_i) = \emptyset$ by Corollary 4.3, so each of the sets H_i has an empty interior. By (ii) we have $\mathbf{K}\left(\bigcup_{n=1}^{\infty} H_i\right) = \emptyset$, so

$$\mathbf{K}\left(\bigcap_{i \geqslant 1} L_i\right) = S - \mathbf{I}\left(S - \bigcap_{i \geqslant 1} L_i\right)$$

$$= S - \mathbf{I}\left(\bigcup_{i \geqslant 1}(S - L_i)\right) = S - \mathbf{I}\left(\bigcup_{i \geqslant 1} H_i\right) = S,$$

which shows that (i) holds. $\qquad\square$

Definition 4.8. A *Baire*[1] *space* is a topological space $(S, \mathcal{O})$ that satisfies one of the equivalent conditions of Theorem 4.11.

Theorem 4.12. *Every open subspace of a Baire space $(S, \mathcal{O})$ is a Baire space.*

---

[1] René-Louis Baire was born on January 21st in Paris and died on July 5th 1932 in Chambery. He was a French mathematician who made important contributions to real analysis. Baire taught at the Universities of Montpellier and at the Faculty of Science in Dijon.

Proof. Let U be an open set in $(S, \mathcal{O})$ and let $\{H_n \mid n \geqslant 1\}$ be a collection of closed sets in U that have empty interiors.

By Theorem 4.4, for each set H_n there is a closed set $\tilde{H}_n$ in S such that $H_n = U \cap \tilde{H}_n$.

If V is a non-empty open set in S contained in $\tilde{H}_n$, then $V \cap H_n \neq \emptyset$. Then, $V \cap U$ is a non-empty open set of U,

$$V \cap H_n = V \cap (U \cap \tilde{H}_n) = V \cap \tilde{H}_n = V,$$

so V is contained in H_n, which contradicts the assumption that H_n has a non-empty interior.

If $\bigcup_{n \geqslant 1} H_n$ contains a non-empty open subset W of U, then $\bigcup_{n \geqslant 1} \tilde{H}_n$ also contains W; W is open in S because it is open in U. Since each set $\tilde{H}_n$ has an empty interior in S, this contradicts the fact that S is a Baire space. $\qquad\square$

Definition 4.9. A subset U of a topological space $(S, \mathcal{O})$ is *nowhere dense* if its closure has an empty interior, that is, $\mathbf{I}(\mathbf{K}(U)) = \emptyset$.

A subset V of S is of *first category* it equals a countable union of nowhere dense sets; a subset is of *second category* if it is not of first category.

Note that U is nowhere dense in $(S, \mathcal{O})$ if and only if its closure $\mathbf{K}(U)$ has the same property.

Theorem 4.13. *The following statements are equivalent:*
  (i) *U is nowhere dense in $(S, \mathcal{O})$;*
  (ii) *$\overline{\mathbf{I}(\mathbf{K}(U))} = S$;*
  (iii) *$\mathbf{K}(\overline{\mathbf{K}(U)}) = S$;*
  (iv) *$\mathbf{I}(\overline{U})$ is dense in S.*

Proof. The equivalence of these statements is an immediate consequence of the definitions. $\qquad\square$

We add now two further characterizations of Baire spaces.

Theorem 4.14. *For a topological space $(S, \mathcal{O})$ the following are equivalent:*
  (i) *$(S, \mathcal{O})$ is a Baire space;*
  (ii) *if $S = \bigcup_{n \geqslant 1} T_n$ and each T_n is closed, then the open set $\bigcup_{n \geqslant 1} \mathbf{I}(T_n)$ is dense in S;*
  (iii) *non-empty open sets are not of first category.*

Proof. (i) implies (ii): Let (T_n) be a sequence of closed sets with $S = \bigcup_{n \geqslant 1} T_n$ and let G be the open set, $G = \bigcup_{n \geqslant 1} \mathbf{I}(T_n)$. For each n

let $V_n = T_n - \mathbf{I}(T_n)$. Note that V_n is a closed set and, furthermore, V_n is nowhere dense. This implies that $V = \bigcup_{n \geqslant 1} V_n$ is nowhere dense.

Since V_n is closed and nowhere dense, each $\overline{V_n}$ is an open dense set. By (i), $\overline{V} = \bigcap_{n \geqslant 1} \overline{V_n}$ is also dense. Note that

$$\overline{G} = \bigcup_{n \geqslant 1} T_n - \bigcup_{n \geqslant 1} \mathbf{I}(T_n) \subseteq \bigcup_{n \geqslant 1} (T_n - \mathbf{I}(T_n)) = V,$$

so $\overline{V} \subseteq G$. Since $\overline{V}$ is dense, so is G.

(ii) implies (iii): Let G be a non-empty open set. Suppose that G is of first category, that is G can be written as a countable union $G = \bigcup_{n \geqslant 1} A_n$, where $\mathbf{I}(\mathbf{K}(A_n)) = \emptyset$. Then $S = \overline{G} \cup \mathbf{K}(A_1) \cup \cdots \cup \mathbf{K}(A_n) \cup \cdots$ is a union of closed sets, so by (ii) the open set

$$\mathbf{I}(\overline{G}) \cup \mathbf{I}(\mathbf{K}(A_1)) \cup \mathbf{I}(\mathbf{K}(A_2)) \cup \cdots = \mathbf{I}(\overline{(G)})$$

is dense in S. Since $\mathbf{I}(\overline{G}) \subseteq \overline{G}$ it follows that $\overline{G}$ is dense in S. This implies $G \cap \overline{G} \neq \emptyset$ which is impossible. Thus, G is not of first category.

(iii) implies (i): If G is an open dense set, then $\overline{G}$ is nowhere dense. Indeed, since $\overline{G}$ is closed it suffices to show that $\mathbf{I}(\overline{G}) = \emptyset$. Since $\mathbf{I}(\overline{G}) = \mathbf{K}(G)$, we have $\mathbf{I}(\overline{G}) = \emptyset$ because G is dense.

Assume that (G_n) is a sequence of open dense subsets of S. Let $A = \bigcap_{n \geqslant 1} G_n$ and assume that $A \cap U = \emptyset$ for some non-empty open set U. Since $S = \overline{A \cap U} = \overline{A} \cup \overline{U}$, we have

$$U = X \cap U = \overline{A} \cap U = \overline{\left(\bigcap_{n \geqslant 1} G_n \right)} \cap U = \bigcup_{n \geqslant 1} (\overline{G_n} \cap U).$$

This shows that U is a first category set, which is not the case. Therefore, A is dense in S. $\qquad\square$

Definition 4.10. Let $(S, \mathcal{O})$ be a topological space. The *boundary* of a set U, where $U \in \mathcal{P}(S)$, is the set $\partial_S U = \mathbf{K}(U) \cap \mathbf{K}(S - U)$.

If S is clear from the context, then we omit the subscript and denote the boundary of U just by ∂U.

The boundary of every set is a closed set as an intersection of two closed sets.

By Corollary 4.3 the boundary of a set can be expressed also in term of interiors:

$$\partial U = (S - \mathbf{I}(S - U)) \cap (S - \mathbf{I}(U)) = S - (\mathbf{I}(S - U) \cup \mathbf{I}(U)). \qquad (4.2)$$

Note that for every set $U \subseteq S$, where $(S, \mathcal{O})$ is a topological space we have $S - \mathbf{K}(U) \subseteq S - U \subseteq \mathbf{K}(S - U)$. Therefore, we have

$$S - U \subseteq \mathbf{K}(S - U) = (S - \mathbf{K}(U)) \cup \partial U. \tag{4.3}$$

Theorem 4.15. *The boundary of a subset U of a topological space $(S, \mathcal{O})$ consists of those elements s of S such that for every open set L that contains s we have both $L \cap U \neq \emptyset$ and $L \cap (S - U) \neq \emptyset$.*

Proof. Let $x \in \partial U$ and let L be an open set such that $x \in L$. By equality(4.2), we have both $x \notin \mathbf{I}(S - U)$ and $x \notin \mathbf{I}(U)$. Therefore, $L \not\subseteq S - U$ and $L \not\subseteq U$, which imply $L \cap U \neq \emptyset$ and $L \cap (S - U) \neq \emptyset$.

Conversely, suppose that, for every open set L that contains s, we have both $L \cap U \neq \emptyset$ and $L \cap (S - U) \neq \emptyset$. This implies $x \notin \mathbf{I}(U)$ and $s \notin \mathbf{I}(S - U)$, so $x \in \partial U$ by equality (4.2). □

Theorem 4.16. *Let $(S, \mathcal{O})$ be a topological space, $(T, \mathcal{O} \restriction_T)$ be a subspace, and W be a subset of S. The boundary $\partial_T(W \cap T)$ of $W \cap T$ in the subspace T is a subset of the intersection $\partial_S(W) \cap T$, where $\partial_S(W)$ is the boundary of W in S.*

Proof. By Definition 4.10, we have

$$\begin{aligned}
\partial_T(W \cap T) &= \mathbf{K}_T(W \cap T) \cap \mathbf{K}_T(T - (W \cap T)) \\
&= \mathbf{K}_T(W \cap T) \cap \mathbf{K}_T(T - W) \\
&\subseteq (\mathbf{K}_S(W) \cap T) \cap \mathbf{K}_T(T - W)
\end{aligned}$$

(by Corollary 4.1).

Again, by Corollary 4.1, we have $\mathbf{K}_T(T - W) = \mathbf{K}_T(T \cap (S - W)) \subseteq \mathbf{K}_S(S - W) \cap T$, and this allows us to write

$$\partial_T(W \cap T) \subseteq (\mathbf{K}_S(W) \cap T) \cap \mathbf{K}_S(S - W) \cap T = \partial_S(W) \cap T,$$

which is the desired conclusion. □

The next statement relates three important sets that we defined for each subset U of a topological space $(S, \mathcal{O})$.

Theorem 4.17. *Let $(S, \mathcal{O})$ be a topological space. For every subset U of S, we have $\boldsymbol{K}(U) = \boldsymbol{I}(U) \cup \partial U$.*

Proof. By equality (4.2), we have $\partial U = (S - \mathbf{I}(S - U)) \cap (S - \mathbf{I}(U))$. Therefore,

$$\partial U \cup \mathbf{I}(U) = (S - \mathbf{I}(S - U)) \cap \mathbf{I}(U)$$

$$\text{(by Corollary 4.3)}$$

$$= \mathbf{K}(U) \cap \mathbf{I}(U)$$

$$\text{(because } \mathbf{I}(U) \subseteq \mathbf{K}(U)\text{)}$$

$$= \mathbf{K}(U).$$

$\square$

Corollary 4.4. *Let* $(S, \mathcal{O})$ *be a topological space and let* $(T, \mathcal{O} \restriction_T)$ *be a subspace of* $(S, \mathcal{O})$. *For any subset* U *of* S, *we have* $\partial_T(U \cap T) \subseteq \partial_S(U)$.

Proof. Let $t \in \partial_T(U \cap T)$. By Theorem 4.15, for every open set $L \in \mathcal{O} \restriction_T$ such that $t \in L$ we have both $L \cap (U \cap T) \neq \emptyset$ and $L \cap (T - (U \cap T)) \neq \emptyset$.

If L_1 is an open set of $(S, \mathcal{O})$ that contains S, then $L_1 \cap T$ is an open set of $(T, \mathcal{O} \restriction_T)$ that contains t, so for L_1 we have both $(L_1 \cap T) \cap (U \cap T) \neq \emptyset$ and $(L_1 \cap T) \cap (T - (U \cap T)) \neq \emptyset$. This immediately implies $L_1 \cap U \neq \emptyset$ and $L_1 \cap (S - U) \neq \emptyset$, that is, $t \in \partial_S(U)$. $\square$

By applying the notations introduced in Section 1.4 we have $\mathcal{O}_\sigma = \mathcal{O}$ and $closed(\mathcal{O})_\delta = closed(\mathcal{O})$. It is clear that $\mathcal{O}_\delta$ is the collection that consists of all countable intersections of open sets and $closed(\mathcal{O})_\sigma$ is the collection that consists of all countable unions of closed sets.

Note that $\mathbb{Q} \in closed(\mathcal{O})_\sigma$, because $\mathbb{Q}$ is the countable union $\mathbb{Q} = \bigcup\{\{x\} \mid x \in qq\}$, and each set $\{x\}$ is closed in $(\mathbb{R}, \mathcal{O})$.

4.4   Neighborhoods

Definition 4.11. Let $(S, \mathcal{O})$ be a topological space. A subset U of S is a *neighborhood* of $x \in S$ if there exists an open set T such that $x \in T \subseteq U$.

The *collection of neighborhoods* of an element x of S is denoted by $neigh_x(\mathcal{O})$.

Equivalently, a subset U of $(S, \mathcal{O})$ is a neighborhood of $x \in S$ if $x \in \mathbf{I}(U)$.

Example 4.8. Let $(\mathbb{R}, \mathcal{O})$ be the topological space introduced in Example 4.2. A neighborhood of $x \in \mathbb{R}$ is a set U such that there exists $\epsilon > 0$ such that $B(x, \epsilon) \subseteq U$.

Indeed, if $U \in neigh_{\mathbb{O}}(x)$, then there is an open set T such that $x \in T \subseteq U$. Since T is an open set and $x \in T$, there exists $\epsilon > 0$ such that $B(x, \epsilon) \subseteq T \subseteq U$, so $B(x, \epsilon) \subseteq U$.

Conversely, if there exists $\epsilon > 0$ such that $B(x, \epsilon) \subseteq U$, then $U \in neigh_x(\mathbb{O})$ because $B(x, \epsilon)$ is an open set that contains x and is included in U.

Theorem 4.18. *Let $(S, \mathbb{O})$ be a topological space. A subset L of S is open if and only if L is a neighborhood of all its points.*

Proof. If L is open, it is immediate that L is a neighborhood of all its points.

Conversely, suppose that L is a neighborhood of all its members. Then, for each $x \in L$ there exists $W_x \in \mathbb{O}$ such that $x \in W_x \subseteq L$. Therefore,

$$L = \bigcup_{x \in L} \{x\} \subseteq \bigcup_{x \in L} W_x \subseteq L,$$

which implies $L = \bigcup_{x \in L} W_x$. This in turn implies $L \in \mathbb{O}$. $\square$

In other words, $L \in \mathbb{O}$ if and only if $L \in \bigcap_{x \in L} neigh_x(\mathbb{O})$. Thus, if $U \in neigh_x(\mathbb{O})$ there exists always an open neighborhood T of x such that $x \in T \subseteq U$.

Theorem 4.19. *Let $(S, \mathbb{O})$ be a topological space. A subset T of S is closed if and only for each $x \in T$ and $V \in neigh_x(\mathbb{O})$ we have $V \cap T \neq \emptyset$.*

Proof. Let T be a closed subset of S and let $x \in T$. The set $S - T$ is open. If V is a neighborhood of x then $V \cap T \neq \emptyset$ because, otherwise, we would have $x \in V \subseteq S - T$, which is a contradiction.

Conversely, suppose that for each $x \in T$ and $V \in neigh_x(\mathbb{O})$ we have $V \cap T \neq \emptyset$. We claim that in this case the set $S - T$ is open. Indeed, let $y \in S - T$. Since $y \notin T$ there exists $W \in neigh_y(\mathbb{O})$ such that $W \cap T = \emptyset$, which is equivalent to $W \subseteq S - T$. Therefore, $S - T$ is a neighborhood of y, so $S - T$ is open by Theorem 4.18, which means that T is closed. $\square$

Corollary 4.5. *Let $\mathbb{O}, \mathbb{O}'$ be two topologies on a set S. The topology $\mathbb{O}'$ is finer than $\mathbb{O}$ if and only if $neigh_x(\mathbb{O}) \subseteq neigh_x(\mathbb{O}')$ for every $x \in S$.*

Proof. This is an immediate consequence of Theorem 4.18. $\square$

Theorem 4.20. *The following statements hold for any topological space $(S, \mathbb{O})$ and $x \in S$:*

    (i) *there exists at least one set in $neigh_x(\mathbb{O})$ for every $x \in S$;*

    (ii) *we have $x \in W$ for every $W \in neigh_x(\mathbb{O})$;*

(iii) *if $U, V \in neigh_x(\mathcal{O})$, then $U \cap V \in neigh_x(\mathcal{O})$;*

(iv) *if $U \in neigh_x(\mathcal{O})$ and $U \subseteq W \subseteq S$, then $W \in neigh_x(\mathcal{O})$;*

(v) *each set $W \in neigh_x(\mathcal{O})$ contains a subset $U \in neigh_x(\mathcal{O})$ such that $U \in neigh_y(\mathcal{O})$ for each $y \in U$.*

Proof.   Part (i) follows from the fact that $S \in neigh_x(\mathcal{O})$ for each $x \in S$. If $U \in neigh_x(\mathcal{O})$ there is $W \in \mathcal{O}$ such that $x \in W \subseteq U$, so $x \in U$, and we obtain part (ii).

The proofs of parts (iii) and (iv) are left to the reader.

For part (v) let $x \in S$ and let $W \in neigh_x(\mathcal{O})$. There exists an open set T such that $x \in T \subseteq W$. Since T is a neighborhood for each of its members, part (v) follows.   □

An alternative technique for introducing topologies starts with families of sets that satisfy characteristic properties of collections of neighborhoods.

Theorem 4.21. *Let S be a set such that for each $x \in S$ there exists a collection $\mathcal{N}_x$ of subsets of S with the following properties:*

(i) *there exists at least one set U in $\mathcal{N}_x$ for every $x \in S$;*

(ii) *we have $x \in W$ for every $W \in \mathcal{N}_x$;*

(iii) *if $U, V \in \mathcal{N}_x$, then $U \cap V \in \mathcal{N}_x$;*

(iv) *if $U \in \mathcal{N}_x$ and $U \subseteq W \subseteq S$, then $W \in \mathcal{N}_x$;*

(v) *each set $W \in \mathcal{N}_x$ contains a subset $U \in \mathcal{N}_x$ such that $U \in \bigcap_{y \in U} \mathcal{N}_y$.*

There exists a unique topology $\mathcal{O}$ on S such that for each $x \in S$, $neigh_x(\mathcal{O}) = \mathcal{N}_x$. A subset L is open if and only if $L \in \mathcal{N}_x$ for each $x \in L$.

Proof.   Define the family of sets

$$\mathcal{O} = \{L \mid L \subseteq S, L \in \mathcal{N}_x \text{ for each } x \in L\}.$$

It is immediate that $\emptyset \in \mathcal{O}$.

Let $x \in S$. By (i) and (ii) there exists $U \in \mathcal{N}_x$ such that $x \in U \subseteq S$ and by (iv), $S \in \mathcal{N}_x$, so $S \in \mathcal{O}$.

Let $\{V_i \mid i \in I\}$ be a family of sets that belong to $\mathcal{O}$ and let $V = \bigcup_{i \in I} V_i$. If $x \in V$, there exists $V_i \in \mathcal{N}_x$ such that $x \in V_i \subseteq V$. By (iv) $V \in \mathcal{N}_x$ and, since this holds for every $x \in V$, we have $V \in \mathcal{O}$.

If V and W are two subsets of S that belong to $\mathcal{O}$, we need to show that for each $x \in V \cap W$ we have $V \cap W \in \mathcal{N}_x$. Note that if $x \in V \cap W$, then $V \in \mathcal{N}_x$ and $W \in \mathcal{N}_x$, so $V \cap W \in \mathcal{N}_x$ by (iii), which implies $V \cap W \in \mathcal{O}$. We conclude that $\mathcal{O}$ is a topology.

We claim that $neigh_x(\mathcal{O}) = \mathcal{N}_x$ for each $x \in S$. Indeed, if U is a neighborhood of x relative to the topology $\mathcal{O}$, there exists an open set $L \in \mathcal{O}$ such that $x \in L \subseteq U$. By the definition of $\mathcal{O}$, $L \in \mathcal{N}_x$, which yields $U \in \mathcal{N}_x$ by (iv). Thus, $neigh_x(\mathcal{O}) \subseteq \mathcal{N}_x$ for each $x \in S$.

Conversely, let $V \in \mathcal{N}_x$. By (v), there is a set $U \in neigh_x(\mathcal{O})$ such that $U \subseteq V$ and $U \in \mathcal{N}_y$ for every $y \in U$. By the definition of $\mathcal{O}$ we have $U \in \mathcal{O}$, so $V \in neigh_x(\mathcal{O})$. This shows that $neigh_x(\mathcal{O}) = \mathcal{N}_x$ for each $x \in S$.

Theorem 4.18 implies the uniqueness of the topology $\mathcal{O}$. □

Example 4.9. Let $\hat{\mathbb{R}} = \mathbb{R} \cup \{-\infty, \infty\}$ be the extended set of real numbers. A neighborhood of ∞ in $\hat{\mathbb{R}}$ is defined as a subset of $\hat{\mathbb{R}}$ that includes a set $(a, \infty]$, where $a \in \mathbb{R}$; similarly, a neighborhood of $-\infty$ in $\hat{\mathbb{R}}$ is a set that includes a set of the form $[-\infty, b)$ for some $b \in \mathbb{R}$. The collection of neighborhoods of ∞ and $-\infty$ are denoted by $\mathcal{N}_\infty$ and $\mathcal{N}_{-\infty}$, respectively.

We claim that the collection $\bigcup_{a \in \mathbb{R}} \mathcal{N}_a \cup \mathcal{N}_\infty \cup \mathcal{N}_{-\infty}$ satisfies the conditions of Theorem 4.21, and thus is defining a unique topology on $\hat{\mathbb{R}}$.

Suppose that $U, V \in \mathcal{N}_\infty$. Then, $(a, \infty] \subseteq$, $(b, \infty] \subseteq V$ for some $a, b \in \mathbb{R}$ and $(\max\{a, b\}, \infty] \subseteq U \cap V$, hence $U \cap V \in \mathcal{N}_\infty$. Similarly, if $U, V \in \mathcal{N}_{-\infty}$, then $U \cap V \in \mathcal{N}_{-\infty}$.

If $U \in \mathcal{N}_\infty$ and $U \subseteq W \subseteq \hat{\mathbb{R}}$ it is immediate that $W \in \mathcal{N}_{-\infty}$; a similar property holds for $\mathcal{N}_{-\infty}$.

Let now W be a set in $\mathcal{N}_\infty$, so there exists $a \in \mathbb{R}$ such that $(a, \infty] \subseteq W$. The role of the set U of the fifth condition of Theorem 4.21 is played by the open set $U = (a, \infty)$. A similar argument works for $W \in \mathcal{N}_{-\infty}$. The topology defined in Theorem 4.21 is the usual topology for $\hat{\mathbb{R}}$.

Note that the set $\mathbb{R}$ is an open set in the topology introduced on $\hat{\mathbb{R}}$. Furthermore, if $T \subseteq \hat{\mathbb{R}}$ is an open in $\hat{\mathbb{R}}$, then $T \cap \mathbb{R}$ is open in $\mathbb{R}$, so the usual topology on $\mathbb{R}$ is the trace of the topology defined on $\hat{\mathbb{R}}$.

Theorem 4.22. *The boundary ∂U of a subset U of a topological space $(S, \mathcal{O})$ consists of those elements x of S such that for every $V \in neigh_s(\mathcal{O})$ that contains x we have both $V \cap U \neq \emptyset$ and $V \cap (S - U) \neq \emptyset$.*

Proof. By Theorem 4.15, $x \in \partial T$ if and only if we have both $L \cap U \neq \emptyset$ and $L \cap (S - U) \neq \emptyset$ for every open set that contains x.

These conditions are equivalent to $V \cap U \neq \emptyset$ and $V \cap (S - U) \neq \emptyset$ for each neighborhood $V \in neigh_x(\mathcal{O})$ because every open set that contains x is a neighborhood of x, and every neighborhood of x contains an open set that contains x. □

Theorem 4.23. *Let $(S, \mathcal{O})$ be a topological space. For every subset U of S the following statements hold:*

(i) $\partial U = \partial(S - U)$;

(ii) $U \in \mathcal{O}$ *if and only if* $\partial U \subseteq S - U$;

(iii) U *is closed if and only if* $\partial U \subseteq U$.

Proof. Definition 4.10, $\partial U = \mathbf{K}(U) \cap \mathbf{K}(S - U)$ implies immediately (i).

For part (ii), if $U \in \mathcal{O}$, $S - U$ is a closed set, so $S - U = \mathbf{K}(S - U)$, which implies $\partial U = \mathbf{K}(U) \cap \mathbf{K}(S - U) \subseteq S - U$.

Conversely, suppose $\partial U \subseteq S - U$ and let $x \in U$, so $x \notin S - U$. Thus, $x \notin \partial U$, which means that there exists $V \in neigh_x(\mathcal{O})$ that does not intersect both U and $S - U$. Since V intersects U, it follows that V does not intersect $S - U$, that is, $V \subseteq U$. Therefore, U is open.

Finally, U is closed, if and only if $S - U$ is open. By part (ii), this is equivalent to $\partial(S - U) \subseteq U$, which by part (i) means that $\partial U \subseteq U$. $\square$

Theorem 4.24. *Let $(S, \mathcal{O})$ be a topological space and let $x \in S$. We have $x \in \mathbf{K}(T)$ if and only if $V \cap T \neq \emptyset$ for every $V \in neigh_x(\mathcal{O})$.*

Proof. Suppose that $x \in \mathbf{K}(T)$. If $x \in \mathbf{I}(T)$, then $x \in T$, so the intersection of every $V \in neigh_x(\mathcal{O})$ with T contains at least x, so it is non-empty.

If $x \in \partial T$, then each $V \in neigh_x(\mathcal{O})$ has a non-empty intersection with both T and $S - T$.

Conversely, suppose that every $V \in neigh_x(\mathcal{O})$ has a non-intersection with T. If some neighborhood is contained in T, then $x \in \mathbf{I}(T) \subseteq \mathbf{K}(T)$. Otherwise, we have $V \cap T \neq \emptyset$ and $V \cap (S - T) \neq \emptyset$, so $x \in \partial T \subseteq \mathbf{K}(T)$. $\square$

Definition 4.12. Let $(S, \mathcal{O})$ be a topological space and let $x \in S$. A family of neighborhoods $\mathcal{L}_x(\mathcal{O})$ of x is a *local basis* (or a *neighborhood basis* at x) if for every neighborhood $V \in neigh_x(\mathcal{O})$ there exists a $L \in \mathcal{L}_x(\mathcal{O})$ such that $x \in L \subseteq V$.

Clearly, $neigh_x(\mathcal{O})$ itself is a local basis at x.

Some authors use the term *fundamental system* of neighborhoods instead of local basis.

Example 4.10. For the set of reals equipped with the usual topology $(\mathbb{R}, \mathcal{O})$ the collection of open intervals $\{(x - 1/n, x + 1/n) \mid n \geqslant 1\}$ is a local basis at x.

In Theorem 4.19 we characterized the points of the closure of a subset T of a topological space $(S, \mathcal{O})$ as those points of S such that each of their neighborhoods has a non-empty intersection with T. Next, we introduce a class of points that satisfy a more stringent condition.

Definition 4.13. Let $(S, \mathcal{O})$ be a topological space and let T be a subset of S.

An element t of S is an *accumulation point*, or a *cluster point*, or a *limit point* of T if, for every $V \in neigh_t(\mathcal{O})$ the set $(T - \{t\}) \cap V$ is not empty.

The set of all accumulation points of a set T is the *derived set* of T and is denoted by T'.

A element u is an *isolated point* of T if there exists $V \in neigh_u(\mathcal{O})$ the set $T \cap V = \{u\}$.

Clearly, any accumulation point of a set T belongs to $\mathbf{K}(T)$. Also, if t is an accumulation point of a set T, then it is also an accumulation point for any set that contains T. In other words, $T_1 \subseteq T_2$ implies $T_1 \subseteq T_2$ for $T_1, T_2 \subseteq S$.

Theorem 4.25. *T is closed if and only if $T' \subseteq T$.*

Proof. T is closed if and only if $S - T$ is open, which is equivalent to saying that each point $x \in S - T$ has a neighborhood W_x included in $S - T$, or equivalently, $W_x \cap T = \emptyset$. Thus, T is closed if and only if for $x \in S$, if every $V \in neigh_x(\mathcal{O})$ has a non-empty intersection with T, then $x \in T$. In other words, every accumulation point of T belongs to T, that is, $T' \subseteq T$. $\square$

Theorem 4.26. *Let $(S, \mathcal{O})$ be a topological space and let T be a subset of S. The set $T \cup T'$ is closed.*

Proof. Let $x \in T \cup T'$ and let $V \in neigh_x(\mathcal{O})$. If $x \in T$, then $x \in V \cap T$, so $V \cap (T \cup T') \neq \emptyset$. If $x \in T'$, then $(T - \{t\}) \cap V \neq \emptyset$ by the definition of accumulation points, so, again $V \cap (T \cup T') \neq \emptyset$. Thus, in either case $V \cap (T \cup T') \neq \emptyset$, which means that $T \cup T'$ is closed. $\square$

Theorem 4.27. *Let $(S, \mathcal{O})$ be a topological space and let T be a subset of S. We have $\mathbf{K}(T) = T \cup T'$.*

Proof. Since $T \cup T'$ is a closed set, it follows that $\mathbf{K}(T) \subseteq T \cup T'$. Conversely, if $x \in T \cup T'$ it follows that every neighborhood of x intersects T, so $x \in \mathbf{K}(T)$, which yields the desired equality. $\square$

4.5   Bases

Definition 4.14. Let $(S, \mathcal{O})$ be a topological space. A collection $\mathcal{B}$ of open sets is a *basis* for $(S, \mathcal{O})$ if every open set is a union of a subcollection of $\mathcal{B}$.

Example 4.11. By Theorem 4.1 a subset U of $\mathbb{R}$ is open in the topological space $(\mathbb{R}, \mathcal{O})$ if and only if it equals the union of a countable collection of disjoint open intervals. This shows that the collection of open intervals is a basis for the $(\mathbb{R}, \mathcal{O})$.

If $\mathcal{B}$ is a basis for $(S, \mathcal{O})$ and T is a subset of S, then the trace $\mathcal{B}_T$ is a basis for the subspace $(T, \mathcal{O}_T)$.

Theorem 4.28. *If $\mathcal{B}$ is a basis for the topological space $(S, \mathcal{O})$, then $\bigcup \mathcal{B} = S$ and for each two sets $B_1, B_2 \in \mathcal{B}$ and each $x \in B_1 \cap B_2$ there exists a set $B \in \mathcal{B}$ such that $x \in B \subseteq B_1 \cap B_2$.*

Proof.   Since S is an open set, the definition of a basis implies $S = \bigcup \mathcal{B}$. Then, if $x \in B_1 \cap B_2$, taking into account that $B_1 \cap B_2$ is an open set, the last part of the theorem is immediate. $\square$

Theorem 4.29. *Let S be a set. A collection $\mathcal{B}$ of subsets of S such that*
   (i) $\bigcup \mathcal{B} = S$, *and*
   (ii) *for each two sets $B_1, B_2 \in \mathcal{B}$ and each $x \in B_1 \cap B_2$ there exists a set $B \in \mathcal{B}$ such that $x \in B \subseteq B_1 \cap B_2$*
is a basis for a topology on S.

Proof.   Let $\mathcal{O}$ be the collection of subsets of S that are unions of a sub-collections of $\mathcal{B}$. It is immediate that the union of any subcollection of $\mathcal{O}$ belongs to $\mathcal{O}$.

Let $U, V \in \mathcal{O}$. If $U \cap V = \emptyset$, then $U \cap V \in \mathcal{O}$ because $\emptyset$ is the union of the empty subcollection of $\mathcal{B}$. Suppose that $x \in U \cup V$. There exist $B_1, B_2 \in \mathcal{B}$ such that $x \in B_1 \subseteq U$ and $x \in B_2 \subseteq V$. By hypothesis, there exists a set B_x with $x \in B_x \subseteq B_1 \cap B_2 \subseteq U \cap V$. Then $\bigcup_{x \in U \cap V} B_x = U \cap V$, so $U \cap V \in \mathcal{O}$.

Now, an immediate argument by induction of n shows that if $U_1, \ldots, U_n \in \mathcal{O}$, then $\bigcap_{i=1}^{n} U_i \in \mathcal{O}$. $\square$

Example 4.12. Consider the collections of subsets of $\hat{\mathbb{R}}$ defined by
$$\mathcal{B} = \{(a, b) \mid -\infty \leqslant a < b \leqslant \infty\},$$
$$\mathcal{B}_{-\infty} = \{[-\infty, b) \mid b \in \mathbb{R}\},$$
$$\mathcal{B}_{\infty} = \{(a, \infty] \mid a \in \mathbb{R}\}.$$

By Theorem 4.29 the collection $\mathcal{B}$ is a basis for a topology on $\hat{\mathbb{R}}$. We refer to this topology as the *usual topology of the extended set of reals*. The restriction of this topology to $\mathbb{R}$ is the usual topology of reals as defined in Example 4.3. In other words, a set U is open in $\mathbb{R}$ if and only if U is open in $\hat{\mathbb{R}}$.

Let $\mathfrak{O} = \{\mathcal{O}_i \mid i \in I\}$ be a family of topologies defined on a set S that contains the discrete topology $\mathcal{P}(S)$. We claim that $\mathfrak{O}$ is a closure system on $\mathcal{P}(S)$. The first condition of Definition 1.34 is satisfied due to the definition of $\mathfrak{O}$. It is easy to verify that for every subfamily $\mathfrak{O}'$ of $\mathfrak{O}$, $\bigcap \mathfrak{O}'$ is a topology, so $\mathfrak{O}$ is indeed a closure system.

Thus, if $\mathcal{S}$ is a family of subsets of S, there exists the smallest topology that includes $\mathcal{S}$.

Theorem 4.30. *The topology $TOP(\mathcal{S})$ generated by a family $\mathcal{S}$ of subsets of S consists of unions of finite intersections of the members of $\mathcal{S}$.*

Proof. Let $\mathcal{E}$ be the collection of all unions of finite intersections of the members of $\mathcal{S}$. It is clear that $\mathcal{S} \subseteq \mathcal{E}$. We claim that $\mathcal{E}$ is a topology that contains $\mathcal{S}$.

Note that the intersection of the empty collection of sets in $\mathcal{S}$ is S, so $S \in \mathcal{E}$; also, the union of an empty collection of finite intersections is $\emptyset$, so $\emptyset \in \mathcal{E}$.

Every $U \in \mathcal{E}$ can be written as $U = \bigcup\{V_j \mid j \in J_U\}$, where the sets V_j are finite intersections of sets of $\mathcal{S}$. Therefore, it is immediate that any union of sets of this form belongs to $\mathcal{E}$.

Suppose that $\{U_i \mid i \in I\}$ is a finite collection of parts of S, where $U_i = \bigcup\{V_j \in \mathcal{S} \mid j \in J_i\}$ and that each V_j can be written as $V_j = \bigcap\{W_{jh} \in \mathcal{S} \mid h \in H_j\}$, where each set H_j is finite. One can prove by induction on $p = |I|$ that $\bigcap\{U_i \mid i \in I\} \in \mathcal{E}$. To simplify the presentation, we discuss here only the case where $|I| = 2$. So, if $U_i = \bigcup\{V_j \in \mathcal{S} \mid j \in J_i\}$ for $i = 1, 2$, we have

$$U_1 \cap U_2 = \bigcup\{V_{j_1} \in \mathcal{S} \mid j_1 \in J_1\} \cap \bigcup\{V_{j_2} \in \mathcal{S} \mid j_2 \in J_2\}$$
$$= \bigcap_{j_1, j_2} (V_{j_1} \cap V_{j_2}).$$

Since each intersection $V_{j_1} \cap V_{j_2}$ is in turn a finite intersection of sets of $\mathcal{S}$, it follows that $U_1 \cap U_2 \in \mathcal{S}$.

Thus, $TOP(\mathcal{S})$ is contained in $\mathcal{E}$ because $TOP(\mathcal{S})$ is the coarsest topology that contains $\mathcal{S}$. This gives the desired conclusion. $\square$

Corollary 4.6. *Let $\mathcal{B}$ be a collection of subsets of the set S such that for every finite subcollection $\mathcal{D}$ of $\mathcal{B}$, $x \in \bigcap \mathcal{D}$ implies the existence of a set $B \in \mathcal{B}$ such that $x \in B \subseteq \bigcap \mathcal{D}$. Then, $TOP(\mathcal{B})$, the topology generated by $\mathcal{B}$, consists of sets that are unions of subcollections of $\mathcal{B}$.*

Proof. By Theorem 4.30, $TOP(\mathcal{B})$ consists of unions of finite intersections of the members of $\mathcal{B}$. Therefore, unions of sets of $\mathcal{B}$ belong to $TOP(\mathcal{B})$.

Conversely, let $U \in \mathcal{B}$, that is, $U = \bigcup \{V_i \mid i \in I\}$, where each V_i is a finite intersection of members of $\mathcal{B}$. For every $x \in V_i$, there exists a set $B_{x,i} \in \mathcal{B}$ such that $x \in B_{x,i} \subseteq V_i$. Therefore, $V_i = \bigcup_{x \in V_i} B_{x,i}$, and this implies that U is indeed a union of sets from $\mathcal{B}$. □

Example 4.13. The collection of open intervals $\{(a,b) \mid a,b \in \mathbb{R} \text{ and } a < b\}$ is a basis for the topological space $(\mathbb{R}, \mathcal{O})$ by Theorem 4.1.

Definition 4.15. Let S be a set. A collection $\mathcal{S}$ of subsets of S is a *sub-basis* for a topology $\mathcal{O}$ if $\mathcal{O} = TOP(\mathcal{S})$.

Theorem 4.31. *The topology $\mathcal{O}$ generated by a sub-basis $\mathcal{S}$ has as a basis the collection $\mathcal{B}(\mathcal{S})$ of intersections of finite subcollections of sets in $\mathcal{S}$.*

Proof. Note that $S \in \mathcal{B}(\mathcal{S})$ as the intersection of the empty subcollection of sets of $\mathcal{S}$.

Let $B_1 = \bigcap \mathcal{S}_1$ and $B_2 = \bigcap \mathcal{S}_2$, where $\mathcal{S}_1, \mathcal{S}_2$ are two finite subcollections of sets in $\mathcal{S}$. If $x \in B_1 \cap B_2$, then x belongs to all sets in $\mathcal{S}_1 \cup \mathcal{S}_2$. Then, if B is the intersection of all sets in $\mathcal{S}_1$ and $\mathcal{S}_2$, we have $x \in B \subseteq B_1 \cap B_2$, so, by Theorem 4.29, $\mathcal{B}(\mathcal{S})$ is a basis of a topology $\mathcal{O}'$.

Since $\mathcal{S} \subseteq \mathcal{B}(\mathcal{S}) \subseteq \mathcal{O}'$, we have $\mathcal{O} \subseteq \mathcal{O}'$ because $\mathcal{O}$ is the smallest topology containing $\mathcal{S}$. Finally, if W is a set in $\mathcal{B}(\mathcal{S})$, since W is the intersection of a finite subcollection of $\mathcal{S}$ and $\mathcal{S} \subseteq \mathcal{O}$, we have $W \in \mathcal{O}$. Thus, $\mathcal{O}' \subseteq \mathcal{O}$. □

Example 4.14. The collection $\mathcal{S} = \{(a, +\infty) \mid a \in \mathbb{R}\} \cup \{(-\infty, b) \mid b \in \mathbb{R}\}$ is a sub-basis of the usual topology on $\mathbb{R}$ because every member (a, b) of the basis can be written as $(a, b) = (-\infty, b) \cap (a, +\infty)$.

Starting from a topology, we find a basis using the following theorem.

Theorem 4.32. *Let $(S, \mathcal{O})$ be a topological space. If $\mathcal{B}$ is a collection of open subsets of S such that for every $x \in S$ and every open set $L \in \mathcal{O}$ there exists a set $B \in \mathcal{B}$ such that $x \in B \subseteq L$, then $\mathcal{B}$ is a basis for $(S, \mathcal{O})$.*

Proof. This statement is an immediate consequence of Definition 4.15. □

Theorem 4.33. *Let $(S, \mathcal{O})$ be a topological space. The following statements involving a family $\mathcal{B}$ of subsets of S are equivalent:*

(i) *$\mathcal{B}$ is a basis for $(S, \mathcal{O})$;*

(ii) *for every $x \in S$ and $U \in neigh_x(\mathcal{O})$, there exists $B \in \mathcal{B}$ such that $x \in B \subseteq U$;*

(iii) *for every open set L, there is a subcollection $\mathcal{C}$ of $\mathcal{B}$ such that $L = \bigcup \mathcal{C}$.*

Proof. (i) implies (ii): Let $\mathcal{B}$ be a basis for $(S, \mathcal{O})$ and let $U \in neigh_x(\mathcal{O})$. There exists an open set L such that $x \in L \subseteq U$. Since $\mathcal{B}$ is a basis, there exists a set $B \in \mathcal{B}$ such that $x \in B \subseteq L \subseteq U$, which is what we aimed to prove.

(ii) implies (iii): Suppose that the second statement holds, and let L be an open set. Since L is a neighborhood for all its elements, for every $x \in L$ there exists $B_x \in \mathcal{B}$ such that $\{x\} \subseteq B_x \subseteq L$. Therefore, $L = \bigcup \{B_x \mid x \in L\}$.

(iii) implies (i): part (iii) implies part (i) immediately. □

Corollary 4.7. *Let U be a subspace of a topological space $(S, \mathcal{O})$. If $\mathcal{B}$ is a basis of $(S, \mathcal{O})$, then $\mathcal{B}_U = \{U \cap B \mid B \in \mathcal{B}\}$ is a basis of the subspace U.*

Proof. Let K be an open subset in the subspace U. There is an open set L in $(S, \mathcal{O})$ such that $K = U \cap L$. Since $\mathcal{B}$ is a basis for $(S, \mathcal{O})$, by the third part of Theorem 4.33, there is a subcollection $\mathcal{C}$ of $\mathcal{B}$ such that $L = \bigcup \mathcal{C}$, which implies $K = \bigcup \{U \cap C \mid C \in \mathcal{C}\}$. Thus, $\mathcal{B}_U$ is a basis for U. □

Definition 4.16. A topological space $(S, \mathcal{O})$ satisfies the *first axiom of countability* if for every $x \in S$ there is a countable local basis of neighborhoods at x.

A topological space satisfies the *second axiom of countability* if it has a countable basis.

It is clear that the second axiom of countability implies the first. Furthermore, by Corollary 4.7, every subspace of a topological space that satisfies the second axiom of countability satisfies this axiom itself.

Theorem 4.34. *Let $(S, \mathcal{O})$ be a topological space. If $(S, \mathcal{O})$ has a countable basis, then $(S, \mathcal{O})$ is separable.*

Proof. Let $\{B_n \mid n \in \mathbb{N}\}$ be a countable basis for $(S, \mathcal{O})$ and let x_n be an element of B_n for $n \in \mathbb{N}$. We claim that $S = \mathbf{K}(\{x_n \mid n \in \mathbb{N}\})$, which is equivalent to $S - \mathbf{K}(\{x_n \mid n \in \mathbb{N}\}) = \emptyset$.

Indeed, observe that $S - \mathbf{K}(\{x_n \mid n \in \mathbb{N}\})$ is a non-empty open set; therefore, there exists $m \in \mathbb{N}$ such that $B_m \subseteq S - \mathbf{K}(\{x_n \mid n \in \mathbb{N}\})$, so $x_m \in S - \mathbf{K}(\{x_n \mid n \in \mathbb{N}\}) \subseteq S - \{x_n \mid n \in \mathbb{N}\}$, which is a contradiction. Therefore, the countable set $\{x_n \mid n \in \mathbb{N}\}$ is dense in $(S, \mathcal{O})$. $\qquad \square$

The notion of an open cover of a topological space is introduced next.

Definition 4.17. A *cover* of a topological space $(S, \mathcal{O})$ is a collection of sets $\mathcal{C}$ such that $\bigcup \mathcal{C} = S$.

If $\mathcal{C}$ is a cover of $(S, \mathcal{O})$ and every set $C \in \mathcal{C}$ is open (respectively, closed), then we refer to $\mathcal{C}$ as an *open cover* (respectively, a *closed cover*).

A *subcover* of an *open cover* $\mathcal{C}$ is a collection $\mathcal{D}$ such that $\mathcal{D} \subseteq \mathcal{C}$ and $\bigcup \mathcal{D} = S$.

Theorem 4.35. *If a topological space $(S, \mathcal{O})$ satisfies the second axiom of countability, then every basis $\mathcal{B}$ for $(S, \mathcal{O})$ contains a countable collection $\mathcal{B}_0$ that is a basis for $(S, \mathcal{O})$.*

Proof.   Let $\mathcal{B}' = \{L_i \mid i \in \mathbb{N}\}$ be a countable basis for $(S, \mathcal{O})$ and let $\mathcal{C}_i$ be the subcollection of $\mathcal{B}$ defined by $\mathcal{C}_i = \{V \in \mathcal{B} \mid V \subseteq L_i\}$ for $i \in \mathbb{N}$. Since $\mathcal{B}$ is a basis for $(S, \mathcal{O})$, it is clear that $\mathcal{C}_i$ is an open cover for L_i; that is, $\bigcup \mathcal{C}_i = L_i$ for every $i \in \mathbb{N}$. Since each subspace L_i has a countable basis, $\mathcal{C}_i$ contains a countable subcover $\mathcal{C}'_i$ of L_i. The collection $\mathcal{B}_0 = \bigcup \{\mathcal{C}'_i \mid i \in \mathbb{N}\}$ is countable and is a basis for $(S, \mathcal{O})$ that is included in $\mathcal{B}$. $\qquad \square$

Theorem 4.36. (Lindelöf's Theorem) *Let $(S, \mathcal{O})$ be a topological space that satisfies the second axiom of countability. If $\mathcal{C}$ is an open cover of $(S, \mathcal{O})$, then $\mathcal{C}$ contains some countable subcover of S.*

Proof.   Let $\mathcal{B}$ be a countable basis of $(S, \mathcal{O})$ and let

$$\mathcal{D} = \{B \in \mathcal{B} \mid B \subseteq C \text{ for some } C \in \mathcal{C}\}.$$

$\mathcal{D}$ is countable since $\mathcal{D} \subseteq \mathcal{B}$. For $D \in \mathcal{D}$ let $C_D \in \mathcal{C}$ be a set such that $D \subseteq C_D$. Note that if $\mathcal{K} = \{C_D \mid D \in \mathcal{D}\}$, then $\mathcal{K}$ is countable because $\mathcal{K} \subseteq \mathcal{C}$.

Let $x \in S$. There exists $C \in \mathcal{C}$ such that $x \in C$. Since $\mathcal{B}$ is a basis, $x \in B \subseteq C$ for some $B \in \mathcal{B}$. Then, $B \in \mathcal{D}$, $C_D \in \mathcal{K}$ and $x \in C_D$, which proves that $\mathcal{K}$ is a countable cover contained in $\mathcal{C}$. $\qquad \square$

Definition 4.18. Let $(S, \mathcal{O})$ be a topological space. A subset U of S is *clopen* if it is both open and closed.

Clearly, in every topological space $(S, \mathcal{O})$, both $\emptyset$ and S are clopen sets.

Example 4.15. Let $\pi = \{B_i \mid i \in I\}$ be a partition of a set S. The *partition topology* on S determined by π is the collection of subsets of S that equal an union of blocks of π, that is, are π-saturated (see Example 1.10).

It is easy to verify that the collection of π-saturated sets is a topology. Moreover, since the complement of a π-saturated set is π-saturated set, it follows that all open sets of this topology are clopen.

Example 4.16. Let a and d be two integers. An *infinite arithmetic progression* on the set $\mathbb{Z}$ is a set of the form

$$P_{a,d} = \{n \in \mathbb{Z} \mid n = a + kd, k \in \mathbb{Z}\}.$$

The number d is the *difference* of this progression.

It is easy to see that we have $P_{a,d} = P_{a',d}$ for every member a' of $P_{a,d}$. Also, note that $P_{0,1} = \mathbb{Z}$.

If $d|d'$, the definition of infinite arithmetic progression implies $P_{a,d'} \subseteq P_{a,d}$.

Let $P_{a,d}$ and $P_{b,e}$ be two arithmetic progressions that have a non-empty intersection. This means that there is $n_0 \in \mathbb{Z}$ such that $n_0 = a + k_0 d = b + h_0 e$ for some $k_0, h_0 \in \mathbb{Z}$. It is clear that $P_{a,d} = P_{n_0,d}$ and $P_{b,e} = P_{n_0,e}$. If r is the least common multiple of d and e, then

$$P_{n_0,r} \subseteq P_{n_0,d} \cap P_{n_0,e} = P_{a,d} \cap P_{b,e}.$$

By Theorem 4.29, the collection of infinite arithmetic progression is a topology basis on $\mathbb{Z}$.

Observe that

$$P_{a,d} = \mathbb{Z} - \bigcup_{i=1}^{d-1} P_{a+i,d}.$$

This shows that every set of this basis is also closed as a complement of a finite union of member of the basis. Therefore, every progression $P_{a,d}$ is a clopen set, which implies that every open set of this topology is clopen.

This topology on $\mathbb{Z}$ was introduced in [61] as a tool for reproving Euclid's result that stipulates that there exists an infinite number of prime numbers.

Note that the single integers that are not divisible by a prime are -1 and 1. Suppose that there exist only a finite number of prime numbers $p_1, \ldots, p_m$. Then $P_{0,p_1} \cup P_{0,p_2} \cup \cdots \cup P_{0,p_m} = \mathbb{Z} - \{-1, 1\}$. Since the sets $P_{0,p_1}, \ldots, P_{0,p_m}$ are clopen, the set $\{-1, 1\}$ is open. This, however is a contradiction since in this topology an open set is either empty or is infinite.

Theorem 4.37. *Let $(S, \mathcal{O})$ be a topological space. A set U is clopen if and only if $\partial U = \emptyset$.*

Proof. Suppose that U is clopen. Then $U = \mathbf{K}(U)$; moreover, $S - U$ is also closed (because U is open) and therefore $S - U = \mathbf{K}(S - U)$. Thus, $\mathbf{K}(U) \cap \mathbf{K}(S - U) = U \cap (S - U) = \emptyset$, so $\partial U = \emptyset$.

Conversely, suppose that $\partial U = \emptyset$. Then, since $\mathbf{K}(U) \cap \mathbf{K}(S - U) = \emptyset$, it follows that $\mathbf{K}(U) \subseteq S - \mathbf{K}(S - U)$. Therefore, $\mathbf{K}(U) \subseteq S - (S - U) = U$, which implies $\mathbf{K}(U) = U$. Thus, U is closed. Furthermore, by equality (4.2), $\partial U = \emptyset$ also implies $\mathbf{I}(S - L) \cup \mathbf{I}(L) = S$, so $S - \mathbf{I}(S - L) \subseteq \mathbf{I}(L)$. By Corollary 4.3, we have $\mathbf{K}(L) \subseteq \mathbf{I}(L)$, so $L \subseteq \mathbf{I}(L)$. Thus, $L = \mathbf{I}(L)$, so L is also an open set. $\qquad\square$

The definition of neighborhoods allows us to introduce the notion of convergent sequence in a topological space.

Definition 4.19. Let $(S, \mathcal{O})$ be a topological space. A sequence $\mathbf{x} = (x_n) \in \mathbf{Seq}(S)$ *converges* to $x \in S$ if for every neighborhood $U \in neigh_x(\mathcal{O})$ there exists a number n_U such that $n \geqslant n_U$ implies $x_n \in U$.

If $\mathbf{x}$ converges to x we say that x is a *limit point* for the sequence (x_n) and that $\mathbf{x}$ is a *convergent sequence*.

Note that can replace $neigh_x(\mathcal{O})$ in Definition 4.19 by a local basis of neighborhoods at x.

Example 4.17. Let $(S, \mathcal{O})$ be a topological space where S is an infinite set and let $\mathcal{O}$ be the cofinite topology introduced in Example 4.4. Let (x_n) be a sequence in S such that $i \neq j$ implies $x_i \neq x_j$. Then, for every $x \in S$ is a limit point for (x_n). Indeed, let $V \in neigh_x(V)$. Note that V contains an open set (which is infinite), so $S - V$ is finite. Thus, there exists $i \in \mathbb{N}$ such that $x_i \notin S - V$ for $j \geqslant i$, which implies $x_i \in V$ for all $j \geqslant i$.

This example also shows that a sequence may converge to more than one element.

Theorem 4.38. *Let $\boldsymbol{x} = (x_0, \dots, x_n, \dots)$ be a sequence in $(\mathbb{R}, \mathcal{O})$, where $\mathcal{O}$ is the usual topology on $\mathbb{R}$.*

If $\boldsymbol{x}$ is an increasing (decreasing) sequence and there exists a number $b \in \mathbb{R}$ such that $x_n \leqslant b$ ($x_n \geqslant b$, respectively), then the sequence $\boldsymbol{x}$ is convergent.

Proof. Since the set $\{x_n \mid n \in \mathbb{N}\}$ is bounded above, its supremum s exists by the Completeness Axiom for $\mathbb{R}$. We claim that $\lim_{n \to \infty} x_n = s$.

Indeed, by Theorem 1.16, for every $\epsilon > 0$ there exists $n_\epsilon \in \mathbb{N}$ such that $s - \epsilon < x_{n_\epsilon} \leqslant s$. Therefore, by the monotonicity of the sequence and its boundedness, we have $s - \epsilon < x_n \leqslant s$ for $n \geqslant n_\epsilon$, so $x_n \in B(x, \epsilon)$, which proves that $\mathbf{x}$ converges to s.

We leave it to the reader to show that any decreasing sequence in $(\mathbb{R}, \mathcal{O})$ that is bounded below is convergent. □

If $\mathbf{x}$ is an increasing sequence and there is no upper bound for $\mathbf{x}$, this means that for every $b \in \mathbb{R}$ there exists a number n_b such that $n \geqslant n_b$ implies $x_n > b$. If this is the case, we say that $\mathbf{x}$ is a sequence *divergent to* $+\infty$ and we write $\lim_{n \to \infty} x_n = +\infty$. Similarly, if $\mathbf{x}$ is a decreasing sequence and there is no lower bound for it, this means that for every $b \in \mathbb{R}$ there exists a number n_b such that $n \geqslant n_b$ implies $x_n < b$. In this case, we say that $\mathbf{x}$ is a sequence *divergent to* $-\infty$ and we write $\lim_{n \to \infty} x_n = -\infty$.

Theorem 4.38 and the notion of a divergent sequence allow us to say that $\lim_{n \to \infty} x_n$ exists for every increasing or decreasing sequence; this limit may be a real number or $\pm\infty$ depending on the boundedness of the sequence.

Theorem 4.39. *Let* $[a_0, b_0] \supseteq [a_1, b_1] \supseteq \cdots \supseteq [a_n, b_n] \supseteq \cdots$ *be a sequence of nested closed intervals of real numbers. There exists a closed interval* $[a, b]$ *such that* $a = \lim_{n \to \infty} a_n$, $b = \lim_{n \to \infty} b_n$, *and*

$$[a, b] = \bigcap_{n \in \mathbb{N}} [a_n, b_n].$$

Proof. The sequence $a_0, a_1, \ldots, a_n, \ldots$ is clearly increasing and bounded because we have $a_n \leqslant b_m$ for every $n, m \in \mathbb{N}$. Therefore, it converges to a number $a \in \mathbb{R}$ and $a \leqslant b_m$ for every $m \in \mathbb{N}$. Similarly, $b_0, b_1, \ldots, b_n, \ldots$ is a decreasing sequence that is bounded below, so it converges to a number b such that $a_n \leqslant b$ for $n \in \mathbb{N}$. Consequently, $[a, b] \subseteq \bigcap_{n \in \mathbb{N}} [a_n, b_n]$.

Conversely, let c be a number in $\bigcap_{n \in \mathbb{N}} [a_n, b_n]$. Since $c \geqslant a_n$ for $n \in \mathbb{N}$, it follows that $c \geqslant \sup\{a_n \mid n \in \mathbb{N}\}$, so $c \geqslant a$. A similar argument shows that $c \leqslant b$, so $c \in [a, b]$, which implies the reverse inclusion $\bigcap_{n \in \mathbb{N}} [a_n, b_n] \subseteq [a, b]$. □

Theorem 4.40. *Let* $(S, \mathcal{O})$ *be a topological space that satisfies the first axiom of countability. For* $T \subseteq S$ *we have* $x \in \mathbf{K}(T)$ *if and only if there exists a sequence* (x_n) *in* T *such that* $\lim_{n \to \infty} x_n = x$.

Proof. Let $x \in T$ and let $\{V_n \mid n \in \mathbb{N}\}$ be a local basis of neighborhoods at x. Note that if $U_n = \bigcup_{k \leqslant n} V_n$, then $\{U_n \mid n \in \mathbb{N}\}$ is again a local basis of neighborhoods at x and $U_0 \supseteq U_1 \cdots \supseteq U_n \supseteq \cdots$ and since each set $U_n \cap T$ is non-empty, there exists $x_n \in U_n \cap T$. The sequence (x_n) converges to x.

Conversely, suppose that (x_n) is a sequence contained in T and $\lim_{n \to \infty} x_n = x$. Then, for every neighborhood $V \in neigh_x(0)$ there exists a number n_V such that $n \geqslant n_V$ implies $x_n \in V$, so $x \in \mathbf{K}(T)$. $\square$

Corollary 4.8. *Let $(S, 0)$ be a topological space that satisfies the first axiom of countability. A subset U of S is closed if and only if for every sequence (x_n) in U that converges to x we have $x \in U$.*

Proof.   Suppose that U is a closed set of $(S, 0)$ and $x \in U$. Since $U = \mathbf{K}(U)$, by Theorem 4.40, there exists a sequence (x_n) in U such that $\lim_{n \to \infty} x_n = x$.

Conversely, if for every sequence (x_n) in U that converges to x we have $x \in U$, it follows that $\mathbf{K}(U) \subseteq U$, so $\mathbf{K}(U) = U$, so U is closed. $\square$

Corollary 4.9. *Let $(S, 0)$ be a topological space that satisfies the first axiom of countability. A subset W of S is open if and only if for every $x \in W$ and sequence (x_n) that converges to x there exists a number $n_W \in \mathbb{N}$ such that $n \geqslant n_W$ implies $x_n \in W$.*

Proof.   Let W be an open subset in S and let $x \in W$. If (x_n) is a sequence that converges to x, since W is a neighborhood of x, the existence on n_W follows immediately.

Conversely, suppose that for every $x \in W$ and sequence (x_n) that converges to x there exists a number $n_W \in \mathbb{N}$ such that $n \geqslant n_W$ implies $x_n \in W$. (y_n) be a sequence in $S - W$ that converges to $y \in S$. Note that y cannot be an element of W because this would imply that the existence of a number n' such that for $n \geqslant n'$ we would have $y_n \in W$. Therefore, $y \in S - W$, so $S - W$ is closed, which means that W is open. $\square$

Theorem 4.40 and Corollaries 4.8 and 4.9 show that sequences as adequate for describing topological spaces that satisfy the first countability axiom. However, they fail to provide descriptions for general topological spaces. A generalization of sequences that overcomes this limitation is described in Section 4.10.

4.6 Compactness

Definition 4.20. Let $(S, \mathcal{O})$ be a topological space. A subset T of S is *compact* if for every collection $\mathcal{C}$ of open sets such that $T \subseteq \bigcup \mathcal{C}$ there exists a finite subcollection $\mathcal{C}'$ of $\mathcal{C}$ such that $T \subseteq \bigcup \mathcal{C}'$.

The topological space $(S, \mathcal{O})$ is *compact* if S itself is compact.

The collection of compact subsets of a topological space $(S, \mathcal{O})$ will de denoted by $COMP(S, \mathcal{O})$.

Example 4.18. Let $(S, \mathcal{O})$ be a topological space. For $x \in S$, the singleton $\{x\}$ is a compact set for if $x \in \bigcup \mathcal{C}$, there exists a set $C \in \mathcal{C}$ such that $\{x\} \subseteq C$. Similarly, any finite subset T of S is compact.

If $\mathcal{C}$ is a cover for a set T and $\mathcal{C}' \subseteq \mathcal{C}$ is a subcollection of $\mathcal{C}$ such that $T \subseteq \bigcup \mathcal{C}'$, we say that $\mathcal{C}'$ is a *subcover* of T.

The compactness can also be characterized in terms of neighborhoods.

Theorem 4.41. *Let $(S, \mathcal{O})$ be a topological space and let T be a subset of S. T is compact if for any collection of neighborhoods $\mathcal{N} = \{U_x \mid x \in T \text{ and } U_x \in neigh_x(\mathcal{O})\}$ there exists a finite subcollection of $\mathcal{N}$ that is a cover of T.*

Proof. Since every open set that contains a point x is a neighborhood of x, the condition of the theorem is clearly sufficient.

Conversely, if T is compact and $\mathcal{N}$ is a cover of T by neighborhoods, $\mathcal{N} = \{U_x \mid x \in T \text{ and } U_x \in neigh_x(\mathcal{O})\}$, let V_x be an open set such that $x \in V_x \subseteq U_x$. Then $\{V_x \mid x \in T\}$ is an open cover of T. The compactness of T implies the existence of a finite open cover of T, $\{V_{x_1}, \ldots, V_{x_n}\}$. This, in turn, implies that $\{U_{x_1}, \ldots, U_{x_n}\}$ is a finite collection of neighborhoods contained in $\mathcal{N}$ that is a cover for T. $\qquad\square$

Theorem 4.42. *Let $(S, \mathcal{O})$ be a topological space and let T be a subset of S. $T \in COMP(S, \mathcal{O})$ if and only if the subspace $(T, \mathcal{O} \restriction_T)$ is a compact space.*

Proof. The argument is immediate. $\qquad\square$

Example 4.19. Every topological space $(S, \mathcal{O})$ where S is a finite set is compact.

If $(S, \mathcal{O})$ is a topological space such that S is infinite set and $\mathcal{O} = \mathcal{P}(S)$, then $(S, \mathcal{O})$ is not compact because the collection $\{\{x\} \mid x \in S\}$ is a finite cover of S that contains no finite subcover.

Definition 4.21. A subset U of a topological space $(S, \mathcal{O})$ is σ-compact if there exists a sequence of compact sets (C_n) in S such that $U = \bigcup_{n \in \mathbb{N}} C_n$.

Another useful concept is the notion of a family of sets with the finite intersection property.

Definition 4.22. A collection $\mathcal{C}$ of subsets of a set S has the *finite intersection property* (f.i.p.) if $\bigcap \mathcal{D} \neq \emptyset$ for every finite subcollection $\mathcal{D}$ of $\mathcal{C}$.

Theorem 4.43. *The following three statements concerning a topological space $(S, \mathcal{O})$ are equivalent:*
   (i) *$(S, \mathcal{O})$ is compact;*
   (ii) *if $\mathcal{D}$ is a family of closed subsets of S such that $\bigcap \mathcal{D} = \emptyset$, then there exists a finite subfamily $\mathcal{D}_0$ of $\mathcal{D}$ such that $\bigcap \mathcal{D}_0 = \emptyset$;*
   (iii) *if $\mathcal{E}$ is a family of closed sets having the f.i.p., then $\bigcap \mathcal{E} \neq \emptyset$.*

Proof.   The argument is left to the reader.   □

Another characterization of compactness that is just a variant of part (iii) of Theorem 4.43 that applies to an arbitrary family of sets (not necessarily closed) is given next.

Theorem 4.44. *A topological space $(S, \mathcal{O})$ is compact if and only if for every family of subsets $\mathcal{C}$ that has the f.i.p. we have $\bigcap \{ \boldsymbol{K}(C) \mid C \in \mathcal{C} \} \neq \emptyset$.*

Proof.   If for every family of subsets $\mathcal{C}$ that has the f.i.p. we have $\bigcap \{ \boldsymbol{K}(C) \mid C \in \mathcal{C} \} \neq \emptyset$, then, in particular, if $\mathcal{C}$ consists of closed sets, it follows that $\bigcap \{ C \mid C \in \mathcal{C} \} \neq \emptyset$, which amounts to part (iii) of Theorem 4.43, so $(S, \mathcal{O})$ is compact.

Conversely, suppose that the space $(S, \mathcal{O})$ is compact, which means that the property of part (iii) of Theorem 4.43 holds. Suppose that $\mathcal{C}$ is an arbitrary collection of subsets of S that has the f.i.p. Then, the collection of closed subsets $\{ \boldsymbol{K}(C) \mid C \in \mathcal{C} \}$ also has the f.i.p. because $C \in \boldsymbol{K}(\mathcal{C})$ for every $C \in \mathcal{C}$. Therefore, $\bigcap \{ \boldsymbol{K}(C) \mid C \in \mathcal{C} \} \neq \emptyset$.   □

Example 4.20. Let $U_1 \supseteq U_2 \supseteq \cdots$ be a descending sequence of nonempty closed subsets of a compact space $(S, \mathcal{O})$. Its intersection $\bigcap_{n \geq 1} U_n$ is non-empty because $(S, \mathcal{O})$ is compact and $\bigcap_{p=1}^{k} U_{i_p} = U_l \neq \emptyset$, where $l = \min\{i_1, \ldots, i_k\}$ for every $k \geq 1$.

Example 4.21. Every closed interval $[x, y]$ of $\mathbb{R}$ is a compact set. Indeed, if $\mathcal{C}$ is an open cover of $[x, y]$ we can assume without loss of generality that $\mathcal{C}$ consists of open intervals $\mathcal{C} = \{(a_i, b_i) \mid i \in I\}$.

Let

$$K = \left\{ c \mid c \in [x, y] \text{ and } [x, c] \subseteq \bigcup_{j \in J} (a_j, b_j) \text{ for some finite } J \subseteq I \right\}.$$

Observe that $K \neq \emptyset$ because $x \in K$. Indeed, we have $[x, x] = \{x\}$ and therefore $[x, x] \subseteq (a_i, b_i)$ for some $i \in I$.

We claim that $y \leqslant w = \sup K$. It is clear that $w \leqslant y$ because y is an upper bound of $[x, y]$ and therefore an upper bound of K. Suppose that $w < y$. Note that in this case there exists an open interval (a_p, b_p) for some $p \in I$ such that $w \in (a_p, b_p)$. By Theorem 1.16, for every $\epsilon > 0$, there is $z \in K$ such that $\sup K - \epsilon < z$. Choose ϵ such that $\epsilon < w - a_p$. Since the closed interval $[x, z]$ is covered by a finite collection of open intervals $[x, z] \subseteq (a_{j_1}, b_{j_1}) \cup \cdots \cup (a_{j_r}, b_{j_r})$, it follows that the interval $[x, w]$ is covered by $(a_{j_1}, b_{j_1}) \cup \cdots \cup (a_{j_r}, b_{j_r}) \cup (a_p, b_p)$. This leads to a contradiction because the open interval (a_p, b_p) contains numbers in K that are greater than w. So we have $w = y$, which shows that $[x, y]$ can be covered by a finite family of open intervals extracted from $\mathcal{C}$.

In Example 4.21, we saw that every closed interval $[a, b]$ of $\mathbb{R}$ is a compact set. This allows us to prove the next statement.

Theorem 4.45. (Bolzano[2]-Weierstrass Theorem) *A bounded sequence of real numbers has a convergent subsequence.*

Proof. Let $\mathbf{x} = (x_0, \ldots, x_n, \ldots)$ be a bounded sequence of real numbers. The boundedness of $\mathbf{x}$ implies the existence of a closed interval $D_0 = [a_0, b_0]$ such that $\{x_n \mid n \in \mathbb{N}\} \subseteq [a_0, b_0]$.

Let $c = \frac{a_0 + b_0}{2}$ be the midpoint of D_0. At least one of the sets $\mathbf{x}^{-1}([a_0, c_0])$, $\mathbf{x}^{-1}([c_0, b_0])$ is infinite. Let $[a_1, b_1]$ be one of $[a_0, c_0]$ or $[c_0, b_0]$, for which $\mathbf{x}^{-1}([a_0, c_0])$, $\mathbf{x}^{-1}([c_0, b_0])$ is infinite.

---

[2]Bernard P. J. N. Bolzano was born on October 5th 1781 in Prague and died in the same city on December 18th 1848. He was a mathematician, philosopher and theologian. Bolzano studied at the University of Prague, where he studied mathematics and philosophy and later, theology. Bolzano taught religion and philosophy. After his dismissal from the University in 1819 by the Austrian government due to his pacifist convictions, he spent his exile writing on philosophical and mathematical matters. Bolzano contributed to the foundation of mathematical analysis.

Suppose that we have constructed the interval $D_n = [a_n, b_n]$ having $c_n = \frac{a_n + b_n}{2}$ as its midpoint such that $\mathbf{x}^{-1}(D_n)$ is infinite. Then, $D_{n+1} = [a_{n+1}, b_{n+1}]$ is obtained from D_n as one of the intervals $[a_n, c_n]$ or $[c_n, b_n]$ that contains x_n for infinitely many n.

Thus, we obtain a descending sequence of closed intervals $[a_0, b_0] \supset [a_1, b_1] \supset \cdots$ such that each interval contains an infinite set of members of the sequence $\mathbf{x}$. By Theorem 4.39, we have $[a, b] = \bigcup_{n \in \mathbb{N}}[a_n, b_n]$, where $a = \lim_{n \to \infty} a_n$ and $b = \lim_{n \to \infty} b_n$. Note that $b_n - a_n = \frac{b_0 - a_0}{2^n}$, so $a = \lim_{n \to \infty} a_n = \lim_{n \to \infty} b_n = b$.

The interval D_0 contains at least one member of $\mathbf{x}$, say x_{n_0}. Since D_1 contains infinitely many members of $\mathbf{x}$, there exists a member x_{n_1} of $\mathbf{x}$ such that $n_1 > n_0$. Continuing in this manner, we obtain a subsequence $x_{n_0}, x_{n_1}, \ldots, x_{n_p}, \ldots$. Since $a_p \leqslant x_{n_p} \leqslant b_p$, it follows that the sequence $(x_{n_0}, x_{n_1}, \ldots, x_{n_p}, \ldots)$ converges to a. $\qquad \square$

Example 4.22. The topological space $(\mathbb{R}, \mathcal{O})$ is not compact because $\bigcap_{n \geqslant 1}[n, \infty) = \emptyset$.

Example 4.23. Let $\mathbb{R}^n = \mathbb{R} \times \cdots \times \mathbb{R}$, where the product involves n copies of $\mathbb{R}$ and $n \geqslant 1$. In Example 4.13, we saw that the collection of open intervals $\{(a, b) \mid a, b \in \mathbb{R} \text{ and } a < b\}$ is a basis for the topological space $(\mathbb{R}, \mathcal{O})$. Therefore, a basis of the topological space $(\mathbb{R}^n, \mathcal{O} \times \cdots \mathcal{O})$ consists of parallelepipeds of the form $(a_1, b_1) \times \cdots \times (a_n, b_n)$, where $a_i < b_i$ for $1 \leqslant i \leqslant n$. This topological space will be denoted by $(\mathbb{R}^n, \mathcal{O}^n)$.

Example 4.24. The open interval $(0, 1)$ is not compact. Indeed, it is easy to see that the collection of open sets $\left\{\left(\frac{1}{n}, 1 - \frac{1}{n}\right)\right\}$ is an open cover of $(0, 1)$. However, no finite subcollection of this collection of sets is an open cover of $(0, 1)$.

Example 4.24 suggests the interest of the following definition.

Definition 4.23. A subset T of a topological space $(S, \mathcal{O})$ is *relatively compact* if $\mathbf{K}(T) \in COMP(S, \mathcal{O})$.

Example 4.25. The set $(0, 1)$ is a relatively compact subset of $\mathbb{R}$ but not a compact one.

Theorem 4.46. *If $(S, \mathcal{O})$ is a compact topological space, any closed subset T of S is compact.*

Proof. Let T be a closed subset of $(S, \mathcal{O})$. We need to show that the subspace $(T, \mathcal{O} \restriction_T)$ is compact. Let $\mathcal{C}$ be an open cover of $(T, \mathcal{O} \restriction_T)$. Then,

$\mathcal{C} \cup \{S - T\}$ is a open cover of $(S, \mathcal{O})$. The compactness of $(S, \mathcal{O})$ means that there exists a finite subcover $\mathcal{D}$ of $(S, \mathcal{O})$ such that $\mathcal{D} \subseteq \mathcal{C} \cup \{S - T\}$. It follows immediately that $\mathcal{D} - \{S - T\}$ is a finite subcover of $\mathcal{C}$ for $(T, \mathcal{O} \restriction_T)$. $\square$

Corollary 4.10. *Let $(S, \mathcal{O})$ be a topological space. If U is a compact set and V is a closed set in $(S, \mathcal{O})$, then $U \cap V$ is a compact set.*

Proof. Note that the set $U \cap V$ is a closed subset of U relative to the subspace determined by U. Therefore, $U \cap V$ is compact in this subspace by Theorem 4.46, and therefore, it is compact in $(S, \mathcal{O})$. $\square$

Bolzano-Weierstrass[3] property can now be formulated in a more general context.

Theorem 4.47. (Bolzano-Weierstrass Theorem) *If $(S, \mathcal{O})$ is a compact topological space, then, for every infinite subset U of S we have $U' \neq \emptyset$ (the* Bolzano-Weierstrass property*).*

Proof. Let $U = \{x_i \mid i \in I\}$ be an infinite subset of S. Suppose that U has no accumulation point. For every $s \in S$, there is an open set L_s such that $s \in L_s$ and $U \cap (L_s - \{s\}) = \emptyset$. Clearly the collection $\{L_s \mid s \in S\}$ is an open cover of S, so it contains a finite subcover $\{L_{s_1}, \ldots, L_{s_p}\}$. Thus, $S = L_{s_1} \cup \cdots \cup L_{s_p}$. Note that each L_{s_i} contains at most one element of U (which happens when $s_i \in U$), which implies that U is finite. This contradiction means that $U' \neq \emptyset$. $\square$

4.7 Separation Hierarchy

Separation properties of topological spaces aim to introduce conditions that ensure that it is possible to distinguish topologically between points or sets. The classes of topological spaces that we are about to present are named T_i after the German word "Trennungsaxiom" (or separation axiom), where $i \in \{0, 1, 2, 3, 4\}$.

---

[3]Karl T. W. Weierstrass was born on October 31st 1815 in Ostenfelde, a Westfalian city and died on February 19th 1897 in Berlin. He studied mathematics in Bonn, then on his own, and at the Academy of Münster, and taught high school. Later he taught at the Technical Institute in Berlin (a precursor of the Technical University) and at the University of Berlin.

Weierstrass is known as the founder of modern analysis. He formalized the notion of continuous function, obtained convergence criteria for series and contributed to the theory of several classes of functions, and the calculus of variations.

Definition 4.24. Let $(S, \mathcal{O})$ be a topological space and let x and y be two arbitrary, distinct elements of S. This topological space is:

    (i) *a T_0 space* if there exists $U \in \mathcal{O}$ such that one member of the set $\{x, y\}$ belongs to U and the other to $S - U$;

    (ii) *a T_1 space* if there exist $U, V \in \mathcal{O}$ such that $x \in U - V$ and $y \in V - U$;

    (iii) *a T_2 space* or a *Hausdorff space* if there exist $U, V \in \mathcal{O}$ such that $x \in U$ and $y \in V$ and $U \cap V = \emptyset$;

    (iv) *a T_3 space* if for every closed set H and $x \in S - H$ there exist $U, V \in \mathcal{O}$ such that $x \in U$ and $H \subseteq V$ and $U \cap V = \emptyset$;

    (v) *a T_4 space* if for all disjoint closed sets H, L there exist two open sets $U, V \in \mathcal{O}$ such that $H \subseteq U$, $L \subseteq V$, and $U \cap V = \emptyset$.

Example 4.26. It is clear that every T_1 space is also a T_0 space; however, there exists T_0 spaces that are not T_1 spaces. For instance, if $S = \{a, b\}$ and $\mathcal{O} = \{\emptyset, \{a\}, \{a, b\}\}$, then $(S, \mathcal{O})$ is a T_0 space but not a T_1 space.

Theorem 4.48. *A topological space $(S, \mathcal{O})$ is a T_1 space if and only if every singleton $\{x\}$ is a closed set.*

Proof. Suppose that $(S, \mathcal{O})$ is a T_1, space and for every $y \in S - \{x\}$ let U_y and V_y be two open sets such as $x \in U_y - V_y$ and $y \in V_y - U_y$. Then, $x \in \bigcup_{y \neq x} U_y$ and $x \notin \bigcup_{y \neq x} V_y$, so $y \in \bigcup_{y \neq x} V_y \subseteq S - \{x\}$. Thus, $S - \{x\}$ is an open set, so $\{x\}$ is closed.

Conversely, suppose that each singleton $\{u\}$ is closed. Let $x, y \in S$ be two distinct elements of S. Note that the sets $S - \{x\}$ and $S - \{y\}$ are open and $x \in (S - \{y\}) - (S - \{x\})$ and $y \in (S - \{x\}) - (S - \{y\})$, which shows that $(S, \mathcal{O})$ is a T_1-space. $\qquad\square$

Theorem 4.49. *$(S, \mathcal{O})$ is a Hausdorff space if and only if for $x, y \in S$ such that $x \neq y$, there exist $U \in \mathrm{neigh}_x(\mathcal{O})$ and $V \in \mathrm{neigh}_y(\mathcal{O})$ such that $U \cap V = \emptyset$.*

Proof. This statement is a direct consequence of Definition 4.24. $\qquad\square$

Theorem 4.50. *Let $(S, \mathcal{O})$ be a T_4-separated topological space. If H is a closed set and L is an open set such that $H \subseteq L$, then there exists an open set U such that $H \subseteq U \subseteq \boldsymbol{K}(U) \subseteq L$.*

Proof. Observe that H and $S - L$ are two disjoint closed sets under the assumptions of the theorem. Since $(S, \mathcal{O})$ is a T_4-separated topological space, there exist $U, V \in \mathcal{O}$ such that $H \subseteq U$, $S - L \subseteq V$ and $U \cap V = \emptyset$. This implies $U \subseteq S - V \subseteq L$. Since $S - V$ is closed, we have

$$H \subseteq U \subseteq \mathbf{K}(U) \subseteq \mathbf{K}(S - V) = S - V \subseteq L,$$

which proves that U satisfies the conditions of the theorem. $\square$

Theorem 4.51 is in some sense a reciprocal result of Theorem 4.46, which holds in the realm of Hausdorff spaces. We need a preliminary result.

Lemma 4.1. *Let* $(S, \mathcal{O})$ *be a Hausdorff topological space. If* H *is a compact subset of* S *and* $x \notin H$, *there exist disjoint open subsets* U, V *of* S *such that* $x \in U$ *and* $H \subseteq V$.

Proof. Since $(S, \mathcal{O})$ is a Hausdorff space, for every $y \in H$ there exist open neighborhoods U_y, V_y of x and y, respectively such that $U_y \cap V_y = \emptyset$. Since $H \subseteq \bigcup_{y \in H} V_y$ and H is compact, it follows that there exists a finite subset $\{y_1, \ldots, y_n\}$ of H such that $H \subseteq \bigcup_{k=1}^{n} V_{y_k}$. Note that $\bigcup_{k=1}^{n} V_{y_k}$ is am open set that contains H. If $U_y = \bigcap_{k=1}^{n} U_{y_k}$, then U_y is an open neighborhood of x that contains x and $U_y \cap (\bigcup_{k=1}^{n} V_{y_k}) = \emptyset$. $\square$

By Lemma 4.1, if H is a compact subset of $(S, \mathcal{O})$, then for every $x \in S - H$ there exists an open set U with $x \in U \subseteq S - H$.

Theorem 4.51. *Each compact subset* H *of a Hausdorff space* $(S, \mathcal{O})$ *is closed. Furthermore, if* $G \subseteq H$, *then* G *is compact if and only if* G *is a closed set in* $(S, \mathcal{O})$.

Proof. By Lemma 4.1 the complement of H can be written as a union of open sets:

$$S - H = \bigcup \{D_x \mid x \in S - H\},$$

so $S - H$ is an open set, which implies that H is closed.

If G is a closed set, then G is compact by Theorem 4.46. Conversely, if G is compact, then by the first part of this theorem, G is closed. $\square$

Corollary 4.11. *In a Hausdorff space* $(S, \mathcal{O})$, *each finite subset is a closed set.*

Proof. Since every finite subset of S is compact, the statement follows immediately from Theorem 4.51. $\square$

Theorem 4.52. *Let* $(S, \mathcal{O})$ *be a Hausdorff space and let* U, W *be disjoint compact subsets of* S. *There exist disjoint open subsets* V_1, V_2 *of* S *such that* $U \subseteq V_1$ *and* $W \subseteq V_2$.

Proof. Let $x \in U$. By Lemma 4.1 there exist disjoint open subsets U_x, V_x of S such that $x \in U_x$ and $W \subseteq V_x$. Since U is compact, there exists a finite set $\{x_1, \ldots, x_n\}$ such that $U \subseteq \bigcup_{i=1}^n U_{x_i}$. Define $V_1 = \bigcup_{i=1}^n U_{x_i}$. Let $V_2 = \bigcap_{i=1}^n V_{x_i}$. Then, V_1 and V_2 are open sets, $U \subseteq V_1$, $W \subseteq V_2$ and $V_1 \cap V_2 = \emptyset$. $\qquad\square$

It is clear that every T_2 space is a T_1 space and each T_1 space is a T_0 space. However, this hierarchy does not hold beyond T_2. This requires the introduction of two further classes of topological spaces.

Definition 4.25. A topological space $(S, \mathcal{O})$ is *regular* if it is both a T_1 and a T_3 space; $(S, \mathcal{O})$ is *normal* if it is both a T_1 and a T_4 space.

Theorem 4.53. *Every normal topological space is a regular one and every regular topological space is a T_2 space.*

Proof. We leave the first part of the theorem to the reader.

Let $(S, \mathcal{O})$ be a topological space that is regular and let x and y be two distinct points in S. By Theorem 4.48, the singleton $\{y\}$ is a closed set. Since $(S, \mathcal{O})$ is a T_3, space, two open sets U and V exist such that $x \in U$, $\{y\} \subseteq V$, and $U \cap V = \emptyset$, so $(S, \mathcal{O})$ is a T_2 space. $\qquad\square$

Theorem 4.54. *Every compact Hausdorff space $(S, \mathcal{O})$ is normal.*

Proof. To prove that $(S, \mathcal{O})$ is normal we need to show that it is a T_4-space, that is, for all disjoint closed sets A, B there exist two disjoint open sets $U, V \in \mathcal{O}$ such that $A \subseteq U$ and $B \subseteq V$.

Suppose initially that $B = \{b\}$. For every $a \in A$ we have the disjoint open sets U_a and V_a such that $a \in U_a$ and $b \in V_a$. Since A is compact and $A \subseteq \bigcup_{a \in A} U_a$, there exists a finite set $\{a_1, \ldots, a_n\}$ such that $A \subseteq U_{a_1} \cup \cdots \cup U_{a_n}$. The statement is proven for this special basis $(B = \{b\})$ where $U = U_{a_1} \cup \cdots \cup U_{a_n}$ and $V = V_{a_1} \cap \cdots \cap V_{a_n}$.

For every $b \in B$, by the previous argument, there exist two disjoint open sets U_b and V_b such that $A \subseteq U_b$ and $b \in V_b$. The set B is compact and $B \subseteq \bigcup \{V_b \mid b \in B\}$, so there exist $b_1, \ldots, b_n$ such that $B \subseteq V_{b_1} \cup \cdots \cup V_{b_n}$. The argument is completed by taking $U = U_{b_1} \cap \cdots \cap U_{b_n}$ and $V = V_{b_1} \cup \cdots \cup V_{b_n}$. $\qquad\square$

Theorem 4.55. *A compact Hausdorff space $(S, \mathcal{O})$ is a Baire space.*

Proof. Let $L_1, \ldots, L_n, \ldots$ be a sequence of dense open subsets of S. By applying Theorem 4.9 we shall prove that $\bigcap_{n \geqslant 1} L_n$ is dense in S by showing that the intersection of this set with an arbitrary non-empty open set U is non-empty.

We construct inductively a sequence of non-empty open sets $U_0, U_1, \ldots, U_n, \ldots$, where $U_0 = U$ such that $\mathbf{K}(U_n) \subseteq L_n \cap U_{n-1}$ and $\mathbf{K}(U_n)$ is compact.

Suppose that the non-empty open set U_{n-1} was constructed. Note that $L_n \cap U_{n-1} \neq \emptyset$ because L_n is dense in S. Therefore, there exists a non-empty open set U_n such that $\mathbf{K}(U_n) \subseteq L_n \cap U_{n-1}$ and $\mathbf{K}(U_n)$ is compact as a closed subset of a compact space (by Theorem 4.46).

Let $H = \bigcap_{n \geqslant 1} \mathbf{K}(U_n)$. The compactness implies that $H \neq \emptyset$. We have $H \subseteq U$ and $H \subseteq L_n$ for each n. Therefore, U has a non-empty intersection with $\bigcap_{n \geqslant 1} L_n$, which implies that $\bigcap_{n \geqslant 1} L_n$ is dense in S. $\qquad \square$

4.8 Locally Compact Spaces

Definition 4.26. A topological space is *locally compact* if it is a Hausdorff space and every point has a local basis consisting of compact sets.

Example 4.27. The topological space $(\mathbb{R}, \mathcal{O})$ is not compact, as we saw in Example 4.22. However, it is locally compact because every $x_0 \in \mathbb{R}$ since the family of sets $\{[x_0 - a, x_0 + a] \mid a \in \mathbb{R}\}$ is a local basis of compact neighborhoods.

Similarly, $(\mathbb{R}^n, \mathcal{O})$ is locally compact.

The next theorem states that every Hausdorff compact space is locally compact.

Theorem 4.56. *Let $(S, \mathcal{O})$ be a Hausdorff space. The following statements are equivalent:*

(i) *$(S, \mathcal{O})$ is locally compact;*

(ii) *for each $U \in neigh_x(\mathcal{O})$ there exists an open neighborhood V of x such that $\mathbf{K}(V)$ is compact and $\mathbf{K}(V) \subseteq U$;*

(iii) *each $x \in S$ has a compact neighborhood.*

Proof. (i) implies (ii): Let $x \in S$ and let $U \in neigh_x(\mathcal{O})$. By (i) there exists a compact neighborhood W of x such that $W \subseteq U$. The set $V = \mathbf{I}(W)$ is an open neighborhood of x. Since W is a compact subset of a Hausdorff space, W is closed. Therefore, $\mathbf{K}(V) \subseteq \mathbf{K}(W) = W \subseteq U$ and $\mathbf{K}(V)$ is compact because it is a closed subset of the compact set W.

(ii) implies (iii): This implication is immediate.

(iii) implies (i): Let $U \in neigh_x(\mathcal{O})$. By (iii) there exists a compact neighborhood C of x. Consider the open neighborhood $W = \mathbf{I}(U \cap C)$ of x. The compactness of C implies that C is a compact Hausdorff space, the set $Y = \mathbf{K}(W)$ is a subspace of C and, therefore, it is a compact Hausdorff space. In this subspace, $Y - W$ is closed and $x \notin Y - W$, so by Lemma 4.1, there are disjoint open sets M, N such that $x \in M$, $Y - W \subseteq N$. Since $x \in M \subseteq V \subseteq W$, V is a neighborhood of x in Y with $V \subseteq U$. Since V is a closed set in the compact space Y, it follows that V is compact. Finally, Y is a neighborhood of x in S because $V \subset W$ and W is open in S. $\square$

Corollary 4.12. *A Hausdorff space is locally compact if each of its points has a compact neighborhood. Furthermore, every compact Hausdorff space is locally compact.*

Proof.   This is an immediate consequence of Theorem 4.56. $\square$

Theorem 4.57. *Let $(S, \mathcal{O})$ be a locally compact topological space. If W is an open or a closed set in this space, the subspace $(W, \mathcal{O} \restriction_W)$ is a locally compact space.*

Proof.   Let $x \in S$ and let $U \in neigh_x(\mathcal{O} \restriction_W)$.

If W is open, any neighborhood $U \in neigh_x(\mathcal{O} \restriction_W)$ is also in $neigh_x(\mathcal{O})$ in S, so there is a compact neighborhood $V \in neigh_x(\mathcal{O})$ with $V \subseteq U$. Since $V \subseteq W$, $V \in neigh_x(W)$.

If W is closed, let $U_0 \in neigh_x(\mathcal{O})$ such that $U = U_0 \cap W$. There is some compact neighborhood $V_0 \in neigh_x(\mathcal{O})$ with $V_0 \subseteq U_0$. Then $V = V_0 \cap W \in neigh_x(\mathcal{O} \restriction_W)$ with $V \subseteq U$. Since W is closed in S, V_0 is compact, hence V is compact. $\square$

Theorem 4.58. *If a topological space $(S, \mathcal{O})$ is locally compact then every neighborhood $U \in neigh_x(\mathcal{O})$ of a point x includes a compact neighborhood of x.*

Proof.   Let T be an open neighborhood of x and let W be a compact neighborhood of x. If $W \subseteq T$, the statement holds. Suppose, therefore, that W is not included in U and let $Z = W \cap \overline{T}$. Since $(S, \mathcal{O})$ is a Hausdorff space there exist $U_z \in neigh_z(\mathcal{O})$ for each $z \in Z$ and W_z, an open neighborhood of x satisfying $W_z \subseteq W$ and $U_z \cap W_z = \emptyset$. Since $Z = W \cap \overline{T}$ is compact (by Corollary 4.10), there exist $z_1, \ldots, z_k \in Z$ such that $Z \subseteq \bigcup_{i=1}^k U_{z_i}$. Let $V = \bigcap_{i=1}^k W_{z_i}$ and $U = \bigcup_{i=1}^k U_{z_i}$. Note that V is an open neighborhood of x. We claim that $\mathbf{K}(V)$ is compact and included in T.

The inclusion $\mathbf{K}(V) \subseteq W$ implies that $\mathbf{K}(V)$ is compact. Since $U, V \in \mathcal{O}$ and $U \cap V = \emptyset$, it follows that $\mathbf{K}(V) \cap U = \emptyset$. From

$$\mathbf{K}(V) \cap \overline{T} = \mathbf{K}(V) \cap (W \cap \overline{T}) = \mathbf{K}(V) \cap A \subseteq \mathbf{K}(V) \cap U = \emptyset,$$

it follows that $\mathbf{K}(V) \cap \overline{T} = \emptyset$, which implies that $\mathbf{K}(V) \subseteq T$. This shows that $\mathbf{K}(V)$ is a compact neighborhood of x. □

Corollary 4.13. *Let $(S, \mathcal{O})$ be a Hausdorff space. The following statements are equivalent:*

(i) *$(S, \mathcal{O})$ is locally compact;*
(ii) *for every $x \in S$ there exists a closed compact neighborhood of x;*
(iii) *for every $x \in S$ there exists a relatively compact neighborhood of x;*
(iv) *every $x \in S$ has a local basis of relatively compact neighborhoods.*

Proof. (i) implies (ii): Since every compact subset in a Hausdorff space is closed, if follows from Theorem 4.58, that every point of a locally compact Hausdorff space has a closed compact neighborhood.

(ii) implies (iii): This implication is immediate because every closed compact set is a relatively compact set.

(iii) implies (iv): By Theorem 4.58 every neighborhood of x includes a relatively compact neighborhood of x; therefore, the collection of relatively compact neighborhoods of x is a local basis at x.

(iv) implies (i): Let U be a relatively compact neighborhood of an arbitrary $x \in S$. The closure $\mathbf{K}(U)$ is a compact neighborhood of x, so $(S, \mathcal{O})$ is locally compact. □

Lemma 4.2. *Let $(S, \mathcal{O})$ be a locally compact space, D be an open set, and let $x \in D$. There exists an open set E such that $\mathbf{K}(E)$ is compact and $x \in E \subseteq \mathbf{K}(E) \subseteq D$.*

Proof. Let T be a compact neighborhood of x. By Theorem 4.51 the set T is closed; furthermore, by Theorem 4.54, T is normal.

Note that the sets $\{x\}$ and $T - D$ are closed in the subspace T. The normality of T implies the existence of the disjoint open sets U and V (in the topology of the subspace T) such that $x \in U$ and $T - D \subseteq V$. By the definition of the topology of the subspace T there exist the open sets $U_0, V_0 \in \mathcal{O}$ such that $U = U_0 \cap T$ and $V = V_0 \cap T$. Define the open set E as $E = \mathbf{I}(U)$.

We have $x \in E$. Since $E \subseteq U \subseteq T$, it follows that $\mathbf{K}(E) \subseteq \mathbf{K}(T) = T$, which implies that E is compact. Finally, we have

$$E \cap V_0 \subseteq U \cap V_0 = (T \cap U_0 \cap V_0 = U \cap V = \emptyset,$$

so $E \subseteq X - V_0$. Since $S - V_0$ is closed, we also have $\mathbf{K}(E) \subseteq S - V_0$. Since $T - D \subseteq V \subseteq V_0$, we obtain

$$\mathbf{K}(E) \subseteq T \cap (S - V_0) \subseteq T \cap (S - (T - D)) = T \cap D \subseteq D. \qquad \square$$

Theorem 4.59. *Let $(S, \mathcal{O})$ be a locally compact space, D be an open set, and let C be a compact set such that $C \subseteq D$. There exists an open set E such that $\mathbf{K}(E)$ is compact and $C \subseteq E \subseteq \mathbf{K}(E) \subseteq D$.*

Proof. By Lemma 4.2, for every $x \in C$ there exists an open set E_x such that $x \in E_x \subseteq \mathbf{K}(E_x) \subseteq D$, where $\mathbf{K}(E_x)$ is compact. Since $C \subseteq \bigcup_{x \in K} E_x$ and C is compact, there exists a finite set $\{x_1, \ldots, x_n\}$ such that $C \subseteq \bigcup_{j=1}^{n} E_{x_j}$. If E is defined as $E = \bigcup_{j=1}^{n} E_{x_j}$, then

$$C \subseteq E \subseteq \mathbf{K}(E) \subseteq \mathbf{K}(E_{x_1}) \cup \cdots \cup \mathbf{K}(E_{x_n}) \subseteq D,$$

which concludes the argument. $\qquad \square$

Theorem 4.60. *Let $(T, \mathcal{O})$ be a non-compact Hausdorff space that is locally compact, and let $s_0 \notin T$. Let $\mathcal{O}'$ be the collection of subsets of the set $S = T \cup \{s_0\}$ that consists of:*
   (i) *the sets in $\mathcal{O}$, and*
   (ii) *the sets of the form $\{s_0\} \cup (T - C)$, where C is a compact subset of T.*
The pair $(S, \mathcal{O}')$ is compact Hausdorff space.

Proof. Note that Let $\mathcal{C}'$ be a collection of subsets of $\mathcal{O}'$. The definition of $\mathcal{C}'$ allows us to write $\mathcal{C}' = \mathcal{C}_1' \cup \mathcal{C}_2'$, where $\mathcal{C}_1' \subseteq \mathcal{O}$ and

$$\mathcal{C}_2' = \{\{s_0\} \cup (T - C_i), C_i \text{ is a compact subset of } T, i \in I\}.$$

It is clear that $\bigcup \mathcal{C}_1'$ is an open set in T. Also,

$$\bigcup \mathcal{C}_2' = \bigcup_{i \in} \{s_0\} \cup (T - C_i)$$

$$= \{s_0\} \cup \left(T - \bigcap_{i \in} C_i \right).$$

The set C_i are closed in $(T, \mathcal{O})$ as in T as compact subsets of a Hausdorff space (by Theorem 4.51), so the set $\tilde{C} = T - \bigcap_{i \in} C_i$ is open in T. Thus,

$$\bigcup \mathcal{C}' = \bigcup \mathcal{C}_1' \cup \{s_0\} \cup \tilde{C},$$

which proves that $\bigcup \mathcal{C}' \in \mathcal{O}'$.

Let U, V two sets in $\mathcal{O}'$. If $U, V \in \mathcal{O}$, then $U \cap V \in \mathcal{O} \subseteq \mathcal{O}'$. Suppose now that $U \in \mathcal{O}$ and $V = \{s_0\} \cup (T - C)$, where C is a compact subset of T. As above, $T - C \in \mathcal{O}$, so $U \cap V = U \cap (\{s_0\} \cup (T - C))) = U \cap (T - V) \in \mathcal{O}$ because $s_0 \notin T$. Finally, if $U = \{s_0\} \cup (T - C_1)$ and $V = \{s_0\} \cup (T - C_2)$, where C_1, C_2 are compact subsets of T, we have

$$U \cap V = (\{s_0\} \cup (T - C_1)) \cap (\{s_0\} \cup (T - C_2))$$
$$= \{s_0\} \cup ((T - C_1) \cap (T - C_2)) \in \mathcal{O}'.$$

This argument can be extended immediately to a finite collection of subsets of $\mathcal{O}'$, so $\mathcal{O}'$ is indeed a topology.

To prove that $(S, \mathcal{O}')$ is a Hausdorff space let $x, y \in S$ be two distinct points in S. If both $x, y \in T$, then it is obviously that the Hausdorff separation is satisfied. Suppose that $x \in T$ and $y = s_0$. Since $(T, \mathcal{O})$ is a Hausdorff locally compact space there exists a neighborhood W of x in T whose closure $\mathbf{K}(W)$ is compact. The set $\{s_0\} \cup (T - \mathbf{K}(W))$ is an open set that contains s_0 and has an empty intersection with W, so $(S, \mathcal{O}')$ is indeed a Hausdorff space.

To prove the compactness of $(S, \mathcal{O}')$ consider an arbitrary open covering $\{U_i \mid \in I\}$ of S and let U_{i_0} be an open set such that $s_0 \in U_{i_0}$. The set $T - U_{i_0}$ is a compact subset of T. Therefore, there exists a finite covering $U_{i_1}, \ldots, U_{i_m}$ of $T - U_{i_0}$, so $U_{i_0}, U_{i_1}, \ldots, U_{i_m}$ is a finite covering of S. $\qquad \square$

The topological space $(S, \mathcal{O}')$ is known as the Alexandrov compactification of $(T, \mathcal{O})$. Note that the mapping $\kappa : T \longrightarrow S$ given by $\kappa(x) = x$ for $x \in T$ is an injection of T in S.

4.9 Limits of Functions

Definition 4.27. Let S be a set. A non-empty collection $\mathcal{F}$ of non-empty subsets of S is a *filter* on S if $U, V \in \mathcal{F}$ implies $U \cap V \in \mathcal{F}$ and $T \in \mathcal{F}$ and $T \subseteq W$ implies $W \in \mathcal{F}$.

A non-empty collection $\mathcal{B}$ of non-empty subsets of S is a *filter basis* on S if $U, V \in \mathcal{B}$ implies $U \cap V \in \mathcal{B}$.

A *filter sub-basis* is a non-empty collection $\mathcal{S}$ of non-empty subsets of S such that the intersection of any finite subcollection of $\mathcal{S}$ is non-empty.

A filter is a filter base; the converse is not true. Note that the set of neighborhoods $neigh_x(\mathcal{O})$ of a point x of a topological space is a filter on S and a local basis at x is a filter basis.

Example 4.28. Let $(\mathbb{R}, \mathcal{O})$ be the set of reals equipped with the usual topology. The following collections of sets are filter bases:

    (i) the collection $\{(x_0 - \delta, x_0 + \delta) \mid \delta > 0\}$;

    (ii) the collection $\{[x_0, x_0 + \delta) \mid \delta > 0\}$;

    (iii) the collection $\{(x_0, x_0 + \delta) \mid \delta > 0\}$;

    (iv) the collection $\{(x_0 - \delta, x_0] \mid \delta > 0\}$;

    (v) the collection $\{(x_0 - \delta, x_0) \mid \delta > 0\}$.

The collections $\{[t, \infty) \mid t \in \mathbb{R}\}$ and $\{(-\infty, t] \mid t \in \mathbb{R}\}$ are also filter bases.

Definition 4.28. Let $(T, \mathcal{O})$ be a topological space, $\mathcal{B}$ a filter base on a set S and let $f : S \longrightarrow T$ be a function. A function $f : S \longrightarrow T$ *tends to* $\ell \in T$ *along* $\mathcal{B}$ if for every $V \in neigh_\ell(\mathcal{O})$ there exists $B \in \mathcal{B}$ such that $f(B) \subseteq V$. The element ℓ of T is the limit of f along the filter base $\mathcal{B}$.

Example 4.29. Suppose that $(S, \mathcal{O}')$ is a topological space and that $\mathcal{B}$ is the filter base $\mathcal{B} = neigh_{x_0}(\mathcal{O}')$. If $(T, \mathcal{O})$ is another topological space and $f : S \longrightarrow T$, then the limit of f along $neigh_{x_0}(\mathcal{O}')$ is ℓ if for every $V \in neigh_\ell(\mathcal{O})$ there exists $W \in neigh_{x_0}(\mathcal{O}')$ such that $x \in W$ implies $f(x) \in V$. This is denoted as $\lim_{x \to x_0} f(x) = \ell$.

Example 4.30. Suppose that $S = T = \mathbb{R}$ and $\mathcal{O}'$ and $\mathcal{O}$ are the usual topologies on $\mathbb{R}$. If $\mathcal{B}$ is the collection $\mathcal{B} = \{(x_0 - \delta, x_0 + \delta) \mid \delta > 0\}$, then ℓ is the limit along $\mathcal{B}$ if, for every $\epsilon > 0$, there exists $\delta > 0$ such that $f(x_0 - \delta, x_0 + \delta) \subseteq (\ell - \epsilon, \ell + \epsilon)$. This is denoted as $\lim_{x \to x_0} f(x) = \ell$.

If $\mathcal{B} = \{(x_0, x_0 + \delta) \mid \delta > 0\}$, then f has the limit ℓ along this filter base, if for every $\epsilon > 0$, there exists $\delta > 0$ such that $f(x_0, x_0 + \delta) \subseteq (\ell - \epsilon, \ell + \epsilon)$. This is denoted as $\lim_{x \to x_0+} f(x) = \ell$ and we say that f has the limit ℓ in x_0 from the right.

Similarly, if $\mathcal{B} = \{(x_0 - \delta, x_0) \mid \delta > 0\}$, then f has the limit ℓ along this filter base, if for every $\epsilon > 0$, there exists $\delta > 0$ such that $f(x_0 + \delta, x_0) \subseteq (\ell - \epsilon, \ell + \epsilon)$. This is denoted as $\lim_{x \to x_0-} f(x) = \ell$. In this case, ℓ is the limit of f in x_0 from the left.

We have $\lim_{x \to x_0} f(x) = \ell$ if and only if $\lim_{x \to x_0+} f(x) = \lim_{x \to x_0-} f(x) = \ell$.

The limits from the left or right of f are collectively known as *lateral limits*.

Definition 4.29. Let $f : X \longrightarrow \mathbb{R}$ be a function, where $X \subseteq \mathbb{R}$. If f is not continuous in x_0 (where $x_0 \in X$), we say that f is *discontinuous* in x_0.

A *first type discontinuity point* is a discontinuity point x_0 such that f has lateral limits in x_0 such that at least one of them is distinct from $f(x_0)$.

A *discontinuity point of the second type* is a discontinuity point for f that is not of the first kind.

The *jump of a function in a discontinuity point* x_0 is the number

$$\text{jump}(f, x_0) = \lim_{x \to x_0+} f(x) - \lim_{x \to x_0-} f(x).$$

Theorem 4.61. *Let $f : X \longrightarrow \mathbb{R}$ be a monotonic function, where $X \subseteq \mathbb{R}$. All its discontinuity points are of the first kind.*

Proof. It is clear that a monotonic function has lateral limits in every point of its definition domain. We need to prove that these lateral limits are finite.

Suppose that f is increasing. Let $u, v \in X$ such that $u < x < v$. By monotonicity we have $f(u) \leqslant f(x) \leqslant f(v)$. This implies $f(u) \leqslant \lim_{t \to x-} f(t) \leqslant \lim_{t \to x+} f(t) \leqslant f(v)$.

The argument for decreasing functions is similar. □

Theorem 4.62. *The set of discontinuity points of a monotonic function is at most countable.*

Proof. Suppose initially that $f : X \longrightarrow \mathbb{R}$, where $X = [a, b]$, and f is increasing. If $a < c < b$ we have

$$
\begin{aligned}
f(a) &\leqslant \lim_{x \to a+} f(x) \\
&\leqslant \lim_{x \to c-} f(x) \leqslant \lim_{x \to c+} f(x) \\
&\leqslant \lim_{x \to b-} f(x) \leqslant f(b),
\end{aligned}
$$

so the jump of f in a discontinuity point of the first kind c is less than $f(b) - f(a)$.

Let $c_1 < c_2 < \cdots < c_n$ be n discontinuity points of f in (a, b) such that $\text{jump}(f, c_i) \geqslant \alpha$, where $\alpha > 0$. We have

$$
\begin{aligned}
f(b) - f(a) &\geqslant \lim_{x \to c_n+} f(x) - \lim_{x \to c_1-} f(x) \\
&= \sum_{i=1}^{n} \text{jump}(f, x_i) + \sum_{i=1}^{n-1} \left(\lim_{x \to x_{i+1}-} f(x) - \lim_{x \to x_i+} f(x) \right) \\
&\geqslant \sum_{i=1}^{n} \text{jump}(f, x_i) \geqslant n\alpha.
\end{aligned}
$$

Thus, $n \leqslant \frac{f(b)-f(a)}{n}$. Therefore, the number of discontinuity points where the jump is larger than α is finite.

Let C_1 be the set of discontinuities of f where the jump is at least equal to 1 and for $n \geqslant 2$ let

$$C_n = \left\{ c \,\middle|\, c \text{ is a discontinuity for } f \text{ and } \frac{1}{n} \leqslant \text{jump}(f,c) \leqslant \frac{1}{n-1} \right\}.$$

Each set C_n is finite, so their union $C = \bigcup_{n \geqslant 1} S_n$ is countable as a countable union of finite sets.

If I is not a closed interval bound and closed, then I can be written as a countable union of closed and bounded intervals, and the same conclusion can be easily reached.   □

4.10   Nets

The notion of net is a generalization of the notion of sequence previously introduced.

Definition 4.30. A *directed set* is a partially ordered set $(I, \leqslant)$ such that for $i, j \in I$ there exists $k \in I$ such that $i \leqslant k$ and $j \leqslant k$.

A subset J of I is *cofinal* if for every $i \in I$ there exists $j \in J$ such that $j \geqslant i$.

Starting from directed sets we can introduce the notion of net on a set.

Definition 4.31. A *I-net* on a set S is a function $\xi : I \longrightarrow S$. For an I-net we denote $\xi(i) \in S$ by x_i and the net itself by $(x_i)_{i \in I}$. If the indexing set I is clear from context, the net will be denoted by (x_i).

The poset $(\mathbb{N}, \leqslant)$ is a directed set. Thus, a sequence a set S is just an $\mathbb{N}$-net $(x_n)_{n \in \mathbb{N}}$.

The notion of *subnet* is a generalization of the notion of subsequence.

Definition 4.32. Let $(I, \leqslant)$ and $(J, \leqslant)$ be two directed partially ordered sets, and let $\xi = (x_i)_{i \in I}$, $\zeta = (z_j)_{j \in J}$ be two nets. The net J-net ζ is a *subnet* of the I-net ξ if there exists a function $h : J \longrightarrow I$ such that

(i) $\zeta = \xi h$, that is, $z_j = x_{h(j)}$ for $j \in J$;

(ii) for each $i \in I$ there exists $j_i \in J$ such that $j \geqslant j_i$ implies $h(j) \geqslant i$.

Note that for a strictly increasing function $h : \mathbb{N} \longrightarrow \mathbb{N}$ and each $n \in \mathbb{N}$ there exists $m \in \mathbb{N}$ such that $n \leqslant h(m)$ because the infinite set

$\{h(\ell) \mid \ell \in \mathbb{N}\}$ cannot be contained in the finite set $\{0, \ldots, n\}$. Thus, if $\mathbf{x} = (x_n)$ is a sequence in $\mathbf{Seq}(S)$ we can regard a subsequence $(x_{h(n)})$ of $\mathbf{x}$ as a subnet of $\mathbf{x}$, where $I = J = \mathbb{N}$.

If (x_i) is an I-net on a poset $(S, \leqslant)$, we say that (x_i) is an *monotonic I-net* if $i \leqslant j$ implies $x_i \leqslant x_j$ for $i, j \in I$; if $i \leqslant j$ implies $x_i \geqslant x_j$ for $i, j \in I$, then the net is an *anti-monotonic I-net*.

Example 4.31. Let $(S, \mathcal{O})$ be a topological space. The set of neighborhoods of $x \in S$, $neigh_x(\mathcal{O})$ is a directed poset ordered by the partial order relation $\supseteq$. Indeed, if U, V are two neighborhoods of x, then $U \cap V$ is also a neighborhood of x, $U \supseteq U \cap V$ and $V \supseteq U \cap V$. Thus, we may consider nets of the form $\xi : neigh_x(\mathcal{O}) \longrightarrow S$ indexed $neigh_x(\mathcal{O})$ such that $\xi(V) \in V$ for $V \in neigh_x(\mathcal{O})$. We denote $\xi(V)$ as x_V.

The notions introduced next allow us to define net convergence as a generalization of sequence convergence.

Definition 4.33. Let U be a subset of a set S and let (x_i) be an I-net on S.

(x_i) is *eventually* in the set U if there exists $i_U \in I$ such that $i \geqslant i_U$ implies $x_i \in U$.

(x_i) is *frequently* in U if for each $i \in I$ there exists a $j \in I$ such that $j \geqslant i$ and $x_j \in U$.

Theorem 4.63. *If an I-net ξ is eventually in a set U, then any subnet ζ of ξ is eventually in U.*

Proof. Suppose that $\zeta = (z_j)_{j \in J}$ is a J-subnet of I-net $(x_i)_{i \in I}$ determined by the function $h : J \longrightarrow I$. We have $z_j = x_{h(j)}$ for every $j \in J$.

Since ξ is eventually in U, there exists i_U such that $i_U \leqslant i$ implies $x_i \in U$. By Definition 4.32 there exists j_U such that $j \geqslant j_U$ implies $h(j) \geqslant i_U$, so $z_j = x_{h(j)} \in U$. Thus, (z_j) is eventually in U. $\square$

Definition 4.34. Let $(S, \mathcal{O})$ be a topological space. An I-net (x_i) on S *converges* to x if for each $V \in neigh_x(\mathcal{O})$ the net is eventually in V. In this case we say that x is a *limit* of the net (x_i) and we write either $x_i \to x$ or $\lim_{i \in I} x_i = x$.

A net (x_i) is *convergent* if it converges to some $x \in S$.

A net (x_i) *clusters* at $x \in S$ when it is frequently in each neighborhood $V \in neigh_x(\mathcal{O})$.

In other words, the net (x_i) clusters at x if for each $V \in neigh_x(\mathcal{O})$ and $i \in I$ exists a $j \in I$ such that $j \geqslant i$ and $x_j \in V$.

Theorem 4.64. *Let $(S, \mathcal{O})$ be a topological space and let T be a subset of S. A point t is an accumulation point of T if and only if there exists an I-net (x_i) in $T - \{t\}$ such that $x_i \to t$.*

Proof. We saw that if t is an accumulation point of the subset T of the topological space $(S, \mathcal{O})$ and $U \in neigh_t(\mathcal{O})$, then $T \cap (U - \{t\}) \neq \emptyset$. Let (x_U) be a net such that $x_U \in T \cap (U - \{t\})$. Clearly, the net (x_U) converges to t.

Conversely, suppose that a net (x_i) in $T - \{t\}$ converges to t, then for every $V \in neigh_t(\mathcal{O})$ the net is eventually in V and the set $T - \{t\}$ intersects each neighborhood V, which means that t is an accumulation point of T. $\square$

A helpful characterization of net convergence is given next.

Theorem 4.65. *Let $(S, \mathcal{O})$ be a topological space having $\mathcal{B}$ as a basis. If (x_i) is an I-net on S we have $x_i \longrightarrow x$ if and only if for every $B \in \mathcal{B}$ such that $x \in B$ the net is eventually in B.*

Proof. Suppose that $x_i \to x$. If $B \in \mathcal{B}$ and $x \in B$ it is clear that B is a neighborhood of x, so (x_i) is eventually in B.

Conversely, suppose that for every set B of the basis that contains x, (x_i) is eventually in B and let $V \in neigh_x(\mathcal{O})$. There is an open set U such that $x \in U \subseteq V$ and, therefore, there exists a set $B \in \mathcal{B}$ such that $x \in B \subseteq U \subseteq V$. This shows that (x_i) is eventually in V, so $x_i \to x$. $\square$

Example 4.32. Monotonic or anti-monotonic nets on $\hat{\mathbb{R}}$ always have limits.

Let (x_i) be a monotonic I-net on $\hat{\mathbb{R}}$. We claim that $x_i \to \sup\{x_i \mid i \in I\}$. Indeed, if $s = \sup\{x_i \mid i \in I\} < \infty$, then for $\epsilon > 0$ there exists $i_0 \in I$ such that $s - \epsilon \leqslant x_{i_0} \leqslant s$. Therefore, by the monotonicity of $(x_i)_{i \in I}$, $i_0 \leqslant i$ implies $s - \epsilon \leqslant x_i \leqslant s$, which shows that $\lim_I x_i = s$. If $s = \infty$, for every $r \in \mathbb{R}$ the net (x_i) is eventually in (r, ∞), so again $x_i \to \infty$, which justifies the claim.

Similarly, if (x_i) is an anti-monotonic net, $x_i \to \inf\{x_i \mid i \in I\}$.

Example 4.33. Let (x_n) be an $\mathbb{N}$-net in a topological space. We have $x_n \to x$ if for every $V \in neigh_x(\mathcal{O})$ there exists n_0 such that $n \geq n_0$ implies $x_n \in V$.

Example 4.34. Let $(S, \mathcal{O})$ be a topological space and let $(x_V)_{V \in neigh_x(\mathcal{O})}$ be the net introduced in Example 4.31. We have $x_V \to x$. Indeed, there exists $V \in neigh_x(\mathcal{O})$ such that for every $V' \subseteq V$ we have $x_{V'} \in V' \subseteq V$.

Theorem 4.66. *Let $(S, \mathcal{O})$ be a topological space and let T be a subset of S. We have $x \in \boldsymbol{K}(T)$ if and only if some net in T converges to x.*

Proof. Suppose that there is an I-net (x_i) with $x_i \to x$. If $V \in neigh_x(\mathcal{O})$, there exists $i \in I$ such that $x_j \in V$ for all j with $j \geqslant i$. Since $i \geqslant i$, we have $x_i \in V \cap T$ and, therefore, $V \cap T \neq \emptyset$. This implies $x \in \boldsymbol{K}(T)$ by Theorem 4.24.

Conversely, let $x \in \boldsymbol{K}(T)$. By Theorem 4.24 we have $V \cap T \neq \emptyset$ for every $V \in neigh_x(\mathcal{O})$. Let $x_V \in V \cap T$. The set $(x_V)_{V \in neigh_x(\mathcal{O})}$ is a net in T that converges to x. $\quad\square$

Corollary 4.14. *Let $(S, \mathcal{O})$ be a topological space and let T be a subset of S. T is closed if and only if for each point t such that $x_i \to t$ for some net (x_i) in T we have $t \in T$.*

T is open if and only if each net that converges to a point $t \in T$ is eventually in T.

Proof. The corollary follows immediately from Theorem 4.66. $\quad\square$

Theorem 4.67. *Nets in Hausdorff spaces may not converge to more than one point.*

Proof. Suppose that (x_i) is a net in a Hausdorff space and we have both $x_i \to x$ and $x_i \to y$ and $x \neq y$. By Theorem 4.49 there exist $U \in neigh_x(\mathcal{O})$ and $V \in neigh_y(\mathcal{O})$ such that $U \cap V = \emptyset$. There exists $i \in I$ such that $j \geqslant i$ implies $x_j \in U$ and there exists $i' \in I$ such that $j \geqslant i'$ implies $x_j \in U$. Since $(I, \leqslant)$ is a directed poset there exists $k \in I$ such that $k \geqslant i$ and $k \geqslant i'$ which implies $x_k \in U \cap V$. This contradicts the disjointness of U and V. $\quad\square$

Theorem 4.68. *Let $(x_i), (y_i), (z_i)$ be three I-nets on $\hat{\mathbb{R}}$ such that $x_i \leqslant y_i \leqslant z_i$ for $i \in I$. If $\lim x_i = \lim z_i = \ell$, then $\lim y_i = \ell$.*

Proof. Let V be an open set of ℓ in $\hat{\mathbb{R}}$. Observe that if $u, v \in V$, then $[u, v] \subseteq V$. Since $\lim x_i = \lim z_i = \ell$, for each open set V that contains ℓ there exist i_0 and j_0 such that $i > i_0$ implies $y_i \in V$ and $i > j_0$ implies $z_i \in V$. Since $(I, \leqslant)$ is a directed poset, there exits $k_0 \in I$ such that $k_0 \geqslant i_0$ and $k_0 \geqslant j_0$. Thus, for $i \geqslant k_0$ we have both $i \geqslant i_0$ and $i \geqslant j_0$. Therefore, if $i > k_0$ we have both $x_i \in V$ and $z_j \in V$, which implies $y_i \in V$. This shows that $y_i \longrightarrow \ell$. $\quad\square$

Example 4.35. Consider now an I-net $(x_i)_{i \in I}$ on the set $\hat{\mathbb{R}}$. By extending Definition 4.34 to $\hat{\mathbb{R}}$, we write $\lim_I x_i = \infty$ if for each $a \in \mathbb{R}$ the net is eventually in (a, ∞). Similarly, $\lim_I x_i = -\infty$ if for each $a \in \mathbb{R}$ the net is eventually in $(-\infty, a)$.

Let $(x_i)_{i \in I}$ be an I-net on the set $\hat{\mathbb{R}}$. For $i \in I$ define the set

$$S_i = \{x_j \mid j \geqslant i\}.$$

It is clear that $i \leqslant k$ implies $S_k \subseteq S_i$ and, therefore, $\inf S_i \leqslant \inf S_k \leqslant \sup S_k \leqslant \sup S_i$.

Define the I-nets (y_i) and (z_i) as $y_i = \inf S_i$ and $z_i = \sup S_i$ for $i \in I$, so $i \leqslant k$ implies $y_i \leqslant y_k \leqslant z_k \leqslant z_i$. Then, (y_i) is a monotonic I-net, while (z_i) is an anti-monotonic I-net. As we observed in Example 4.32, $y_i \to \sup\{y_i \mid i \in I\}$ and $z_i \to \inf\{z_i \mid i \in I\}$. We define $\liminf x_i$ and $\limsup x_i$ as

$$\liminf x_i = \lim_I y_i = \sup\{y_i \mid i \in I\}$$
$$= \sup\{\inf S_i \mid i \in I\},$$
$$\limsup x_i = \lim_I z_i = \inf\{z_i \mid i \in I\}$$
$$= \inf\{\sup S_i \mid i \in I\}.$$

In Example 4.31 we saw that for $x_0 \in S$ we can define a net (x_V) indexed by $neigh_{x_0}(0)$. In this case $S_V = \{x_U \mid V \subseteq U\}$ and we have

$$\liminf x_V = \sup \inf\{S_V \mid V \in neigh_{x_0}(0)\},$$
$$\limsup x_V = \inf \sup\{S_V \mid V \in neigh_{x_0}(0)\}.$$

Theorem 4.69. *For every I-net (x_i) on $\hat{\mathbb{R}}$ we have*

$$\liminf x_i \leqslant \limsup x_i.$$

Proof. The theorem is a direct consequence of Theorem 1.21. $\square$

The convergence of an I-net on $\hat{\mathbb{R}}$ can be expressed using the sets S_i. Namely, we have $x_i \to \ell$ if and only if for every neighborhood V of ℓ there exists a set S_i that is included in V.

Theorem 4.70. *Let (x_i) be an I-net on $\hat{\mathbb{R}}$. We have $\liminf x_i = \limsup x_i = \ell$ if and only if $\lim x_i = \ell$.*

Proof. Note that if $a \in \hat{\mathbb{R}}$ and $a > \liminf x_i$, then a cannot be the limit of the net (x_i). Indeed, suppose that $x_i \to a$ and let b such that

$\liminf x_i < b < a$. Thus, $(b, \infty]$ is a neighborhood of a. For every $i \in I$ there is j such that $i < j$ such that $x_j < b$, and so for no $i \in I$ the set S_i is contained in the neighborhood $(b, \infty]$ of a, which prevents a from being a limit of (x_i).

Similarly, if $a \in \hat{\mathbb{R}}$ and $a < \limsup x_i$ then a cannot be the limit of the net x_i. This shows that if $\liminf x_i < \limsup x_i$ the limit of x_i cannot exist. Thus, if $\lim x_i$ exists we must have $\liminf x_i = \limsup x_i$.

Conversely, suppose that $\liminf x_i = \limsup x_i$. Note that for $i \in I$ we have $y_i \leqslant x_i \leqslant z_i$, where $y_i = \inf S_i$ and $z_i = \sup S_i$. Since $y_i \to \liminf x_i$ and $z_i \to \limsup x_i$, the equality $\liminf x_i = \limsup x_i$ implies

$$x_i \to \liminf x_i = \limsup x_i,$$

by Theorem 4.68. □

In topological spaces that satisfy the first axiom of countability the characterization of the points in the closure of a set contained in Theorem 4.66 may be reformulated by replacing nets with sequences.

Theorem 4.71. *Let $(S, \mathcal{O})$ be a topological space that satisfies the first axiom of countability and let T be a subset of S. We have $x \in \mathbf{K}(T)$ if and only if there exists a sequence in T that converges to x.*

Proof. Assume that $x \in \mathbf{K}(T)$. We have $V \cap T \neq \emptyset$ for every $V \in neigh_x(\mathcal{O})$. Since $(S, \mathcal{O})$ satisfies the first countability axiom there exist a countable local basis of neighborhoods at x, $\{V_0, V_1, \ldots, V_n, \ldots\}$. We have $\bigcap_{k=1}^{n} V_k \cap T \neq \emptyset$. If $x_n \in \bigcap_{k=1}^{n} V_k \cap T$, it follows that $x_n \to x$.

Conversely, suppose that there exists a sequence (x_n) in T that converges to x. If $V neigh_x(T)$ there exists n_V such that $n \geqslant n_V$ implies $x_n \in V$, hence $x_n \in V \cap T$. Thus, $x \in \mathbf{K}(T)$. □

The next statement is a characterization of compact spaces that uses nets.

Theorem 4.72. *A topological space $(S, \mathcal{O})$ is compact if and only if each net $(x_i)_{i \in I}$ in S clusters at some point of S.*

Proof. Suppose that $(S, \mathcal{O})$ is compact and let $(x_i)_{i \in I}$ be a net in S. Define the collection $\mathcal{A}$ of subsets of S as $\mathcal{A} = \{A_i \mid i \in I\}$ by $A_i = \{x_j \mid j \in I, j \leqslant i\}$.

Let J be a non-empty and finite subset of I. Since I is directed, there exists $k \in I$ such that $j \leqslant k$ for every $j \in J$, so $A_k \subseteq \bigcap_{j \in J} A_j \subseteq \bigcap_{j \in J} \mathbf{K}(A_j)$. Thus, the collection $\{\mathbf{K}(A_i) \mid i \in I\}$ has the f.i.p. so there exists

$x \in \bigcap\{\mathbf{K}(A_i) \mid i \in I\}$. We claim that (x_i) clusters at x. Let $V \in neigh_x(\mathbb{O})$ and let $i \in I$. Since $x \in \mathbf{K}(A_i)$ we have $V \cap A_i \neq \emptyset$, so $x_j \in V$ for some $j \geqslant i$.

Conversely, assume that each net (x_i) clusters at some point of S. Let $\mathcal{D}$ be a collection of closed subsets of S that has the f.i.p..

Let I consist of all pairs $(\mathcal{E}, x)$ such that $\mathcal{E}$ is a non-empty finite subcollection of $\mathcal{D}$ and $x \in \bigcap \mathcal{E}$. Define $(\mathcal{E}, x) \leqslant (\mathcal{E}', x')$ if and only if $\mathcal{E} \subseteq \mathcal{E}'$. It is easy to see that I is a directed partial order for, if $(\mathcal{E}_1, x_1), (\mathcal{E}_2, x_2) \in I$, then $\mathcal{E}_1 \cup \mathcal{E}_2$ is a non-empty finite subcollection of $\mathcal{D}$ and there exists $x \in \bigcap(\mathcal{E}_1 \cup \mathcal{E}_2)$, so $(\mathcal{E}_1 \cup \mathcal{E}_2, x) \in I$ and $(\mathcal{E}_1, x_1) \leqslant (\mathcal{E}_1 \cup \mathcal{E}_2, x)$, $(\mathcal{E}_2, x_2) \leqslant (\mathcal{E}_1 \cup \mathcal{E}_2, x)$.

For $i = (\mathcal{E}, x)$, define x_i as $x_i = x$.

We show that if (x_i) clusters at some x, then $x \in \bigcap \mathcal{D}$. Let D be a closed set in $\mathcal{D}$ and let $V \in neigh_x(\mathbb{O})$. If $y \in D$, then $(\{D\}, y) \in I$, so there exists $(\mathcal{E}, z) \in I$ such that $(\{D\}, y) \leqslant (\mathcal{E}, z)$ and $z \in V$. Since $D \in \mathcal{D}$, it follows that $z \in \bigcap \mathcal{E} \subseteq D$, so $z \in V \cap D$. This shows that $x \in \bigcup \mathcal{D}$. $\square$

By Theorem 4.63, a topological space $(S, \mathbb{O})$ is compact if and only if each net in S has some convergent subnet.

4.11 Continuous Functions

Definition 4.35. Let $(S_1, \mathbb{O}_1)$ and $(S_2, \mathbb{O}_2)$ be two topological spaces. A function $f : S_1 \longrightarrow S_2$ is *continuous* at $x_0 \in S$ if, for every $V \in neigh_{f(x_0)}(\mathbb{O}_2)$ there exists $U \in neigh_{x_0}(\mathbb{O}_1)$ such that $f(U) \subseteq V$.

Example 4.36. Let $(\mathbb{R}, \mathbb{O})$ be the topological space introduced in Example 4.2.

Choose $V \in neigh_{x_0}(\mathbb{O})$ as $V = B(f(x_0), \epsilon)$. The existence of $U \in neigh_{x_0}(\mathbb{O})$ such that $f(U) \subseteq B(f(x_0), \epsilon)$ implies the existence of $\delta > 0$ such that $B(x_0, \delta) \subseteq U$, hence $f(B(x_0, \delta)) \subseteq B(f(x_0), \epsilon)$.

Conversely, suppose that for every $\epsilon > 0$ there exists $\delta > 0$ such that $f(B(x_0, \delta)) \subseteq B(f(x_0), \epsilon)$. Let V be a neighborhood of $f(x_0)$. There exists $\epsilon > 0$ such that $B(f(x_0), \epsilon) \subseteq V$. We can choose $U = B(x_0, \delta)$ because

$$f(U) = f(B(x_0, \delta)) \subseteq B(f(x_0), \epsilon) \subseteq V.$$

Thus, the continuity of f at x_0 can be formulated in the "δ,ϵ"-language, well-known from calculus.

Definition 4.36. The function $f : \mathbb{R} \longrightarrow \mathbb{R}$ is *right-continuous* in x_0 if $\lim_{x \to x_0-} f(x) = f(x_0)$; f is *left-continuous* in x_0 if $\lim_{x \to x_0+} f(x) = f(x_0)$.

Definition 4.36 implies that $f : \mathbb{R} \longrightarrow \mathbb{R}$ is continuous in x_0 if and only if it is both right- and left-continuous.

Example 4.37. Define the function $f : \mathbb{R} \longrightarrow \mathbb{R}$ as

$$f(x) = \begin{cases} 1 & \text{if } x \geqslant 3, \\ 0 & \text{otherwise.} \end{cases}$$

Since $f(3) = 1$ and $\lim_{x \to 3+} f(x) = 1$, the function is right-continuous in 3. On other hand $\lim_{x \to 3-} f(x) = 0$, so the function has only lateral limits in 3. Therefore, f is not continuous in 3.

Example 4.38. Let $(S, \mathcal{O}_1)$ be a topological space, and let $(\mathbb{R}, \mathcal{O})$ be the topological space of real numbers equipped with the usual topology. A function $f : S \longrightarrow \mathbb{R}$ is continuous in $x_0 \in S$ if for every neighborhood $V \in neigh_{f(x_0)}(\mathcal{O})$ there exists $U \in neigh_{x_0}(\mathcal{O}_1)$ such that $f(U) \subseteq V$.

If $c < f(x_0)$, the set (c, ∞) is a neighborhood of $f(x_0)$ in $(\mathbb{R}, \mathcal{O})$. Therefore, there exists a neighborhood U of x_0 in $(S, \mathcal{O}_1)$ such that $f(U) \subseteq (c, \infty)$. In other words, for every $x \in U$ we have $c < f(x)$.

Similarly, if $f(x_0) < d$, the set $(-\infty, d)$ is a neighborhood of $f(x_0)$ in $\mathbb{R}$ and therefore, there exists a neighborhood W of x_0 in $(S, \mathcal{O}_1)$ such that $f(W) \subseteq (-\infty, d)$. In other words, for every $x \in W$ we have $f(x) < d$.

This discussion shows that if f is continuous in x_0, then there exists a neighborhood Y of x_0 such that f is bounded in Y.

Conversely, suppose that the following conditions are satisfied:

    (i) if $c < f(x_0)$ there exists a neighborhood U of x_0 in $(S, \mathcal{O}_1)$ such that for every $x \in U$ we have $c < f(x)$;

    (ii) if $f(x_0) < d$ there exists a neighborhood W of x_0 in $(S, \mathcal{O}_1)$ such that for every $x \in W$ we have $f(x) < d$,

the function f is continuous in x_0.

Indeed, let $x_0 \in S$ and let (c, d) be an interval that includes $f(x_0)$. Since $c < f(x_0)$, there exists a neighborhood U of x_0 in $(S, \mathcal{O}_1)$ such that $x \in U$ implies $c < f(x)$. Similarly, there exists a neighborhood W of x_0 in $(S, \mathcal{O}_1)$ such that for every $x \in W$ we have $f(x) < d$. It is clear that $Z = U \cap W$ is a neighborhood of x_0 and $x \in Z$ implies $c < f(x) < d$, or $f(Z) \subseteq (c, d)$, hence f is continuous in x_0.

In particular, if $f : S \longrightarrow \mathbb{R}$ is a continuous function in x_0 and $f(x_0) > 0$, then there exists a neighborhood U of x_0 such that $f(x) > 0$ when

$x \in U$; this follows by taking $c = 0$ in the previous argument. Similarly, if $f(x_0) < 0$, there exists a neighborhood V of x_0 such that $f(x) < 0$ when $x \in V$.

Using the characterization of real-valued continuous function defined on a topological space $(S, \mathcal{O})$ discussed in Example 4.38 it is possible to establish certain closure properties of the set of these functions.

Theorem 4.73. *Let $(S, \mathcal{O})$ be a topological space and let $C(S)$ be the set of bounded real-valued continuous functions of the form $f : S \longrightarrow \mathbb{R}$.*

If $f, g \in C(S)$ then for every $a, b \in \mathbb{R}$ we have $af + bg \in C(S)$, where $(af + bg)(x) = af(x) + bg(x)$ for $x \in S$. Also, the product fg defined by $(fg)(x) = f(x)g(x)$ for $x \in S$ belongs to $C(S)$.

Proof. We prove only the closure of $C(S)$ relative to the product. Suppose that f, g are continuous in x_0. Since

$$f(x)g(x) - f(x_0)g(x_0) = (f(x) - f(x_0))g(x) + f(x_0)(g(x) - g(x_0)),$$

it follows that

$$|f(x)g(x) - f(x_0)g(x_0)| \leqslant |f(x) - f(x_0)| \, g(x) + |f(x_0)| \, |g(x) - g(x_0)|.$$

By the continuity of f, there exists a neighborhood U of x_0 in $(S, \mathcal{O})$ such that $x \in U$ implies $|f(x) - f(x_0)| < \frac{\epsilon}{2M}$, where $M = \sup\{|g(x)| \mid x \in Y\}$, where Y is a neighborhood of x_0 on which g is bounded. If $f(x_0) = 0$ the continuity of fg in x_0 is immediate, so we may assume that $f(x_0) \neq 0$. The continuity of g, implies the existence of a neighborhood T of x_0 such that $x \in T$ implies $|g(x) - g(x_0)| < \frac{\epsilon}{2|f(x_0)|}$, which allows us to conclude that if x belongs to the neighborhood $U \cap Y \cap T$ of x_0, then

$$|f(x)g(x) - f(x_0)g(x_0)| < \frac{\epsilon}{2M} M + |f(x_0)| \frac{\epsilon}{2|f(x_0)|} = \epsilon,$$

which implies the continuity of fg in x_0. $\qquad\square$

Note that $f(U) \subseteq V$ is equivalent to $U \subseteq f^{-1}(V)$. This allows us to formulate an equivalent condition for continuity.

Theorem 4.74. *Let $(S_1, \mathcal{O}_1)$ and $(S_2, \mathcal{O}_2)$ be two topological spaces. A function $f : S_1 \longrightarrow S_2$ is continuous at $x_0 \in S_1$ if for each neighborhood $V \in neigh_{f(x_0)}(\mathcal{O}_2)$ the set $f^{-1}(V)$ belongs to $neigh_{x_0}(\mathcal{O}_1)$.*

Proof. Suppose that f is continuous at $x_0 \in S_1$. Then, for every $V \in neigh_{f(x_0)}(\mathcal{O}_2)$ there exists $U \in neigh_{x_0}(\mathcal{O}_1)$ such that $U \subseteq f^{-1}(V)$, which implies that $f^{-1}(V)$ is a neighborhood of x_0.

Conversely, if $f^{-1}(V)$ is a neighborhood of x_0 for each $V \in neigh_{f(x_0)}(\mathcal{O}_2)$ the continuity of f in x_0 is immediate. $\qquad\square$

Theorem 4.75. *Let $(S_1, \mathcal{O}_1)$ and $(S_2, \mathcal{O}_2)$ be two topological spaces having the closure operators $\mathbf{K}_1$ and $\mathbf{K}_2$, respectively. If $f : S_1 \longrightarrow S_2$ is continuous at $x_0 \in S_1$, then $x_0 \in \mathbf{K}_1(T)$ for some subset T of S_1 implies $f(x_0) \in \mathbf{K}_2(f(T))$.*

Proof. Let T be a subset of S_1, $x_0 \in T$, and let V be a neighborhood of $f(x_0)$ in S_2. Since f is continuous at x_0, $f^{-1}(V)$ is a neighborhood of x_0 in S_1. Therefore, by Theorem 4.24, $f^{-1}(V) \cap T \neq \emptyset$, which implies that $V \cap f(T) \neq \emptyset$. By the same Theorem 4.24, this implies $f(x_0) \in \mathbf{K}_2(f(T))$. $\qquad\square$

Theorem 4.76. *For $1 \leqslant i \leqslant 3$ let $(S_i, \mathcal{O}_i)$ be three topological spaces. If $f : S_1 \longrightarrow S_2$ is continuous at x_0, where $x_0 \in S_1$ and $g : S_2 \longrightarrow S_3$ is continuous at $f(x_0)$, then the function $gf : S_1 \longrightarrow S_3$ is continuous at x_0.*

Proof. Let $W \in neigh_{g(f(x_0))}(\mathcal{O}_3)$. Since g is continuous at $f(x_0)$ we have $g^{-1}(W) \in neigh_{f(x_0)}(\mathcal{O}_2)$. The continuity of f in x_0 implies, in turn, that $f^{-1}(g^{-1}(W)) \in neigh_{x_0}(\mathcal{O}_1)$. The continuity of gf follows by observing that $(gf)^{-1}(W) = f^{-1}(g^{-1}(W))$. $\qquad\square$

Definition 4.37. Let $(S_1, \mathcal{O}_1)$ and $(S_2, \mathcal{O}_2)$ be two topological spaces. A function $f : S_1 \longrightarrow S_2$ is *continuous* if it is continuous at each point x of S_1.

Theorem 4.77. *Let $(S_1, \mathcal{O}_1)$ and $(S_2, \mathcal{O}_2)$ be two topological spaces having the closure operators $\mathbf{K}_1$ and $\mathbf{K}_2$, respectively, and let $f : S_1 \longrightarrow S_2$ be a function. The following statements are equivalent:*

   (i) *f is continuous;*
   (ii) *$f(\mathbf{K}_1(T)) \subseteq \mathbf{K}_2(f(T))$ for every subset T of S_1;*
   (iii) *if L is a closed set in $(S_2, \mathcal{O}_2)$, then $f^{-1}(L)$ is a closed set in $(S_1, \mathcal{O}_1)$;*
   (iv) *if V is an open set in $(S_2, \mathcal{O}_2)$, then $f^{-1}(V)$ is an open set in $(S_1, \mathcal{O}_1)$.*

Proof. (i) implies (ii): This implication follows from Theorem 4.75.

(ii) implies (iii): Let L be a closed set in $(S_2, \mathcal{O}_2)$. By (ii) we have $f(\mathbf{K}_1(f^{-1}(L))) \subseteq \mathbf{K}_2(f(f^{-1}(L))$. Taking into account that $f(f^{-1}(L)) = L$ it follows that $f(\mathbf{K}_1(f^{-1}(L))) \subseteq \mathbf{K}_2(L) = L$, so $\mathbf{K}_1(f^{-1}(L)) \subseteq f^{-1}(L)$, which implies the equality $\mathbf{K}_1(f^{-1}(L)) = f^{-1}(L)$. This shows that $f^{-1}(L)$ is a closed set.

(iii) implies (iv): Let V be an open set in $(S_2, \mathcal{O}_2)$. This means that $S_2 - V$ is a closed set, so by (iii), $f^{-1}(S_2 - V) = S_1 - f^{-1}(V)$ is a closed set in $(S_1, \mathcal{O}_1)$. This means that $f^{-1}(V)$ is an open set in this space.

(iv) implies (i): Let $x \in S_1$ and let $V \in neigh_{f(x)}(\mathcal{O}_2)$. There exists an open set $U \in \mathcal{O}_2$ such that $f(x) \in U \subseteq V$, so $x \in f^{-1}(U) \subseteq f^{-1}(V)$. By (iv) $f^{-1}(U)$ is open in $(S_1, \mathcal{O}_1)$, which implies that $f^{-1}(V) \in neigh_x(\mathcal{O}_1)$. Since $f(f^{-1}(V)) = V$, it follows that f is continuous at an arbitrary $x \in S_1$, that is, f is continuous in S_1. $\square$

If $f : S_1 \longrightarrow S_2$ is a continuous function between the topological spaces $(S_1, \mathcal{O}_1)$ and $(S_2, \mathcal{O}_2)$ and $\mathcal{O}_1'$ and $\mathcal{O}_2'$ are topologies on S_1 and S_2, respectively, such that $\mathcal{O}_2' \subseteq \mathcal{O}_2$ and $\mathcal{O}_1 \subseteq \mathcal{O}_1'$, then f is also a continuous function between the topological spaces $(S_1, \mathcal{O}_1')$ and $(S_2, \mathcal{O}_2')$. Therefore, any function defined on the topological space $(S, \mathcal{P}(S))$ (equipped with the discrete topology) with values in an arbitrary topological space $(S', \mathcal{O}')$ is continuous; similarly, any function $f : S \longrightarrow S'$ between a topological space $(S, \mathcal{O})$ and $(S', \{\emptyset, S'\})$ (equipped with the discrete topology) is continuous.

Theorem 4.78. *Let $(S_1, \mathcal{O}_1)$ and $(S_2, \mathcal{O}_2)$ be two topological spaces and let $\mathcal{S}_2$ be a sub-basis of the topology $\mathcal{O}_2$. A function $f : S_1 \longrightarrow S_2$ is continuous if and only if for set $S \in \mathcal{S}_2$, we have $f^{-1}(S) \in \mathcal{O}_1$.*

Proof.   Let T be an open set in $\mathcal{O}_2$. Then T is a union of finite intersections of members of $\mathcal{S}_2$, that is, $T = \bigcup\{V_j \mid j \in J\}$, where $V_j = \bigcap_{i \in I_j} S_i$, each I_j is a finite set and each S_i belongs to $\mathcal{S}_2$. Since $f^{-1}(T) = \bigcup_{j \in J} \bigcap_{i \in I_j} f^{-1}(S_i)$ and each of the sets $f^{-1}(S_i)$ is open, it follows that $f^{-1}(T)$ is open, so f is continuous.

Conversely, if f is continuous each of the sets $f^{-1}(S)$ is open. $\square$

Theorem 4.79. *Let $(S_1, \mathcal{O}_1)$ and $(S_2, \mathcal{O}_2)$ be two topological spaces and let $\mathcal{B}_2$ be a basis of the topology $\mathcal{O}_2$. A function $f : S_1 \longrightarrow S_2$ is continuous if and only if for set $B \in \mathcal{B}_2$, we have $f^{-1}(B) \in \mathcal{O}_1$.*

Proof.   The proof is similar to the argument of Theorem 4.78. $\square$

Example 4.39. Let $(S, \mathcal{O})$ be a topological space and let $f : S \longrightarrow \mathbb{R}$ be a continuous function, where $\mathbb{R}$ is equipped with the usual topology introduced in Example 4.3. Recall that the collection of open intervals of $\mathbb{R}$ is a basis for $\mathbb{R}$, so the continuity of f is equivalent to the fact that for every $a, b \in \mathbb{R}$, $f(x) \in (a, b)$ implies that $f^{-1}(a, b)$ is an open set that contains x.

Function continuity can be formulated using nets.

Theorem 4.80. *Let $(S_1, \mathcal{O}_1)$ and $(S_2, \mathcal{O}_2)$ be two topological spaces. A function $f : S_1 \longrightarrow S_2$ is continuous at $x \in S_1$ if and only if for each net $(x_i)_{i \in I}$ such that $x_i \to x$ we have $f(x_i) \to f(x)$.*

Proof. Let f be a function continuous at x and let $(x_i)_{i \in I}$ be a net such that $x_i \to x$. If $V \in neigh_{f(x)}(\mathcal{O}_2)$, then $f^{-1}(V) \in neigh_x(\mathcal{O}_1)$, so there exists $i \in I$ such that $x_j \in f^{-1}(V)$ for $j \geqslant i$. This implies $f(x_j) \in V$ for $j \geqslant i$, so $f(x_i) \to f(x)$.

Conversely, assume that for each net $(x_i)_{i \in I}$ such that $x_i \to x$ we have $f(x_i) \to f(x)$. Suppose that there exists $V' \in neigh_{f(x)}(\mathcal{O}_2)$ such that $f^{-1}(V') \notin neigh_x(\mathcal{O}_1)$. For each $U \in neigh_x(\mathcal{O}_1)$ there exists $x_U \in U$ such that $x_U \notin f^{-1}(V')$. This yields a net (x_U) with $x_U \to x$ in $(S_1, \mathcal{O}_1)$, which, by hypothesis, implies $f(x_U) \to f(x)$, so $f(x_U) \in V'$ for some $U \in neigh_x(\mathcal{O}_1)$, so $x_U \in f^{-1}(V')$. This contradiction shows that f is continuous at x. $\qquad \square$

Compactness is preserved by continuous functions as we show next.

Theorem 4.81. *Let $(S, \mathcal{O})$ and $(T, \mathcal{O}')$ be two topological spaces and let $f : S \longrightarrow T$ be a continuous function. If $(S, \mathcal{O})$ is compact, then $f(S)$ is compact in $(T, \mathcal{O}')$.*

Proof. Let $\mathcal{D} = \{D_i \mid i \in I\}$ be an open cover of $f(S)$. Then $f^{-1}(D_i)$ is an open set in $(S, \mathcal{O})$ because f is continuous and the collection $\mathcal{C} = \{f^{-1}(D_i) \mid i \in I\}$ is an open cover of S. Since $(S, \mathcal{O})$ is compact, there exists a finite subcover $\mathcal{C}_1 = \{f^{-1}(D_i) \mid i \in I_1\}$ of S (I_1 is a finite subset of I). Since $S = \bigcup\{f^{-1}(D_i) \mid i \in I_1\}$, we have

$$f(S) = f\left(\bigcup\{f^{-1}(D_i) \mid i \in I_1\}\right)$$
$$= \bigcup\{f(f^{-1}(D_i)) \mid i \in I_1\} = \bigcup\{D_i \mid i \in I_1\},$$

which shows that $\mathcal{D}$ contains a finite subcover of $f(S)$. $\qquad \square$

Corollary 4.15. *Let $(S, \mathcal{O})$ and $(T, \mathcal{O}')$ be two topological spaces and let $f : S \longrightarrow T$ be a continuous function. If U is a compact subset of S, then $f(U)$ is compact in $(T, \mathcal{O}')$.*

Proof. This statement is an immediate consequence of Theorem 4.81. $\square$

Definition 4.38. Let $(S, \mathcal{O})$ be a topological space and let $f : S \longrightarrow \mathbb{R}$ be a function. The *support* of f is the closed set

$$supp(f) = \mathbf{K}(\{x \in S \mid f(x) \neq 0\}).$$

The set of continuous functions $f : S \longrightarrow \mathbb{R}$ such that $supp(f)$ is a compact set is denoted by $\mathcal{F}_c(S, \mathcal{O})$.

Theorem 4.82. *Let $(S, \mathcal{O})$ and $(T, \mathcal{O}')$ be two topological spaces and let $f : S \longrightarrow T$ be a continuous function in $\mathcal{F}_c(S, \mathcal{O})$. Then, the range of f is a compact subset of T.*

Proof. Note that the range of f, that is, the set $f(S)$, can be written as $f(S) = f(supp(f)) \cup \{0\}$. Since $supp(f)$ is compact, the set $f(supp(S))$ is compact. Therefore, the range $f(S)$ of f is compact. ☐

Theorem 4.83. (Uryson's Lemma for Normal Spaces) *Let $(S, \mathcal{O})$ be a normal topological space and let A, B be two disjoint closed sets. There exists a continuous function $f : S \longrightarrow [0, 1]$ such that $f(x) = 0$ for $x \in A$ and $f(x) = 1$ for $x \in B$.*

Proof. Consider the following sequence that consists of rational numbers in $[0, 1]$ expressed as irreducible fractions:

$$1, 0, \frac{1}{2}, \frac{1}{3}, \frac{2}{3}, \frac{1}{4}, \frac{3}{4}, \frac{1}{5}, \frac{2}{5}, \frac{3}{5}, \frac{4}{5}, \frac{1}{6}, \dots . \tag{4.4}$$

We define a sequence of open subsets (U_p) of a normal topological space $(S, \mathcal{O})$, where p is a member of the above sequence such that $U_1 = S - B$ and U_p is defined inductively such that

$$p < q \text{ implies } \mathbf{K}(U_p) \subseteq U_q. \tag{4.5}$$

Since $A \cap B = \emptyset$ we have $A \subseteq U_1$. By Theorem 4.50 the normality of S implies the existence of an open set U_0 such that $A \subseteq U_0 \subseteq \mathbf{K}(U_0) \subseteq U_1$.

Let P_n be the set of the first n rational numbers in the above sequence. Suppose that the open set U_p is constructed for all numbers p in P_n such that $p < q$ implies $\mathbf{K}(U_p) \subseteq U_q$. If r is the $(n+1)^{\text{st}}$ rational number in the sequence (4.4) and $P_{n+1} = P_n \cup \{r\}$, then there exists a largest number p and a smallest number q in P_n such that $p < r < q$. The sets U_p and U_q are already defined and $\mathbf{K}(U_p) \subseteq U_q$ by the inductive hypothesis. Since $(S, \mathcal{O})$ is normal, $\mathbf{K}(U_p)$ is a closed set and U_q is an open set, by Theorem 4.50, there exists an open set U_r such that $\mathbf{K}(U_p) \subseteq U_r \subseteq \mathbf{K}(U_r) \subseteq U_q$.

Property (4.5) holds for P_{n+1}. Indeed, if $p, q \in P_n$, the property holds by inductive hypothesis. Suppose that one of the numbers p, q is r and let $s \in P_n$. Then, either $s \leqslant p < r$ or $r < q \leqslant s$. In the first case, $\mathbf{K}(U_s) \subseteq \mathbf{K}(U_p) \subseteq U_r$; in the second case, $\mathbf{K}(U_r) \subseteq U_q \subseteq U_s$, so property (4.5) holds for P_{n+1}.

Starting from the collection

$$\{U_p \mid p \text{ is a rational number in } [0, 1]\},$$

we extend this notation to $\mathbb{Q}$ by defining

$$U_p = \begin{cases} \emptyset & \text{if } p < 0, \\ S & \text{if } p > 1. \end{cases}$$

With this extended notation property (4.5) still holds.

Let $x \in S$. Define the set

$$Q(x) = \{p \in \mathbb{Q} \mid x \in U_p\}.$$

The set $Q(x)$ is lower bounded because $x \notin U_p$ for $p < 0$. Note also, that $x \in U_p$ for $p > 1$, This allows us to define a function $f : S \longrightarrow [0,1]$ as $f(x) = \inf Q(x)$. We claim that f is the function whose existence is affirmed by the theorem.

If $x \in A$, then $x \in U_p$ for every $p \geqslant 0$, so $f(x) = 0$. If $x \in B$, then $x \notin U_p$ for every $p \leqslant 1$, so $f(x) = 1$.

Note that

(i) If $x \in \mathbf{K}(U_r)$, then $f(x) \leqslant r$.

Indeed, if $x \in \mathbf{K}(U_r)$, then $x \in U_s$ for every $s > r$, so $Q(x)$ contains all rational number greater than r and, therefore, $f(x) = \inf Q(x) \leqslant r$.

(ii) If $x \notin U_r$, then $f(x) \geqslant r$.

Indeed, since $x \notin U_r$, we have $x \notin U_s$ for $s < r$, so $Q(x)$ contains no rational number less than r which implies $f(x) = \inf Q(x) \geqslant r$.

To prove the continuity of f in x_0 we show that if $f(x_0) \in (c, d)$, then there exists a neighborhood U of x_0 such that $f(U) \subseteq (c, d)$. Let p, q be rational numbers such that $c < p < f(x_0) < q < d$.

Let U be the open set $U = U_q - \mathbf{K}(U_p)$. Note that $x_0 \in U$ because $f(x_0) < q$ implies $x_0 \in U_q$ and $f(x_0) > p$ implies $x_0 \notin \mathbf{K}(U_p)$, as we saw previously.

If $x \in U$, then $x \in U_q \subseteq \mathbf{K}(U_q)$, so $f(x) \leqslant q$. Also, $x \notin \mathbf{K}(U_p)$, so $x \notin U_p$, which implies $f(x) \geqslant p$. Thus, $f(x) \in [p, q] \subseteq (c, d)$, so f is continuous. $\qquad \square$

Corollary 4.16. *Let $(S, \mathcal{O})$ be a normal topological space and let K, T be two sets such that K is compact, T is open and $K \subseteq T$. There exists a continuous function $f : S \longrightarrow [0, 1]$ such that $1_K \leqslant f \leqslant 1_T$.*

Proof. Since the sets K and $S - T$ are closed and disjoint, by Uryson's Lemma (Theorem 4.83), there exists a continuous function $f : S \longrightarrow [0, 1]$ on S such that $f(x) = 0$ if $x \in S - T$ and $f(x) = 1$ if $x \in K$. This is equivalent to $1_K \leqslant f \leqslant 1_T$. $\qquad \square$

Note that if K_1, K_2 are two compact and disjoint subsets of normal topological space $(S, \mathcal{O})$, we have $K_1 \subseteq S - K_2$, and $S - K_2$ is open. Thus, by Corollary 4.16, there exists a continuous function $f : S \longrightarrow [0, 1]$ such that $1_{K_1} \leqslant f \leqslant 1_{S - K_2} = 1 - 1_{K_2}$.

Theorem 4.84. *Any locally compact topological space is a subspace of a compact Hausdorff space.*

Proof. This follows directly from Theorem 4.60. $\square$

Definition 4.39. A Hausdorff topological space $(S, calo)$ is *completely regular* if for every point $x \in S$ and every closed set W such that $y \notin W$ there exists a continuous function $f : S \longrightarrow \mathbb{R}$ such that $f(y) = 0$ and $f(w) = 1$ for every $x \in W$.

Complete regularity of topological spaces is hereditary; in other words, if $(S, \mathcal{O})$ is a completely regular topological space then any of its subspaces is also completely regular.

Theorem 4.85. *Any normal space is completely regular.*

Proof. This follows immediately from Uryson's Lemma (Theorem 4.83). $\square$

Theorem 4.86. *Any locally compact topological space $(S, \mathcal{O})$ is completely regular.*

Proof. $(s, \mathcal{O})$ is a subspace of a compact Hausdorff space, which is a normal space and therefore a completely regular space. Therefore, by heredity, $(S, \mathcal{O})$ is completely regular. $\square$

4.12 Homeomorphisms

Definition 4.40. Let $(S, \mathcal{O})$ and $(T, \mathcal{O}')$ be two topological spaces. A bijection $f : S \longrightarrow T$ is a *homeomorphism* if both f and its inverse f^{-1} are continuous functions.

If a homeomorphism exists between the topological spaces $(S, \mathcal{O})$ and $(S, \mathcal{O}')$, we say that these spaces are *homeomorphic*.

Two homeomorphic topological spaces are essentially identical from a topological point of view.

Example 4.40. The identity map 1_S of any topological space $(S, \mathcal{O})$ is a homeomorphism.

Example 4.41. Consider the subsets $[0, 1)$ of $\mathbb{R}$ and $S_2(\mathbf{0}_2, 1) = \{\mathbf{x} \in \mathbb{R}_2 \mid x_1^2 + x_2^2 = 1\}$. The function $f : [0, 1) \longrightarrow S_2(\mathbf{0}_2, 1)$ given by

$$f(a) = \begin{pmatrix} \cos(2\pi a) \\ \sin(2\pi a) \end{pmatrix}$$

for $a \in [0, 1)$ is bijective and continuous, but it is not a homeomorphism. Indeed, its inverse $f^{-1} : S_2(\mathbf{0}_2, 1) \longrightarrow [0, 1)$ is not continuous at $\binom{1}{0}$. Observe that $f^{-1}\binom{1}{0} = 0$. However, for a neighborhood V of $\binom{1}{0}$ in $S_2(\mathbf{0}_2, 1)$ and $\mathbf{y} \in V$, $f^{-1}(\mathbf{y})$ is not necessarily located in a neighborhood of 0.

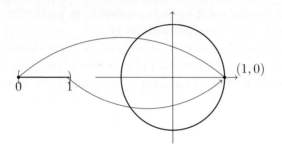

Fig. 4.1 A continuous and bijective functions which is not a homeomorphism.

Theorem 4.87. *A bijection* $f : S \longrightarrow T$ *between two topological spaces* $(S, \mathcal{O})$ *and* $(T, \mathcal{O}')$ *is a homeomorphism if and only if* $U \in \mathcal{O}$ *is equivalent to* $f(U) \in \mathcal{O}'$.

Proof. Suppose that f is a homeomorphism between $(S, \mathcal{O})$ and $(T, \mathcal{O}')$. If $U \in \mathcal{O}$ the continuity of f^{-1} implies that $(f^{-1})^{-1}(U) = f(U) \in \mathcal{O}'$; on the other hand, if $f(U) \in \mathcal{O}'$, then, since $U = f^{-1}(f(U))$, the continuity of f yields $U \in \mathcal{O}$.

Conversely, suppose that for the bijection $f : S \longrightarrow T$, $U \in \mathcal{O}$ if and only if $f(U) \in \mathcal{O}'$. Suppose that $V \in \mathcal{O}'$; since f is a bijection, there is $W \subseteq S$ such that $V = f(W)$ and $W \in \mathcal{O}$ by hypothesis. Observe that $f^{-1}(V) = W$, so f is continuous. To prove that f^{-1} is continuous, note that we need to verify that $(f^{-1})^{-1}(Z)$ is an open set in $(S, \mathcal{O})$ for any set $Z \in \mathcal{O}'$, which is effectively the case because $(f^{-1})^{-1}(Z) = f(Z)$. $\qquad \square$

Any property of $(S, \mathcal{O})$ that can be expressed using the open sets of this topological space is preserved in topological spaces $(T, \mathcal{O}')$ that are homeomorphic to $(S, \mathcal{O})$. Therefore, such a property is said to be *topological*.

The collection of all pairs of topological spaces that are homeomorphic is an equivalence relation on the class of topological spaces as can be easily shown.

Example 4.42. All open intervals of $\mathbb{R}$, bounded or not, are homeomorphic.

Let (a, b) and (c, d) be two bounded intervals of $\mathbb{R}$ and let $f : (a, b) \longrightarrow (c, d)$ be the linear function defined by $f(x) = px + q$, where $p = \frac{d-c}{b-a}$ and $q = \frac{bc - ad}{b-a}$. It is easy to verify that f is a homeomorphism, so any two bounded intervals of $\mathbb{R}$ are homeomorphic; in particular, any bounded interval (a, b) is homeomorphic with $(0, 1)$.

Any two unbounded intervals (a, ∞) and (b, ∞) are homeomorphic; the mapping $g(x) = \frac{b}{a}x$ is a homeomorphism between these sets. Similarly, any two unbounded intervals of the form $(-\infty, a)$ and $(-\infty, b)$ are homeomorphic, and so are (a, ∞) and $(-\infty, b)$.

The function $h : (0, 1) \longrightarrow (0, \infty)$ defined by $h(x) = \tan \frac{\pi x}{2}$ is a homeomorphism, whose inverse mapping is $h^{-1}(x) = \frac{2}{\pi} \arctan x$ so $(0, 1)$ is homeomorphic with $(0, \infty)$. Finally, $(-1, 1)$ is homeomorphic to $(-\infty, \infty)$ since the mapping $h_1 : (-1, 1) \longrightarrow (-\infty, \infty)$ defined by $h(x) = \tan \frac{\pi x}{2}$ for $x \in (-1, 1)$ is a homeomorphism.

Definition 4.41. Let S be a set and let $\mathcal{F} = \{f_\alpha \mid \alpha \in A, f_\alpha : S \longrightarrow T_\alpha\}$ be a family of functions indexed by the set A, where $(T_\alpha, \mathcal{O}_\alpha)$ is a topological space for each $\alpha \in A$.

The *weak topology* on S induced by $\mathcal{F}$ is the topology $\mathcal{O}_\mathcal{F}$ generated by the collection $\mathcal{S} = \{f_\alpha^{-1}(U) \mid U \in \mathcal{O}_\alpha \text{ for } \alpha \in A\}$.

This definition means that the weak topology on S induced by $\mathcal{F}$ has $\mathcal{S}$ as a sub-basis.

Note that each function f_α is continuous when regarded as functions between $(S, \mathcal{O}_\mathcal{F})$ and $(T_\alpha, \mathcal{O}_\alpha)$. Furthermore, $\mathcal{O}_\mathcal{F}$ is the least topology on S that makes all functions f_α continuous.

A basis for the weak topology $\mathcal{O}_\mathcal{F}$ consists of finite intersections of the form $\bigcap_{k=1}^m f_{\alpha_k}^{-1}(U_{\alpha_k})$, where $U_{\alpha_k} \in \mathcal{O}_{\alpha_k}$.

Theorem 4.88. *Let* $\{(T_\alpha, \mathcal{O}_\alpha) \mid \alpha \in A\}$ *be a collection of topological spaces,* S *be a set, and let*

$$\mathcal{F} = \{f_\alpha \mid \alpha \in A, f_\alpha : S \longrightarrow T_\alpha\}$$

be a family of functions. Suppose that $(x_i)_{i \in I}$ be a net in the topological space $(S, \mathcal{O}_{\mathcal{F}})$ equipped with the weak topology generated by $\mathcal{F}$.

We have $x_i \to x$ in $(S, \mathcal{O}_{\mathcal{F}})$ if and only if $f_\alpha(x_i) \longrightarrow f_\alpha(x)$ for each $\alpha \in A$.

Proof. Since each function f_α is continuous, $x_i \to x$ implies immediately $f_\alpha(x_i) \longrightarrow f_\alpha(x)$ for each $\alpha \in A$.

Conversely, suppose that $f_\alpha(x_i) \longrightarrow f_\alpha(x)$ for each $\alpha \in A$ and let $B = \bigcap_{k=1}^{m} f_{\alpha_k}^{-1}(U_{\alpha_k})$ be a set in the basis in $(S, \mathcal{O}_{\mathcal{F}})$.

For each k there exists i_{α_k} such that $j \geqslant i_{\alpha_k}$ implies $f_\alpha(x_j) \in U_{\alpha_k}$. Let i be such that $i \geqslant i_{\alpha_k}$ for $1 \leqslant k \leqslant m$. Then, $x_i \in \bigcap_{k=1}^{m} f_{\alpha_k}^{-1}(U_{\alpha_k}) = B$, so $x_i \to x$ by Theorem 4.65. $\qquad\square$

Definition 4.42. Let $(S_1, \mathcal{O}_1)$ and $(S_2, \mathcal{O}_2)$ be two topological spaces and let $f : S_1 \longrightarrow S_2$ be a function.

The function f is *open* if $f(L)$ is open for every open set L, where $L \in \mathcal{O}_1$; the function f is *closed* if $f(H)$ is closed for every closed set H in S_1.

Theorem 4.89. Let $(S_1, \mathcal{O}_1)$ and $(S_2, \mathcal{O}_2)$ be two topological spaces, let $\boldsymbol{K}_i$ and $\boldsymbol{I}_i$ be the closure and interior operators of the space S_i for $i = 1, 2$, and let $f : S_1 \longrightarrow S_2$ be a function. The following statements hold:

  (i) f is open if and only if $f(\boldsymbol{I}_1(U)) \subseteq \boldsymbol{I}_2(f(U))$ for every $U \in \mathcal{P}(S_1)$;

  (ii) f is closed if and only if $\boldsymbol{K}_2(f(U)) \subseteq f(\boldsymbol{K}_1(U))$ for every $U \in \mathcal{P}(S_1)$;

  (iii) a bijection $f : S_1 \longrightarrow S_2$ is open if and only if it is closed.

Proof. Part (i): Suppose that f is open. Since $\boldsymbol{I}_1(U)$ is an open set, it follows that $f(\boldsymbol{I}_1(U))$ is open. Note that $f(\boldsymbol{I}_1(U))$ is included in $f(U)$ and, since $\boldsymbol{I}_2(f(U)$ is the largest open set included in $f(U)$ it follows that $f(\boldsymbol{I}_1(U)) \subseteq \boldsymbol{I}_2(f(U))$ for every $U \in \mathcal{P}(S_1)$.

Conversely, suppose that $f(\boldsymbol{I}_1(U)) \subseteq \boldsymbol{I}_2(f(U))$ for every $U \in \mathcal{P}(S_1)$. If U is an open set, then $\boldsymbol{I}_1(U) = U$, so $f(U) \subseteq \boldsymbol{I}_2(f(U))$, which implies $f(U) = \boldsymbol{I}_2(f(U)$. Therefore, $f(U)$ is an open set, so f is an open function.

Part (ii) is has a similar argument.

Part (iii): Let f be a bijection. Suppose that f is open and let U be a closed set in $(S_1, \mathcal{O}_1)$. Then $S_1 - U$ is open and, therefore, the set $f(S_1 - U)$ is open in S_2. Since f is a bijection we have $f(S_1 - U) = S_2 - f(U)$, so $f(U)$ is closed. Thus, f is a closed mapping. In a similar manner we can show that if f is closed, then f is open. $\qquad\square$

4.13   Connected Topological Spaces

This chapter is dedicated to the formalization of the notion of an "one-piece" topological space.

Theorem 4.90. *Let $(S, \mathcal{O})$ be a topological space. The following statements are equivalent:*

(i) *there exists a clopen subset K of S such that $K \notin \{\emptyset, S\}$;*

(ii) *there exist two non-empty open subsets L, L' of S that are complementary;*

(iii) *there exist two non-empty closed subsets H, H' of S that are complementary.*

Proof. (i) implies (ii): If K is clopen and $K \notin \{\emptyset, S\}$, then both K and $\bar{K}$ are non-empty open sets.

(ii) implies (iii): Suppose that L and L' are two non-empty complementary open subsets of S. Then, L and L' are in the same time closed because the complements of each set is open.

(iii) implies (i): If H and H' are complementary closed sets, then each of them is also open because the complements of each set is closed. Thus, both sets are clopen.   □

Definition 4.43. A topological space $(S, \mathcal{O})$ is *disconnected* if it satisfies any of the equivalent conditions of Theorem 4.90. Otherwise, $(S, \mathcal{O})$ is said to be *connected*.

A subset T of a connected topological space is *connected* if the subspace T is connected.

Theorem 4.91. *Let T be a subset of S, where $(S, \mathcal{O})$ is a topological space. The following statements are equivalent:*

(i) *T is connected;*

(ii) *there are no open sets L_1, L_2 in $(S, \mathcal{O})$ such that $T \subseteq L_1 \cup L_2$, and $T \cap L_1$, and $T \cap L_2$ are non-empty and disjoint;*

(iii) *there are no closed sets H_1, H_2 in $(S, \mathcal{O})$ such that $T \subseteq H_1 \cup H_2$, and $T \cap H_1$ and $T \cap H_2$ are non-empty and disjoint;*

(iv) *there is no clopen set in $(S, \mathcal{O})$ that has a non-empty intersection with T.*

Proof.   The equivalence of the statements follows immediately from the definition of the subspace topology.   □

Theorem 4.92. *Let* $\mathcal{C} = \{C_i \mid i \in I\}$ *be a family of connected subsets of a topological space* $(S, \mathcal{O})$. *If* $C_i \cap C_j \neq \emptyset$ *for every* $i, j \in I$ *such that* $i \neq j$, *then* $\bigcup \mathcal{C}$ *is connected.*

Proof. Suppose that $C = \bigcup \mathcal{C}$ is not connected. Then C contains two complementary open subsets L' and L''. For every $i \in I$, the sets $C_i \cap L'$ and $C_i \cap L''$ are complementary and open in C_i. Since each C_i is connected, we have either $C_i \cap L' = \emptyset$ or $C_i \cap L'' = \emptyset$ for every $i \in I$. In the first case, $C_i \subseteq L''$, while in the second, $C_i \subseteq L'$. Thus, the collection $\mathcal{C}$ can be partitioned into two subcollections, $\mathcal{C} = \mathcal{C}' \cup \mathcal{C}''$, where $\mathcal{C}' = \{C_i \in \mathcal{C} \mid C_i \subseteq L'\}$ and $\mathcal{C}'' = \{C_i \in \mathcal{C} \mid C_i \subseteq L''\}$. Clearly, two sets $C_i \in \mathcal{C}'$ and $C_j \in \mathcal{C}''$ are disjoint because the sets L' and L'' are disjoint, and this contradicts the hypothesis. $\square$

Corollary 4.17. *Let* $(S, \mathcal{O})$ *be a topological space and let* $x \in S$. *The collection* $\mathcal{C}_x$ *of connected subsets of* S *that contain* x *has* $K_x = \bigcup \mathcal{C}_x$ *as its largest element.*

Proof. This follows immediately from Theorem 4.92. $\square$

We refer to K_x as *the connected component* of x.

Theorem 4.93. *Let* T *be a connected subset of a topological space* $(S, \mathcal{O})$, *and suppose that* W *is a subset of* S *such that* $T \subseteq W \subseteq \boldsymbol{K}(T)$. *Then* W *is connected.*

Proof. Suppose that W is not connected (that is, $W = U \cup U'$, where U and U' are two non-empty, disjoint, and open sets in W). There exist two open sets L, L' in S such that $U = W \cap L$ and $U' = W \cap L'$. Since $T \subseteq W$, the sets $T \cap U$ and $T \cap U'$ are open in T, disjoint, and their union equals T. Thus, we have either $T \cap U = \emptyset$ or $T \cap U' = \emptyset$ because T is connected.

If $T \cap U = \emptyset$, then $T \cap L = (T \cap W) \cap L = T \cap (W \cap L) = T \cap U = \emptyset$, so $T \subseteq \bar{L}$. Since $\bar{L}$ is closed, $\boldsymbol{K}(T) \subseteq \bar{L}$, which implies $W \subseteq \bar{L}$, which implies $U = W \cap L = \emptyset$. This contradicts the assumption made earlier about U. A similar contradiction follows from $T \cap U' = \emptyset$. Thus, W is connected. $\square$

Corollary 4.18. *If* T *is a connected subset of a topological space* $(S, \mathcal{O})$, *then* $\boldsymbol{K}(T)$ *is also connected.*

Proof. This statement is a special case of Theorem 4.17. $\square$

Theorem 4.94. *Let* $(S, \mathcal{O})$ *be a topological space. The collection of all connected components of* S *is a partition of* S *that consists of closed sets.*

Proof. Corollary 4.18 implies that each connected component K_x is closed. Suppose that K_x and K_y are two connected components that are not disjoint. Then, by Theorem 4.92, $K_x \cup K_y$ is connected. Since $x \in K_x \cup K_y$, it follows that $K_x \cup K_y \subseteq K_x$ because K_x is the maximal connected set that contains x, so $K_y \subseteq K_x$. Similarly, $K_x \subseteq K_y$, so $K_x = K_y$. □

Theorem 4.95. *The image of a connected topological space through a continuous function is a connected set.*

Proof. Let $(S_1, \mathcal{O}_1)$ and $(S_2, \mathcal{O}_2)$ be two topological spaces and let $f : S_1 \longrightarrow S_2$ be a continuous function, where S_1 is connected. If $f(S_1)$ were not connected, we would have two non-empty open subsets L and L' of $f(S_1)$ that are complementary. Then, $f^{-1}(L)$ and $f^{-1}(L')$ would be two non-empty, open sets in S_1 which are complementary, which contradicts the fact that S_1 is connected. □

A characterization of connected spaces is given next.

Theorem 4.96. *Let $(S, \mathcal{O})$ be a topological space and let $(\{0, 1\}, \mathcal{P}(\{0, 1\}))$ be a two-element topological space equipped with the non-discrete topology. Then, S is connected if and only if every continuous application $f : S \longrightarrow \{0, 1\}$ is constant.*

Proof. Suppose that S is connected. Both $f^{-1}(0)$ and $f^{-1}(1)$ are clopen sets in S because both $\{0\}$ and $\{1\}$ are clopen in the discrete topology. Thus, we have either $f^{-1}(0) = \emptyset$ and $f^{-1}(1) = S$, or $f^{-1}(0) = S$ and $f^{-1}(1) = \emptyset$. In the first case, f is the constant function $f(x) = 1$; in the second, it is the constant function $f(x) = 0$.

Conversely, suppose that the condition is satisfied for every continuous function $f : S \longrightarrow \{0, 1\}$ and suppose $(S, \mathcal{O})$ is not connected. Then, there exist two non-empty disjoint open subsets L and L' that are complementary. Let $f = 1_L$ be the characteristic function of L, which is continuous because both L and L' are open. Thus, f is constant and this implies either $L = \emptyset$ and $L' = S$ or $L = S$ and $L' = \emptyset$, so S is connected. □

Example 4.43. The topological space $(\mathbb{R}, \mathcal{O})$ is connected. Suppose that K is a clopen set in $\mathbb{R}$ distinct from $\mathbb{R}$ and $\emptyset$, and let $x \in \mathbb{R} - K$.

Suppose that the set $K \cap [x, \infty)$ is non-empty. Then, this set is closed and bounded below and therefore has a least element u. Since $K \cap [x, \infty) = K \cap (x, \infty)$ is also open, there exists $\epsilon > 0$ such that $(u - \epsilon, u + \epsilon) \subseteq K \cap [x, \infty)$, which contradicts the fact that u is the least element of $K \cap [x, \infty)$. A similar contradiction is obtained if we assume that $K \cap (-\infty, x] \neq \emptyset$, so $\mathbb{R}$ cannot contain a clopen set distinct from $\mathbb{R}$ or $\emptyset$.

Example 4.44. Theorem 4.96 allows us to prove that the connected subsets of $\mathbb{R}$ are exactly the intervals.

Suppose that T is a connected subset of S but is not an interval. Then, there are three numbers x, y, z such that $x < y < z$, $x, z \in T$ but $y \notin T$. Define the function $f : T \longrightarrow \{0, 1\}$ by $f(u) = 0$ if $u < y$ and $f(u) = 1$ if $y < u$. Clearly, f is continuous but is not constant, and this contradicts Theorem 4.96. Thus, T must be an interval.

Suppose now that T is an open interval of $\mathbb{R}$. We saw that T is homeomorphic to $\mathbb{R}$ (see Example 4.42), so T is indeed connected. If T is an arbitrary interval, its interior $\mathbf{I}(T)$ is an open interval and, since $\mathbf{I}(T) \subseteq T \subseteq \mathbf{K}(\mathbf{I}(T))$, it follows that T is connected.

Definition 4.44. A topological space $(S, \mathcal{O})$ is *totally disconnected* if, for every $x \in S$, the connected component of x is $K_x = \{x\}$.

Example 4.45. Any topological space equipped with the discrete topology is totally disconnected.

Theorem 4.97. *Let $(S, \mathcal{O})$ be a topological space and let T be a subset of S.*

If for every pair of distinct points $x, y \in T$ there exist two disjoint closed sets H_x and H_y such that $T \subseteq H_x \cup H_y$, $x \in H_x$, and $y \in H_y$, then T is totally disconnected.

Proof. Let K_x be the connected component of x, and suppose that $y \in K_x$ and $y \neq x$, that is, $K_x = K_y = K$. Then, $K \cap H_x$ and $K \cap H_y$ are non-empty disjoint closed sets and $K = (K \cap H_x) \cup (K \cap H_y)$, which contradicts the connectedness of K. Therefore, $K_x = \{x\}$ for every $x \in T$ and T is totally disconnected. $\square$

4.14 Products of Topological Spaces

Theorem 4.98. *Let $\{(S_i, \mathcal{O}_i) \mid i \in I\}$ be a family of topological spaces indexed by the set I. Define on the set $S = \prod_{i \in I} S_i$ the collection of sets $\mathcal{B} = \{\bigcap_{j \in J} p_j^{-1}(L_j) \mid L_j \in \mathcal{O}_j \text{ and } J \text{ finite}\}$. Then, $\mathcal{B}$ is a basis for a topology.*

Proof. Note that every set $\bigcap_{j \in J} p_j^{-1}(L_j)$ has the form $\prod_{i \in I-J} \times \prod_{j \in J} L_j$. We need to observe only that a finite intersection of sets in $\mathcal{B}$ is again a set in $\mathcal{B}$. Therefore, $\mathcal{B}$ is a basis. $\quad\square$

Definition 4.45. The topology $TOP(\mathcal{B})$ generated on the set $S = \prod_{i \in I} S_i$ by $\mathcal{B}$ is called the *product of the topologies* $\mathcal{O}_i$ and is denoted by $\prod_{i \in I} \mathcal{O}_i$.

The topological space $(\prod_{i \in I} S_i, \prod_{i \in I} \mathcal{O}_i)$ is the *product of the collection of topological spaces* $\{(S_i, \mathcal{O}_i) \mid i \in I\}$.

The product of the topologies $\{\mathcal{O}_i \mid i \in I\}$ can be generated starting from the sub-basis $\mathcal{S}$ that consists of sets of the form $D_{j,L} = \{t \mid t \in \prod_{i \in I} \mid t(j) \in L\}$, where $j \in I$ and L is an open set in $(S_j, \mathcal{O}_j)$. It is easy to see that any set in the basis $\mathcal{B}$ is a finite intersection of sets of the form $D_{j,L}$.

Theorem 4.99. *Let* $\{(S_i, \mathcal{O}_i) \mid i \in I\}$ *be a collection of topological spaces. Each projection* $p_\ell : \prod_{i \in I} S_i \longrightarrow S_\ell$ *is a continuous function for* $\ell \in I$. *Moreover, the product topology is the coarsest topology on S such that projections are continuous.*

Proof. Let L be an open set in $(S_\ell, \mathcal{O}_\ell)$. We have

$$p_\ell^{-1}(L) = \left\{ t \in \prod_{i \in I} S_i \mid t(\ell) \in L \right\},$$

which has the form $\prod_{i \in I} K_i$, where each set K_i is open because

$$K_i = \begin{cases} S_i & \text{if } i \neq \ell, \\ L & \text{if } i = \ell, \end{cases}$$

for $i \in I$. Thus, $p_\ell^{-1}(L)$ is open and p_ℓ is continuous.

The proof of the second part of the theorem is left to the reader. $\quad\square$

Theorem 4.100. *Let* $\{(S_i, \mathcal{O}_i) \mid i \in I\}$ *be a collection of topological spaces and let* $x = (x_i) \in \prod_{i \in I} S_i$. *Then, a subset V of* $\prod_{i \in I} S_i$ *is a neighborhood of x if and only if V contains a set of the form* $\prod_{i \in I} V_i$, *where V_i is a neighborhood of x_i for every $i \in I$, and $V_i = S_i$ for almost all $i \in I$.*

Proof. If $V \in neigh_x (\prod_{i \in I} \mathcal{O}_i)$ there exists a set B in the basis $\mathcal{B}$ of the product topology (defined in Theorem 4.98) such that $x \in B \subseteq V$ and B is a set that satisfies the condition of the theorem.

Conversely, suppose that $\{V_i \mid i \in I\}$ is a collection such that $V_i \in neigh_{x_i}(\mathcal{O}_i)$ and $J = \{i \in I \mid V_i \neq S_i\}$ is a finite set. For each i, V_i contains an open neighborhood U_i of x_i, where $U_i = S_i$ for $i \notin J$. Then, $B = \prod_{i \in I}$ is a open set with $x \in B \subseteq \prod_{i \in I} V_i \subseteq V$, so $V \in neigh_x (\prod_{i \in I} \mathcal{O}_i)$. $\quad\square$

Note that if I is a finite set, $I = \{1, \ldots, n\}$ a neighborhood of $x = (x_1, \ldots, x_n)$ is any subset of $S_1 \times \cdots \times S_n$ containing a product $V_1 \times \cdots \times V_n$, where $V_i \in neigh_{x_i}(\mathcal{O}_i)$ for $1 \leqslant i \leqslant n$.

Let $\{(S_i, \mathcal{O}_i) \mid i \in I\}$ be a collection of topological spaces and let $x = (x_i) \in \prod_{i \in I} S_i$. If $f : S \longrightarrow \prod_{i \in I} S_i$ is a mapping, then its ith coordinate mappings is the mapping $f_i : S \longrightarrow S_i$ defined by $f_i(x) = p_i(f(x))$ for $x \in S$.

Theorem 4.101. *Let $\{(S_i, \mathcal{O}_i) \mid i \in I\}$ be a finite collection of topological spaces. If $(S, \mathcal{O})$ is a topological space and $f : S \longrightarrow \prod_{i \in I} S_i$, then f is continuous if and only if each component f_i is continuous.*

Proof. Since $f_i = p_i f$, it is clear that the continuity of f implies the continuity of all its components.

Conversely, suppose that each f_i is continuous at $x_0 \in S$. If $U = \prod_{i \in I} U_i$ is an open set containing $f(x_0)$, where $U_i \in \mathcal{O}_i$ for $i \in I$, $f_i^{-1}(U_i)$ is a neighborhood of x_0 in S and, therefore, $f^{-1}(U) = \bigcap_{i \in I} f_i^{-1}(U_i)$ is also a neighborhood of x_0. Since every neighborhood V of $f(x_0)$ in S contains an open set containing $f(x_0)$ it follows that $f^{-1}(V)$ (which contains $f^{-1}(U)$) is a neighborhood of x_0, so f is continuous. $\square$

Theorem 4.102. *Let $\{(S_i, \mathcal{O}_i) \mid i \in I\}$ be a collection of topological spaces. If each of the spaces S_i are Hausdorff spaces, then $\prod_{i \in I} S_i$ is a Hausdorff space.*

Proof. Let $x = (x_i), y = (y_i) \in \prod_{i \in I} S_i$. There exists $i \in I$ such that $x_i \neq y_i$. By Theorem 4.49, there exist $U \in neigh_{x_i}(\mathcal{O}_i)$ and $V \in neigh_{y_i}(\mathcal{O}_i)$ such that $U \cap V = \emptyset$. Thus, x and y have disjoint neighborhoods in the product space, which implies that $\prod_{i \in I} S_i$ is a Hausdorff space. $\square$

Theorem 4.103. *If $(S, \mathcal{O})$ is a Hausdorff space, then the diagonal set*

$$D_S = \{(x, x) \mid x \in S\}$$

is closed in the topological space $(S \times S, \mathcal{O} \times \mathcal{O})$.

Proof. Let x, y be two distinct points in S. Then, $(x, y) \notin D \times D$. Since x and y are distinct and S is a Hausdorff space, by Theorem 4.49 there exist $U \in neigh_x(\mathcal{O})$ and $V \in neigh_y(\mathcal{O})$ such that $U \cap V = \emptyset$.

Thus, the set $U \times V$ is a neighborhood of (x, y) that does not intersect D. This implies that $S \times S - D$ is an open set, which shows that D is a closed set. $\square$

Corollary 4.19. *Let $(S, \mathcal{O})$ be a topological space, $(T, \mathcal{O}')$ be a Hausdorff topological space, and let $f, g : S \longrightarrow T$ be two continuous functions. The set $EQ(f, g) = \{x \in S \mid f(x) = g(x)\}$ is a closed subset of S.*

Proof. Let $h : S \longrightarrow S \times T \times T$ be the mapping defined by $h(x) = (f(x), g(x))$ for $x \in S$. It is clear that h is continuous. The set $D = \{(t, t) \mid t \in T\}$ is closed by Theorem 4.103 and so is the set $h^{-1}(D) = \{x \in S \mid f(x) = g(x)\}$. $\qquad\square$

Corollary 4.20. *Let $(S, \mathcal{O})$ be a topological space, $(T, \mathcal{O}')$ be a Hausdorff topological space, and let $f : S \longrightarrow T$ be a continuous function. The set $\{(x, y) \in S \times T \mid y = f(x)\}$ is a closed subset of $S \times T$.*

Proof. Note that the mappings $\phi : S \times T \longrightarrow T$ and $\psi : S \times T \longrightarrow T$ defined by $\phi(x, y) = y$ and $\psi(x, y) = f(x)$ are continuous. Therefore, since $EQ(\phi, \psi) = \{(x, y) \in S \mid y = f(x)\}$, by Corollary 4.19, the set $\{(x, y) \in S \times T \mid y = f(x)\}$ is closed. $\qquad\square$

Corollary 4.21. *Let $(S, \mathcal{O})$ be a topological space, $(T, \mathcal{O}')$ be a Hausdorff topological space, and let $f, g : S \longrightarrow T$ be two continuous functions. If the set $EQ(f, g) = \{x \in S \mid f(x) = g(x)\}$ is dense in S, then $f = g$.*

Proof. If $E(f, g)$ is dense in S we have $\mathbf{K}(EQ(f, g)) = S$. Since $EQ(f, g)$ is closed, it follows that $EQ(f, g) = S$, hence $f = g$. $\qquad\square$

Lemma 4.3. *Let $\mathcal{C}$ be a collection of subsets of $S = \prod_{i \in I} S_i$ such that $\mathcal{C}$ has the f.i.p. and $\mathcal{C}$ is maximal with this property.*

We have $\bigcap \mathcal{D} \in \mathcal{C}$ for every finite subcollection $\mathcal{D}$ of $\mathcal{C}$. Furthermore, if $T \cap C \neq \emptyset$ for every $C \in \mathcal{C}$, then $T \in \mathcal{C}$.

Proof. Let $\mathcal{D} = \{D_1, \ldots, D_n\}$ be a finite subcollection of $\mathcal{C}$ and let $D = \bigcap \mathcal{D} \neq \emptyset$. Note that the intersection of every finite subcollection of $\mathcal{C} \cup \{D\}$ is also non-empty. The maximality of $\mathcal{C}$ implies $D \in \mathcal{C}$, which proves the first part of the lemma.

For the second part of the lemma, observe that the intersection of any finite subcollection of $\mathcal{D} \cup \{T\}$ is not empty. Therefore, as above, $T \in \mathcal{C}$. $\qquad\square$

In the proof of the next theorem we use a fundamental assumption in mathematics known as *Zorn's lemma*, that states that if every chain of a partially ordered set $(S, \leqslant)$ has an upper bound, then S has a maximal element. This is equivalent to saying that S contains a chain that is maximal with respect to set inclusion.

Theorem 4.104. (Tychonoff's Theorem) *Let* $\{(S_i, \mathcal{O}_i) \mid i \in I\}$ *be a collection of topological spaces such that* $S_i \neq \emptyset$ *for every* $i \in I$. *Then,* $(\prod_{i \in I} S_i, \prod_{i \in I} \mathcal{O}_i)$ *is compact if and only if each topological space* $(S_i, \mathcal{O}_i)$ *is compact for* $i \in I$.

Proof. If $(\prod_{i \in I} S_i, \mathcal{O})$ is compact, then, by Theorem 4.81, it is clear that each of the topological spaces $(S_i, \mathcal{O}_i)$ is compact because each projection p_i is continuous.

Conversely, suppose that each of the topological spaces $(S_i, \mathcal{O}_i)$ is compact.

Let $\mathcal{E}$ be a family of sets in $S = \prod_{i \in I} S_i$ that has the f.i.p. and let $(\mathfrak{C}, \subseteq)$ be the partially ordered set whose elements are collections of subsets of S that have the f.i.p. and contain the family $\mathcal{E}$.

Let $\{\mathcal{C}_i \mid i \in I\}$ be a chain in $(\mathfrak{C}, \subseteq)$. It is easy to verify that $\bigcup\{\mathcal{C}_i \mid i \in I\}$ has the f.i.p., so every chain in $(\mathfrak{C}, \subseteq)$ has an upper bound.

Therefore, by Zorn's Lemma, the poset $(\mathfrak{C}, \subseteq)$ contains a maximal collection $\mathcal{C}$ that has the f.i.p. and contains $\mathcal{E}$. We aim to find an element $t \in \prod_{i \in I} S_i$ that belongs to $\bigcap\{\mathbf{K}(C) \mid C \in \mathcal{C}\}$ because, in this case, the same element belongs to $\bigcap\{\mathbf{K}(C) \mid C \in \mathcal{E}\}$ and this would imply, by Theorem 4.44, that $(S, \mathcal{O})$ is compact.

Let $\mathcal{C}_i$ be the collection of closed subsets of S_i defined by

$$\mathcal{C}_i = \{\mathbf{K}_i(p_i(C)) \mid C \in \mathcal{C}\}$$

for $i \in I$, where $\mathbf{K}_i$ is the closure of the topological space $(S_i, \mathcal{O}_i)$.

It is clear that each collection $\mathcal{C}_i$ has the f.i.p. in S_i. Indeed, since $\mathcal{C}$ has the f.i.p., if $\{C_1, \ldots, C_n\} \subseteq \mathcal{C}$ and $x \in \bigcap_{k=1}^n C_k$, then $p_i(x) \in \bigcap_{k=1}^n \mathbf{K}(p_i(C_k))$, so $\mathcal{C}_i$ has the f.i.p. Since $(S_i, \mathcal{O}_i)$ is compact, we have $\bigcap \mathcal{C}_i \neq \emptyset$, by part (iii) of Theorem 4.43. Let $t_i \in \bigcap \mathcal{C}_i = \bigcap\{\mathbf{K}_i(p_i(C)) \mid C \in \mathcal{C}\}$ and let $t \in S$ be defined by $t(i) = t_i$ for $i \in I$.

Let $D_{j,L} = \{u \mid u \in \prod_{i \in I} \mid u(j) \in L\}$, a set of the sub-basis of the product topology that contains t, defined earlier, where L is an open set in $(S_j, \mathcal{O}_j)$. Since $g(j) \in L$, the set L has a non-empty intersection with every set $\mathbf{K}_i(p_i(C))$, where $C \in \mathcal{C}$. On the other hand, since $p_i(D_{j,L}) = S_i$ for $i \neq j$, it follows that for every $i \in I$ we have $p_i(D_{j,L}) \cap \bigcap_{C \in \mathcal{C}} \mathbf{K}_i(p_i(C)) \neq \emptyset$. Therefore, $p_i(D_{j,L})$ has a non-empty intersection with every set of the form $\mathbf{K}_i(p_i(C))$, where $C \in \mathcal{C}$. By the contrapositive of Theorem 4.6, this means that $p_i(D_{j,L}) \cup p_i(C) \neq \emptyset$ for every $i \in I$ and $C \in \mathcal{C}$. This in turn means that $D_{j,L} \cup C \neq \emptyset$ for every $C \in \mathcal{C}$. By Lemma 4.3, it follows that $D_{j,L} \in \mathcal{C}$. Since every set that belongs to the basis of the product topology is a finite intersection of sets of the form $D_{j,L}$, it follows that any member of the basis

has a non-empty intersection with every set of $\mathcal{C}$. This implies that g belongs to $\bigcup \{ \mathbf{K}(C) \mid C \in \mathcal{C} \}$, which implies the compactness of $(\prod_{i \in I} S_i, \prod_{i \in I} \mathcal{O}_i)$.
$\square$

Example 4.46. In Example 4.21, we have shown that every closed interval $[x, y]$ of $\mathbb{R}$ where $x < y$ is compact. By Theorem 4.104, any subset of $\mathbb{R}^n$ of the form $[x_1, y_1] \times \cdots \times [x_n, y_n]$ is compact.

4.15   Semicontinuous Functions

We saw that a function $f : S \longrightarrow \hat{\mathbb{R}}$ defined on a topological space $(S, \mathcal{O})$ is continuous in $\mathbf{x}_0 \in S$ if and only if the following conditions
   (i) if $c < f(x_0)$ there exists a neighborhood U of x_0 in $(S, \mathcal{O})$ such that for every $x \in U$ we have $c < f(x)$;
   (ii) if $f(x_0) < d$ there exists a neighborhood W of x_0 in $(S, \mathcal{O})$ such that for every $x \in W$ we have $f(x) < d$
are satisfied.

If only one of these conditions are satisfied, we say that f is *semicontinuous* in $\mathbf{x}_0$. Specifically, we have the following definition.

Definition 4.46. Let $(S, \mathcal{O})$ be a topological space. A function $f : S \longrightarrow \hat{\mathbb{R}}$ is *lower semicontinuous* at $x_0 \in S$ if for every $c < f(x_0)$ there is a neighborhood U of x_0 such that for every $x \in U$ we have $c < f(x)$;

The function f is *upper semicontinuous* at $x_0 \in S$ if for every $d > f(x_0)$ there is a neighborhood W of x_0 such that for every $x \in W$ we have $d > f(x)$.

The function f is lower semicontinuous (upper-semicontinuous) on S if it is lower semicontinuous (upper semicontinuous) at every point of S.

Observe that the function f is lower semicontinuous at x_0 if for every $c < f(x_0)$ the set $f^{-1}(c, \infty]$ is a neighborhood of x_0. Similarly, f is upper semicontinuous at x_0 if the set $f^{-1}[-\infty, d)$ is a neighborhood of x_0 for each $d > f(x_0)$.

Since $(-f)^{-1}(c, \infty] = \{ x \in S \mid -f(x) > c \} = \{ x \in S \mid f(x) < -c \} = f^{-1}[-\infty, -c)$, it follows that $-f$ is upper semicontinuous if and only if f is lower semicontinuous.

Example 4.47. Let $f : \mathbb{R} \longrightarrow \hat{\mathbb{R}}$ be the function
$$f(x) = \begin{cases} -1 & \text{if } x < 0, \\ 1 & \text{if } x \geqslant 0 \end{cases}$$

for $x \in \mathbb{R}$. Observe that

$$\{x \in \mathbb{R} \mid f(x) < d\} = \begin{cases} \emptyset & \text{if } d \leqslant -1, \\ \mathbb{R}_{<0} & \text{if } -1 < d \leqslant 1, \\ \mathbb{R} & \text{if } d > 1. \end{cases}$$

In each case, the set $\{x \in \mathbb{R} \mid f(x) < d\}$ is open in $(\mathbb{R}, \mathcal{O})$, so f is upper semicontinuous.

Example 4.48. Let $\lfloor x \rfloor$ be the largest integer less or equal to x and let $\lceil x \rceil$ be the least integer greater or equal to x. The function $f : \mathbb{R} \longrightarrow \hat{\mathbb{R}}$ defined by $f(x) = \lfloor x \rfloor$, is upper semicontinuous because

$$\{x \in \mathbb{R} \mid \lfloor x \rfloor \leqslant t\} = (-\infty, t]$$

is closed for any $t \in \mathbb{R}$.

Lemma 4.4. *Let $f : S \longrightarrow \hat{\mathbb{R}}$ and $g : S \longrightarrow \hat{\mathbb{R}}$ be two functions and let $h = f + g$. For $r, s \in \mathbb{R}$ define the set*

$$W_{r,s} = \{x \in S \mid f(x) < r\} \cap \{x \in S \mid g(x) < s\}.$$

If $t \in \mathbb{R}$ we have:

$$\{x \in S \mid f(x) + g(x) < t\} = \bigcup_{r+s=t} W_{r,s}.$$

Proof. If $x \in \bigcup_{r+s=t} W_{r,s}$ there exists a pair of numbers (r, s) such that $r + s = t$, $f(x) < r$, and $g(x) < s$. This implies $f(x) + g(x) < r + s = t$, so $x \in \{x \in S \mid f(x) + g(x) < t\}$.

Conversely, suppose that $f(x) + g(x) < t$. We need to show that there exist r, s such that $f(x) < r$, $g(x) < s$, and $r + s = t$. Let $r = t - g(x)$ and $s = t - f(x)$. It is clear that $f(x) < r$ and $g(x) < s$, so $x \in W_{r,s}$ and, therefore, $x \in \bigcup_{r+s=t} W_{r,s}$. $\square$

Theorem 4.105. *Let $(S, \mathcal{O})$ be a topological space and let $f, g : S \longrightarrow \hat{\mathbb{R}}$ be two upper semicontinuous functions. Their sum $h : S \longrightarrow \hat{\mathbb{R}}$ is upper semicontinuous.*

Proof. Since f, g are upper semicontinuous, the sets $\{x \in S \mid f(x) < r\}$ and $\{x \in S \mid g(x) < s\}$ are open for each r and s. Therefore, using the notations of Lemma 4.4, each sets $W_{r,s}$ is open as the intersection of two open sets. Consequently, by the same lemma, the set $\{x \in S \mid f(x) + g(x) < t\}$ is open for every t, so $f + g$ is upper semicontinuous. $\square$

Example 4.49. Let $(S, \mathcal{O})$ be a topological space. The characteristic function 1_U of a subset U of S is lower semicontinuous if and only if U is open. Indeed, since

$$(1_U)^{-1}(t, \infty] = \begin{cases} S & \text{if } t < 0, \\ U & \text{if } 0 \leqslant t < 1, \\ \emptyset & \text{if } t \geqslant 1, \end{cases}$$

it follows that $(1_U)^{-1}(t, \infty] \in \mathcal{O}$ for each $t \in \mathbb{R}$ if and only if $U \in \mathcal{O}$.

The characteristic function 1_W of a set W is upper semicontinuous if and only if W is a closed set. Indeed, let W be a set such that 1_W is upper semicontinuous. This means that the function -1_W is lower semicontinuous and, therefore, the function $1 - 1_W$ is lower semicontinuous. Since $1_{S-W} = 1 - 1_W$, it follows that 1_{S-W} is lower semicontinuous, so $S - W$ is an open set, which is equivalent to W being closed.

The limits superior and inferior defined for nets allow us to apply these concepts for functions having numerical values.

Let $(S, \mathcal{O})$ be a topological space and let $f : S \longrightarrow \hat{\mathbb{R}}$ be a function. If $x_0 \in S$ and (x_V) is a net indexed by $neigh_{x_0}(\mathcal{O})$ we focus our attention on the numerical net $(f(x_V))$ indexed by the same $neigh_{x_0}(\mathcal{O})$.

Definition 4.47. Let $f : S \to \hat{\mathbb{R}}$ be a real-valued function defined on the topological space $(S, \mathcal{O})$. The *limit inferior* of f in x_0 and the limit superior of f in x_0 are the numbers $\liminf_{x \to x_0} f$ and $\limsup_{x \to x_0} f$ given by

$$\liminf_{x \to x_0} f = \sup \inf \{ f(V) \mid V \in neigh_{x_0}(\mathcal{O}) \}, \tag{4.6}$$

$$\limsup_{x \to x_0} f = \inf \sup \{ f(V) \mid V \in neigh_{x_0}(\mathcal{O}) \}, \tag{4.7}$$

respectively.

Note that if $r > 0$ then $\liminf_{x \to x_0} a f(x) = a \liminf_{x \to x_0} f(x)$.

Example 4.50. If $f : \mathbb{R} \longrightarrow \hat{\mathbb{R}}$, then

$$\liminf_{x \to x_0} f = \sup_{r > 0} \inf \{ f(x) \mid |x - x_0| < r \}, \tag{4.8}$$

$$\limsup_{x \to x_0} f = \inf_{r > 0} \sup \{ f(x) \mid |x - x_0| < r \}. \tag{4.9}$$

Theorem 4.106. *If* $f, g : S \longrightarrow \hat{r}r$ *are two functions (such that the additions in the equality below are defined), then*

$$\liminf_{x \to x_0} (f + g)(x) \geqslant \liminf_{x \to x_0} f(x) + \liminf_{x \to x_0} g(x).$$

Proof. If $\liminf_{x \to x_0} f(x) = -\infty$ or $\liminf_{x \to x_0} g(x) = -\infty$ the inequality is immediate. Otherwise, if $a < \liminf_{x \to x_0} f(x)$ and $b < \liminf_{x \to x_0} g(x)$ there exist $U, V \in neigh_{x_0}(\mathcal{O})$ such that $\inf f(U) > a$ and $\inf g(V) > b$, so $\inf(f + g)(U \cap V) > a + b$. This implies $\liminf_{x \to x_0} (f + g)(x) \geqslant a + b$. $\qquad \square$

Theorem 4.107. *Let $(S, \mathcal{O})$ be a topological space and let $f : S \longrightarrow \hat{\mathbb{R}}$ be a function. Then, f is lower semicontinuous if and only if $(x_i)_{i \in I}$ being a convergent net in S with $x_i \to x$ implies that*

$$f(x) \leqslant \liminf f(x_i).$$

Proof. Suppose that f is lower semicontinuous and let $t \in \mathbb{R}$ such that $t < f(x)$. Then, the set $f^{-1}(t, \infty]$ is open and $x \in f^{-1}(t, \infty]$.

Let (x_i) be a net such that and $x_i \to x$. Since $x_i \to x$, there is some i_t such that $i \geqslant i_t$ implies $x_i \in f^{-1}(t, \infty]$. In other words, $i \geqslant i_t$ implies $f(x_i) > t$. This implies $\liminf f(x_i) \geqslant t$. Since this holds for all $t < f(x)$, it follows that $f(x) \leqslant \liminf f(x_i)$.

Conversely, suppose that $x_i \to x$ implies $f(x) \leqslant \liminf f(x_i)$. Let $T = f^{-1}(-\infty, t]$, where $t \in \mathbb{R}$. If $x \in \mathbf{K}(T)$, by Theorem 4.66, there is a net (x_i) in T such that $x_i \to x$. By hypothesis, $f(x) \leqslant \liminf f(x_i)$. The definition of T implies that $f(x_i) \leqslant t$ for $i \in I$, hence $f(x) \leqslant t$. This means that $x \in T$, so T is closed and $S - T = f^{-1}(t, \infty]$ is open, which means that f is lower semicontinuous. $\qquad \square$

Theorem 4.108. *Let $(S, \mathcal{O})$ be a topological space and let $\{f_j \mid f_j : X \longrightarrow \hat{\mathbb{R}} \text{ for } j \in J\}$ be a collection of lower semicontinuous functions. Then, the function $f : S \longrightarrow \hat{\mathbb{R}}$ defined by $f(x) = \sup\{f_j(x) \mid j \in J\}$ is a lower semicontinuous function.*

Proof. Note that

$$\{x \in S \mid f(x) \leqslant t\} = \bigcap_{j \in J} \{x \in S \mid f_j(x) \leqslant t\}.$$

Since each f_j is lower semicontinuous, each set $\{x \in S \mid f_j(x) \leqslant t\}$ is closed, so $\{x \in S \mid f(x) \leqslant t\}$ is closed, which allows us to conclude that f is lower semicontinuous. $\qquad \square$

Corollary 4.22. *Let $(S, \mathcal{O})$ be a topological space and let $\{f_j \mid f_j : X \longrightarrow \hat{\mathbb{R}} \text{ for } j \in J\}$ be a collection of upper semicontinuous functions. Then, the function $f : S \longrightarrow \hat{\mathbb{R}}$ defined by $f(x) = \inf\{f_j(x) \mid j \in J\}$ is an upper semicontinuous function.*

Proof. This statement follows by applying Theorem 4.108 to the collection of lower semicontinuous functions $\{-f_j \mid f_j : X \longrightarrow \hat{\mathbb{R}} \text{ for } j \in J\}$. $\square$

Theorem 4.109. *Let $(S, \mathcal{O})$ be a compact topological space and let $f : S \longrightarrow \hat{\mathbb{R}}$ be a lower semicontinuous function. The function f attains its minimum and the non-empty set of minimizers is compact.*

Proof. For $a \in f(S)$ let $F_a = \{x \in S \mid f(x) \leqslant a\}$. Since f is lower semicontinuous the non-empty set F_a is closed.

Note that the set of minimizers of f is

$$M = \bigcap_{a \in f(S)} F_a.$$

The collection $\{F_a \mid a \in f(S)\}$ has the f.i.p. because $\bigcap_{r=1}^n F_{a_i} = F_{\min_{1 \leqslant r \leqslant n} a_r}$. Since $(S, \mathcal{O})$ is compact the set M is a compact and non-empty set. $\square$

Corollary 4.23. *Let $(S, \mathcal{O})$ be a compact topological space and let $f : S \longrightarrow \hat{\mathbb{R}}$ be a upper semicontinuous function. The function f attains its maximum and the non-empty set of maximizers is compact.*

Proof. This statement follows by applying Theorem 4.109 to the lower semicontinuous functions $-f$. $\square$

Using semicontinuous functions it is possible to prove a form of Uryson's lemma for locally compact spaces.

Let $(S, \mathcal{O})$ be a locally compact topological space and let $\mathcal{F}_c(S, \mathcal{O})$ be the set of continuous functions $f : S \longrightarrow \mathbb{R}$ such that $\mathbf{K}(\{x \in S \mid f(x) \neq 0\})$ is a compact set.

Lemma 4.5. *Let $(S, \mathcal{O})$ be a locally compact topological space. The set $\mathcal{F}_c(S, \mathcal{O})$ is a linear space.*

Proof. Note that $supp(f + g) \subseteq supp(f) \cup supp(g)$ and $supp(f) \cup supp(g)$ is compact, hence $supp(f + g)$ is compact. Thus, $f + g \in \mathcal{F}_c(S, \mathcal{O})$. The remaining argument follows immediately. $\square$

For an open set V of a topological space $(S, \mathcal{O})$ we define the set

$$\mathcal{F}_{c,V}(S, \mathcal{O}) = \{f \in \mathcal{F}_c(S, \mathcal{O}) \mid f(x) \in [0, 1] \text{ for } x \in S$$
$$\text{and } supp(f) \subseteq V\}. \tag{4.10}$$

If C is a compact set in the same topological space, we also define

$$\mathcal{F}_{C,c}(S, \mathcal{O}) = \{f \in \mathcal{F}_c(S, \mathcal{O}) \mid f(x) \in [0, 1] \text{ for } x \in S$$
$$\text{and } f(x) = 1 \text{ for } x \in C\}. \tag{4.11}$$

Theorem 4.110. (Uryson's Lemma for locally compact spaces) *Let $(S, \mathcal{O})$ be a locally compact, C be a compact subset, and V be an open subset such that $C \subseteq V$. Then, $\mathcal{F}_{c,V}(S, \mathcal{O}) \cap \mathcal{F}_{C,c}(S, \mathcal{O}) \neq \emptyset$.*

Proof. The set $\mathbb{Q} \cap \{0, 1\}$ is countable. Let $r_0 = 0$ and $r_1 = 1$ and let $r_2, r_3, \ldots$ be a list of rational numbers in $(0, 1)$. By Theorem 4.59 there exists open sets V_0 and V_1 such that $C \subseteq V_1 \subseteq \mathbf{K}(V_1) \subseteq V_0 \subseteq \mathbf{K}(V_0) \subseteq V$.

Suppose that $n \geqslant 2$ and $V_{r_1}, \ldots, V_{r_n}$ are such that $r_p < r_q$ implies $\mathbf{K}(V_{r_q}) \subseteq V_{r_p}$. Let

$$r_i = \max\{r_\ell \mid 1 \leqslant \ell \leqslant n \text{ and } r_i < r_{n+1}\},$$
$$r_j = \min\{r_\ell \mid 1 \leqslant \ell \leqslant n \text{ and } r_i > r_{n+1}\}.$$

By Theorem 4.59 there exists an open set $V_{r_{n+1}}$ such that $\mathbf{K}(V_{r_j}) \subseteq V_{r_{n+1}} \subseteq \mathbf{K}(V_{r_{n+1}}) \subseteq V_{r_i}$. This process produces a collection of open sets indexed by the rational numbers $r \in [0, 1]$ such that $C \subseteq V_1$, $\mathbf{K}(V_0) \subseteq V$, each set $\mathbf{K}(V_r)$ is compact, and $s > r$ implies $\mathbf{K}(V_s) \subseteq V_r$.

For $r, s \in \mathbb{Q} \cap [0, 1]$ define the functions $f_r : S \longrightarrow [0, 1]$ and $g_s : S \longrightarrow [0, 1]$ by

$$f_r(x) = \begin{cases} r & \text{if } x \in V_r, \\ 0 & \text{otherwise,} \end{cases}$$

and

$$g_s(x) = \begin{cases} 1 & \text{if } x \in \mathbf{K}(V_s), \\ s & \text{otherwise,} \end{cases}$$

for $x \in S$. The functions $f, g : S \longrightarrow [0, 1]$ are defined as

$$f \sup_r f_r \text{ and } g = \inf_s g_s.$$

We show next that f is the function whose existence is asserted by the theorem.

Example 4.49 implies that the functions f_r are lower semicontinuous and g_s are upper semicontinuous. By Theorem 4.108 and Corollary 4.22, f is a lower semicontinuous function and g is an upper semicontinuous function.

Suppose that $f_r(x) > g_s(x)$ for some $x \in S$. We have $r > s$, $x \in V_r$, and $x \notin \mathbf{K}(V_s)$. This leads to a contradiction because $r > s$ implies $V_r \subseteq V_s$. Therefore, we have $f_r(x) \leqslant g_s(x)$ for all r, s, so $f \leqslant g$.

Suppose that there exists x such that $f(x) < g(x)$. Let $r, s \in \mathbb{Q} \cap [0, 1]$ such that $f(x) < r < s < g(x)$. Since $f(x) < r$, we have $x \notin V_r$. Since $g(x) > s$, we have $x \in \mathbf{K}(V_s)$, which is a contradiction. This $f = g$. Note that the function f satisfies the conditions of the theorem. Indeed, since $f = g$, f is both lower and upper semicontinuous, so it is a continuous function. Furthermore, $f(x) \in [0, 1]$, $f(x) = 1$ if $x \in C$ and $\mathbf{K}(\{x \mid f(x) \neq 0\}) \subseteq V$, so $f \in \mathcal{F}_{c,V}(S, \mathcal{O}) \cap \mathcal{F}_{C,c}(S, calo)$. $\qquad \square$

Corollary 4.24. *Let $(S, \mathcal{O})$ be a locally compact topological space, and let C_1, C_2 be two disjoint compact subsets of S. There exists a function $f \in \mathcal{F}_c(S, \mathcal{O})$ such that $f(x) \in [0, 1]$ for $x \in S$, $f(x) = 1$ for $x \in C_1$, and $f(x) = 0$ for $x \in C_2$.*

Proof. Since $(S, \mathcal{O})$ is a Hausdorff space, by Theorem 4.51, C_2 is closed. Thus, $S - C_2$ is an open set and $C_1 \subseteq S - C_2$. By Uryson's Lemma, there exists a function $f \in \mathcal{F}_{c,S-C_2}(S, \mathcal{O}) \cap \mathcal{F}_{C_1,c}(S, \mathcal{O})$. Therefore, $f(x) = 1$ for $x \in C_1$ and $supp(f) \subseteq S - C_2$. The last inclusion means that $f(x) = 0$ for $x \in C_2$. $\qquad \square$

Theorem 4.111. (Partition of Unity Theorem) *Let $(S, \mathcal{O})$ be a locally compact space and let $V_1, \ldots, V_n$ a collection of open sets. If C is a compact set such that $C \subseteq \bigcup_{i=1}^n V_n$, there exist n continuous functions $h_1, \ldots, h_n$ in $\mathcal{F}_c(S, \mathcal{O})$ such that $h_i(x) \in [0, 1]$, $supp(h_i) \subseteq V_i$ and $h_1(x) + \cdots + h_n(x) = 1$ for $x \in C$.*

Proof. Since $(S, \mathcal{O})$ is a locally compact space, by Theorem 4.59, for each $x \in C$ there exists a neighborhood W_x such that $\mathbf{K}(W_x) \subseteq V_i$. The compactness of C means that there exist $x_1, \ldots, x_n$ such that $C \subseteq W_{x_1} \cup \cdots \cup W_{x_n}$. Let $H_i = \bigcup \{\mathbf{K}(W_{x_j}) \mid \mathbf{K}(W_{x_j}) \subseteq V_i\}$.

By Uryson's Lemma for locally compact spaces (Theorem 4.110) there exist continuous functions g_i such that $g(x) \in [0, 1]$ for $x \in S$, $\mathbf{K}(\{x \mid g_i(x) \neq 0\})$ is compact and included in V_i and $g(x) = 1$ for $x \in H_i$. Define $h_1, \ldots, h_n$ as

$$h_1 = g_1$$

$$h_2 = (1 - g_1)g_2$$

$$\vdots$$

$$h_n = (1 - g_1)(1 - g_2) \cdots (1 - g_{xn-1})g_n.$$

Note that for each of the functions h_i we have $0 \leqslant h_i(x) \leqslant 1$ for $x \in S$. Also, $\{x \mid h_i(x) \neq 0\} \subseteq \{x \mid g_i(x) \neq 0\}$, hence $\mathbf{K}(\{x \mid h_i(x) \neq 0\}) \subseteq V_i$.

It is easy to see that

$$h_1 + h_2 + \cdots + h_n = 1 - (1 - g_1)(1 - g_2) \cdots (1 - g_n).$$

Since $C \subseteq H_1 \cup H_2 \cup \cdots \cup H_n$, there exists i such that $g_i(x) = 1$ if $x \in C$, hence $h_1(x) + \cdots + h_n(x) = 1$ for $x \in C$. $\qquad \square$

4.16 The Epigraph and the Hypograph of a Function

Definition 4.48. Let $(S, \mathcal{O})$ be a topological space and let $f : S \longrightarrow \hat{\mathbb{R}}$ be a function. Its *epigraph* is the set

$$\mathsf{epi}(f) = \{(x, y) \in S \times \mathbb{R} \mid f(x) \leqslant y\}.$$

The *hypograph* of f is the set

$$\mathsf{hyp}(f) = \{(x, y) \in S \times \mathbb{R} \mid y \leqslant f(\mathbf{x})\}.$$

The epigraph of a function $f : \mathbb{R} \longrightarrow \mathbb{R}$ is the dotted area in $\mathbb{R}^2$ located above the graph of the function f and it is shown in Figure 4.2(a); the hypograph of f is the dotted area below the graph shown in Figure 4.2(b).

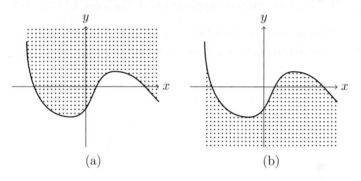

(a)　　　　　　　　　　　(b)

Fig. 4.2　Epigraph (a) and hypograph (b) of a function $f : \mathbb{R} \longrightarrow \mathbb{R}$.

Note that the intersection

$$\mathsf{epi}(f) \cap \mathsf{hyp}(f) = \{(x, y) \in S \times \mathbb{R} \mid y = f(x)\}$$

is the graph of the function f.

If $f(x) = \infty$, then $(x, \infty) \notin \mathsf{epi}(f)$. Thus, for the function f_∞ defined by $f_\infty(x) = \infty$ for $x \in S$ we have $\mathsf{epi}(f_\infty) = \emptyset$.

Theorem 4.112. *Let $(S, \mathcal{O})$ be a topological space and let $f : S \longrightarrow \hat{\mathbb{R}}$ be a function. Then, f is lower semicontinuous if and only if $\mathsf{epi}(f)$ is a closed set in $S \times \mathbb{R}$.*

Proof. Suppose that f is a lower semicontinuous function and let $(x_i, a_i)_{i \longrightarrow I}$ be a set in $\mathsf{epi}(f)$ such that $\lim_I (x_i, a_i) = (x, a)$. We have $\lim_I x_i = x$ and $\lim_I a_i = a$. By the definition of $\mathsf{epi}(f)$ we have $f(x_i) \leqslant a_i$ for $i \in I$.

By Theorem 4.107, if $(x_i)_{i \in I}$ is a convergent net in S with $x_i \to x$, then $f(x) \leqslant \liminf f(x_i)$, hence $f(x) \leqslant \lim_I a_i = a$. Thus, $(x, a) \in \mathsf{epi}(f)$, so $\mathsf{epi}(f)$ is closed.

Conversely, suppose that $\mathsf{epi}(f)$ is closed in $S \times \mathbb{R}$. By a previous remark it suffices to show that the set $U_t = \{x \in S \mid f(x) \leqslant t\}$ is closed for any $t \in \mathbb{R}$. Let (x_i) be a net in U_t such that $x_i \to x$. Since $f(x_i) \leqslant t$, we have $(x_i, t) \in \mathsf{epi}(f)$ for $i \in I$. Since $\mathsf{epi}(f)$ is closed and $(x_i, t) \to (x, t)$, we have $(x, t) \in \mathsf{epi}(f)$ so $f(x) \leqslant t$, which implies that U_t is closed for each t. $\qquad \square$

Corollary 4.25. *Let $(S, \mathcal{O})$ be a topological space and let $f : S \longrightarrow \hat{\mathbb{R}}$ be a function. Then, f is upper semicontinuous if and only if $\mathsf{hyp}(f)$ is a closed set in $S \times \mathbb{R}$.*

Proof. This follows from an application of Theorem 4.112 to $-f$. $\qquad \square$

The notion of level set of a function to be introduced next allows yet another characterization of semicontinuous functions.

Definition 4.49. *Let $(S, \mathcal{O})$ be a topological space, $f : S \longrightarrow \hat{\mathbb{R}}$ be a function and let $a \in \hat{\mathbb{R}}$. The level set for f at a is the set*

$$L_{f,a} = \{x \in S \mid f(x) \leqslant a\}.$$

Theorem 4.113. *Let $(S, \mathcal{O})$ be a topological space and let $f : S \longrightarrow \hat{\mathbb{R}}$ be a function. The following statements are equivalent:*

   (i) *f is lower semicontinuous on S;*
   (ii) *for each $a \in \mathbb{R}$ the level set $L_{f,a}$ is closed;*
   (iii) *if (x_i) is a net such that $x_i \to x$ then $f(x) \leqslant \liminf f(x_i)$.*

Proof. (i) implies (ii): Let f be a lower semicontinuous function on S. Since $L_{f,a} \times \{a\} = \mathsf{epi}(f) \cap (S \times \{a\})$, $L_{f,a} \times \{a\}$ is closed because $S \times \{a\}$ is closed in $S \times \mathbb{R}$. This implies that $L_{f,a}$ is closed.

(ii) implies (iii): Suppose that for every $a \in \mathbb{R}$, the set $L_{f,a}$ is closed and let (x_i) be a sequence such that $x_i \to x$. Since $f(x_i) \leqslant \liminf f(x_i)$, it follows that $x_i \in L_{f, \liminf f(x_i)}$. Taking into account that $L_{f, \liminf f(x_i)}$ is a closed set, it follows that $x \in L_{f, \liminf f(x_i)}$ because $x_i \to x$. Consequently, $f(x) \leqslant \liminf f(x_i)$.

(iii) implies (i): Let (x_i, y_i) be a net in $\mathsf{epi}(f)$ such that $x_i \to x$ and $y_i \to y$. By (iii), we have $f(x) \leqslant \liminf f(x_i)$. Since $(x_i, y_i) \in \mathsf{epi}(f)$ we have $f(x_i) \leqslant y_i$, so $\liminf f(x_i) \leqslant \liminf y_i = y$. Thus, $f(x) \leqslant y$, so $(x, y) \in \mathsf{epi}(f)$. This proves that $\mathsf{epi}(f)$ is closed. $\qquad \square$

A similar statement that involves hypographs is given next.

Theorem 4.114. *Let $(S, \mathcal{O})$ be a topological space and let $f : S \longrightarrow \hat{\mathbb{R}}$ be a function. The following statements are equivalent:*

(i) *f is upper semicontinuous on S;*
(ii) *for each $a \in \mathbb{R}$ the set $L_{-f,a}$ is closed relative to S;*
(iii) *if (x_i) is a sequence such that $x_i \to x$ and the limit of the sequence $(f(\boldsymbol{x}_n))$ exists, then $\limsup f(x_i) \leqslant f(\boldsymbol{x})$.*

Proof. The proof is similar to the proof of Theorem 4.113. □

Exercises and Supplements

(1) Prove that the family of subsets $\{(-n, n) \mid n \in \mathbb{N}\} \cup \{\emptyset, \mathbb{R}\}$ is a topology on $\mathbb{R}$.

(2) Let S be a set and let s_0 be an element of S. Prove that the family of subsets $\mathcal{O}_{s_0} = \{L \in \mathcal{P}(S) \mid s_0 \in L\} \cup \{\emptyset\}$ is a topology on S.

(3) Let S be a set and let s_0 be such that $s_0 \notin S$. Prove that:
   (a) the family of subsets $\mathcal{O}^{s_0} = \{L \in \mathcal{P}(S \cup \{s_0\}) \mid s_0 \in L\} \cup \{\emptyset\}$ is a topology on S;
   (b) the singleton $\{s_0\}$ is compact but not closed in this topology.

(4) Let $(S, \mathcal{O})$ be a topological space, L be an open set in $(S, \mathcal{O})$, and H be a closed set.
   (a) Prove that a set V is open in the subspace $(L, \mathcal{O} \restriction_L)$ if and only if V is open in $(S, \mathcal{O})$ and $V \subseteq L$;
   (b) Prove that a set W is closed in the subspace $(H, \mathcal{O} \restriction_H)$ if and only if W is closed in $(S, \mathcal{O})$ and $W \subseteq H$.

(5) Let $(S, \mathcal{O})$ be a topological space where $\mathcal{O} = \{\emptyset, U, V, S\}$, where U and V are two subsets of S. Prove that either $\{U, V\}$ is a partition of S or one of the sets $\{U, V\}$ is included in the other.

(6) Let $\mathcal{S}$ be the set of subsets of $\mathbb{R}$ such that, for every $U \in \mathcal{S}$, $x \in U$ implies $-x \in U$. Prove that $\{\emptyset\} \cup \mathcal{S}$ is a topology on $\mathbb{R}$.

(7) Let $(S, \mathcal{O})$ be a topological space, T be a set, and let $f : T \longrightarrow S$ be a function. Prove that the collection $f^{-1}(\mathcal{O})$ defined by $f^{-1}(\mathcal{O}) = \{f^{-1}(X) \mid X \in \mathcal{O}\}$ is a topology on T; furthermore, prove that $f^{-1}(\mathcal{O})$ is the weakest topology $\mathcal{O}'$ on T such that f is a continuous function between $(T, \mathcal{O}')$ and $(S, \mathcal{O})$. The topology $f^{-1}(\mathcal{O})$ is known as the *pullback topology* induced by f.

   Solution: It is easy to verify that $f^{-1}(\mathcal{O})$ is indeed a topology on T. Suppose that f is a continuous function between the topological spaces $(T, \mathcal{O}')$ and $(S, \mathcal{O})$. Then, for $Y \in \mathcal{O}$, $f^{-1}(Y) \in \mathcal{O}'$, so $f^{-1}(\mathcal{O}) \subseteq \mathcal{O}'$.

(8) Let $(S, \mathcal{O})$ be a topological space, T be a set, and let $f : S \longrightarrow T$ be a function. Prove that the collection $\mathcal{O}' = \{V \mid V \subseteq T, f^{-1}(V) \in \mathcal{O}\}$ is a topology on T; furthermore, prove that $\mathcal{O}'$ is the finest topology on T such that f is a continuous function between and $(S, \mathcal{O})$ and $(T, \mathcal{O}')$. The topology $f^{-1}(\mathcal{O})$ is known as the push-forward topology induced by f.

    Solution: Since $f^{-1}(V_1) \cap f^{-1}(V_2) = f^{-1}(V_1 \cap V_2)$, it follows that $V_1 \in \mathcal{O}'$ and $V_2 \in \mathcal{O}'$ imply $V_1 \cap V_2 \in \mathcal{O}'$. Also, if $\{V_i \mid i \in I\} \subseteq \mathcal{O}'$ we have $f^{-1}(V_i) \in \mathcal{O}$ for $i \in I$, which means that $f^{-1}\left(\bigcup_{i \in I} V_i\right) \bigcup_{i \in I} f^{-1}(V_i) \in \mathcal{O}$. This implies $\bigcup_{i \in I} V_i \in \mathcal{O}'$, so $\mathcal{O}'$ is indeed a topology.

    Suppose that $\mathcal{O}_1$ is a topology on T such that $f : S \longrightarrow T$ is a continuous function between the topological spaces $(S, \mathcal{O})$ and $(T, \mathcal{O}_1)$. Then, for every open set $W \in \mathcal{O}_1$ we have $f^{-1}(W) \in \mathcal{O}$, so $W \in \mathcal{O}'$. This shows that $\mathcal{O}_1 \subseteq \mathcal{O}'$, which shows that $\mathcal{O}'$ is the finest topology on T such that f is a continuous function.

Theorem 4.1 allows the introduction the notion of *size of an open set* in $\mathbb{R}$.

Let U be an open set in $\mathbb{R}$, which is a union of open intervals, $U = \bigcup_{j \in J} I_j$ (here J may be a finite set, or the entire set $\{n \mid n \geqslant 1\}$). Its size $\ell(U)$ is defined as $\sum_{j \in J} l(I_j)$, where $l(I_j)$ is the length of the open interval $I_j = (a_j, b_j)$, that is, $l(I_j) = b_j - a_j$. Since the terms of the sum are positive, the value of this sum is independent of the order of its terms. We have $0 \leqslant \ell(U) \leqslant \infty$ and $\ell(\emptyset) = 0$. Note that for an open interval $I = (a, b)$ we have $\ell(I) = l(I) = b - a$.

(9) Prove that the size of the open subset $U = \bigcup_{n \geqslant 1}(n, n + \frac{1}{n})$ of $\mathbb{R}$ is infinite.

(10) Prove that if U is a bounded open set and $U \subseteq (a, b)$, then $\ell(U) \leqslant b - a$.

(11) Prove that the open set $W = \bigcup_{n \geqslant 1}(n + \frac{1}{2^{n+1}}, n + \frac{1}{2^n})$ in $\mathbb{R}$ has finite size but is not bounded.

(12) Let U, V be two open sets in $\mathbb{R}$ such that $U \subseteq V$. Prove that $\ell(U) \leqslant \ell(V)$ and that $\ell(U) + \ell(V) = \ell(U \cup V) + \ell(U \cap V)$.

(13) Prove that if $(U_n)_{n \geqslant 1}$ is an increasing chain of open sets in $\mathbb{R}$ and $U = \bigcup_{n \in \mathbb{N}} U_n$, then $\ell(U) = \sup\{\ell(U_n) \mid n \geqslant 1\}$.

    Solution: Since $U_n \subseteq U$ for $n \in \mathbb{N}$, we have $\ell(U_n) \leqslant \ell(U)$, so $\sup\{\ell(U_n) \mid n \geqslant 1\} \leqslant \ell(U)$.

    Suppose that $U = \bigcup\{I_j \mid j \in J\}$, where $\{I_j \mid j \in J\}$ is a finite or infinite sequence of disjoint and open intervals and let $\epsilon > 0$.

    If $\ell(U)$ is finite, then there exists $h \in \mathbb{N}$ such that $\sum_{j=1}^{h} \ell(I_j) \geqslant \ell(U) - \frac{\epsilon}{2}$. Let $\eta > 0$ be such that $\eta < \frac{\epsilon}{4h}$ and $\eta < \frac{b_j - a_j}{2}$ for $1 \leqslant j \leqslant h$. Define $L_j = (a_j + \eta, b_j - \eta)$ and $K_j = [a_j + \eta, b_j - \eta]$ for $1 \leqslant j \leqslant k$, and $L = \bigcup_{j=1}^{h} L_j$, $K = \bigcup_{j=1}^{h} K_j$. The set K is a compact set in $\mathbb{R}$ that is covered by $\{U_n \mid n \geqslant 1\}$. Thus, there exists $m \in \mathbb{N}$ such that

$L \subseteq K \subseteq U_m$. If $n \geqslant m$, then

$$\ell(U_n) \geqslant \ell(U_m) \leqslant \ell(L) = \sum_{j=1}^{h}(b_j - a_j - 2\eta)$$

$$\geqslant \sum_{j=1}^{h}(b_j - a_j) - \frac{\epsilon}{2} \geqslant \ell(U) - \epsilon.$$

This shows that $\ell(U) = \sup\{\ell(U_n) \mid n \geqslant 1\}$. The case when $\ell(U) = \infty$ is left to the reader.

(14) Let U_1, U_2 be two bounded open sets in $\mathbb{R}$ and let K be a compact subset of $\mathbb{R}$ such that $K \subseteq U_1 \cap U_2$. Prove that $\ell(U_1) - \ell(U_1 - K) = \ell(U_2) - \ell(U_2 - K)$.

Solution: Note that $U_1 - K, U_2 - K$ and $(U_1 \cap U_2) - K$ are open sets. It is clear that

$$U_1 \cup (U_2 - K) = U_1 \cup U_2, \text{ and}$$
$$U_1 \cap (U_2 - K) = (U_1 \cap U_2) - K.$$

Therefore,

$$\ell(U_1 \cup U_2) = \ell(U_1 \cup (U_2 - K))$$
$$= \ell(U_1) + \ell(U_2 - K) - \ell(U_1 \cap (U_2 - K)$$
$$= \ell(U_1) + \ell(U_2 - K) - \ell((U_1 \cap U_2) - K),$$

hence $\ell(U_1) + \ell(U_2 - K) = \ell(U_1 \cup U_2) + \ell((U_1 \cap U_2) - K)$. Similarly, $\ell(U_2) + \ell(U_1 - K) = \ell(U_1 \cup U_2) + \ell((U_1 \cap U_2) - K)$, hence $\ell(U_1) + \ell(U_2 - K) = \ell(U_2) + \ell(U_1 - K)$.

(15) Let K be a compact subset of $\mathbb{R}$. Supplement 14 shows that the number $s(K) = \ell(U) - \ell(U \cap K)$ is the same for every open set in $\mathbb{R}$ that contains K. Prove that

   (a) $s([a, b]) = b - a$;
   (b) if K_1, K_2 are compact subsets of $\mathbb{R}$, then $K_1 \subseteq K_2$ implies $s(K_1) \leqslant s(K_2)$;
   (c) if (K_n) is a decreasing sequence of compact subsets of $\mathbb{R}$ and $K = \bigcap_{n \geqslant 1} K_n$, then $s(K) = \lim_{n \to \infty} s(K_n)$;
   (d) if K_1, K_2 are compact subsets of $\mathbb{R}$, then $s(K_1 \cup K_2) + s(K_1 \cap K_2) = s(K_1) + s(K_2)$.

(16) Prove that if U is a closed set in a topological space $(S, \mathcal{O})$ then $\mathbf{I}(S - U) = S - U$.

(17) Let S be a set and let $\mathbf{H} : \mathcal{P}(S) \longrightarrow \mathcal{P}(S)$ be a mapping. Prove that $\mathbf{H}$ is a closure operator on S if and only if

$$U \cup \mathbf{H}(U) \cup \mathbf{H}(\mathbf{H}(V)) = \mathbf{H}(U \cup V) - \mathbf{H}(\emptyset)$$

for all $U, V \in \mathcal{P}(S)$.

(18) Let $(S, \mathcal{O})$ be a topological space and let $\mathbf{I}$ be its interior operator. Prove that the poset of open sets $(\mathcal{O}, \subseteq)$ is a complete lattice, where $\sup \mathcal{L} = \bigcup \mathcal{L}$ and $\inf \mathcal{L} = \mathbf{I}(\bigcap \mathcal{L})$ for every family of open sets $\mathcal{L}$.

(19) Let $(S, \mathcal{O})$ be a topological space, let $\mathbf{K}$ be its interior operator and let $\mathcal{K}$ be its collection of closed sets. Prove that $(\mathcal{K}, \subseteq)$ is a complete lattice, where $\sup \mathcal{L} = \mathbf{K}(\bigcup \mathcal{L})$ and $\inf \mathcal{L} = \bigcap \mathcal{L}$ for every family of closed sets.

(20) Prove that if U, V are two subsets of a topological space $(S, \mathcal{O})$, then $\mathbf{K}(U \cap V) \subseteq \mathbf{K}(U) \cap \mathbf{K}(V)$. Formulate an example where this inclusion is strict.

(21) Let T be a subspace of the topological space $(S, \mathcal{O})$. Let $\mathbf{K}_S, \mathbf{I}_S$, and ∂_S be the closure, interior and boundary operators associated to S and $\mathbf{K}_T, \mathbf{I}_T$ and ∂_T the corresponding operators associated to T. Prove that

    (a) $\mathbf{K}_T(U) = \mathbf{K}_S(U) \cap T$,
    (b) $\mathbf{I}_S(U) \subseteq \mathbf{I}_T(U)$, and
    (c) $\partial_T U \subseteq \partial_S U$

for every subset U of T.

(22) Let $(S, \mathcal{O})$ be a topological space and let $\mathbf{K}$ and $\mathbf{I}$ be its associated closure and interior operator, respectively. Define the mappings $\phi, \psi : \mathcal{P}(S) \longrightarrow \mathcal{P}(S)$ by $\phi(U) = \mathbf{I}(\mathbf{K}(U))$ and $\psi(U) = \mathbf{K}(\mathbf{I}(U))$ for $U \in \mathcal{P}(S)$.

    (a) Prove that $\phi(U)$ is an open set and $\psi(U)$ is a closed set for every set $U \in \mathcal{P}(S)$.
    (b) Prove that $\psi(H) \subseteq H$ for every closed set H and $L \subseteq \phi(L)$ for every open set L.
    (c) Prove that $\phi(\phi(U)) = \phi(U)$ and $\psi(\psi(U)) = \psi(U)$ for every $U \in \mathcal{P}(S)$.
    (d) Let $(\mathbf{J}_1, \ldots, \mathbf{J}_n)$ be a sequence such that $\mathbf{J}_i \in \{\mathbf{K}, \mathbf{I}\}$. Prove that there are at most seven distinct sets of the form $\mathbf{J}_n(\cdots (\mathbf{J}_1(U)) \cdots)$ for every set $U \in \mathcal{P}(S)$, and give an example of a topological space $(S, \mathcal{O})$ and a subset U of S such that these seven sets are pairwise distinct.

(23) Let $(S, \mathcal{O})$ be a topological space. The subsets X and Y are said to be *separated* if $X \cap \mathbf{K}(Y) = \mathbf{K}(X) \cap Y = \emptyset$.

    (a) Prove that X and Y are separated sets in $(S, \mathcal{O})$ if and only if they are disjoint and clopen in the subspace $X \cup Y$.
    (b) Prove that two disjoint open sets or two disjoint closed sets in $(S, \mathcal{O})$ are separated.

(24) Let $(S, \mathcal{O})$ be a topological space and let X, Y be two closed sets such that $\mathbf{I}(X \cup Y) \neq \emptyset$. Prove that at least one of the sets $\mathbf{I}(X)$ or $\mathbf{I}(Y)$ is non-empty.

  Solution: Suppose that X and Y are two closed sets such that both $\mathbf{I}(X) = \mathbf{I}(Y) = \emptyset$. By the second part of Theorem 4.11, we have $\mathbf{I}(X \cup Y) = \emptyset$. Since this is not the case, at least one of the sets $\mathbf{I}(X)$ or $\mathbf{I}(Y)$ must be non-empty.

(25) Let $(S, \mathcal{O})$ be a topological space. Prove that

  - $\partial(\partial U) \subseteq \partial U$ for every $U \subseteq S$;
  - if U is open or closed, then $\partial(\partial U) = \partial U$;
  - for every subset U of S we have $\partial(\partial(\partial U)) = \partial(\partial U)$.

(26) Let $(S, \mathcal{O})$ is a topological space. Prove that a subset T of S is closed if and only for each $x \in S$ and $V \in neigh_x(\mathcal{O})$, $V \cap T \neq \emptyset$ implies $x \in T$.

(27) Prove that if U, V are two subsets of a topological space $(S, \mathcal{O})$, then $\mathbf{K}(U \cap V) \subseteq \mathbf{K}(U) \cap \mathbf{K}(V)$. Formulate an example where this inclusion is strict.

(28) Let $(S, \mathcal{O})$ be a topological space. Prove that for every subset T of S we have
$$S = \mathbf{I}(T) \cup \mathbf{I}(S - T) \cup \partial_S T.$$

(29) Let $(S, \mathcal{O})$ be a topological space and let $\mathbf{K}$ and $\mathbf{I}$ be its associated closure and interior operator, respectively. Define the mappings $\phi, \psi : \mathcal{P}(S) \longrightarrow \mathcal{P}(S)$ by $\phi(U) = \mathbf{I}(\mathbf{K}(U))$ and $\psi(U) = \mathbf{K}(\mathbf{I}(U))$ for $U \in \mathcal{P}(S)$.

  (a) Prove that $\phi(U)$ is an open set and $\psi(U)$ is a closed set for every set $U \in \mathcal{P}(S)$.
  (b) Prove that $\psi(H) \subseteq H$ for every closed set H and $L \subseteq \phi(L)$ for every open set L.
  (c) Prove that $\phi(\phi(U)) = \phi(U)$ and $\psi(\psi(U)) = \psi(U)$ for every $U \in \mathcal{P}(S)$.
  (d) Let $(\mathbf{J}_1, \ldots, \mathbf{J}_n)$ be a sequence such that $\mathbf{J}_i \in \{\mathbf{K}, \mathbf{I}\}$. Prove that there are at most seven distinct sets of the form $\mathbf{J}_n(\cdots (\mathbf{J}_1(U)) \cdots)$ for every set $U \in \mathcal{P}(S)$, and give an example of a topological space $(S, \mathcal{O})$ and a subset U of S such that these seven sets are pairwise distinct.

(30) Let $(S, \mathcal{O})$ be a topological space, and U and U' be two subsets of S.
  (a) Prove that $\partial(U \cup V) \subseteq \partial U \cup \partial V$.
  (b) Prove that $\partial U = \partial(S - U)$.

(31) Let $\mathcal{B}$ be a basis for a topological space $(S, \mathcal{O})$. Prove that if $\mathcal{B}'$ is a collection of subsets of S such that $\mathcal{B} \subseteq \mathcal{B}' \subseteq \mathcal{O}$, then $\mathcal{B}'$ is a basis for $\mathcal{O}$.

(32) Let $S = \{a, b, c\}$ and let $\mathcal{S} = \{\{a, b\}, \{a, c\}\}$. Determine the topology generated by the collection $\mathcal{S}$.

(33) Let $\mathcal{C}$ be the family of open intervals $\mathcal{C} = \{(a, b) \mid a, b \in \mathbb{R} \text{ and } ab > 0\}$. Prove that:

    (a) Every open set L of $(\mathbb{R}, \mathcal{O})$ contains a member of $\mathcal{C}$.

    (b) $\mathcal{C}$ is not a basis for the topology $\mathcal{O}$.

(34) Let $\mathcal{C}$ be a chain of subsets of a set S such that $\bigcup \mathcal{C} = S$. Prove that $\mathcal{C}$ is the basis of a topology.

(35) Let $\mathcal{B}$ be a basis for a topological space $(S, \mathcal{O})$. Prove that if $\mathcal{B}'$ is a collection of subsets of S such that $\mathcal{B} \subseteq \mathcal{B}' \subseteq \mathcal{O}$, then $\mathcal{B}'$ is a basis for $\mathcal{O}$.

(36) Let $(S, \mathcal{O})$ be a topological space, U and U' two subsets of S, and $\mathcal{B}$ and $\mathcal{B}'$ two bases in the subspaces $(U, \mathcal{O} \upharpoonright_U)$ and $(U', \mathcal{O} \upharpoonright_{U'})$, respectively. Prove that $\mathcal{B} \vee \mathcal{B}'$ is a basis in the subspace $U \cup U'$.

    Solution: Let M be an open set in the subspace $U \cup V$. By the definition of the subspace topology, there exists an open set $L \in \mathcal{O}$ such that $M = L \cap (U \cup V) = (L \cap U) \cup (L \cap V)$, so L is the union of two open sets, $L \cap U$ and $L \cap U'$, in the subspaces U and U'. Since $\mathcal{B}$ is a basis in U, there is a subcollection $\mathcal{B}_1$ such that $L \cap U = \bigcup \mathcal{B}_1$. Similarly, $\mathcal{B}'$ contains a subcollection $\mathcal{B}'_1$ such that $L \cap U = \bigcup \mathcal{B}'_1$. Therefore, $M = \bigcup \mathcal{B}_1 \cup \bigcup \mathcal{B}'_1 = \bigcup \mathcal{B}_1 \vee \mathcal{B}'_1$.

(37) Let S be an uncountable set and let $(S, \mathcal{O})$ be the cofinite topology on S.

    (a) Prove that every non-finite set is dense.

    (b) Prove that there is no countable basis for this topological space. What does this say about Theorem 4.34?

(38) Prove that if $(S, \mathcal{O})$ is a topological space such that $\mathcal{O}$ is finite, then $(S, \mathcal{O})$ is compact.

(39) Let $(S, \mathcal{O})$ be a compact space and let $\mathbf{H} = (H_0, H_1, \ldots)$ be a non-increasing sequence of non-empty and closed subsets of S. Prove that $\bigcap_{i \in \mathbb{N}} H_i$ is non-empty.

(40) Let $U = \{\mathbf{u} \in \mathbb{R}^2 \mid u_1 > 0 \text{ and } u_2 \geqslant \frac{1}{u_1}\}$ and $V = \{\mathbf{v} \in \mathbb{R}^2 \mid v_1 < 0 \text{ and } v_2 \geqslant -\frac{1}{v_1}\}$. Prove that:

    (a) both U and V are closed subsets of $\mathbb{R}^2$;

    (b) the set $U + V = \{\mathbf{u} + \mathbf{v} \mid \mathbf{u} \in U \text{ and } \mathbf{v} \in V\}$ is not closed in $\mathbb{R}^2$.

(41) Let U, V be two subsets of $\mathbb{R}^2$ such that U is compact and V is closed. Prove that the set $U + V$ is closed.

    Solution: Let $(\mathbf{x}_n)$ be a sequence in $U + V$ such that $\lim_{n \to \infty} \mathbf{x}_n = \mathbf{x}$. There exist the sequences $(\mathbf{u}_n)$ in U and $(\mathbf{v}_n)$ in V such that $\mathbf{x}_n = \mathbf{u}_n + \mathbf{v}_n$. Since U is compact there exists a subsequence $(\mathbf{u}_{n_j})$ of $(\mathbf{u}_n)$ such that $\lim_{j \to \infty} \mathbf{u}_{n_j} = \mathbf{u} \in U$. This implies $\lim_{j \to \infty} \mathbf{v}_{n_j} = \lim_{j \to \infty} (\mathbf{x}_{n_j} - \mathbf{u}_{n_j}) = \mathbf{x} - \mathbf{u} \in V$, hence $\mathbf{x} \in U + V$, which proves that $U + V$ is closed.

(42) Let $(S, \mathcal{O})$ be a compact topological space and let $f : S \longrightarrow T$ be a continuous bijection between $(S, \mathcal{O})$ and a Hausdorff topological space

$(T, \mathcal{O}')$. Prove that the inverse function $f^{-1} : T \longrightarrow S$ is continuous, that is, f is a homeomorphism.

Solution: We shall prove that for every open subset U of S, the set $(f^{-1})^{-1}(U) = f(U)$ is open in $(T, \mathcal{O})$. Since $U \in \mathcal{O}$, $\overline{U}$ is a closed set; since $(S, \mathcal{O})$ is compact, $\overline{U}$ is compact by Theorem 4.46. Theorem 4.81 implies that $f(\overline{U})$ is compact because f is continuous. Therefore, this set is closed in $(T, \mathcal{O}')$ by Theorem 4.51. Since f is a bijection, $f(U)$ is the complement of $f(\overline{U})$, and therefore it is open in $(T, \mathcal{O})$.

(43) Let $(\{x_1, x_2, x_3, x_4\}, \mathcal{O})$ be a topological space where

$$\mathcal{O} = \{\emptyset, \{x_1, x_2\}, \{x_1, x_2, x_3\}, \{x_1, x_2, x_4\}, \{x_1, x_2, x_3, x_4\}\}.$$

Prove that this topological space satisfies none of the separation axioms T_i, where $0 \leqslant i \leqslant 4$.

(44) Let $(S, \mathcal{O})$ be a topological space, where S is an infinite set and $\mathcal{O}$ is the cofinite topology. Prove that $(S, \mathcal{O})$ is a T_1 space but not a T_2-space.

Solution: Let x, y be two distinct points in x. Since $S - \{x\}$ is open and contains y but not x, it follows that $(S, \mathcal{O})$ is a T_1-space.

Since S is infinite, it contains two distinct elements x, y. Suppose that U, V are two disjoint open sets such that $x \in U$ and $y \in V$. Then $U \subseteq S - V$, which is finite, so U is also finite. This is contradictory, because $S - U$ is finite, and this would imply that S is finite. Thus, $(S, \mathcal{O})$ is not a T_2-space.

(45) Let U be an open set in a Hausdorff topological space and let K be a compact set in the same space. Prove that $S - K$ is an open set.

(46) Let $(S, \mathcal{O})$ be a Hausdorff space and let $\{K_i \mid i \geqslant I\}$ be a collection of compact subsets of S. Prove that the set $\bigcap_{i \in I} K_i$ is compact.

Solution: By Theorem 4.51 every set K_i is closed, so $\bigcap_{i \in I} K_i$ is closed; by the same theorem, $\bigcap_{i \in I} K_i$ is compact.

(47) Let $(S, \mathcal{O})$ be a T_0 topological space. Define the relation "$\leqslant$" on S by $x \leqslant y$ if $x \in \mathbf{K}(\{y\})$. Prove that $\leqslant$ is a partial order.

(48) Let $(S, \mathcal{O})$ be a T_4 topological space.

  (a) Let H and H' be two closed sets and L be an open set such that $H \cap H' \subseteq L$. Prove that there exists two open sets U and U' such that $H \subseteq U$, $H' \subseteq U'$, and $L = U \cap U'$.
  (b) If $\{H_1, \ldots, H_p\}$ is a collection of closed sets such that $p \geqslant 2$ and $\bigcap_{i=1}^{p} H_i = \emptyset$, prove that there exists a family of open sets $\{U_1, \ldots, U_p\}$ such that $\bigcap_{i=1}^{p} U_i = \emptyset$ and $H_i \subseteq U_i$ for $1 \leqslant i \leqslant p$.

Solution: Observe that the sets $H - L$ and $H' - L$ are closed and disjoint sets. Since $(S, \mathcal{O})$ is T_4, there are two disjoint open sets V and V' such that $H - L \subseteq V$ and $H' - L \subseteq V'$. Define the open sets U

and U' as $U = V \cup L$ and $U' = V' \cup L$. It is clear that U and U' satisfy the requirements of the statement.

The second part is an extension of Definition 4.24. The argument is by induction on p. The base case, $p = 2$, follows immediately from the definition of T_4 spaces.

Suppose that the statement holds for p, and let $\{H_1, \ldots, H_{p+1}\}$ be a collection of closed sets such that $\bigcap_{i=1}^{p+1} H_i = \emptyset$.

By applying the inductive hypothesis to the collection of p closed sets $\{H_1, \ldots, H_{p-1}, H_p \cap H_{p+1}\}$, we obtain the existence of the open sets $U_1, \ldots, U_{p-1}, U$ such that $H_i \subseteq U_i$ for $1 \leqslant i \leqslant p-1$, $H_p \cap H_{p+1} \subseteq U$, and $\left(\bigcap_{j=1}^{p-1} U_j\right) \cap U = \emptyset$. By the first part of this supplement, we obtain the existence of two open sets U_p and U_{p+1} such that $H_p \subseteq U_p$, $H_{p+1} \subseteq U_{p+1}$, and $U = U_p \cap U_{p+1}$. Note that $\bigcap_{j=1} U_j = \emptyset$, which concludes the argument.

(49) Let $(S, \mathcal{O})$ be a Hausdorff space and let C be a compact subset of S. Suppose that U and V are two open sets such that $C \subseteq U \cup V$. Prove that there exist two compact sets D and E such that $D \subseteq U$, $E \subseteq V$ such that $C = D \cup E$.

Solution: Since C is a compact subset of S, C is closed. By Theorem 4.51 C is a closed set, which implies that the disjoint sets $C - U$ and $C - V$ are also closed (as intersection of C and the closed set $S - U$ and $S - V$, respectively). Consequently, by Theorem 4.52, there exist two disjoint open sets U_1 and V_1 such that $C - U \subseteq U_1$ and $C - V \subseteq V_1$. Define $D = C - U_1$ and $E = C - V_1$. We have:

$$D = C - U_1 \subseteq C - (C \cap \overline{U})$$
$$= C \cap \overline{(C \cap \overline{U})} = C \cap U \subseteq U,$$

hence $D \subseteq U$ and, similarly $E \subseteq V$. The sets D and E are compact because they are closed subsets of a compact set. Since $U_1 \cap V_1 = \emptyset$ we have

$$D \cup E = (C - U_1) \cup (C - V_1) = C - (U_1 \cap V_1) = C.$$

(50) Let $(S, \mathcal{O})$ be a T_4 topological space and let $\mathcal{L} = \{L_1, \ldots, L_p\}$ be an open cover of S.

(a) Prove that for every k, $1 \leqslant k \leqslant p$ there exist k open sets $V_1, \ldots, V_k$ such that the collection $\{S - \mathbf{K}(V_1), \ldots, S - \mathbf{K}(V_k), L_{k+1}, \ldots, L_p\}$ is an open cover of S and for the closed sets $H_j = S - V_j$ we have $H_j \subseteq L_j$ for $1 \leqslant j \leqslant k$.

(b) Conclude that for every open cover $\mathcal{L} = \{L_1, \ldots, L_p\}$ of S there is a closed cover $\mathcal{H} = \{H_1, \ldots, H_p\}$ of S such that $H_i \subseteq L_i$ for $1 \leqslant i \leqslant p$.

Solution: The proof of the first part is by induction on k, $1 \leqslant k \leqslant p$. For the base case, $k = 1$, observe that $S - L_1 \subseteq \bigcup_{j=2}^{p} L_j$ because $\mathcal{L}$ is a cover. Since $(S, \mathcal{O})$ is a T_4 space, there exists an open set V_1 such that $S - L_1 \subseteq V_1 \subseteq \mathbf{K}(V_1) \subseteq \bigcup_{j=2}^{p} L_j$. For $H_1 = S - V_1$, it is clear that $H_1 \subseteq L_1$ and $\{S - \mathbf{K}(V_1), L_2, \ldots, L_p\}$ is an open cover of S.

Suppose that the statement holds for k. This implies

$$S - L_{k+1} \subseteq \bigcup_{j=1}^{k}(S - \mathbf{K}(V_j)) \cup \bigcup_{j=k+2}^{p} L_j.$$

Again, by the property of T_4 spaces, there is an open set V_{k+1} such that

$$S - L_{k+1} \subseteq V_{k+1} \subseteq \mathbf{K}(V_{k+1}) \bigcup_{j=1}^{k}(S - \mathbf{K}(V_j)) \cup \bigcup_{j=k+2}^{p} L_j.$$

Thus, $\{S - \mathbf{K}(V_1), \ldots, S - \mathbf{K}(V_k), S - \mathbf{K}(V_{K+1}), L_{k+2}, \ldots, L_p\}$ is an open cover of S and $H_{k+1} = S - V_{k+1} \subseteq L_{k+1}$, which concludes the inductive step.

The second part follows immediately from the first by taking $k = p$. Indeed, since $\{S - \mathbf{K}(V_1), \ldots, S - \mathbf{K}(V_p)\}$ is a cover of S and $S - \mathbf{K}(V_i) \subseteq H_i$ for $1 \leqslant i \leqslant p$, it follows immediately that $\mathcal{H}$ is a cover of S.

(51) Let $(S, \mathcal{O})$ and $(Z, \mathcal{O}')$ be two topological spaces, such that $(Z, \mathcal{O}')$ is a Hausdorff space and let $f, g : S \longrightarrow Z$ be two continuous functions. If the set $X = \{x \in S \mid f(x) = g(x)\}$ is dense in $(S, \mathcal{O})$, then $f = g$.

Solution: Suppose that $f \neq g$, that is, there exists $t \in S$ such that $f(t) \neq g(t)$. Since Z is a Hausdorff space, there exists two open subsets U and V of Z such that $f(t) \in U$ and $g(t) \in V$. This implies $t \in f^{-1}(U) \cap g^{-1}(V)$, so $W = f^{-1}(U) \cap g^{-1}(V)$ is a non-empty open subset of S.

Since X is dense in S, by Theorem 4.9, $X \cap W \neq \emptyset$, so there exists $y \in X \cap W$. We have $f(x) = g(x)$ because $y \in X$. On the other hand, since $y \in W$, we obtain the existence of $u \in U$ and $v \in V$ such that $y = f(u) \in U$ and $y = g(y) \in V$, which leads to a contradiction because U and V are disjoint.

(52) If $(S, \mathcal{O})$ is a locally compact space and $U = V \cap W$, where V is open set and W is a closed set, then U is locally compact.

(53) Prove that if a subspace U of a Hausdorff space $(S, \mathcal{O})$ is locally compact, then there exists an open set V and a closed set W in S such that $U = V \cap W$.

(54) Let $(S, \mathcal{O})$ be a Hausdorff topological space. Prove that $(S, \mathcal{O})$ is locally compact if for every $x \in S$ and $U \in neigh_x(S, \mathcal{O})$, there exists $V \in neigh_x(S, \mathcal{O})$ such that $\mathbf{K}(V)$ is compact and $\mathbf{K}(V) \subseteq U$.

(55) Let $(S, \mathcal{O})$ be a Hausdorff locally compact topological space. Prove that if T is open or closed in $(S, \mathcal{O})$, then $(T, \mathcal{O} \restriction_T)$ is locally compact.

(56) Prove that the topological space $(S, \mathcal{O})$ is homeomorphic to an open subspace of a compact Hausdorff space $(S', \mathcal{O}')$ if and only if $(S, \mathcal{O})$ is locally compact and Hausdorff.

(57) Let $(S, \mathcal{O})$ be a topological space. Prove that $neigh_x(\mathcal{O})$ is a filter and that $\{V \mid \mathcal{O} \cap neigh_x(\mathcal{O})\}$ is a filter basis that generates the filter $neigh_x(\mathcal{O})$.

(58) Let $\mathbb{N}_k = \{n \in \mathbb{N} \mid n \geqslant k\}$. Prove that the collection $\mathcal{S} = \{\mathbb{N}_{2^p} \mid p \in \mathbb{N}\}$ is a filter basis in $\mathbb{N}$.

(59) Let S be an infinite set. Prove that the collection of all cofinite subsets of S is a filter on S.

(60) Let (x_i) be an I-net on a set S and let $T_j = \{x_i \mid i \geqslant j\}$, where $j \in I$. Prove that the collection $\{T_j \mid j \in I\}$ is a filter basis on S.

(61) Let $\mathcal{B}$ be a filter basis on a set S and $\mathcal{S}$ is a filter sub-basis on S. Prove that:

    (a) the collection $\{F \in \mathcal{P}(S) \mid$ there exists $B \in \mathcal{B}, B \subseteq F\}$ is a filter on S;

    (b) the collection of all finite intersections of $\mathcal{S}$ is a filter basis.

(62) Let (x_i) be a net of real numbers in the topological space $(\mathbb{R}, \mathcal{O}_u)$. We have $x_i \to x$ if and only if $\limsup x_i \geqslant x$.

(63) Let (x_i) and (y_i) be two I-nets in the topological space $(\mathbb{R}, \mathcal{O})$. Define the I-nets (u_i) and (v_i) as $u_i = x_i + y_i$ and $v_i = x_i y_i$ for $i \in I$. Prove that if $x_i \to x$ and $y_i \to y$, then $u_i \to x + y$ and $v_i \to xy$.

(64) Let $f : \mathbb{R}^n \longrightarrow \mathbb{R}$ be a continuous function and let $S \subseteq \mathbb{R}^n$. Prove that:

$$\sup\{f(\mathbf{x}) \mid \mathbf{x} \in S\} = \sup\{f(\mathbf{x}) \mid \mathbf{x} \in \mathbf{K}(S)\},$$
$$\inf\{f(\mathbf{x}) \mid \mathbf{x} \in S\} = \inf\{f(\mathbf{x}) \mid \mathbf{x} \in \mathbf{K}(S)\}.$$

Solution: Since $\mathbf{K}(\emptyset) = \emptyset$, it is clear that the statement holds for $S = \emptyset$. Thus, we may assume that $S \neq \emptyset$.

Since $S \subseteq \mathbf{K}(S)$, it follows that

$$\sup\{f(\mathbf{x}) \mid \mathbf{x} \in S\} \leqslant \sup\{f(\mathbf{x}) \mid \mathbf{x} \in \mathbf{K}(S)\}.$$

Suppose now that $r = \sup\{f(\mathbf{x}) \mid \mathbf{x} \in \mathbf{K}(S)\}$. We need to show only that $r \leqslant \sup\{f(\mathbf{x}) \mid \mathbf{x} \in S\}$.

Let ϵ be a positive number. There exists $\mathbf{x}_0 \in bf{K}(S)$ such that $f(\mathbf{x}_0) \geqslant r - \frac{\epsilon}{2}$. Since f is continuous, there exists $\delta > 0$ such that if $\mathbf{x} \in B(\mathbf{x}_0, \delta)$ then $-\frac{\epsilon}{2} < f(\mathbf{x}) - f(\mathbf{x}_0) < \frac{\epsilon}{2}$. Since $\mathbf{x}_0 \in \mathbf{K}(S)$, there exists $\mathbf{x}_1 \in S$ such that $\mathbf{x}_1 \in B(\mathbf{x}_0, \delta)$, so

$$-\frac{\epsilon}{2} < f(\mathbf{x}_1) - f(\mathbf{x}_0) < \frac{\epsilon}{2}$$

for some $\mathbf{x}_1 \in S$. Therefore, $f(\mathbf{x}_1) > f(\mathbf{x}_0) - \frac{\epsilon}{2} \geqslant r - \epsilon$ for every $\epsilon > 0$, which implies the reverse inequality.

If $\sup\{f(\mathbf{x}) \mid \mathbf{x} \in \mathbf{K}(S)\} = \infty$ and let $a \in \mathbb{R}$. There exists $\mathbf{x}_0 \in \mathbf{K}(S)$ such that $f(\mathbf{x}_0) \geqslant a + 1$. Since f is continuous, there exists $\delta > 0$ such that if $\|\mathbf{x} - \mathbf{x}_0\| < \delta$, we have $-1 < f(\mathbf{x}) - f(\mathbf{x}_0) < 1$. Since $\mathbf{x}_0 \in \mathbf{K}(S)$ there exists $\mathbf{x}_1 \in S$, so such that $\|\mathbf{x} - \mathbf{x}_0\| < \delta$, so $f(\mathbf{x}_1) > f(\mathbf{x}_0) - 1 \geqslant a$, so $\sup\{f(\mathbf{x}) \mid \mathbf{x} \in S\} = \infty$.

The proof of the remaining equality is left to the reader.

(65) Let $(S, \mathcal{O}_{s_0})$ be the topological space defined in Exercise 2, where $s_0 \in S$. Prove that any continuous function $f : S \longrightarrow \mathbb{R}$ is a constant function.

(66) Let $(S_1, \mathcal{O}_1)$ and $(S_2, \mathcal{O}_2)$ be two topological spaces and let $f : S_1 \longrightarrow S_2$ be a continuous surjective function. Prove that if $(S_2, \mathcal{O}_2)$ is compact, then $(S_1, \mathcal{O}_1)$ is compact.

(67) Let $f : \mathbb{R} \longrightarrow \mathbb{R}$ be a continuous function defined on the topological space $(\mathbb{R}, \mathcal{O})$. Prove that if $f(q) = 0$ for every $q \in \mathbb{Q}$, then $f(x) = 0$ for every $x \in \mathbb{R}$.

(68) Let $f : \mathbb{R} \longrightarrow \mathbb{R}$ be a continuous function in x_0. Prove that if $f(x_0) > 0$, then there exists an open interval (a, b) such that $x_0 \in (a, b)$ and $f(x) > 0$ for every $x \in (a, b)$.

(69) Let $(S, \mathcal{O})$ and $(T, \mathcal{O}')$ be two topological spaces and let $\mathcal{B}'$ be a basis of $(T, \mathcal{O}')$. Prove that $f : S \longrightarrow T$ is continuous if and only if $f^{-1}(B) \in \mathcal{O}$ for every $B \in \mathcal{B}'$.

(70) Let $(S, \mathcal{O})$ be a topological space and let $f : S \longrightarrow \mathbb{R}$. Prove that a function is continuous at $\mathbf{x}_0 \in S$ if and only if the following conditions are satisfied:

    (a) for every $s < f(x_0)$ there is $U \in neigh_{x_0}(\mathcal{O})$ such that for every $x \in U$ we have $s < f(x)$;

    (b) for every $t > f(x_0)$ there is $V \in neigh_{x_0}(\mathcal{O})$ such that for every $x \in V$ we have $t > f(x)$.

(71) Prove that a function $f : S \longrightarrow T$ is open if there is some basis $\mathcal{B}$ of the topological space $(S, \mathcal{O})$ such that $f(B)$ is open for each $B \in \mathcal{B}$.

(72) Prove that a bijection $f : S \longrightarrow T$ is an open function if and only if it is a closed mapping.

    Hint: Use the identity $T - f(U) = f(S - U)$ satisfied by any bijection $f : S \longrightarrow T$ for each $U \in \mathcal{P}(S)$.

(73) Prove that the function $f : \mathbb{R} \longrightarrow \mathbb{R}$ defined by $f(x) = x^2$ for $x \in \mathbb{R}$ is continuous but not open.

(74) Prove that if $a < b$ and $c < d$, then the subspaces $[a, b]$ and $[c, d]$ of $(\mathbb{R}, \mathcal{O})$ are homeomorphic.

(75) Let $(S, \mathcal{O})$ and $(T, \mathcal{O}')$ be two topological spaces and let $f : S \longrightarrow T$ be a bijection. Prove that

    (a) f is a closed function if and only if it is an open function;

    (b) f is a homeomorphism if and only if f is an open function.

(76) Let $(S, \mathcal{O})$ and $(T, \mathcal{O}')$ be two topological spaces and let $\mathcal{B}$ be a basis for $(S, \mathcal{O})$. Prove that if f is a homeomorphism, then $f(\mathcal{B})$ is a basis for $(T, \mathcal{O}')$.

(77) Let $(S, \mathcal{O})$ be a connected topological space and $f : S \longrightarrow \mathbb{R}$ be a continuous function. Prove that if $x, y \in S$, then for every $r \in [f(x), f(y)]$ there is $z \in S$ such that $f(z) = r$.

(78) Let a and b be two real numbers such that $a \leqslant b$. Prove that if $f : [a, b] \longrightarrow [a, b]$ is a continuous function, then there is $c \in [a, b]$ such that $f(c) = c$.

(79) Prove that a topological space $(S, \mathcal{O})$ is connected if and only if $\partial T = \emptyset$ implies $T \in \{\emptyset, S\}$ for every $T \in \mathcal{P}(S)$.

Let $(S, \mathcal{O})$ be a topological space and let x and y be two elements of S. A *continuous path* between x and y is a continuous function $f : [0, 1] \longrightarrow S$ such that $f(0) = x$ and $f(1) = y$. We refer to x as the *origin* and to y as the *destination* of f.

    $(S, \mathcal{O})$ is said to be *arcwise connected* if any two points x and y are the origin and destination of a continuous path.

(80) Prove that any arcwise connected topological space is connected.

(81) Prove that, for a topological space $(S, \mathcal{O})$, the following statements are equivalent:

    (a) $(S, \mathcal{O})$ is connected.

    (b) If $S = L_1 \cup L_2$ and $L_1 \cap L_2 = \emptyset$, where L_1 and L_2 are open, then $L_1 = \emptyset$ or $L_2 = \emptyset$.

    (c) If $S = H_1 \cup H_2$ and $H_1 \cap H_2 = \emptyset$, where H_1 and H_2 are closed, then $H_1 = \emptyset$ or $H_2 = \emptyset$.

    (d) If K is a clopen set, then $K = \emptyset$ or $K = S$.

(82) Prove that any subspace of a totally disconnected topological space is totally disconnected, and prove that a product of totally disconnected topological spaces is totally disconnected.

(83) Let $(S, \mathcal{O})$ be a connected topological space and $f : S \longrightarrow \mathbb{R}$ be a continuous function. Prove that if $x, y \in S$, then for every $r \in [f(x), f(y)]$ there is $z \in S$ such that $f(z) = r$.

(84) Prove that, for a topological space $(S, \mathcal{O})$, the following statements are equivalent:

    (a) $(S, \mathcal{O})$ is connected.

    (b) If $S = L_1 \cup L_2$ and $L_1 \cap L_2 = \emptyset$, where L_1 and L_2 are open, then $L_1 = \emptyset$ or $L_2 = \emptyset$.

(c) If $S = H_1 \cup H_2$ and $H_1 \cap H_2 = \emptyset$, where H_1 and H_2 are closed, then $H_1 = \emptyset$ or $H_2 = \emptyset$.

(d) If K is a clopen set, then $K = \emptyset$ or $K = S$.

(85) Prove that any subspace of a totally disconnected topological space is totally disconnected, and prove that a product of totally disconnected topological spaces is totally disconnected.

(86) Prove that if $(S, \mathcal{P}(S))$ and $(S', \mathcal{P}(S'))$ are two discrete topological spaces, then their product is a discrete topological space.

(87) Let $(S, \mathcal{O}), (S, \mathcal{O}')$ be two topological spaces. Prove that the collection

$$\{S \times L' \mid L' \in \mathcal{O}'\} \cup \{L \times S' \mid L \in \mathcal{O}\}$$

is a sub-basis for the product topology $\mathcal{O} \times \mathcal{O}'$.

(88) Let $\{(S_i, \mathcal{O}_i) \mid i \in I\}$ be a collection of topological spaces. Prove that each projection $p_j : \prod_{i \in I} S_i \longrightarrow S_j$ is a open mapping.

(89) Prove that the following classes of topological spaces are closed with respect to the product of topological spaces:

(a) the class of spaces that satisfy the first axiom of countability;

(b) the class of spaces that satisfy the second axiom of countability;

(c) the class of separable spaces.

(90) Let $\{(S_i, \mathcal{O}_i) \mid i \in I\}$ be a family of topological spaces indexed by the set I and let (x_j) be a J-net on $S = \prod_{i \in I} S_i$ so that $x_j = (x_{ji})$ for $i \in I$. Prove that if $y = (y_i) \in \prod_{i \in I} S_i$, then $x_j \to y$ in S if and only if $x_{ji} \to y_i$ in S_i for every $i \in I$.

(91) Let $(S, \mathcal{O}), (S, \mathcal{O}')$ be two topological spaces and let $(S \times S', \mathcal{O} \times \mathcal{O}')$ be their product.

(a) Prove that for all sets T, T' such that $T \subseteq S$ and $T' \subseteq S'$, $\mathbf{K}(T \times T') = \mathbf{K}(T) \times \mathbf{K}(T')$ and $\mathbf{I}(T \times T') = \mathbf{I}(T) \times \mathbf{I}(T')$.

(b) Prove that $\partial(T \times T') = (\partial(T) \times \mathbf{K}(T')) \cup (\mathbf{K}(T) \times \partial T')$.

(92) Let S be a subset of $\mathbb{R}^n$. Prove that if S is closed, then its characteristic function 1_S is upper semicontinuous on $\mathbb{R}^n$; also, if S is open, then 1_S is lower semicontinuous on $\mathbb{R}^n$.

Solution: Let S be an open subset of $\mathbb{R}^n$. Note that

$$L_{1_S,a} = \{\mathbf{x} \in S \mid 1_S(\mathbf{x}) \leqslant a\}$$
$$= \begin{cases} \emptyset & \text{if } a < 0, \\ \mathbb{R}^n - S & \text{if } 0 \leqslant a < 1, \\ \mathbb{R}^n & \text{if } 1 \leqslant a. \end{cases}$$

Thus, in every case, a level set $L_{1_S,a}$ is closed. By Theorem 4.113, 1_S is lower semicontinuous on S.

The argument for the case when S is closed is similar.

(93) Let a and b be two real numbers such that $a \leqslant b$. Prove that if $f :$ $[a, b] \longrightarrow [a, b]$ is a continuous function, then there is $c \in [a, b]$ such that $f(c) = c$.

A function $f : \mathbb{R}^n \longrightarrow \mathbb{R}$ is *coercive* if for any number $M > 0$ there exists a number r_M such that $\|\mathbf{x}\| > r_M$ implies $f(\mathbf{x}) > M$. In other words, f is coercive if $\lim_{\|\mathbf{x}\| \to \infty} f(\mathbf{x}) = \infty$.

(94) Prove that a lower semicontinuous and coercive function $f : \mathbb{R}^n \longrightarrow \mathbb{R}$ attains its infimum and is bounded below.

   Solution: Let $(\mathbf{x}_m)$ be a sequence such that $\lim_{m \to \infty} f(\mathbf{x}_m) = \inf f(\mathbf{x})$. Such a sequence exists because for every $m \geqslant 1$ there exists $\mathbf{x}_m$ such that $f(\mathbf{x}_m) < \inf f + \frac{1}{m}$. Since f is coercive, the sequence $(\mathbf{x}_m)$ is bounded, so it contains a convergent subsequence $(\mathbf{x}_{m_k})$. Let $\mathbf{x} = \lim_{k \to \infty} f(\mathbf{x}_{m_k})$. By part (iii) of Theorem 4.113 we have $f(\mathbf{x}) \leqslant \lim_{k \to \infty} f(\mathbf{x}_{m_k}) = \inf f$, hence $f(x) = \inf f$.

(95) Prove that the function $g : \mathbb{R}^2 \longrightarrow \mathbb{R}$ given by $g(\mathbf{x}) = x_1^2 + x_2^2$ for $\mathbf{x} \in \mathbb{R}^2$ is coercive.

(96) Prove that the function $h : \mathbb{R}^2 \longrightarrow \mathbb{R}$ given by $h(\mathbf{x}) = (x_1 - x_2)^2$ for $\mathbf{x} \in \mathbb{R}^2$ is not coercive.

(97) Let p be a polynomial,

$$p(x) = a_0 x^n + a_1 x^{n-1} + \cdots + a_n,$$

where $a_i \in \mathbb{R}$ for $0 \leqslant i \leqslant n$. Prove that the function $f : \mathbb{R} \longrightarrow \mathbb{R}$ defined by $f(x) = |p(x)|$ is coercive.

(98) Let $f : \mathbb{R}^n \longrightarrow \mathbb{R}$ be a continuous function. Prove that f is coercive if and only if each level set $L_{f,a}$ is compact.

   Solution: Since f is continuous each level set $L_{f,a}$ is closed. Thus, it suffices to show that each level set is bounded. Suppose that there exists a such that $L_{f,a}$ is unbounded. Then, there exists a sequence $(\mathbf{x}_n)$ in $L_{f,a}$ such that $\lim_{n \to \infty} \|\mathbf{x}_n\| = \infty$. The coercivity of f implies that $\lim_{n \to \infty} f(\mathbf{x}_n) = \infty$, which contradicts the fact that $f(\mathbf{x}_n) \leqslant a$. Thus, each level set $L_{f,a}$ is closed and bounded and is, therefore, compact.

   Conversely, suppose that each level set $L_{f,a}$ is compact and, therefore, is bounded. To prove that f is coercive it suffices to show that for a sequence $(\mathbf{x}_n)$ such that $\lim_{n \to \infty} \|\mathbf{x}_n\| = \infty$, the sequence $(f(\mathbf{x}_n))$ contains no bounded subsequence. Suppose that the sequence $(f(\mathbf{x}_n))$ contains a bounded subsequence $(f(\mathbf{x}_{n_i}))_{i \in I}$ and let b be an upper bound of this sequence. Then, $\{\mathbf{x}_{n_i} \mid i \in I\} \subseteq L_{f,b}$, which is contradictory because no subsequence of $(\mathbf{x}_n)$ can be bounded.

(99) Let $f : \mathbb{R}^n \longrightarrow \mathbb{R}$ be a continuous function. Prove that if f is coercive, then f has a global minimum.

Solution: Let $L_{f,a}$ be a level set that is non-empty. Since f is coercive, $L_{f,a}$ is compact. By Corollary 5.11 f attains a minimum in some $\mathbf{x}_0 \in L_{f,a}$. It follows that $\mathbf{x}_0$ is a global minimum for f.

Bibliographical Comments

There are several excellent classic references on general topology ([89, 42, 47, 43, 135]). A very readable introduction to topology is [53]. Pioneering work in applying topology in data mining has been done in [109, 92].

The one-axiom for closure operators given in Exercise 17 was obtained in [110].

Supplements from 9 to 15 which offer a modality to introduce the Lebesgue measure on $\mathbb{R}$ originate in [63].

A modern, up-to-date introduction is [2].

Chapter 5

Metric Space Topologies

5.1 Introduction

In this chapter we study an hierarchy of topological spaces that comprises topological metric spaces, topological normed spaces, and topological inner product spaces. This hierarchy is based on the fact that metric spaces can be equipped with topologies; since norms generate metrics and inner products generate norms, increasingly specialized topologies can be defined on normed spaces and on inner product spaces.

Theorem 5.1. *Let (S, d) be a metric space. The collection $\mathcal{O}_d$ defined by*

$$\mathcal{O}_d = \{L \in \mathcal{P}(S) \mid \text{ for each } x \in L \text{ there exists } \epsilon > 0 \text{ such that } B(x, \epsilon) \subseteq L\}$$

is a topology on the set S.

Proof. We have $\emptyset \in \mathcal{O}_d$ because there is no x in $\emptyset$, so the condition of the definition of $\mathcal{O}_d$ is vacuously satisfied. The set S belongs to $\mathcal{O}_d$ because $B(x, \epsilon) \subseteq S$ for every $x \in S$ and every positive number ϵ.

If $\{U_i \mid i \in I\} \subseteq \mathcal{O}_d$ and $x \in \bigcup\{U_i \mid i \in I\}$, then $x \in U_j$ for some $j \in I$. Then, there exists $\epsilon > 0$ such that $B(x, \epsilon) \subseteq U_j$ and therefore $B(x, \epsilon) \subseteq \bigcup\{U_i \mid i \in I\}$. Thus, $\bigcup\{U_i \mid i \in I\} \in \mathcal{O}_d$.

Finally, let $U, V \in \mathcal{O}_d$ and let $x \in U \cap V$. Since $U \in \mathcal{O}_d$, there exists $\epsilon > 0$ such that $B(x, \epsilon) \subseteq U$. Similarly, there exists ϵ' such that $B(x, \epsilon') \subseteq V$. If $\epsilon_1 = \min\{\epsilon, \epsilon'\}$, then $B(x, \epsilon_1) \subseteq B(x, \epsilon) \cap B(x, \epsilon') \subseteq U \cap V$, so $U \cap V \in \mathcal{O}_d$. This concludes the argument. $\square$

Theorem 5.1 implies that the collection of spheres $\{B(x, \epsilon) \mid \epsilon > 0\}$ is a local basis at x for any point x of a metric space (S, d).

Definition 5.1. Let d be a metric on a set S. The *topology induced by d* is the family of sets $\mathcal{O}_d$.

We refer to the pair $(S, \mathcal{O}_d)$ as a *topological metric space*.

Example 5.1. The usual topology of the set of real numbers $\mathbb{R}$ introduced in Example 4.3 is actually induced by the metric $d : \mathbb{R} \times \mathbb{R} \longrightarrow \mathbb{R}_{\geqslant 0}$ given by $d(x, y) = |x - y|$ for $x, y \in \mathbb{R}$. Recall that, by Theorem 4.1, every open set of this space is the union of a countable set of disjoint open intervals.

The corresponding metric topology of complex numbers $\mathbb{C}$ has a similar definition using $d(z_1, z_2) = |z_1 - z_2|$ for $z_1, z_2 \in \mathbb{C}$.

Example 5.2. The topology on $\mathbb{R}^n$ induced by the metric d defined by

$$d(\mathbf{x}, \mathbf{y}) = \sqrt{\sum_{j=1}^{n} (x_j - y_j)^2}$$

for $\mathbf{x}, \mathbf{y} \in \mathbb{R}^n$ is known as the *Euclidean topology* on $\mathbb{R}^n$.

A topological space $(S, \mathcal{O})$ is *metrizable* if there exists a metric $d : S \times S \longrightarrow \mathbb{R}_{\geqslant 0}$ such that $\mathcal{O} = \mathcal{O}_d$.

The next statement explains the terms "open sphere" and "closed sphere," which we have used previously.

Theorem 5.2. *Let $(S, \mathcal{O}_d)$ be a topological metric space. If $t \in S$ and $r > 0$, then any open sphere $B(t, r)$ is an open set and any closed sphere $B[t, r]$ is a closed set in the topological space $(S, \mathcal{O}_d)$.*

Proof. Let $x \in B(t, r)$, so $d(t, x) < r$. Choose ϵ such that $\epsilon < r - d(t, x)$. We claim that $B(x, \epsilon) \subseteq B(t, r)$. Indeed, let $z \in B(x, \epsilon)$. We have $d(x, z) < \epsilon < r - d(t, x)$. Therefore, $d(z, t) \leqslant d(z, x) + d(x, t) < r$, so $z \in B(t, r)$, which implies $B(x, \epsilon) \subseteq B(t, r)$. We conclude that $B(t, r)$ is an open set.

To show that the closed sphere $B[t, r]$ is a closed set, we will prove that its complement $S - B[t, r] = \{u \in S \mid d(u, t) > r\}$ is an open set. Let $v \in S - B[t, r]$. Now choose ϵ such that $\epsilon < d(v, t) - r$. It is easy to see that $B(v, \epsilon) \subseteq S - B[t, r]$, which proves that $S - B[t, r]$ is an open set. $\square$

Corollary 5.1. *The collection of all open spheres in a topological metric space $(S, \mathcal{O}_d)$ is a basis for this topological space.*

Proof. This statement follows immediately from Theorem 5.2. $\square$

Note that every metric space $(S, \mathcal{O}_d)$ satisfies the first axiom of countability because for every $x \in S$ the countable family of open sets $\{B(x, 1/n) \mid n \geqslant 1\}$ satisfies the requirements of Definition 4.16. This is not the case with the second axiom as we show later in Theorem 5.23.

As we have shown in Chapter 4, sequences are adequate for studying topological metric spaces.

The definition of open sets in a topological metric space implies that a subset U of a topological metric space $(S, \mathcal{O}_d)$ is closed if and only if for every $x \in S$ such that $x \notin U$ there is $\epsilon > 0$ such that $B(x, \epsilon)$ is disjoint from U. Thus, if $B(x, \epsilon) \cap U \neq \emptyset$ for every $\epsilon > 0$ and U is a closed set, then $x \in U$.

Theorem 5.3. *In a topological metric space $(S, \mathcal{O}_d)$ the closed sets are $(\mathcal{O}_d)_\delta$ sets and the open sets are $(\mathcal{F}_d)_\sigma$ sets, where $\mathcal{F}_d$ is the collection of closed sets of $(S, \mathcal{O}_d)$.*

Proof. Let U be a closed set in $(S, \mathcal{O}_d)$. Define $V_n = \{x \in S \mid d(x, y) \leqslant \frac{1}{n}$ for some $y \in U\}$. Clearly, each of the sets V_n is open because $V_n = \bigcup_{y \in U} B\left(y, \frac{1}{n}\right)$. Note that if $U = \emptyset$, then $V_n = \emptyset$. It is immediate that $U \subseteq \bigcap_{n \geqslant 1} V_n$. Conversely, if $x \in \bigcap_{n \geqslant 1} V_n$ then for each $n \geqslant 1$, there exists $y \in U$ such that $y \in B\left(x, \frac{1}{n}\right)$, which implies $x \in U$. Thus, $U = \bigcap_{n \geqslant 1} V_n$.

If V is an open set, then $\overline{V} = S - V$ is a closed set. By the first part of the theorem, there exists a countable collection of open sets (W_n) such that $S - V = \bigcap_{n \geqslant 1} W_n$, which means that $V = \bigcup_{n \geqslant 1} (S - W_n)$. Since each set $S - W_n$ is closed, it follows that V is a union of closed sets, that is, a $(\mathcal{F}_d)_\sigma$-set. $\qquad\square$

The closure and the interior operators $\mathbf{K}$ and $\mathbf{I}$ in a topological metric space $(S, \mathcal{O}_d)$ are described next.

Theorem 5.4. *In a topological metric space $(S, \mathcal{O}_d)$, we have*

$$\mathbf{K}(U) = \{x \in S \mid B(x, \epsilon) \cap U \neq \emptyset \text{ for every } \epsilon > 0\}$$

and

$$\mathbf{I}(U) = \{x \in S \mid B(x, \epsilon) \subseteq U \text{ for some } \epsilon > 0\}$$

for every $U \in \mathcal{P}(S)$.

Proof. If $B(x, \epsilon) \cap U \neq \emptyset$ for every $\epsilon > 0$, then clearly $B(x, \epsilon) \cap \mathbf{K}(U) \neq \emptyset$ for every $\epsilon > 0$ and therefore $x \in \mathbf{K}(U)$ by a previous observation.

Now let $x \in \mathbf{K}(U)$ and let $\epsilon > 0$. Suppose that $B(x, \epsilon) \cap U = \emptyset$. Then, $U \subseteq S - B(x, \epsilon)$ and $S - B(x, \epsilon)$ is a closed set. Therefore, $\mathbf{K}(U) \subseteq S - B(x, \epsilon)$. This is a contradiction because $x \in \mathbf{K}(U)$ and $x \notin S - B(x, \epsilon)$.

The second part of the theorem follows from the first part and from Corollary 4.3. $\qquad\square$

Corollary 5.2. *The subset U of the topological metric space $(S, \mathcal{O}_d)$ is closed if and only if $B(x, \epsilon) \cap U \neq \emptyset$ for every $\epsilon > 0$ implies $x \in U$.*

The border of a set U, ∂U is given by

$$\partial U = \{x \in S \mid \text{ for every } \epsilon > 0, B(x, \epsilon) \cap U \neq \emptyset \text{ and } B(x, \epsilon) \cap (S - U) \neq \emptyset\}.$$

Proof.　This corollary follows immediately from Theorem 5.4.　　　□

Recall that the notion of diameter of a subset of a metric space was introduced in Definition 1.50.

Theorem 5.5. *Let T be a subset of a topological metric space $(S, \mathcal{O}_d)$. We have $diam(\boldsymbol{K}(T)) = diam(T)$.*

Proof.　Since $T \subseteq \boldsymbol{K}(T)$, it follows immediately that $diam(T) \leqslant diam(\boldsymbol{K}(T))$, so we have to prove only the reverse inequality.

Let $u, v \in \boldsymbol{K}(T)$. For every positive number ϵ, we have $B(u, \epsilon) \cap T \neq \emptyset$ and $B(v, \epsilon) \cap T \neq \emptyset$. Thus, there exists $x, y \in T$ such that $d(u, x) < \epsilon$ and $d(v, y) < \epsilon$. Thus, $d(u, v) \leqslant d(u, x) + d(x, y) + d(y, v) \leqslant 2\epsilon + diam(T)$ for every ϵ, which implies $d(u, v) \leqslant diam(T)$ for every $u, v \in \boldsymbol{K}(T)$. This yields $diam(\boldsymbol{K}(T)) \leqslant diam(T)$.　　　□

Example 5.3. Let $\mathbb{C}$ be the set of complex numbers,

$$\mathbb{C} = \{a + ib \mid a, b \in \mathbb{R}\}.$$

A metric $d : \mathbb{C} \times \mathbb{C} \longrightarrow \mathbb{R}_{\geqslant 0}$ can be defined on $\mathbb{C}$ as

$$d(u, v) = |u - v| = \sqrt{(u_1 - v_1)^2 + (u_2 - v_2)^2},$$

where $u = u_1 + iu_2$ and $v = v_1 + iv_2$. Thus, an open sphere $B(u_0, r)$ is given by

$$B(u_0, r) = \{z \in \mathbb{C} \mid |z - u_0| < r\}.$$

A subset U of $\mathbb{C}$ is open if for every $u \in U$ there is a sphere $B(u, r)$ that is included in U.

The *extended set of complex numbers* is obtained by adding the infinity symbol ∞ to $\mathbb{C}$ and define the extended set of complex numbers $\hat{\mathbb{C}} = \mathbb{C} \cup \{\infty\}$. Note that unlike the extended set of real numbers, the extended set of complex numbers contains a unique element at infinity. As we did in the case of real numbers we add the following supplementary rules:

    (i)　$\infty + c = c + \infty = \infty$ for $c \in \mathbb{C}$;

    (ii)　if $c \neq 0$, then $c\infty = \infty c = \infty\infty = \infty$;

    (iii)　if $c \neq 0$, then $\frac{c}{\infty} = 0$ and $\frac{c}{0} = \infty$.

Theorem 5.6. *Let d and d' be two metrics defined on a set S. The metric topology $\mathcal{O}_d$ is finer than $\mathcal{O}'_d$, that is, $\mathcal{O}_{d'} \subseteq \mathcal{O}$ if and only if for each $x \in S$ and $r' > 0$ there exists $r > 0$ such that $B_d(x, r) \subseteq B_{d'}(x, r')$.*

Proof. Suppose that $\mathcal{O}_d$ is finer than $\mathcal{O}_{d'}$. Since $B_{d'}(x, r)$ is an open set in $\mathcal{O}_{d'}$, it follows that it is an open set in $\mathcal{O}_d$. This implies the existence of a sphere $B_d(x, r)$ such that $B_d(x, r) \subseteq B_{d'}(x, r')$.

Conversely, suppose the condition of the theorem holds and let U' be an open set in $\mathcal{O}_{d'}$. If $x \in U'$ there exists a sphere $B_{d'}(x, r')$ included in U'. By hypothesis, there exists $r > 0$ such that $B_d(x, r) \subseteq B_{d'}(x, r')$, so $B_d(x, r) \subseteq U'$, which means that $U' \in \mathcal{O}$. □

A metric topology can be defined, as we shall see, by more than one metric.

Definition 5.2. Two metrics d and d' defined on a set S are *topologically equivalent* if the topologies $\mathcal{O}_d$ and $\mathcal{O}_{d'}$ are equal.

Theorem 5.7. *Let d and d' be two metrics defined on a set S. If there exist two numbers $a, b \in \mathbb{R}_{>0}$ such that $a\, d(x, y) \leqslant d'(x, y) \leqslant b\, d(x, y)$, for $x, y \in S$, then $\mathcal{O}_d = \mathcal{O}_{d'}$.*

Proof. Let $B_d(x, r)$ be an open sphere centered in x, defined by d. The previous inequalities imply

$$B_d\left(x, \frac{r}{b}\right) \subseteq B_{d'}(x, r) \subseteq B_d\left(x, \frac{r}{a}\right).$$

Let $L \in \mathcal{O}_d$. By Definition 5.1, for each $x \in L$ there exists $\epsilon > 0$ such that $B_d(x, \epsilon) \subseteq L$. Then, $B_{d'}(x, a\epsilon) \subseteq B_d(x, \epsilon) \subseteq L$, which implies $L \in \mathcal{O}_{d'}$. We leave it to the reader to prove the reverse inclusion $\mathcal{O}_{d'} \subseteq \mathcal{O}_d$. □

Example 5.4. By Corollary 2.8, any two Minkowski metrics d_p and d_q on $\mathbb{R}^n$, with $p, q \geqslant 1$ are topologically equivalent. Thus, the Euclidean topology on $\mathbb{R}^n$ is induced not only by d_2, but also by d_1 and by d_∞.

Similarly, we can examine equivalence of norms on linear spaces. If ν and ν' are norms defined on a linear space L, then the corresponding metrics d and d' are equivalent if and only if there exist two numbers $a, b \in \mathbb{R}_{>0}$ such that $a\, \nu(x) \leqslant \nu'(x) \leqslant b\nu'(x)$, for $x, y \in L$.

Definition 5.3. A topological space $(S, \mathcal{O})$ is *metrizable* if there exists a metric d on S such that $\mathcal{O} = \mathcal{O}_d$.

5.2   Sequences in Metric Spaces

Since topological metric spaces satisfy the first axiom of countability, open and closed sets in these spaces can be described in terms of sequences.

As we saw in Corollaries 4.9 and 4.8, a subset T of a topological space $(S, \mathcal{O})$ that satisfies the first axiom of countability is open if for every $x \in T$ and sequence (x_n) that converges to x there exists a number $n_T \in \mathbb{N}$ such that $n \geqslant n_T$ implies $x_n \in T$. Therefore, this characterization of open sets is valid in the case of topological metric spaces.

Let U be a closed set in the topological metric space $(S, \mathcal{O}_d)$ and let (x_n) be a sequence in U such that $\lim_{n \to \infty} x_n = x$. Then, we have $x \in U$. Indeed, if this is not the case, that is, $x \in S - U$, we would have a number n_T such that $n \geqslant n_T$ would imply $x_n \in S - U$ because $S - T$ is an open subset of S. This contradiction means that $x \in U$.

Conversely, let U be a subset of S such that for every sequence (x_n) in U such that $\lim_{n \to \infty} x_n = x$, we have $x \in U$. Suppose that U is not closed, so $S - U$ is not open. This means that there exists $z \in S - U$ and a sequence (z_n) in $S - U$ such that if $\lim_{n \to \infty} z_n = z$ such that for every $m \in \mathbb{N}$ there exists z_n with $n > m$ such that $z_n \notin S - U$, that is, $z_n \in U$. This contradiction means that U is closed.

Definition 5.4. A sequence $\mathbf{x} = (x_0, \ldots, x_n, \ldots)$ of elements in a metric space (S, d) *converges* to an element x of S if for every $\epsilon > 0$ there exists $n_\epsilon \in \mathbb{N}$ such that $n \geqslant n_\epsilon$ implies $x_n \in B(x, \epsilon)$.

If there exists $x \in S$ such that $\mathbf{x}$ converges to x, we say that the sequence $\mathbf{x}$ is *convergent*.

Theorem 5.8. *Let $(S, \mathcal{O}_d)$ be a topological metric space and let $\boldsymbol{x} = (x_0, \ldots, x_n, \ldots)$ be a sequence in $\mathbf{Seq}_\infty(S)$. If $\boldsymbol{x}$ is convergent, then there exists a unique x such that $\boldsymbol{x}$ converges to x.*

Proof. Suppose that there are two distinct elements x and y of the set S that satisfy the condition of Definition 5.4. We have $d(x, y) > 0$. Define $\epsilon = \frac{d(x,y)}{3}$. By definition, there exists n_ϵ such that $n \geqslant n_\epsilon$ implies $d(x, x_n) < \epsilon$ and $d(x_n, y) < \epsilon$. By applying the triangular inequality, we obtain

$$d(x, y) \leqslant d(x, x_n) + d(x_n, y) < 2\epsilon = \frac{2}{3} d(x, y),$$

which is a contradiction. $\square$

If the sequence $\mathbf{x} = (x_0, \ldots, x_n, \ldots)$ converges to x, this is denoted by $\lim_{n \to \infty} x_n = x$ or by $x_n \to x$.

An important special case is the metric space $(\mathbb{R}, \mathcal{O}_d)$, where d is the usual metric on $\mathbb{R}$ defined by $d(x, y) = |x - y|$ for $x, y \in \mathbb{R}$.

Definition 5.5. A sequence of real numbers (x_n) *converges to x from the left* if $x_n \leqslant x$ for $n \in \mathbb{N}$ and $x_n \to x$. Similarly, (x_n) converges to x from the right if $x_n \geqslant x$ for $n \in \mathbb{N}$ and $x_n \to x$.

Example 5.5. The sequence of real numbers (u_n) defined by $u_n = \left(1 + \frac{1}{n}\right)^n$ converges to e from the left, while the sequence (v_n) given by $v_n = \left(1 + \frac{1}{n}\right)^{n+1}$ converges to e from the right, as it is well-known from calculus.

5.3 Limits of Functions on Metric Spaces

Definition 5.6. Let $(S, \mathcal{O}_d)$ and $(T, \mathcal{O}_e)$ be two topological metric spaces, X be subset of S, and let a an accumulation point of X.

A function $f : X \longrightarrow T$ *has the limit* $b \in T$ *in* a if for every $V \in neigh_b(\mathcal{O}_e)$ there exists a neighborhood $U \in neigh_a(\mathcal{O}_d)$ such that $f(U) \subseteq V$.

This is denoted by $\lim_{x \to a} f(x) = b$.

Note that in order to consider the existence of a limit in a it is not necessary for f to be defined in a; it suffices for a to be an accumulation point of the definition domain of f.

Theorem 5.9. *Let $(S, \mathcal{O}_d)$ and $(T, \mathcal{O}_e)$ be two topological metric spaces, X be a subset of S and let a be an accumulation point of X. If a function $f : X \longrightarrow T$ has a limit in a, then this limit is unique.*

Proof. Suppose that we have $\lim_{x \to a} f(x) = b_1$ and $\lim_{x \to a} f(x) = b2$. Consider the neighborhoods $B(b_1, r_1)$ and $B(b_2, r_2)$ such that $r_1 + r_2 < e(y_1, y_2)$. The open spheres $B(b_1, r_1)$ and $B(b_2, r_2)$ are disjoint. By hypothesis, there exists $U_1, U_2 \in neigh_a(\mathcal{O}_d)$ such that $f(U_1) \subseteq B(y_1, r_1)$ and $f(U_2) \subseteq B(y_2, r_2)$, which implies $f(U_1) \cap f(U_2) = \emptyset$. Since $f(U_1 \cap U_2) \subseteq f(U_1) \cap f(U_2)$, it follows that $f(U_1 \cap U_2) = \emptyset$. This contradicts the fact that $f(a) \in f(U_1 \cap U_2)$. $\qquad\square$

Example 5.6. In the special case of functions of the form $f : X \longrightarrow \mathbb{C}$ the definition of the limit of f in a can be formulated in an $\epsilon - \delta$ language. Namely, for an accumulation point a of X, we have $\lim_{x \to a} f(x) = b$ if for every $\epsilon > 0$, there exists $\delta > 0$ (which depends on both a and ϵ) such that $|x - a| < \delta$ implies $|f(x) - b| < \epsilon$.

The same description works for real-valued limits of real-valued functions,

Next we extend the notion of neighborhood to the points ∞ and $-\infty$ of $\hat{R}$.

Definition 5.7. A subset V of $\hat{R}$ is a *neighborhood of* ∞ if it has the form (a, ∞) for some $a \in \mathbb{R}$; V is a *neighborhood of* $-\infty$ if $V = (-\infty, a)$ for some $a \in \mathbb{R}$.

The collection of neighborhoods of ∞ and $-\infty$ will be denoted by $\mathcal{N}_\infty$ and $\mathcal{N}_{-\infty}$, respectively.

Using Definition 5.7, it is possible to extend the notion of limit to functions of the form $f : \mathbb{R} \longrightarrow T$, where $(T, \mathcal{O}_e)$ is a topological metric space. Thus, we write $\lim_{x \to \infty} f(x) = b$ if for every $V \in neigh_b(\mathcal{O}_e)$ there exists $a \in \mathbb{R}$ such that $x > a$ implies $f(x) \in V$. Similarly, $\lim_{x \to -\infty} f(x) = b$ if for every $V \in neigh_b(\mathcal{O}_e)$ there exists $a \in \mathbb{R}$ such that $x < a$ implies $f(x) \in V$.

Definition 5.8. Let $X \subset \mathbb{R}$, $f : X \longrightarrow (S, d)$ be a function of a real argument ranging over a metric space (S, d), and let a be an accumulation point of the set $X \cap (-\infty, a)$.

An element $b \in S$ is the *left limit* of f in a if for every $V \in neigh_b(\mathcal{O}_d)$ there exists $U \in neigh_a(\mathcal{O})$ (where $\mathcal{O}$ is the usual topology on $\mathbb{R}$) such that $x \in U \cap X$ and $x < a$ imply $f(x) \in V$.

This is denoted by $\lim_{x \to a-} f(x) = b$.

Definition 5.9. Let $X \subset \mathbb{R}$, $f : X \longrightarrow (S, d)$ be a function of a real argument ranging over a metric space (S, d), and let a be an accumulation point of the set $X \cap (a, \infty)$.

An element $b \in S$ is the *right limit* of f in a if for every $V \in neigh_b(\mathcal{O}_d)$ there exists $U \in neigh_a(\mathcal{O})$ (where $\mathcal{O}$ is the usual topology on $\mathbb{R}$) such that $x \in U \cap X$ and $x > a$ imply $f(x) \in V$.

This is denoted by $\lim_{x \to a+} f(x) = b$.

The function $f : X \longrightarrow \mathbb{R}$ has the left limit b in a (where a is an accumulation point of the set $X \cap (-\infty, a)$ and $b \in \mathbb{R}$) if for every sequence (x_n) such that $x_n < a$ and $\lim_{n \to \infty} x_n = a$ we have $\lim_{n \to \infty} f(x_n) = b$.

The function f has the right limit b in $a \in I$ (where a is an accumulation point of the set $X \cap (a, \infty)$ and $b \in \mathbb{R}$) if for every sequence (x_n) such that $x_n > a$ and $\lim_{n \to \infty} x_n = a$ we have $\lim_{n \to \infty} f(x_n) = b$.

Example 5.7. Let $f : \mathbb{R} \longrightarrow \mathbb{R}$ be the function defined by $f(x) = n$ if $x \in [n, n+1)$ for $x \in \mathbb{R}$ and $n \in \mathbb{N}$. This is the well-known floor function. Note that $\lim_{x \to n-} f(x) = n-1$ and $\lim_{x \to n+} f(x) = n$.

Theorem 5.10. *Let X be a subset of $\mathbb{R}$ and let $f : X \longrightarrow (S, d)$ be a function of a real argument ranging over a metric space (S, d). The function has a limit ℓ in a (where a is an accumulation point of X in the topological space $(\mathbb{R}, \mathcal{O})$) if and only if the lateral limits $\lim_{x \to a-} f(x), \lim_{x \to a+} f(x)$ exists and are equal.*

Proof. By Definition 5.6 it is clear if $\lim_{x \to a} f(x)$ exists, then both lateral limits in a exist and are equal.

Conversely, suppose that both lateral limits in a exist and are equal to b. Let $V \in neigh_b(\mathcal{O}_d)$. Since $b = \lim_{x \to a-} f(x)$ there exists a neighborhood U_1 of a such that if $x \in U_1 \cap X$ and $x < a$, then $f(x) \in U_1$. Also, since $b = \lim_{x \to a+} f(x)$, there exists a neighborhood U_2 of a such that if $x \in U_2 \cap X$ and $x > a$, $f(x) \in U_2$.

Let $U = U_1 \cap U_2$. We have $U \cap X \subseteq U_1 \cap X$ and $U \cap X \subseteq U_2 \cap X$ and $U \in neigh_a(\mathcal{O})$. If $x \neq a$ and $x \in U \cap X$, then $x \in U_1 \cap X$ and $x \in U_2 \cap X$. If $x < a$, then $f(x) \in V$ (because $x \in U_1 \cap X$); if $x > a$, then we also have $f(x) \in V$. Thus, for any $x \neq a$, we have $f(x) \in V$, so $\lim_{x \to a} f(x) = b$. $\square$

Theorem 5.11. *Let X be a subset of $\mathbb{R}$ and let $f : X \longrightarrow \mathbb{R}$ be a monotonic function. Then, f has lateral limits in every accumulation point of X.*

Proof. Suppose that f is an increasing function and let (x_n) be an arbitrary increasing sequence (x_n) such that $\lim_{n \to \infty} x_n = a$ and $x_n < a$ for $n \in \mathbb{N}$. Since f is increasing, the sequence $(f(x_n))$ is increasing and has a limit (finite or not), so the left limit of f in a exists.

Similarly, for every decreasing sequence (x_n) such that $\lim_{n \to \infty} x_n = a$, the sequence $(f(x_n))$ has a limit. The argument for decreasing functions is similar. $\square$

It is possible that a function has no lateral limits in a particular point, or even in any point, as the next example shows.

Example 5.8. The function $f : \mathbb{R} - \{0\} \longrightarrow \mathbb{R}$ defined by $f(x) = \sin \frac{1}{x}$ for $x \neq 0$ has no limit in 0. Indeed, let $x_n = \frac{2}{n\pi}$. We have $\lim_{n \to \infty} x_n = 0$ and

$x_n > 0$ for $n \in \mathbb{N}$. The sequence $(f(x_n))$ is

$$0, 1, 0, -1, 0, 1, \ldots,$$

so f has no right limit in 0. Choosing $x_n = -\frac{2}{n\pi}$ we have $\lim_{n\to\infty} x_n = 0$ and $x_n < 0$; again, the sequence $(f(x_n))$ is

$$0, -1, 0, 1, 0, -1, \ldots,$$

and f has no left limit in 0.

5.4   Continuity of Functions between Metric Spaces

For functions between topological metric spaces we can formulate specific characterizations of continuity.

Theorem 5.12. *Let $(S, \mathcal{O}_d)$ and $(T, \mathcal{O}_e)$ be two topological metric spaces. The following statements concerning a function $f : S \longrightarrow T$ are equivalent:*
   (i) *f is a continuous function;*
   (ii) *for every $\epsilon > 0$ and $x \in S$ there exists $\delta > 0$ such that $f(B_d(x, \delta)) \subseteq B_e(f(x), \epsilon)$.*

Proof.   (i) implies (ii): Suppose that f is a continuous function. Since $B_e(f(x), \epsilon)$ is an open set in $(T, \mathcal{O}_e)$, the set $f^{-1}(B_e(f(x), \epsilon)$ is an open set in $(S, \mathcal{O}_d)$. Clearly, $x \in f^{-1}(B_e(f(x), \epsilon))$, so by the definition of the metric topology there exists $\delta > 0$ such that $B_d(x, \delta) \subseteq f^{-1}(B_e(f(x), \epsilon)$, which yields $f(B_d(x, \delta)) \subseteq B_e(f(x), \epsilon)$.

(ii) implies (i): Let V be an open set of $(T, \mathcal{O}_e)$. If $f^{-1}(V)$ is empty, then it is clearly open. Therefore, we may assume that $f^{-1}(V)$ is not empty. Let $x \in f^{1-}(V)$. Since $f(x) \in V$ and V is open, there exists $\epsilon > 0$ such that $B_e(f(x), \epsilon) \subseteq V$. By part (ii) of the theorem, there exists $\delta > 0$ such that $f(B_d(x, \delta)) \subseteq B_e(f(x), \epsilon)$, which implies $x \in B_d(x, \delta) \subseteq f^{-1}(V)$. This means that $f^{-1}(V)$ is open, so f is continuous. $\square$

Theorem 5.13. *Let $(S, \mathcal{O}_d)$ and $(T, \mathcal{O}_e)$ be two topological metric spaces, X be a subset of S, and let $a \in S$ be an accumulation point of X. We have $\lim_{x\to a} f(x) = b$ if for every sequence (x_n) such that $\lim_{n\to\infty} x_n = a$ we have $\lim_{n\to\infty} f(x_n) = b$.*

Proof.   Suppose that $\lim_{n\to\infty} f(x_n) = b$ and let $\epsilon > 0$. By Theorem 5.12, there exists $\delta > 0$ such that $f(B(a, \delta)) \subseteq B(b, \epsilon)$. Let $\mathbf{x} = (x_0, \ldots, x_n, \ldots)$ be a sequence such that $\lim_{n\to\infty} x_n = a$. Since $\lim_{n\to\infty} x_n = a$, there exists

n_δ such that $n \geq n_\delta$ implies $x_n \in B(a, \delta)$. Then, $f(x_n) \in f(B(a, \delta)) \subseteq B(b, \epsilon)$. This shows that $\lim_{n \to \infty} f(x_n) = b$.

Conversely, suppose that for every sequence $\mathbf{x} = (x_0, \dots, x_n, \dots)$ such that $\lim_{n \to \infty} x_n = a$, we have $\lim_{n \to \infty} f(x_n) = b$. If f were not continuous in a, we would have an $\epsilon > 0$ such that for all $\delta > 0$ we would have $y \in B(a, \delta)$ but $f(y) \notin B(f(a), \epsilon)$. Choosing $\delta = \frac{1}{n}$, let $y_n \in S$ such that $y_n \in B\left(x, \frac{1}{n}\right)$ and $f(y_n) \notin B(b, \epsilon)$. This yields a contradiction because we should have $\lim_{n \to \infty} f(y_n) = b$. $\qquad \square$

A local continuity property is introduced next.

Definition 5.10. Let $(S, \mathcal{O}_d)$ and $(T, \mathcal{O}_e)$ be two topological metric spaces and let $x \in S$.

A function $f : S \longrightarrow T$ is *continuous in* x if for every $\epsilon > 0$ there exists $\delta > 0$ such that $f(B(x, \delta)) \subseteq B(f(x), \epsilon)$.

It is clear that f is continuous if it is continuous in every $x \in S$.

The definition of continuity in a point can be restated by saying that f is continuous in x if for every $\epsilon > 0$ there is $\delta > 0$ such that $d(x, y) < \delta$ implies $e(f(x), f(y)) < \epsilon$.

We saw that a function $f : S \longrightarrow T$ between two topological metric spaces $(S, \mathcal{O}_d)$ and $(T, \mathcal{O}_e)$ is continuous if and only if for every $\epsilon > 0$ and every $x \in S$ there exists $\delta > 0$ such that $f(B_d(x, \delta)) \subseteq B_e(f(x), \epsilon)$.

Definition 5.11. A function $f : S \longrightarrow T$ between two topological metric spaces $(S, \mathcal{O}_d)$ and $(T, \mathcal{O}_e)$ is *uniformly continuous* if and only if for every $\epsilon > 0$, there exists $\delta > 0$ such that for every $x \in S$ we have $f(B_d(x, \delta)) \subseteq B_e(f(x), \epsilon)$.

Note that the definition of uniform continuity is obtained from the second part of the characterization of continuous function by inverting the order of the expressions "for every $x \in S$" and "there exists $\delta > 0$". Thus, for a continuous function f from $(S, \mathcal{O}_d)$ and $(T, \mathcal{O}_e)$, the number δ introduced in the definition of local continuity depends both on x and on ϵ. If δ is dependent only on ϵ (as in Definition 5.11) we obtain the stronger property of uniform continuity.

Example 5.9. The function $f : \mathbb{R} \longrightarrow \mathbb{R}$ given by $f(x) = x \sin x$ is continuous but not uniformly continuous. Indeed, let $u_n = n\pi$ and $v_n = n\pi + \frac{1}{n}$. Note that $\lim_{n \to \infty} |u_n - v_n| = 0$, $f(u_n) = 0$, and

$f(v_n) = (n\pi + \frac{1}{n})\sin(n\pi + \frac{1}{n}) = (n\pi + \frac{1}{n})(-1)^n \sin\frac{1}{n}$. Therefore,

$$\lim_{n \to \infty} |f(u_n) - f(v_n)| = \lim_{n \to \infty} \left(n\pi + \frac{1}{n}\right)\sin\frac{1}{n} = \pi \lim_{n \to \infty} \frac{n}{\sin\frac{1}{n}} = \pi,$$

so f is not uniformly continuous.

Theorem 5.14. *Let $(S, \mathcal{O}_d)$ and $(T, \mathcal{O}_e)$ be two topological metric spaces, $f : S \longrightarrow T$ be a function, and let $\boldsymbol{u} = (u_0, u_1, \ldots)$ and $\boldsymbol{v} = (v_0, v_1, \ldots)$ in $\mathbf{Seq}_\infty(S)$. The following statements are equivalent:*

    (i) *f is uniformly continuous;*

    (ii) *if $\lim_{n \to \infty} d(u_n, v_n) = 0$, then $\lim_{n \to \infty} e(f(u_n), f(v_n)) = 0$;*

    (iii) *if $\lim_{n \to \infty} d(u_n, v_n) = 0$, we have $\lim_{k \to \infty} e(f(u_{n_k}), f(v_{n_k})) = 0$, where $(u_{n_0}, u_{n_1}, \ldots)$ and $(v_{n_0}, v_{n_1}, \ldots)$ are two arbitrary subsequences of $\boldsymbol{u}$ and $\boldsymbol{v}$, respectively.*

Proof. (i) implies (ii): For $\epsilon > 0$, there exists δ such that $d(u, v) < \delta$ implies $e(f(u), f(v)) < \epsilon$. Therefore, if $\boldsymbol{u}$ and $\boldsymbol{v}$ are sequences as above, there exists n_δ such that $n > n_\delta$ implies $d(u_n, v_n) < \delta$, so $e(f(u_n), f(v_n)) < \epsilon$. Thus, $\lim_{n \to \infty} e(f(u_n), f(v_n)) = 0$.

(ii) implies (iii): This implication is obvious.

(iii) implies (i): Suppose that f satisfies (iii) but is not uniformly continuous. Then, there exists $\epsilon > 0$ such that for every $\delta > 0$ there exist $u, v \in X$ such that $d(u, v) < \delta$ and $e(f(u), f(v)) > \epsilon$. Let u_n, v_n be such that $d(u_n, v_n) < \frac{1}{n}$ for $n \geqslant 1$. Then, $\lim_{n \to \infty} d(u_n, v_n) = 0$ but $e(f(u_n), f(v_n))$ does not converge to 0. $\qquad\square$

Next we discuss extensions of the notion of distance between points to dissimilarities between points and sets and between subsets of metric spaces.

Definition 5.12. Let (S, d) be a metric space and let U be a subset of S. The *distance from an element x to U* is the number

$$d(x, U) = \inf\{d(x, u) \mid u \in U\}.$$

Note that if $x \in U$, then $d(x, U) = 0$.

Theorem 5.15. *Let (S, d) be a metric space and let U be a subset of S. The function $f : S \longrightarrow \mathbb{R}$ given by $f(x) = d(x, U)$ for $x \in S$ is continuous.*

Proof. Since $d(x, z) \leqslant d(x, y) + d(y, z)$, we have $d(x, U) \leqslant d(x, y) + d(y, U)$. By exchanging x and y we also have $d(y, U) \leqslant d(x, y) + d(x, U)$ and, together, these inequalities yield the inequality

$$|d(x, U) - d(y, U)| \leqslant d(x, y). \tag{5.1}$$

Therefore, if $d(x, y) < \epsilon$, it follows that $|d(x, U) - d(y, U)| \leqslant \epsilon$, which implies the continuity of $d(x, U)$. $\square$

Theorem 5.16. *Let (S, d) be a metric space. The following statements hold:*

    (i) $d(u, V) = 0$ if and only if $u \in \boldsymbol{K}(V)$, and
    (ii) $d(u, V) = d(u, \boldsymbol{K}(V))$
for every $u, u' \in S$ and $V \subseteq S$.

Proof. Suppose that $d(u, V) = 0$. Again, by the definition of $d(u, V)$, for every $\epsilon > 0$ there exists $v \in V$ such that $d(u, v) < \epsilon$, which means that $B(u, \epsilon) \cap V \neq \emptyset$. By Theorem 5.4, we have $u \in \boldsymbol{K}(V)$. The converse implication is immediate, so (i) holds.

To prove (ii), observe that $V \subseteq \boldsymbol{K}(V)$ implies that $d(u, \boldsymbol{K}(V)) \leqslant d(u, V)$, so we need to show only the reverse inequality.

Let w be an arbitrary element of $\boldsymbol{K}(V)$. By Theorem 5.4, for every $\epsilon > 0$, $B(w, \epsilon) \cap V \neq \emptyset$. Let $v \in B(w, \epsilon) \cap V$. We have

$$d(u, v) \leqslant d(u, w) + d(w, v) \leqslant d(u, w) + \epsilon,$$

so $d(u, V) \leqslant d(u, w) + \epsilon$. Since this inequality holds for every ϵ, $d(u, V) \leqslant d(u, w)$ for every $w \in \boldsymbol{K}(V)$, so $d(u, V) \leqslant d(u, \boldsymbol{K}(V))$. This allows us to conclude that $d(u, V) = d(u, \boldsymbol{K}(V))$. $\square$

Corollary 5.3. *If V is a closed subset of a metric space (S, d) and $d(u, V) > 0$, then $v \in S - V$.*

Proof. This is an immediate consequence of Theorem 5.16. $\square$

Theorem 5.16 can be restated using the function $d_U : S \longrightarrow \mathbb{R}_{\geqslant 0}$ defined by $d_U(x) = d(x, U)$ for $u \in S$. Thus, for every subset U of S and $x, y \in S$, we have $|d_U(x) - d_U(y)| \leqslant d(x, y)$, $d_U(x) = 0$ if and only if $x \in \boldsymbol{K}(U)$, and $d_U = d_{\boldsymbol{K}(V)}$. The function d_U is continuous.

A dissimilarity $d : S \times S \longrightarrow \hat{\mathbb{R}}_{\geqslant 0}$ can be extended to the set of subsets of S by defining $d(U, V)$ as

$$d(U, V) = \inf\{d(u, v) \mid u \in U \text{ and } v \in V\}$$

for $U, V \in \mathcal{P}(S)$. The resulting extension is also a dissimilarity. However, even if d is a metric, then its extension to subsets of S is not, in general, a metric on $\mathcal{P}(S)$ because it does not satisfy the triangular inequality. Instead, we prove that if d is a metric, then for every U, V, W we have

$$d(U, W) \leqslant d(U, V) + diam(V) + d(V, W).$$

Indeed, by the definition of $d(U,V)$ and $d(V,W)$, for every $\epsilon > 0$, there exist $u \in U$, $v, v' \in V$, and $w \in W$ such that

$$d(U,V) \leqslant d(u,v) \leqslant d(U,V) + \tfrac{\epsilon}{2},$$
$$d(V,W) \leqslant d(v',w) \leqslant d(V,W) + \tfrac{\epsilon}{2}.$$

By the triangular axiom, we have $d(u,w) \leqslant d(u,v) + d(v,v') + d(v',w)$. Hence, $d(u,w) \leqslant d(U,V) + diam(V) + d(V,W) + \epsilon$, which implies $d(U,W) \leqslant d(U,V) + diam(V) + d(V,W) + \epsilon$ for every $\epsilon > 0$. This yields the needed inequality.

Definition 5.13. Let (S,d) be a metric space. The sets $U, V \in \mathcal{P}(S)$ are *separate* if $d(U,V) > 0$.

The notions of an open sphere and a closed sphere in a metric space (S,d) are extended to the space of subsets of S by defining the sets $B(T,r)$ and $B[T,r]$ as

$$B(T,r) = \{u \in S \mid d(u,T) < r\},$$
$$B[T,r] = \{u \in S \mid d(u,T) \leqslant r\},$$

for $T \in \mathcal{P}(S)$ and $r \geqslant 0$, respectively.

The next statement is a generalization of Theorem 5.2.

Theorem 5.17. *Let $(S, \mathcal{O}_d)$ be a topological metric space. For every set T, $T \subseteq S$, and every $r > 0$, $B(T,r)$ is an open set and $B[T,r]$ is a closed set in $(S, \mathcal{O}_d)$.*

Proof. Let $u \in B(T,r)$. We have $d(u,T) < r$, or, equivalently, $\inf\{d(u,t) \mid t \in T\} < r$. We claim that if ϵ is a positive number such that $\epsilon < \tfrac{r}{2}$, then $B(u,\epsilon) \subseteq B(T,r)$.

Let $z \in B(u,\epsilon)$. For every $v \in T$, we have $d(z,v) \leqslant d(z,u) + d(u,v) < \epsilon + d(u,v)$. From the definition of $d(u,T)$ as an infimum, it follows that there exists $v' \in T$ such that $d(u,v') < d(u,V) + \tfrac{\epsilon}{2}$, so $d(z,v') < d(u,T) + \epsilon < r + \epsilon$. Since this inequality holds for every $\epsilon > 0$, it follows that $d(z,v') < r$, so $d(z,T) < r$, which proves that $B(u,\epsilon) \subseteq B(T,r)$. Thus, $B(T,r)$ is an open set.

Suppose now that $s \in \mathbf{K}(B[T,r])$. By part (ii) of Theorem 5.16, we have $d(s, B[T,r]) = 0$, so $\inf\{d(s,w) \mid w \in B[T,r]\} = 0$. Therefore, for every $\epsilon > 0$, there is $w \in B[T,r]$ such that $d(s,w) < \epsilon$. Since $d(w,T) \leqslant r$, it follows from the first part of Theorem 5.16 that $|d(s,T) - d(w,T)| \leqslant d(s,w) < \epsilon$ for every $\epsilon > 0$. This implies $d(s,T) = d(w,T)$, so $s \in B[T,r]$. This allows us to conclude that $B[T,r]$ is indeed a closed set. $\square$

To introduce a metric structure on a quotient space of a linear space we need to limit ourselves to considering only closed subspaces.

Let M be a subspace of a normed linear space L and let $[x], [y] \in L/M$. The dissimilarity between the classes $[x]$ and $[y]$ is

$$d([x], [y]) = \inf\{\|u - v\| \mid u \in [x] \text{ and } v \in [y]\}.$$

The distance between x and $[y]$ is

$$d(x, [y]) = \inf\{\|x - w\| \mid w \in [y]\},$$

and we have $d(x, [y]) = d([x], [y])$ because

$$\begin{aligned}
\{u - v \mid u \in [x], v \in [y]\} &= \{(x + z_1) - (y + z_2) \mid z_1, z_2 \in M\} \\
&= \{x - (y - z_1 + z_2) \mid z_1, z_2 \in M\} \\
&= \{x - (y + z) \mid z \in M\} \\
&= \{x - w \mid w \in M\}.
\end{aligned}$$

Note that $M = [0_L]$. By Theorem 5.16 if $x \in \mathbf{K}(M) - M$, then $d(x, [0]_L) > 0$. On other hand, $d([x], [0_L]) = 0$ even though $[x] \neq [0_L]$. Therefore, if we assume that d is a metric on L/M we must have $\mathbf{K}(M) = M$, that is, we need to consider only quotient spaces relative to closed subspaces.

Definition 5.14. Let M be a subspace of a normed linear space L. The quotient norm on L/M is given by $\|[x]\| = d([x], [0_L])$.

Theorem 5.18. (Lebesgue's Lemma) *Let $(S, \mathcal{O}_d)$ be a compact topological metric space and let $\mathcal{C}$ be an open cover of this space. There exists $r \in \mathbb{R}_{>0}$ such that for every subset U with $diam(U) < r$ there is a set $L \in \mathcal{C}$ such that $U \subseteq L$.*

Proof. Suppose that the statement is not true. Then, for every $k \in \mathbb{P}$, there exists a subset U_k of S such that $diam(U_k) < \frac{1}{k}$ and U_k is not included in any of the sets L of $\mathcal{C}$. Since $(S, \mathcal{O}_d)$ is compact, there exists a finite subcover $\{L_1, \ldots, L_p\}$ of $\mathcal{C}$.

Let x_{ik} be an element in $U_k - L_i$. For every two points x_{ik}, x_{jk}, we have $d(x_{ik}, x_{jk}) \leqslant \frac{1}{k}$ because both belong to the same set U_k. By Theorem 5.43, the compactness of S implies that any sequence $\mathbf{x}_i = (x_{i1}, x_{i2}, \ldots)$ contains a convergent subsequence. Denote by x_i the limit of this subsequence, where $1 \leqslant i \leqslant p$. The inequality $d(x_{ik}, x_{jk}) \leqslant \frac{1}{k}$ for $k \geqslant 1$ implies that $d(x_i, x_j) = 0$ so $x_i = x_j$ for $1 \leqslant i, j \leqslant p$. Let x be their common value. Then x does not belong to any of the sets L_i, which contradicts the fact that $\{L_1, \ldots, L_p\}$ is an open cover. $\square$

5.5   Separation Properties of Metric Spaces

Theorem 5.19. *Every topological metric space* $(S, \mathcal{O}_d)$ *is a Hausdorff space.*

Proof. Let x and y be two distinct elements of S, so $d(x, y) > 0$. Choose $\epsilon = \frac{d(x,y)}{3}$. It is clear that for the open spheres $B(x, \epsilon)$ and $B(y, \epsilon)$, we have $x \in B(x, \epsilon)$, $y \in B(y, \epsilon)$, and $B(x, \epsilon) \cap B(y, \epsilon) = \emptyset$, so $(S, \mathcal{O}_d)$ is indeed a Hausdorff space. $\square$

Corollary 5.4. *Every compact subset of a topological metric space is closed and bounded.*

Proof. By Theorem 4.51 every compact subset of a Hausdorff space is closed. Furthermore, if C is a compact subset of $(S, \mathcal{O}_d)$, then from the fact that $C \subseteq \bigcup \{B(x, r) \mid x \in C\}$ it follows that $C \subseteq \bigcup_{i=1}^{n} B(x_i, r)$ for a finite subset $\{x_1, \ldots, x_n\}$ of C, which shows that C is bounded. $\square$

Corollary 5.5. *If S is a finite set and d is a metric on S, then the topology $\mathcal{O}_d$ is the discrete topology.*

Proof. Let $S = \{x_1, \ldots, x_n\}$ be a finite set. We saw that every singleton $\{x_i\}$ is a closed set. Therefore, every subset of S is closed as a finite union of closed sets. $\square$

Theorem 5.20. *Every topological metric space* $(S, \mathcal{O}_d)$ *is a T_4 space.*

Proof. We need to prove that for all disjoint closed sets H_1 and H_2 of S there exist two open disjoint sets V_1 and V_2 such that $H_1 \subseteq V_1$ and $H_2 \subseteq V_2$.

Let $x \in H_1$. Since $H_1 \cap H_2 = \emptyset$, it follows that $x \notin H_2 = \mathbf{K}(H_2)$, so $d(x, H_2) > 0$ by part (ii) of Theorem 5.16. By Theorem 5.17, the set $B\left(H_1, \frac{d(x,L)}{3}\right)$ is an open set and so is

$$Q_H = \bigcup \left\{ B\left(H_1, \frac{d(x, L)}{3}\right) \,\middle|\, x \in H_1 \right\}.$$

The open set Q_{H_2} is defined in a similar manner as

$$Q_{H_2} = \bigcup \left\{ B\left(H_2, \frac{d(y, H_1)}{3}\right) \,\middle|\, y \in H_2 \right\}.$$

The sets Q_{H_1} and Q_{H_2} are disjoint because $t \in Q_{H_1} \cap Q_{H_2}$ implies that there is $x_1 \in H_1$ and $x_2 \in H_2$ such that $d(t, x_1) < \frac{d(x_1, H_2)}{3}$ and $d(t, x_2) < \frac{d(x_2, H_1)}{3}$. This, in turn, would imply

$$d(x_1, x_2) < \frac{d(x_1, H_2) + d(x_2, H_1)}{3} \leqslant \frac{2}{3} d(x_1, x_2),$$

which is a contradiction. Therefore, $(S, \mathcal{O}_d)$ is a T_4 topological space. $\qquad \square$

Corollary 5.6. *Every metric space is normal.*

Proof. By Theorem 5.19, a metric space is a T_2 space and therefore a T_1 space. The statement then follows directly from Theorem 5.20. $\qquad \square$

Corollary 5.7. *Let H be a closed set and L be an open set in a topological metric space $(S, \mathcal{O}_d)$ such that $H \subseteq L$. Then, there is an open set V such that $H \subseteq V \subseteq \mathbf{K}(V) \subseteq L$.*

Proof. The closed sets H and $S - L$ are disjoint. Therefore, since $(S, \mathcal{O})$ is normal, there exist two disjoint open sets V and W such that $H \subseteq V$ and $S - L \subseteq W$. Since $S - W$ is closed and $V \subseteq S - W$, it follows that $\mathbf{K}(V) \subseteq S - W \subseteq L$. Thus, we obtain $H \subseteq V \subseteq \mathbf{K}(V) \subseteq L$. $\qquad \square$

A stronger form of Theorem 5.20, where the disjointness of the open sets is replaced by the disjointness of their closures, is given next.

Theorem 5.21. *Let $(S, \mathcal{O}_d)$ be a metric space. For all disjoint closed sets H_1 and H_2 of S, there exist two open sets V_1 and V_2 such that $H_1 \subseteq V_1$, $H_2 \subseteq V_2$, and $\mathbf{K}(V_1) \cap \mathbf{K}(V_2) = \emptyset$.*

Proof. By Theorem 5.20, we obtain the existence of the disjoint open sets Q_{H_1} and Q_{H_2} such that $H_1 \subseteq Q_{H_1}$ and $H_2 \subseteq Q_{H_2}$. We claim that the closures of these sets are disjoint.

Suppose that $s \in \mathbf{K}(Q_{H_1}) \cap \mathbf{K}(Q_{H_2})$. Then, we have $B\left(s, \frac{\epsilon}{12}\right) \cap Q_{H_1} \neq \emptyset$ and $B\left(s, \frac{\epsilon}{12}\right) \cap Q_{H_2} \neq \emptyset$. Thus, there exist $t \in Q_{H_1}$ and $t' \in Q_{H_2}$ such that $d(t, s) < \frac{\epsilon}{12}$ and $d(t', s) < \frac{\epsilon}{12}$.

As in the proof of the previous theorem, there is $x_1 \in H_1$ and $y_1 \in H_2$ such that $d(t, x_1) < \frac{d(x_1, H_2)}{3}$ and $d(t', y_1) < \frac{d(y_1, H_1)}{3}$. Choose t and t' above for $\epsilon = d(x_1, y_1)$. This leads to a contradiction because

$$d(x_1, y_1) \leqslant d(x_1, t) + d(t, s) + d(s, t') + d(t', y_1) \leqslant \frac{5}{6} d(x_1, y_1). \qquad \square$$

Corollary 5.8. *Let $(S, \mathcal{O}_d)$ be a metric space. If $x \in L$, where L is an open subset of S, then there exists two open sets V_1 and V_2 in S such that $x \in V_1$, $S - L \subseteq V_2$, and $\mathbf{K}(V_1) \cap \mathbf{K}(V_2) = \emptyset$.*

Proof.   The statement follows by applying Theorem 5.21 to the disjoint closed sets $H_1 = \{x\}$ and $H_2 = S - L$. $\square$

Recall that the Bolzano-Weierstrass property of topological spaces was introduced in Theorem 4.47. Namely, a topological space $(S, \mathcal{O})$ has the Bolzano-Weierstrass property if every infinite subset T of S has at least one accumulation point, that is, if $T' \neq \emptyset$. For metric spaces, this property is equivalent to compactness, as we show next.

Theorem 5.22. *Let $(S, \mathcal{O}_d)$ be a topological metric space. The following three statements are equivalent:*
   (i) *$(S, \mathcal{O}_d)$ is compact;*
   (ii) *$(S, \mathcal{O}_d)$ has the Bolzano-Weierstrass property;*
   (iii) *every countable open cover of $(S, \mathcal{O}_d)$ contains a finite subcover.*

Proof.   (i) implies (ii): by Theorem 4.47.

(ii) implies (iii): Let $\{L_n \mid n \in \mathbb{N}\}$ be a countable open cover of S. Without loss of generality, we may assume that none of the sets L_n is included in $\bigcup_{p=1}^{n-1} L_p$; indeed, if this is not the case, we can discard L_n and still have a countable open cover. Let $x_n \in L_n - \bigcup_{p=1}^{n-1} L_p$ and let $U = \{x_n \mid n \in \mathbb{N}\}$. Since $(S, \mathcal{O}_d)$ has the Bolzano-Weierstrass property, we have $U' \neq \emptyset$, so there exists an accumulation point z of U. In every open set L that contains z, there exists $x_n \in U$ such that $x_n \neq z$.

Since $\{L_n \mid n \in \mathbb{N}\}$ is an open cover, there exists L_m such that $z \in L_m$. Suppose that the set L_m contains only a finite number of elements $x_{n_1}, \ldots, x_{n_k}$, and let $d = \min\{d(z, x_{n_i}) \mid 1 \leqslant i \leqslant k\}$. Then, $L_m \cap B\left(z, \frac{d}{2}\right)$ is an open set that contains no elements of U with the possible exception of z, which contradicts the fact that z is an accumulation point. Thus, L_m contains an infinite subset of U, which implies that there exists $x_q \in L_m$ for some $q > m$. This contradicts the definition of the elements x_n of U. We conclude that there exists a number r_0 such that $L_r - \bigcup_{i=0}^{r-1} L_i = \emptyset$ for $r \geqslant r_0$, so $S = L_0 \cup \cdots \cup L_{r_0-1}$, which proves that $L_0, \ldots, L_{r_0-1}$ is a finite subcover.

(iii) implies (i). Let ϵ be a positive number. Suppose that there is an infinite sequence $\mathbf{x} = (x_0, \ldots, x_n, \ldots)$ such that $d(x_i, x_j) > \epsilon$ for every $i, j \in \mathbb{N}$ such that $i \neq j$. Consider the open spheres $B(x_i, \epsilon)$ and the set

$$C = S - \mathbf{K}\left(\bigcup_{i \in \mathbb{N}} B\left(x_i, \frac{\epsilon}{2}\right)\right).$$

We will show that $\{C\} \cup \{B(x_i, \epsilon) \mid i \in \mathbb{N}\}$ is a countable open cover of S.

Suppose that $x \in S - C$; that is $x \in \mathbf{K}\left(\bigcup_{i \in \mathbb{N}} B\left(x_i, \frac{\epsilon}{2}\right)\right)$. We have either that $x \in \bigcup_{i \in \mathbb{N}} B\left(x_i, \frac{\epsilon}{2}\right)$ or x is an accumulation point of that set.

In the first case, $x \in \bigcup_{i \in \mathbb{N}} B(x_i, \epsilon)$ because $B\left(x_i, \frac{\epsilon}{2}\right) \subseteq B(x_i, \epsilon)$. If x is an accumulation point of $\bigcup_{i \in \mathbb{N}} B\left(x_i, \frac{\epsilon}{2}\right)$, given any open set L such that $x \in L$, then L must intersect at least one of the spheres $B\left(x_i, \frac{\epsilon}{2}\right)$. Suppose that $B\left(x, \frac{\epsilon}{2}\right) \cap B\left(x_i, \frac{\epsilon}{2}\right) \neq \emptyset$, and let t be a point that belongs to this intersection. Then, $d(x, x_i) < d(x, t) + d(t, x_i) < \frac{\epsilon}{2} + \frac{\epsilon}{2} = \epsilon$, so $x \in B(x_i, \epsilon)$.

Therefore, $\{C\} \cup \{B(x_i, \epsilon) \mid i \in \mathbb{N}\}$ is a countable open cover of S. Since every countable open cover of $(S, \mathcal{O}_d)$ contains a finite subcover, it follows that this open cover contains a finite subcover. Observe that there exists an open sphere $B(x_i, \epsilon)$ that contains infinitely many x_n because none of these elements belongs to C. Consequently, for any two of these points, the distance is less than ϵ, which contradicts the assumption we made initially about the sequence $\mathbf{x}$.

Choose $\epsilon = \frac{1}{k}$ for some $k \in \mathbb{N}$ such that $k \geq 1$. Since there is no infinite sequence of points such that every two distinct points are at a distance greater than $\frac{1}{k}$, it is possible to find a finite sequence of points $\mathbf{x} = (x_0, \ldots, x_{n-1})$ such that $i \neq j$ implies $d(x_i, x_j) > \frac{1}{k}$ for $0 \leqslant i, j \leqslant n - 1$ and for every other point $x \in S$ there exists x_i such that $d(x_i, x) \leqslant \frac{1}{k}$.

Define the set $L_{k,m,i}$ as the open sphere $B\left(x_i, \frac{1}{m}\right)$, where x_i is one of the points that belongs to the sequence above determined by k and $m \in \mathbb{N}$ and $m \geqslant 1$. The collection $\{L_{k,m,i} \mid m \geqslant 1, 0 \leqslant i \leqslant n - 1\}$ is clearly countable. We will prove that each open set of $(S, \mathcal{O}_d)$ is a union of sets of the form $L_{k,m,i}$; in other words, we will show that this family of sets is a basis for $(S, \mathcal{O}_d)$.

Let L be an open set and let $z \in L$. Since L is open, there exists $\epsilon > 0$ such that $z \in B(z, \epsilon) \subseteq L$. Choose k and m such that $\frac{1}{k} < \frac{1}{m} < \frac{\epsilon}{2}$. By the definition of the sequence $\mathbf{x}$, there is x_i such that $d(z, x_i) < \frac{1}{k}$. We claim that

$$L_{k,m,i} = B\left(x_i, \frac{1}{m}\right) \subseteq L.$$

Let $y \in L_{k,m,i}$. Since $d(z, y) \leqslant d(z, x_i) + d(x_i, y) < \frac{1}{k} + \frac{1}{m} < \epsilon$, it follows that $L_{k,m,i} \subseteq B(z, \epsilon) \subseteq L$. Since $d(y, z) < \frac{1}{k} < \frac{1}{m}$, we have $z \in L_{k,m,i}$. This shows that L is a union of sets of the form $L_{k,m,i}$, so this family of sets is a countable open cover of S. It follows that that there exists a finite open cover of $(S, \mathcal{O}_d)$ because every countable open cover of $(S, \mathcal{O}_d)$ contains a finite subcover. $\square$

In Section 4.2, we saw that if a topological space has a countable basis, then the space is separable (Theorem 4.34) and each open cover of the basis contains a countable subcover (Theorem 4.36). For metric spaces, these properties are equivalent, as we show next.

Theorem 5.23. *Let $(S, \mathcal{O}_d)$ be a topological metric space. The following statements are equivalent:*

    (i) *$(S, \mathcal{O}_d)$ satisfies the second axiom of countability, that is, it has a countable basis;*

    (ii) *$(S, \mathcal{O}_d)$ is a separable;*

    (iii) *every open cover of $(S, \mathcal{O}_d)$ contains a countable subcover.*

Proof. By Theorems 4.34 and 4.36, the first statement implies (ii) and (iii). Therefore, it suffices to prove that (iii) implies (ii) and (ii) implies (i).

To show that (iii) implies (ii), suppose that every open cover of $(S, \mathcal{O}_d)$ contains a countable subcover. The collection of open spheres $\{B\left(x, \frac{1}{n}\right) \mid x \in S, n \in \mathbb{N}_{>0}\}$ is an open cover of S and therefore there exists a countable set $T_n \subseteq S$ such that $\mathcal{C}_n = \{B\left(x, \frac{1}{n}\right) \mid x \in T_n, n \in \mathbb{N}_{>0}\}$ is an open cover of S. Let $C = \bigcup_{n \geqslant 1} T_n$. Thus, C is a countable set.

We claim that C is dense in $(S, \mathcal{O}_d)$. Indeed, let $s \in S$ and choose n such that $n > \frac{1}{\epsilon}$. Since $\mathcal{C}_n$ is an open cover of S, there is $x \in T_n$ such that $s \in B\left(x, \frac{1}{n}\right) \subseteq B\left(x, \epsilon\right)$. Since $T_n \subseteq C$, it follows that C is dense in $(S, \mathcal{O}_d)$. Thus, $(S, \mathcal{O}_d)$ is separable.

To prove that (ii) implies (i), let $(S, \mathcal{O}_d)$ be a separable space. There exists a countable set U that is dense in $(S, \mathcal{O}_d)$. Consider the countable collection

$$\mathcal{C} = \left\{ B\left(u, \frac{1}{n}\right) \middle| u \in U, n \geqslant 1 \right\}.$$

If L is an open set in $(S, \mathcal{O}_d)$ and $x \in L$, then there exists $\epsilon > 0$ such that $B(x, \epsilon) \subseteq L$. Let n be such that $n > \frac{2}{\epsilon}$. Since U is dense in $(S, \mathcal{O}_d)$, we know that $x \in \mathbf{K}(U)$, so there exists $y \in S(x, \epsilon) \cap U$ and $x \in B\left(y, \frac{1}{n}\right) \subseteq B\left(x, \frac{2}{n}\right) \subseteq B(x, \epsilon) \subseteq L$. Thus, $\mathcal{C}$ is a countable basis. $\square$

Theorem 5.24. *Let $(S, \mathcal{O}_d)$ be a topological metric space. Every closed set of this space is a countable intersection of open sets, and every open set is a countable union of closed sets.*

Proof. Let H be a closed set and let U_n be the open set

$$U_n = \bigcup_{n \geqslant 1} \left\{ B\left(x, \frac{1}{n}\right) \middle| x \in F \right\}.$$

It is clear that $H \subseteq \bigcap_{n \geqslant 1} U_n$. Now let $u \in \bigcap_{n \geqslant 1} U_n$ and let ϵ be an arbitrary positive number. For every $n \geqslant 1$, there is an element $x_n \in H$

such that $d(u, x_n) < \frac{1}{n}$. Thus, if $\frac{1}{n} < \epsilon$, we have $x_n \in H \cap B(u, \epsilon)$, so $B(u, \epsilon) \cap H \neq \emptyset$. By Corollary 5.2, it follows that $u \in H$, which proves the reverse inclusion $\bigcap_{n \geqslant 1} U_n \subseteq H$. This shows that every closed set is a countable union of open sets.

If L is an open set, then its complement is closed and, by the first part of the theorem, it is a countable intersection of open sets. Thus, L itself is a countable union of closed sets. $\square$

Definition 5.15. Let $(S, \mathcal{O}_d)$ be a topological metric space. A G_δ-*set* is a countable intersection of open sets. An F_σ-*set* is a countable union of open sets.

Now, Theorem 5.24 can be restated by saying that every closed set of a topological metric space is a G_δ-set and every open set is an F_σ-set.

For a topological space $(S, \mathcal{O})$, using the notations introduced in Section 1.4, the collections F_σ and G_δ can be written as $F_\sigma = \mathcal{O}_\sigma$ and $G_\delta = closed(\mathcal{O})_\delta$. The notation F_σ is suggested by the term "fermé" (closed, in French) and by the term "somme" (sum, in the same language); the notation G_δ originates in German: G stands for "Gebiet" (region) and δ is suggested by the word "Durchschnitt" (intersection).

Theorem 5.25. *Let U be a G_δ-set in the topological metric space $(S, \mathcal{O}_d)$. If T is a G_δ-set in the subspace U, then T is a G_δ-set in S.*

Proof. Since T is a G_δ-set in the subspace U, we can write $T = \bigcap_{n \in \mathbb{N}} L_n$, where each L_n is an open set in the subspace U. By the definition of the subspace topology, for each L_n there exists an open set in S such that $L_n = L'_n \cap U$, so

$$T = \bigcap_{n \in \mathbb{N}} L_n = \bigcap_{n \in \mathbb{N}} (L'_n \cap U) = U \cap \bigcap_{n \in \mathbb{N}} L'_n.$$

Since U is a countable intersection of open sets of S, the last equality shows that T is a countable intersection of open sets of S and hence a G_δ-set in S. $\square$

5.6 Completeness of Metric Spaces

Let $\mathbf{x} = (x_0, \ldots, x_n, \ldots)$ be a sequence in the topological metric space $(S, \mathcal{O}_d)$ such that $\lim_{n \to \infty} x_n = x$. If $m, n > n_{\frac{\epsilon}{2}}$, we have $d(x_m, x_n) \leqslant d(x_m, x) + d(x, x_n) < \frac{\epsilon}{2} + \frac{\epsilon}{2} = \epsilon$. In other words, if $\mathbf{x}$ is a sequence that converges to x, then given a positive number ϵ we have members of the sequence closer than ϵ if we go far enough in the sequence. This suggests the following definition.

Definition 5.16. A sequence $\mathbf{x} = (x_0, \ldots, x_n, \ldots)$ in the topological metric space $(S, \mathcal{O}_d)$ is a *Cauchy sequence* if for every $\epsilon > 0$ there exists $n_\epsilon \in \mathbb{N}$ such that $m, n \geqslant n_\epsilon$ implies $d(x_m, x_n) < \epsilon$.

Theorem 5.26. *Every convergent sequence in a topological metric space* $(S, \mathcal{O}_d)$ *is a Cauchy sequence.*

Proof. Let $\mathbf{x} = (x_0, x_1, \ldots)$ be a convergent sequence and let $x = \lim_{n \to \infty} \mathbf{x}$. There exists $n'_{\frac{\epsilon}{2}}$ such that if $n > n'_{\frac{\epsilon}{2}}$, then $d(x_n, x) < \frac{\epsilon}{2}$. Thus, if $m, n \geqslant n_\epsilon = n'_{\frac{\epsilon}{2}}$, it follows that

$$d(x_m, x_n) \leqslant d(x_m, x) + d(x, x_n) < \frac{\epsilon}{2} + \frac{\epsilon}{2} = \epsilon,$$

which means that $\mathbf{x}$ is a Cauchy sequence. $\qquad\square$

Definition 5.17. A topological metric space is *complete* if every Cauchy sequence is convergent.

Example 5.10. The converse of Theorem 5.26 is not true, in general, as we show next.

Let $((0, 1), d)$ be the metric space equipped with the metric $d(x, y) = |x - y|$ for $x, y \in (0, 1)$. The sequence defined by $x_n = \frac{1}{n+1}$ for $n \in \mathbb{N}$ is a Cauchy sequence. Indeed, it suffices to take $m, n \geqslant \frac{1}{\epsilon} - 1$ to obtain $|x_n - x_m| < \epsilon$; however, the sequence x_n is not convergent to an element of $(0, 1)$. This also shows that $((0, 1), \mathcal{O}_d)$ is not complete.

Example 5.11. The topological metric space $(\mathbb{R}, \mathcal{O}_d)$, where $d(x, y) = |x - y|$ for $x, y \in \mathbb{R}$, is complete.

Let $\mathbf{x} = (x_0, x_1, \ldots)$ be a Cauchy sequence in $\mathbb{R}$. For every $\epsilon > 0$, there exists $n_\epsilon \in \mathbb{N}$ such that $m, n \geqslant n_\epsilon$ implies $|x_m - x_n| < \epsilon$. Choose $m_0 \in \mathbb{N}$ such that $m_0 \geqslant n_\epsilon$. Thus, if $n \geqslant n_\epsilon$, then $x_{m_0} - \epsilon < x_n < x_{m_0} + \epsilon$, which means that $\mathbf{x}$ is a bounded sequence. By Theorem 4.45, the sequence $\mathbf{x}$ contains a bounded subsequence $(x_{i_0}, x_{i_1}, \ldots)$ that is convergent. Let $l = \lim_{k \to \infty} x_{i_k}$. It is not difficult to see that $\lim_{x_n} x_n = l$, which shows that $(\mathbb{R}, \mathcal{O}_d)$ is complete.

Example 5.12. The space $\mathbb{R}^n$ is complete. Indeed, let $(\mathbf{x}_n)$ be a Cauchy sequence in $\mathbb{R}^n$. Since $|(\mathbf{x}_n)_i - (\mathbf{x}_m)_i| \leqslant \|\mathbf{x}_n - \mathbf{x}_m\|$, each coordinate sequence $((\mathbf{x}_n)_i)$ is a Cauchy sequence in $\mathbb{R}$. By the completeness of $\mathbb{R}$, it must have a limit x_i. Therefore,

$$\mathbf{x} = \begin{pmatrix} x_1 \\ \vdots \\ x_n \end{pmatrix}$$

is the limit of $(\mathbf{x}_n)$.

Theorem 5.27. *There is no clopen set in the topological space $(\mathbb{R}, \mathcal{O})$ except the empty set and the set $\mathbb{R}$.*

Proof. Suppose that L is a clopen subset of $\mathbb{R}$ that is distinct from $\emptyset$ and $\mathbb{R}$. Then, there exist $x \in L$ and $y \notin L$. Starting from x and y, we define inductively the terms of two sequences $\mathbf{x} = (x_0, \dots, x_n, \dots)$ and $\mathbf{y} = (y_0, \dots, y_n, \dots)$ as follows. Let $x_0 = x$ and $y_0 = y$. Suppose that x_n and y_n are defined. Then,

$$x_{n+1} = \begin{cases} \dfrac{x_n + y_n}{2} & \text{if } \dfrac{x_n + y_n}{2} \in L, \\ x_n & \text{otherwise,} \end{cases}$$

and

$$y_{n+1} = \begin{cases} \dfrac{x_n + y_n}{2} & \text{if } \dfrac{x_n + y_n}{2} \notin L, \\ y_n & \text{otherwise.} \end{cases}$$

It is clear that $\{x_n \mid n \in \mathbb{N}\} \subseteq L$ and $\{y_n \mid n \in \mathbb{N}\} \subseteq \mathbb{R} - L$. Moreover, we have

$$|y_{n+1} - x_{n+1}| = \frac{|y_n - x_n|}{2} = \cdots = \frac{|y - x|}{2^{n+1}}.$$

Note that

$$|x_{n+1} - x_n| \leqslant |y_n - x_n| \leqslant \frac{|y - x|}{2^n}.$$

This implies that $\mathbf{x}$ is a Cauchy sequence and therefore there is $x = \lim_{n \to \infty} x_n$; moreover, the sequence $\mathbf{y}$ also converges to x, so x belongs to ∂L, which is a contradiction. $\square$

Theorem 5.28. *Let $\mathbf{x} = (x_0, \dots, x_n, \dots)$ be a Cauchy sequence in the topological metric space $(S, \mathcal{O}_d)$. If $\mathbf{x}$ contains a convergent subsequence*

$$(x_{p_0}, \dots, x_{p_r}, \dots),$$

then the sequence $\mathbf{x}$ converges and its limit is the same as the limit of the subsequence.

Proof.   Since (x_n) is a Cauchy sequence for $\epsilon > 0$ there exists n_ϵ such that $d(x_n, x_m) < \frac{\epsilon}{2}$. Since (x_{p_r}) is convergent to x there exists n'_ϵ such that $r \geqslant n'_\epsilon$ implies $d(x_{p_r}, x) < \frac{\epsilon}{2}$. Therefore, if $p_r \geqslant m \leqslant n_\epsilon$ we have:

$$d(x_n, x) \leqslant d(x_n, x_{p_r}) + d(x_{p_r}, x) < \epsilon,$$

so $\lim_{n \to \infty} x_n = x$.   □

Theorem 5.29. *Let $(S, \mathcal{O}_d)$ be a complete topological metric space. If T is a closed subset of S, then the subspace T is complete.*

Proof.   Let T be a closed subset of S and let $\mathbf{x} = (x_0, x_1, \ldots)$ be a Cauchy sequence in this subspace. The sequence $\mathbf{x}$ is a Cauchy sequence in the complete space S, so there exists $x = \lim_{n \to \infty} x_n$. Since T is closed, we have $x \in T$, so T is complete.

Conversely, suppose that T is complete. Let $x \in \mathbf{K}(T)$. There exists a sequence $\mathbf{x} = (x_0, x_1, \ldots) \in \mathbf{Seq}_\infty(T)$ such that $\lim_{n \to \infty} x_n = x$. Then, $\mathbf{x}$ is a Cauchy sequence in T, so there is a limit t of this sequence in T. The uniqueness of the limit implies $x = t \in T$, so T is a closed set.   □

Theorem 5.30. *In a complete topological metric space $(S, \mathcal{O}_d)$, every descending sequence of closed sets $V_0 \supset \cdots \supset V_n \supset V_{n+1} \supset \cdots$ such that $\lim_{n \to \infty} diam(V_n) = 0$ has a non-empty intersection that consists of a single point of S.*

Proof.   A sequence (x_n) in S such that $x_n \in V_n$ is a Cauchy sequence. Indeed, let $\epsilon > 0$. Since $\lim_{n \to \infty} diam(V_n) = 0$, there exists n_ϵ such that if $m, n > n_\epsilon$ we have $x_m, x_n \in V_{\min\{m,n\}}$. Since $\min\{m, n\} \geqslant n_\epsilon$, it follows that $d(x_m, x_n) \leqslant diam(V_{\min m,n}) < \epsilon$. The completeness of $(S, \mathcal{O}_d)$ is implies that there exists $x \in S$ such that $\lim_{n \to \infty} x_n = x$. Note that all members of the sequence belong to V_m, with the possible exception of the first m members. Therefore $x \in V_m$, so $x \in \bigcap_{n \in \mathbb{N}} V_n$, which implies that $\bigcap_{n \in \mathbb{N}} V_n \neq \emptyset$.

Suppose that $y \in \bigcap_{n \in \mathbb{N}} V_n$. Since $d(y, x) \leqslant diam(V_n)$ it follows that $d(y, x) = 0$, so $y = x$, which allows us to conclude that the intersection $\bigcap_{n \in \mathbb{N}} V_n = \{x\}$.   □

Theorem 5.31. (Baire's Theorem for Complete Metric Spaces) *Every non-empty complete topological metric space is a Baire space.*

Proof.   We prove that if $(S, \mathcal{O}_d)$ is non-empty and complete, then it satisfies the first condition of Theorem 4.11.

Let $L_1, \ldots, L_n, \ldots$ be a sequence of open subsets of S that are dense in S and let L be an open, non-empty subset of S. We construct inductively a sequence of closed sets $H_1, \ldots, H_n, \ldots$ that satisfy the following conditions:

  (i) $H_1 \subseteq L_0 \cap L$,
  (ii) $H_n \subseteq L_n \cap H_{n-1}$ for $n \geqslant 2$,
  (iii) $\mathbf{I}(H_n) \neq \emptyset$, and
  (iv) $diam(H_n) \leqslant \frac{1}{n}$

for $n \geqslant 2$.

Since L_1 is dense in S, by Theorem 4.9, $L_1 \cap L \neq \emptyset$, so there is a closed sphere of diameter less than 1 enclosed in $L_1 \cap L$. Define H_1 as this closed sphere.

Suppose that H_{n-1} was constructed. Since $\mathbf{I}(H_{n-1}) \neq \emptyset$, the open set $L_n \cap \mathbf{I}(H_{n-1})$ is not empty because L_n is dense in S. Thus, there is a closed sphere H_n included in $L_n \cap \mathbf{I}(H_{n-1})$, and therefore included in $L_n \cap H_{n-1}$, such that $diam(H_n) < \frac{1}{n}$. Clearly, we have $\mathbf{I}(H_n) \neq \emptyset$. By applying Theorem 5.30 to the descending sequence of closed sets $H_1, \ldots, H_n, \ldots$, the completeness of the space implies that $\bigcap_{n \geqslant 1} H_n \neq \emptyset$. If $s \in \bigcap_{n \geqslant 1} H_n$, then it is clear that $x \in \bigcap_{n \geqslant 1} L_n$ and $x \in L$, which means that the set $\bigcap_{n \geqslant 1} L_n$ has a non-empty intersection with every open set L. This implies that $\bigcap_{n \geqslant 1} L_n$ is dense in S. $\qquad \square$

Corollary 5.9. *Let $(S, \mathcal{O}_d)$ be a complete topological metric space. If $S = \bigcup_{i \geqslant 1} H_i$ is a countable union of closed sets, then there exists i such that H_i contains a open sphere $B(x, \epsilon)$, or equivalently, $\mathbf{I}(H_i) \neq \emptyset$.*

Proof.   Suppose that $S = \bigcup_{i \geqslant 1} H_i$, where each set H_i has an empty interior. Let $L_i = S - H_i$ for $i \geqslant 1$. Each of open sets L_i is dense in S because, by Theorem 4.10, $\mathbf{K}(L_i) = \mathbf{K}(S - H_i) = S - \mathbf{I}(H_i) = S$. Therefore, by Baire's Theorem, $\bigcap_{i \geqslant 1} L_i$ is dense, which means that $\bigcap_{i \geqslant 1} L_i \neq \emptyset$.

Thus, there exists $x \in \bigcap_{i \geqslant 1} L_i = \bigcap_{i \geqslant 1}(S - H_i) = S - \bigcup_{i \geqslant 1} H_i$, which contradicts the hypothesis. $\qquad \square$

Theorem 5.32. *Let $(S, \mathcal{O}_d)$ be a topological metric space and let T be a subset of S that is dense in this space. If the subspace $(T, \mathcal{O}_d)$ is complete, then $(S, \mathcal{O}_d)$ is complete.*

Proof.   Let $\epsilon > 0$ and let $\mathbf{x}$ be a Cauchy sequence in S. For each x_n there exists $y_n \in B(x_n, \epsilon/3) \cap T$ because T is dense in S. Since $\mathbf{x}$ is a Cauchy sequence, there exists n_ϵ such that $n, m \geqslant n_\epsilon$ implies $d(x_m, x_n) < \epsilon/3$. Therefore, taking into account that

$$d(y_m, y_n) \leqslant d(y_m, x_m) + d(x_m, x_n) + d(x_n, y_n) < \epsilon$$

when $m, n \geqslant n_\epsilon$, it follows that $\mathbf{y}$ is a Cauchy sequence. By the completeness of T, there exists $t \in T$ such that $\lim_{n \to \infty} y_n = t$. Thus, there exists m_ϵ such that $n \geqslant m_\epsilon$ implies $|y_n - t| < \frac{2}{3}\epsilon$, which imply

$$|x_n - t| < |x_n - y_n| + |y_n - t| < \epsilon,$$

so $\lim_{n \to \infty} x_n = t$ and $(S, \mathcal{O}_d)$ is complete. $\square$

Let $\mathsf{Cauchy}(S, \mathcal{O}_d)$ be the set of Cauchy sequences on a topological metric space $(S, \mathcal{O}_d)$. Define the relation $\sim$ on $\mathsf{Cauchy}(S, \mathcal{O}_d)$ as $\mathbf{x} \sim \mathbf{y}$ if $\lim_{n \to \infty} d(x_n, y_n) = 0$. It is easy to verify that $\sim$ is an equivalence on $\mathsf{Cauchy}(S, \mathcal{O}_d)$. This allows us to consider the quotient set $\mathsf{Cauchy}(S, \mathcal{O}_d)/\sim$, where the equivalence class of the Cauchy sequence $\mathbf{x}$ is denoted by $[\mathbf{x}]$, and to introduce a metric e on $\mathsf{Cauchy}(S, \mathcal{O}_d)/\sim$ by

$$e([\mathbf{x}], [\mathbf{y}]) = \lim_{n \to \infty} d(x_n, y_n).$$

We need to show that e is well-defined. Let $\mathbf{x}' \in [\mathbf{x}]$ and $\mathbf{y}' \in [\mathbf{y}]$. We have

$$d(x_n, y_n) \leqslant d(x_n, x_n') + d(x_n', y_n') + d(y_n', y_n),$$
$$d(x_n', y_n') \leqslant d(x_n', x_n) + d(x_n, y_n) + d(y_n, y_n'),$$

which imply

$$|d(x_n, y_n) - d(x_n', y_n')| \leqslant d(x_n, x_n') + d(y_n, y_n').$$

Therefore, $\lim_{n \to \infty} |d(x_n, y_n) - d(x_n', y_n')| = 0$. Since both $d(x_n, y_n)$ and $d(x_n', y_n')$ are convergent, it follows that $\lim_{n \to \infty} d(x_n, y_n) = \lim_{n \to \infty} d(x_n', y_n')$, so e is well-defined.

Next, we show that e is a metric on $\mathsf{Cauchy}(S, \mathcal{O}_d)$. Let $\mathbf{x} = (x_n)$, $\mathbf{y} = (y_n)$, and $\mathbf{z} = (z_n)$ be three Cauchy sequences.

We have $e([\mathbf{x}], [\mathbf{y}]) = 0$ if and only if $\lim_{n \to \infty} d(x_n, y_n) = 0$, so $\mathbf{x} \sim \mathbf{y}$, which amounts to $[\mathbf{x}] = [\mathbf{y}]$. The symmetry of e is immediate.

The inequality $d(x_n, z_n) \leqslant d(x_n, y_n) + d(y_n, z_n)$ implies

$$\lim_{n \to \infty} d(x_n, z_n) \leqslant \lim_{n \to \infty} d(x_n, y_n) + \lim_{n \to \infty} d(y_n, z_n),$$

which yields $e([\mathbf{x}], [\mathbf{z}]) \leqslant d([\mathbf{x}], [\mathbf{y}]) + d([\mathbf{y}], [\mathbf{z}])$, so e is a metric.

For $x \in S$ consider the sequence

$$\tilde{\mathbf{x}} = (x, x, \ldots, x, \ldots).$$

Define the mapping $h : S \longrightarrow \mathsf{Cauchy}(S/\sim, \mathcal{O}_e)$ as $h(x) = [\tilde{\mathbf{x}}]$. For $x, y \in S$ we have

$$e(h(x), h(y)) = e([\tilde{\mathbf{x}}], [\tilde{\mathbf{y}}]) = \lim_{n \to \infty} d(x, y) = d(x, y),$$

so e is an isometry between $(S, \mathcal{O}_d)$ and $\mathsf{Cauchy}(S/\sim, \mathcal{O}_e)$.

Theorem 5.33. *Let $h : S \longrightarrow \mathsf{Cauchy}(S/ \sim, \mathcal{O}_e)$ be the isometry defined above. The set $h(S)$ is dense in $\mathsf{Cauchy}(S, / \sim, \mathcal{O}_e)$ and the metric space $\mathsf{Cauchy}(S/ \sim, \mathcal{O}_e)$ is complete.*

Proof. Let $[\mathbf{x}] \in \mathsf{Cauchy}(S/ \sim, \mathcal{O}_e)$ and let ϵ be a positive number. Since $\mathbf{x} = (x_n)$ is a Cauchy sequence, there exists n_ϵ such that $m, n > n_\epsilon$ implies $d(x_m, x_n) < \frac{\epsilon}{2}$. Let $z = x_{n_\epsilon}$. Then, $[\tilde{\mathbf{z}}] \in h(S)$ and

$$e([\mathbf{x}], [\tilde{\mathbf{z}}]) = \lim_{n \to \infty} d(x_n, z) = \lim_{n \to \infty} d(x_n, x_{n_\epsilon}) \leqslant \frac{\epsilon}{2} < \epsilon,$$

which shows that $[\tilde{\mathbf{z}}] \in B([\mathbf{x}], e) \cap h(S)$. Thus, $h(S)$ is dense in S.

By Theorem 5.32 it suffices to show that $h(S)$ is complete to obtain the completeness of $\mathsf{Cauchy}(S/ \sim, \mathcal{O}_e)$.

Let $[\widetilde{\mathbf{z}_k}]$ be an element in $S/ \sim$, where $\widetilde{\mathbf{z}_k} = (z_k, z_k, \ldots)$ such that $([\widetilde{z_n}])$ is a Cauchy sequence in $\mathsf{Cauchy}(S/ \sim, \mathcal{O}_e)$. We have $d(z_n, z_m) = e([\widetilde{z_n}], [\widetilde{z_m}])$ because h is an isometry, so $\mathbf{z}$ is a Cauchy sequence in $(S, \mathcal{O}_d)$. We claim that the sequence $([\widetilde{z_n}])$ converges to $[\mathbf{z}]$. Let $\epsilon > 0$. There is a n_ϵ such that $k, n \geqslant n_\epsilon$ implies $d(z_k, z_n) < \frac{\epsilon}{2}$. Hence, for $k \geqslant n_\epsilon$,

$$e([\widetilde{z_k}], [\mathbf{z}]) = \lim_{n \to \infty} d(z_k, z_n) \leqslant \frac{\epsilon}{2} < \epsilon,$$

which shows that

$$\lim_{n \to \infty} ([\widetilde{z_n}]) = [\mathbf{z}]. \qquad \square$$

Theorem 5.34. *Let $(S, \mathcal{O})$ be a topological space, $(T, \mathcal{O}_d)$ be a complete metric topological space, and let $C(X, Y)$ be the set of continuous function from S to T equipped with the metric $d_\infty(f, g) = \sup_{x \in S} \min\{d(f(x), g(x)), 1\}$. Then $C(X, Y)$ is a complete metric space.*

Proof. Let (f_n) be a Cauchy sequence in $C(X, Y)$. Then, for each $x \in S$ the sequence $(f_n(x))$ is a Cauchy sequence in $(T, \mathcal{O}_d)$, so we have a function $f : S \longrightarrow T$ defined by $f(x) = \lim_{n \to \infty} f_n(x)$. By the definition of d_∞ for each $\epsilon > 0$ there exists n_ϵ such that $n > n_\epsilon$ implies $d_\infty(f_n, f) < \epsilon$.

If (x_i) is a net in S that converges to x, then for $n > n_\epsilon$ we have

$$d(f(x_i), f(x)) \leqslant d(f(x_i), f_n(x_i)) + d(f_n(x_i), f_n(x)) + d(f_n(x), f(x))$$
$$\leqslant 2d_\infty(f_n, f) + d(f_n(x_i), f_n(x))$$
$$\leqslant 2\epsilon + d(f_n(x_i), f_n(x)).$$

Since f_n is continuous we have eventually $d(f(x_i), f(x)) < 3\epsilon$, so f is continuous in x. Thus, $C(X, Y)$ is complete. $\qquad \square$

For $Y = \mathbb{C}$ we denote the space $C(X, \mathbb{C})$ by $C(X)$.

Theorem 5.35. (Tietze's Theorem) *Let $(S, \mathcal{O})$ be a normal topological space and let U be a closed subset of S. Each bounded continuous function $f : U \longrightarrow \mathbb{R}$ has an extension to a bounded continuous function defined on the entire space S.*

Proof. Since f is bounded, we may assume without loss of generality that $\|f\|_\infty = 1$. Thus, $f(U) \subseteq [-1, 1]$. Let

$$A = f^{-1}\left(\left[-1, -\frac{1}{3}\right]\right), B = f^{-1}\left(\left[\frac{1}{3}, 1\right]\right).$$

In other words, $x \in A$ if and only if $-1 \leqslant f(x) \leqslant -\frac{1}{3}$ and $x \in B$ if and only if $\frac{1}{3} \leqslant f(x) \leqslant 1$.

By Uryson's Lemma, there exists a continuous function $f_1 : S \longrightarrow [-\frac{1}{3}, \frac{1}{3}]$ such that

$$f_1(x) = \begin{cases} -\frac{1}{3} & \text{if } x \in A, \\ \frac{1}{3} & \text{if } x \in B. \end{cases}$$

This implies $|f(x) - f_1(x)| \leqslant \frac{2}{3}$ for $x \in U$.

Applying the same argument to the function $(f - f_1)\restriction_U$ produces a continuous function $f_2 : S \longrightarrow [-\frac{2}{3^2}, \frac{2}{3^2}]$ on S such that $|f_2(x)| \leqslant \frac{2}{3^2}$ such that

$$|f(x) - f_1(x) - f_2(x)| \leqslant \left(\frac{2}{3}\right)^2$$

when $x \in U$. Thus, we build a sequence of continuous functions (f_n) defined on S such that $|f_n(x)| \leqslant \frac{2^{n-1}}{3^n}$ and

$$\left| f(x) - \sum_{k=1}^n f_k(x) \right| \leqslant \left(\frac{2}{3}\right)^n$$

for $x \in U$. Define the function $g : S \longrightarrow \mathbb{R}$ as

$$g(x) = \sum_{n=1}^\infty f_n(x)$$

for $x \in S$. We have

$$|g(x)| \leqslant \sum_{k=1}^\infty \frac{2^{n-1}}{3^n} = 1,$$

for $x \in S$, and $g\restriction_U = f$. The continuity of g follows from Theorem 5.34.

$\square$

5.7 Pointwise and Uniform Convergence

Definition 5.18. Let X be a set and let (T, d) be a metric space.

A sequence of functions (f_n), where $f_n : X \longrightarrow T$ *converges pointwise* to a function $f : X \longrightarrow T$ if for every $x \in X$ the sequence $(f_n(x))$ converges to $f(x)$. In other words, the following formula is valid:

$$(\forall \epsilon > 0)(\forall x \in X)(\exists n_{\epsilon,x})(n \geqslant n_{\epsilon,x} \Rightarrow d(f_n(x), f(x)) < \epsilon).$$

The sequence (f_n) *converges uniformly* to f if

$$\lim_{n \to \infty} \sup_{x \in X} d(f_n(x), f(x)) = 0,$$

that is, the following first-order formula is valid:

$$(\forall \epsilon > 0)(\exists n_\epsilon)(\forall x \in X)(n \geqslant n_\epsilon \Rightarrow d(f_n(x), f(x)) < \epsilon).$$

Note the difference in the order of the quantifier symbols in the above formulas. In the case of the pointwise convergence the number $n_{\epsilon,x}$ depends both on ϵ and on x; in the case of the uniform convergence the similar number depends only on ϵ.

Example 5.13. Let $f_n : [0, 1] \longrightarrow \mathbb{R}$ be the function defined by

$$f_n(x) = \begin{cases} |nx - 1| & \text{if } 0 \leqslant x \leqslant \frac{2}{n}, \\ 1 & \text{if } \frac{2}{n} < x \leqslant 1 \end{cases}$$

for $x \in [0, 1]$. The graph of f_n is shown in Figure 5.1.

The sequence of functions (f_n) converges pointwise to the constant function $f : [0, 1] \longrightarrow [0, 1]$ given by $f(x) = 1$, with the usual metric on $\mathbb{R}$. Indeed, we have:

$$|f_n(x) - f(x)| = \begin{cases} 1 - |nx - 1| & \text{if } 0 \leqslant x \leqslant \frac{2}{n}, \\ 0 & \text{if } \frac{2}{n} < x \leqslant 1 \end{cases}$$

$$= \begin{cases} nx & \text{if } 0 \leqslant x \leqslant \frac{1}{n}, \\ 2 - nx & \text{if } \frac{1}{n} < x \leqslant \frac{2}{n}, \\ 0 & \text{if } \frac{2}{n} < x \leqslant 1. \end{cases}$$

Thus, given x and $\epsilon > 0$, if $n \geqslant \lceil 2/x \rceil$ we shall have $|f_n(x) - f(x)| < \epsilon$.

However, the convergence of (f_n) to f is *not* uniform. Indeed, it is impossible to find a number n_ϵ independent of x such that $|f_n(x) - f(x)| < \epsilon$ because $|f_n(1/n) - f(1/n)| = 1$ for $n \geqslant 1$.

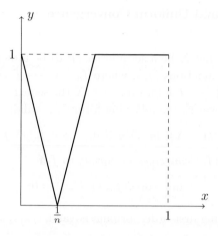

Fig. 5.1   Continuous function on $[0, 1]$.

Theorem 5.36. *Let $(S, \mathcal{O}_d)$ and $(T, \mathcal{O}_e)$ be two topological metric spaces. If (f_n) a sequence of continuous functions from S to T that converges uniformly to a function $f : S \longrightarrow T$ then f is continuous.*

Proof.   Let ϵ be a positive number. Since (f_n) converges uniformly to f there exists a natural number n_ϵ such that $n \geqslant n_\epsilon$ implies $e(f_n(s), f(s)) < \frac{\epsilon}{3}$ for every $s \in S$.

Since f_{n_ϵ} is a continuous function there exists a $\delta > 0$ such that $d(s, s') < \delta$ implies $e(f_{n_\epsilon}(s), f_{n_\epsilon}(s')) < \frac{\epsilon}{3}$, Thus, if $d(s, s') < \delta$ we have

$$e(f(s), f(s')) \leqslant e(f(s), f_{n_\epsilon}(s)) + e(f_{n_\epsilon}(s), f_{n_\epsilon}(s')) + e(f_{n_\epsilon}(s'), f(s')) < \epsilon,$$

which shows that f is continuous.   □

Theorem 5.37. (Dini's[1] Theorem) *Let $(S, \mathcal{O}_d)$ be a compact metric space and let (f_n) be a sequence of continuous functions $f_n : S \longrightarrow \mathbb{R}$ for $n \in \mathbb{N}$ that converges pointwise to $f : S \longrightarrow \mathbb{R}$ such that $f_n(x) \geqslant f_{n+1}(x)$ for all $x \in S$ and $n \in \mathbb{N}$. Then (f_n) converges uniformly to f.*

Proof.   Let $g_n : S \longrightarrow \mathbb{R}$ be defined as $g_n(x) = f_n(x) - f(x)$ for $n \in \mathbb{N}$ and $x \in S$. Then (g_n) converges pointwise to the constant function 0, $g_n(x) \geqslant g_{n+1}(x) \geqslant 0$ for $x \in S$ and $n \in \mathbb{N}$. Define $M_n = \sup\{g_n(x) \mid x \in S\}$.

---

[1] Ullise Dini was born in Pisa, Italy, on November 14th 1845 and died on October 28th 1918. He is known for his contribution to real analysis. Dini served as rector of the Pisa University, and of the Scuola Normale Superiore and was active in Italian politics.

Define the set $T_n = g_n^{-1}(-\infty, \epsilon)$ for some positive ϵ. Since g_n is continuous, T_n is an open set. Also $T_n \subseteq T_{n+1}$.

For each $x \in S$, $\lim_{n\to\infty} g_n(x) = 0$, so there exists $n \in \mathbb{N}$ such that $g_n(x) < \epsilon$, hence $x \in T_n$. Thus, $S = \bigcup_{n\in\mathbb{N}} T_n$. Since S is compact, there exists a finite subcover $\{T_{i_1}, \ldots, T_{i_m}\}$ of S with $i_1 \leqslant \cdots \leqslant i_m$. Since $T_{i_1} \subseteq \cdots \subseteq T_{i_m}$ of S, this finite subcover reduces to T_{i_m}. This means that $g_{i_m}(x) < \epsilon$ for all $x \in S$. Thus, $M_{i_m} \leqslant \epsilon$ for all $x \in S$. Since M_n decreases with n and every $M_n \geqslant 0$, it follows that $\lim_{n\to\infty} M_n = 0$. $\qquad\square$

If any of the conditions of Dini's theorem fails the convergence of f_n to f may not be uniform.

Example 5.14. Let $f_n(x) = x^n$ be functions defined on the non-compact set $S = (0, 1)$. The sequence (f_n) converges pointwise to 0. However, the convergence is not uniform because $\sup\{x^n \mid x \in (0,1)\} = 1$ for $n \in \mathbb{N}$.

Let $S = [0, 1]$ be compact and let f_n be defined as

$$f_n(x) = \begin{cases} 1 - nx & \text{if } 0 \leqslant x \leqslant \frac{1}{n}, \\ 1 & \text{if } \frac{1}{n} \leqslant x \leqslant 1. \end{cases}$$

It is clear that (f_n) converges pointwise to the function f given by

$$f(x) = \begin{cases} 1 & \text{if } x = 0, \\ 0 & \text{if } 0 < x \leqslant 1, \end{cases}$$

which is discontinuous in 0. The convergence of (f_n) to f is not uniform because $\sup\{f_n(x) - f(x) \mid x \in [0,1]\} = 1$.

Theorem 5.38. *Let $(S, \mathcal{O}_d)$ and $(T, \mathcal{O}_e)$ be two topological metric spaces. Suppose that $(T, \mathcal{O}_e)$ is complete. The sequence of functions (f_n) converges uniformly on S if and only if for every $\epsilon > 0$ there exists n_ϵ such that $m, n \geqslant n_\epsilon, x \in S$ imply $e(f_n(x), f_m(x)) < \epsilon$.*

Proof. Suppose that (f_n) converges uniformly on S and let $f = \lim_{n\to\infty} f_n$. There is $n_{\epsilon/2}$ such that $n > n_{\epsilon/2}$ implies $e(f_n(x), f(x)) < \frac{\epsilon}{2}$, hence $m, n > n_{\epsilon/2}$ imply

$$e(f_n(x), f_m(x)) \leqslant e(f_n(x), f(x)) + e(f(x), f_m(x)) < \epsilon.$$

Conversely, suppose that the condition of the theorem holds. Since $(T, \mathcal{O}_e)$ is complete, the sequence $(f_n(x))$ converges for every x. Define $f(x) = \lim_{n\to\infty} f_n(x)$. Let $n_\epsilon \in \mathbb{N}$ be such that $m, n > n_\epsilon$ implies $e(f_m(x), f_n(x)) < \epsilon$. For any $n > n_\epsilon$ we have $\lim_{m\to\infty} e(f_m(x), f_n(x)) = e(f(x), f_n(x)) < \epsilon$ for every $n > n_\epsilon$, hence (f_n) converges uniformly to f. $\qquad\square$

Let $C(S)$ be the linear space of real-valued bounded continuous functions of the form $f : S \longrightarrow \mathbb{R}$, where $(S, \mathcal{O})$ is a topological space. For $f \in C(S)$ define $\|f\|_\infty = \sup\{|f(x)| \mid x \in S\}$.

We claim that $\|\cdot\|_\infty$ is a norm on $C(S)$.

Since f is bounded, $\|f\|_\infty < \infty$. If $\|f\|_\infty = 0$, it is clear that $f(x) = 0$ for every $x \in S$. Note that $h = f + g$ implies

$$|h(x)| \leqslant |f(x)| + g(x) \leqslant \|f\|_\infty + \|g\|_\infty,$$

hence $\|h\|_\infty \leqslant \|f\|_\infty + \|g\|_\infty$, that is $\|f + g\|_\infty \leqslant \|f\|_\infty + \|g\|_\infty$, so $\|\cdot\|_\infty$ is indeed a norm. This implies that $d_\infty : C(S)^2 \longrightarrow \mathbb{R}$ defined by $d_\infty(f, g) = \|f - g\|_\infty$ for $f, g \in C(S)$ is a metric on $C(S)$.

We shall refer to $\|f\|_\infty$ as the *supremum norm* of a function $f \in C(S)$. An alternative term used for $\|\cdot\|_\infty$ is the *uniform convergence norm*. This is motivated by the fact that if $\lim_{n\to\infty} \|f_n - f\|_\infty = 0$, then f_n converges uniformly to f on S.

If $(S, \mathcal{O})$ is compact, we have $\|f\|_\infty(f) = \max\{|f(x)| \mid x \in S\}$.

Theorem 5.39. *The metric space $(C(S), d_\infty)$ is complete.*

Proof. Let (f_n) be a Cauchy sequence in $C(S)$. This implies that for every $\epsilon > 0$ there exists n_ϵ such that $m, n > n_\epsilon$ implies $|f_n(x) - f_m(x)| < \epsilon$. Since $\mathbb{R}$ is complete, by Theorem 5.38 there exists a function $f : S \longrightarrow \mathbb{R}$ such that (f_n) converges uniformly to f. By Theorem 5.36, f is continuous. Furthermore, f is bounded because there is n_1 such that $|f_{n_1}(x) - f(x)| < 1$ for $x \in S$. Thus, $f \in C(S)$ and $\lim_{n\to\infty} \|f - f_n\|_\infty = 0$. $\square$

5.8 The Stone-Weierstrass Theorem

Theorem 4.73 shows that the set of real-valued continuous functions defined on a topological space $(S, \mathcal{O})$ is an algebra.

Definition 5.19. A subset $\mathcal{U}$ of $C(S)$ *separates points* if for every $x, y \in S$ such that $x \neq y$ there exists a function $f \in \mathcal{U}$ such that $f(u) \neq f(v)$.

Example 5.15. The algebra of all polynomials defined on an interval $[a, b]$ separates points. Indeed, let $c, d \in [a, b]$ with $c \neq d$ and p be the polynomial $p(x) = \frac{1}{c-d}(x - d)$ for $x \in [a, b]$. Since $p(c) = 1$ and $p(d) = 0$, the algebra of all polynomials separates points.

On other hand the set of even functions on $[-1, 1]$ is an algebra, but it does not separate points because $f(-x) = f(x)$ for $x \in [-1, 1]$.

The Stone-Weierstrass theorem shows that the continuous functions of the form $f : S \longrightarrow \mathbb{R}$ (where $(S, \mathcal{O})$ is a compact topological space) can be uniformly approximated by the functions that belong to a subalgebra $\mathcal{U}$ of $C(S)$ that has certain properties. The next two lemmas are preliminaries to an elementary proof of this important result.

In the next lemma we make use of Bernoulli's inequality (Exercise 49 of Chapter 1).

Lemma 5.1. *Let $(S, \mathcal{O})$ be a compact topological space, U be an open subset in this space, and let $t_0 \in U$.*

If $\mathcal{U}$ is a subalgebra of $C(S)$ that contains the constant functions and separates points, then there exists $V \in neigh_{t_0}(\mathcal{O})$, $V \subseteq U$ such that for every $\epsilon > 0$ there exists $f \in \mathcal{U}$ that satisfies the following conditions:

    (i) *for every $x \in S$, $0 \leqslant f(x) \leqslant 1$;*

    (ii) *$f(x) < \epsilon$ for $x \in V$;*

    (iii) *$f(x) > 1 - \epsilon$ for $x \in S - U$.*

Proof. Let c_a be the constant function in $\mathcal{U}$ whose value is a.

Let $t \in S - U$. Then, since $t \neq t_0$ and $\mathcal{U}$ separates points, there exists a function $g_t \in \mathcal{U}$ such that $g_t(t) \neq g_t(t_0)$. Then, the function h_t defined by

$$h_t = g_t - g_t(t_0) \cdot c_1$$

belongs to $\mathcal{U}$ and $h_t(t) = g_t(t) - g_t(t_0) \neq h_t(t_0) = 0$.

Define

$$\nu(f) = \sup\{|f(x)| \mid x \in S\}. \tag{5.2}$$

Let p_t be the function given by $p_t = \frac{1}{\nu(h_t)^2}(h_t)^2$. Observe that $p_t \in \mathcal{U}$, $p_t(t_0) = 0$, and $p_t(t) > 0$. In addition, $c_0 \leqslant p_t \leqslant c_1$.

The set $U(t) = \{s \in S \mid p_t(s) > 0\}$ is an open neighborhood of t. Since $(S, \mathcal{O})$ is compact and U is open, $S - U$ is closed and, therefore, it is compact (by Theorem 4.46). The compactness of $S - U$ implies the existence of a finite number of points $t_1, \ldots, t_m$ in $S - U$ such that $S - U = \bigcup_{i=1}^m U(t_i)$.

Let p be the function defined by $p(t) = \frac{1}{m}\sum_{i=1}^m p_{t_i}$. Then $p \in \mathcal{U}$, $c_0 \leqslant p \leqslant c_1$, $p(t_0) = 0$ and $p(t) > 0$ for $t \in S - U$.

Since $S - U$ is compact, there exists $\delta \in (0, 1)$ such that $p(t) \geqslant \delta$ for $t \in S - U$. Let V be the set defined by $V = \{t \in S \mid p(t) < \frac{\delta}{2}\}$. Then V is an open neighborhood of t_0 and $V \subseteq U$.

Let k be the smallest integer that is greater than $\frac{1}{\delta}$. Then, $k - 1 \leqslant \frac{1}{\delta}$, hence $k \leqslant \frac{1+\delta}{\delta} < \frac{2}{\delta}$. Thus, $1 < k\delta < 2$.

For $n \in \mathbb{N}$ and $n \geqslant 1$ consider the functions q_n defined by

$$q_n(t) = (1 - p^n(t))^{k^n}.$$

We have $q_n \in \mathcal{U}$, $c_0 \leqslant q_n \leqslant c_1$ and $q_n(t_0) = 1$. For $t \in V$ we have $kp(t) \leqslant k\frac{\delta}{2} < 1$, so

$$q_n(t) \geqslant 1 - (kp(t))^n \geqslant 1 - \left(\frac{k\delta}{2}\right)^n.$$

Thus, $\lim_{n \to \infty} q_n(t) = 1$ uniformly on V.

For $t \in S - U$, $kp(t) \geqslant k\delta > 1$ and, by Bernoulli's inequality:

$$
\begin{aligned}
q_n(t) &= \frac{1}{k^n p^n(t)} (1 - p^n(t))^{k^n} k^n p^n(t) \\
&\leqslant \frac{1}{(kp(t))^n} (1 - p^n(t))^{k^n} (1 + k^n p^n(t)) \\
&\leqslant \frac{1}{(kp(t))^n} (1 - p^n(t))^{k^n} (1 + p^n(t))^{k^n} \\
&= \frac{1}{(kp(t))^n} (1 - p^{2n}(t))^{k^n} \leqslant \frac{1}{(k\delta)^n}.
\end{aligned}
$$

Therefore, $\lim_{n \to \infty} q_n(t) = 0$, and this happens uniformly on $S - U$. Thus, for n sufficiently large, q_n has the property that $c_0 \leqslant q_n \leqslant c_1$, $q_n(t) < \epsilon$ on $S - U$ and $q(t) > 1 - \epsilon$ on V. The Lemma follows by taking $f = c_1 - q_n$. $\square$

Lemma 5.2. *Let $(S, \mathcal{O})$ be a compact topological space, $t_0 \in S$, and let U be an open set in $(S, \mathcal{O})$ that contains t_0.*

If $\mathcal{U}$ is a subalgebra of $C(S)$ that contains the constant functions and separates points, and A, B are two closed and disjoint subsets of S, then there exists $f \in \mathcal{U}$ such that:

(i) $0 \leqslant f(t) \leqslant 1$ *for $t \in S$;*
(ii) $f(t) < \epsilon$ *for $t \in A$;*
(iii) $f(t) > 1 - \epsilon$ *for $t \in B$.*

Proof. Let $U = S - B$. Since B is closed, U is an open set.

For each $t \in A$ chose the open set $V(t)$ that contains t as in Lemma 5.1. There exists a finite set of points $\{t_1, \ldots, t_m\} \subseteq A$ such that $A \subseteq \bigcup_{i=1}^{m} V(t_i)$. By the choice of $V(t_i)$, there exist $f_i \in \mathcal{U}$ for $1 \leqslant i \leqslant m$ such that $c_0 \leqslant f_i \leqslant c_1$, $f_i(x) < \frac{\epsilon}{m}$ when $x \in V(t_i)$ and $f_i(x) > 1 - \frac{\epsilon}{m}$ when $x \in S - U = B$. Then, the function $f = \prod_{i=1}^{m} f_i$ belongs to $\mathcal{U}$, $c_0 \leqslant f \leqslant c_1$, $f(x) < \frac{\epsilon}{m} \leqslant \epsilon$ when $x \in \bigcup_{i=1}^{m} \supseteq A$ and, by Bernoulli's inequality $f(x) > \left(1 - \frac{\epsilon}{m}\right)^m > 1 - \epsilon$ on B. $\square$

Theorem 5.40. (Stone-Weierstrass Theorem) *If $(S, \mathcal{O})$ is a compact topological space and $\mathcal{U}$ is a subalgebra of $C(S)$ that satisfies the following conditions:*

   (i) *$\mathcal{U}$ contains the constant functions;*
   (ii) *$\mathcal{U}$ separates points.*

Then for every element $f \in C(S)$ and $\epsilon > 0$, there exists $g \in \mathcal{U}$ such that $\sup_{x \in S} |f(x) - g(x)| < \epsilon$.

Proof.   By replacing f by $f + \nu(f)$, where ν was defined in equality (5.2) we can assume that $f(x) \geqslant 0$ for $x \in S$. We can assume that $\epsilon < \frac{1}{3}$. Let n be an integer such that $(n-1)\epsilon \geqslant \nu(f)$. For $j \in \mathbb{N}$ define the sets

$$A_j = \left\{ x \in S \mid f(x) \leqslant \left(j - \frac{1}{3} \right) \epsilon \right\} \text{ and } B_j = \left\{ x \in S \mid f(x) \geqslant \left(j + \frac{1}{3} \right) \epsilon \right\}.$$

The sets A_j and B_j are disjoint and

$$\emptyset = A_0 \subset A_1 \subset \cdots \subset A_n = S \text{ and } B_0 \supset B_1 \supset \cdots \supset B_n = \emptyset.$$

Lemma 5.2 implies the existence of $f_j \in \mathcal{U}$, such that $0 \leqslant f_j(t) \leqslant 1$ for $t \in S$, $f_j(t) < \frac{\epsilon}{3}$ for $t \in A_j$ and $f_j(t) > 1 - \frac{\epsilon}{n}$ for $t \in B_j$. The function $g = \epsilon \sum_{i=0}^{n} f_i$ belongs to $\mathcal{U}$. For $t \in S$ we have $t \in A_j - A_{j-1}$ for some $j \geqslant 1$, which implies

$$\left(j - \frac{4}{3} \right) \epsilon < f(t) < \left(j - \frac{1}{3} \right) \epsilon \tag{5.3}$$

and

$$f_i(t) < \frac{\epsilon}{n} \tag{5.4}$$

for every $i \geqslant j$. Also, $t \in B_i$ for $i \leqslant j - 2$ which implies

$$f_i(t) > 1 - \frac{\epsilon}{n} \tag{5.5}$$

for every $i \leqslant j - 2$. Using inequalities (5.4) we obtain

$$g(t) = \epsilon \sum_{i=0}^{j-1} f_i(t) + \epsilon \sum_{i=j}^{n} f_i(t)$$
$$\leqslant j\epsilon + \epsilon(n - j + 1)\frac{\epsilon}{n}$$
$$\leqslant j\epsilon + \epsilon^2 < \left(j + \frac{1}{3} \right) \epsilon.$$

Using inequalities (5.5) we obtain for $j \geqslant 2$:

$$g(t) \geqslant \epsilon \sum_{i=0}^{j-2} f_i(t) \geqslant (j-1)\epsilon \left(1 - \frac{\epsilon}{n}\right)$$

$$= (j-1)\epsilon - ((j-1)/n)\epsilon^2 > (j-1)\epsilon - \epsilon^2 > \left(j - \frac{4}{3}\right)\epsilon.$$

The inequality $g(t) > (j - 4/3)\epsilon$ is trivially true for $j = 1$. Thus,

$$|f(t) - g(t)| \leqslant \left(j + \frac{1}{3}\right)\epsilon - \left(j - \frac{4}{3}\right)\epsilon < 2\epsilon. \qquad \square$$

Stone-Weierstrass Theorem can be extended to algebras of complex continuous functions by adding a supplemental requirement.

Theorem 5.41. (Complex Stone-Weierstrass Theorem) *Let $(S, \mathcal{O})$ be a compact topological space and $\mathcal{U}$ be an algebra of complex continuous functions that satisfies the following conditions:*

   (i) *$\mathcal{U}$ contains the constant functions;*
   (ii) *$\mathcal{U}$ separates points;*
   (iii) *for every $f \in \mathcal{U}$ its complex conjugate $\overline{f}$ defined as $\overline{f}(x) = \overline{f(x)}$ for $x \in S$ belongs to $\mathcal{U}$.*

Then for every complex continuous function $f \in C(S)$ and $\epsilon > 0$, there exists $g \in \mathcal{U}$ such that $\sup_{x \in S} |f(x) - g(x)| < \epsilon$.

Proof. Let $\mathcal{U}_r$ be the set of all real-valued functions on S that belong to $\mathcal{U}$. If $f \in \mathcal{U}$ we have $\overline{f} \in \mathcal{U}$ and since the function $h = \frac{1}{2}(f + \overline{f})$ is real-valued, we have $h \in \mathcal{U}_r$. It is immediate that $\mathcal{U}_r$ is an algebra that contains the real-valued constant functions.

Since $\mathcal{U}$ separates points, if $c, d \in S$ and $c \neq d$, there exists a function $\ell \in \mathcal{U}$ such that $\ell(c) \neq \ell(d)$. Since $\mathcal{U}$ is an algebra that contains constants, the function f defined by $f(x) = \frac{\ell(x) - \ell(c)}{\ell(d) - \ell(c)}$ also belongs to $\mathcal{U}$ and, $f(c) = 0$ and $f(d) = 1$. Then $h(c) = 0$ and $h(d) = 1$, which shows that $\mathcal{U}_r$ also separates points.

The algebra $\mathcal{U}_r$ satisfies the conditions of Theorem 5.40, so for every real-valued continuous function $h \in C(S)$ and $\epsilon > 0$, there exists $g \in \mathcal{U}$ such that $\sup_{x \in S} |h(x) - g(x)| < \epsilon$. If $f : S \longrightarrow \mathbb{C}$ is a complex valued continuous functions, then for the real-valued functions $f_1 = \Re(f)$ and $f_2 = \Im(f)$ there exist $g_1, g_2 \in \mathcal{U}_r$ such that $\sup_{x \in S} |f_1(x) - g_1(x)| < \frac{\epsilon}{2}$ and $\sup_{x \in S} |f_2(x) - g_2(x)| < \frac{\epsilon}{2}$. Define $g = g_1 + ig_2$. We have

$$\begin{aligned}
|f(x) - g(x)| &= |f_1(x) + if_2(x) - g_1(x) - ig_2(x)| \\
&= |f_1(x) - g_1(x) + i(f_2(x) - g_2(x))| \\
&\leqslant |f_1(x) - g_1(x)| + |f_2(x) - g_2(x)| < \epsilon. \qquad \square
\end{aligned}$$

5.9 Totally Bounded Metric Spaces

Definition 5.20. An *r-net* for a subset T of a metric space $(S, \mathcal{O}_d)$ is a subset U of S such that for every $x \in T$ there exists $u \in U$ such that $x \in B(u, r)$.

A *finite r-net* is an *r-net* U such that U is a finite set.

This definition allows us to introduce the notion of totally bounded or precompact set.

Definition 5.21. A subset T of a metric space $(S, \mathcal{O}_d)$ is *totally bounded* (or *precompact*) if, for every positive number r there exists an *r-net* for T.

If S is totally bounded or precompact, we say that $(S, \mathcal{O}_d)$ is totally bounded or precompact.

$(S, \mathcal{O}_d)$ is compact, then it is totally bounded.

Next, we show that total boundedness is inherited by subsets.

Theorem 5.42. *If $(S, \mathcal{O}_d)$ is a totally bounded topological metric space and $T \subseteq S$, then the subspace $(T, \mathcal{O}_d \restriction_T)$ is also totally bounded.*

Proof. Since $(S, \mathcal{O}_d)$ is totally bounded, for every $r > 0$ there exists a finite open cover $\mathcal{C}_{r/2} = \{B\left(s_i, \frac{r}{2}\right) \mid s_i \in S, 1 \leqslant i \leqslant n\}$. Let $\mathcal{C}' = \{B\left(s_{i_j}, \frac{r}{2}\right) \mid 1 \leqslant j \leqslant m\}$ be a minimal subcollection of $\mathcal{C}_{r/2}$ that consists of those open spheres that cover T; that is,

$$T \subseteq \bigcup \left\{ B\left(s_{i_j}, \frac{r}{2}\right) \middle| 1 \leqslant j \leqslant m \right\}.$$

The minimality of $\mathcal{C}'$ implies that each set $B\left(s_{i_j}, \frac{r}{2}\right)$ contains an element y_j of T. We have $B\left(s_{i_j}, \frac{r}{2}\right) \subseteq B(y_j, r)$ and this implies that the set $\{y_1, \ldots, y_m\}$ is an *r-net* for the set T. $\qquad\square$

If the subspace $(T, \mathcal{O}_d \restriction_T)$ of $(S, \mathcal{O}_d)$ is totally bounded, we say that the set T is *totally bounded*.

Example 5.16. In Example 4.21 we saw that the metric space $([0, 1], d)$, where d is the usual metric on $[0, 1]$ is compact. However, the set $(0, 1)$ is not compact, but it is totally bounded (or, precompact).

The next corollary shows that there is no need to require the centers of the spheres involved in the definition of the total boundedness of a subspace to be located in the subspace.

Corollary 5.10. *Let $(S, \mathcal{O}_d)$ be a topological metric space (not necessarily totally bounded) and let T be a subset of S. The subspace $(T, \mathcal{O}_d \upharpoonright_T)$ is totally bounded if and only if for every positive number r there exists a finite subcover $\{B(x_1, r), \dots, B(x_n, r) \mid x_i \in S \text{ for } 1 \leqslant i \leqslant n\}$.*

Proof.   The argument has been made in the proof of Theorem 5.42.   □

The next theorem adds two further equivalent characterizations of compact metric spaces to the ones given in Theorem 5.22.

Theorem 5.43. *Let $(S, \mathcal{O}_d)$ be a topological metric space. The following statements are equivalent.*

(i) *$(S, \mathcal{O}_d)$ is compact;*
(ii) *every sequence $\boldsymbol{x} \in \mathbf{Seq}_\infty(S)$ contains a convergent subsequence;*
(iii) *$(S, \mathcal{O}_d)$ is totally bounded and complete.*

Proof.   (i) implies (ii): Let $(S, \mathcal{O}_d)$ be a compact topological metric space and let $\mathbf{x}$ be a sequence in $\mathbf{Seq}_\infty(S)$. By Theorem 5.22, $(S, \mathcal{O}_d)$ has the Bolzano-Weierstrass property, so the set $\{x_n \mid n \in \mathbb{N}\}$ has an accumulation point t. For every $k \geqslant 1$, the set $\{x_n \mid n \in \mathbb{N}\} \cap B\left(t, \frac{1}{k}\right)$ contains an element x_{n_k} distinct from t. Since $d(t, x_{n_k}) < \frac{1}{k}$ for $k \geqslant 1$, it follows that the subsequence $(x_{n_1}, x_{n_2}, \dots)$ converges to t.

(ii) implies (iii): Suppose that every sequence $\mathbf{x} \in \mathbf{Seq}_\infty(S)$ contains a convergent subsequence and that $(S, \mathcal{O}_d)$ is not totally bounded. Then, there exists a positive number r such that S cannot be covered by any collection of open spheres of radius r.

Let x_0 be an arbitrary element of S. Note that $B(x_0, r) - S \neq \emptyset$ because otherwise the $B(x_0, r)$ would constitute an open cover for S. Let x_1 be an arbitrary element in $B(x_0, r) - S$. Observe that $d(x_0, x_1) \geqslant r$. The set $(B(x_0, r) \cup B(x_1, r)) - S$ is not empty. Thus, for any $x_2 \in (B(x_0, r) \cup B(x_1, r)) - S$, we have $d(x_0, x_2) \geqslant r$ and $d(x_0, x_1) \geqslant r$, etc. We obtain in this manner a sequence $x_0, x_1, \dots, x_n, \dots$ such that $d(x_i, x_j) \geqslant r$ when $i \neq j$. Clearly, this sequence cannot contain a convergent sequence, and this contradiction shows that the space must be totally bounded.

To prove that $(S, \mathcal{O}_d)$ is complete, consider a Cauchy sequence $\mathbf{x} = (x_0, x_1, \dots, x_n, \dots)$. By hypothesis, this sequence contains a convergent subsequence $(x_{n_0}, x_{n_1}, \dots)$. Suppose that $\lim_{k \to \infty} x_{n_k} = l$. Since $\mathbf{x}$ is a Cauchy sequence, there is $n'_{\frac{\epsilon}{2}}$ such that $n, n_k \geqslant n'_{\frac{\epsilon}{2}}$ implies $d(x_n, x_{n_k}) < \frac{\epsilon}{2}$. The convergence of the subsequence $(x_{n_0}, x_{n_1}, \dots)$ means that there exists $n''_{\frac{\epsilon}{2}}$ such that $n_k \geqslant n''_{\frac{\epsilon}{2}}$ implies $d(x_{n_k}, l) < \frac{\epsilon}{2}$. Choosing $n_k \geqslant n''_{\frac{\epsilon}{2}}$, if

$n \geqslant n'_{\frac{\epsilon}{2}} = n_\epsilon$, we obtain

$$d(x_n, l) \leqslant d(x_n, x_{n_k}) + d(x_{n_k}, l) < \frac{\epsilon}{2} + \frac{\epsilon}{2} = \epsilon,$$

which proves that $\mathbf{x}$ is convergent. Consequently, $(S, \mathcal{O}_d)$ is both totally bounded and complete.

(iii) implies (i): Suppose that $(S, \mathcal{O}_d)$ is both totally bounded and complete but not compact, which means that there exists an open cover $\mathcal{C}$ of S that does not contain any finite subcover.

Since $(S, \mathcal{O}_d)$ is totally bounded, there exists a $\frac{1}{2}$-net, $\{x_1^1, \ldots, x_{n_1}^1\}$. For each of the closed spheres $B[x_i^1, \frac{1}{2}]$, $1 \leqslant i \leqslant n_1$, the trace collection $\mathcal{C}_{B[x_i^1, \frac{1}{2}]}$ is an open cover. There is a closed sphere $B[x_j^1, \frac{1}{2}]$ such that the open cover $\mathcal{C}_{B[x_j^1, \frac{1}{2}]}$ does not contain any finite subcover of $B[x_j^1, \frac{1}{2}]$ since $(S, \mathcal{O}_d)$ was assumed not to be compact. Let $z_1 = x_j^1$.

By Theorem 5.42, the closed sphere $B[z_1, \frac{1}{2}]$ is totally bounded. Thus, there exists a $\frac{1}{2^2}$-net $\{x_1^2, \ldots, x_{n_2}^2\}$ of $B[z_1, \frac{1}{2}]$. There exists a closed sphere $B[x_k^2, \frac{1}{2^2}]$ such that the open cover $\mathcal{C}_{B[x_k^2, \frac{1}{2^2}]}$ does not contain any finite subcover of $B[x_k^2, \frac{1}{2^2}]$. Let $z_2 = x_k^2$; note that $d(z_1, z_2) \leqslant \frac{1}{2}$.

Thus, we construct a sequence $\mathbf{z} = (z_1, z_2, \ldots)$ such that $d(z_{n+1}, z_n) \leqslant \frac{1}{2^n}$ for $n \geqslant 1$.

Observe that

$$d(z_{n+p}, z_n) \leqslant d(z_{n+p}, z_{n+p-1}) + d(z_{n+p-1}, z_{n+p-2}) + \cdots + d(z_{n+1}, z_n)$$

$$\leqslant \frac{1}{2^{n+p-1}} \frac{1}{2^{n+p-2}} + \cdots + \frac{1}{2^n}$$

$$= \frac{1}{2^{n-1}} \left(1 - \frac{1}{2^p}\right).$$

Thus, the sequence $\mathbf{z}$ is a Cauchy sequence and there exists $z = \lim_{n \to \infty} z_n$, because $(S, \mathcal{O}_d)$ is complete.

Since $\mathcal{C}$ is an open cover, there exists a set $L \in \mathcal{C}$ such that $z \in L$. Let r be a positive number such that $B(z, r) \subseteq L$. Let n_0 be such that $d(z_n, z) < \frac{r}{2}$ and $\frac{1}{2^n} \leqslant \frac{r}{2}$. If $x \in B[z_n, \frac{1}{2^n}]$, then $d(x, z) \leqslant d(x, z_n) + d(z_n, z) < \frac{1}{2^n} + \frac{r}{2} \leqslant r$, so $B[z_n, \frac{1}{2^n}] \subseteq B(z, r) \subseteq L$. This is a contradiction because the spheres $B[z_n, \frac{1}{2^n}]$ were defined such that $\mathcal{C}_{B[z_n, \frac{1}{2^n}]}$ did not contain any finite subcover. Thus, $(S, \mathcal{O}_d)$ is compact. $\qquad\square$

Theorem 5.44. (Heine-Borel Theorem) *A subset T of $(\mathbb{R}^n, \mathcal{O})$ is compact if and only if it is closed and bounded.*

Proof. Let T be a compact set. By Corollary 5.4. T is closed. Let r be a positive number and let $\{B(t, r) \mid t \in T\}$ be a cover of T. Since

T is compact, there exists a finite collection $\{B(t_i, r) \mid 1 \leqslant i \leqslant p\}$ such that $T \subseteq \bigcup\{B(t_i, r) \mid 1 \leqslant i \leqslant p\}$. Therefore, if $x, y \in T$, we have $d(x, y) \leqslant 2 + \max\{d(t_i, t_j) \mid 1 \leqslant i, j \leqslant p\}$, which implies that T is also bounded.

Conversely, suppose that T is closed and bounded. The boundedness of T implies the existence of a parallelepiped $[x_1, y_1] \times \cdots \times [x_n, y_n]$ that includes T, and we saw in Example 4.46 that this parallelepiped is compact. Since T is closed, it is immediate that T is compact by Theorem 4.46. $\qquad \square$

Corollary 5.11. *Let $(S, \mathcal{O})$ be a compact topological space and let $f : S \longrightarrow \mathbb{R}$ be a continuous function, where $\mathbb{R}$ is equipped with the usual topology. Then, f is bounded and there exist $u_0, u_1 \in S$ such that $f(u_0) = \inf_{x \in S} f(x)$ and $f(u_1) = \sup_{x \in S} f(x)$. In other words, f attains its maximum and minimum.*

Proof.   Since S is compact and f is continuous, the set $f(S)$ is a compact subset of $\mathbb{R}$ and, by Theorem 5.44, is bounded and closed.

Both $\inf_{x \in S} f(x)$ and $\sup_{x \in S} f(x)$ are cluster points of $f(S)$; therefore, both belong to $f(S)$, which implies the existence of u_0 and u_1. $\qquad \square$

We shall describe the existence of u_0 (and u_1) as established in Corollary 5.11 by saying that f *attains* its infimum in u_0 (and that it *attains* its supremum in u_1).

Example 5.17. Let $f : \mathbb{R} \longrightarrow \mathbb{R}$ be the function defined by $f(x) = x$ for $x \in \mathbb{R}$. It is clear that $\inf_{x \in S} f(x) = -\infty$ and $\sup_{x \in S} f(x) = \infty$. Note that the conditions of Corollary 5.11 are violated since the $\mathbb{R}$ is not compact.

Example 5.18. Let S be the compact subset $[-1, 1]$ of $\mathbb{R}$ and let $f : S \longrightarrow \mathbb{R}$ be defined by

$$f(x) = \begin{cases} 0 & \text{if } x \in \{-1, 1\}, \\ x & \text{if } x \in (-1, 1). \end{cases}$$

Observe that $\inf_{x \in S} f(x) = -1$ and $\sup_{x \in S} f(x) = 1$, and there is no $u_0 \in S$ such that $f(u_0) = -1$ and there is no $u_1 \in S$ such that $f(u_0) = 1$. The hypothesis of Corollary 5.11 is violated because f is not continuous on S.

The converse of Corollary 5.11 is false. Compactness and continuity are sufficient for attainability of the supremum and infimum but they are not necessary as the next example shows.

Example 5.19. Let $f : \mathbb{R} \longrightarrow \mathbb{R}$ be given by

$$f(x) = \begin{cases} 1 & \text{if } x \text{ is rational,} \\ 0 & \text{if } x \text{ is irrational.} \end{cases}$$

The definition domain $\mathbb{R}$ of f is not compact and f is discontinuous at every point of its domain. However, $\inf_{x \in \mathbb{R}} f(x) = 0$ and $\sup_{x \in S} f(x) = 1$ and we have $f(u_0) = 0$ for each irrational u_0 and $f(u_1) = 1$ for each rational u_1.

Theorem 5.45. (Heine's Theorem) *Let $(S, \mathcal{O}_d)$ be a compact topological metric space and let $(T, \mathcal{O}_e)$ be a metric space. Every continuous function $f : S \longrightarrow T$ is uniformly continuous on S.*

Proof. Let $\mathbf{u} = (u_0, u_1, \ldots)$ and $\mathbf{v} = (v_0, v_1, \ldots)$ be two sequences in $\mathbf{Seq}_\infty(S)$ such that $\lim_{n \to \infty} d(u_n, v_n) = 0$. By Theorem 5.43, the sequence $\mathbf{u}$ contains a convergent subsequence $(u_{p_0}, u_{p_1}, \ldots)$. If $x = \lim_{n \to \infty} u_{p_n}$, then $\lim_{n \to \infty} v_{p_n} = x$. The continuity of f implies that $\lim_{n \to \infty} e(f(u_{p_n}), f(v_{p_n})) = e(f(x), f(x)) = 0$, so f is uniformly continuous by Theorem 5.14. $\square$

Theorem 5.46. *Let (S, d) be a totally bounded metric space. Then (S, d) satisfies the second axiom of countability.*

Proof. By Theorem 5.23 it suffices to show that (S, d) is separable. For each positive $n \in \mathbb{N}$ there exists a finite subset $F_n = \{x_1, \ldots, x_n\}$ of S such that $S = \bigcup_{i=1}^{n} S(x_i, \frac{1}{n})$. Then $\bigcup_{n \geqslant 1} F_n$ is a countable set that is dense in S. $\square$

5.10 Contractions and Fixed Points

Definition 5.22. Let (S, d) and (T, d') be two metric spaces. A function $f : S \longrightarrow T$ is a *similarity* if there exists a number $c > 0$ for which $d'(f(x), f(y)) = cd(x, y)$ for every $x, y \in S$. If the two metric spaces coincide, we refer to f as a *self-similarity of (S, d)*.

The number c is called the *ratio* of the similarity f and is denoted by *ratio(f)*.

Note that an isometry is a similarity of ratio 1.

Example 5.20. Let $(\mathbb{R}, d)$ be the metric space defined by $d(x, y) = |x - y|$. Any linear mapping (that is, any mapping of the form $f(x) = ax + b$ for $x \in \mathbb{R}$) is a similarity having ratio a.

Definition 5.23. Let (S, d) and (T, d') be two metric spaces. If there exists $c > 0$ such that

$$d'(f(x), f(y)) \leqslant cd(x, y) \tag{5.6}$$

for all $x, y \in S$, then we say that f is a *Lipschitz function*.[2]

A number c that occurs in inequality (5.6) is a *Lipschitz constant* for f. If there exists a Lipschitz constant $c < 1$ for f, then f is a *contraction* with the *contraction constant* c.

A function $f : S \longrightarrow T$ is *locally Lipschitz* at $x_0 \in S$ if there exists $c > 0$ such that $d'(f(x_0), f(y)) \leqslant cd(x_0, y)$ for every $y \in S$.

Theorem 5.47. *Let $(S, \mathcal{O}_d)$ and $(T, \mathcal{O}_{d'})$ be two metric spaces. Every Lipschitz function $f : S \longrightarrow T$ is uniformly continuous.*

Proof. Suppose that $d'(f(x), f(y)) \leqslant cd(x, y)$ for $x, y \in S$ and let ϵ be a positive number. Define $\delta = \frac{\epsilon}{c}$. If $z \in f(B(x, \delta))$, there exists $y \in B(x, \delta)$ such that $z = f(y)$. This implies $d'(f(x), z) = d(f(x), f(y)) < cd(x, y) < c\delta = \epsilon$, so $z \in B(f(x), \epsilon)$. Thus, $f(B(x, \delta)) \subseteq B(f(x), \epsilon)$, which means that f is uniformly continuous. $\qquad\square$

It is easy to see, using a similar argument, that a locally Lipschitz function at x_0 is continuous in x_0.

Example 5.21. Let $a > 0$ and let $f : (0, a) \longrightarrow \mathbb{R}$ be the function defined by $f(x) = x^2$. We have

$$|f(x) - f(y)| = |x^2 - y^2| = (x + y)|x - y|$$
$$\leqslant 2a|x - y|,$$

so f is a Lipschitz function with the constant $2a$. Therefore, f is uniform continuous on $(0, a)$.

---

[2]Rudolf Lipschitz was born near Königsberg, Germany (now Kaliningrad, Russia) on May 14th 1832 and died in Bonn, Germany on October 7th 1903. He studied mathematics at the University of Königsberg and obtained his doctorate at the University of Berlin in 1857. Lipschitz taught at universities of Berlin, Breslau and Bonn. He has important contributions in number theory, Fourier series, differential equations, and in analytical mechanics.

A function f may be uniformly continuous on a set without being a Lipschitz function as the next example shows.

Example 5.22. Let $f : (0, \infty) \longrightarrow \mathbb{R}$ be the function defined by $f(x) = \sqrt{x}$ for $x > 0$. Suppose that f satisfies a Lischitz condition, that is, there exists $c > 0$ such that $|\sqrt{x} - \sqrt{y}| \leqslant c|x - y|$. This is equivalent to $1 \leqslant c(\sqrt{x} + \sqrt{y})$ for every $x, y > 0$. Choosing $x = y = \frac{1}{9c^2}$ leads to a contradiction.

On other hand, f is uniformly continuous. Indeed, note that for every $u, v \geqslant 0$ we have $\sqrt{u + v} \leqslant \sqrt{u} + \sqrt{v}$. If $|x - y| < \epsilon^2$, then either $x \leqslant y < x + \epsilon^2$ or $y \leqslant x < y + \epsilon^2$. The first inequality implies

$$\sqrt{x} \leqslant \sqrt{y} < \sqrt{x + \epsilon^2} \leqslant \sqrt{x} + \epsilon.$$

The second implies

$$\sqrt{y} \leqslant \sqrt{x} < \sqrt{y + \epsilon^2} \leqslant \sqrt{y} + \epsilon,$$

so, in either case, $|\sqrt{x} - \sqrt{y}| < \epsilon$, which shows that f is uniformly convergent on $(0, \infty)$.

A generalization of the class of Lipschitz functions is given next.

Definition 5.24. Let (S, d) and (T, d') be two metric spaces. If there exists $c > 0$ and $a \in (0, 1]$ such that $d'(f(x), f(y)) \leqslant cd(x, y)^a$ for all $x, y \in S$, then we say that f is an *a-Hölder function* on S.

Note that if $a, b \in (0, 1]$, where $a \leqslant b$, and $f : S \longrightarrow T$ is a b-Hölder function, then f is also an a-Hölder function. In general, Lipschitz functions are a-Hölder functions for $a \leqslant 1$, which are, in turn uniformly continuous on S.

Theorem 5.47 implies that every similarity is uniformly continuous.

Let $f : S \longrightarrow S$ be a function. We define inductively the functions $f^{(n)} : S \longrightarrow S$ for $n \in \mathbb{N}$ by

$$f^{(0)}(x) = x$$

and

$$f^{(n+1)}(x) = f(f^{(n)}(x))$$

for $x \in S$. The function $f^{(n)}$ is the nth *iteration of the function f*.

Example 5.23. Let $f : \mathbb{R} \longrightarrow \mathbb{R}$ be the function defined by $f(x) = ax + b$ for $x \in \mathbb{R}$, where $a, b \in \mathbb{R}$ and $a \neq 1$. It is easy to verify that $f^{(n)}(x) = a^n x + \frac{a^n - 1}{a - 1} \cdot b$ for $x \in \mathbb{R}$.

Definition 5.25. Let $f : S \longrightarrow S$ be a function. A *fixed point of f is a* member x of the set S that satisfies the equality $f(x) = x$.

Example 5.24. The function f defined in Example 5.23 has the fixed point $x_0 = \frac{b}{1-a}$.

Theorem 5.48. (Banach Fixed Point Theorem) *Let $(S, \mathcal{O}_d)$ be a complete topological metric space and let $f : S \longrightarrow S$ be a contraction on S having the contraction ratio c. There exists a unique fixed point $u \in S$ for f, and for any $x \in S$ we have $\lim_{n \to \infty} f^{(n)}(x) = u$. Moreover, we have*

$$d(f^{(n)}(x), u) \leqslant \frac{c^n}{1 - c} d(x, f(x))$$

for $x \in S$ and $n \in \mathbb{N}$.

Proof. Since f is a contraction, there exists a positive number $c \in (0, 1)$, such that $d(f(x), f(y)) \leqslant cd(x, y)$ for $x, y \in S$. Note that each such function has at most one fixed point. Indeed, suppose that we have both $u = f(u)$ and $v = f(v)$ and $u \neq v$, so $d(u, v) > 0$. Then, $d(f(u), f(v)) = d(u, v) \leqslant cd(u, v)$, which is absurd because $c < 1$.

The sequence $\mathbf{s} = (x, f(x), \ldots, f^{(n)}(x), \ldots)$ is a Cauchy sequence. Indeed, observe that

$$d(f^{(n)}(x), f^{(n+1)}(x)) \leqslant c\, d(f^{(n-1)}(x), f^{(n)}(x)) \leqslant \cdots \leqslant c^n d(x, f(x)).$$

For $n \leqslant p$, this implies

$$\begin{aligned}
d(f^{(n)}(x), f^{(p)}(x)) &\leqslant d(f^{(n)}(x), f^{(n+1)}(x)) + d(f^{(n+1)}(x), f^{(n+2)}(x)) \\
&\quad + \cdots + d(f^{(p-1)}(x), f^{(p)}(x)) \\
&\leqslant c^n d(x, f(x)) + \cdots + c^{p-1} d(x, f(x)) \\
&\leqslant \frac{c^n}{1 - c} d(x, f(x)),
\end{aligned}$$

which shows that the sequence $\mathbf{s}$ is indeed a Cauchy sequence. By the completeness of $(S, \mathcal{O}_d)$, there exists $u \in S$ such that $u = \lim_{n \to \infty} f^{(n)}(x)$. The continuity of f implies

$$u = \lim_{n \to \infty} f^{(n+1)}(x) = \lim_{n \to \infty} f(f^{(n)}(x)) = f(u),$$

so u is a fixed point of f.

Since $d(f^{(n)}(x), f^{(p)}(x)) \leqslant \frac{c^n}{1-c} d(x, f(x))$, we have

$$\lim_{p \to \infty} d(f^{(n)}(x), f^{(p)}(x)) = d(f^{(n)}(x), u) \leqslant \frac{c^n}{1 - c} d(x, f(x))$$

for $n \in \mathbb{N}$. $\qquad\square$

Theorem 5.49. *Let $B[x_0, r]$ be a closed sphere in a complete metric space $(S, \mathcal{O}_d)$ and let $f : B[x_0, r] \longrightarrow S$ be a contraction with a contraction constant c, $c \in (0, 1)$, such that $d(f(x_0), x_0) \leqslant (1 - c)r$. Then, f has a unique fixed point u in $B[x_0, r]$ and*

$$d(f^{(n)}(x), u) \leqslant rc^n d(x, f(x_0))$$

for $x \in B[x_0, r]$ and $n \in \mathbb{N}$.

Proof. Let $x \in B[x_0, r]$. We have

$$\begin{aligned}
d(f(x), x_0) &\leqslant d(f(x), f(x_0)) + d(f(x_0), x_0) \\
&\leqslant cd(x, x_0) + (1 - c)r \\
&\leqslant cr + (1 - c)r = r.
\end{aligned}$$

This shows that $f(B[x_0, r]) \subseteq B[x_0, r]$, hence f is a transformation of $B[x_0, r]$. The statement now follows immediately from the Banach Fixed Point Theorem (Theorem 5.48). $\qquad\square$

Corollary 5.12. *Let $B(x_0, r)$ be an open sphere in a complete metric space $(S, \mathcal{O}_d)$. If $f : B(x_0, r) \longrightarrow S$ is a contraction with the contraction constant c, $c \in (0, 1)$, such that $d(f(x_0), x_0) < (1 - c)r$, then f has a unique fixed point in $B(x_0, r)$.*

Proof. Let $B(x_0, r)$ be an open sphere and let sphere $B[x_0, r - \epsilon]$ be a closed sphere included in $B(x_0, r)$. By Theorem 5.49, f has a unique fixed point $u \in B[x_0, r - \epsilon]$ such that

$$d(f^{(n)}(x), u) \leqslant (r - \epsilon)c^n d(x, f(x_0))$$

for $x \in B[x_0, r - \epsilon]$ and $n \in \mathbb{N}$. Thus, the fixed point belongs to $B(x_0, r)$. $\qquad\square$

Theorem 5.50. *Let $(S, \mathcal{O}_d)$ be a complete topological metric space, $f : S \longrightarrow S$ be a contraction on S having the contraction ratio $c \in (0, 1)$ and let $x \in S$. If u is the unique fixed point of f, then*

$$d(x, u) \leqslant \frac{d(f(x), x)}{1 - c}.$$

Proof. Consider the closed sphere $B\left[x, \frac{d(f(x), x)}{1 - c}\right]$. By Theorem 5.49 applied to the restriction of f to this closed sphere, it follows that u belongs to this sphere. $\qquad\square$

Theorem 5.51. *Let $(S, \mathcal{O}_d)$ be a complete topological metric space and let (T, e) be any metric space. Suppose that $h : T \times S \longrightarrow S$ is a function such that $d(h(t, x), h(t, y)) \leqslant cd(x, y)$ (uniformly relative to $t \in T$), where $c \in (0, 1)$, for $t \in T$ and $x, y \in S$. Furthermore, assume that $h(t, x)$ is continuous in t for each fixed $x \in S$.*

For each $t \in T$ define $\psi(t)$ to be the unique fixed point u_t satisfying $h(t, u_t) = u_t$. The mapping ψ is continuous.

Proof.   Let $s \in T$ and let ϵ be a positive number. By the continuity of h there exists $\delta > 0$ such that $e(t, s) < \delta$ implies $d(h(t, u_s), h(s, u_s)) < \epsilon$. Since $h(s, u_s) = u_s$, we have $d(h(t, u_s), u_s) < \epsilon$, so u_s is moved at most ϵ by $h(t, \cdot)$. Thus, by Theorem 5.50, we have $d(u_t, u_s) \leqslant \frac{\epsilon}{1-\epsilon}$, which shows that ψ is continuous. $\qquad\square$

Corollary 5.13. *Let $(S, \mathcal{O}_d)$ be a complete topological metric space, (T, e) be any metric space and let $B(x, r)$ be an open sphere in S. Suppose that $h : T \times B(x, r) \longrightarrow S$ is a function such that $d(h(t, x), h(t, y)) \leqslant cd(x, y)$ (uniformly relative to $t \in T$), where $c \in (0, 1)$, for $t \in T$ and $x, y \in B(x, r)$. Furthermore, assume that $h(t, x)$ is continuous in t for each fixed $x \in S$ and that $d(h(t, x), x) < (1 - c)r$ for every $t \in T$.*

There exists a continuous mapping $\psi : T \longrightarrow B(x, r)$ such that for each $t \in T$ $h(t, \psi(t)) = \psi(t)$.

Proof.   This statement follows from Theorems 5.51 and 5.50. $\qquad\square$

5.11   The Hausdorff Metric Hyperspace of Compact Subsets

Lemma 5.3. *Let (S, d) be a metric space and let U and V be two subsets of S. If $r \in \mathbb{R}_{\geqslant 0}$ is such that $U \subseteq B(V, r)$ and $V \subseteq B(U, r)$, then we have $|d(x, U) - d(x, V)| \leqslant r$ for every $x \in S$.*

Proof.   Since $U \subseteq B(V, r)$, for every $u \in U$ there is $v \in V$ such that $d(u, v) < r$. Therefore, by the triangular inequality, it follows that for every $u \in U$ there is $v \in V$ such that $d(x, u) < d(x, v) + r$, so $d(x, U) < d(x, v) + r$. Consequently, $d(x, U) \leqslant d(x, V) + r$. In a similar manner, we can show that $V \subseteq B(U, r)$ implies $d(x, V) \leqslant d(x, U) + r$. Thus, $|d(x, U) - d(x, V)| \leqslant r$ for every $x \in S$. $\qquad\square$

Let $(S, \mathcal{O}_d)$ be a topological metric space. Denote by $\mathcal{K}(S, \mathcal{O}_d)$ the collection of all non-empty, compact subsets of $(S, \mathcal{O}_d)$, and define the mapping

$\delta : \mathcal{K}(S, \mathcal{O}_d)^2 \longrightarrow \mathbb{R}_{\geqslant 0}$ by

$$\delta(U, V) = \inf\{r \in \mathbb{R}_{\geqslant 0} \mid U \subseteq B(V, r) \text{ and } V \subseteq B(U, r)\}$$

for $U, V \in \mathcal{K}(S, \mathcal{O}_d)$.

Lemma 5.4. *Let U and V be two compact subsets of a topological metric space $(S, \mathcal{O}_d)$. We have*

$$\sup_{x \in S} |d(x, U) - d(x, V)| = \max\left\{\sup_{x \in V} d(x, U), \sup_{x \in U} d(x, V)\right\}.$$

Proof. Let $x \in S$. There is $v_0 \in V$ such that $d(x, v_0) = d(x, V)$ because V is a compact set. Then, the compactness of U implies that there is $u_0 \in U$ such that $d(u_0, v_0) = d(v_0, U)$. We have

$$\begin{aligned}
d(x, U) - d(x, V) &= d(x, U) - d(x, v_0) \\
&\leqslant d(x, u_0) - d(x, v_0) \\
&\leqslant d(u_0, v_0) \leqslant \sup_{x \in V} d(U, x).
\end{aligned}$$

Similarly, $d(x, U) - d(x, V) \leqslant \sup_{x \in U} d(x, V)$, which implies

$$\sup_{x \in S} |d(x, U) - d(x, V)| \leqslant \max\left\{\sup_{x \in V} d(x, U), \sup_{x \in U} d(x, V)\right\}.$$

On the other hand, since $U \subseteq S$, we have

$$\sup_{x \in S} |d(x, U) - d(x, V)| \geqslant \sup_{x \in U} |d(x, U) - d(x, V)| = \sup_{x \in U} d(x, V)$$

and, similarly, $\sup_{x \in S} |d(x, U) - d(x, V)| \geqslant \sup_{x \in V} d(x, U)$, and these inequalities prove that

$$\sup_{x \in S} |d(x, U) - d(x, V)| \geqslant \max\left\{\sup_{x \in V} d(x, U), \sup_{x \in U} d(x, V)\right\},$$

which concludes the argument. $\qquad\square$

An equivalent useful definition of δ is given in the next theorem.

Theorem 5.52. *Let (S, d) be a metric space and let U and V be two compact subsets of S. We have the equality*

$$\delta(U, V) = \sup_{x \in S} |d(x, U) - d(x, V)|.$$

Proof. Observe that we have both $U \subseteq B(V, \sup_{x \in U} d(x, V))$ and $V \subseteq B(U, \sup_{x \in V} d(x, U))$. Therefore, we have

$$\delta(U, V) \leqslant \max\left\{\sup_{x \in V} d(x, U), \sup_{x \in U} d(x, V)\right\}.$$

Combining this observation with Lemma 5.4 yields the desired equality.

$\qquad\square$

Theorem 5.53. *Let $(S, \mathcal{O}_d)$ be a complete topological metric space. The mapping $\delta : \mathcal{K}(S, \mathcal{O}_d)^2 \longrightarrow \mathbb{R}_{\geqslant 0}$ is a metric on $\mathcal{K}(S, \mathcal{O}_d)$.*

Proof. It is clear that $\delta(U, U) \geqslant 0$ and that $\delta(U, V) = \delta(V, U)$ for every $U, V \in \mathcal{K}(S, \mathcal{O}_d)$. Suppose that $\delta(U, V) = 0$; that is, $d(x, U) = d(x, V)$ for every $x \in S$. If $x \in U$, then $d(x, U) = 0$, so $d(x, V) = 0$. Since V is closed, by part (ii) of Theorem 5.16, we have $x \in V$, so $U \subseteq V$. The reverse inclusion can be shown in a similar manner.

To prove the triangular inequality, let $U, V, W \in \mathcal{K}(S, \mathcal{O}_d)$. Since

$$|d(x, U) - d(x, V)| \leqslant |d(x, U) - d(x, V)| + |d(x, V) - d(x, W)|,$$

for every $x \in S$, we have

$$\sup_{x \in S} |d(x, U) - d(x, V)| \leqslant \sup_{x \in S} \left(|d(x, U) - d(x, V)| + |d(x, V) - d(x, W)| \right)$$

$$\leqslant \sup_{x \in S} |d(x, U) - d(x, V)| + \sup_{x \in S} |d(x, V) - d(x, W)|,$$

which implies the triangular inequality

$$\delta(U, V) \leqslant \delta(U, W) + \delta(W, V). \qquad \square$$

The metric δ is known as the *Hausdorff metric*, and the metric space $(\mathcal{K}(S, \mathcal{O}_d), \delta)$ is known as the *Hausdorff metric hyperspace* of $(S, \mathcal{O}_d)$.

Theorem 5.54. *If $(S, \mathcal{O}_d)$ is a complete topological metric space, then so is the Hausdorff metric hyperspace $(\mathcal{K}(S, \mathcal{O}_d), \delta)$.*

Proof. Let $\mathbf{U} = (U_0, U_1, \ldots)$ be a Cauchy sequence in $(\mathcal{K}(S, \mathcal{O}_d), \delta)$ and let $U = \mathbf{K}(\bigcup_{n \in \mathbb{N}} U_n)$. It is clear that U consists of those elements x of S such that $x = \lim_{n \to \infty} x_n$ for some sequence $\mathbf{x} = (x_0, x_1, \ldots)$, where $x_n \in U_n$ for $n \in \mathbb{N}$.

The set U is totally bounded. Indeed, let $\epsilon > 0$ and let n_0 be such that $\delta(U_n, U_{n_0}) \leqslant \epsilon$ for $n \geqslant n_0$. Let N be an ϵ-net for the compact set $H = \bigcup_{n \leqslant n_0} U_n$. Clearly, $H \subseteq B(N, \epsilon)$. Since $\delta(U_n, U_{n_0}) \leqslant \epsilon$, it follows that $U \subseteq B(H, \epsilon)$, so $U \subseteq B(N, 2\epsilon)$. This shows that U is totally bounded. Since U is closed in the complete space $(S, \mathcal{O}_d)$, it follows that U is compact.

Let ϵ be a positive number. Since $\mathbf{U}$ is a Cauchy sequence, there exists $n_{\frac{\epsilon}{2}}$ such that $m, n \geqslant n_{\frac{\epsilon}{2}}$ implies $\delta(U_m, U_n) < \frac{\epsilon}{2}$; that is, $\sup_{s \in S} |d(s, U_m) - d(s, U_n)| < \frac{\epsilon}{2}$. In particular, if $x_m \in U_m$, then $d(x_m, U_n) = \inf_{y \in U_m} d(x, y) < \frac{\epsilon}{2}$, so there exists $y \in U_n$ such that $d(x_m, y) < \frac{\epsilon}{2}$.

For $x \in U$, there exists a sequence $\mathbf{x} = (x_0, x_1, \ldots)$ such that $x_n \in U_n$ for $n \in \mathbb{N}$ and $\lim_{n \to \infty} x_n = x$. Therefore, there exists a number $n'_{\frac{\epsilon}{2}}$ such that

$p \geqslant n'_{\frac{\epsilon}{2}}$ implies $d(x, x_p) < \frac{\epsilon}{2}$. This implies $d(x, y) \leqslant d(x, x_p) + d(x_p, y) \leqslant \epsilon$ if $n \geqslant \max\{n_{\frac{\epsilon}{2}}, n'_{\frac{\epsilon}{2}}\}$, and therefore $U \subseteq B(U_n, \epsilon)$.

Let $y \in U_n$. Since $\mathbf{U}$ is a Cauchy sequence, there exists a subsequence $\mathbf{U}' = (U_{k_0}, U_{k_1}, \ldots)$ of $\mathbf{U}$ such that $k_0 = q$ and $\delta(U_{k_j}, U_n) < 2^j \epsilon$ for all $n \geqslant k_j$.

Define the sequence $\mathbf{z} = (z_0, z_1, \ldots)$ by choosing z_k arbitrarily for $k < q$, $z_q = y$, and $z_k \in U_k$ for $k_j < k < k_{j+1}$ such that $d(z_k, z_{k_j}) < 2^{-j}\epsilon$. The sequence $\mathbf{z}$ is a Cauchy sequence in S, so there exists $z = \lim_{k \to \infty} z_k$ and $z \in U$. Since $d(y, z) = \lim_{k \to \infty} d(y, z_k) < \epsilon$, it follows that $y \in B(U, \epsilon)$. Therefore, $\delta(U, U_n) < \epsilon$, which proves that $\lim_{n \to \infty} U_n = U$. We conclude that $(\mathcal{K}(S, \mathcal{O}_d), \delta)$ is complete. $\qquad\square$

5.12   The Topological Space $(\mathbb{R}, \mathcal{O})$

Let $\mathbf{x} = (x_0, \ldots, x_n, \ldots)$ be a sequence of real numbers. Consider the sequence of sets (S_n), where $S_n = \{x_n, x_{n+1}, \ldots\}$ for $n \in \mathbb{N}$. It is clear that $S_0 \supseteq S_1 \supseteq \cdots \subseteq S_n \supseteq \cdots$. Therefore, we have the increasing sequence of numbers $\inf S_0 \leqslant \inf S_1 \leqslant \cdots \leqslant \inf S_n \leqslant \cdots$ and the decreasing sequence of numbers $\sup S_0 \geqslant \sup S_1 \geqslant \cdots \geqslant \sup S_n \geqslant \cdots$.

We define $\liminf \mathbf{x}$ as $\lim_{n \to \infty} \inf S_n$ and $\limsup \mathbf{x}$ as $\lim_{n \to \infty} \sup S_n$. The number $\liminf \mathbf{x}$ is referred to as the *limit inferior* of the sequence $\mathbf{x}$, while $\limsup x_n$ is referred to as the *limit superior* of $\mathbf{x}$.

Example 5.25. Let $\mathbf{x}$ be the sequence defined by $x_n = (-1)^n$ for $n \in \mathbb{N}$. It is clear that $\sup S_n = 1$ and $\inf S_n = -1$. Therefore, $\limsup \mathbf{x} = 1$ and $\liminf \mathbf{x} = -1$.

Theorem 5.55. *For every sequence $\boldsymbol{x}$ of real numbers, we have* $\liminf \boldsymbol{x} \leqslant \limsup \boldsymbol{x}$.

Proof.   Let $S_n = \{x_n, x_{n+1}, \ldots\}$, $y_n = \inf S_n$, and $z_n = \sup S_n$ for $n \in \mathbb{N}$.

If $p \geqslant n$, we have $S_p \subseteq S_n$, so $y_n \leqslant y_p \leqslant z_p \leqslant z_n$, so $y_n \leqslant z_p$ for every n, p such that $p \geqslant n$. Therefore, $\limsup \mathbf{x} = \lim_{p \to \infty} z_p \geqslant y_n$ for every $n \in \mathbb{N}$, which in turn implies $\liminf \mathbf{x} = \lim_{n \to \infty} y_n \leqslant \limsup \mathbf{x}$. $\qquad\square$

Corollary 5.14. *Let $\boldsymbol{x} = (x_0, x_1, \ldots, x_n, \ldots)$ be a sequence of real numbers. We have $\liminf x_n = \limsup x_n = \ell$ if and only if $\lim_{n \to \infty} x_n = \ell$.*

Proof.   Suppose that $\liminf \mathbf{x}_n = \limsup \mathbf{x}_n = \ell$ and that it is not the case that $\lim_{n \to \infty} x_n = \ell$. This means that there exists $\epsilon > 0$ such that, for every $m \in \mathbb{N}$, $n \geqslant m$ implies $|x_n - \ell| \geqslant \epsilon$, which is equivalent to $x_n \geqslant \ell + \epsilon$ or $x_n \leqslant \ell - \epsilon$. Thus, at least one of the following cases occurs:

(i) there are infinitely many n such that $x_n \geqslant \ell + \epsilon$, which implies that $\limsup x_n \geqslant \ell + \epsilon$, or

(ii) there are infinitely many n such that $x_n \leqslant -\epsilon$, which implies that $\liminf x_n \geqslant \ell - \epsilon$.

Either case contradicts the hypothesis, so $\lim_{n \to \infty} x_n = l$.

Conversely, suppose that $\lim_{n \to \infty} x_n = \ell$. There exists n_ϵ such that $n \geqslant n_\epsilon$ implies $\ell - \epsilon < x_n < \ell + \epsilon$. Thus, $\sup\{x_n \mid n \geqslant n_\epsilon\} \leqslant \ell + \epsilon$, so $\limsup \mathbf{x} \leqslant \ell + \epsilon$. Similarly, $y - \epsilon \leqslant \liminf \mathbf{x}$ and the inequality

$$\ell - \epsilon \leqslant \liminf \mathbf{x} \leqslant \limsup \mathbf{x} \leqslant \ell + \epsilon,$$

which holds for every $\epsilon > 0$, implies $\liminf \mathbf{x}_n = \limsup \mathbf{x}_n = \ell$. $\square$

The notion of limit inferior and limit superior can be extended to nets of real numbers.

Let $(x_i)_{i \in I}$ is a bounded net of $\mathbb{R}$ and let $S_i = \{x_p \mid p \geqslant i\}$. If $i \leqslant j$, $j \leqslant k$ implies $i \leqslant k$, so $S_j \subseteq S_i$. Therefore,

$$\inf S_i \leqslant \inf S_j \leqslant \sup S_j \leqslant \sup S_i.$$

Let $y_i = \inf S_i$ and $z_i = \sup S_i$ for $i \in I$. Then, $i \leqslant j$ implies

$$y_i \leqslant y_j \leqslant z_j \leqslant z_i,$$

so $y_j \leqslant z_i$ for every i, j such that $i \leqslant j$. Define $\liminf(x_i)_{i \in I} = \lim_I(y_i)$ and $\limsup(x_i)_{i \in I} = \lim_I(z_i)$. We have

$$\limsup(x_i)_{i \in I} = \lim_I(z_i) \geq y_i$$

for every $i \in I$, which, in turn implies $\limsup(x_i)_{i \in I} \geqslant \lim_I(y_i) = \liminf(x_i)_{i \in I}$.

In Example 4.21, we saw that every closed interval $[a, b]$ of $\mathbb{R}$ is a compact set. This allows us to prove the next statement.

Theorem 5.56. *Let $f : (a, b) \longrightarrow \mathbb{R}$ be a function that is continuous at $x_0 \in (a, b)$ and $f(x_0) \neq 0$. There exists an open sphere $B(x_0, r)$ such that $f(x)$ has the same sign as $f(x_0)$ for $x \in B(x_0, r)$.*

Proof. Suppose that $f(x_0) > 0$. Since f is continuous in x_0 for every positive ϵ there exists a positive δ such that $x \in B(x_0, \delta) \cap (a, b)$ implies $f(x_0) - \epsilon < f(x) < f(x_0) + \epsilon$. If δ corresponds to $\epsilon = \frac{f(x_0)}{2}$, then

$$\frac{f(x_0)}{2} < f(x) < \frac{3f(x_0)}{2},$$

so $f(x)$ has the same sign as $f(x_0)$ when $x \in B(x_0, \delta)$.

The argument is similar when $f(x_0) < 0$. $\square$

Theorem 5.57. (Bolzano's Theorem) *Let $f : [a, b] \longrightarrow \mathbb{R}$ be a function continuous on $[a, b]$ and suppose that $f(a)$ and $f(b)$ have opposite signs. There exists $c \in (a, b)$ such that $f(c) = 0$.*

Proof. Suppose that $f(a) > 0$ and $f(b) < 0$ and let $T = \{x \in [a, b] \mid f(x) \geqslant 0\}$. Since $a \in T$ it follows that $T \neq \emptyset$ and b is an upper bound of T. If $c = \sup T$, then $a < c < b$.

If $f(c) \neq 0$, by Theorem 5.56 there exists a $\delta > 0$ such that $c - \delta < x < c + \delta$ implies that $f(x)$ has the same sign as $f(c)$. If $f(c) > 0$, there exists $x > c$ such that $f(x) > 0$ contradicting the definition of c. If $f(c) < 0$, then $c - \frac{\delta}{2}$ is an upper bound for T, again contradicting the definition of c. Therefore, $f(c) = 0$. $\square$

Definition 5.26. Let S be a subset of $\mathbb{R}$. A function $f : S \longrightarrow \mathbb{R}$ has the *Darboux property on S* if for any $a, b \in S$ and any y between $f(a)$ and $f(b)$ there exists $c \in [a, b]$ such that $f(c) = y$.

Theorem 5.58. (Intermediate Value Theorem) *If $f : [a, b] \longrightarrow \mathbb{R}$ is continuous on $[a, b]$, then f has the Darboux property on S.*

Proof. Suppose that $f(a) < f(b)$ and let y be a number such that $f(a) < y < f(b)$. Note that for the function $g(x) = f(x) - y$ we have $g(a) < 0$ and $g(b) > 0$. By Bolzano's theorem, there exists $c \in [a, b]$ such that $g(c) = 0$, which is equivalent to $f(c) = y$. $\square$

The converse of the intermediate value theorem is false as the next example shows.

Example 5.26. Let $S = [0, 1)$ and let $f : S \longrightarrow \mathbb{R}$ be the function given by

$$f(x) = \begin{cases} \sin \frac{1}{x} & \text{if } x > 0, \\ 0 & \text{if } x = 0. \end{cases}$$

Since the limit of f in 0 does not exist the function is not continuous on S; however, it is easy to see that the function has the Darboux property.

Let $(S, \mathcal{O})$ be a topological space and let $C(S, \mathcal{O})$ be the set of continuous functions of the form $f : S \longrightarrow \mathbb{R}$. This set is a real linear space relative to the sum defined as $(f + g)(x) = f(x) + g(x)$ and the scalar multiplication defined as $(cf)(x) = cf(x)$ for $x \in S$.

The set $C_b(S, \mathcal{O})$ of continuous and bounded functions of the form $f : S \longrightarrow \mathbb{R}$ is a subspace of $C(S, \mathcal{O})$.

The linear space $C(S, \mathcal{O})$ is not finitely dimensional. Indeed, the infinite set of function $\{p_n \mid n \in \mathbb{N}\}$ in $C[a, b]$, where $p_n(x) = x^n$ is linearly independent.

A norm ν can be defined on $C(S, \mathcal{O})$ as $\nu(f) = \sup\{|f(x)| \mid x \in S\}$. Since $|f(x)| \leqslant \nu(f)$ and $|g(x)| \leqslant \nu(g)$ for $x \in S$, it follows that $|(f+g)(x)| \leqslant |f(x)| + |g(x)| \leqslant \nu(f) + \nu(g)$. Thus, $\nu(f + g) \leqslant \nu(f) + \nu(g)$. We leave to the reader the verification of the remaining properties of norms.

If (f_n) is a sequence of functions in $C_b(S, \mathcal{O})$ equipped with the norm ν_{sup} such that $\lim_{n \to \infty} f_n = f$, then the metric generated by this norm is denoted by d_{sup}.

Note that the function $z : S \longrightarrow \mathbb{R}$ defined as $z(x) = 0$ for $x \in S$ belongs to $C_b(S, \mathcal{O})$. If $f \in C_b(S, \mathcal{O})$, then $d(z, f) = \max\{|f(x)| \mid x \in S\} < \infty$.

The next statement shows that the $C_b(S, \mathcal{O})$ equipped with the topology induced by the metric d_{sup} is complete.

Theorem 5.59. *Let (f_n) be a sequence of functions in $C_b(S, \mathcal{O})$ such that $\lim_{n \to \infty} f_n = f$ (in the sense of d_{sup}). Then $f \in C_b(S, \mathcal{O})$.*

Proof. Let ϵ be a positive number and let n_ϵ be such that $d_{\text{sup}}(f_n, f) < \frac{\epsilon}{3}$. Since each of the functions f_n is continuous, there exists $U \in neigh_x(S, \mathcal{O})$ such that $|f_n(x) - f_n(y)| < \frac{\epsilon}{3}$ for every $y \in U$. Thus, if $n > n_\epsilon$ we have:

$$|f(x) - f(y)| \leqslant |f(x) - f_n(x)| + |f_n(x) - f_n(y)|$$
$$+ |f_n(y) - f(y)| < \epsilon,$$

which implies the continuity of f. Further, since $d(z, f) \leqslant d(z, f_n) + d(f_n, f)$, it follows that z is a bounded function, so $f \in C_b(S, \mathcal{O})$. $\square$

For nets whose set of values is $\hat{R}$ we can prove a variant of Cauchy's criterion that is less general but is easier to verify.

Theorem 5.60. *Every isotonic net of $\hat{\mathbb{R}}$ has a limit (finite or infinite).*

Proof. Let $(x_i)_{i \in I}$ be an isotonic map and let $X = \{x_i \mid i \in I\}$. Suppose that there exists $M = \sup X$ and let $m \in \mathbb{R}$ such that $m < M$. By the definition of $\sup X$ there exists x_{i_0} such that $m < x_{i_0} \leqslant M$. Since (x_i) is isotonic, $j > i_0$ implies $x_j \geqslant x_{i_0} > m$, which means that $\lim_I x_i = M$.

If X has no upper bound, then for any $a > 0$ there exists $x_{i_0} > a$. Since $i \geqslant i_0$ implies $x_i \geqslant x_{i_0}$, we have $x_i > a$ for $i \geqslant i_0$, so $\lim x_i = \infty$. $\square$

Every norm on a linear space generates a metric and, therefore, a metric topology. Therefore, topologies of normed linear spaces enjoy the properties previously discussed for metric spaces.

5.13 Series and Schauder Bases

Definition 5.27. A sequence of numbers $\mathbf{s} = (s_n)$ is a *numerical series* in $\mathbb{R}$, or just a *series*, if there exists a sequence (x_n) in $\mathbb{R}$ such that

$$s_n = x_0 + x_1 + \cdots + x_n$$

for $n \in \mathbb{N}$. The numbers x_n are the *terms* of the series $\mathbf{s}$, while the elements s_n are the *partial sums* of $\mathbf{s}$.

If the sequence (s_n) is convergent, then we say that the series $\mathbf{s}$ is *convergent*, or that the set $\{x_n \mid n \in \mathbb{N}\}$ is *summable*. If $s = \lim_{n \to \infty}(x_0 + \cdots + x_n)$ we often written

$$s = x_0 + \cdots + x_n + \cdots .$$

Thus $x_0 + \cdots + x_n + \cdots$ is defined as $\lim_{n \to \infty}(x_0 + \cdots + x_n)$.

If $\lim_{n \to \infty} s_n = s$, then s is the *sum* of the series $\mathbf{s}$ and we write $s = \sum_{n \in \mathbb{N}} x_n$.

The number $s_n = \sum_{i=0}^{n} x_i$ is the nth *partial sum* of the series $\mathbf{s}$.

If $\mathbf{s}$ is not convergent, then we say that it is *divergent*.

Note that the series $x_0 + x_1 + \cdots$ and $x_k + x_{k+1} + \cdots$ are convergent or divergent in the same time.

A series $s_n = \sum_{i \leqslant n} x_i$ is convergent if and only if for every $\epsilon > 0$ there exists a number n_ϵ such that for $n \geqslant n_\epsilon$ and $p \in \mathbb{N}$ we have:

$$\|s_{n+p} - s_n\| = \|x_{n+1} + \cdots + x_{n+p}\| \leqslant \epsilon.$$

This is a mere restatement of the completeness property of $\mathbb{R}$.

Note that if a series $\mathbf{s}$ is convergent then we have $\lim_{n \to \infty} x_n = \lim_{n \to \infty}(s_n - s_{n-1}) = 0$.

Theorem 5.61. *If (x_n) and (y_n) are two convergent series, then $(x_n + y_n)$ is a convergent series and $\sum_{n \in \mathbb{N}}(x_n + y_n) = \sum_{n \in \mathbb{N}} x_n + \sum_{n \in \mathbb{N}} y_n$. Also, for any $a \in \mathbb{R}$ the series (ax_n) converges and $\sum_{n \in \mathbb{N}} ax_n = a \sum_{n \in \mathbb{N}} x_n$.*

Proof. The statements of the theorem follow immediately from Definition 5.27. □

Theorem 5.62. *Let $\mathbf{s}$ be a convergent series having sum s. We have* $\lim_{n \to \infty} \|x_n\| = 0$.

Proof. For $\epsilon > 0$ there exists a number n_ϵ such that for $n \geqslant n_\epsilon$ and for $p \in \mathbb{N}$ we have $|s_{n+p} - s_n| = |x_{n+1} + \cdots + x_{n+1}| \leqslant \epsilon$. In particular $|s_{n+1} - s_n| = |x_{n+1}| < \epsilon$, which implies $\lim_{n \to \infty} |x_n| = 0$. □

Note that the converse of Theorem 5.62 is false. Indeed, consider the series $1 + \frac{1}{2} + \cdots + \frac{1}{n} + \cdots$, where $x_n = \frac{1}{n}$. Clearly, $\lim_{n \to \infty} |x_n| = \lim_{n \to \infty} \frac{1}{n} = 0$. However this series (called the *harmonic series*) is divergent. Indeed, note that

$$
\begin{aligned}
s_{2n} - s_n &= \frac{1}{n+1} + \frac{1}{n+2} + \cdots + \frac{1}{2n} \\
&> \frac{1}{2n} + \frac{1}{2n} + \cdots + \frac{1}{2n} > \frac{1}{2},
\end{aligned}
$$

which contradicts the convergence of (s_n).

Definition 5.28. A series $s = x_0 + \cdots + x_n + \cdots$ is *absolutely convergent* (or the sequence (x_n) is *absolutely summable*) if the series of non-negative numbers $|x_0| + \cdots + |x_n| + \cdots$ is convergent.

Theorem 5.63. *An absolutely convergent series is convergent.*

Proof. Let $s = \sum x_n$ be an absolutely convergent series. In other word, the sequence of partial sums (z_n), where $z_n = |x_0| + \cdots + |x_n|$ for $n \in \mathbb{N}$ is convergent. We have

$$
|s_{n+p} - s_n| \leqslant |x_{n+1}| + \cdots + |x_{n+p}| \leqslant z_{n+p} - z_n.
$$

The desired conclusion follows immediately. $\square$

Definition 5.29. A series $s = \sum x_n$ is *semiconvergent* if it is convergent but the series $\sum |x_n|$ is divergent.

Theorem 5.64. (Leibniz' Theorem) *Let (x_n) be a sequence of positive numbers and let s be the series $x_0 - x_1 + x_2 - x_3 + \cdots + x_{2n} - x_{2n+1} + \cdots$. If $x_0 > x_1 > \cdots > x_n > x_{n+1} > \cdots$ and $\lim_{n \to \infty} x_n = 0$, then s is a convergent series.*

Proof. Consider separately the sequence of even ranked partial sums $s_0, s_2, s_4, \ldots$ and $s_1, s_3, s_5, \ldots$. Note that the first sequence is decreasing, while the second is increasing. Moreover, since

$$
s_{2n} = x_0 - x_1 + x_2 - \cdots - x_{2n-1} + x_{2n} \geqslant s_1,
$$
$$
s_{2n-1} = x_0 - x_1 + x_2 - \cdots x_{2n-2} - x_{2n-1} \leqslant x_0,
$$

it follows that both sequences are convergent. Furthermore, from the equality $s_{2n} = s_{2n-1} + x_{2n}$, it follows that $\lim_{n \to \infty} s_{2n} = \lim_{n \to \infty} s_{2n-1}$, so the sequence of all partial sums is convergent. $\square$

A series of the form $x_0 - x_1 + x_2 - \cdots$, where $x_n > 0$ for $n \in \mathbb{N}$ is an *alternate series*.

Example 5.27. By Leibniz' Theorem the alternate series

$$1 - \frac{1}{2} + \frac{1}{3} - \cdots + (-1)^n \frac{1}{n+1} + \cdots$$

is convergent. However, it is not absolutely convergent because the series

$$1 + \frac{1}{2} + \frac{1}{3} + \cdots + \frac{1}{n+1} + \cdots$$

is the divergent harmonic series, which shows that the series considered is semiconvergent. Thus, the reciprocal of Theorem 5.63 is false.

Theorem 5.65. *Let $\sum x_n$ and $\sum y_n$ be two series with positive terms. If $x_n \leqslant y_n$ for $n \in \mathbb{N}$, then the convergence of $\sum y_n$ implies the convergence of $\sum x_n$; further, if $\sum x_n$ is divergent, then $\sum y_n$ is divergent.*

Proof. Let $s_n = x_0 + \cdots + x_n$ and $z_n = y_0 + \cdots + y_n$ be the partial sums of order n. Since $x_n \leqslant y_n$, it follows that $s_n \leqslant z_n$ for $n \in \mathbb{N}$. If (s_n) is divergent, then so is (z_n).

Suppose that (z_n) is convergent and let $z = \lim_{n \to \infty} z_n$. Since $s_n \leqslant z_n < z$ it follows that the sequence (s_n) is monotonic and has an upper bound. Thus, (s_n) is a convergent sequence. $\qquad \square$

Theorem 5.66. *Let $\sum x_n$ and $\sum y_n$ be two series with positive terms. If*

$$\frac{x_{n+1}}{x_n} < \frac{y_{n+1}}{y_n}$$

for $n \in \mathbb{N}$, then the convergence of $\sum y_n$ implies the convergence of $\sum x_n$ and the divergence of $\sum x_n$ implies the divergence of $\sum y_n$.

Proof. The inequalities that exist by hypothesis imply

$$\frac{x_0}{y_0} > \frac{x_1}{y_1} > \cdots > \frac{x_n}{y_n} > \cdots .$$

If $k = \frac{x_0}{y_0}$ we have

$$x_1 < ky_1, x_2 < ky_2, \ldots, x_n < ky_n, \ldots .$$

The desired conclusion follows immediately from Theorem 5.65. $\qquad \square$

Theorem 5.67. *Let $\sum x_n$ and $\sum y_n$ be two series with positive terms. If*

$$0 < \liminf \frac{x_n}{y_n} \leqslant \limsup \frac{x_n}{y_n} < \infty,$$

then both series $\sum x_n$ and $\sum y_n$ are either convergent or divergent.

Proof. Let a, b be two positive numbers such that

$$a < \liminf \frac{x_n}{y_n} \leqslant \limsup \frac{x_n}{y_n} < b.$$

There exists a number n_0 such that if $n \geqslant n_0$ then $ay_n < x_n < by_n$, which implies the statement of the theorem. $\qquad\square$

Let $\sigma : \mathbb{N} \longrightarrow \mathbb{N}$ be a bijection and let $x_0 + x_1 + \cdots + x_n + \cdots$ be a series that is absolutely convergent. The series obtained by permuting this series using σ is the series $x_{\sigma(0)} + x_{\sigma(1)} + \cdots + x_{\sigma(n)} + \cdots$.

Theorem 5.68. *If $s = x_0 + x_1 + \cdots + x_n + \cdots$ is an absolutely convergent series and $\sigma : \mathbb{N} \longrightarrow \mathbb{N}$ be a bijection, then the series $x_{\sigma(0)} + x_{\sigma(1)} + \cdots + x_{\sigma(n)} + \cdots$ is absolutely convergent and the sums of these series are equal.*

Proof. Let $s_n = x_0 + x_1 + \cdots + x_n$ and let $z_n = |x_0| + |x_1| + \cdots + |x_n|$. Since $x_0 + x_1 + \cdots + x_n + \cdots$ is absolutely convergent, for every $\epsilon > 0$ there exists n_ϵ such that $|z_{n_\epsilon+p} - z_{n_\epsilon+q}| < \frac{\epsilon}{2}$ for every $p, q \in \mathbb{N}$. If $q > p$ this means that $|x_{n_\epsilon+p+1}| + \cdots + |x_{n_\epsilon+q}| < \frac{\epsilon}{2}$.

Since the series $x_0 + x_1 + \cdots$ is convergent we may assume that we also have $|s_n - s| < \frac{\epsilon}{2}$ if $n \geqslant n_\epsilon$. There exists n' (which depends on n_ϵ) such that if $m > n'$, z_m contains all terms of n_ϵ and terms that follow these terms in the original series $x_{n'+k_0}, x_{n'+k_1}, \ldots$. This implies $|z_m - s_n| < \frac{\epsilon}{2}$. Since $s - z_m = (s - s_{n_\epsilon}) + (s_{n_\epsilon} - z_m)$, it follows that $|s - z_m| < \epsilon$ if $m > n'$, which shows that the series $x_{\sigma(0)} + x_{\sigma(1)} + \cdots + x_{\sigma(n)} + \cdots$ is convergent and its sum is s. $\qquad\square$

Lemma 5.5. *Let $\sum x_n$ be a semiconvergent series, and let a_n and $-b_n$ the sums of the positive terms and the sum of the negative terms contained in the first n terms of the series $\sum x_n$, respectively. We have $\lim_{n\to\infty} a_n = \lim_{n\to\infty} b_n = \infty$.*

Proof. Let $s_n = x_0 + x_1 + \cdots + x_n$ and let $z_n = |x_0| + |x_1| + \cdots + |x_n|$. We have $s_n = a_n - b_n$ and $z_n = a_n + b_n$, so $a_n = \frac{1}{2}(s_n + z_n)$ and $b_n = \frac{1}{2}(z_n - s_n)$. Since $\lim_{n\to\infty} s_n$ is finite and $\lim_{n\to\infty} z_n = \infty$, it follows that $\lim_{n\to\infty} a_n = \lim_{n\to\infty} b_n = \infty$. $\qquad\square$

Theorem 5.69. (**Riemann's**[3] **Theorem**) *Let $\sum x_n$ be a semiconvergent series. For any number $r \in \mathbb{R}$ there exists a bijection σ of $\mathbb{N}$ such that the*

---

[3]Georg Riemann (Sept. 17th 1826–July 20th 1866) was a very influential German mathematician who made lasting contributions to analysis, number theory, and differential geometry. He served as a Professor and Chair of Mathematics at Göttingen.

series $\sum x_{\sigma(n)}$ *converges to* r*; Furthermore, there exists a bijection* σ *of* $\mathbb{N}$ *such that the series* $\sum x_{\sigma(n)}$ *is divergent.*

Proof. We rearrange the terms of the series $\sum x_n$ as follows. First, we consider the shortest sequence of positive terms in the order they appear in $\sum x_n$ such that their sum exceeds r; then, we will continue with the shortest sequence of negative terms in the order they appear in $\sum x_n$ such that the sum of the terms is less than r. Then, we continue with the shortest sequence of remaining positive term until the sum exceeds r, etc. This rearrangement is possible because, as we saw in Lemma 5.5, we have $\lim_{n\to\infty} a_n = \lim_{n\to\infty} b_n = \infty$.

We shall prove that the series obtained in this manner is convergent and its sum is r. Let $r_0, r_1, \ldots, r_n, \ldots$ be the partial sums of the new series and let t_n be the number of terms (positive and negative) considered in the first n rearranging operations.

If n is even, then $r_{t_n} > r$ and $r_{t_n} - x_{t_n-1} < r$, hence $0 < r_{t_n} - r < x_{t_n-1}$. (Note that the term of the original series is x_{t_n-1} because the terms of the series are numbered beginning with 0.)

If n is odd then $r_{t_n} < r$ and $r_{t_n} - x_{t_n-1} > r$, hence $x_{t_n-1} < r_{t_n} - r < 0$. Thus, for any $n \in \mathbb{N}$ we have $|r - r_{t_n}| < |x_{t_n-1}|$. Since $p_n \geq n$, we have $\lim_{n\to\infty} p_n = \infty$. The convergence of $\sum x_n$ implies $\lim_{n\to\infty} x_{t_n-1} = 0$, hence $\lim_{n\to\infty} r_{t_n} = r$, which proves the first part of the theorem.

For the second part, we rearrange the terms of the series by choosing the least number of positive terms whose sum exceeds 1, followed by the least number of negative terms that makes the sum less than 1, then the least number of positive terms that yields a sum greater than 2, etc. In the $2n - 1^{\text{st}}$ rearranging we select the least amount of positive terms that gives a sum that exceeds n; in the $2n^{\text{th}}$ rearranging we select the least number of negative terms that results in a partial sum less than n.

Let p_n be the number of terms selected in the first $2n - 1$ operations and let q_n be the number of terms selected in the first $2n$ operations. We have as above $0 < r_{p_n} - n < x_{p_n}$ and $0 < n - r_{q_n} < -x_{q_n}$. Recall that $\lim_{n\to\infty} x_{p_n} = \lim_{n\to\infty} x_{q_n} = 0$.

Let $a > 0$ and let $m \in \mathbb{N}$ be such that for $n > m$ we have

$$a + 1 < n, |x_{p_n}| < 1, |x_{q_n}| < 1.$$

It is clear that $r_{p_n} > n > a$. The choice of n implies $a < n - 1 < r_{q_n}$, so for $n > m$ we have both $r_{p_n} > a$ and $r_{q_n} > a$, which implies $\lim_{n\to\infty} r_{p_n} = \lim_{n\to\infty} r_{q_n} = \infty$.

To complete the proof, let c, d be two numbers such that $c < d$. This time we rearrange the terms of the series by choosing first the least number of positive terms such that their sum exceeds d; then select the least number of terms such that the sum is below c. Then, add the least number of positive terms such that the sum exceeds d, etc. If p_n is the number of terms considered in the nth operation, then the sequence $r_{p_1}, r_{p_3}, r_{p_5}, \ldots$ tends towards d, while the sequence $r_{p_2}, r_{p_4}, r_{p_6}, \ldots$ tends towards c, so the sequence $r_1, r_2, \ldots$ cannot be convergent. $\qquad\square$

The notion of series in normed linear spaces is a generalization of the notion of numerical series. The notations introduced for numerical series are extended naturally.

Definition 5.30. Let $(S, \|\cdot\|)$ be a normed linear space. A sequence $\mathbf{s} = (s_n)$ is a *series* in S if there exists a sequence (x_n) in this space such that

$$s_n = x_0 + x_1 + \cdots + x_n$$

for $n \in \mathbb{N}$. The elements x_n are the *terms* of the series $\mathbf{s}$, while the elements s_n are the *partial sums* of $\mathbf{s}$.

If the sequence (s_n) is convergent, then we say that the series $\mathbf{s}$ is *convergent* and for the limit s of this sequence we can write $s = \lim_{n\to\infty}(x_0 + \cdots + x_n)$. This equality is often written as

$$s = x_0 + \cdots + x_n + \cdots,$$

which amounts to defining $x_0 + \cdots + x_n + \cdots$ as $\lim_{n\to\infty}(x_0 + \cdots + x_n)$.

If $\lim_{n\to\infty} s_n = s$, then s is the *sum* of the series $\mathbf{s}$ and we write $s = \sum_{n\in\mathbb{N}} x_n$.

The nth *partial sum* of the series $\mathbf{s}$ is $s_n = \sum_{i=0}^{n} x_i$.

If $\mathbf{s}$ is not convergent, then we say that it is *divergent*.

Note that the series $x_0 + x_1 + \cdots$ and $x_k + x_{k+1} + \cdots$ are convergent or divergent in the same time.

Let $(S, \|\cdot\|)$ be a complete normed space. A series $s_n = \sum_{i\leqslant n} x_i$ is convergent if and only if for every $\epsilon > 0$ there exists a number n_ϵ such that for $n \geqslant n_\epsilon$ and for $p \in \mathbb{N}$ we have

$$\|s_{n+p} - s_n\| = \|x_{n+1} + \cdots + x_{n+1}\| \leqslant \epsilon.$$

If a series $\mathbf{s}$ in a normed space $(S, \|\cdot\|)$ is convergent then we have:

$$\lim_{n\to\infty} x_n = \lim_{n\to\infty} (s_n - s_{n-1}) = 0.$$

Theorem 5.70. *If (x_n) and (y_n) are two convergent series in a normed space $(S, \| \cdot \|)$, then $(x_n + y_n)$ is a convergent series and $\sum_{n \in \mathbb{N}} (x_n + y_n) = \sum_{n \in \mathbb{N}} x_n + \sum_{n \in \mathbb{N}} y_n$. Also, for any scalar a the series (ax_n) converges and $\sum_{n \in \mathbb{N}} ax_n = a \sum_{n \in \mathbb{N}} x_n$.*

Proof. The statements of the theorem follow immediately from Definition 5.30. $\qquad\square$

Theorem 5.71. *Let $s = x_0 + x_1 + \cdots$ be a convergent series having sum s in a normed space $(S, \| \cdot \|)$. We have $\lim_{n \to \infty} \|x_n\| = 0$.*

Proof. For $\epsilon > 0$ there exists a number n_ϵ such that for $n \geqslant n_\epsilon$ and for $p \in \mathbb{N}$ we have $\|s_{n+p} - s_n\| = \|x_{n+1} + \cdots + x_{n+1}\| \leqslant \epsilon$. In particular $\|s_{n+1} - s_n\| = \|x_{n+1}\| < \epsilon$, which implies $\lim_{n \to \infty} \|x_n\| = 0$. $\qquad\square$

Definition 5.31. A series $s = x_0 + \cdots + x_n + \cdots$ in a normed space $(S, \| \cdot \|)$ is *absolutely convergent* if the series of non-negative numbers $\|x_0\| + \cdots + \|x_n\| + \cdots$ is convergent.

Alternatively, we say that the sequence (x_n) is *absolutely summable*.

Theorem 5.72. *A normed space $(S, \| \cdot \|)$ is complete if and only if every absolutely convergent series $s = x_0 + \cdots + x_n + \cdots$ is convergent.*

Proof. Suppose that every absolutely convergent series in S converges. Let (x_n) be a Cauchy sequence. For each $j \geqslant 1$ there exists n_j such that $m, n \geqslant n_j$ implies $\|x_n - x_m\| \leqslant 2^{-j}$. Let $z_0 = n_0$ and $z_j = x_{n_j} - x_{n_{j-1}}$ for $j \geqslant 1$. Since $\|z_j\| \leqslant 2^{-j}$ the series (z_j) is absolutely convergent, and so it is convergent. Note that for the partial sum $u_j = \sum \{z_i \mid i < j\}$ we have $u_j = x_{n_j}$. Since (u_j) is convergent it follows that the subsequence (x_{n_j}) is convergent, so the sequence (x_n) is convergent by Theorem 5.28. Thus, $(S, \| \cdot \|)$ is complete.

Conversely, let $(S, \| \cdot \|)$ be complete and let $s = x_0 + \cdots + x_n + \cdots$ be an absolutely convergent series. Let $t_n = \sum_{i=0}^{n} \|x_i\|$ for $n \in \mathbb{N}$. If $m < n$ we have

$$\|s_n - s_m\| = \left\| \sum_{k=m+1}^{n} x_i \right\| \leqslant \sum_{k=m+1}^{n} \|x_i\| = t_n - t_m.$$

The sequence of real numbers (t_n) is a Cauchy sequence because of the convergence of $\sum_{i=0}^{\infty} \|x_i\|$. Therefore, the sequence of partial sums (s_n) is a Cauchy sequence in $(S, \| \cdot \|)$, hence the series $\sum_{n=0}^{\infty} x_n$ is convergent. $\qquad\square$

Definition 5.32. Let $(S, \| \cdot \|)$ be an $\mathbb{F}$-normed linear space. A sequence (e_n) of distinct elements of S is a *Schauder basis* if every $x \in S$ can be uniquely represented as $x = \sum_{n \in \mathbb{N}} a_i e_i$, where $a_i \in \mathbb{F}$ for $i \in \mathbb{N}$.

Theorem 5.73. *A normed linear space that has a Schauder basis is separable.*

Proof. Let (e_n) be a Schauder basis of a normed linear space $(S, \| \cdot \|)$. The set C that consists of elements of S of the form $x = \sum_{i=1}^{n} r_i e_i$, where $r_i \in \mathbb{Q}$ for $1 \leqslant i \leqslant n$ is countable. We claim that C is dense in S.

Let x be an arbitrary element of S that can be written as $x = \sum_{i \geqslant 1} a_i e_i$. For $x_n = \sum_{i=1}^{n} a_i e_i$ we have $\lim_{n \to \infty} x_n = x$.

For every $n \geqslant 1$ consider a sequence of rational numbers $(r_{n1}, \ldots, r_{nn})$ such that $|r_{ni} - a_i| < \frac{1}{n^2 \|e_i\|}$ for $1 \leqslant i \leqslant n$. Define $y_n = \sum_{i=1}^{n} r_{ni} e_i \in C$ and

$$
\left\| y_n - \sum_{i=1}^{n} a_i x_i \right\| = \left\| \sum_{i=1}^{n} r_{ni} e_i - \sum_{i=1}^{n} a_i x_i \right\|
$$

$$
= \left\| \sum_{i=1}^{n} (r_{ni} - a_i) e_i \right\| \leqslant \sum_{i=1}^{n} |r_{ni} - a_i| \|e_i\|
$$

$$
\leqslant \sum_{i=1}^{n} \frac{1}{n^2 \|e_i\|} \|e_i\| \leqslant \frac{1}{n}.
$$

Since $\|y_n - x\| \leqslant \|y_n - x_n\| + \|x_n - x\|$ and $\lim_{n \to \infty} \|y_n - x_n\| = \lim_{n \to \infty} \|x_n - x\| = 0$, it follows that $\lim_{n \to \infty} \|y_n - x\| = 0$, which concludes the argument. $\square$

Example 5.28. Let $\mathbf{e}_i = (0, 0, \ldots, 0, 1, 0, \ldots)$ be an infinite sequence of real numbers that consists of 0s with the exception of the ith component which equals 1. The normed space $(\ell^1(\mathbb{R}), \| \cdot \|)$ is separable because the sequence $(\mathbf{e}_n)$ is a Schauder basis of this space.

Let $(f_n)_{n \geqslant 1}$ be a sequence of real-valued functions defined on a metric space $(S, \| \cdot \|)$. Define the sequence of partial sums (s_n) as consisting of functions $s_n : S \longrightarrow \mathbb{R}$ given by $s_n(x) = \sum_{j=1}^{n} f_j(x)$ for $x \in S$. If the sequence (s_n) converges pointwise (uniformly) to s, we say that the series $\sum_{n \geqslant 1} f_n(x)$ converges pointwise (uniformly) to s. In either case, we write $s = \sum_{n \geqslant 1} f_n$.

It is immediate that uniform convergence of a series of functions implies pointwise convergence.

Theorem 5.74. (Weierstrass M-test) *Let $(f_n)_{n \geqslant 1}$ be a series of real-valued functions defined on a normed space $(S, \|\cdot\|)$. If there exists a convergent series $\sum_{n \geqslant 1} M_n$ of non-negative real numbers such that $|f_n(x)| \leqslant M_n$ for $n \geqslant 1$ and $x \in S$, the series $\sum_{n \geqslant 1} f_n$ converges uniformly.*

Proof. Let ϵ be a positive number. Since the series $\sum_{n \geqslant 1} M_n$ converges, there exists n_ϵ such that $m, p > n_\epsilon$ implies $\sum_{n=m}^{p} M_n < \epsilon$. Therefore, for every $x \in S$ and $m, p > n_\epsilon$ we have $|\sum_{n=m}^{p} f_n(x)| \leqslant \sum_{n=m}^{p} |f_n(x)| \leqslant < \epsilon$, so the series $\sum_{n \geqslant 1} f_n$ converges uniformly. $\qquad\square$

5.14 Equicontinuity

Definition 5.33. Let (S, d) and (T, e) be two metric spaces. A collection of functions $\mathcal{F} = \{f_i \mid i \in I\}$ is *equicontinuous* at x_0 (where $x_0 \in S$) if for every $\epsilon > 0$ there exists $\delta > 0$ such that for every $f_i \in \mathcal{F}$, $d(x, x_0) < \delta$ implies $e(f_i(x), f_i(x_0)) < \epsilon$.

$\mathcal{F}$ is *equicontinuous* if it is equicontinuous at every $x_0 \in S$.

Note that if $\mathcal{F}$ is an equicontinuous family at x_0, the positive number δ is the same for every function f that is a member of $\mathcal{F}$; thus, δ depends on x_0 and on ϵ.

Theorem 5.75. *Let (S, d) and (T, e) be two metric spaces and let $\mathcal{F} = \{f_n : S \longrightarrow T \mid n \in \mathbb{N}\}$ be a countable equicontinuous collection of functions. If (T, e) is complete and $(f_n(z))$ converges for all $z \in D$, where D is a dense subset of (S, d), then $(f_n(x))$ converges for all $x \in S$.*

Proof. Since D is dense in S for every $x \in S$ and every $\delta > 0$ there exists $z \in D$ such that $d(z, x) < \delta$.

The equicontinuity of $\mathcal{F}$ means that there exists δ such that for every f_n, $d(z, x) < \delta$ implies $e(f_n(z), f_n(x)) < \frac{\epsilon}{3}$ for $z \in D$ and $x \in S$.

Since $(f_n(z))$ converges for all $z \in D$ there exists n_ϵ such that $n, m \geqslant n_\epsilon$ implies $e(f_n(z), f_m(z)) < \frac{\epsilon}{3}$. Therefore, if $n, m \geqslant n_\epsilon$ we have

$$e(f_n(x), f_m(x)) \leqslant e(f_n(x), f_n(z)) + e(f_n(z), f_m(z)) + e(f_m(z), f_m(x))$$
$$< 3\frac{\epsilon}{3} = \epsilon.$$

This means that $(f_n(x))$ is a Cauchy sequence in (T, e) and, since T is complete, it converges. Thus, $(f_n(x))$ converges for every x. $\qquad\square$

Theorem 5.76. *Let (S, d) and (T, e) be two metric spaces and let $\mathcal{F} = \{f_n : S \longrightarrow T \mid n \in \mathbb{N}\}$ be a countable equicontinuous collection of functions. If*

$f : S \longrightarrow T$ *is a function such that* $\lim_{n \to \infty} f_n(x) = f(x)$ *for* $x \in S$, *then* f *is a continuous function. Furthermore,* $\mathcal{F} \cup \{f\}$ *is also an equicontinuous collection of functions.*

Proof.   For $\epsilon > 0$ and $x, y \in S$ there exists $\delta > 0$ such that $d(x, y) < \delta$ implies $e(f_n(x), f_n(y)) < \frac{\epsilon}{3}$ for $n \in \mathbb{N}$ because $\mathcal{F}$ is equicontinuous.

Since $\lim_{n \to \infty} f_n(x) = f(x)$ there exists n_ϵ such that $n \geqslant n_\epsilon$ implies $e(f(x), f_n(x)) < \frac{\epsilon}{3}$ and $e(f(y), f_n(y)) < \frac{\epsilon}{3}$. Then, $n \geqslant n_\epsilon$ and $d(x, y) < \delta$ imply

$$e(f(x), f(y)) \leqslant e(f(x), f_n(x)) + e(f_n(x), f_n(y)) + e(f_n(y), f(y))$$
$$\leqslant \epsilon,$$

which shows that f is a continuous function. The equicontinuity of $\mathcal{F} \cup \{f\}$ follows from the fact that $d(x, y) < \delta$ implies $e(f_n(x), f_n(y)) < \epsilon$, which in turn, yields $e(f(x), f(y)) < \epsilon$, due to the continuity of the metric e.   □

A stronger property is given next.

Definition 5.34. Let (S, d) and (T, e) be two metric spaces. A collection of functions $\mathcal{F} = \{f_i \mid i \in I\}$ is *uniformly equicontinuous* if for every $\epsilon > 0$ there exists $\delta > 0$ such that $d(x, x') < \delta$ implies $e(f_i(x), f_i(x')) < \epsilon$ for every $x, x' \in S$ and $i \in I$.

Example 5.29. Let M be a positive number and let $\mathcal{F}_M$ be the family of functions

$$\mathcal{F}_M = \{f : \mathbb{R} \longrightarrow \mathbb{R} \mid |f(x) - f(x')| \leqslant M|x - x'| \text{ for } x, x' \in \mathbb{R}\},$$

where $\mathbb{R}$ is equipped with the metric defined by $d(x, x') = |x - x'|$ for $x, x' \in \mathbb{R}$.

$\mathcal{F}_M$ is uniformly equicontinuous. Indeed, if $\epsilon > 0$ it suffices to take $\delta = \frac{\epsilon}{M}$ to obtain

$$|f(x) - f(x')| \leqslant M|x - x'| < M \cdot \frac{\epsilon}{M} = \epsilon$$

for every $f \in \mathcal{F}_M$.

Theorem 5.77. *Let* $(S, \mathcal{O}_d)$ *and* $(T, \mathcal{O}_e)$ *be two topological metric spaces and let* $\mathcal{F} = \{f_i : S \longrightarrow T \mid i \in I\}$ *be an equicontinuous family of functions. If* $(S, \mathcal{O}_d)$ *is compact, then* $\mathcal{F}$ *is uniformly equicontinuous.*

Proof.   Let $\epsilon > 0$. By Theorem 5.45 each function f_i is uniformly continuous on S. In other words, for every $i \in I$ there exists $\delta_i > 0$ such that $d(x, x') < \delta_i$ implies $e(f_i(x), f_i(x')) < \frac{\epsilon}{2}$ for every $x, x' \in S$.

It is clear that the collection of spheres $\{B(x, \delta_i) \mid x \in S, i \in I\}$ is a cover of S. Since S is compact, it is possible to extract a finite subcollection of spheres $B(x_1, \delta_{i_1}), \ldots, B(x_n, \delta_{i_n})$ that is itself a cover of S.

Let $\delta = \frac{1}{2} \min\{\delta_{i_1}, \ldots, \delta_{i_n}\} > 0$. Suppose that $d(x, x') < \delta$. There exists a sphere $B(x_j, \delta_{i_j})$ such that $x' \in B(x_j, \delta_{i_j})$.

Let $x', x'' \in S$ be such that $d(x', x'') < \delta$.

Since x' belongs to an open sphere $B(x_j, \delta_{i_j})$, we have $d(x_j, x') < \frac{\delta_{i_j}}{2}$, which, in turn implies $e(f(x_j), f(x')) < \frac{\epsilon}{2}$.

We have

$$d(x_j, x'') \leqslant d(x_j, x') + d(x', x'') < \frac{\delta_{i_j}}{2} + \delta \leqslant \delta_{i_j},$$

which yields $e(f(x''), f(x_i)) \leqslant \frac{\epsilon}{2}$.

This implies $e(f_i(x), f_i(x')) < \epsilon$ for every $x, x' \in S$ and $i \in I$. $\qquad \square$

Theorem 5.78. *Let $(S, \mathcal{O}_d)$ and $(T, \mathcal{O}_e)$ be two topological metric spaces such that $(S, \mathcal{O}_d)$ is compact, and let $\mathcal{F} = \{f_i : S \longrightarrow T \mid i \in I\}$ be a uniformly equicontinuous family of functions such that $\lim_{n \to \infty} f_n(x) = f(x)$ for $x \in S$. Then, the convergence of (f_n) to f is uniform.*

Proof. By Theorem 5.76, the function f is continuous and $\mathcal{F} \cup \{f\}$ is equicontinuous. For every $\epsilon > 0$ there exists $\delta > 0$ such that $d(x, y) < \delta$ implies $e(f(x), f(y)) < \frac{\epsilon}{3}$ and $e(f_n(x), f_n(y)) < \frac{\epsilon}{3}$ for all $n \in \mathbb{N}$.

The compactness of $(S, \mathcal{O}_d)$ implies the existence of a finite subset $\{u_1, \ldots, u_m\}$ of S such that for every $x \in S$ there is u_j such that $x \in S(u_j, \delta)$. Therefore, $e(f(x), f(u_j)) < \frac{\epsilon}{3}$ and $e(f_n(x), f_n(u_j)) < \frac{\epsilon}{3}$.

There exists n_ϵ (dependent only on ϵ) such that $n \geqslant n_\epsilon$ implies $e(f(u_j), f_n(u_j)) < \frac{\epsilon}{3}$. Therefore, if $n > n_\epsilon$ we have

$$e(f(x), f_n(x))$$
$$\leqslant e(f(x), f(u_j)) + e(f(u_j), f_n(u_j)) + e(f_n(u_j), f_n(x)) < \epsilon,$$

which shows that (f_n) converges uniformly to f. $\qquad \square$

Theorem 5.79. (Arzelà-Ascoli Theorem) *Let $(S, \mathcal{O}_d)$ be a compact topological metric space, and let $\mathcal{F} = \{f_i : S \longrightarrow \mathbb{C} \mid i \in I\}$ be a uniformly equicontinuous family of functions that is uniformly bounded, that is, there exists $c > 0$ such that $|f_n(x)| \leqslant c$ for $n \in \mathbb{N}$ and $x \in S$. Then, $\mathcal{F}$ is totally bounded in $C(S)$ and every sequence in $\mathcal{F}$ contains a uniformly convergent subsequence.*

Proof. Since $\mathcal{F} = \{f_i \mid i \in I\}$ is uniformly equicontinuous, for every $\epsilon > 0$ there exists $\delta > 0$ such that $d(x, x') < \delta$ implies $|f_i(x) - f_i(x')| < \frac{\epsilon}{3}$ for every $x, x' \in S$ and $i \in I$.

The compactness of $(S, \mathcal{O}_d)$ means that there exists a finite set $\{x_1, \ldots, x_n\}$ such that $S \subseteq \bigcup_{i=1}^{n} B(x_i, \delta)$. We associate to each function $f \in \mathcal{F}$ the vector $\wp(f) = \begin{pmatrix} f(x_1) \\ \vdots \\ f(x_n) \end{pmatrix} \in \mathbb{C}^n$.

Note that $\wp(f) \in D^n$, where $D = \{a \in \mathbb{C} \mid |a| < c\}$. Since D_n is a finite union of sets of diameter less than ϵ there exist $f_1, \ldots, f_m$ such that $\wp(f) \in B(\wp(f_k), \epsilon)$ for some k, $1 \leqslant k \leqslant m$.

If $f \in \mathcal{F}$ there exists k such that $|f(x_i) - f_k(x_i)| < \frac{\epsilon}{3}$ for $1 \leqslant k \leqslant m$. Every $x \in S$ lies in some sphere $B(x_i, \delta)$ and therefore, $|f(x) - f(x_i)| < \frac{\epsilon}{3}$ and $f_k(x) - f_k(x_i)| < \frac{\epsilon}{3}$. Thus, $|f(x) - f_k(x)| < \epsilon$ for every $x \in S$. Since ϵ is arbitrary $\mathcal{F}$ is totally bounded.

Since $C(S)$ is complete, the closure of $\mathcal{F}$ is compact and thus, every sequence in $\mathcal{F}$ contains an uniformly convergent subsequence. $\qquad \square$

Exercises and Supplements

(1) Prove that every metric defined on a set S is equivalent to a bounded metric.

(2) Let $f : \hat{\mathbb{R}} \longrightarrow [-1, 1]$ be the function defined by

$$f(x) = \begin{cases} \frac{x}{1+|x|} & \text{if } x \in \mathbb{R}, \\ 1 & \text{if } x = \infty, \\ -1 & \text{if } x = -\infty. \end{cases}$$

Prove that

(a) f is a bijection between $\hat{\mathbb{R}}$ and $[-1, 1]$;
(b) the mapping $d : (\hat{\mathbb{R}})^2 \longrightarrow \mathbb{R}_{\geq 0}$ defined by $d(x, y) = |f(x) - f(y)|$ for $x, y \in \hat{\mathbb{R}}$ is a bounded metric on $\hat{\mathbb{R}}$;
(c) the restriction d' of d to $\mathbb{R}$ is equivalent to the usual distance on $\mathbb{R}$.

(3) Let (x_n) be a sequence in $\mathbb{R}$. If $a = \liminf x_n$ prove that there may be infinitely many terms x_n that are less than a; also, for every $\epsilon > 0$ there exist only a finite number of terms x_n that are less than $a - \epsilon$. Formulate and prove a similar statement for $b = \limsup x_n$.

(4) Let (x_n) be a sequence in $\mathbb{R}$ and let L be the set of all numbers that are limits of some subsequences of (x_n). Prove that:

(a) $\liminf x_n = \inf L$ and $\limsup x_n = \sup L$;

(b) the set L has both a least element and a greatest element, that is, $\sup L \in L$ and $\inf L \in L$.

(5) Let (x_n) be a sequence in $\mathbb{R}$ and let (x_{n_i}) be a subsequence of (x_n). Prove that

$$\liminf x_n \leqslant \liminf x_{n_i} \leqslant \limsup x_{n_i} \leqslant \limsup x_n.$$

(6) Let (u_n) and (v_n) be two sequences in $\mathbb{R}$. Prove that

$$\limsup(x_n + y_n) \leqslant \limsup x_n + \limsup y_n,$$
$$\liminf(x_n + y_n) \geqslant \liminf x_n + \liminf y_n,$$

where $\{\limsup x_n, \limsup y_n\} \neq \{\infty, -\infty\}$ for the first inequality and $\{\liminf x_n, \liminf y_n\} \neq \{\infty, -\infty\}$ for the second inequality.

(7) Let (x_n) be a sequence in $\mathbb{R}$. If $a = \liminf x_n$, $b = \limsup x_n$, prove that there exists $n_0 \in \mathbb{N}$ such that $n \geqslant n_0$ implies $a < x_n < b$.

(8) Let (S, d) be a metric space. A d-point for a function $h : S \longrightarrow \mathbb{R}$ is a point x_0 of S such that, for every other $x \in S$ we have $h(x_0) - h(x) < d(x, x_0)$.

Prove that:

(a) If (S, d) is complete then any lower semicontinuous function $f : S \longrightarrow \mathbb{R}$ which is bounded below has a d-point.

(b) If (S, d) is not complete, there exists a uniformly continuous function $f : S \longrightarrow \mathbb{R}$ which is bounded below but has no d-point.

(9) Let $(\mathbf{x}^m)$ be a sequence in $\mathbb{R}^n$. Prove that $\lim_{m \to \infty} \mathbf{x}^m = \mathbf{0}_n$ if and only if for each j, $1 \leqslant j \leqslant n$ we have $\lim_{m \to \infty} x_j^m = 0$.

Solution: The statement follows immediately from the inequalities:

$$\max\{|x_j^m| \mid 1 \leqslant j \leqslant n\} \leqslant \|\mathbf{x}^m\| \leqslant \sum_{j=1}^{n} |x_j^m|.$$

(10) Let (S, d) be a metric space, $x_0 \in S$, and let r be a positive number. Prove that there exists a continuous function $f : S \longrightarrow \mathbb{R}$ such that $f(x) \in [0, 1]$, $f(x) = 1$ for every $x \in B(x_0, r)$ such that $\{x \in S \mid f(x) \neq 0\} \subseteq B(x_0, 2r)$.

Solution: Let $g : \mathbb{R} \longrightarrow \mathbb{R}$ be the continuous function defined by

$$g(t) = \begin{cases} 1 & \text{if } 0 \leqslant t \leqslant r, \\ 1 - 2\left(\frac{t}{r} - 1\right) & \text{if } r < t \leqslant \frac{3r}{2} \\ 0 & \text{if } t > \frac{3r}{2}. \end{cases}$$

The desired function is $f(x) = g(d(x, x_0))$ for $x \in S$.

(11) Let $(S, \mathcal{O}_d)$ be a metric space and let U, V be two subsets of S such that U is compact, V is open and $U \subseteq V$. Prove that:

    (a) there exists a continuous function $f : S \longrightarrow [0,1]$ such that $f(x) = 0$ for $x \in U$ and $f(x) = 1$ if $x \notin V$;

    (b) there exists a continuous function $g : S \longrightarrow [0,1]$ such that $g(x) = 1$ for $x \in U$ and $\{x \in S \mid g(x) \neq 0\} \subseteq V$.

Solution: By Corollary 5.4 U is a closed set; furthermore, the closed sets U and $S - V$ are disjoint. Since every topological metric space is normal (by Corollary 5.6), by Uryson's Lemma (Theorem 4.83), there exists a continuous function $f : S \longrightarrow [0,1]$ such that $f(x) = 0$ for $x \in U$ and $f(x) = 1$ for $x \in S - V$.

For the second part of the supplement take $g(x) = 1 - f(x)$ for $x \in S$.

(12) Let $(S, \mathcal{O}_d)$ be a metric space, $\{U_1, \dots, U_n\}$ be a partition of S that consists of compact sets, and let $a_1, \dots, a_n \in \mathbb{R}$. Prove that the function $f : S \longrightarrow \mathbb{R}$ defined as $f(x) = \sum_{j=1}^{n} a_j 1_{U_j}(x)$ is continuous and $\|f\|_\infty \leqslant \max\{|a_j| \mid 1 \leqslant j \leqslant n\}$.

(13) Let (S, d_S) and (T, d_T) be two metric spaces. A function $f : S \longrightarrow T$ is bounded $f(S) \subseteq B_{d_T}[y_0, r]$ for some $y_0 \in T$. Let The set of bounded functions between these metric spaces is denoted by $B(S, T)$; the set of bounded and continuous functions is denoted by $C(X, Y)$. For $f, g \in B(S, T)$ define $d : B(S, T) \times B(S, T) \longrightarrow \mathbb{R}_{\geqslant 0}$ as $d(f, g) = \sup\{d_T(f(x), g(x)) \mid x \in S\}$.

Prove that

    (a) $(B(S, T), d)$ is a metric space;

    (b) if (f_n) be a sequence of functions in $B(S, T)$ and $f \in B(S, T)$, the sequence (f_n) converges uniformly to f if and only if f_n converges to f in the metric space $(B(S, T), d)$;

    (c) the set $C(S, T)$ is closed in $B(S, T)$;

    (d) if (T, d_T) is complete, then $C(S, T)$ is a complete subspace of $B(S, T)$.

A *continuity modulus* is a function $\omega : \mathbb{R}_{\geqslant 0} \cup \infty \longrightarrow \mathbb{R}_{\geqslant 0} \cup \infty$ such that $\lim_{x \downarrow 0} \omega(x) = \omega(0) = 0$.

Let (S, d_S) and (T, d_T) be two metric spaces. A function $f : S \longrightarrow T$ admits ω as its continuity modulus at $x_0 \in S$ if $d_T(f(x_0), f(x)) \leqslant \omega(d_S(x_0, x))$ for every $x \in S$. The function f admits ω as its continuity modulus if $d_T(f(x_1), f(x_2)) \leqslant \omega(d_S(x_1, x_2))$ for every $x_1, x_2 \in S$. Note that f is a Lipschitz function having the Lipschitz constant c if and only if it admits the function $\omega(t) = ct$ as a continuity modulus.

(14) Prove that if $f : S \longrightarrow T$ is a function between two metric spaces (S, d_S) and (T, d_T) that admits a continuity modulus ω on S that is monotone increasing, then f is uniformly continuous on S.

(15) Let (S, d_S), (T, d_T) and (U, d_U) be three metric spaces and let $f : S \longrightarrow T$ and $g : T \longrightarrow U$ be functions that admit continuity moduli ω_1 and ω_2, respectively. Prove that $gf : S \longrightarrow U$ admits $\omega_2\omega_1$ as a continuity modulus.

(16) Let $(S, \mathcal{O}_d)$ and $(T, \mathcal{O}_e)$ be two topological metric spaces, $f : S \longrightarrow T$ be an uniformly continuous function, and let $\omega : \mathbb{R}_{\geqslant 0} \cup \infty \longrightarrow \mathbb{R}_{\geqslant 0} \cup \infty$ be defined as
$$\omega(t) = \sup\{e(f(x), f(y)) \mid d(x, y) = t\}$$
for $t \leqslant 0$. Prove that ω is the minimal continuity modulus for f.

(17) Consider the polynomials $B_{n,k}(x) = \binom{n}{k}x^k(1-x)^{n-k}$ for $n \geqslant 0$, $0 \leqslant k \leqslant n$ and $x \in [0, 1]$. Prove that

   (a) $\sum_{k=0}^{n} B_{n,k}(x) = 1$;
   (b) $\sum_{k=0}^{n} k B_{n,k}(x) = nx$;
   (c) $\sum_{k=0}^{n} k^2 B_{n,k}(x) = n(n-1)x^2 + nx = n^2x^2 - nx^2 + nx$;
   (d) $\sum_{k=0}^{n} (k - nx)^2 B_{n,k}(x) = nx(1-x)$;
   (e) $\sum_k \{B_{n,k}(x) \mid |k - nx| \geqslant \lambda\} \leqslant \frac{nx(1-x)}{\lambda^2}$.

   Solution: Consider the function $h(t) = (xt + 1 - x)^n$ for $t \in \mathbb{R}$ and observe that $h(1) = 1$. We have
$$h(t) = \sum_{k=0}^{n} \binom{n}{k} t^k x^k (1-x)^{n-k} = \sum_{k=0}^{n} t^k B_{n,k}(x),$$
   hence $h(1) = 1 = \sum_{k=0}^{n} B_{n,k}(x)$.

   Differentiating h with respect to t yields
$$nx(xt + 1 - x)^{n-1} = \sum_{k=0}^{n} k t^{k-1} B_{n,k}(x)$$
   and the second equality follows by taking $t = 1$. One more differentiation allows us to write
$$n(n-1)x^2(xt + 1 - x)^{n-2} = \sum_{k=0}^{n} k(k-1)t^{k-2} B_{n,k}(x),$$
   hence $n(n - 1)x^2 = \sum_{k=0}^{n}(k^2 - k)B_{n,k}(x)$, which implies $\sum_{k=0}^{n} k^2 B_{n,k}(x) = n(n - 1)x^2 + nx$. For the fourth equality we have:
$$\sum_{k=0}^{n}(k - nx)^2 B_{n,k}(x) = \sum_{k=0}^{n}(k^2 - 2nxk + n^2x^2)B_{n,k}(x)$$
$$= n^2x^2 - nx^2 + nx - 2n^2x^2 + n^2x^2$$
$$= nx - nx^2 = nx(1 - x).$$

The last equality implies

$$nx(1-x) = \sum_{k=0}^{n}(k-nx)^2 B_{n,k}(x)$$

$$\geqslant \sum\{(k-nx)^2 \mid |k-nx| \geqslant \lambda\}$$

$$\geqslant \lambda^2 \sum_k\{B_{n,k}(x) \mid |k-nx| \geqslant \lambda\}.$$

Next we prove directly an approximation result implied by Stone-Weierstrass Theorem.

(18) Let $f : [0,1] \longrightarrow \mathbb{R}$ be a continuous function. Prove that for every $\epsilon > 0$ there exists a polynomial p on $[0,1]$ such that $\sup_{x \in [0,1]} |f(x) - p(x)| < \epsilon$.

Solution: Since f is continuous on $[0,1]$, it is uniformly continuous on this interval (by Heine's Theorem, that is, Theorem 5.45), hence there is a $\delta > 0$ such that $|x - y| < \delta$ implies $|f(x) - f(y)| < \epsilon$. The function f is also bounded, so $|f(x)| < M$ for some number M and for $x \in [0,1]$. Let p be defined as $p(x) = \sum_{k=0}^{n} f\left(\frac{k}{n}\right) B_{n,k}(x)$ for $x \in [0,1]$. We have

$$|f(x) - p(x)|$$

$$= \sum_{k=0}^{n} \left|f(x) - f\left(\frac{k}{n}\right)\right| B_{n,k}(x)$$

$$= \sum_{|x-\frac{k}{n}|<\delta} \left|f(x) - f\left(\frac{k}{n}\right)\right| B_{n,k}(x) + \sum_{|x-\frac{k}{n}|\geqslant\delta} \left|f(x) - f\left(\frac{k}{n}\right)\right| B_{n,k}(x)$$

$$< \frac{\epsilon}{2} \sum_{k=0}^{n} B_{n,k}(x) + 2M \sum\{B_{n,k}(x) \mid |k-nx| \geqslant n\delta\}$$

$$< \frac{\epsilon}{2} + \frac{2M}{n\delta^2}.$$

It suffices to take $n > \frac{4M}{\epsilon\delta^2}$ to obtain $|f(x) - p(x)| < \epsilon$.

(19) Let $(S, \mathcal{O})$ be a topological space. A subalgebra $\mathcal{U}$ of $C(S)$ *vanishes nowhere* if $\bigcap\{f^{-1}(0) \mid f \in \mathcal{U}\} = \emptyset$. Prove that if $\mathcal{U}$ contains the constant function k_1 defined by $k_1(x) = 1$ for $x \in S$, then $\mathcal{U}$ vanishes nowhere. Give an example of a subalgebra $\mathcal{U}$ of $C(S)$ such that the reverse implication fails.

(20) Let $(S, \mathcal{O})$ be a topological space. Prove that if there exists an algebra of real-valued continuous function defined on S that separates points, then $(S, \mathcal{O})$ is a Hausdorff space.

(21) Prove that a sequence $\mathbf{x} = (x_n)$ in a metric space (S, d) is a Cauchy sequence if and only if the series $\sum_{n \geqslant 1} d(x_n, x_{n+1})$ is convergent.

Solution: Suppose that $\mathbf{x}$ is a Cauchy sequence. Then, for each $\epsilon > 0$ there exists n_ϵ such that $m, n \geqslant n_\epsilon$ implies $d(x_n, x_m) < \epsilon$; in particular, there exists n_0 such that $n \geqslant n_0$ implies $d(x_n, x_{n+1}) < \frac{1}{2^n}$. By Theorem 5.65, the series $\sum_{n \geqslant 1} d(x_n, x_{n+1})$ is convergent.

Conversely, suppose that the series $\sum_{n \geqslant 1} d(x_n, x_{n+1})$ is convergent. Then, every $\epsilon > 0$ there exists a number n_ϵ such that for $n \geqslant n_\epsilon$ and $p \in \mathbb{N}$ we have $d(x_n, x_{n+1}) + d(x_{n+1}, x_{n+2}) + \cdots + d(x_{n+p-1}, x_{n+p}) < \epsilon$. This, in turn implies $d(x_{n+p}, x_n) < \epsilon$, so (x_n) is a Cauchy sequence.

(22) Let $(S, \mathcal{O})$ be a normal topological space, U be a closed subset of S and let $f : U \longrightarrow \mathbb{R}$ be a bounded continuous function. Prove that if $g : S \longrightarrow \mathbb{R}$ is the extension of f to a bounded continuous function defined on the entire space S (whose existence is established by Tietze's Theorem (Theorem 5.35), then $\|g\|_\infty \leqslant \|f\|_\infty$.

Solution: In the proof of Tietze's Theorem we made an assumption that implies $\|f\|_\infty \leqslant 1$. If this is not the case, we can apply the same argument to the function $f_1 = \frac{1}{\|f\|_\infty} f$ and obtain the existence of a function g_1 such that $\|g_1\|_\infty \leqslant 1$. Then, the function $g = \|f\|_\infty g_1$ satisfies the condition.

(23) Let $(S, \mathcal{O})$ be a compact metric space and let L_1, L_2 be two closed sets that are disjoint. Prove that for every $a_1, a_2 \in \mathbb{R}$ and every $\epsilon > 0$, there exists a function g such that $\|g\|_\infty < \max\{a_1 + a_2\} + \epsilon$ and $\|g - a_1 1_{L_1} - a_2 1_{L_2}\|_\infty < \epsilon$.

(24) Let $(S, \mathcal{O})$ be a compact metric space, $L_1, \ldots, L_n$ be n disjoint closed sets, and let $L = \bigcup_{i=1}^{n} L_i$. If $a_1, \ldots, a_n \in \mathbb{R}$, then for every $\epsilon > 0$ there exists a continuous function $g : L \longrightarrow \mathbb{R}$ such that $\|g\|_\infty \leqslant \max\{|a_i| \mid 1 \leqslant i \leqslant n\}$ and $\|g - \sum_{i=1}^{n} a_i 1_{L_i}\|_\infty < \epsilon$.

(25) Let $f : \mathbb{R}^n \longrightarrow \mathbb{R}$ be defined as $f(\mathbf{x}) = \mathbf{a}'\mathbf{x} + b$. Prove that f is a Lipschitz function.

(26) Let $(S, d), (T, d'), (U, d'')$ be three metric spaces and let $f : S \longrightarrow T$ and $g : T \longrightarrow U$ be two Lipschitz functions. Prove that gf is a Lipschitz function.

(27) Let $(x_n), (y_n), (z_n)$ be three sequences of real numbers such that $x_n \leqslant y_n \leqslant z_n$ for $n \in \mathbb{N}$. If $\lim_{n \to \infty} x_n = \lim_{n \to \infty} z_n = \ell$, prove that $\lim_{n \to \infty} y_n = \ell$.

(28) Let $(u_n)_{n \geqslant 1}$ and $(v_n)_{\geqslant 1}$ be the sequences defined by

$$u_n = \left(1 + \frac{1}{n}\right)^n \text{ and } v_n = \left(1 + \frac{1}{n}\right)^{n+1}$$

for $n \geqslant 1$. Prove that:

(a) $(u_n)_{n \geqslant 1}$ is an increasing sequence, $(v_n)_{n \geqslant 1}$ is a decreasing sequence;

(b) $2 \leqslant u_n \leqslant v_n \leqslant 3$;

(c) $\lim_{n \to \infty} u_n = \lim_{n \to \infty} v_n$.

Solution: Observe that u_n can be written as a sum of n terms:

$$u_n = \left(1 + \frac{1}{n}\right)^n = 1 + \binom{n}{1}\frac{1}{n} + \binom{n}{2}\frac{1}{n^2} + \cdots + \binom{n}{n}\frac{1}{n^n}$$

$$= 2 + \frac{1}{2!}\left(1 - \frac{1}{n}\right) + \cdots + \frac{1}{n!}\left(1 - \frac{1}{n}\right)\left(1 - \frac{2}{n}\right)\cdots\left(1 - \frac{n-1}{n}\right).$$

Similarly, u_{n+1} can be written as a sum $n+1$ terms:

$$u_{n+1} = 2 + \frac{1}{2!}\left(1 - \frac{1}{n+1}\right)$$

$$+ \cdots + \frac{1}{(n+1)!}\left(1 - \frac{1}{n+1}\right)\left(1 - \frac{2}{n+1}\right)\cdots\left(1 - \frac{n}{n+1}\right),$$

and each of the first n terms of u_{n+1} is at least as large as the corresponding term of u_n. Therefore, $u_n \leqslant u_{n+1}$. A similar argument can be used to show that $v_n \geqslant v_{n+1}$.

It is clear that $u_n \geqslant 2$. Note that

$$u_n \leqslant 2 + \frac{1}{2!} + \cdots + \frac{1}{n!}$$
$$\leqslant 2 + \frac{1}{2} + \cdots + \frac{1}{2^{n+1}} \leqslant 3,$$

We leave to the reader to prove that $2 \leqslant v_n \leqslant 3$. Since $v_n = u_n(1 + \frac{1}{n+1})$, the second part follows immediately.

It is immediate that both sequences are convergent. Let $\ell_1 = \lim_{n \to \infty} u_n$ and $\ell_2 = \lim_{n \to \infty} v_n$. It is clear that $\ell_1 \leqslant \ell_2$. Since $v_n - u_n = \frac{1}{n}u_n$ it follows that $\ell_1 = \ell_2$.

(29) Let $(x_0, x_1, \ldots)$ be a sequence in $\mathbb{R}$ such that $\lim_{n \to \infty} = x$. Prove that the sequence of averages (a_n) defined by

$$a_n = \frac{1}{n}\sum_{j=0}^{n-1} x_j$$

is also convergent and $\lim_{n \to \infty} a_n = x$.

Solution: Note that $a_n - x = \frac{(x_0 - x) + (x_1 - x) + \cdots + (x_{n-1} - x)}{n}$ Since $\lim_{j \to \infty} x_j = x$, for every $\epsilon > 0$ there exists $n_\epsilon \in \mathbb{N}$ such that $n > n_\epsilon$

implies $|x_n - x| < \epsilon$. Consequently,

$$|a_n - x| \leqslant \frac{1}{n}\left(\sum_{j=1}^{n_\epsilon}|x_j - x| + \sum_{n_\epsilon+1}^{n-1}|x_j - x|\right)$$

$$< \frac{1}{n}\sum_{j=1}^{n_\epsilon}|x_j - x| + \epsilon.$$

Since $\lim_{n\to\infty}\frac{1}{n}\sum_{j=1}^{n_\epsilon}|x_j - x| = 0$, the desired conclusion follows immediately.

A sequence (x_n) of complex numbers *converges in Cesàro*[4] *sense* to ℓ if the sequence of arithmetic averages (a_n) converges to ℓ.

For series $s_n = \sum_{j=1}^{n}x_j$ define $\sigma_n = \frac{1}{n}\sum_{j=1}^{n}s_j$. The series (s_n) is Cesàro summable and its sum is s if $\lim_{n\to\infty}\sigma_n = s$.

(30) Let (x_n) be the sequence of defined by $x_n = (-1)^n$ Prove that although (x_n) is not convergent in the usual sense, it is convergent in Cesàro sense.

(31) Let $z = \cos\alpha + i\sin\alpha$, where $\alpha \neq 0$. Prove that the series $s_n = \sum_{j=0}^{n-1} z^j$ is not convergent but it is Cesàro summable.

   Solution: Since $\sum_{j=0}^{n-1} z^j = \frac{z^n - 1}{z - 1} = \frac{1}{z-1}(\cos n\alpha + \sin n\alpha - 1)$ it is clear that the series (s_n) is not convergent. On other hand,

$$\lim_{n\to\infty}\sigma_n = \frac{1}{z - 1}.$$

(32) Let L be a normed linear space. Prove that L is homeomorphic to $S(0_L, 1)$.

   Hint: Let $f : S(0_L, 1) \longrightarrow L$ be the function $f(x) = \tan\left(\frac{\pi}{2}\|x\|\right)$ for $x \in S(0_L, 1)$. Prove that f is the desired homeomorphism.

(33) Let L be a real normed linear space. If U is a subset of L and let V be an open subset in L, prove that the Minkowski sum $U + V$ is an open set in L.

   Solution: Note that for every $u \in U$, $t_u(V) = u + V$ is open by Theorem 6.4, and we can write $U + V = \bigcup_{u\in U} t_u(V)$. Therefore, $U + V$ is open.

(34) Let $(S, \|\cdot\|)$ be a normed linear space, $x \in S$, $U \subseteq S$ and let d be the metric induced by the norm on S. Prove that $d(ax, U) = |a|d(x, U)$.

---

[4]Ernesto Cesàro, was born in Naples on March 12th and died on September 12, 1906 in Torre Annunziata. Cesàro graduated from the University of Rome and taught ar the Sapienza University. His main contributions are in differential geometry and is known for his averaging method.

Solution: By Definition 5.12 we have

$$
\begin{aligned}
d(ax, U) &= \inf\{d(ax, u) \mid u \in U\} \\
&= \inf\{\|ax - u\| \mid u \in U\} \\
&= |a|\inf\left\{\left\|x - \frac{1}{a}u\right\| \mid u \in U\right\}.
\end{aligned}
$$

Since every $v \in U$ can be written as $\frac{1}{a}u$ for some $u \in U$ it follows that $d(ax, U) = |a|d(x, U)$.

(35) Prove that each closed sphere $B[\mathbf{0}_m, r]$ in the normed linear space $(\mathbb{R}^m, \|\cdot\|_\infty)$ is compact.

   Solution: Let $(\mathbf{x}_n)_{n\in\mathbb{N}}$ be a sequence included in $B[\mathbf{0}_m, r]$, that is, $\|\mathbf{x}_n\|_\infty \leqslant r$, which means that $-r \leqslant (\mathbf{x}_n)_i \leqslant r$ for $1 \leqslant i \leqslant m$.

   Since $[-r, r]$ is a compact subset of $\mathbb{R}$ it follows that there exists a subset N_1 of $\mathbb{N}$ such that $\lim((\mathbf{x}_n)_{n\in N_1})_1 = a_1$ exists. Then, by the same compactness property, a subset N_2 of N_1 such that $\lim((\mathbf{x}_n)_{n\in N_2})_2 = a_2$ exists, etc. At the mth step of the process we have constructed a sequence of sets $N_1 \supseteq N_2 \supseteq \cdots \subseteq N_m$ such that $\lim((\mathbf{x}_n)_{n\in N_m})_m = a_m$ exists.

   Thus, $\lim((\mathbf{x}_n)_{n\in N_m})_k = a_k$ exists for $1 \leqslant k \leqslant m$. If $\mathbf{a} = \begin{pmatrix} a_1 \\ \vdots \\ a_m \end{pmatrix}$ we have $\lim\{\mathbf{x}_n \mid n \in N_m\} = \mathbf{a}$, which shows that $B[\mathbf{0}_m, r]$ is compact.

(36) Let L be a real linear space and let T be a subspace of L such that $\mathbf{K}(T) \neq L$. Prove that there exists a non-zero linear functional f on L such that $f(x) = 0$ for every $x \in T$.

(37) Let $(S, \mathcal{O}_d)$ be a metric space. Prove that the family of Lipschitz functions

$$
\mathcal{F}_c = \{f : S \longrightarrow \mathbb{R} \mid |f(x) - f(y)| \leqslant cd(x, y) \text{ for all } x, y \in S\}
$$

is equicontinuous.

(38) Let (f_n) be a sequence of functions, where $f_n : [a, b] \longrightarrow \mathbb{R}$. If (f_n) converges to a function f pointwise, and the family $\{f_n \mid n \in \mathbb{N}\}$ is equicontinuous, prove that the convergence to f is uniform.

   Extend the previous statement by replacing the interval $[a, b]$ by a compact set in a metric space (S, d).

(39) Let P_n be the family of polynomials of the form $p(x) = \sum_{i=0}^{n} a_i x^i$ for $x \in [a, b]$ such that $|a_i| \leqslant 1$ for $0 \leqslant i \leqslant n$. Prove that P_n is uniformly bounded and equicontinuous on $[a, b]$.

Bibliographical Comments

Pioneering work in applying topology in data mining has been done in [109, 92].

Chapter 6

Topological Linear Spaces

6.1 Introduction

In this chapter we present the interaction between the structure of a linear space and a topology defined on such a space assuming that the topological structure is compatible with the pre-existing linear structure. Linear spaces equipped with topologies are the main objects of functional analysis.

We also discuss topological properties of convex sets.

6.2 Topologies of Linear Spaces

Definition 6.1. Let $\mathbb{F}$ be the real or complex field. A *topological $\mathbb{F}$-linear space* is an $\mathbb{F}$-linear space $(L, +, \cdot)$ equipped with a topology $\mathcal{O}$ such that the addition in L and the scalar multiplication are continuous operations.

A topological linear space is denoted by $(L, \mathcal{O})$, or just by L if there is no ambiguity.

The collection of neighborhoods of a point x of a topological linear space $(L, \mathcal{O})$ is denoted by $neigh_x(L, \mathcal{O})$.

If U, V are subsets of a linear space, their *Minkowski sum* is the set

$$U + V = \{u + v \mid u \in U, v \in V\}.$$

Let L be an $\mathbb{F}$-linear space. The addition in L is continuous in (x, y) if for every neighborhood W of $x + y$ there exist neighborhoods $U \in neigh_x(L, \mathcal{O})$ and $V \in neigh_y(L, \mathcal{O})$ such that for $u \in U$ and $v \in V$ we have $u + v \in W$.

Similarly, scalar multiplication is continuous in (a, x) if for every neighborhood W of ax there exists $U \in neigh_x(L, \mathcal{O})$ and a positive number δ such that if $|b - a| < \delta$ and $u \in U$ imply $bu \in W$.

For the *translation* $t_z : L \longrightarrow L$ generated by $z \in L$ defined as $t_z(x) = x + z$ we have the following theorem.

Theorem 6.1. *Let L be a topological $\mathbb{F}$-linear space. Every translation t_z of L is a homeomorphism of L.*

Proof. It is immediate that every translation is a bijective mapping on L. The continuity of t_z and of its inverse, t_{-z} follows from the continuity of addition in L. $\square$

Theorem 6.2. *Let $(L, \mathcal{O})$ a topological linear space. If T is an open subset and $R \subseteq L$, the set $T + R$ is an open subset of L.*

Proof. Since t_r is a homeomorphism of L for every $r \in L$, $t_r(T)$ is an open subset of L. Therefore, taking into account that $T+R = \bigcup\{t_r(T) \mid r \in T\}$, it follows that $T + R$ is open. $\square$

For a homothety $h_a : L \longrightarrow L$ of L defined as $h_a(x) = ax$ we have the next statement:

Theorem 6.3. *Let L be a topological $\mathbb{F}$-linear space. If $a \neq 0$, then the homothety h_a is a homeomorphism of L.*

Proof. The continuity of h_a and of its inverse $h_{\frac{1}{a}}$ follows from the continuity of scalar multiplication. $\square$

Theorem 6.4. *Let L be a topological $\mathbb{F}$-linear space. If U is an open subset of L, then $t_z(L)$ and $h_a(L)$ are open sets for every translation t_z and every homothety h_a of L.*

Proof. This statement is an immediate consequence of Theorems 6.1 and 6.3. $\square$

Theorem 6.5. *Let $(L, \mathcal{O})$ be a topological linear space. The closure $\boldsymbol{K}(U)$ of a set U is given by*

$$\boldsymbol{K}(U) = \bigcap\{U + V \mid V \in neigh_{0_L}(L, \mathcal{O})\}.$$

Proof. Let $x \in \mathbf{K}(U)$. Since $x+V \in neigh_x(L, \mathcal{O})$, we have $(x+V) \cap U \neq \emptyset$, so $x \in U - V$. Therefore, $x \in \bigcap\{U - V \mid V \in neigh_{0_L}(L, \mathcal{O})\} = \bigcap\{U + V \mid V \in neigh_0(L, \mathcal{O})\}$.

Suppose now that $x \notin \mathbf{K}(U)$. There exists $V \in neigh_0(L, \mathcal{O})$ such that $(x + V) \cap U = \emptyset$, so $x \notin U - V$, hence $x \notin \bigcap\{U + V \mid V \in neigh_{0_L}(L, \mathcal{O})\}$, which proves that $\bigcap\{U + V \mid V \in neigh_{0_L}(L, \mathcal{O})\} \subseteq \mathbf{K}(U)$. $\square$

Theorem 6.6. *Let $(L, \mathcal{O})$ be a topological linear space. For any subsets U and W of L we have*

$$\boldsymbol{K}(U) + \boldsymbol{K}(W) \subseteq \boldsymbol{K}(U + W).$$

Proof. Let $u \in \mathbf{K}(U)$ and $w \in \mathbf{K}(W)$. Since addition is continuous, for every $V \in neigh_{u+v}(L, \mathcal{O})$ there exist $V' \in neigh_u(L, \mathcal{O})$ and $V'' \in neigh_w(L, \mathcal{O})$ such that $V' + V'' \subseteq V$. By Theorem 4.24 there exist $x \in V' \cap U$ and $y \in V'' \cap W$, hence $x + y \in U + W$ and $x + y \in V' + V''$. Thus, every neighborhood of $u + w$ intersects $U + W$, which implies $u + w \in \mathbf{K}(U + W)$. This yields the desired inclusion. $\square$

Theorem 6.7. *Let L be an $\mathbb{F}$-topological linear space. If U is a subspace of L, then $\boldsymbol{K}(U)$ is also a subspace of L.*

Proof. Since U is a subspace we have $U + U \subseteq U$ and $aU \subseteq U$ for $a \in \mathbb{F}$. By Theorem 6.6 we have $\mathbf{K}(U) + \mathbf{K}(U) \subseteq \mathbf{K}(U + U) \subseteq \mathbf{K}(U)$.

Since h_a is a homeomorphism for $a \neq 0$, $a\mathbf{K}(U) = \mathsf{h}_a(\mathbf{K}(U)) = \mathbf{K}(\mathsf{h}_a(U)) \subseteq \mathbf{K}(U)$, which allows us to conclude that $\mathbf{K}(U)$ is indeed a subspace. $\square$

Theorem 6.8. *Let $(L, \mathcal{O})$ be a topological linear space. Every maximal subspace S in L is either closed or dense in L.*

Proof. Since $\mathbf{K}(S)$ is a subspace of L and $S \subseteq \mathbf{K}(S) \subseteq L$, the maximality of S leaves two alternatives: either $S = \mathbf{K}(S)$, which means that S is closed, or $\mathbf{K}(S) = L$, which means that S is dense in L. $\square$

Corollary 6.1. *Let L be a topological linear space. Every hyperplane in L is either closed or dense in L.*

Proof. Since a hyperplane H is the translate of a maximal subspace of L, the statement follows from Theorem 6.8. $\square$

Corollary 6.2. *Every affine subset of $\mathbb{R}^n$ is closed.*

Proof. This statement follows from Theorem 3.11 and Corollary 6.2. $\square$

Theorem 6.9. *Let $(L, \mathcal{O})$ be a topological linear space. If K is a compact subset of L and C is a closed subset of L and $K \cap C = \emptyset$, then there exists $V \in neigh_{0_L}(L, \mathcal{O})$ such that $(K + V) \cap (C + V) = \emptyset$.*

Proof. If $K = \emptyset$ the conclusion is immediate because $K + C = \emptyset$. Thus, we need to consider only the case when $K \neq \emptyset$.

Let $x \in K$. Since $x \notin C$ and C is closed, there exists a neighborhood W_x of x such that $W_x \cap C = \emptyset$. Since $\mathcal{O}$ is a linear topology there is a neighborhood Z_x of 0_L such that $W_x = x + Z_x$; furthermore, by Supplement 6, there exists a symmetric neighborhood U_x of 0_L such that $U_x + U_x + U_x \subseteq Z_x$, hence $x + U_x + U_x + U_x \subseteq x + Z_x = W_x$.

Since W_x is disjoint from C, $x + U_x + U_x$ is disjoint from $C + U_x$.

The collection of neighborhoods $\{x + U_x \mid x \in K\}$ is a cover of K. Since K is compact, there exists a finite cover of K of the form $\{x_1 + U_{x_1}, \ldots, x_n + U_{x_n}\}$.

Note that the set $V = \bigcap_{i=1}^n U_{x_i}$ is a neighborhood of 0_L. We have

$$K + V \subseteq \bigcup_{i=1}^n (x_i + U_{x_i} + V) \subseteq \bigcup_{i=1}^n (y_{x_i}(x_i + U_{x_i} + U_{x_i}).$$

Since no set $x_i + U_{x_i} + U_{x_i}$ has a non-empty intersection with $C + V$ it follows that $(K + V) \cap (C + V) = \emptyset$. $\qquad\square$

Corollary 6.3. *Let* $(L, \mathcal{O})$ *be a topological linear space. If for every* $x \in L$ *the set* $\{x\}$ *is closed, then* $(L, \mathcal{O})$ *is a Hausdorff space.*

Proof. Let $x, y \in L$ be two distinct point. The singleton $K = \{x\}$ is a compact set (see Example 4.18) and $\{y\}$ is a closed set. Thus, by Theorem 6.9 there exists $V \in neigh_{0_L}(L, \mathcal{O})$ such that $(x + V) \cap (y + V) = \emptyset$. Since $x + V$ and $y + V$ are disjoint neighborhoods of x and y, respectively, it follows that there exists two open sets $V_1, V_2 \in \mathcal{O}$ such that $x \in V_1 \subseteq x + V$ and $y \in V_2 \subseteq y + V$, which means that $(L, \mathcal{O})$ is a Hausdorff space. $\qquad\square$

Corollary 6.4. *Let* $(L, \mathcal{O})$ *be a topological linear space. If* K *is a compact subset of* L *and* C *is a closed subset of* L *and* $K \cap C = \emptyset$, *then there an open subset* $U \in \mathcal{O}$ *such that* $0_L \in U$ *and* $(K + U) \cap (C + U) = \emptyset$.

Proof. By Theorem 6.9 there exists $V \in neigh_{0_L}(L, \mathcal{O})$ such that $(K + U) \cap (C + U) = \emptyset$. Therefore, there exists an open set U such that $0_L \in U \subseteq V$, and this implies $(K + U) \cap (C + U) = \emptyset$. $\qquad\square$

A stronger form of Corollary 6.4 is given as follows.

Corollary 6.5. *Let* $(L, \mathcal{O})$ *be a topological linear space. If* K *is a compact subset of* L *and* C *is a closed subset of* L *and* $K \cap C = \emptyset$, *then there an open subset* $U \in \mathcal{O}$ *such that* $0_L \in U$ *and* $\mathbf{K}(K + U) \cap (C + U) = \emptyset$.

Proof. Note that $C + U$ is an open set and that $K + U \subseteq \overline{C + U}$. Since $\overline{C + U}$ is closed, it follows that $\mathbf{K}(K + U) \subseteq \overline{C + U}$, or $\mathbf{K}(K + U) \cap (C + U) = \emptyset$. $\qquad\square$

If we have $K = \{0_L\}$ it follows that for any closed subset C of L, it follows that there exists an open subset U of L such that $\mathbf{K}(U) \cap (C+U) = \emptyset$. Since $C + U$ is an open set, $\overline{C + U}$ is closed and, therefore $\mathbf{K}(U) \subseteq \overline{C + U}$.

Definition 6.2. A subset U of a topological $\mathbb{F}$-linear space L is *bounded* if there exists a neighborhood W of 0_L and $a \in \mathbb{F}$ such that $U \subseteq aW$.

The next definition is a generalization of the notion of Cauchy sequence.

Definition 6.3. Let $(L, \mathcal{O})$ be a topological linear space. A *Cauchy net* is a net $(x_i)_{i \in I}$ such that for every $U \in neigh_{0_L}(L, \mathcal{O})$ there exists $i \in I$ such that $j, k > i$ implies $x_j - x_k \in U$.
$(L, \mathcal{O})$ is

  (i) *complete* if every Cauchy net is convergent;

  (ii) *quasi-complete* if every bounded Cauchy net is convergent;

  (iii) *sequentially complete* if every Cauchy sequence is convergent.

A net $(x_i)_{i \in I}$ is *eventually bounded* if there exists a neighborhood $W \in neigh_{0_L}(L, \mathcal{O})$ and $i_W \in I$ such that $i \geqslant i_W$ implies $x_i \in W$.

Next we show that in a topological linear the set of neighborhoods of a point x is a translation of the set of neighborhoods of 0_L.

Theorem 6.10. *Let $(L, \mathcal{O})$ be a topological linear space. If $V \in neigh_{0_L}(L, \mathcal{O})$, where $\mathcal{O}$ is the topology defined on L, then $t_x(V) = x + V \in neigh_x(L, \mathcal{O})$. Conversely, for every $W \in neigh_x(L, \mathcal{O})$ we have $W = t_x(V) = x + V$, where $V \in neigh_{0_L}(L, \mathcal{O})$.*

Proof. Let $V \in neigh_{0_L}(L, \mathcal{O})$. There exists an open subset T of L such that $0_L \in T \subseteq V$. Since $x + T$ is an open set and $x \in x + T \subseteq x + V$ it follows that $x + V$ is a neighborhood of x.

If W is a neighborhood of x, following a similar argument, it follows that $-x + W \in neigh_{0_L}(L, \mathcal{O})$ and, since $W = t_x(-x + W)$, the second part of the theorem is proven. $\qquad\square$

Thus a topology of a linear space L is defined by the collection of neighborhoods of 0_L.

Theorem 6.11. *A linear topological space is Hausdorff if and only if for every $x \in L - \{0_L\}$, there exists $U \in neigh_{0_L}(L, \mathcal{O})$ such that $x \notin U$.*

Proof. Suppose that $(L, \mathcal{O})$ is Hausdorff. Then, there exist $U \in neigh_{0_L}(L, \mathcal{O})$ and $V \in neigh_x(L, \mathcal{O})$ such that $U \cap V = \emptyset$. In particular, $x \notin U$.

Conversely, suppose that the condition holds and let $x, y \in L$ with $x \neq y$, that is, $x - y \neq 0_L$. There exists $U \in neigh_{0_L}(L, \mathcal{O})$ such that $x - y \notin U$. By the continuity of subtraction there exists $V \in neigh_{0_L}$ such that $V - V \subseteq U$. Suppose that $(V + x) \cap (V + y) \neq \emptyset$. There exists $z \in (V + x) \cap (V + y)$, that is, $z = u + x = v + y$ for some $u, v \in V$. Then, $x - y = v - u \in V - V \subseteq U$, so $x - y \in U$, which is a contradiction. Hence, $(V + x) \cap (V + y) = \emptyset$, hence $(L, \mathcal{O})$ is a Hausdorff space. $\qquad\square$

Theorem 6.12. *Let $(L, \mathcal{O})$ be a topological linear space. $(L.\mathcal{O})$ is a Hausdorff space if and only if $\bigcap neigh_{0_L} = \{0_L\}$.*

Proof. Let $x, y \in L$ be such that $x - y \neq 0_L$ and let $W \in neigh_{0_L}$ be such that $x - y \notin W$. By the continuity of subtraction, there exists $V \in neigh_{0_L}$ such that $V - V \subseteq W$. Then $x + V$ is disjoint from $y + V$. Indeed, if we would have $z \in (x + V) \cap (y + V)$ we could write $z = x + x_1 = y + y_1$, where $x_1, y_1 \in V$. Then, $x - y = y_1 - x_1 \in V - V \subseteq W$, which is a contradiction. Thus, L is a Hausdorff space.

Conversely, let $(L, \mathcal{O})$ be a Hausdorff topological linear space. Clearly, $0_L \in \bigcap neigh_{0_L}(L, \mathcal{O})$. Suppose that $x \neq 0_L$ also belongs to $\bigcap neigh_{0_L}(L, \mathcal{O})$. By Theorem 6.11, there exists $U \in neigh_{0_L}(L, \mathcal{O})$ such that $x \notin U$, which is a contradiction. $\qquad\square$

Theorem 6.13. *Let L be an real linear space. If S is a balanced subset of L, then so is $\mathbf{K}(S)$; furthermore, if $0_L \in \mathbf{I}(S)$, then $\mathbf{I}(S)$ is balanced.*

Proof. Since h_a is a homeomorphism for $a \neq 0$, $\mathsf{h}_a(\mathbf{K}(S)) = \mathbf{K}(\mathsf{h}_a(S))$. Taking into account that S is balanced we have for $a \in F$ and $|a| \leqslant 1$, $\mathsf{h}_a(\mathbf{K}(S)) = \mathbf{K}(\mathsf{h}_a(S)) \subseteq \mathbf{K}(S)$, so $\mathbf{K}(S)$ is balanced.

Again, since h_a is a homeomorphism for $a \neq 0$, we have $\mathsf{h}_a(\mathbf{I}(S)) = \mathbf{I}(\mathsf{h}_a(S)) \subseteq \mathbf{I}(S)$. Note that for $a = 0$, $aS = \{0\}$, so we must require that $0 \in \mathbf{I}(S)$ in order for $\mathbf{I}(S)$ to be balanced. $\qquad\square$

Theorem 6.14. *Let L be an real linear space. If S is an absorbing subset of L, then so is $\mathbf{K}(S)$.*

Proof. Since $S \subseteq \mathbf{K}(S)$, it is immediate that $\mathbf{K}(S)$ is absorbing because every set that includes an absorbing set is itself absorbing. $\qquad\square$

Theorem 6.15. *In a topological real linear space $(L, \mathcal{O})$, there exists a local basis $\mathcal{L}_{0_L}$ of neighborhoods of 0_L that satisfies the following conditions:*

    (i) *each $V \in \mathcal{L}_{0_L}$ is balanced and absorbing;*

    (ii) *for each $V \in \mathcal{L}_{0_L}$, there exists $W \in \mathcal{L}_{0_L}$ such that $W + W \subseteq V$;*

    (iii) *each $V \in \mathcal{L}_{0_L}$ is closed.*

Proof. For every neighborhood $V \in neigh_{0_L}(L, \mathcal{O})$ there are a number $\delta > 0$ and $W \in neigh_{0_L}(L, \mathcal{O})$ such that $aW \subseteq W$ for all a such that $|a| < \delta$ because multiplication by scalars is continuous. Then $U = \bigcup \{aW \mid |a| < \delta\}$ is a balanced neighborhood.

Since vector addition is continuous in $(0_L, 0_L)$ there exist $W \in neigh_{0_L}(L, \mathcal{O})$ such that $x, y \in W$ implies $x + y \in V$, that is, $W + W \subseteq V$. If $x \in \mathbf{K}(W)$, $x - W$ is a neighborhood of x, hence $(x - W) \cap W \neq \emptyset$, implies $x \in W + W \subseteq V$, so $\mathbf{K}(W) \subseteq V$.

Since $\mathbf{K}(W)$ is the closure of an balanced and absorbing set remains balanced and absorbing (by Theorems 6.13 and 6.14), this shows that there exists a local base at 0_L that satisfies the above conditions. $\qquad\square$

Theorem 6.16. *Let L be a real linear space and let $\mathcal{L}$ be a collection of subsets of L such that $\emptyset \notin \mathcal{L}$, for $A, B \in \mathcal{L}$ there exists $C \in \mathcal{L}$ such that $C \subset A \cap B$, and $\mathcal{L}$ satisfies the first two conditions mentioned in Theorem 6.15, that is,*

(i) *each $V \in \mathcal{L}$ is balanced and absorbing;*

(ii) *for each $V \in \mathcal{L}$, there exists $W \in \mathcal{L}$ such that $W + W \subseteq V$.*

Then, there exists a linear space topology $\mathcal{O}$ on L such that $\mathcal{L} = neigh_{0_L}(L, \mathcal{O})$.

Proof. Define $\mathcal{O}$ as the collection of all subsets U such that

$$U = \{x \in U \mid x + V \subseteq U \text{ for some } V \in \mathcal{L}\}.$$

It is immediate that $\emptyset$ and L belong to $\mathcal{O}$ and that if $\{U_i \mid i \in I\}$ is a collection of sets with the above property, then $\bigcup_{i \in I} U_i$ enjoys the same property.

Suppose that U_1, U_2 are two sets in $\mathcal{O}$ and $x \in U_1 \cap U_2$. Since $x \in U_i$ there exists $V_i \in \mathcal{L}$ such that $x + V_i \subseteq U_i$ for $i = 1, 2$. By hypothesis, there exists $V \in \mathcal{L}$ such that $V \subseteq V_1 \cap V_2$. Since $x + V_1 \cap V_2 \subseteq U_1 \cap U_2$, it follows that $U_1 \cap U_2 \in \mathcal{O}$, hence $\mathcal{O}$ is indeed a topology.

For the interior $\mathbf{I}(T)$ of a subset T of L relative to the topology $\mathcal{O}$ we have

$$\mathbf{I}(T) = \{x \in T \mid x + V \subseteq T \text{ for some } V \in \mathcal{L}\}. \tag{6.1}$$

Indeed, if $x \in \mathbf{I}(T)$, since $\mathbf{I}(T)$ is open, there exists $V \in \mathcal{L}$ such that $x + V \subseteq \mathbf{I}(T) \subseteq T$, so we have $\mathbf{I}(T) \subseteq \{x \in T \mid x + V \subseteq T \text{ for some } V \in \mathcal{L}\}$. Next, we show that $\{x \in T \mid x + V \subseteq T \text{ for some } V \in \mathcal{L}\} \in \mathcal{O}$.

Let $y \in T$ such that $y + V \subseteq T$ for some $V \in \mathcal{L}$. By hypothesis, there exists $W \in \mathcal{L}$ such that $W + W \subseteq V$. If $w \in W$, then

$$y + w + W \subseteq y + W + W \subseteq y + V \subseteq T,$$

hence $y + w \in \mathbf{I}(T)$, hence the set $\{x \in T \mid x + V \subseteq T$ for some $V \in \mathcal{L}\}$ is open. This implies equality (6.1). Therefore, the collection $\{x + V \mid V \in V \in \mathcal{L}\}$ is a local base at x.

It remains to prove the continuity of vector addition and multiplication by scalars.

Let $x_0, y_0 \in L$ and let $V \in \mathcal{L}$. By hypothesis, there exists $U \in \mathcal{L}$ such that $U + U \subseteq W$. If $x \in x_0 + U$ and $y \in y_0 + U$, then $x + y \in x_0 + y_0 + U + U \subseteq x_0 + y_0 + V$, which implies that vector addition is continuous.

To prove the continuity of scalar multiplication let $a_0 \in \mathbb{R}$, $x_0 \in L$, and $V \in \mathcal{L}$. Let $W \in \mathcal{L}$ be such that $W + W \subseteq V$. Since W is absorbing, there exists $\delta > 0$ such that $|a| \leqslant \delta$ implies $ax \in W$. Let $n \in \mathbb{N}$ be such that $|a_0| + \delta < n$. If $|a - a_0| < \delta$, then $||a| - |a_0|| \leqslant |a - a_0| < \delta$, which implies

$$\left| \frac{a}{n} \right| \leqslant \frac{|a_0| + \delta}{n} < 1.$$

Since W is balanced, for each $a \in \mathbb{R}$ and $|a - a_0| < \delta$ and $x \in x_0 + \frac{1}{n}W$ we have:

$$
\begin{aligned}
ax &= a_0 x_0 + (a - a_0) x_0 + a(x - x_0) \\
&\in a_0 x_0 + W + \frac{a}{n} W \\
&\subseteq a_0 x_0 + W + W \subseteq a_0 x_0 + V,
\end{aligned}
$$

which shows that scalar multiplication is continuous. $\qquad\square$

Theorem 6.17. *A Hausdorff topological $\mathbb{F}$-linear space $(L, \mathcal{O})$ is locally compact if and only if it is finite dimensional.*

Proof.   If L is finite dimensional, then L is homeomorphic to $\mathbb{F}^n$ and therefore, it is locally compact.

Let L be a Hausdorff topological $\mathbb{F}$-linear space that is locally compact. Let $V \in neigh_{0_L}(L, \mathcal{O})$ be a compact neighborhood of 0_L. Note that $V \subseteq \bigcup \{x + 0.5V \mid x \in V\}$, hence there exists a finite subset $\{x_1, \ldots, x_n\}$ of V such that $V \subseteq \bigcup_{j=1}^{n} (x_j + 0.5V) \subseteq \{x_1, \ldots, x_n\} + 0.5V$. Let $Y = \langle x_1, \ldots, x_n \rangle$. It is clear that $V \subseteq Y + 0.5V$, hence

$$0.5V \subseteq 0.5(Y + 0.5V) = Y + 0.5^2 V.$$

Thus, $V \subseteq Y + Y + 0.5^2 V = Y + 0.5^2 V$, etc. This shows that $V \subseteq Y + 0.5^n V$ for every n.

For $x \in V$ there exists $y_n \in Y$ and $v_n \in 0.5^n V$ such that $x = y_n + 0.5^n v_n$. Since V is compact, there exists a subnet (v_{n_j}) of (v_n) such that $\lim_{j \in J} v_{n_j} = v$. Therefore, for the net (y_{n_j}) we have

$$\lim_{j \in J} y_{n_j} = \lim_{j \in J}(x - 0.5^{n_j} v_{n_j}) = x.$$

Since Y is a closed subspace, we have $x \in Y$, that is $V \subseteq Y$. Since V is an absorbing set, it follows that $L = Y$, hence L is finite dimensional. $\qquad \square$

6.3 Topologies on Inner Product Spaces

Inner product spaces are naturally equipped with norms induced by inner products, and normed spaces, in turn, are special metric spaces, where the metrics are induced by norms. Thus, properties of topological metric spaces and normed linear spaces transfer to inner product spaces.

Inner product in topological inner product spaces is continuous as we show next.

Theorem 6.18. *Let (x_n) and (y_n) be two sequences in a inner product space $(L, (\cdot, \cdot))$. If $\lim x_n = x$ and $\lim y_n = y$, then $\lim(x_n, y_n) = (x, y)$.*

Proof. Since $x_n \to x$ the set $\{x_n \mid n \in \mathbb{N}\}$ is bounded and we have $\|x_n\| \leqslant m$, and

$$\begin{aligned}
|(x_n, y_n) - (x, y)| &= |(x_n, y_n) - (x_n, y) + (x_n, y) - (x, y)| \\
&\leqslant |(x_n, y_n) - (x_n, y)| + |(x_n, y) - (x, y)| \\
&= |(x_n, y_n - y)| + |(x_n - x, y)| \\
&\leqslant \|x_n\| \|y_n - y\| + \|x_n - x\| \|y\| \\
&\qquad \text{(by Cauchy-Schwarz Inequality)} \\
&\leqslant m \|y_n - y\| + \|x_n - x\| \|y\|,
\end{aligned}$$

which implies that $\lim(x_n, y_n) = (x, y)$. $\qquad \square$

Corollary 6.6. *The norm induced by the inner product of a inner product space is continuous.*

Proof. This statement is an immediate consequence of Theorem 6.18 because $\|x\| = \sqrt{(x, x)}$ for every $x \in L$. $\qquad \square$

Properties of orthogonal complements in inner product spaces can be sharpened when the inner product space is equipped with a topology. For example, the next statement is a strengthening of Theorem 2.41.

Theorem 6.19. *If T is a subset of a inner product space $(L, (\cdot, \cdot))$, then $T^{\perp}$ is a closed subspace of L.*

Proof. We have already seen in Theorem 2.41 that $T^{\perp}$ is a subspace of L. Let (x_n) be a convergent sequence in T such that $\lim_{n \to \infty} x_n = x$. By the continuity of the inner product, for $t \in T$ we have $(t, x) = \lim_{n \to \infty} (t, x_n) = 0$, so $x \in T^{\perp}$. Therefore, $T^{\perp}$ is a closed subspace of L. $\square$

6.4 Locally Convex Linear Spaces

Definition 6.4. A *locally convex linear space* is a topological linear space L such that every $x \in L$ has a local basis of convex neighborhoods.

Let ν be a seminorm on the linear space L. We saw that the collection of open spheres of the form $B_{\nu}(x_0, r)$ is a local basis in x_0 for the topology defined by ν.

Theorem 6.20. *Let L be a linear space and let $\mathcal{N}$ be a collection of seminorms on L. The collection $\mathfrak{T}$ of all finite intersections of the form $B_{i_1,\ldots,i_m}(x, r) = \bigcap_{k=1}^{m} B_{\nu_{i_k}}(x, r)$ is a local basis at 0_L for a linear space topology $\mathcal{O}_{\mathcal{N}}$.*

The topology $\mathcal{O}_{\mathcal{N}}$ consists of those subsets U of L such that for every $x \in U$ there exists $T \in \mathfrak{T}$ such that $x + T \subseteq U$.

If $I = \{i_1, \ldots, i_k\}$, we denote the set $B_{i_1,\ldots,i_m}(x, r) = \bigcap_{k=1}^{m} B_{\nu_{i_k}}(x, r)$ by $B_I(x, r)$. With this notation we have

$$B_I(x, r) \cap B_J(x, r) = B_{I \cup J}(x, r).$$

Proof. It is immediate that $\emptyset$ and L are open sets. Also, if $\mathcal{U} \subseteq \mathcal{O}_{\mathcal{N}}$, then $\bigcup \mathcal{U}$ is an open set.

Let U_1, U_2 be two open sets and let $x \in U_1 \cap U_2$. There exists a finite intersection of the form $B_J(x, r)$ included in U_1 and a finite intersection of the form $B_K(x, s)$ included in U_2. Therefore,

$$x \in B_{J \cup K}(x, r) \subseteq U_1 \cap U_2,$$

so $\mathcal{U}$ is closed with respect to finite intersections and is, therefore, a topology.

Next, we show that the addition and the scalar multiplication are continuous in this topology.

To prove that addition of elements of L is continuous it suffices to show that given $U \in \mathcal{T}$ and $x, y \in L$ there are $U_1, U_2 \in \mathcal{T}$ such that $(x + U_1) + (y + U_2) \subseteq (x + y) + U$.

For each seminorm ν_i we have $B_{\nu_i}(0_L, r_1) + B_{\nu_i}(0_L, r_2) \subseteq B_{\nu_i}(0_L, r_1 + r_2)$, by the triangular inequality for ν_i. Therefore, $(x + B_{\nu_i}(0_L, r_1)) + (y + B_{\nu_i}(0_L, r_2)) \subseteq x + y + B_{\nu_i}(0_L, r_1 + r_2)$. Thus, for $W = B_{\nu_{i_1}}(0_L, r_1) \cap \cdots \cap B_{\nu_{i_k}}(0_L, r_k)$ we can take $U_1 = U_2 = B_{\nu_{i_1}}(0_L, r_1/2) \cap \cdots \cap B_{\nu_{i_k}}(0_L, r_k/2)$. Thus, addition in L is continuous.

To prove the continuity of multiplication by scalars, we need to show that given $a \in \mathbb{R}$, $x \in L$ and $U \in \mathcal{T}$ there is $\delta > 0$ and $V \in \mathcal{T}$ such that $(a + B(0, \delta))(x + U) \subseteq ax + U$.

Suppose initially that $U = B_{\nu_i}(0_L, r)$. If $|a - a'| < \delta$ and $x - x' \in B(0_L, r)$ we have

$$\begin{aligned}
\nu_i(ax - a'x') &= \nu_i((a - a')x + a'(x - x')) \\
&\leqslant \nu_i((a - a')x) + \nu_i(a'(x - x')) \\
&= |a - a'|\nu_i(x) + |a'|\nu_i(x - x') \\
&\leqslant |a - a'|\nu_i(x) + (|a| + \delta)\nu_i(x - x') \\
&\leqslant \delta(\nu_i(x) + |a| + \delta).
\end{aligned}$$

Thus, if $\delta(\nu_i(x) + |a| + \delta) < r$, the desired continuity of scalar multiplication follows. These observations can be readily extended to finite intersections as needed. $\qquad\square$

Note that the local basis at $x \in L$ defined above consists of convex sets. For this reason, topological spaces defined in this manner are said to be *locally convex*.

Definition 6.5. Let $\mathcal{N} = \{\nu_i \mid i \in I\}$ be a collection of seminorms defined on a linear space L The collection $\mathcal{N}$ is *separating* if for every $x \in L - \{0_L\}$ there exists $\nu_i \in \mathcal{N}$ such that $\nu_i(x) \neq 0$.

Theorem 6.21. *Let L be a linear space and let $\mathcal{N}$ be a collection of seminorms on L. The locally convex topological space $(L, \mathcal{O}_{\mathcal{N}})$ is a Hausdorff space if and only if $\mathcal{N}$ is a separate collection of seminorms.*

Proof. Suppose that $(L, \mathcal{O}_{\mathcal{N}})$ is a Hausdorff space. Suppose that for $x \neq 0_L$ we would have $\nu(x) = 0$ for every $\nu \in \mathcal{N}$. This would imply that $x \in B_I(0_L, r)$, so x belongs to all neighborhoods of 0_L, which contradicts the separation property of Hausdorff spaces.

If x and y are two distinct elements of L, we have $x - y \neq 0_L$, so there exists a seminorm $\nu \in \mathcal{N}$ such that $\nu(x_0 - y_0) = d > 0$. This is why $B_\nu(x, d/3) \cap B_\nu(y, d/3) = \emptyset$. Indeed, if we would have $z \in B_\nu(x, d/3) \cap B_\nu(y, d/3)$ this would imply $d = \nu(x - y) \leqslant \nu(x - z) + \nu(z - y) < 2d/3$, which is a contradiction. $\qquad\square$

Let $(L, \|\cdot\|)$ be a normed linear topological space and let V be a neighborhood of 0_L. There exists an open set included in V and therefore, there is an open sphere $B(0_L, r)$ included in V. Thus, every neighborhood of 0_L contains an open, convex, and balanced neighborhood C of 0_L. By Theorem 3.32, the Minkowski functional m_C is a seminorm.

Let L be a locally convex topological space. The topology of L is defined by the collection of seminorms defined by a local basis at 0_L that consists of convex and balanced open sets that contain 0_L.

6.5　Continuous Linear Operators

The set of linear operators between two $\mathbb{F}$-linear spaces L, K is denoted by $\mathfrak{L}(L, K)$; if L and K are equipped with topologies then the set of continuous linear operators between these spaces is denoted by $\mathfrak{L}_c(L, K)$.

If $L = K$ we write $\mathfrak{L}(L)$ and $\mathfrak{L}_c(L)$ for these sets, respectively. Then $\mathfrak{L}(L)$ is an algebra relative to operator sum, product of a scalar with an operator, and operator composition.

Theorem 6.22. *Let $(L, \mathcal{O})$ and $(K, \mathcal{O}')$ be two topological linear spaces having the zero elements 0_L and 0_K, respectively. A linear operator $h : L \longrightarrow K$ is continuous in $x \in L$ if and only if it is continuous in 0_L.*

Proof.　Let $h : L \longrightarrow K$ be a linear operator that is continuous in x_0 and let $V \in neigh_{0_K}(\mathcal{O}')$. Then $h(x_0) + V \in neigh_{h(x_0)}(\mathcal{O}')$. By the continuity of h in x_0 there exists $U \in neigh_{x_0}(L, \mathcal{O})$ such that $x \in U$ implies $h(x) \in h(x_0) + V$. Since $-x_0 + U \in neigh_{0_L}(L, \mathcal{O})$ and $x \in -x_0 + U$, we have $x + x_0 \in U$. Therefore, by the linearity of h, we have $h(x + x_0) = h(x) + h(x_0) \in h(x_0) + V$, that is, $h(x) \in V$. This yields the continuity of h in 0_L.

Conversely, suppose that h is continuous in 0_L. Let $x \in L$ and let $V \in neigh_{h(x_0)}(\mathcal{O}')$. Note that $-h(x_0) + V$ is a neighborhood of 0_K. The continuity of h in 0_L implies that there is $U \in neigh_{0_L}(L, \mathcal{O})$ such that $x \in U$ implies $h(x) \in -h(x_0) + V$.

Since $x_0 + U$ is a neighborhood of x_0 and $x \in x_0 + U$ (equivalent to $x - x_0 \in U$), we have $h(x - x_0) \in -h(x_0) + V$, which is equivalent to $h(x) \in V$ by the linearity of h. Thus h is continuous in x_0. $\square$

Corollary 6.7. *Let $(L, \mathcal{O})$ and $(K, \mathcal{O}')$ be two topological linear spaces. A linear operator $h : L \longrightarrow K$ is either continuous everywhere in L or is not continuous in any $x \in L$.*

Proof. This is a direct consequence of Theorem 6.22. $\square$

Theorem 6.23. *The set $\mathfrak{L}_c(L)$ of continuous linear operators defined on a topological linear space L is an algebra relative to operator sum, product of a scalar with an operator, and operator composition.*

Proof. This follows immediately from the corresponding results for linear operators and for continuous functions. $\square$

For a subspace U of a linear space L the mapping $h_U : L \longrightarrow L/U$ is a surjective linear operator (see, for example [121]). In the presence of a topology on L we can prove a stronger result. Recall that the push-forward topology was introduced in Supplement 8 of Chapter 4.

Theorem 6.24. *Let U be a subspace of the topological linear space $(L, \mathcal{O})$ and let $h_U : L \longrightarrow L/H$. If L/U is equipped with the push-forward topology induced by h_U, then $h_U : L \longrightarrow L/U$ is an open mapping.*

Proof. If X is an open subset in L and U is a subset of L, then the set $X + U = \bigcup_{u \in U} t_u(X)$ is an open set as a union of open sets. The set $h_U(X)$ is open in L/H because $h_U^{-1}(h_U(X)) = X + U$. $\square$

6.6 Linear Operators on Normed Linear Spaces

Next we discuss linear operators between topological linear spaces whose topologies are induced by norms.

Theorem 6.25. *Let $(L, \| \cdot \|)$ and $(K, \| \cdot \|)$ be two normed linear spaces. A linear operator $h : L \longrightarrow K$ is continuous if and only it is bounded, that is, there exists a number $c > 0$ such that $\|h(x)\| \leqslant c\|x\|$ for all $x \in L$.*

Proof. Suppose that h is continuous, and therefore, continuous at 0. There exists $\delta > 0$ such that $\|x\| \leqslant \delta$ implies $\|h(x)\| \leqslant 1$. If $\|\mathbf{x}\| \leqslant 1$, then $\|\delta x\| \leqslant \delta$, so $h(\delta x) \leqslant 1$, which implies $h(x) \leqslant \frac{1}{\delta}$, which shows that h is bounded.

Conversely, suppose that h is bounded, that is, $\|x\| \leqslant 1$ implies $\|h(x)\| \leqslant c$. Then, if $\|\mathbf{x}\| \leqslant \frac{\epsilon}{c}$, we have $\left\| \frac{c}{\epsilon} x \right\| \leqslant 1$, which yields $\left\| h \left(\frac{c}{\epsilon} x \right) \right\| \leqslant c$, so $\|h(x)\| \leqslant \epsilon$. Thus, h is continuous at 0, which implies its continuity. $\qquad\square$

Corollary 6.8. *A functional $f : L \longrightarrow \mathbb{R}$ is continuous if and only if it is bounded.*

Proof.   This is an immediate consequence of Theorem 6.25. $\qquad\square$

The set of bounded linear operators between the normed spaces $(L, \|\cdot\|)$ and $(K, \|\cdot\|)$ will be denoted by $\mathfrak{B}(L, K)$.

Definition 6.6. Let $(L, \|\cdot\|)$ and $(K, \|\cdot\|)$ be two normed linear spaces and let $h : L \longrightarrow K$ be a linear and continuous operator between these spaces. The norm of h is the number $\|h\|$ given by

$$\|h\| = \sup\{\|h(x)\| \mid x \in B[0_L, 1]\}.$$

The existence of the number $\|h\|$ follows from the fact that for $\|x\| = 1$ we have $\|h(x)\| \leqslant c$, where c was introduced in Definition 6.6.

The homogeneity of linear operators implies that the norm of a linear and continuous operator h is also given by

$$\|h\| = \sup\left\{ \frac{\|h(x)\|}{\|x\|} \,\middle|\, x \neq 0_L \right\}. \tag{6.2}$$

Note that $\|h\|$ is the least number c such that $\|h(x)\| \leqslant c\|x\|$.

The number $\|h\|$ is indeed a norm on $\mathfrak{L}_c(L, K)$, the linear space of continuous linear operators between L and K.

If $\|h\| = 0$, the inequality $\|h(x)\| \leqslant \|h\|\|x\|$ implies $\|h(x)\| = 0$ for every $x \in L$, hence h is the zero operator.

If $h_1, h_2 \in \mathfrak{L}_c(L, K)$ we can write

$$\begin{aligned}
\|(h_1 + h_2)(x)\| &= \|h_1(x) + h_2(x)\| \leqslant \|h_1(x)\| + \|h_2(x)\| \\
&\leqslant \|h_1\|\|x\| + \|h_2\|\|x\| \\
&= (\|h_1\| + \|h_2\|)\|x\|,
\end{aligned}$$

hence $h_1 + h_2 \in \mathfrak{L}_c(L, K)$ and $\|h_1 + h_2\| \leqslant \|h_1\| + \|h_2\|$.

Furthermore, if $h \in \mathfrak{L}_c(L, K)$, then

$$\|(ah)(x)\| = \|ah(x)\| = |a|\|h(x)\| \leqslant (|a|\|h\|)\|x\|,$$

which means that $ah \in \mathfrak{L}_c(L, K)$ and $\|ah\| \leqslant |a|\|h\|$. We conclude that $\|\cdot\|$ is indeed a norm on $\mathfrak{L}_c(L, K)$.

Definition 6.7. A sequence of linear operators (h_n) in $\mathfrak{L}_c(L, K)$ *converges uniformly* to an operator $h \in \mathfrak{L}_c(L, K)$ if $\lim_{n \to \infty} \|h_n - h\| = 0$.

If $\lim_{n \to \infty} h_n(x) = h(x)$ for every $x \in L$, we say that (h_n) converges to h *pointwise*.

Since

$$\|h_n(x) - h(x)\| = \|(h_n - h)(x)\| \leqslant \|h_n - h\| \, \|\mathbf{x}\|,$$

it is clear that uniform convergence implies pointwise convergence.

Theorem 6.26. *If K is a complete linear space, then $\mathfrak{L}_c(L, K)$ is complete.*

Proof. Suppose that (h_n) is a Cauchy sequence, that is, for every $\epsilon > 0$ there exists n_ϵ such that $m, n \geqslant n_\epsilon$ implies $\|h_n - h_m\| < \epsilon$. Since

$$\|h_n(x) - h_m(x)\| = \|(h_n - h_m)(x)\| \leqslant \|h_n - h_m\| \, \|x\|,$$

then $(h_n(x))$ is a Cauchy sequence, hence there exists $\lim_{n \to \infty} h_n(x)$. If we denote this limit by $h(x)$, this defines a linear operator h. To prove that is bounded, note that $\|h_n - h_n\| < \epsilon$ for $m, n \geqslant n_\epsilon$ implies $\|h_n(x) - h_m(x)\| \leqslant \epsilon \|x\|$ for $m, n \geqslant n_\epsilon$. For $m \to \infty$ we obtain $\|h_n(x) - h(x)\| \leqslant \epsilon \|x\|$ for $n \geqslant n_\epsilon$, hence $h_n - h \in \mathfrak{L}_c(L, K)$. Since $h = h_n - (h_n - h)$, it follows that $h \in \mathfrak{L}_c(L, K)$ and $\lim_{n \to \infty} h_n = h$. $\qquad \square$

Theorem 6.27. *Let $h, g : L \longrightarrow L$ be two linear operators on a normed linear space L. We have $\|gh\| \leqslant \|g\| \|h\|$.*

Proof. For $x \in L$ we have

$$\|gh(x)\| = \|g(f(x))\| \leqslant \|g\| \|f(x)\|$$
$$\leqslant \|g\| \|f\| \|x\|.$$

Since $\|gh\|$ is the least number c such that $\|gh(x)\| \leqslant c \|x\|$, it follows that $\|gh(x)\| \leqslant \|g\| \|h\|$. $\qquad \square$

Corollary 6.9. *Let $h : L \longrightarrow L$ be a linear operators on a normed linear space L. We have $\|h^n\| \leqslant (\|h\|)^n$ for $n \in \mathbb{N}$.*

Proof. This follows immediately from Theorem 6.27. $\qquad \square$

Observe that if $h : L \longrightarrow K$ is a linear bounded operator, and, therefore, a continuous operator, the unit sphere $B[0_L, 1]$ is mapped by h to a bounded set. Operators that map the unit sphere to a set whose closure is compact posses a property stronger than continuity, because this property implies their continuity. This is formalized in the next definition.

Definition 6.8. Let $(L, \|\cdot\|)$ and $(K, \|\cdot\|)$ be two normed linear spaces. A linear operator $h : L \longrightarrow K$ is *compact* if it maps $B[0_L, 1]$ into a set whose closure is compact.

Since $f, g \in \mathfrak{L}_c(L, K)$ imply $f + g \in \mathfrak{L}_c(L, K)$ and $af \in \mathfrak{L}_c(L, K)$ it follows that $\mathfrak{L}_c(L, K)$ is a linear subspace of the linear space of linear operators between L and K.

Theorem 6.28. *Let (h_n) be a sequence of operators in $\mathfrak{L}_c(L, K)$, where $(L, \|\cdot\|)$ and $(K, \|\cdot\|)$ are two normed linear spaces. The sequence (h_n) converges in norm to $h \in \mathfrak{L}_c(L, K)$ if and only if for any bounded subset X of L the sequence $(h_n(x))$ converges uniformly to $h(x)$.*

Proof. Suppose that (h_n) converges in norm to h, that is, $\lim_{n \to \infty} \|h_n - h\| = 0$ and let X be a bounded subset of L such that $\|x\| \leqslant r$. For $\epsilon > 0$ there exists $n_\epsilon \in \mathbb{N}$ such that $n \geqslant n_\epsilon$ implies $\|h_n - h\| \leqslant \frac{\epsilon}{r}$. Therefore, for $x \in X$ and $n \geqslant n_\epsilon$ we have

$$\|h_n(x) - h(x)\| = \|(h_n - h)(x)\| \leqslant \|h_n - h\| \cdot \|x\| < \epsilon,$$

which means that (h_n) converges uniformly on X.

Conversely, suppose that (h_n) converges uniformly on every bounded subset X of L. In particular, this takes place on the sphere $B[0_L, 1]$. Therefore, for $\frac{\epsilon}{2}$ there is $n_\epsilon \in \mathbb{N}$ such that $n \geqslant n_\epsilon$ implies $\|h_n(x) - h(x)\| \leqslant \frac{\epsilon}{2}$ for $\|x\| \leqslant 1$. Therefore, $\|h_n - h\| \leqslant \frac{\epsilon}{2} \leqslant \epsilon$, which concludes the proof. $\square$

The notion of pointwise convergence introduced in Definition 5.18 is applicable to linear operators between normed linear spaces. Namely, a sequence of linear operators (h_n) in $\mathfrak{L}(L, K)$ (where L and K be two normed $\mathbb{F}$–linear spaces) is *pointwise convergent* if for every $x \in L$ the sequence $(h_n(x))$ is convergent in K.

If (h_n) is a pointwise convergent sequence of linear operators, it is possible to define a operator $h : L \longrightarrow K$ as $h(x) = \lim_{n \to \infty} f(x)$. The mapping h is linear because

$$h(ax + by) = \lim_{n \to \infty} h_n(ax + by) = \lim_{n \to \infty} (ah_n(x) + bh_n(y)) = ah(x) + bh(y)$$

for $a, b \in \mathbb{F}$ and $x, y \in L$.

Theorem 6.29. *If (h_n) is a sequence of linear operators in $\mathfrak{L}(L, K)$ that converges in norm to a linear operator $h : L \longrightarrow K$, that is, $\lim_{n \to \infty} \|h_n - h\| = 0$, then (h_n) converges pointwise to h, that is, $\lim_{n \to \infty} h_n(x) = h(x)$ for every $x \in L$.*

Proof. The statement follows from

$$\|h_n(x) - h(x)\| = \|(h_n - h)(x)\| \leqslant \|h_n - h\|\|x\|.$$

$\square$

Theorem 6.30. *Let L and K be two normed $\mathbb{F}$-linear spaces. and let $h : L \longrightarrow K$ be a linear operator. There exists a linear and continuous left inverse h^{-1} of h if and only if there exists $M > 0$ such that $\|h(x)\| \geqslant M\|x\|$ for every $x \in L$. In this case, $\|h^{-1}\| \leqslant \frac{1}{M}$.*

Proof. Suppose that g is a linear and continuous left inverse of h. By Theorem 6.25, g is bounded, so there exists $k > 0$ such that $\|g(y)\| \leqslant k\|y\|$ for $y \in K$. If $y = h(x)$, then $\|x\| = \|g(h(x))\| \leqslant k\|h(x)\|$, so $\|h(x)\| \geqslant \frac{1}{k}\|x\|$, which shows that the inequality of the theorem is satisfied with $M = \frac{1}{k}$.

Conversely, suppose that $\|h(x)\| \geqslant M\|x\|$ for every $x \in L$. Note that if $x \in \mathsf{Null}(h)$ we have $h(x) = 0$, which implies $\|x\| = 0$, that is, $x = 0_L$. Thus, h is injective, hence there exists a left inverse $g : \mathsf{Img}(h) \longrightarrow L$.

Note that for $y \in \mathsf{Img}(h)$ such that $y = h(x)$ we have

$$\|g(y)\| = \|x\| \leqslant \frac{1}{M}\|h(x)\| = \frac{1}{M}\|y\|,$$

which shows that g is continuous. $\square$

Theorem 6.31. *Let L be a normed space and let $h : L \longrightarrow L$ be a linear continuous operator on L. If 1_L is the identity operator on L and $\|h\| \leqslant r < 1$, then $1_L - h$ has an continuous left inverse operator $(1_L - h)^{-1}$ and $\|(1_L - h)^{-1}\| \leqslant \frac{1}{1-\|h\|}$.*

Proof. We have

$$\|(1_L - h)x\| = \|x - h(x)\| \geqslant \|x\| - \|h(x)\| \geqslant \|x\| - r\|x\| = (1 - r)\|x\|.$$

By Theorem 6.30, $1_L - h$ has a continuous left inverse operator $(1_L - h)^{-1}$ and $\|(1_L - h)^{-1}\| \leqslant \frac{1}{1-\|h\|}$. $\square$

Corollary 6.10. *Let L and K be two normed $\mathbb{F}$-linear spaces and let $h : L \longrightarrow K$ be a surjective linear operator. The spaces L and K are homeomorphic if and only if there exists $m, M \in \mathbb{F}$ such that $m\|x\| \leqslant \|h(x)\| \leqslant M\|x\|$ for every $x \in L$.*

Proof. This statement is a consequence of Theorem 6.30. $\square$

Theorem 6.32. *Let L be a real finite-dimensional normed linear space. If U is a closed and bounded subset of L, then U is a compact set.*

Proof. Let $\{x_1, \ldots, x_m\}$ be a basis in L. Define $f : \mathbb{R}^m \longrightarrow L$ as $f(\mathbf{a}) = a_1 x_1 + \cdots + a_m x_m$ for $\mathbf{a} \in \mathbb{R}^m$. We have

$$\|f(\mathbf{a}) - f(\mathbf{b})\| = \left\| \sum_{i=1}^{m} (a_i - b_i) x_i \right\| \leqslant \sum_{i=1}^{m} |a_i - b_i| \|x_i\|$$

$$\leqslant \max_{1 \leqslant i \leqslant m} |a_i - b_i| \sum_{i=1}^{m} \|x_i\| = \|\mathbf{a} - \mathbf{b}\|_\infty \sum_{i=1}^{m} \|x_i\|.$$

Let $W = f^{-1}(U) \subseteq \mathbb{R}^m$. By Theorem 4.77, W is a closed set.

We claim that W is bounded. Indeed, note that the set $\{\mathbf{a} \in \mathbb{R}^m \mid \|\mathbf{a}\|_\infty = 1\}$ is a closed and bounded subset of $\mathbb{R}^m$, and therefore, this set is compact. Thus, f achieves $\mu = \inf\{\|f(\mathbf{a})\| \mid \|\mathbf{a}\|_\infty = 1\}$ in some $\mathbf{b} \in \mathbb{R}^m$. In other words, there exists $\mathbf{b} \in \mathbb{R}^m$ with $\|\mathbf{b}\|_\infty = 1$ such that $f(\mathbf{b}) = \sum_{i=1}^{m} b_i x_i = \mu$. Clearly, we have $\mathbf{b} \neq \mathbf{0}_m$. This implies $f(\mathbf{b}) \neq 0$ because, otherwise, we would have $\sum_{i=1}^{m} b_i \mathbf{x}_i = 0$ and this would imply $b_i = 0$ for $1 \leqslant i \leqslant m$ by the linear independence if $x_1, \ldots, x_m$. Therefore, $\|f(\mathbf{b})\| \neq 0$, which allows to conclude that $\mu = f(\mathbf{b}) > 0$.

Since U is bounded we have $\|\mathbf{x}\| \leqslant c$ for $\mathbf{x} \in U$.

Let $\mathbf{a} \in \mathbb{R}^m$. If $\mathbf{a} \neq \mathbf{0}_m$, we have $\left\| \frac{1}{\|\mathbf{a}\|} \mathbf{a} \right\| = 1$. Therefore,

$$\left\| f\left(\frac{1}{\|\mathbf{a}\|_\infty} \mathbf{a} \right) \right\| \geqslant \mu,$$

or $\|f(\mathbf{a})\| \geqslant \mu \|\mathbf{a}\|_\infty$. This inequality also holds for $\mathbf{a} = \mathbf{0}_m$, so it holds for $\mathbf{a} \in \mathbb{R}^m$.

For $\mathbf{a} \in W$ we have $f(\mathbf{a}) \in U$, hence $\|\mathbf{a}\|_\infty \leqslant \frac{c}{\mu}$ and

$$\mu \|\mathbf{a}\|_\infty \leqslant \|f(\mathbf{a})\| \leqslant c,$$

which implies that W is bounded. $\qquad\square$

Theorem 6.33. *A real finite-dimensional normed linear space is complete.*

Proof. Let L be a real finite-dimensional normed linear space and let (x_n) be a Cauchy sequence in L. Let $n_1 \in \mathbb{N}$ be a number such that $i, j \leqslant n_1$ implies $\|x_i - x_j\| < 1$. Thus, $i \geqslant n_1$ implies $\|x_i\| \leqslant \|x_i - x_{n_1}\| + \|x_{n_1}\| \leqslant 1 + \|x_{n_1}\|$. Therefore, $\|x_i\| \leqslant 1 + \|x_1\| + \cdots + \|x_{n_1}\| = k$ for $i \in \mathbb{N}$. We conclude that the set $\{x_i \mid i \in \mathbb{N}\} \subseteq B[0, k]$, so $\{x_i \mid i \in \mathbb{N}\}$ is bounded.

By Theorem 6.32 the set $B[0, k]$ is compact. Thus, (x_n) must contain a convergent subsequence (x_{n_i}). By Theorem 5.28 the sequence (x_n) converges and its limit is the same as the limit of the subsequence. $\qquad\square$

Theorem 6.34. *Every finite-dimensional subspace of a normed linear space is closed.*

Proof. Let U be a finite-dimensional subspace of a normed linear space L and let (u_n) be a sequence in U such that $\lim_{n\to\infty} u_n = u$. Thus, (u_n) is a Cauchy sequence and, by the completeness of U established in Theorem 6.33, we have $u \in U$. This shows that U is closed. □

Theorem 6.35. (Riesz' Lemma) *Let L be a normed linear space and let U be a proper and closed subspace of L. If $r \in (0,1)$ there exists $y \in L$ such that $\|y\| = 1$ and $\inf\{\|y - u\| \mid u \in U\} \geqslant r$.*

Proof. If $z \in L - U$ we have $d(z, U) > 0$ by Theorem 5.16 because $U = \mathbf{K}(U)$.

Let $a = \inf\{\|z - u\| \mid u \in U\} > 0$. Since $\frac{a}{r} > a$, there exists $u_1 \in U$ such that $\|z - u_1\| < \frac{a}{r}$. Then, we have for all $u \in U$:

$$\left\| \frac{z - u_1}{\|z - u_1\|} - u \right\| = \frac{1}{\|z - u_1\|} \|z - (u_1 + \|z - u_1\|u)\|$$
$$\geqslant \frac{r}{a} a = r,$$

because $u_1 + \|z - u_1\|u \in U$. Thus $y = \frac{z - u_1}{\|z - u_1\|}$ is the desired element. □

The next statement offers a characterization of finite-dimensional normed linear spaces.

Theorem 6.36. *Let L be a normed linear space. L is finite-dimensional if and only if its unit ball $B[0, 1]$ is compact.*

Proof. If L is finite-dimensional, taking into account that $B[0, 1]$ is bounded and closed, it follows that $B[0, 1]$ is compact by Theorem 6.32.

Conversely, suppose that $B[0, 1]$ is compact but L is not finite-dimensional. Consider a sequence (x_n) defined inductively as follows.

Let x_0 be such that $\|x_0\| = 1$. Suppose that we defined $x_0, x_1, \ldots, x_n$ and let U_n be the subspace generated by these elements. Since U_n is finite-dimensional it follows that it is closed. By Riesz' Lemma we select x_{n+1} such that $\|x_{n+1}\| = 1$ and $d(x_{n+1}, U_n) > \frac{1}{2}$. Then, $\|x_n - x_i\| \geqslant \frac{1}{2}$ for $i < n$ and, therefore, (x_n) cannot have a convergent subsequence, which contradicts the compactness of $B[0, 1]$. □

The notion of separability of topological spaces is applicable to normed linear space.

Example 6.1. Any finite dimensional normed real linear space L is separable. Indeed, if $B = \{e_1, \ldots, e_m\}$ is a basis in L, then for every $x \in L$ we have $x = \sum_{i=1}^{m} a_i e_i$. Each of the numbers a_i is the limit of a sequence of rational numbers $a_i = \lim_{n \to \infty} r_{ni}$. If $x_n = \sum_{i=1}^{m} r_{ni} e_i$, then it is easy to see that $x = \lim_{n \to \infty} x_n$, which shows that the set of elements of L with rational coefficients in dense in L. Therefore, L is separable.

6.7 Topological Aspects of Convex Sets

Theorem 6.37. *Let C be a convex set in a real linear space L. Both $\boldsymbol{K}(C)$ and $\boldsymbol{I}(C)$ are convex sets.*

Proof. The convexity of C implies $(1 - a)C + aC \subseteq C$ for $a \in [0, 1]$. Since h_a is a homeomorphism of L we have $(1 - a)\boldsymbol{K}(C) \subseteq \boldsymbol{K}((1 - a)C)$ and $a\boldsymbol{K}(C) \subseteq \boldsymbol{K}(aC)$. Therefore,

$$(1-a)\boldsymbol{K}(C)+a\boldsymbol{K}(C) \subseteq \boldsymbol{K}((1-a)C)+\boldsymbol{K}(aC) \subseteq \boldsymbol{K}((1-a)C+aC)) \subseteq \boldsymbol{K}(C),$$

which implies that $\boldsymbol{K}(C)$ is convex.

If $u, w \in \boldsymbol{I}(C)$, there exist $U, W \in neigh_{0_L}(L, \mathcal{O})$ such that $u + U \subseteq C$ and $v + V \subseteq C$. The convexity of C implies

$$(1 - a)(u + U) + a(v + V) = (1 - a)u + av + (1 - a)U + aV \subseteq C,$$

so $\boldsymbol{I}(C)$ is convex. $\qquad\square$

Theorem 6.38. *Let C be a non-empty convex set in a normed real linear space L such that $\boldsymbol{I}(C) \neq \emptyset$. If $x \in \boldsymbol{I}(C)$ and $y \in \boldsymbol{K}(C)$, then $[x, y) \subseteq \boldsymbol{I}(C)$.*

Proof. Since $x \in \boldsymbol{I}(C)$, there exists $r_0 > 0$ such that $B(x, r_0) \subseteq C$.

To show that $[x, y) \subseteq \boldsymbol{I}(C)$ it suffices to prove that for every $z \in (x, y) \subseteq C$ there exists $r > 0$ such that $B(z, r) \subseteq C$. Since $z \in (x, y)$, there exists $a \in (0, 1)$ such that $z = (1 - a)x + ay$.

Since $y \in \boldsymbol{K}(C)$, for every $r_1 > 0$, we have $B(y, r_1) \cap C \neq \emptyset$, so there exists $w_1 \in C$ such that $\|y - w_1\| < r_1$.

If $r < \frac{1}{2}((1 - a)r_0 + ar_1)$, we claim that $B(z, r) \subseteq C$. Indeed, let $w \in B(z, r)$. We have $\|z - w\| < r$ If w_2 is defined such that w is a convex combination of w_1 and w_2, that is, $w = (1 - a)w_2 + aw_1$, then

$$x - w_2 = x - \frac{1}{1 - a}w - \frac{a}{1 - a}w_1,$$

so

$$\|x - w_2\| = \left\| x - \frac{1}{1-a}w + \frac{a}{1-a}w_1 \right\|$$

$$= \left\| \frac{1}{1-a}z - \frac{a}{1-a}y - \frac{1}{1-a}w + \frac{a}{1-a}w_1 \right\|$$

$$\leqslant \frac{1}{1-a}\|z - w\| + \frac{a}{1-a}\|y - w_1\|$$

$$\leqslant \frac{1}{1-a}r + \frac{a}{1-a}r_1.$$

Since $r < \frac{1}{2}((1-a)r_0 + ar_1)$, we have

$$\frac{1}{1-a}r + \frac{a}{1-a}r_1 < \frac{1}{2}r_0 + \frac{3}{2}\frac{a}{1-a}r_1.$$

Choosing r_1 such that $r_1 < \frac{1-a}{3a}r_0$, it follows that $\|x - w_2\| < r_0$, so $w_2 \in B(x, r_0) \subseteq C$, hence $w_2 \in C$. Since w is a convex combination of two elements of C, if follows that $w \in C$, so $B(z, r) \subseteq C$, which shows that $z \in \mathbf{I}(C)$, that is, $[x, y) \subseteq \mathbf{I}(C)$. $\qquad\square$

Theorem 6.39. *If C is a convex subset of a normed real linear space L such that $\mathbf{I}(C) \neq \emptyset$, then $\mathbf{K}(\mathbf{I}(C)) = \mathbf{K}(C)$ and $\mathbf{I}(\mathbf{K}(C)) = \mathbf{I}(C)$.*

Proof. Note that, since $\mathbf{I}(C) \subseteq C$, we have $\mathbf{K}(\mathbf{I}(C)) \subseteq \mathbf{K}(C)$.

Conversely, let $x \in \mathbf{K}(C)$. Since $\mathbf{I}(C) \neq \emptyset$, there exists $y \in \mathbf{I}(C)$ such that $z_a = (1-a)x + ay \in \mathbf{I}(C)$. Since $\lim_{a \to 1} z_a = x$, it follows that $x \in \mathbf{K}(\mathbf{I}(C))$, so $\mathbf{K}(C) \subseteq \mathbf{K}(\mathbf{I}(C))$.

For the second equality observe that $C \subseteq \mathbf{K}(C)$ implies $\mathbf{I}(C) \subseteq \mathbf{I}(\mathbf{K}(C))$.

Let $u \in \mathbf{I}(\mathbf{K}(C))$. There exists $\epsilon > 0$ such that $B(u, \epsilon) \subseteq \mathbf{K}(C)$. Let $v \in \mathbf{I}(C)$, where $v \neq u$ and let $y = (1+d)u - dv$, where $d = \frac{\epsilon}{2\|u-v\|}$.

We have

$$\|y - u\| = d\|u - v\| \leqslant \frac{\epsilon}{2},$$

it follows that $y \in \mathbf{K}(C)$. Since

$$u = \frac{1}{1+d}y + \frac{d}{1+d}v,$$

$y \in \mathbf{K}(C)$ and $v \in \mathbf{I}(C)$, it follows that $u \in \mathbf{I}(C)$ by Theorem 6.38, so $\mathbf{I}(\mathbf{K}(C)) \subseteq \mathbf{I}(C)$. $\qquad\square$

Theorem 6.40. *Let $T_{n+1} = \{(t_1, \ldots, t_{n+1}) \mid \sum_{i=1}^{n+1} t_i = 1, t_i \geqslant 0 \text{ for } 1 \leqslant i \leqslant n+1\}$. The topological subspace $(T_{n+1}, \mathcal{O}^n)$ of the topological space $(\mathbb{R}^{n+1}, \mathcal{O}^{n+1})$ is homeomorphic to any simplex $S[\boldsymbol{x}_1, \ldots, \boldsymbol{x}_n, \boldsymbol{x}_{n+1}]$ in $\mathbb{R}^n$, where the vectors $\boldsymbol{x}_1, \ldots, \boldsymbol{x}_n, \boldsymbol{x}_{n+1}$ are in general position.*

Proof.   Let $f : T_{n+1} \longrightarrow S[\mathbf{x}_1, \ldots, \mathbf{x}_n, \mathbf{x}_{n+1}]$ be the function defined by

$$f(t_1, \ldots, t_n, t_{n+1}) = t_1 \mathbf{x}_1 + \cdots + t_n \mathbf{x}_n + t_{n+1} \mathbf{x}_{n+1}$$

for

$$\mathbf{t} = \begin{pmatrix} t_1 \\ \vdots \\ t_n \\ t_{n+1} \end{pmatrix},$$

where $\sum_{i=1}^{n+1} t_i = 1$ and $t_i \geqslant 0$. The uniqueness of the barycentric coordinates (Theorem 3.34) implies that f is a bijection. Observe that we have

$$f(\mathbf{t}) = (\mathbf{x}_1 \; \cdots \; \mathbf{x}_n \; \mathbf{x}_{n+1})\mathbf{t} = \mathbf{X}\mathbf{t},$$

where $\mathbf{X} = (\mathbf{x}_1 \; \cdots \; \mathbf{x}_n \; \mathbf{x}_{n+1}) \in \mathbb{R}^{n \times (n+1)}$ and $\mathbf{t} = \begin{pmatrix} t_1 \\ \vdots \\ t_k, t_{k+1} \end{pmatrix}$. Thus, f is

also continuous as a linear mapping.

The inverse of f is also continuous. Indeed, note that if $t_1 \mathbf{x}_1 + \cdots + t_n \mathbf{x}_n + t_{n+1} \mathbf{x}_{n+1} = \mathbf{y}$, then

$$t_1(\mathbf{x}_1 - \mathbf{x}_{n+1}) + \cdots + t_n(\mathbf{x}_n - \mathbf{x}_{n+1}) = \mathbf{y} - \mathbf{x}_n.$$

Since $\mathbf{x}_1, \ldots, \mathbf{x}_n, \mathbf{x}_{n+1}$ are in general position, the vectors $\mathbf{x}_1 - \mathbf{x}_{n+1}, \ldots, \mathbf{x}_n - \mathbf{x}_{n+1}$ are linearly independent and the matrix $V = (\mathbf{x}_1 - \mathbf{x}_{n+1} \; \cdots \; \mathbf{x}_n - \mathbf{x}_{n+1})$ is invertible. This yields

$$\begin{pmatrix} t_1 \\ \vdots \\ t_n \end{pmatrix} = V^{-1}(\mathbf{y} - \mathbf{x}_{n+1}).$$

Therefore,

$$\begin{pmatrix} t_1 \\ \vdots \\ t_n \\ t_{n+1} \end{pmatrix} = \begin{pmatrix} I_n & \mathbf{0}_n \\ -\mathbf{1}'_n & 1 \end{pmatrix} (V'(\mathbf{y} - \mathbf{x}_{n+1}) \; 1),$$

which implies that the inverse of f is also continuous. $\square$

We shall refer to the homeomorphism f defined in Theorem 6.40 as the *canonical homeomorphism* T_{n+1} and $S[\mathbf{x}_1, \ldots, \mathbf{x}_n, \mathbf{x}_{n+1}]$. The existence of this homeomorphism between T_{n+1} and $S[\mathbf{x}_1, \ldots, \mathbf{x}_n, \mathbf{x}_{n+1}]$ allows us to transfer topological properties to simplexes. An example is given in the next corollary.

Corollary 6.11. *Every simplex $S[\boldsymbol{x}_1, \ldots, \boldsymbol{x}_n, \boldsymbol{x}_{n+1}]$ in $\mathbb{R}^n$ is a compact set.*

Proof. Since T_{n+1} is a closed and bounded set of $\mathbb{R}^n$, it follows that T_{n+1} is compact. The property of $S[\mathbf{x}_1, \ldots, \mathbf{x}_n, \mathbf{x}_{n+1}]$ follows from the previous theorem. □

Theorem 6.41. *The set*

$$\{\boldsymbol{x} \in S[\boldsymbol{x}_1, \ldots, \boldsymbol{x}_n, \boldsymbol{x}_{n+1}] \mid a_i(x) > 0 \text{ for } 1 \leqslant i \leqslant n+1\}$$

is an open set in $S[\boldsymbol{x}_1, \ldots, \boldsymbol{x}_n, \boldsymbol{x}_{n+1}]$. *Furthermore,* $\boldsymbol{x} \in \partial S[\boldsymbol{x}_1, \ldots, \boldsymbol{x}_n, \boldsymbol{x}_{n+1}]$ *if and only if* $a_i(\boldsymbol{x}) = 0$ *for some* i, $1 \leqslant i \leqslant n+1$.

Proof. Consider the open sets $U_i = \{\mathbf{t} \in \mathbb{R}^{n+1} \mid t_i > 0\}$, where $1 \leqslant i \leqslant n + 1$. Note that

$$\{\mathbf{t} \in T_{n+1} \mid t_i > 0 \text{ for } 1 \leqslant i \leqslant n+1\} = T_{n+1} \cap \bigcap_{i=1}^{n+1} U_i,$$

which implies that $\{\mathbf{t} \in T_{n+1} \mid t_i > 0 \text{ for } 1 \leqslant i \leqslant n + 1\}$ is an open set in T_{n+1}. Its image through the canonical homeomorphism f is the set $\{\mathbf{x} \in S[\mathbf{x}_1, \ldots, \mathbf{x}_n, \mathbf{x}_{n+1}] \mid a_i(x) > 0 \text{ for } 1 \leqslant i \leqslant n+1\}$, so this latest set is open in $S[\mathbf{x}_1, \ldots, \mathbf{x}_n, \mathbf{x}_{n+1}]$.

Note that $T_{n+1} \subseteq H_{\mathbf{1}_n, 1}$. The canonical homeomorphism f can be extended to the hyperplane $H_{\mathbf{1}_n, 1}$ as $f(\mathbf{t}) = t_1 \mathbf{x}_1 + \cdots + t_n \mathbf{x}_n + t_{n+1} \mathbf{x}_{n+1}$; the points in ∂T_{n+1} (which must have some t_i equal to 0) are mapped by this extension into points in $\partial S[\mathbf{x}_1, \ldots, \mathbf{x}_n, \mathbf{x}_{n+1}]$.

If $\mathbf{x} \in \partial S[\mathbf{x}_1, \ldots, \mathbf{x}_n, \mathbf{x}_{n+1}]$, any open set that contains $\mathbf{x}$ intersects $\mathbb{R}^{n+1} - S[\mathbf{x}_1, \ldots, \mathbf{x}_n, \mathbf{x}_{n+1}]$, so it contains points in $f(H_{\mathbf{1}_{n+1}, 1})$ with negative coordinates. This implies that some t_j is 0. □

Theorem 6.42. *Every point located in* $\boldsymbol{I}(S[\boldsymbol{x}_1, \ldots, \boldsymbol{x}_n, \boldsymbol{x}_{n+1}])$ *belongs to the interior of a unique subsimplex of* $S[\boldsymbol{x}_1, \ldots, \boldsymbol{x}_n, \boldsymbol{x}_{n+1}]$.

Proof. If $\mathbf{x} \in \mathbf{I}(S[\mathbf{x}_1, \ldots, \mathbf{x}_k, \mathbf{x}_{k+1}])$ then we can write $\mathbf{x} = a_{i_1}(\mathbf{x})\mathbf{x}_{i_1} + \cdots + a_{i_m}(\mathbf{x})\mathbf{x}_{i_m}$, where $\{i_1, \ldots, i_m\}$ is the set of subscripts that correspond to non-zero barycentric coordinates. Since these coordinates are uniquely determined by $\mathbf{x}$, it follows that $\mathbf{x}$ belongs to the interior of a unique subsimplex of $S[\mathbf{x}_1, \ldots, \mathbf{x}_n, \mathbf{x}_{n+1}]$. □

6.8 The Relative Interior

Consider the uni-dimensional simplex S in $\mathbb{R}^2$ generated by the points $\mathbf{x}_1 = \binom{1}{0}$ and $\mathbf{x}_2 = \binom{0}{1}$. The interior $\mathbf{I}(S)$ is empty since no two-dimensional sphere centered in a point of S is included in S. However, there exists a continuous bijection h between the interval $[0,1]$ (which has a non-empty interior in $\mathbb{R}^1$) and S, defined by $h(r) = \begin{pmatrix} r \\ 1-r \end{pmatrix}$, and this suggests that the notion of interior of a set should be adapted to accommodate this situation. This can be achieved by relaxing the defining condition for interior points of C that requires for $\mathbf{x} \in \mathbf{I}(C)$ the existence of a positive number r such that $B(\mathbf{x}, r) \cap C \neq \emptyset$. Instead, we define a point $\mathbf{x}$ to be *relatively interior* to C if the intersection with C of each line through $\mathbf{x}$ contains an open interval about $\mathbf{x}$. Equivalently, $\mathbf{x}$ is relatively interior to C if given $\mathbf{y} \in C$, there is an $r > 0$ such that $\mathbf{x} + t\mathbf{y} \in C$ for all t with $|t| < r$.

Definition 6.9. Let C be a convex set, $C \subseteq \mathbb{R}^n$. The *relative interior* $\mathbf{RI}(C)$ of C consists of all relatively interior points of C:

$$\mathbf{RI}(C) = \{\mathbf{x} \in C \mid B(\mathbf{x}, r) \cap \mathbf{K}_{\mathrm{aff}}(C) \subseteq C \text{ for some } r > 0\}.$$

A set S is *relatively open* is $S = \mathbf{RI}(S)$.

It is clear that $\mathbf{I}(C) \subseteq \mathbf{RI}(C) \subseteq C$ for each convex set C.

Example 6.2. Let $C = \{\mathbf{x}_0\}$ be an one-point subset of $\mathbb{R}^n$. It is immediate that $\mathbf{I}(C) = \emptyset$, since there is no open sphere $B(\mathbf{x}_0, r)$ with $r > 0$ included in C. On the other hand, $\mathbf{RI}(C) = \{\mathbf{x}_0\}$.

Example 6.3. Let $C = \{\mathbf{x} \in \mathbb{R}^3 \mid x_1^2 + x_2^2 \leqslant 1, x_3 = 0\}$. We have $\mathbf{I}(C) = \emptyset$. However, since $\mathbf{K}_{\mathrm{aff}}(C) = \{(x_1, x_2, 0) \mid x_1, x_2 \in \mathbb{R}\}$, the relative interior of C is

$$\mathbf{RI}(C) = \{\mathbf{x} \in \mathbb{R}^3 \mid x_1^2 + x_2^2 < 1, x_3 = 0\}.$$

If C is a convex subset of $\mathbb{R}^n$ that contains a non-empty open set D, then $\mathbf{RI}(C) \neq \emptyset$. Indeed, in this case, for $x \in D$ there exists $r > 0$ such that $B(x, r) \subseteq D$. Therefore,

$$B(x, r) \cap \mathbf{K}_{\mathrm{aff}}(C) \subseteq D \cap \mathbf{K}_{\mathrm{aff}}(C) \subseteq C \cap \mathbf{K}_{\mathrm{aff}}(C) = C,$$

which implies $x \in C$. Thus, $\mathbf{RI}(C)$ is non-empty. This observation is applied in the next example.

Example 6.4. Let $S[\mathbf{x}_1, \ldots, \mathbf{x}_k, \mathbf{x}_{k+1}]$ be the k-dimensional simplex in $\mathbb{R}^n$ generated by the affinely independent points $\mathbf{x}_1, \ldots, \mathbf{x}_k, \mathbf{x}_{k+1}$. Thus, $\mathbf{K}_{\mathrm{aff}}$ consists of those points $\mathbf{x}$ that are affine combinations of the form

$$\mathbf{x} = a_1\mathbf{x}_1 + \cdots + a_k\mathbf{x}_k + a_{k+1}\mathbf{x}_{k+1},$$

where $a_1 + \cdots + a_k + a_{k+1} = 1$ and the coefficients $a_1, \ldots, a_k, a_{k+1}$ are uniquely determined by $\mathbf{x}$.

Note that

$$S[\mathbf{x}_1, \ldots, \mathbf{x}_k, \mathbf{x}_{k+1}] = \mathbf{K}_{\text{conv}}(\{\mathbf{x}_1, \ldots, \mathbf{x}_k, \mathbf{x}_{k+1}\}) \subseteq \mathbf{K}_{\text{aff}}(\{\mathbf{x}_1, \ldots, \mathbf{x}_k, \mathbf{x}_{k+1}\}).$$

Let $h : \mathbf{K}_{\text{aff}}(S) \longrightarrow \mathbb{R}^{k+1}$ be the affine and continuous mapping defined as

$$h(\mathbf{x}) = \begin{pmatrix} a_1 \\ \vdots \\ a_k \\ a_{k+1} \end{pmatrix}$$

for $\mathbf{x} \in \mathbf{K}_{\text{aff}}(S)$.

Define the K_i as

$$K_i = \mathbb{R} \times \cdots \times \mathbb{R}_{>0} \times \cdots \mathbb{R},$$

where the ith component of each vector of K_i is positive, for $1 \leqslant i \leqslant k+1$. Each set K_i is open, and therefore, each set $h^{-1}(K_i)$ is an open non-empty subset of $\mathbf{K}_{\text{aff}}(S)$. This implies that $\bigcap_{i=1}^{k+1} h^{-1}(K_i)$ is open. Furthermore, we have

$$\bigcap_{i=1}^{k+1} h^{-1}(K_i) = \{a_1\mathbf{x}_1 + \cdots + a_k\mathbf{x}_k + a_{k+1}\mathbf{x}_{k+1} \mid a_i > 0 \text{ for } 1 \leqslant i \leqslant k+1\}$$

$$\subseteq \mathbf{K}_{\text{conv}}(\{x_1, \ldots, x_k, x_{k+1}\}) = S[\mathbf{x}_1, \ldots, \mathbf{x}_k, \mathbf{x}_{k+1}].$$

Thus, $\mathbf{K}_{\text{aff}}(\{\mathbf{x}_1, \ldots, \mathbf{x}_k, \mathbf{x}_{k+1}\})$ contains a non-empty open set, so the relative interior of $S[\mathbf{x}_1, \ldots, \mathbf{x}_k, \mathbf{x}_{k+1}]$ is non-empty.

In the special case of uni- and bi-dimensional simplexes we have $S[\mathbf{x}_1, \mathbf{x}_2] \subseteq S[\mathbf{x}_1, \mathbf{x}_2, \mathbf{x}_3]$. Note, however, that

$$\mathbf{RI}(S[\mathbf{x}_1, \mathbf{x}_2]) = \{(1 - a)\mathbf{x}_1 + a\mathbf{x}_2 \mid a \in (0, 1)\},$$

while

$$\mathbf{RI}(S[\mathbf{x}_1, \mathbf{x}_2, \mathbf{x}_3]) = \{(1 - a - b)\mathbf{x}_1 + a\mathbf{x}_2 + b\mathbf{x}_3 \mid a, b \in (0, 1)\}.$$

This shows that the relative interior operation is not monotonic. Indeed, we actually have:

$$\mathbf{RI}(S[\mathbf{x}_1, \mathbf{x}_2]) \cap \mathbf{RI}(S[\mathbf{x}_1, \mathbf{x}_2, \mathbf{x}_3]) = \emptyset.$$

Theorem 6.43. *If C is a non-empty convex subset of $\mathbb{R}^n$, then $\mathbf{RI}(C) \neq \emptyset$.*

Proof.   Let m be the dimension of $\mathbf{K}_{\mathrm{aff}}(C)$. There is an affinely independent set $\{\mathbf{x}_1, \ldots, \mathbf{x}_{m+1}\}$ of points from C, where m is maximal with this property. The set $S = \mathbf{K}_{\mathrm{conv}}(\{\mathbf{x}_1, \ldots, \mathbf{x}_{m+1}\})$ is a simplex contained in C. As we saw in Example 6.4, S has a non-empty relative interior. Since $\mathbf{K}_{\mathrm{aff}}(S) \subseteq \mathbf{K}_{\mathrm{aff}}(C)$ and $\dim(\mathbf{K}_{\mathrm{aff}}(S)) = m = \dim(\mathbf{K}_{\mathrm{aff}}(C))$, it follows that $\mathbf{K}_{\mathrm{aff}}(S) = \mathbf{K}_{\mathrm{aff}}(C)$. Thus, S has a non-empty relative interior. $\square$

Theorem 6.44. *Let C be a non-empty convex set in $\mathbb{R}^n$. If $\boldsymbol{x} \in \boldsymbol{RI}(C)$ and $\boldsymbol{y} \in \boldsymbol{K}(C)$, then $[\boldsymbol{x}, \boldsymbol{y}) \subseteq \boldsymbol{RI}(C)$.*

Proof.   Suppose initially that $\mathbf{y} \in C$. Since $\mathbf{x} \in \mathbf{RI}(C)$, there exists $r > 0$ such that such that $B(\mathbf{x}, r) \cap \mathbf{K}_{\mathrm{aff}}(C) \subseteq C$.

Let $\mathbf{x}_a = (1 - a)\mathbf{x} + a\mathbf{y}$ for $0 \leqslant a < 1$, so $\mathbf{x}_a \in [\mathbf{x}, \mathbf{y})$, and let $\mathbf{z} \in B(\mathbf{x}_a, (1-a)r) \cap \mathbf{K}_{\mathrm{aff}}(C)$.

Define $\mathbf{w} = \mathbf{x} + \frac{1}{1-a}(\mathbf{z} - \mathbf{x}_a)$. We have $\|\mathbf{w} - \mathbf{x}\| = \frac{1}{1-a}\|\mathbf{z} - \mathbf{x}_a\| < r$, so $\mathbf{w} \in B(\mathbf{x}, r)$. Also,

$$\mathbf{w} = \mathbf{x} + \frac{1}{1-a}(\mathbf{z} - (1-a)\mathbf{x} - a\mathbf{y}) = \frac{1}{1-a}\mathbf{z} - \frac{a}{1-a}\mathbf{y} \in \mathbf{K}_{\mathrm{aff}}(C),$$

so $\mathbf{w} \in B(\mathbf{x}, r) \cap \mathbf{K}_{\mathrm{aff}}(C)$, which shows that $\mathbf{z}$ is a convex combination of some point of $\mathbf{w} \in B(\mathbf{x}, r) \cap \mathbf{K}_{\mathrm{aff}}(C) \subseteq C$ and of $\mathbf{y}$. Since C is convex, $\mathbf{x}_a \in \mathbf{RI}(C)$.

Suppose now that $\mathbf{y} \in \mathbf{K}(C) - C$. Consider a sequence $(\mathbf{y}_k)$ of elements of C such that $\lim_{k \to \infty} \mathbf{y}_k = \mathbf{y}$ and let $\mathbf{y}_{k,a} = (1 - a)\mathbf{x} + a\mathbf{y}_k$.

Let r be a positive number such that $B(\mathbf{x}, r) \cap \mathbf{K}_{\mathrm{aff}}(C) \subset C$. Then, $B(\mathbf{y}_{k,a}, (1-a)r) \cap \mathbf{K}_{\mathrm{aff}}(C) \subseteq C$ for all k. Since $\lim_{k \to \infty} \mathbf{y}_{k,a} = \mathbf{y}_a$, if k is sufficiently large, we have $B(\mathbf{y}_a, \frac{(1-a)r}{2}) \subseteq B(\mathbf{y}_{k,a}, (1-a)r)$. Therefore, $B(\mathbf{y}_a, \frac{(1-a)r}{2}) \cap \mathbf{K}_{\mathrm{aff}}(C) \subseteq C$, so $\mathbf{y}_a \in \mathbf{RI}(C)$. $\square$

Corollary 6.12. *If C is a convex subset of $\mathbb{R}^n$, then $\boldsymbol{RI}(C)$ is a convex set.*

Proof.   This follows immediately from Theorem 6.44 by taking $\mathbf{y} \in \mathbf{RI}(C)$. $\square$

Theorem 6.45. (Prolongation Theorem) *Let C be a non-empty convex subset of $\mathbb{R}^n$. We have $z \in \boldsymbol{RI}(C)$ if and only if for every $x \in C$, there exists $a > 1$ such that $(1 - a)x + az \in C$.*

Proof.   Let $z_a = (1 - a)x + az$ for $a \in \mathbb{R}$. It is clear that $z_a \in \mathbf{K}_{\mathrm{aff}}\{x, z\}$. If $a = 0$ we have $z_a = x$ and if $a = 1$, $z_1 = z$. Therefore, if $a > 1$, z_a is located on the prolongation of the segment $[x, z]$ (which explains the name given to this theorem).

Suppose that $z \in \mathbf{RI}(C)$. Since

$$\|z - z_a\| = \|(1 - a)(z - x)\| = |1 - a| \|z - x\|,$$

it suffices to take $|1 - a| < \frac{r}{\|z - x\|}$, to obtain $z_a \in B(z, r)$. Since $z_a \in \mathbf{K}_{\mathrm{aff}}[x, z] \subseteq \mathbf{K}_{\mathrm{aff}}(C)$, it follows that $z_a \in C$.

Conversely, suppose that for every $x \in C$, there exists $a > 1$ such that $(1 - a)x + az \in C$. Since $\mathbf{RI}(C) \neq \emptyset$, there exits $x \in \mathbf{RI}(C)$. By hypothesis, there exists $y_a = (1 - a)x + az$ with $a > 1$ such that $y_a \in C$. Then,

$$z = \frac{a - 1}{a}x + \frac{1}{a},$$

where $\frac{a-1}{a}, \frac{1}{a} \in (0, 1)$. This implies $z \in \mathbf{RI}(C)$. $\square$

Theorem 6.46. *Let C be a convex subset of $\mathbb{R}^n$. The relative interior $\mathbf{RI}(C)$ is a relatively open subset of $\mathbb{R}^n$.*

Proof. We need to show that $\mathbf{RI}(\mathbf{RI}(C)) = \mathbf{RI}(C)$. Suppose that $\mathbf{x} \in \mathbf{RI}(\mathbf{RI}(C))$. Then for every $\mathbf{u} \in \mathbf{RI}(C)$ there exist $\mathbf{v} \in \mathbf{RI}(C)$ and $a \in [0, 1)$ such that $\mathbf{x} = (1 - a)\mathbf{u} + a\mathbf{v}$.

Also, since $\mathbf{u}, \mathbf{v} \in \mathbf{RI}(C)$, then for every $\mathbf{s}, \mathbf{t} \in C$, there exist $\mathbf{p}, \mathbf{q} \in C$ and $\mu, \nu \in [0, 1)$ such that $\mathbf{u} = (1 - \mu)\mathbf{s} + \mu\mathbf{p}$ and $\mathbf{v} = (1 - \nu)\mathbf{t} + \nu\mathbf{q}$. This allows us to write

$$\mathbf{x} = (1 - a)\mathbf{u} + a\mathbf{v} = (1 - a)((1 - \mu)\mathbf{s} + \mu\mathbf{p}) + a((1 - \nu)\mathbf{t} + \nu\mathbf{q})$$
$$= (1 - a)(1 - \mu)\mathbf{s} + (1 - a)\mu\mathbf{p} + a(1 - \nu)\mathbf{t} + a\nu\mathbf{q},$$

which shows that $\mathbf{x}$ can be expressed as a convex combination of $\mathbf{s}, \mathbf{p}, \mathbf{t}$, and $\mathbf{q}$. $\square$

Definition 6.10. Let C be a convex set in $\mathbb{R}^n$. The *relative border* of C is the set $\partial^r(C) = \mathbf{K}(C) - \mathbf{RI}(C)$.

Theorem 6.47. *Let C be a non-empty, convex, and closed subset of a complete normed real linear space L. For each $x \in L$ there is a unique $t \in C$ that is closest to x.*

Proof. Let $d = d(x, C)$ and let (y_n) be a sequence in C such that $\|y_n - x\| = d$. We claim that (y_n) is a Cauchy sequence.

Note that $\frac{1}{2}y_n + \frac{1}{2}y_m \in C$ because C is convex. Therefore, $\left\| \frac{1}{2}y_n + \frac{1}{2}y_m - x \right\| \geqslant d$. We have

$$
\begin{aligned}
\|y_n - y_m\|^2 &= \|(y_n - x) - (y_m - x)\|^2 \\
&= 2\|y_n - x\|^2 + 2\|y_m - x\|^2 - \|y_n + y_m - 2x\|^2 \\
&\quad \text{(by the Parallelogram Equality)} \\
&= 2\|y_n - x\|^2 + 2\|y_m - x\|^2 - 4\left\| \frac{y_n + y_m}{2} - x \right\|^2 \\
&\leqslant 2\|y_n - x\|^2 + 2\|y_m - x\|^2 - 4d^2,
\end{aligned}
$$

which shows that (y_n) is indeed a Cauchy sequence. Due to the completeness of L there exists $y = \lim_{n \to \infty} y_n$. By the continuity of the norm,

$$
\|x - y\| = \|x - \lim_{n \to \infty} y_n\| = \lim_{n \to \infty} \|x - y_n\| = d.
$$

Suppose that both $u, v \in C$ are such that $\|x - u\| = \|x - v\| = d$. If $\lim_{n \to \infty} y_n = u$ and $\lim_{m \to \infty} y_m = v$ in the inequality

$$
\|y_n - y_m\|^2 \leqslant 2\|y_n - x\|^2 + 2\|y_m - x\|^2 - 4d^2,
$$

it follows that

$$
\|u - v\|^2 \leqslant 0,
$$

which implies $u = v$. $\qquad\square$

Corollary 6.13. *If T is a closed subspace of a complete normed real linear space L, then T is an approximating subspace of L and $L = T \boxplus T^{\perp}$.*

Proof.   The statement follows immediately from Theorem 6.47 by observing that every subspace is a non-empty convex set. The second part of the corollary follows from Theorem 2.46. $\qquad\square$

6.9   Separation of Convex Sets

Definition 6.11. Let L be a real linear space and let f be a linear functional defined on L. A hyperplane $H = \{x \in L \mid f(x) = a\}$ *separates* two subsets C, D of L if $f(x) \leqslant a$ for every $x \in C$ and $f(x) \geqslant a$ for every $x \in D$.

If a separating hyperplane H exists for two subsets C, D of L we say that C, D are *separable*.

In other words, C and D are separated by a hyperplane H if C and D are located in distinct closed half-spaces associated to H. The sets C and D are *linearly separable* if there exists a hyperplane that separates them.

Definition 6.12. The subsets C and D of a real linear space L are *strictly separated* by a hyperplane $H = \{x \in L \mid f(x) = a\}$ if we have either $f(x) > a > f(y)$ for $x \in C$ and $y \in D$, or $f(y) > a > f(x)$ for $x \in C$ and $y \in D$. The sets C and D are *strictly linearly separable* if there exists a hyperplane that strictly separates them.

Theorem 6.48. (Geometric Version of Hahn-Banach Theorem) *Let C be a convex subset of a real normed linear space L such that $\mathbf{I}(C) \neq \emptyset$ and let V be an affine subspace such that $V \cap \mathbf{I}(C) = \emptyset$.*

There exists a closed hyperplane H in L and a linear functional $\ell \in L^*$ such that

(i) *$V \subseteq H$ and $H \cap \mathbf{I}(C) = \emptyset$, and*

(ii) *there exists $c \in \mathbb{R}$ such that $\ell(x) = c$ for all $x \in V$ and $\ell(x) < c$ for all $x \in \mathbf{I}(C)$.*

Proof. Suppose initially that $0_L \in \mathbf{I}(C)$ and let S be the subspace generated by V, $S = \langle V \rangle$. Thus, V is a hyperplane in S and, by Theorem 2.55 there exists a linear functional f on S such that $V = \{x \in S \mid f(x) = 1\}$.

Since $V \cap \mathbf{I}(C) = \emptyset$ we have $f(x) = 1 \leqslant \mathsf{m}_C(x)$ for $x \in V$. Since f is linear, if $a > 0$ we have $f(ax) = a \leqslant \mathsf{m}_C(ax)$ for $x \in V$; if $a < 0$, $f(ax) \leqslant 0 \leqslant \mathsf{m}_C(ax)$, so we have $f(ax) \leqslant \mathsf{m}_C(ax)$ for every a.

By Hahn-Banach Theorem (Theorem 2.19) there exists an extension ℓ of f to L such that $\ell(x) \leqslant \mathsf{m}_C(x)$ for $x \in L$. Define H as the hyperplane $H = \{x \mid \ell(x) = 1\}$.

Since $\ell(x) \leqslant \mathsf{m}_C(x)$ for $x \in L$ and m_C is continuous, ℓ is continuous, $\ell(x) < 1$ for $x \in \mathbf{I}(C)$, so H is the desired closed hyperplane.

If $0_L \notin \mathbf{I}(C)$ let $x_0 \in \mathbf{I}(C)$. Then, the previous argument applied to the set $C - x_0$ yields the same conclusion. $\square$

Definition 6.13. Let C be a convex set in a linear space L. A hyperplane H in L is said to be a *supporting hyperplane of C* if the following conditions are satisfied:

(i) H is closed;

(ii) C is included in one of the closed half-spaces determined by H;

(iii) $H \cap \mathbf{K}(C) \neq \emptyset$.

Theorem 6.49. *Let C be a convex set in a linear space L. If $\mathbf{I}(C) \neq \emptyset$ and $x_0 \in \partial C$, then there exists a supporting hyperplane H of C such that $x_0 \in H$.*

Proof. Let V be affine subspace $V = \{x_0\}$. Since $x_0 \in \partial C$ it is clear that $\{x_0\} \cap \mathbf{I}(C) = \emptyset$. By Theorem 6.48 there exists a closed hyperplane H in L and a linear functional $F \in L^*$ such that

(i) $x_0 \in H$ and $H \cap \mathbf{I}(C) = \emptyset$, and
(ii) there exists $c \in \mathbb{R}$ such that $F(x_0) = c$ for all and $F(x) < c$ for all $x \in \mathbf{I}(C)$.

Furthermore, $C \subseteq \{x \in L \mid F(x) \leqslant c\}$. $\qquad\square$

Note that the support hyperplane is not unique, in general.

The next statement establishes that under certain conditions two convex subsets of a real linear space are separated by a hyperplane. It was proven in [46].

Theorem 6.50. (Separation Theorem) *Let L be a real linear space and let C_1, C_2 be two non-empty convex sets in L such that $\mathbf{I}(C_1) \neq \emptyset$ and $C_2 \cap \mathbf{I}(C_1) = \emptyset$.*

There exists a closed hyperplane H separating C_1 and C_2. In other words, there exists a linear functional $f \in L^*$ such that

$$\sup\{f(x) \mid x \in C_1\} \leqslant \inf\{f(x) \mid x \in C_2\},$$

which means that C_1 and C_2 are located in distinct half-spaces determined by H.

Proof. Let $C = C_1 - C_2$. We have $\mathbf{I}(C) \neq \emptyset$ and $0_L \notin C$. By Theorem 6.49 there exists a linear functional f in L^* that is not equal to 0 such that $f(x) \leqslant 0$ for $x \in C$. Therefore, $f(x_1) \leqslant f(x_2)$ for $x_1 \in C_1$ and $x_2 \in C_2$, which implies the existence of $c \in \mathbb{R}$ such that

$$\sup\{f(x_1) \mid x_1 \in C_1\} \leqslant c \leqslant \inf\{f(x_2) \mid x_2 \in C_2\}.$$

The desired hyperplane is $H = \{x \in L \mid f(x) = c\}$. $\qquad\square$

Corollary 6.14. *Let C_1, C_2 be two disjoint subsets of a locally convex linear topological space. If C_1 is open, then C_1 and C_2 are separable, that is, there exists a linear functional $f \in L^*$ such that*

$$\sup\{f(x) \mid x \in C_1\} \leqslant \inf\{f(x) \mid x \in C_2\},$$

Theorem 6.51. *Let L be a linear normed space. For every $x_0 \in L$ there exists a linear functional $\ell : L \longrightarrow \mathbb{R}$ such that $\|\ell\| = 1$ and $\ell(x_0) = \|x_0\|$.*

Proof. For $x_0 = 0_L$ the existence of ℓ is immediate. So let $x_0 \neq 0_L$ and let $C_1 = B[0_L, \|x_0\|]$ and $C_2 = \{x_0\}$. Since $I(C_1) \cap C_2 = \emptyset$, by Theorem 6.50 there exists a linear functional ℓ_1 and $a \in \mathbb{R}$ such that $\ell_1(s) \leqslant a \leqslant \ell_1(x)$ for all $s \in C_1$. Define $\ell = \frac{1}{\|\ell_1\|}\ell_1$. We have $\|\ell\| = 1$ and $\ell(s) \leqslant \ell(x)$ for all $x \in C_1$. Then,

$$\|x\| = \|x\| \sup\{|\ell(y)| \mid \|y\| \leqslant 1\}$$
$$= \sup\{|\ell(\|x\| y)| \mid \|y\| \leqslant 1\}$$
$$= \sup\{|\ell(s)| \mid s \in C_1\}$$
$$= \sup\{\ell(s) \mid s \in C_1\} \leqslant \ell(x).$$

Since $\|\ell\| = 1$ we have $\sup\left\{\frac{|\ell(y)|}{\|y\|} \mid y \neq 0_L\right\} = 1$, which implies $\ell(y) \leqslant \|y\|$ for all $y \in L$. This, in turn yields $\ell(x) \leqslant \|x\|$, hence $\ell(x) = \|x\|$. □

Proof. Since C_1 is open, $\mathbf{I}(C_1) = C_1 \neq \emptyset$. Therefore, by Theorem 6.50, the sets C_1, C_2 are separable. □

Theorem 6.52. *Let C be an open convex set in a real linear space L and let $f : L \longrightarrow \mathbb{R}$ be a non-zero linear continuous functional. Then, the set $f(C)$ is an open subset of $\mathbb{R}$.*

Proof. If $t \in f(C)$, then there exists $y \in C$ such that $f(y) = t$. Let $x_0 \in L$ be such that $f(x_0) \neq 0$. The set $U_0 = \{t \in \mathbb{R} \mid y + tx_0 \in C\}$ contains 0 and is open in $\mathbb{R}$ because $t \in U_0$ implies $t \in \frac{1}{f(x_0)}(C - y)$, hence $U_0 = \frac{1}{f(x_0)}(C - y)$. Since $f(y) + U_0$ is an open set that contains $t = f(y)$ and is included in $f(C)$ it follows that $f(C)$ is open. □

Corollary 6.15. *Let C_1, C_2 be two disjoint open subsets of a locally convex linear topological space. The sets C_1, C_2 are strictly separable.*

Proof. By Corollary 6.14, the sets C_1, C_2 are separable, so there exists a non-zero linear functional ℓ such that $\sup\{f(x) \mid x \in C_1\} \leqslant a$ and $a \leqslant \inf\{f(x) \mid x \in C_2\}$. By Theorem 6.52, $f(C_1) \subseteq (-\infty, a)$ and $f(C_2) \subseteq (a, \infty)$, hence C_1, C_2 are strictly separable. □

Theorem 6.53. *Let C_1, C_2 be two disjoint closed subsets of a locally convex linear topological space L. If C_2 is compact, then there exist disjoint open convex sets D_1, D_2 in L such that $C_1 \subseteq D_1$ and $C_2 \subseteq D_2$.*

Proof. Let $C = C_1 - C_2$ and let $(x_i)_{i \in I}$ be a net in C that converges to x. Then $x_i = y_i - z_i$, where $(y_i)_{i \in I}$ is a net in C_1 and $(z_i)_{i \in I}$ is a net in C_2. Since C_2 is compact, there exists a subnet $(z_{i_j})_{j \in J}$ that is convergent, $z_{i_j} \to z$. Since the subnet $(x_{i_j})_{j \in J}$ converges to x, the net $(y_{i_j})_{j \in J}$ converges to $x + z \in C_1$ because C_1 is closed. Therefore, $y - z \in C$, hence C is closed.

Since C_1, C_2 are disjoint, $0_L \notin C$, hence there exists a balanced and convex neighborhood W of 0_L such that $W \cap C = \emptyset$. The sets $U = C_1 + 0.5C_1$ and $V = C_2 + 0.5W$, then $U \cap V = \emptyset$ and U, V are open and convex. $\qquad \square$

Corollary 6.16. *Let C_1, C_2 be two disjoint closed subsets of a locally convex linear topological space L. If C_2 is compact, then C_1, C_2 are strictly separable.*

Proof.   This follows from Theorem 6.53. $\qquad \square$

Theorem 6.54. *Let C be a closed and convex subset of a real normed linear space L. If $x \in L - C$, there exists a closed half-space U in L such that $C \subseteq U$ and $x \notin U$.*

Proof.   Since C is a closed set, $d(\{x\}, K) > 0$. By Theorem 6.50 applied to the sets C and $B[x, \frac{d}{2}]$, there exists a hyperplane separating these sets. Then U is the half-space determined by this hyperplane that contains C. $\qquad \square$

Corollary 6.17. *Let C be a closed and convex subset of a real normed linear space L. Then C equals the intersection of all closed half-spaces that contain C.*

Proof.   It is clear that C is included into the intersection T of all closed half-spaces that contain C. Suppose that this inclusion is strict, that is, there $x \in T - C$. By Theorem 6.54 there exists a half-space U such that $x \notin U$ and $C \subseteq U$. This leads to a contradiction, hence $C = T$. $\qquad \square$

Next, we discuss the separation of convex subsets of $\mathbb{R}^n$.

Let C, D be two disjoint subsets of $\mathbb{R}^n$. If $\mathbf{w}'\mathbf{x} \leqslant a \leqslant \mathbf{w}'\mathbf{y}$ for all $\mathbf{x} \in C$ and $\mathbf{y} \in D$, it follows that

$$\sup\{\mathbf{w}'\mathbf{x} \mid \mathbf{x} \in C\} \leqslant \inf\{\mathbf{w}'\mathbf{y} \mid \mathbf{y} \in D\},$$

for some $\mathbf{w} \neq \mathbf{0}$. It is easy to see that this inequality is sufficient for the existence of a hyperplane that separates C and D.

Lemma 6.1. *Let C be a non-empty and closed convex set, $C \subseteq \mathbb{R}^n$ and let $\boldsymbol{x}_0 \notin C$. There exists a unique point $\boldsymbol{u} \in C$ such that $\|\boldsymbol{u} - \boldsymbol{x}_0\|$ is the minimal distance from $\boldsymbol{x}_0$ to C.*

Proof.   Let $\mu = \min\{\|\mathbf{x} - \mathbf{x}_0\| \mid \mathbf{x} \in C\}$. There exists a sequence of elements in C, $(\mathbf{z}_n)$ such that $\lim_{n \to \infty} \|\mathbf{z}_n - \mathbf{x}_0\| = \mu$. By the law of the parallelogram, $\|\mathbf{z}_k - \mathbf{z}_m\|^2 = 2\|\mathbf{z}_k - \mathbf{x}_0\|^2 + 2\|\mathbf{z}_m - \mathbf{x}_0\|^2 - 4\|\frac{\mathbf{x}_k + \mathbf{x}_m}{2} - \mathbf{x}_0\|^2$.

Since C is convex, we have $\frac{\mathbf{x}_k + \mathbf{x}_m}{2} \in C$; the definition of μ implies that

$$\left\| \frac{\mathbf{x}_k + \mathbf{x}_m}{2} - \mathbf{x}_0 \right\|^2 \geqslant \mu^2,$$

so

$$\|\mathbf{z}_k - \mathbf{z}_m\|^2 \leqslant 2\|\mathbf{z}_k - \mathbf{x}_0\|^2 + 2\|\mathbf{z}_m - \mathbf{x}_0\|^2 - 4\mu^2.$$

Since $\lim_{n\to\infty} \|\mathbf{z}_n - \mathbf{x}_0\| = \mu$, for every $\epsilon > 0$, there exists n_ϵ such that $k, m > n_\epsilon$ imply $\|\mathbf{z}_k - \mathbf{x}_0\| < \mu\epsilon$ and $\|\mathbf{z}_m - \mathbf{x}_0\| < \mu\epsilon$. Therefore, if $k, m > n_\epsilon$, it follows that

$$\|\mathbf{z}_k - \mathbf{z}_m\|^2 \leqslant 4\mu^2(\epsilon^2 - 1).$$

Thus, $(\mathbf{z}_n)$ is a Cauchy sequence. If $\lim_{n\to\infty} \mathbf{z}_n = \mathbf{u}$, then $\mathbf{u} \in C$ because C is a closed set.

Suppose $\mathbf{v} \in C$ with $\mathbf{v} \neq \mathbf{v}$ and $\|\mathbf{v} - \mathbf{x}_0\| = \|\mathbf{u} - \mathbf{x}_0\|$. Since C is convex, $\mathbf{w} = \frac{1}{2}(\mathbf{u} + \mathbf{v}) \in C$ and we have

$$\left\| \frac{1}{2}(\mathbf{u} + \mathbf{v}) - \mathbf{x}_0 \right\| \leqslant \frac{1}{2}\|\mathbf{u} - \mathbf{x}_0\| + \frac{1}{2}\|\mathbf{v} - \mathbf{x}_0\| = \mu.$$

If $\left\| \frac{1}{2}(\mathbf{u} + \mathbf{v}) - \mathbf{x}_0 \right\| < \mu$, the definition of μ is violated. Therefore, we have

$$\left\| \frac{1}{2}(\mathbf{u} + \mathbf{v}) - \mathbf{x}_0 \right\| = \mu,$$

which implies $\mathbf{u} - \mathbf{x}_0 = k(\mathbf{v} - \mathbf{x}_0)$ for some $k \in \mathbb{R}$. This, in turn, implies $|k| = 1$. If $k = 1$ we would have $\mathbf{u} - \mathbf{x}_0 = \mathbf{v} - \mathbf{x}_0$, so $\mathbf{u} = \mathbf{v}$, which is a contradiction. Therefore, $a = 1$ and this implies $\mathbf{x}_0 = \frac{1}{2}(\mathbf{u} + \mathbf{v}) \in C$, which is again a contradiction. This implies that $\mathbf{u}$ is indeed unique. □

The point $\mathbf{u}$ whose existence and uniqueness is established by Lemma 6.1 (see Figure 6.1) is the *C-proximal point* to $\mathbf{x}_0$.

Lemma 6.2. *Let C be a non-empty and closed convex set, $C \subseteq \mathbb{R}^n$ and let $\boldsymbol{x}_0 \notin C$. Then $\boldsymbol{u} \in C$ is the C-proximal point to $\boldsymbol{x}_0$ if and only if for all $\boldsymbol{x} \in C$ we have*

$$(\boldsymbol{x} - \boldsymbol{u})'(\boldsymbol{u} - \boldsymbol{x}_0) \geqslant 0.$$

Proof. Let $\mathbf{x} \in C$. Since

$$\begin{aligned}
\|\mathbf{x} - \mathbf{x}_0\|^2 &= \|\mathbf{x} - \mathbf{u} + \mathbf{u} - \mathbf{x}_0\|^2 \\
&= \|\mathbf{x} - \mathbf{u}\|^2 + \|\mathbf{u} - \mathbf{x}_0\|^2 + 2(\mathbf{x} - \mathbf{u})'(\mathbf{u} - \mathbf{x}_0),
\end{aligned}$$

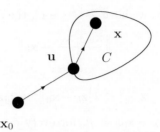

Fig. 6.1 $\mathbf{u}$ is the proximal point to $\mathbf{x}_0$ in the convex set C.

$\|\mathbf{u} - \mathbf{x}_0\|^2 \geqslant 0$ and $(\mathbf{x} - \mathbf{u})'(\mathbf{u} - \mathbf{x}_0) \geqslant 0$, it follows that $\|\mathbf{x} - \mathbf{x}_0\| \geqslant \|\mathbf{x} - \mathbf{u}\|$, which means that $\mathbf{u}$ is the closest point in C to $\mathbf{x}_0$, and the condition of the lemma is sufficient.

Conversely, suppose that $\mathbf{u}$ is the proximal point in C to $\mathbf{x}_0$, that is, $\|\mathbf{x} - \mathbf{x}_0\| \geqslant \|\mathbf{x}_0 - \mathbf{u}\|$ for $\mathbf{x} \in C$. If t is positive and sufficiently small, then $\mathbf{u} + t(\mathbf{x} - \mathbf{u}) \in C$ because $\mathbf{x} \in C$. Consequently,

$$\|\mathbf{x}_0 - \mathbf{u} - t(\mathbf{x} - \mathbf{u})\|^2 \geqslant \|\mathbf{x}_0 - \mathbf{u}\|^2.$$

Since

$$\|\mathbf{x}_0 - \mathbf{u} - t(\mathbf{x} - \mathbf{u})\|^2 = \|\mathbf{x}_0 - \mathbf{u}\|^2 - 2t(\mathbf{x}_0 - \mathbf{u})'(\mathbf{x} - \mathbf{u}) + t^2\|\mathbf{x} - \mathbf{u}\|^2,$$

it follows that

$$-2t(\mathbf{x}_0 - \mathbf{u})'(\mathbf{x} - \mathbf{u}) + t^2\|\mathbf{x} - \mathbf{u}\|^2 \geqslant 0,$$

for $t > 0$ and t sufficiently small. This is equivalent to

$$2(\mathbf{x} - \mathbf{u})'(\mathbf{u} - \mathbf{x}_0) + t\|\mathbf{x} - \mathbf{u}\|^2 \geqslant 0,$$

which holds for $t > 0$ and t sufficiently small. This implies $(\mathbf{x} - \mathbf{u})'(\mathbf{u} - \mathbf{x}_0) \geqslant 0$. $\qquad\square$

Theorem 6.55. *Let C be a non-empty and closed convex set, $C \subseteq \mathbb{R}^n$ and let $\boldsymbol{x}_0 \notin C$. There exists $\boldsymbol{w} \in \mathbb{R}^n - \{\boldsymbol{0}_n\}$ and $a \in R$ such that $a < \boldsymbol{w}'\boldsymbol{x}_0$ and $a \geqslant \boldsymbol{w}'\boldsymbol{x}$ for $\boldsymbol{x} \in C$.*

Proof.   By Lemmas 6.1 and 6.2 there exists a unique proximal point to $\mathbf{x}_0$, $\mathbf{u} \in C$, such that

$$(\mathbf{x} - \mathbf{u})'(\mathbf{u} - \mathbf{x}_0) \geqslant 0 \tag{6.3}$$

for every $\mathbf{x} \in C$. Let $\mathbf{w} = \mathbf{x}_0 - \mathbf{u}$. The inequality (6.3) is equivalent to $\mathbf{x}'\mathbf{w} \leqslant \mathbf{u}'\mathbf{w}$ for $\mathbf{x} \in C$ and we can write

$$
\begin{aligned}
\|\mathbf{w}\|^2 = \|\mathbf{x}_0 - \mathbf{u}\|^2 &= \mathbf{x}_0'(\mathbf{x}_0 - \mathbf{u}) - \mathbf{u}'(\mathbf{x}_0 - \mathbf{u}) \\
&= \mathbf{x}_0'\mathbf{w} - \mathbf{u}'\mathbf{w} \\
&= \mathbf{w}'\mathbf{x}_0 - \mathbf{u}'\mathbf{w} \\
&\leqslant \mathbf{w}'\mathbf{x}_0 - \mathbf{x}'\mathbf{w},
\end{aligned}
$$

which implies $\mathbf{x}'\mathbf{w} \leqslant \mathbf{w}'\mathbf{x}_0 - \|\mathbf{w}\|^2$ for every $\mathbf{x} \in C$. Therefore, if $a = \sup\{\mathbf{w}'\mathbf{x} \mid \mathbf{x} \in C\}$ we have

$$
a \leqslant \mathbf{w}'\mathbf{x}_0 - \|\mathbf{w}\|^2.
$$

Since $\mathbf{w} \neq \mathbf{0}_n$, it follows that $a < \mathbf{w}'\mathbf{x}_0$.

The inequality $\mathbf{w}'\mathbf{x} \leqslant a$ for $\mathbf{x} \in C$ follows from the definition of a. $\square$

A variation of the previous theorem, where C is just a convex set (not necessarily closed) is given next.

Theorem 6.56. *Let C be a non-empty convex set, $C \subseteq \mathbb{R}^n$ and let $\boldsymbol{x}_0 \in \partial C$. There exists $\boldsymbol{w} \in \mathbb{R}^n - \{\boldsymbol{0}_n\}$ such that $\boldsymbol{w}'(\boldsymbol{x} - \boldsymbol{x}_0) \leqslant 0$ for $\boldsymbol{x} \in \boldsymbol{K}(C)$.*

Proof. Since $\mathbf{x}_0 \in \partial C$, there exists a sequence $(\mathbf{z}_m)$ such that $\mathbf{z}_m \notin \mathbf{K}(C)$ and $\lim_{m \to \infty} \mathbf{z}_m = \mathbf{x}_0$. By Theorem 6.55 for each $m \in \mathbb{N}$ there exists $\mathbf{w}_m \in \mathbb{R}^n - \{\mathbf{0}_n\}$ such that $\mathbf{w}_m'\mathbf{z}_m > \mathbf{w}_m'\mathbf{x}$ for each $\mathbf{x} \in \mathbf{K}(C)$. Without loss of generality we may assume that $\|\mathbf{w}_m\| = 1$. Since the sequence $(\mathbf{w}_m)$ is bounded, it contains a convergent subsequence $\mathbf{w}_{i_p}$ such that $\lim_{p \to \infty} \mathbf{w}_{i_p} = \mathbf{w}$ and we have $\mathbf{w}_{i_p}'\mathbf{z}_{i_p} > \mathbf{w}_{i_p}'\mathbf{x}$ for each $\mathbf{x} \in \mathbf{K}(C)$. Taking $p \to \infty$ we obtain $\mathbf{w}'\mathbf{x}_0 > \mathbf{w}'\mathbf{x}$ for $\mathbf{x} \in \mathbf{K}(C)$. $\square$

Theorem 6.57. *Let C be a non-empty convex set, $C \subseteq \mathbb{R}^n$ and let $\boldsymbol{x}_0 \notin \boldsymbol{I}(C)$. There exists $\boldsymbol{w} \in \mathbb{R}^n - \{\boldsymbol{0}_n\}$ such that $\boldsymbol{w}'(\boldsymbol{x} - \boldsymbol{x}_0) \leqslant 0$ for $\boldsymbol{x} \in \boldsymbol{K}(C)$.*

Proof. If $\mathbf{x} \notin \mathbf{K}(C)$, the statement follows from Theorem 6.55. Otherwise, $\mathbf{x}_0 \in \mathbf{K}(C) - C \subseteq \partial C$, so $\mathbf{x}_0 \in \partial C$ and the statement is a consequence of Theorem 6.56. $\square$

Corollary 6.18. *Let C be a non-empty convex set, $C \subseteq \mathbb{R}^n$ and let $\boldsymbol{x}_0 \notin \boldsymbol{I}(C)$. There exists $\tilde{\boldsymbol{w}} \in \mathbb{R}^n - \{\boldsymbol{0}_n\}$ such that $\tilde{\boldsymbol{w}}'(\boldsymbol{x} - \boldsymbol{x}_0) \geqslant 0$ for $\boldsymbol{x} \in \boldsymbol{K}(C)$.*

Proof. Define $\tilde{\mathbf{w}}$ as $\tilde{\mathbf{w}} = -\mathbf{w}$, where $\mathbf{w}$ is the vector whose existence was established in Theorem 6.57. Clearly, $\tilde{\mathbf{w}} \in \mathbb{R}^n - \{\mathbf{0}_n\}$ and $\tilde{\mathbf{w}}'(\mathbf{x} - \mathbf{x}_0) \geqslant 0$ for $\mathbf{x} \in \mathbf{K}(C)$. $\square$

The existence of a supporting hyperplane for a non-empty convex set and a point located on its border can be shown directly for $\mathbb{R}^n$.

Theorem 6.58. *Let $C \subseteq \mathbb{R}^n$ be a non-empty convex set and let $\mathbf{x}_0 \in \partial C$. There exists a supporting hyperplane of C at $\mathbf{x}_0$.*

Proof. Since $\mathbf{x}_0 \in \partial C$, there exists a sequence $(\mathbf{z}_n)$ of elements of $\mathbb{R}^n - C$ such that $\lim_{n \to \infty} \mathbf{z}_n = \mathbf{x}_0$.

By Theorem 6.55 for each $\mathbf{z}_n$ there exists $\mathbf{w}_n$ such that $\mathbf{w}_n' \mathbf{z}_n > a$ and $\mathbf{w}_n' \mathbf{x} \leqslant a$ for $\mathbf{x} \in C$. Without loss of generality we may assume that $\|\mathbf{w}_n\| = 1$. Since the sequence $(\mathbf{w}_n)$ is bounded, it contains a convergent subsequence $(\mathbf{w}_{i_m})$ such that $\lim_{m \to \infty} \mathbf{w}_{i_m} = \mathbf{w}$.

For this subsequence we have $\mathbf{w}' \mathbf{z}_{i_m} > a$ and $\mathbf{w}' \mathbf{x} \leqslant a$. Taking $m \to \infty$ we obtain $\mathbf{w}' \mathbf{x}_0 > a$ and $\mathbf{w}' \mathbf{x} \leqslant a$ for all $\mathbf{x} \in C$, which means that $H_{\mathbf{w},a}$ is a support plane of C at $\mathbf{x}_0$. $\qquad \square$

Theorem 6.59. *Let S, T be two non-empty convex subsets of $\mathbb{R}^n$ that are disjoint. There exists $\mathbf{w} \in \mathbb{R}^n - \{\mathbf{0}_n\}$ such that*

$$\inf\{\mathbf{w}'\mathbf{s} \mid \mathbf{s} \in S\} \geqslant \sup\{\mathbf{w}'\mathbf{t} \mid \mathbf{t} \in T\}.$$

Proof. It is easy to see that the set $S - T$ defined by

$$S - T = \{\mathbf{s} - \mathbf{t} \mid \mathbf{s} \in S \text{ and } \mathbf{t} \in T\}$$

is convex. Furthermore $\mathbf{0}_n \notin S - T$ because the sets S and T are disjoint. Thus, there exists in $S - T$ a proximal point $\mathbf{w}$ to $\mathbf{0}_n$, for which we have $(\mathbf{x} - \mathbf{w})' \mathbf{w} \geqslant 0$ for every $\mathbf{x} \in S - T$, that is, $(\mathbf{s} - \mathbf{t} - \mathbf{w})' \mathbf{w} \geqslant 0$, which is equivalent to

$$\mathbf{s}'\mathbf{w} \geqslant \mathbf{t}'\mathbf{w} + \|\mathbf{w}\|^2$$

for $\mathbf{s} \in S$ and $\mathbf{t} \in T$. This implies the inequality of the theorem. $\qquad \square$

Corollary 6.19. *For any two non-empty convex subsets that are disjoint, there exists a non-zero vector $\mathbf{w} \in \mathbb{R}^n$ such that*

$$\inf\{\mathbf{w}'\mathbf{s} \mid \mathbf{s} \in S\} \geqslant \sup\{\mathbf{w}'\mathbf{t} \mid \mathbf{t} \in \mathbf{K}(T)\}.$$

Proof. This statement follows from Theorem 6.59 and from Supplement 64 of Chapter 4. $\qquad \square$

Definition 6.14. A subset C of $\mathbb{R}^n$ is *bounded from below* if $\inf\{x_j \mid \mathbf{x} \in C\} > -\infty$ for every j, $1 \leqslant j \leq n$.

Example 6.5. The set $(\mathbb{R}^n)_{\geq 0}$ and any of its subsets are bounded from below.

Theorem 6.60. *Let C be a closed and convex subset of $\mathbb{R}^n$ that is bounded from below. Then every supporting hyperplane of C contains an extreme point of C.*

Proof. Let $\mathbf{x}_0 \in \partial C$. By Theorem 6.58 there exists a supporting hyperplane $H_{\mathbf{w},a}$ of C at $\mathbf{x}_0$. Define $Z = H_{\mathbf{w},a} \cap C$.

Note that $Z \neq \emptyset$ because $\mathbf{x}_0 \in H_{\mathbf{w},a}$ and $\mathbf{x}_0 \in C$.

Every extreme point $\mathbf{z}$ of Z is also an extreme point of C, which is equivalent to showing that if $\mathbf{z}$ is not an extreme point of C, then it cannot be an extreme point of Z.

Let $\mathbf{z}$ is a point in C that is not an extreme point of this set. If $\mathbf{z} \notin Z$, then $\mathbf{z}$ cannot be an extreme point of Z. If $\mathbf{z} \in Z$ we have $\mathbf{z} \in C$. We may assume that $C \subseteq \{\mathbf{x} \mid \mathbf{w}'\mathbf{x} \geq a\}$. Since $\mathbf{z}$ is not an extreme point in C, there exist $\mathbf{x}_1, \mathbf{x}_2 \in C$ with $\mathbf{x}_1 \neq \mathbf{x}_2$ such that $\mathbf{z} = (1-t)\mathbf{x}_1 + t\mathbf{x}_2$ for some $t \in (0,1)$. Since $\mathbf{w}'\mathbf{z} = a = (1-t)\mathbf{w}'\mathbf{x}_1 + t\mathbf{w}'\mathbf{x}_2$ and $C \subseteq \{\mathbf{x} \mid \mathbf{w}'\mathbf{x} \geq a\}$ it follows that $\mathbf{w}'\mathbf{x}_1 = a = \mathbf{w}'\mathbf{x}_2$, hence $\mathbf{x}_1, \mathbf{x}_2 \in Z$. Thus, $\mathbf{z}$ is not an extreme point of Z.

We show next that Z contains an extreme point. Define

$$
\mathbf{z}^1 = \begin{pmatrix} z_1^1 \\ z_2^1 \\ \vdots \\ z_n^1 \end{pmatrix}
$$

such that $z_1^1 = \inf\{z_1 \mid \mathbf{z} \in Z\}$. Since $Z \subseteq C$ and C is bounded from below, z_1^1 is well-defined. If $\mathbf{z}^1$ is unique, we will show next that it is an extreme point.

If $\mathbf{z}^1$ is not unique, we can define $\mathbf{z}^2$ such that

$$
\mathbf{z}^2 = \begin{pmatrix} z_1^2 \\ z_2^2 \\ \vdots \\ z_n^2 \end{pmatrix}
$$

such that $z_1^2 = z_1^1$ and

$$
z_2^2 = \inf\left\{ z_2 \;\middle|\; \begin{pmatrix} z_1^1 \\ z_2 \\ \vdots \\ z_n \end{pmatrix} \in Z \right\}.
$$

Since $C \subseteq \mathbb{R}^n$ this process will stop at most after n steps. Let $\mathbf{z}^j$ be the point where the process stops. For all k, $1 \leqslant k \leqslant j$, we have

$$z_k^j = \inf \left\{ z_k \;\middle|\; \mathbf{z} = \begin{pmatrix} t_1 \\ t_2 \\ \vdots \\ t_n \end{pmatrix}, z_i = z_i^j \text{ for } 1 \leqslant i \leqslant k-1 \right\}.$$

Suppose $\mathbf{z}^j$ is not an extreme point of Z. Then, there exist two distinct points $\mathbf{u}, \mathbf{v} \in Z$ such that $\mathbf{z}^j = (1-t)\mathbf{u} + t\mathbf{v}$ for some $t \in (0,1)$. Thus, $z_i^j = (1-t)u_i + tv_i$ for $1 \leqslant i \leqslant n$. For $1 \leqslant i \leqslant j$, since z_i^j is the infimum, $z_i^j \leqslant u_i$ and $z_i^j \leqslant v_i$, which implies $z_i^j = u_i = v_i$ for $1 \leqslant i \leqslant j$, which contradicts the uniqueness of $\mathbf{z}^j$. □

6.10   Theorems of Alternatives

Separation results have two important consequences for optimization theory, namely Farkas' and Gordan's alternative theorems.

Theorem 6.61. (Farkas' Theorem) *Let $A \in \mathbb{R}^{m \times n}$ and let $\mathbf{c} \in \mathbb{R}^n$. Exactly one of the following linear systems has a solution:*

(i) $A\mathbf{x} \leqslant \mathbf{0}_m$ and $\mathbf{c}'\mathbf{x} > 0$;

(ii) $A'\mathbf{y} = \mathbf{c}$ and $\mathbf{y} \geqslant \mathbf{0}_m$.

Proof. If the second system has a solution, then $A'\mathbf{y} = \mathbf{c}$ and $\mathbf{y} \geqslant \mathbf{0}_m$ for some $\mathbf{y} \in \mathbb{R}^m$. Suppose that $\mathbf{x}$ is a solution of the first system. Then, $\mathbf{c}'\mathbf{x} = \mathbf{y}'A\mathbf{x} \leqslant 0$, which contradicts the inequality $\mathbf{c}'\mathbf{x} > 0$. Thus, if the second system has a solution, the first system has no solution.

Suppose now that the second system has no solution. Note that the set $S = \{\mathbf{x} \in \mathbb{R}^n \mid \mathbf{x} = A'\mathbf{y}, \mathbf{y} \geqslant \mathbf{0}_m\}$ is a closed convex set. Furthermore, $\mathbf{c} \notin S$ because, otherwise, $\mathbf{c}$ would be a solution of the second system. Thus, by Theorem 6.55, there exists $\mathbf{w} \in \mathbb{R}^n - \{\mathbf{0}_n\}$ and $a \in R$ such that $\mathbf{w}'\mathbf{c} > a$ and $\mathbf{w}'\mathbf{x} \leqslant a$ for $\mathbf{x} \in S$. In particular, since $\mathbf{0}_n \in S$ we have $a \geqslant 0$ and, therefore, $\mathbf{w}'\mathbf{c} > 0$. Also, for $\mathbf{y} \geqslant \mathbf{0}_m$ we have $a \geqslant \mathbf{w}'A'\mathbf{y} = \mathbf{y}'A\mathbf{w}$. Since $\mathbf{y}$ can be made arbitrarily large we must have $A\mathbf{w} \leqslant \mathbf{0}_m$. Then $\mathbf{w}$ is a solution of the first system. □

Theorem 6.62. (Gordan's Alternative Theorem) *Let $A \in \mathbb{R}^{m \times n}$ be a matrix. Exactly one of the following linear systems has a solution:*

(i) $A\mathbf{x} < \mathbf{0}_m$ for $\mathbf{x} \in \mathbb{R}^n$;

(ii) $A'\mathbf{y} = \mathbf{0}_n$ and $\mathbf{y} \geq \mathbf{0}_m$ for $\mathbf{y} \in \mathbb{R}^m$.

Proof. Let A be a matrix such that the first system, $A\mathbf{x} < \mathbf{0}_m$ has a solution $\mathbf{x}_0$. Suppose that a solution $\mathbf{y}_0$ of the second system exists. Since $A\mathbf{x}_0 < \mathbf{0}_m$ and $\mathbf{y}_0 \geq \mathbf{0}_m$ (which implies that at least one component of $\mathbf{y}_0$ is positive) it follows that $\mathbf{y}_0'A\mathbf{x}_0 < 0$, which is equivalent to $\mathbf{x}_0'A'\mathbf{y} < 0$. This contradicts the assumption that $A'\mathbf{y} = \mathbf{0}_n$. Thus, the second system cannot have a solution if the first has one.

Suppose now that the first system has no solution and consider the non-empty convex subsets S, T of $\mathbb{R}^m$ defined by

$$S = \{\mathbf{s} \in \mathbb{R}^m \mid \mathbf{s} = A\mathbf{x}, \mathbf{x} \in \mathbb{R}^n\} \text{ and } T = \{\mathbf{t} \in \mathbb{R}^m \mid \mathbf{t} < \mathbf{0}_m\}.$$

These sets are disjoint by the previous supposition. Then, by Theorem 6.59, there exists $\mathbf{w} \neq \mathbf{0}_m$ such that $\mathbf{w}'A\mathbf{s} \geq \mathbf{w}'\mathbf{t}$ for $\mathbf{s} \in S$ and $\mathbf{t} \in \mathbf{K}(T)$. This implies that $\mathbf{w} \geq \mathbf{0}_m$ because otherwise the components of $\mathbf{t}$ that correspond to a negative component of $\mathbf{w}$ could be made arbitrarily negative (and large in absolute value) and this would contradict the above inequality. Thus, $\mathbf{w} \geq \mathbf{0}_m$.

Since $\mathbf{0}_m \in \mathbf{K}(T)$, we also have $\mathbf{w}'A\mathbf{s} \geq 0$ for every $\mathbf{s} \in \mathbb{R}^m$. In particular, for $\mathbf{s} = -A'\mathbf{w}$ we obtain $\mathbf{w}'A(-A'\mathbf{w}) = -\|A'\mathbf{w}\|^2 = 0$, so $A'\mathbf{w} = \mathbf{0}_m$, which means that the second system has a solution. $\qquad\square$

The next definition comes from [27] where a study of consistency of linear inequality systems was developed.

Definition 6.15. A linear system is *consistent* or *inconsistent* according as solution of the system do or do not exist.

Example 6.6. An inequality $\sum_{j=1}^{n} a_j x_j + b > 0$ is inconsistent only when $a_1 = \cdots = a_n = 0$ and $b \leq 0$.

Definition 6.16. A system of inequalities is *minimally inconsistent* or *irreducibly inconsistent* if removing one of its conditions renders the system consistent.

A single inequality is minimally inconsistent if it is inconsistent.

Lemma 6.3. Let $\{\ell_i \mid 1 \leq i \leq k\}$ be a set of k linear functionals on a real linear space L. The set

$$L_x = \{\mathbf{y} \in \mathbb{R}^k \mid y_i = \ell_i(x) \text{ for } 1 \leq i \leq k\}$$

is a linear subspace of $\mathbb{R}^k$; furthermore, L_x is a proper subspace of $\mathbb{R}^k$ for every $x \in L$ if and only if the set $\{\ell_i \mid 1 \leq i \leq k\}$ is linearly dependent.

Proof. It is immediate that L_x is a linear subspace due to the linearity of the functionals $\{\ell_i \mid 1 \leqslant i \leqslant k\}$. The subspace L_x is non-trivial if and only if there exists a non-zero vector $\mathbf{w} \in \mathbb{R}^k$ such that $\mathbf{w} \perp \mathbf{z}$ for every $\mathbf{z} \in L_x$, that is, $\sum_{i=1}^{k} w_i \ell_i(x) = 0$ for every $x \in L$, which is equivalent to the linear dependence of the set $\{\ell_i \mid 1 \leqslant i \leqslant k\}$. $\square$

Lemma 6.4. *Let L be a linear space, let $\ell : L \longrightarrow \mathbb{R}$ be a linear functional, and let $x_t = (1 - t)a + tb$ be a point on the segment $[a, b] \subseteq L$, where $t \in [0, 1]$. If $\ell(a) < 0$ and $\ell(b) \geqslant 0$, then $t < \frac{-\ell(a)}{\ell(b)-\ell(a)}$ implies $\ell(x_t) < 0$.*

Proof. The inequality $\ell(x_t) < 0$ is equivalent to $(1 - t)\ell(a) + t\ell(b) < 0$, which, in turn, is equivalent to $t < \frac{-\ell(a)}{\ell(b)-\ell(a)}$. In other words, if x_t is sufficiently close to a, $\ell(x_t)$ is negative. $\square$

The next result is a general alternative theorem. We follow the presentation of [71].

Theorem 6.63. (Motzkin's Transposition Theorem) *Let L be a real linear space, and let $\{\ell_i \mid i \in I\}$, $\{\ell_j \mid j \in J\}$, and $\{\ell_k \mid k \in K\}$, be three families of real-valued linear functionals defined on L, where I, J and K are finite sets. Then exactly one if the linear systems*

$$\ell_i(x) < 0 \text{ for } i \in I, \ell_j(x) \leqslant 0 \text{ for } j \in J, \text{ and } \ell_k(x) = 0 \text{ for } k \in K, \quad (6.4)$$

and

$$\begin{aligned} \sum_{i \in I} y_i \ell_i + \sum_{j \in J} z_j \ell_j + \sum_{k \in K} u_k \ell_k = 0, \\ \mathbf{y} \geqslant \mathbf{0}_n, \mathbf{y} \neq \mathbf{0}_n, \text{ and } \mathbf{z} \geqslant \mathbf{0}_q, \end{aligned} \quad (6.5)$$

where $|I| = n$, $|J| = p$, and $|K| = q$, is consistent.

Proof. Suppose that system (6.4) has a solution $\mathbf{x}$. If system (6.5) has a solution $\mathbf{y}, \mathbf{z}, \mathbf{u}$, then

$$\left(\sum_{i \in I} y_i \ell_i + \sum_{j \in J} z_j \ell_j + \sum_{k \in K} u_k \ell_k \right) (x) = 0.$$

On other hand,

$$\sum_{i \in I} y_i \ell_i(x) + \sum_{j \in J} z_j \ell_j(x) + \sum_{k \in K} u_k \ell_k(x) \leqslant \sum_{i \in I} y_i \ell_i(x) < 0.$$

This contradiction shows that system (6.5) is inconsistent.

Conversely, if system (6.4) is inconsistent, then system (6.5) has a solution.

Without loss of generality we may take $K = \emptyset$, because each equality $\ell_k(x) = 0$ can be replaced by a pair of inequalities $\ell_k(x) \leqslant 0$ and $-\ell_k(x) \leqslant 0$. Also, we may assume that the system

$$\ell_i(x) < 0 \text{ for } i \in I, \ell_j(x) \leqslant 0 \text{ for } j \in J \qquad (6.6)$$

is minimally inconsistent.

We may also assume that there exists only one strict inequality in the system (6.6), that is, $|I| = 1$. Indeed, suppose that $|I| > 1$ and let $p \in I$. Consider the system obtained by replacing all inequalities $\ell_i(x) < 0$ by $\ell_i(x) \leqslant 0$ for $i \neq p$:

$$\ell_p(x) < 0, \ell_i(x) \leqslant 0 \text{ for } i \in I - \{p\}, \ell_j(x) \leqslant 0 \text{ for } j \in J. \qquad (6.7)$$

Since system (6.4) is minimally inconsistent, there exists $a \in L$ such that

$$\ell_p(a) < 0, \ell_i(a) \leqslant 0 \text{ for } i \in I - \{p\}, \ell_j(a) \leqslant 0 \text{ for } j \in J.$$

Since system (6.6) is minimally inconsistent, there exists $b \in L$ such that

$$\ell_p(b) \geqslant 0, \ell_i(b) < 0 \text{ for } i \in I - \{p\}, \ell_j(b) \leqslant 0 \text{ for } j \in J.$$

By Lemma 6.4 this implies that there exists a point c that is sufficiently close to a that satisfies system (6.6) which is a contradiction. This proves that system (6.7) is minimally inconsistent because system (6.4) is minimally inconsistent.

The minimal inconsistency of the system

$$\ell(x) < 0, \ell_j(x) \leqslant 0 \text{ for } j \in J \qquad (6.8)$$

implies that for any two distinct $r, k \in J$, there exist $a, b \in L$ such that

$$\ell(a) < 0, \ell_r(a) > 0, \ell_k(a) \leqslant 0, \ell_j(a) \leqslant 0 \text{ for } j \in J - \{r, k\},$$
$$\ell(b) < 0, \ell_r(b) \leqslant 0, \ell_k(b) > 0, \ell_j(a) \leqslant 0 \text{ for } j \in J - \{r, k\}.$$

This implies the existence of $c \in [a, b]$ such that $\ell_k(c) = 0$. Thus, c satisfies the inequalities

$$\ell(c) < 0, \ell_r(c) > 0, \ell_k(c) = 0, \ell_j(c) < 0 \text{ for } j \in J - \{r, k\},$$

where $\ell_r(c) > 0$ follows from the fact that system (6.8) is inconsistent.

Consider two consistent systems like the previous one,

$$\ell(x) < 0, \ell_r(x) > 0, \ell_{k_1}(x) = 0, \ell_{k_2}(x) \leqslant 0,$$
$$\ell_j(x) \leqslant 0 \text{ for } j \in J - \{r, k_1, k_2\},$$
$$\ell(x) < 0, \ell_r(x) \leqslant 0, \ell_{k_1}(x) > 0, \ell_{k_2}(x) > 0,$$
$$\ell_j(x) \leqslant 0 \text{ for } j \in J - \{r, k_1, k_2\}.$$

that yield a consistent system

$$\ell(x) < 0,\, \ell_r(x) > 0,\, \ell_{k_1}(x) = 0,\, \ell_{k_2}(x) = 0,$$
$$\ell_j(x) \leqslant 0 \text{ for } j \in J - \{r, k_1, k_2\}.$$

By repeatedly applying this argument and replacing one of the non-strict inequalities, we obtain a consistent system

$$\ell(x) < 0,\, \ell_k(x) > 0,\, \ell_j(x) = 0 \text{ for } j \in J - \{k\}. \tag{6.9}$$

Since system (6.8) is inconsistent, the set of linear functional $\{\ell\} \cup \{\ell_j \mid j \in J\}$ is linearly dependent, which implies the existence of y and z_j for $j \in J$ such that $y\ell + \sum\{z_j\ell_j \mid j \in J\} = 0$. At least two multipliers are non-zero and we may assume that $z_r > 0$ for some $r \in J$.

If $a \in L$ satisfies system (6.9) for $k = r$, then $y\ell(a) = -z_r\ell_r(a) < 0$. Since $\ell(a) < 0$ we have $y > 0$.

For an arbitrary $s \in J$ and a $b \in L$ that satisfies system (6.9) for $k = s$, then $\mu_s\ell_s(b) = -y\ell(b) > 0$ and since $\ell_s(b) > 0$, we have $\mu_s > 0$, which completes the argument. $\qquad\square$

6.11 The Contingent Cone

Definition 6.17. Let L be a normed real linear space and let S be a subset of L. If $z \in \mathbf{K}(S)$, then $h \in L$ is a *tangent vector* to S at z if there is a sequence (x_n) in S such that $\lim_{n\to\infty} x_n = x$ and a sequence $(a_n) \in \mathbf{Seq}(\mathbb{R}_{\geqslant 0})$ such that $h = \lim_{n\to\infty} a_n(x_n - z)$.

The set $T(S, z)$ of all tangent vector to S at z is the *contingent cone* to S at z.

It is easy to verify that $T(S, z)$ is indeed a cone.

Theorem 6.64. *Let L be a normed real linear space and let S be a non-empty subset of L. If S is local convex at $z \in S$, then $\mathbf{K}_{cone}(S - \{z\}) \subseteq T(S, z)$.*

Proof. Suppose that S is local convex at $z \in S$. Let $x \in S$ be an arbitrary element and let $x_n = z + \frac{1}{n}(x - z)$. It is clear that $\lim_{n\to\infty} x_n = z$. Furthermore, since $x_n = \left(1 - \frac{1}{n}\right)z + \frac{1}{n}x$ and S is locally convex at z it follows that $x_n \in S$.

Note that $n(x_n - z) = x - z$, so $x - z$ is a tangent vector to S for every $x \in S$, which implies $S - \{z\} \subseteq T(S, z)$. Since $T(S, z)$ is a cone, it follows that $\mathbf{K}_{cone}(S - \{z\}) \subseteq T(S, z)$. $\qquad\square$

Theorem 6.65. *Let L be a normed real linear space and let S be a non-empty subset of L. For every $z \in S$ we have*

$$T(S, z) \subseteq \boldsymbol{K}(\boldsymbol{K}_{cone}(S - \{z\})).$$

Proof. This statement follows immediately from Definition 6.17. □

Corollary 6.20. *Let L be a normed real linear space and let S be a non-empty subset of L. If S is local convex at $z \in S$, then*

$$\boldsymbol{K}_{cone}(S - \{z\}) \subseteq T(S, z).$$

Proof. The corollary follows from Theorems 6.64 and 6.65. □

Theorem 6.66. *Let L be a normed real linear space and let S be a non-empty subset of L. For every $z \in S$ the contingent cone $T(S, z)$ is closed.*

Proof. Let (h_n) be a sequence of vectors in $T(S, z)$ such that $\lim_{n \to \infty} h_n = h$. For each h_n there exists a sequence $(x_{n,m})$ such that $\lim_{m \to \infty} x_{n,m} = z$ and a sequence of scalars $(a_{n,m})$ such that $h_n = \lim_{m \to \infty} a_{n,m}(x_{n,m} - z)$. Therefore, for each $n \in \mathbb{N}$ there exists $M(n) \in \mathbb{N}$ such that if $m \geqslant M(n)$ we have $\|x_{n,m} - z\| \leqslant \frac{1}{n}$ and $\|a_{n,m}(x_{n,m} - z)\| \leqslant \frac{1}{n}$.

Let $y_n = x_{n,n}$ and $b_n = a_{n,n}$. It is clear that $\lim_{n \to \infty} y_n = z$ and

$$
\begin{aligned}
\|b_n(y_n - z) - h\| &= \|a_{n,n}(x_{n,n} - z) - h\| \\
&\leqslant \|a_{n,n}(x_{n,n} - z) - h_n\| + \|h_n - h\| \\
&\leqslant \frac{1}{n} + \|h_n - h\|,
\end{aligned}
$$

which means that $h = \lim_{n \to \infty} b_n(y_n - z)$, so $h \in T(S, z)$. This shows that $T(S, z)$ is closed. □

Corollary 6.21. *Let L be a normed real linear space and let S be a non-empty subset of L. If S is locally convex at z, then*

$$T(S, z) = \boldsymbol{K}(\boldsymbol{K}_{cone}(S - \{z\})).$$

Proof. Recall that $T(S, z) \subseteq \boldsymbol{K}(\boldsymbol{K}_{cone}(S - \{z\}))$ by Theorem 6.65. Since $\boldsymbol{K}_{cone}(S - \{z\}) \subseteq T(S, z)$ by Corollary 6.20, it follows that

$$\boldsymbol{K}(\boldsymbol{K}_{cone}(S - \{z\})) \subseteq T(S, z)$$

because $T(S, z)$ is closed. This completes the argument. □

Theorem 6.67. *The contingent cone $T(S, z)$ of a non-empty convex subset S of a real linear space L is convex for every z.*

Proof. Let $h, k \in T(S, z)$. We have $h = \lim_{n\to\infty} a_n(x_n - z)$ and $k = \lim_{n\to\infty} b_n(y_n - z)$, where $\lim_{n\to\infty} x_n = \lim_{n\to\infty} y_n$ for some sequences of real numbers (a_n) and (b_n).

Let $c_n = a_n + b_n$ and

$$z_n = \frac{a_n x_n + b_n y_n}{c_n}$$

$$= \frac{a_n}{a_n + b_n} x_n + \frac{b_n}{a_n + b_n} y_n$$

define the sequences (c_n) and (z_n). Note that $z_n \in S$ because S is convex. Since

$$z_n = \frac{a_n}{c_n}(x_n - z) + \frac{b_n}{c_n}(y_n - z) + z,$$

it follows that $\lim_{n\to\infty} z_n = z$. The desired conclusion follows from the fact that

$$\begin{aligned} h + k &= \lim_{n\to\infty} a_n(x_n - z) + \lim_{n\to\infty} b_n(y_n - z) \\ &= \lim_{n\to\infty} a_n x_n + b_n y_n - c_n z) \\ &= \lim_{n\to\infty} c_n(z_n - z). \end{aligned}$$
□

Recall that a face of a convex set C is a convex subset of C such that $(u, v) \subseteq C$ and $\{u, v\} \cap (C - F) \neq \emptyset$ implies $(u, v) \subseteq C - F$; the face F of C is proper if $F \neq C$.

Theorem 6.68. *Let C be a convex set in a real linear space L. A face F of C is included in ∂C.*

If L is locally convex and $\mathbf{I}(C) \neq \emptyset$ then any $x \in C \cap \partial C$ belongs to a proper face.

Proof. Let $x \in F$ and let $y \in C - F$. We have:

$$[0, 1] \subseteq \{a \mid (1 - a)x + ay \in C\}.$$

However, if $a < 0$, $z = (1 - a)x + ay \notin C$, because otherwise we would have

$$x = \frac{1}{1 - a} z + \frac{-a}{1 - a} y$$

and this would mean that $x \in (z, y)$, where we have $z \in C$, $y \in C - F$ and $x \in F$, which contradicts Definition 3.13.

Define $z_n = \frac{n+1}{n} x - \frac{1}{n} y$. We have $\lim_{n\to\infty} n = x$, hence x is a limit point of a sequence of points not in C. This shows that $x \in \mathbf{K}(C) \cap \mathbf{K}(L - C)$, so $x \in \partial C$.

Suppose now that $x \in C \cap \partial C$. Let $D = \mathbf{I}(C)$. Since D is open, by Corollary 6.14 there exists a continuous, non-zero linear functional ℓ such that $c = \sup\{f(y) \mid y \in D\} \leqslant \ell(x)$. Since $x \in C$, $\ell(x) = c$. Since D is open, $\ell(D)$ is an open set by Theorem 6.52, so the hyperplane $H = \{y \mid \ell(y) = c\}$ is disjoint from D. Thus, x belongs to the proper face $H \cap C$. $\qquad\square$

6.12 Extreme Points and Krein-Milman Theorem

The notion of supporting set of a convex set generalizes the notion of extreme point.

Definition 6.18. Let C be a convex subset of a real linear space L. A set S is a *supporting set* of C if the following conditions are satisfied:

(i) $S \subseteq C$;

(ii) S is closed and convex, and

(iii) if $u, v \in C$ and $\mathbf{I}([u, v]) \cap S \neq \emptyset$, then $[u, v] \subseteq S$.

Any extreme point x of a convex set can be regarded as a supporting set $S_x = \{x\}$. Moreover, if a supporting set for C consists of one point, $S = \{x\}$, then x is an extreme point of C.

Lemma 6.5. *Let C be a convex subset of a real linear space L. The intersection of a family of supporting sets of C is a supporting set of C.*

Proof. The lemma is an immediate consequence of Definition 6.18. $\qquad\square$

Lemma 6.6. *Let C be a convex subset of a real linear space L and let S be a supporting set of C. If T is a supporting set of S, then T is a supporting set of C.*

Proof. It is clear that $T \subseteq S \subseteq C$ and that T is convex and closed by Theorem 4.4. Suppose now that if $u, v \in C$ and $x \in \mathbf{I}([u, v]) \cap T$. Then $x \in \mathbf{I}([u, v]) \cap S$, hence $[u, v] \subseteq S$. Since T is a support set for S, it follows that $[u, v] \subseteq T$. Thus, T is a supporting set of C. $\qquad\square$

Lemma 6.7. *Let C be a compact and convex subset of a real linear space L and let f be a continuous linear functional on L such that $m = \max\{f(x) \mid x \in C\}$. The set $S = \{x \in C \mid f(x) = m\}$ is a supporting hyperplane for C.*

Proof. Suppose that $x, y \in S$, that is, $f(x) = f(y) = m$. Then, $f((1 - a)x + ay) = m$ for $a \in [0, 1]$, so S is convex. If $[x, y] \subseteq C$, $z \in \mathbf{I}([x, y])$, and

$f(z) = m$, then $m = f((1-a)x + ay)$ and since $f(x) \leqslant m$ and $f(y) \leqslant$ we must have $f(x) = f(y) = m$. This implies $[x, y] \subseteq S$. $\qquad\square$

Lemma 6.8. *Let L be a locally convex linear topological space and let U be a closed convex set such that $0_L \notin U$. There exists a continuous linear functional f on L such that $\inf\{f(u) \mid u \in U\} > 0$.*

Proof. Since $0_L \notin U$, there exists an open set V such that $0_L \in V$ and $U \cap V = \emptyset$. Let $W = V \cap (-V)$. Then, W is an open convex set that contains 0_L, $-W = W$, and $W \cap U = \emptyset$. Since $0_L \in \mathbf{RI}(W)$, there exists a non-zero linear functional f such that

$$\sup\{f(u) \mid u \in W\} \leqslant \inf\{f(u) \mid u \in U\} = a.$$

Thus, $f(u) \leqslant a$ for every $u \in W$ and, since $u \in W$ implies $-u \in W$, we also have $-f(u) \leqslant a$ for $u \in W$, hence $|f(u)| \leqslant a$ for $x \in W$. Therefore, for any $c > 0$ we have $|f(u)| < c$ for $u \in \frac{c}{a}W$. Since $W_1 = \frac{c}{a}W$ is an open set containing 0_L it follows that f is continuous at 0_L.

To show that $a > 0$, note that there exists u_0 such that $f(u_0) > 0$ because f is a non-zero functional. Since $0_L \in \mathbf{RI}(W)$, there exists $t > 0$ so that $tu \in W$. This implies $0 < tf(u) = f(tu) \leqslant a$. $\qquad\square$

Lemma 6.9. *Let L be a locally convex linear topological space and let U be a closed convex set such that $x_0 \notin U$. There exists a continuous linear functional f on L such that $\inf\{f(x) \mid x \in U\} > f(x_0)$.*

Proof. Since $x_0 \notin U$, it follows that $0_L \notin \mathsf{t}_{-x_0}(U)$ and it is clear that $\mathsf{t}_{-x_0}(U)$ is a closed convex set. Thus Lemma 6.8 is applicable, and it implies that there exists a continuous linear functional f on L such that $\inf\{f(z) \mid z \in \mathsf{t}_{-x_0}(U)\} > 0$. Since $z \in \mathsf{t}_{-x_0}(U)$, it follows that $x = z + x_0 \in U$, hence $\inf\{f(x) \mid x \in U\} > f(x_0)$. $\qquad\square$

Krein and Milman theorem is a generalization of a result of Carathéodory (see Theorem 3.25) to locally convex linear topological spaces.

Theorem 6.69. (Krein-Milman Theorem) *Let L be a locally convex Hausdorff linear topological space and let C be a non-empty compact and convex subset of L. We have:*

$$C = \mathbf{K}(\mathbf{K}_{\mathrm{conv}}(extr(C))).$$

Proof. We saw that the intersection of supporting sets for C is a supporting set for C and that a support set of a support set of C is itself a support set for C.

The collection $\mathcal{S}$ of supporting sets of C is a partially ordered set (relative to set inclusion). Therefore, by Hausdorff maximality principle (Theorem 1.23) there exists a maximal chain $\mathcal{C}$ of supporting sets for C. Since C is compact, the intersection T of all non-empty supporting sets of C is non-empty and, also, is a supporting set for C. It is also a minimal non-empty supporting set of C, because if T would contain a strictly smaller supporting set, this would contradict the maximality of the chain $\mathcal{C}$.

A minimal supporting M set may contain only one point and such a point must be an extreme point. Indeed, if a supporting set S contains two distinct points x and y, then there exists a continuous linear functional f such that $f(x) > f(y)$. Then, the subset of S where f attains its maximum is a supporting subset of S and, therefore of C. Since C is compact, it is a non-empty supporting set of C that does not contain y.

If a supporting set consists of one point x, x must be extreme. Thus, every non-empty supporting set contains an extreme point. The maximum of a continuous linear functional f on C is equal to the maximum on the set $\mathsf{extr}(C)$ because the subset of C where a linear functional assumes its maximum is a non-empty supporting set.

Let $D = \mathbf{K}(\mathbf{K}_{\mathrm{conv}}(\mathsf{extr}(C)))$. Since $\mathsf{extr}(C) \subseteq C$, it follows that $\mathbf{K}_{\mathrm{conv}}(\mathsf{extr}(C))) \subseteq C$ because C is convex. Thus, $D = \mathbf{K}(\mathbf{K}_{\mathrm{conv}}(\mathsf{extr}(C))) \subseteq \mathbf{K}(C) = C$. Suppose that $x \notin D$. By Lemma 6.9 there is a continuous linear functional f such that $f(x) > \max\{f(y) \mid y \in D\} = \max\{f(y) \mid y \in C\}$. Thus, $x \notin C$, and $C \subseteq D$, which implies $C = D$. $\qquad\square$

Exercises and Supplements

(1) Prove that a subset U of a real topological linear space L is open if and only $\mathbf{t}_z(U)$ is open for every $z \in L$.

(2) Prove that in a topological linear space $(L, \mathcal{O})$ for every $U \in neigh_{0_L}(L, \mathcal{O})$ there exists a balanced neighborhood $W \in neigh_{0_L}(L, \mathcal{O})$ such that $W \subseteq U$.

   Solution: The continuity of scalar multiplication implies that there exists $\epsilon > 0$ and $V \in neigh_{0_L}(L, \mathcal{O})$ such that $rV \subseteq U$ if $|r| < \epsilon$. Define $W = \bigcup\{rV \mid |r| < \epsilon\}$. It is clear that $W \in neigh_{0_L}(L, \mathcal{O})$, W is balanced and $W \subseteq U$.

(3) Prove that in a topological linear space $(L, \mathcal{O})$ for every convex neighborhood $U \in neigh_{0_L}(L, \mathcal{O})$ there exists a convex balanced neighborhood $W \in neigh_{0_L}(L, \mathcal{O})$ such that $W \subseteq U$.

Solution: The set $Z = \bigcap\{rU \mid |r| \leqslant 1\}$ is convex as an intersection of convex sets. Moreover, Z is a balanced set. Indeed, for $|t| \leqslant 1$ we have $tZ = \bigcap\{trU \mid |r| \leqslant 1\} \subseteq \bigcap\{rU \mid |r| \leqslant 1\} = Z$. Thus, by Theorem 6.13, $\mathbf{I}(Z)$ is a balanced set.

By Supplement 2 there exists a balanced neighborhood W such that $W \subseteq U$. We have $\frac{1}{r}W = W$ if $|r| = 1$ because W is balanced, hence $W \subseteq rU$, which implies $W \subseteq Z$. This implies $\mathbf{I}(Z) \in neigh_{0_L}(L, \mathcal{O})$; also $\mathbf{I}(Z)$ is convex by Theorem 6.37, and, as we saw above, a balanced set.

(4) Let L be a real topological linear space. If $U \subseteq \mathbb{R}$ is a closed set of scalars such that $0 \notin U$ and T is a closed subset of L such that $0_L \notin T$, then $\bigcup\{h_a(T) \mid a \in U\}$ is a closed set.

(5) Let U, V be two compact subsets of a real topological linear space L. Prove that $U + V$ is compact.

(6) Let L be a topological linear space. Prove that:

   (a) if $V \in neigh_{0_L}(L, \mathcal{O})$, then $\hat{V} = V \cap h_{-1}(V)$ is a symmetric neighborhood of 0_L;
   (b) if $W \in neigh_{0_L}(L, \mathcal{O})$ there exists a symmetric neighborhood U of 0_L such that $U + U \subseteq W$;
   (c) if $W \in neigh_{0_L}(L, \mathcal{O})$ for each $k \geqslant 2$ there exist symmetric neighborhoods $U_1, U_2, \ldots, U_k$ of 0_L such that $U_1 + U_2 + \cdots + U_k \subseteq W$.

Solution: The first part is immediate. By the continuity of addition in L there exist $V_1, V_2 \in neigh_{0_L}(L, \mathcal{O})$ such that $V_1 + V_2 \subseteq W$. Then, $U = \hat{V}_1 \cap \hat{V}_2$ is a symmetric neighborhood of 0_L and $U + U \subseteq W$.

For the last part by applying m times the second statement one could construct a sequence $U_1, U_2, \ldots, U_{2^m}$ of symmetric neighborhoods of 0_L such that $U_1 + U_2 + \cdots + U_{2^m} \subseteq W$. Choosing m such that $k \leqslant 2^m$ we obtain $U_1 + \cdots + U_k \subseteq U_1 + \cdots + U_k + \cdots + U_{2^m} \subseteq W$.

(7) Prove that a subset U of a linear space L is bounded if and only if for every sequence (x_n) in U we have $\lim_{n \to \infty} \frac{1}{n} x_n = 0$.

(8) Let $f : L \longrightarrow \mathbb{R}$ be a linear functional defined on the real topological linear space L such that f is not identically 0 on L. Prove that the following statements are equivalent:

   (a) f is continuous;
   (b) the set $\{x \in L \mid f(x) = 0\}$ is closed;
   (c) the set $\{x \in L \mid f(x) = 0\}$ is not dense in L.

(9) Let $(L, \mathcal{O})$ be a real linear space. Prove that for every subset T of L we have $\mathbf{K}(T) = \bigcap\{T + V \mid v \in neigh_{0_L}(L, \mathcal{O})\}$.

Solution: We have $x \in \mathbf{K}(T)$ if and only if $x + V \cap T \neq \emptyset$ for every $V \in neigh_{0_L}(L, \mathcal{O})$. This is equivalent to $x \in T - V$. Since $-V \in$

$neigh_{0_L}(L, \mathcal{O})$ if and only if $V \in neigh_{0_L}(L, \mathcal{O})$, the desired equality follows.

(10) Let $(L, \mathcal{O})$ be a topological $\mathbb{F}$-linear space. Prove that if U is an open set in L and W is a subset of L, then $\mathbf{K}(W) + U = W + U$.

Solution: The inclusion $W + U \subseteq \mathbf{K}(W) + U$ is immediate.

To prove the reverse inclusion let $y \in \mathbf{K}(W) + U$. We have $y = x + u$, where $x \in \mathbf{K}(W)$ and $u \in U$. There exists $V \in neigh_{0_L}(L, \mathcal{O})$ such that $u + V \subseteq U$ because U is an open set. Since $x \in \mathbf{K}(W)$, taking into account that $x - V \in neigh_x(L, \mathcal{O})$, there exists some $z \in W \cap (x - V)$. Then, $y = x + u = z + u + (x - z) \in z + u + V \subseteq U + V$.

(11) Let $(L, \mathcal{O})$ be a topological $\mathbb{F}$-linear space. Prove that if U is a compact subset of L and W is a closed subset of L, then $U + W$ is closed.

Solution: By Theorem 4.63, since U is compact if and only if each net in S has some convergent subnet. Suppose that a net in U clusters to x and let (x_i) be a subnet in U such that $x_i \to u$.

Let (y_i) be a net in W such that $x_i + y_i \to z$. Since $y_i = (x_i + y_i) - x_i \to z - x = y$ and W is closed, we have $y \in W$, so $z = x + y \in U + W$, which implies that $U + W$ is closed by Corollary 4.14.

(12) Let $(L, \mathcal{O})$ be a Hausdorff topological linear space. Prove that every finite dimensional subspace of L is closed.

(13) Corollary 6.1 shows that a hyperplane H in a topological linear space L is either closed or dense in L. If $H = \{x \in L \mid f(x) = 0\}$, where f is a linear functional, prove that H is closed if and only if f is continuous, and H is dense if and only if f is discontinuous.

(14) Prove that a product of locally convex linear spaces is locally convex.

(15) Let L be a linear space. Prove that the product topology on $\mathbb{R}^L$ is a locally convex Hausdorff topology.

(16) Let f be a linear functional defined on a normed real linear space $(L, \|\cdot\|)$. Prove that:

(a) f is continuous if and only if $f^{-1}(0)$ is a closed subspace;
(b) we have $\|f\| = \frac{1}{d(0_L, M_f)}$, where $M_f = f^{-1}(1)$.

In the special case, when $f = 0$ we have $M_f = \emptyset$ and $d(0_L, M_f) = \infty$.

Solution: It is clear that if f is continuous, then $f^{-1}(0)$ is a closed subspace of L. Conversely, suppose that $f^{-1}(0)$ is a closed subspace and let $x_0 \in L - f^{-1}(0)$ such that $f(x_0) = 1$. Since $x_0 \notin f^{-1}(0)$ we have $d(x_0, f^{-1}(0)) > 0$. Every $x \in L$ can be uniquely written as $x = ax_0 + z$

with z in the subspace $f^{-1}(0)$ and

$$\|x\| = d(x, 0_L)$$

$$\text{(because } d \text{ is induced by the norm)}$$
$$\geqslant d(x, f^{-1}(0))$$
$$\text{(because } 0_L \in f^{-1}(0))$$
$$= |a| d(x_0, f^{-1}(0))$$

and $f(x) = a$, hence $|f(x)| \leqslant \frac{1}{d(x_0, f^{-1}(0))} \|x\|$, hence f is continuous. When f is continuous we have

$$\|f\| = \sup_{x \neq 0_L} \frac{|f(x)|}{\|x\|} = \frac{1}{\inf_{x \mid f(x) \neq 0} \frac{\|x\|}{|f(x)|}}$$

$$= \frac{1}{\inf_{x \mid f(x)=1} \|x\|} = \frac{1}{d(0_L, M_f)}.$$

(17) Let $(L, \|\cdot\|)$ be a normed real linear space. If M is a closed proper linear subspace of L and $x_0 \in L - M$, prove that:

  (a) there exists a linear functional f with $\|f\| = 1$ such that $f(y) = 0$ for every $y \in M$ and $f(x_0) = d(x_0, M)$;

  (b) for each $x_0 \in L - \{0_L\}$ there exists a linear functional f with $\|f\| = 1$ and $f(x_0) = \|x_0\|$;

  (c) if U is a closed subspace of L such that every linear functional g such that $g(u) = 0$ for every $u \in U$ is 0, then U is dense in L.

Solution: Note that the linear subspace M_1 generated by M and x_0 consists of linear combinations of the form $y + ax_0$, where $y \in M$ and $a \in \mathbb{R}$. Define the linear functional f_1 on M as $f_1(y + a\mathbf{x}_0) = a$. Clearly, $f_1(y) = 0$ for every $y \in M$ and $f_1(x_0) = 1$.

Note that $f_1^{-1}(1) = \{y + x_0 \mid y \in M\}$. This implies that $\|f_1\| = \frac{1}{d(x_0, M)}$. By Hahn-Banach theorem, f_1 can be extended to a linear functional $\tilde{f}$ on the entire space L with $\|\tilde{f}\| = \frac{1}{d(x_0, M)}$, which shows that $f = d(x_0, M)\tilde{f}$ is the needed functional.

The last two parts follow immediately from the first.

(18) A subset S of $\mathbb{R}^n$ is *midpoint convex* if $\mathbf{x}, \mathbf{y} \in S$ implies $\frac{1}{2}(\mathbf{x} + \mathbf{y}) \in S$. Prove that if S is closed and mid-point convex, then it is convex.

Solution: Let $\mathbf{x}, \mathbf{y} \in S$ and let $\mathbf{z}$ be a vector in the segment $[\mathbf{x}, \mathbf{y}]$. Construct the sequences of vectors $(\mathbf{x}_n)$ and $(\mathbf{y}_n)$ as $\mathbf{x}_0 = \mathbf{x}$, $\mathbf{y}_0 = \mathbf{y}$,

$$\mathbf{x}_{n+1} = \frac{1}{2}(\mathbf{x}_n + \mathbf{z}), \text{ and } \mathbf{y}_{n+1} = \frac{1}{2}(\mathbf{y}_n + \mathbf{z}).$$

If $\mathbf{z}_n = \frac{1}{2}(\mathbf{x}_n + \mathbf{y}_n)$ for $n \geqslant 0$ then $\|\mathbf{z}_n - \mathbf{z}\| \leqslant \frac{1}{2^n}\|\mathbf{x} - \mathbf{y}\|$. Therefore, $\lim_{n \to \infty} z_n = z$. By mid-point convexity we have $\mathbf{z}_i \in S$ and because S is closed, we have $\mathbf{z} \in S$. Thus, C is indeed convex.

(19) Prove that the set of rational numbers $\mathbb{Q}$ is mid-point convex but not convex.

(20) If U is a compact subset of $\mathbb{R}^n$, prove that its convex closure $\mathbf{K}_{\text{conv}}(U)$ is a compact set.

Solution: Let $\mathbf{x} \in \mathbf{K}_{\text{conv}}(U)$. By Carathéodory's Theorem (Theorem 3.25) we have $\mathbf{x} = \sum_{i=1}^{n+1} a_i \mathbf{u}_i$, where $\mathbf{u}_i \in U$, $a_i \geqslant 0$ for $1 \leqslant i \leqslant n+1$, and $\sum_{i=1}^{n+1} a_i = 1$.

Let $(\mathbf{x}_p)$ be a sequence in $\mathbf{K}_{\text{conv}}(U)$. Each $\mathbf{x}_p$ can be written as $\mathbf{x}_p = \sum_{j-1}^{n+1} c_{p,j} \mathbf{u}_{(p,j)}$, where $c_{p,j} \geqslant 0$, $\sum_{j=1}^{n+1} c_{p,j} = 1$, and $\mathbf{u}_{(p,j)} \in U$.

Note that the vectors $\begin{pmatrix} c_{p,1} \\ \vdots \\ c_{p,n+1} \end{pmatrix}$ belong to a simplex in $\mathbb{R}^{n+1}$ which is compact (by Corollary 6.11). Since U is compact too, there exists a sequence $p_1, p_2, \ldots$ in $\mathbb{N}$ such that $(c_{p_j,1})$ and $(\mathbf{u}_{p_j,n+1})$ are convergent subsequences of the sequences $(c_{p,j})$ and $(\mathbf{u}_{p,j})$. Suppose that $\lim_{j \to \infty} c_{p_j,k} = c_k$ and $\lim_{j \to \infty} \mathbf{u}_{p_j,k} = \mathbf{u}_k$ for $1 \leqslant k \leqslant n+1$. Therefore, the sequence $(\mathbf{x}_{p_j})$ is a convergent subsequence of $(\mathbf{x}_p)$, hence $\mathbf{K}_{\text{conv}}(U)$ is compact.

(21) Let C be a compact subset of $\mathbb{R}^n$. Prove that $\mathbf{0}_n \in \mathbf{K}_{\text{conv}}(C)$ if and only the set $\{\mathbf{h} \in \mathbb{R}^n \mid \mathbf{x}'\mathbf{h} < 0\}$ is empty.

Solution: If $\mathbf{0}_n \in \mathbf{K}_{\text{conv}}(C)$ then $\mathbf{0}_n$ is a convex combination $\mathbf{0}_n = \sum_{i=1}^{n} a_i \mathbf{x}_i$ for some $\mathbf{x}_i \in C$. Then, $\sum_{i=1}^{n} a_i(\mathbf{x}_i, \mathbf{h}) = 0$ and this contradicts the fact that $\mathbf{x}_i'\mathbf{h} < 0$. This implies that $\{\mathbf{h} \in \mathbb{R}^n \mid \mathbf{x}'\mathbf{h} < 0\}$ is empty.

Conversely, suppose that $\mathbf{0}_n \in \mathbf{K}_{\text{conv}}(C)$. Since $\mathbf{K}_{\text{conv}}(C)$ is compact by Supplement 20, there exists $\mathbf{h} \in \mathbb{R}^n$ such that $\mathbf{x}'\mathbf{h} < 0$ for all $\mathbf{x} \in \mathbf{K}_{\text{conv}}(C)$, hence $\mathbf{x}'\mathbf{h} < 0$ for $\mathbf{x} \in C$.

(22) Show that Farkas' Theorem (Theorem 6.61) follows from Supplement 26.

Solution: Let $A \in \mathbb{R}^{m \times n}$ be a matrix and let $\mathbf{b} \in \mathbb{R}^n$ be a vector. Since $C = \{A'\mathbf{y} \mid \mathbf{y} \in \mathbb{R}^m, \mathbf{y} \geqslant \mathbf{0}_m\}$ is a closed convex cone in $\mathbb{R}^n$, by Supplement 26 we have $C = (C^*)^*$.

By Supplement 25 the polar cone C^* is given by $C^* = \{\mathbf{p} \in \mathbb{R}^n \mid A\mathbf{p} \leqslant \mathbf{0}_m\}$. Thus, we have $\mathbf{c} \in (C^*)^*$ if and only if $\mathbf{c}'\mathbf{x} \leqslant 0$ for all $\mathbf{x} \in C^*$, that is, $A\mathbf{x} \leqslant \mathbf{0}_m$ implies $\mathbf{c}'\mathbf{x} \leqslant 0$. Therefore, $A'\mathbf{x} \leqslant \mathbf{0}_m$ implies $\mathbf{c}'\mathbf{x} \leqslant 0$ is equivalent to the existence of $\mathbf{x} \in \mathbb{R}^n$ such that

$$\mathbf{c} = A\mathbf{x} \text{ and } \mathbf{x} \leqslant \mathbf{0}_n.$$

This allows us to conclude that

$$A'\mathbf{x} \geqslant \mathbf{0}_m \text{ implies } \mathbf{c}'\mathbf{x} \geqslant 0$$

is equivalent to the existence of $\mathbf{x} \in \mathbb{R}^n$ such that

$$\mathbf{c} = A\mathbf{x} \text{ and } \mathbf{x} \geqslant \mathbf{0}_n,$$

which is the statement of Theorem 6.61.

(23) Let $P \subseteq \mathbb{R}^n$ be a polytope and let $\{F_i \mid 1 \leqslant m \leqslant m\}$ be the set of its faces. Prove that if $H_{\mathbf{w}_i,a_i}$ is a hyperplane that supports P such that $F_i = P \cap H^{\geqslant}_{\mathbf{w}_i,a_i}$ for $1 \leqslant i \leqslant m$, then $P = \bigcap_{i=1}^m H^{\geqslant}_{\mathbf{w}_i,a_i}$.

Let T be a subset of $\mathbb{R}^n$. Define the set T^* as

$$T^* = \begin{cases} \{\mathbf{p} \in \mathbb{R}^n \mid \mathbf{p}'\mathbf{x} \leqslant 0 \text{ for all } \mathbf{x} \in T\} & \text{if } T \neq \emptyset, \\ \mathbb{R}^n & \text{if } T = \emptyset. \end{cases}$$

(24) Prove that for every subsets T, T_1, T_2 of $\mathbb{R}^n$ we have:

   (a) T^* is a closed convex cone with vertex $\mathbf{0}_n$ for every $T \subseteq \mathbb{R}^n$. The set T^* is known as the *polar cone* of T.
   (b) $T_1 \subseteq T_2$ implies $(T_2)^* \subseteq (T_1)^*$;
   (c) $T \subseteq (T^*)^*$.

(25) Let $A \in \mathbb{R}^{m \times n}$ and let $C = \{A'\mathbf{y} \mid \mathbf{y} \geqslant \mathbf{0}_m\}$. Prove that C is a closed and convex cone and that $C^* = \{\mathbf{x} \in \mathbb{R}^n \mid A\mathbf{x} \leqslant \mathbf{0}_m\}$.

   Solution: We leave it to the reader to show that C is a closed and convex cone. If $\mathbf{z} \in C^*$ we have $\mathbf{z}'A'\mathbf{y} \leqslant 0$, or $\mathbf{y}'A\mathbf{z} \leqslant 0$ for every $\mathbf{y} \geqslant \mathbf{0}$. This is equivalent to $A\mathbf{z} \leqslant \mathbf{0}_m$, which gives the desired equality for C^*.

(26) Prove that if C is a convex and closed cone in $\mathbb{R}^n$ having the vertex $\mathbf{0}_n$, then $C = (C^*)^*$.

   Solution: By Part (b) of Exercise 24 we have $C \subseteq (C^*)^*$; this leaves us to prove the reverse inclusion.

   Suppose that $\mathbf{x} \in (C^*)^*$ but $\mathbf{x} \notin C$. By the Separation Theorem (Theorem 6.55) there exists $\mathbf{w} \in \mathbb{R}^n - \{\mathbf{0}_n\}$ such that $\mathbf{w}'\mathbf{y} \leqslant a$ for every $\mathbf{y} \in C$ and $\mathbf{w}'\mathbf{x} > a$.

   Since $\mathbf{0}_n \in C$, it follows that $0 \leqslant a$, that is, that a is a non-negative number, so $\mathbf{w}'\mathbf{x} > 0$.

   We claim that $\mathbf{w} \in C^*$. If this is not the case, there exists a $\tilde{\mathbf{y}} \in C$ such that $\mathbf{w}'\tilde{\mathbf{y}} > 0$. Therefore, choosing k an arbitrarily large number, the number $\mathbf{w}'(k\tilde{\mathbf{y}})$ can be made arbitrarily large, which contradicts the fact that $\mathbf{w}'\mathbf{y} \leqslant a$ for all $\mathbf{y} \in C$. Therefore, we have $\mathbf{w} \in C^*$. Since

$\mathbf{x} \in (C^*)^*$, $\mathbf{w}'\mathbf{x} \leqslant 0$, which contradicts the fact that $\mathbf{w}'\mathbf{x} > 0$. Thus, $\mathbf{x} \in C$.

(27) Prove that if C is an open set in $\mathbb{R}^n$, then $\mathbf{K}_{\mathrm{conv}}(C)$ is open.

(28) Let U be a subset of $\mathbb{R}^n$. Prove that:
   (a) We have $\mathbf{K}_{\mathrm{conv}}(\mathbf{K}(U)) \subseteq \mathbf{K}(\mathbf{K}_{\mathrm{conv}}(U))$;
   (b) if U is bounded, then $\mathbf{K}_{\mathrm{conv}}(\mathbf{K}(U)) = \mathbf{K}(\mathbf{K}_{\mathrm{conv}}(U))$;
   (c) if U is both bounded and closed, then $\mathbf{K}_{\mathrm{conv}(U)}$ is a closed set.

(29) Give an example of a non-bounded and closed subset U of $\mathbb{R}^n$ such that $\mathbf{K}_{\mathrm{conv}}(U)$ is not closed.

(30) Let C be a convex subset of $\mathbb{R}^n$. Prove that:
   (a) $\mathbf{RI}(C)$ is a convex subset of $\mathbb{R}^n$;
   (b) $\mathbf{K}(\mathbf{RI}(C)) = \mathbf{K}(C)$;
   (c) $\mathbf{RI}(\mathbf{K}(C)) = \mathbf{RI}(C) = \mathbf{RI}(\mathbf{RI}(C))$.

(31) Let C be a convex subset of $\mathbb{R}^n$. Prove that

$$\mathbf{K}_{\mathrm{aff}}(C) = \mathbf{K}_{\mathrm{aff}}(\mathbf{K}(C)) = \mathbf{K}_{\mathrm{aff}}(\mathbf{RI}(C)).$$

Bibliographical Comments

The standard reference for topological linear space is [90].

The books [111, 23, 15, 18, 99] contain a vast amount of results in convexity theory. References that focus on geometric aspects are [69, 115].

We followed [85] in the presentation of contingent cones.

PART III

Measure and Integration

Chapter 7

Measurable Spaces and Measures

7.1 Introduction

Measure theory is an area of mathematical analysis that seeks to formalize a generalization of the notion of body volume. The relevant mathematical structures (algebras and σ-algebras of sets) have been presented in Chapter 1. In this chapter we discuss measurable spaces, Borel sets in topological spaces and several classes of functions that are naturally related to the notion of measure. Then, we focus on outer measures, on Lebesgue measures on $\mathbb{R}^n$, and on signed and complex measures. The chapter concludes with some applications of measure theory to probabilities.

7.2 Measurable Spaces

Definition 7.1. A *measurable space* is a pair $(S, \mathcal{E})$, where S is a non-empty set and $\mathcal{E}$ is a σ-algebra of subsets of S.

The sets that belong to $\mathcal{E}$ are referred to as *measurable sets*.

For a measurable space $(S, \mathcal{E})$ and a set $T \in \mathcal{E}$ we denote

$$\mathcal{E}[T] = \{U \in \mathcal{E} \mid U \subseteq T\}.$$

It is immediate to verify that $\mathcal{E}[T]$ is a σ-algebra for every $T \in \mathcal{E}$.

If $(S, \mathcal{E})$ is a measurable space then $\mathcal{E}_\sigma \subseteq \mathcal{E}$. Moreover, by part (ii) of Theorem 1.12, we also have $\mathcal{E}_\delta \subseteq \mathcal{E}$.

Definition 7.2. Let $(S, \mathcal{E})$ be a measurable space. An *$\mathcal{E}$-partition* (or a *measurable partition* of $(S, \mathcal{E})$) is a partition $\pi \in PART(S)$ such that $B \in \mathcal{E}$ for every $B \in \pi$.

The set of *finite* $\mathcal{E}$-partitions of a set $T \in \mathcal{E}$ is denoted by $PART_{\mathcal{E}}(T)$.

If π is a $\mathcal{E}$-measurable partition, then $\mathcal{E}_\pi \subseteq \mathcal{E}$.

Definition 7.3. Let $\{(S_i, \mathcal{E}_i) \mid i \in I\}$ be a family of measurable spaces and let $p_i : \prod_{i \in I} S_i \longrightarrow S_i$ be the ith projection.

The *product σ-algebra* on the set $\prod_{i \in I} S_i$ is the collection of subsets of $\prod_{i \in I} S_i$ generated by the sets of the form $p_i^{-1}(E_i)$, where $E_i \in \mathcal{E}_i$ for $i \in I$. This σ-algebra will be denoted by $\prod_{i \in I} \mathcal{E}_i$.

The pair $(\prod_{i \in I} S_i, \prod_{i \in I} \mathcal{E}_i)$ is the *product measurable space* of the family $\{(S_i, \mathcal{E}_i) \mid i \in I\}$ of measurable spaces.

Theorem 7.1. *Let I be a countable set and let $\{(S_i, \mathcal{E}_i) \mid i \in I\}$ be a countable family of measurable spaces indexed by I. Then, the product σ-algebra $\prod_{i \in I} \mathcal{E}_i$ is generated by the sets of the form $\prod_{i \in I}\{E_i \in \mathcal{E}_i \mid i \in I\}$.*

Proof.   If $E_i \in \mathcal{E}_i$ we have $p_i^{-1}(E_i) = \prod_{j \in I} C_j$, where

$$C_j = \begin{cases} S_j & \text{if } j \neq i, \\ E_i & \text{if } j = i. \end{cases}$$

Therefore, we have

$$\prod_{i \in I} E_i = \bigcap_{i \in I} p_i^{-1}(E_i)$$

and the theorem follows because the previous equality involves a countable intersection.   □

Theorem 7.2. *Let $\{(S_i, \mathcal{E}_i) \mid i \in I\}$ be a family of measurable spaces indexed by the set I, where each σ-algebra $\mathcal{E}_i$ is generated by a collection $\mathcal{C}_i$, that is, $\mathcal{E}_i = \mathbf{K}_{\sigma\text{-alg}}(\mathcal{C}_i)$. Then, we have*

$$\mathbf{K}_{\sigma\text{-alg}}\left(\{p_i^{-1}(C_i) \mid C_i \in \mathcal{C}_i, i \in I\}\right) = \prod_{i \in I} \mathcal{E}_i.$$

Proof.   Let $\mathcal{C}$ be the collection of subsets of $\prod_{i \in I} S_i$ defined by

$$\mathcal{C} = \{p_i^{-1}(C_i) \mid C_i \in \mathcal{C}_i, i \in I\}.$$

It is clear that $\mathbf{K}_{\sigma\text{-alg}}(\mathcal{C}) \subseteq \prod_{i \in I} \mathcal{E}_i$.

For each $i \in I$ the collection $\{C \mid C \in \mathcal{E}_i \text{ and } p_i^{-1}(C) \in \mathbf{K}_{\sigma\text{-alg}}(\mathcal{C})\}$ is a σ-algebra on S_i that contains $\mathcal{C}_i$ and, therefore $\mathcal{E}_i$. In other words, $p_i^{-1}(C) \in \mathbf{K}_{\sigma\text{-alg}}(\mathcal{C})$ for all $C \in \mathcal{E}_i$, $i \in I$, and, therefore $\prod_{i \in I} \mathcal{E}_i \subseteq \mathbf{K}_{\sigma\text{-alg}}(\mathcal{C})$.   □

Corollary 7.1. *Let $\{(S_i, \mathcal{E}_i) \mid i \in I\}$ be a family of measurable spaces indexed by the set I, where each σ-algebra $\mathcal{E}_i$ is generated by a collection $\mathcal{C}_i$.*

If I is countable and $S_i \in \mathcal{C}_i$ for $i \in I$, then

$$K_{\sigma\text{-alg}}\left(\left\{\prod_{i \in I} C_i \mid C_i \in \mathcal{C}_i, i \in I\right\}\right) = \prod_{i \in I} \mathcal{E}_i.$$

Proof. The argument is based on the observation that

$$\prod_{i \in I}\{C_i \in \mathcal{C}_i, i \in I\} = \bigcap_{i \in I} p_i^{-1}(C_i)$$

and on the fact that I is countable. □

Definition 7.4. Let S, T be two sets and let U be a subset of S and V be a subset of T. The set $U \times V$ is a *rectangle* on $S \times T$.

Example 7.1. If $(S, \mathcal{E}), (T, \mathcal{E}')$ are two measurable spaces. Denote by $p_1 : S \times T \longrightarrow S$, $p_2 : S \times T \longrightarrow T$ the projection function. Then, by Definition 7.3, the product σ-algebra on $S \times T$, denoted here by $\mathcal{E} \times \mathcal{E}'$, is generated by sets of the form $p_1^{-1}(U) = U \times T$ and $p_2^{-1}(V) = S \times V$.

By Theorem 7.1, the same σ-algebra is generated by rectangles of the form $U \times V$, where $U \in \mathcal{E}$ and $V \in \mathcal{E}'$.

Theorem 7.3. *Let $f : S \longrightarrow T$ be a function. If $\mathcal{E}'$ is a σ-algebra on the set T, then $\{f^{-1}(V) \mid V \in \mathcal{E}'\}$ is a σ-algebra on S.*

Proof. Suppose that $U = f^{-1}(V)$ for some $V \in \mathcal{E}'$. Since $S - U = f^{-1}(T - V)$ by Theorem 1.6, the first condition of the definition of σ-algebras is satisfied.

If $\{A_i \mid i \in \mathbb{N}\}$ is a countable collection of subsets of S such that $A_i = f^{-1}(V_i)$ where $V_i \in \mathcal{E}'$, then

$$\bigcup_{i \in \mathbb{N}} A_i = \bigcup_{i \in \mathbb{N}} f^{-1}(V_i) = f^{-1}\left(\bigcup_{i \in \mathbb{N}} V_i\right).$$

Since $\bigcup_{i \in \mathbb{N}} V_i \in \mathcal{E}'$, the second condition of the definition of σ-algebras is satisfied. □

7.3 Borel Sets

Definition 7.5. Let $(S, \mathcal{O})$ be a topological space. The *Borel sets* of $(S, \mathcal{O})$ are the sets in $\mathbf{K}_{\sigma\text{-alg}}(\mathcal{O})$. The σ-algebra of Borel sets $\mathbf{K}_{\sigma\text{-alg}}(\mathcal{O})$ is denoted by $\mathbb{B}(S, \mathcal{O})$, or just by $\mathbb{B}(S)$ if the topology $\mathcal{O}$ is clear from context.

Theorem 7.4. *Let $(S, \mathcal{O})$ be a topological space. We have*
  (i) *if $U_0, U_1, \ldots, U_n, \ldots$ are open subsets of S, then $\bigcap_{n \in \mathbb{N}} U_n$ is a Borel set;*
 (ii) *all closed sets are Borel sets;*
(iii) *if $V_0, V_1, \ldots, V_n, \ldots$ are closed sets, then $\bigcup_{n \in \mathbb{N}} V_n$ is a Borel set.*

Proof. These statements follow immediately from Definition 7.5. $\qquad\square$

Example 7.2. We identify several families of Borel subsets of the topological space $(\mathbb{R}, \mathcal{O})$.

Every open interval (a, b) and every set (a, ∞) or $(-\infty, a)$ is a Borel set for $a, b \in \mathbb{R}$, because they are open sets. The closed intervals of the form $[a, b]$ are Borel sets because they are closed sets in the topological space.

Since $[a, b) = (-\infty, b) - (-\infty, a)$ it follows that the half-open intervals of this form are also Borel sets.

For every $a \in \mathbb{R}$ we have $\{a\} \in \mathbb{B}(\mathbb{R}, \mathcal{O})$ because $\{a\} = [a, b) - (a, b)$ for every $b \in \mathbb{R}$ such that $b > a$. Therefore, every countable subset $\{a_n \mid n \in \mathbb{N}\}$ of $\mathbb{R}$ is a Borel set.

Theorem 7.5. *The Borel σ-algebra $\mathbb{B}(\mathbb{R}, \mathcal{O})$ equals the σ-algebra generated by any of the following families of subsets of $\mathbb{R}$:*
   (i) *all open intervals (a, b), where $a < b$;*
  (ii) *all closed intervals $[a, b]$, where $a \leqslant b$;*
 (iii) *all half-open intervals $[a, b)$, where $a < b$;*
 (iv) *all rays of the form (a, ∞);*
  (v) *all rays of the form $(-\infty, b)$;*
 (vi) *all rays of the form $[a, \infty)$;*
(vii) *all rays of the form $(-\infty, b]$.*

Proof. Since every open set in $\mathbb{R}$ is a countable union of open intervals it follows that the family of Borel sets of $\mathbb{R}$ coincides with the σ-algebra $\mathbb{B}(\mathbb{R}, \mathcal{O})$ generated by the family of open intervals (a, b), where $a < b$.

Let $\mathcal{B}'$ be the Borel σ-algebra generated by the family of half-open intervals $[a, b)$, where $a < b$. Note that a half-open interval $[a, b)$ can be written as

$$[a, b) = \bigcap_{n=1}^{\infty} (a - 1/n, b),$$

which implies that $[a, b) \in \mathcal{B}$ for all $a, b \in \mathbb{R}$ with $a < b$. Therefore, $\mathcal{B}' \subseteq \mathcal{B}$.
Conversely, observe that

$$(a, b) = \bigcup_{n=1}^{\infty} [a + 1/n, b),$$

which implies that $(a, b) \in \mathcal{B}'$ and, therefore, $\mathcal{B} \subseteq \mathcal{B}'$. This allows us to conclude that $\mathcal{B} = \mathcal{B}'$.

We leave the proofs of the remaining parts to the reader. $\qquad\square$

The next theorem shows that the Borel sets of a subspace T of a topological space S are the intersections of the Borel sets of S with T.

Theorem 7.6. *Let T be a non-empty subset of a topological space $(S, \mathcal{O})$ equipped with the topology $\mathcal{O}_T = \mathcal{O} \restriction_T$. We have*

$$\mathbb{B}(T, \mathcal{O}_T) = \{U \cap T \mid U \in \mathbb{B}(S, \mathcal{O})\}.$$

Proof. By Corollary 1.3 we have

$$\begin{aligned}
\mathbb{B}(T, \mathcal{O}_T) &= \mathbf{K}_{\sigma\text{-alg}}(\mathbb{B}(S, \mathcal{O}) \restriction_T) \\
&= \mathbf{K}_{\sigma\text{-alg}}(\mathbb{B}(S, \mathcal{O})) \restriction_T \\
&= \mathbb{B}(S, \mathcal{O}) \restriction_T = \{U \cap T \mid U \in \mathbb{B}(S, \mathcal{O})\}. \qquad\square
\end{aligned}$$

Corollary 7.2. *The collection of Borel subsets of $\mathbb{R}$ is given by $\mathbb{B}(\mathbb{R}) = (\mathbb{B}(\hat{\mathbb{R}})) \restriction_{\mathbb{R}}$, where $\hat{\mathbb{R}}$ is equipped with the topology defined in Example 4.9.*

Proof. This is an immediate consequence of Theorem 7.6. $\qquad\square$

Theorem 7.7. *The collection $\mathbb{B}(\hat{\mathbb{R}}, \mathcal{O})$ of Borel sets on the extended set of real numbers $\hat{\mathbb{R}}$ equipped with the topology introduced in Example 4.9 equals the σ-algebra $\tilde{\mathcal{E}}$ generated by all intervals of the form $(a, \infty]$, where $a \in \mathbb{R}$.*

Proof. Since $\hat{\mathbb{R}} - (a, \infty] = [-\infty, a]$, we have $[-\infty, a] \in \tilde{\mathcal{E}}$ for $a \in \mathbb{R} \cup \{-\infty\}$. Thus, $(a, \infty] \cap [-\infty, b] = (a, b] \in \tilde{\mathcal{E}}$, so $\tilde{\mathcal{E}}$ contains the σ-algebra containing sets of the form $(a, b]$, which is $\mathbb{B}(\mathbb{R}, \mathcal{O})$. Also, $\tilde{\mathcal{E}}$ contains $\{\infty\} = \bigcap_{n \in \mathbb{N}}(n, \infty]$ and $\{-\infty\} = \bigcap_{n \in \mathbb{N}}[-\infty, n]$. This implies that $\tilde{\mathcal{E}}$ contains the smallest σ-algebra containing $\mathbb{B}(\mathbb{R}, \mathcal{O}) \cup \{-\infty, \infty\}$, so $\mathbb{B}(\hat{\mathbb{R}}, \mathcal{O}) \subseteq \tilde{\mathcal{E}}$.

Since $(a, \infty] = \bigcup_{n \in \mathbb{N}}(a, n) \cup \{\infty\} \in \mathbb{B}(\hat{\mathbb{R}}, \mathcal{O})$, the smallest σ-algebra containing sets of the form $(a, \infty]$ must be included in any other σ-algebra containing these sets, so $\tilde{\mathcal{E}} \subseteq \mathbb{B}(\hat{\mathbb{R}}, \mathcal{O})$. We conclude that $\tilde{\mathcal{E}} = \mathbb{B}(\hat{\mathbb{R}}, \mathcal{O})$. $\qquad\square$

A similar argument shows that $\mathbb{B}(\hat{\mathbb{R}}, \mathcal{O})$ is generated by sets of the form $[a, \infty]$, $[-\infty, a]$, or $[-\infty, a)$, where $a \in \mathbb{R}$.

We can restrict a, b in the equivalent descriptions of the σ-algebra $\mathbb{B}(\mathbb{R})$ of Borel sets of $\mathbb{R}$ given in Theorem 7.5 to belong to the set $\mathbb{Q}$ of rational numbers. We show here, as an example, that $\mathbb{B}(\mathbb{R})$ equals the σ-algebra $\mathbf{K}_{\sigma\text{-alg}}(\mathcal{D})$, where $\mathcal{D}$ is the collection of the sets of the form $(-\infty, a]$ with $a \in \mathbb{Q}$.

Since each set $(-\infty, a]$ is closed and, therefore, Borelian, we have $\mathbf{K}_{\sigma\text{-alg}}(\mathcal{D}) \subseteq \mathbb{B}(\mathbb{R})$. To prove the reverse inclusion let (a, b) be an open interval in $\mathbb{R}$ and let $a_n = a + \frac{1}{n}$ and $b_n = b - \frac{1}{n}$ for $n \geqslant 1$. We have

$$(a, b) = \bigcup_{n=1}^{\infty} (a_n, b_n] = \bigcup_{n=1}^{\infty} ((-\infty, b_n] \cap \overline{(-\infty, a_n]}),$$

which show that $(a, b) \in \mathbf{K}_{\sigma\text{-alg}}(\mathcal{D})$. This implies the reverse inclusion $\mathbb{B}(\mathbb{R}) \subseteq \mathbf{K}_{\sigma\text{-alg}}(\mathcal{D})$, so $\mathbb{B}(\mathbb{R}) = \mathbf{K}_{\sigma\text{-alg}}(\mathcal{D})$.

Theorem 7.8. *Let $\mathcal{C}_n$ be the closed sets of the topological space $(\mathbb{R}^n, \mathcal{O})$. We have $\mathbb{B}(\mathbb{R}^n) = \mathbf{K}_{\sigma\text{-alg}}(\mathcal{O}) = \mathbf{K}_{\sigma\text{-alg}}(\mathcal{C}_n) = \mathbf{K}_{\sigma\text{-alg}}(COMP(\mathbb{R}^n, \mathcal{O})).$*

Proof. Since compact subsets of $\mathbb{R}^n$ are closed, we have $COMP(\mathbb{R}^n, \mathcal{O}) \subseteq \mathcal{C}_n$, hence $\mathbf{K}_{\sigma\text{-alg}}(COMP(\mathbb{R}^n, \mathcal{O})) \subseteq \mathbf{K}_{\sigma\text{-alg}}(\mathcal{C}_n)$.

If $C \in \mathcal{C}_n$ and $k \in \mathbb{N}$, the set $C_k = C \cap B[\mathbf{0}_n, k]$ is closed and bounded, so $C_k \in COMP(\mathbb{R}^n, \mathcal{O})$. Since $C = \bigcup_{k \in \mathbb{N}} C_k$, it follows that $C \in \mathbf{K}_{\sigma\text{-alg}}(COMP(\mathbb{R}^n, \mathcal{O}))$, so $\mathcal{C}_n \subseteq \mathbf{K}_{\sigma\text{-alg}}(COMP(\mathbb{R}^n, \mathcal{O}))$, which, in turn yields $\mathbf{K}_{\sigma\text{-alg}}(\mathcal{C}_n) \subseteq \mathbf{K}_{\sigma\text{-alg}}(COMP(\mathbb{R}^n, \mathcal{O}))$. Thus, $\mathbf{K}_{\sigma\text{-alg}}(\mathcal{C}_n) = \mathbf{K}_{\sigma\text{-alg}}(COMP(\mathbb{R}^n, \mathcal{O}))$. Since $\mathbf{K}_{\sigma\text{-alg}}(\mathcal{O}) = \mathbf{K}_{\sigma\text{-alg}}(\mathcal{C}_n)$, the statement of the theorem follows. $\square$

Let $\mathbf{a}, \mathbf{b} \in \mathbb{R}^n$. The *closed interval* of $\mathbb{R}^n$ determined by $\mathbf{a}, \mathbf{b}$ is the set

$$K = [a_1, b_1] \times \cdots \times [a_n, b_n].$$

Similarly, the *open* interval, *open-closed*, and *closed-open* intervals of $\mathbb{R}^n$ are the sets:

$$I = (a_1, b_1) \times \cdots \times (a_n, b_n),$$
$$G = (a_1, b_1] \times \cdots \times (a_n, b_n],$$
$$H = [a_1, b_1) \times \cdots \times [a_n, b_n),$$

respectively. It is immediate to verify that $\mathcal{K}, \mathcal{I}, \mathcal{G}$ and $\mathcal{H}$ are π-systems.

An analogue of Theorem 7.5 for $\mathbb{R}^n$ is given next:

Theorem 7.9. *The σ-algebra of Borel subsets of $(\mathbb{R}^n, \mathcal{O})$ is generated by each of the following collections of sets:*

(i) *the collection $\mathcal{I}$ of all open intervals of $\mathbb{R}^n$;*

(ii) *the collection $\mathcal{H}$ of all closed-open intervals of $\mathbb{R}^n$;*

(iii) *the collection $\mathcal{I}_r$ of all open intervals of $\mathbb{R}^n$ with rational endpoints;*

(iv) *the collection $\mathcal{H}_r$ of all closed-open intervals of $\mathbb{R}^n$ with rational endpoints.*

Proof. Since $\mathcal{I}_r \subseteq \mathcal{I} \subseteq \mathcal{O}$, we have $\mathbf{K}_{\sigma\text{-alg}}(\mathcal{I}_r) \subseteq \mathbf{K}_{\sigma\text{-alg}}(\mathcal{I}) \subseteq \mathbf{K}_{\sigma\text{-alg}}(\mathcal{O}) = \mathbb{B}(\mathbb{R}^n)$.

Let U be an open set in $\mathbb{R}^n$. We claim that

$$U = \bigcup\{I \in \mathcal{I}_r \mid I \subseteq U\}.$$

It is clear that $\bigcup\{I \in \mathcal{I}_r \mid I \subseteq U\} \subseteq U$. To prove the converse inclusion let $\mathbf{x} \in U$. There exists a cube with rational endpoints that contains $\mathbf{x}$ and is included in U. Since the set of all such cubes is countable, we have $U \subseteq \mathbf{K}_{\sigma\text{-alg}}(\mathcal{I}_r)$, so $\mathbf{K}_{\sigma\text{-alg}}(\mathcal{O}) \subseteq \mathbf{K}_{\sigma\text{-alg}}(\mathcal{I}_r)$. Thus, $\mathbf{K}_{\sigma\text{-alg}}(\mathcal{I}_r) = \mathbf{K}_{\sigma\text{-alg}}(\mathcal{I}) = \mathbf{K}_{\sigma\text{-alg}}(\mathcal{O}) = \mathbb{B}(\mathbb{R}^n)$.

If $H \in \mathcal{H}$ we can write

$$H = [a_1, b_1) \times \cdots \times [a_n, b_n) = \bigcap_{k \geqslant 1} \left(a_1 - \frac{1}{k}, b_1\right) \times \cdots \times \left(a_n - \frac{1}{k}, b_n\right),$$

which implies $\mathcal{H} \subseteq \mathbf{K}_{\sigma\text{-alg}}(\mathcal{I})$; in particular, this also implies $\mathcal{H}_r \subseteq \mathbf{K}_{\sigma\text{-alg}}(\mathcal{I}_r)$. These inclusions imply

$$\mathbf{K}_{\sigma\text{-alg}}(\mathcal{H}) \subseteq \mathbf{K}_{\sigma\text{-alg}}(\mathcal{I}) \text{ and } \mathbf{K}_{\sigma\text{-alg}}(\mathcal{H}_r) \subseteq \mathbf{K}_{\sigma\text{-alg}}(\mathcal{I}_r).$$

Every $I \in \mathcal{I}$ can be written as:

$$I = (a_1, b_1) \times \cdots \times (a_n, b_n) = \bigcup_{k \geqslant 1} \left[a_1 + \frac{1}{k}, d_1\right) \times \cdots \times \left[a_n + \frac{1}{k}, d_n\right),$$

which yields $\mathcal{I} \subseteq \mathbf{K}_{\sigma\text{-alg}}(\mathcal{H})$, and also, $\mathcal{I}_r \subseteq \mathbf{K}_{\sigma\text{-alg}}(\mathcal{H}_r)$. Therefore,

$$\mathbf{K}_{\sigma\text{-alg}}(\mathcal{I}) \subseteq \mathbf{K}_{\sigma\text{-alg}}(\mathcal{H}) \text{ and } \mathbf{K}_{\sigma\text{-alg}}(\mathcal{I}_r) \subseteq \mathbf{K}_{\sigma\text{-alg}}(\mathcal{H}_r).$$

This allows us to conclude that

$$\mathbf{K}_{\sigma\text{-alg}}(\mathcal{I}) = \mathbf{K}_{\sigma\text{-alg}}(\mathcal{H}) = \mathbf{K}_{\sigma\text{-alg}}(\mathcal{I}_r) = \mathbf{K}_{\sigma\text{-alg}}(\mathcal{H}_r) = \mathbb{B}(\mathbb{R}^n). \qquad \square$$

7.4   Measurable Functions

The notion of measurable functions is similar to the notion of continuous function is topology and is used in the definition of the Lebesgue integral that we present in the next chapter. We begin with a study of simple functions as a first step in the construction of the Legesgue integral.

Definition 7.6. A *simple function on a set S* is a function $f : S \longrightarrow \mathbb{R}$ that has a finite range.

The set of simple functions on the set S is denoted by $\mathsf{SF}(S)$; also, the set of non-negative simple functions on the same set is denoted by $\mathsf{SF}_+(S)$.

Simple functions are linear combinations of characteristic functions.

Theorem 7.10. *Let $f \in \mathsf{SF}(S)$ such that $\mathsf{Ran}(f) = \{y_1, \dots, y_n\} \subseteq \mathbb{R}$. Then, $f = \sum_{i=1}^{n} y_i 1_{f^{-1}(y_i)}$.*

Proof.   Let $x \in S$. If $f(x) = y_j$, then

$$1_{f^{-1}(y_\ell)}(x) = \begin{cases} 1 & \text{if } \ell = j, \\ 0 & \text{otherwise.} \end{cases}$$

Thus, $\left(\sum_{i=1}^{n} y_i 1_{f^{-1}(y_i)}\right)(x) = y_j$, which shows that $f(x) = \left(\sum_{i=1}^{n} y_i 1_{f^{-1}(y_i)}\right)(x)$. $\square$

Theorem 7.11. *Let $f_1, \dots, f_k$ be k simple functions defined on a set S. If $g : \mathbb{R}^k \longrightarrow \mathbb{R}$ is an arbitrary function, then $g(f_1, \dots, f_k)$ is a simple function on S and we have:*

$$g(f_1, \dots, f_k)(x) = \sum_{p_1=1}^{m_1} \cdots \sum_{p_k=1}^{m_k} g(y_{1p_1}, \dots, y_{kp_k}) 1_{f_1^{-1}(y_{1p_1}) \cap \cdots \cap f_k^{-1}(y_{kp_k})}(x)$$

for every $x \in S$, where $\mathsf{Ran}(f_i) = \{y_{i1}, \dots, y_{im_i}\}$ for $1 \leqslant i \leqslant k$.

Proof.   The function $g(f_1, \dots, f_k)$ is a simple function because it has a finite range. Moreover, if $\mathsf{Ran}(f_i) = \{y_{i1}, \dots, y_{im_i}\}$, then the values of $g(f_1, \dots, f_k)$ have the form $g(y_{1p_1}, \dots, y_{kp_k})$ and $g(f_1, \dots, f_k)$ can be written as:

$$g(f_1, \dots, f_k)(x)$$
$$= \sum_{p_1=1}^{m_1} \cdots \sum_{p_k=1}^{m_k} g(y_{1p_1}, \dots, y_{kp_k}) 1_{f_1^{-1}(y_{1p_1})}(x) \cdots 1_{f_k^{-1}(y_{kp_k})}(x)$$
$$= \sum_{p_1=1}^{m_1} \cdots \sum p_k = 1^{m_k} g(y_{1p_1}, \dots, y_{kp_k}) 1_{f_1^{-1}(y_{1p_1}) \cap \cdots \cap f_k^{-1}(y_{kp_k})}(x)$$

for $x \in S$. $\square$

Corollary 7.3. *If $f_i \in \mathsf{SF}(S)$ for $1 \leqslant i \leqslant k$ then*

$$\max\{f_1(x), \ldots, f_k(x)\},$$
$$\min\{f_1(x), \ldots, f_k(x)\},$$
$$f_1(x) + \cdots + f_k(x),$$
$$f_1(x) \cdot \ldots \cdot f_k(x)$$

belong to $\mathsf{SF}(S)$.

Proof. The statement follows immediately from Theorem 7.11. ∎

Definition 7.7. Let $f : S \longrightarrow \mathbb{R}$ be a simple function such that $\mathsf{Ran}(f) = \{y_1, \ldots, y_n\}$. A finite partition of S is *related* to f if for every block B of π there exists $y \in \mathsf{Ran}(f)$ such that $f(x) = y$ for every $x \in B$.

It is easy to see that the largest partition in $(PART(S), \leqslant)$ related to a simple f whose range is $\{y_1, \ldots, y_n\}$ is $\{f^{-1}(y_1), \ldots, f^{-1}(y_n)\}$.

Definition 7.8. Let $(S, \mathcal{D})$ and $(T, \mathcal{E})$ be two measurable spaces. A function $f : S \longrightarrow T$ is said to be *measurable* if $f^{-1}(V) \in \mathcal{D}$ for every $V \in \mathcal{E}$.

Example 7.3. Every constant function $f : S \longrightarrow T$ between two measurable spaces $(S, \mathcal{D})$ and $(T, \mathcal{E})$ is measurable because $f^{-1}(V)$ is either $\emptyset$ or S for every $V \in \mathcal{E}$.

Lemma 7.1. *Let $(S, \mathcal{E})$ be a measurable space and let $f : S \longrightarrow S'$ be a function. The collection $\mathcal{E}_1 = \{W \in \mathcal{P}(S') \mid f^{-1}(W) \in \mathcal{E}\}$ is a σ-algebra on S'.*

Proof. If $f^{-1}(W) \in \mathcal{E}$, then $f^{-1}(S' - W) = f^{-1}(S') - f^{-1}(W) = S - f^{-1}(W) \in \mathcal{E}$, hence $S' - W \in \mathcal{E}_1$.

Let $\{W_n \mid n \in \mathbb{N}\}$ be a countable collection of subsets of S' such that $f^{-1}(W_n) \in \mathcal{E}$ for $n \in \mathbb{N}$. Since $f^{-1}\left(\bigcup_{n \in \mathbb{N}} W_n\right) = \bigcup_{n \in \mathbb{N}} f^{-1}(W_n) \in \mathcal{E}$, it follows that $\bigcup_{n \in \mathbb{N}} W_n \in \mathcal{E}_1$, so $\mathcal{E}_1$ is indeed a σ-algebra on S'. ∎

Theorem 7.12. *Let $(S, \mathcal{E})$ and $(S', \mathcal{E}')$ be two measurable spaces and let $\mathcal{C}'$ a collection of generators for $\mathcal{E}'$. A function $f : S \longrightarrow S'$ is measurable if and only if $f^{-1}(C') \in \mathcal{E}$ for every $C' \in \mathcal{C}'$.*

Proof. The necessity of the condition is immediate. Suppose now that $f^{-1}(C') \in \mathcal{E}$ for every $C' \in \mathcal{C}'$, where $\mathbf{K}_{\sigma\text{-alg}}(\mathcal{C}') = \mathcal{E}'$.

We have $\mathcal{C}' \subseteq \mathcal{E}_1$, where $\mathcal{E}_1 = \{W \in \mathcal{P}(S') \mid f^{-1}(W) \in \mathcal{E}\}$ is a σ-algebra by Lemma 7.1. Therefore, $\mathcal{E}' = \mathbf{K}_{\sigma\text{-alg}}(\mathcal{C}') \subseteq \mathbf{K}_{\sigma\text{-alg}}(\mathcal{E}_1) = \mathcal{E}_1$, and this means that the pre-images of each set in $\mathcal{E}'$ under f belong to $\mathcal{E}$. Therefore, f is measurable. ∎

Given a measurable space $(S, \mathcal{E})$ and a function $f : S \longrightarrow S'$, $\mathcal{E}_1$ is the least σ-algebra that can be defined on S' such that the function $f : S \longrightarrow S'$ is measurable.

Theorem 7.13. *Let $(S, \mathcal{O})$, $(S', \mathcal{O}')$ be two topological spaces and let $f : S \longrightarrow S'$ be a continuous function. Then, f is measurable relative to the measurable spaces $(S, \mathbb{B}(S))$ and $(S', \mathbb{B}(S'))$, where $\mathbb{B}(S)$ and $\mathbb{B}(S')$ are the collection of Borel sets in $(S, \mathcal{O})$ and $(S', \mathcal{O}')$, respectively.*

Proof.   By Lemma 7.1 the collection of sets $\mathcal{E}_1 = \{W \in \mathcal{P}(S') \mid f^{-1}(W) \in \mathbb{B}(S)\}$ is a σ-algebra on S'. Since f is continuous, $\mathcal{E}_1$ contains every open set in $\mathcal{O}'$, so the σ-algebra of Borel sets $\mathbb{B}(T)$ that is generated by $\mathcal{O}'$ is contained in $\mathcal{E}_1$. Thus, for every Borel set U in S', $f^{-1}(U) \in \mathbb{B}(S)$, which implies that f is indeed measurable. $\square$

We refer to a measurable function between $(S, \mathbb{B}(S))$ and $(T, \mathbb{B}(T))$ as a *Borel measurable function*. Thus, Theorem 7.13 establishes that a continuous function between two topological spaces is a Borel measurable function.

Example 7.4. Not every measurable function is continuous. Indeed, let $f : \mathbb{R} \longrightarrow \mathbb{R}$ be the function defined as

$$f(x) = \begin{cases} 1 & \text{if } 0 \leqslant x \leqslant 1, \\ 0 & \text{otherwise.} \end{cases}$$

It is clear that f is a measurable function between $(\mathbb{R}, \mathbb{B}(\mathbb{R}))$ and itself; however f is not continuous.

We focus now on functions defined on a measurable space and ranging over $\hat{\mathbb{R}}$, the extended set of reals (equipped with the σ-algebra of Borel subsets of $\hat{\mathbb{R}}$). We will refer to measurable functions between the measurable spaces $(S, \mathcal{E})$ and $(\hat{\mathbb{R}}, \mathbb{B}(\hat{\mathbb{R}}))$ as *measurable functions*.

Theorem 7.14. *Let $(S, \mathcal{E})$ be a measurable space and let $f, g : S \longrightarrow \hat{\mathbb{R}}$ be two measurable functions. If $U \in \mathcal{E}$, then the sets $\{x \in U \mid f(x) < g(y)\}$, $\{x \in U \mid f(x) \leqslant g(y)\}$, and $\{x \in U \mid f(x) = g(y)\}$ belong to $\mathcal{E}$.*

Proof.   We have $f(x) < g(x)$ if and only if there exists a rational number r such that $f(x) < r < g(x)$. This allows us to write:

$$\{x \in U \mid f(x) < g(x)\}$$
$$= \bigcup_{r \in \mathbb{Q}} \left(\{x \in U \mid f(x) < r\} \cap \{x \in U \mid r < g(x)\} \right).$$

Since f and g are measurable, we have $\{x \in U \mid f(x) < r\} \in \mathcal{E}$ and $\{x \in U \mid r < g(x)\} \in \mathcal{E}$, so $\{x \in U \mid f(x) < r\} \cap \{x \in U \mid r < g(x)\} \in \mathcal{E}$, which implies that $\{x \in U \mid f(x) < g(x)\} \in \mathcal{E}$ as a countable union of sets in $\mathcal{E}$. Obviously, we also have $\{x \in U \mid g(x) < f(x)\}$ belongs to $\mathcal{E}$.

Since
$$\{x \in U \mid f(x) \leqslant g(x)\} = U - \{x \in U \mid g(x) < f(x)\},$$
it follows that $\{x \in U \mid f(x) \leqslant g(x)\} \in \mathcal{E}$.

The equality
$$\{x \in U \mid f(x) = g(x)\} = \{x \in U \mid f(x) \leqslant g(x)\} - \{x \in U \mid f(x) < g(x)\}$$
implies that $\{x \in U \mid f(x) = g(x)\} \in \mathcal{E}$. $\qquad\square$

Theorem 7.15. *Let $(S, \mathcal{E})$ be a measurable space and let $\boldsymbol{f} = (f_n)$ be a sequence of measurable functions between $(S, \mathcal{E})$ and $(\hat{\mathbb{R}}, \mathbb{B}(\hat{\mathbb{R}}))$. The functions $h_n = \sup\{f_1, \ldots, f_n\}$ and $g_n = \inf\{f_1, \ldots, f_n\}$ are measurable.*

Also, the functions p and q defined by $p(x) = \sup\{f_i(x) \mid i \geqslant 1\}$ and $q(x) = \inf\{f_i(x) \mid i \geqslant 1\}$ are measurable, as well as the functions l, u given by $u(x) = \limsup f_n(x)$ and $l(x) = \liminf f_n(x)$ for $x \in S$.

Proof. Since
$$\{x \in S \mid h_n(x) > t\} = \bigcup_{i=1}^{n} \{x \in S \mid f_i(x) > t\},$$
$$\{x \in S \mid g_n(x) < t\} = \bigcup_{i=1}^{n} \{x \in S \mid f_i(x) < t\},$$
the measurability of f_i for $1 \leqslant i \leqslant n$ implies that h_n and g_n are measurable.

For the functions p and q we have
$$\{x \in S \mid p(x) > t\} = \bigcup_{i=1}^{\infty} \{x \in S \mid f_i(x) > t\},$$
$$\{x \in S \mid q(x) < t\} = \bigcup_{i=1}^{\infty} \{x \in S \mid f_i(x) < t\},$$
which prove that p and q are measurable.

Finally, note that $u(x) = \inf_n \sup_{k \geqslant n} f_k(x)$ and $l(x) = \sup_n \inf_{k \geqslant n} f_k(x)$ for $x \in S$. The measurability of u and k follows from previous parts of this theorem. $\qquad\square$

Corollary 7.4. *Let $(S, \mathcal{E})$ be a measurable space and let $\boldsymbol{f} = (f_n)$ be a sequence of measurable functions between $(S, \mathcal{E})$ and $(\mathbb{R}, \mathbb{B}(\mathbb{R}))$. If the sequence $\boldsymbol{f}$ converges pointwise to a function f, then f is measurable.*

Proof. If $\lim_{n \to \infty} f_n(x) = f(x)$, then $f(x) = \limsup f_n(x) = \liminf f_n(x)$ for $x \in S$ and the measurability of f follows immediately from Theorem 7.14. $\qquad \square$

Lemma 7.2. *Let $(S, \mathcal{E})$ be a measurable space. The following statements that concern a function $f : S \longrightarrow \hat{\mathbb{R}}$ are equivalent:*

  (i) *for each $t \in \mathbb{R}$ the set $f^{-1}([-\infty, t]) \in \mathcal{E}$;*
  (ii) *for each $t \in \mathbb{R}$ the set $f^{-1}([-\infty, t)) \in \mathcal{E}$;*
  (iii) *for each $t \in \mathbb{R}$ the set $f^{-1}([t, \infty]) \in \mathcal{E}$;*
  (iv) *for each $t \in \mathbb{R}$ the set $f^{-1}((t, \infty]) \in \mathcal{E}$.*

Proof.   Since

$$f^{-1}([-\infty, t)) = \bigcup_{n \in \mathbb{N}} f^{-1}((-\infty, t - 1/n]),$$

it follows that (i) implies (ii).

Note that

$$f^{-1}([t, \infty]) = S - f^{-1}([-\infty, t)),$$

which shows that (ii) implies (iii).

The fact that (iii) implies (iv) follows from the fact that

$$f^{-1}((t, \infty]) = \bigcap_{n \in \mathbb{N}} f^{-1}([t + 1/n, \infty]).$$

Finally, (iv) implies (i) because

$$f^{-1}([-\infty, t]) = S - f^{-1}((t, \infty]). \qquad \square$$

Theorem 7.16. *Let $(S, \mathcal{E})$ be a measurable space. The following statements that concern a function $f : S \longrightarrow \hat{\mathbb{R}}$ are equivalent:*

  (i) *any of the equivalent conditions of Lemma 7.2 hold for f;*
  (ii) *for each Borel subset B of $\hat{\mathbb{R}}$, $f^{-1}(B) \in \mathcal{E}$;*
  (iii) *for each open subset U of $\hat{\mathbb{R}}$, $f^{-1}(U) \in \mathcal{E}$;*
  (iv) *for each closed subset V of $\hat{\mathbb{R}}$, $f^{-1}(V) \in \mathcal{E}$.*

Proof.   (i) implies (ii): Suppose that f satisfies any of the equivalent conditions of Lemma 7.2. Since the Borel algebra $\mathbb{B}(\hat{\mathbb{R}})$ is generated by the sets of the form $(t, \infty]$ it follows that $f^{-1}(B) \in \mathcal{E}$ for each Borel subset B of $\hat{\mathbb{R}}$.

(ii) implies (iii) and (iv): Any open subset of $\hat{\mathbb{R}}$ and any closed subset of $\hat{\mathbb{R}}$ are members of $\mathbb{B}(\hat{\mathbb{R}})$, so the implications follow immediately.

(iii) implies (i) because the set $[-\infty, t)$ is an open set in $\hat{\mathbb{R}}$.

(iv) implies (i) because the set $[-\infty, t]$ is a closed set in $\hat{\mathbb{R}}$. $\qquad \square$

Corollary 7.5. *Let $(S, \mathcal{E})$ be a measurable space. A function $f : S \longrightarrow \hat{\mathbb{R}}$ is measurable (considered as a function between $(S, \mathcal{E})$ and $(\hat{\mathbb{R}}, \mathbb{B}(\hat{\mathbb{R}})$ if and only if it satisfies any of the equivalent conditions of Theorem 7.16.*

Proof. This statement is follows immediately from Theorem 7.16. □

Corollary 7.6. *Let $(S, \mathcal{E})$ be a measurable space. A simple function $f : S \longrightarrow \hat{\mathbb{R}}$ is measurable if for every $y \in \mathsf{Ran}(f)$, $f^{-1}(y) \in \mathcal{E}$. In particular, for $T \in \mathcal{E}$, the characteristic function 1_T is a measurable simple function because $1_T^{-1}(1) = T$ and $1_T^{-1}(0) = S - T$. Furthermore, f is a linear combination of characteristic functions of sets in $\mathcal{E}$.*

Proof. These statements follow from Theorems 7.10 and 7.16. □

It is easy to verify that if f is a measurable function between $(S, \mathcal{E})$ and $(T, \mathcal{E}')$ and g is a measurable function between $(T, \mathcal{E}')$ and $(U, \mathcal{E}'')$, then gf is a measurable function between $(S, \mathcal{E})$ and $(U, \mathcal{E}'')$.

Theorem 7.17. *Let J be an interval of $\mathbb{R}$ and let $f : J \longrightarrow \mathbb{R}$ be a function that has a countable set of discontinuities of the first kind on J. Then, f is a measurable function between the measurable spaces $(J, \mathbb{B}(J))$ and $(\mathbb{R}, \mathbb{B}(\mathbb{R}))$.*

Proof. It suffices to show that for every $c \in \mathbb{R}$, the set $f^{-1}(-\infty, c)$ is a Borel set. Let U be the open set $U = \mathbf{I}(f^{-1}(-\infty, c))$; since U is open, it is $\mathbb{B}(J)$-measurable. Define V as

$$V = f^{-1}(-\infty, c) - U = f^{-1}(-\infty, c) - \mathbf{I}(f^{-1}(-\infty, c)).$$

We shall prove that every $x \in V$ is a discontinuity point of the first kind for f. Since $x \in V$, it follows that $x \notin U = \mathbf{I}(f^{-1}(-\infty, c))$. Note that $x \in V$ implies $f(x) < c$.

By Theorem 5.4, for every $r > 0$, there exists $y \in B(x, r)$ such that $y \notin f^{-1}(-\infty, c)$ (which amounts to $f(y) \geqslant c$). Since $f(x) < c$, x is a discontinuity point of the first kind for f. Therefore, V is at most countable because f has a countable set of discontinuities of the first kind. Thus, V is a Borel set. Since $f^{-1}(-\infty, c) = U \cup V$ it follows that $f^{-1}(-\infty, c)$ is a Borel set. □

Corollary 7.7. *Let J be an interval of $\mathbb{R}$ and let $f : J \longrightarrow \mathbb{R}$ be a monotonic function. Then, f is a measurable function between the measurable spaces $(J, \mathbb{B}(J))$ and $(\mathbb{R}, \mathbb{B}(\mathbb{R}))$.*

Proof. This follows from Theorems 4.61 and 7.17. □

The notion of measurability can be extended to complex-valued functions.

Definition 7.9. Let $(S, \mathcal{E})$ be a measurable space and let $f : S \longrightarrow \mathbb{C}$ be a complex-valued function, where $f(x) = u(x) + iv(x)$ for $x \in S$, where u and v are real-valued functions. The function f is *measurable* if and only if both u and v are measurable.

7.5 Measures and Measure Spaces

Definition 7.10. Let $\mathcal{E}$ be a σ-algebra of subsets of a set S. A *measure* is a function $m : \mathcal{E} \longrightarrow \hat{\mathbb{R}}_{\geqslant 0}$ that satisfies the following conditions:

(1) $m(\emptyset) = 0$;
(2) for every countable collection $\{U_0, U_1, \ldots\}$ of sets in $\mathcal{E}$ that are pairwise disjoint such that $\bigcup_{n \in \mathbb{N}} U_n \in \mathcal{E}$ we have:

$$
m\left(\bigcup_{n \in \mathbb{N}} U_n \right) = \sum_{n \in \mathbb{N}} m(U_n)
$$

(the *countable additivity property*).

If the σ-algebra $\mathcal{E}$ is replaced by an algebra and the countable additive property by simple additivity, then we obtain the notion of *premeasure*.

Note that a premeasure on an algebra $\mathcal{E}$ is supposed to satisfy the same conditions as a measure; however, in the case of a premeasure, the countable union $\bigcup_{n \in \mathbb{N}}$ may not belong to $\mathcal{E}$.

A *measure space* is a triple $(S, \mathcal{E}, m)$, where $(S, \mathcal{E})$ is a measurable space and m is a measure.

Example 7.5. If $(S, \mathcal{E})$ is a measurable space the mapping $m : \mathcal{E} \longrightarrow \mathbb{R}$ given by $m(U) = 0$ for every $U \in \mathcal{E}$ is a measure.

Example 7.6. Let S be a set and let s be a fixed element of S. Define the mapping $\delta_s : \mathcal{P}(S) \longrightarrow \hat{\mathbb{R}}_{\geqslant 0}$ by

$$
\delta_s(U) = \begin{cases} 1 & \text{if } s \in U \\ 0 & \text{otherwise} \end{cases} = 1_U(s),
$$

for $U \in \mathcal{P}(S)$.

It is easy to verify that δ_s is a measure defined on $\mathcal{P}(S)$. Indeed, we have $\delta_s(\emptyset) = 0$. If $U_0, U_1, \ldots$ is a countable collection of pairwise disjoint sets, then s may belong to at most one of these sets. If there is a set U_i such that $s \in U_i$, $s \in \bigcup_{n \in \mathbb{N}} U_i$, so $\delta_s \left(\bigcup_{n \in \mathbb{N}} U_n \right) = \sum_{n \in \mathbb{N}} \delta_s(U_n) = 1$. If no such set U_i exists, then $\delta_s \left(\bigcup_{n \in \mathbb{N}} U_n \right) = \sum_{n \in \mathbb{N}} \delta_s(U_n) = 0$. In either case, the countable additivity property is satisfied. The measure δ_s is known as the *Dirac measure concentrated as s*.

Example 7.7. Let S be a finite set and let $\mathcal{E} = \mathcal{P}(S)$. The mapping $m : \mathcal{P}(S) \longrightarrow \mathbb{R}$ given by $m(U) = |U|$ is a measure on $\mathcal{P}(S)$, as can be verified immediately. Note that $m(T) = \sum \{\delta_u(T) \mid u \in S\}$.

This measure can be extended to arbitrary sets S by defining

$$m(T) = \begin{cases} |T| & \text{if } T \text{ is finite,} \\ \infty & \text{otherwise,} \end{cases}$$

for $T \in \mathcal{P}(S)$. We refer to m as the *counting measure* on $\mathcal{P}(S)$.

Theorem 7.18. *Let $(S, \mathcal{E}, m)$ be a measure space, $(T, \mathcal{E}')$ be a measurable space and let $f : S \longrightarrow T$ be a measurable function. The mapping $m' : \mathcal{E}' \longrightarrow \mathbb{R}$ defined by $m'(V) = m(f^{-1}(V))$ for $V \in \mathcal{E}'$ is a measure on $(T, \mathcal{E}')$.*

Proof. If $V = \emptyset$, $f^{-1}(\emptyset) = \emptyset$, so $m'(\emptyset) = 0$. If $\{V_n \mid n \in \mathbb{N}\}$ is a family of pairwise disjoint sets in $\mathcal{E}'$ we have

$$m' \left(\bigcup_{n \in \mathbb{N}} U_n \right) = m \left(f^{-1} \left(\bigcup_{n \in \mathbb{N}} U_n \right) \right)$$

$$= m \left(\bigcup_{n \in \mathbb{N}} f^{-1} U_n \right) = \sum_{n \in \mathbb{N}} m(f^{-1}(U_n)) = \sum_{n \in \mathbb{N}} m'(U_n),$$

which shows that m' is indeed a measure on $\mathcal{E}'$. $\square$

The measure m' introduced in Theorem 7.18 is the *image measure* of m under f.

For a finite collection of n pairwise disjoint sets $\{U_0, U_1, \ldots, U_{n-1}\}$ in a measure space $(S, \mathcal{E}, m)$ we have the *finite additivity property*:

$$m(U_0 \cup U_1 \cup \cdots \cup U_{n-1}) = \sum_{i=0}^{n-1} m(U). \tag{7.1}$$

Observe that in a measure space $(S, \mathcal{E}, m)$, if $U, V \in \mathcal{E}$ and $U \subseteq V$, then $V = U \cup (V - U)$, so by the finite additivity property,

$m(V) = m(U) + m(V - U) \geqslant m(U)$. This shows that $U \subseteq V$ implies $m(U) \leqslant m(V)$ (the *monotonicity* of measures).

Definition 7.11. Let $(S, \mathcal{E}, m)$ be a measure space. If $m(S)$ is finite (which implies that $m(U)$ is finite for all $U \in \mathcal{E}$) we say that m is a *finite measure*.

If S equals a countable union of sets U_n in $\mathcal{E}$, that is, $S = \bigcup_{n \in \mathbb{N}} U_n$ such that each $m(U_n)$ is finite, then m is a *σ-finite measure*.

The measure m is *semi-finite* if for each $U \in \mathcal{E}$ with $m(U) = \infty$, there exists $V \in \mathcal{E}$ such that $V \subseteq U$ and $0 < m(V) < \infty$.

If $U \in \mathcal{E}$ and $S = \bigcup_{n \in \mathbb{N}} U_n$ such that each $m(U_n)$ is finite, then $U = \bigcup_{n \in \mathbb{N}} (U \cap U_n)$, where $U \cap U_n \in \mathcal{E}$ and $m(U \cap U_n)$ is finite.

Every finite measure is clearly σ-finite. Also, every σ-finite measure is semi-finite. Indeed, let m be a σ-finite measure and let $W \in \mathcal{E}$ be a subset of S such that $m(W) = \infty$. Since m is σ-finite, $W = \bigcup_{n \in \mathbb{N}} W_n$, where $W_n \in \mathcal{E}$ and $m(W_n)$ is finite for $n \in \mathbb{N}$. There exists at least one set W_n such that $m(W_n) > 0$ because, otherwise, we would have $m(W) = 0$. This shows that m is semi-finite.

Example 7.8. Let $(S, \mathcal{P}(S))$ be a measure space and let $f : S \longrightarrow [0, \infty]$. Define $m_f : \mathcal{P}(S) \longrightarrow [0, \infty]$ as

$$m_f(U) = \sup_{T \subseteq U, T \text{ finite}} \sum \{f(x) \mid x \in T\}.$$

Then m_f is a semi-finite measure if and only if $f(x) < \infty$ for every $x \in S$. Furthermore, m_f is σ-finite if and only if m_f is semi-finite and the set $\{x \mid f(x) > 0\}$ is countable. Observe that if $f(x) = 1$, then m_f is the counting measure introduced in Example 7.7.

Let $(S, \mathcal{E}, m)$ be a measure space and let $X, Y \in \mathcal{E}$. Since $X \cup Y = X \cup (Y - X)$, $Y = (Y - X) \cup (Y \cap X)$ and the pairs of sets $X, (Y - X)$ and $(Y - X), (Y \cap X)$ are disjoint, we can write

$$m(X \cup Y) = m(X) + m(Y - X)$$
$$= m(X) + m(Y) - m(X \cap Y). \tag{7.2}$$

The resulting equality:

$$m(X \cup Y) + m(X \cap Y) = m(X) + m(Y) \tag{7.3}$$

for $X, Y \in \mathcal{E}$ is known as the *modularity property* of measures.

If the sets U_i of a countable collection $\{U_0, U_1, \ldots\}$ of sets in $\mathcal{E}$ are not disjoint, then instead of the additivity property we have the *subadditive inequality*:

$$m\left(\bigcup_{n \in \mathbb{N}} U_n\right) \leqslant \sum_{n \in \mathbb{N}} m(U_n). \qquad (7.4)$$

By Theorem 1.33 there exists a family of sets $\{V_i \in \mathcal{E} \mid i \in \mathbb{N}\} \subseteq \mathcal{E}$ that are pairwise disjoint such that $V_i \subseteq U_i$ for $i \in \mathbb{N}$ and $\bigcup\{V_i \mid i \in \mathbb{N}\} = \bigcup\{U_i \mid i \in \mathbb{N}\}$. This implies $m(V_i) \leqslant m(U_i)$ and

$$\begin{aligned}
m\left(\bigcup_{n \in \mathbb{N}} U_n\right) &= m\left(\bigcup_{n \in \mathbb{N}} V_n\right) \\
&= \sum_{n \in \mathbb{N}} m(V_n) \leqslant \sum_{n \in \mathbb{N}} m(U_n),
\end{aligned}$$

which gives the desired subadditivity property of measures.

Definition 7.12. Let $(S, \mathcal{E}, m)$ be a measure space. A *null set* is a subset U of S such that $U \in \mathcal{E}$ and $m(U) = 0$.

A countable union of null sets in a measure space $(S, \mathcal{E}, m)$ is a null set due to the subadditivity of measures. Note that if U is a null set in $(S, \mathcal{E}, m)$ and $V \subseteq U$, it does not follow that $V \in \mathcal{E}$. However, if $V \in \mathcal{E}$, then, of course V is a null set.

Definition 7.13. A *property of the elements of a measure space* $(S, \mathcal{E}, m)$ is a measurable subset R of S. If $m(S - R) = 0$ we say that the property R holds *m-almost everywhere*, or that R *holds m-a.e.*

If m is clear from context we refer to R as an *a.e. property*.

Definition 7.14. The measure space $(S, \mathcal{E}, m)$ is *complete* (and m is a *complete measure*) if

$$W \in \mathcal{E}, m(W) = 0, U \subseteq W \text{ imply } U \in \mathcal{E}.$$

Definition 7.15. Let $(S, \mathcal{E}, m)$ be a measure space. The *completion* of $(S, \mathcal{E}, m)$ is the collection $\mathcal{E}_m$ of subsets of S that consists of those subsets T of S such that there exist $U, V \in \mathcal{E}$ such that $U \subseteq T \subseteq V$, and $m(V - U) = 0$.

If $U, V \in \mathcal{E}$ are two sets in $\mathcal{E}$ that satisfy the conditions of Definition 7.15, we have $m(U) = m(V)$. Moreover, if $Z \subseteq T$ and $Z \in \mathcal{E}$, then $m(Z) \leqslant m(U) = m(V)$. Therefore,

$$\sup\{m(Z) \mid Z \in \mathcal{E} \text{ and } Z \subseteq T\} \leqslant m(V).$$

Actually, we have the equality

$$\sup\{m(Z) \mid Z \in \mathcal{E} \text{ and } Z \subseteq T\} = m(V)$$

because $m(U)$ is one of the numbers that occurs in the set of the left side of the previous inequality. We infer that the value $m(V) = m(U)$ depends only on the set T and the measure m.

These considerations allow us to define a function $\tilde{m} : \mathcal{E}_m \longrightarrow \hat{\mathbb{R}}_{\geqslant 0}$ where $\tilde{m}(T)$ is the common value of $m(U)$ and $m(V)$, when these sets are introduced as above. The function $\tilde{m}$ is the *completion* of m.

Theorem 7.19. *Let $(S, \mathcal{E}, m)$ be a measure space. The collection $\mathcal{E}_m$ is a σ-algebra on S that includes $\mathcal{E}$, $\tilde{m}$ is a measure on $\mathcal{E}_m$ that is complete, and $\tilde{m} \restriction_{\mathcal{E}} = m$.*

Proof. Let $T \in \mathcal{E}$. By taking $U = T$ and $V = T$, it follows that $\mathcal{E} \subseteq \mathcal{E}_m$. Since $U \subseteq T \subseteq V$ for some $U, V \in \mathcal{E}$, we also have $\overline{V} \subseteq \overline{T} \subseteq \overline{U}$ and $m(\overline{U} - \overline{V}) = 0$. Therefore, $\overline{T} \in \mathcal{E}_m$.

Suppose that (T_n) is a sequence of sets in $\mathcal{E}_m$. Let U_n and V_n be two sets in $\mathcal{E}$ such that $U_n \subseteq T_n \subseteq V_n$ and $m(V_n - U_n) = 0$ for $n \in \mathbb{N}$. Then $\bigcup_{n \in \mathbb{N}} U_n$ and $\bigcup_{n \in \mathbb{N}} V_n$ belong to $\mathcal{E}$, $\bigcup_{n \in \mathbb{N}} U_n \subseteq \bigcup_{n \in \mathbb{N}} T_n \subseteq \bigcup_{n \in \mathbb{N}} V_n$, and

$$m\left(\bigcup_{n \in \mathbb{N}} V_n - \bigcup_{n \in \mathbb{N}} U_n\right) \leqslant m\left(\bigcup_{n \in \mathbb{N}} (V_n - U_n)\right)$$

$$\leqslant \sum_{n \in \mathbb{N}} m(V_n - U_n) = 0,$$

so $\bigcup_{n \in \mathbb{N}} T_n \in \mathcal{E}_m$. Thus, $\mathcal{E}_m$ is a σ-algebra on S that includes $\mathcal{E}$.

It is clear that $\tilde{m}$ is an extension of m because, if $T \in \mathcal{E}$, we obtain $m(T) = \tilde{m}(T)$ by taking $U = T = V$. We need to prove that $\tilde{m}$ is countable additive.

Let (T_n) be a sequence of pairwise disjoint sets and let U_n, V_n be sets in $\mathcal{E}$ such that $U_n \subseteq T_n \subseteq V_n$, and $m(V_n - U_n) = 0$. It is immediate that the sequence (U_n) also consists of disjoint sets. Therefore,

$$\tilde{m}\left(\bigcup_{n \in \mathbb{N}} T_n\right) = m\left(\bigcup_{n \in \mathbb{N}} U_n\right) = \sum_{n \in \mathbb{N}} m(E_n) = \sum_{n \in \mathbb{N}} \tilde{m}(E_n),$$

so $\tilde{m}$ is a measure.

To show that $\tilde{m}$ is a complete measure let $W \in \mathcal{E}_m$ be a subset of S such that $\tilde{m}(W) = 0$ and let $R \subseteq W$. Since $W \in \mathcal{E}_m$, there exist $U, V \in \mathcal{E}$, such that $U \subseteq W \subseteq V$ and $m(U) = m(V)$. It is clear that $m(U) = m(W) = m(V) = 0$, so $W \in \mathcal{E}_m$. □

Theorem 7.20. *Let $(S, \mathcal{E})$ be a complete measurable space. If $f : S \longrightarrow \hat{\mathbb{R}}$ is a measurable function and $f = g$ a.e., where $g : S \longrightarrow \hat{\mathbb{R}}$ then g is a measurable function.*

Proof. Let D be the subset of S defined by $D = \{x \in S \mid f(x) \neq g(x)\}$. By hypothesis, we have $m(D) = 0$. Since

$$\{x \in S \mid g(x) > t\} = (\{x \in S \mid f(x) > t\} \cup \{x \in D \mid g(x) > t\})$$
$$- \{x \in D \mid g(x) \leqslant t\},$$

taking into account that $\{x \in S \mid f(x) > t\}$ is measurable because f is measurable, it follows that the sets $\{x \in D \mid g(x) > t\}$ and $\{x \in D \mid g(x) \leqslant t\}$ are measurable as subsets of D. This implies the measurability of g. □

Definition 7.16. Let $(S, \mathcal{E}_1, m_1)$ and $(S, \mathcal{E}_2, m_2)$ be two measure spaces on a set S. $(S, \mathcal{E}_2, m_2)$ is an *extension* of $(S, \mathcal{E}_1, m_1)$ if $\mathcal{E}_1 \subseteq \mathcal{E}_2$ and $m_2 \restriction_{\mathcal{E}_1} = m_1$.

The fact that $(S, \mathcal{E}_2, m_2)$ is an extension of $(S, \mathcal{E}_1, m_1)$ is denoted by $(S, \mathcal{E}_1, m_1) \leqslant (S, \mathcal{E}_2, m_2)$.

Theorem 7.21. *Let $(S, \mathcal{E}, m)$ be a measure space. There exists a unique measure space $(S, \mathcal{E}', m')$ that is an extension of $(S, \mathcal{E}, m)$, is complete, and for any other complete extension $(S, \mathcal{E}'', m'')$ then $(S, \mathcal{E}', m') \leqslant (S, \mathcal{E}'', m'')$.*

Proof. The collection $\mathcal{E}'$ defined as

$$\mathcal{E}' = \{U \cup L \mid U \in \mathcal{E}, L \subseteq M \text{ for some } M \in \mathcal{E} \text{ with } m(M) = 0\}$$

is a σ-algebra. Note that $\emptyset \in \mathcal{E}'$, so $\mathcal{E}'$ is a non-empty collection.

Suppose that $T \in \mathcal{E}'$, so $T = U \cup L$, where $U \in \mathcal{E}$ and $L \subseteq M$ for some $M \in \mathcal{E}$ with $m(M) = 0$. We have:

$$\overline{T} = \overline{U} \cap \overline{L} = \overline{U} \cap (\overline{M} \cap \overline{L})$$
$$= \overline{U} \cap (\overline{M} \cup (M \cap \overline{L})) = (\overline{U} \cap \overline{M}) \cup (M \cap \overline{U} \cap \overline{L})$$
$$= \overline{U \cup M} \cup (M - (U \cup L)),$$

and, since $\overline{U \cup M} \in \mathcal{E}$ and $(M - (U \cup L)) \subseteq M$, it follows that $\overline{T} \in \mathcal{E}'$.

Suppose now that $T_1, T_2, \ldots$ belong to $\mathcal{E}'$, that is, $T_j = U_j \cup L_j$, where $U_j \in \mathcal{E}$ and $L_j \subseteq M_j$ for some $M_j \in \mathcal{E}$ and $m(M_j) = 0$. This implies $\bigcup_{j \geqslant 1} T_j = \bigcup_{j \geqslant 1} U_j \cup \bigcup_{j \geqslant 1} M_j$, where $\bigcup_{j \geqslant 1} U_j \in \mathcal{E}$ and $\bigcup_{j \geqslant 1} L_j \subseteq \bigcup_{j \geqslant 1} M_j$. Since $\bigcup_{j \geqslant 1} M_j \in \mathcal{E}$ and $m(\bigcup_{j \geqslant 1} M_j) = 0$, it follows that $\bigcup_{j \geqslant 1} T_j \in \mathcal{E}'$. This shows that $\mathcal{E}'$ is indeed, a σ-algebra.

For $T \in \mathcal{E}'$ define $m'(T)$ as $m'(T) = m(U)$, where $T = U \cup L$, $L \subseteq M$ for a set $M \in \mathcal{E}$ with $m(M) = 0$. Then, m' is well-defined. Indeed, suppose that $T = U_1 \cup L_1$ such that $L_1 \subseteq M_1$ for a set $M_1 \in \mathcal{E}$ with $m(M_1) = 0$. Since $T = U \cup L = U_1 \cup L_1$ we have $U \subseteq T = U_1 \cup L_1$, so $m(U) \leqslant m(u_1) + m(L_1) = m(U_1)$; reversing the roles of U and U_1 we have $m(U_1) \leqslant m(U)$, hence $m(U_1) = m(U)$, which shows that $m'(T)$ is well-defined.

We claim that m' is a measure on $\mathcal{E}'$. It is immediate that $m'(\emptyset) = 0$. Let $\{T_0, T_1, \ldots\}$ be a countable collection of pairwise disjoint sets in $\mathcal{E}'$. There exist $U_1, U_2, \ldots$ in $\mathcal{E}$ and $L_1, L_2, \ldots$ such that $T_j = U_j \cup L_j$ and $L_j \subseteq M_j$, where $M_j \in \mathcal{E}$ and $m(M_j) = 0$ for $j \geqslant 1$. Note that the sets U_j are also pairwise disjoint. Since $\bigcup_{j \geqslant 1} T_j = \bigcup_{j \geqslant 1} U_j \cup \bigcup_{j \geqslant 1} L_j$, $\bigcup_{j \geqslant 1} L_j \subseteq \bigcup_{j \geqslant 1} M_j$, and $m(\bigcup_{j \geqslant 1} M_j) = 0$, it follows that

$$m'\left(\bigcup_{j \geqslant 1} T_j\right) = m\left(\bigcup_{j \geqslant 1} U_j\right) = \sum_{j \geqslant 1} m(U_j) = \sum_{j \geqslant 1} m'(T_j).$$

To prove that m' is complete let $T \in \mathcal{E}'$ with $m'(T) = 0$ and let Z be a subset of T. We have $T = U \cup L$, where $U \in \mathcal{E}$ and $L \subseteq M$, where $m(M) = 0$. Note that $m(U) = m'(T) = 0$. For $M' = U \cup M$ we have $m(M') \leqslant m(U) + m(M) = 0$. By taking $Z = U' \cup L'$, where $U' = \emptyset \in \mathcal{E}$ and $L' = Z \subseteq M'$ we have $Z \in \mathcal{E}'$.

It is immediate that $\mathcal{E} \subseteq \mathcal{E}'$ and that $U \in \mathcal{E}$ implies $m(U) = m'(U)$, so $(S, \mathcal{E}', m')$ is indeed a complete extension of $(S, \mathcal{E}, m)$. This extension is unique for if $(S, \mathcal{E}'', m'')$ is another complete extension of $S, cale, m)$ and $T \in \mathcal{E}'$ we have $T = U \cup L$, where $U \in \mathcal{E}$, $L \subseteq M$ for some $M \in \mathcal{E}$ with $m(M) = 0$. This implies $U, M \in \mathcal{E}''$ and $m''(M) = m(M) = 0$. Since m'' is complete, we obtain $L \in \mathcal{E}''$, hence $T \in \mathcal{E}''$. Also, $m''(U) \leqslant m''(T) \leqslant m''(U) + m''(L) = m''(U)$, hence $m''(T) = m''(U) = m(U) = m'(T)$. $\square$

The smallest complete extension of a measure space $(S, \mathcal{E}, m)$ whose existence is proven in Theorem 7.21 is called the *completion* of $(S, \mathcal{E}, m)$.

Lemma 7.3. *Let $(S, \mathcal{E}, m)$ and $(S, \mathcal{E}, m')$ be two measure spaces on S that have the same collection of measurable sets $\mathcal{E}$ and $m(S) = m'(S)$. The collection $\mathcal{D} = \{C \in \mathcal{E} \mid m(C) = m'(C)\}$ is a Dynkin system.*

Proof. By hypothesis, $S \in \mathcal{D}$, so the first condition of Definition 1.45 is satisfied.

Suppose that $U, V \in \mathcal{D}$, that is, $m(U) = m'(U)$, $m(V) = m'(V)$ and $U \subseteq V$. Then,

$$m(V - U) = m(V) - m(U) = m'(V) - m'(U) = m'(V - U),$$

hence $V - U \in \mathcal{D}$.

Finally, let $\mathbf{T} = (T_0, T_1, \dots)$ is an increasing sequence of subsets of S such that $m(T_i) = m'(T_i)$ for $i \in \mathbb{N}$. We have

$$m\left(\bigcup_{i \in \mathbb{N}} T_i\right) = \lim_{n \to \infty} m(T_i) = \lim_{n \to \infty} m(T_i') = m\left(\bigcup_{i \in \mathbb{N}} T_i\right),$$

so $\bigcup_{i \in \mathbb{N}} T_i \in \mathcal{D}$. $\qquad\square$

Theorem 7.22. *Let $(S, \mathcal{E}, m)$ and $(S, \mathcal{E}, m')$ be two measure spaces on S that have the same collection of measurable sets $\mathcal{E}$, where $\mathcal{E} = \mathbf{K}_{\sigma\text{-alg}}(\mathcal{C})$ for some π-system $\mathcal{C}$ of subsets of S.*

If m and m' are finite measures such that
(i) $m(S) = m'(S)$, and
(ii) $m(C) = m'(C)$ for every $C \in \mathcal{C}$,
then $m = m'$.

Proof. Let $\mathcal{D} = \{C \in \mathcal{E} \mid m(C) = m'(C)\}$. We prove the theorem by showing that $\mathcal{E} \subseteq \mathcal{D}$.

By hypothesis, $\mathcal{C} \subseteq \mathcal{D}$, so $\mathbf{K}_{\text{Dyn}}(\mathcal{C}) \subseteq \mathbf{K}_{\text{Dyn}}(\mathcal{D}) = \mathcal{D}$, taking into account that $\mathcal{D}$ is a Dynkin system (by Lemma 7.3). Since $\mathcal{C}$ is a π-system we have $\mathbf{K}_{\sigma\text{-alg}}(\mathcal{C}) = \mathbf{K}_{\text{Dyn}}(\mathcal{C})$ by Theorem 1.42. Since $\mathcal{E} = \mathbf{K}_{\sigma\text{-alg}}(\mathcal{C})$, it follows that $\mathcal{E} \subseteq \mathcal{D}$. $\qquad\square$

Corollary 7.8. *Let $(S, \mathcal{E}, m)$ and $(S, \mathcal{E}, m')$ be two measure spaces on S that have the same collection of measurable sets $\mathcal{E}$, where $\mathcal{E} = \mathbf{K}_{\sigma\text{-alg}}(\mathcal{C})$ for some π-system $\mathcal{C}$ of subsets of S.*

If the following conditions:
(i) $m(C) = m'(C)$ for $C \in \mathcal{C}$;
(ii) there exists a increasing sequence of sets in $\mathcal{C}$, $\mathbf{C} = (C_n)$, such that $\bigcup_{n \in \mathbb{N}} C_n = S$, where $m(C_i)$ and $m'(C_i)$ are finite for $i \in \mathbb{N}$,
then $m = m'$.

Proof.   For $n \in \mathbb{N}$ define the measures m_n and m'_n as

$$m_n(T) = m(T \cap C_n) \text{ and } m'_n(T) = m'(T \cap C_n)$$

for $T \in \mathcal{E}$ and $n \in \mathbb{N}$. By Theorem 7.22 we have $m_n = m'_n$. Therefore,

$$m(T) = \lim_{n \to \infty} m_n(T) = \lim_{n \to \infty} m'_n(T) = m'(T)$$

for $T \in \mathcal{E}$, so $m = m'$.   □

The modularity property of measures can be extended to the *inclusion-exclusion* equality given next.

Theorem 7.23. (The Inclusion-Exclusion Equality) *Let m be a measure defined on a ring of subsets $\mathcal{E}$ of a set S. If $U_1, \ldots, U_n$ are n members of $\mathcal{E}$ and $n \geqslant 2$, then*

$$m\left(\bigcup_{i=1}^{n} U_i\right) = \sum_{i=1}^{n} m(U_i) - \sum_{i_1 < i_2} m(U_{i_1} \cap U_{i_2})$$
$$+ \sum_{i_1 < i_2 < i_3} m(U_{i_1} \cap U_{i_2} \cap U_{i_3})$$
$$+ \cdots + (-1)^{n+1} m(U_1 \cap U_2 \cap \cdots \cap U_n).$$

Proof.   For $n = 2$ the inclusion-exclusion equality amounts to the modularity property of m. The proof is by induction on $n \geqslant 2$ and the base step of the argument holds by this fact.

Define

$$s_p = m\left(\bigcup_{i=1}^{p} U_i\right)$$

for $2 \leqslant p \leqslant n$. We have

$$s_{p+1} = m\left(\bigcup_{i=1}^{p+1} U_i\right) = m\left(\bigcup_{i=1}^{p} U_i \cup U_{p+1}\right)$$
$$= m\left(\bigcup_{i=1}^{p} U_i\right) + m(U_{p+1}) - m\left(\bigcup_{i=1}^{p}(U_i \cap U_{p+1})\right).$$

Note now that both $\bigcup_{i=1}^{p} U_i$ and $\bigcup_{i=1}^{p}(U_i \cap U_{p+1})$ involve unions of p sets. Therefore, by applying the inductive hypothesis we can write:

$$
\begin{aligned}
s_{p+1} = \sum_{i=1}^{p} m(U_i) &- \sum_{i_1 < i_2} m(U_{i_1} \cap U_{i_2}) + \sum_{i_1 < i_2 < i_3} m(U_{i_1} \cap U_{i_2} \cap U_{i_3}) \\
&+ \cdots + (-1)^{p+1} m(U_1 \cap U_2 \cap \cdots \cap U_p) + m(U_{p+1}) \\
&- \sum_{i=1}^{p} m(U_i \cap U_{p+1}) + \sum_{i_1 < i_2} m(U_{i_1} \cap U_{i_2} \cap U_{p+1}) \\
&- \sum_{i_1 < i_2 < i_3} m(U_{i_1} \cap U_{i_2} \cap U_{i_3} \cap U_{p+1}) \\
&+ \cdots + (-1)^{p+2} m(U_1 \cap U_2 \cap \cdots \cap U_p \cap U_{p+1}),
\end{aligned}
$$

which justifies the desired equality. $\qquad \square$

Theorem 7.24. *If m_1, m_2 are two measures on the measurable space $(S, \mathcal{E})$, $\mathcal{F}$ is an algebra that generates the σ-algebra $\mathcal{E}$, and $m_1(T) = m_2(T)$ for every $T \in \mathcal{F}$, then $m_1 = m_2$.*

Proof. Observe that the collection $\mathcal{D} = \{U \in \mathcal{E} \mid m_1(U) = m_2(U)\}$ is a monotone collection that contains the algebra $\mathcal{F}$. Since $\mathcal{F} \subseteq \mathcal{D}$, it follows that $\mathbf{K}_{\mathrm{mon}}(\mathcal{F}) = \mathbf{K}_{\mathrm{mon}}(\mathcal{D}) = \mathcal{D}$. By Theorem 1.39, $\mathbf{K}_{\mathrm{mon}}(\mathcal{F}) = \mathbf{K}_{\sigma\text{-alg}}(\mathcal{F}) = \mathcal{E}$, hence $\mathcal{D} = \mathcal{E}$. Therefore, $m_1 = m_2$. $\qquad \square$

Theorem 7.25. *Let $(S, \mathcal{E}, m)$ be a measure space and let $f : S \longrightarrow \mathbb{R}$ be a simple measurable function. If $\pi = \{B_1, \ldots, B_n\}$ and $\sigma = \{C_1, \ldots, C_n\}$ are two partitions in $\mathrm{PART}_{\mathrm{fin}}(S)$ related to f such that $f(x) = y_i$ for $x \in B_i$ and $f(x) = z_j$ for $x \in C_j$ for $1 \leqslant i \leqslant n$ and $1 \leqslant j \leqslant m$, then*

$$
\sum_{i=1}^{n} y_i m(B_i) = \sum_{j=1}^{m} z_j m(C_j). \tag{7.5}
$$

Proof. Since $f(x) = \sum_{i=1}^{n} y_i 1_{B_i}(x) = \sum_{j=1}^{m} z_j 1_{C_j}(x)$, it is clear that if $B_i \cap C_j \neq \emptyset$, then $y_i = z_j$. Consider the $n \times m$ matrix $\mathbf{U} = (u_{ij})$ defined by

$$
u_{ij} = \begin{cases} y_i = z_j & \text{if } B_i \cap C_j \neq \emptyset, \\ 0 & \text{if } B_i \cap C_j = \emptyset, \end{cases}
$$

for $1 \leqslant i \leqslant n$ and $1 \leqslant j \leqslant m$. Then, we have

$$\sum_{i=1}^{n}\sum_{j=1}^{m} u_{ij} m(B_i \cap C_j) = \sum_{i=1}^{n}\sum_{j=1}^{m} u_{ij}\{m(B_i \cap C_j) \mid B_i \cap C_j \neq \emptyset\}$$

$$= \sum_{i=1}^{n} y_i \sum_{j=1}^{m}\{m(B_i \cap C_j) \mid B_i \cap C_j \neq \emptyset\}$$

$$= \sum_{i=1}^{n} y_i m(B_i),$$

and, similarly,

$$\sum_{i=1}^{n}\sum_{j=1}^{m} u_{ij} m(B_i \cap C_j) = \sum_{j=1}^{m} z_j m(C_j),$$

which justifies our claim. □

As we shall see, equality (7.5) will play an important role in integration theory.

Theorem 7.26. *Let $(S, \mathcal{E})$ be a measurable space. Any non-negative measurable function $f : S \longrightarrow \hat{\mathbb{R}}_{\geqslant 0}$ between the measurable spaces $(S, \mathcal{E})$ and $(\hat{\mathbb{R}}_{\geqslant 0}, \mathbb{B}(\hat{\mathbb{R}}_{\geqslant 0}))$ is the pointwise limit of a non-decreasing sequence of non-negative measurable simple functions (f_n). Moreover, for each $r < \infty$ the sequence (f_n) converges uniformly to f on the set $S_r = f^{-1}((-\infty, r])$.*

Proof. Consider the partition of $\mathbb{R}_{>0}$ that consists of the Borel sets

$$V_{j,n} = \left(\frac{j}{2^n}, \frac{j+1}{2^n}\right],$$

where $1 \leqslant j \leqslant n2^n - 1$, and $V_n = (n, \infty)$, and the sets $E_{j,n} = f^{-1}(V_{j,n})$ and $E_n = f^{-1}(V_n)$ (see Figure 7.1). Since f is measurable each of the sets $E_{j,n}$ or E_n is measurable. Therefore, the simple function $f_n : S \longrightarrow \mathbb{R}_{\geqslant 0}$ defined by

$$f_n(x) = \sum_{j=1}^{n2^n - 1} \frac{j}{2^n} 1_{E_{j,n}}(x) + n 1_{E_n}(x)$$

is measurable. If $x \in E_{j,n}$ for some j, $1 \leqslant j \leqslant n \cdot 2^n - 1$, then we have $f_n(x) = \frac{j}{2^n}$. Also, if $x \in E_n$ (that is, $f(x) > n$), we have $f_n(x) = n$. Thus, for every $x \in \hat{\mathbb{R}}_{\geqslant 0}$ we have $f_n(x) \leqslant f(x)$. Also, if $x \leqslant 2^n$, we have $f(x) - f_n(x) \leqslant \frac{1}{2^n}$, which shows that the convergence of f_n to f is uniform on bounded sets.

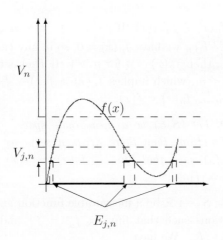

Fig. 7.1 The sets $V_{j,n}$ and $E_{j,n}$ defined in the proof of Theorem 7.26.

The definition of the functions f_n depends on the function f. In particular, for $f(x) = x$, we denote the corresponding sequence of simple measurable functions by $(h_1, \ldots, h_n, \ldots)$. In this case, $E_{j,n} = V_{j,n}$ and $E_n = V_n$, so

$$h_n(x) = \sum_{j=1}^{n2^n - 1} \frac{j}{2^n} 1_{V_{j,n}}(x) + n1_{V_n}(x)$$

$$= \begin{cases} \dfrac{j}{2^n} & \text{if } \dfrac{j}{2^n} < x \leqslant \dfrac{j+1}{2^n}, \\ n & \text{if } x > n. \end{cases}$$

Note that $f_n(x) = h_n(f(x))$ for $x \in \mathbb{R}_{\geqslant 0}$.

The sequence of functions $(f_1(x), f_2(x), \ldots)$ is non-decreasing. Indeed, observe that

$$E_{2j,n+1} \cup E_{2j+1,n+1} = f^{-1}(V_{2j,n+1}) \cup f^{-1}(V_{2j+1,n+1})$$
$$= f^{-1}(V_{2j,n+1} \cup V_{2j+1,n+1})$$
$$= f^{-1}\left(\left(\frac{2j}{2^{n+1}}, \frac{2j+1}{2^{n+1}} \right] \cup \left(\frac{2j+1}{2^{n+1}}, \frac{2j+2}{2^{n+1}} \right] \right)$$
$$= f^{-1}\left(\left(\frac{j}{2^n}, \frac{j+1}{2^n} \right] \right)$$
$$= E_{j,n}.$$

If $x \in E_{n,j}$ two cases may occur because of the previous observation. If $x \in E_{2j,n+1}$, $f_{n+1}(x) = \frac{j}{2^n} = f_n(x)$; otherwise, $x \in E_{2j+1,n+1}$, $f_{n+1}(x) =$

$\frac{2j+1}{2 \cdot 2^n} > \frac{j}{2^n}$, so $f_n(x) \leqslant f_{n+1}(x)$. If $x \in E_n$, $f_n(x) = n \leqslant f_{n+1}(x)$. Finally, if $x \notin E_n \cup \bigcup_{j=1}^{n2^n-1} E_{j,n}$ we have $f_n(x) = 0$, so in any case, $f_n(x) \leqslant f_{n+1}(x)$.

If $f(x) = \infty$, then $f_n(x) = n$ for $n \geqslant 1$. If $f(x)$ is finite, there exists m such that $f(x) < m$, which implies $f_n(x) \geqslant f(x) - \frac{1}{2^n}$ if $n \geqslant m$. Thus, in either case, $\lim_{n \to \infty} f_n(x) = f(x)$. $\square$

Corollary 7.9. *Let $(S, \mathcal{E})$ be a measurable space. If $f : S \longrightarrow \mathbb{C}$ is a measurable function, then there exists a sequence of measurable simple functions (f_n) such that $\lim_{n \to \infty} f_n(x) = f(x)$ for all $x \in S$ and $\lim_{n \to \infty} |f_n(x)| = |f|$.*

Proof. Let $f : S \longrightarrow \mathbb{R}$ be a measurable function and let (f_n^+) and (f_n^-) be simple functions such that $\lim_{n \to \infty} f_n^+ = f^+$ and $\lim_{n \to \infty} f_n^- = f^-$. Define $f_n = f_n^+ - f_n^-$. We have

$$|f_n| = f_n^+ + f_n^- \leqslant f_{n+1}^+ + f_{n+1}^- = |f_{n+1}|$$

and $\lim_{n \to \infty} |f_n| = |f|$.

Let now $f : S \longrightarrow \mathbb{C}$ be a complex-valued measurable function. There exist two sequences (g_n) and (h_n) of simple measurable functions such that $\lim_{n \to \infty} u_n = \Re(f)$, $\lim_{n \to \infty} v_n = \Im(f)$. If $f_n = g_n + ih_n$ we can write $|f_n(x)|^2 = |g_n(x)|^2 + |h_n(x)|^2$, and $\lim_{n \to \infty} |f_n(x)| = f(x)$. $\square$

Theorem 7.27. *Let $h : \mathbb{R}^2 \longrightarrow \mathbb{R}$ be a continuous function. If $(S, \mathcal{E})$ is a measurable space and $f, g : S \longrightarrow \mathbb{R}$ are two measurable functions, then the function $\ell : S \longrightarrow \mathbb{R}$ defined by $\ell(x) = h(f(x), g(x))$ for $x \in S$ is measurable.*

Proof. Recall that the collection of subsets $\{(a, \infty) \mid a \in \mathbb{R}\}$ generates the family of Borel subsets of $\mathbb{R}$.

Since $U = h^{-1}(a, +\infty)$ is an open set in $\mathbb{R}^2$, by Example 4.23, it follows that U it is a countable union of rectangles, $U = \bigcup_{n \in \mathbb{N}} (a_n, b_n) \times (c_n, d_n)$. Therefore, to prove this statement it suffices to prove that U is a measurable set. This follows from the equality

$$U = \bigcup_{n \in \mathbb{N}} \left(f^{-1}(a_n, b_n) \cap g^{-1}(c_n, d_n) \right).$$

$\square$

Corollary 7.10. *Let $(S, \mathcal{E})$ be a measurable space. If $f : S \longrightarrow \mathbb{R}$ and $g : S \longrightarrow \mathbb{R}$ are measurable functions, then so are $f + g$ and fg.*

Proof. By taking h as $h(x, y) = x + y$ and $h(x, y) = xy$ for $x, y \in \mathbb{R}$, where h is the continuous function considered in Theorem 7.27, the corollary follows immediately. $\square$

Corollary 7.11. *Let $(S, \mathcal{E})$ be a measurable space. The set of measurable functions of the form $f : S \longrightarrow \mathbb{R}$ is a real linear space.*

Proof. Every constant function $h_c : S \longrightarrow \mathbb{R}$ given by $h_c(x) = c$ for every $x \in S$ is measurable. Therefore if $f : S \longrightarrow \mathbb{R}$ is a measurable function, then cf is a measurable function. $\qquad\qquad\square$

Definition 7.17. Let $f : S \longrightarrow \hat{\mathbb{R}}$ be a function ranging over the set $\hat{\mathbb{R}}$. The *positive* and the *negative* parts of f are the functions f^+ and f^-, respectively, defined as:

$$f^+(x) = \max\{f(x), 0\} \text{ and } f^- = -\min\{f(x), 0\} = \max\{-f(x), 0\}$$

for $x \in S$.

It is easy to see that $f(x) = f^+(x) - f^-(x)$ for $x \in \hat{\mathbb{R}}$. Furthermore, we have:

$$f^+(x) = \frac{|f(x)| + f(x)}{2} \text{ and } f^-(x) = \frac{|f(x)| - f(x)}{2},$$

and

$$f(x) = f^+(x) - f^-(x) \text{ and } |f(x)| = f^+(x) + f^-(x),$$

for every $x \in S$.

Note that

$$|f|^+ = |f| \text{ and } |f|^- = 0.$$

Since $f = f^+ - f^-$ and $g = g^+ - g^-$, it follows that $f + g = f^+ + g^+ - f^- - g^-$. Therefore,

$$(f + g)^+ - (f + g)^- = f^+ + g^+ - f^- - g^-,$$

which implies

$$(f + g)^+ f^- + g^- = (f + g)^- + f^+ + f^+. \qquad\qquad (7.6)$$

Theorem 7.28. *Let $f, g : S \longrightarrow \mathbb{R}$ be two functions. We have:*

$$(f + g)^+ \leqslant f^+ + g^+ \text{ and } (f + g)^- \leqslant f^- + g^-.$$

Proof. By the definition of f^+ we have $f(x) \leqslant f^+(x)$ for $x \in S$, so $f \leqslant f^+$. Therefore, $f + g \leqslant f^+ + g^+$, which implies $(f + g)^+ \leqslant f^+ + g^+$.

To prove the second inequality note that

$$(f + g)^- = (f + g)^+ - (f + g) \leqslant f^+ + g^+ - (f + g)$$
$$= f^+ - f + g^+ - g = f^- + g^-. \qquad\qquad\square$$

Theorem 7.29. *Let $(S, \mathcal{D})$ be a measurable space. A function $f : S \longrightarrow \mathbb{R}$ is measurable if and only if both f^+ and f^- are measurable functions.*

Proof. Suppose that f is a measurable function. Then, the sets $U = f^{-1}(0, \infty)$ and $W = f^{-1}(-\infty, 0]$ are a measurable subsets of S. Therefore, the characteristic functions 1_U and 1_W are measurable and, by Corollary 7.10, the functions $f1_U$ and $f1_W$ are measurable. These functions are exactly f^+ and f^-, respectively.

Conversely, suppose that both f^+ and f^- are measurable functions. Then, since $f(x) = f^+(x) - f^-(x)$, by Corollary 7.11, the function f is measurable. $\qquad\square$

Corollary 7.12. *Let $(S, \mathcal{D})$ be a measurable space. If $f : S \longrightarrow \mathbb{R}$ is a measurable function, then so is $|f|$.*

Proof. If f is measurable, then so are f^+ and f^-. Since $|f(x)| = f^+(x) + f^-(x)$ for $x \in S$, it follows that $|f|$ is also measurable. $\qquad\square$

Example 7.9. The converse of the statement of Corollary 7.12 is not true, in general. In other words, it is possible that $|f|$ is a measurable function without f being one. Consider, for instance, a subset U of S such that $U \notin \mathcal{E}$. Its complement, $\overline{U}$ does not belong to $\mathcal{E}$ either. Consider the function $f : S \longrightarrow \mathbb{R}$ given by

$$f(x) = \begin{cases} 1 & \text{if } x \in U, \\ -1 & \text{if } x \notin U, \end{cases}$$

for $x \in S$. Note that the function $|f|$ is a constant function, $|f|(x) = 1$ for $x \in S$ and, therefore, it is measurable. However, $f^+ = 1_U$ and this function is not measurable because $U \notin \mathcal{E}$. Therefore, f is not measurable.

Theorem 7.26 can be extended to functions that range over the entire set $\hat{\mathbb{R}}$.

Corollary 7.13. *Let $(S, \mathcal{E})$ be a measurable space. Any measurable function $f : S \longrightarrow \hat{\mathbb{R}}$ between the measurable spaces $(S, \mathcal{E})$ and $(\hat{\mathbb{R}}, \mathbb{B}(\hat{\mathbb{R}}))$ is the limit of a sequence of simple measurable functions.*

Proof. This statement follows immediately by applying Theorem 7.26 to the functions f^+ and f^-. $\qquad\square$

If f is a bounded measurable function, a stronger statement holds.

Corollary 7.14. *If $(S, \mathcal{E})$ is a measurable space and $f : S \longrightarrow \mathbb{R}$ is a bounded measurable function, then f is the uniform limit of a sequence of simple measurable functions.*

Proof. This statement can be easily obtained by modifying the proof of Theorem 7.26. $\square$

Lemma 7.4. *Let $(S, \mathcal{E})$ be a measurable space and let $\boldsymbol{f} = (f_0, f_1, \dots, f_n, \dots)$ be a sequence of real-valued functions, $f_i : S \longrightarrow \hat{\mathbb{R}}$. We have*

$$\{x \in S \mid (\sup_{n \geqslant k} f_n)(x) > a\} = \bigcup_{n \geqslant k} \{x \in S \mid f_n(x) > a\},$$

$$\{x \in S \mid (\inf_{n \geqslant k} f_n)(x) > a\} = \bigcap_{n \geqslant k} \{x \in S \mid f_n(x) > a\}$$

for every $k \in \mathbb{N}$.

Proof. Let $x \in S$ be such that $(\sup_{n \geqslant k} f_n)(x) = \sup\{f_n(x) \mid n \in \mathbb{N}, n \geqslant k\} > a$ for $n \geqslant k$. By the definition of the supremum, there exists $m \geqslant k$ such that $f_m(x) > a$. Therefore, $x \in \bigcup_{n \geqslant k} \{x \in S \mid f_n(x) > a\}$. Conversely, suppose that there exists $m \geqslant k$ such that $f_m(x) > a$. This implies immediately that $(\sup_{n \geqslant k} f_n)(x) > a$, which justifies the first equality of the lemma.

We omit the proof of the second equality. $\square$

Theorem 7.30. *Let $(S, \mathcal{E})$ be a measurable space and let*

$$\boldsymbol{f} = (f_0, f_1, \dots, f_n, \dots)$$

be a sequence of real-valued functions, $f_i : S \longrightarrow \mathbb{R}$. If the functions f_n are measurable, then so are the functions $\sup_n f_n$, $\inf_n f_n$, $\limsup_{n \to \infty} f_n$ and $\liminf_{n \to \infty} f_n$.

Proof. The conclusion follows immediately from Lemma 7.4 and from the equalities

$$\limsup_{n \to \infty} f_n = \inf_{n \geqslant 1} \sup_{m \geqslant n} f_m$$

and

$$\liminf_{n \to \infty} f_n = \sup_{n \geqslant 1} \inf_{m \geqslant n} f_m. \qquad \square$$

Corollary 7.15. *Let $(S, \mathcal{E})$ be a measurable space and let*

$$\boldsymbol{f} = (f_0, f_1, \ldots, f_n, \ldots)$$

be a sequence of real-valued functions, $f_i : S \longrightarrow \mathbb{R}$ such that $\lim_{n\to\infty} f_n(x)$ exists for $x \in S$. If the functions f_n are measurable, then $f : S \longrightarrow \hat{R}$ defined by $f(x) = \lim_{n\to\infty} f_n(x)$ for $x \in S$ is a measurable function.

Proof. This statement is an immediate consequence of Theorem 7.30.

$\square$

We extend the notion of measurability to functions with complex values.

Definition 7.18. Let $(S, \mathcal{O})$ be a measurable space. A function $f : S \longrightarrow \mathbb{C}$ is *measurable* if assuming that $f(x) = u(x) + iv(x)$, u and v are both real-valued measurable functions.

Note that if $f : S \longrightarrow \mathbb{C}$ is measurable, then $|f|$ is also measurable because $|f| = \sqrt{u^2 + v^2}$.

Let $(S, \mathcal{O})$ be a topological space and let $f : S \longrightarrow \mathbb{C}$ be a complex-valued function. Its *support* is the set $supp(f) = \mathbf{K}(\{x \in S \mid f(x) \neq 0\})$. The set of continuous complex-valued functions whose support is compact is denoted by $C_c(S)$.

Note that $C_c(S)$ is a linear space. Recall that a locally compact topological space is automatically a Hausdorff space (see Definition 4.26).

Theorem 7.31. (Uniqueness of Measures Theorem) *Let $(S, \mathcal{E})$ be a measurable space such that $\mathcal{E} = \boldsymbol{K}_{\sigma\text{-alg}}(\mathcal{G})$ such that*

(i) *if $G, H \in \mathcal{G}$, then $G \cap H \in \mathcal{G}$, and*

(ii) *there exists a increasing sequence of sets (G_n) in $\mathcal{G}$ such that $\bigcup_{n \in \mathbb{N}} G_n = S$.*

If m_1, m_2 are two measures such that $m_1(G) = m_2(G)$ for every $G \in \mathcal{G}$ and both $m_1(G_n)$ and $m_2(G_n)$ are finite for $n \in \mathbb{N}$, then $m_1(U) = m_2(U)$ for every $U \in \mathcal{E}$.

Proof. For each of the sets G_n let $\mathcal{D}_n$ be the collection

$$\mathcal{D}_n = \{U \in \mathcal{E} \mid m_1(G_n \cap U) = m_2(G_n \cap U)\}.$$

We show that each $\mathcal{D}_n$ is a Dynkin system by proving that $\mathcal{D}_n$ satisfies the conditions of Theorem 1.41.

Note that $S \in \mathcal{D}_n$ because $m_1(G) = m_2(G)$ for each set $G \in \mathcal{G}$. If $U \in \mathcal{D}_n$, then

$$m_1(G_n \cap \overline{U}) = m_1(G_n) - m_1(G_n \cap U)$$
$$= m_2(G_n) - m_2(G_n \cap U) = m_2(G_n \cap \overline{U}),$$

hence $\overline{U} \in \mathcal{D}_n$.

Finally, let (U_p) be a sequence of pairwise disjoint sets in $\mathcal{D}_n$. We have:

$$m_1\left(G_n \cap \bigcup_{p \in \mathbb{N}} U_p\right) = m_1\left(\bigcup_{p \in \mathbb{N}}(G_n \cap U_p)\right)$$

$$= \sum_{p \in \mathbb{N}} m_1(G_n \cap U_p) = \sum_{p \in \mathbb{N}} m_2(G_n \cap U_p)$$

$$= m_2\left(\bigcup_{p \in \mathbb{N}}(G_n \cap U_p)\right) = m_2\left(G_n \cap \bigcup_{p \in \mathbb{N}} U_p\right),$$

hence $\bigcup_{p \in \mathbb{N}} U_p \in \mathcal{D}_n$.

Since $\mathcal{G}$ is a π-system, it follows that $\mathbf{K}_{\mathrm{Dyn}}(\mathcal{G}) = \mathbf{K}_{\sigma\text{-alg}}(\mathcal{G})$ by Theorem 1.42. Thus, $\mathcal{G} \subseteq \mathcal{D}_n$ implies $\mathbf{K}_{\sigma\text{-alg}}(\mathcal{G}) \subseteq \mathbf{K}_{\sigma\text{-alg}}(\mathcal{G}) \subseteq \mathcal{D}_n$ for $n \in \mathbb{N}$.

Since $\mathcal{E} = \mathbf{K}_{\sigma\text{-alg}}(\mathcal{G}) \subseteq \mathcal{D}_n \subseteq \mathcal{E}$, it follows that $\mathcal{E} = \mathcal{D}_n$ for all $n \in \mathbb{N}$, hence $m_1(G_n \cap U) = m_2(G_n \cap U)$ for $n \in \mathbb{N}$ and $U \in \mathcal{E}$.

By the continuity property of measures we have:

$$m_1(U) = \lim_{n \to \infty} m_1(G_n \cap U) = \lim_{n \to \infty} m_2(G_n \cap U) = m_2(U)$$

for every $U \in \mathcal{E}$ which concludes the argument. $\qquad\square$

The behavior of measures with respect to limits of sequences of sets is discussed next.

Theorem 7.32. (Measure Continuity Theorem) *Let $(S, \mathcal{E}, m)$ be a measure space and let $(U_0, U_1, \ldots)$ be a sequence of sets.*

   (i) *if $(U_0, U_1, \ldots)$ is an increasing sequence, then $m(\lim U_n) = \lim m(U_n)$ (continuity from below).*

   (ii) *if $(U_0, U_1, \ldots)$ is a decreasing sequence and there exists a set U_i such that $m(U_i)$ is finite, then $m(\lim U_n) = \lim m(U_n)$ (continuity from above).*

Proof. Suppose that $U_0 \subset U_1 \subset \cdots$ is an increasing sequence, so $m(\lim U_n) = m(\bigcup_n U_n)$.

By Theorem 1.33 there exists a sequence $V_0 \subset V_1 \subset \cdots$ of disjoint sets in $\mathcal{E}$ such that $\bigcup U_n = \bigcup V_n$ and $V_0 = U_0$, and $V_n = U_n - V_{n-1}$ for $n \geqslant 1$. Then,

$$m(\lim U_n) = m\left(\bigcup_n V_n\right) = m(V_0) + \sum_{n \geqslant 1} m(V_n)$$

$$= \lim_{n \to \infty}\left(m(V_0) + \sum_{i=1}^{n} m(V_i)\right)$$

$$= \lim_{n \to \infty} m \left(V_0 \cup \left(\bigcup_{i=1}^{n} V_i \right) \right)$$

$$= \lim_{n \to \infty} m(U_i).$$

Suppose now that $U_0 \supset U_1 \supset \cdots$ is a decreasing sequence of sets, so $m(\lim U_n) = m(\bigcap_n U_n)$. Also, suppose that $m(U_0)$ is finite.

Define the sequence of sets $W_0, W_1, \ldots$ by $W_n = U_0 - U_n$ for $n \in \mathbb{N}$. Since this sequence is increasing, we have $m(\bigcup_{n \in \mathbb{N}} W_n) = \lim m(W_n)$ by the first part of the theorem. Thus, we can write:

$$m \left(\bigcup_{n \in \mathbb{N}} W_n \right) = \lim m(W_n) = m(U_0) - \lim m(U_n).$$

Since

$$m \left(\bigcup_{n \in \mathbb{N}} W_n \right) = m \left(\bigcup_{n \in \mathbb{N}} (U_0 - U_n) \right)$$

$$= m \left(U_0 - \bigcap_{n \in \mathbb{N}} U_n \right)$$

$$= m(U_0) - m \left(\bigcap_{n \in \mathbb{N}} U_n \right),$$

it follows that

$$m(\lim U_n) = m \left(\bigcap_{n \in \mathbb{N}} U_n \right) = \lim m(U_n),$$

because U_0 is finite. □

Theorem 7.33. (Borel-Cantelli Lemma) *Let $(S, \mathcal{E}, m)$ be a measure space. If $\mathbf{S} = (S_0, S_1, \ldots)$ is a sequence of sets such that $\sum_i m(S_i) < \infty$, then $m(\limsup \mathbf{S}) = 0$.*

Proof.   Let $T_p = \bigcup_{i=p}^{\infty} S_i$ for $p \in \mathbb{N}$. By the subadditivity of m we have $m(T_p) \leqslant \sum_{i=p}^{\infty} m(S_i)$ and, therefore $\lim_{p \to \infty} m(T_p) = 0$ because of the convergence of the series $\sum_i m(S_i)$.

Since $\limsup \mathbf{S} = \bigcap_{p=0}^{\infty} \bigcup_{i=p}^{\infty} S_i = \bigcap_{p=0}^{\infty} T_p$, it follows that $m(\limsup \mathbf{S}) \leqslant m(T_p)$ for every $p \in \mathbb{N}$, so $m(\limsup \mathbf{S}) \leqslant \inf_p m(T_p) = 0$, which implies $m(\limsup \mathbf{S}) = 0$. □

7.6 Outer Measures

Definition 7.19. Let S be a set. An *outer measure* on S is a function $\mu : \mathcal{P}(S) \longrightarrow \hat{\mathbb{R}}_{\geqslant 0}$ such that:
  (i) $\mu(\emptyset) = 0$;
  (ii) μ is countably subadditive, that is,

$$\mu\left(\bigcup_{n \in \mathbb{N}} U_n\right) \leqslant \sum \{\mu(U_n) \mid n \in \mathbb{N}\}$$

  for every countable family $\{U_n \in \mathcal{P}(S) \mid n \in \mathbb{N}\}$ of subsets of S;
  (iii) μ is monotonic, that is, if $U, V \subseteq S$ such that $U \subseteq V$, then $\mu(U) \leqslant \mu(V)$.

Clearly, every measure on S is an outer measure on the same set. The reverse is false, as the next example shows.

Example 7.10. Let $S = \{s_0, s_1, s_2\}$ be a set. Define the function $\mu : \mathcal{P}(S) \longrightarrow \hat{\mathbb{R}}_{\geqslant 0}$ by

$$\mu(X) = \begin{cases} 0 & \text{if } X = \emptyset, \\ 2 & \text{if } X = S, \\ 1 & \text{otherwise.} \end{cases}$$

For the disjoint sets $X_0 = \{s_0\}$ and $X_1 = \{s_1\}$ we have $\mu(X_1 \cup X_2) = 1$ and $\mu(X_1) + \mu(X_2) = 2$, so μ is not a measure.

To show that μ is an outer measure we need to verify only is countable subadditivity for the other properties are immediate. Let $\{U_n \in \mathcal{P}(S) \mid n \in \mathbb{N}\}$ be a countable family of subsets of S. Three cases need to be considered depending on the set $U = \bigcup_{n \in \mathbb{N}} U_n$:
  (i) If $U = \emptyset$, then $U_n = \emptyset$ for every $n \in \mathbb{N}$ and the subadditivity is immediate.
  (ii) If $U = S$, then $\mu(U) = 2$. If there is a set U_n such that $U_n = S$, the subadditivity follows. If none of sets U_n equals S, there must be least two non-empty distinct sets U_j and U_k among the members of the family $\{U_n \mid n \in \mathbb{N}\}$. For these sets $\mu(U_j) = \mu(U_k) = 1$ and the subadditivity follows.
  (iii) If U is neither $\emptyset$ nor S, then $\mu(U) = 1$. Clearly, at least one of the sets U_n is non-empty which implies the subadditivity.

Example 7.11. For $U \subseteq \mathbb{R}$ define the collection C_U of sequences of open intervals of $\mathbb{R}$ of the form $((a_n, b_n))_{n \geqslant 1}$ such that $U \subseteq \bigcup_{n=1}^{\infty}(a_n, b_n)$. Let $\mu_L : \mathcal{P}(\mathbb{R}) \longrightarrow \hat{\mathbb{R}}_{\geqslant 0}$ be defined as:

$$\mu_L(U) = \inf \left\{ \sum_{n \geqslant 1}(b_n - a_n) \mid ((a_n, b_n))_{n \geqslant 1} \in C_U \right\}.$$

We claim that μ_L is an outer measure on $\mathbb{R}$.

It is easy to see that $\mu_L(\emptyset) = 0$. If $C_U = \emptyset$ define $\mu_L(U) = \infty$.

Let $U, V \subseteq \mathbb{R}$ be such that $U \subseteq V$. Then $C_V \subseteq C_U$ and this implies $\mu_L(U) \leqslant \mu_L(V)$.

To prove the countable subadditivity of μ_L let $(U_n)_{n \geqslant 1}$ be a countable family of subsets of $\mathbb{R}$. If $\sum_{n \geqslant 1} \mu_L(U_n) = \infty$, the subadditivity follows immediately. Suppose that $\sum_{n \geqslant 1} \mu_L(U_n)$ is finite and let $\epsilon > 0$. Let $((a_n^j, b_n^j))_{n \geqslant 1} \in C_{U_j}$ and

$$\sum_{n \geqslant 1}(b_n^j - a_n^j) < \mu_L(U_j) + \frac{\epsilon}{2^j}.$$

If $((a_j, b_j))_{j \geqslant 1}$ is a sequence constructed by amalgamating the sequences $((a_n^j, b_n^j))_{n \geqslant 1}$ (see Supplement 13 of Chapter 1), it follows that $\bigcup_{j \geqslant 1} U_j \subseteq \bigcup_{j \geqslant 1}(a_j, b_j)$ and

$$\sum_{j \geqslant 1}(b_j - a_j) < \sum_{j \geqslant 1}\left(\mu_L(U_j) + \frac{\epsilon}{2^j}\right)$$
$$= \sum_{j \geqslant 1}\mu_L(U_j) + \epsilon,$$

hence $\mu_L(\bigcup_{j \geqslant 1} U_j) \leqslant \sum_{j \geqslant 1} \mu_L(U_j)$. Thus, μ_L is indeed an outer measure. This measure is referred to as the *Lebesgue outer measure* on $\mathbb{R}$.

Example 7.12. Example 7.11 can be generalized to a collection $\mathcal{C} = \{C_1, \ldots, C_n, \ldots\}$ of subsets of a set S such that $\emptyset \in \mathcal{C}$, and a function $\phi : \mathcal{C} \longrightarrow \hat{\mathbb{R}}_{\geqslant 0}$ such that $\phi(\emptyset) = 0$.

For $U \in \mathcal{P}(S)$ define

$$\mu_\phi(U) = \inf \left\{ \sum_{j \geqslant 1}\phi(C_j) \mid C_1, \ldots, C_j, \ldots \in \mathcal{C} \text{ and } U \subseteq \bigcup_{j \geqslant 1} C_j \right\}.$$

If $\inf \emptyset$ is defined as ∞ then μ_ϕ is an outer measure on S.

Suppose that $U \subseteq V \subseteq S$. If there is no sequence (C_n) in $\mathcal{C}$ such that $V \subseteq \bigcup_{n \geqslant 1} C_n$, then $\mu_\phi(V) = \infty$, and we have the inequality $\mu_\phi \leqslant \mu_\phi(V)$.

Otherwise, every cover of V is also a cover of U, which again, implies $\mu_\phi(U) \leqslant \mu_\phi(V)$.

If $\sum_{n \geqslant 1} \mu_\phi(U_n) = \infty$, then $\mu_\phi(\bigcup_{n \geqslant 1} U_n) \leqslant \sum_{n \geqslant 1} \mu_\phi(U_n)$. Therefore, we may assume that $\sum_{n \geqslant 1} \mu_\phi(U_n)$ is finite, hence $\mu_\phi(U_n)$ is finite for $n \geqslant 1$. By the definition of $\mu_\phi(U_n)$, for every $\epsilon > 0$, there exist $C_{n1}, C_{n2}, \ldots$ in $\mathcal{C}$ such that $U_n \subseteq \bigcup_{p \geqslant 1} C_{np}$ and $\sum_{p \geqslant 1} \phi(C_{np}) \leqslant \mu_\phi(U_n) + \frac{\epsilon}{2^n}$. This implies $\bigcup_{n \geqslant 1} U_n \subseteq \bigcup_{n \geqslant 1} \bigcup_{p \geqslant 1} C_{np}$, hence

$$\mu_\phi\left(\bigcup_{n \geqslant 1} U_n\right) \leqslant \sum_{n \geqslant 1} \sum_{p \geqslant 1} \phi(C_{np}) < \sum_{n \geqslant 1} \left((\mu_\phi(U_n) + \frac{\epsilon}{2^n}\right) < \sum_{n \geqslant 1} \mu_\phi(U_n) + \epsilon,$$

which implies $\mu_\phi(\bigcup_{n \geqslant 1} U_n) \leqslant \sum_{n \geqslant 1} \mu_\phi(U_n)$.

An outer measure on a set defines a class of subsets introduced next.

Definition 7.20. Let $\mu : \mathcal{P}(S) \longrightarrow \hat{\mathbb{R}}_{\geqslant 0}$ be an outer measure on S.

A subset T of S is μ-*measurable* if $\mu(H) = \mu(H \cap T) + \mu(H \cap \bar{T})$ for every set $H \in \mathcal{P}(S)$.

Lemma 7.5. *Let S be a set and let μ be an outer measure on a set S. A set T is μ-measurable if and only if*

$$\mu(H) \geqslant \mu(H \cap T) + \mu(H \cap \bar{T})$$

for every $H \in \mathcal{P}(S)$ such that $\mu(H) < \infty$.

Proof. The necessity of the condition is obvious. Suppose, therefore, that the condition is satisfied. Since μ is subadditive, we have

$$\mu(H) \leqslant \mu(H \cap T) + \mu(H \cap \bar{T}),$$

which implies $\mu(H) = \mu(H \cap T) + \mu(H \cap \bar{T})$. $\qquad\square$

Example 7.13. Let $\mu : \mathcal{P}(S) \longrightarrow \hat{\mathbb{R}}_{\geqslant 0}$ be an outer measure on S and let T be a subset of S such that $\mu(T) = 0$. The set T is μ-measurable.

Indeed, let $H \in \mathcal{P}(S)$. Since $H \cap T \subseteq T$ we have $\mu(H \cap T) \leqslant \mu(T) = 0$, so $\mu(H \cap T) = 0$. Also, $H \cap \bar{T} \subseteq H$, hence $\mu(H \cap \bar{T}) \leqslant \mu(H)$. This allows us to conclude that $\mu(H) \geqslant \mu(H \cap \bar{T}) + \mu(H \cap T)$, which implies that T is μ-measurable by Lemma 7.5.

It follows that the sets $\emptyset$ and S are μ-measurable for any outer measure μ. Also, for any outer measure μ on a set S, the measure space $(S, \mathcal{E}_\mu, \mu)$ is complete.

Theorem 7.34. *Let S be a set and let μ be an outer measure on S. If $\mu(U) = 0$, then U is μ-measurable.*

Proof. Let T be a subset of S. Since $T \cap U \subseteq U$, we have $\mu(T \cap U) \leqslant \mu(U) = 0$. Also, $T \cap \overline{U} \subseteq T$, hence $\mu(T) \geqslant \mu(T \cap olU) = \mu(T \cap olU) + \mu(T \cap U)$, hence U is measurable. □

Theorem 7.35. (Carathéodory Outer Measure Theorem) *Let μ be an outer measure on a set S. The collection of μ-measurable sets is a σ-algebra $\mathcal{E}_\mu$ on S. The restriction $m_\mu = \mu \restriction_{\mathcal{E}_\mu}$ to the σ-algebra $\mathcal{E}_\mu$ is a measure and $(S, \mathcal{E}_\mu, m_\mu)$ is a complete measure space.*

Proof. If U is a μ-subset we have $\mu(H) = \mu(H \cap U) + \mu(H \cap \overline{U})$. Since this inequality remains the same when we exchange U with $\overline{U}$, it follows that $\overline{U}$ is μ-measurable, so the collection of μ-measurable set is closed with respect to complementation.

Next, we show that the set of μ-measurable sets is closed with respect to finite unions. Let $T_1, \ldots, T_n$ be a sequence of μ-measurable sets. We prove, by induction on $n \in \mathbb{N}$ that $\bigcup_{j=1}^n T_j$ is μ-measurable.

The base step, $n = 0$, is immediate. Suppose that w is μ-measurable and let $H \in \mathcal{P}(S)$. By the inductive hypothesis we have:

$$\mu(H) = \mu\left(H \cap \bigcup_{j=1}^n T_j\right) + \mu\left(\overline{H \cap \bigcup_{j=1}^n T_j}\right)$$

$$= \mu\left(H \cap \bigcup_{j=1}^n T_j\right) + \mu\left(H \cap \bigcap_{j=1}^n \overline{T_j}\right)$$

for every $H \in \mathcal{P}(S)$. Substituting $H \cap T_{n+1}$ for H and $H \cap \overline{T_{n+1}}$ in the above equality yields

$$\mu(H \cap T_{n+1}) = \mu\left((H \cap T_{n+1}) \cap \bigcup_{j=1}^n T_j\right) + \mu\left((H \cap T_{n+1}) \cap \bigcap_{j=1}^n \overline{T_j}\right)$$

$$\mu(H \cap \overline{T_{n+1}}) = \mu\left((H \cap \overline{T_{n+1}}) \cap \bigcup_{j=1}^n T_j\right) + \mu\left((H \cap \overline{T_{n+1}}) \cap \bigcap_{j=1}^n \overline{T_j}\right).$$

Note that

$$(T_{n+1} \cap T_j) \cup (T_{n+1} \cap \overline{T_j}) \cup (\overline{T_{n+1}} \cap T_j) = T_{n+1} \cup T_j$$

for $1 \leqslant j \leqslant n$. Therefore,

$$H \cap \bigcup_{j=1}^{n+1} T_j = \left((H \cap T_{n+1}) \cap \bigcup_{j=1}^{n} T_j \right) \cup \left((H \cap T_{n+1}) \cap \bigcap_{j=1}^{n} \overline{T_j} \right)$$
$$\cup \left((H \cap \overline{T_{n+1}}) \cap \bigcup_{j=1}^{n} T_j \right),$$

hence

$$\mu \left(H \cup \bigcup_{j=1}^{n} T_j \right)$$
$$\leqslant \mu \left((H \cap T_{n+1}) \cap \bigcup_{j=1}^{n} T_j \right) + \mu \left((H \cap T_{n+1}) \cap \bigcap_{j=1}^{n} \overline{T_j} \right)$$
$$+ \mu \left((H \cap \overline{T_{n+1}}) \cap \bigcup_{j=1}^{n} T_j \right).$$

The measurability of T_{n+1} implies

$$\mu(H) = \mu(H \cap T_{n+1}) + \mu(H \cap \overline{T_{n+1}})$$
$$\geqslant \mu \left((H \cap T_{n+1}) \cap \bigcup_{j=1}^{n} T_j \right) + \mu \left((H \cap T_{n+1}) \cap \bigcap_{j=1}^{n} \overline{T_j} \right)$$
$$+ \mu \left((H \cap \overline{T_{n+1}}) \cap \bigcup_{j=1}^{n} T_j \right) + \mu \left((H \cap \overline{T_{n+1}}) \cap \bigcap_{j=1}^{n} \overline{T_j} \right)$$
$$\geqslant \mu \left(H \cup \bigcup_{j=1}^{n+1} T_j \right) + \mu \left(H \cap \overline{\bigcup_{j=1}^{n+1} T_j} \right),$$

which proves that $\bigcup_{j=1}^{n} T_j$ is μ-measurable for $n \in \mathbb{N}$.

Thus, the collection of μ-measurable sets is an algebra, and, therefore is also closed under finite intersections and set difference.

If U_0, U_1 are two disjoint μ-measurable sets, then

$$\mu(H \cap (U_0 \cup U_1)) = \mu(H \cap U_0) + \mu(H \cap U_1),$$

for every H. Again, an inductive argument allows us to show that if $T_0, \ldots, T_n$ are pairwise disjoint μ-measurable sets then

$$\mu \left(H \cap \bigcup_{i=0}^{n} U_i \right) = \sum_{i=0}^{n} \mu(H \cap U_i). \tag{7.7}$$

Define $W_n = \bigcup_{i=0}^{n} T_i$. We have seen that W_n is μ-measurable for every $n \in \mathbb{N}$. Thus, we have

$$\mu(H) = \mu(H \cap W_n) + \mu(H \cap \overline{W_n})$$

$$= \mu\left(H \cap \left(\bigcup_{i=0}^{n} T_i\right)\right) + \mu(H \cap \overline{W_n})$$

$$\geqslant \mu\left(H \cap \left(\bigcup_{i=0}^{n} T_i\right)\right) + \mu(H \cap \overline{W}),$$

where $W = \bigcup_{i \geqslant 0} T_i$. By equality (7.7) we have

$$\mu(H) \geqslant \sum_{i \geqslant 0}^{n} \mu(H \cap T_i) + \mu(H \cap \overline{W}), \tag{7.8}$$

for every $n \in \mathbb{N}$. Therefore,

$$\mu(H) \geqslant \sum_{i \geqslant 0}^{\infty} \mu(H \cap T_i) + \mu(H \cap \overline{W}),$$

hence $\mu(H) \geqslant \mu(H \cap W) + \mu(H \cap \overline{W})$. By Lemma 7.5, the set W is μ-measurable. Note also that we have shown that

$$\mu(H) = \sum_{i \geqslant 0}^{n} \mu(H \cap T_i) + \mu(H \cap \overline{W}) = \mu(H \cap W) + \mu(H \cap \overline{W}). \tag{7.9}$$

Suppose now that the sets $T_0, T_1, \ldots$ are not disjoint. Consider the sequence of pairwise disjoint sets $V_0, V_1, \ldots$ defined by:

$$V_0 = T_0,$$

$$V_n = T_n - \bigcup_{i=0}^{n-1} T_i,$$

for $n \geqslant 1$. The measurability of each set V_n is immediate and, by the previous argument, $\bigcup_{n \in \mathbb{N}} V_n$ is μ-measurable. Since $\bigcup_{n \in \mathbb{N}} V_n = \bigcup_{n \in \mathbb{N}} T_n$, it follows that $\bigcup_{n \in \mathbb{N}} T_n$ is μ-measurable. We conclude that the collection of μ-measurable sets is actually a σ-algebra.

Let $T_0, T_1, \ldots$ a sequence of sets in $\mathcal{E}_\mu$ that are pairwise disjoint. Choosing $H = W$ in equality (7.9) we have:

$$\mu(W) = \sum_{i \geqslant 0}^{n} \mu(T_i),$$

which proves that $m_\mu = \mu \restriction_{\mathcal{E}_\mu}$ is indeed a measure.

Let $W \in \mathcal{E}_\mu$ such that $m_\mu(W) = 0$ and let $U \subseteq W$. Note that $\mu(U) \leqslant \mu(W) = m_\mu(W) = 0$. For every $T \subseteq S$ we have $\mu(T \cap U) + \mu(T \cap \overline{U}) \leqslant \mu(U) + \mu(T) = \mu(T)$, so $U \in \mathcal{E}_\mu$, which shows that $(S, \mathcal{E}_\mu, m_\mu)$ is a complete measure space. $\qquad\square$

If μ_ϕ is the outer measure that is generated by a mapping $\phi : \mathcal{C} \longrightarrow \hat{\mathbb{R}}_{\geqslant 0}$ such that $\phi(\emptyset) = 0$ (as discussed in Example 7.12), we will denote by m_ϕ the measure m_{μ_ϕ}.

Corollary 7.16. *Let μ be an outer measure and let $U_0, U_1, \ldots$ be a sequence of μ-measurable sets. Then, both $\liminf U_n$ and $\limsup U_n$ are μ-measurable sets.*

Proof. This statement follows immediately from Theorems 7.35 and 7.52.

$\square$

Definition 7.21. Let μ_L be the Lebesgue outer measure on $\mathbb{R}$ introduced in Example 7.11.

A *Lebesgue measurable set* is a subset U of $\mathbb{R}$ that is μ_L-measurable.

Theorem 7.36. *Every Borel set $B \in \mathbb{B}(\hat{\mathbb{R}})$ is a Lebesgue measurable set.*

Proof. The argument is based on the fact that the σ-algebra of Borel sets of reals is generated by intervals of the form $(-\infty, b]$, as we saw in Theorem 7.5. It would suffice to show that each such interval is μ_L-measurable to show that $\mathbb{B}(\mathbb{R}) \subseteq \mathcal{E}_{\mu_L}$.

We need to prove that for every subset T of $\mathbb{R}$ such that $\mu_L(T)$ is finite we have:
$$\mu_L(T) \geqslant \mu_L(T \cap (-\infty, a]) + \mu_L(T \cap (a, \infty)).$$
Let $((a_n, b_n))_{n \geqslant 1}$ be a sequence of open interval such that $T \subseteq \bigcup_{n \geqslant 1}(a_n, b_n)$ and $\sum_{n \geqslant 1}(b_n - a_n) < \mu_L(T) + \epsilon$.

Observe that the sets $(a_n, b_n) \cap (-\infty, b]$ and $(a_n, b_n) \cap (b, \infty)$ are disjoint.

Define the intervals (s_n, t_n) and (u_n, v_n) such that the following conditions are satisfied:

(i) $(a_n, b_n) \cap (-\infty, a] \subseteq (s_n, t_n)$,

(ii) $(a_n, b_n) \cap (a, \infty) \subseteq (u_n, v_n)$, and

(iii) $t_n - s_n + v_n - u_n \leqslant b_n - a_n + \frac{\epsilon}{2^n}$.

Since
$$T \cap (-\infty, a] \subseteq \bigcup_{n \geqslant 1}(s_n, t_n),$$
$$T \cap (a, \infty) \subseteq \bigcup_{n \geqslant 1}(u_n, v_n),$$
it follows that
$$\mu_L(T \cap (-\infty, a]) \leqslant \sum_{n \geqslant 1}(t_n - s_n),$$
$$\mu_L(T \cap (a, \infty)) \leqslant \sum_{n \geqslant 1}(v_n - u_n).$$

Taking into account that

$$\sum_{n \geqslant 1} (t_n - s_n + v_n - u_n) \leqslant \sum_{n \geqslant 1} (b_n - a_n) + \epsilon,$$

it follows that

$$\mu_L(T \cap (-\infty, a]) + \mu_L(T \cap (a, \infty)) \leqslant \sum_{n \geqslant 1} (b_n - a_n) + \epsilon < \mu_L(T) + 2\epsilon.$$

Since this holds for every positive ϵ it follows that

$$\mu_L(T \cap (-\infty, a]) + \mu_L(T \cap (a, \infty)) \leqslant \mu_L(T),$$

so $(-\infty, a]$ is μ_L-measurable. □

Corollary 7.17. *Every open set and every closed set in $\mathbb{R}$ is measurable.*

Proof. Since $(-\infty, a] = \mathbb{R} - (a, \infty)$, each set $(-\infty, a]$ is measurable. In turn, this implies that $(-\infty, b) = \bigcup_{n \geqslant 1} (-\infty, b - 1/n]$ is measurable. Therefore, each open interval (a, b) is measurable because $(a, b) = (-\infty, b) \cap (a, \infty)$. Since each open set is a countable union of open intervals, it follows that open sets are measurable. □

We revisit the construction of an outer measure discussed in Example 7.12 to better relate the outer measure μ to the function $\phi : \mathcal{C} \longrightarrow \hat{\mathbb{R}}_{\geqslant 0}$ that generated the measure.

Example 7.12 shows that a premeasure on S induces an outer measure on S.

Theorem 7.37. *Let ϕ be a premeasure on an algebra $\mathcal{E}$ of subsets of a set S and let μ_ϕ is the outer measure defined by:*

$$\mu_\phi(U) = \inf \left\{ \sum_{j \geqslant 1} \phi(U_j) \mid U_j \in \mathcal{E} \text{ for } j \geqslant 1 \text{ and } U \subseteq \bigcup_{j \geqslant 1} U_j \right\}.$$

For every $T \in \mathcal{E}$ we have $\mu_\phi(T) = \phi(T)$ and every set in $\mathcal{E}$ is μ_ϕ-measurable.

Proof. Note that $\mu_\phi(T) \leqslant \phi(T)$ for all $T \in \mathcal{E}$ because $\{T\}$ is a cover for T.

Suppose $T \in \mathcal{E}$ and $T \subseteq \bigcup_{j \geqslant 1} U_j$. Let $\{V_j \mid j \geqslant 1\}$ be the collection of disjoint members of $\mathcal{E}$ defined by $V_j = T \cap (U_j - \bigcup_{k < j} U_k)$ for $j \geqslant 1$. Note that $T = \bigcup_{j \geqslant 1} V_j$. Thus, by the definition of premeasures

$$\phi(T) = \sum_{j \geqslant 1} \phi(V_j) \leqslant \sum_{j \geqslant 1} \phi(U_j),$$

hence $\phi(T) \leqslant \mu_\phi(T)$. This shows that if $T \in \mathcal{E}$ we have $\mu_\phi(T) = \phi(T)$.

To prove that each $T \in \mathcal{E}$ is μ_ϕ-measurable consider a subset H of S.

For $\epsilon > 0$ there exists a sequence $\{W_j \mid j \geqslant 1\}$ of sets in $\mathcal{E}$ such that $H \subset_{j \geqslant 1} W_j$ and $\sum_{j \geqslant 1} \phi(W_j) \leqslant \mu_\phi(H) + \epsilon$. The additivity of ϕ on $\mathcal{E}$ implies:

$$\mu_\phi(H) + \epsilon \geqslant \sum_{j \geqslant 1} \phi(W_j \cap T) + \sum_{j \geqslant 1} \phi(W_j \cap \overline{T})$$
$$\geqslant \mu_\phi(H \cap T) + \mu_\phi(H \cap \overline{T}), \tag{7.10}$$

because $\{W_j \cap T \mid j \geqslant 1\}$ is a cover of $H \cap T$ by sets in $\mathcal{E}$ and $\{W_j \cap \overline{T} \mid j \geqslant 1\}$ is a cover of $H \cap \overline{T}$ by sets in $\mathcal{E}$. Since inequality (7.10) holds for every positive ϵ we have $\mu_\phi(H) \geqslant \mu_\phi(H \cap T) + \mu_\phi(H \cap \overline{T})$, which implies that T is μ_ϕ-measurable. $\qquad\square$

Theorem 7.38. *Let ϕ be a premeasure defined on an algebra $\mathcal{E}$ and let $\mathcal{E}' = \boldsymbol{K}_{\sigma\text{-alg}}(\mathcal{E})$ be the σ-algebra generated by $\mathcal{E}$. There exists a measure m_ϕ on $\mathcal{E}'$ whose restriction to $\mathcal{E}$ equals ϕ, namely, the restriction of the outer measure μ_ϕ to $\mathcal{E}'$.*

Proof. This statement follows from Theorem 7.37. $\qquad\square$

Theorem 7.39. (Carathéodory Extension Theorem) *Let $\mathcal{E}$ be an algebra of subsets of a set S, $\mathcal{E}' = \boldsymbol{K}_{\sigma\text{-alg}}(\mathcal{E})$ be the σ-algebra generated by $\mathcal{E}$, ϕ be a premeasure on $\mathcal{E}$, and let m_ϕ be the measure on $\mathcal{E}'$ whose restriction to $\mathcal{E}$ equals ϕ.*

If $\tilde{m}$ is another measure on $\mathcal{E}'$ such that $\tilde{m}(T) = m_\phi(T)$ for $T \in \mathcal{E}$, then for all $U \in \mathcal{E}'$ we have $\tilde{m}(U) \leqslant m_\phi(U)$; also if $m_\phi(U)$ is finite, then $\tilde{m}(U) = m_\phi(U)$.

If there exists a countable cover of S, $\{U_j \mid j \geqslant 1, U_j \in \mathcal{E}$ and $m_\phi(U_j) < \infty\}$, then $\tilde{m}(U) \leqslant m_\phi(U)$ for all $U \in \mathcal{E}'$.

Proof. Let $T \in \mathcal{E}'$ such that $T \subseteq \bigcup_{j \geqslant 1} U_j$, where $U_j \in \mathcal{E}$. We have $\tilde{m}(T) \leqslant \sum_{j \geqslant 1} \tilde{m}(U_j) = \sum_{j \geqslant 1} \phi(U_j)$, which implies $\tilde{m}(T) \leqslant m_\phi(T)$ for every $T \in \mathcal{E}'$.

Let $T \in \mathcal{E}'$ with $m_\phi(T) < \infty$. There exists a cover of T, $\{U_j \mid j \geqslant 1\}$ such that $\sum_{j \geqslant 1} m_\phi(U_j) < m_\phi(T) + \epsilon$.

Define the increasing sequence of sets (W_n) by $W_n = \bigcup_{j=1}^{n} U_j$ and let $W = \bigcup_{n \geqslant 1} W_n$. We have $\tilde{m}(W) = \lim_{n \to \infty} \tilde{m}(W_n) = \lim_{n \to \infty} m_\phi(W_n) = m_\phi(W)$.

Suppose now that $T \in \mathcal{E}'$ and $m_\phi(T)$ is finite. Let ϵ be a positive number and let $\{U_j \mid j \geqslant 1\}$ be a cover of T such that $\sum_{j \geqslant 1} m_\phi(U_j) < m_\phi(T) + \epsilon$. This implies $m_\phi(W) \leqslant m_\phi(T) + \epsilon$, so $m_\phi(W - T) < \epsilon$, hence $\tilde{m}(W - T) < \epsilon$.

Since $\tilde{m}(W) = m_\phi(W)$, we have

$$m_\phi(T) \leqslant m_\phi(W) = \tilde{m}(W) = \tilde{m}(T) + \tilde{m}(W - T) \leqslant \tilde{m}(T) + \epsilon,$$

for every $\epsilon > 0$, hence $m_\phi(T) \leqslant \tilde{m}(T)$ because $m_\phi(T)$ is finite, hence $m_\phi(T) = \tilde{m}(T)$.

If $\{U_j \mid U_j \in \mathcal{E}, j \geqslant 1$ and $m_\phi(U_j) < \infty\}$, we may assume that the collection $\{U_1, U_2, \ldots\}$ is a partition of S. If $T \in \mathcal{E}'$, T can be written as the disjoint union $T = \bigcup_{j \geqslant 1} T \cap U_j$. Since $m_\phi(U_j) = \tilde{m}(U_j)$, then $m_\phi(T) = \tilde{m}(T)$. $\square$

Definition 7.22. An outer measure on a set S is *regular* if given any subset T of S, there exists a μ-measurable set U such that $T \subseteq U$ and $\mu(T) = \mu(U)$.

The regularity of an outer measure ensures that it is possible to determine the outer measure of any subset T of S by considering only the subsets in $\mathcal{E}_\mu$.

Theorem 7.40. *Let S be a set and let $(S_0, S_1, \ldots)$ a sequence of subsets of S. If μ is a regular outer measure on S, then*

$$\mu\left(\liminf_n S_n\right) \leqslant \liminf_n \mu(S_n).$$

Proof. Since μ is regular, for each $n \in \mathbb{N}$ there exists a μ-measurable set U_n such that $S_n \subseteq U_n$ and $\mu(S_n) = \mu(U_n)$. Then, $\liminf_n \mu(S_n) \liminf_n \mu(U_n)$. Since $\liminf_n \mu(U_n)$ is measurable (by Corollary 7.16) we have:

$$\mu\left(\liminf_n S_n\right) \leqslant \mu\left(\liminf_n U_n\right) \leqslant \liminf_n \mu(U_n) = \liminf_n \mu(S_n)). \quad \square$$

Corollary 7.18. *Let μ be an outer measure on a set S. If $\mathbf{S} = (S_0, S_1, \ldots)$ is an expanding sequence of subsets of S, then $\mu(\lim_n S_n) = \lim_n \mu(S_n)$.*

Proof. Since $\mathbf{S}$ is an expanding sequence $\lim_n S_n = \bigcup_n S_n$, so $\mu(\lim_n S_n) \geqslant \mu(S_n)$ for $n \in \mathbb{N}$, so $\mu(\lim_n S_n) \geqslant \lim_n \mu(S_n)$. On the other hand, Theorem 7.40 implies $\mu(\lim S_n) \leqslant \lim \mu(S_n)$, which gives the desired equality. $\square$

For finite regular outer measures the measurability condition can be simplified as shown next.

Theorem 7.41. *Let μ a regular outer measure on a set S such that $\mu(S)$ is finite. A subset T of S is measurable if and only if $\mu(S) = \mu(T) + \mu(\overline{T})$, where $\overline{T} = S - T$.*

Proof. The condition is clearly necessary. To prove its sufficiency, let T be a subset of S such that $\mu(S) = \mu(T) + \mu(\overline{T})$. By Lemma 7.5, to prove that T is measurable it suffices to show that if H is a set with $\mu(H) < \infty$, then $\mu(H) \geqslant \mu(H \cap T) + \mu(H \cap \overline{T})$.

The regularity of μ implies the existence of a μ-measurable set K such that $H \subseteq K$ and $\mu(H) = \mu(K)$. Since K is measurable, we have

$$\mu(H) = \mu(H \cap K) + \mu(H \cap \overline{K}),$$
$$\mu(\overline{H}) = \mu(\overline{H} \cap K) + \mu(\overline{H} \cap \overline{K}).$$

This implies

$$\mu(S) = \mu(T) + \mu(\overline{T})$$
$$= \mu(T \cap K) + \mu(T \cap \overline{K}) + \mu(\overline{T} \cap K) + \mu(\overline{T} \cap \overline{K})$$
$$\geqslant \mu(K) + \mu(\overline{K}) = \mu(S).$$

Thus,

$$\mu(T \cap K) + \mu(T \cap \overline{K}) + \mu(\overline{T} \cap K) + \mu(\overline{T} \cap \overline{K}) = \mu(K) + \mu(\overline{K}) = \mu(S).$$

Since $\mu(\overline{K}) \leqslant \mu(T \cap \overline{K}) + \mu(\overline{T} \cap \overline{K})$, it follows that $\mu(K \cap T) + \mu(K \cap \overline{T}) \leqslant \mu(K)$. Since $H \cap T \subseteq K \cap T$ and $H \cap \overline{T} \subseteq K \cap \overline{T}$, we have $\mu(H \cap T) + \mu(H \cap \overline{T}) \leqslant \mu(K) = \mu(H)$, which shows that T is indeed, μ-measurable. $\square$

7.7 The Lebesgue Measure on $\mathbb{R}^n$

Let $K = [a_1, b_1] \times \cdots \times [a_n, b_n]$ be a closed interval of $\hat{\mathbb{R}}^n$, $I = (a_1, b_1) \times \cdots \times (a_n, b_n)$, an open interval, $G = (a_1, b_1] \times \cdots \times (a_n, b_n]$ an open-closed interval, and $H = [a_1, b_1) \times \cdots \times [a_n, b_n)$ a closed-open interval of $\mathbb{R}^n$, where $a_1, \ldots, a_n, b_1, \ldots, b_n \in \hat{\mathbb{R}}$.

The collections of closed, open, open-closed and closed-open intervals of $\mathbb{R}^n$ are denoted by $\mathcal{K}_n, \mathcal{I}_n, \mathcal{G}_n$ and $\mathcal{H}_n$, respectively.

If U is any of the above intervals its *volume* is:

$$vol(U) = \prod_{j=1}^{n} (b_j - a_j).$$

Theorem 7.42. *The set $\mathcal{E}$ of finite unions of disjoint open-closed intervals is an algebra of sets.*

Proof. Let $G = (a_1, b_1] \times \cdots \times (a_n, b_n]$ and $G' = (a_1', b_1'] \times \cdots \times (a_n', b_n']$ be two open-closed intervals in $\hat{\mathbb{R}}^n$.

We begin by showing that $\mathcal{E}$ is closed with respect to finite intersections. We have $G \cap G' = \emptyset$ if there exists j, $1 \leqslant j \leqslant n$ such that $(a_n, b_n] \cap (a'_n, b'_n] = \emptyset$. In this case, $G \cap G' \in \mathcal{E}$.

Suppose now that $G \cap G' \neq \emptyset$. We have $(a_j, b_j] \cap (a'_j \cap b_j] \neq \emptyset$ for $1 \leqslant j \leqslant n$, which is possible if and only if $\max\{a_j, a'_j\} \leqslant \min\{b_j, b'_j\}$; in this case $(a_j, b_j] \cap (a'_j \cap b_j] = (\max\{a_j, a'_j\}, \min\{b_j, b'_j\}]$ and

$$G \cap G' = \prod_{j=1}^{n} (\max\{a_j, a'_j\}, \min\{b_j, b'_j\}],$$

so $\mathcal{E}$ is closed with respect to finite intersections.

To show that $\mathcal{E}$ is closed with respect to complements consider an open-closed interval $G = (a_1, b_1] \times \cdots \times (a_n, b_n]$. Note that $\hat{\mathbb{R}} - (a_j, b_j] = (-\infty, a_j) \cup (b_j, \infty]$. By applying the second equality of Supplement 7 of Chapter 1 we have:

$$\hat{\mathbb{R}}^n - ((a_1, b_1] \times (a_2, b_2] \times \cdots \times (a_n, b_n])$$
$$= ((\hat{\mathbb{R}} - (a_1, b_1]) \times \hat{\mathbb{R}}^{n-1})$$
$$\cup ((a_1, b_1] \times (\hat{\mathbb{R}} - (a_2, b_2]) \times \hat{\mathbb{R}}^{n-2})$$
$$\cup ((a_1, b_1] \times \cdots \times (a_{k-1}, b_{k-1}] \times (\hat{\mathbb{R}} - (a_k, b_k]) \times \hat{\mathbb{R}}^{n-k})$$
$$\cup ((a_1, b_1] \times (a_2, b_2] \times \cdots \times (a_{n-1}, b_{n-1}] \times (\hat{\mathbb{R}} - (a_n, b_n])).$$

Since $\hat{\mathbb{R}} - (a_j, b_j] = (-\infty, a] \cup (b_j, \infty]$ for $1 \leqslant j \leqslant n$, by applying the distributivity of set product with respect to union it follows that the complement of G, $\hat{\mathbb{R}}^n - ((a_1, b_1] \times (a_2, b_2] \times \cdots \times (a_n, b_n])$ is an union of open-closed intervals, so it belongs to $\mathcal{E}$.

If $E \in \mathcal{E}$ is the union of disjoint open-closed intervals in $\mathcal{G}_n$, $E = G_1 \cup \cdots \cup G_m$. Then $\overline{E} = \bigcap_{j=1}^{m} \overline{G_j}$. Each complement $\overline{G_j}$ belongs to $\mathcal{E}$ as we saw above, and since $\mathcal{E}$ is closed with respect to finite intersections, $\overline{E} \in \mathcal{E}$ so $\mathcal{E}$ is closed with respect to complementation.

Finally, since $\mathcal{E}$ is closed with respect to finite intersection and complementation, it follows that $\mathcal{E}$ is closed with respect to finite unions, so it is an algebra of sets. $\square$

Corollary 7.19. *If $G, G_1, \ldots, G_m$ are pairwise disjoint open-closed intervals, there exist pairwise disjoint open-closed intervals $G'_1, \ldots, G'_q$ such that $G - \bigcup_{j=1}^{m} G_j = G'_1 \cup \cdots \cup G'_q$.*

Proof. This follows from the fact that an algebra of sets is closed with respect to set difference. $\square$

Corollary 7.20. *If $G_1, \ldots, G_m$ are open-closed intervals then there exist pairwise disjoint open-closed intervals $G'_1, \ldots, G'_q$ such that $G_1 \cup \cdots \cup G_m = G'_1 \cup \cdots \cup G'_q$.*

Proof. Let $\mathcal{E}$ be the algebra of finite unions of disjoint open-closed intervals in $\hat{\mathbb{R}}^n$. Consider the sequence of open-closed interval $(G_1, \ldots, G_m)$. We have shown that the complement $\overline{G_j}$ of any of these intervals belongs to $\mathcal{E}$.

For each $x \in \bigcup_{j=1}^n$ there is a least j such that $x \in G_j$. Thus, $x \in G'_j$, where $G'_j = G_j \cap \overline{G_1} \cup \cdots \cup \overline{G_{j-1}})$. Note that if $j \neq k$, then $G'_j \cap C_k = \emptyset$, the sets $G'_1, G'_2, \ldots, G'_m$ belong to $\mathcal{E}$, and that $G_1 \cup \cdots \cup G_m = G'_1 \cup \cdots \cup G'_q$. $\qquad \square$

Lemma 7.6. *Let $G \in \mathcal{G}_n$ be a closed-open interval, $G = (a_1, b_1] \times \cdots \times (a_n, b_n]$. Suppose that for each interval $(a_j, b_j]$ there is a subdivision $\Delta_j = \{a_j^0, a_j^1, \ldots, a_j^{m_j}\}$ such that $a_j = a_j^0 < a_j^1 < \cdots < a_j^{m_j} = b_j$. Let $G^{i_1 i_2 \cdots i_n}$ be the open-closed interval given by*
$$G^{i_1 i_2 \cdots i_n} = (a_1^{i_1-1}, a_1^{i_1}] \times \cdots \times (a_n^{i_n-1}, a_n^{i_n}].$$
Then,
$$vol(G) = \sum \{vol(G^{i_1 i_2 \cdots i_n}) \mid 1 \leqslant i_1 \leqslant m_1, \ldots, 1 \leqslant i_n \leqslant m_n\}.$$

Proof. Note that
$$\sum \{vol(G^{i_1 i_2 \cdots i_n}) \mid 1 \leqslant i_1 \leqslant m_1, \ldots, 1 \leqslant i_n \leqslant m_n\}$$
$$= \sum \{(a_1^{i_1} - a_1^{i_1-1}) \cdots (a_n^{i_n} - a_n^{i_n-1}) \mid 1 \leqslant i_1 \leqslant m_1, \ldots, 1 \leqslant i_n \leqslant m_n\}$$
$$= \sum \{(a_1^{i_1} - a_1^{i_1-1}) \mid 1 \leqslant i_1 \leqslant m_1\} \cdots \sum \{(a_n^{i_n} - a_n^{i_n-1}) \mid 1 \leqslant i_1 \leqslant m_1\}$$
(by the distributivity property)
$$= (b_1 - a_1) \cdots (b_n - a_n) = vol(G),$$
which concludes the argument. $\qquad \square$

Theorem 7.43. *Let $G = (a_1, b_1] \times \cdots \times (a_n, b_n]$. If $\pi = \{G_1, \ldots, G_\ell\}$ is a partition of G that consists of open-closed intervals in $\mathcal{G}_n$, then $vol(G) = \sum_{k=1}^{\ell} vol(G_k)$.*

Proof. The idea of the proof is to show that both G and each of the sets $G_1, \ldots, G_\ell$ can be decomposed into a union of pairwise open-closed intervals.

Let $p_j : \mathbb{R}^n \longrightarrow \mathbb{R}$ be the jth projection defined by $p_j(\mathbf{x}) = x_j$ for $\mathbf{x} \in \mathbb{R}^n$, where $1 \leqslant j \leqslant n$. Consider the partition
$$\pi_j = \{(a_j^0, a_j^1], \ldots, (a_j^{m_j-1}, a_j^{m_j}]\},$$

of the interval $(a_j, b_j]$ generated by the collection $\{p_j(G_1), \ldots, p_j(G_\ell)\}$ as defined in Supplement 6 of Chapter 1. We have $a_j^0 = a_j$ and $a_j^{m_j} = b_j$.

Each set $p_j(G_k)$ is π_j-saturated, that is, each set $p_j(G_k)$ is an union of a collection $\mathcal{G}_{kj}$ of r_{jk} one-dimensional open-closed intervals G_{jk}^h, where $1 \leqslant h \leqslant r_{jk}$,

$$p_j(G_k) = \bigcup_{h=1}^{r_{jk}} G_{jk}^h.$$

Therefore, by Lemma 7.6, we have

$$G_k = \prod_{j=1}^n p_j(G_k) = \prod_{j=1}^n \bigcup_{h=1}^{r_{jk}} G_{jk}^h$$

for $1 \leqslant j \leqslant$. Thus, we have

$$G = \bigcup_{k=1}^\ell G_k = \bigcup_{k=1}^\ell \prod_{j=1}^n \bigcup_{h=1}^{r_{jk}} G_{jk}^h$$

and the intervals G_{jk}^h are pairwise disjoint. An application of Lemma 7.6 leads to the desired conclusion.   □

Theorem 7.44. *Let $G_1, \ldots, G_m$ be m pairwise disjoint open-closed intervals in $\hat{\mathbb{R}}^n$. If $\bigcup_{j=1}^m G_j \subseteq G$, where G is an open-closed interval in $\hat{\mathbb{R}}^n$, then $vol(G_1) + \cdots + vol(G_n) \leqslant vol(G)$.*

Proof.   By Theorem 7.42, $G_1 \cup \cdots \cup G_m$ belongs to the algebra $\mathcal{E}$ of unions of families of disjoint open-closed intervals. Therefore, $G - \bigcup_{j=1}^m G_j$ belongs to the same algebra and, thus it can be written as a union of disjoint open-closed intervals $G_1', \ldots, G_p'$. Thus, $G = G_1 \cup \cdots \cup G_m \cup G_1' \cup \cdots \cup G_p'$, hence $vol(G) = \sum_{j=1}^m vol(G_j) + \sum_{k=1}^p vol(G_k')$, by Theorem 7.43. Thus, $\sum_{j=1}^m vol(G_j) \leqslant vol(G)$.   □

Theorem 7.45. *Let $G_1, \ldots, G_m$ be m open-closed intervals in $\hat{\mathbb{R}}^n$. If $G \subseteq \bigcup_{j=1}^m G_j$, where G is an open-closed interval in $\hat{\mathbb{R}}^n$, then $vol(G) \leqslant vol(G_1) + \cdots + vol(G_n)$.*

Proof.   Since $G \subseteq \bigcup_{j=1}^m G_j$, we have $G = \bigcup_{j=1}^m G_j'$, where $G_j' = G \cap G_j$ are open-closed intervals. G can be written as a union of disjoint members of the algebra $\mathcal{E}$ of unions of disjoint open-closed intervals:

$$G = G_1' \cup (G_2' - G_1') \cup \cdots \cup \left(G_m' - \bigcup_{j=1}^{m-1} G_j' \right).$$

Thus,

$$vol(G) = vol(G_1') + vol(G_2' - G_1') + \cdots + vol\left(G_m' - \bigcup_{j=1}^{m-1} G_j'\right)$$

$$\leqslant \sum_{j=1}^{m} vol(G_j).$$

$\square$

Theorem 7.46. *Let $I_1, \ldots, I_m$ be m open intervals in $\hat{\mathbb{R}}^n$, where $I_j = (c_{j1}, d_{j1}) \times (c_{jn}, d_{jn})$ for $1 \leqslant j \leqslant m$. If $K = [a_1, b_1] \times \cdots \times [a_n, b_n]$ is a closed interval in $\hat{\mathbb{R}}^n$ such that $K \subseteq \bigcup_{j=1}^{m} I_j$, then $vol(K) \leqslant vol(I_1) + \cdots + vol(I_m)$.*

Proof. Consider the open-closed intervals $G = (a_1, b_1] \times \cdots \times (a_n, b_n]$ and $G_j = (c_{j1}, d_{j1}] \times (c_{jn}, d_{jn}]$ for $1 \leqslant j \leqslant m$. We have:

$$G \subseteq K \subseteq I_1 \cup \cdots \cup I_m \subseteq G_1 \cup \cdots \cup G_m,$$

hence

$$vol(K) = vol(G) \leqslant vol(G_1) + \cdots + vol(G_m)$$
$$\text{(by Theorem 7.45)}$$
$$= vol(I_1) + \cdots + vol(I_m).$$

$\square$

Theorem 7.37 allows the introduction of an outer measure on $\mathbb{R}^n$ as

$$\mu_n(U) = \inf\left\{\sum_{j \geqslant 1} vol(I_j) \mid I_j \in \mathcal{I}(\mathbb{R}^n) \text{ for } j \geqslant 1 \text{ and } U \subseteq \bigcup_{j \geqslant 1} I_j\right\}$$

for $U \subseteq \mathbb{R}^n$. The collection $\mathcal{E}_{\mu_n}$ of μ_n-measurable sets defines a complete measure space $(\mathbb{R}^n, \mathcal{E}_{\mu_n}, m_{\mu_n})$.

Definition 7.23. The collection $\mathcal{E}_{\mu_n}$ is the σ-algebra $\mathbb{L}_n$ of *Lebesgue measurable sets* in $\mathbb{R}^n$ and m_{μ_n} is the *n-dimensional Lebesgue measure* on $\mathbb{R}^n$.

Since the dimension of the ambient space $\mathbb{R}^n$ is usually clear from context, we use the notation m_L for the n-dimensional Lebesgue measure m_{μ_n}.

Theorem 7.47. *For every type of interval U (open, closed, open-closed, or closed-open) we have $m_L(U) = vol(U)$; also, each interval is a m_L-measurable set.*

Proof. Let K be a closed interval, $K = [a_1, b_1] \times \cdots \times [a_n, b_n]$. For every $\epsilon > 0$ we have;

$$K \subseteq (a_1 - \epsilon, b_1 + \epsilon) \times \cdots \times (a_n - \epsilon, b_n + \epsilon).$$

Therefore, by the definition of μ_n we have:

$$\mu_n(K) \leqslant vol((a_1 - \epsilon, b_1 + \epsilon) \times \cdots \times (a_n - \epsilon, b_n + \epsilon)) = \prod_{j=1}^{n}(b_j - a_j + 2\epsilon)$$

for every $\epsilon > 0$. Therefore, $\mu_n(K) \leqslant vol(K)$.

Let $\{I_j \mid j \in J\}$ be a cover of K by open intervals. Since K is compact, there exists a finite subcollection of this collection of open intervals such that $K \subseteq I_{j_1} \cup \cdots \cup I_{j_k}$, hence

$$vol(K) \leqslant vol(I_{j_1}) + \cdots + vol(I_{j_k})$$
$$\leqslant \sum_{j \in J} vol(I_j).$$

This implies $vol(K) \leqslant \mu_n(K)$ (since $\mu_n(K)$ was defined as an infimum). Therefore, $vol(K) = \mu_n(K)$.

Let W be an interval delimited by $a_1, b_1, \ldots, a_n, b_n$ and let K_1, K_2 be

$$K_1^\epsilon = [a_1 - \epsilon, b_1 + \epsilon] \times \cdots \times [a_n - \epsilon, b_n + \epsilon],$$
$$K_2^\epsilon = [a_1 + \epsilon, b_1 - \epsilon] \times \cdots \times [a_n + \epsilon, b_n - \epsilon].$$

Since $K_2^\epsilon \subseteq W \subseteq K_1^\epsilon$, it follows that $\mu_n(K_2^\epsilon) \leqslant \mu_n(W) \leqslant \mu_n(K_1^\epsilon)$ for every $\epsilon > 0$. Thus, $\mu_n(W) = vol(W)$.

Next, we show that every open-closed interval $G = (a_1, b_1] \times \cdots \times (a_n, b_n]$ is μ_n-measurable.

Let $I = (c_1, d_1) \times \cdots \times (c_n, d_n)$ and let $G_I = (c_1, d_1] \times \cdots \times (c_n, d_n]$. Then, $\mu_n(G \cap I) \leqslant \mu_n(G \cap G_I) = vol(G \cap G_I)$ and $\mu_n(\overline{G} \cap I) \leqslant \mu_n(\overline{G} \cap G_I)$.

By Corollary 7.19 we have

$$G_I \cap \overline{G} = G_I - G = G_1' \cup \cdots \cup G_k'$$

for some pairwise disjoint open-closed intervals $G_1', \ldots, G_k'$. This implies

$$\mu_n(I \cup \overline{G}) \leqslant \mu_n(G_1') + \cdots + \mu_n(G_k')$$
$$= vol(G_1') + \cdots + vol(G_k') = vol(G_I) = vol(I).$$

We may conclude that $\mu_n(I \cap G) + \mu_n(I \cap \overline{G}) \leqslant vol(I)$.

Let E be a subset of $\hat{\mathbb{R}}^n$ with $\mu_n(E) < \infty$. Consider a cover of E that consists of open intervals, $E \subseteq \bigcup_{j \geqslant 1} I_j$ such that $\sum_{j \geqslant 1} vol(I_j) < \mu_n(E) + \epsilon$. If G is an open-closed interval, then

$$\mu_n(E \cap G) + \mu_n(E \cap \overline{G})$$
$$\leqslant \sum_{j \geqslant 1} \mu_n(I_j \cap G) + \sum_{j \geqslant 1} \mu_n(I_j \cap \overline{G})$$
$$= \sum_{j \geqslant 1} (\mu_n(I_j \cap G) + \mu_n(I_j \cap \overline{G})) \leqslant \sum_{j \geqslant 1} vol(I_j) < \mu_n(E) + \epsilon.$$

Therefore, $\mu_n(E \cap G) + \mu_n(E \cap \overline{G}) \leqslant \mu_n(E)$, hence G is μ_n-measurable, that is, $G \in \mathbb{L}_n$.

For any interval V that has an edge that consists of a single point we have $\mu_n(V) = 0$ and, therefore, by the completeness of μ_n, V is a Lebesgue measurable set. Since every open, closed, or closed-open interval differs from an open-closed interval G with the same sides by finitely many intervals of measure 0, any such interval is also a Lebesgue measurable set.

□

The Lebesgue measure m_L on $\hat{\mathbb{R}}^n$ is σ-finite because $\hat{\mathbb{R}}^n = \bigcup_{k=1}^{n} [-k, k]^n$ and $m_L([-k, k]^n) = \mu_n([-k, k]^n) = vol([-k, k]^n) = (2k)^n$ for $k \in \mathbb{N}$ and $k \leqslant 1$. On the other hand, $m_L(\hat{\mathbb{R}}^n)$ is not finite.

Theorem 7.48. *Every Borel set in $\mathbb{R}^n$ is a Lebesgue measurable set.*

Proof. This follows from the fact that $\mathbb{B}(\hat{\mathbb{R}}^n)$ is generated by the set of intervals and each interval is a Lebesgue measurable set. □

The next two theorems offer characterizations of μ_n-measurable sets relative to certain topologically defined subsets of $\hat{\mathbb{R}}^n$.

Theorem 7.49. *Let $(\hat{\mathbb{R}}^n, \mathcal{O})$ be the usual topological space on $\hat{\mathbb{R}}^n$. A subset U of $\hat{\mathbb{R}}^n$ is Lebesgue measurable if and only if there exists $A \in \mathcal{O}_\delta$ such that $U \subseteq A$ and $\mu_n(A - U) = 0$.*

Proof. Suppose that there exists $A \in \mathcal{O}_\delta$ such that $U \subseteq A$ and $\mu_n(A - U) = 0$. By the completeness of m_L the set $A - U$ is Lebesgue measurable and, therefore $U = A - (A - U)$ is Lebesgue measurable.

Conversely, suppose that U is Lebesgue measurable. There exists a sequence $(V_1, V_2, \ldots)$ of Lebesgue measurable sets such that $\mu_n(V_j) < \infty$ and $\hat{\mathbb{R}}^n = \bigcup_{j \geqslant 1} V_j$. Therefore, $U = \bigcup_{j \geqslant 1} (U \cap V_j)$ and $\mu_n(U \cap V_j) < \infty$ for $j \geqslant 1$.

The definition of μ_n as an infimum implies a collection of open intervals $I_j^{k,l}$ such that $U_k \subseteq \bigcup_{j \geqslant 1} I_j^{(k,l)}$ and $\sum_{j \geqslant 1} vol(I_j^{(k,l)}) \leqslant \mu_n(U_k) + \frac{1}{2^k l}$.

Let $W^{(k,l)} = \bigcup_{j \geqslant 1} I_j^{(k,l)}$. Then, $U_k \subseteq W^{k,l}$ and $\mu_n(W^{(k,l)}) \leqslant \mu_n(U_k) + \frac{1}{2^k l}$. Therefore, $\mu_n(W^{(k,l)} - U_k) < \frac{1}{l 2^k}$. If $Z^{(l)} = \bigcup_{k \geqslant 1} W^{(k,l)}$, then $Z^{(l)}$ is open, $U \subseteq Z^{(l)}$, and $Z^{(l)} - U \subseteq \bigcup_{k \geqslant 1} (W^{(k,l)} - U_k)$. This implies

$$\mu_n(Z^{(l)} - U) \leqslant \sum_{k \geqslant 1} \mu_n(W^{(k,l)} - U_k) < \sum_{k \geqslant 1} \frac{1}{l 2^k} = \frac{1}{l}.$$

If $A = \bigcap_{l \geqslant 1} Z^{(l)}$, we have $U \subseteq A$ and $\mu_n(A - U) \leqslant \mu_n(Z^{(l)} - U) < \frac{1}{l}$ for every $l \geqslant 1$, hence $\mu_n(A - U) = 0$. □

Theorem 7.50. *Let* $(\hat{\mathbb{R}}^n, \mathcal{O})$ *be the usual topological space on* $\hat{\mathbb{R}}^n$. *A subset* U *of* $\hat{\mathbb{R}}^n$ *is Lebesgue measurable if and only if there exists* $C \in COMP(\hat{\mathbb{R}}^n, \mathcal{O})_\sigma$ *such that* $C \subseteq U$ *and* $\mu_n(U - C) = 0$.

Proof. Suppose that B is a union of compact sets such that $B \subseteq U$ and $\mu_n(U - B) = 0$. The completeness of m_L implies that $U - B$ is Lebesgue measurable. Since $U = B \cup (U - B)$, it follows that U is Lebesgue measurable.

Conversely, suppose that U is Lebesgue measurable. Since $\overline{U}$ is Lebesgue measurable, by Theorem 7.48 there exists $A \in \mathcal{O}_\delta$ such that $\overline{U} \subseteq A$ and $\mu_n(A - \overline{U}) = 0$. The set $C = \overline{A}$ is a countable union of closed sets, $C = \bigcup_{j \geqslant 1} T_j$. The sets $T_{j,k} = T_j \cap [-k, k]^n$ are compact because they are closed and bounded and $C = \bigcup_{j \geqslant 1} \bigcup_{k \geqslant 1} T_{j,k}$ belongs to $COMP(\hat{\mathbb{R}}^n, \mathcal{O})_\sigma$. ☐

Corollary 7.21. *Every Lebesgue set in* $\hat{\mathbb{R}}^n$ *is almost equal to a Borel set.*

Proof. This follows from Theorems 7.48 and 7.49. ☐

Theorem 7.51. *If* $m : \mathbb{B}(\hat{\mathbb{R}}^n) \longrightarrow \hat{\mathbb{R}}_{\geqslant 0}$ *is a measure such that* $m(G) = \mathrm{vol}(G)$ *for every open-closed interval* G, *then* $m = m_L$.

Proof. Let G is an unbounded open-closed interval and let $(G_1, G_2, \ldots)$ be an increasing sequence of bounded open-closed intervals such that $\bigcup_{j \geqslant 1} G_j = G$. Since $\lim_{n \to \infty} m(G_i) = m(G)$, it follows that $m(G) = \infty$.

If $G_1, \ldots, G_m$ are pairwise disjoint open-closed intervals we have

$$m \left(\bigcup_{j=1}^m G_j \right) = \sum_{j=1}^m m(G_j) = \sum_{j=1}^m m_L(G_j) = m_L \left(\bigcup_{j=1}^m G_j \right),$$

hence m and m_L are equal on the algebra that consists of unions of pairwise disjoint open-closed intervals. Since these unions generate the σ-algebra of Borel sets, we have $m = m_L$. ☐

Theorem 7.52. *The measure space* $(\hat{\mathbb{R}}^n, \mathbb{L}_n, m_L)$ *is the completion of the measure space* $(\hat{\mathbb{R}}^n, \mathbb{B}(\hat{\mathbb{R}}^n), m_L)$.

Proof. Since every Borel subset of $\mathbb{R}^n$ is a Lebesgue measurable set we have $\mathbb{B}(\hat{\mathbb{R}}^n) \subseteq \mathbb{L}_n$.

Let U be a Lebesgue measurable set. By Theorem 7.49 there exists an $A \in \mathcal{O}_\delta \subseteq \mathbb{B}(\hat{\mathbb{R}}^n)$ such that $U \subseteq A$ and $\mu_n(A - U) = 0$. Note that A is a Borel set.

By Theorem 7.49 there exists $C \in COMP(\hat{\mathbb{R}}^n, \mathcal{O})_\sigma$ such that $C \subseteq U$ and $\mu_n(U - C) = 0$ and, again C is a Borel set.

Note that $m(A - C) \leqslant m(A - U) + m(U - C) = 0$, so $m(A - C) = 0$, which shows that $\mathbb{L}_n$ is indeed the completion of $\mathbb{B}(\hat{\mathbb{R}}^n)$. $\qquad\square$

Next we examine the behavior of the Lebesgue measures on $\hat{\mathbb{R}}^n$ with respect to linear and affine transformations.

Note that a translation $h_{\mathbf{x}}$ of $\hat{\mathbb{R}}^n$ transforms every interval (open, closed, open-closed, or closed-open) into an interval of the same nature with the same volume.

A homothety h_a transforms any interval into an interval of the same nature; the volume this time changes. Indeed, let $G = (a_1, b_1] \times (a_n, b_n]$ be an open-closed interval. Since

$$\mathsf{h}_a(G) = (aa_1, ab_1] \times (aa_n, ab_n],$$

we have $vol(\mathsf{h}_a(G)) = a^n vol(G)$. This is the *homogeneity property of volume.*

The image of G under reflection is a closed open interval

$$\mathsf{r}(G) = [-b_1, -a_1) \times \cdots [-b_n, a_n)$$

and $vol(\mathsf{r}(G)) = vol(G)$.

We conclude that the volumes of intervals in $\hat{\mathbb{R}}^n$ are invariant under translations and reflections; with respect to homotheties, the volume is a homogenous function of degree n.

Theorem 7.53. *The set $\mathbb{L}_n$ of Lebesgue measurable sets in $\hat{\mathbb{R}}^n$ is closed with respect to translations, reflections and homotheties. Furthermore, $m_L(t_{\boldsymbol{x}}(U)) = m_L(U)$, $m_L(\mathsf{s}(U)) = m_L(U)$, and $\mu_L(\mathsf{h}_a(U)) = a^n m_(U)$ for every Lebesgue measurable set U, $\boldsymbol{x} \in \mathbb{R}^n$ and $a > 0$.*

Proof. Let U be a subset of $\hat{\mathbb{R}}^n$ and let $\{I_1, I_2, \ldots\}$ be a collection of open intervals such that $U \subseteq \bigcup_{j \geqslant 1} I_j$. It follows that

$$t_{\mathbf{x}}(U) \subseteq \bigcup_{j \geqslant 1} t_{\mathbf{x}}(I_j),$$

hence

$$\mu_n(t_{\mathbf{x}}(U)) \leqslant \sum_{j \geqslant 1} vol(t_{\mathbf{x}}(I_j)) = \sum_{j \geqslant 1} vol(I_j),$$

hence $\mu_n(t_{\mathbf{x}}(U)) \leqslant \mu_n(U)$. Therefore, $\mu_n(U) = \mu_n(t_{-\mathbf{x}}(t_{\mathbf{x}}(U))) \leqslant \mu_n(t_{\mathbf{x}}(U))$, which implies $\mu_n(t_{\mathbf{x}}(U)) = \mu_n(U)$.

Since $r(U) \subseteq \bigcup_{j \geqslant 1} r(I_j)$, we have $\mu_n(r(U)) \leqslant \sum_{j \geqslant 1} vol(r(I_j)) = \sum_{j \geqslant 1} vol(I_j)$, which implies $\mu_n(r(U)) \leqslant \mu_n(U)$. By replacing U with $r(U)$ in the last inequality we obtain $\mu_n(U) \leqslant \mu_n(r(U))$, so $\mu_n(U) = \mu_n(r(U))$.

Since $h_a(U) \subseteq \bigcup_{j \geqslant 1} h_a(I_j)$, we have

$$\mu_n(h_a(U)) \leqslant \sum_{j \geqslant 1} vol(h_a(I_j)) = a^n \sum_{j \geqslant 1} vol(I_j),$$

hence $\mu_n(h_a(U)) \leqslant a^n \mu_n(U)$. Substituting $h_a(U)$ for U and $\frac{1}{a}$ for a in previous inequality yields

$$\mu_n(h_{\frac{1}{a}}(h_a(U))) \leqslant \frac{1}{a^n} \mu_n(h_a(U)),$$

which amounts to $a^n \mu_n(U) \leqslant \mu_n(h_a(U))$. Thus, $a^n \mu_n(U) = \mu_n(h_a(U))$.

Since $t_{\mathbf{x}}, h_a$ and r are bijections on $\hat{\mathbb{R}}^n$, by Corollary 1.2, we have

$$\overline{t_{\mathbf{x}}(S)} = t_{\mathbf{x}}(\overline{S}), \overline{h_a(S)} = h_a(\overline{S}), \text{ and } \overline{r(S)} = r(\overline{S}),$$

for every subset S of $\hat{\mathbb{R}}^n$.

Let $T \in \mathbb{L}_n$ and let U be a subset of $\hat{\mathbb{R}}^n$. We have

$$\mu_n(U \cap t_{\mathbf{x}}(T)) + \mu_n(U \cap \overline{t_{\mathbf{x}}(T)})$$
$$= \mu_n(U \cap t_{\mathbf{x}}(T)) + \mu_n(U \cap t_{\mathbf{x}}(\overline{T})) = \mu_n(U),$$

which implies that $t_{\mathbf{x}}(T) \in \mathbb{L}_n$.

Similar arguments show that $h_a(T) \in \mathbb{L}_n$ and $r(T) \in \mathbb{L}_n$. $\qquad \square$

Theorem 7.54. *Let* $h : \hat{\mathbb{R}}^n \longrightarrow \hat{\mathbb{R}}^n$ *be a invertible linear operator. If* $T \in \mathbb{L}_n$*, then* $h(T) \in \mathbb{L}_n$ *and* $m_L(h(T)) = |\det(A_h)| m_L(T)$*.*

Proof. An injective linear transformation can be expressed as a composition of three types of linear transforms whose matrices are $T^{(i) \leftrightarrow (j)}$, $T^{a(i)}$ with $a \neq 0$, and $T^{(i)+1(j)}$ (see [121]).

Since

$$T^{(i) \leftrightarrow (j)} \begin{pmatrix} x_1 \\ \vdots \\ x_i \\ \vdots \\ x_j \\ \vdots \\ x_n \end{pmatrix} = \begin{pmatrix} x_1 \\ \vdots \\ x_j \\ \vdots \\ x_i \\ \vdots \\ x_n \end{pmatrix},$$

we have

$$h_{T^{(i)\leftrightarrow(j)}}(G) = (a_1, b_1] \times \cdots \times (a_j, b_j] \times \cdots \times (a_i, b_i] \times \cdots \times (a_n, b_n],$$

hence $h_{T^{(i)\leftrightarrow(j)}}(G)$ is an open-closed interval with the same volume as G and we have

$$vol(h_{T^{(i)\leftrightarrow(j)}}(G)) = |\det(A_{h_{T^{(i)\leftrightarrow(j)}}})|vol(G)$$

because $\det(A_{h_{T^{(i)\leftrightarrow(j)}}}) = -1$.

The effect of $h_{T^{a(i)}}$ on $\mathbf{x}$ is

$$T^{a(i)} \begin{pmatrix} x_1 \\ \vdots \\ x_i \\ \vdots \\ x_n \end{pmatrix} = \begin{pmatrix} x_1 \\ \vdots \\ ax_i \\ \vdots \\ x_n \end{pmatrix}.$$

We have for $a > 0$:

$$h_{T^{a(i)}}(G) = (a_1, b_1] \times \cdots \times (aa_i, ab_i] \times \cdots (a_n, b_n],$$

and for $a < 0$,

$$h_{T^{a(i)}}(G) = (a_1, b_1] \times \cdots \times (ab_i, aa_i] \times \cdots (a_n, b_n],$$

hence $h_{T^{a(i)}}(G)$ is an open-closed interval, $vol(h_{T^{a(i)}}(G)) = |a|vol(G)$, and

$$vol(h_{T^{a(i)}}(G)) = |\det(A_{h_{T^{a(i)}}})|vol(G)$$

because $\det(A_{h_{T^{(i)\leftrightarrow(j)}}}) = a$.

Finally, for $T^{(i)+1(j)}$ we have

$$T^{(i)+1(j)} \begin{pmatrix} x_1 \\ \vdots \\ x_i \\ \vdots \\ x_j \\ \vdots \\ x_n \end{pmatrix} = \begin{pmatrix} x_1 \\ \vdots \\ x_i + x_j \\ \vdots \\ x_j \\ \vdots \\ x_n \end{pmatrix}.$$

Therefore, if $\mathbf{y} \in G' = h_{T^{(i)+1(j)}}(G)$ we have $y_k \in (a_k, b_k]$ for $k \neq i$ and $y_i - y_j \in (a_i, b_i]$.

Consider the open-closed interval

$$G'' = (a_1, b_1] \times \cdots \times (a_{i-1}, b_{i-1}] \times (a_i + a_j, b_i + a_j] \times (a_{i+1}, b_{i+1}] \times \cdots (a_n, b_n]$$

and the sets

$$M' = \{\mathbf{y} \in \hat{\mathbb{R}}^n \mid y_k \in (a_k, b_k) \text{ if } k \neq i \text{ and } a_i + a_j < y_i \leqslant a_i + y_j\},$$
$$M'' = \{\mathbf{y} \in \hat{\mathbb{R}}^n \mid y_k \in (a_k, b_k) \text{ if } k \neq i \text{ and } b_i + a_j < y_i \leqslant b_i + y_j\}.$$

It is clear that the sets G', G'', M' and M'' are Borel sets and, therefore, are Lebesgue measurable. Note that $M'' = \mathbf{t}_u(M')$, where $\mathbf{u} = (b_i - a_i)\mathbf{e}_i$. Therefore, by Theorem 7.53 we have $m_L(M') = m_L(M'')$.

The sets G' and M' are disjoint for the defining conditions of these sets imply $y_i - y_j > a_i$ and $y_i - y_j \leqslant a_i$ which cannot be satisfied simultaneously.

Similarly, the sets G'' and M'' are disjoint because their defining conditions imply $y_i \leqslant b_i + a_j$ and $y_i > b_i + a_j$, respectively, and these conditions are incompatible.

On other hand we have $G' \cup M' = G'' \cup M''$. Indeed, if $\mathbf{y} \in G' \cup M'$ then

$$a_i < y_i - y_j \leqslant b_i \text{ or } a_i + a_j < y_i \leqslant a_i + y_j.$$

If $\mathbf{y} \in G'' \cup M''$ we have, then

$$a_i + a_j < y_i \leqslant b_i + a_j \text{ or } b_i + a_j < y_i \leqslant b_i + y_j.$$

Since $a_i < y_i \leqslant b_i$ and $a_j < y_j \leqslant b_j$ the two systems of inequalities are equivalent, so $G' \cup M' = G'' \cup M''$. This implies

$$m_L(G') + m_L(M') = m_L(G'') + m_L(M''),$$

hence

$$m_L(h_{T^{(i)+1(j)}}(G)) = m_L(G')$$
$$= m_L(G) = |\det(A_{T^{(i)+1(j)}})|m_L(G).$$

We have shown that for every elementary transformation h we have $m_L(h(G)) = |\det(A_h)|m_L(G)$ for any open-closed interval G.

If I is an open interval, it is immediate that $h(I)$ is a Borel set. For $I = (a_1, b_1) \times \cdots \times (a_n, b_n)$ consider the open-closed intervals

$$G_1 = (a_1, b_1] \times \cdots \times (a_n, b_n],$$
$$G_2^\epsilon = (a_1, b_1 - \epsilon] \times \cdots \times (a_n, b_n - \epsilon].$$

Since $G_2^\epsilon \subseteq I \subseteq G_1$, we have $h(G_2^\epsilon) \subseteq h(I) \subseteq h(G_1)$, so

$$|\det(A_h)|m_L(G_2) \leqslant m_L(h(I)) \leqslant |\det(A_h)|m_L(G_1).$$

Taking $\epsilon \to 0$ we have $m_L(h(I)) = |\det(A_h)|m_L(I)$ for every open interval I.

Let h be an elementary linear transformation. If $U \subseteq \hat{\mathbb{R}}^n$ and suppose that $\{I_1, I_2, \ldots\}$ is a cover of U. We have $h(I) \subseteq \bigcap_{j \geqslant 1} h(I_j)$, hence

$$\mu_n(h(U)) \leqslant \sum_{j \geqslant 1} m_L(h(I_j)) = |\det(A_h)| \sum_{j \geqslant 1} m_L(I_j).$$

This implies $\mu_n(h(U)) \leqslant |\det(A_h)| \mu_n(U)$.

Since every linear transformation h is a superposition of elementary transformations, $h = h_1 h_2 \cdots h_q$, we have

$$\mu_n(h(U)) \leqslant |\det(A_{h_1})| \cdots |\det(A_{h_q})| \mu_n(U) = |\det(A_h)| \mu_n(U)$$

for every $U \subseteq \hat{\mathbb{R}}^n$. Since h is invertible we also have

$$\mu_n(U) \leqslant |\det(A_{h^{-1}})| \mu_n(h(U)) = \frac{1}{|\det(A_h)|} \mu_n(h(U),$$

that is, $\mu_n(h(U)) \geqslant |\det(A_h)| \mu_n(U)$. Thus, we have $\mu_n(h(U)) = |\det(A_h)| \mu_n(U)$.

Let now $T \in \mathbb{L}_n$. We claim that if h is an invertible linear operator, then $h(T) \in \mathbb{L}_n$. Indeed, let U be a subset of $\hat{\mathbb{R}}^n$. We have:

$$\begin{aligned}
&\mu_n(U \cap h(T)) + \mu_n(U \cap \overline{h(T)}) \\
&= \mu_n(h(h^{-1}(U)) \cap h(T)) + \mu_n(h(h^{-1}(U)) \cap \overline{h(T)}) \\
&= \mu_n(h(h^{-1}(U \cap T) + \mu_n(h(h^{-1}(U) \cap \overline{T})) \\
&= |\det(A_h)|(\mu_n(h^{-1}(U \cap T)) + \mu_n(h^{-1}(U) \cap \overline{T}) \\
&= |\det(A_h)| \mu_n(h^{-1}(U)) = \mu_n(U),
\end{aligned}$$

hence $h(T) \in \mathbb{L}_n$. Furthermore,

$$m_L(h(T)) = \mu_n(h(T)) = |\det(A_h)| \mu_n(T) = |\det(A_h)| m_L(T). \qquad \square$$

Theorem 7.55. *A subspace V of $\mathbb{R}^n$ with $\dim(V) < n$ is Lebesgue measurable and $m_L(V) = 0$.*

Proof. Let $\{\mathbf{v}_1, \ldots, \mathbf{v}_m\}$ be a basis in V, where $m \leqslant n - 1$. This basis can be extended to a basis of $\mathbb{R}^n$ (see [121]), $\{\mathbf{v}_1, \ldots, \mathbf{v}_m, \mathbf{v}_{m+1}, \ldots, \mathbf{v}_n\}$. If $\mathbf{x} \in \mathbb{R}^n$ we have $\mathbf{x} = x_1 \mathbf{v}_1 + \cdots + x_n \mathbf{v}_n$ and the function $g : \mathbb{R}^n \longrightarrow \mathbb{R}^n$ defined by

$$g(\mathbf{x}) = \begin{pmatrix} x_1 \\ \vdots \\ x_n \end{pmatrix}$$

is invertible and

$$g(V) = \left\{ \begin{pmatrix} \mathbf{v} \\ \mathbf{0}_{n-m} \end{pmatrix} \Bigg| \, \mathbf{v} \in V \right\}.$$

For $r \in \mathbb{N}$ define the m-dimensional cube K_r as

$$K_r = \underbrace{[-r, r] \times \cdots \times [-r, r]}_{m} \times \{0\} \times \{0\} \cdots \times \{0\}.$$

Clearly, $K_r \in \mathbb{L}_n$ and $m_L(K_r) = 0$. Since $g(V) \subseteq \bigcup_{r \geqslant 1} K_r$, by the completeness of the Lebesgue measure, it follows that $g(V) \in \mathbb{L}_n$ and $m_L(g(V)) = 0$. $\qquad \square$

Theorem 7.56. *Let* $h : \hat{\mathbb{R}}^n \longrightarrow \hat{\mathbb{R}}^n$ *be a linear operator such that* $\det(A_h) = 0$. *Then,* $\mathsf{Img}(h)$ *is a Lebesgue measurable set with* $m_L(\mathsf{Img}(h)) = 0$.

Proof. If $\det(A_h) = 0$, h is not invertible and $V = \mathsf{Img}(h)$ is a subspace that is at most $(n-1)$-dimensional. Thus, by Theorem 7.55, $\mathsf{Img}(h)$ is a Lebesgue measurable set with $m_L(\mathsf{Img}(h)) = 0$. $\qquad \square$

The remainder of this section focuses on null sets in $(\mathbb{R}, \mathbb{B}(\mathbb{R}), m_L)$.

We introduced the notion of null set in a measure space $(S, \mathcal{E}, m)$ in Definition 7.12. In the specific case of $(\mathbb{R}, \mathbb{L}, m_L)$ we have the following alternative characterization:

Theorem 7.57. *A Lebesgue measurable subset U of $\mathbb{R}$ is a null set in* $(\mathbb{R}, \mathbb{L}, m_L)$ *if for every $\epsilon > 0$ there exists a countable collection of intervals* (a_i, b_i) *for $i \in \mathbb{N}$ such that* $U \subseteq \bigcup_{i \in \mathbb{N}}(a_i, b_i)$ *and* $\sum_{i \in \mathbb{N}} \ell(a_i, b_i) < \epsilon$.

Proof. Suppose that U is a null set in $(\mathbb{R}, \mathbb{B}(\mathbb{R}), m_L)$, hence U is m_L-measurable and $m_L(U) = 0$. We have

$$m_L(U) = \mu_L(U) = \inf \left\{ \sum_{n \geqslant 1} (b_n - a_n) \mid ((a_n, b_n))_{n \geqslant 1} \in C_U \right\} = 0,$$

hence for every $\epsilon > 0$, there exists a collection of intervals $\{(a_n, b_n) \mid n \geqslant 1\}$ such that

$$U \subseteq \bigcup_{i \in \mathbb{N}} (a_i, b_i) \text{ and } \sum_{i \in \mathbb{N}} \ell(a_i, b_i) < \epsilon.$$

Conversely, suppose that for a set $U \in \mathbb{L}$ and every $\epsilon > 0$ there exists a countable collection of intervals (a_i, b_i) for $i \in \mathbb{N}$ such that $U \subseteq \bigcup_{i \in \mathbb{N}}(a_i, b_i)$ and $\sum_{i \in \mathbb{N}} \ell(a_i, b_i) < \epsilon$. Then, $m_L(U) \leqslant \sum_{i \in \mathbb{N}} \ell(a_i, b_i) < \epsilon$, hence $m_L(U) = 0$. $\qquad \square$

By a previous observation the open intervals can be replaced by closed intervals or by semi-closed (or semi-open) intervals without affecting the definition of null set.

Example 7.14. Every one-element subset $\{x\}$ of $\mathbb{R}$ is a null set because we have $\{x\} \subseteq (x - \frac{\epsilon}{2}, x + \frac{\epsilon}{2})$ for every $\epsilon > 0$.

Theorem 7.58. *A countable union of null subsets of $\mathbb{R}$ is a null set.*

Proof. Let $\{U_n \mid n \in \mathbb{N}\}$ be a countable collection of null sets and let ϵ be a positive number. For a set U_n there exists a countable collection of intervals $\mathfrak{I}_n = \{I_n^m \mid m \in \mathbb{N}\}$ such that $U_n \subseteq \bigcup \mathfrak{I}_n$ and $\sum_{m \in \mathbb{N}} \ell(I_n^m) < \frac{\epsilon}{2^{n+1}}$. The total length of all intervals can be bounded by

$$\sum_{n \in \mathbb{N}} \sum_{m \in \mathbb{N}} \ell(I_n^m) < \sum_{n \in \mathbb{N}} \frac{\epsilon}{2^{n+1}} = \epsilon.$$

Since $\bigcup_{n \in \mathbb{N}} \mathfrak{I}_n$ is a countable collection of intervals such that $\bigcup \{U_n \mid n \in \mathbb{N}\} \subseteq \bigcup_{n \in \mathbb{N}} \bigcup \mathfrak{I}_n$, it follows that $\bigcup \{U_n \mid n \in \mathbb{N}\}$ is a null set. $\square$

Corollary 7.22. *The set of rational numbers $\mathbb{Q}$ is a null set.*

Proof. Since $\mathbb{Q}$ is a countable set, we can regard it as the countable union of singleton sets $\{q\}$ for $q \in \mathbb{Q}$. The statement follows immediately from Theorem 7.58. $\square$

Null sets that are uncountable also exist. We introduce a special uncountable subset of the set of real numbers that is a null set.

Let $v_n : \{0, 1\}^n \longrightarrow \mathbb{N}$ be the function defined by

$$v_n(b_0, b_1, \ldots, b_{n-1}) = 2^{n-1} b_0 + \cdots + 2 b_{n-2} + b_{n-1}$$

for every sequence $(b_0, \ldots, b_n) \in \{0, 1\}^n$. Clearly, $v_n(b_0, \ldots, b_{n-2}, b_{n-1})$ yields the number designated by the binary sequence $(b_0, \ldots, b_{n-2}, b_{n-1})$. For example, $v_3(110) = 2^2 \cdot 1 + 2^1 \cdot 1 + 0 = 6$.

Similarly, let $w_n : \{0, 1, 2\}^n \longrightarrow \mathbb{N}$ be the function defined by

$$w_n(b_0, b_1, \ldots, b_{n-1}) = 3^{n-1} b_0 + \cdots + 3 b_{n-2} + b_{n-1}$$

for every sequence $(b_0, \ldots, b_n) \in \{0, 1, 2\}^n$. Then, $w_n(b_0, \ldots, b_{n-2}, b_{n-1})$ is the number designated by the ternary sequence $(b_0, \ldots, b_{n-2}, b_{n-1})$. For example, $w_3(110) = 3^2 \cdot 1 + 3^1 \cdot 1 + 0 = 12$.

Consider a sequence of subsets of $\mathbb{R}$, $E^0, E^1, \ldots$, where $E^0 = [0, 1]$ and E^1 is obtained from E^0 by removing the middle third $(1/3, 2/3)$ of E^0.

If the remaining closed intervals are E_0^1 and E_1^1, then E^1 is defined by $E^1 = E_0^1 \cup E_1^1$.

By removing the middle intervals from the sets E_0^1 and E_1^1, four new closed intervals $E_{00}^2, E_{01}^2, E_{10}^2, E_{11}^2$ are created. Let $E^2 = E_{00}^2 \cup E_{01}^2 \cup E_{10}^2 \cup E_{11}^2$.

E^n is constructed from E^{n-1} by removing 2^{n-1} disjoint middle third intervals from E^{n-1} (see Figure 7.2). Namely, if $E_{i_0 \cdots i_{n-1}}^n$ is an interval of the set E^n, by removing the middle third of this interval, we generate two closed intervals $E_{i_0 \cdots i_{n-1} 0}^{n+1}$ and $E_{i_0 \cdots i_{n-1} 1}^{n+1}$.

In general, E_n is the union of 2^n closed intervals

$$E^n = \bigcup_{i_0,\ldots,i_{n-1}} \{E_{i_0,\ldots,i_{n-1}}^n \mid (i_0,\ldots,i_{n-1}) \in \{0,1\}^n\},$$

for $n \geqslant 0$.

An argument by induction on $n \in \mathbb{N}$ shows that

$$E_{i_0 \cdots i_{n-1}}^n = \left[\frac{2w_n(i_0,\ldots,i_{n-1})}{3^n}, \frac{2w_n(i_0,\ldots,i_{n-1})+1}{3^n} \right].$$

Indeed, the equality above holds for $n = 0$. Suppose that it holds for n, and denote by a and b the endpoints of the interval $E_{i_0 \cdots i_{n-1}}^n$; that is,

$$a = \frac{2w_n(i_0,\ldots,i_{n-1})}{3^n},$$

$$b = \frac{2w_n(i_0,\ldots,i_{n-1})+1}{3^n}.$$

By the inductive hypothesis, the points that divide $E_{i_0 \cdots i_{n-1}}^n$ are

$$\frac{2a+b}{3} = \frac{6w_n(i_0,\ldots,i_{n-1})+1}{3^{n+1}}$$
$$= \frac{2w_{n+1}(i_0,\ldots,i_{n-1},0)+1}{3^{n+1}}$$

and

$$\frac{a+2b}{3} = \frac{6w_n(i_0,\ldots,i_{n-1})+2}{3^{n+1}}$$
$$= \frac{2w_{n+1}(i_0,\ldots,i_{n-1},1)}{3^{n+1}}.$$

Thus, the remaining left third of $E_{i_0 \cdots i_{n-1}}^n$ is

$$E_{i_0 \cdots i_{n-1} 0}^{n+1} = \left[\frac{2w_n(i_0,\ldots,i_{n-1})}{3^n}, \frac{2w_{n+1}(i_0,\ldots,i_{n-1},0)+1}{3^{n+1}} \right]$$
$$= \left[\frac{2w_{n+1}(i_0,\ldots,i_{n-1},0)}{3^{n+1}}, \frac{2w_{n+1}(i_0,\ldots,i_{n-1},0)+1}{3^{n+1}} \right],$$

while the remaining right third is

$$E^{n+1}_{i_0 \cdots i_{n-1} 1} = \left[\frac{2w_{n+1}(i_0, \ldots, i_{n-1}, 1)}{3^{n+1}}, \frac{2w_n(i_0, \ldots, i_{n-1}) + 1}{3^n} \right]$$

$$= \left[\frac{2w_{n+1}(i_0, \ldots, i_{n-1}, 1)}{3^{n+1}}, \frac{2w_{n+1}(i_0, \ldots, i_{n-1}, 1) + 1}{3^{n+1}} \right],$$

which concludes the inductive argument.

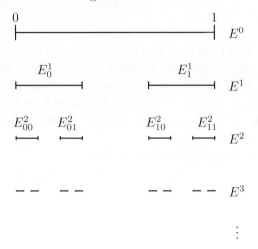

Fig. 7.2   Construction of the Cantor dust.

Each number x located in the leftmost third $E^1_0 = [0, 1/3]$ of the set $E_0 = [0, 1]$ can be expressed in base 3 as a number of the form $x = 0.0d_2d_3 \cdots$; the number $1/3$, the right extreme of this interval, can be written either as $x = 0.1$ or $x = 0.022 \cdots$. We adopt the second representation which allows us to say that all numbers in the rightmost third $E^1_1 = [2/3, 1]$ of E^0 have the form $0.2d_2d_3 \cdots$ in the base 3.

The argument applies again to the intervals $E^2_{00}, E^2_{01}, E^2_{10}, E^2_{11}$ obtained from the set E^1. Every number x in the interval E^2_{ij} can be written in base 3 as $x = 0.i'j' \cdots$, where $i' = 2i$ and $j' = 2j$.

The Cantor set is the intersection

$$C = \bigcap \{ E^n \mid n \geqslant 0 \}.$$

Let us evaluate the total length of the intervals of which a set of the form E_n consists. There are 2^n intervals of the form $E^n_{i_0 \cdots i_{n-1}}$, and the length of each of these intervals is $\frac{1}{3^n}$. Therefore, the length of E^n is $(2/3)^n$, so this length tends toward 0 when n tends towards infinity. This implies that the Cantor set is a null set.

Despite its sparsity, surprisingly, the Cantor set is equinumerous with the interval $[0, 1]$, so it is uncountable. To prove this fact, observe that the Cantor set consists of the numbers x that can be expressed as

$$x = \sum_{n=1}^{\infty} \frac{a_n}{3^n},$$

where $a_n \in \{0, 2\}$ for $n \geqslant 1$. For example, $1/4$ is a member of this set because $1/4$ can be expressed in base 3 as $0.020202\cdots$. Define the function $g : C \longrightarrow [0, 1]$ by $g(x) = y$ if $x = 0.a_1 a_2 \cdots$ (in base 3), where $a_i \in \{0, 2\}$ for $i \geqslant 1$ and $y = 0.b_1 b_2 \cdots$ (in base 2), where $b_i = a_i/2$ for $i \geqslant 1$. It is easy to see that this is a bijection between C and $[0, 1]$, which shows that these sets are equinumerous.

We now examine the behavior of the sets

$$E_{i_0 \cdots i_{n-1}}^n = \left[\frac{2 w_n(i_0, \ldots, i_{n-1})}{3^n}, \frac{2 w_n(i_0, \ldots, i_{n-1}) + 1}{3^n} \right]$$

relative to two mappings $f_0, f_1 : [0, 1] \longrightarrow [0, 1]$ defined by

$$f_0(x) = \frac{x}{3} \text{ and } f_1(x) = \frac{x+2}{3}$$

for $x \in [0, 1]$.

Note that

$$
\begin{aligned}
f_0(E_{i_0 \cdots i_{n-1}}^n) &= \left[\frac{2 w_n(i_0, \ldots, i_{n-1})}{3^{n+1}}, \frac{2 w_n(i_0, \ldots, i_{n-1}) + 1}{3^{n+1}} \right] \\
&= \left[\frac{2 w_{n+1}(0 i_0, \ldots, i_{n-1})}{3^{n+1}}, \frac{2 w_{n+1}(0 i_0, \ldots, i_{n-1}) + 1}{3^{n+1}} \right] \\
&= E_{0 i_0 \cdots i_{n-1}}^{n+1}.
\end{aligned}
$$

Similarly,

$$f_1(E_{i_0 \cdots i_{n-1}}^n) = E_{1 i_0 \cdots i_{n-1}}^{n+1}.$$

Thus, in general, we have $f_i(E_{i_0 \cdots i_{n-1}}^n) = E_{i i_0 \cdots i_{n-1}}^{n+1}$ for $i \in \{0, 1\}$.

This allows us to conclude that $E^{n+1} = f_0(E^n) \cup f^1(E^n)$ for $n \in \mathbb{N}$.

Since both f_0 and f_1 are injective, it follows that

$$C = \bigcap_{n \geqslant 1} E^n = \bigcap_{n \geqslant 0} E^{n+1}$$

$$= \bigcap_{n \geqslant 0} [f_0(E^n) \cup f_1(E^n)]$$

$$= \left(\bigcap_{n \geqslant 0} f_0(E^n) \right) \cup \left(\bigcap_{n \geqslant 0} f_1(E^n) \right)$$

$$= f_0 \left(\bigcap_{n \geqslant 0} E^n \right) \cup f_1 \left(\bigcap_{n \geqslant 0} E^n \right).$$

In Figure 7.3 we show how sets of the form E_{ij}^2 are mapped into sets of the form E_{ijk}^3 by f_0 (represented by plain arrows) and f_1 (represented by dashed arrows).

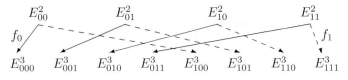

Fig. 7.3   Mapping sets E_{ij}^2 into sets E_{ijk}^3.

Definition 7.24. Let $(S, \mathcal{E}, m)$ be a measure space and let $f : S \longrightarrow \mathbb{R}$ be a function. An *upper bound* for f is a number $a \in \mathbb{R}$ such that $f(x) \leqslant a$ for $x \in S$. A *lower bound* for f is a number $b \in \mathbb{R}$ such that $b \leqslant f(x)$ for $x \in S$.

Equivalently, a is an upper found for f if $f^{-1}(a, \infty) = \emptyset$. Similarly, b is a lower bound for f if $f^{-1}(-\infty, b) = \emptyset$.

Let U_f the set of upper bounds for f and let L_f the set of lower bounds for the same function.

Definition 7.25. The *supremum* of f is the number $\sup f$ defined by

$$\sup f = \begin{cases} \inf U_f & \text{if } U_f \neq \emptyset, \\ \infty & \text{if } U_f = \emptyset. \end{cases}$$

The *infimum* of f is the number $\inf f$ defined by

$$\inf f = \begin{cases} \sup L_f & \text{if } L_f \neq \emptyset, \\ -\infty & \text{if } L_f = \emptyset. \end{cases}$$

If the function f is measurable, then we can define the essential supremum and the essential infimum of f that are similar to $\sup f$ and $\inf f$.

Definition 7.26. Let $(S, \mathcal{E}, m)$ be a measure space and let $f : S \longrightarrow \mathbb{R}$ be a measurable function. An *essential upper bound* of f is a number a such that $m(f^{-1}(a, \infty)) = 0$. An *essential lower bound* of f is a number b such that $m(f^{-1}(-\infty, b)) = 0$.

The sets of essential upper bounds and essential lower bounds for f are denoted by U_f^{ess} and L_f^{ess}, respectively.

The *essential supremum* for f is $\operatorname{ess\,sup} f$ given by

$$\operatorname{ess\,sup} f = \begin{cases} \inf U_f^{\text{ess}} & \text{if } U_f^{\text{ess}} \neq \emptyset, \\ \infty & \text{otherwise.} \end{cases}$$

The *essential infimum* for f is the number $\operatorname{ess\,inf} f$ given by

$$\operatorname{ess\,inf} f = \begin{cases} \sup L_f^{\text{ess}} & \text{if } L_f^{\text{ess}} \neq \emptyset, \\ -\infty & \text{otherwise.} \end{cases}$$

Note that if the function f is modified on a null set, then $\operatorname{ess\,sup} f$ and $\operatorname{ess\,inf} f$ do not change.

Example 7.15. Le $f : \mathbb{R} \longrightarrow \mathbb{R}$ be the function given by:

$$f(x) = \begin{cases} 2 & \text{if } x \in \mathbb{Q}, \\ \arctan x & \text{if } x \in \mathbb{R} - \mathbb{Q}. \end{cases}$$

It is immediate that $\sup f = 2$, $\operatorname{ess\,sup} f = \frac{\pi}{2}$ and $\inf f = \operatorname{ess\,inf} f = -\frac{\pi}{2}$.

Note that $\operatorname{ess\,sup} f \leqslant \sup |f|$.

Theorem 7.59. *Let $(I, \mathbb{L}_I, m_L)$ be a measure space where I is an interval of $\mathbb{R}$ and let $f : I \longrightarrow \mathbb{R}$ be a continuous function. Then $\operatorname{ess\,sup} f = \sup_I |f|$.*

Proof. Since $\operatorname{ess\,sup} f \leqslant \sup_I |f|$ we need to prove only that $\sup_I |f| \leqslant \operatorname{ess\,sup} f$. If $c \in \mathbb{R}$ and $c < \sup_I |f|$ there exists $x_0 \in I$ such that $c < |f(x_0)|$. Since f is continuous, there exists $\delta > 0$ such that $(x_0 - \delta, x_0 + \delta) \cap I \subseteq \{x \in I \mid |f(x)| > c\}$, hence

$$0 < m_L((x_0 - \delta, x_0 + \delta) \cap I) \leqslant m_L(\{x \in I \mid |f(x)| > c\}),$$

hence $c \leqslant \sup \operatorname{ess} f$. This implies $\sup_I |f| \leqslant \operatorname{ess\,sup} f$. $\qquad \square$

Theorem 7.60. *Let $(S, \mathcal{E}, m)$ be a measure space. The collection $\mathcal{E}^*$ defined as*

$$\mathcal{E}^* = \{T \in \mathcal{P}(S) \mid U \subseteq T \subseteq W \text{ where } U, W \in \mathcal{E} \text{ and } m(W - U) = 0\}.$$

is a σ-algebra; furthermore, if $T \in \mathcal{E}^*$ and $m^*(T)$ equals $m(U)$, then $(S, \mathcal{E}^*, m^*)$ is a measure space.

Proof. It is clear that $\mathcal{E} \subseteq \mathcal{E}^*$ and $S \in \mathcal{E}^*$.

The measure m^* is well-defined. Indeed, suppose that we have both $U \subseteq T \subseteq W$ and $U_1 \subseteq T \subseteq W_1$, where $U, U_1, W, W_1 \in \mathcal{E}$ and $m(W_1 - U_1) = m(W - U) = 0$. Since $U - U_1 \subseteq T - U_1 \subseteq W_1 - U_1$, we have $m(U - U_1) = 0$, hence $\mu(U) = m(U \cap U_1)$. Similarly, $m(U_1) = m(U \cap U_1)$, so $m(U_1) = m(U)$.

If $U \subseteq T \subseteq W$, then $S - W \subseteq S - T \subseteq S - U$. Since $(S - U) - (S - W) = W - U$, it follows that $S - T \in \mathcal{E}^*$.

Suppose that $U_n \subseteq T_n \subseteq W_n$, where $U_n, W_n \in \mathcal{E}$ and $m(W_n - U_n) = 0$ for $n \in \mathbb{N}$. If $U = \bigcup_{n \in \mathbb{N}} U_n$, $W = \bigcup_{n \in \mathbb{N}} W_n$, and $T = \bigcup_{n \in \mathbb{N}} T_n$, then $U \subseteq T \subseteq W_n$, $U, W \in \mathcal{E}$ and

$$W - U = W - \bigcup_{n \in \mathbb{N}} U_n = \bigcup_{n \in \mathbb{N}} (W - U_n),$$

so $m(W - U) = 0$ because a countable union of sets of measure 0 has measure 0. Thus, $T \in \mathcal{E}^*$.

If the sets T_n are disjoint, the same is true for the sets U_n, hence $m^*(T) = m(U) = \sum_{n \in \mathbb{N}} m(U_n) = \sum_{n \in \mathbb{N}} m^*(T_n)$, hence m^* is a measure on $\mathcal{E}^*$. $\qquad\square$

Theorem 7.61. (Regularity Theorem for Measures on $\mathbb{R}^n$) *Let $(\mathbb{R}^n, \mathbb{B}(\mathbb{R}^n), m)$ be a measure space defined on $\mathbb{R}^n$ such that if $U \in \mathbb{B}(\mathbb{R}^n)$ is bounded then $m(U) < \infty$.*

If $U \in \mathbb{B}(\mathbb{R}^n)$ and $\epsilon > 0$, there exists a closed set C and an open set V such that $C \subseteq U \subseteq V$ and $m(V - C) < \epsilon$.

If $U \in \mathbb{B}(\mathbb{R}^n)$ and $m(U) < \infty$, then

$$m(U) = \sup\{m(K) \mid K \text{ is compact and } K \subseteq U\}.$$

Proof. Consider the open-closed interval $G = (a_1, b_1] \times \cdots \times (a_n, b_n]$. The set $I_k = (a_1, b_1 + \frac{1}{k}) \times \cdots \times (a_n, b_n + \frac{1}{k})$ is open and $\lim_{k \to \infty} I_k = G$. Since $m(I_1)$ is finite, by the Measure Continuity Theorem (Theorem 7.32) it follows that $m(I_k - G) < \epsilon$ when k is sufficiently large, which proves the first part of the theorem for open-closed intervals.

We saw that open-closed intervals form a semi-ring (by Supplement 35 of Chapter 1). For an arbitrary set $U \in \mathbb{B}(\mathbb{R}^n)$ there exist open-closed intervals G_k such that $U \subseteq \bigcup_k G_k$ and $m\left(\bigcup_k G_k - G\right) < \epsilon$. Choose open sets V_k such that $V_k \subseteq G_k$ and $m(G_k - V_k) < \frac{\epsilon}{2^k}$. Then $V = \bigcup_k V_k$ is open and $m(V - U) < 2\epsilon$. This proves the first part of the theorem which concerns open sets. The case of the closed sets can be shown by taken the complementary sets.

Since $m(U) < \infty$, $m(U - U_0) < \epsilon$ for some bounded subset U_0 of S and, then, by the first part that $m(U - K) < \epsilon$ for a closed subset of U_0. Since K is bounded and closed in $\mathbb{R}^n$, it is compact. $\qquad\square$

Definition 7.27. A collection of intervals $\mathcal{C}$ of $\mathbb{R}$ is a *Vitali*[1] *cover* of a subset X of $\mathbb{R}$ if for every $\epsilon > 0$ and $x \in X$ there exists $I \in \mathcal{C}$ such that $x \in I$ and $m_L(I) < \epsilon$.

Theorem 7.62. (Vitali Theorem) *Let X be a non-empty subset of $\mathbb{R}$ and let $\mathcal{K}$ be a Vitali cover of X that consists of non-trivial closed intervals (that is, of intervals that do not consist of one point). For every $\epsilon > 0$ there exists a finite or infinite sequence of disjoint intervals $(K_1, \ldots, K_n, \ldots)$ in $\mathcal{K}$ such that $\mu_L(X - \bigcup_{i \geqslant 1} K_i) < \epsilon$.*

Proof. Suppose initially that X is bounded. Let U be a bounded open set such that $X \subseteq U$ and let $\mathcal{K}_0$ be the collection of closed intervals of $\mathcal{K}$ that are included in U. It is clear that $\mathcal{K}_0$ is a Vitali covering of X. Define $s_1 = \sup\{m_L(K) \mid K \in \mathcal{K}_0\}$.

We proceed to construct inductively a sequence of closed intervals (K_n) in $\mathcal{K}_0$. Since $X \neq \emptyset$ we have $0 < s_1 < \infty$ and we can select an interval $K_1 \in \mathcal{K}_0$ that satisfies $m_L(K_1) > \frac{s_1}{2}$.

If $X \subseteq \bigcup_{j=1}^{n} K_j$, the construction is completed. Otherwise, there exists $x \in X - \bigcup_{j=1}^{n} K_j$ and, therefore, since $\bigcup_{j=1}^{n} K_j$ is closed, and $\mathcal{K}_0$ is a Vitali covering of X, there exists an interval in $\mathcal{K}_0$ that contains x and is disjoint from $\bigcup_{j=1}^{n} K_j$. Define

$$s_{n+1} = \sup\left\{m_L(K) \;\middle|\; K \in \mathcal{K}_0 \text{ and } K \cap \bigcup_{j=1}^{n} K_j = \emptyset\right\}.$$

---

[1] Giuseppe Vitali (26th of August 1875–29th of February 1932) was an Italian mathematician who worked in mathematical analysis. Vitali studied at the Scuola Normale Superiore in Pisa and graduated to the University of Pisa in 1899. After teaching in secondary schools he became a professor of calculus at the University of Modena in 1923. He also taught at the Universities of Padua and Bologna.

We have $0 < s_{n+1} < \infty$ and we can choose an interval K_{n+1} such that

$$m_L(K_{n+1}) > \frac{s_{n+1}}{2} \text{ and } K_{n+1} \cap \bigcup_{j=1}^{n} K_j = \emptyset.$$

If this process ends in p steps, then $X \subseteq \bigcup_{j=1}^{p} K_j$ and $(K_1, \ldots, K_p)$ is the required sequence. Otherwise, that is, if the process does not terminate in a finite number of steps, the series $\sum_{j=1}^{\infty} m_L(K_j)$ must be convergent because the intervals $K_1, \ldots, K_n, \ldots$ are disjoint and included in the bounded set U. Therefore, $\lim_{n \to \infty} m_L(K_n) = 0$ and, consequently, $\lim_{n \to \infty} s_n = 0$.

For each n let $\hat{K}_n$ be the interval in $\mathcal{K}$ with the same center as K_n such that $m_L(\hat{K}_n) = 5\, m_L(K_n)$ (see Figure 7.4). Since $m_L(\hat{K}_n) = 5 m_L(K_n)$, the series $\sum_{j=1}^{\infty} m_L(\hat{K}_n)$ is also convergent.

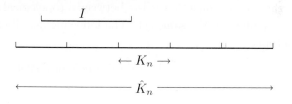

Fig. 7.4   When $I \cap K_n \neq \emptyset$ and $m_L(K_n) > \frac{1}{2} m_L(I)$ then $I \subseteq \hat{K}_n$.

Let $x \in X - \bigcup_{j=1}^{p} K_j$. Since $\bigcup_{j=1}^{p} K_j$ is closed and and $\mathcal{K}_0$ is a Vitali cover of X, there are intervals in $\mathcal{K}_0$ that contain x and are disjoint from $\bigcup_{j=1}^{p} K_j$. Let I be such an interval. Since $m_L(I) < s_{k+1}$ holds for each k such that $I \cap \bigcup_{n=1}^{k} K_n = \emptyset$, and $\lim_{k \to \infty} s_k = 0$, if follows that $I \cap \bigcup_{j=1}^{k} K_j \neq \emptyset$ when k is sufficiently large. Let k_0 be the smallest k such that $I \cap \bigcup_{j=1}^{k} K_j \neq \emptyset$. Then $m_L(I) \leqslant s_{k_0}$ and, therefore, $m_L(I) \leqslant 2m_L(K_{k_0})$ because $s_{k_0}/2 \leqslant m_L(K_{k_0})$. Since $I \cap K_{k_0} \neq \emptyset$, the definition of the intervals $\hat{K}_n$ implies that $I \subseteq \hat{K}_{k_0}$. Since I is disjoint from $\bigcup_{j=1}^{p} K_j$, it follow that $k_0 \geqslant p+1$. Thus, $x \in I \subseteq \hat{K}_{k_0} \subseteq \bigcup_{n=N+1}^{\infty} \hat{K}_n$. Since x was an arbitrary element of $X - \bigcup_{n=1}^{p} K_n$, it follows that

$$X - \bigcup_{n=1}^{p} K_n \subseteq \bigcup_{n=p+1}^{\infty} \hat{K}_n$$

for every positive integer p. Therefore,

$$\mu_L \left(X - \bigcup_{n=1}^{\infty} K_n \right) \leqslant \mu_L \left(X - \bigcup_{n=1}^{p} K_n \right) \leqslant \sum_{n=p+1}^{\infty} m_L(\hat{K}_n).$$

Since the convergence of the series $\sum_{n=1}^{\infty} m_L(\hat{K}_n)$ implies that $\lim_{p\to\infty} \sum_{n=p+1}^{\infty} m_L(\hat{K}_n) = 0$, it follows that $\mu_L(X - \bigcup_{n=1}^{\infty} K_n) = 0$, so (K_n) is the required sequence. This concludes the argument when X is bounded.

When X is not bounded, for each m such that $X_m = X \cap (-m, m) \neq \emptyset$, we can apply the previous argument and find a sequence of disjoint intervals K_k^m that belong to $\mathcal{K}$ such that $\bigcup_j K_j^m \subseteq (-m, m)$ and contains almost every point in $X \cap (-k, k)$. Merging these sequences results in a sequence for X. $\qquad\square$

7.8 Measures on Topological Spaces

We examine the relationships that exists between a topological space and a measure space defined on the same set. The following definition comprises the main concepts:

Definition 7.28. Let $(S, \mathcal{O})$ be a Hausdorff topological space, $\mathbb{B}(S)$ be the σ-algebra of Borel sets, and let $(S, \mathbb{B}(S, \mathcal{O}), m)$ be a measure space. The measure m is:

  (i) a *Borel measure* if $m(C) < \infty$ for every $C \in COMP(S, \mathcal{O})$;
  (ii) a *locally finite measure* if for every $x \in S$ there exists $U \in neigh_x(\mathcal{O})$ such that $m(U) < \infty$;
  (iii) a *inner regular measure* if for every $U \in \mathbb{B}(S, \mathcal{O})$ we have:
$$m(U) = \sup\{m(C) \mid C \in COMP(S, \mathcal{O}), C \subseteq U\};$$
  (iv) an *outer regular measure* if for every $U \in \mathbb{B}(S, \mathcal{O})$ we have:
$$m(U) = \inf\{m(D) \mid D \in \mathcal{O}, U \subseteq D\}.$$

Theorem 7.63. *Every locally finite measure is a Borel measure.*

Proof. Let $C \in COMP(S, \mathcal{O})$. Each $x \in C$ has an open neighborhood V_x with $m(V_x) < \infty$. Since C is compact there exists a finite family $V_{x_1}, \ldots, V_{x_n}$ such that $C \subseteq \bigcup_{j=1}^{n} V_{x_j}$. Therefore, $m(C) \leqslant m(\bigcup_{j=1}^{n} V_{x_j}) \leqslant \sum_{j=1}^{n} m(V_{x_j}) < \infty$. $\qquad\square$

Definition 7.29. Let $(S, \mathcal{O})$ be a Hausdorff topological space. A measure defined on $\mathbb{B}(S, \mathcal{O})$ is a *Radon measure* if it is locally finite and inner regular.

Theorem 7.64. *Let $(S, \mathcal{O})$ be a Hausdorff topological space. If every point has a countable neighborhood basis, every inner regular Borel measure m is also locally finite, and therefore, is a Radon measure.*

Proof. Suppose that m is not local finite. This means that there exists $x \in S$ such that $m(V) = \infty$ for every open neighborhood V of x. Since x has a countable neighborhood basis $(V_n)_{n \geqslant 1}$ that consists of open sets, we have a countable neighborhood basis (V_n') such that $V_n' = \bigcap_{j=1}^n V_n$ such that $m(V_n') = \infty$ for $n \geqslant 1$ and $\bigcup_{n \geqslant 1} V_n' = \{x\}$.

Since $m(V_n') = \infty$ and m is inner regular, there exists a compact set C_n such that $C_n \subseteq V_n'$ such that $m(C_n) > n$ for every $n \geqslant 1$. Let $C = \{x\} \cup \bigcup_{n \geqslant 1} C_n$.

The set C is compact. Indeed, suppose that $\mathcal{C}$ is an open cover of C. There exists some $U \in \mathcal{C}$ such that $x \in U$. Since $\{V_n' \mid n \geqslant 1\}$ is a neighborhood basis at x, there exists n_0 such that $V_{n_0}' \subseteq U$ for some $n_0 \geqslant 1$. Then, $C_n \subseteq V_n' \subseteq V_{n_0}' \subseteq U$ for $n \geqslant n_0$. Since $C_1 \cup \cdots \cup C_{n_0}$ is a compact subset of C, it is covered by finitely many sets in $\mathcal{C}$. These sets together with U constitute a finite covering of C. Thus, we have $m(C) < \infty$ because m is a Borel measure, and, since $C_n \subseteq C$, $m(C) \geqslant m(C_n) > n$ for every $n \geqslant 1$, which is a contradiction. $\qquad\square$

Let $(S, \mathcal{O})$ be a topological space and let $C(S, \mathbb{R})$ be the set of continuous functions from S to $\mathbb{R}$. Denote by $\mathcal{F}_{cb}(S, \mathbb{R})$ the subset of $C(S, \mathbb{R})$ that consists of continuous bounded functions. Note that for any measurable space $(S, \mathcal{E})$ the following hold:

  (i) the function $\phi : C(S, \mathbb{R}) \longrightarrow \mathcal{F}_{cb}(S, \mathbb{R})$ defined by $\phi(f) = \arctan f$ is injective;

 (ii) $\phi(f)$ is continuous if and only if f is continuous;

(iii) $\phi(f)$ is measurable as a function between $(S, \mathcal{E})$ and $(\mathbb{R}, \mathbb{B}(\mathbb{R}))$ if and only if f is measurable as a function between the same measurable spaces.

The second point follows immediately from the equalities

$$\phi(f) = \arctan f \text{ and } f = \tan \phi.$$

To prove the third point let B be a Borel set in $\mathbb{R}$. We have $\phi(f)^{-1}(B) = f^{-1}(\{\tan(x) \mid x \in B\})$ and $f^{-1}(B) = (\phi(f))^{-1}(\{\arctan(x) \mid x \in B\})$. Note that both $\{\tan(x) \mid x \in B\}$ and $\{\arctan(x) \mid x \in B\}$ are Borel sets (by Theorem 7.13), so the equivalence of the measurability of f and $\phi(f)$ follows.

Definition 7.30. Let $(S, \mathcal{O})$ be a topological space. The *σ-algebra of Baire sets* is the smallest σ-algebra $\mathbb{BA}(S)$ such that all functions $f \in \mathcal{F}_{cb}(S, \mathbb{R})$ are measurable as functions between the measurable spaces $(S, \mathbb{BA}(S))$ and $(\mathbb{R}, \mathbb{B}(\mathbb{R}))$.

We have $\mathbb{BA}(S) \subseteq \mathbb{B}(S)$.

Theorem 7.65. *In a topological metric space* $(S, \mathcal{O}_d)$ *we have* $\mathbb{BA}(S) = \mathbb{B}(S)$.

Proof.   Let V be a closed set in $(S, \mathcal{O})$ and let $f : S \longrightarrow \mathbb{R}$ be the function defined by

$$f(x) = d(x, V) = \inf\{d(x, v) \mid v \in V\}.$$

The inequality (5.1), $|d(x, V) - d(y, V)| \leqslant d(x, y)$, implies the continuity of f; moreover, $V = f^{-1}(\{0\})$, so V is a Baire set. Since all closed subsets of $(S, \mathcal{O}_d)$ are Baire set, it follows that all Borel sets are Baire sets and, so $\mathbb{B}(S) \subseteq \mathbb{BA}(S)$. Coupled with the reverse inclusion stated above, we have $\mathbb{BA}(S) = \mathbb{B}(S)$. $\square$

Definition 7.31. Let $(S, \mathcal{O})$ be a topological space and let $(S, \mathcal{E}, m)$ be a measure space on the same set S.

A subset $U \in \mathcal{E}$ is *regular* if

$$m(U) = \sup\{m(C) \mid C \in COMP(S, \mathcal{O}) \cap \mathcal{E} \text{ and } C \subseteq U\}.$$

The measure m is *tight* if

$$m(S) = \sup\{m(C) \mid C \in COMP(S, \mathcal{O}) \cap \mathcal{E}\}.$$

If $U \in \mathcal{E}$ is regular, then $m(C) \leqslant m(U)$ for any compact set included in U; also, for every $\epsilon > 0$ there exists a compact set C such that $m(U) - \epsilon \leqslant m(C) \leqslant m(U)$.

Theorem 7.66. *Let* $(S, \mathcal{O})$ *be a Hausdorff topological space and let* $(S, \mathcal{E}, m)$ *be a measure space on the same set* S, *where* m *is finite and tight. The collection*

$$\mathcal{F} = \{F \in \mathcal{E} \mid \text{both } F \text{ and } S - F \text{ are regular}\}$$

is a σ-*algebra.*

Proof.   Since m is tight, S is regular; also, we have $\emptyset \in \mathcal{F}$, hence $S \in \mathcal{F}$.

Let $U_1, U_2, \ldots, U_n, \ldots$ be a countable collection of sets in $\mathcal{F}$ and let $U = \bigcup_{n \in \mathbb{N}} U_n$.

For each $n \geqslant 1$, both U_n and $S - U_n$ are regular sets, so

$$m(U_n) = \sup\{m(C) \mid C \in C(S, \mathcal{O}) \cap \mathcal{E} \text{ and } C \subseteq U_n\} \text{ and}$$
$$m(S - U_n) = \sup\{m(D) \mid D \in C(S, \mathcal{O}) \cap \mathcal{E} \text{ and } D \subseteq S - U_n\}.$$

Let $\epsilon > 0$. For $n \geqslant 1$ there exist disjoint compact sets C_n and D_n such that $C_n \subseteq U_n$ and $D_n \subseteq S - U_n$,

$$m(U_n - C_n) < \frac{\epsilon}{2^n}, \text{ and } m((S - U_n) - D_n) < \frac{\epsilon}{2^n}.$$

There exists m_ϵ such that:

$$m\left(\bigcup_{1 \leqslant n \leqslant m_\epsilon} C_n \right) > m(U) - \frac{\epsilon}{2}.$$

The set $C = \bigcup_{n \leqslant m_\epsilon} C_n$ is compact, $C \subseteq U$ and $m(C) \geqslant m(U) - \epsilon$.

The set $D = \bigcap_{n \in \mathbb{N}} D_n$ is compact, $m((S - U) - D) \leqslant \sum_{n \geqslant 1} \frac{\epsilon}{2^n} = \epsilon$.

Thus, C and $S - C$ are regular, so $\mathcal{F}$ is a σ-algebra. $\qquad\square$

7.9 Measures in Metric Spaces

In this section we discuss the interaction between metrics and measures defined on metric spaces.

Recall that the dissimilarities between subsets of a metric space was introduced in Section 5.4.

Definition 7.32. Let (S, d) be a metric space. A *Carathéodory outer measure* on (S, d) is an outer measure on S, $\mu : \mathcal{P}(S) \longrightarrow \hat{\mathbb{R}}_{\geqslant 0}$ such that for every two subsets U, V of S such that $d(U, V) > 0$ we have $\mu(U \cup V) = \mu(U) + \mu(V)$.

Theorem 7.67. *Let (S, d) be a metric space. An outer measure μ on S is a Carathéodory outer measure if and only if every closed set of $(S, \mathcal{O}_d)$ is μ-measurable.*

Proof. Suppose that every closed set is μ-measurable and let U, V be two subsets of S such that $d(U, V) > 0$.

Consider the closed set $\mathbf{K}(B(U, r))$, where $r = \frac{d(u,v)}{2}$. Clearly, we have

$$U \subseteq \mathbf{K}(B(U, r)) \text{ and } V \subseteq S - \mathbf{K}(B(U, r)).$$

Since $\mathbf{K}(B(U, r))$ is a μ-measurable set, we have:

$$\mu(U \cup V) = \mu((U \cup V) \cap \mathbf{K}(B(U, r))) + \mu((U \cup V) \cap \overline{\mathbf{K}(B(U, r))}) = \mu(U) + \mu(V),$$

so μ is a Carathéodory outer measure.

Conversely, suppose that μ is a Carathéodory outer measure, that is, $d(U, V) > 0$ implies $\mu(U \cup V) = \mu(U) + \mu(V)$.

Let U be an open set, L be a subset of U, and let $L_1, L_2, \ldots$ be a sequence of sets defined by:

$$L_n = \left\{ t \in L \,\middle|\, d(t, \mathbf{K}(U)) \geqslant \frac{1}{n} \right\},$$

for $n \geqslant 1$. Observe that $L_1, L_2, \ldots$ is an increasing sequence of sets, so the sequence $\mu(L_1), \mu(L_2), \ldots$ is increasing. Therefore, $\lim_{n \to \infty} \mu(L_i)$ exists and $\lim_{n \to \infty} \mu(L_i) \leqslant \mu(L)$. We claim that $\lim_{n \to \infty} \mu(L_i) = \mu(L)$.

Since every set L_n is a subset of L, it follows that $\bigcup_{n \geqslant 1} L_n \subseteq L$. Let $t \in L \subseteq U$. Since U is an open set, there exists $\epsilon > 0$ such that $B(t, \epsilon) \subseteq U$, so $d(t, \mathbf{K}(U)) \geqslant \frac{1}{n}$ if $n > \frac{1}{\epsilon}$. Thus, for sufficiently large values of n, we have $t \in L_n$, so $L \subseteq \bigcup_{n \geqslant 1} L_n$. This shows that $L = \bigcup_{n \geqslant 1} L_n$.

Consider the sequence of sets $M_n = L_{n+1} - L_n$ for $n \geqslant 1$. Clearly, we can write:

$$L = L_{2n} \cup \bigcup_{k=2n}^{\infty} M_k = L_{2n} \cup \bigcup_{p=n}^{\infty} M_{2p} \cup \bigcup_{p=n}^{\infty} M_{2p+1},$$

so

$$\mu(L) \leqslant \mu(L_{2n}) + \sum_{p=n}^{\infty} \mu(M_{2p}) + \sum_{p=n}^{\infty} \mu(M_{2p+1}),$$

If both series $\sum_{p=1}^{\infty} \mu(M_{2p})$ and $\sum_{p=1}^{\infty} \mu(M_{2p+1})$ are convergent, then

$$\lim_{n \to \infty} \sum_{p=n}^{\infty} \mu(M_{2p}) = 0 \text{ and } \lim_{n \to \infty} \sum_{p=n}^{\infty} \mu(M_{2p+1}) = 0,$$

and so $\mu(L) \leqslant \lim_{n \to \infty} \mu(L_{2n})$.

If the series $\sum_{p=n}^{\infty} \mu(M_{2p})$ is divergent, let $t \in M_{2p} \subseteq L_{2p+1}$. If $z \in \mathbf{K}(U)$, then $d(t, z) \geqslant \frac{1}{2p+1}$ by the definition of L_{2p+1}. Let $y \in M_{2p+2} \subseteq L_{2p+3}$. We have

$$\frac{1}{2p+2} > d(y, z) > \frac{1}{2p+3},$$

so

$$d(t, y) \geqslant t(t, z) - d(y, z) \geqslant \frac{1}{2p+1} - \frac{1}{2p+2},$$

which means that $d(M_{2p}, M_{2p+2}) > 0$ for $p \geqslant 1$. Since μ is a Carathéodory outer measure, we have:

$$\sum_{p=1}^{n} \mu(M_{2p}) = \mu \left(\bigcup_{p=1}^{n} M_{2p} \right) \leqslant \mu(L_{2n}).$$

This implies $\lim_{n\to\infty} \mu(L_n) = \lim_{n\to\infty} \mu(L_{2n}) = \infty$, so we have in all cases $\lim_{n\to\infty} \mu(A_n) = \mu(L)$.

Let F be a closed set in $(S, \mathcal{O}_d)$ and let V be an arbitrary set. The set $V \cup \mathbf{K}(F)$ is contained in the set $\mathbf{K}(F) = F$, so, by the previous argument, there exists a sequence of sets L_n such that $d(L_n, F) \geqslant \frac{1}{n}$ for each n and $\lim_{n\to\infty} \mu(L_n) = \mu(V \cap \mathbf{K}(F))$. Consequently, $\mu(V) \geqslant \mu((V \cap F) \cup L_n) = \mu(V \cup F) + \mu(L_n)$. Taking the limit we obtain $\mu(V) \geqslant \mu(V \cap F) + \mu(V \cap \mathbf{K}(F))$, which proves that F is μ-measurable. $\qquad\square$

Corollary 7.23. *Let (S, d) be a metric space. An outer measure on S is a Carathéodory outer measure if and only if every Borel subset of S is μ-measurable.*

Proof. This statement is an immediate consequence of Theorem 7.67. $\qquad\square$

Let (S, d) be a metric space and let $\mathcal{C}$ be a countable collection of subsets of S. Define

$$\mathcal{C}_r = \{C \in \mathcal{C} \mid diam(C) < r\}$$

and assume that for every $x \in S$ and $r > 0$ there exists $C \in \mathcal{C}_r$ such that $x \in C$. Let $\phi : \mathcal{C} \to \hat{\mathbb{R}}_{\geqslant 0}$ be a function and let $\mu_{\phi,r}$ be the outer measure constructed using the method described in Example 7.12.

This construction yields an outer measure that is not necessarily a Carathéodory outer measure. When r decreases, $\mu_{\phi,r}$ increases. This allows us to define

$$\hat{\mu}_\phi = \lim_{r\to 0} \mu_{\phi,r}.$$

We shall prove that the measure $\hat{\mu}_\phi$ is a Carathéodory outer measure.

Since each measure $\mu_{\phi,r}$ is an outer measure, it follows immediately that $\hat{\mu}_\phi$ is an outer measure.

Theorem 7.68. *Let (S, d) be a metric space, $\mathcal{C}$ be a countable collection of subsets of S, and $f : \mathcal{C} \to \hat{\mathbb{R}}_{\geqslant 0}$. Then, $\hat{\mu}_\phi$ is a Carathéodory outer measure.*

Proof. Let U, V be two subsets of S such that $d(U, V) > 0$. We need to show only that $\hat{\mu}_\phi(U \cup V) \geqslant \hat{\mu}_\phi(U) + \hat{\mu}_\phi(V)$.

Choose r such that $0 < r < d(U, V)$ and let $\mathcal{D}$ be an open cover of $U \cup V$ that consists of sets of $\mathcal{C}_r$. Each set of $\mathcal{D}$ can intersect at most one of the set U and V. Therefore, $\mathcal{D}$ is a disjoint union of two collections, $\mathcal{D} = \mathcal{D}_U \cup \mathcal{D}_V$, where $\mathcal{D}_U$ is an open cover for U and $\mathcal{D}_V$ is an open cover for V. Then,

$$\sum\{\phi(D) \mid D \in \mathcal{D}\} = \sum\{\phi(D) \mid D \in \mathcal{D}_U\} + \sum\{\phi(D) \mid D \in \mathcal{D}_V\}$$
$$\geqslant \mu_{\phi,r}(U) + \mu_{\phi,r}(V).$$

This implies $\mu_{\phi,r}(U \cup V) \geqslant \mu_{\phi,r}(U) + \mu_{\phi,r}(V)$, which yields $\hat{\mu}_\phi(U \cup V) \geqslant \hat{\mu}_\phi(U) + \hat{\mu}_\phi(V)$ by taking the limit for $r \to 0$. $\qquad\square$

7.10 Signed and Complex Measures

The notion of measure can be extended by allowing a measure to range over the extended set of real numbers.

Definition 7.33. Let $(S, \mathcal{E})$ be a measurable space. A *signed measure* is a function $m : \mathcal{E} \longrightarrow \hat{\mathbb{R}}$ that satisfies the following conditions:

(i) $m(\emptyset) = 0$;
(ii) $\mathsf{Ran}(m)$ contains only one of the values ∞ and $-\infty$;
(iii) for every countable collection $\{U_0, U_1, \ldots\}$ of sets in $\mathcal{E}$ that are pairwise disjoint one of the following cases may occur:

(a) if $m(\bigcup_{n \in \mathbb{N}})$ is finite, then the series $\sum_{n \in \mathbb{N}} m(U_i)$ is absolutely convergent and

$$m\left(\bigcup_{n \in \mathbb{N}} U_n\right) = \sum_{n \in \mathbb{N}} m(U_n);$$

(b) if $m(\bigcup_{n \in \mathbb{N}})$ is not finite, then the series $\sum_{n \in \mathbb{N}} m(U_n)$ is divergent

(the *additivity property of signed measures*).

We refer to the triple $(S, \mathcal{E}, m)$ as a *signed measure space*.

The set of signed, real-valued measures over a measurable space $(S, \mathcal{E})$ is denoted by $\mathsf{RM}(S, cale)$.

The set $\mathsf{RM}(S, \mathcal{E})$ is a real linear space relative the addition of real-valued measures and multiplication by scalars.

Example 7.16. Let $(S, \mathcal{E})$ be a measurable space and let m_1, m_2 be two measures defined on $\mathcal{E}$ such that at least one of these measures is finite. Then, the function $m : \mathcal{E} \longrightarrow \hat{\mathbb{R}}$ given by $m(U) = m_1(U) - m_2(U)$ for $U \in \mathcal{E}$ is a signed measure.

The requirement that at least one of m_1, m_2 is finite ensures that m is well-defined.

Definition 7.34. Let $(S, \mathcal{E}, m)$ be a signed measure space. A set $U \in \mathcal{E}$ is *positive* if for every set W such that $W \in \mathcal{E}$ and $W \subseteq U$ we have $m(W) \geqslant 0$. Similarly, $U \in \mathcal{E}$ is *negative* if for every set W such that $W \in \mathcal{E}$ and $W \subseteq U$ we have $m(W) \leqslant 0$.

A set $U \in \mathcal{E}$ is an *m-null* for a signed measure m if it is both positive and negative.

Both positivity and negativity are hereditary properties; in other words, if a set is positive (negative), then so is any of its measurable subsets.

Note that the requirement that a set is m-null, where m is a signed measure, is more stringent than the usual definition of null sets for measures.

A set U is m-null if and only if *for each of its measurable subsets W we have $m(W) = 0$.* It is clear that for every m-null set U we have $m(U) = 0$. However, the inverse is not true: a set of measure 0 is not necessarily an m-null set in the sense of Definition 7.34 as the next example shows.

Example 7.17. Let $(S, \mathcal{P}(S))$ be a measurable space and let x_1 and x_2 be two distinct elements of S. Consider the Dirac measures δ_{x_1} and δ_{x_2} defined on $\mathcal{P}(S)$ (as introduced in Example 7.6). It is easy to verify that $m : \mathcal{P}(S) \longrightarrow \hat{\mathbb{R}}$ defined by $m(U) = \delta_{x_1}(U) - \delta_{x_2}(U)$ is a signed measure on $\mathcal{P}(S)$, so $(S, \mathcal{P}(S), m)$ is a signed measure space. Then, we have

$$m(\{x_1, x_2\}) = \delta_{x_1}(\{x_1, x_2\}) - \delta_{x_2}(\{x_1, x_2\}) = 1 - 1 = 0.$$

However, $\{x_1, x_2\}$ is not an m-null set because for its subsets $\{x_1\}$ and $\{x_2\}$ we have $m(\{x_1\}) = 1$ and $m(\{x_2\}) = -1$.

Theorem 7.69. *Let $(S, \mathcal{E}, m)$ a signed measure space and let $\boldsymbol{U} = (U_0, \ldots, U_n, \ldots)$ be a sequence of positive (negative) sets. Then, $U = \bigcup_{n \in \mathbb{N}} U_n$ is a positive (negative) set.*

Proof. Let W be a subset of U. Define the sequence of sets $\boldsymbol{V} = (V_0, \ldots, V_n, \ldots)$ as

$$V_n = W \cap U_n \cap \bigcap_{i=0}^{n-1} \overline{U_i},$$

for $n \geqslant 0$.

Any set V_n is a measurable subset of U_n and, therefore, $m(V_n) \geqslant 0$. Furthermore, since the sets V_n are pairwise disjoint and $W = \bigcup_{n \in \mathbb{N}} V_n$, it follows that $m(W) = \sum_{n \in \mathbb{N}} m(V_n) \geqslant 0$, so U is indeed a positive set. The argument for the union of negative set is similar. $\qquad \square$

Theorem 7.70. *Let* $(S, \mathcal{E}, m)$ *a signed measure space and let* $U \in \mathcal{E}$ *be a set such that* $0 < m(U) < \infty$. *Then,* U *contains a positive subset* T *such that* $m(T) > 0$.

Proof. If U itself is positive, then we can take $T = U$. Therefore, we need to consider only the case when U is not positive, that is, the case when U contains some subsets of negative measure.

We construct inductively a sequence of sets $\mathbf{V} = (V_0, V_1, \ldots, V_n, \ldots)$ as follows.

By the assumption made above there exists a subset V_0 of U such that $m(V_0) < 0$. Let n_0 be the least natural number such that $m(V_0) \leqslant -\frac{1}{n_0}$.

Suppose that we constructed the sets $V_0, \ldots, V_{i-1}$. Let n_i be the least natural number such that there exists a set $W_i \in \mathcal{E}$ such that $W_i \subseteq U - \bigcup_{j=1}^{i-1} W_j$ and $m(W_i) < -\frac{1}{n_i}$.

Define $T = U - \bigcup_{i=0}^{\infty} W_i$. We have

$$U = T \cup \bigcup_{i=0}^{\infty} W_i,$$

and the sets and since the sets W_i are are pairwise disjoint, this implies

$$m(U) = m(T) + \sum_{i=0}^{\infty} m(W_i).$$

The finiteness of $m(U)$ means that the series $\sum_{i=0}^{\infty} m(W_i)$ is absolutely convergent. Since $\frac{1}{n_i} < |m(W_i)|$, the series $\sum_{i=0}^{\infty} \frac{1}{n_i}$ is convergent which, in turn, implies $\lim_{i \to \infty} n_i = \infty$. Further, we have $m(T) > 0$.

To show that T is a positive set let ϵ be a positive number. We shall prove that T contains no measurable subset Z such that $m(Z) < -\epsilon$.

Suppose that such a set Z exists. Choose k such that

$$\frac{1}{n_k - 1} < \epsilon$$

and observe that $T \subseteq U - \bigcup_{i=0}^{k-1} W_i$. If such a set Z would exist we would have

$$m(Z) < -\epsilon < -\frac{1}{n_k - 1},$$

and this would contradict the definition of n_k as the least natural number such that there exists a subset of $U - \bigcup_{j=0}^{k-1} W_j$ whose measure is less than $-\frac{1}{n_k}$. Since this is true for every $\epsilon > 0$, it follows that T contains no subsets of negative measure, so T is positive. $\qquad\square$

Theorem 7.71 (Hahn Decomposition Theorem). *Let $(S, \mathcal{E}, m)$ be a signed measure space. There exists a two-block partition of S, $\pi = \{B_+, B_-\}$ such that $B_+ \in \mathcal{E}$ is a positive set for m and $B_- \in \mathcal{E}$ is a negative set.*

Proof. Suppose that ∞ is not in the range of m. Define

$$M = \sup\{m(U) \mid U \in \mathcal{E} \text{ and } m(U) \geqslant 0\}.$$

We have $M \geqslant 0$ because $m(\emptyset) = 0$.

Let $\mathbf{U} = (U_0, \ldots, U_n, \ldots)$ be a sequence of sets in $\mathcal{E}$ such that $\lim_{n \to \infty} m(U_n) = M$ and let $U = \bigcup_{n=0}^{\infty} m(U_i) \in \mathcal{E}$. We claim that $m(U) = M$.

By Theorem 7.69, U is a positive set, so $m(U) \leqslant M$. Since $U - U_n$ is a subset of U, it follows that $m(U - U_n) \geqslant 0$. Consequently, $m(U) = m(U_n) + m(U - U_n) \geqslant m(U_n)$, which implies $m(U) \geqslant m(U_n)$ for $n \in \mathbb{N}$. Therefore, $m(U) = M$, which justifies the previous claim. In addition, this means that $M < \infty$.

Consider now the set $V = S - U$. We claim now that V is a negative set. Suppose that V is not negative. Then it contains a positive set W. Since W is disjoint from U, it follows that $U \cup W$ is a positive set, so $M \geqslant m(U \cup W) = m(U) + m(W) > M + m(W)$, which is impossible. Thus, V is a negative set. The partition π is obtained now as $B_+ = U$ and $B_- = V$. $\square$

The two-block partition π whose existence was established in Theorem 7.71 is known as a *Hahn decomposition* of the signed measure space $(S, \mathcal{E}, m)$. The Hahn decomposition is not unique as the next example shows.

Example 7.18. Let $(S, \mathcal{P}(S), m)$ be the signed measure space introduced in Example 7.17, where we have the *strict* inclusion $\{x_1, x_2\} \subset S$. The range of m is the set $\{-1, 0, 1\}$.

Define $B_+ = S - \{x_2\}$ and $B_- = \{x_2\}$. The partition $\{B_+, B_-\}$ is a Hahn decomposition for $(S, \mathcal{P}(S), m)$. On the other hand, if $B'_+ = \{x_1\}$ and $B'_- = S - \{x_1\}$, then $\{B'_+, B'_-\}$ is a distinct Hahn decomposition of this signed measure space.

Definition 7.35. Let $(S, \mathcal{E})$ be a measurable space and let $m_0, m_1 : \mathcal{E} \longrightarrow \hat{\mathbb{R}}_{\geqslant 0}$ be two measures. The measures m_0 and m_1 are *mutually singular* if there exists a subset $T \in \mathcal{E}$ such that $m_0(T) = m_1(S - T) = 0$. This is denoted by $m_0 \perp m_1$.

Theorem 7.72. (Jordan's Decomposition Theorem) *A Hahn decomposition of a signed measure space $(S, \mathcal{E}, m)$ generates a unique pair of mutually singular measures such that m is the difference of these mutually singular measures.*

Any two mutually singular measures on $(S, \mathcal{E}, m)$ generate a Hahn decomposition of a signed measure space.

Proof. Let $\pi = \{B_+, B_-\}$ be a Hahn decomposition of $(S, \mathcal{E}, m)$. Define the measures

$$m_+(U) = m(U \cap B_+),$$
$$m_-(U) = -m(U \cap B_-),$$

for $U \in \mathcal{E}$. Observe that the measures m_+ and m_- are mutually singular because $m_+(B_-) = 0$ and $m_-(S - B_-) = m_-(B_+) = 0$, which shows that the role of the set T can be played by the set B_-. Moreover, we have

$$m(U) = m(U \cap B_+) + m(U \cap B_-) = m_+(U) - m_-(U),$$

for every $U \in \mathcal{E}$. This shows that we can decompose any signed measure into the difference of two measures.

Conversely, suppose that q_0, q_1 are two mutually singular measures on the measurable space $(S, \mathcal{E})$ such that $q_0(T) = q_1(S - T) = 0$ and let $q : \mathcal{E} \longrightarrow \hat{\mathbb{R}}$ be the signed measure $q(U) = q_0(U) - q_1(U)$ for $U \in \mathcal{E}$. We claim that $\{S - T, T\}$ is a Hahn decomposition of the signed measure space $(S, \mathcal{E}, q)$.

Note that $q(T) = -q_1(T) \leqslant 0$ and $q(S - T) = q_0(S - T) \geqslant 0$. Suppose that Z is a subset of T. Since q_0 and q_1 are measures, we have $q_0(Z) \leqslant q_0(T) = 0$ and $q_1(Z) \leqslant q_1(T)$. Therefore, $q_0(Z) = 0$ and $q(Z) = q_0(Z) - q_1(Z) \leqslant 0$, so T is a negative set. If $Y \subseteq S-T$, then $q_1(Y) \leqslant q_1(S-T) = 0$, so $q_1(Y) = q_0(Y) - q_1(Y) \geqslant 0$, which proves that $S - T$ is a positive set. Thus, $\{S - T, T\}$ is indeed a Hahn decomposition of the signed measure space $(S, \mathcal{E}, q)$. Moreover,

$$q_0(U) = q_0(U \cap T) + q_0(U \cap (S-T)) = q_0(U \cap (S-T)) = q(U \cap (S-T)) = q_+(U)$$

and

$$q_1(U) = q_1(U \cap T) + q_1(U \cap (S - T)) = q_1(U \cap T) = -q(U \cap T) = q_-(U).$$

$\square$

The decomposition of a signed measure m as a difference of two mutually singular measures is known as the *Jordan decomposition* of the signed measure m.

Definition 7.36. The measure $|m|$ defined by $m(U) = m_+(U) + m_-(U)$ is called the *absolute value* or the *total variation* of m.

A signed measure m is *finite* (σ-*finite*) if $|m|$ is finite (σ-finite).

Theorem 7.73. *Let* $(S, \mathcal{E}, m)$ *be a signed measure space. The following statements hold for a set* $T \in \mathcal{E}$:

(i) $|m|(T) = \sup\{\sum_{k=1}^{n} |m(T_j)| \mid \{T_1, \ldots, T_n\} \in PART_{\mathcal{E}}(T)\}$;

(ii) $\sup\{|m(U)| \mid U \in \mathcal{E}[T]\} \leqslant |m|(T) \leqslant 2\sup\{|m(U)| \mid U \in \mathcal{E}[T]\}$;

(iii) *for every positive measure* m_1 *such that* $|m(T)| \leqslant m_1(T)$ *we have* $|m| \leqslant m_1$.

Proof. Let $\{T_1, \ldots, T_n\} \in PART_{\mathcal{E}}(T)\}$. We have

$$|m|(T) = \sum_{j=1}^{n} |m|(T_j) = \sum_{j=1}^{n} (m_-(T_j) + m_+(T_j))$$

$$\geqslant \sum_{j=1}^{n} (m_-(T_j) - m_+(T_j)) = \sum_{j=1}^{n} |m(T_j)|. \tag{7.11}$$

If $\{B_+, B_-\}$ is a Hahn decomposition theorem of S, $\{T \cap B_+, T \cap B_-\} \in PART_{\mathcal{E}}(T)$ and

$$|m(T \cap B_+)| + |m(T \cap B_-)| = m(T \cap B_+) - m(T \cap B_-)$$
$$= m_+(T) + m_-(T) = |m|(T).$$

Therefore,

$$|m|(T) \leqslant \sum \{\sum_{k=1}^{n} |m(T_j)| \mid \{T_1, \ldots, T_n\} \in PART_{\mathcal{E}}(T)\}.$$

This and inequality (7.11) imply the equality of the first part.

If $T \in \mathcal{E}$ and $U \in \mathcal{E}[T]$ we have $\{U, T - U\} \in PART_{\mathcal{E}}(T)$ and therefore,

$$|m|(T) \geqslant |m(U)| + |m(T - U)| \geqslant |m(U)|.$$

Consequently, $\sup\{|m(U)| \mid U \in \mathcal{E}[T]\} \leqslant |m|(T)$.

If $\{B_+, B_-\}$ is a Hahn decomposition for S we have

$$|m|(T) = m_+(T) + m_-(T) = m(T \cap B_+) - m(T \cap B_-)$$
$$= |m(T \cap B_+)| + |m(T \cap B_-)| \leqslant 2\sup\{|m(U)| \mid U \in \mathcal{E}[T]\},$$

which proves the second part of the theorem.

Since $\sup\{|m(U)| \mid U \in \mathcal{E}[T]\} \leqslant |m|(T)$, we have $|m|$ is a positive measure with $|m(T)| \leqslant |m|(T)$ for $T \in \mathcal{E}$.

Let m_1 be a positive measure m_1 such that $|m(T)| \leqslant m_1(T)$ for every $T \in \mathcal{E}$ and let $\{B_+, B_-\}$ be a Hahn decomposition of S relative to m. Then,

$$|m|(U) = m(U \cap B_+) - m(U \cap B_-) = |m(U \cap B_+)| + |m(U \cap B_-)|$$
$$\leqslant m_1(U \cap B_+) + m_1(U \cap B_-) = m_1(U),$$

for every $U \in \mathcal{E}$, hence $|m| \leqslant m_1$. □

Theorem 7.74. *Let $(S, \mathcal{E}, m)$ be a signed measure space. We have $m(T) = 0$ for some $T \in \mathcal{E}$ (that is, T is an m-null set) if and only if $|m|(T) = 0$.*

Proof. Note that T is a m-null set if and only if $m(U) = 0$ for every $U \in \mathcal{E}[T]$, which means that $\sup\{m(U) \mid U \in \mathcal{E}[T]\} = 0$. By Theorem 7.73, $|m|(T) = 0$. □

The next definition further extends the notion of measure to include measures whose values are complex numbers.

Definition 7.37. Let $(S, \mathcal{E})$ be a measurable space. A *complex measure* on $\mathcal{E}$ is a complex function $m : \mathcal{E} \longrightarrow \mathbb{C}$ such that

(i) $m(\emptyset) = 0$, and
(ii) $m(\bigcup_{j=1}^{\infty} E_j) = \sum_{j=1}^{\infty} m(E_j)$ for every infinite sequence (E_n) of disjoint sets in $\mathcal{E}$.

Note that a complex measure has no infinite values. Thus, a real measure can be regarded as a complex measure only if its values are finite.

Jordan's Decomposition Theorem can be naturally extended to complex measures. Suppose that m is a complex measure on S. We can write $m(E) = m_1(E) + im_2(E)$, where m_1, m_2 are signed measures on S. Further, by Jordan's decomposition theorem there exists mutually singular measures m_1', m_1'' and m_2', m_2'' such that $m_1 = m_1' - m_1''$ and $m_2 = m_2' - m_2''$. This allows us to write

$$m(E) = m_1' - m_1'' + i(m_2' - m_2''),$$

where $m_1' - m_1''$ and $m_2' - m_2''$ are signed measures.

For a complex measure on a measurable space $(S, \mathcal{E})$ let $|m| : \mathcal{E} \longrightarrow \mathbb{R}$ be the real-valued function defined by:

$$|m|(E) = \sup\left\{\sum_{i=1}^{n} |m(E_i)| \mid \{E_1, \dots, E_n\}\right.$$

$$\left. \text{is a partition of } E \text{ with } E_i \in \mathcal{E}\right\}.$$

Theorem 7.75. *For every measure space* $(S, \mathcal{E}, m)$, *where* m *is a complex measure* $m : \mathcal{E} \longrightarrow \mathbb{C}$, *the mapping* $|m| : \mathcal{E} \longrightarrow \mathbb{R}$ *is a finite measure on* $(S, \mathcal{E})$.

Proof. Observe that $|m|(\emptyset) = 0$. Since m is a complex measure on S, as we shown before, can write $m(E) = m_1(E) + im_2(E)$, where m_1, m_2 are signed measures on S. Furthermore, there exist mutually singular measures m'_1, m''_1 and m'_2, m''_2 such that $m_1 = m'_1 - m''_1$ and $m_2 = m'_2 - m''_2$, hence

$$m(E) = m'_1(E) - m''_1(E) + i(m'_2(E) - m''_2(E)).$$

Let $C, D \in \mathcal{E}$, where $C \cap D = \emptyset$, and let $\{B_1, \dots, B_n\}$ be a finite partition of $C \cup D$, where $B_j \in \mathcal{E}$ for $1 \leqslant j \leqslant n$. We have

$$\sum_{j=1}^{n} |m(B_j)| \leqslant \sum_{j=1}^{n} |m(B_j \cap C)| + \sum_{j=1}^{n} |m(B_j \cap D)|$$
$$\leqslant |m|(C) + |m|(D).$$

Since

$$|m|(C \cup D) = \sup\{\sum_{j=1}^{n} |m(B_j)| \mid \{B_1, \dots, B_n\} \text{ is a partition of } C \cup D \},$$

it follows that $|m|(C \cup D) \leqslant |m|(C) + |m|(D)$.

To prove the reverse inequality, let $\{B_1, \dots, B_p\}$ be a finite partition of C and let $\{B'_1, \dots, B'_q\}$ be a partition of D. Since C and D are disjoint, $\{B_1, \dots, B_p, B'_1, \dots, B'_q\}$ is a partition of $C \cup D$. Thus,

$$|m|(C \cup D) \geqslant \sup\left\{ \sum_{j=1}^{p} |m(B_j)| + \sum_{j=1}^{q} |m(B'_j)| \right\}$$

$$= \sup\left\{ \sum_{j=1}^{p} |m(B_j)| \mid \{B_1, \dots, B_p\} \text{ is a partition of } C \right\}$$

$$+ \sup\left\{ \sum_{j=1}^{q} |m(B'_j)| \mid \{B'_1, \dots, B'_q\} \text{ is a partition of } D \right\}$$

$$= |m|(C) + |m|(D).$$

Therefore $|m|(C \cup D) = |m|(C) + |m|(D)$, so m is finitely additive.

By Jordan's decomposition theorem we have

$$|m|(E) \leqslant m'_1(E) + m''_1(E) + m'_2(E)' + m''_2(E),$$

which implies that $|m|$ is finite.

If $(U_n)_{n \geqslant 1}$ is a decreasing sequence of measurable sets such that $\bigcap U_n = \emptyset$, then for $m' \in \{m'_1, m''_1, m'_2, m''_2\}$ we have $\lim_{n \to \infty} m'(U_n) = 0$, hence $\lim_{n \to \infty} |m|(U_n) = 0$. Thus, by Supplement 46, $|m|$ is countably additive. $\qquad \square$

For a complex measure m the measure $|m|$ is known as the *variation* of m. The number $|m|(S)$ is known as the *total variation* of m and is denoted by $\|m\|$.

Let $\mathsf{CM}(S, \mathcal{E})$ be the collection of all complex measures on the measure space $(S, \mathcal{E})$. The set $\mathsf{CM}(S, \mathcal{E})$ is a complex linear space relative the addition of complex-valued measures and multiplication by scalars. Furthermore, the total variation is a norm over this space.

If $m_1, m_2 \in \mathsf{CM}(S, \mathcal{E})$ the sum $m_1 + m_2$ and product with a scalar $c \in \mathbb{C}$ are defined as

$$(m_1 + m_2)(U) = m_1(U) + m_2(U),$$
$$(am_1)(U) = am_1(U)$$

for each $U \in \mathcal{E}$. The set $\mathsf{CM}(S, \mathcal{E})$ becomes a complex linear space and this space can be equipped with the norm $\| \cdot \|$ defined as $\|m\| = |m|(S)$.

7.11 Probability Spaces

Definition 7.38. A *probability space* is a measure space $(\Omega, \mathcal{E}, P)$, where $P : \mathcal{E} \longrightarrow [0, 1]$ is a measure such that $P(\Omega) = 1$.

We will refer to P as a *probability measure* or, simply, as a *probability*.

In the context of probability spaces we refer to the subsets of Ω that belong to $\mathcal{E}$ as *events*.

Example 7.19. Probability spaces formalize the notion of sets of experiments. Consider, for instance, throwing a coin. There are two possible outcomes, head or tail, denoted by $\mathbf{h}$ and $\mathbf{t}$. If we define $\Omega = \{\mathbf{h}, \mathbf{t}\}$, $\mathcal{E} = \mathcal{P}(\Omega)$ and $P(\mathbf{h}) = P(\mathbf{t}) = \frac{1}{2}$ we obtain the probability space that describes the coin throwing experiment.

Let $(\Omega, \mathcal{E}, P)$ and $(\Omega, \mathcal{E}, Q)$ be two probability spaces that share the same Ω and σ-algebra of events $\mathcal{E}$ that is generated by a π-system $\mathcal{C}$. If $P(A) = Q(A)$ for all $A \in \mathcal{C}$, then $P(A) = Q(A)$ for all $A \in \mathcal{E}$. This follows from Corollary 7.8 because both P and Q are finite measures.

If A is an event of a probability space $(\Omega, \mathcal{E}, P)$ and $P(A) = 1$ we say that A occurs *almost surely*.

Theorem 7.76. *Let $(\Omega, \mathcal{E}, P)$ be a probability space and let $B \in \mathcal{E}$ be an event such that $P(B) > 0$. Define the* probability conditioned by the event B, $P(\cdot|B) : \mathcal{E} \upharpoonright_B \longrightarrow [0,1]$ *as*

$$P(A|B) = \frac{P(A \cap B)}{P(B)}.$$

The triple $(B, \mathcal{E} \upharpoonright_B, P(\cdot|B))$ is a probability space.

Proof. Let $\{A_n \mid n \in \mathbb{N}\}$ be a sequence of pairwise disjoint events in $(\Omega, \mathcal{E}, P)$. We have:

$$P\left(\bigcup_{n\in\mathbb{N}} A_n \Big| B\right) = \frac{P\left(\left(\bigcup_{s\in\mathbb{N}} A_n\right) \cap B\right)}{P(B)}$$

$$= \frac{P\left(\bigcup_{s\in\mathbb{N}}(A_n \cap B)\right)}{P(B)}$$

$$= \frac{\sum_{n\in\mathbb{N}} P(A_n \cap B)}{P(B)} = \sum_{n\in\mathbb{N}} P(A_n|B),$$

so P is countably additive. Since $P(B|B) = 1$, $(B, \mathcal{E} \upharpoonright_B, P(\cdot|B))$ is a probability space. $\qquad\square$

Let $\mathcal{E}_1 = \{B \in \mathcal{E} \mid P(B) > 0\}$. The function $P(\cdot|\cdot) : \mathcal{E} \times \mathcal{E}' \longrightarrow [0,1]$ given by $P(A|B) = \frac{P(A\cap B)}{P(B)}$, where $A \in \mathcal{E}$ and $B \in \mathcal{E}'$ is the *conditional probability defined by P.*

Theorem 7.77. (Total Probability Theorem) *Let $\{B_n \mid n \in \mathbb{N}\}$ be a family of pairwise disjoint events in the probability space $(\Omega, \mathcal{E}, P)$ such that $\bigcup_{n\in\mathbb{N}} B_n = \Omega$ and $P(B_n) \neq 0$ for $n \in \mathbb{N}$. We have*

$$P(A) = \sum_{n\in\mathbb{N}} P(A|B_n)P(B_n).$$

Proof. Note that the family of events $\{A \cap B_n \mid n \in \mathbb{N}\}$ is a partition of A. This allows us to write

$$A = A \cap \Omega = A \cap \left(\bigcup_{n\in\mathbb{N}} B_n\right)$$

$$= \bigcup_{n\in\mathbb{N}} (A \cap B_n).$$

Since the events of the form $A \cap B_n$ are pairwise disjoint, it follows that

$$P(A) = \sum_{n\in\mathbb{N}} P(A \cap B_n) = \sum_{n\in\mathbb{N}} P(A|B_n)P(B_n). \qquad\square$$

Definition 7.39. Let $(\Omega, \mathcal{E}, P)$ be a probability space and let $A, B \in \mathcal{E}$. The events A and B are *independent* if $P(A \cap B) = P(A)P(B)$.

Note that if A, B are events and $P(B) \ne 0$, then A, B are independent if $P(A) = P(A|B)$.

If $A \cap B = \emptyset$, then A and B are independent if at least of them equals $\emptyset$. If $A \subseteq B$, then A, B are independent if $A = \emptyset$ or $B = \Omega$.

Example 7.20. Consider the probability space $([0, 1], \mathbb{B}([0, 1]), P)$, where P is obtained by defining $P([a, b]) = b - a$. If $0 \leqslant a \leqslant c \leqslant b \leqslant d \leqslant 1$, the independence condition for the events $[a, b]$ and $[c, d]$

$$P([a, b] \cap [c, d]) = P([a, b]) \cdot P([c, d])$$

amounts to

$$(b - c) = (b - a)(d - c).$$

The concept of independent events can be extended to any finite collection of events.

Definition 7.40. Let $(\Omega, \mathcal{E}, P)$ be a probability space and let $A_1, \ldots, A_n$ be events in $\mathcal{E}$. These events are independent if for every k such that $2 \leqslant k \leqslant n$ we have the equalities

$$P(A_{i_1} \cap A_{i_2} \cap \cdots \cap A_{i_k}) = P(A_{i_1})P(A_{i_2}) \cdots P(A_{i_k}).$$

Example 7.21. Three events A_1, A_2, A_3 are independent if each of the following equalities

$$P(A_1 \cap A_2) = P(A_1)P(A_2), \tag{7.12}$$

$$P(A_2 \cap A_3) = P(A_2)P(A_3), \tag{7.13}$$

$$P(A_1 \cap A_3) = P(A_1)P(A_3), \tag{7.14}$$

$$P(A_1 \cap A_2 \cap A_3) = P(A_1)P(A_2)P(A_3). \tag{7.15}$$

It interesting to note that the satisfaction of equalities (7.12) - (7.14) is independent of the satisfaction of equality (7.15). Consider, for example, the events $A_1 = [a, b]$, $A_2 = [c, d]$, and $A_3 = [c, e] \cup [k, h]$, where $a < c < b < e < d < k < h$.

If $(b - c) = (b - a)(d - c)$, A_1 and A_2 are independent. Since $A_1 \cap A_3 = [c, b]$ and $A_2 \cap A_3 = [c, e]$, A_1 and A_3 are independent if $(b - c) = (b - a)[(e - c) + (h - k)]$; also, A_2 and A_3 are independent if $(e - c) = (d - c)[(e - c) + (h - k)]$. The first two conditions imply $d = e + h - k$. Thus, the events A_1, A_2, A_3 are pairwise independent if and only if $b-c = (b-a)(d-c)$, $e - c = (d - c)^2$, and $d = e + h - k$.

Note that equality (7.15) amounts to

$$b - c = (b - a)(d - c)[(e - c) + h - k].$$

In view of the fact that $d = e + h_k$ this equality becomes

$$b - c = (d - c)^2. \tag{7.16}$$

If $(d - c) \neq (d - c)^2$, then equality (7.16) cannot be satisfied. Thus, also A_1, A_2, A_3 are pairwise independent, the collection $\{A_1, A_2, A_3\}$ is not independent.

The σ-algebra generated by an event A, $\sigma(A) = \{\emptyset, A, \Omega - A, \Omega\}$ was introduced in Example 1.25. If A, B are independent events in the probability space, then any pair of events in $\{A, \Omega - A\} \times \{B, \Omega - B\}$ is independent.

Indeed, note that

$$P(A \cap (\Omega - B)) = P(A - (A \cap B))$$
$$= P(A) - P(A \cap B) = P(A) - P(A)P(B)$$
$$= P(A)(1 - P(B)) = P(A)P(\Omega - B),$$

so A and $\Omega - B$ are independent events. Similar computations for the remaining pairs of $\{A, \omega - A\} \times \{B, \Omega - B\}$ lead to the conclusion that these pairs of events are independent.

Thus, the notion of independence can be defined for σ-algebras.

Definition 7.41. The collection of σ-algebras $\{\mathcal{E}_i \mid 1 \leqslant i \leqslant n\}$ on Ω, where $(\Omega, \mathcal{E}_i, P)$ are probability spaces is *independent* if every set of n events $A_1, \ldots, A_n$ where $A_i \in \mathcal{E}_i$ for $1 \leqslant i \leqslant n$ is independent.

In the language of probabilities a measurable function between a probability space $(\Omega, \mathcal{E}, P)$ and $(\mathbb{R}, \mathbb{B}(\mathbb{R}), m_L)$ is known as a *random variable*.[2] We denote such random variables using capital letters $X, Y, \ldots$.

Since random variables are special measurable functions, previous facts relevant to such functions apply to random variables. For instance, if $X : \Omega \longrightarrow \mathbb{R}$ is a random variable defined on a probability space $(\Omega, \mathcal{E}, P)$, the *σ-algebra generated by X* is the collection $\mathcal{E}_X = \{X^{-1}(B) \mid B \in \mathbb{B}(\mathbb{R})\}$, as we have shown in Theorem 7.3.

---

[2] A random variable is clearly a function rather than a variable; however, the term "variable" was adopted broadly in probability theory, and we will continue to use it in this context.

Example 7.22. The constant function $X : \mathcal{E} \longrightarrow \mathbb{R}$ defined as $X(\omega) = c$ is a random variable for any probability space $(\Omega, \mathcal{E}, P)$ because

$$X^{-1}(B) = \begin{cases} \Omega & \text{if } c \in B, \\ \emptyset & \text{otherwise,} \end{cases}$$

and the fact that $\{\emptyset, \Omega\} \subseteq \mathcal{E}$. Thus, $\mathcal{E}_X = \{\Omega, \emptyset\}$.

Example 7.23. Suppose now that $\mathsf{Ran}(X) = \{a, b\}$. The σ-algebra $\mathcal{E}_X$ consists of $\{\Omega, \emptyset, X^{-1}(a), X^{-1}(b)\}$.

Let X, Y are two random variable defined on a probability space $(\Omega, \mathcal{E}, P)$. Since $|X - Y|$ is a random variable, $|X - Y|^{-1}(\{0\}) \in \mathcal{E}$. If $P(|X - Y|^{-1}(\{0\}) = 1$, the random variables are equal almost surely. In this case, we say that X and Y are *versions* of each other.

Definition 7.42. Let $(\Omega, \mathcal{E}, P)$ be a probability space and let X, Y be random variables defined on that space. The random variables X and Y are *independent* if the σ-algebras $\mathcal{E}_X$ and $\mathcal{E}_Y$ they generate respectively are independent.

Example 7.24. Let $([0, 1], \mathbb{B}([0, 1]), m_L)$ be a probability space and let $a, b \in [0, 1]$, where $a < b$. The σ-algebra generated by the random variable $X_{[a,b]} = 1_{[a,b]}$ is $\mathcal{E}_X = \{[0, 1], \emptyset, [a, b], [0, a) \cup (b, 1]\}$. If $c, d \in [0, 1]$ and $c < d$, consider the random variable $X_{[c,d]} = 1_{[c,d]}$.

If $a < b \leqslant c < d$, $m_L([a, b] \cap [c, d]) = 0$ and $X_{[a,b]}, X_{c,d}$ are not independent because $m_L([a, b]) = b - a > 0$, $m_L([c, d]) = d - c$, and $m_L([a, b] \cap [c, d]) = 0$.

Thus, it is necessary for independence to have $[a, b] \cap [c, d] \neq \emptyset$. If one of the interval is included in the other, it is easily seen that the independence condition is violated.

Thus, the to obtain independence, the intersection $[a, b] \cap [c, d]$ must be a non-empty interval $[p, q]$, and we must have $(b - a)(d - c) = (q - p)$. Note that if $a \leqslant c \leqslant b \leqslant q$, then $p = c$ and $q = b$, hence we must have $(b - a)(d - c) = b - c$. By Exercise 48, this condition suffices for the independence of $X_{[a,b]}$ and $X_{[c,d]}$.

The alternative, $c \leqslant a \leqslant d \leqslant b$ implies $(b - a)(d - c) = d - a$.

Definition 7.43. A *statement* on a probability space $(\Omega, \mathcal{E}, P)$ is a radom variable $S : \Omega \longrightarrow \{0, 1\}$. If $S(\omega) = 1$ we say that the statement holds on ω.

A statement is true *almost surely* (a.s.) if $F_S = \{\omega \in \Omega \mid S(\omega) = 1\}$ belongs to $\mathcal{E}$ and $P(F_S) = 1$.

Theorem 7.78. *Let* $X : \Omega \longrightarrow \mathbb{R}$ *be a random variable on the probability space* $(\Omega, \mathcal{E}, P)$. *If* $h : \mathbb{R} \longrightarrow \mathbb{R}$ *is a Borel measurable function, then* $Y = hX$ *is a random variable on the same probability space.*

Proof. The statement follows from the equality $Y^{-1}(U) = X^{-1}(f^{-1}(U))$ that holds for every Borel subset U of $\mathbb{R}$. $\qquad \square$

Theorem 7.79. *Let* $X_1, X_2, \ldots$ *be random variables on a probability space* $(\Omega, \mathcal{E}, P)$. *The following are random variables on the same probability space:*
   (i) $\max\{X_1, X_2\}$ *and* $\min\{X_1, X_2\}$;
   (ii) $\sup_n X_n$ *and* $\inf_n X_n$;
   (iii) $\limsup_{n \to \infty} X_n$ *and* $\liminf_{n \to \infty} X_n$ *and*

Proof. Observe that

$$\{\omega \in \Omega \mid \max\{X_1, X_2\}(\omega) \leqslant x\}$$
$$= \{\omega \in \Omega \mid X_1(\omega) \leqslant x\} \cap \{\omega \in \Omega \mid X_1(\omega) \leqslant x\},$$
$$\{\omega \in \Omega \mid \min\{X_1, X_2\}(\omega) \leqslant x\}$$
$$= \{\omega \in \Omega \mid X_1(\omega) \leqslant x\} \cup \{\omega \in \Omega \mid X_1(\omega) \leqslant x\}$$

for every $x \in \hat{\mathbb{R}}$, which proves the first part.

The second part follows from the fact that

$$\{\omega \in \Omega \mid (\sup X_n)(\omega) \leqslant x\} = \bigcap_{n \in \mathbb{N}} \{\omega \in \Omega \mid X_n \leqslant x\} \in \mathcal{E}$$

and

$$\{\omega \in \Omega \mid (\inf X_n)(\omega) \leqslant x\} = \bigcup_{n \in \mathbb{N}} \{\omega \in \Omega \mid X_n \leqslant x\} \in \mathcal{E}.$$

Finally, since

$$\limsup_{n \to \infty} X_n = \inf_m \sup_{n \geqslant m} X_n$$

and

$$\liminf_{n \to \infty} X_n = \sup_m \inf_{n \geqslant m} X_n,$$

the last part follows. $\qquad \square$

Corollary 7.24. *If* $(X_n(\omega))$ *converges for almost every* ω, *then* $\lim_{n \to \infty} X_n$ *is a random variable.*

Proof. This statement follows from the fact that $\lim_{n \to \infty} X_n = \limsup_{n \to \infty} X_n = \liminf_{n \to \infty} X_n$. $\qquad\square$

The conditional probability can be extended to involve an event in a probability space $(\Omega, \mathcal{E}, P)$ and a σ-algebra $\mathcal{G}$ included in $\mathcal{F}$.

Fix $A \in \mathcal{F}$ and define a measure m on $\mathcal{G}$ be $m(B) = P(B \cap A)$ for $B \in \mathcal{G}$. If $P(B) = 0$ then $m(B) = 0$, hence $m \ll P$. By Radon-Nikodym theorem (Theorem 8.58), there exists a $\mathcal{G}$-measurable function f that is integrable relative to P such that $P(A \cap B) = m(B) = \int_B f \, dP$. The function f is a random variable, is referred to as the *conditional probability of A on the σ-algebra $\mathcal{G}$*, and will denoted by $P(A|\mathcal{G})$. Thus, we can write

$$P(A \cap B) = \int_B P(A|\mathcal{G}) \, dP \qquad (7.17)$$

for $B \in \mathcal{G}$.

Example 7.25. Let $(\Omega, \mathcal{E}, P)$ be a probability space and let $\pi = \{B_1, B_2, \ldots\}$ be a partition of Ω that consists of sets in $\mathcal{E}$. If $\mathcal{G}$ is the σ-algebra generated by the sets in π, the function $f : \Omega \longrightarrow \mathbb{R}$ defined by

$$f(\omega) = \frac{P(A \cap B_i)}{P(B_i)} \text{ if } \omega \in B_i$$

is measurable relative to the σ-algebra $\mathcal{G}$. If $G \in \mathcal{G}$, then G is a union of blocks of π, $G = \bigcup_{j \in J} B_{i_j}$, hence $P(AG) = \sum_{l \in J} \mathcal{P}(A|\mathcal{B}_{\rangle_l})\mathcal{P}(\mathcal{B}_{\rangle_l})$.

Example 7.26. Let $(\Omega, \mathcal{E}, P)$ be a probability space. For $A \in \mathcal{E}$ we have $P(A|\mathcal{E}) = 1_A$ with probability 1 because 1_A satisfies equality (7.17).

If $\mathcal{G} = \{\emptyset, \Omega\}$, then $P(A|\mathcal{E}) = P(A)$ with probability 1 because every $\mathcal{G}$-measurable function must be a constant.

Exercises and Supplements

(1) Let $(S, \mathcal{E})$ and $(T, \mathcal{F})$ be two measurable spaces such that $S \cap T = \emptyset$. Prove that the collection $\mathcal{E} \vee \mathcal{F}$ is a σ-algebra on the set $S \cup T$. Furthermore, we have $\mathbf{K}_{\sigma\text{-alg}}(\mathcal{E} \cup \mathcal{F}) = \mathcal{E} \vee \mathcal{F}$.

Solution: If $B \in \mathcal{E} \vee \mathcal{F}$, we have $B = C \cup D$, where $C \in \mathcal{E}$ and $D \in \mathcal{F}$. Then, $(S \cup T) - B = (S - C) \cup (T - D)$, $S - C \in \mathcal{E}$ because $\mathcal{E}$ is a σ-algebra, and $T - D \in \mathcal{F}$, hence $(S \cup T) - B \in \mathcal{E} \vee \mathcal{F}$. Thus, $\mathcal{E} \vee \mathcal{F}$ is closed with respect to complement.

Let now $\{B_n \mid n \in \mathbb{N}\}$ be a countable family of sets in $\mathcal{E} \vee \mathcal{F}$. We can write $B_n = C_n \cup D_n$, where $C_n \in \mathcal{E}$ and $D_n \in \mathcal{F}$ for $n \in \mathbb{N}$. Since

$$\bigcup_{n \in \mathbb{N}} B_n = \bigcup_{n \in \mathbb{N}} (C_n \cup D_n) = \left(\bigcup_{n \in \mathbb{N}} C_n \right) \cup \left(\bigcup_{n \in \mathbb{N}} D_n \right),$$

it follows that $\mathcal{E} \vee \mathcal{P}(A)$ is indeed a σ-algebra because $\bigcup_{n \in \mathbb{N}} C_n \in \mathcal{E}$ and $\bigcup_{n \in \mathbb{N}} D_n \in \mathcal{F}$.

The equality $\mathbf{K}_{\sigma\text{-alg}}(\mathcal{E} \cup \mathcal{F}) = \mathcal{E} \vee \mathcal{F}$ follows immediately.

(2) Let $(S, \mathcal{E})$ be a measurable space and let (U_n) be a sequence of subsets in $\mathcal{E}$. Prove that there exists a sequence (V_n) of pairwise disjoint subsets of S such that $V_n \subseteq U_n$ and $\bigcup_n V_n = \bigcup_n U_n$.

(3) Let $\mathcal{F}$ and $\mathcal{O}$ be the collection of closed and open set of a topological metric space. Consider the sequences $\mathbf{u}_n = (\sigma, \delta, \sigma, \cdots)$ and $\mathbf{v}_n = (\delta, \sigma, \delta, \cdots)$ of length n that consist of alternating symbols σ and δ, and the collections $\mathcal{F}_{\mathbf{u}_n} = (\cdots ((\mathcal{F}_\sigma)_\delta)_\sigma \cdots)$ and $\mathcal{O}_{\mathbf{v}_n} = (\cdots ((\mathcal{O}_\delta)_\sigma)_\delta \cdots)$.

    (a) Prove that $\mathcal{F}_{\mathbf{u}_{n-1}} \subseteq \mathcal{F}_{\mathbf{u}_n}$, $\mathcal{O}_{\mathbf{v}_{n-1}} \subseteq \mathcal{O}_{\mathbf{v}_n}$, $\mathcal{F}_{\mathbf{u}_{n-1}} \subseteq \mathcal{O}_{\mathbf{v}_n}$, and $\mathcal{O}_{\mathbf{v}_{n-1}} \subseteq \mathcal{F}_{\mathbf{u}_n}$, for every $n \geqslant 1$.

    (b) Prove that for every $n \in \mathbb{N}$ the collections $\mathcal{F}_{\mathbf{u}_n}$ and $\mathcal{O}_{\mathbf{v}_n}$ consist of Borel sets.

(4) A σ-algebra on S is *separable* if it is generated by a countable collection of subsets of S. Prove that the σ-algebra of Borel subsets of $\mathbb{R}$ is separable.

(5) Let $(S, \mathcal{E})$ be a measurable space and let $f, g : S \longrightarrow \mathbb{R}$ be two simple measurable functions. Prove that if $a \in \mathbb{R}$ the set $\{x \in S \mid af(x) \leqslant g(x)\}$ belongs to $\mathcal{E}$.

    Solution: It is easy to see that $g - af$ is a simple measurable function and $\{x \in S \mid af(x) \leqslant g(x)\} = (g - af)^{-1}(\mathbb{R}_{\geqslant 0})$, the statement follows.

(6) Let $\{(S_i, \mathcal{E}_i) \mid i \in I\}$ be a family of measurable spaces, $(S, \mathcal{E})$ be a measurable space and let $\{f_i \mid i \in I\}$ be a collection of functions $f_i : S \longrightarrow S_i$ for $i \in I$. Let $\mathcal{E}$ be the σ-algebra on S generated by the collection $\bigcup_{i \in I} f_i^{-1}(\mathcal{E}_i)$.

Let $(S_0, \mathcal{E}_0)$ be a measurable space and let $f : S_0 \longrightarrow S$ be a function. Prove that f is measurable (as a function between the measurable spaces $(S_0, \mathcal{E}_0)$ and $(S, \mathcal{E})$) if and only if each function $g_i = f_i f$ is a measurable function between the measurable spaces $(S_0, \mathcal{E}_0)$ and $(S_i, \mathcal{E}_i)$ (see diagram below).

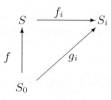

Solution: Since the composition of two measurable mappings is measurable, the condition is necessary.

Conversely, suppose that each function $g_i = f_i f$ is measurable and let $U \in \mathcal{E}$.

Since $\mathcal{E}$ is the σ-algebra generated by the collection $\bigcup_{i \in I} f_i^{-1}(\mathcal{E}_i)$, to prove that f is measurable it would suffice to show that $f^{-1}(D) \in \mathcal{E}_0$ for every D of the form $D = f_i^{-1}(E)$, where $E \in f_i^{-1}(\mathcal{E}_i)$. Since $f_i f$ is measurable, it follows $(f_i f)^{-1}(E) \in \mathcal{E}_0$. Note that

$$f^{-1}(D) = f^{-1}(f_i^{-1}(E)) = (f_i f)^{-1}(E) \in \mathcal{E}_0,$$

which implies that f is measurable.

(7) Prove that if $f : \mathbb{R} \longrightarrow \mathbb{R}$ is a monotonic function, then f is measurable relative to $(\hat{\mathbb{R}}, \mathbb{B}(\hat{\mathbb{R}}))$.

(8) Let $\mathbf{f} = (f_0, f_1, \dots)$ be a sequence of measurable real-valued functions defined on the measurable space $\mathfrak{S} = (S, \mathcal{E})$. The sets

$$U = \left\{ x \in S \,\middle|\, \lim_{n \to \infty} f(x) \text{ exists and is finite} \right\}$$

$$U_+ = \left\{ x \in S \,\middle|\, \lim_{n \to \infty} f(x) = \infty \right\}$$

$$U_- = \left\{ x \in S \,\middle|\, \lim_{n \to \infty} f(x) = -\infty \right\}$$

belong to $\mathcal{E}$.

(9) Let $(S, \mathcal{E})$ be a measurable space. Prove that if $f : S \longrightarrow \hat{\mathbb{R}}$ is a measurable function, then the set

$$M_{f,t} = \{ x \in S \mid f(x) = t \}$$

is measurable for every $t \in \hat{\mathbb{R}}$.

Solution: Since

$$L_{f,t} = \{x \in S \mid f(x) \geqslant t\} \cap \{x \in S \mid f(x) \leqslant t\},$$

the statement follows.

(10) Let $\{B(x_i, r_i) \mid 1 \leqslant i \leqslant N\}$ be a finite collection of open spheres in $\mathbb{R}^n$ and let $W = \bigcup_{i=1}^{N} B(x_i, r_i)$. Prove that there exists a set $I \subseteq \{1, \ldots, N\}$ so that the spheres of the collection $\{B(x_i, r_i) \mid i \in I\}$ are disjoint, $W \subseteq \bigcup_{i \in I} B(x_i, 3r_i)$ and $m_L(W) \leqslant 3^n \sum_{i \in I} m(B(x_i, r_i))$.

Solution: Suppose without loss of generality that $r_1 \geqslant r_2 \geqslant \cdots \geqslant r_N$. Let $i_1 = 1$. Discard all $B(x_i, r_i)$ that intersect $B(i_1, r_1)$ and let $B(x_{i_2}, r_{i_2})$ the first of the remaining spheres, etc. The process halts after a finite number of steps and yields $I = \{i_1, i_2, \ldots\}$. The spheres $\{B(x_i, r_i) \mid i \in I\}$ are clearly disjoint. Each discarded $B(x_i, r_i)$ is a subset of of $B(x_i, 3r_i)$ for some $i \in I$ because if $r' \leqslant r$ and $B(x', r') \cap B(x, r)$, then $B(x', r') \subseteq B(x, 3r)$. This proves the second claim. Finally, the third claim follows from the second because $m_L(B(x, 3r)) \leqslant 3^n m_L(B(x, r))$.

(11) Let $(S, \mathcal{E}, m)$ be a measure space and let $(f_n)_{n \geqslant 1}$ be a sequence of functions, where $f_n : S \longrightarrow T$, where (T, d) is a metric space. Suppose that $A \in \mathcal{E}$ is a set with $m(A) < \infty$ such that $\lim_{n \to \infty} f_n = f$ a.e. on A. Prove that for every $\epsilon > 0$ there exists a subset B of A such that $m(B) < \epsilon$ and (f_n) converges uniformly to f on the set $A - B$.

Solution: Let $U_{n,k} = \bigcup_{m \geqslant n}\{x \in A \mid |f_m(x) - f(x)| \geqslant 1/k\}$. For a fixed k, the sequence $(U_{n,k})$ is clearly decreasing.

If $x \in A$ is such that $\lim_{n \to \infty} f_n(x) = f(x)$, then $x \notin \bigcup_{n \geqslant 1} E_{n,k}$, which implies that $m\left(\bigcap_{n \geqslant 1} U_{n,k}\right) = 0$. Since $m(A) < \infty$, by the continuity from above (Theorem 7.32), it follows that for each k there exists a number n_k such that $m(U_{n_k,k}) < \frac{\epsilon}{2^k}$. If $B = \bigcup_{k \geqslant 1} U_{n_k,k}$, on the set $A - B$ the sequence (f_n) converges uniformly to f and

$$m(B) \leqslant \sum_{k \geqslant 1} m(E_{n_k,k}) < \sum_{k \geqslant 1} \frac{\epsilon}{2^k} = \epsilon.$$

The statement proved here is known as the *Severini-Egorov Theorem*.

(12) Let $f : \mathbb{R} \longrightarrow \mathbb{C}$ be a complex-valued Lebesgue measurable function of a real variable. We say that f is a member of the space M if the number $\mathfrak{l}(f)$ defined as

$$\mathfrak{l}(f) = \inf\{\epsilon \mid m_L(\{x \mid |f(x)| > \epsilon\}) \leqslant \epsilon\},$$

is finite. Prove that $\lambda = \mathfrak{l}(f)$ if and only if the following conditions:

(a) $m_L(\{x \mid |f(x)| > \lambda\}) \leqslant \lambda$, and

(b) $m_L(\{x \mid |f(x)| > \lambda - \delta\}) > \lambda - \delta$ for each $\delta > 0$

are satisfied.

Solution: Suppose that $\lambda = \mathfrak{l}(f)$. By the definition of infimum the second condition is met.

Again, by definition,

$$m_L(\{x \mid |f(x)| > \mathfrak{l}(f) + \epsilon\}) \leqslant \mathfrak{l}(f) + \epsilon$$

for each $\epsilon > 0$. When $\epsilon \to 0$, the set $\{x \mid |f(x)| > \mathfrak{l}(f) + \epsilon\}$ expands toward the limit set $\{x \mid |f(x)| > \mathfrak{l}(f)\}$, hence $m_L(\{x \mid |f(x)| > \lambda\}) \leqslant \lambda$ due to the continuity property of measures.

Conversely, let λ satisfy the two requirements. By definition, $\lambda - \delta < \mathfrak{l}(f) \leqslant \lambda$ for each $\delta > 0$. This is possible only if $\lambda = \mathfrak{l}(f)$.

(13) Prove that $\mathfrak{l}(f) \geqslant 0$.

Solution: Note that the inequality $m_L(\{\mathbf{x} \mid |f(\mathbf{x})| > \epsilon\}) \leqslant \epsilon$ can be satisfied only by non-negative values of ϵ since the values of m_L are non-negative. Thus, $\mathfrak{l}(f) \geqslant 0$.

(14) Prove that $\mathfrak{l}(f) = 0$ if and only if $f = 0$ almost everywhere.

Solution: By Supplements 12 and 13, a necessary and sufficient condition for $\mathfrak{l}(f) = 0$ is $m_L(\{x \mid |f(x)| > 0\}) = 0$, which means that $f = 0$ almost everywhere.

(15) Let $f, g : \mathbb{R} \longrightarrow \mathbb{R}$ be Lebesgue measurable functions. Prove that

$$\mathfrak{l}(f + g) \leqslant \mathfrak{l}(f) + \mathfrak{l}(g).$$

Solution: If $\mathbf{x}$ is such that $|f(\mathbf{x}) + g(\mathbf{x})| > \mathfrak{l}(f) + \mathfrak{l}(g)$, then at least one of the inequalities $|f(\mathbf{x})| > \mathfrak{l}(f)$, $|g(\mathbf{x})| > \mathfrak{l}(g)$ must be satisfied. Therefore,

$$\begin{aligned}
m_L(\{\mathbf{x} \mid |f(\mathbf{x}) + g(\mathbf{x})| &> \mathfrak{l}(f) + \mathfrak{l}(g)\}) \\
&\leqslant m_L(\{\mathbf{x} \mid |f(\mathbf{x})| > \mathfrak{l}(f)\}) + m_L(\{\mathbf{x} \mid |g(\mathbf{x})| > \mathfrak{l}(g)\}) \\
&\leqslant \mathfrak{l}(f) + \mathfrak{l}(g),
\end{aligned}$$

by Supplement 1. Therefore, $\mathfrak{l}(f + g) \leqslant \mathfrak{l}(f) + \mathfrak{l}(g)$.

(16) Let $f : \mathbb{R} \longrightarrow \mathbb{R}$ be a Lebesgue measurable function. Prove that if $|a| \geqslant 1$, then $\mathfrak{l}(af) \leqslant |a|\mathfrak{l}(f)$.

Solution: By Supplement 1, if $|a| > 1$, we have

$$\begin{aligned}
m_L(\{\mathbf{x} \mid |af(\mathbf{x})| &> |a|\mathfrak{l}(f)\}) \\
&= m_L(\{\mathbf{x} \mid |f(\mathbf{x})| > \mathfrak{l}(f)\}) \leqslant \mathfrak{l}(f) \leqslant |a|\mathfrak{l}(f),
\end{aligned}$$

which implies $\mathfrak{l}(af) \leqslant |a|\mathfrak{l}(f)$.

(17) Let M be the set of Lebesgue measurable functions $f : \mathbb{R} \longrightarrow \mathbb{R}$ such that $\mathfrak{l}(f)$ exists and is finite. Prove that if (f_n) is a sequence of functions in M such that $\lim_{m,n\to\infty} \mathfrak{l}(f_m - f_n) = 0$, then there exists a function $f \in M$ such that $\lim_{n\to\infty} \mathfrak{l}(f_n - f) = 0$.

Solution: Let (f_n) be a sequence of functions such that $\lim_{m,n\to\infty} \mathfrak{l}(f_m - f_n) = 0$. We seek to determine a subsequence (f_{n_k}) such that $\mathfrak{l}(f_m - f_n) < 2^{-k}$ when $m \geqslant n_k$ and $n \geqslant n_k$, where $k \geqslant 1$. By Supplement 1 we have

$$m_L(\{\mathbf{x} \mid |f_{n_k+1}(\mathbf{x}) - f_{n_k}(\mathbf{x})| > 2^{-k}\}) \leqslant 2^{-k}.$$

Let $E_k = \bigcup_{j=k}^{\infty}\{\mathbf{x} \mid |f_{n_k+1}(\mathbf{x}) - f_{n_k}(\mathbf{x})| > 2^{-j}\}$. It is clear that $E_{k+1} \subseteq E_k$ and that $m_L(E_k) \leqslant 2^{1-k}$. The series

$$f_{n_1} + (f_{n_2} - f_{n_1}) + (f_{n_3} - f_{n_2}) + \cdots$$

converges uniformly over any set $\mathbb{R} - E_k$ and, therefore, it converges for almost all $\mathbf{x}$ to some function f. If $x \in \mathbb{R}^r - E_k$ we have $|f(\mathbf{x}) - f_{n_k}(\mathbf{x})| \leqslant 2^{1-k}$, hence

$$m_L(\{\mathbf{x} \mid |f(\mathbf{x}) - f_{n_k}(\mathbf{x})| > 2^{1-k}\}) \leqslant m_L(E_k) \leqslant 2^{1-k},$$

which implies $\mathfrak{l}(f - f_{n_k}) \leqslant 2^{1-k}$. By Supplement 15,

$$\limsup \mathfrak{l}(f - f_n)$$
$$\leqslant \mathfrak{l}(f - f_n) + \limsup \mathfrak{l}(f_n - f_{n_k}) \leqslant 2^{1-k} + 2^{-k},$$

which is possible only if $\lim_{n\to\infty} \mathfrak{l}(f - f_n) = 0$. Since $f - f_n \in M$ and $f_n \in M$, it follows that $f \in M$.

(18) Let M^r be the set of Lebesgue measurable functions of the form $f : \mathbb{R}^r \longrightarrow \mathbb{R}$, where $\mathfrak{l}(f)$ exists and is finite. Prove that $\nu : M^r \longrightarrow \mathbb{R}$ defined as $\nu(f) = \mathfrak{l}(f)$ is a seminorm; consequently, $\mathfrak{d} : M \times M \longrightarrow \mathbb{R}_{\geqslant 0}$ defined by

$$\mathfrak{d}(f,g) = \mathfrak{l}(f - g) = \inf\{\epsilon \mid m_L(\{x \mid |f(x) - g(x)| > \epsilon\}) \leqslant \epsilon\}$$

is a semimetric on M. Two functions f, g are close relative to this semimetric if the measure of the set on which they differ signficantly is small.

(19) Let $(S, \mathcal{E})$ be a measurable space and let $f : S \longrightarrow \mathbb{R}$ be a bounded function. Prove that for every $\epsilon > 0$ there are simple functions h_ϵ and g_ϵ defined on S such that $h_\epsilon(x) \leqslant f(x) \leqslant g_\epsilon(x)$ and $0 \leqslant h_\epsilon(x) - g_\epsilon(x) < \epsilon$. This statement is known as the *simple approximation lemma*.

Solution: Since f is bounded, $\mathsf{Ran}(f)$ is contained in some interval (c, d). Let $(y_0, y_1, \ldots, y_n)$ be a sequence of numbers in (c, d) such that

$c = y_0 < y_1 < \cdots < y_n = d$ and $y_k - y_{k-1} < \epsilon$. Define $I_k = [y_{k-1}, y_k)$ and $E_k = f^{-1}(I_k)$ for $1 \leqslant k \leqslant n$. Since f is a measurable function, each set E_k is a measurable set. Define the simple functions h_ϵ and g_ϵ to be

$$h_\epsilon = \sum_{k=1}^{n} y_{k-1} 1_{E_k} \text{ and } g_\epsilon = \sum_{k=1}^{n} y_k 1_{E_k}.$$

Note that $h_\epsilon(x) \leqslant f(x) \leqslant g_\epsilon(x)$ and $0 \leqslant h_\epsilon(x) - g_\epsilon(x) < \epsilon$.

(20) Prove Corollary 7.14 starting with the simple approximation lemma.

(21) Let $f : S \longrightarrow \hat{\mathbb{R}}$ be a function. Prove that $f^+ = f 1_{\hat{\mathbb{R}}_{\geqslant 0}}$ and $f^- = -f 1_{\hat{\mathbb{R}}_{\leqslant 0}}$.

(22) Let S be a set and let $\mathcal{E}$ be a σ-algebra. Define the function $m : \mathcal{E} \longrightarrow \hat{\mathbb{R}}_{\geqslant 0}$ by

$$m(U) = \begin{cases} |U| & \text{if } U \text{ is finite,} \\ \infty & \text{otherwise} \end{cases}$$

for $U \in \mathcal{P}(S)$. Prove that m is a measure.

(23) A function $m : \mathcal{P}(S) \longrightarrow \hat{\mathbb{R}}_{\geqslant 0}$ is continuous if for every ascending sequence of subsets of S, (U_n), we have $\lim_{n \to \infty} m(U_n) = m\left(\bigcup_{n \in \mathbb{N}} U_n\right)$.

Prove that the second condition in the definition of a measure $m : S \longrightarrow \hat{\mathbb{R}}_{\geqslant 0}$ is equivalent to finite additivity and the continuity property.

(24) Let μ be an outer measure on the set S. Prove that $|\mu(U) - \mu(V)| \leqslant \mu(U \oplus V)$ for every $U, V \in \mathcal{P}(S)$ such that $\mu(U) < \infty$ or $\mu(V) < \infty$.

(25) Let $\mu : \mathcal{P}(S) \longrightarrow \hat{\mathbb{R}}_{\geqslant 0}$ be an outer measure such that $\mathsf{Ran}(\mu) = \{0, \infty\}$. Prove that every subset of S is μ-measurable.

(26) Let $\mathcal{C}$ be a collection of sets such that $\emptyset \in \mathcal{C}$, every subset of a set in $\mathcal{C}$ also belongs to $\mathcal{C}$, and for every sequence $(S_0, S_1, \ldots, S_i, \ldots)$ of sets in $\mathcal{C}$ we have $\bigcup_{i \in \mathbb{N}} S_i \in \mathcal{C}$. Prove that

   (a) the function $\mu : \mathcal{P}(S) \longrightarrow \hat{\mathbb{R}}_{\geqslant 0}$ defined by

   $$\mu(U) = \begin{cases} 0 & \text{if } U \in \mathcal{C}, \\ 1 & \text{otherwise} \end{cases}$$

   is an outer measure.

   (b) The function $\mu_\infty : \mathcal{P}(S) \longrightarrow \hat{\mathbb{R}}_{\geqslant 0}$ defined by

   $$\mu_\infty(U) = \begin{cases} 0 & \text{if } U \in \mathcal{C}, \\ \infty & \text{otherwise} \end{cases}$$

   is an outer measure.

(27) Let μ be an outer measure on a set S. Prove that if one of the subsets U, V of S is μ-measurable, then

$$\mu(U \cup V) + \mu(U \cap V) = \mu(V) + \mu(V).$$

(28) Let $\mathcal{S}$ be a semiring of subsets of a set S and let $m : \mathcal{S} \longrightarrow \hat{\mathbb{R}}_{\geq 0}$ such that $m(\emptyset) = 0$, m is finitely additive and countable subadditive. Prove that m can be extended to a measure on $\mathbf{K}_{\sigma\text{-alg}}(\mathcal{S})$.

Solution: Note that m is monotonic. Indeed, if $U, V \in \mathcal{S}$ and $V \subseteq U$, taking into account that $U - V = \bigcup \mathcal{U}$, where $\mathcal{U}$ is a finite collection $\mathcal{U}$ of pairwise disjoint sets in $\mathcal{S}$, it follows that $m(U) \geqslant m(V)$, by the finite additivity of m. Define $\mu(U) = \inf \sum_n m(U_n)$, where the infimum extends to all covers of U by sets in $\mathcal{S}$

The argument of Example 7.12 shows that m can be extended to an outer measure μ on S such that the sets in $\mathcal{S}$ are μ-measurable.

If U and U_n belong to $\mathcal{S}$ for $n \in \mathbb{N}$ and $U \subseteq \bigcup_n U_n$, then $m(U) \leqslant \sum_n m(U \cap U_n) \leqslant \sum_n m(U_n)$. Therefore, $m(U) \leqslant \mu(U)$. Since $\mu(U) \leqslant m(U)$ because $U \in \mathcal{S}$, we have $m(U) = \mu(U)$ for $U \in \mathcal{S}$. Since $\mathcal{S} \subseteq \mathbf{K}_{\sigma\text{-alg}}(\mathcal{S}) \subseteq \mathcal{E}_\mu$ and μ is σ-additive on $\mathcal{E}_\mu$, it follows that μ is σ-additive on $\mathbf{K}_{\sigma\text{-alg}}(\mathcal{S})$.

(29) Let $(S, \mathcal{E}, m)$ be a measure space such that m is σ-finite. Suppose that $\mathcal{S}$ is a semi-ring on S such that $\mathbf{K}_{\sigma\text{-alg}}(\mathcal{S}) = \mathcal{E}$. Prove that:

(a) if $U \in \mathcal{E}$ and $\epsilon > 0$ there exists a sequence of pairwise disjoint sets $V_1, V_2, \ldots$ in $\mathcal{S}$ such that $U \subseteq \bigcup_n V_n$ and

$$m \left(\bigcup_n V_n - U \right) < \epsilon; \tag{7.18}$$

(b) if $m(U)$ is finite there exists a sequence as above such that $m \left(\bigcup_n V_n \oplus U \right) < \epsilon$.

Solution: By Supplement 28, m can be extended to an outer measure μ on $\mathbf{K}_{\sigma\text{-alg}}(\mathcal{S}) = \mathcal{E}$. Thus, $m(T) = \mu(T)$ for every $T \in \mathcal{S}$ and $\mathcal{E} \subseteq \mathcal{E}_\mu$.

Suppose that $U \in \mathcal{E}$ and $m(U) < \infty$. There exists a sequence of sets $(V_1, V_2, \ldots)$ in $\mathcal{S}$ such that $m \left(\bigcup_k V_k \right) \leqslant \sum_k m(V_k) < m(T) + \epsilon$, which implies $m \left(\bigcup_n V_n - U \right) < \epsilon$. The sequence $(V_1, V_2, \ldots)$ can be replaced by a sequence of pairwise sequence of disjoint sets of the form $V_k \cap \bigcap_{j=1}^{k-1} \overline{V_j}$.

If $U \in \mathcal{E}$ and $m(U) = \mu(U) = \infty$, since m is σ-finite, there exists a sequence of sets (W_p) in $\mathcal{S}$ such that $S = \bigcup_p W_p$ and $m(W_p) < \infty$. Consequently, there exist Z_{pq} in $\mathcal{S}$ such that $U \cap W_p \subseteq \bigcup_q Z_{pq}$ and $m \left(\bigcup_q Z_{pq} - (U \cap W_p) \right) < \frac{\epsilon}{2^m}$. The sequence (Z_{pq}) constitute a sequence of sets in $\mathcal{S}$ that satisfies Condition (7.18). As before, the sequence (Z_{pq}) can be replaced with a sequence of pairwise disjoint sets.

The second part follows immediately from the first.

(30) Let $\mathcal{S}$ be a semi-ring on a set S such that S is a countable union of sets from $\mathcal{S}$ such that $(S, \mathcal{E}, m_1)$ and $(S, \mathcal{E}, m_2)$ are measure spaces such that $\mathcal{E} = \mathbf{K}_{\sigma\text{-alg}}(\mathcal{S})$ and both $m_1(S)$ and $m_2(S)$ are finite. Prove that:

   (a) if $m_1(T) \leqslant m_2(T)$ for each $T \in \mathcal{S}$, then $m_1(U) \leqslant m_2(U)$ for every $U \in \mathcal{E}$;

   (b) if $m_1(T) = m_2(T)$ for each $T \in \mathcal{S}$, then $m_1(U) = m_2(U)$ for every $U \in \mathcal{E}$.

   Solution: By Supplement 29, let (V_k) be a sequence of disjoint sets in $\mathcal{S}$ such that $U \subseteq \bigcup_n V_n$ and $\sum_k m_2(V_k) < m_2(U) + \epsilon$. Then, $m_1(U) \leqslant \sum_k m_1(V_k) \leqslant \sum_k m_2(V_k) < m_2(V_k) + \epsilon$.

   The second part is an immediate consequence of the first.

(31) Let G, G' be two extended open-closed intervals of $\mathbb{R}^n$. Prove that $G \cap G'$ is an extended open-closed interval of $\mathbb{R}^n$.

   Solution: Let $G = (a_1, b_1] \times \cdots \times (a_n, b_n]$ and $G' = (a'_1, b'_1] \times \cdots \times (a'_n, b'_n]$ be two extended open-closed intervals. We have $\mathbf{x} \in G \cap G'$ if and only if $\max\{a_i, a'_i\} < x_i \leqslant \min\{b_i, b'_i\}$ for $1 \leqslant i \leqslant n$, hence

$$G \cap G' = \prod_{j=1}^{n} (\max\{a_i, a'_i\}, \min\{b_i, b'_i\}].$$

(32) Let $G = (a_1, b_1] \times \cdots \times (a_n, b_n]$ be an extended open-closed interval in $\mathbb{R}^n$. Prove that $\mathbb{R}^n - G$ is a union of at most $2n$ disjoint extended open-closed intervals.

   Solution: For an extended open-closed interval $(a, b]$ of $\mathbb{R}$ consider the disjoint extended open-closed intervals $(a, b]^l = (-\infty, a]$ and $(a, b]^r = (b, \infty]$. Then, $\mathbb{R} - (a, b] = (a, b]^l \cup (a, b]^r$.

   If $\mathbf{x} \notin G$ at least one of the inequalities $a_i < x_i \leqslant b_i$ must fail, so

$$\mathbb{R}^n - G$$
$$= \bigcup_{i=1}^{n} (a_1, b_1] \times \cdots \times (a_{i-1}, b_{i-1}] \times ((a_i, b_i]^l \cup (a_i, b_i]^r) \times \cdots \times (a_n, b_n]$$
$$= \bigcup_{i=1}^{n} (a_1, b_1] \times \cdots \times (a_{i-1}, b_{i-1}] \times (a_i, b_i]^l \times \cdots \times (a_n, b_n]$$
$$\cup \bigcup_{i=1}^{n} (a_1, b_1] \times \cdots \times \times (a_i, b_i]^r \times \cdots \times (a_n, b_n]$$

and some of the $2n$ pairwise disjoint sets that occur on the right side of the equality may be empty.

(33) Let S be a bounded Borel subset of $\mathbb{R}$ and let $\mathfrak{I}$ be a collection of open intervals in $\mathbb{R}$ such that $S \subseteq \bigcup \mathfrak{I}$. Prove that $\mathfrak{I}$ contains a finite disjoint subcollection $\{I_1, \ldots, I_k\}$ such that $\sum_{i=1}^{k} m_L(I_k) \geqslant \frac{1}{6} m_L(S)$.

Solution: By Theorem 7.61 S contains a compact subset K such that $m_L(K) \geqslant \frac{1}{2} m_L(S)$. Let $\mathfrak{I}_0$ be a subcollection of $\mathfrak{I}$ that covers K and let $I_0 \in \mathfrak{I}_0$ be an interval of maximal length in $\mathfrak{I}_0$. Let $\mathfrak{I}_1$ the collection obtained from $\mathfrak{I}_0$ by discarding I_0 and all intervals that intersect it. Repeat the process; to obtain $\mathfrak{I}_2$ discard from $\mathfrak{I}_1$ an interval I_1 of maximal length and all intervals that intersect it, etc., until no more intervals in $\mathfrak{I}_0$ are left. The intervals I_i are disjoint, and each interval I_i together with the intervals that intersect it is included in an interval J_i with the same midpoint as I_i and with $m_L(J_i) = 3 m_L(I_i)$. Thus, the family of intervals $\{J_i\}$ covers K and $\sum_{i=1}^{k} m_L(I_i) = \sum \frac{m_L(J_i)}{3} \geqslant \frac{m(K)}{3} \geqslant \frac{m_L(S)}{6}$.

(34) Let $G = (a_1, b_1] \times \cdots \times (a_n, b_n]$ and $G' = (c_1, d_1] \times \cdots \times (c_n, d_n]$ be two extended open-closed intervals in $\mathbb{R}^n$. Prove that $G' - G$ is a union of at most $2n$ disjoint extended open-closed intervals.

Solution: Note that $G' - G = G' \cap (\mathbb{R}^n - G)$. By Supplement 32, $\mathbb{R}^n - G$ is is a union of at most $2n$ disjoint extended open-closed intervals, $\mathbb{R}^n - G = G_1 \cup \cdots \cup G_p$, hence

$$G' - G = G' \cap (\mathbb{R}^n - G) = G' \cap (G_1 \cup \cdots \cup G_p) = \bigcup_{k=1}^{p} (G' \cap G_k).$$

By Supplement 31, each set $G' \cap G_k$ is an extended open-closed interval of $\mathbb{R}^n$; moreover, the sets $G' \cap G_1, \ldots, G' \cap G_k$ are pairwise disjoint because $G_1, \ldots, G_k$ are pairwise disjoint.

(35) Let $\mathcal{E}$ be the collection of subsets of $\mathbb{R}^n$ that are unions of finite collections of pairwise disjoint open-closed extended intervals. Prove that $\mathcal{E}$ is an algebra of subsets of $\mathbb{R}^n$.

Solution: If $U, V \in \mathcal{E}$ we have $U = \bigcup_{j=1}^{m} G_j$ and $V = \bigcup_{k=1}^{p} G'_k$, where $G_1, \ldots, G_m$ are pairwise disjoint open-closed extended intervals and $G'_1, \ldots, G'_p$ are sets that satisfy the same description. Then,

$$U \cap V = \bigcup_{j=1}^{m} \bigcup_{k=1}^{p} G_j \cap G'_k$$

and $G_j \cap G'_k$ are extended open-closed intervals that are pairwise disjoint, so $\mathcal{E}$ is closed under finite intersections.

Supplement 32 shows that the complement of an extended open-closed interval is an union of at most $2n$ disjoint extended open-closed intervals. Since $\mathcal{E}$ is closed to finite intersections it follows that $\mathcal{E}$ is indeed an algebra.

(36) Prove that if μ_L is the Lebesgue outer measure on $\mathbb{R}$ and F is a finite subset of $\mathbb{R}$, then $\mu_L(F) = 0$.

(37) Let $\mathbf{a}, \mathbf{a}_1, \cdots, \mathbf{a}_n$ be vectors in $\mathbb{R}^n$. The *parallelepiped* determined by these vectors is the set $P = \{\mathbf{x} \in \mathbb{R}^n \mid \mathbf{x} = \mathbf{a} + \alpha_1 \mathbf{a}_1 + \cdots + \alpha_n \mathbf{a}_n, 0 \leqslant \alpha_j \leqslant 1 \text{ for } 1 \leqslant j \leqslant n\}$. Prove that:

(a) if $K_1 = [0,1]^n$ is the n-dimensional unit cube, then there exists a linear transformation h on $\mathbb{R}^n$ such $P = \mathbf{t_b}(h(K_1))$, where the columns of A_h are $\mathbf{a}_1, \ldots, \mathbf{a}_n$;

(b) P is a Lebesgue set and $m_L(P) = |\det(A_h)|$.

Solution: Let $h : \mathbb{R}^n \longrightarrow \mathbb{R}^n$ be the linear operator defined as

$$h(\mathbf{x}) = \sum_{i=1}^n x_i \mathbf{b}_i$$

for $\mathbf{x} \in \mathbb{R}^n$. The equality $P = \mathbf{t_b}(h(K_1))$ follows immediately. $P \in \mathbb{L}_n$ by Theorem 7.53 and $m_L(P) = m_L(\mathbf{t_b}(h(K_1))) = m_L(h(K_1)) = |\det(A_h)| m_L(K_1) = |\det(A_h)|$.

(38) Let $(S, \mathcal{E}, m)$ be a measure space such that $\mathcal{E} = \mathbf{K}_{\sigma\text{-alg}}(\mathcal{A})$, where $m : \mathcal{E} \longrightarrow \hat{\mathbb{R}}_{\geqslant 0}$ is a measure that is σ-finite on $\mathcal{A}$.

Prove that:

(a) for every $U \in \mathcal{E}$ we have $m(U) = \inf\{m(V) \mid U \subseteq V \text{ and } V \in \mathcal{A}_\sigma\}$;

(b) if $U \in \mathcal{E}$ and $\epsilon > 0$ then there exist $V \in \mathcal{A}_\sigma$ such that $U \subseteq V$ and $m(V - U) < \epsilon$.

Solution: Let $m' : \mathcal{P}(S) \longrightarrow \hat{\mathbb{R}}_{\geqslant 0}$ be defined as:

$$m'(L) = \inf\{m(M) \mid L \subseteq M \text{ and } M \in \mathcal{A}_\sigma\}.$$

Suppose initially that m is finite, that is $m(S) < \infty$.

Define the collection $\mathcal{F} = \{V \in \mathcal{E} \mid m'(V) = m(V)\}$. It is immediate that $\mathcal{A} \subseteq \mathcal{F} \subseteq \mathcal{E}$. We claim that $\mathcal{F}$ is a monotone collection.

Let (V_n) be an ascending chain of sets in $\mathcal{F}$ such that $\bigcup_{n \in \mathbb{N}} V_n = V$. Note that $m'(V_n) = m(V_n)$ for $n \in \mathbb{N}$ by the definition of $\mathcal{F}$. Since $m'(V_n)$ is defined by an infimum, for every $\epsilon > 0$ there exists $U_n \in \mathcal{A}_\sigma$ such that $V_n \subseteq U_n$ and $m(U_n) \leqslant m(V_n) + \frac{\epsilon}{2^n}$, or $m(U_n - V_n) \leqslant \frac{\epsilon}{2^n}$.

If $U = \bigcup_{n \in \mathbb{N}} U_n \in \mathcal{A}_\sigma$, we have $V \subseteq U$ and

$$m(U - V) = m\left(\bigcup_{n \in \mathbb{N}} (U_n - V)\right) \leqslant \sum_{n \in nn} m(U_n - V)$$

$$\leqslant \sum_{n \geqslant 1} m(U_n - V_n) \leqslant \sum_{n \geqslant 1} \frac{\epsilon}{2^n} = 2\epsilon,$$

hence $m'(V) \leqslant m(U) < m(V) + 2\epsilon$. Therefore, $B \in \mathcal{F}$. The argument for a descending chain is similar, so $\mathcal{F}$ is a monotone collection, which means that $\mathcal{F} = \mathbf{K}_{\mathrm{mon}}(\mathcal{F})$.

Since $\mathcal{A} \subseteq \mathcal{F} \subseteq \mathcal{E}$, it follows that $\mathbf{K}_{\mathrm{mon}}(\mathcal{A}) \subseteq \mathbf{K}_{\mathrm{mon}}(\mathcal{F}) \subseteq \mathbf{K}_{\mathrm{mon}}(\mathcal{E})$. By Theorem 1.39 we have $\mathcal{E} = \mathbf{K}_{\sigma\text{-alg}}(\mathcal{A}) = \mathbf{K}_{\mathrm{mon}}(\mathcal{A})$, which implies $\mathcal{E} \subseteq \mathcal{F} \subseteq \mathcal{E}$, hence $\mathcal{F} = \mathcal{E}$, which, in turn, shows that $m' = m$ on $\mathcal{E}$.

If m is σ-finite let (S_n) be a sequence of subsets of S such that $S = \bigcup_{n \in \mathbb{N}} S_n$ and $m(S_n) < \infty$.

Define the finite measure m_n on $\mathcal{E}$ as $m_n(U) = m(U \cap S_n)$ for $U \in \mathcal{E}$. By the previous argument, for every $U \in \mathcal{E}$ and $\epsilon > 0$ there exists $V_n in \mathcal{A}_\sigma$ such that $U \subseteq V_n$ and $m((V_n \cap S_n) - (U \cap S_n)) = m_n(V_n - U) \leqslant \frac{\epsilon}{2^n}$. Since $S_n \in \mathcal{A}_\sigma$ we have $V_n \cap S_n \in \mathcal{A}_\sigma$ and the set $V = \bigcup_{n \in \mathbb{N}}(V_n \cap S_n) \in \mathcal{A}_\sigma$. Furthermore, $U \subseteq V$ and

$$
\begin{aligned}
m(V - U) &\leqslant \sum_{n \in \mathbb{N}} m((V_n \cap S_n) - U) \\
&\leqslant \sum_{n \in \mathbb{N}} m((V_n \cap S_n) - (U \cap S_n)) \\
&\leqslant \sum_{n \in \mathbb{N}} \frac{\epsilon}{2^n} = 2\epsilon,
\end{aligned}
$$

which implies $m(U) \leqslant m(V) \leqslant m(U) + 2\epsilon$, so $m(U) = \inf\{m(V) \mid U \subseteq V \text{ and } V \in \mathcal{A}_\sigma\}$.

(39) Let $(S, \mathcal{E}, m)$ be a measure space, where m is a finite signed measure. Prove that $m_+(T) = \sup\{m(U) \mid U \in \mathcal{E} \text{ and } U \subseteq T\}$ and $m_-(T) = -\inf\{m(U) \mid U \in \mathcal{E} \text{ and } U \subseteq T\}$.

Solution: For $T \in \mathcal{E}$, $T \subseteq U$, and any Hahn decomposition $\{B_+, B_-\}$ we have:

$$
m(T) = m_+(T) - m_-(T) \leqslant m_+(T) \leqslant m_+(U) = m(U \cap B_+) \subseteq m(U),
$$

by the definition of m_+ given in Theorem 7.72. Similarly,

$$
m(T) = m_+(T) - m_-(T) \leqslant m_+(T) \geqslant -m_-(U) = -m(U \cap B_-).
$$

(40) This supplement shows that the Jordan decomposition of a signed measure has a minimal character. Let $(S, \mathcal{E}, m)$ be a measure space, where m is a finite signed measure such that $m(T) = m_1(T) - m_2(T)$ for $T \in \mathcal{E}$, where m_1 and m_2 are non-negative measures. Prove that $m_1 \geqslant m_+$ and $m_2 \geqslant m_-$.

Solution: Assume that for some $T \in \mathcal{E}$ we have $m_1 < m_+$. Therefore, $m_1(T \cap B_+) + m_1(T \cap B_-) < m_+(T \cap B_+) + m_+(T \cap B_-)$. It follows that $m_1(T \cap B_+) < m_+(T \cap B_+)$ because $m_+(T \cap B_-) = 0$ and $m_1(T \cap B_-) \geqslant 0$.

The inequality $m_1(T \cap B_+) < m_+(T \cap B_+)$ implies $m_2(T \cap B_+) < m_-(T \cap B_+) = 0$, which contradicts the fact that m_2 is non-negative.

(41) Let $(S, \mathcal{E})$ be a measurable space and let m, m_1, m_2 be complex measures on this space. Prove that:

(a) $|m_1 + m - 2| \leqslant |m_1| + |m_2|$;

(b) $|cm| = |c|\,|m|$ for $c \in \mathbb{C}$;

(c) $\max\{\Re(m), \Im(m)\} \leqslant |m| \leqslant |\Re(m)| + |\Im(m)|$.

(42) Let $(S, \mathcal{E})$ be a measurable space and let m be a complex measure on this space. Prove that the following statements are equivalent:

(a) U is a null set for m;

(b) U is a null set for both $\Re(m)$ and $\Im(m)$;

(c) U is a null set for $|m|$.

(43) Let $(S, \mathcal{E}, m)$ be a measure space, where m is a complex measure. Prove that $m_1, m_2 : \mathcal{E} \longrightarrow \mathbb{R}$ defined by $m_1(U) = \Re(m(U))$ and $m_2(U) = \Im(m(U))$ are finite signed measures.

(44) Let m, m' be signed measures. Prove that the following are equivalent:

(a) $m \perp m'$;

(b) $|m| \perp m'$;

(c) $m \perp |m'|$;

(d) $|m| \perp |m'|$.

Solution: Suppose that $m \perp m'$, that is, there exists $T \in \mathcal{E}$ such that $m(T) = m'(S - T) = 0$. We have $|m|(T) = 0$, so T is an $|m|$-null set and $|m| \perp m'$.

Suppose now that $|m| \perp m'$, so that $|m|(V) = m'(S - V) = 0$ for some $V \in \mathcal{E}$. Since $m_+ \leqslant |m|$ and $m_- \leqslant |m|$, T is both m_+-null and m_--null. Therefore, $m_+ \perp m'$ and $m_- \perp m'$.

Finally, suppose that $m_+ \perp m'$ and $m_- \perp m'$. Then, there are two subsets X, Y in S such that $m_+(X) = m'(S - X)$ and $m_-(Y) = m'(S - Y)$. Note that $(S - X) \cup Y$ is m'-null because every subset of $(S - X) \cup Y = (S - X) \cup (Y - (S - X))$ is the disjoint union of two m'-null sets. Furthermore, $S - ((S - X) \cup (S - Y)) = X \cap Y$, which is both m_+- and m_--null, hence m-null. This shows that $m \perp m'$.

(45) Let m_1, m_2 be positive measures such that at least one of the measures m_1, m_2 is finite and let $m = m_1 - m_2$ be a signed measure on a set S. Prove that $m_1 \geqslant m_+$ and $m_2 \geqslant m_-$.

(46) Let $(S, \mathcal{E})$ be a measurable space. Prove that if $m : \mathcal{E} \longrightarrow \mathbb{R}$ is a finitely additive function such that for every decreasing sequence of sets $(U_n)_{n \geqslant 1}$ where $U_n \in \mathcal{E}$ and $\bigcap_{n \geqslant 1} U_n = \emptyset$ we have $\lim_{n \to \infty} m(U_n) = 0$, then m is a measure.

Solution: Define $W_n = U_n - U_{n+1}$ for $n \geqslant 1$. Then, $U_n = \bigcup_{k \leqslant n} W_k$ for $n \in \mathbb{N}$. Since $\bigcup_{j=1}^{\infty} W_j = \bigcup_{j=1}^{k} W_j + \bigcup_{j=k+1}^{\infty} W_j$, the finite additivity of m implies

$$m\left(\bigcup_{j=1}^{\infty} W_j\right) = m\left(\bigcup_{j=1}^{k} W_j\right) + m(U_{k+1})$$

$$= \sum_{j=1}^{k} m(W_j) + m(U_{k+1}).$$

Since $\lim_{k\to\infty} m(U_{k+1}) = 0$, we have $m\left(\bigcup_{j=1}^{\infty} W_j\right) = \sum_{j=1}^{\infty} m(W_j)$.

(47) Let $(S, \mathcal{E})$ be a measurable space and let m be a complex measure on this space. Prove that for every real-valued measure m' on the same measure space such that $|m(E)| \leqslant m'(E)$ for $E \in \mathcal{E}$, we have $|m|(E) \leqslant m'(E)$ for $E \in \mathcal{E}$. In other words, prove that the variation $|m|$ of m is the smallest of all real measures m' such that $|m(E)| \leqslant m'(E)$.

Solution: Let m' be a measure space such that $|m(E)| \leqslant m'(E)$ for $E \in \mathcal{E}$. For $E \in \mathcal{E}$ we have:

$$|m|(E) = \sup\left\{\sum_{i=1}^{n} |m(E_i)| \mid \{E_1, \dots, E_n\}\right.$$

$$\left. \text{is a partition of } E \text{ with } E_i \in \mathcal{E}\right\}$$

$$\leqslant \sup\left\{\sum_{i=1}^{n} m'(E_i) \mid \{E_1, \dots, E_n\}\right.$$

$$\left. \text{is a partition of } E \text{ with } E_i \in \mathcal{E}\right\}$$

$$= m'(E).$$

(48) Prove that if A, B are two independent events, then the pairs of events $(A, \overline{B})$, $(\overline{A}, B)$, and $(\overline{A}, \overline{B})$ are independent.

Let A be a Lebesgue measurable subset of $\mathbb{R}$. A function $f : \mathbb{R} \longrightarrow \mathbb{R}$ is *measurable Lebesgue on* A if $f^{-1}(-\infty, a) \in \mathbb{L}$ for every $a \in A$.

(49) Prove that the characteristic function 1_B of a subset B of $\mathbb{R}$ is measurable Lebesgue on $\mathbb{R}$ if and only if $B \in \mathbb{L}$.

Solution: Suppose that 1_B is measurable Lebesgue on $\mathbb{R}$. Then, $\overline{B} = \mathbb{R} - B = 1_B^{-1}(-\infty, 1/2) \in \mathbb{L}$, hence $B \in \mathbb{L}$. Conversely, if $B \in \mathbb{L}$, then

$$1_B^{-1}(-\infty, b) = \begin{cases} \emptyset & \text{if } b \leqslant 0, \\ \overline{B} & \text{if } 0 < b \leqslant 1, \\ \mathbb{R} & \text{if } 1 < b \end{cases}$$

for every $b \in \mathbb{R}$, hence 1_B is measurable Lebesgue on $\mathbb{R}$.

Bibliographical Comments

Our presentation of product measure space follows [32]. The results in Supplements 12-18 belong to [11].

Chapter 8

Integration

8.1 Introduction

The Lebesgue integral is the cornerstone of integration theory and offers a far-reaching generalization of the Riemann integral that is applicable to a broad class of function. This chapter begins with the gradual introduction of the Lebesgue integral starting with simple measurable real functions and extending the integral to measurable non-negative functions, and ending with the integral of real-valued measurable functions. A further extension to complex-valued functions follows. Fundamental results of integration theory such as the monotone convergence theorem, Fatou's lemma, the dominated convergence theorem, etc., which have frequent applications in practice are also discussed.

We review the basics of Riemann integration and analyze the relationship between the class of Lebesgue-integrable functions and the class of Riemann integrable function. This is especially interesting because, although the class of Lebesgue-integrable functions is broader than the class of Riemann-integrable functions, the value of a Riemann integral is easier to compute and, in many cases, the value of these integrals are the same.

The notions of absolute continuity of measures and the Radon-Nikodym theorem that leads to the notion of Radon-Nikodym derivative and to the Lebesgue decomposition theorem are presented. Finally, we discuss properties of L^p spaces and certain aspects of probability theory.

8.2 The Lebesgue Integral

The construction of the integral is done in several stages. We begin by defining the integral for simple measurable functions, then extend this definition to non-negative measurable function. After introducing the notion of integrable real-valued function, the notion of integral for arbitrary real-valued measurable functions is introduced. Finally, we present the construction of the integral for complex-valued functions.

8.2.1   *The Integral of Simple Measurable Functions*

Recall that the set of simple, non-negative functions was denoted by $\mathsf{SF}_+(S)$.

Let $(S, \mathcal{E}, m)$ be a measure space and let $f \in \mathsf{SF}_+(S)$ be a non-negative simple measurable function between the measurable spaces $(S, \mathcal{E})$ and $(\mathbb{R}, \mathbb{B}(\mathbb{R}))$. By Theorem 7.10 the function f can be written as

$$f(x) = \sum_{i=1}^{n} y_i 1_{f^{-1}(y_i)}(x),$$

for $x \in S$, where $\mathsf{Ran}(f) = \{y_1, \ldots, y_n\} \subseteq \mathbb{R}_{\geqslant 0}$. We have $f^{-1}(y_i) \in \mathcal{E}$ because f is a measurable function.

Definition 8.1. Let $(S, \mathcal{E}, m)$ be a measure space and let $f \in \mathsf{SF}_+(S)$ be a simple measurable function given by $f(x) = \sum_{i=1}^{n} y_i 1_{f^{-1}(y_i)}(x)$ for $x \in S$.

The *Lebesgue integral* of f on S is the number $\int_S f \, dm$ defined as

$$\int_S f \, dm = \sum_{i=1}^{n} y_i m(f^{-1}(y_i)),$$

where we assume that $0 \cdot \infty = 0$ in order to accommodate the case when $m(f^{-1}(y_i)) = \infty$.

Note that if $y_i = 0$, the contribution of the term $y_i m(f^{-1}(y_i))$ is zero even when $m(f^{-1}(y_i)) = \infty$, due to the convention established earlier that $0 \cdot \infty = 0$.

Example 8.1. Let $(S, \mathcal{E}, m)$ be a measure space and let $U \in \mathcal{E}$. The characteristic function 1_U belongs to SF_+ and we have

$$\int_S 1_U \, dm = m(U).$$

Example 8.2. Let $(S, \mathcal{E}, m)$ be a measure space and let δ_{s_0} be a Dirac measure. If $f \in \mathsf{SF}_+(S)$, where $f(x) = \sum_{i=1}^{n} y_i I_{f^{-1}(y_i)}(x)$, then

$$\int_S f \, d\delta_{s_0} = \sum_{i=1}^{n} y_i \delta_{s_0}(f^{-1}(y_i)) = y_i$$

if $f(s_0) = y_i$. In other words, $\int_S f \, d\delta_{s_0} = f(s_0)$.

As Theorem 7.25 shows, we could use any partition of a set S related to a simple measurable function $f \in \mathsf{SF}_+(S)$ to define $\int_S f \, dm$. In other words, if $\pi = \{B_1, \ldots, B_\ell\}$ is any partition of S related to f, then

$$\int_S f \, dm = \sum_{k=1}^{\ell} y_k m(B_k), \tag{8.1}$$

where $f(x) = y_k$ for every $x \in B_k$ for $1 \leqslant k \leqslant \ell$.

Theorem 8.1. *Let $(S, \mathcal{E}, m)$ be a measure space and let $f, g \in \mathsf{SF}_+(S)$ be such that $f(x) \leqslant g(x)$ for every $x \in S$. We have:*

$$\int_S f \, dm \leqslant \int_S g \, dm.$$

Proof. Let $\pi = \{B_1, \ldots, B_n\}$ and $\sigma = \{C_1, \ldots, C_m\}$ be two partitions of S related to f and g, respectively. Then, the partition $\pi \wedge \sigma$ that consists of the non-empty sets of the form $B_i \cap C_j$ is related to both f and g and we have

$$\int_S f \, dm = \sum_{i=1}^{n} \sum_{j=1}^{m} \{u_{ij} m(B_i \cap C_j) \mid B_i \cap C_j \neq \emptyset\},$$

$$\int_S g \, dm = \sum_{i=1}^{n} \sum_{j=1}^{m} \{v_{ij} m(B_i \cap C_j) \mid B_i \cap C_j \neq \emptyset\},$$

where $u_{ij} = f(x)$ and $v_{ij} = g(x)$ if $x \in B_i \cap C_j$. Since $0 \leqslant u_{ij} \leqslant v_{ij}$ whenever $B_i \cap C_j \neq \emptyset$, the inequality $\int_S f \, dm \leqslant \int_S g \, dm$ follows immediately.

$\square$

Let $(S, \mathcal{E}, m)$ be a measure space. The integral of a non-negative simple measurable function f relative to a subset T of S that belongs to $\mathcal{E}$ is defined by

$$\int_T f \, dm = \int_S f 1_T \, dm.$$

If f is a simple non-negative measurable function, then so is $f 1_T$. Furthermore, the function $f 1_T$ is zero outside the set T.

If $f(x) = \sum_{i=1}^{n} y_i 1_{f^{-1}(y_i)}(x)$ for $x \in S$ and T is a subset of S that belongs to $\mathcal{E}$, then $f 1_T(x) = \sum_{i=1}^{n} y_i 1_{f^{-1}(y_i) \cap T}(x)$ for $x \in S$. Therefore, we have

$$\int_T f \, dm = \int_S f 1_T \, dm = \sum_{i=1}^{n} y_i m(f^{-1}(y_i) \cap T). \tag{8.2}$$

Theorem 8.2. *Let $(S, \mathcal{E}, m)$ be a measure space and let U, V be two disjoint subsets of S. If $f \in \mathsf{SF}_+(S)$ then*

$$\int_{U \cup V} f \, dm = \int_U f \, dm + \int_V f \, dm.$$

Proof. Suppose that $\mathsf{Ran}(f) = \{y_1, \ldots, y_n\}$. We have

$$m(f^{-1}(y_i) \cap (U \cup V)) = m(f^{-1}(y_i) \cap U) + m(f^{-1}(y_i) \cap V),$$

because the sets U and V are disjoint. Therefore, we have

$$
\begin{aligned}
\int_{U \cup V} f \, dm &= \sum_{i=1}^{n} y_i m(f^{-1}(y_i) \cap (U \cup V)) \\
&= \sum_{i=1}^{n} m(f^{-1}(y_i) \cap U) + \sum_{i=1}^{n} m(f^{-1}(y_i) \cap V) \\
&= \int_U f \, dm + \int_V f \, dm,
\end{aligned}
$$

which concludes the argument. $\qquad\square$

Theorem 8.3. *Let $(S, \mathcal{E}, m)$ be a measure space and let $f, g \in \mathsf{SF}_+(S)$. Then,*

$$\int_S (af + bg) \, dm = a \int_S f \, dm + b \int_S g \, dm,$$

for every $a, b \in \mathbb{R}_{\geqslant 0}$.

Proof. Let $\pi = \{B_1, \ldots, B_n\}$ and $\sigma = \{C_1, \ldots, C_m\}$ be two measurable partitions of S related to f and g, respectively. Suppose that the infimum of these two partitions in $(PART(S), \leqslant)$ is $\tau = \pi \wedge \sigma$, where $\tau = \{D_1, \ldots, D_r\}$. The partition τ is related to both f and g and, therefore, there exist $u_1, \ldots, u_r$ and $v_1, \ldots, v_r$ in $\mathbb{R}$ such that $f(x) = u_i$ and $g(x) = v_i$ for every $x \in D_i$ and $1 \leqslant i \leqslant r$. Furthermore, τ is related to $af + bg$ as well because $(af + bg)(x) = au_i + bv_i$ for every $x \in D_i$. Thus,

$$
\begin{aligned}
\int_S (af + bg) \, dm &= \sum_{i=1}^{r} (au_i + bv_i) m(D_i) \\
&= a \sum_{i=1}^{r} u_i m(D_i) + b \sum_{i=1}^{r} v_i m(D_i) \\
&= a \int_S f \, dm + b \int_S g \, dm,
\end{aligned}
$$

which is the desired equality. $\qquad\square$

Corollary 8.1. *Let $(S, \mathcal{E}, m)$ be a measure space and let $f \in \mathsf{SF}_+(S)$. Then, the mapping $m_f : \mathcal{E} \longrightarrow \hat{\mathbb{R}}_{\geqslant 0}$ defined by $m_f(U) = \int_U f \, dm$ is a measure on $\mathcal{E}$.*

Proof. It is clear that $\int_\emptyset f \, dm = 0$. Thus, we need to prove only the additivity:

$$m_f \left(\bigcup_{n \in \mathbb{N}} U_n \right) = \sum_{n \in \mathbb{N}} m_f(U_n),$$

that is,

$$\int_{\bigcup_{n \in \mathbb{N}} U_n} f \, dm = \sum_{n \in \mathbb{N}} \int_{U_n} f \, dm \tag{8.3}$$

for every countable collection $\{U_0, U_1, \ldots\}$ of sets in $\mathcal{E}$ that are pairwise disjoint.

Consider the case when f is the characteristic function of a set $W \in \mathcal{E}$, that is, $f = 1_W$. In this case, equality (8.3) amounts to

$$m \left(W \cap \bigcup_{n \in \mathbb{N}} U_n \right) = \sum_{n \in \mathbb{N}} m(W \cap U_n),$$

which holds by the distributivity of the intersection over the countable union and the additivity of measures.

Since every simple non-negative function is a linear combination of characteristic functions, the additivity of m_f follows immediately. $\qquad \square$

Example 8.3. Note that for $x \in \mathbb{R}$ the interval $[x - 1, x)$ contains exactly one integer k, denoted by $\lfloor x \rfloor$. Consider the simple function measurable $f : [0, 3] \longrightarrow \mathbb{R}$ given by $f(x) = \lfloor x^2 \rfloor$. The range of this function is the set $\{0, 1, 4, 9\}$ and we have

$$f^{-1}(0) = [0, 1), \; f^{-1}(1) = [1, 2),$$
$$f^{-1}(4) = [2, 3), \; f^{-1}(9) = \{3\}.$$

Thus, if m is the Lebesgue measure we have

$$\int_{[0,3]} f \, dm = 0 \cdot m([0, 1)) + 1 \cdot m([1, 2)) + 4 \cdot m([2, 3)) + 9 \cdot m(\{3\})$$
$$= 0 \cdot 1 + 1 \cdot 1 + 4 \cdot 1 + 9 \cdot 0 = 5.$$

Theorem 8.4. *Let $(S, \mathcal{E}, m)$ be a measure space and let $f, g \in \mathsf{SF}_+(S)$ such that $f(x) \leqslant g(x)$ for $x \in S$. Then, $\int_S f \, dm \leqslant \int_S g \, dm$.*

Proof. Let $f(x) = \sum_{i=1}^n y_i 1_{f^{-1}(y_i)}(x)$ and $g(x) = \sum_{j=1}^m z_j 1_{g^{-1}(z_j)}(x)$ for $x \in S$. If $f^{-1}(y_i) \cap g^{-1}(z_j) \neq \emptyset$, then for $x \in f^{-1}(y_i) \cap g^{-1}(z_j)$ we have

$y_i = f(x) \leqslant g(x) = z_j$. This allows us to write

$$\int_S f \, dm = \sum_{i=1}^{n} y_i m(f^{-1}(y_i))$$

$$= \sum_{i=1}^{n} \sum_{j=1}^{m} y_i m(f^{-1}(y_i) \cap g^{-1}(z_j))$$

(because only terms with $f^{-1}(y_i) \cap g^{-1}(z_j) \neq \emptyset$ contribute)

$$\leqslant \sum_{i=1}^{n} \sum_{j=1}^{m} z_j m(f^{-1}(y_i) \cap g^{-1}(z_j))$$

$$= \sum_{j=1}^{m} z_j m(f^{-1}(z_j)) = \int_S g \, dm.$$

$\square$

Theorem 8.5. *Let $(S, \mathcal{E}, m)$ be a measure space and let $f \in \mathsf{SF}_+(S)$. If (U_n) is an increasing sequence of subsets of S with $\bigcup_{n \geqslant 1} U_n = S$, then $\int_S f \, 1_U \, dm = \lim_{n \to \infty} \int_S f \, 1_{U_n} \, dm$.*

Proof. Since $f \in SF_+(S)$ we have $f(x) = \sum_{i=1}^{n} y_i 1_{f^{-1}(y_i)}(x)$. Then $(f \, 1_U)(x) = \sum_{i=1}^{n} y_i 1_{f^{-1}(y_i)}(x) 1_U(x) = \sum_{i=1}^{n} y_i 1_{f^{-1}(y_i) \cap U}(x)$. Therefore, $\int_S f \, 1_U \, dm = \sum_{i=1}^{n} y_i m(f^{-1}(y_i) \cap U)$.

Note that $\lim_{n \to \infty} m(f^{-1}(y_i) \cap U_n) = m(f^{-1}(y_i) \cap U)$. Therefore, $\lim_{n \to \infty} \int_S f \, 1_{U_n} \, dm = \int_S f \, 1_U \, dm$. $\square$

Theorem 8.6. *Let $f = (f_n)_{n \geqslant 1}$ be a sequence on non-negative simple measurable functions defined on the measure space $(S, \mathcal{E}, m)$ such that $f_n(x) \leqslant f_{n+1}(x)$ for all $x \in S$ and $n \geqslant 1$. Also, let f be a non-negative simple measurable function on the same space. The following statements hold:*

    (i) *if $\lim_{n \to \infty} f_n(x) \leqslant f(x)$ for $x \in S$, then $\lim_{n \to \infty} \int_S f_n \, dm \leqslant \int_S f \, dm$;*

    (ii) *if $\lim_{n \to \infty} f_n(x) \geqslant f(x)$ for $x \in S$, then $\lim_{n \to \infty} \int_S f_n \, dm \geqslant \int_S f \, dm$.*

Proof. Theorem 8.4 implies that $\int_S f_n \, dm \leqslant \int_S f_{n+1} \, dm$ for $n \geqslant 1$ and therefore $\lim_{n \to \infty} f_n \, dm$ exists in $[0, \infty]$. By the same theorem, $\int_S f_n \, dm \leqslant \int_S f \, dm$, hence $\lim_{n \to \infty} \int_S f_n \, dm \leqslant \int_S f \, dm$, which proves part (i).

To prove part (ii), suppose that $\lim_{n \to \infty} f_n(x) \geqslant f(x)$ for $x \in S$. By Supplement 5 of Chapter 7 the set $S_{n,a} = \{x \in S \mid af(x) \leqslant f_n(x)\}$ is measurable for every $a \in [0, 1)$. The sequence of sets $(S_{n,a})_{n \geqslant 1}$ is increasing.

We claim that $\bigcup_{n \geqslant 1} S_{n,a} = S$. Suppose that this is not the case, that is, there exists $x \in S$ such that $x \notin \bigcup_{n \geqslant 1} S_{n,a}$. Then $af(x) > f_n(x)$ for $n \geqslant 1$, hence $af(x) \geqslant f(x) > 0$, which contradicts the assumption that $a \in [0, 1)$. We have $af(x)1_{S_{n,a}}(x) \leqslant f(x)$ for $x \in S$. Therefore,

$$a \int_S f \, dm = \int_S af \, dm$$
$$= \lim_{n \to \infty} \int_S af 1_{S_{n,a}} \, dm$$
$$\text{(by Theorem 8.4)}$$
$$\leqslant \lim_{n \to \infty} \int_S f_n \, dm$$
$$\text{(by Theorem 8.5)}.$$

Since this inequality holds for $a \in [0, 1)$ it follows that $\int_S f \, dm \leqslant \lim_{n \to \infty} \int_S f_n \, dm$. $\qquad \square$

Theorem 8.7. *Let $(S, \mathcal{E})$ be a measure space and let $(f_n)_{n \geqslant 1}$ and $(g_n)_{n \geqslant 1}$ be two increasing sequences of functions in $\mathsf{SF}_+(S)$. If $\lim_{n \to \infty} f_n(x) = \lim_{n \to \infty} g_n(x)$ for $x \in S$, then $\lim_{n \to \infty} \int_S f_n \, dm = \lim_{n \to \infty} \int_S g_n \, dm$.*

Proof. We have $f_p \leqslant \lim_{n \to \infty} g_n(x)$ for $x \in S$ and $p \geqslant 1$. Therefore, the second part of Theorem 8.6 implies $\int_S f_p \, dm \leqslant \lim_{n \to \infty} \int_S g_n \, dm$ for every $p \geqslant 1$, hence $\lim_{n \to \infty} \int_S f_n \, dm \leqslant \lim_{n \to \infty} \int_S g_n \, dm$. The reverse inequality has a similar proof. $\qquad \square$

8.2.2 The Integral of Non-negative Measurable Functions

The extension of integral to non-negative measurable functions is based on the fact (shown in Theorem 7.26) that a non-negative measurable function is the pointwise limit of a sequence of measurable simple non-negative functions.

Definition 8.2. Let $(S, \mathcal{E}, m)$ be a measure space, $f : S \longrightarrow [0, \infty]$ be a non-negative measurable function. The *Lebesgue integral* of f on S, denoted by $\int_S f \, dm$, is defined as:

$$\int_S f \, dm = \lim_{n \to \infty} \int_S f_n \, dm,$$

where (f_n) is any sequence of non-negative simple functions such that $\lim_{n \to \infty} f_n = f$.

The non-negative measurable function f is *m-integrable*, or just *integrable* if $\int_S f \, dm$ is finite.

By Theorem 8.7, $\int_S f \, dm$ is well-defined because its value is independent of the choice made for the sequence of non-negative simple functions that converges to f.

Theorem 8.8. *Let $(S, \mathcal{E}, m)$ be a measure space, $f, g : S \longrightarrow [0, \infty]$ be non-negative measurable functions. We have:*

$$\int_S (f + g) \, dm = \int_S f \, dm + \int_S g \, dm$$

$$\int_S af \, dm = a \int_S f \, dm$$

for every $a \geqslant 0$.

Proof. Let $(f_n)_{n \geqslant 1}$ and $(g_n)_{n \geqslant 1}$ be two sequences of non-negative measurable simple functions such that $\lim_{n \to \infty} f_n = f$ and $\lim_{n \to \infty} g_n = g$. Then, $(f_n + g_n)_{n \geqslant 1}$ is a sequence of non-negative measurable simple functions that converges to $f + g$, hence

$$
\begin{aligned}
\int_S (f + g) \, dm &= \lim_{n \to \infty} \int_S (f_n + g_n) \, dm \\
&= \lim_{n \to \infty} \left(\int_S f_n \, dm + \int_S g_n \, dm \right) \\
&= \text{(by Theorem 8.3)} \\
&= \lim_{n \to \infty} \int_S f_n \, dm + \lim_{n \to \infty} \int_S g_n \, dm \\
&= \int_S f \, dm + \int_S g \, dm.
\end{aligned}
$$

Since $a \geqslant 0$, $(af_n)_{n \geqslant 1}$ is a sequence of non-negative measurable simple functions such that $\lim_{n \to \infty} af_n = af$. By Theorem 8.3,

$$
\begin{aligned}
\int_S af \, dm &= \lim_{n \to \infty} \int_S af_n \, dm \\
&= \lim_{n \to \infty} a \int_S f_n \, dm \\
&= a \lim_{n \to \infty} \int_S f_n \, dm = a \int_S f \, dm. \qquad \square
\end{aligned}
$$

Theorem 8.9. *Let $(S, \mathcal{E}, m)$ be a measure space, and let f and g be two non-negative measurable functions such that $f(x) \leqslant g(x)$ for $x \in S$. We have $\int_S f \, dm \leqslant \int_S g \, dm$.*

Proof. Let (f_n) and (g_n) be two sequences of non-negative increasing functions such that $\lim_{n \to \infty} f_n = f$ and $\lim_{n \to \infty} g_n = g$. Since

$$f_n \leqslant f \leqslant g = \lim_{n \to \infty} g_n,$$

we have

$$\int_S f_n \, dm \leqslant \lim_{n \to \infty} \int_S g_n \, dm = \int_S g \, dm,$$

by the second part of Theorem 8.6. The inequality $\int_S f_n \, dm \leqslant \int_S g \, dm$ implies $\int_S f \, dm \leqslant \int_S g \, dm$. □

Theorem 8.10. *Let $(S, \mathcal{E}, m)$ be a measure space, and let $f, g : S \longrightarrow \hat{\mathbb{R}}_{\geqslant 0}$ be two non-negative measurable functions. The following statements hold:*

    (i) *we have $\int_S f \, dm = 0$ if and only if $f = 0$ a.e.;*

    (ii) *if $f = g$ a.e., then $\int_S f \, dm = \int_S g \, dm$.*

Proof. Suppose that $\int_S f \, dm = 0$ and let $U_n = f^{-1} \left[\frac{1}{n}, \infty \right]$ for $n \geqslant 1$. We have $\frac{1}{n} 1_{U_n} \leqslant f$, which implies

$$\frac{1}{n} m(U_n) = \int_S \frac{1}{n} 1_{U_n} \, dm \leqslant \int_S f \, dm = 0$$

by Theorem 8.9. Thus, $m(U_n) = 0$ for $n \geqslant 1$. Since $\{x \in S \mid f(x) \neq 0\} = \bigcup_{n \geqslant 1} U_n$, it follows that $\{x \in S \mid f(x) \neq 0\} = 0$, so $f = 0$ a.e.

Conversely, suppose that $f = 0$ a.e. Let (f_n) be an increasing sequence of non-negative measurable simple functions such that $\lim_{n \to \infty} f_n = f$. We have $f_n = 0$ a.e., hence $\int_S f_n \, dm = 0$ for $n \geqslant 1$, which implies $\int_S f \, dm = 0$.

For the second part let $V = \{x \in S \mid f(x) = g(x)\} \in \mathcal{E}$. There exists $W \in \mathcal{E}$ such that $S - V \subseteq W$ and $m(W) = 0$. Let $Y = S - W \subseteq V$. The functions $f 1_Y$ and $g 1_Y$ are measurable and $f 1_Y = g 1_Y$. Also, note that $f 1_W = 0$ a.e and $g 1_W = 0$ a.e. on S.

The first part implies $\int_S f 1_W \, dm = \int_S g 1_W \, dm = 0$. Theorem 8.8 implies:

$$\int_S f \, dm = \int_S (f 1_W + f 1_Y) \, dm$$

$$= \int_S f 1_W \, dm = \int_S g 1_W \, dm$$

$$= \int_S (g 1_W + g 1_Y) \, dm = \int_S g \, dm.$$

□

The next theorem shows that *pointwise* convergence of a sequence of non-negative functions allows us to permute integration and limit.

Theorem 8.11. (The Monotone Convergence Theorem) *Let f be a non-decreasing sequence of non-negative and measurable functions, $\boldsymbol{f} = (f_n)$ such that $\lim_{n\to\infty} f_n(x)$ exists for every $x \in S$. If $f : S \longrightarrow \hat{\mathbb{R}}_{\geqslant 0}$ is the function defined by $f(x) = \lim_{n\to\infty} f_n(x)$ for $x \in S$, then f is a non-negative measurable function and*

$$\int_S f \, dm = \lim_{n\to\infty} \int_S f_n \, dm.$$

Proof. Since $\boldsymbol{f}$ is a nondecreasing sequence, $\lim_{n\to\infty} f_n(x)$ exists, finite or not. Therefore, by Corollary 7.15, the function f is measurable. By the hypothesis of the theorem, $\int_S f_n \, dm \leqslant \int_S f \, dm$.

The sequence $\mathbf{v} = (v_0, \ldots, v_n, \ldots)$ given by $v_n = \int_S f_n \, dm$ for $n \in \mathbb{N}$ is increasing. Let $v \in \hat{\mathbb{R}}_{\geqslant 0}$ be $v = \lim_{n\to\infty} v_n \leqslant \int_S f \, dm$, so $\lim_{n\to\infty} \int_S f_n \, dm \leqslant \int_S f \, dm$.

To prove the reverse inequality, $\int_S f \, dm \leqslant \lim_{n\to\infty} \int_S f_n \, dm$, let h be a simple non-negative function such that $h \leqslant f$. For $\alpha \in (0,1)$ and $n \in \mathbb{N}$ consider the sets $U_n^\alpha = \{x \in S \mid f_n(x) \geqslant \alpha h(x)\}$.

We claim that the sequence of sets $\mathbf{U} = (U_0^\alpha, \ldots, U_n^\alpha, \ldots)$ is nondecreasing and

$$S = \bigcup_{n\in\mathbb{N}} U_n^\alpha.$$

Thus, $\lim_{n\to\infty} U_n^\alpha = S$ and $\lim_{n\to\infty} I_{U_n^\alpha}(x) = 1$ for $x \in S$ and $\alpha \in (0,1)$.

Let $x \in U_n^\alpha$. We have $f_n(x) \geqslant \alpha h(x)$ and, since $f_{n+1}(x) \geqslant f_n(x)$, it follows that $x \in U_{n+1}^\alpha$. Thus, $U_n^\alpha \subseteq U_{n+1}^\alpha$, so $\mathbf{U}$ is indeed a non-decreasing sequence of sets.

Let x be an element of S. If we would have $f_n(x) < \alpha h(x)$ for every $n \in \mathbb{N}$ this would imply that $f(x) = \lim_{n\to\infty} f_n(x) < \alpha h(x) < h(x)$, which contradicts the definition of h. Therefore, there exists $n \in \mathbb{N}$ such that $f_n(x) \geqslant \alpha h(x)$, so $x \in U_n^\alpha$, which justifies our claim.

We have

$$\int_S f_n \, dm \geqslant \int_{U_n^\alpha} f_n \, dm \geqslant \alpha \int_{U_n^\alpha} h \, dm = \alpha m_h(U_n^\alpha).$$

Thus,

$$\lim_{n\to\infty} \int_S f_n \, dm \geqslant \lim_{n\to\infty} \alpha m_h(U_n^\alpha) = \alpha m_h \left(\lim_{n\to\infty} U_n^\alpha \right) = \alpha m_h(S),$$

by Theorem 7.32. Therefore,

$$\lim_{n \to \infty} \int_S f_n \, dm \geqslant \lim_{\alpha \to 1} \alpha m_h(S),$$

for every non-negative simple function h such that $h \leqslant f$. We conclude that $\lim_{n \to \infty} \int_S f_n \, dm \geqslant \int_S \, dm$. □

Theorem 8.12. (Fatou's Lemma) *Let* $(S, \mathcal{E}, m)$ *be a measure space and let* $\boldsymbol{f}$ *be a sequence of non-negative measurable functions,* $\boldsymbol{f} = (f_0, f_1, \ldots, f_n, \ldots)$ *such that* $f_i : S \longrightarrow \mathbb{R}_{\geqslant 0}$. *We have the inequality*

$$\int_S \liminf_{n \to \infty} f_n \, dm \leqslant \liminf_{n \to \infty} \int_S f_n \, dm.$$

Proof. If $k \leqslant j$, then $\inf_{n \geqslant k} f_n \leqslant f_j$. Therefore, $\int_S \inf_{n \geqslant k} f_n \, dm \leqslant \int_S f_j \, dm$, which implies $\int_S \inf_{n \geqslant k} f_n \, dm \leqslant \inf_{k \leqslant j} \int_S f_j \, dm$.

The sequence of functions $(\inf_{n \geqslant k} f_n)$ is nondecreasing and

$$\lim_{k \to \infty} \inf_{n \geqslant k} f_n = \liminf_{n \to \infty} f_n.$$

By the Monotone Convergence Theorem we have

$$\int_S \liminf_{n \to \infty} f_n \, dm = \lim_{k \to \infty} \int_S \inf_{n \geqslant k} f_n \leqslant \liminf_{j \to \infty} \int_S f_j \, dm.$$ □

Example 8.4. The inequality in Fatou's Lemma may be strict. Consider, for example the sequence of functions $\mathbf{f} = (f_0, f_1, \ldots, f_n, \ldots)$, where

$$f_n(x) = \begin{cases} 1 & \text{if } n \leqslant x \leqslant n+1, \\ 0 & \text{otherwise.} \end{cases}$$

It is clear that $\liminf_{n \to \infty} f_n = \lim_{n \to \infty} f_n = 0$, so $\int_{\mathbb{R}} \liminf_{n \to \infty} f_n \, dm = 0$. On another hand, $\int_{\mathbb{R}} f_n \, dm = 1$ for $n \in \mathbb{N}$. Therefore, $\liminf_{n \to \infty} \int_{\mathbb{R}} f_n \, dm = 1$.

Lemma 8.1. *Let* $(S, \mathcal{E}, m)$ *be a measure space and let* $\boldsymbol{f}$ *be a sequence of non-negative measurable functions,* $\boldsymbol{f} = (f_1, \ldots, f_n, \ldots)$. *We have*

$$\int_S \sum_{j=1}^{\infty} f_j \, dm = \sum_{j=1}^{\infty} \int_S f_j \, dm.$$

Proof. Since $\mathbf{f}$ consists of non-negative functions, the sequence of functions $\mathbf{g} = (g_0, g_1, \ldots, g_n, \ldots)$ given by $g_n = \sum_{j=1}^{n} f_j$ is non-decreasing and $\lim_{n \to \infty} g_n = \sum_{j=1}^{\infty} f_j$.

The Monotone Convergence Theorem (Theorem 8.11) implies

$$\int_S \lim_{n \to \infty} g_n \, dm = \lim_{n \to \infty} \int_S g_n \, dm.$$

By the definition of (g_n) this means that

$$\int_S \sum_{j=1}^{\infty} f_j \, dm = \lim_{n \to \infty} \int_S \left(\sum_{j=1}^{n} f_j \right) dm$$

$$= \lim_{n \to \infty} \sum_{j=1}^{n} \int_S f_j \, dm = \sum_{j=1}^{\infty} \int_S f_j \, dm,$$

which concludes the argument. $\qquad\square$

Note that both sides of the equality of Lemma 8.1 may be infinite.

Theorem 8.13. *Let $(S, \mathcal{E}, m)$ be a complete measure space, $E \in \mathcal{E}$ be a set of finite measure and let $f : S \longrightarrow \mathbb{R}$ be a bounded function. We have*

$$\inf \left\{ \int_E h \, dm \,\middle|\, h \in \mathsf{SF}(E) \text{ and } h \geqslant f \right\}$$

$$= \sup \left\{ \int_E g \, dm \,\middle|\, g \in \mathsf{SF}(E) \text{ and } g \leqslant f \right\}$$

if and only if f is measurable.

Proof. Suppose that $f(x) < M$ when $x \in E$. Since f is measurable, for $-n \leqslant k \leqslant n$ the sets

$$E_k = \left\{ x \in E \,\middle|\, \frac{(k-1)M}{n} < f(x) \leqslant \frac{kM}{n} \right\}$$

form a partition of the set E, so $m(E) = \sum_{k=-n}^{k=n} m(E_k)$.

Let h_n, g_n be the simple functions defined by:

$$h_n(x) = \frac{M}{n} \sum_{k=-n}^{n} k 1_{E_k}(x),$$

$$g_n(x) = \frac{M}{n} \sum_{k=-n}^{n} (k-1) 1_{E_k}(x).$$

We have

$$g_n(x) \leqslant f(x) \leqslant h_n(x).$$

Therefore,

$$\inf \left\{ \int_E h \, dm \mid h \in \mathsf{SF}(E), h \leqslant f \right\} \leqslant \int_E h_n \, dm = \frac{M}{n} \sum_{k=-n}^{k=n} k m(E_k)$$

and

$$\sup\left\{\int_E g \, dm \mid g \in \mathsf{SF}(E), g \geqslant f\right\} \geqslant \int_E g_n \, dm = \frac{M}{n} \sum_{k=-n}^{k=n} (k-1)m(E_k).$$

Consequently,

$$0 \leqslant \inf\left\{\int_E h \, dm \mid h \in \mathsf{SF}(E), h \leqslant f\right\}$$

$$- \sup\left\{\int_E g \, dm \mid g \in \mathsf{SF}(E), g \geqslant f\right\}$$

$$\leqslant \frac{M}{n} \sum_{k=-n}^{n} m(E_k) = \frac{M}{n}m(E),$$

for $n \geqslant 1$, which implies the equality of the theorem.

Conversely, suppose that

$$\inf\left\{\int_E h \, dm \,\middle|\, h \in \mathsf{SF}(E) \text{ and } h \geqslant f\right\}$$

$$= \sup\left\{\int_E h \, dm \,\middle|\, g \in \mathsf{SF}(E) \text{ and } g \leqslant f\right\}.$$

For every $n \in \mathbb{N}$ there are simple functions g_n and h_n such that $g_n(x) \leqslant f(x) \leqslant h_n(x)$ and $\int_S h_n \, dm - \int_S g_n \, dm < \frac{1}{n}$. Therefore, the functions $p = \sup h_n$ and $q = \inf g_n$ are measurable and $p \leqslant f \leqslant g^*$.

Observe that

$$\{x \in S \mid p(x) < q(x)\} = \bigcup_{m \geqslant 1}\left\{x \in S \mid p(x) < q(x) - \frac{1}{m}\right\}.$$

Since

$$\left\{x \in S \mid p(x) < q(x) - \frac{1}{m}\right\} \subseteq \left\{x \in S \mid h_n(x) < g_n(x) - \frac{1}{m}\right\},$$

for every n and $m\left(\{x \in S \mid h_n(x) < g_n(x) - \frac{1}{m}\}\right) < \frac{m}{n}$ for every $n \geqslant 1$. Therefore, we have $m\left(\{x \in S \mid h_n(x) < g_n(x) - \frac{1}{m}\}\right) = 0$ and $p = f$ almost everywhere. Thus, f is measurable. $\square$

Theorem 8.14. *Let $(S, \mathcal{E}, m)$ be a measure space and let $f, g : S \longrightarrow \hat{\mathbb{R}}_{\geqslant 0}$. If $f(x) \leqslant g(x)$ for $x \in S$ and $\int_S f \, dm$, $\int_S g \, dm$ exist, then $\int_S f \, dm \leqslant \int_S g \, dm$.*

Proof. It is easy to see that $f(x) \leqslant g(x)$ for $x \in S$ implies $f^+(x) \leqslant g^+(x)$ and $f^-(x) \leqslant g^-(x)$ for $x \in S$. We have the inequalities $\int_S f^+ \, dm \leqslant \int_S g^+ \, dm$ and $\int_S f^- \, dm \geqslant \int_S g^- \, dm$. and all four previously mentioned integrals are finite due to the integrability of f and g. Therefore,

$$\int_S f \, dm = \int_S f^+ \, dm - \int_S f^- \, dm \leqslant \int_S g^+ \, dm - \int_S g^- \, dm = \int_S g \, dm.$$

$\square$

Theorem 8.15. *Let f be a non-negative function defined on the measure space $(S, \mathcal{E}, m)$. The function f is zero a.e. if and only if $\int_S f \, dm = 0$.*

Proof. Suppose that f is zero a.e.. If h is a simple function such that $0 \leqslant h \leqslant f$, then $h = 0$ almost everywhere. Thus, $\int_S h \, dm = 0$ for all such simple function, hence $\int_S f \, dm = 0$.

Suppose now that $\int_S f \, dm = 0$ and let $T = \{x \in S \mid f(x) > 0\}$. Let

$$T_n = \left\{ x \in S \,\middle|\, \frac{1}{n} \leqslant x < \infty \right\} = f^{-1}\left(\left[\frac{1}{n}, \infty\right)\right).$$

The sequence (T_n) is increasing and $T = \bigcup\{T_n \mid 1 \leqslant n \leqslant \infty\}$.

Consider the simple function $h_n = \frac{1}{n} 1_{T_n}$. We have $h_n \leqslant f$ and $\int_{\mathbb{R}} h_n \, dm = \frac{1}{n} m(T_n) \leqslant \int_{\mathbb{R}} f \, dm = 0$, hence $m(T_n) = 0$ for all n. By Theorem 7.32 it follows that $m(T) = 0$, so f is 0 a.e. $\qquad\square$

Theorem 8.16. *Let $(S, \mathcal{E}, m)$ be a measure space and let $f, g : S \longrightarrow \hat{\mathbb{R}}_{\geqslant 0}$ be two measurable functions defined on S. If $f \leqslant g$ almost everywhere in the sense of the measure m and $\int_S f \, dm$, $\int_S g \, dm$ exist, then $\int_S f \, dm \leqslant \int_S g \, dm$.*

Proof. Let $U = \{x \in S \mid f(x) \leqslant g(x)\}$. Then $S - U$ is a null set. The inequality $f 1_U \leqslant g 1_U$ implies $\int_S f 1_U \, dm \leqslant \int_S g 1_U \, dm$. Since $S - U$ is null, $\int_{S-U} f 1_A \, dm = \int_{S-U} g 1_A \, dm = 0$, so

$$\int_S f \, dm = \int_U f \, dm + \int_{S-U} f \, dm = \int_U f \, dm$$
$$\leqslant \int_U g \, dm = \int_U g \, dm + \int_{S-U} g \, dm = \int_S g \, dm. \qquad\square$$

Corollary 8.2. *Let $(S, \mathcal{E}, m)$ be a measure space and let $f, g : S \longrightarrow \hat{\mathbb{R}}_{\geqslant 0}$ be two non-negative measurable functions defined on S. If $f = g$ a.e., then $\int_S f \, dm = \int_S g \, dm$.*

Proof. This follows immediately from Theorem 8.16. $\qquad\square$

Theorem 8.17. *Let $(S, \mathcal{E}, m)$ be a measure space. If $f : S \longrightarrow \hat{\mathbb{R}}_{\geqslant 0}$ is an integrable function then f is finite almost everywhere.*

Proof. Let Y be the set $Y = \{x \in \mathbb{R} \mid f(y) = \infty\}$. For the simple function $g_n = n I_Y$ we have $g_n \leqslant f$. Since $\int g_n \, dm = nm(A)$, we have $\sup \int g_n \, dm = \infty$, it follows that $\int f \, dm = \infty$, which contradicts the fact that f is integrable. Thus, $m(Y) = 0$, so f is finite almost everywhere. $\qquad\square$

Theorem 8.18. (Mean Value Theorem for Lebesgue Integrals) *Let*
$(S, \mathcal{E}, m)$ *be a measure space and* $U \in \mathcal{E}$. *If* $f : S \longrightarrow \hat{\mathbb{R}}_{\geqslant 0}$ *is an integrable*
function and $U \in \mathcal{E}$, *then*

$$m(U) \inf\{f(x) \mid x \in U\} \leqslant \int_U f \, dm \leqslant m(U) \sup\{f(x) \mid x \in U\}.$$

Proof. Let $(S, \mathcal{E}, m)$ be a measure space and let g and h be the simple
functions defined on S by $g = \inf\{f(x) \mid x \in S\} I_U$ and $h = \sup\{f(x) \mid x \in S\} I_U$, then

$$\int_U g \, dm = \inf\{f(x) \mid x \in S\} \int_U I_U \, dm = \inf\{f(x) \mid x \in S\} m(U),$$

$$\int_U h \, dm = \sup\{f(x) \mid x \in S\} \int_U I_U \, dm = \inf\{f(x) \mid x \in S\} m(U).$$

Since $\int_U g \, dm \leq \int_U f \, dm \leq \int_U h \, dm$, the double inequality of the theorem
follows immediately. $\qquad\square$

Theorem 8.19. *Let* $(S, \mathcal{E}, m)$ *be a measure space and let* $f : S \longrightarrow \mathbb{R}_{\geqslant 0}$ *be*
a non-negative function. If $\int f \, dm = 0$, *then* $f(x) = 0$ *almost everywhere.*

Proof. For $n \geqslant 1$, define $U_n = \{x \in S \mid f(x) \geqslant \frac{1}{n}\}$. Clearly, U_n is
measurable and so is $U = \bigcup_{n \geqslant 1} U_n$. We have $f(x) = 0$ if $x \notin U$.

Let h_n be the simple function defined by

$$h_n(x) = \begin{cases} \dfrac{1}{n} & \text{if } f(x) \geqslant \dfrac{1}{n}, \\ 0 & \text{otherwise.} \end{cases}$$

Clearly, we have $h_n \leqslant f$, so $\int h_n \, dm \leqslant \int f \, dm = 0$, so $h_n \leqslant f$, so
$\int h_n \, dm = 0$, which implies $\frac{1}{n} m(U_n) = 0$ for $n \in \mathbb{N}$. Since U_n is a monotonic
sequence, $m(U) = \lim m(U_n) = 0$, and f is zero outside the null set U. $\quad\square$

Definition 8.3. Let $(S, \mathcal{E}, m)$ be a measure space and let $f : S \longrightarrow \hat{\mathbb{R}}_{\geqslant 0}$ be
a measurable non-negative function. The *integral on a measurable subset*
$U \in \mathcal{E}$ of f is defined as

$$\int_U f \, dm = \int_S f 1_U \, dm.$$

Theorem 8.20. *Let* $(S, \mathcal{E}, m)$ *be a measure space, and let* U *and* V *two*
disjoint subsets of S *such that* $U, V \in \mathcal{E}$. *If* f *is a non-negative measurable*
function, then

$$\int_{U \cup V} f \, dm = \int_U f \, dm + \int_V f \, dm.$$

Proof. By Definition 8.2, $\int_{U \cup V} f \, dm$ is the supremum of the set that consists of numbers of the form $\int_{U \cup V} h \, dm$, h is a non-negative simple measurable function such that $h(x) \leqslant f(x)$ for $x \in U \cup V$. By Theorem 8.2 we have $\int_{U \cup V} h \, dm = \int_U h \, dm + \int_V h \, dm$, which implies

$$\int_{U \cup V} h \, dm \leqslant \int_U f \, dm + \int_V f \, dm.$$

Therefore,

$$\int_{U \cup V} f \, dm \leqslant \int_U f \, dm + \int_V f \, dm.$$

To prove the converse inequality, let h_1, h_2 be two simple functions on S such that $h_1(x) = 0$ if $x \notin U$, $h_2(x) = 0$ if $x \notin V$, and $\max\{h_1(x), h_2(x)\} \leqslant f(x)$ for $x \in U \cup V$. Define the non-negative simple function $h : S \longrightarrow \mathbb{R}$ as

$$h(x) = \begin{cases} h_1(x) & \text{if } x \in U, \\ h_2(x) & \text{if } x \in U, \\ 0 & \text{if } x \in S - (U \cup V). \end{cases}$$

Clearly, we have $h(x) \leqslant f(x)$ for $x \in S$. We have

$$\int_U h_1 \, dm + \int_V h_2 \, dm = \int_U h \, dm + \int_V h \, dm = \int_{U \cup V} h \, dm \leqslant \int_{U \cup V} f \, dm.$$

Consequently,

$$\int_U f \, dm + \int_V f \, dm \leqslant \int_{U \cup V} f \, dm,$$

which concludes the argument. $\qquad\qquad\square$

Theorem 8.21. *Let $(S, \mathcal{E}, m)$ be a measure space, and let f be a non-negative measurable function. If U and V are two subsets of S such that $U \subseteq V$, then $\int_U f \, dm \leqslant \int_V f \, dm$.*

Proof. Note that $U \subseteq V$ implies $I_U(x) \leqslant I_V(x)$ for $x \in S$. Therefore, $fI_U \leqslant fI_V$. This implies $\int_U f \, dm = \int_S fI_U \, dm \leqslant \int_S fI_V \, dm = \int_V f \, dm$. $\qquad\square$

8.2.3 The Integral of Real-Valued Measurable Functions

The definition of Lebesgue integral is extended now to real-valued functions that range over the extended set of real numbers $\hat{\mathbb{R}}$.

Definition 8.4. Let $(S, \mathcal{E}, m)$ be a measure space. A measurable function $f : S \longrightarrow \hat{\mathbb{R}}$ is *m-integrable*, or just *integrable* if both $\int_S f^+ \, dm$ and $\int_S f^- \, dm$ are finite.

If at least one of the integrals $\int_S f^+ \, dm$ or $\int_S f^- \, dm$ is finite, then we say that *the integral $\int_S f \, dm$ exists* is defined as:

$$\int_S f \, dm = \int_S f^+ \, dm - \int_S f^- \, dm.$$

Note that the integral $\int_S f \, dm$ may exist (and be ∞ or $-\infty$) even if the function f is not integrable.

The set of all real-valued integrable functions on the measure space $(S, \mathcal{E}, m)$ is denoted by $\mathcal{L}^1(S, \mathcal{E}, m)$, or just $\mathcal{L}^1(S)$ when the measure space is understood from context.

Theorem 8.22. *Let $(S, \mathcal{E}, m)$ be a measure space. A function $f : S \longrightarrow \mathring{\mathbb{R}}$ is integrable if and only if $|f|$ is integrable.*

Proof. Suppose that f is integrable, so $\int_S f^+ \, dm$ and $\int_S f^- \, dm$ are finite. Since $|f| = f^+(x) + f^-(x)$ for $x \in S$, it follows that $\int_S |f| \, dm = \int_S f^+ \, dm + \int_S f^- \, dm$, so $|f|$ is integrable.

Conversely, suppose that $|f|$ is integrable, that is both $\int_S |f|^+ \, dm$ and $\int_S |f|^- \, dm$ are finite. Since $|f|^+ = |f|$, if follows that $\int_S |f| \, dm$ is finite. This implies that both $\int_S f^+ \, dm$ and $\int_S f^- \, dm$ are finite, which implies that f is integrable. $\square$

Theorem 8.23. *Let $(S, \mathcal{E}, m)$ be a measure space and $f : S \longrightarrow \mathring{\mathbb{R}}$ be a measurable function. If $\int_S f \, dm$ is defined, and $c \in \mathbb{R}$, then $\int_S cf \, dm$ is defined and $\int_S cf \, dm = c \int_S f \, dm$.*

If f is integrable, then cf is also integrable and, again, $\int_S cf \, dm = c \int_S f \, dm$.

Proof. If $c = -1$, then $cf = -f$, so $(cf)^+ = f^-$ and $(-f)^- = f^+$. Therefore,

$$\int_S f \, dm = \int_S f^+ \, dm - \int_S f^- \, dm = \int_S (-f)^- \, dm - \int_S (-f)^+ \, dm$$
$$= - \left(\int_S (-f)^+ \, dm - \int_S (-f)^- \, dm \right)$$
$$= - \int_S (-f) \, dm.$$

Thus,

$$\int_S (-f) \, dm = - \int_S f \, dm.$$

If $c \geqslant 0$ we need to consider two subcases: $c = 0$ and $c > 0$. In the first subcase, we have $cf = 0$, so $\int_S cf \, dm = \int_S 0 \, dm = 0 = 0 \cdot \int_S f \, dm$, because we adopted the convention that $0\infty = 0(-\infty) = 0$.

Suppose now that $c > 0$. We have $(cf)^+ = cf^+$, $(cf)^- = cf^-$. Thus, if $\int_S cf \, dm$ exists we have

$$\int_S cf \, dm = \int_S (cf)^+ \, dm - \int_S (cf)^- \, dm = \int_S cf^+ \, dm - \int_S cf^- \, dm. \quad (8.4)$$

Since $f^+ \geqslant 0$, by Theorem 7.26, there exists a non-decreasing sequence of non-negative simple measurable functions (f_n) whose limit is f^+. Thus, $\lim_{n\to\infty} cf_n(x) = cf^+(x)$. Since $\int_S cf_n \, dm = c \int_S f_n \, dm$, we have $\int_S cf^+ \, dm = c \int_S f^+ \, dm$. Similarly, we have $\int_S cf^- \, dm = c \int_S f^- \, dm$ and the desired result follows from equality (8.4).

For the remaining case, $c < 0$, we have

$$\int_S cf \, dm = \int_S (-1)(cf) \, dm = -\int_S (-c)f \, dm = -(-c) \int_S f \, dm$$

by the previous arguments. Thus, in all cases, the desired conclusion follows.

If f is integrable, then $|f|$ is integrable (by Theorem 8.22), so $\int_S |cf| \, dm = |c| \int_S |f| \, dm < \infty$, so cf is also integrable and $\int_S cf \, dm = c \int_S f \, dm$ by the first part of the theorem. $\qquad\square$

Theorem 8.24. *Let $(S, \mathcal{E}, m)$ be a measure space and let $f, g : S \longrightarrow \hat{\mathbb{R}}$ be two measurable functions such that $f \leqslant g$ and both $\int_S f \, dm$ and $\int_S g \, dm$ are defined. Then $\int_S f \, dm \leqslant \int_S g \, dm$.*

Proof. Since $f(x) \leqslant g(x)$ we have

$$f^+(x) = \max\{f(x), 0\} \leqslant \max\{g(x), 0\} = g^+(x),$$
$$g^-(x) = -\min\{g(x), 0\} \leqslant -\min\{f(x), 0\} = f^-(x),$$

which implies $\int_S f^+ \, dm \leqslant \int_S g^+ \, dm$ and $\int_S g^- \, dm \leqslant \int_S f^- \, dm$. In turn, this yields

$$\int_S f \, dm = \int_S f^+ \, dm - \int_S f^- \, dm \leqslant \int_S g^+ \, dm - \int_S g^- \, dm = \int_S g \, dm.$$

$\qquad\square$

Theorem 8.25. *Let $f : S \longrightarrow \hat{\mathbb{R}}$ be an integrable function on the measure space $(S, \mathcal{E}, m)$. We have:*

$$\left| \int f \, dm \right| \leqslant \int |f| \, dm.$$

Proof. By Theorem 8.22, $|f|$ is integrable. Since $-|f| \leqslant f \leqslant |f|$, we have $-\int |f|\, dm \leqslant \int f\, dm \leqslant \int |f|\, dm$. This implies the desired inequality. $\qquad\square$

Theorem 8.26. *Let $(S, \mathcal{E}, m)$ be a measure space and let $f : S \longrightarrow \hat{\mathbb{R}}$ be a measurable function that is integrable. Then $f(x) \in \mathbb{R}$ a.e. and the set $U = \{x \in S \mid f(x) \neq 0\}$ is of σ-finite measure m.*

Proof. Since f is integrable, we have $\int_S |f|\, dm$ is finite by Theorem 8.22. Let $T = \{x \in S \mid f(x) = \infty\}$. If $r > 0$ we have $r 1_T(x) \leqslant |f|(x)$ for $x \in S$, hence

$$r\, m(T) = \int_S r 1_T\, dm \leqslant \int_S |f|\, dm < \infty.$$

Therefore, $m(T) \leqslant \frac{1}{r} \int_S |f|\, dm$ for every r, so $m(T) = 0$.

Let $U = \{x \in S \mid f(x) \neq 0\}$ and $U_n = \{x \in S \mid |f(x)| \geqslant \frac{1}{n}\}$ for $n \geqslant 1$. Note that $U = \bigcup_{n \geqslant 1} U_n$.

We have $\frac{1}{n} 1_{U_n}(x) \leqslant |f(x)|$, hence

$$\frac{1}{n} m(U_n) = \int_S \frac{1}{n} 1_{U_n}\, dm \leqslant \int_S |f|\, dm < \infty.$$

Thus, $m(A_n)$ is finite for every n, hence U is of σ-finite measure m. $\qquad\square$

Corollary 8.3. *Let $(S, \mathcal{E}, m)$ be a measure space and let $f : S \longrightarrow \hat{\mathbb{R}}$ be a measurable function that is integrable. There exists a function $g : S \longrightarrow \mathbb{R}$ such that $f = g$ a.e. and $\int_S g\, dm = \int_S f\, dm$.*

Proof. It suffices to define $g = f 1_{S-T}$, where $T = \{x \in S \mid f(x) = \infty\}$ is the set defined in the proof of Theorem 8.26. $\qquad\square$

Theorem 8.27. *Let $(S, \mathcal{E}, m)$ be a measure space and let $f, g : S \longrightarrow \hat{\mathbb{R}}$ be two functions such that $f = g$ almost everywhere. If $\int_S f\, dm$ is defined, then $\int_S g\, dm$ is defined and the two integrals are equal.*

Proof. If $f = g$ a.e., then $f^+ = g^+$ and $f^- = g^-$ a.e., so $\int_S f^+\, dm = \int_S g^+\, dm$ and $\int_S f^-\, dm = \int_S g^-\, dm$ by Corollary 8.2. Furthermore, $\int_S f^+\, dm$ is finite if and only if $\int_S g^+\, dm$ is finite and, similarly $\int_S f^-\, dm$ is finite if and only if $\int_S g^-\, dm$ is finite. The conclusion follows immediately. $\qquad\square$

If $f, g : S \longrightarrow \hat{\mathbb{R}}$ are two functions such that there exists x such that $\{f(x), g(x)\} = \{-\infty, \infty\}\}$ we will assume that $f(x) + g(x) = 0$.

Theorem 8.28. *Let $(S, \mathcal{E}, m)$ be a measure space and let $f, g : S \longrightarrow \hat{\mathbb{R}}$ be two measurable functions. If both $\int_S f\, dm$ and $\int_S g\, dm$ are defined and*

$\{\int_S f\, dm, \int_S g\, dm\} \neq \{-\infty, \infty\}$, then $\int_S (f+g)\, dm$ is defined and

$$\int_S (f+g)\, dm = \int_S f\, dm + \int_S g\, dm. \tag{8.5}$$

If both f, g are integrable, then so is $f + g$ and equality (8.5) holds.

Proof. Assume that $\int_S f\, dm$ and $\int_S g\, dm$ are defined. Therefore, out of the four values

$$\int_S f^+\, dm, \int_S f^-\, dm, \int_S g^+\, dm, \int_S g^-\, dm,$$

at most $\int_S f^+\, dm, \int_S g^+\, dm$ or $\int_S f^-\, dm, \int_S g^-\, dm$ may be infinite.

Suppose that $\int_S f^-\, dm < \infty$ and $\int_S g^-\, dm < \infty$. Then, if $T = \{x \in S \mid f(x) \neq -\infty$ and $g(x) \neq -\infty\}$, $m(S - T) = 0$.

Define the measurable functions $\phi, \psi : S \longrightarrow (-\infty, \infty]$ as $\phi = f 1_T$ and $\psi = g 1_T$. We have $\phi = f$ and $\psi = g$ almost everywhere on S and $\phi + \psi = f + g$ almost everywhere on S.

By Theorem 7.28 we have $\phi(x) + \psi(x) \leqslant \phi^-(x) + \psi^-(x)$, so $\int_S (\phi + \psi)\, dm \leqslant \int_S \phi^-\, dm + \int_S \psi^-\, dm$, so $\int_S (\phi + \psi)\, dm$ is defined. Equality (7.6) and Theorem 8.8 imply

$$\int_S (\phi + \psi)^+\, dm + \int_S \phi^-\, dm + \int_S \psi^-\, dm$$

$$= \int_S (\phi + \psi)^-\, dm + \int_S \phi^+\, dm + \int_S \psi^+\, dm.$$

Since $\int_S (\phi + \psi)^-\, dm, \int_S \phi^-\, dm$, and $\int_S \psi^-\, dm$ are finite we have

$$\int_S (\phi + \psi)\, dm = \int_S (\phi + \psi)^+\, dm - \int_S (\phi + \psi)^-\, dm$$

$$= \int_S \phi^+\, dm + \int_S \psi^+\, dm - \int_S \phi^-\, dm - \int_S \psi^-\, dm$$

$$= \int_S f\, dm + \int_S g\, dm.$$

A similar argument can be used for the case when $\int_S f^+\, dm < \infty$ and $\int_S g^+\, dm < \infty$. In either case, the equality of the theorem follows immediately. $\qquad\square$

Theorem 8.29. *Let $(S, \mathcal{E}, m)$ be a measure space, $U, V \in \mathcal{E}$ such that $U \cap V = \emptyset$, and let $f : S \longrightarrow \hat{\mathbb{R}}$ be a measurable function. If $\int_{U \cup V} f\, dm$ exists, then both $\int_U f\, dm$ and $\int_V f\, dm$ exist and $\int_{U \cup V} f\, dm = \int_U f\, dm + \int_V f\, dm$.*

If $\int_U f\, dm$ and $\int_V f\, dm$ and are defined, then $\int_{U \cup V} f\, dm$ exists and $\int_{U \cup V} f\, dm = \int_U f\, dm + \int_V f\, dm$.

Proof. This theorem follows immediately from the corresponding result for non-negative functions (Theorem 8.20). $\qquad\square$

8.2.4 The Integral of Complex-Valued Measurable Functions

Definition 8.5. Let $(S, \mathcal{E}, m)$ be a measure space and let $f : S \longrightarrow \hat{\mathbb{C}}$ be a measurable function. The function f is *integrable* on S with respect to m if $\int_S |f|\, dm$ is finite.

The set of all complex-valued integrable functions on the measure space $(S, \mathcal{E}, m)$ is $\mathcal{L}^1(S, \mathcal{E}, m)$; the ambiguity introduced by this notation (the same as the one used for real-valued integrable functions) will be resolved in the context of the specific situation.

Theorem 8.30. *Let $(S, \mathcal{E}, m)$ be a measure space and let $f \in \mathcal{L}^1(S, \mathcal{E}, m)$ be a complex-valued integrable function. Then $f(x) \in \mathbb{C}$ a.e., and the set $\{x \in S \mid f(x) \neq 0\}$ is σ-finite relative to m.*

Proof. This statement follows by applying Theorem 8.26 to $|f|$. □

Let $(S, \mathcal{E}, m)$ be a measure space and let $f : S \longrightarrow \hat{\mathbb{C}}$ be an integrable function and let $D_f = \{x \in S \mid f(x) \in \mathbb{C}\}$. We have:

$$(f 1_{D_f})(x) = \begin{cases} f(x) & \text{if } x \neq \infty, \\ 0 & \text{if } x = \infty. \end{cases}$$

Thus, the value of $(f 1_{D_f})$ is defined for all $x \in S$, including those x for which $f(x) = \infty$. Additionally, we have

$$|\Re(f 1_{D_f})| \leqslant |f 1_{D_f}| \leqslant |f| \text{ and } |\Im(f 1_{D_f})| \leqslant |f 1_{D_f}| \leqslant |f|,$$

which shows that for an integrable complex-valued function f both $\Re(f 1_{D_f})$ and $\Im(f 1_{D_f})$ are integrable real-valued functions. As follows from the next definition, the integral of a complex-valued function is defined only if f is integrable. Its value is a finite complex number.

Definition 8.6. Let $(S, \mathcal{E}, m)$ be a measure space and let $f : S \longrightarrow \hat{\mathbb{C}}$ be an integrable function and let $D_f = \{x \in S \mid f(x) \in \mathbb{C}\}$. The integral $\int_S f\, dm$ is defined as:

$$\int_S f\, dm = \int_S \Re(f 1_{D_f})\, dm + i \int_S \Im(f 1_{D_f})\, dm.$$

Theorem 8.31. *Let $(S, \mathcal{E}, m)$ be a measure space and let $f : S \longrightarrow \hat{\mathbb{C}}$ be an integrable function. There exists an integrable function $g : S \longrightarrow \mathbb{C}$ such that $f = g$ a.e. and $\int_S f\, dm = \int_S g\, dm$.*

Proof. Note that $f = f1_{D_f}$ a.e. because $\{x \in S \mid f(x) \neq (f1_{D_f})(x)\} = \{x \in S \mid f(x) = 0\}$ and $m(\{x \in S \mid f(x) = 0\}) = 0$. Thus, if we take $g = f1_{D_f}$ the requirements of the theorem are satisfied. $\qquad\square$

Corollary 8.4. *Let $(S, \mathcal{E}, m)$ be a measure space and let $f : S \longrightarrow \hat{\mathbb{C}}$ be a measurable function that is integrable. There exists a function $g : S \longrightarrow \mathbb{C}$ such that $f = g$ a.e. and $\int_S g\, dm = \int_S f\, dm$.*

Proof. The function g is $g = f1_{D_f}$. $\qquad\square$

Theorem 8.10 can be extended to functions that range over $\hat{\mathbb{C}}$.

Theorem 8.32. *Let $(S, \mathcal{E}, m)$ be a measure space, and let $f, g : S \longrightarrow \hat{\mathbb{C}}$ be two complex-valued measurable functions. If $f = g$ a.e. then, if one of $\int_S f\, dm$ or $\int_S g\, dm$ is defined, the other is also defined and $\int_S f\, dm = \int_S g\, dm$.*

Proof. If f is integrable and $f = g$ a.e., then $|f| = |g|$ a.e., hence $\int_S |f|\, dm = \int_S |g|\, dm < \infty$, so g is also integrable.

By Theorem 8.31, there exist integrable functions $f_1, g_1 : S \longrightarrow \mathbb{C}$ such that $f = f_1$ a.e., and $g = g_1$ a.e. such that $\int_S f\, dm = \int_S f_1\, dm$ and $\int_S g\, dm = \int_S g_1\, dm$. Since $f = g$ a.e., $f_1 = g_1$ a.e., hence $\Re(f_1) = \Re(g_1)$ a.e. and $\Im(f_1) = \Im(g_1)$. Theorem 8.10 implies $\int_S \Re(f_1)\, dm = \int_S \Re(g_1)\, dm$ and $\int_S \Im(f_1)\, dm = \int_S \Im(g_1)\, dm$. Therefore, $\int_S f\, dm = \int_S g\, dm$. $\qquad\square$

Theorem 8.33. *Let $(S, \mathcal{E}, m)$ be a measure space, and let $f : S \longrightarrow \hat{\mathbb{C}}$ be a measurable function. The following statements are equivalent:*

(i) $\int_S |f|\, dm = 0$;
(ii) $f = 0$ a.e. on S;
(iii) $\int_S f1_E\, dm = 0$ for every $E \in \mathcal{E}$.

Proof. (i) implies (ii): If $\int_S |f|\, dm = 0$, we have $|f| = 0$ a.e. on S by Theorem 8.10.

(ii) implies (iii): If $f = 0$ a.e. on S then $f1_E = 0$ a.e. on S for all $E \in \mathcal{E}$, so $\int_S f1_E\, dm = 0$ for every $E \in \mathcal{E}$.

(iii) implies (i): Suppose that $\int_S f1_E\, dm = 0$ for every $E \in \mathcal{E}$. For $E = S$ we have $\int_S f\, dm = 0$, so f is integrable. Let $g : S \longrightarrow \mathbb{C}$ such that $f = g$ a.e. For every $E \in \mathcal{E}$ we have $f1_E = g1_E$ and $\int_S g1_E\, dm = \int_S f1_E\, dm = 0$. This yields

$$\int_S \Re(g)1_E\, dm = \int_S \Re(g1_E)\, dm = \Re\left(\int_S g1_E\, dm\right) = 0,$$

and, therefore $\Re(g) = 0$ a.e. on S. Similarly, $\Im(g) = 0$ a.e., so $g = 0$ a.e. on S. Therefore, $f = 0$ a.e. on S. $\qquad\square$

Theorem 8.34. *Let $(S, \mathcal{E}, m)$ be a measure space and let $f, g : S \longrightarrow \hat{\mathbb{C}}$ be two functions such that $f = g$ almost everywhere. If $\int_S f\, dm$ is defined, then $\int_S g\, dm$ is defined and the two integrals are equal.*

Proof. If f is integrable, then $|f| = |g|$ a.e. and, since $|f|, |g|$ are nonnegative, it follows that $\int_S |f|\, dm = \int_S |g|\, dm$, hence g is also integrable.

By Corollary 8.4, there exist $\phi, \psi : S \longrightarrow \mathbb{C}$ such that $f = \phi$ a.e., $g = \psi$ a.e., $\int_S f\, dm = \int_S \phi\, dm$, and $\int_S g\, dm = \int_S \psi\, dm$. Since $\phi = \psi$ a.e. we have $\Re(\phi) = \Re(\psi)$ a.e., and $\Im(\phi) = \Im(\psi)$, hence $\int_S \Re(\phi)\, dm = \int_S \Re(\psi)\, dm$ and $\int_S \Im(\phi)\, dm = \int_S \Im(\psi)\, dm$, which implies

$$\int_S f\, dm = \int_S \phi\, dm = \int_S \Re(\phi)\, dm + i \int_S \Im(\phi)\, dm$$
$$= \int_S \Re(\psi)\, dm + i \int_S \Im(\psi)\, dm = \int_S g\, dm. \qquad\square$$

Theorem 8.35. *Let $(S, \mathcal{E}, m)$ be a measure space, and let $f : S \longrightarrow \hat{\mathbb{C}}$ be a measurable function. If f is integrable and $c \in \mathbb{C}$, then λf is integrable and $\int_S cf\, dm = c \int_S f\, dm$.*

Proof. Let $\phi : S \longrightarrow \mathbb{C}$ such that $\phi(x) = f(x)$ almost everywhere on S. Then $c\phi = cf$ a.e., $\int_S c\phi\, dm = \int_S cf\, dm$ and $\int_S \phi\, dm = \int_S f\, dm$ by Theorem 8.32. Thus, it suffices to prove that $\int_S c\phi\, dm = c \int_S \phi\, dm$.

Suppose that $c = a + ib$, where $a = \Re(c)$ and $b = \Im(c)$. Since

$$c\phi(x) = (a + ib)(\Re(\phi)(x) + i\Im(\phi)(x))$$
$$= (a\Re(\phi)(x) - b\Im(\phi)(x)) + i(b\Re(\phi)(x) + a\Im(\phi)(x)),$$

we have, by Theorem 8.23:

$$\int_S \Re(c\phi)\, dm = a \int_S \Re(\phi)\, dm - b \int_S \Im(\phi)\, dm,$$
$$\int_S \Im(c\phi)\, dm = a \int_S \Im(\phi)\, dm + b \int_S \Re(\phi)\, dm.$$

These equalities imply

$$\int_S c\phi\, dm = c \int_S \Re(\phi)\, dm + ic \int_S \Im(\phi)\, dm = c \int_S \phi\, dm. \qquad\square$$

An analog of Theorem 8.28 for complex measurable function is given next.

Theorem 8.36. *Let* $f, g : S \longrightarrow \hat{\mathbb{C}}$ *be two integrable functions on the measure space* $(S, \mathcal{E}, m)$ *ranging over the extended set of complex numbers* $\hat{\mathbb{C}}$. *Then* $f + g$ *is also integrable and*

$$\int_S (f + g) \, dm = \int_S f \, dm + \int_S g \, dm.$$

Proof. If both f and g are integrable, by Theorem 8.31 there exist two integrable functions $f_1, g_1 : S \longrightarrow \mathbb{C}$ such that $f = f_1$ a.e., $g = g_1$ a.e., $\int_S f \, dm = \int_S f_1 \, dm$, and $\int_S g \, dm = \int_S g_1 \, dm$. Therefore, $f + g = f_1 + g_1$ a.e., and it suffices to show that $f_1 + g_1$ is integrable and $\int_S (f_1 + g_1) \, dm = \int_S f_1 \, dm + \int_S g_1 \, dm$. Since $\int_S |f_1 + g_1| \, dm \leqslant \int_S |f_1| \, dm + \int_S |g_1| \, dm$, hence $f_1 + g_1$ is integrable.

By Theorem 8.28 we have:

$$\int_S \Re(f_1 + g_1) \, dm = \int_S \Re(f_1) \, dm + \int_S \Re(g_1) \, dm,$$

$$\int_S \Im(f_1 + g_1) \, dm = \int_S \Im(f_1) \, dm + \int_S \Im(g_1) \, dm,$$

hence $\int_S (f_1 + g_1) \, dm = \int_S f_1 \, dm + \int_S g_1 \, dm$. □

8.3   The Dominated Convergence Theorem

Theorem 8.37. (The Dominated Convergence Theorem) *Let* $(S, \mathcal{E}, m)$ *be a measure space and let* $\boldsymbol{f} = (f_0, f_1, \dots)$ *be a sequence of functions such that* $|f_i| < g$ *a.e., where* g *is an integrable function. If* $f(x) = \lim_{n \to \infty} f_n(x)$ *for every* $x \in S$, *then* f *is integrable and*

$$\lim_{n \to \infty} \int_S f_n \, dm = \int_S f \, dm.$$

Proof. Suppose initially that the functions f_n are non-negative. By Fatou's Lemma (Theorem 8.12) we have

$$\int_S f \, dm = \int_S \liminf_{n \to \infty} f_n \, dm \leqslant \liminf_{n \to \infty} \int_S f_n \, dm.$$

Thus, it suffices to show that $\limsup_{n \to \infty} \int_S f_n \, dm \leqslant \int_S f \, dm$.

An application of Fatou's Lemma to the sequence of non-negative functions $(g - f_1, g - f_2, \ldots)$ yields

$$\int_S \lim_{n \to \infty} (g - f_n) \, dm \leq \lim_{n \to \infty} \inf \int_S (g - f_n) \, dm.$$

Note that

$$\int_S \lim_{n \to \infty} (g - f_n) \, dm = \int_S (g - f) \, dm = \int_S g \, dm - \int_S f \, dm.$$

Also,

$$\lim_{n \to \infty} \inf \int_S (g - f_n) \, dm = \lim_{n \to \infty} \inf \left(\int_S g \, dm - \int_S f_n \, dm \right)$$

$$= \int_S g \, dm - \lim_{n \to \infty} \sup \int_S f_n \, dm.$$

Thus, we have

$$\int_S g \, dm - \int_S f \, dm \leq \int_S g \, dm - \lim_{n \to \infty} \sup \int_S f_n \, dm.$$

Since g is integrable, $\int_S g \, dm$ is finite, so $\lim\sup_{n \to \infty} \int_S f_n \, dm \leq \int_S f \, dm$, which gives the needed equality for non-negative functions.

If $f_0, f_1, \ldots$ are general measurable functions (that is, not necessarily non-negative), since $|f_n| \leq g$, it follows that $0 \leq f_n(x) + g(x) \leq 2g(x)$ for $x \in S$. Then, the sequence of non-negative functions $f_n + g$ is dominated by the integrable function $2g$, and we apply the first part of the argument, so

$$\lim_{n \to \infty} \int_S (f_n + g) \, dm = \int_S (f + g) \, dm,$$

which gives the equality in the general case. $\square$

Theorem 8.38. *Let $(S, \mathcal{E}, m)$ be a measure space. If (f_n) is a sequence of measurable functions on S such that $\sum_{n \geq 1} \int_S |f_n| \, dm < \infty$, then $\sum_{n \geq 1} f_n(x)$ exists a.e. on S. If $f = \sum_{n \geq 1} f_n$ a.e., then $\int_S f \, dm = \sum_{n \geq 1} \int_S f_n \, dm$.*

Proof. Let $g : S \longrightarrow \hat{\mathbb{R}}_{\geq 0}$ be the function defined by $g = \sum_{n \geq 1} |f_n|$. Lemma 8.1 implies that $\int_S g \, dm = \sum_{n \geq 1} \int_S |f_n| \, dm < \infty$, hence $g < \infty$ a.e. on S. Therefore, the series $\sum_{n \geq 1} f_n(x)$ converges absolutely, hence it converges a.e. on S.

Let $s_n = \sum_{m=1}^n f_m$ be a partial sum of the series $\sum_{m \geq 1} f_m$. Then, $\lim_{n \to \infty} s_n = f$ a.e. on S and $|s_n| \leq g$. The Dominated Convergence Theorem implies

$$\lim_{n \to \infty} \int_S s_n \, dm = \int_S f \, dm. \qquad \square$$

Theorem 8.39. (Beppo Levi's Theorem) *Let $(S, \mathcal{E}, m)$ be a measure space and let $\boldsymbol{f} = (f_0, f_1, \ldots, f_n, \ldots)$ be a sequence of measurable functions. If the series $\sum_{n \in \mathbb{N}} \int_S |f_n| \, dm$ is convergent, then $\sum_{n=1}^{n} f_n(x)$ converges a.e., its sum $f(x) = \sum_{n=1}^{n} f_n(x)$ is integrable, and*

$$\int_S f \, dm = \sum_{n \in \mathbb{N}} \int_S f_n \, dm.$$

Proof.   The function $h(x) = \sum_{n \in \mathbb{N}} |f_n(x)|$ is non-negative, measurable, and

$$\int_S h \, dm = \sum_{n \in \mathbb{N}} \int_S |f_n| \, dm,$$

by Lemma 8.1. Since $\sum_{n \in \mathbb{N}} \int_S |f_n| \, dm$ is finite, h is integrable, which implies that h is finite almost everywhere. Define the function ϕ as

$$\phi(x) = \begin{cases} \sum_{n \in \mathbb{N}} f_n(x) & \text{if } \sum_{n \in \mathbb{N}} f(x) \text{ exists}, \\ 0 & \text{otherwise.} \end{cases}$$

Note that the set on which $\sum_{n \in \mathbb{N}} f_n(x)$ is null.

We have $|\sum_{k \leqslant n} f_k(x)| \leqslant \phi(x)$. By the Dominated Convergence Theorem (Theorem 8.37) we obtain

$$\int f \, dm = \int \lim_{n \to \infty} \sum_{k \leqslant n} f_k \, dm = \lim_{n \to \infty} \int \sum_{k \leqslant n} f_k \, dm$$

$$= \lim_{n \to \infty} \sum_{k \leqslant n} \int f_k \, dm = \sum_{k \in n} \int f_k \, dm,$$

which concludes the argument. $\square$

Theorem 8.40. *Let $f : S \longrightarrow \hat{\mathbb{R}}$ and $g : S \longrightarrow \hat{\mathbb{R}}$ be two measurable functions relative to the measure space $(S, \mathcal{E}, m)$ such that $f(x) = g(x)$ a.e. Then, if one of $\int_S f \, dm$ or $\int_S g \, dm$ exists the other exists and they are equal.*

Proof.   We need to deal only with the case when both f and g are non-negative. If this is not the case, the same conclusion can be reached by decomposing f and g into their positive and negative components.

Let $A = \{x \in S \mid f(x) \neq g(x)\}$. By hypothesis, $m(A) = 0$.

If $h_n = n 1_A$ we have $\int_S h_n \, dm = 0$, so $\int_S I_A \, dm = 0$ because $\lim_{n \to \infty} h_n = I_A$, where I_A is the indicator function of A (introduced in Definition 1.14).

Note that we have both $f \leqslant g + I_A$ and $g \leqslant f + I_A$, so $\int_S f \, dm \leqslant \int_S g \, dm$ and $\int_S g \, dm \leqslant \int_S f \, dm$. Therefore, $\int_S f \, dm = \int_S g \, dm$. $\square$

Theorem 8.41. (Markov's Inequality) *Let* $(S, \mathcal{E}, m)$ *be a measure space,* $f : S \longrightarrow \mathbb{R}_{\geqslant 0}$ *be a measurable function, and let a be a positive number. We have:*

$$m(\{x \in S \mid f(x) \geqslant a\}) \leqslant \frac{1}{a} \int_S f \, dm.$$

Proof. Since $f(x) \geqslant 0$, we have for $T = \{x \in S \mid f(x) \geqslant a\}$:

$$\int_S f \, dm \geqslant \int_T f \, dm \geqslant am(T),$$

which implies the desired inequality. $\qquad\square$

Let $f : S \longrightarrow \mathbb{R}_{\geqslant 0}$ be a measurable function on the measure space $(S, \mathcal{E}, m)$ and let $E(f) = \int_S f \, dm$. Define the measurable function $g : S \longrightarrow \mathbb{R}$ by $g(x) = (f - E(f))^2$. The *variance of* f, $var(f)$ is the number $E(g)$.

By Markov's inequality applied to g and to $a = (kvar(f))^2$ we have

$$m(\{x \in S \mid (f(x) - E(f))^2 \geqslant (kvar(f))^2\}) \leqslant \frac{1}{(kvar(f))^2} E(g),$$

which now becomes

$$m(\{x \in S \mid |f(x) - E(f)| \geqslant kvar(f)\}) \leqslant \frac{1}{k^2}. \tag{8.6}$$

This inequality is known as *Chebyshev's inequality*.

Corollary 8.5. *Let* $f : S \longrightarrow \mathbb{R}$ *be an integrable function defined on the measure space* $(S, \mathcal{E}, m)$. *The set* $\{x \in S \mid f(x) \neq 0\}$ *is σ-finite relative to m.*

Proof. By applying Markov's inequality to the function $|f|$ we have

$$m(\{x \in S \mid |f(x)| \geqslant \frac{1}{n}\}) \leqslant n \int_S |f| \, dm, \tag{8.7}$$

which means that each set $\{x \in S \mid |f(x)| \geqslant \frac{1}{n}\}$ has a finite measure. The statement follows by observing that

$$\{x \in S \mid f(x) \neq 0\} = \{x \in S \mid |f(x)| > 0\}$$
$$= \bigcup_{n \geqslant 1} \left\{ x \in S \mid |f(x)| \geqslant \frac{1}{n} \right\}.$$

$\qquad\square$

Corollary 8.6. *Let* $f : S \longrightarrow \hat{\mathbb{R}}$ *be an integrable function defined on the measure space* $(S, \mathcal{E}, m)$. *If* $\int_S |f| \, dm = 0$, *then* $f(x) = 0$ *a.e. on S.*

Proof. By inequality (8.7), the hypothesis implies $m(\{x \in S \mid |f(x)| \geq \frac{1}{n}\}) = 0$ for $n \geq 1$. Furthermore, since

$$\{x \in S \mid f(x) \neq 0\} = \bigcup_{n \geq 1} \left\{ x \in S \,\middle|\, |f(x)| \geq \frac{1}{n} \right\},$$

by the subadditivity of m it follows that $m(\{x \in S \mid f(x) \neq 0\}) = 0$, so $f(x) = 0$ a.e. on S. $\qquad\square$

Corollary 8.7. *Let $f : S \longrightarrow \hat{\mathbb{R}}$ be an integrable function defined on the measure space $(S, \mathcal{E}, m)$. Then $|f(x)| < \infty$ a.e. on S.*

Proof. An application of Markov's Inequality yields

$$m(\{x \in S \mid |f(x)| \geq n\}) \leq \frac{1}{n} \int_S |f| \, dm$$

for each $n \geq 1$. Therefore,

$$m(\{x \in S \mid |f(x)| = \infty\}) \leq m(\{x \in S \mid |f(x)| \geq n\})$$
$$\leq \frac{1}{n} \int_S |f| \, dm$$

for every $n \geq 1$, which implies $m(\{x \in S \mid |f(x)| = \infty\}) = 0$, a statement equivalent to what we aim to prove. $\qquad\square$

Corollary 8.8. *Let $(S, \mathcal{E}, m)$ be a measure space and let $f : S \longrightarrow \hat{\mathbb{R}}$ be a measurable function on this space ranging in $\hat{\mathbb{R}}$. Then f is integrable if and only if there exists a function $g : S \longrightarrow \mathbb{R}$ that is integrable such that $f(x) = g(x)$ a.e.*

Proof. If there exists a function $g : S \longrightarrow \mathbb{R}$ that is integrable such that $f(x) = g(x)$ a.e., then f is integrable by Theorem 8.40.

Conversely, suppose that f is integrable and let $A = \{x \in S \mid |f(x)| = \infty\}$. By Corollary 8.7, $m(A) = 0$, and $f_0 = f1_A$ equals f a.e. The function $f_0 : S \longrightarrow \mathbb{R}$ is integrable. $\qquad\square$

8.4 Functions of Bounded Variation

In Chapter 4 we have shown that for monotonic functions all discontinuity points are of first kind, that is, the function has lateral limits in such points (see Theorem 4.61). Next, we show that if $f : [a, b] \longrightarrow \mathbb{R}$ is an increasing function, then f is differentiable a.e.

Let $f : [a, b]$ and let $x \in (a, b)$. The derivatives of f in x are

$$D^+ f(x) = \limsup_{h \downarrow 0} \frac{f(x+h) - f(x)}{h}, \quad D_+ f(x) = \liminf_{h \downarrow 0} \frac{f(x+h) - f(x)}{h},$$
$$D^- f(x) = \limsup_{h \uparrow 0} \frac{f(x+h) - f(x)}{h}, \quad D_- f(x) = \liminf_{h \uparrow 0} \frac{f(x+h) - f(x)}{h}.$$

It is immediate that $D^+ f(x) \geqslant D_+ f(x)$ and $D^- f(x) \geqslant D_- f(x)$.

Definition 8.7. A function $f : [a, b]$ is differentiable in $x \in (a, b)$ if $D^+ f(x) = D_+ f(x) = D^- f(x) = D_- f(x)$. In this case the common value of these derivatives is denoted by $f'(x)$.

If $D^+ f(x) = D_+ f(x)$, we say that f has a *right derivative* in x and we denote their common value by $f'(x+)$; if $D^- f(x) = D_- f(x)$, we say that f has a *left derivative* and their common value is denoted by $f'(x-)$.

If f is continuous on $[a, b]$ and one of its derivatives is non-negative on (a, b), then f is non-decreasing on $[a, b]$. For example, if $D^+ f(x) > 0$ for $x \in (a, b)$, we have $\limsup_{h \downarrow 0} \frac{f(x+h) - f(x)}{h} > 0$, which means that

$$\inf_{r > 0} \sup \left\{ \frac{f(x+h) - f(x)}{h} \mid 0 < h < r \right\} > 0,$$

by Example 4.50. This implies $f(x+h) \geqslant f(x)$, so f is non-decreasing on (a, b) and, by continuity, on $[a, b]$.

Theorem 8.42. *Let $f : [a, b] \longrightarrow \mathbb{R}$ be an increasing function. The set where any two derivatives of f are distinct have measure 0.*

Proof. Let

$$E = \{ x \in [a, b] \mid D^+ f(x) > D_- f(x) \}.$$

For $u, v \in \mathbb{Q}$ define $E_{u,v} = \{ x \mid D^+ f(x) > u > v > D_- f(x) \}$. Clearly, E is the countable union of sets $E_{u,v}$, hence it suffices to prove that $\mu_L(E_{u,v}) = 0$.

For $\epsilon > 0$ there exists an open set U such that $m_L(U) < \mu_L(E_{u,v}) + \epsilon$. For each $x \in E_{u,v}$ there exists $[x - h, x] \subseteq U$ such that $f(x) - f(x - h) < vh$.

By Vitali's Theorem (Theorem 7.62) there exists a collection of such intervals $[x_1 - h_1, x_1], \ldots, [x_N - h_N, x_N]$ whose interiors cover a subset A of $E_{u,v}$ and $f(x_n) - f(x_n - h_n) < \epsilon$ such that $\mu_L(A) > \mu_L(E_{u,v}) - \epsilon$. This implies

$$\sum_{n=1}^{N} (f(x_n) - f(x_n - h_n)) < v \sum_{n=1}^{N} h_n < v m_L(U) < v(\mu(E_{u,v}) + \epsilon).$$

For $y \in A$ there exists an interval $(y, y + k)$ that is contained in some interval $[x_n - h_n, x_n]$ such that $f(y + k) - f(y) > uk$. By Vitali's Theorem, there exists a collection $(y_1, y_1+k_1), \ldots, (y_M, y_M+k_M)$ such that $\bigcup_{i=1}^{M} (y_i, y_i+k_i)$ contains a subset C of A with $\mu_L(C) > m_L(E_{u,v}) - 2\epsilon$. This implies

$$\sum_{i=1}^{M} (f(y_i + k_i) - f(y_i)) > u \sum_{i=1}^{M} k_i > u(m_L(E_{u,v}) - 2\epsilon).$$

Since each interval $(y_i, y_i + k_i)$ is contained in some interval $(x_j - h_j, x_j)$ and f is increasing, we have

$$\sum \{f(y_i + k_i) - f(y_i)) \mid (y_i, y_i+k_i) \subseteq (x_n - h_n, x_n)\} \leqslant f(x_n) - f(x_n - h_n).$$

Therefore,

$$\sum_{n=1}^{N} (f(x_n) - f(x_n - h_n)) \geqslant \sum_{i=1}^{M} (f(y_i + k_i) - f(y_i)),$$

hence $v(m_L(E_{u,v}) + \epsilon) \geqslant u(m_L(E_{u,v}) - 2\epsilon)$ for every positive ϵ, that is, $vm_L(E_{u,v}) \geqslant um_L E_{u,v}$. Since $u > v$, this implies $m_L(E_{u,v}) = 0$. Thus, $g(x) = \lim_{h \to 0} \frac{f(x+h)-f(x)}{h}$ is defined a.e. and that f is differentiable if g is finite. $\qquad\square$

Corollary 8.9. *Let $f : [a, b] \longrightarrow \mathbb{R}$ be an increasing function. The derivative f' is measurable and $\int_a^b f' \, dm_L \leqslant f(b) - f(a)$.*

Proof. By Theorem 8.42 f is differentiable a.e. Let $g(x) = \lim_{h \to 0} \frac{f(x+h)-f(x)}{h}$ and let $g_n(x) = \frac{f(x+\frac{1}{n})-f(x)}{\frac{1}{n}}$. Define $f(x) = f(b)$ for $x \geqslant b$. We have $g_n(x) \geqslant 0$ because f is increasing and $\lim_{n \to \infty} g_n(x) = g(x)$ a.e., so g is measurable. By Fatou's Lemma (Theorem 8.12) we have

$$\int_a^b g \, dm_L = \int_a^b \lim_{n \to \infty} g_n \, dm_L$$

$$\leqslant \liminf \int_a^b g_n \, d_{;L} = \liminf n \int_a^b (f(x + 1/n) - f(x)) \, dm_L$$

$$= \liminf \left(n \int_b^{b+1/n} f \, dm_L - \int_a^{a+1/n} dm_L \right)$$

$$= \liminf \left(f(b) - n \int_a^{a+1/n} f \, dm_L \right) \leqslant f(b) - f(a).$$

Therefore, g is integrable and finite a.e. Thus, f is differentiable and $g = f'$ a.e. $\qquad\square$

Definition 8.8. Let $[a, b]$ be an interval on $\mathbb{R}$; a *subdivision* of $[a, b]$ is a finite set $\Delta = \{x_0, x_1, \ldots, x_n\}$ such that $a = x_0 < a_1 < \cdots < x_n = b$. The members of Δ are the *subdivision points* of $[a, b]$.

We denote

$$\nu(\Delta) = \max\{a_i - a_{i-1} \mid 1 \leqslant i \leqslant n\}.$$

The set of subdivisions of $[a, b]$ is denoted by $\mathsf{SUBD}[a, b]$.

A subdivision $\Delta' = \{a'_0, a'_1, \ldots, a'_m\}$ of $[a, b]$ is a *refinement* of a subdivision $\Delta = \{a_0, a_1, \ldots, a_n\}$ of the same interval if $\Delta \subseteq \Delta'$. This is denoted by $\Delta \leqslant \Delta'$.

It is clear that $\Delta \leqslant \Delta'$ implies $\nu(\Delta') \leqslant \nu(\Delta)$.

Definition 8.9. Let $f : [a, b] \longrightarrow \mathbb{R}$ be a real-valued function and let $\Delta = \{x_0, x_1, \ldots, x_n\} \in \mathsf{SUBD}[a, b]$.

The *variation* of f on the interval $[a, b]$ with the subdivision Δ is the number $\mathbf{V}_a^b(f, \Delta)$ defined as

$$\mathbf{V}_a^b(f, \Delta) = \sum_{i=1}^n |f(x_i) - f(x_{i-1})|.$$

The *positive variation* of f with the subdivision Δ is

$$\overset{+}{\mathbf{V}}{}_a^b (f, \Delta) = \sum_{i=1}^n \max\{f(x_i) - f(x_{i-1}), 0\}.$$

Similarly, the *negative variation* of f with the subdivision Δ is

$$\overset{-}{\mathbf{V}}{}_a^b (f, \Delta) = \sum_{i=1}^n - \min\{f(x_i) - f(x_{i-1}), 0\}.$$

It is easy to verify that $\max\{r, 0\} - \min\{r, 0\} = |r|$ and $\max\{r, 0\} + \min\{r, 0\} = r$ for every $r \in \mathbb{R}$. Therefore, we have

$$\overset{+}{\mathbf{V}}{}_a^b (f, \Delta) + \overset{-}{\mathbf{V}}{}_a^b (f, \Delta) = \mathbf{V}_a^b(f, \Delta), \tag{8.8}$$

$$\overset{+}{\mathbf{V}}{}_a^b (f, \Delta) - \overset{-}{\mathbf{V}}{}_a^b (f, \Delta) = \sum_{i=1}^n (f(x_i) - f_{x_{i-1}}) = f(b) - f(a), \tag{8.9}$$

and these equalities imply

$$\overset{+}{\mathbf{V}}{}_a^b (f, \Delta) = \frac{1}{2}(\mathbf{V}_a^b(f, \Delta) + f(b) - f(a)), \tag{8.10}$$

$$\overset{-}{\mathbf{V}}{}_a^b (f, \Delta) = \frac{1}{2}(\mathbf{V}_a^b(f, \Delta) - f(b) + f(a)). \tag{8.11}$$

Equalities (8.10) and (8.11) imply

$$\overset{+}{\mathbf{V}}{}_a^b (f, \Delta) + \overset{-}{\mathbf{V}}{}_a^b (f, \Delta) = \mathbf{V}_a^b(f, \Delta).$$

Note that if $\Delta, \Delta' \in \mathsf{SUBD}[a,b]$ and $\Delta \subseteq \Delta'$, then $\mathbf{V}_a^b(f, \Delta) \leqslant$ $\mathbf{V}_a^b(f, \Delta')$, $\overset{+}{\mathbf{V}}_a^b(f, \Delta) \leqslant \overset{+}{\mathbf{V}}_a^b(f, \Delta')$, and $\overset{-}{\mathbf{V}}_a^b(f, \Delta) \leqslant \overset{-}{\mathbf{V}}_a^b(f, \Delta')$.

Definition 8.10. Let $f : [a, b] \longrightarrow \mathbb{R}$ be a real-valued function. The *variation* of f on the interval $[a, b]$ is the number $\mathbf{V}_a^b f$ defined as

$$\mathbf{V}_a^b f = \sup\{\mathbf{V}_a^b(f, \Delta) \mid \Delta \in \mathsf{SUBD}[a, b]\}.$$

The *positive variation* of f on $[a, b]$ is

$$\overset{+}{\mathbf{V}}_a^b f = \sup\{\overset{+}{\mathbf{V}}_a^b(f, \Delta) \mid \Delta \in \mathsf{SUBD}[a, b]\}.$$

Similarly, the *negative variation* of f on $[a, b]$ is the number

$$\overset{-}{\mathbf{V}}_a^b f = \sup\{\overset{-}{\mathbf{V}}_a^b(f, \Delta) \mid \Delta \in \mathsf{SUBD}[a, b]\}.$$

The function is of *bounded variation* over $[a, b]$ if $\mathbf{V}_a^b f$ is finite.

From equalities (8.8) and (8.9) it follows that

$$\overset{+}{\mathbf{V}}_a^b f = \frac{1}{2}(\mathbf{V}_a^b f + f(b) - f(a)), \tag{8.12}$$

$$\overset{-}{\mathbf{V}}_a^b f = \frac{1}{2}(\mathbf{V}_a^b f - f(b) + f(a)), \tag{8.13}$$

and $\overset{+}{\mathbf{V}}_a^b f + \overset{-}{\mathbf{V}}_a^b f = \mathbf{V}_a^b f$.

Theorem 8.43. *A function $f : [a, b] \longrightarrow \mathbb{R}$ is of bounded variation if and only it equals the difference of two monotone increasing real-valued functions on $[a, b]$.*

Proof. Let f be a function of bounded variation. Define the functions $g, h : [a, b] \longrightarrow \mathbb{R}$ as $g(x) = \overset{+}{\mathbf{V}}_a^x f$ and $h(x) = \overset{-}{\mathbf{V}}_a^x f$. Both g and h are monotone increasing. Since $\mathbf{V}_a^b f$ is finite, both g and h are finite.

Conversely, if $f = g - h$, where g, h are monotone increasing functions on $[a, b]$, then for any $\Delta = \{x_0, x_1, \dots, x_n\} \in \mathsf{SUBD}[a, b]$ we have

$$\mathbf{V}_a^b(f, \Delta) = \sum_{i=1}^{n} |f(x_i) - f(x_{i-1})|$$

$$\leqslant \sum_{i=1}^{n} (g(x_i) - g(x_{i-1})) + \sum_{i=1}^{n} (h(x_i) - h(x_{i-1}))$$

$$= g(b) - g(a) + h(b) - h(a),$$

hence $\mathbf{V}_a^b f \leqslant g(b) - g(a) + h(b) - h(a)$. $\square$

Definition 8.11. A function $f : [a, b] \longrightarrow \mathbb{R}$ is *absolutely continuous* on $[a, b]$ if for each $\epsilon > 0$ there exists $\delta > 0$ such that for every finite collection of pairwise disjoint intervals $\{(u_i, v_i) \mid 1 \leqslant i \leqslant n\}$ such that $\sum_{i=1}^{n} (v_i - u_i) < \delta$ we have $\sum_{i=1}^{n} |f(v_i) - f(u_i)| < \epsilon$.

Theorem 8.44. *If a function* $f : [a, b] \longrightarrow \mathbb{R}$ *is absolutely continuous then it of bounded variation on* $[a, b]$.

Proof. Let Δ be a subdivision of $[a, b]$ and let $\epsilon > 0$. There exists $\delta > 0$ and a refinement Δ' of Δ such that $\nu(\Delta') < \delta$, which implies $\mathbf{V}_a^b(f, \Delta') < \epsilon$. Thus, $\mathbf{V}_a^b(f, \Delta) < \epsilon$ for any Δ, hence $\mathbf{V}_a^b f < \epsilon$. $\qquad \square$

8.5 Riemann Integral vs. Lebesgue Integral

We present the fundamentals of Riemann integration, a topic that is usually presented in basic calculus. As we shall see, the class of Lebesgue-integrable functions is broader than the class of Riemann-integrable functions; in many cases, the value of the integrals are the same. However, computing effectively the Lebesgue integral is difficult and Riemann integration benefits from the multitude of integration techniques developed in classical analysis. Therefore, it is important to elucidate the relationships that exists between these types of integration.

Recall that the notion of subdivision of an interval was introduced in Definition 8.8.

If $f : [a, b]$ is a bounded function on $[a, b]$ and $\Delta = \{a_0, a_1, \ldots, a_n\} \in$ SUBD$[a, b]$ define $m_i = \inf\{f(x) \mid x \in [a_{i-1}, a_i]\}$, and $M_i = \sup\{f(x) \mid x \in [a_{i-1}, a_i]\}$ for $1 \leqslant i \leqslant n$.

The *lower Darboux sum* and *upper Darboux sum* for f and Δ are given by

$$s(f, \Delta) = \sum_{i=1}^{n} m_i(a_i - a_{i-1}) \text{ and } S(f, \Delta) = \sum_{i=1}^{n} M_i(a_i - a_{i-1}),$$

respectively. These sums coincide with the Lebesgue integrals of the simple functions $L_{f,\Delta} = \sum_{i=1}^{n} m_i 1_{[a_{i-1}, a_i]}$ and $U_{f,\Delta} = \sum_{i=1}^{n} M_i 1_{[a_{i-1}, a_i]}$, respectively, that is,

$$s(f, \Delta) = \int_{[a,b]} L_{f,\Delta} \, dm \text{ and } S(f, \Delta) = \int_{[a,b]} U_{f,\Delta} \, dm.$$

For a subdivision Δ of $[a, b]$ let $\Xi = \{\xi_1, \ldots, \xi_n\}$ be a set of numbers such that $\xi_i \in [a_{i-1}, a_i]$ for $1 \leqslant i \leqslant n$. The *Riemann sum* that corresponds to Ξ is the number $\sigma(f, \Delta, \Xi)$ given by

$$\sigma(f, \Delta, \Xi) = \sum_{i=1}^{n} f(\xi_i)(a_i - a_{i-1}). \tag{8.14}$$

If $m = \inf\{f(x) \mid x \in [a,b]\}$ and $M = \sup\{f(x) \mid x \in [a,b]\}$, then we have

$$m(b-a) \leqslant s(f, \Delta) \leqslant \sigma(f, \Delta, \Xi) \leqslant S(f, \Delta) \leqslant M(b-a).$$

Indeed, we have $m \leqslant m_i \leqslant f(\xi_i) \leqslant M_i \leqslant m$ for every $\xi \in [a_{i-1}, a_i]$, which implies immediately the desired inequality.

It is easy to verify that

$$s(f, \Delta) = \inf_{\Xi} \sigma(f, \Delta, \Xi) \text{ and } S(f, \Delta) = \sup_{\Xi} \sigma(f, \Delta, \Xi).$$

Moreover, we can prove a stronger claim.

Theorem 8.45. *Let* $\Delta, \Delta' \in SUBD[a,b]$ *such that* $\Delta \leqslant \Delta'$. *For any bounded function* f *on* $[a,b]$ *we have*

$$s(f, \Delta) \leqslant s(f, \Delta') \leqslant S(f, \Delta') \leqslant S(f, \Delta).$$

Proof.   Let $\Delta = \{a_0, a_1, \ldots, a_n\}$ be a subdivision of $[a,b]$ and let Δ' be a subdivision of the same interval such that $\Delta < \Delta'$ and Δ' is given by $\Delta' = \{a_0, a_1, \ldots, a_i, c, a_{i+1}, \ldots, a_n\}$, where $a_0 < a_1 < \cdots < a_i < c < a_{i+1} < \cdots < a_n$. For $m_i = \inf\{f(x) \mid x \in [a_{i-1}, a_i]\}$, $m_i' = \inf\{f(x) \mid x \in [a_{i-1}, c]\}$, and $m_i'' = \inf\{f(x) \mid x \in [c, a_i]\}$ we obviously have $m_i \leqslant m_i'$ and $m_i \leqslant m''$. Therefore,

$$m_i(a_i - a_{i-1}) \leqslant m_i'(c - a_{i-1}) + m_i''(a_i - c).$$

Thus, $s(f, \Delta) \leqslant s(f, \Delta')$ and this inequality clearly holds when Δ' has more division points in the interval $[a_{i-1}, a_i]$. This leads to the inequality $s(f, \Delta) \leqslant s(f, \Delta')$.

The inequality $S(f, \Delta') \leqslant S(f, \Delta)$ can be shown in a similar manner noting that if $M_i = \sup\{f(x) \mid x \in [a_{i-1}, a_i]\}$, $M_i' = \sup\{f(x) \mid x \in [a_{i-1}, c]\}$, and $M_i'' = \sup\{f(x) \mid x \in [c, a_i]\}$, we have $M_i' \leqslant M_i$ and $M_i'' \leqslant M_i$. Since the inequality $s(f, \Delta') \leqslant S(f, \Delta')$ obviously holds, the lemma is proven. $\square$

Theorem 8.46. *Let* $\Delta_1, \Delta_2 \in SUBD[a,b]$. *For any bounded function* f *on* $[a,b]$ *we have*

$$s(f, \Delta_1) \leqslant S(f, \Delta_2).$$

Proof. Let $\hat{\Delta}$ be the subdivision of $[a, b]$ whose set of points is the union of the sets of points of Δ_1 and Δ_2. Clearly, we have $\Delta_1 \leqslant \hat{\Delta}$ and $\Delta_2 \leqslant \hat{\Delta}$. Therefore, by Theorem 8.45 we have

$$s(f, \Delta_1) \leqslant s(f, \hat{\Delta}) \leqslant S(f, \hat{\Delta}) \leqslant S(f, \Delta_1), \text{ and}$$
$$s(f, \Delta_2) \leqslant s(f, \hat{\Delta}) \leqslant S(f, \hat{\Delta}) \leqslant S(f, \Delta_2).$$

These inequalities give the desired inequality. $\qquad\square$

Theorem 8.47. *For any bounded function f on $[a, b]$ we have:*

$$\sup\{s(f, \Delta) \mid \Delta \in SUBD(\Delta)\} \leqslant \inf\{S(f, \Delta) \mid \Delta \in SUBD(\Delta)\}.$$

Proof. Let Δ_0 be a subdivision of $[a, b]$. For any $\Delta \in \mathsf{SUBD}[a, b]$ we have $s(f, \Delta) \leqslant S(f, \Delta_0)$, so $S(f, \Delta_0)$ is an upper bound of the set $\{s(f, \Delta) \mid \Delta \in \mathsf{SUBD}(\Delta)\}$. Therefore, $\sup\{s(f, \Delta) \mid \Delta \in \mathsf{SUBD}(\Delta)\}$ exists and

$$\sup\{s(f, \Delta) \mid \Delta \in \mathsf{SUBD}(\Delta)\} \leqslant S(f, \Delta_0).$$

Since this inequality holds for every Δ_0, it follows that

$$\sup\{s(f, \Delta) \mid \Delta \in \mathsf{SUBD}(\Delta)\} \leqslant \inf\{S(f, \Delta) \mid \Delta \in \mathsf{SUBD}(\Delta)\}. \qquad\square$$

The *lower Riemann integral* of f on $[a, b]$ is defined as

$$\underline{\int_a^b} f \, dx = \sup\{s(f, \Delta) | \Delta \in \mathsf{SUBD}([a, b])\}.$$

Similarly, the *upper Riemann integral* is

$$\overline{\int_a^b} f \, dx = \inf\{S(f, \Delta) | \Delta \in \mathsf{SUBD}([a, b])\}.$$

Theorem 8.47 means that for every $\Delta \in \mathsf{SUBD}([a, b])$ we have

$$s(f, \Delta) \leqslant \underline{\int_a^b} f \, dx \leqslant \overline{\int_a^b} f \, dx \leqslant S(f, \Delta).$$

Definition 8.12. A function $f : [a, b] \longrightarrow \mathbb{R}$ is *Riemann integrable* if $\underline{\int_a^b} f \, dx = \overline{\int_a^b} f \, dx$.

Example 8.5. The function $f : [0, 1] \longrightarrow \mathbb{R}$ defined by

$$f(x) = \begin{cases} 1 & \text{if } x \in \mathbb{Q} \cap [0, 1], \\ 0 & \text{otherwise,} \end{cases}$$

is not integrable Riemann because $\underline{\int_0^1} f \, dx = 0$ while $\overline{\int_0^1} f \, dx = 1$. This is inconvenient because f is 0 a.e. (the set of rational numbers in $[0, 1]$ is a null set by Corollary 7.22).

However, f is Lebesgue integrable on $[0, 1]$. Since the set $\mathbb{Q}_1 = \{x \in \mathbb{Q} \cap [0, 1]\}$ is countable, we can write $\mathbb{Q}_1 = \{q_1, q_2, \ldots\}$. Let

$$I_n = \left(q_n - \frac{\epsilon}{2^{n+1}}, q_n + \frac{\epsilon}{2^{n+1}} \right)$$

be an open interval of length $\frac{\epsilon}{2^n}$ centered in q_n for $n \geqslant 1$. Thus, $\mathbb{Q}_1 \subseteq S_\epsilon$, where $S_\epsilon = \bigcup_{n \geqslant 1} I_n$ is a Lebesgue measurable set. Note that $1_{\mathbb{Q}_1} \leqslant 1_{S_\epsilon}$. Since

$$m_L(S_\epsilon) \int_{[0,1]} 1_{S_\epsilon} \, dm_L \leqslant \epsilon \sum_{n \geqslant 1} \frac{\epsilon}{2^n} < \epsilon,$$

it follows that $\int_{[0,1]} f \, dm_L \leqslant \int_{[0,1]} 1_{S_\epsilon} \, dm_L < \epsilon$, for every $\epsilon > 0$, which implies $\int_{[0,1]} f \, dm_L = 0$.

The next statement shows that the Lebesgue integral is a generalization of the Riemann integral.

Theorem 8.48. *Let $f : [a, b] \longrightarrow \mathbb{R}$ be a bounded function defined on $[a, b]$. If f is Riemann integrable on $[a, b]$, then it is measurable, and $\int_a^b f(x) \, dx = \int_a^b f \, dm$.*

Proof.   We have the obvious inequalities

$$\underline{\int_a^b} f \, dx = \sup\{L_{f,\Delta} | \Delta \in \mathsf{SUBD}([a, b])\}$$

$$\leqslant \inf\{U_{f,\Delta} | \Delta \in \mathsf{SUBD}([a, b])\} = \overline{\int_a^b} f \, dx.$$

Since f is Riemann integrable, we have $\underline{\int_a^b} f \, dx = \overline{\int_a^b} f \, dx$, which implies the Lebesgue integrability of f and the equality of the theorem. $\square$

Theorem 8.49. *Let $f : [a, b] \longrightarrow \mathbb{R}$ be a continuous function. Then f is Lebesgue integrable on $[a, b]$. Furthermore, the function $F : [a, b] \longrightarrow \mathbb{R}$ defined by $F(x) = \int_{[a,x]} f(x) \, dm$ is differentiable on (a, b) and its derivative is $F'(x) = f(x)$ for $x \in (a, b)$.*

Proof.   Since continuous functions are measurable and f is bounded on $[a, b]$, the integral $\int_{[a,b]} |f| \, dm$ exists.

Let x and h be such that $a < x < x + h < b$. We have

$$F(x + h) - F(x) = \int_{[x, x+h]} f \, dm.$$

Let $m = \inf\{f(t) \mid t \in [x, x+h]\}$ and $M = \sup\{f(t) \mid t \in [x, x+h]\}$. Both m and M are attained (by Theorem 4.109), so there exist $t_1, t_2 \in [x, x+h]$ such that $m = f(t_1)$ and $M = f(t_2)$. By the Mean Value Theorem for Lebesgue Integrals (Theorem 8.18) we have $f(t_1) \leqslant \frac{1}{h} \int_{[x, x+h]} f \, dm \leqslant f(t_2)$. Therefore,

$$f(t_1) \leqslant \frac{F(x + h) - F(x)}{h} \leqslant f(t_2).$$

The Intermediate Value Theorem (Theorem 5.58) implies the existence of $\theta \in [0, 1]$ such that $f(x + \theta h) = \frac{F(x+h) - F(x)}{h}$. Taking $\lim_{h \to 0}$ we obtain that $f(x) = F'(x)$. $\qquad\square$

Let (Δ_n) be a sequence of subdivisions of the interval $[a, b]$. Note that the set of all subdivision points $\bigcup_{n \in \mathbb{N}} \Delta_n$ is a countable set and, therefore, a null set.

Theorem 8.50. *Let $f : [a, b] \longrightarrow \mathbb{R}$ be a bounded functions and let (Δ_n) a sequence of subdivisions of $[a, b]$ with $\lim_{n \to \infty} \nu(\Delta_n) = 0$.*

For $x \in [a, b] - \bigcup_{n \in \mathbb{N}} \Delta_n$ define $l(x) = \sup L_{f, \Delta_n}(x)$ and $u(x) = \inf U_{f, \Delta_n}(x)$. The function f is continuous in x if and only if $u(x) = f(x) = l(x)$.

Proof. Suppose that f is continuous on $[a, b]$. Since x is not a subdivision point, we have

$$L_{f, \Delta_0}(x) \leqslant L_{f, \Delta_1}(x) \leqslant \cdots \leqslant f(x) \leqslant \cdots \leqslant U_{f, \Delta_1}(x) \leqslant U_{f, \Delta_0}.$$

By Theorem 7.15 both $l = \lim_{n \to \infty} L_{f, \Delta_n}$ and $u = \lim_{n \to \infty}$ are measurable functions. $\qquad\square$

Theorem 8.51. *Let $f : [a, b] \longrightarrow \mathbb{R}$ be a bounded function. The, f is Riemann-integrable if and only if f is a.e. continuous relative to the Lebesgue measure on $[a, b]$.*

If f is Riemann-integrable, then f is Lebesgue-integrable and the two integrals are equal.

Proof. Suppose that f is Riemann-integrable. There exists a chain of subdivisions $\Delta_1 \leqslant \cdots \leqslant \Delta_n \leqslant \cdots$ such that $S(f, \Delta_n) - s(f, \Delta_n) < \frac{1}{n}$ for $n \geqslant 1$.

For each subdivision Δ_n define the simple functions g_{Δ_n} and $_h\Delta_n$ on $[a, b]$ such that $g_{\Delta_n}(a) = h_{\Delta_n}(a) = f(a)$ and

$$g_{\Delta_n}(x) = \inf\{f(x) \mid x \in [a_{i-1}, a_i]\} \text{ if } x \in (a_{i-1}, a_i]$$

and

$$h_{\Delta_n}(x) = \sup\{f(x) \mid x \in [a_{i-1}, a_i]\} \text{ if } x \in (a_{i-1}, a_i].$$

Since f is bounded, the terms of the sequences (g_{Δ_n}) and (h_{Δ_n}) are bounded. Furthermore, (g_{Δ_n}) is an non-decreasing sequence of functions, (h_{Δ_n}) is an non-increasing sequence of simple functions, $g_{\Delta_n} \leqslant f \leqslant h_{\Delta_n}$, and

$$\int_{[a,b]} g_{\Delta_n} \, dm_L = s(f, \Delta_n), \int_{[a,b]} h_{\Delta_n} \, dm = S(f, \Delta_n).$$

The functions $g = \lim_{n\to\infty} g_{\Delta_n}$ and $h = \lim_{n\to\infty} h_{\Delta_n}$ are measurable,

$$\int_{[a,b]} g \, dm_L = \lim_{n\to\infty} s(f, \Delta_n) \text{ and } \int_{[a,b]} h \, dm_L = \lim_{n\to\infty} S(f, \Delta_n)$$

by the Dominated Convergence Theorem (Theorem 8.37). Therefore,

$$\int_{[a,b]} g \, dm_L = \int_{[a,b]} h \, dm_L = \int_a^b f \, dx.$$

Consequently, $\int_{[a,b]} (h - g) \, dm_L = 0$. Since $h - g \geqslant 0$, it follows that $g = h$ a.e. in $[a, b]$ by Corollary 8.6.

If $g(x) = f(x)$ and $x \in [a, b] - \bigcup_{n\geqslant 1} \Delta_n$, then f is continuous x, and therefore, it is a.e. continuous relative to the Lebesgue measure on $[a, b]$.

Since $g(x) \leqslant f(x) \leqslant h(x)$, it follows that $f(x) = g(x)$ a.e. Thus, f is Lebesgue integrable by Theorem 8.40 and the Riemann integral equals the Lebesgue integral.

Suppose that f is continuous a.e. in $[a, b]$. Let now Δ_n be the subdivision of $[a, b]$ which divides $[a, b]$ is equal subintervals of length $\frac{b-a}{n}$. At each x where f is continuous we have

$$\lim_{n\to\infty} g_{\Delta_n} = \lim_{n\to\infty} h_{\Delta_n} = f(x),$$

hence there equalities hold a.e. on $[a, b]$. Thus, we have $\lim_{n\to\infty}(h_{\Delta_n} - g_{\Delta_n}) = 0$ a.e. on $[a, b]$. Since

$$\int_{[a,b]} g_{\Delta_n} \, dm = s(f, \Delta_n), \int_{[a,b]} h_{\Delta_n} \, dm = S(f, \Delta_n),$$

it follows that $\lim_{n\to\infty}(S(f, \Delta_n) - s(f, \Delta_n)) = 0$, which implies that f is Riemann integrable. $\qquad\square$

Definition 8.13. Let $f : (a, b) \longrightarrow \mathbb{R}$ be a function, where $a, b \in \hat{\mathbb{R}}$ such that f is Riemann integrable on all intervals $[c, d]$ included in (a, b). If both $\lim_{t \to a, t \geqslant a} \int_t^c f(x) \ dx$ and $\lim_{t \to b, t \leqslant b} \int_c^t f(x) \ dx$ exist, then $\int_a^b f(x) \ dx$ is called a *convergent improper integral*; its value is defined as:

$$\int_a^b f(x) \ dx = \lim_{t \to a, t \geqslant a} \int_t^c f(x) \ dx + \lim_{t \to b, t \leqslant b} \int_c^t f(x) \ dx.$$

Note that the choice of c is immaterial to the convergence or the value of the convergent improper integral. If f is integrable over $[a, b]$, then the value of the improper integral exists and is equal to the Riemann integral.

Example 8.6. Consider the Riemann integral $\int_{-\infty}^{\infty} e^{-|x|} \ dx$. Choosing $c = 0$ and taking into account that $\lim_{t \to -\infty} e^t = 0$ we have

$$\lim_{t \to -\infty} \int_t^0 e^{-|x|} \ dx = \lim_{t \to -\infty} \int_t^0 e^x \ dx = \lim_{t \to -\infty} e^x |_t^0 = 1,$$

$$\lim_{t \to \infty} \int_0^t e^{-|x|} \ dx = \lim_{t \to \infty} \int_0^t e^{-x} \ dx = \lim_{t \to \infty} -e^{-x}|_0^t = 1,$$

hence $\int_{-\infty}^{\infty} e^{-|x|} \ dx = 2$, which shows that $\int_{-\infty}^{\infty} e^{-|x|} \ dx$ is convergent.

If $f : [a, \infty) \longrightarrow \mathbb{R}$ is Riemann integrable on every interval $[a, b]$, and $\lim_{t \to \infty} \int_a^t f(x) \ dx$ exists, then we have the one-sided improper integral $\int_a^{\infty} f(x) \ dx$ defined as $\int_a^{\infty} f(x) \ dx = \lim_{t \to \infty} \int_a^t f(x) \ dx$. Similarly, the one-sided improper integral $\int_{-\infty}^n f(x) \ dx$ exists if $f(x)$ is Riemann integrable on $[a, b]$ and $\lim_{a \to -\infty} \int_a^b f(x) \ dx$ exists. In this case, $\int_{-\infty}^n f(x) \ dx = \lim_{a \to -\infty} \int_a^b f(x) \ dx$.

Example 8.7. Consider the continuous function $f : \mathbb{R} \longrightarrow \mathbb{R}$ defined by

$$f(x) = \begin{cases} \dfrac{\sin x}{x} & \text{if } x \neq 0, \\ 1 & \text{otherwise} \end{cases}$$

and the integral $\int_0^t f(x) \ dx$. Integrating by parts yields

$$\int_a^t f(x) \ dx = \left. \frac{-\cos x}{x} \right|_a^t - \int_a^t -\frac{-\cos x}{x^2} \ dx$$

$$= \frac{\cos a}{a} - \frac{\cos t}{t} - \int_a^t \frac{\cos x}{x^2} \ dx$$

for $t \geqslant a$. Since $\lim_{t \to \infty} \frac{\cos t}{t} = 0$, $\left| \int_a^t \frac{\cos x}{x^2} \ dx \right| \leqslant \int_a^t \frac{1}{x^2} \ dx$, and the fact that $\int_a^t \frac{1}{x^2} \ dx$ is convergent, it follows that $\int_a^t \frac{\cos x}{x^2} \ dx$ is convergent.

Note that

$$\int_{\pi}^{(n+1)\pi} \left| \frac{\sin x}{x} \right| dx = \sum_{k=1}^{n} \int_{k\pi}^{(k+1)\pi} \left| \frac{\sin x}{x} \right| dx$$

$$= \sum_{k=1}^{n} \int_{0}^{\pi} \frac{|\sin(t+k\pi)|}{t+k\pi} dt = \sum_{k=1}^{n} \int_{0}^{\pi} \frac{|\sin t|}{t+k\pi} dt$$

$$\geqslant \sum_{k=1}^{n} \frac{1}{(k+1)\pi} \int_{0}^{\pi} |\sin t| \, dt = \frac{2}{\pi} \sum_{k=1}^{n} \frac{1}{k+1},$$

which shows that $\int_{0}^{\infty} \left| \frac{\sin x}{x} \right| dx$ is not convergent, because the harmonic series is not convergent. This, in turn, implies that the function f is not Lebesgue integrable (by Theorem 8.22). However, the Riemann integral $\int_{0}^{\infty} \frac{\sin x}{x} dx$ exists.

Example 8.7 shows that the existence of improper Riemann integrals *does not* necessarily entail the existence of the corresponding Lebesgue integral. However, if f is non-negative this implication holds as we show next.

Theorem 8.52. *If $f : \mathbb{R} \longrightarrow \mathbb{R}$ is Riemann-integrable on $\mathbb{R}$ and $f(x) \geqslant 0$ for $x \in \mathbb{R}$, then f is Lebesgue-integrable on the same set and*

$$\int_{\mathbb{R}} f(x) dx = \int_{\mathbb{R}} f \, dm.$$

Proof.   Let (f_n) be the sequence of functions defined by $f_n = f1_{[-n,n]}$ for $n \geqslant 1$. Observe that for every $x \in \mathbb{R}$ we have $f_n(x) \leqslant f_{n+1}(x)$ for $n \geqslant 1$, so (f_n) is a monotonic sequence and $\lim_{n \to \infty} f_n = f$. Since each f_n is Riemann integrable on $[-n, n]$ we have $\int_{[-n,n]} f_n \, dm = \int_{-n}^{n} f \, dx$, so $f_n \in \mathcal{L}_1(\mathbb{R})$ for $n \geqslant 1$. By definition, $\int_{\mathbb{R}} f \, dx = \lim_{n \to \infty} \int_{-n}^{n} f \, dx$. By (Theorem 8.11) we have

$$\int_{\mathbb{R}} f \, dm = \lim_{n \to \infty} \int_{\mathbb{R}} f_n \, dm$$

(by the Monotone Convergence Theorem)

$$= \lim_{n \to \infty} \int_{\mathbb{R}} f_n \, dx = \int_{\mathbb{R}} f \, dx,$$

hence $f \in \mathcal{L}^1(\mathbb{R})$ and proof is complete.   □

In general, we use Lebesgue integrals. When integrating continuous functions, the use of Lebesgue integrals causes no problem since, in this case, the Riemann and Lebesgue integrals coincide.

8.6 The Radon-Nikodym Theorem

Definition 8.14. Let $(S, \mathcal{E}, m)$ be a measure space and let m' be a signed measure defined on $\mathcal{E}$. The measure m' is *absolutely continuous* with respect to the measure m if $m(T) = 0$ implies $m'(T) = 0$ for every $T \in \mathcal{E}$. This is denoted by $m' \ll m$.

We have $m' \ll m$ if and only if $|m'|(T) = 0$ for every $T \in \mathcal{E}$ with $m(T) = 0$.

Example 8.8. Let $(S, \mathcal{E})$ be a measurable space and let m, m' be two measures defined on $\mathcal{E}$ such that $m'(U) \leqslant m(U)$ for every $U \in \mathcal{E}$. Then, $m' \ll m$.

Theorem 8.53. *Let m' be a signed finite measures on the measurable space $(S, \mathcal{E})$. We have $m' \ll m$ if and only if for every positive number ϵ there exists a positive number δ such that if $T \in \mathcal{E}$, then $m(T) < \delta$ implies $|m'|(T) < \epsilon$.*

Proof. To establish that the condition is sufficient let $T \in \mathcal{E}$ be a set such that $m(T) = 0$. Then $m(T) < \delta$, hence $|m'|(T) < \epsilon$ for every positive ϵ. Therefore, $|m'|(T) = 0$, hence $m' \ll m$.

To establish that the condition is necessary, suppose that $m' \ll m$. and the ϵ, δ-condition is not true. Then, there exists a positive number ϵ and a sequence of sets $(T_1, T_2, \ldots)$ in $\mathcal{E}$ such that $m(T_n) < \frac{1}{2^n}$ and $m'(T_n) \geqslant \epsilon$ for every $n \geqslant 1$. Define $T = \limsup T_n = \bigcap_{n=1}^{\infty} \bigcup_{i \geqslant n} T_i$.

We have

$$m(T) \leqslant m\left(\bigcup_{i \geqslant n} T_i\right) \leqslant \sum_{i \geqslant n} m(T_i) < \sum_{i=n}^{\infty} \frac{1}{2^i} = \frac{1}{2^{n-1}},$$

for every $n \geqslant 1$, which implies $m(T) = 0$, hence $|m'|(T) = 0$

Since m' is finite, it follows that $|m'|$ is finite, hence $|m'|(\bigcup_{i \geqslant n} T_i) < \infty$. Since the sequence $(\bigcup_{i \geqslant n} T_n)$ is increasing, by Theorem 7.32 we have

$$|m'|(T) = |m'|\left(\lim \bigcup_{i \geqslant n} T_i\right) = \lim |m'|\left(\bigcup_{i \geqslant n} T_i\right) > \epsilon,$$

which contradicts the absolute continuity of m' with respect to m. $\qquad \square$

Theorem 8.54. *Let $(S, \mathcal{E}, m)$ be a measure space and let m' be a signed measure defined on $\mathcal{E}$. The following statements are equivalent:*
   (i) $m' \ll m$;
   (ii) $|m'| \ll m$;
   (iii) $m'_+ \ll m$ and $m'_- \ll m$.

Proof.   (i) implies (ii): Since the absolute value of $|m'|$ is the same as $|m'|$, this implication follows immediately.

(ii) implies (iii): $|m'| \ll m$ implies $m'_+ + m'_- \ll m$. Since m'_+, m'_- and m are positive measures, we obtain (iii).

(iii) implies (i): Suppose that $m(T) = 0$. We have $m'_+ \ll m$ and $m'_- \ll m$, hence $m'_+(t) = m'_-(T) = 0$. Thus, $|m'|(T) = 0$ and $m' \ll m$. $\square$

Lemma 8.2. *Let $(S, \mathcal{E}, m)$ be a measure space such that $m(S)$ is finite and let m' be a measure defined on $\mathcal{E}$ such that $m'(T) \leqslant m(T)$ for every $T \in \mathcal{E}$.*

For a $\mathcal{E}$-partition π of S, $\pi = \{L_1, \ldots, L_p\}$ define the simple function $f_\pi : S \longrightarrow \mathbb{R}$ by

$$f_\pi(x) = \begin{cases} \dfrac{m'(L_i)}{m(L_i)} & \text{if } x \in L_i \text{ and } m(L_i) > 0, \\ 0 & \text{otherwise.} \end{cases}$$

If π_1 and π_2 are two $\mathcal{E}$-partitions on S such that $\pi_2 \leqslant \pi_1$, then

$$\int_S f_{\pi_2}^2 \, dm \geqslant \int_S f_{\pi_1}^2 \, dm.$$

Proof.   It is easy to see that $0 \leqslant f_\pi(x) \leqslant 1$ for all $x \in S$.

We have $m'(L_i) = \int_{L_i} f_\pi \, dm$ for every $L_i \in \pi$; furthermore, if $I \subseteq \{1, \ldots, n\}$ and $K = \bigcup_{i \in I} L_i$, then

$$m'(K) = \sum_{i \in I} m'(L_i)$$

$$= \sum_{i \in I} \left\{ \frac{m'(L_i)}{m(L_i)} m(L_i) \,\middle|\, i \in I, m(L_i) > 0 \right\}$$

$$= \sum \left\{ \int_{L_i} f_\pi \, dm \,\middle|\, i \in I, m(L_i) > 0 \right\} = \int_K f_\pi \, dm.$$

Suppose that $\pi_1 = \{B_1, \ldots, B_n\}$ and $\pi_2 = \{C_1, \ldots, C_m\}$. Since $\pi_2 \leqslant \pi_1$, for each block B_i of π_1 there exists a family of blocks $\{C_j \mid j \in J_i\}$ such that $B_i = \bigcup\{C_j \mid j \in J_i\}$. If $m(C_j) = 0$, then $m'(C_j) = 0$. Consequently, we have

$$\int_{B_i} f_{\pi_1} \, dm = m'(B_i) = \sum_{j \in J_i} m'(C_j) = \sum \left\{ \frac{m'(C_j)}{m(C_j)} m(C_j) \,\middle|\, j \in J_i, m(C_j) > 0 \right\}$$

$$= \sum \left\{ \int_{C_j} f_{\pi_2} \, dm \,\middle|\, j \in J_i \right\}$$

$$= \sum \left\{ \int_{C_j} f_{\pi_2} \, dm \,\middle|\, j \in J_i \right\} = \int_{B_i} f_{\pi_2} \, dm.$$

Let B_i be a block of the partition π_1 such that $m(B_i) > 0$. We can write

$$\int_{B_i} f_{\pi_1} f_{\pi_2} \, dm = \frac{m'(B_i)}{m(B_i)} \int_{B_i} f_{\pi_2} \, dm$$

$$\text{(because } f_{\pi_1}(x) \text{ is constant on } B_i\text{)}$$

$$= \frac{(m'(B_i))^2}{m(B_i)} \int_{B_i} f_{\pi_2} \, dm$$

$$= \int_{B_i} \left(\frac{m'(B_i)}{m(B_i)} \right)^2 dm = \int_{B_i} f_{\pi_1}^2 \, dm,$$

which implies $\int_{B_i} f_{\pi_1}(f_{\pi_1} - f_{\pi_2}) \, dm = 0$ for every block B_i of π_1. Consequently,

$$\int_S f_{\pi_1}(f_{\pi_1} - f_{\pi_2}) \, dm = \sum_{i=1}^{n} \int_{B_i} f_{\pi_1}(f_{\pi_1} - f_{\pi_2}) \, dm = 0.$$

Therefore,

$$\int_S (f_{\pi_1} - f_{\pi_2})^2 \, dm = \int_S (f_{\pi_1}^2 - 2f_{\pi_1} f_{\pi_2} + f_{\pi_2}^2) \, dm$$

$$= \int_S (-f_{\pi_1}^2 + 2f_{\pi_1}^2 - 2f_{\pi_1} f_{\pi_2} + f_{\pi_2}^2) \, dm$$

$$= \int_S (-f_{\pi_1}^2 + 2f_{\pi_1}^2 - 2f_{\pi_1} f_{\pi_2} + f_{\pi_2}^2) \, dm$$

$$= \int_S (-f_{\pi_1}^2 + 2f_{\pi_1}(f_{\pi_1} - f_{\pi_2}) + f_{\pi_2}^2) \, dm$$

$$= \int_S (f_{\pi_2}^2 - f_{\pi_1}^2) \, dm + 2 \int_S f_{\pi_1}(f_{\pi_1} - f_{\pi_2}) \, dm$$

$$= \int_S (f_{\pi_2}^2 - f_{\pi_1}^2) \, dm = \int_S f_{\pi_2}^2 \, dm - \int_S f_{\pi_1}^2 \, dm,$$

which shows that

$$\int_S (f_{\pi_1} - f_{\pi_2})^2 \, dm = \int_S f_{\pi_2}^2 \, dm - \int_S f_{\pi_1}^2 \, dm. \tag{8.15}$$

Since $\int_S (f_{\pi_1} - f_{\pi_2})^2 \, dm \geqslant 0$, the desired conclusion follows. $\qquad \square$

Lemma 8.3. *Let $(S, \mathcal{E}, m)$ be a measure space such that $m(S)$ is finite. If m_1 is a finite measure defined on $\mathcal{E}$ such that $m_1(T) \leqslant m(T)$ for every $T \in \mathcal{E}$, then there exists a non-negative measurable function $f : S \longrightarrow \mathbb{R}$ such that $m_1(T) = \int_T f \, dm$ for every set $T \in \mathcal{E}$.*

Proof.	Without loss of generality we may assume that $m(S) = 1$. Let $I = \sup \left\{ \int_S f_\pi^2 \, dm \mid \pi \in PART_{\text{fin}}(S) \right\}$. Since $f_\pi(x) \in [0, 1]$ for all $x \in S$, it follows that $0 \leqslant I \leqslant 1$.

By the definition of the supremum, for every $n \geqslant 1$, there exists a partition $\pi_n \in PART_{\text{fin}}(S)$ such that

$$I - \frac{1}{4^n} < \int_S f_\pi^2 \, dm.$$

Define the finite partition σ_n as $\sigma_n = \bigcap_{l=1}^n \pi_l$. Since $\sigma_{n+1} \leqslant \sigma_n \leqslant \pi_n$, by Lemma 8.2 we have

$$I - \frac{1}{4^n} < \int_S f_{\pi_n}^2 \, dm \leqslant \int_S f_{\sigma_n}^2 \, dm \leqslant \int_S f_{\sigma_{n+1}}^2 \, dm \leqslant I. \qquad (8.16)$$

Using equality (8.15) we have

$$\int_S (f_{\sigma_{n+1}} - f_{\sigma_n})^2 \, dm = \int_S f_{\sigma_{n+1}}^2 \, dm - \int_S f_{\sigma_n}^2 \, dm < \frac{1}{4^n}.$$

By the Cauchy-Schwartz inequality applied to the functions $f = f_{\sigma_{n+1}} - f_{\sigma_n}$ and $g = 1$ we obtain

$$\int_S |f_{\sigma_{n+1}} - f_{\sigma_n}| \, dm < \frac{1}{2^n}.$$

Since $\int_S |f_{\sigma_{n+1}} - f_{\sigma_n}| \, dm$ is finite, by Beppo Levi's Theorem, the telescopic series $\sum_{n \geqslant 1} (f_{\sigma_{n+1}} - f_{\sigma_n})$ is m-convergent a.e., so the function f given by series

$$f = f_{\sigma_1} + \sum_{n \geqslant 1} (f_{\sigma_{n+1}} - f_{\sigma_n})$$

is defined a.e. with respect to m. On the m-null set we set $f(x) = 0$.

We claim that the function f satisfies the conditions of the theorem.

Consider the two-block $\mathcal{E}$-partition $\theta = \{T, S - T\}$ of S and let $\zeta_n = \sigma_n \wedge \theta$. We have $m_1(T) = \int_T f_{\zeta_n} \, dm$ because T is a ζ_n-saturated set. Moreover, we have

$$I - \frac{1}{4^n} < \int_S f_{\sigma_n}^2 \, dm \leqslant \int_S f_{\zeta_n}^2 \, dm \leqslant I.$$

Therefore, as before, we have $\int_S (f_{\zeta_n} - f_{\sigma_n})^2 \, dm < \frac{1}{4^n}$. By Cauchy-Schwartz inequality applied to the functions $f_{\zeta_n} - f_{\sigma_n}$ and I_T we have

$$\left| \int_T (f_{\zeta_n} - f_{\sigma_n}) \, dm \right| \leq |f_{\zeta_n} - f_{\sigma_n}| < \frac{1}{2^n}.$$

Observe that

$$m_1(T) = \int_T f_{\zeta_n} \, dm = \int_T (f_{\zeta_n} - f_{\sigma_n}) \, dm + \int_T f_{\sigma_n} \, dm$$

for every $n \geqslant 1$. Since $\lim_{n \to \infty} \int_T (f_{\zeta_n} - f_{\sigma_n}) \, dm = 0$, and $\lim_{n \to \infty} \int_T f_{\sigma_n} \, dm = \int_T f \, dm$ by the Dominated Convergence Theorem (Theorem 8.37) because $0 \leqslant f_{\sigma_n} \leqslant 1$, we have $m_1(T) = \int_T f \, dm$.	$\square$

Corollary 8.10. *Let $(S, \mathcal{E}, m)$ be a measure space such that $m(S)$ is finite and $m(S) > 0$. If m_1 is a finite measure defined on $\mathcal{E}$ such that $m_1(T) \leqslant m(T)$ for every $T \in \mathcal{E}$, then there exists a non-negative measurable function $f : S \longrightarrow \mathbb{R}$ such that $m_1(T) = \int_T f \, dm$ for every set $T \in \mathcal{E}$.*

Proof. Consider the measure space $(S, \mathcal{E}, m_1)$, where $m_1(T) = \frac{m(T)}{m(S)}$. Define m_1' by $m_1'(T) = \frac{m_1(T)}{m(S)}$. Clearly, we have $m_1'(T) \leqslant m_1(T)$ for every $T \in \mathcal{E}$. By Lemma 8.3, there exists a non-negative measurable function f such that $m_1'(T) = \int_T f \, dm_1$ for every set $T \in \mathcal{E}$. This implies immediately $m_1(T) = \int_T f \, dm$ for every set $T \in \mathcal{E}$. □

Theorem 8.55. *Let $(S, \mathcal{E}, m)$ be a measure space such that $m(S)$ is finite and $m(S) > 0$ and let m_1 is a finite measure defined on $\mathcal{E}$ such that $m_1(T) \leqslant m(T)$ for every $T \in \mathcal{E}$. If f_1 is a measurable function $f : S \longrightarrow \mathbb{R}$ such that $m_1(T) = \int_T f_1 \, dm$ for every set $T \in \mathcal{E}$, then for every non-negative measurable function $g : S \longrightarrow \mathbb{R}$ we have $\int_S g \, dm_1 = \int_S g f_1 \, dm$.*

Proof. Suppose initially that $g = I_W$, where W is a set in $\mathcal{E}$. Then, $\int_S g \, dm_1 = m_1(W) = \int_W f_1 \, dm$.

If g is a simple function, then, by Theorem 7.10, g can be written as a linear combination of indicator functions of sets $W_1, \ldots, W_n$ in $\mathcal{E}$,

$$g = \sum_{i=1}^{n} y_i I_{W_i},$$

which implies

$$\int_S g \, dm_1 = \sum_{i=1}^{n} y_i m_1(W_i) = \sum_{i=1}^{n} y_i \int_{W_i} f_1 \, dm$$

$$= \sum_{i=1}^{n} y_i \int_S I_{W_i} f_1 \, dm = \int_S \left(\sum_{i=1}^{n} y_i I_{W_i} \right) f_1 \, dm = \int_S g f_1 \, dm.$$

By Theorem 7.26, if g is a non-negative measurable function, then g is the limit of a non-decreasing sequence of simple measurable functions $(g_1, \ldots, g_n, \ldots)$. By the previous argument, we have $\int_S g_n \, dm_1 = \int_S g_n f_1 \, dm$. Since $0 \leqslant f_1(x) \leqslant 1$, the sequence $g_n f_1(x)$ increases to $g f_1(x)$, so $\lim_{n \to \infty} \int_S g_n f_1 \, dm = \int_S g f_1 \, dm$. Therefore,

$$\int_S g \, dm_1 = \lim_{n \to \infty} \int_S g_n \, dm_1 = \lim_{n \to \infty} \int_S g_n f_1 \, dm$$

$$= \int_S \lim_{n \to \infty} g_n f_1 \, dm = \int_S g f_1 \, dm.$$

Finally, if g is not non-negative the result follows from a separate application to the functions g^+ and g^-. □

By relaxing the requirement imposed on the finite measures m and m_1 in Lemma 8.3 we obtain the next statement.

Theorem 8.56. *Let $(S, \mathcal{E}, m)$ be a measure space such that m is finite and $m(S) > 0$. If m_1 is a finite measure defined on $\mathcal{E}$ such that $m_1 \ll m$, then there exists a non-negative measurable function $f : S \longrightarrow \mathbb{R}$ such that $m_1(T) = \int_T f \, dm$ for every set $T \in \mathcal{E}$.*

Proof. Let m_2 be the measure defined by $m_2 = m + m_1$. We have both $m(T) \leq m_2(T)$ and $m_1(T) \leqslant m_2(T)$ for every $T \in \mathcal{E}$. Therefore, by Corollary 8.10, there exist two measurable functions f and f_1 such that

$$m(T) = \int_T f \, dm_2 \text{ and } m_1(T) = \int_T f_1 \, dm_2.$$

Consider the sets $U = \{x \in S \mid f(x) > 0\}$ and $V = \{x \in S \mid f(x) = 0\}$. We have $m(V) = \int_V f \, dm = 0$, so $m_1(V) = 0$ because $m_1 \ll m$, so both m and m_1 are null on V.

Define the function h by $h(x) = \frac{f_1(x)}{f(x)} \cdot I_U(x)$. If $T \subseteq U$, then $m_1(T) = \int_T f_1 \, dm_2 = \int_T hf \, dm_2 = \int_S hf I_T dm_2$. By Theorem 8.55 applied to the function $g = hI_T$ we have

$$\int_S hI_T \, dm = \int_S hI_T f \, dm_2,$$

so $m_1(T) = \int_S hI_T \, dm = \int_T h \, dm$. $\square$

A more general result can be obtained by allowing m to be σ-finite.

Theorem 8.57. *Let $(S, \mathcal{E}, m)$ be a measure space such that m is σ-finite and $m(S) > 0$. If m_1 is a finite measure defined on $\mathcal{E}$ such that $m_1 \ll m$, then there exists a non-negative measurable function $f : S \longrightarrow \mathbb{R}$ such that $m_1(T) = \int_T f \, dm$ for every set $T \in \mathcal{E}$.*

Proof. Let (S_n) be a increasing sequence of sets in $\mathcal{E}$ such that $\bigcup_{n \in \mathbb{N}} S_n = S$ and $m(S_n) < \infty$ for $n \in \mathbb{N}$. Let m_n, m'_n be defined as $m_n(B) = m(B \cap S_n)$ and $m'_n(B) = m'(B \cap S_n)$. Since $m'_n \ll m_n$, by Theorem 8.56, there exists a sequence of functions (f_n) that are positive and m_n-integrable such that $m'_n(B) = \int_B f_n \, dm_n$ for $n \in \mathbb{N}$ and $B \subseteq S_n$. Note that $m_n(B) = m(B)$ and $m'_n(B) = m'(B)$ for every $B \in \mathcal{E}$ and $B \subseteq S_n$, and $m_n(B) = m'_n(B) = 0$ for every $B \subseteq S - S_n$. Thus, if $B \in \mathcal{E}$ and $B \subseteq S_n \subseteq S_{n+1}$ we have

$$\int_B (f_{n+1} - f_n) \, dm = \int_B f_{n+1} \, dm - \int_B f_n \, dm$$
$$= m'_{n+1}(B) - m_n(B) = m'(B) - m'(B) = 0.$$

Thus, $f_{n+1} = f_n$ a.e. on B_n. Also, and m_n-integrable function is m-integrable, hence $f_n \in \mathcal{L}^1(S)$. Now we can define a function $f : S \longrightarrow \mathbb{R}$ as $f(x) = f_n(x)$ if $x \in B_n$. We have $f^{-1}(-\infty, a) = \bigcup_{n \in \mathbb{N}} f_n^{-1}(-\infty, a)$, hence f is positive and measurable. By the upward continuity of measures we obtain

$$\int_B f \, dm = \lim_{n \to \infty} \int_{B \cap S_n} f \, dm = \lim_{n \to \infty} \int_{B \cap S_n} f_n \, dm$$
$$= \lim_{n \to \infty} m_n'(B \cap S_n) = \lim_{n \to \infty} m_n(B \cap S_n) = m'(B).$$

In particular, $\int_S f \, dm = m'(S) < \infty$, hence $f \in \mathcal{L}^1(S)$. $\qquad\square$

Finally, the next statement extends Theorem 8.57 by allowing m_1 to be a real measure.

Theorem 8.58. (The Radon-Nikodym Theorem) *Let $(S, \mathcal{E}, m)$ be a measure space such that m is σ-finite and $m(S) > 0$. If m_1 is a real finite measure defined on $\mathcal{E}$ such that $m_1 \ll m$, then there exists a non-negative measurable function $f : S \longrightarrow \mathbb{R}$ such that $m_1(T) = \int_T f \, dm$ for every set $T \in \mathcal{E}$. The function f is uniquely determined up to a μ-null set.*

Proof. Since m_1 is a real and finite, by Jordan's Decomposition Theorem, we can write $m_1 = m_{1+} - m_{1-}$. It is immediate that $m_{1+} \ll m$ and $m_{1-} \ll m$. By Theorem 8.57, there exist $g, h \in \mathcal{L}^1(S)$ such that $m_{1+}(T) = \int_T g \, dm$ and $m_{1-}(T) = \int_T h \, dm$. The function $f = g - h$ satisfies the condition of the theorem.

If $f_1, f_2 \in \mathcal{L}^1(S)$ such that $m_1(T) = \int_T f_1 \, dm = \int_T f_2 \, dm$, we have $\int_T (f_1 - f_2) \, dm = 0$, hence $f_1 = f_2$ a.e. $\qquad\square$

Definition 8.15. Let $(S, \mathcal{E}, m)$ be a measure space such that m is σ-finite and $m(S) > 0$. If m_1 is a real finite measure defined on $\mathcal{E}$ such that $m_1 \ll m$, the function $f \in \mathcal{L}^1(S)$ that satisfies the equality $m_1(T) = \int_T f \, dm$ for every set $T \in \mathcal{E}$ is the *Radon-Nikodym derivative* of m relative to m'.

We will denote f by $\frac{dm_1}{dm}$.

Lemma 8.4. *Let $(S, \mathcal{E}, m)$ be a measure space and let $f, g : S \longrightarrow \hat{\mathbb{R}}_{\geqslant 0}$ be measurable functions. We have $\int_S g \, dm_f = \int_S gf \, dm$, where m_f is the indefinite integral of f relative to m.*

Proof. Suppose initially that $g = 1_T$ for some $T \in \mathcal{E}$. We have

$$\int_S 1_T \, dm_f = m_f(T) = \int_T f \, dm = \int_S 1_T f \, dm,$$

which show that the equality of the lemma holds for characteristic functions. This can be extended, by linearity to measurable non-negative simple functions, and, then, by the Monotone Convergence Theorem, to measurable functions. □

Theorem 8.59. *Let $(S, \mathcal{E}, m)$ be a measure space and let $f : S \longrightarrow \hat{\mathbb{R}}$ be a measurable function such that $\int_S f \, dm$ is defined. Consider the signed measure m_f, that is, the indefinite integral of f relative to m.*

A measurable function $g : S \longrightarrow \hat{\mathbb{R}}$ is integrable over S with respect to m_f if and only if gf is integrable over S relative to m, in which case $\int_S g \, dm_f = \int_S gf \, dm$.

Proof. By Lemma 8.4 we have $\int_S |g| \, dm_{|f|} = \int_S |gf| \, dm$. This equality shows that g is integrable over S with respect to $m_{|f|}$ if and only if gf is integrable over S with respect to m. The equality of the theorem follows now from Lemma 8.4. □

Theorem 8.60. *Let $(S, \mathcal{E}, m)$ be a measure space, where m is a σ-finite measure. If m_1, m_2 are σ-finite measures on $(S, \mathcal{E})$ such that $m_1 \ll m$, $m_2 \ll m$, $m_1 + m_2$ is defined, then $m_1 + m_2 \ll m$ and*

$$\frac{d(m_1 + m_2)}{ddm} = \frac{dm_1}{ddm} + \frac{dm_2}{ddm} \quad (a.e.).$$

Proof. We have

$$\int_T \frac{d(m_1 + m_2)}{ddm} \, dm = (m_1 + m_2)(T)$$

$$= \int_T \frac{dm_1}{dm} \, dm + \int_T \frac{dm_2}{dm} \, dm$$

$$= \int_T \left(\frac{dm_1}{dm} + \frac{dm_2}{dm} \right) \, dm,$$

which implies the conclusion. □

Theorem 8.61. *Let $(S, \mathcal{E}, m)$ be a measure space, where m is a σ-finite measure. If m_1 is a σ-finite measures on $(S, \mathcal{E})$ such that $m_1 \ll m$, then for every $k \in \mathbb{R}$ we have:*

$$\frac{dkm_1}{ddm} = k \frac{dm_1}{ddm} \quad (a.e.).$$

Proof. We have $(km_1)(T) = k \int_T \frac{dm_1}{dm} \, dm = \int_T \left(k \frac{dm_1}{dm} \right) \, dm$ for all $T \in \mathcal{E}$, so $\frac{dkm_1}{ddm} = k \frac{dm_1}{ddm}$ a.e. □

Theorem 8.62. (Chain Rule for Radon-Nikodym Derivatives) *Let m_1, m, m' be σ-finite signed measures such that $m_1 \ll m'$ and $m' \ll m$. Then $m_1 \ll m$ and*

$$\frac{dm_1}{dm} = \frac{dm_1}{dm'} \frac{dm'}{dm} \quad a.e. \text{ with respect to } m.$$

Proof. If $T \in \mathcal{E}$ is such that $m(T) = 0$, then $m'(T) = 0$, hence $m_1(T) = 0$. Therefore, $m_1 \ll m$.

Theorem 8.59 implies that

$$m_1(T) = \int_T \frac{dm_1}{dm'} \, dm' = \int_T \frac{dm_1}{dm'} \frac{dm'}{dm} \, dm$$

for every $T \in \mathcal{E}$, which gives the conclusion of the theorem. $\qquad \square$

Theorem 8.63. (Lebesgue Decomposition Theorem) *Let $(S, \mathcal{E}, m)$ be a measure space such that m is finite and $m(S) > 0$. If $\tilde{m}$ is a finite measure defined on $\mathcal{E}$ then there exist two measures m_0 and m_1 on $\mathcal{E}$ such that $m_0 \perp m$ and m_1 is absolutely continuous with respect to m such that $\tilde{m} = m_0 + m_1$.*

Proof. Since both m and $\tilde{m}$ are finite measures, so is the measure $m' = m + \tilde{m}$. By Radon-Nikodym Theorem, there exist non-negative measurable functions f, g such that for each $U \in \mathcal{E}$, we have $m(U) = \int_U f \, dm'$ and $\tilde{m}(U) = \int_U g \, dm'$ because both m and $\tilde{m}$ are absolutely continuous relative to m'.

Let $V = \{x \in S \mid f(x) > 0\}$ and $W = \{x \in S \mid f(x) = 0\}$. Then S is the disjoint union of V and W, where $m(W) = 0$.

Define m_0 by $m_0(U) = \tilde{m}(U \cap W)$. We have $m_0(V) = 0$, so $m_0 \perp m$.

Let m_1 be defined by $m_1(U) = \tilde{m}(U \cap V) = \int_{U \cap V} g \, dm$.

We have $\tilde{m} = m_0 + m_1$ and we need to show only that $m_1 \ll m$. Let T be a set such that $m(T) = 0$. Then $0 = m(T) = \int_T f \, dm'$ and $f = 0$ a.e. relative to m'. Since $f > 0$ on $U \cap V$ we have $m'(U \cap V) = 0$. Thus, $\tilde{m}(U \cap V) = 0$, so $m_1(U) = U \cap V = 0$, which concludes the argument. $\quad \square$

8.7 Integration on Products of Measure Spaces

Let $(S, \mathcal{E})$ and $(T, \mathcal{E}')$ be two measurable spaces. For a set $E \subseteq S \times T$, $s \in S$, and $t \in T$, subset E_s of T and the subset E^t of S are defined as:

$$E_s = \{t \in T \mid (s, t) \in E\},$$
$$E^t = \{s \in S \mid (s, t) \in E\}.$$

The sets E_s and E^t are referred to as the *s-section* and the *t-section* of E, respectively.

Let $E = U \times V$ be a rectangle in $S \times T$. We have

$$(U \times V)_s = \begin{cases} V & \text{if } s \in U, \\ \emptyset & \text{if } s \notin U \end{cases} \quad \text{and} \quad (U \times V)^t = \begin{cases} U & \text{if } t \in V, \\ \emptyset & \text{if } t \notin V \end{cases}$$

for $s \in S$ and $t \in T$, respectively.

Is immediate that $(\overline{E})_s = \overline{E_s}$ and

$$\left(\bigcup_{i \in I} E_i \right)_s = \bigcup_{i \in I} (E_i)_s,$$

for any collection $\{E_i \mid i \in I\}$ of subsets of $S \times T$.

If $f : S \times T \longrightarrow Z$, then the *section* f_s is the function $f_s : T \longrightarrow Z$ that depends on the argument t and is given by $f_s(t) = f(s,t)$; similarly, the *section* f^t is the function f^t that depends on s and is given by $f^t(s) = f(s,t)$ for $(s,t) \in S \times T$.

For every $D \subseteq S \times T$ we have the equalities

$$(f_s)^{-1}(D) = (f^{-1}(D))_s, \tag{8.17}$$
$$(f^t)^{-1}(D) = (f^{-1}(D))^t. \tag{8.18}$$

Theorem 8.64. *Let $(S, \mathcal{E})$ and $(T, \mathcal{E}')$ be two measurable spaces and let $(S \times T, \mathcal{E} \times \mathcal{E}')$ be their product. If $E \in \mathcal{E} \times \mathcal{E}'$, then $E_s \in \mathcal{E}'$ and $E^t \in \mathcal{E}$ for $s \in S$ and $t \in T$.*

If $f : S \times T \longrightarrow \hat{\mathbb{R}}$ is $\mathcal{E} \times \mathcal{E}'$-measurable, then each section f_s is $\mathcal{E}'$-measurable and each f^t is $\mathcal{E}$-measurable.

Proof.   Let $\mathcal{F}$ be the collection of subsets of $S \times T$ defined by

$$\mathcal{F} = \{E \subseteq S \times T \mid \text{ for all } s \in S, E_s \in \mathcal{E}'\}.$$

$\mathcal{F}$ contains all rectangles of the form $U \times V$ such that $U \in \mathcal{E}$ and $V \in \mathcal{E}'$. In particular, $S \times T \in \mathcal{F}$. Since $\mathcal{F}$ is closed under complementation and countable unions, it follows that $\mathcal{F}$ is a σ-algebra. Therefore, $\mathcal{E} \times \mathcal{E}' \subseteq \mathcal{F}$ and $E_s \in \mathcal{E}'$, whenever $E \in \mathcal{E} \times \mathcal{E}'$. Similarly, $E^t \in \mathcal{E}$ whenever $E \in \mathcal{E} \times \mathcal{E}'$. This proves the first part of the theorem.

The second part of the theorem is an immediate consequence of equalities (8.17) and (8.18). $\square$

If $(S, \mathcal{E}, m)$ and $(T, \mathcal{E}', m')$ are two σ-finite measure spaces then

$$m'((U \times V)_s) = m'(V)1_U(s), \tag{8.19}$$
$$m((U \times V)^t) = m(U)1_V(t) \tag{8.20}$$

for $s \in S$ and $t \in T$.

Theorem 8.65. *Let $(S, \mathcal{E}, m)$ and $(T, \mathcal{E}', m')$ be two σ-finite measure spaces and let $E \in \mathcal{E} \times \mathcal{E}'$. The functions $f_E : S \longrightarrow \hat{\mathbb{R}}$ and $g_E : T \longrightarrow \hat{\mathbb{R}}$ defined by $f_E(s) = m'(E_s)$ and $g_E(t) = m(E^t)$ are Borel-measurable.*

Proof. Suppose initially that the measure m is finite.

We claim that the collection

$$\mathcal{F} = \{E \in \mathcal{E} \times \mathcal{E}' \mid f_E \text{ is measurable}\}$$

is a Dynkin system.

The definitions of the functions f_E and g_E mean that equalities (8.19) and (8.20) can be written as

$$f_{U \times V}(s) = m'(V)1_U(s),$$
$$g_{U \times V}(t) = m(U)1_V(t),$$

for $U \in \mathcal{E}$, $V \in \mathcal{E}'$, $s \in S$ and $t \in T$. Therefore, $U \times V \in \mathcal{F}$ and, in particular, $S \times T \in \mathcal{F}$.

If $P, Q \subseteq S \times T$ and $P \subseteq Q$, we have $m'((Q - P)_s) = m'(Q_s) - m'(P_s)$, or equivalently, $f_{Q-P} = f_Q - f_P$. Therefore, under these assumptions, $P, Q \in \mathcal{F}$ and $P \subseteq Q$ imply $Q - P \in \mathcal{F}$.

Also, if (E_n) is an increasing sequence of subsets in $\mathcal{E} \times \mathcal{E}'$ and $E = \bigcup_{n \in \mathbb{N}} E_n$, then

$$f_E(s) = m'(E_s) = \lim_{n \to \infty} f_{E_n}(s).$$

Thus, $\mathcal{F}$ is indeed a Dynkin system.

Let now $U_1, U_2 \in \mathcal{E}$ and $V_1, V_2 \in \mathcal{E}'$. Since

$$(U_1 \times V_1) \cap (U_2 \times V_2) = (U_1 \cap U_2) \times (V_1 \cap V_2),$$

it follows that $\mathcal{F}$ is also a π-system and, therefore, $\mathcal{F}$ is a σ-algebra by Theorem 1.43. Since the set of rectangles $U \times V$ with $U \in \mathcal{E}$ and $V \in \mathcal{E}'$ is included in $\mathcal{F}$, it follows that $\mathcal{F} = \mathcal{E} \times \mathcal{E}'$, so f_E is measurable for every $E \in \mathcal{E} \times \mathcal{E}'$.

Suppose now that m is σ-finite. Let (D_n) be a sequence of pairwise disjoint sets in $\mathcal{E}'$ such that $\bigcup_{n \in \mathbb{N}} D_n = T$ and $m'(D_n)$ is finite for $n \in \mathbb{N}$. Define a finite measure $m_n(B) = m(B \cap D_n)$ for $B \in \mathcal{E}'$. By the first part of the argument, the function $f_{E,n}$ defined by $f_{E,n}(s) = m_n(E_s \cap D_n)$ is $\mathcal{E}$-measurable. Since $f_E(s) = \sum_{n \in \mathbb{N}} f_{E,n}(s)$, it follows that f_E is measurable. The treatment for g_E is similar. $\qquad\square$

Suppose that $(S, \mathcal{E}, m)$ and $(T, \mathcal{E}', m')$ are two measure spaces and $h : S \times T \longrightarrow \hat{\mathbb{R}}$. Then, for each $s \in S$ there exists a function $h(s, \cdot) : T \longrightarrow \hat{\mathbb{R}}$, such $h(s, \cdot)(t) = h(s, t)$. If the function $h(s, \cdot)$ is m'-integrable, its m'-integral is denoted by $\int_T h(s, \cdot) \, dm'$ or by $\int_T h(s, t) \, dm'(t)$. Similarly, for each $t \in T$ there exists a function $h(\cdot, t) : S \longrightarrow \hat{\mathbb{R}}$. If $h(\cdot, t)$ is m-integrable, its m-integral is denoted by $\int_S h(\cdot, t) \, dm$ or by $\int_S h(s, t) \, dm(s)$. The symbol

s in $\int_S h(s,t)\ dm(s)$ or the symbol t in $\int_T h(s,t)\ dm'(t)$ designates the component that is involved in the integration process.

Theorem 8.66. *Let $(S, \mathcal{E}, m)$ and $(T, \mathcal{E}', m')$ be two σ-finite measure spaces. There is a unique measure $m \times m'$ on the σ-algebra $\mathcal{E} \times \mathcal{E}'$ such that $(m \times m')(A \times B) = m(A)m'(B)$ for $A \in \mathcal{E}$ and $B \in \mathcal{E}'$.*
If $E \in \mathcal{E} \times E'$ we have

$$(m \times m')(E) = \int_S m(E_s)\ dm(s) = \int_T m(E^t)\ dm'(t).$$

Proof. Theorem 8.65 implies that the functions $f_E : S \longrightarrow \hat{\mathbb{R}}$ and $g_E : T \longrightarrow \hat{\mathbb{R}}$ defined by $f_E(s) = m'(E_s)$ and $g_E(t) = m(E^t)$ are Borel-measurable. This allows us to define the functions $(m \times m')_1$ and $(m \times m')_2$ on $\mathcal{E} \times \mathcal{E}'$ as

$$(m \times m')_1(E) = \int_T m(E^t)\ dm'(t),$$

$$(m \times m')_2(E) = \int_S m'(E_s)\ dm(s).$$

It is clear that

$$(m \times m')_1(\emptyset) = (m \times m')_2(\emptyset) = 0.$$

Let (E_n) be a sequence of pairwise disjoint sets in $\mathcal{E} \times \mathcal{E}'$ and let $E = \bigcup_{n \in \mathbb{N}} E_n$. For $t \in T$, (E_n^t) is a sequence of pairwise disjoint sets in $\mathcal{E}$ such that $E^t = \bigcup E_n^t$ and $m(E^t) = \sum_{n \in \mathbb{N}} m(E_n^t)$. By Beppo Levi's Theorem (Theorem 8.39), we have:

$$(m \times m')_1(E) = \int_T m(E^t)\ dm'(t),$$

$$= \sum_{n \in \mathbb{N}} \int_T m'(E_n^t)\ dm'(t),$$

$$= \sum_{n \in \mathbb{N}} (m \times m')_1(E_n),$$

which means that $(m \times m')_1$ is σ-additive.

Similarly, $(m \times m')_2$ is σ-additive. Furthermore,

$$(m \times m)_1(U \times V) = m(U)m'(V) = (m \times m')_2(U \times V).$$

for $U \in \mathcal{E}$ and $V \in \mathcal{E}'$. Thus, $(m \times m')_1$ and $(m \times m')_2$ are measures on $\mathcal{E} \times \mathcal{E}'$.

The uniqueness of $m \times m'$ follows from Corollary 7.8. Thus, $(m \times m')_1 = (m \times m')_2$, which yields the equality of the theorem. $\qquad\square$

The assumption of σ-finiteness for m and m' is essential.

The next two theorems establish sufficient conditions for the existence of integrals of the form $\int_{S \times T} f \, d(m \times m')$ as iterated integrals of the sections of the function f. The first result, known as Tonelli's Theorem shows that this is always possible for non-negative functions (and possibly obtain ∞ as a value). The second result known as Fubini's Theorem applies to more general real-valued functions but requires the iterated integrals to be finite.

Theorem 8.67. (Tonelli's[1] Theorem) *Let $(S, \mathcal{E}, m)$ and $(T, \mathcal{E}', m')$ be two σ-finite measure spaces and let $f : S \times T \longrightarrow \hat{\mathbb{R}}_{\geqslant 0}$ be an $(S \times T)$-measurable function.*

The function $\phi : S \longrightarrow \hat{\mathbb{R}}_{\geqslant 0}$ defined by $\phi(s) = \int_T f_s \, dm'(t)$ is $\mathcal{E}'$-measurable and the function $\psi : T \longrightarrow \hat{\mathbb{R}}_{\geqslant 0}$ defined as $\psi(t) = \int_S f^t \, dm(s)$ is $\mathcal{E}$-measurable. Furthermore, we have:

$$\int_{S \times T} f \, d(m \times m') = \int_T \left(\int_S f^t \, dm(s) \right) dm'(t) = \int_S \left(\int_T f_s \, dm'(t) \right) dm(s)$$

Proof. Let $E \in \mathcal{E} \times \mathcal{E}'$. The sections $(1_E)_s$ and $(1_E)^t$ of its characteristic function 1_E are equal to the characteristic functions 1_{E_s} and 1_{E^t}, respectively. Thus, for every $s \in S$ and $t \in T$ we have:

$$\int_T 1_{E_s} \, dm'(t) = m'(E_s) \text{ and } \int_S 1_{E^t} \, dm(s) = m(E^t).$$

Furthermore,

$$\int_S \left(\int_T 1_{E_s} \, dm'(t) \right) dm(s) = \int_T \left(\int_S 1_{E^t} \, dm(s) \right) dm'(t)$$

$$= \int_{S \times T} 1_E \, d(m \times m')$$

because $\int_S \left(\int_T 1_{E_s} \, dm'(t) \right) dm(s) = \int_S m'(E_s) \, dm(s) = (m \times m')(E) = \int_{S \times T} 1_E \, d(m \times m')$ and

$$\int_T \left(\int_S 1_{E^t} \, dm(s) \right) dm'(t) = \int_T m(E^t) \, dm(t) = (m \times m')(E)$$

$$= \int_{S \times T} 1_E \, d(m \times m').$$

---

[1]Leonida Tonelli was born on April 19th 1885 in Gallipoli, Apulia, Italy and died on March 12th 1946 in Pisa. Tonelli studied at the University of Bologna with Cesare Arzelà and Salvatore Pincherle, where he obtained his doctorate in 1907. He taught at the Universities of Cagliari, Parma, Bologna and, after 1930 ar the University of Pisa. Tonelli has been a member of Accademia Nazionale dei Lincei. His contribution are in the calculus of variations, integration theory, and is considered one of the founders of the modern theory of functions of real variables.

This shows that the theorem holds for characteristic functions, and, therefore, for simple measurable functions on $\mathcal{E} \times \mathcal{E}'$. This, in turn, imply that the theorem holds for arbitrary non-negative measurable functions.   □

If positivity and measurability of f is replaced by $m \times m'$-integrability we obtain a variant of the previous result.

Theorem 8.68. (Fubini's[2] Theorem) *Let $(S, \mathcal{E}, m)$ and $(T, \mathcal{E}', m')$ be two σ-finite measure spaces and let $f : S \times T \longrightarrow \hat{\mathbb{R}}$ be an $(S \times T)$-measurable function that is $m \times m'$-integrable.*

The section f_s is m'-integrable a.e. for $s \in S$ and f^t is m-integrable a.e. for $t \in T$. Furthermore, the functions $I_f : S \longrightarrow \mathbb{R}$ and $J_f : T \longrightarrow \mathbb{R}$ defined by:

$$I_f(s) = \begin{cases} \displaystyle\int_T f_s \, dm' & \textit{if } f_s \textit{ is } m'\textit{-integrable,} \\ 0 & \textit{otherwise} \end{cases}$$

and

$$J_f(t) = \begin{cases} \displaystyle\int_S f^t \, dm(s) & \textit{if } f^t \textit{ is } m\textit{-integrable,} \\ 0 & \textit{otherwise} \end{cases}$$

belong to $\mathcal{L}^1(S, \mathcal{E}, m)$ and $\mathcal{L}^1(T, \mathcal{E}', m')$ respectively and we have:

$$\int_{S \times T} f \, d(m \times m') = \int_S I_f \, dm = \int_T J_f \, dm'.$$

Proof.   The section f_s and its positive and its negative part $(f^+)_s, (f^-)_s$ of f, are measurable and, therefore, the functions $\phi : S \longrightarrow \hat{\mathbb{R}}$ and $\psi : S \longrightarrow \hat{\mathbb{R}}$ defined by $\phi(s) = \int (f^+)_s \, dm'$ and $\psi(s) = \int (f^-)_s \, dm'$ are $\mathcal{E}$-measurable and m-integrable. Thus, by Theorem 8.17, they are finite almost everywhere in the sense of the measure m.

Let

$$Z = \{s \in S \mid \phi(s) = \infty \text{ or } \psi(s) = \infty\}.$$

---

[2]Guido Fubini was born on January 19th 1879 in Venice, Italy. In 1896 Fubini began his studies at Scuola Normale Superiore di Pisa where he studies with Ulisse Dini and Luigi Bianchi. He defended his doctoral thesis in 1900 and began teaching at the University of Catania in Sicily, moved to the University of Genoa, and in 1908 he moved to the Politecnico in Turin, and then the University of Turin. After Mussolini adopted racial policies in 1939, Fubini, who was Jewish, accepted an invitation by Princeton University to teach there; he died in New York City on June 6th 1943 in New York. Fubini's contributions are in functional analysis, complex analysis, and the calculus of variations.

We have $Z \in \mathcal{E}$ and

$$I_f(s) = \begin{cases} \int_T (f^+)_s \, dm' - \int_T (f^-)_s \, dm' & \text{if } s \notin Z, \\ 0 & \text{if } s \in Z. \end{cases}$$

Therefore, I_f is integrable.

By Tonneli's Theorem (Theorem 8.67) we have:

$$\int f \, d(m \times m') = \int f^+ \, d(m \times m') - \int f^- \, d(m \times m')$$

$$= \int \left(\int (f^+)_s \, dm' \right) dm(s) - \int \left(\int (f^+)_s \, dm' \right) dm(s)$$

$$= \int I_f \, dm.$$

Similar arguments work for f^t and J_f. $\qquad\qquad \square$

Lebesgue measurable functions need to be defined a.e. Two functions which are equal a.e. will be identified.

Example 8.9. Note that

$$\int_0^t e^{-ax} \sin x \, dx = \frac{1}{1+a^2} \left(1 - e^{-at}(a \sin t + \cos t) \right).$$

Since

$$\int_0^t \left(\int_0^\infty |e^{-ax} \sin x| \, da \right) dx = \int_0^t |\sin x| \frac{1}{x} \, dx \leqslant t < \infty.$$

Fubini's Theorem can be applied for $x \in (0,t)$ and $a \in (0,\infty)$ and this yields:

$$\int_0^t \frac{\sin x}{x} \, dx = \int_0^t \sin x \left(\int_0^\infty e^{-ax} \, da \right) dx$$

$$= \int_0^\infty \left(\int_0^t e^{-ax} \sin x \, dx \right) da$$

$$= \int_0^\infty \frac{1}{1+a^2} \, da - \int_0^\infty \frac{e^{-at}}{1+a^2} (a \sin t + \cos t) \, da$$

$$= \frac{\pi}{2} - \int_0^\infty \frac{e^{-at}}{1+a^2} (a \sin t + \cos t) \, da.$$

If we apply the change of variable $a = \frac{s}{t}$ the last integral becomes

$$\int_0^\infty \frac{e^{-st^2}}{1+s^2} (a \sin t + \cos t) \, da = \int_0^\infty e^{-s} \frac{s \sin t + t \cos t}{s^2 + t^2} \, ds = 0,$$

hence $\int_0^\infty \frac{\sin x}{x} \, dx = \frac{\pi}{2}$.

8.8   The Riesz-Markov-Kakutani Theorem

In this section we present a Riesz's representation result for a class of linear functionals defined on a certain linear space of continuous functions. This theorem is known also as the Riesz-Markov[3]-Kakutani[4] theorem or the RMK theorem, and is named after the discover of the result and the mathematicians who gave important extensions of this result.

We follow the outline of the proof given in [114]. The proof contains a series of lemmas that use consistent notations introduced gradually.

Recall that for a topological space $(S, \mathcal{O})$ we defined $\mathcal{F}_c(S, \mathcal{O})$ as the set of continuous functions $f : S \longrightarrow \mathbb{R}$ such that $supp(f)$ is a compact set. Also, for an open set V and a compact set C we defined the families of functions:

$$\mathcal{F}_{c,V}(S, \mathcal{O}) = \{f \in \mathcal{F}_c(S, \mathcal{O}) \mid f(x) \in [0, 1] \text{ for } x \in S$$
$$\text{and } supp(f) \subseteq V\},$$
$$\mathcal{F}_{C,c}(S, \mathcal{O}) = \{f \in \mathcal{F}_c(S, \mathcal{O}) \mid f(x) \in [0, 1] \text{ for } x \in S$$
$$\text{and } f(x) = 1 \text{ for } x \in C\}.$$

Definition 8.16. A *positive linear functional* is a linear functional ℓ defined on $\mathcal{F}_c(S, \mathcal{O})$ such that $f \geqslant 0$ implies $\ell(f) > 0$.

Lemma 8.5. *Let $(S, \mathcal{O})$ be a locally compact topological space and let ℓ be a positive linear functional on the linear space $\mathcal{F}_c(S, \mathcal{O})$.*

If $\mathcal{E}$ is a σ-algebra $\mathcal{E}$ on S such that $\mathbb{B}(S) \subseteq \mathcal{E}$, then there exists at most one measure m on $\mathcal{E}$ such that:

(i) *$m(C)$ is finite for every compact subset C of S;*
(ii) *we have $\ell(f) = \int_S f \, dm$ for $f \in \mathcal{F}_c(S, \mathcal{O})$;*
(iii) *for every $E \in \mathcal{E}$ we have*

---

[3]A. A. Markov was born on June 14th, 1856 and died on July 20th was a Russian mathematician best known for his work on stochastic processes. A primary subject of his research later became known as Markov chains and Markov processes. Markov studied at Petersburg University, where among his professors was Chebyshev. Markov his got his doctorate in 1885 and became a professor in 1894. He extended Riesz' Theoremto the case of bounded positive real functional.

[4]Shizuo Kakutani was born on August 28, 1911 in Osaka and died on August 17, 2004 in New Haven, Connecticut. Kakutani was a Japanese-American mathematician, best known for his contributions to functional analysis. Kakutani attended Tohoku University in Sendai and spent two years at the Institute for Advanced Study in Princeton. He received his Ph.D. in 1941 from Osaka University. After the war he returned to the Institute for Advanced Study in 1948, and was appointed a professor at Yale in 1949. He extended Riesz' theorem to locally compact spaces.

$$m(E) = \inf\{m(V) \mid E \subseteq V, V \in \mathcal{O}\};$$

(iv) *we have*

$$m(E) = \sup\{m(C) \mid C \subseteq E, C \text{ is compact}\},$$

where E is an open set, or a member of $\mathcal{E}$ with $m(E) < \infty$.

Proof. Let m_1 and m_2 be two measures such that $m_1(C) = m_2(C)$ for all compact subsets of S that belong to $\mathcal{E}$.

Let C be a compact subset such that $C \in \mathcal{E}$ and let $\epsilon > 0$. Since $m_2(C) = \inf\{m_2(V) \mid C \subseteq V, V \in \mathcal{O}\}$ and $m_2(C)$ is finite, it follows that there exists an open set V such that $m_2(V) < m_2(C) + \epsilon$. By Uryson's Lemma for locally compact spaces (Theorem 4.110) there exists a continuous function $f \in \mathcal{F}_{c,V}(S, calo) \cap \mathcal{F}_{C,c}(S, \mathcal{O})$. Therefore,

$$m_1(C) = \int_S 1_C \, dm_1 \leqslant \int_S f \, dm_1 = \ell(f)$$
$$= \int_S f \, dm_2 \leqslant \int_S 1_V \, dm_2 = m_2(V) < m_2(C) + \epsilon,$$

hence $m_1(C) \leqslant m_2(C)$. By swapping m_1 and m_2 we obtain the reverse inequality, hence m_1 and m_2 are equal on all compact subsets of $\mathcal{E}$. By (iv) we have $m_1(E) = m_2(E)$ for every $E \in \mathcal{E}$, so $m_1 = m_2$. $\square$

Let $(S, \mathcal{O})$ be a locally compact topological space and let ℓ be a positive linear functional on $\mathcal{F}_c(S, \mathcal{O})$. For $V \in \mathcal{O}$ define $m_\ell(V)$ as

$$m_\ell(V) = \sup\{\ell(f) \mid f \in \mathcal{F}_{c,V}(S, \mathcal{O})\}. \tag{8.21}$$

If $V_1 \subseteq V_2$ we have $m_\ell(V_1) \leqslant m_\ell(V_2)$. The definition of m_ℓ is extended to $\mathcal{P}(S)$ as

$$m_\ell(E) = \inf\{m_\ell(V) \mid E \subseteq V, V \in \mathcal{O}\} \tag{8.22}$$

for every subset E of S.

Let $\tilde{\mathcal{E}}$ be the set of all subsets E of S such that $m_\ell(E)$ is finite and $m_\ell(E) = \sup\{m_\ell(C) \mid C \subseteq E \text{ and } C \text{ is compact}\}$. Define $\mathcal{E}$ as

$$\mathcal{E} = \{E \mid E \subseteq S, E \cap C \in \tilde{\mathcal{E}} \text{ for every compact subset } C\}. \tag{8.23}$$

Lemma 8.6. *The function m_ℓ defined by equality (8.22) is monotonic and $m_\ell(E) = 0$ implies $E \in \tilde{\mathcal{E}}$.*

Proof. Suppose that $E_1 \subseteq E_2$. Then,

$$\{V \in \mathcal{O} \mid E_2 \subseteq V\} \subseteq \{V \in \mathcal{O} \mid E_1 \subseteq V\},$$

which implies

$$\inf\{m_\ell(V) \in \mathcal{O} \mid E_1 \subseteq V\} \leqslant \{m_\ell(V) \in \mathcal{O} \mid E_2 \subseteq V\},$$

which shows that m is monotonic.

If $m_\ell(E) = 0$ it is immediate that $E \in \tilde{\mathcal{E}}$ and $E \in \mathcal{E}$. $\square$

The positive linear functional ℓ is monotonic because for $f, g \in \mathcal{F}_c(S, \mathcal{O})$ such that $f \leqslant g$ we have $g - f \geqslant 0$, hence $\ell(g) = \ell(f) + \ell(g - f) \geqslant \ell(f)$.

Note that m_ℓ was defined for all subsets of S. This allows us to formulate the following preliminary result:

Lemma 8.7. *The function m_ℓ defined by equality (8.22) is subadditive on $\mathcal{P}(S)$, that is, if $E_1, \dots, E_n, \dots$ are subsets of S, then $m_\ell \left(\bigcup_{i=1}^\infty E_i \right) \leqslant \sum_{i=1}^\infty m_\ell(E_i)$.*

Proof. We prove by induction on $n \geqslant 2$ that if $V_1, \dots, V_n$ are open sets, and g is a function such that $0 \leqslant g(x) \leqslant 1$ and $supp(g) \subseteq \bigcup_{i=1}^n V_i$, then $\ell(g) \leqslant \sum_{i=1}^n m_\ell(V_i)$.

For the base case, $n = 2$, let $V_1, V_2 \in \mathcal{O}$ and let g be a function such that $0 \leqslant g(x) \leqslant 1$ and $supp(g) \subseteq V_1 \cup V_2$. An application of the Partition of Unity Theorem (Theorem 4.111) to the compact set $supp(g)$ implies the existence of two continuous functions h_1, h_2 in $\mathcal{F}_c(S, \mathcal{O})$ such that $h_1(x), h_2(x) \in [0, 1]$, $supp(h_1) \subseteq V_1$, $supp(h_2) \subseteq V_2$, and $h_1(x) + h_2(x) = 1$ for $x \in supp(g)$. Therefore, $g = h_1 \cdot g + h_2 \cdot g$, hence $supp(h_1 \cdot g) \subseteq V_1$, $supp(h_2 \cdot g) \subseteq V_2$ and, therefore, $\ell(g) = \ell(h_1 \cdot g) + \ell(h_2 \cdot g) \leqslant m_\ell(V_1) + m_\ell(V_2)$. Since this inequality holds for every g such that $g(x) \in [0, 1]$ and $supp(g) \subseteq V_1 \cup V_2$ it follows that $m_\ell(V_1 \cup V_2) \leqslant m_\ell(V_1) + m_\ell(V_2)$.

If there exists E_i such that $m_\ell(E_i) = \infty$, the inequality of the lemma obviously holds. Suppose therefore that $m_\ell(E_1), \dots, m_\ell(E_n)$ are finite. Since $m_\ell(E) = \inf\{m_\ell(V) \mid E \subseteq V \text{ and } V \in \mathcal{O}\}$, there exist open sets $V_1, \dots, V_n$ such that $m_\ell(V_i) < m_\ell(E_i) + \frac{\epsilon}{2^i}$ for $1 \leqslant i \leqslant n$. Let V be the open set $V = \bigcup_{n=1}^\infty V_i$ and let f be a function such that $f(x) \in [0, 1]$ for $x \in S$ and $supp(f) \subseteq V$. Since $supp(f)$ is a compact set, there exists n such that $supp(f) \subseteq V_1 \cup \dots \cup V_n$. By the induction hypothesis,

$$\ell(f) \leqslant m_\ell(V_1 \cup \dots \cup V_n) \leqslant m_\ell(V_1) + \dots + m_\ell(V_n) \leqslant \sum_{i=1}^\infty m_\ell(V_i) + \epsilon.$$

Since this holds for every f such that $f(x) \in [0, 1]$ and $supp(f) \subseteq V$ and $\bigcup_{n=1}^\infty E_i \subseteq V$, it follows that

$$m_\ell \left(\bigcup_{i=1}^\infty E_i \right) \leqslant m_\ell(V) \leqslant \sum_{i=1}^\infty m_\ell(E_i) + \epsilon,$$

which completes the argument. $\qquad \square$

Lemma 8.8. *Let C be a compact subset of a locally compact topological space $(S, \mathcal{O})$. We have $C \in \tilde{\mathcal{E}}$ and*

$$m_\ell(C) = \inf\{\ell(f) \mid f \in \mathcal{F}_{C,c}(S, \mathcal{O})\}.$$

Proof. Let $f \in \mathcal{F}_{C,c}(S,\mathcal{O})\}$ and let $a \in (0,1)$. The set $V_a = \{x \mid f(x) > a\} = f^{-1}(a, \infty)$ is open and $C \subseteq V_a$ because $f(x) = 1$ for $x \in C$.

If $g \in \mathcal{F}_{c,V_a}$, then $ag \leqslant f$, hence

$$m_\ell(C) \leqslant m_\ell(V_a) = \sum \{\ell(g) \mid g \in \mathcal{F}_{c,V_a}(S,\mathcal{O})\} \leqslant \frac{1}{a}\ell(f).$$

When $a \to 1$ we have $m_\ell(C) \leqslant \ell(f)$, hence $m_\ell(C)$ is finite. Thus, $C \in \tilde{\mathcal{E}}$.

For $\epsilon > 0$ there exists an open set V such that $C \subseteq V$ and $m_\ell(V) < m_\ell(C) + \epsilon$. By Uryson's Lemma for locally compact spaces, there exists f in $\mathcal{F}_{C,c}(S,\mathcal{O}) \cap \mathcal{F}_{c,V}(S,\mathcal{O})$. Thus, $\ell(f) \leqslant m_\ell(V) < m_\ell(C) + \epsilon$. This gives the equality of the lemma. $\qquad\square$

Let $f \in \mathcal{F}_c(S,\mathcal{O})$. Since $supp(f)$ is a compact set, by the last lemma we have:

$$m_\ell(supp(f)) = \inf\{\ell(f) \mid f \in \mathcal{F}_{supp(f),c}(S,\mathcal{O}). \qquad (8.24)$$

Lemma 8.9. *Let $(S,\mathcal{O})$ be a locally compact topological space, ℓ be a positive linear functional on $\mathcal{F}_c(S,\mathcal{O})$. For every open set V we have:*

$$m_\ell(V) = \sup\{m_\ell(C) \mid C \subseteq V \text{ and } C \text{is compact}\}.$$

Proof. The extended definition of m_ℓ in equality (8.21), for a compact set C we have $m_\ell(C) = \inf\{m_\ell(V) \mid E \subseteq V, V \in \mathcal{O}\}$. Thus, for every compact set C included in an open set V we have $m_\ell(C) \leqslant m_\ell(V)$. This entails the inequality

$$\sup\{m_\ell(C) \mid C \subseteq V \text{and} C \text{is compact}\} \leqslant m_\ell(V),$$

hence $m_\ell(V)$ is an upper bound of the set $\{m_\ell(C) \mid C \subseteq V$ and C is compact$\}$.

To prove the reverse inequality, we need to show that there exists a compact set C included in V such that $m_\ell(V) \leqslant m_\ell(C)$.

Let a be a number such that $a < m_\ell(V) = \sup\{\ell(f) \mid f \in \mathcal{F}_{c,V}(S,\mathcal{O})\}$. To prove that $m_\ell(V) = \sup\{m_\ell(C) \mid C \subseteq V$ and C is compact$\}$, by Supplement 16 of Chapter 1 it suffices to show that

$$a \leqslant \sup\{m_\ell(C) \mid C \subseteq V \text{ and } C \text{is compact}\}.$$

By the definition of $m_\ell(V)$ there exists $f \in \mathcal{F}_{c,V}(S,\mathcal{O})$ such that $a < \ell(f)$.

If W is an open set such that $supp(f) \subseteq W$, then $f \in \mathcal{F}_{c,W}(S,\mathcal{O})$, hence $\ell(f) \leqslant m_\ell(W)$, because $m_\ell(W) = \sup\{\ell(f) \mid f \in \mathcal{F}_{c,W}(S,\mathcal{O})\}$. Thus, $\ell(f) \leqslant m_\ell(supp(f))$. The set $supp(f)$ is a compact set, $supp(f) \subseteq V$ and $a < m_\ell(supp(f))$, which implies the reverse inequality. $\qquad\square$

The previous lemma shows that $\tilde{\mathcal{E}}$ contains every open set V such that $m_\ell(V)$ is finite.

Lemma 8.10. *Let $(E_n)_{n \geqslant 1}$ be a sequence of pairwise disjoint sets in $\tilde{\mathcal{E}}$ and let $E = \bigcup_{n \geqslant 1} E_n$. We have*

$$m_\ell(E) = \sum_{n=1}^{\infty} m_\ell(E_n).$$

If $m_\ell(E)$ is finite, then $E \in \tilde{\mathcal{E}}$.

Proof. Let C_1, C_2 be two disjoint compact subsets of S. Corollary 4.24, there exists a function $f \in \mathcal{F}$ such that $f(x) = 1$ for $x \in C_1$, $f(x) = 0$ for $x \in C_2$ and $f(x) \in [0,1]$ for $x \in S$. By Lemma 8.8 for every $\epsilon > 0$ there exists $g \in \mathcal{F}_{C_1 \cup C_2, c}(S, \mathcal{O})$ such that $\ell(g) < m_\ell(C_1 \cup C_2) + \epsilon$.

Note that $fg \in \mathcal{F}_{C_1, c}(S, \mathcal{O})$ and $(1 - f)g \in \mathcal{F}_{C_2, c}(S, \mathcal{O})$. Since ℓ is linear we have

$$m_\ell(C_1) + m_\ell(C_2) \leqslant \ell(fg) + \ell(g - fg) = \ell(g) < m_\ell(C_1 \cup C_2) + \epsilon.$$

By Lemma 8.7, we have $m_\ell(C_1 \cup C_2) = m_\ell(C_1) + m_\ell(C_2)$.

If $m_\ell(E)$ is infinite, the equality follows from Lemma 8.7.

Suppose now that $m_\ell(E)$ is finite and let ϵ be a positive number. Since $E_i \in \tilde{\mathcal{E}}$ there are compact subsets D_i of E_i with $m_\ell(D_i) > m_\ell(E_i) - \frac{\epsilon}{2^i}$. If $C_i = D_1 \cup \cdots \cup D_i$ we have

$$m_\ell(E) \geqslant m_\ell(C_n) = \sum_{i=1}^{n} m_\ell(D_i) > \sum_{i=1}^{n} m_\ell(E_i) - \epsilon.$$

Since this holds for every $n \in \mathbb{N}$ and $\epsilon > 0$, $m_\ell(E) \geqslant \sum_{n=1}^{\infty} m_\ell(E_n)$ and the equality follows from Lemma 8.7.

If $m_\ell(E)$ is finite and $\epsilon > 0$, there exists N such that $m_\ell(E) < \sum_{i=1}^{N} m_\ell(E_i) + \epsilon$, so $m_\ell(E) \leqslant m_\ell(C_N) + 2\epsilon$, hence $E \in \tilde{\mathcal{E}}$. $\qquad\square$

Lemma 8.11. *Let $E \in \tilde{\mathcal{E}}$ and $\epsilon > 0$. There exist a compact set C and an open set V such that $C \subseteq E \subseteq V$ and $m_\ell(V - C) < \epsilon$.*

Proof. Since $E \in \tilde{\mathcal{E}}$, $m_\ell(E) = \sup\{m_\ell(C) \mid C$ is compact and $C \subseteq E\}$ and $m_\ell(E)$ is finite. Therefore, there exists a compact set C such that $m_\ell(E) < m_\ell(C) + \frac{\epsilon}{2}$.

Since we have $m_\ell(E) = \inf\{m_\ell(V) \mid V \in \mathcal{O}$ and $E \subseteq V\}$, there exists an open set V such that $m_\ell(V) - \frac{\epsilon}{2} < m_\ell(E)$.

Since $V - C$ is an open set, we have $V - C \in \tilde{\mathcal{E}}$ by Lemma 8.9. Therefore,

$$m_\ell(C) + m_\ell(V - C) = m_\ell(V) < m_\ell(C) + \epsilon,$$

by Lemma 8.8. $\qquad\square$

Lemma 8.12. *If* $A, B \in \tilde{\mathcal{E}}$, *then* $A - B, A \cup B$, *and* $A \cap B$ *belong to* $\tilde{\mathcal{E}}$.

Proof. By Lemma 8.11, there exists compact sets C_1, C_2 and open sets V_1, V_2 such that $C_1 \subseteq A \subseteq V_1$, $m_\ell(V_1 - C_1) < \epsilon$, and $C_2 \subseteq B \subseteq V_2$, $m_\ell(V_2 - C_2) < \epsilon$. Since

$$A - B \subseteq V_1 - C_2 \subseteq (V_1 - C_1) \cup (C_1 - V_2) \cup (V_2 - C_2),$$

we have, by the subadditivity of m_ℓ shown in Lemma 8.7:

$$m_\ell(A - B) \leqslant \epsilon + m_\ell(C_1 - V_2) + \epsilon.$$

Since $C_1 - V_2$ is a compact subset of $A - B$ we have $A - B \in \tilde{\mathcal{E}}$ by Lemma 8.9.

Since $A \cup B = (A - B) \cup B$, $A \cup B \in \tilde{\mathcal{E}}$ by Lemma 8.10. $A \cap B \in \tilde{\mathcal{E}}$ because $A \cap B = A - (A - B)$. $\square$

Lemma 8.13. *Let* $(S, \mathcal{O})$ *be a topological space. The collection* $\mathcal{E}$ *defined by equality (8.23) is a* σ-*algebra such that* $\mathbb{B}(S, \mathcal{O}) \subseteq \mathcal{E}$.

Proof. Let $E \in \mathcal{E}$. Then $E \cap C \in \tilde{\mathcal{E}}$ for every compact subset C of S. This implies

$$(S - E) \cap C = C - (E \cap C),$$

hence $S - E$ is the difference of two sets in $\tilde{\mathcal{E}}$ because $C \in \tilde{\mathcal{E}}$ by Lemma 8.8. Therefore, $(S - E) \cap C \in \tilde{\mathcal{E}}$, hence $E \in \mathcal{E}$ implies $\overline{E} = S - E \in \mathcal{E}$.

Suppose that $(A_i)_{i \geqslant 1}$ is a sequence of sets in $\mathcal{E}$ and let $A = \bigcup_{i \geqslant 1} A_i$. Define the sequence of sets $(B_i)_{i \geqslant 1}$ as

$$B_1 = A_1 \cap C,$$
$$B_n = (A_n \cap c) - (B_1 \cup \cdots \cup B_{n-1}) \text{ for } n \geqslant 2.$$

The sets in the sequence $(B_i)_{i \geqslant 1}$ are disjoint sets in $\tilde{\mathcal{E}}$ by Lemma 8.12. Also, $A \cap C = \bigcup_{n \geqslant 1} B_n$. Therefore, $A \cap C \in \tilde{\mathcal{E}}$ by Lemma 8.10, hence $A \in \mathcal{E}$.

If H is closed, then $H \cap C$ is compact, hence $H \cap C \in \tilde{\mathcal{E}}$, so $H \in \mathcal{E}$. Therefore $S \in \mathcal{E}$.

Since $\mathcal{E}$ is a σ-algebra in S that contains all closed subsets of S, it follows that $\mathcal{E}$ contains $\mathbb{B}(S, \mathcal{O})$. $\square$

Lemma 8.14. *The collection* $\tilde{\mathcal{E}}$ *equals the collection of sets* E *in* $\mathcal{E}$ *such that* $m_\ell(E)$ *is finite.*

Proof. Let $E \in \tilde{\mathcal{E}}$. By Lemma 8.8, for each compact set C we have $C \in \tilde{\mathcal{E}}$, so $E \cap C \in \tilde{\mathcal{E}}$ by Lemma 8.12. Therefore, $E \in \mathcal{E}$.

Suppose now that $E \in \mathcal{E}$ and $m_\ell(E)$ is finite. There exists an open set V such that $C \subseteq V$ and $m_\ell(V)$ is finite. By Lemmas 8.9 and 8.11, there exists a compact set C such that $C \subseteq V$ and $m_\ell(V - C) < \epsilon$. Since $E \cap C \in \tilde{\mathcal{E}}$, for $\epsilon > 0$ there is a compact set C_1 such that $C_1 \subseteq E \cap C$ with $m_\ell(E \cap C) < m_\ell(C_1) + \epsilon$. Since $E \subseteq (E \cap C) \cup (V - K)$, it follows that $m_{ell}(E) \leqslant m_{ell}(E \cap C) + m_{ell}(V - C) < m_{ell}(C_1) + 2\epsilon$, hence $E \in \tilde{\mathcal{E}}$. $\square$

Theorem 8.69. (The Riesz-Markov-Kakutani Theorem) *Let $(S, \mathcal{O})$ be a locally compact space, and let ℓ be a positive linear functional on $\mathcal{F}_c(S, \mathcal{O})$. There exists a measurable space $(S, \mathcal{E})$ such that $\mathbb{B}(S, \mathcal{O}) \subseteq \mathcal{E}$ and a unique positive measure m_ℓ on $\mathcal{E}$ such that*

(i) $\ell(f) = \int_S f \, dm_\ell$;

(ii) $m_\ell(C)$ *is finite for every compact subset of S;*

(iii) *for every $E \in \mathcal{E}$ we have $m_\ell(E) = \inf\{m_\ell(V) \mid E \subseteq V \text{ and } V \in \mathcal{O}\}$;*

(iv) *for every $E \in \mathcal{E}$ such that $m_\ell(E)$ is finite, and for every E that is open we have $m_\ell(E) = \sup\{m_\ell(C) \mid C \subseteq E \text{ and } C \text{ is compact }\}$;*

(v) *the measure space $(S, \mathcal{E}, m_\ell)$ is complete.*

Proof.   Note that m_ℓ is a measure on $\mathcal{E}$ by Lemmas 8.10 and 8.14. To prove (i) it suffices to prove that for real-valued functions we have $\ell(f) \leqslant \int_S f \, dm_\ell$. Indeed, if this is the case, we also have

$$-\ell(f) = \ell(-f) \leqslant \int_S (-f) \, dm_\ell = -\int_S f \, dm_\ell,$$

which implies $\ell(f) \geqslant \int_S f \, dm_\ell$. Therefore, if $\ell(f) \leqslant \int_S f \, dm_\ell$ holds, then $\ell(f) = \int_S f \, dm_\ell$.

Let $f \in \mathcal{F}_c(S, \mathcal{O})$ and let $[a, b]$ be an interval such that $supp(f) \subseteq [a, b]$. Choose $y_0, y_1, \ldots, y_n$ such that $y - 0 = a$, $y_0 < y_1 < \cdots < y_{n-1} < y_n$, and $y_n = b$, and let $E_i = \{x \mid y_{i-1} < f(x) \leqslant y_i\} \cap supp(f)$ for $1 \leqslant i \leqslant n - 1$. Since f is continuous, f is Borel measurable, so the sets $E_1, \ldots, E_n$ are disjoint Borel sets that partition $supp(f)$. Let V_i be open sets such that $E_i \subseteq V_i$ and $m_\ell(V_i) < m_\ell(E_i) + \frac{\epsilon}{n}$ and $f(x) < y_i + \epsilon$ for $x \in V_i$ and for $1 \leqslant i \leqslant n$. By the Partition of Unity Theorem, there are $h_i \in \mathcal{F}_{c, V_i}(S, \mathcal{O})$ such that $\sum h_i = 1$, hence $f = \sum_i h_i f$. By Lemma 8.8 we have $m_\ell(supp(f)) < \ell\left(\sum_i h_i\right) = \sum_i \ell(h_i)$.

Since $h_i f \leqslant (y_i + \epsilon) h_i$ and $y_i - \epsilon < f(x)$ when $x \in E_i$, we have

$$\ell(f) = \sum_{i=1}^{n} \ell(h_i f) \leqslant \sum_{i=1}^{n} (y_i + \epsilon) \ell(h_i)$$

$$= \sum_{i=1}^{n} (|a| + y + i + \epsilon) \ell(h_i) - |a| \sum_{i=1}^{n} \ell(h_i)$$

$$\leqslant \sum_{i=1}^{n} (|a| + y_i + \epsilon) \left(m_\ell(E_i) + \frac{\epsilon}{n} \right) - |a| m_\ell(supp(f))$$

$$= \sum_{i=1}^{n} (y_i - \epsilon) m_\ell(E_i) + 2\epsilon m_\ell(supp(f)) + \frac{\epsilon}{n} \left(\sum_{i=1}^{n} (|a| + y_i + \epsilon) \right)$$

$$\leqslant \int_S f \, dm_\ell + \epsilon(2 m_\ell(supp(f)) + |a| + b + \epsilon),$$

which implies the desired inequality.

It is immediate that m_ℓ is monotone and that $m_\ell(E) = 0$ implies $E \in \tilde{\mathcal{E}}$ and, therefore $E \in \mathcal{E}$. This shows that condition (v) is satisfied.

By Lemma 8.8, part (ii) holds. Part (iii) follows from the definition of m_ℓ for open set given in equality (8.21) and its extension to $\mathcal{P}(S)$ given in equality (8.22).

The argument for part (iv) is given by Lemma 8.10.

Lemma 8.5 establishes the uniqueness of a measure for which conditions (i)-(v) are satisfied. □

8.9 Integration Relative to Signed Measures and Complex Measures

Definition 8.17. Let $(S, \mathcal{E}.m)$ be a measure space, where m is a signed measure. The *integral* $\int_S f \, dm$ of a measurable function $f : S \longrightarrow \bar{\mathbb{R}}$ is defined if both $\int_S f \, dm^+$ and $\int_S f \, dm^-$ are defined and at least one of then is neither ∞ or $-\infty$. If this is the case,

$$\int_S f \, dm = \int_S f \, dm^+ - \int_S f \, dm^-.$$

The function f is *integrable* if $\int_S f \, dm$ is finite.

Theorem 8.70. *Let $(S, \mathcal{E}.m)$ be a measure space, where m is a signed measure. The following statements concerning a measurable function $f : S \longrightarrow \hat{\mathbb{R}}$ are equivalent:*

(i) *f is integrable with respect to m;*
(ii) *f is integrable with respect to both m^+ and m^-;*
(iii) *f is integrable with respect to $|m|$.*

Proof. Note that $\int_S f \, dm$ is finite if and only if $\int_S f \, dm^+$ and $\int_S f \, dm^-$ are finite, so (i) is equivalent to (ii).

The second statement is equivalent to the finiteness of $\int_S |f| \, dm^+$ and $\int_S |f| \, dm^-$, or with $\int_S |f| \, d|m| < \infty$, which is equivalent to (iii). $\qquad\square$

Theorem 8.71. *Let m_1, m_2 be two measures on the measurable space $(S, \mathcal{E})$ such that $m_1 \leqslant m_2$. For every non-negative measurable function $f : S \longrightarrow \hat{\mathbb{R}}_{\geqslant 0}$ we have $\int_S f \, dm_1 \leqslant \int_S f \, dm_2$.*

Proof. Suppose that f is a non-negative simple measurable function $f = \sum_{i=1}^n y_i \mathbf{1}_{f^{-1}(y_i)}$. Then, $\int_S f \, dm_1 = \sum_{i=1}^n y_i m_1(f^{-1}(y_i)) \leqslant \sum_{i=1}^n y_i m_2(f^{-1}(y_i)) = \int_S f \, dm_2$.

If f is a non-negative measurable function and (f_n) is a sequence of measurable non-negative simple functions such that $\lim_{n \to \infty} f_n = f$, the Monotone Convergence Theorem implies the desired inequality. $\qquad\square$

Theorem 8.72. *Let $(S, \mathcal{E}, m)$ be a measure space and let $f : S \longrightarrow \mathbb{C}$ be a complex-valued function such that $f(x) = u(x) + iv(x)$ for $x \in S$. We have $\int_S |f| \, dm < \infty$ if and only if $\int_S |f| \, dm < \infty$ and $\int_S |f| \, dm < \infty$.*

Proof. Observe that $|f(x)| = \sqrt{u^2(x) + v^2(x)} \leqslant |u(x)| + |v(x)|$, so $\int_S |f| \, dm < \infty$ and $\int_S |f| \, dm < \infty$ implies $\int_S |f| \, dm < \infty$.

Since $\int_S |f| \, dm \geqslant \int_S |u| \, dm$ and $\int_S |f| \, dm \geqslant \int_S |v| \, dm$, it is clear that $\int_S |f| \, dm < \infty$ implies $\int_S |f| \, dm < \infty$ and $\int_S |f| \, dm < \infty$. $\qquad\square$

Definition 8.18. Let $(S, \mathcal{E}, m)$ be a measure space and let $f : S \longrightarrow \mathbb{C}$ be a complex-valued function. The function f is *integrable* if $\int_S |f| \, dm < \infty$.

If $f = u + iv$, the integral $\int_S f \, dm$ is the complex number $\int_S u \, dm + i \int_S v \, dm$.

If $(S, \mathcal{E}, m)$ is a measure space, where m is a complex measure and $f : S \longrightarrow \mathbb{C}$ is a complex bounded function defined on S, the Jordan decomposition of m can be used to define $\int_S f \, dm$. Namely, if $m = m_1' - m_1'' + i(m_2' - m_2'')$, $\int_S f \, dm$ is defined as

$$\int_S f \, dm = \int_S f \, dm_1' - \int_S f \, dm_1'' + i \left(\int_S f \, dm_2' - \int_S f \, dm_2'' \right).$$

Theorem 8.73. *Let $B(S, \mathcal{E}, m)$ the set of complex-valued bounded and measurable functions on $(S, \mathcal{E}, m)$ and let*

$$\|f\|_\infty = \text{ess sup}\{|f(x)| \mid x \in S\}$$

for $f \in B(S, \mathcal{E}, m)$. We have:

$$\left| \int f \, dm \right| \leqslant \|f\|_\infty \, \|m\|.$$

Proof. Let f be a simple measurable function on S with $f(S) = \{a_1, \ldots, a_n\}$. If $A_i = f^{-1}(a_i)$ for $1 \leqslant i \leqslant n$, then

$$\left| \int_S f \, dm \right| = \left| \sum_{j=1}^n a_j m(A_j) \right| \leqslant \sum_{j=1}^n |a_j| |m(A_j)| \leqslant \sum_{j=1}^n \|f\|_\infty |m(A_j)|,$$

hence $|\int f \, dm| \leqslant \|f\|_\infty \, \|m\|$.

Since every bounded function f is the limit of a sequence of simple functions that converges uniformly to f (see Corollary 7.14), the desired conclusion follows. □

8.10 Indefinite Integral of a Function

Theorem 8.74. *Let $(S, \mathcal{E}, m)$ be a measure space and $f : S \longrightarrow \hat{\mathbb{R}}$ be a measurable function. If the integral $\int_S f \, dm$ exists, then $\int_S f 1_U \, dm$ is defined for every $U \in \mathcal{E}$.*

Proof. Observe that $(f 1_U)^+ = f^+ 1_U \leqslant f^+$ and $(f 1_U)^- = f^- 1_U \leqslant f^-$. Since $\int_S f \, dm$ exists, at least one of the integrals $\int_S f \, dm^+$ or $\int_S f \, dm^-$ is finite. Since $\int_S (f 1_U)^+ \, dm =\leqslant \int_S f^+ \, dm$ and $\int_S (f 1_U)^- \, dm =\leqslant \int_S f^- \, dm$, it follows that at least one of $\int_S (f 1_U)^+ \, dm$, $\int_S (f 1_U)^- \, dm$ is finite, which means that $\int_S f 1_U \, dm$ exists. □

Definition 8.19. Let $(S, \mathcal{E}, m)$ be a measure space and $f : S \longrightarrow \hat{\mathbb{R}}$ be a measurable function. The *indefinite integral of f with respect to m* is the function $\phi : \mathcal{E} \longrightarrow \hat{\mathbb{R}}$ defined by

$$\phi(U) = \int_S f 1_U \, dm$$

for $U \in \mathcal{E}$.

If $f \geqslant 0$ a.e. on S, then ϕ is a measure; we denote it by fm.

Theorem 8.75. *Let $(S, \mathcal{E}, m)$ be a measure space and $f : S \longrightarrow \hat{\mathbb{R}}$ be a function such that $\int_S f \, dm$ is defined. If $U \in \mathcal{E}$ and $m(U) = 0$, then $\int_U f \, dm = 0$.*

Proof. This statement follows from the fact that $f1_U = 0$ almost everywhere on S. $\qquad\square$

Theorem 8.76. *Let $(S, \mathcal{E}, m)$ be a measure space and $f : S \longrightarrow \hat{\mathbb{R}}$ be a function such that $\int_S f \, dm$ is defined. If $(U_1, U_2, \ldots)$ is a sequence of pairwise disjoint sets in $\mathcal{E}$ and $U = \bigcup_{n \geqslant 1} U_n$, then*

$$\int_U f \, dm = \sum_{n \geqslant 1} \int_{U_n} f \, dm.$$

Proof. Since the sets $U_1, U_2, \ldots$ are pairwise disjoint, $1_U = \sum_{n \geqslant 1} 1_{U_n}$, hence $f1_U = \sum_{n \geqslant 1} f1_{U_n}$. This, in turn, implies $\int_U f \, dm = \sum_{n \geqslant 1} \int_{U_n} f \, dm$. $\qquad\square$

Theorem 8.77. *Let $(S, \mathcal{E}, m)$ be a measure space and $f : S \longrightarrow \hat{\mathbb{R}}$ be a function such that $\int_S f \, dm$ is defined. If $(U_1, U_2, \ldots)$ is an increasing sequence of sets and $U = \bigcup_{n \geqslant 1} U_n$, then $\lim_{n \to \infty} \int_{U_n} f \, dm = \int_U f \, dm$.*

If $(U_1, U_2, \ldots)$ is a decreasing sequence of sets and $U = \bigcap_{n \geqslant 1} U_n$ such that $\int_{U_1} f \, dm$ is finite, then $\lim_{n \to \infty} \int_{U_n} f \, dm = \int_U f \, dm$.

Proof. For an increasing sequence of sets $(U_1, U_2, \ldots)$ and $U = \bigcup_{n \geqslant 1} U_n$, the set U can be written as the union of a pairwise disjoint sequence, $U = U_1 \cup (U_2 - U_1) \cup (U_3 - U_2) \cup \cdots$. By Theorem 8.76,

$$\int_U f \, dm = \int_{U_1} f \, dm + \sum_{n \geq 2} \int_{U_n - U_{n-1}} f \, dm$$

$$= \int_{U_1} f \, dm + \lim_{n \to \infty} \sum_{m=2}^{n} \int_{U_m - U_{m-1}} f \, dm$$

$$= \lim_{n \to \infty} \int_{U_n} f \, dm.$$

For a decreasing sequence of sets $(U_1, U_2, \ldots)$ we have $U_1 - U = \bigcup_{n=1}^{\infty}(U_1 - U_n)$, where $(U_1 - U_n)$ is an increasing sequence of sets. By the first part of the theorem we have $\lim_{n \to \infty} \int_{U_1 - U_n} f \, dm = \int_{U_1 - U} f \, dm$. Since $\int_{U_1 - U} f \, dm + \int_U f \, dm = \int_{U_1} f \, dm$, taking into account that $\int_{U_1} f \, dm$ is finite, it follows that $|\int_U f \, dm|$ is finite and $\int_{U_1 - U} f \, dm = \int_{U_1} f \, dm - \int_U f \, dm$. Similarly, $\int_{U_1 - U_n} f \, dm = \int_{U_1} f \, dm - \int_{U_n} f \, dm$, hence $\lim_{n \to \infty} (\int_{U_1} f \, dm - \int_{U_n} f \, dm) = 0$ because $|\int_{U_1} f \, dm|$ is finite. This yields $\lim_{n \to \infty} \int_{U_n} f_n \, dm = \int_U f \, dm$. $\qquad\square$

Theorem 8.78. *Let $(S, \mathcal{E}, m)$ be a measure space and let $f : S \longrightarrow \hat{\mathbb{R}}$ be a measurable function such that $\int_S f \, dm$ is defined. Then, the function*

$m_f : \mathcal{E} \longrightarrow \hat{\mathbb{R}}$ *defined by* $m_f(U) = \int_U f \, dm$ *is a signed measure on the measurable space* $(S, \mathcal{E})$.

Proof. Since $(f1_U)^+ = f^+1_U \leqslant f^+$ and $(f1_U)^- = f^-1_U \leqslant f^-$, either $\int_S (f1_U)^+ \, dm \leqslant \int_S f^+ < \infty$ or $\int_S (f1_U)^- \, dm \leqslant \int_S f^- < \infty$, which means that $\int_S f1_U \, dm$ is defined and, therefore $\int_U f \, dm$ is defined.

We claim that either $\int_U f \, dm > -\infty$ for every $U \in \mathcal{E}$, or $\int_U f \, dm < \infty$ for every $U \in \mathcal{E}$.

Suppose that $\int_S f^- \, dm < \infty$. Then, $\int_S (f1_U)^- \, dm \leqslant \int_S f^- \, dm < \infty$, hence $\int_U f \, dm = \int_S f1_U \, dm > -\infty$ for $U \in \mathcal{E}$. Similarly, if $\int_S f^+ \, dm < \infty$, then $\int_U f \, dm < \infty$ for all $U \in \mathcal{E}$. The conclusion then follows from the last part of Theorem 8.77. $\square$

Let $(S, \mathcal{E}, m)$ be a measure space and let $f : S \longrightarrow \mathbb{R}_{\geqslant 0}$ be a non-negative function that is not necessarily integrable relative to m. Define the measure m_f on $m_f(U) = \int_U f \, dm$. Note that $m_f(U) = 0$ implies $m(U) = 0$; m_f is finite if and only if f is integrable. The measure m_f is said to have f as *density* with respect to m.

Note that if $m_f = m_g$, then $f = g$ almost everywhere.

Theorem 8.79. *Let* $(S, \mathcal{E}, m)$ *be a measure space,* $f : S \longrightarrow \mathbb{R}_{\geqslant 0}$ *be a non-negative function that is not necessarily integrable relative to* m, *and let* $h : S \longrightarrow \mathbb{R}_{\geqslant 0}$. *We have* $\int h \, dm_f = \int hf \, dm$.

A function $h : S \longrightarrow \mathbb{R}$, *not necessarily non-negative, is integrable with respect to* m_f *if and only if* hf *is integrable with respect to* m. *In this case,* $\int h \, dm_f = \int hf \, dm$ *and* $\int_U h \, dm_f = \int_U hf \, dm$.

Proof. If $h = 1_U$ for $U \in \mathcal{E}$, then $\int h \, dm_f = m_f(U)$, so the equality $\int h \, dm_f = \int hf \, dm$ amounts to $m_f(U) = \int 1_U f \, dm = \int_U f \, dm$, which clearly holds. Thus, by linearity, the first equality of the theorem holds for simple non-negative functions, hence by passing to limit the equality holds for non-negative measurable functions.

If h is not non-negative, the first equality applied to $|h|$ implies that h is integrable with respect to m_f if and only hf is integrable with respect to m. If h is integrable, the first equality follows by applying this argument to h^+ and h^-. Substituting h by $h1_U$ gives the second equality. $\square$

8.11 Convergence in Measure

We have seen (Corollary 7.4) that if a sequence of measurable $\mathbf{f} = (f_n)_{n \geqslant 1}$ converges pointwise to a function f, then f is measurable. The same holds when $\mathbf{f}$ converges to f a.e.

Theorem 8.80. *Let $(S, \mathcal{E}, m)$ be a complete measure space and let $\boldsymbol{f} = (f_1, f_2, \ldots)$ be a sequence of measurable functions such that $\lim_{n \to \infty} f_n(x) = f(x)$ a.e. Then, f is a measurable function.*

Proof. This statement follows immediately from Theorem 7.15. $\qquad\square$

Definition 8.20. Let $(S, \mathcal{E}, m)$ be a measure space and let $\boldsymbol{f} = (f_n)$ be a sequence of measurable functions that are finite a.e, where $f_n : S \longrightarrow \hat{\mathbb{R}}$. The sequence $\boldsymbol{f}$ *converges in measure* to the measurable function $f : S \longrightarrow \hat{\mathbb{R}}$ that is finite a.e. if for every $\epsilon > 0$, $\lim_{n \to \infty} m(\{x \in S \mid |f_n(x) - f(x)| \geqslant \epsilon\}) = 0$.

Note that the definition of convergence in measure makes no use of a norm or a metric.

Theorem 8.81. *Let $(S, \mathcal{E}, m)$ be a measure space and let $\boldsymbol{f} = (f_n)$ be a sequence of measurable functions that are finite a.e, where $f_n : S \longrightarrow \hat{\mathbb{R}}$.*

If $\boldsymbol{f}$ converges in measure to f and $f = g$ a.e., then the sequence $\boldsymbol{f}$ also converges to g in measure.

Proof. For $\epsilon > 0$ we have

$$\{x \in S \mid |f_n(x) - f(x)| < \epsilon\} - \{x \in S \mid |f_n(x) - g(x)| < \epsilon\}$$
$$\subseteq \{x \in S \mid f(x) \neq g(x)\},$$

hence $m(\{x \in S \mid |f_n(x) - f(x)| < \epsilon\}) - m(\{x \in S \mid |f_n(x) - g(x)| < \epsilon\}) \leqslant m(\{x \in S \mid f(x) \neq g(x)\}) = 0$. Therefore, $\lim_{n \to \infty} m(\{x \in S \mid |f_n(x) - f(x)| < \epsilon\}) \leqslant \lim_{n \to \infty} m(\{x \in S \mid |f_n(x) - g(x)| < \epsilon\})$. By reversing the roles of f and g we obtain $\lim_{n \to \infty} m(\{x \in S \mid |f_n(x) - f(x)| < \epsilon\}) = \lim_{n \to \infty} m(\{x \in S \mid |f_n(x) - g(x)| < \epsilon\})$. Therefore, $\boldsymbol{f} = (f_n)_{n \geqslant 1}$ converges in measure to f if and only if it converges in measure to g. $\qquad\square$

Theorem 8.82. *Let $(S, \mathcal{E}, m)$ be a measure space and let $\boldsymbol{f} = (f_n)$ be a sequence of measurable functions that are finite a.e, where $f_n : S \longrightarrow \hat{\mathbb{R}}$.*

The sequence $\boldsymbol{f}$ converges in measure to f if for every $\epsilon > 0$, there exists $n_\epsilon \in \mathbb{N}$ such that $n > n_\epsilon$ implies $m(\{x \in S \mid |f_n(x) - f(x)| \geqslant \epsilon\}) < \epsilon$.

Proof. Suppose that $\boldsymbol{f}$ converges in measure to f, that is, $\lim_{n \to \infty} m(\{x \in S \mid |f_n(x) - f(x)| \geqslant \epsilon\}) = 0$ for every $\epsilon > 0$. For every $n_0 \geqslant 1$ there exists n_1 such that $n \geqslant n_1$ implies $m(\{x \in S \mid |f_n(x) - f(x)| \geqslant \epsilon\}) \leqslant \frac{1}{n_0}$. Choose n_0 such that $\frac{1}{n_0} < \epsilon$. Then, $m(\{x \in S \mid |f_n(x) - f(x)| \geqslant \epsilon\}) \leqslant \epsilon$.

Conversely, suppose that for every $\epsilon > 0$, there exists $n_\epsilon \in \mathbb{N}$ such that $n > n_\epsilon$ implies $m(\{x \in S \mid |f_n(x) - f(x)| \geqslant \epsilon\}) < \epsilon$. Choose m such that

$\epsilon < \frac{1}{m}$. Then $n > n_{\frac{1}{m}}$ implies $m(\{x \in S \mid |f_n(x) - f(x)| \geqslant \epsilon\}) < m(\{x \in S \mid |f_n(x) - f(x)| \geqslant \frac{1}{m}\}) < \frac{1}{m}$, hence $\lim_{n\to\infty} m(\{x \in S \mid |f_n(x) - f(x)| \geqslant \epsilon\}) = 0$. $\square$

Let $(S, \mathcal{E}, m)$ be a measure space and let $f, g : S \longrightarrow \mathbb{R}_{\geqslant 0}$ be two measurable functions. We have:

$$\{x \in S \mid f(x) + g(x) \geqslant 2\epsilon\} \subseteq \{x \in S \mid f(x) \geqslant \epsilon\} \cup \{x \in S \mid g(x) \geqslant \epsilon\},$$

which implies

$$m(\{x \in S \mid f(x) + g(x) \geqslant 2\epsilon\}) \leqslant m(\{x \in S \mid f(x) \geqslant \epsilon\}) \\ + m(\{x \in S \mid g(x) \geqslant \epsilon\}).$$

Theorem 8.83. *Let $(S, \mathcal{E}, m)$ be a measure space and let $\boldsymbol{f} = (f_n)$ be a sequence of measurable functions that converges in measure to both f and g. Then, $f = g$ a.e.*

Proof. Let $\epsilon > 0$. Since

$$m(\{x \in S \mid |f(x) - g(x)| \geqslant \epsilon\}) \leqslant m\left(\left\{x \in S \mid |f(x) - f_n(x)| \geqslant \frac{\epsilon}{2}\right\}\right) \\ + m\left(\left\{x \in S \mid |f_n(x) - g(x)| \geqslant \frac{\epsilon}{2}\right\}\right),$$

and $\lim_{n\to\infty} m(\{x \in S \mid |f(x) - f_n(x)| \geqslant \frac{\epsilon}{2}\}) = \lim_{n\to\infty} m(\{x \in S \mid |f(x) - f_n(x)| \geqslant \frac{\epsilon}{2}\}) = 0$, it follows that $m(\{x \in S \mid |f(x) - g(x)| \geqslant \epsilon\}) = 0$. Thus, for $n \geqslant 1$, the set $U_n = \{x \in S \mid |f(x) - g(x)| \geqslant \frac{1}{n}\}$ is a null set, hence $U = \bigcap_{n\geqslant 1} U_n$ is a null set. Thus, for $x \in U$ we have $|f(x) - g(x)| < \frac{1}{n}$ for all $n \geqslant 1$, hence $f = g$ a.e. $\square$

Definition 8.21. Let $(S, \mathcal{E}, m)$ be a measure space and let $\boldsymbol{f} = (f_n)$ be a sequence of measurable functions that are finite a.e., where $f_n : S \longrightarrow \hat{\mathbb{R}}$. The sequence $\boldsymbol{f}$ is a *Cauchy sequence in measure* if every $\epsilon > 0$ there exists $n_\epsilon \in \mathbb{N}$, such that $m, n \geqslant n_\epsilon$ implies $m(\{x \in S \mid |f_n(x) - f_m(x)|\}) < \epsilon$.

Theorem 8.84. (Riesz' Theorem) *Let $(S, \mathcal{E}, m)$ be a measure space. If $\boldsymbol{f} = (f_n)$ is a Cauchy sequence in measure, then $\boldsymbol{f}$ has an almost everywhere uniformly convergent subsequence.*

Proof. Suppose that $\boldsymbol{f} = (f_n)$ is a Cauchy sequence in measure, which means that for every $\epsilon > 0$ there exists $n_\epsilon \in \mathbb{N}$, such that $m, n \geqslant n_\epsilon$ implies $m(\{x \in S \mid |f_n(x) - f_m(x)|\}) < \epsilon$.

This generates a sequence of numbers $n_0, n_1, \ldots, n_m, \ldots$ defined as follows:

- for $\epsilon = 1$ there exists k_0 such that $k > k_0$ implies $m(|f_k - f_{k_0}| \geqslant 1) < 1$;
- for $\epsilon = \frac{1}{2}$ there exists $k_1 > k_0$ such that $k > k_1$ implies $m(|f_k - f_{k_1}| \geqslant 2^{-1}) < 2^{-1}$;
- $\cdots$;
- for $\epsilon = \frac{1}{2^n}$ there exists $k_n > k_{n-1}$ such that $k > k_n$ implies $m(|f_k - f_{k_1}| \geqslant 2^{-n}) < 2^{-n}$;
- $\cdots$

The last statement implies $m(|f_{k_{n+1}} - f_{k_n}| \geqslant 2^{-n}) < 2^{-n}$.

Let $B_n = \bigcup_{i=n}^{\infty} (|f_{k_{i+1}} - f_{k_i}| \geqslant 2^{-i})$. Note that

$$m(B_n) \leqslant \sum_{i=n}^{\infty} m(|f_{k_{i+1}} - f_{k_i}| \geqslant 2^{-i})$$

$$< \sum_{i=n}^{\infty} 2^{-i} = 2^{-(n-1)}.$$

If $B = \bigcap_{n=1}^{\infty} B_n$, then $m(B) \leqslant m(B_n) < 2^{-(n-1)}$, hence $m(B) = 0$.

For every $x \in S - B = \bigcup_{n=1}^{\infty} (S - B_n)$ there exists n_0 such that $x \in S - B_{n_0}$. Therefore, if $n \geqslant n_0$, $|f_{k_{n+1}} - f_{k_n}| < 2^{-n}$. Then, for every $n > m \geqslant n_0$ we have

$$|f_{k_n}(x) - f_{k_m}(x)| \leqslant |f_{k_n}(x) - f_{k_{n-1}}(x)| + \cdots + \leqslant |f_{k_{m+1}}(x) - f_{k_m}(x)|$$
$$< 2^{-(n-1)} + \cdots + 2^{-m} < 2^{-(m-1)}.$$

Thus, (f_{k_n}) is a Cauchy sequence, hence there the limit $\lim_{n \to \infty} f_{k_n}(x)$ in $\mathbb{R}$.

Let $f : S \longrightarrow \mathbb{R}$ be the measurable function defined as

$$f(x) = \begin{cases} \lim_{n \to \infty} f_{k_n}(x) & \text{if } x \in S - B, \\ 0 & \text{if } x \in B. \end{cases}$$

For every $\epsilon > 0$ there exists n_0 such that $2^{-(n_0-1)} < \epsilon$. Then, $m(B_{n_0}) < 2^{-(n_0-1)} < \epsilon$. We claim that (f_{k_n}) converges almost uniformly to f on $S - B_{n_0}$.

If $x \in S - B_{n_0} = \bigcap_{n=n_0}^{\infty} (|f_{k_{n+1}} - f_{k_n}| \leqslant 2^{-n}$ we have $|f_{k_{n+1}}(x) - f_{k_n}(x)| < 2^{-n}$ when $n \geqslant n_0$. Then, as above, $n > m \geqslant n_0$ implies $f_{k_n}(x) - f_{k_m}(x)| < 2^{-(m-1)}$. Note that $x \in S - B_{n_0} \subseteq S - B$, hence $\lim_{n \to \infty} f_{k_n}(x) = f(x)$. If we take $n \to \infty$ we obtain $|f(x) - f_{k_m}(x)| < 2^{-(m-1)}$ for every $m \geqslant n_0$ and $x \in S - B_{n_0}$, which yields the desired conclusion. $\qquad \square$

Theorem 8.85. *Let* $(S, \mathcal{E}, m)$ *be a measure space and let* $\boldsymbol{f} = (f_1, \ldots, f_n, \ldots)$ *be a Cauchy sequence in measure. If* $\boldsymbol{f}$ *contains a subsequence* (f_{n_j}) *that converges in measure to a function* f, *then* $\boldsymbol{f}$ *converges in measure to the same* f.

Proof. Define the sequence of non-negative functions $\mathbf{h} = (h_n)$ as $h_n = |f_n - f|$ for $n \geqslant 1$. Since (f_n) is a Cauchy sequence in measure, for every $\epsilon > 0$ there is $n_\epsilon \in \mathbb{N}$ such that $m, n \geqslant n_\epsilon$ implies $m(\{x \in S \mid |f_n(x) - f_m(x)|\}) < \epsilon$. Since

$$|h_n(x) - h_m(x)| = ||f_n - f| - |f_m - f|| \leqslant |f_n - f_m| < \epsilon,$$

the sequence (h_n) is a again a Cauchy sequence and (h_{n_j}) is a subsequence of (h_n).

Since (h_{n_j}) converges in measure to 0 there exists $k_\epsilon \in \mathbb{N}$ such that $k > k_\epsilon$ $m(\{x \in S \mid h_{n_j} \geqslant \epsilon\}) < \epsilon$ for $j \geqslant k_\epsilon$. Let $p \geqslant k$. Since $n_p \geqslant n$ we have $n_p \geqslant k_0$, hence

$$m(\{x \in S \mid h_n > 2\epsilon\}) \leqslant m(\{x \in S \mid |h_n - h_{n_p}| \geqslant \epsilon\})$$
$$+ m(\{x \in S \mid h_{n_p} \geqslant \epsilon\}) < 2\epsilon,$$

hence h_n converges to 0 in measure. Thus, f_n converges in measure to f. $\square$

Theorem 8.86. (Completeness of Convergence in Measure) *Let* $(S, \mathcal{E}, m)$ *be a measure space and let* $\boldsymbol{f} = (f_1, \ldots, f_n, \ldots)$ *be a Cauchy sequence in measure. Then* $\boldsymbol{f}$ *converges in measure.*

Proof. Since $\mathbf{f}$ is a Cauchy sequence, there is a subsequence (f_{n_j}) constructed as in the proof of Theorem 8.84 such that for $g_j = f_{n_j}$ for $j \geqslant 1$ and $S_j = \{x \in S \mid |g_{j+1}(x) - g_j(x)| \geqslant \frac{1}{2^j}\}$ we have $m(S_j) \leqslant 2^{-j}$. Let $H_k = \bigcup_{j=k}^{\infty} S_j$. We have $m(H_k) \leqslant \sum_{j=k}^{\infty} \frac{1}{2^j} = \frac{1}{2^{k-1}}$. Let $W = \bigcap_{k=1}^{\infty} H_k = \bigcap_{k=1}^{\infty} \bigcup_{j=k}^{\infty} S_j = \limsup S_j$. Since $W \subseteq H_k$ for every k, we have $m(W) = 0$.

Let $x \notin W$. Then, $x \notin H_k$ for some k and, therefore, $x \notin S_j$ for $j \geqslant k$. Therefore, for $k \leqslant j \leqslant m$ we have

$$|g_j(x) - g_m(x)| \leqslant \sum_{i=1}^{m-1} |g_{i+1}(x) - g_i(x)| \leqslant \sum_{i=1}^{m-1} \frac{1}{2^i} \leqslant \frac{1}{2^{j-1}}.$$

The sequence of real numbers $(g_j(x))$ is a Cauchy sequence and, therefore, it is convergent. Let $f : S \longrightarrow \mathbb{R}$ be the function defined as

$$f(x) = \begin{cases} \lim_{j \to \infty} g_j(x) & \text{if the limit exists,} \\ 0 & \text{otherwise,} \end{cases}$$

then f is measurable and, since the limit exists for every $x \notin W$, it follows that (g_j) converges pointwise to f almost everywhere.

If $x \notin H_j$, then $|g_j(x) - g_m(x)| \leqslant \frac{1}{2^{j-1}}$ for $m \geqslant j$. Therefore,

$$|g_j(x) - f(x)| = \lim_{m \to \infty} |g_j(x) - g_m(x)| \leqslant \frac{1}{2^{j-1}},$$

which implies $\{x \in S \mid |g_j(x) - f(x)| \geqslant \frac{1}{2^{j-1}}\} \subseteq H_k$. Therefore

$$m(\{x \in S \mid |g_j(x) - f(x)| \geqslant \frac{1}{2^{j-1}}\}) \leqslant m(H_k) \leqslant \frac{1}{2^{j-1}}.$$

Therefore, (g_j) converges in measure to f. By Theorem 8.85 if follows that (f_n) converges in measure to f. $\qquad\square$

8.12 $\mathcal{L}^p$ and L^p Spaces

Let $(S, \mathcal{E}, m)$ be a measure space. Denote by $\mathcal{L}^p(S, \mathcal{E}, m)$ the set of all measurable complex-valued function $f : S \longrightarrow \hat{\mathbb{C}}$ such that $\int_S |f|^p \, dm < \infty$. If $(S, \mathcal{E}, m)$ is understood from context we write just $\mathcal{L}^p$ instead of $\mathcal{L}^p(S, \mathcal{E}, m)$.

The same notation is used for the set of real-valued function $f : S \longrightarrow \hat{\mathbb{R}}$ such that $\int_S |f|^p \, dm < \infty$.

Observe that by Theorem 8.22 for a function $f : S \longrightarrow \hat{\mathbb{C}}$ we have $f \in \mathcal{L}^p$ if and only if $|f|^p \in \mathcal{L}_1$.

Theorem 8.87. *For every measure space $(S, \mathcal{E}, m)$ the set of complex-valued functions $\mathcal{L}^p(S, \mathcal{E}, m)$ is a linear space.*

Proof.   Let $f, g \in \mathcal{L}^p(S, \mathcal{E}, m)$. Both f and g are finite a.e. on S, hence $f + g$ is defined a.e on S.

If a, b are two complex numbers we have $|a| + |b| \leqslant 2 \max\{|a|, |b|\}$, hence

$$(|a| + |b|)^p \leqslant 2^p \max\{|a|^p, |b|^p\} \leqslant 2^p(|a|^p + |b|^p).$$

Thus, $|(f + g)(x)|^p \leqslant 2^p(|f(x)|^p + |g(x)|^p)$ a.e. on S and, therefore

$$\int_S |(f + g)(x)|^p \, dm \leqslant 2^p \left(\int_S |f(x)|^p \, dm + \int_S |g(x)|^p \, dm \right) < \infty,$$

hence $f + g \in \mathcal{L}^p(S, \mathcal{E}, m)$.

Also, we have

$$\int_S |af|^p \, dm = |a|^p \int_S |f|^p \, dm < \infty,$$

hence $af \in \mathcal{L}^p(S, \mathcal{E}, m)$. $\qquad\square$

For $f \in \mathcal{L}^p$ and $p \geqslant 1$ let $\nu_p(f)$ be the number

$$\nu_p(f) = \left(\int_S |f|^p \, dm \right)^{\frac{1}{p}}.$$

It is immediate that $\nu_p(af) = |a|\nu_p(f)$ for every $a \in \mathbb{R}$.

Theorem 8.88. (Hölder's Inequality for Functions) *Let $(S, \mathcal{E}, m)$ be a measure space and let $f \in \mathcal{L}^p(S, \mathcal{E}, m)$ and $g \in \mathcal{L}^q(S, \mathcal{E}, m)$ be two functions, where p, q are two numbers such that $\frac{1}{p} + \frac{1}{q} = 1$ and $p, q > 1$. We have $\nu_1(fg) \leqslant \nu_p(f)\nu_q(g)$.*

Proof.   Observe that if $\nu_p(f) = 0$, by Theorem 8.15, $|f|^p = 0$ a.e., so the function fg is 0 a.e., which implies $\int_S fg \, dm = 0$. The same holds if $\nu_q(g) = 0$, so in either case the inequality of the theorem holds. Therefore, without loss of generality we may assume that $\nu_p(f) \neq 0$ and $\nu_q(g) \neq 0$.

Suppose initially that $\nu_p(f) = \nu_q(f) = 1$. By Lemma 2.1, if $p, q \in \mathbb{R} - \{0, 1\}$ are two numbers such that $\frac{1}{p} + \frac{1}{q} = 1$ and $p > 1$, then, for every $a, b \in \mathbb{R}_{\geqslant 0}$, we have

$$|f(x)g(x)| \leqslant \frac{|f(x)|^p}{p} + \frac{|g(x)|^q}{q}.$$

By integrating we have

$$\nu_1(fg) = \int_S |fg| \, dm$$
$$\leqslant \frac{1}{p} \int_S |f|^p \, dm + \frac{1}{q} \int_S |g|^q \, dm$$
$$= \frac{1}{p} + \frac{1}{q} = 1.$$

If $\nu_p(f) \neq 1$ or $\nu_q(f) \neq 1$ we apply the inequality obtained above to the functions $\tilde{f} = \frac{1}{\nu_p(f)}f$ and $\tilde{g} = \frac{1}{\nu_q(g)}g$. Since $\nu_1(\tilde{f}\tilde{g}) \leqslant 1$, it follows that $\nu_1(fg) \leqslant \nu_p(f)\nu_q(f)$. $\square$

The equality $\frac{1}{p} + \frac{1}{q} = 1$ implies $q = \frac{p}{p-1}$. Therefore, $\lim_{p \to 1, p > 1} q = \infty$. We show that Hölder's Inequality can be extended to the case when $p = 1$ and $q = \infty$ by adopting the special definitions

$$\mathcal{L}^\infty(S, \mathcal{E}, m) = \{g \mid g \text{ is bounded a.e}\}$$

and

$$\nu_\infty(g) = \inf\{a \in \mathbb{R} \mid |g(x)| \leqslant a \text{ a.e.}\}.$$

For this special case let $\nu_\infty(g) = a_0 \geqslant 0$ and note that $fg \leqslant fa_0$ a.e. Therefore,

$$\nu_1(fg) \leqslant \nu_1(fa_0) = a_0\nu_1(f) = \nu_1(f)\nu_\infty(g),$$

which shows that Hölder's Inequality holds for $p = 1$ and $q = \infty$.

Theorem 8.89. *For every $f \in \mathcal{L}^\infty(S, \mathcal{E}, m)$ we have*

$$\nu_\infty(f) = \operatorname{ess\,sup}|f|,$$

and $\{x \in \mathbb{R} \mid f > \nu_\infty(f)\}$ is a null set.

Proof.　　This follows immediately from the definitions.　　□

Corollary 8.11. (Cauchy-Schwarz Inequality) *Let $(S, \mathcal{E}, m)$ be a measure space and let $f, g \in \mathcal{L}^2(S, \mathcal{E}, m)$ be two functions. We have $\nu_1(fg) \leqslant \nu_2(f)\nu_2(g)$.*

Proof.　　The desired inequality follows from Theorem 8.88 by taking $p = q = 2$.　　□

Theorem 8.90. (Minkowski's Inequality for Functions) *Let $(S, \mathcal{E}, m)$ be a measure space and let $f, g \in \mathcal{L}^p(S, \mathcal{E}, m)$ be two functions, where $p \geqslant 1$. We have*

$$\nu_p(f + g) \leqslant \nu_p(f) + \nu_p(q).$$

Proof.　　For $p = 1$, observe that $|(f + g)(x)| \leqslant |f(x)| + |g(x)|$ for $x \in S$, hence

$$\int_S |f + g|\, dm \leqslant \int_S |f|\, dm + \int_S |g|\, dm,$$

which gives the desired inequality for $p = 1$.

Suppose now that $1 < p < \infty$. Since

$$|f + g|^p \leqslant (|f| + |g|)^p \leqslant 2^p \max\{|f|^p + |g|^p\}$$
$$\leqslant 2^p(|f|^p + |g|^p),$$

we get that $|f + g|^p \in \mathcal{L}^1$, or $|f + g| \in \mathcal{L}^p$. Furthermore, we have

$$(\nu_p(f + g))^p = \int_S |f + g|^p\, dm = \int_S |f + g| \cdot |f + g|^{p-1}\, dm$$
$$\leqslant \int_S |f| \cdot |f + g|^{p-1}\, dm + \int_S |g| \cdot |f + g|^{p-1}\, dm$$
$$\leqslant \nu_p(f)\nu_q(|f + g|^{p-1}) + \nu_p(g)\nu_q(|f + g|^{p-1})$$

by Hölder inequality. This implies

$$\frac{(\nu_p(f+g))^p}{\nu_q(|f+g|^{p-1})} \leqslant \nu_p(f) + \nu_p(g). \tag{8.25}$$

Taking into account that $p = (p-1)q$, it follows that

$$\nu_q(|f+g|^{p-1}) = \left(\int_S \left(|f+g|^{p-1} \right)^q \, dm \right)^{\frac{1}{q}}$$

$$= \left(\int_S |f+g|^p \, dm \right)^{\frac{1}{q}} = (\nu_p(f+g))^{\frac{p}{q}}.$$

Substituting this expression in equality (8.25) leads to

$$\nu_p(f+g)^{p-\frac{p}{q}} \leqslant \nu_p(f) + \nu_q(g).$$

Since $p - \frac{p}{q} = 1$, Minkowski's inequality follows.

For $p = \infty$ let k_0, k_1 be two constants such that $|f(x)| \leqslant k_0$ (a.e.) and $|g(x)| \leqslant k_1$ (a.e.). Then, $|f(x) + g(x)| \leqslant k_0 + k_1$ (a.e.), so $f + g \in \mathcal{L}^\infty$. This implies $\nu_\infty(f+g) \leqslant \nu_\infty(f) + \nu_\infty(g)$ by an application of the definition of ν_∞. □

The previous results imply that ν_p is a seminorm on $\mathcal{L}^p$. However, ν_p is not a norm because $\nu_p(f) = 0$ only implies that $f = 0$ a.e., but not $f = 0$.

Theorem 8.91. *Let $(S, \mathcal{E}, m)$ be a measure space. The measurable simple functions in $\mathcal{L}^p(S, \mathcal{E}, m)$, where $1 \leqslant p \leqslant \infty$, form a dense set in this space.*

Proof. Consider the case when $1 \leqslant p < \infty$. Let $f \in \mathcal{L}^p(S, \mathcal{E}, m)$. By Theorem 7.26 there exist two non-decreasing sequences of non-negative simple measurable functions $(\hat{f}_n)$ and $(\check{f}_n)$ such that $f^+ = \lim_{n\to\infty} \hat{f}_n$ and $f^- = \lim_{n\to\infty} \check{f}_n$. The sequence (f_n) defined by $f_n = \hat{f}_n - \check{f}_n$ consists of simple functions such that $|f_n| \leqslant |f|$. Therefore, $f_n \in \mathcal{L}^p(S, \mathcal{E}, m)$.

Since $|f_n(x) - f(x)| \leqslant |f(x)|$ and $\lim_{n\to\infty} |f_n(x) - f(x)| = 0$ for every $x \in S$, by the Dominated Convergence Theorem (Theorem 8.37) applied to the functions $|f_n - f|$ we obtain $\lim_{n\to\infty} \|f_n - f\|_p = 0$, which concludes the proof when $1 \leqslant p < \infty$.

For $p = \infty$, let $f \in \mathcal{L}^\infty$. Then, $-\|f\|_\infty \leqslant f(x) \leqslant \|f\|_\infty$. If $\epsilon > 0$ consider the numbers $a_0 < a_1 < \cdots < a_k$ such that $a_{m+1} - a_m < \epsilon$ for $1 \leqslant m \leqslant k - 1$ and $\bigcup_{m=1}^{k-1} (a_m, a_{m+1}] = [-\|f\|_\infty, \|f\|_\infty]$. The function $f_\epsilon = \sum_{m=1}^{k-1} a_i 1_{(a_m, a_{m+1}]}$ is a simple measurable function and $\|f_\epsilon - f\|_\infty \leqslant \epsilon$, which gives the desired argument. □

A special type of simple functions is introduced next.

Definition 8.22. A *step function* on the closed interval $[a, b]$ is a function $f : [a, b] \longrightarrow \mathbb{R}$ such that:

(i) there exist $a_0, a_1, \ldots, a_n \in [a, b]$ where $a = a_0 < a_1 < \cdots < a_n = b$;

(ii) f is constant on each interval (a_{i-1}, a_i).

Each step function is a simple measurable function between the measure spaces $([a, b], \mathbb{B}([a, b]))$ and $(\mathbb{R}, \mathbb{B}(\mathbb{R}))$.

Lemma 8.15. *Let U be a Borel subset of $[a, b]$. For every $\epsilon > 0$ there exists a step function f on the measure space $([a, b], \mathbb{B}([a, b]), m_L)$ such that $\|1_U - f\|_p < \epsilon$.*

Proof. If U is a Borel subset of $\mathbb{R}$ then there exists a collection of open intervals (a_n, b_n) such that $U \subseteq \bigcup (a_n, b_n)$ and $\sum_{n \in \mathbb{N}} (b_n - a_n) < m_L(U) + \epsilon$.

Let n_ϵ be a positive integer such that $\sum_{n > n_\epsilon} (b_n - a_n) < \epsilon$.

Let $G = [a, b] \cap \bigcup_{n < n_\epsilon} (a_n, b_n)$ and $K = [a, b] \cap \bigcup_{n \in \mathbb{N}} (a_n, b_n)$. Then, $G \subseteq K$, 1_G is a step function and

$$\|1_U - 1_G\|_p \leqslant \|1_U - 1_K\|_p + \|1_K - 1_G\|_p$$

$$\leqslant \left(m_L \left(\bigcup_{n \in \mathbb{N}} (a_n, b_n) - U \right) \right)^{\frac{1}{p}}$$

$$+ \left(m_L \left(\bigcup_{n \geqslant n_\epsilon} (a_n, b_n) \right) \right)^{\frac{1}{p}}$$

$$\leqslant \epsilon^{\frac{1}{p}} + \epsilon^{\frac{1}{p}} = 2\epsilon^{\frac{1}{p}}.$$

This concludes the proof. $\qquad\qquad\square$

Theorem 8.92. *The subspace of $\mathcal{L}^p([a, b])$ determined by the step functions defined on $[a, b]$ is dense in $\mathcal{L}^p([a, b])$ for $1 \leqslant p < \infty$.*

Proof. Theorem 8.91 implies that the set of Borel-measurable simple functions in $\mathcal{L}^p(S, \mathcal{E}, m)$, where $1 \leqslant p \leqslant \infty$ is a dense set in this space. To complete the argument we need to show that the set of step function is dense in the set of Borel-measurable simple functions.

Let U be a Borel subset of $[a, b]$ and let $\epsilon > 0$. By Lemma 8.15, for every $\epsilon > 0$ there exists a step function g on the measure space $([a, b], \mathbb{B}([a, b]), m_L)$ such that $\|1_U - g\|_p < \epsilon$.

If f is a Borel simple function on $[a, b]$ and $\mathsf{Ran}(f) = \{y_1, \ldots, y_k\}$, then $f(x) = \sum_{i=1}^{k} y_i 1_{f^{-1}(y_i)}$. Each of the sets $f^{-1}(y_i)$ is a Borel subset of $[a, b]$

and $1_{f^{-1}(y_i)}$ can be approximated by a step function g_i; in other words, for every $\epsilon' > 0$ we have $\|1_{f^{-1}(y_i)} - g_i\|_p < \epsilon'$. It is clear that $\sum_{i=1}^{k} y_i g_i$ is a step function.

Let $\epsilon' = \frac{\epsilon}{\sum_{i=1}^{k} |y_i|}$. We have

$$\left\| f - \sum_{i=1}^{k} y_i g_i \right\|_p = \left\| \sum_{i=1}^{k} y_i 1_{f^{-1}(y_i)} - \sum_{i=1}^{k} y_i g_i \right\|_p$$

$$\leqslant \sum_{i=1}^{k} |y_i| \|1_{f^{-1}(y_i)} - g_i\|_p \leqslant \epsilon' \sum_{i=1}^{k} |y_i| \leqslant \epsilon,$$

which completes the argument. $\qquad\square$

Lemma 8.16. *Let* $f : [a, b] \longrightarrow \mathbb{R}$ *be a step function such that* $M = \sup\{f(x) \mid x \in [a, b]\}$. *For every* $\delta > 0$ *there exists a continuous function* $g : [a, b] \longrightarrow \mathbb{R}$ *such that* $\sup\{g(x) \mid x \in [a, b]\} = M$ *and* $m_L(\{x \in [a, b] \mid f(x) \neq g(x)\}) < \delta$.

Proof. Since f is a step function there exist $a_0, a_1, \ldots, a_n \in [a, b]$ and $y_0, \ldots, y_{n-1} \in \mathbb{R}$ such that $a = a_0 < a_1 < \cdots < a_n = b$ and $f(x) = y_i$ for $x \in (a_i, a_{i+1})$ for $0 \leqslant i \leqslant n - 1$.

Let $\epsilon > 0$ be a number such that $\epsilon < \min\{\frac{a_{i+1} - a_i}{2} \mid 1 \leqslant i \leqslant n - 1\}$. Define the continuous function g as:

$$g(x) = \begin{cases} \frac{y_0}{\epsilon}(x - a_0) & \text{if } a_0 \leqslant x \leqslant a_0 + \epsilon, \\ y_{i-1} & \text{if } a_{i-1} + \epsilon \leqslant x \leqslant a_i - \epsilon, \\ y_{i-1} + \frac{y_i - y_{i-1}}{2\epsilon}(x - a_i + \epsilon) & \text{if } a_i - \epsilon \leqslant x \leqslant a_i + \epsilon, \\ \frac{y_{n-1}}{\epsilon}(a_n - x) & \text{if } a_n - \epsilon \leqslant x \leqslant a_n. \end{cases}$$

We have:

$$\{x \in [a, b] \mid f(x) \neq g(x)\}$$

$$= [a_0, a_0 + \epsilon] \bigcup_{i=1}^{n-1} [a_i - \epsilon, a_i + \epsilon] \cup [a_n - \epsilon, a_n]$$

$$= 2\epsilon(n + 1).$$

Note that $\sup\{g(x) \mid x \in [a, b]\} = M$. Choosing $\epsilon < \frac{\delta}{2(n+1)}$ we have $m_L(\{x \in [a, b] \mid f(x) \neq g(x)\}) < \delta$. $\qquad\square$

Theorem 8.93. *The subspace of* $\mathcal{L}^p([a, b])$ *determined by the continuous functions defined on* $[a, b]$ *is dense in* $\mathcal{L}^p([a, b])$ *for* $1 \leqslant p < \infty$.

Proof. Each continuous function belongs to $\mathcal{L}^p([a,b])$. Since the step functions form a dense subset of $\mathcal{L}^p([a,b])$ it suffices to show that for every $\epsilon > 0$ and every step function f on $[a,b]$ there is a continuous function g such that $\|f - g\|_p < \epsilon$. If g is constructed as in Lemma 8.16 we have

$$\int_{[a,b]} |f - g|^p \, dm_L \leqslant (2M)^p m_L(\{x \in [a,b] \mid f(x) \neq g(x)\}) < (2M)^p \delta.$$

Since δ is arbitrary we obtain the desired conclusion. $\qquad\square$

Theorem 8.94. *Let $(S, \mathcal{E}, m)$ be a measure space. If there exists a countable collection $\mathcal{B} = \{B_k \mid k \in \mathbb{N}\}$ such that for every $\epsilon > 0$ and for every set $A \in \mathcal{E}$ there exists $B_k \in \mathcal{B}$ such that $m(A \oplus B_k) < \epsilon$, then the space $\mathcal{L}^p(S, \mathcal{E}, m)$ is separable.*

Proof. Since $m(A \oplus B_k) < \epsilon$, we have

$$\|1_A - 1_{B_k}\|_p = (m(A \oplus B_k))^{\frac{1}{p}} < \epsilon^{\frac{1}{p}}.$$

It follows that each m-integrable function can be approximated in $\mathcal{L}^p(S, \mathcal{E}, m)$ with any degree of accuracy by a simple function of the form $f(x) = \sum_{k=1}^{n} y_k 1_{B_k}(x)$. Therefore, we have a countable collection $\mathcal{F}$ of such functions dense in the set of m-integrable functions, which means that $\mathcal{F}$ is dense in $\mathcal{L}^p(S, \mathcal{E}, m)$. $\qquad\square$

Definition 8.23. Two functions $f, g \in \mathcal{L}^p(S, \mathcal{E}, m)$ are *equivalent* if $\{x \in S \mid f(x) \neq g(x)\}$ is a null set.

If f, g are equivalent we denote this by $f \sim g$. It easy to verify that this is indeed an equivalence relation. We denote by $[f]_p$ the equivalence class of $f \in \mathcal{L}^p(S, \mathcal{E}, m)$; the quotient space $\mathcal{L}^p(S, \mathcal{E}, m)/\sim$ is denoted by $L^p(S, \mathcal{E}, m)$, or just by L^p when there is no risk of confusion.

Then L^p is a normed space, with the norm given by

$$\|[f]\|_p = \inf\{\nu_p(h) \mid h \in \hat{\mathcal{L}}^p, h \sim f\}.$$

Actually, $\|[f]\|_p = \nu_p(f)$.

Observe that if $f : S \longrightarrow \hat{\mathbb{R}}$ and $\int_S |f|^p \, dm < \infty$, then

$$m(\{x \in S \mid f(x) = \infty\}) = m(\{x \in S \mid |f(x)|^p = \infty\})$$

$$= m\left(\bigcap_{j \in \mathbb{N}} \{x \in S \mid |f(x)|^p > j\}\right)$$

$$= \lim_{j \to \infty} m(\{x \in S \mid |f(x)|^p > j\})$$

$$\leqslant \lim_{j \to \infty} \int_S |f|^p \, dm,$$

by Markov's Inequality.

Theorem 8.95. (Riesz-Fischer Theorem) *Let* $(S, \mathcal{E}, m)$ *be a measure space. For each* p, $1 \leqslant p \leqslant \infty$ *the space* $L^p(S, \mathcal{E}, m)$ *is complete.*

Proof. By Theorem 5.72 it suffices to show that every absolutely convergent series in $L^p(S, \mathcal{E}, m)$ is convergent.

Suppose initially that $1 \leqslant p < \infty$. Let $\mathbf{f} = (f_n)$ be a sequence of functions in $L^p(S, \mathcal{E}, m)$ that is absolutely convergent. In other words, $\sum_{n=0}^{\infty} \|f_n\|_p < \infty$. Let $g : S \longrightarrow [0, \infty]$ be the function

$$g(x) = \left(\sum_{k=0}^{\infty} |f_k(x)| \right)^p = \lim_{n \to \infty} \left(\sum_{k=0}^{n} |f_k(x)| \right)^p.$$

By Minkowski's inequality we have

$$\left(\int_S \left(\sum_{k=0}^{n} |f_k| \right)^p dm \right)^{\frac{1}{p}} = \left\| \sum_{k=0}^{n} |f_k| \right\|_p \leqslant \sum_{k=0}^{n} \|f_k\|_p$$

for every $n \in \mathbb{N}$. Therefore, by the Monotone Convergence Theorem (theorem 8.11), we have

$$\int_S g \, dm = \lim_{n \to \infty} \int_S \left(\sum_{k=0}^{n} |f_k| \right)^p dm \leqslant \left(\sum_{k=0}^{\infty} \|f_k\|_p \right)^p,$$

hence g is integrable. Thus, by Theorem 8.17, g is finite a.e., and the series $f_0(x) + f_1(x) + \cdots$ is absolutely convergent and, therefore, convergent a.e.

Let $f : S \longrightarrow \hat{\mathbb{R}}$ be the function defined by

$$f(x) = \begin{cases} \sum_{k=0}^{\infty} f_k(x) & \text{if } g(x) < \infty, \\ 0 & \text{otherwise.} \end{cases}$$

Then, f is measurable and $|f|^p \leqslant g$, so $f \in L^p(S, \mathcal{E}, m)$.

Note that

$$\lim_{n \to \infty} \left| \sum_{k=0}^{n} f_k(x) - f(x) \right| = 0$$

holds a.e.; also, $|\sum_{k=0}^{n} f_k(x) - f(x)|^p \leqslant g(x)$ holds a.e. By the Dominated Convergence Theorem (theorem 8.37),

$$\lim_{n \to \infty} \left\| \sum_{k=0}^{n} f_k - f \right\|_p = 0.$$

Thus, the absolutely convergent series $\mathbf{f}$ is convergent, and we conclude that $L^p(S, \mathcal{E}, m)$ is complete.

For the case $p = \infty$ let $\mathbf{f}$ be a sequence of functions in $L^\infty(S, \mathcal{E}, m)$ that is absolutely convergent, that is, $\sum_{k=0}^\infty \|f_k\|_\infty < \infty$.

Define the null set $U_k = \{x \in S \mid |f_k(x)| > \|f_k\|_\infty\}$ and let $U = \bigcup_{k=0}^\infty U_k$. The series $\sum_{k=0}^\infty f_k(x)$ converges at each $x \in S - U$, and the function f given by

$$f(x) = \begin{cases} \sum_{k=0}^\infty f_k(x) & \text{if } g(x) < \infty, \\ 0 & \text{otherwise.} \end{cases}$$

is bounded and measurable. Since $\bigcup_{k \in \mathbb{N}} U_k$ is null, we have

$$\left\| f - \sum_{k=0}^n f_k \right\|_\infty \leqslant \sum_{k=n+1}^\infty \|f_k\|_\infty$$

for each n. Therefore,

$$\lim_{n \to \infty} \left\| f - \sum_{k=0}^n f_k \right\| \leqslant \lim_{n \to \infty} \sum_{k=n+1}^\infty \|f_k\|_\infty = 0.$$

Again, this shows that $L^\infty(S, \mathcal{E}, m)$ is complete.   □

Let $c_1 \in \mathcal{F}_c(S, \mathcal{O})$ be the constant function defined by $c_1(x) = 1$ for $x \in S$. If ℓ is a bounded positive functional on $\mathcal{F}_c(S, \mathcal{O})$ and $f \in \mathcal{F}_c(S, \mathcal{O})$ is such that $\|f\|_1 \leqslant 1$, then $|\ell(f)| \leqslant \ell(|f|) \leqslant \ell(c_1)$, hence $\|\ell\|_1 = \ell(c_1)$.

Theorem 8.96. *Let L be a linear space of bounded real-valued functions defined on a set S, such that*

(i) *the constant function c_1 belongs to L;*

(ii) *if $f, g \in L$, then the functions $f \vee g$ and $f \wedge g$ given by $(f \vee g)(x) = \max\{f(x), g(x)\}$ and $(f \wedge g)(x) = \min\{f(x), g(x)\}$, respectively, for $x \in S$ belong to L.*

If ℓ is a bounded linear functional on L, there exist two positive linear functionals ℓ_+ and ℓ_- such that $\ell = \ell_+ - \ell_-$, and $\|\ell\| = \ell_+(c_1) + \ell_-(c_1)$.

Proof.   For a non-negative function $f \in L$ let ℓ_+ be defined as

$$\ell_+(f) = \sup\{\ell(h) \mid 0 \leqslant h \leqslant f\}.$$

We have $\ell_+(f) \geqslant 0$ and $\ell(f) \leqslant \ell_+(f)$.

Note that $a \geqslant 0$ implies $\ell_+(af) = a\ell_+(f)$.

We claim that for two non-negative functions $f, g \in L$ we have $\ell_+(f + g) = \ell_+(f) + \ell_+(g)$.

If $0 \leqslant h_1 \leqslant f$ and $0 \leqslant h_2 \leqslant g$, then $0 \leqslant h_1 + h_2 \leqslant f + g$, which implies $\ell_+(f) + \ell_+(g) \leqslant \ell_+(f + g)$.

If $0 \leqslant h \leqslant f + g$, then $0 \leqslant h \wedge f \leqslant f$, hence $0 \leqslant h - (h \wedge f) \leqslant g$ and, therefore,

$$\ell(h) = \ell(h \wedge f) + \ell(h - (h \wedge f)) \leqslant \ell_+(f) + \ell_+(g).$$

By the definition of ℓ_+, this implies $\ell_+(f + g) \leqslant \ell_+(f) + \ell_-(g)$, hence $\ell_+(f + g) = \ell_+(f) + \ell_-(g)$.

Note that the previous considerations are developed for non-negative functions in L. We need to extend these observations to the entire function space L.

Let $f \in L$ be an arbitrary function in L. Since the functions of this space are bounded there exist two non-negative constants k_1, k_2 such that both $f + k_1$ and $f + k_2$ are non-negative. We have

$$\ell_+(f + k_1 + k_2) = \ell_+(f + k_1) + \ell_+(k_2)$$
$$= \ell_+(f + k_2) + \ell_+(k_1),$$

hence $\ell_+(f + k_1) - \ell_+(k_1) = \ell_+(f + k_2) - \ell_+(k_2)$. Therefore, the value of $\ell_+(f + k) - \ell_+(k)$ is independent of k. Now, the value of $\ell_+(f)$ is extended to the entire space L by choosing k such that $f + k$ is non-negative and defining $\ell_+(f)$ as $\ell_+(f+k) - \ell_+(k)$. Now we have $\ell_+(f+g) = \ell_+(f) + \ell_-(g)$ and $\ell_+(af) = a\ell_+(f)$ for every $f, g \in L$ and $a \geqslant 0$. Furthermore, since $\ell_+(-f) + \ell_+(f) = \ell_+(0) = 0$, we have $\ell_+(-f) = -\ell_+(f)$, hence $\ell_+(af) = a\ell_+(f)$ for $a \in \mathbb{R}$, so ℓ_+ is a linear functional on L. Since $\ell_= \ell_+ - \ell$, and $\ell(f) \leqslant \ell_+(f)$, it follows that ℓ_- is a positive linear functional.

Note that $\|\ell\| \leqslant \|\ell_+\| + \|\ell_-\| = \ell_+(c_1) + \ell_-(c_1)$.

If $f \in L$ is a function such that $0 \leqslant f(x) \leqslant 1$, then $|2f(x) - 1| \leqslant 1$, and $\|\ell\| \geqslant \ell(2f - 1) = 2\ell(f) - \ell(c_1)$. Therefore, $\|\ell\| \geqslant 2\ell_+(c_1) - \ell(c_1) = \ell_+(c_1) + \ell_-(c_1)$, hence $\|\ell\| = \ell_+(c_1) + \ell_-(c_1)$. $\qquad\square$

8.13 Fourier Transforms of Measures

Define the function $\mathsf{s} : \mathbb{R}_{\geqslant 0} \longrightarrow \mathbb{R}$ as:

$$\mathsf{s}(t) = \int_0^t \frac{\sin x}{x} \, dx.$$

We have shown in Example 8.9 that $\lim_{t \to \infty} \mathsf{s}(t) = \frac{\pi}{2}$. It is easy to verify that

$$\int_0^t \frac{\sin t\theta}{t} \, dt = sign(\theta)\mathsf{s}(t|\theta|) \qquad (8.26)$$

for $\theta \in \mathbb{R}$.

Definition 8.24. Let m be a finite measure on $\mathbb{R}^n$. The *Fourier transform* of m is the function $\hat{m} : \mathbb{R}^n \longrightarrow \mathbb{R}^n$ defined as:

$$\hat{m}(\mathbf{t}) = \int_{\mathbb{R}^n} e^{i(\mathbf{t},\mathbf{x})} \, dm_{\mathbf{x}}.$$

Recall that the sphere $B_\infty(\mathbf{0}_n, r)$ in $(\mathbb{R}^n, d_\infty)$ is:

$$B_\infty(\mathbf{0}_n, r) = \{\mathbf{x} \in \mathbb{R}^n \mid -r < x_k < r \text{ for } 1 \leqslant k \leqslant n\}.$$

In the next theorem we prove that the Fourier transform of a measure m defines the values of the measure m on open-closed intervals of $\mathbb{R}^n$ whose border is a null set. Since the family of open-closed intervals in $\mathbb{R}^n$ is a semi-ring of sets that generates the σ-algebra $\mathbb{B}(\mathbb{R})$ (by Supplement 30 of Chapter 7), it follows that two measures that have the same Fourier transforms must be equal.

Theorem 8.97. (The Inversion Theorem) *Let $G = (a_1, b_1] \times \cdots \times (a_n, b_n]$ be a bounded open-close interval and let m be a measure on $\mathbb{R}^n$ such that $m(\partial G) = 0$. We have:*

$$m(G) = \lim_{r \to \infty} \frac{1}{(2\pi)^n} \int_{B_\infty(\mathbf{0}_n, r)} \prod_{k=1}^n \frac{e^{-it_k a_k} - e^{-it_k b_k}}{it_k} \hat{m}(\mathbf{t}) \, d\mathbf{t},$$

where $d\mathbf{t}$ denotes $dt_1 \cdots dt_n$.

Proof. We have

$$\frac{1}{(2\pi)^n} \int_{B_\infty(\mathbf{0}_n, r)} \prod_{k=1}^n \frac{e^{-it_k a_k} - e^{-it_k b_k}}{it_k} \hat{m}(\mathbf{t}) \, d\mathbf{t}$$

$$= \frac{1}{(2\pi)^n} \int_{B_\infty(\mathbf{0}_n, r)} \prod_{k=1}^n \frac{e^{-it_k a_k} - e^{-it_k b_k}}{it_k} \left(\int_{\mathbb{R}^n} e^{i(\mathbf{t},\mathbf{x})} \, dm_{\mathbf{x}} \right) d\mathbf{t}$$

$$= \frac{1}{(2\pi)^n} \int_{\mathbb{R}^n} \left(\int_{B_\infty(\mathbf{0}_n, r)} \prod_{k=1}^n \frac{e^{-it_k a_k} - e^{-it_k b_k}}{it_k} e^{i(\mathbf{t},\mathbf{x})} \, d\mathbf{t} \right) dm_{\mathbf{x}}.$$

Next, the inner integral can be evaluated using Fubini's theorem as:

$$\int_{B_\infty(\mathbf{0}_n, r)} \prod_{k=1}^n \frac{e^{-it_k a_k} - e^{-it_k b_k}}{it_k} e^{i(\mathbf{t},\mathbf{x})} \, d\mathbf{t}$$

$$= \int_{B_\infty(\mathbf{0}_n, r)} \prod_{k=1}^n \frac{e^{-it_k a_k + it_k x_k} - e^{-it_k b_k + it_k x_k}}{it_k} \, d\mathbf{t}$$

$$= \int_{-r}^{r} \cdots \int_{-r}^{r} \prod_{k=1}^{n} \frac{e^{it_k(x_k-a_k)} - e^{it_k(x_k-b_k)}}{it_k} \, d\mathbf{t}$$

$$= \prod_{k=1}^{n} \int_{-r}^{r} \frac{e^{it_k(x_k-a_k)} - e^{it_k(x_k-b_k)}}{it_k} \, dt_k.$$

The integral $\int_{-r}^{r} \frac{e^{it_k(x_k-a_k)} - e^{it_k(x_k-b_k)}}{it_k} \, dt_k$ can be rewritten as

$$\int_{-r}^{r} \frac{e^{it_k(x_k-a_k)} - e^{it_k(x_k-b_k)}}{it_k} \, dt_k$$

$$= \int_{-r}^{0} \frac{e^{it_k(x_k-a_k)} - e^{it_k(x_k-b_k)}}{it_k} \, dt_k + \int_{0}^{r} \frac{e^{it_k(x_k-a_k)} - e^{it_k(x_k-b_k)}}{it_k} \, dt_k$$

$$= \int_{r}^{0} \frac{e^{-it_k(x_k-a_k)} - e^{-it_k(x_k-b_k)}}{it_k} + \int_{0}^{r} \frac{e^{it_k(x_k-a_k)} - e^{it_k(x_k-b_k)}}{it_k}$$

(by changing the variable t in the first integral to $-t$)

$$= \int_{r}^{0} (e^{it_k(x_k-a_k)} - e^{it_k(x_k-b_k)} + e^{-it_k(x_k-b_k)} - e^{-it_k(x_k-a_k)} \, it_k)$$

$$= 2 \int_{0}^{r} \frac{\sin t_k(x_k - a_k) - \sin t_k(x_k - b_k)}{t_k} \, dt_k$$

$$= 2(sign(x_k - a_k)\mathbf{s}(t \cdot |x_k - a_k|) - sign(x_k - b_k)\mathbf{s}(t \cdot |x_k - b_k|)).$$

This allows us to write

$$\frac{1}{(2\pi)^n} \int_{B_\infty(\mathbf{0}_n, r)} \prod_{k=1}^{n} \frac{e^{-it_k a_k} - e^{-it_k b_k}}{it_k} \hat{m}(\mathbf{t}) \, d\mathbf{t}$$

$$= \frac{1}{(2\pi)^n} \int_{\mathbb{R}^n} 2^n \prod_{k=1}^{n} (sign(x_k - a_k)\mathbf{s}(t \cdot |x_k - a_k|)$$

$$- sign(x_k - b_k)\mathbf{s}(t \cdot |x_k - b_k|)) dm_{\mathbf{x}}$$

$$= \frac{1}{\pi^n} \int_{\mathbb{R}^n} \prod_{k=1}^{n} (sign(x_k - a_k)\mathbf{s}(t \cdot |x_k - a_k|)$$

$$- sign(x_k - b_k)\mathbf{s}(t \cdot |x_k - b_k|)) dm_{\mathbf{x}}$$

$$= \frac{1}{\pi^n} \prod_{k=1}^{n} \int_{-\infty}^{\infty} (sign(x_k - a_k)\mathbf{s}(t \cdot |x_k - a_k|)$$

$$- sign(x_k - b_k)\mathbf{s}(t \cdot |x_k - b_k|)) dx_k.$$

Let $\gamma_{a,b,t}(x) = \frac{1}{\pi}(sign(x-a)\mathbf{s}(t \cdot |x-a|) - sign(x-b)\mathbf{s}(t \cdot |x-b|))$. The function $\gamma_{a,b,t}$ is bounded and $\lim_{t\to\infty} \gamma_{a,b,t}(x) = \xi_{a,b}(x)$, where

$$\xi_{a,b}(x) = \begin{cases} 0 & \text{if } x < a, \\ \frac{1}{2} & \text{if } x = a, \\ 1 & \text{if } a < x < b, \\ \frac{1}{2} & \text{if } x = b, \\ 0 & \text{if } x > b. \end{cases}$$

Therefore, $\int_{-\infty}^{\infty} \xi_{a,b}(x)\ dx = m((a,b]) + \frac{1}{2}m(\{a\}) + \frac{1}{2}m(\{b\}) = m((a,b])$ because $m(\{a\}) = m(\{b\}) = 0$. Consequently,

$$\lim_{r\to\infty} \frac{1}{(2\pi)^n} \int_{B_\infty(\mathbf{0}_n,r)} \prod_{k=1}^{n} \frac{e^{-it_k a_k} - e^{-it_k b_k}}{it_k} \hat{m}(\mathbf{t})\ dt,$$

$$= \prod_{k=1}^{n} m((a_k, b_k]) = m(G).$$

$\square$

Corollary 8.12. (Cramér-Wold Theorem) *The values of a finite measure m on $\mathbb{R}^n$ on every half-space of $\mathbb{R}^n$ determine completely the measure m.*

Proof. Let $H_{\mathbf{w},a}^{\leqq}$ be a half-space of $\mathbb{R}^n$. If m is a measure on $\mathbb{R}^n$, the measure of this half-space is $m(H_{\mathbf{w},a}) = m(f^{-1}(-\infty, a))$, where $f : \mathbb{R}^n \longrightarrow \mathbb{R}$ is the linear functional defined by $f(\mathbf{x}) = (\mathbf{w}, \mathbf{x})$ for $\mathbf{x} \in \mathbb{R}^n$. The Fourier transform of the measure mf^{-1} on $\mathbb{R}$ is $\int_{\mathbb{R}} e^{isa}\ d(mf^{-1})$. Applying a transformation of variables we obtain:

$$\int_{\mathbb{R}} e^{isa}\ d(mf^{-1}) = \int_{\mathbb{R}^n} e^{is(\mathbf{t}, \mathbf{x})}\ dm_x = \hat{m}(s\mathbf{t}).$$

In particular, $\hat{m}(\mathbf{t}) = \int_{\mathbb{R}} e^{ia}\ d(mf^{-1})$. Thus, the values of m on half-spaces in $\mathbb{R}^n$ determine completely the measure m. $\square$

Corollary 8.13. *The values of a finite signed measure m on $\mathbb{R}^n$ on every half-space of $\mathbb{R}^n$ determine completely the signed measure m.*

Proof. Let $m = m_+ - m_-$ be the Jordan decomposition of m as a difference of two measures (established in Theorem 7.72). The measure m determines uniquely the measures m_+ and m_- and these measures are, in turn determined uniquely by their values on half-spaces. $\square$

8.14   Lebesgue-Stieltjes Measures and Integrals

We start from the fact that the set $\mathcal{F}$ of unions of finite collections of disjoint open-closed intervals of $\mathbb{R}$ is an algebra of sets.

Theorem 8.98. *Let $F : \mathbb{R} \longrightarrow \mathbb{R}$ be an increasing and right-continuous function. The function $\phi^F : \mathcal{F} \longrightarrow \mathbb{R}$ defined by*

$$\phi^F \left(\bigcup_{j=1}^{n} (a_j, b_j] \right) = \sum_{j=1}^{n} (F(b_j) - F(a_j))$$

is a premeasure on $\mathcal{F}$.

Proof. A sequence of open-closed intervals $((c_1, d_1], \ldots, (c_m, d_m])$ is connected if $d_k = c_{k+1}$ for $1 \leqslant k \leqslant m - 1$. For such a sequence we have $\phi^F((c, d]) = \sum_{j=1}^{m} \phi^F((c_j, d_j])$. In this situation we refer to $((c_1, d_1], \ldots, (c_m, d_m])$ as a sequence subordinated to $(c, d]$.

Note that in the definition of ϕ^F the contribution of an open-closed interval can be replaced with the sum of the contributions of any subordinated sequence of open-closed intervals without changing the valued of ϕ^F. Thus, ϕ^F is well-defined. This also shows that ϕ^F is finitely additive.

We need to verify that if $\{U_n \mid n \geqslant 1\}$ is a sequence of pairwise disjoint sets in $\mathcal{F}$ such that $T = \bigcup_{n \geqslant 1} U_n \in \mathcal{F}$, then $\phi^F(T) = \sum_{n \geqslant 1} \phi^F(U_n)$.

Since $T \in \mathcal{F}$, T is a finite union of pairwise disjoint open-closed intervals, $T = \bigcup_{p=1}^{m} W_p$, we have $\phi^F(T) = \sum_{p=1}^{m} \phi^F(W_p)$. Therefore, the family $\{U_n \mid n \geqslant 1\}$ can be partitioned into a finite number of disjoint subfamilies $\mathcal{W}_1, \ldots, \mathcal{W}_m$ such that $W_i = \bigcup \{U \mid U \in \mathcal{W}_i\}$ for $1 \leqslant i \leqslant m$.

Suppose that $\mathcal{W}_i = \{U_k \mid k \in \mathbb{N}\}$. Since $\phi^F(W_i) \geqslant \phi^F\left(\bigcup_{k=1}^{n} U_k\right) = \sum_{k=1}^{n} \phi^F(U_K)$ for $n \leqslant 1$, it follows that $\phi^F(W_i) \geqslant \sum_{k=1}^{\infty} \phi^F(U_k)$.

Conversely, suppose that $W_i = (a, b]$, where $a, b \in \mathbb{R}$ and that $U_k = (a_k, b_k)$ for $k \geqslant 1$. Since F is right-continuous, for every $\epsilon > 0$ there exists δ such that $F(a + \delta) - F(a) < \epsilon$ and for each $k \geqslant 1$, there exists δ_k such that $F(b_k + \delta_k) - F(b_k) < \frac{\epsilon}{2^k}$.

Since $(a, b] = \bigcup_{k \geqslant 1} (a_k, b_k)$, we have $[a + \delta, b] = \bigcup_{k \geqslant 1} (a_k, b_k + \delta_j)$. The compactness of $[a+\delta, b]$ implies that there exists a finite subcover of $[a+\delta, b]$ by intervals of the form $(a_k, b_k + \delta_j)$. Keeping only those open intervals that are maximal we obtain the intervals $(a_1, b_1 + \delta_1), \ldots, (a_q, b_q + \delta_q)$ that cover

$[a + \delta, b]$, where $b_k + \delta_k \in (a_{k+1}, b_{k+1} + \delta_{k+1})$ for $1 \leqslant k \leqslant q - 1$. We have

$$\phi^F((a, b]) = F(b) - F(a) < F(b) - F(a + \delta) + \epsilon$$
$$\text{(because } F(a + \delta) - F(a) < \epsilon)$$
$$\leqslant F(b_n + \delta_q) - F(a_1) + \epsilon$$
$$= F(b_n + \delta_q) - F(a_q) + \sum_{k=1}^{q-1}(F(a_{j+1}) - F(a_j)) + \epsilon$$
$$\leqslant F(b_n + \delta_q) - F(a_q) + \sum_{k=1}^{q-1}(F(b_j + \delta_j) - F(a_j)) + \epsilon$$
$$< \sum_{j=1}^{q}(F(b_j) + \frac{\epsilon}{2^j} - F(a_j)) + \epsilon < \sum_{j \geqslant 1} \phi^F((a_j, b_j]) + 2\epsilon.$$

Since ϵ is arbitrary, this implies $\phi^F \leqslant \sum_{j \geqslant 1} \phi^F((a_j, b_j])$.

If $a = -\infty$, then the intervals $(a_j, b_j + \delta_j)$ cover $[-t, b]$ for every finite t, which imply $F(b) - F(-t) \leqslant \sum_{j \geqslant 1} \phi^F((a_j, b_j]) + 2\epsilon$, as above.

If $b = \infty$, $F(t) - F(a) \leqslant \sum_{j \geqslant 1} \phi^F((a_j, b_j]) + 2\epsilon$. Since this holds for arbitrary ϵ and t, we get the reverse inequality. □

Theorem 8.99. *Let $F : \mathbb{R} \longrightarrow \mathbb{R}$ be an increasing and right-continuous function. There exists a unique measure m^F on $\mathbb{R}$ such that $m^F((a, b]) = F(b) - F(a)$ for all $a, b \in \mathbb{R}$. If G is another such function, then $m^F = m_G$ if and only $F - G$ is a constant.*

Conversely, if m is a measure on $\mathbb{B}(\mathbb{R})$ that is finite on all bounded Borel sets, then the function $F : \mathbb{R} \longrightarrow \mathbb{R}$ defined by

$$F(x) = \begin{cases} m((0, x]) & \text{if } x > 0, \\ 0 & \text{if } x = 0, \\ -m((x, 0]) & \text{if } x < 0, \end{cases}$$

is an increasing and right-continuous function and $m = m^F$.

Proof. Let ϕ^F be the premeasure on the algebra $\mathcal{F}$ of unions of finite collections of disjoint open-closed intervals of $\mathbb{R}$. If $F - G$ is a constant, then it is immediate that $\phi^F = \phi^G$. Moreover, ϕ^F is σ-finite. The first part of the theorem follows from Carathéodory Extension Theorem (Theorem 7.39).

The monotonicity of m implies the monotonicity of F; also, and the continuity properties of m^F (Theorem 7.32) imply the right continuity of F. Since $m = m^F$ on $\mathcal{F}$, the equality of these measures on $\mathbb{B}(\mathbb{R})$ follows. □

The measure m^F introduced above is the *Lebesgue-Stieltjes* measure defined by F.

Example 8.10. For $F(x) = x$, m^F is the usual Lebesgue measure on $\mathbb{R}$. If F is defined as

$$F(x) = \begin{cases} 1 & \text{if } x \geqslant x_0, \\ 0 & \text{if } x < x_0, \end{cases}$$

then the Lebesgue-Stieltjes measure is the Dirac measure concentrated at x_0, δ_{x_0}.

Definition 8.25. A function $F : \mathbb{R} \longrightarrow \mathbb{R}$ is *absolutely continuous* on an interval $[a, b]$ if for every $\epsilon > 0$ there exists $\delta > 0$ such that for every finite collection of disjoint open intervals $\{(x_j, y_j) \mid (x_j, y_j) \subseteq [a, b] \text{ for } 1 \leqslant j \leqslant n\}$ with $\sum_{j=1}^{n}(y_j - x_j) < \delta$ we have $\sum_{j=1}^{n} |F(x_j) - F(y_j)| < \epsilon$.

Example 8.11. Let $h \in L^1([a, b])$ be a finite function. Then the function $f_h : \mathbb{R} \longrightarrow \mathbb{R}$ defined by $f_h(x) = \int_a^x h \, dm_L$ is absolutely continuous. Indeed, let $\{(x_j, y_j) \mid (x_j, y_j) \subseteq [a, b] \text{ for } 1 \leqslant j \leqslant n\}$ be a finite collection and let $E = \bigcup_{j=1}^{n}(x_j, y_j)$. We have:

$$\sum_{j=1}^{n} |f_h(y_j) - f_h(x_j)| = \sum_{j=1}^{n} \left| \int_{x_j}^{y_j} h \, dm_L \right| \leqslant \sum_{j=1}^{n} \int_{x_j}^{y_j} |h| \, dm_L = \int_E |h| \, dm_L.$$

Since $h \in L^1([a, b])$, the measure $m(E) = \int_E |h| \, dm_L$ is absolutely continuous with respect to m_L and, therefore, by Theorem 8.53, there exists $\delta > 0$ such that $m_L(E) < \delta$ implies $m(E) < \epsilon$. If the total length $\sum_{j=1}^{n}(y_j - x_j) < \delta$, then $m(E) < \epsilon$.

Theorem 8.100. *Let $F : \mathbb{R} \longrightarrow \mathbb{R}$ be a monotone and absolutely continuous on $\mathbb{R}$ and let m^F be the Lebesgue-Stieltjes measure generated by F. Then every Lebesgue measurable set is m^F-measurable and $m^F \ll m_L$.*

Proof. Let B be a Borel set such that $m_L(B) = 0$. We claim that $m^F(B) = 0$. There exists a sequence of open sets $U_1 \supseteq U_2 \supseteq \cdots \supseteq B$ such that $m_L(U_1) < \delta$ and thus, $m_L(U_j) < \delta$ for all $j \in \mathbb{N}$. Also, $\lim_{n \to \infty} m^F(U_j) = m^F(B)$.

By Theorem 4.1 an open set U_j can be written as a union of disjoint open intervals $U_j = \bigcup_{k \in \mathbb{N}}(a_j^k, b_j^k)$; therefore,

$$\sum_{k=1}^{n} |m^F(a_j^k, b_j^k)| \leqslant \sum_{k=1}^{n} |F(b_j^k) - F(a_j^k)| \leqslant \epsilon.$$

When $n \to \infty$ we obtain $|m^F(U_j)| < \epsilon$, hence $|m^F(B)| \leqslant \epsilon$. Since ϵ is arbitrary, $m^F(B) = 0$, hence $m^F \ll m_L$. $\qquad \square$

8.15 Distributions of Random Variables

Definition 8.26. Let $X : \Omega \longrightarrow \mathbb{R}$ be a random variable on a probability space $(\Omega, \mathcal{E}, P)$. The Lebesgue integral $\int_\Omega X \, dP$ is the *expectation* of X or the *mean value* of X and it is denoted by $E(X)$.

Markov's inequality (Theorem 8.41) applied to a random variables X becomes

$$P(X \geqslant a) \leqslant \frac{1}{a} E(X).$$

The number $\int_\Omega (X - E(X))^2 \, dP$ is the *variance* of X and is denoted by $var(X)$.

Chebyshev's Inequality (inequality (8.6)) can be written as:

$$P(|X - E(X)| > k \sqrt{var(X)}) \leqslant \frac{1}{k^2}.$$

Definition 8.27. The *distribution* of a random variable $X : \Omega \longrightarrow \mathbb{R}$ is the measure P_X on $\mathbb{B}(\hat{\mathbb{R}})$ defined by:

$$P_X(U) = P(X^{-1}(U)) = P(\{\omega \in \Omega \mid X(\omega) \in U\}),$$

for every Borel subset U of $\mathbb{R}$.

The triple $(\mathbb{R}, \mathbb{B}(\mathbb{R}), P_X)$ is itself a probability space referred to as the *probability space induced by* X. Instead of writing $P_X(U)$ we may write $P(X \in U)$ for any Borel subset U of $\mathbb{R}$.

Example 8.12. A *discrete random variable* is a random variable $X : \Omega \longrightarrow \mathbb{R}$ that is a measurable function between a probability space $(\Omega, \mathcal{E}, P)$ and $(\mathbb{R}, \mathbb{B}(\mathbb{R}), m_L)$ such that $\mathsf{Ran}(X) = \{x_1, \ldots, x_n, \ldots\}$ is a countable set. The partition of Ω related to X is $\{X^{-1}(x_1), \ldots, X^{-1}(x_n), \ldots\}$. The number $p_j = P(X^{-1}(x_j)$ is the *point mass* in x_j.

Note that $\sum_{j \geq 1} p_j = 1$.

Definition 8.28. Let X, Y be two random variables on the measure space $(\Omega, \mathcal{E}, P)$. X and Y are *equal in distribution* if $P_X = P_Y$.

X and Y are *pointwise equal* if $P(\{\omega \in \Omega \mid X(\omega) = Y(\omega)\}) = 1$.

If X, Y are pointwise equal, then they are equal in distribution. The reverse is false as the next example shows.

Example 8.13. Let $(\Omega, \mathcal{E}, P)$ be the probability space introduced in Example 7.19 that describes the coin throwing experiment. Define X, Y as

$$X(\omega) = \begin{cases} 1 & \text{if } \omega = \mathbf{h}, \\ 0 & \text{if } \omega = \mathbf{t} \end{cases} \quad \text{and } Y(\omega) = \begin{cases} 1 & \text{if } \omega = \mathbf{t}, \\ 0 & \text{if } \omega = \mathbf{h}. \end{cases}$$

X and Y are equal on distribution; however, $X(\omega) \neq Y(\omega)$ for every $\omega \in \Omega = \{\mathbf{h}, \mathbf{t}\}$.

$X : \Omega \longrightarrow \mathbb{R}$ is a random variable on the probability space $(\Omega, \mathcal{E}, P)$ if and only if for every Borel set A, we have $X^{-1}(A) \in \mathcal{E}$. Since the Borel σ-algebra $\mathbb{B}(\mathbb{R})$ is generated by sets of the form $(-\infty, x]$ (by Theorem 7.5) it suffices to have $X^{-1}((-\infty, x]) = \{\omega \in \Omega \mid X(\omega) \leqslant x\} \in \mathbb{B}(\mathbb{R})$ for every $x \in \mathbb{R}$ for X to be a random variable.

Definition 8.29. Let $X : \Omega \longrightarrow \mathbb{R}$ be a random variable on the probability space $(\Omega, \mathcal{E}, P)$. The *distribution function* of X is the function $F_X : \mathbb{R} \longrightarrow [0, 1]$ defined by $F_X(x) = P(\{\omega \mid X(\omega) \leqslant x\})$ for $x \in \mathbb{R}$.

To simplify notation we will denote $P(\{\omega \mid X(\omega) \leqslant x\})$ by $P(X \leqslant x)$.

Example 8.14. The distribution function of a discrete random variable X with $\mathsf{Ran}(X) = \{x_1, \ldots, x_n, \ldots\}$ is $F_X(x) = \sum\{p_j \mid x_j \leqslant x\}$.

Definition 8.30. A random variable X is
  (i) *continuous* if F_X is continuous;
  (ii) *absolutely continuous* if there exists a non-negative Lebesgue integrable function f such that $F_X(b) - F_X(a) = \int_a^b f \, dm_L$;
  (iii) *singular* if F' exists and $F'(x) = 0$ a.e.

Example 8.15. If X is a discrete random variable, then X is singular.

Theorem 8.101. *Let $F_X : \mathbb{R} \longrightarrow [0, 1]$ be a distribution function of a random variable X. Then F_X is non-decreasing function that is monotonic, $0 \leqslant F_X(x) \leqslant 1$, F_X is right-continuous, $\lim_{x \to -\infty} F_X(x) = 0$, and $\lim_{x \to \infty} F_X(x) = 1$.*

Proof. F_X is clearly monotonic and $0 \leqslant F_X(x) \leqslant 1$.

Let (u_n) be a decreasing sequence in $\mathbb{R}$ such that $\lim_{n \to \infty} u_n = x_0$. The sequence of events (U_n) defined by $U_n = \{\omega \in \Omega \mid X(\omega) \leqslant u_n\}$ is decreasing and $\bigcap_{n \in \mathbb{N}} U_n = U$, where $U = \{\omega \in \Omega \mid X(\omega) \leqslant x\}$. Therefore, by the continuity from above shown in Theorem 7.32,

$$F_X(x_0) = P(\lim U_n) = \lim_{n \to \infty} P(U_n) = \lim_{n \to \infty} F_X(u_n),$$

which shows that $F_X(x_0) = \lim x \to x_0 + F_X(x)$, that is, F_X is right-continuous. By the continuity from below, it follows that if $\lim_{x \to x_0-} F_X(x) = P(\{\omega \in \Omega \mid X(\omega) < x_0\}$. It is clear that $\lim_{x \to -\infty} F_X(x) = 0$, and $\lim_{x \to \infty} F_X(x) = 1$. $\quad\square$

Corollary 8.14. *A distribution function F_X of a random variable X has at most a countable set of discontinuity points.*

Proof. Since

$$\text{jump}(F_X, x_0) = \lim_{x \to x_0+} F_X(x) - \lim_{x \to x_0-} F_X(x) = P(\{\omega \in \Omega \mid X(\omega) = x_0\}).$$

Therefore, by Theorem 4.62, F_X can have at most a countable set of discontinuity points. $\quad\square$

Theorem 8.102. *If $F : \mathbb{R} \longrightarrow [0,1]$ is non-decreasing function that is monotonic, $0 \leqslant F(x) \leqslant 1$, F is right-continuous, $\lim_{x \to -\infty} F(x) = 0$, and $\lim_{x \to \infty} F_X(x) = 1$, then there exists a random variable X such that $F = F_X$.*

Proof. Consider the probability space $([0,1], \mathbb{B}([0,1], P)$, where P is the Lebesgue measure m_L restricted to $[0,1]$.

Suppose initially that F is continuous and strictly increasing. Thus, F is invertible. Define the random variable X as $X(a) = F^{-1}(a)$ for $a \in [0,1]$. Since F^{-1} is increasing, X is measurable. We have

$$P(\{a \in [0,1] \mid X(a) \leqslant x\})$$
$$= m_L(\{a \in [0,1] \mid F^{-1}(a) \leqslant x\}) = m_L(\{a \in [0,1] \mid a \leqslant F(x)\}) = F(x).$$

If F is not strictly increasing let h be the function defined as $h(a) = \inf\{x \mid a \leqslant F(x)\}$. Note that the set $\{x \mid a \leqslant F(x)\}$ has the form $[h(a), \infty)$ because F is right-continuous. This implies $h(a) \leqslant x$ if and only if $a \leqslant F(x)$. Thus, if X is defined as $X(a) = h(a)$ for $0 < a < 1$, then X is a random variable and $m_L(\{a \mid X(a) \leqslant x\}) = F(x)$, hence $m_L(a, b] = F(b) - F(a)$. $\quad\square$

Definition 8.31. An absolutely continuous random variable X on a probability space $(\Omega, \mathcal{E}, P)$ has *a probability density function* (pdf) f if $f : \mathbb{R} \longrightarrow \mathbb{R}_{\geqslant 0}$ is a measurable function such that for every $U \in \mathbb{B}(\mathbb{R})$ we have $P(\{\omega \in \Omega \mid X(\omega) \in U\}) = \int_U f(x) \, dx$.

If f is a random variable density of a random variable X, then $f(x) \geqslant 0$ and $\int_{\mathbb{R}} f(x) \, dx = 1$. It is clear that the probability density function is not unique for a random variable. Indeed if f is a density for X and $f = g$ a.e., then g is also a density for X.

If F_X is a distribution functions having the pdf f, we have

$$F_X(x) = P_X(X \leqslant x) = \int_{-\infty}^{x} f(t) \, dt.$$

Example 8.16. Let $a, b \in \mathbb{R}$ be such that $a < b$. A random variable X whose range is $[a, b]$ has a *uniform distribution* if its pdf is

$$f(x) = \begin{cases} \dfrac{1}{b-a} & \text{if } x \in [a, b], \\ 0 & \text{otherwise.} \end{cases}$$

The corresponding distribution function is

$$F_X(x) = \int_{-\infty}^{x} f(t) \, dt = \begin{cases} 0 & \text{if } x < a, \\ \dfrac{x-a}{b-a} & \text{if } a \leqslant x < b, \\ 1 & \text{if } b \leqslant x. \end{cases}$$

Uniformly distributed random variable play an important role highlighted by the following statement:

Theorem 8.103. *Let X be a random variable that has a continuous distribution function F_X. The random variable $Y = F_X(X)$ has a uniform distribution on $[0, 1]$.*

Proof. Since $0 \leqslant F_X(x) \leqslant 1$ if follows that $P(Y < 0) = P(Y > 1) = 0$.

Let $y \in (0, 1)$. If F_X is strictly increasing there is a unique x_0 such that $F_X(x_0) = y$. Then $F_Y(y) = P(Y \leqslant y) = P(X \leqslant x_0) = F_X(x_0) = y$ for $y \in (0, 1)$, which means that Y is uniformly distributed in $[0, 1]$. If F_X is not strictly increasing, then x_0 can be arbitrarily chosen such that $F_X(x_0) = y$. $\square$

Theorem 8.103 is useful for generating random variables with a prescribed distribution function starting with a random variable distributed uniformly. Indeed, if we seek to generate values of a random variable X with an invertible distribution function F_X, taking into account that $Y = F_X(X)$ is uniformly distributed on $[0, 1]$ we obtain $X = F_X^{-1}(Y)$.

Example 8.17. The random variable X has a *normal distribution* with parameters m, σ if it has the pdf

$$f_{m,\sigma}(x) = \frac{1}{\sigma\sqrt{2\pi}} e^{-\left(\frac{x-m}{\sigma}\right)^2}$$

for $x \in \mathbb{R}$. Note that $f(x) > 0$ for $x \in \mathbb{R}$.

To show that f is a pdf we need to verify that $\int_{\mathbb{R}} f_{m,\sigma}(x)\, dx = 1$. Let $y = \frac{x-m}{\sigma}$. We have:

$$\int_{\mathbb{R}} f_{m,\sigma}(x)\, dx = \int_{\mathbb{R}} \frac{1}{\sqrt{2\pi}} e^{-\frac{1}{2}y^2}\, dy.$$

Define $I = \int_{\mathbb{R}} e^{-\frac{1}{2}y^2}\, dy$. Then, we can write

$$I^2 = \int_{\mathbb{R}} e^{-\frac{1}{2}y^2}\, dy \int_{\mathbb{R}} e^{-\frac{1}{2}z^2}\, dz = \int_{\mathbb{R}} e^{-\frac{1}{2}(y^2+z^2)}\, dy\, dz.$$

Changing the variables to polar coordinates $y = r\cos\theta$ and $z = r\sin\theta$ we obtain

$$I^2 = \int_0^{2\pi} \int_0^{\infty} e^{-\frac{r^2}{2}} r\, dr\, d\theta = 2\pi,$$

which shows that $f_{m,\sigma}$ is indeed a pdf.

The class of random variables with parameters m, σ is denoted by $\mathcal{N}(m,\sigma)$. If X belongs to this class we will write $X \sim \mathcal{N}(m,\sigma)$.

If $X : \Omega \longrightarrow \mathbb{R}$ is random variable and $h : \mathbb{R} \longrightarrow \mathbb{R}$ is a Borel measurable function, then $Y = hX$ is a random variable by Theorem 7.78. Suppose that h is a monotonic and invertible function having the inverse g. The distribution of Y is

$$P_Y(U) = P(hX \in U) = P(X \in h^{-1}(U)). \tag{8.27}$$

The distribution function of Y is:

$$F_Y(t) = P(Y \leqslant t) = P(hX \leqslant t) = P(X \leqslant g(t)) = F_X(g(t)).$$

Thus, $F_Y(t) = F_X(g(t))$ for $t \in \mathbb{R}$.

If F_X has a density that allow us to write $F_X' = f$, then the density of F_Y is $F_Y'(t) = F_X'(g(t))g'(t) = f(g(t))g'(t)$ for $t \in \mathbb{R}$.

Example 8.18. Suppose that $h(t) = at+b$ for $t \in \mathbb{R}$, where $a > 0$. Then h is monotonic and invertible and for $Y = aX + b$ we have $F_Y(t) = F_X\left(\frac{t-b}{a}\right)$. If F_X has a density, then the density of F_Y is

$$F_Y'(t) = \frac{1}{a} F_X'\left(\frac{t-b}{a}\right).$$

For example, if $X \sim \mathcal{N}(m,\sigma)$, then $F_Y'(t) = \frac{1}{a\sigma\sqrt{2\pi}} e^{-\frac{(t-(am+b))^2}{a^2\sigma^2}}$, hence $Y \in \mathcal{N}(am+b, a\sigma)$.

8.16 Random Vectors

Definition 8.32. An n-dimensional *random vector* is a measurable function $\mathbf{X}$ from a probability space $(\Omega, \mathcal{E}, P)$ into $(\mathbb{R}^n, \mathbb{B}(\mathbb{R}^n))$.

The *distribution* of $\mathbf{X}$ is the measure $P_{\mathbf{X}}$ on $\mathbb{R}^n$ defined by $P_X(U) = P(\{\omega \in \Omega \mid \mathbf{X}(\omega) \in U\})$ for $U \in \mathbb{B}(\mathbb{R}^n)$.

Let $p_j : \mathbb{R}^n \longrightarrow \mathbb{R}$ be the jth projection, $p_j : \mathbb{R}^n \longrightarrow \mathbb{R}$, where $1 \leqslant j \leqslant n$. The random variable $X_j = p_j \mathbf{X}$ is the jth component of $\mathbf{X}$.

The *joint distribution function* of $\mathbf{X}$ is the function $F_{\mathbf{X}} : \mathbb{R}^n \longrightarrow \mathbb{R}$ defined by

$$F_{\mathbf{X}}(x_1, \ldots, x_n) = P\left(\bigcap_{j=1}^{n} \{\omega \in \Omega \mid X_j \leqslant x_j\}\right).$$

Note that $F_{\mathbf{X}}(\mathbf{x}) = P\left(\bigcap_{i=1}^{n}(X_i \leqslant x_i)\right)$ for $\mathbf{x} \in \mathbb{R}^n$. The *marginal distributions* of the distribution function $F_{\mathbf{X}}$ are the distribution functions F_{X_i}.

Let $\mathbf{X} : \Omega \longrightarrow \mathbb{R}^n$ be a random vector and let $\mathbf{h} : \mathbb{R}^n \longrightarrow \mathbb{R}^k$ is a measurable function between $(\mathbb{R}^n, \mathbb{B}(\mathbb{R}^n), m_L)$ and $(\mathbb{R}^m, \mathbb{B}(\mathbb{R}^m), m_L)$. Then, using an argument similar to the one of Theorem 7.78, it follows that $\mathbf{Y} = \mathbf{h}\mathbf{X}$ is an m-dimensional random vector.

Definition 8.33. Let $X_1, \ldots, X_n$ be n random variables on a probability space $(\Omega, \mathcal{E}, P)$. $X_1, \ldots, X_n$ are *independent* if for any sets $U_1, \ldots, U_n \in \mathbb{B}(\mathbb{R})$ we have

$$P\left(\bigcap_{i=1}^{n} X_i \in U_i\right) = \prod_{i=1}^{n} P(X_i \in U_i).$$

Theorem 8.104. *The random variables $X_1, \ldots, X_n$ are independent if $F_X(x_1, \ldots, x_n) = \prod_{i=1}^{n} F_{X_i}(x_i)$.*

Proof. The necessity of the condition of the theorem follows by taking $U_i = (-\infty, x_i]$ for $1 \leqslant n$ in Definition 8.33.

The sufficiency of follows from Theorem 7.22 and the fact that sets of the form $(-\infty, x]$ form a π-system that generates $\mathbb{B}(\mathbb{R})$. $\qquad\square$

Let $X_1, \ldots, X_n$ be n independent random variables. If F_{X_i} has the density f_i for $1 \leqslant i \leqslant n$, then Fubini's Theorem implies that $\int_{-\infty}^{x_1} \cdots \int_{-\infty}^{x_n} f_1 \cdots f_n \, dm_L = F_{X_1}(x_1) \cdots F_{X_n}(x_n)$, so the distribution function $F_{\mathbf{X}}$ of the random vector $\mathbf{X}$ having components $X_1, \ldots, X_n$ has the density $f_{\mathbf{X}}$ given by $f_{\mathbf{X}}(\mathbf{x}) = f_{X_1}(x_1) \cdots f_{X_n}(x_n)$ for $\mathbf{x} \in \mathbb{R}^n$.

Theorem 8.105. *The random variables* X_1, X_2 *on the probability space* $(\Omega, \mathcal{E}, P)$ *are independent if and only if* $E(f(X_1)g(X_2)) = E(f(X_1))E(g(X_2))$ *for all Borel measurable bounded functions* f, g.

Proof. We first show that the condition is sufficient. If we choose $f = 1_{B_1}$ and $g = 1_{B_2}$, where B_1, B_2 are two Borel sets, we have

$$P((X_1 \in B_1) \cap (X_2 \in B_2)) = \int_\Omega 1_{B_1 \times B_2}(X_1(\omega), X_2(\omega))\, dP$$

$$= \int_\Omega 1_{B_1}(X_1(\omega)) 1_{B_2}(X_2(\omega))\, dP$$

$$= \int_\Omega 1_{B_1}(X_1(\omega))\, dP \int_\Omega 1_{B_2}(X_2(\omega))\, dP$$

$$= P(X_1 \in B_1) P(X_2 \in B_2),$$

which show that X_1, X_2 are indeed independent.

To prove that the necessity suppose that X_1, X_2 are independent. The equality of the theorem holds for the Borel sets B_1, B_2, $f = 1_{B_1}, g = 1_{B_2}$ as we saw.

If f, g are simple measurable functions, then f and g are linear combinations of characteristic functions of sets in $\mathcal{E}$,

$$f = \sum_{i=1}^n b_i 1_{B_i}, g = \sum_{j=1}^m c_j 1_{C_j}.$$

This allows us to write

$$E(f(X_1)g(X_2)) = E\left(\sum_{i=1}^n b_i 1_{B_i} \sum_{j=1}^m c_j 1_{C_j}\right)$$

$$= \sum_{i=1}^n b_i c_j \sum_{j=1}^m E(1_{B_i}(X_1) 1_{C_j}(X_2))$$

$$= \sum_{i=1}^n b_i c_j \sum_{j=1}^m E(1_{B_i}(X_1)) E(1_{C_j}(X_2))$$

$$= \sum_{i=1}^n b_i E(1_{B_i}(X_1)) \sum_{j=1}^m E(1_{C_j}(X_2))$$

$$= E(f(X_1)) E(g(X_2)).$$

Consider now two measurable bounded functions. Since every bounded measurable function f is the limit of a sequence of simple measurable functions, by the Dominated Convergence Theorem the result follows. $\qquad \square$

Definition 8.34. Let X_1, X_2 be two random variables. The *correlation coefficient* of X_1 and X_2 is the number:

$$\rho_{X_1, X_2} = \frac{cov(X_1, X_2)}{\sqrt{var(X_1)var(X_2)}}.$$

We have $|\rho_{X_1, X_2}| \leqslant 1$. The random variables X_1, X_2 are *uncorrelated* if $\rho_{X_1, X_2} = 0$.

Theorem 8.106. *Let X_1, X_2 be two random variables. If X_1, X_2 are independent, then they are uncorrelated, that is, $cov(X_1, X_2) = 0$.*

Proof. Let f, g be the functions defined by $f(x) = x - E(X_1)$ and $g(x) = x - E(X_2)$ in Theorem 8.105. Since X_1, X_2 are independent we have

$$cov(X_1, X_2) = E(f(X_1)g(X_2)) = E((X_1 - E(X_1))(X_2 - E(X_2)))$$
$$= E(X_1 - E(X_1))E(X_2 - E(X_2)) = 0$$

because $E(X_1 - E(X_1)) = E(X_2 - E(X_2)) = 0$. $\square$

Definition 8.35. Let $\mathbf{X}$ be a random vector ranging in $\mathbb{R}^n$. The *mean vector* of $\mathbf{X}$ is the vector $\mathbf{m} = E(\mathbf{X}) \in \mathbb{R}^n$ having the components $m_j = E(X_j)$ for $1 \leqslant j \leqslant n$.

The *covariance matrix* of $\mathbf{X}$ is the matrix $cov(\mathbf{X})$, where $(cov(\mathbf{X}))_{ij} = E((X_i - E(X_i))(X_j - E(X_j)))$.

Observe that

$$cov(\mathbf{X})_{ij} = \begin{cases} var(X_i) & \text{if } i = j, \\ cov(X_i, X_j) & \text{if } i \neq j. \end{cases}$$

Theorem 8.107. *The covariance matrix of a random vector is positive semi-definite.*

Proof. Let $\mathbf{X}$ be a random vector ranging in $\mathbb{R}^n$. Since $cov(X_i, X_j) = cov(X_j, X_i)$ for $1 \leqslant i, j \leqslant n$, it follows that $cov(\mathbf{X})$ is symmetric.

Moreover, we have

$$\mathbf{y}' cov(\mathbf{X})\mathbf{y} = \sum_i \sum_j y_i cov(X_i, X_j) y_j$$

$$= cov\left(\sum_i y_i X_i, \sum_j y_j X_j\right) = var(Z) \geqslant 0,$$

where $Z = \sum_j y_j X_j$. $\square$

If $rank(cov(\mathbf{X})) = n$ then $\mathbf{X}$ is a *non-degenerate n-dimensional random vector*.

If $\mathbf{X}$ is an n-dimensional random vector, the random vector $\tilde{X} = X - E(X)$ is said to be *centered*. This is justified by the fact that $E(\tilde{X}) = 0$. The covariance matrix of $\mathbf{X}$ can now be written as $cov(\mathbf{X}) = E(\tilde{\mathbf{X}}\tilde{\mathbf{X}}')$.

Theorem 8.108. *Let $(\omega, \mathcal{E}, P)$ be a probability space, X be an integrable random variable, and let $\mathcal{G}$ be a σ-algebra on Ω such that $\mathcal{G} \subseteq \mathcal{E}$. There exists an integrable random variable $Y : \Omega \longrightarrow \mathbb{R}$ on $(\Omega, \mathcal{G}, P)$ such that $\int_G Y \, dP = \int_G X \, dP$ for every $G \in \mathcal{G}$.*

Proof. Suppose initially that X is non-negative. Define the measure $m(G) = \int_G X \, dP$. Since X is integrable, m is finite and $m \ll P$. By Radon-Nikodym Theorem (Theorem 8.58) there exists a $\mathcal{G}$-measurable function f such that $m(G) = \int_G f \, dP$. Then, we can define $Y = f$.

If X is not non-negative, the same argument can be applied separately to X^+ and X^-. If Y^+ and Y^- are the resulting random variables, Y can be defined as $Y = Y^+ - Y^-$. $\square$

The random variable Y constructed in the proof of Theorem 8.108 is not unique (there could be several such random variables that may differ on $\mathcal{G}$-null sets). If Y_1 and Y_2 are two random variables that satisfy the condition of Theorem 8.108, then $P(Y_1 = Y_2) = 1$.

Definition 8.36. Let $(\omega, \mathcal{E}, P)$ be a probability space, X be an integrable random variable and let $\mathcal{G}$ be a σ-algebra on Ω such that $\mathcal{G} \subseteq \mathcal{E}$.

A *conditional expectation* of X generated by the σ-algebra $\mathcal{G}$ is a random variable Y introduced as in Theorem 8.108.

With the notation introduced here we have:

$$\int_G E(X|\mathcal{G}) \, dP = \int_G X \, dP$$

for every $G \in \mathcal{G}$.

Example 8.19. Let $(\omega, \mathcal{E}, P)$ be a probability space, X be an integrable random variable, and let $\mathcal{G} = \{\emptyset, \Omega\}$. We have $E(X|\mathcal{G}) = E(X)$.

If X is $\mathcal{G}$-measurable, then for every Borel set $B \in \mathbb{B}(\mathbb{R})$ we have $X^{-1} \in \mathcal{G}$. Therefore, $\int_G E(X|\mathcal{G}) \, dP = \int_G X \, dP$ for every $G \in \mathcal{G}$ and we have $E(X|\mathcal{G}) = X$ almost surely.

Example 8.20. If $X^{-1}(\mathbb{B}(\mathbb{R}))$ and $\mathcal{G}$ are independent, then $E(X|\mathcal{G}) = E(X)$. Indeed, note that $\{1_G \mid G \in \mathcal{G}\}$ are independent random variables, hence

$$\int_G X \, dP = E(1_G X) = E(X)E(1_G) = \int_G E(X) \, dP,$$

hence $E(X)$ a version of $E(X|\mathcal{G})$. Since $E(X)$ is constant, the equality holds.

Example 8.21. Let $(\Omega, \mathcal{E}, P)$ be a probability space, $\pi = \{B_i \mid i \in I\}$ be a countable partition of Ω that consists of members of $\mathcal{E}$, and let $\mathcal{G} = \mathcal{E}_\pi$ (see Theorem 1.34). The random variable $Y = E(X|\mathcal{G})$ has the value a_i over B_i, hence $a_i P(B_i) = \int_{B_i} X \, dP$. Thus, if $P(B_i) > 0$ and $\omega \in B_i$ we have

$$Y(\omega) = \frac{1}{P(B_i)} \int_{B_i} X \, dP.$$

If $P(B_i) = 0$, the value of $Y(\omega)$ is constant on B_i (but arbitrary).

Definition 8.37. Let $(\Omega, \mathcal{E}, P)$ be a probability space, Y be an integrable random variable on this space and let X be another random variable on the same space. Define the conditional expectation $E(Y|X)$ as $E(Y|\mathcal{E}_X)$.

Conditional expectation is linear, that is, $E(aX + bY|\mathcal{G}) = aE(X|\mathcal{G}) + bE(Y|\mathcal{G})$ for $a, b \in \mathbb{R}$. The random variable $aE(X|\mathcal{G}) + bE(Y|\mathcal{G})$ is $\mathcal{G}$-measurable. If $A \in \mathcal{G}$, then by the linearity of the integral we have

$$\int_A (aE(X|\mathcal{G}) + bE(Y|\mathcal{G})) \, dP = a \int_A E(X|\mathcal{G}) \, dP + b \int_A E(Y|\mathcal{G}) \, dP$$

$$= a \int_A X \, dP + b \int_A Y \, dP = \int_A (aX + bY) \, dP.$$

If $X \leqslant Y$, then $E(X|\mathcal{G}) \leqslant E(Y|\mathcal{G})$. Indeed, we have

$$\int_A E(X|\mathcal{G}) \, dP = \int_A X \, dP \leqslant \int_A Y \, dP = \int_A E(Y|\mathcal{G}),$$

which implies $P(E(X|\mathcal{G}) - E(Y|\mathcal{G}) > 0) = 0$, which yields the conclusion.

Theorem 8.109. (The Tower Property) *Let $(\Omega, \mathcal{E}, P)$ be a probability space, and let $\mathcal{G}_1, \mathcal{G}_2$ be two σ-algebras on Ω such that $\mathcal{G}_1 \subseteq \mathcal{G}_2 \subseteq \mathcal{E}$. If X is a random variable such that $E(X) < \infty$ then*

$$E(E(X|\mathcal{G}_2)|\mathcal{G}_1) = E(X|\mathcal{G}_1).$$

Proof. We have $\int_{G_2} E(X|\mathcal{G}_2) \, dP = \int_{G_2} X \, dP$ for $G_2 \in \mathcal{G}_2$ and $\int_{G_1} E(X|\mathcal{G}_1) \, dP = \int_{G_1} X \, dP$ for $G_1 \in \mathcal{G}_1 \subseteq \mathcal{G}_2$. Therefore, for $G_1 \in \mathcal{G}_1$ we obtain

$$\int_{G_1} E(X|\mathcal{G}_2) \, dP = \int_{G_1} E(X|\mathcal{G}_1) \, dP.$$

Thus, $E(X|\mathcal{G}_1)$ satisfies the condition defining the conditional expectation of $E(X|\mathcal{G}_2)$ with respect to $\mathcal{G}_1$, and the equality of the theorem follows.

$\square$

Corollary 8.15. *Let $(\Omega, \mathcal{E}, P)$ be a probability space, and let X, Y be two random variables defined on this space, where X is integrable (that is, $E(X) < \infty$). We have $E(E(X|Y)) = E(X)$.*

Proof. If $\mathcal{G}_1 = \{\emptyset, \Omega\}$ and $\mathcal{G}_2 = \mathcal{E}_Y$ we have $\mathcal{G}_1 \subseteq \mathcal{G}_2$. The equality of theorem 8.109 amounts to the equality to be shown here. $\qquad\square$

Exercises and Supplements

(1) Let $f : \mathbb{R}^r \longrightarrow \mathbb{R}$ be a Lebesgue measurable function such that

$$\mathfrak{l}(f) = \inf\{\epsilon \mid m_L(\{\mathbf{x} \mid |f(\mathbf{x})| > \epsilon\}) \leqslant \epsilon\}$$

is finite.
Prove that:
(a) We have $\lambda = \mathfrak{l}(f)$ if and only if
    i. $m_L(\{\mathbf{x} \mid |f(\mathbf{x})| > \lambda\}) \leqslant \lambda$, and
    ii. $m_L(\{\mathbf{x} \mid |f(\mathbf{x})| > \lambda - \delta\}) > \lambda - \delta$ for each $\delta > 0$.
 Solution: Suppose that $\lambda = \mathfrak{l}(f)$. By the definition of $\mathfrak{l}(f)$ we have $m_L(\{\mathbf{x} \mid |f(\mathbf{x})| > \mathfrak{l}(f) - \delta\}) > \mathfrak{l}(f) - \delta$ for each $\delta > 0$, so the second condition of the first part is satisfied by λ. By the same reason,

$$m_L(\{\mathbf{x} \mid f(\mathbf{x}) > \mathfrak{l}(f) + \epsilon\}) \leqslant \mathfrak{l}(f) + \epsilon$$

for each $\epsilon > 0$. As $\epsilon \to 0$, the set $\{\mathbf{x} \mid f(\mathbf{x}) > \mathfrak{l}(f) + \epsilon\}$ expands towards $\{\mathbf{x} \mid f(\mathbf{x}) > \mathfrak{l}(f)\}$. Thus,

$$\lim_{\epsilon \to 0} m_L(\{\mathbf{x} \mid f(\mathbf{x}) > \mathfrak{l}(f) + \epsilon\}) = m_L\left(\lim_{\epsilon \to 0}\{\mathbf{x} \mid f(\mathbf{x}) > \mathfrak{l}(f) + \epsilon\}\right).$$

We conclude that $m_L(\{\mathbf{x} \mid |f(\mathbf{x})| > \mathfrak{l}(f)\}) \leqslant \mathfrak{l}(f)$, so the first condition is satisfied.
 Conversely, suppose that both conditions are satisfied by λ. By the definition of infimum we have $\lambda - \delta < \mathfrak{l}(f) \leqslant \lambda$ for each $\delta > 0$, which is possible only if $\lambda = \mathfrak{l}(f)$.

(2) Let $(S, \mathcal{E}, m)$ be a measure space and let $f : S \longrightarrow \hat{\mathbb{R}}_{\geqslant 0}$. Prove that

$$\int_S f \, dm = \sup\left\{\int_S h \, dm \mid h \in \mathsf{SF}_+(S) \mid h(x) \leqslant f(x) \text{ for } x \in S\right\}.$$

(3) Let $(S, \mathcal{E}, m)$ be a measure space and let $f, g : S \longrightarrow \hat{\mathbb{R}}$ be two measurable functions such that $f(x) = g(x)$ a.e.
If one of the integrals $\int_S f \, dm$ or $\int_S g \, dm$ exists, then both exist and are equal.

Solution: Suppose initially that both f and g are non-negative. Define $\Delta(f,g) = \{x \in S \mid f(x) \neq g(x)\}$ and observe that $m(\Delta(f,g)) = 0$. Define $h : S \longrightarrow \hat{\mathbb{R}}$ as

$$h(x) = \begin{cases} \infty & \text{if } x \in \Delta(f,g), \\ 0 & \text{if } x \notin \Delta(f,g). \end{cases}$$

Note that we have both

$$f \leqslant g + h \text{ and } g \leqslant f + h. \tag{8.28}$$

Let (h_n) be the sequence of functions given by $h_n = n 1_{\Delta(f,g)}$ for $n \in \mathbb{N}$. We have $\int_S h \, dm = \lim_{n \to \infty} \int_S h_n \, dm = 0$. Inequalities (8.28) imply $\int_S f \, dm \leqslant \int_S g \, dm$ and $\int_S g \, dm \leqslant \int_S f \, dm$, hence $\int_S f \, dm = \int_S g \, dm$.

If the non-negativity of f and g is dropped, the same result can be obtained by applying the previous argument to the positive and negative parts of these functions.

(4) Let $\mathbf{f}$ be a non-decreasing sequence of non-negative functions, $\mathbf{f} = (f_n)$ such that $\lim_{n \to \infty} f_n(x) = f(x)$ a.e., where f is a measurable function. Prove that

$$\int_T f \, dm = \lim_{n \to \infty} \int_T f_n \, dm$$

for all measurable T.

Solution: Let $A = \{x \mid \lim_{n \to \infty} f_n(x) = f(x)\}$. We have $\overline{A}$ is null. If

$$g_n(x) = \begin{cases} f_n(x) & \text{if } x \in A, \\ 0 & \text{if } x \in \overline{A}, \end{cases} \quad \text{and} \quad g(x) = \begin{cases} f(x) & \text{if } x \in A, \\ 0 & \text{if } x \in \overline{A}, \end{cases}$$

then

$$\int_T g_n \, dm = \int_{T \cap A} f_n \, dm + \int_{T \cap \overline{A}} 0 \, dm$$

$$= \int_{T \cap A} f_n \, dm + \int_{T \cap \overline{A}} f_n \, dm = \int_T f_n \, dm.$$

Thus, $\lim_{n \to \infty} g_n(x) = g(x)$ everywhere, so $\lim_{n \to \infty} \int_T g_n \, dm = \int_T g \, dm$ by the Monotone Convergence Theorem.

(5) Let $(S, \mathcal{E}, m)$ be a measure space and let $f : S \longrightarrow \mathbb{R}$ be a Borel measurable function. Prove that if $U \in \mathcal{E}$ is a null set, then $\int_U f \, dm = 0$.

Hint: Prove the statement starting with simple measurable functions.

(6) Let $(S, \mathcal{E}, m)$ be a measure space and let $\mathbf{f} = (f_n)$ be a sequence of functions, where $f_n : S \longrightarrow \hat{\mathbb{R}}_{\geqslant 0}$ for $n \geqslant 1$. Suppose that $\lim_{n \to \infty} f_n(x) = f(x)$ and $\int_S f \, dm = \lim_{n \to \infty} \int_S f_n \, dm < \infty$. Prove that if $U \in \mathcal{E}$, then $\lim_{n \to \infty} \int_U f_n \, dm = \int_U f \, dm$.

Solution: Let $U \in \mathcal{E}$. We have:

$$\int_U f \, dm = \int f 1_U \, dm = \int \lim_{n \to \infty} \inf f_n 1_U \, dm$$

$$\leqslant \lim_{n \to \infty} \inf \int f_n 1_E \, dm$$

(by Fatou's Lemma (Theorem 8.12))

$$= \lim_{n \to \infty} \inf \int_U f_n \, dm.$$

Similarly, we have $\int_{\overline{U}} f \, dm \leqslant \lim \inf_{n \to \infty} \int_{\overline{U}} f_n \, dm$. Since $1_U + 1_{\overline{U}} = 1$, we have $\int_{\overline{U}} f \, dm = \int f \, dm - \int_U f \, dm$ and $\int_{\overline{U}} f_n \, dm = \int f_n \, dm - \int_U f_n \, dm$, which implies

$$\int f \, dm - \int_U f \, dm = \int_{\overline{U}} f \, dm$$

$$\leqslant \lim_{n \to \infty} \inf \left(\int_{\overline{U}} f_n \, dm - \int_U f_n \, dm \right)$$

$$= \int f \, dm - \lim_{n \to \infty} \sup \int_U f_n \, dm.$$

Therefore,

$$\lim_{n \leqslant \infty} \sup \int_U f_n \, dm \leqslant \int_U f \, dm \leqslant \lim_{n \to \infty} \inf \int_U f_n \, dm,$$

hence $\int_U f \, dm = \lim_{n \to \infty} \int_U f_n \, dm$.

(7) Let $(\mathbb{P}, \mathcal{P}(\mathbb{P}), m)$ be a measure space defined on the set of positive natural numbers $\mathbb{P}$, where m is the counting measure. Let $\mathbf{f} = (f_n)_{n \geqslant 1}$ be the sequence of functions defined by $f_n = 1_{\{n\}}$. Prove that:

(a) if $g : \mathbb{P} \longrightarrow \mathbb{P}$ is a function such that $f_n(x) \leqslant g(x)$ for every $x \in \mathbb{P}$, then $\int_{\mathbb{P}} g \, dm = \infty$;

(b) each function f_n is measurable;

(c) verify that $\lim_{n \to \infty} \int_{pp} f_n \, dm = 1$ and $\int_{\mathbb{P}} \lim_{n \to \infty} f_n \, dm = 0$; why is the dominated convergence theorem not applicable?

Hint: We have $\lim_{n \to \infty} f_n = 0$, so $\int_{\mathbb{P}} \lim_{n \to \infty} f_n \, dm = 0$; on other hand, $\int_{\mathbb{P}} f_n \, dm = 1$ for every $n \geqslant 1$, hence $\lim_{n \to \infty} \int_{pp} f_n \, dm = 1$.

(8) Prove that an absolutely continuous function on $[a, b]$ is uniformly continuous on $[a, b]$. Also, prove that if f is a Lipschitz function on $[a, b]$, then f is absolutely continuous on this interval.

(9) Prove that if $f, g : [a, b] \longrightarrow \mathbb{R}$ are absolutely continuous on $[a, b]$, then so are $f + g$ and fg.

(10) Prove that if h is Riemann integrable on $[a, b]$, then the function f defined as

$$f(x) = \int_a^x h(x)\, dx$$

for $a \leqslant x \leqslant b$ is absolutely continuous on $[a, b]$.

(11) Define the relation "$\sim$" on the set of measures on a set S as $m \sim m'$ if $m \ll m'$ and $m' \ll m$. Prove that "$\sim$" is an equivalence relation.

(12) Let $(S, \mathcal{E}, m)$ be a measure space and let $U \in \mathcal{E}$. Define $m_U : \mathcal{E} \longrightarrow \hat{\mathbb{R}}_{\geqslant 0}$ as $m_U(T) = m(T \cap U)$ for every $T \in \mathcal{E}$. Prove that m_U is a measure on $\mathcal{E}$. Furthermore, $m_T \ll m_V$ if and only if $m(T - V) = 0$.

(13) Let m, m' be two σ-finite measure on $(S, \mathcal{E})$. If $m \ll m'$ and $m' \ll m$, prove that $\frac{dm}{dm'} \frac{dm'}{dm} = 1$ a.e. on S.

(14) Let m be a σ-finite measure on $(S, \mathcal{E})$. Prove that $m \ll |m|$ and $\left| \frac{dm}{d|m|} \right| = 1$ a.e. on S.

(15) Let $(\mathbb{N}, \mathcal{P}(\mathbb{N}), m)$ be the measure space defined by $m(A) = |A|$ for every $A \subseteq \mathbb{N}$. For a function $f : \mathbb{N} \longrightarrow \mathbb{R}$ show that $\int_{\mathbb{N}} f\, dm$ as $\sum_{n \in \mathbb{N}} (f(n))^+ - \sum_{n \in \mathbb{N}} (f(n))^-$. If this difference is not defined (because both sums are ∞) the integral does not exist.

(16) Let (f_n) be a sequence of functions in $L^2(S, \mathcal{E}, m)$ such that $\lim_{n \to \infty} \|f_n - f\|_2 = 0$. Prove that for every function $g \in L^2(S, \mathcal{E}, m)$ we have $\lim_{n \to \infty} (f_n, g) = (f, g)$.

(17) Let $f : \mathbb{R}_{>0} \longrightarrow \mathbb{R}_{>0}$ be defined as $f(x) = \frac{1}{e^x \sqrt{x}}$ for $x > 0$. Prove that $f \in \mathcal{L}^1(\mathbb{R}_{>0}, \mathbb{B}(\mathbb{R}_{>0}), m_L)$ but $f \notin \mathcal{L}^2(\mathbb{R}_{>0}, \mathbb{B}(\mathbb{R}_{>0}), m_L)$.

(18) Prove that if $a, b \geqslant 0$, then $(a + b)^p \geqslant 2^{p-1}(a^p + b^p)$ for $p \geqslant 1$. Use this fact to show that a sequence (f_n) in $L^p(\mathbb{R}_{>0})$ converges to $f \in L^p(\mathbb{R}_{>0})$ relative to the norm $\|\cdot\|_p$ if and only if $\lim_{n \to \infty} \|f_n\|_p = \|f\|_p$.

(19) Let $(f_n)_{\geqslant 1}$ be sequence in $L^p(S, \mathcal{E}, m)$ such that $\lim_{n \to \infty} f_n = f$ in the sense of the norm $\|\cdot\|_p$. Prove that the sequence f_n converges to f in measure.

Solution: This fact follows from the Chebyshev's Inequality applied to the function $|f_n - f|$.

(20) Let $(f_n)_{\geqslant 1}$ be a Cauchy sequence in $L^p(S, \mathcal{E}, m)$. Prove that $(f_n)_{\geqslant 1}$ is a Cauchy sequence in measure, that is, for every $\epsilon > 0$ we have $\lim_{m,n \to \infty} m(\{x \in S \mid |f_n(x) - f_m(x)| > \epsilon\}) = 0$.

(21) Let S, T be two sets and let E be a subset of $S \times T$. Prove that $(1_E)s = 1_{E_s}$ and $(1_E)^t = 1_{E^t}$ for every $s \in S$ and $t \in T$.

(22) Let S, T be two sets and let $f : S \longrightarrow T$. Prove that for every subset V of T we have $1_{f^{-1}(V)} = 1_V f$.

Let S be a set and let $f : S \longrightarrow \{0, 1\}$ be a function. The set defined by f is $T_f = \{x \in S \mid f(x) = 1\}$. It is clear that $f = 1_{T_f}$.

If $z : S \longrightarrow \{0, 1\}$ is the constant function defined by $z(x) = 0$, the set T_z is the empty set. The set of characteristic functions of the collection $\mathcal{S}$ of subsets of S is denoted by $I_\mathcal{S}$.

(23) Let $f, g \in I_{\mathcal{P}(S)}$. Prove that:

    (a) if $fg = z$, then $f + g \in I_{\mathcal{P}(S)}$;

    (b) $1_S - f = 1_{S - T_f}$.

(24) Prove that $\mathcal{S}$ is a semiring of sets if and only if the following conditions are satisfied by $I_\mathcal{S}$:

    (a) $z \in I_\mathcal{S}$;

    (b) $f, g \in I_\mathcal{S}$ implies $fg \in I_\mathcal{S}$;

    (c) for every $f, g \in I_\mathcal{S}$ there exists a finite collection $\{h_1, \ldots, h_p\} \subseteq I_\mathcal{S}$ such that for every i, j, $1 \leqslant i, j \leqslant p$, $i \neq j$ implies $h_i h_j = z$ and $f(I_S - g) = h_1 + \cdots + h_p$.

(25) Let $f : S \longrightarrow \mathbb{R}$ be a simple function on S such that $\mathsf{Ran}(f) = \{y_1, \ldots, y_n\}$. If $T \subset S$, and $g(x) = f(x)I_T(x)$ for $x \in S$, prove that $\mathsf{Ran}(g) = \{y \in \mathsf{Ran}(f) \mid f^{-1}(y) \cap T \neq \emptyset\} \cup \{0\}$.

Also, prove that if $y \in \mathsf{Ran}(g)$, then $g^{-1}(y) = f^{-1}(y) \cap T$.

(26) Let $(\mathcal{E}_0, \mathcal{E}_1, \ldots)$ be a sequence of algebras (σ-algebras) on a set S such that $\mathcal{E}_n \subseteq \mathcal{E}_{n+1}$ for $n \in \mathbb{N}$. Prove that $\bigcup_{n \in \mathbb{N}} \mathcal{E}_n$ is an algebra (a σ-algebra, respectively) on S.

(27) Let S be an infinite set.

    (a) Prove that the collection of all subsets U of S such that U is finite or $S - U$ is finite is an algebra but not a σ-algebra.

    (b) Prove that the collection $\mathcal{E}$ of all subsets of S defined by

$$\mathcal{E} = \{U \in \mathcal{P}(S) \mid U \text{ is countable or } S - U \text{ is countable}\}$$

    is a σ-algebra on S.

    (c) Suppose that S is uncountable. Prove that there exists a subset W of S that does not belong to the σ-algebra $\mathcal{E}$ defined above. Prove that the σ-algebra $\mathcal{E}$ is not closed with respect to arbitrary unions.

(28) Prove that any σ-algebra $\mathcal{E}$ contains the empty set; further, prove that if $\mathbf{s} = (S_0, S_1, \ldots)$ is a sequence of sets of $\mathcal{E}$, then both $\liminf \mathbf{s}$ and $\limsup \mathbf{s}$ belong to $\mathcal{E}$.

(29) Let $A \subseteq \mathbb{N}$ be a set. Define the function $d_A : \mathbb{N}_1 \longrightarrow \mathbb{R}$ as

$$d_A(n) = \frac{|A \cap \{1, \ldots, n\}|}{n}$$

for $n \geqslant 1$. The *upper asymptotic density of A* is $\overline{d}(A) = \limsup d_A(n)$, while the *lower asymptotic density of A* is $\underline{d}(A) = \liminf d_A(n)$. The set A has *asymptotic density* $d(A)$ if $\overline{d}(A) = \underline{d}(A) = d(A)$.

(a) Prove that if A has asymptotic density $d(A)$, then $\mathbb{N} - A$ has asymptotic density $1 - d(A)$.

(b) Compute the asymptotic density of the set $A_3 = \{3k \mid k \in \mathbb{N}\}$.

(c) Prove that for any finite subset A of $\mathbb{N}$, $d(A) = 0$.

(d) Compute the asymptotic density of the set $P_k = \{n^k \mid n \in \mathbb{N}\}$.

(e) Let $A = \bigcup_{m=0}^{\infty} \{2^{2m}, \ldots, 2^{2m+1} - 1\}$ be the set of numbers whose binary expression contains a number of odd digits. Prove that A does not have an asymptotic density.

(f) Let C be a subset of $\mathbb{N}$ and let $B = \{b_p \mid p \in \mathbb{N}\}$ be a set such that

$$
b_p = \begin{cases} 3p & \text{if } p \in C, \\ 3p + 1 & \text{otherwise.} \end{cases}
$$

Prove that B has asymptotic density equal to $1/3$ regardless of whether C has an asymptotic density and that $A_3 \cap B = \{3m \mid m \in C\}$.

(g) Prove that the collection of sets that have an asymptotic density is not an algebra.

Hint for Part (e): Note that each set of the form $\{2^{2m}, \ldots, 2^{2m+1} - 1\}$ contains 2^{2m} elements and that

$$
A \cap \{1, \ldots n\} = \bigcup_{m=0}^{p} \{2^{2m}, \ldots, 2^{2m+1} - 1\},
$$

where p is the largest number such that $2^{2p+1} - 1 \leqslant n$. Thus, $p = \lfloor \frac{1}{2} \log_2 \frac{n+1}{2} \rfloor$ and the set $A \cap \{1, \ldots n\}$ contains $\sum_{m=0}^{p} 2^{2m} = \frac{2^{2p+2} - 1}{3}$ numbers.

If n has the form $n = 2^{2m+1}$, then $p = m$ and the set A contains $\frac{2^{2m+2} - 1}{3}$ elements. Then

$$
\lim_{m \to \infty} \frac{2^{2m+2} - 1}{3 \cdot 2^{2m+1}} = \frac{2}{3}.
$$

On the other hand, if $n = 2^{2m+2}$, then $2^{2p+1} \leqslant 2^{2m+2} + 1$, so again $p = m$ and

$$
\lim_{m \to \infty} \frac{2^{2m+2} - 1}{3 \cdot 2^{m+2}} = \frac{1}{3}.
$$

We conclude that $\overline{d}_A \neq \underline{d}_A$, so A has no asymptotic density.

(30) Let $x, y, a_1, b_1, \ldots, a_n, b_n$ be n real numbers such that $x \leqslant y$ and $a_i \leqslant b_i$ for $1 \leqslant i \leqslant n$. Prove, by induction on n, that if $[x, y] \subseteq \bigcup_{i=1}^{n} (a_i, b_i)$, then $y - x \leqslant \sum_{i=1}^{n} (b_i - a_i)$.

(31) Let I be a bounded interval of $\mathbb{R}$. Prove that if K is a compact subset of $\mathbb{R}$ such that $K \subseteq I$, then $m_L(I) = m_L(K) + m_L(I - K)$, where m_L is the Lebesgue measure.

(32) Let $(S, \mathcal{E})$ be a measurable space and let $m : \mathcal{E} \longrightarrow \hat{r}\hat{r}_{\geqslant 0}$ be a measure. Prove that the d_m defined by $d_m(U, V) = m(U \oplus V)$ is a semi-metric on $\mathcal{E}$.

(33) Let $\{(S_i, \mathcal{E}_i, m_i) \mid i \in I\}$ be a collection of measure spaces such that $S_i S_| = \emptyset$ if $i \neq j$ for $i, j \in I$. Define the triplet $(\bigcup_{i \in I} S_i, \mathcal{E}, m)$, where

$$\mathcal{E} = \left\{ U \,\middle|\, U \subseteq \bigcup_{i \in I} S_i, U \cap S_i \in \mathcal{E} \text{ for } i \in I \right\},$$

and $m : \mathcal{E} \longrightarrow \hat{\mathbb{R}}_{\geqslant 0}$ is given by $m(U) = \sum_{i \in I} m_i(U \cap S_i)$ for $U \in \mathcal{E}$. Prove that $(\bigcup_{i \in I} S_i, \mathcal{E}, m)$ is a measure space and that $m(U)$ is finite if and only if there exists a countable subset J of I such that if $j \in J$, then μ_j is finite and $\mu_i = 0$ if $i \in I - J$.

(34) Prove that if U is a subset of $\mathbb{R}^n$ that is Lebesgue measurable, then

$$m_L(U) = \inf\{m_L(W) \mid U \subseteq W, W \text{ is open in } \mathbb{R}^n\}. \tag{8.29}$$

Solution: The monotonicity of m_L implies $m_L(U) \leqslant \inf\{m_L(W) \mid U \subseteq W, W \text{ is open }\}$.

If $m_L(U) = \infty$ the reverse inequality is obvious. Suppose, therefore, that $m_L(U) < \infty$. We have:

$$m_L(U) = \inf\left\{ \sum vol(I_j) \mid j \in J, U \subseteq \bigcup_{j \in J} I_j \right\},$$

so there exists a collection of n-dimensional open intervals $\{I_j \mid j \in \mathbb{N}\}$ such that $\sum_{j \in \mathbb{N}} m_L(I_j) < m_L(U) + \epsilon$. Thus, $m_L(U) = \inf\{m_L(W) \mid U \subseteq W, W \text{ is open in } \mathbb{R}^n\}$.

(35) Let $U \subseteq \mathbb{R}^n$ be a Lebesgue measurable set. For every $\epsilon > 0$ there exists an open set V in $\mathbb{R}^n$ such that $m_L(V - U) < \epsilon$.

Solution: If U is a subset of $\mathbb{R}^n$ that is Lebesgue measurable, then $m_L(U) = \inf\{m_L(W) \mid U \subseteq W, W \text{ is open }\}$. Therefore, for every $\epsilon > 0$ there exists a open subset W of $\mathbb{R}^n$ such that

$$m_L(U) \leqslant m_L(W) \leqslant m_L(U) + \epsilon,$$

which implies

$$m_L(W - V) \leqslant m_L(W) - m_L(V) < \epsilon.$$

If $m_L(U) = \infty$, define $U_k = U \cap [-k, k]$ for $k \in snn$ and $k \geqslant 1$. We have $m_L(U_k) \leqslant m_L([-k, k]) = (2k)^n < \infty$ for $k \geqslant 1$. Thus, by the first part of the proof, for every $k \geqslant 1$ there exists an open set W_k such that $U_k \subseteq W_k$ and $m_L(W_k - U_k) < \frac{\epsilon}{2^k}$. Define $W = \bigcup_{k \geqslant 1} W_k$. Note that $U = \bigcup_{k \geqslant 1} W_k \subset W$ and $W - U \subseteq \bigcup_{k \geqslant 1} (W_k - U_k)$. Then, $m_L(W - U) \leqslant m_L(\bigcup_{k \geqslant 1} W_k - U_k) \leqslant \sum_{k \geqslant 1} \frac{\epsilon}{2^k} = \epsilon$.

(36) Prove that a subset U of $\mathbb{R}^n$ is Lebesgue measurable if and only if for every $\epsilon > 0$ there exist an open set L and a closed set H such that $H \subseteq U \subseteq L$ and $m_L(L - H) < \epsilon$.

Let $\mathcal{C}$ be a collection of sets. A function $f : \mathcal{C} \longrightarrow \mathbb{R}$ is said to be *additive* if for every finite collection of disjoint sets $\mathcal{D} = \{D_1, \ldots, D_n\} \subseteq \mathcal{C}$ such that $\bigcup \mathcal{D} \in \mathcal{C}$ we have

$$f\left(\bigcup \mathcal{D}\right) = \bigcup_{i=1}^{n} f(D_i).$$

(37) Let $f : \mathcal{S} \longrightarrow \mathbb{R}$ be an additive set function on an algebra of sets $\mathcal{S}$. Prove that the following properties are equivalent:
   (a) the function f is countably additive;
   (b) if $U_n \in \mathcal{S}$ and $U_{n+1} \subseteq U_n$ for $n \geqslant 1$, and $\bigcap_{n=1}^{\infty} U_n = \emptyset$, then $\lim_{n \to \infty} f(U_n) = 0$;
   (c) if $V_n \in \mathcal{S}$ and $V_n \subseteq V_{n+1}$ for $n \geqslant 1$, and $\bigcup_{n=1}^{\infty} V_n \in \mathcal{C}$, then $\lim_{n \to \infty} f(U_n) = f\left(\bigcup_{i=1}^{\infty} V_i\right)$.

(38) Let $(U_1, \ldots, U_n, \ldots)$ be an increasing or a decreasing sequence of sets in a semiring such that $\lim_{n \longrightarrow \infty} U_n = U \in \mathcal{S}$. Prove that if $f : \mathcal{S} \longrightarrow \mathbb{R}_{\geqslant 0}$ is a countably additive function on $\mathcal{S}$, then $\lim_{n \to \infty} f(U_n) = f(U)$

(39) Prove that the collection

$$\mathcal{S}_r = \{\emptyset\} \cup \{(a, b] \mid a, b \in \mathbb{Q}, 0 \leqslant a < b \leqslant 1\}$$

is a semiring and that the function $f : \mathcal{S}_r \longrightarrow \mathbb{R}$ given by $f((a, b]) = b - a$ is an additive function but not a countably additive one.

(40) Let $(S, \mathcal{E}, m)$ be a measure space and let $\mathbf{f} = (f_0, \ldots, f_n, \ldots)$ be a sequence of functions such that $f_n : S \longrightarrow \hat{\mathbb{R}}$ for $n \in \mathbb{N}$. If there exists a non-negative integrable function $g : S \longrightarrow \hat{\mathbb{R}}_{\geqslant 0}$ such that $f_n \leqslant g$ for $n \in \mathbb{N}$, prove that

$$\int_S \limsup_{n \to \infty} f_n \, dm \geqslant \limsup_{n \to \infty} \int_S f_n \, dm.$$

This statement is known as the *reverse Fatou Lemma*.

Hint: Apply Fatou's Lemma to the sequence $(g - f_0, \ldots, g - f_n, \ldots)$.

(41) Let $(S, \mathcal{E}, m)$ be a measure space and let $f : S \longrightarrow \mathbb{R}$ be a measurable function. Prove that

$$\inf f \leqslant \operatorname{ess\,inf} f \leqslant \operatorname{ess\,sup} f \leqslant \sup f.$$

(42) Let $\mathfrak{S} = ([0, 1], \mathcal{B}([0, 1]), m)$ and $\mathfrak{T} = ([0, 1], \mathcal{B}([0, 1]), m')$ be two measure spaces, where m is the Lebesgue measure and m' is the counting measure. Let $D = \{(x, x) \mid x \in [0, 1]\}$. Prove that:

   (a) $(m \times m')(D) = \int_{S \times S} 1_D \, d(m \times m') = \infty$;
   (b) $\int_{[0,1]} (\int_{[0,1]} 1_D dm) dm' = 0$;
   (c) $\int_{[0,1]} (\int_{[0,1]} 1_D dm') dm = 1$.

(43) Let $(S, \mathcal{E}, m)$ be a measure space. Prove that a sequence of measurable functions $(f_1, f_2, \ldots)$ converges to a measurable function f if and only if for each $\epsilon > 0$ and each $\eta > 0$ there exists $n_0 \in \mathbb{N}$ such that $n \geqslant n_0$ implies $m(\{x \in S \mid |f_n(x) - f(x)| \geqslant \eta\}) < \epsilon$.

(44) Let Y be a random variable that takes values in $[0, 1]$ such that $E(Y) = m$. Prove that for any $a \in (0, 1)$ we have $P(Y > 1 - a) \geqslant \frac{m-1+a}{a}$.

   Hint: Apply Markov's inequality to the random variable $X = 1 - Y$.

(45) Let $X_1, \ldots, X_n$ be a sequence of independent and identically distributed random variables with $E(Z_i) = m$ and $var(Z_i) \leqslant 1$ for $1 \leqslant i \leqslant n$. Prove that for any $\delta \in (0, 1)$,

$$P\left(\left|\frac{1}{n}\sum_{i=1}^{n} X_i - m\right| \leqslant \sqrt{\frac{1}{\delta n}}\right) > 1 - \delta.$$

   Solution: Let Y be the random variable $Y = \frac{1}{n}\sum_{i=1}^{n} X_i$. We have $E(Y) = m$ and $var(Y) = \frac{1}{n} var(X_i)$.

   By applying Chebyshev's Inequality (inequality (8.6)) to the variable Y we have $P(|Y - m| > a) \leqslant \frac{var(X_i)}{a^2}$ or $P(|Y - m| \leqslant a) > 1 - \frac{1}{na^2}$.

   If $1 - \frac{1}{na^2} = 1 - \delta$, then $a = \sqrt{\frac{1}{\delta n}}$ and the inequality follows immediately.

(46) Let X be a non-negative random variable on the probability space $(\Omega, \mathcal{E}, P)$ and let $\mathcal{G}$ be a σ-algebra such that $\mathcal{G} \subseteq \mathcal{E}$. Prove that $E(X|\mathcal{G}) \geqslant 0$ a.e.

   Solution: Let $k \geqslant 1$ and let $A_k = \{\omega \in \Omega \mid E(X|\mathcal{G}) < -\frac{1}{k}\} \in \mathcal{G}$. Note that $\int_{A_k} E(X|\mathcal{G}) \, dP < -\frac{1}{k}P(A_k)$. On other hand, $\int_{A_k} X \, dP \geqslant 0$.

Since $\int_{A_k} X \, dP = \int_{A_k} E(X|\mathcal{G}) \, dP$, we have $P(A_k) = 0$ for $k \geqslant 1$, which implies $P(E(X|\mathcal{G}) < 0) = P\left(bigcup_{k\geqslant 1} A_k\right) = 0$. Thus, $E(X|\mathcal{G}) \geqslant 0$ a.e.

(47) Let $(S, \mathcal{O})$ be a normal topological space and let $(S, \mathbb{B}(S), m)$ be the corresponding Borel measurable space, where m is a regular measure. Prove that if $f : S \longrightarrow \mathbb{C}$ is a complex-valued measurable function on $(S, \mathbb{B}(S), m)$ and $\delta > 0$, then there exists a continuous complex-valued function $g : S \longrightarrow \mathbb{C}$ such that $m(\{x \in S \mid f(x) \neq g(x)\}) < \delta$. Moreover, prove that it is possible to choose g such that $\sup_{x \in S} |g(x)| \leqslant \sup_{x \in S} |f(x)|$.

Solution: Assume initially that f is real valued and $f(x) \in [0, 1)$ for $x \in S$. Define the sequence of simple, increasing non-negative functions $(h_n)_{n \geqslant 0}$ as $h_0(x) = 0$ and

$$
h_n(x) = \begin{cases} \dfrac{k-1}{2^n} & \text{if } \dfrac{k-1}{2^n} \leqslant f(x) < \dfrac{k}{2^n} \text{ and } 1 \leqslant k \leqslant n2^n, \\ n & \text{when } f(x) \geqslant n. \end{cases}
$$

for $n \geqslant 1$.

Let $(f_n)_{n \geqslant 1}$ be the sequence defined by $f_n(x) = h_n(x) - h_{n-1}(x)$ for $n \geqslant 1$ and $x \in [0, 1]$. Note that a function f_n has only two possible values, 0 and 2^{-n}. We have $f = \sum_{n=1}^{\infty} f_n$. Indeed, as shown next

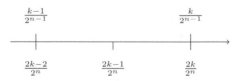

if $\frac{k-1}{2^{n-1}} \leqslant f(x) < \frac{k}{2^{n-1}}$ we have $h_{n-1}(x) = \frac{k-1}{2^{n-1}}$. One of the following two cases may occur: either $\frac{2k-2}{2^n} \leqslant f(x) < \frac{2k-1}{2^n}$, or $\frac{2k-1}{2^n} \leqslant f(x) < \frac{2k}{2n}$. In the first case $h_n(x) = \frac{2k-2}{2^n}$ and $h_n(x) = h_{n-1}(x)$; in the second case, $h_n(x) = \frac{2k-1}{2^n}$ and $h_n(x) - h_{n-1}(x) = 2^{-n}$.

Let $A_n = \{x \in S \mid f_n(x) \neq 0\}$. Denote by C_n a closed subset of A_n and by V_n an open superset of A_n such that $m(V_n - C_n) < \frac{\delta}{2^n}$. Since $(S, \mathcal{O})$ is normal there exists a continuous function $g : S \longrightarrow [0, 1]$ such that $g(x) = 1$ on C_n and $g(x) = 0$ for $x \in S - V_n$.

Let $g = \sum_{n=1}^{\infty} 2^{-n} g_n$. By Weierstrass M-test, g is a continuous map of S into $[0, 1]$. Note that the set $T = \bigcup_{n \geqslant 1}(V_n - C_n)$ we have $m(T) < \delta$ and if $x \in T$, then $f(x) = g(x)$. Indeed, observe that for each $n \geqslant 1$, $x \in C_n$, or $x \notin V_n$. If $x \in C_n \subseteq A_n$, then $2^{-n} g_n(x) = 2^{-n} = f_n(x)$; if $x \notin V_n$, $2^{-n} g_n(x) = 0 = f_n(x)$ because $x \notin A_n$. These considerations prove the existence of g when f is a real-valued function with $f(x) \in [0, 1)$.

Suppose now that f is a complex-valued measurable function.

If f is unbounded we can write $f = f_1 + f_2$, where $f_1 = f1_{\{x \in S \,|\, |f(x)| < n\}}$ and $f_2(x) = f1_{\{x \in S \,|\, |f(x)| \geqslant n\}}$. The function f is bounded and $m(\{x \mid f_2(x) \neq 0\})$ can be made less than $\frac{\delta}{2}$ for sufficiently large n. If g is continuous and $m(\{x \mid f_1(x) \neq g\}) < \frac{\delta}{2}$, then $m(\{x \mid f(x) \neq g\}) < \delta$.

If f is bounded, $|f(x)| \leqslant M < \infty$, and g approximates f as above, let g_1 be defined as

$$g_1(x) = \begin{cases} g(x) & \text{if } |g(x)| \leqslant M, \\ M\dfrac{g(x)}{|g(x)|} & \text{if } |g(x)| > M. \end{cases}$$

Then, g_1 is continuous, $|g_1(x)| \leqslant M$ and $f(x) = g(x)$ implies $g(x) \leqslant M$; hence $g_1(x) = g(x) = f(x)$. Therefore,

$$m(\{x \mid f(x) \neq g_1(x)\}) \leqslant m(\{x \mid f(x) \neq g(x)\}) < \delta.$$

(48) Let $(S, \mathcal{O})$ be a normal topological space and let $(S, \mathbb{B}(S), m)$ be the corresponding Borel measurable space, where m is a regular measure. Prove that if $f : S \longrightarrow \mathbb{C}$ is a complex-valued measurable function on $(S, \mathbb{B}(S), m)$ there is a sequence of continuous complex-valued functions converging almost everywhere to f, with $|f_n(x)| \leqslant \sup\{f(x) \mid x \in S\}$.

Solution: By Supplement 47 there is a continuous function f_n such that $|f_n| \leqslant M = \sup|f|$ and $m(\{x \in S \mid f_n(x) \neq f(x)\}) < 2^{-n}$. If $A_n = \{x \mid f_n(x) \neq f(x)\}$, and $A = \limsup A_n$, then $m(A) = 0$ by Borel-Cantelli Lemma (Theorem 7.33). The statement follows from the fact that $x \notin A$ implies $f_n(x) = f(x)$ for sufficiently large n.

(49) Let $(S, \mathcal{O})$ be a normal topological space, $(S, \mathbb{B}(S), m)$ be the corresponding Borel measurable space, where m is a regular measure, and let $f : S \longrightarrow \mathbb{C}$ be a measurable function. Prove that for $\epsilon > 0$ there exists a closed subset C of S, a continuous function $g : S \longrightarrow \mathbb{C}$ such that $g(x) = f(x)$ for $x \in C$. Thus, the restriction of f to C is continuous.

If $m(A) = \sup\{m(K) \mid K \text{ is compact }, K \subseteq A\}$ for each $A \in \mathbb{B}(S)$, then C may be assumed to be compact.

The statement contained by this supplement is known as *Lusin's Theorem*.

Solution: By Supplement 47 there exists a continuous g such that $m(\{x \in S \mid f(x) \neq g(x)\}) < \frac{\epsilon}{2}$. Since m is regular, there exists a closed set C, $C \subseteq \{x \in S \mid f(x) = g(x)\}$ with $m(C) \geqslant m(\{x \in S \mid f(x) = g(x)\}) - \frac{\epsilon}{2}$, hence C has the desired properties. For the second part of the argument replace closedness of C with compactness.

Bibliographical Comments

Our presentation of product measure space follows [32].

Supplement 42 originates in [57]. The proof of Theorem 8.42 follows [113]. The sequence of Supplements 47-49 that culminates with Lusin's Theorem follow [3].

PART IV

Functional Analysis and Convexity

PART IV

Functional Analysis and Convexity

Chapter 9

Banach Spaces

9.1 Introduction

Definition 9.1. A *Banach*[1] *space* is a normed linear space $(L, \|\cdot\|)$ that is complete when regarded as a metric space through the metric induced by the norm $\|\cdot\|$.

Results presented for complete metric spaces in Chapter 4 can be applied to Banach spaces, where the metric is induced by the norm defined on this space. For example, Theorem 5.72 stipulates that a normed space is a Banach space if and only if every absolutely convergent series is convergent.

9.2 Banach Spaces — Examples

A typical example of a Banach space is $\mathbb{R}^n$ equipped with the Euclidean metric (as we saw in Example 5.12).

Example 9.1. Every finite-dimensional normed space is a Banach space, as Theorem 6.33 implies. Thus, $\mathbb{R}^n$ equipped with the Euclidean form is a Banach space.

Example 9.2. The space $C[a, b]$ equipped with the norm $\|\cdot\|_\infty$ is a Banach space, where $\|f\|_\infty = \sup\{|f(x)| \mid x \in [a, b]\}$ for $f \in C[a, b]$.

Let (f_n) be a Cauchy sequence of functions in $C[a, b]$. For each $x \in [a, b]$ the sequence $(f_n(x))$ is a Cauchy sequence in $\mathbb{R}$. Since $\mathbb{R}$ is complete, the sequence $(f_n(x))$ converges to a real number denoted by $f(x)$. We need to

---

[1] This type of spaces that is fundamental in functional analysis are named after Stefan Banach (March 30, 1892–August 31, 1945), a Polish mathematician who is one of the founders of modern functional analysis

show that the function f defined in this manner is continuous on $[a, b]$ and that $\lim_{n \to \infty} \|f_n - f\|_\infty = 0$.

For $x, z \in [a, b]$ we have:

$$|f(x) - f(z)| \leqslant |f(x) - f_n(x)| + |f_n(x) - f_n(z)| + |f_n(z) - f(z)|. \quad (9.1)$$

Since (f_n) is a Cauchy sequence, for every $\epsilon > 0$ there exists a number n_0 such that $\|f_n - f_m\|_\infty < \frac{\epsilon}{3}$ if $m, n \geqslant n_0$, which yields $|f_n(x) - f_m(x)| \leqslant \frac{\epsilon}{3}$ for each $x \in [a, b]$. This implies $|f_n(x) - f(x)| \leqslant \frac{\epsilon}{3}$ for all $x \in [a, b]$ when $m \to \infty$. Similarly, $|f_n(z) - f(z)| \leqslant \frac{\epsilon}{3}$, which also shows that $\lim_{n \to \infty} \|f_n - f\| = 0$.

Since the functions f_n are continuous, there exists $\delta > 0$ such that $|x - z| < \delta$ implies $|f_n(x) - f_n(z)| < \frac{\epsilon}{3}$. By inequality (9.1), $|f(x) - f(z)| < \epsilon$ whenever $|x - z| < \delta$, so $f \in C[a, b]$.

Example 9.3. Let $BF(X, T)$ be the set of bounded functions defined on a set X and ranging over a normed space $(T, \| \cdot \|)$. The set of all bounded functions from X to T is denoted by $BF(X, T)$.

$BF(X, T)$ is a linear space because

$$\sup\{\|(f + g)(x)\| \mid x \in X\} \leqslant \sup\{\|f(x)\| + \|g(x)\| \mid x \in M\}$$
$$\leqslant \sup\{\|f(x)\| \mid x \in M\}$$
$$+ \sup\{\|g(x)\| \mid x \in M\}.$$

Note that $\sup\{\|f(x)\| \mid x \in X\}$ is a norm on $BF(X, T)$.

If $(T, \| \cdot \|)$ is a Banach space, then $BF(X, T)$ is a Banach space. Indeed, let (f_n) be a sequence of functions in $BF(X, T)$. For every $\epsilon > 0$ there exists n_ϵ such that $m, n \geqslant n_\epsilon$ imply $\|f_m - f_n\| < \epsilon$. Therefore, for each $x \in X$, $m, n \geqslant n_\epsilon$ imply $\|f_m(x) - f_n(x)\| < \epsilon$. Since $(T, \| \cdot \|)$ is a Banach space the sequence $(f_n(x))$ converges to an element $g(x) \in T$, which implies $\|f_m(x) - g(x)\| < \epsilon$ for $m \geqslant n_\epsilon$ and $x \in X$. Thus, $\|g\| \leqslant \|f_m\| + \epsilon$, so g is bounded, that is, $g \in BF(X, T)$. Since $\|f_m(x) - g(x)\| < \epsilon$ for $n \geqslant n_\epsilon$ it follows that the sequence (f_n) converges to g, so $BF(X, T)$ is a Banach space.

Example 9.4. For a measure space $(S, \mathcal{E}, m)$, the space $L^p(S, \mathcal{E}, m)$ is complete by Riesz-Fischer Theorem (Theorem 8.95) and, therefore, it is a Banach space relative to the norm $\| \cdot \|_p$. Important special cases are the spaces of random variables of the form $L^p(\Omega, \mathcal{E}, P)$ for $p = 1$ and $p = 2$.

Note that for a random variable $X \in L^1(\Omega, \mathcal{E}, P)$ we have:

$$\|X\|_1 = \int_\Omega |X| \, dP = E(|X|).$$

Example 9.5. Note that the completeness of spaces $\ell^p(\mathbb{R})$ follows from the completeness of spaces $L^p(S, \mathcal{E}, m)$. Indeed, let $S = \mathbb{R}$, $\mathcal{E} = \mathcal{P}(\mathbb{R})$ and let $m : \mathcal{P}(\mathbb{R}) \longrightarrow \hat{\mathbb{R}}_{\geqslant 0}$ be the measure defined by $m(U) = |U \cap \mathbb{N}|$. Then, a sequence (x_n) belongs to $\ell^p(\mathbb{R})$ if and only the function $f : \mathbb{R} \longrightarrow \mathbb{R}$ defined by

$$f(t) = \begin{cases} |x_i|^p & \text{if } t = i \in \mathbb{N}, \\ 0 & \text{otherwise} \end{cases}$$

is integrable. Therefore, the linear spaces $\ell^p(\mathbb{R})$ are Banach spaces.

In a similar manner, the set of sequences $\mathbf{x} \in \mathbf{Seq}_\infty(\mathbb{C})$ such that $\|\mathbf{x}\|_p$ is finite is a complex normed linear space relative to the norm $\nu_p(\mathbf{x}) = \sum_n |x_n|^p$. We will use the same notation, $\ell^p(\mathbb{R})$ to designate this space, if the type of the space is clear from context.

Theorem 9.1. *Let $(L, \|\cdot\|)$ be a normed $\mathbb{C}$-linear space and let $(T, \|\cdot\|)$ be a complex Banach space. The set of linear operators $\mathfrak{L}(L, T)$ is a Banach space.*

Proof. We saw that $\mathfrak{L}(L, T)$ is a normed linear space. We need to show only its completeness. Let (h_n) be a Cauchy sequence in $\mathfrak{L}(L, T)$. Since

$$\|h_n(x) - h_m(x)\| = \|(h_n - h_m)(x)\| \leqslant \|h_n - h_m\| \, \|x\|,$$

we have a Cauchy sequence $(h_n(x))$ in $(T, \|\cdot\|)$. Since T is a Banach space we can define the operator $h : S \longrightarrow T$ as $h(x) = \lim_{n \to \infty} h_n(x)$. The linearity of h follows immediately from the equality

$$h_n(ax + by) = ah_n(x) + bh_n(y)$$

for $n \in \mathbb{N}$ and $a, b \in \mathbb{C}$. Since (h_n) is a Cauchy sequences the norms of the operators h_n are bounded, that is $\|h_n\| \leqslant M$. Then, $\|h_n(x)\| \leqslant M\|x\|$ for all $x \in S$, which implies $\|h(x)\| \leqslant M\|x\|$. Since (h_n) is a Cauchy sequence, for every positive ϵ there exists n_ϵ such that $m, n \geqslant n_\epsilon$ implies $\|h_n - h_m\| < \epsilon$. Thus, if $\|x\| = 1$, we have $\|h_n(x) - h_m(x)\| < \epsilon$ when $m, n \geqslant n_\epsilon$. This means that $\|h_n(x) - h(x)\| \leqslant \epsilon$, so $\|h_n - h\| \leqslant \epsilon$ when $n \geqslant n_\epsilon$. $\square$

Theorem 9.2. *Let $h : L \longrightarrow L$ be a bounded linear operator on the Banach space L. If $\|h\| < 1$, the operator $1_L - h$ is invertible and $(1_L - h)^{-1} = \sum_{m=0}^{\infty} h^m$.*

Proof.   Define the sequence of linear operators (g_p) as $g_p = \sum_{m=0}^{p} h^m$ for $p \in \mathbb{N}$. Note that

$$\|g_p - g_q\| = \left\| \sum_{k=q+1}^{p} h^k \right\| \leqslant \sum_{k=q+1}^{p} \|h^k\|$$

$$\leqslant \sum_{k=q}^{\infty} \|h\|^k = \frac{\|h\|^q}{1 - \|h\|}.$$

Therefore, (g_p) is Cauchy sequence in $\mathfrak{B}(L, L)$. Since $\mathbf{B}(L, L)$ is complete, there exists a bounded linear operator $g : L \longrightarrow L$ such that $\lim_{p \to \infty} g_p = g$ (which means that $g = \sum_{m=0}^{\infty} h^m$). We have $(1_L - h)g_p = g_p - hg_p = \sum_{m=0}^{p} h^m - \sum_{m=1}^{p+1} h^m = 1_L - h^{p+1}$. Taking $p \to \infty$ we obtain $(1_L - h)g = g$. In the similar manner, we can show that $g(1_L - h) = 1_L$, hence $(1_L - h)^{-1} = g$. $\square$

Theorem 9.3. *If $1 \leqslant p < \infty$, the space $\ell^p(\mathbb{R})$ is separable. In contrast, the space $\ell^\infty(\mathbb{R})$ is not separable.*

Proof.   The separability of $\ell^p(\mathbb{R})$ with $1 \leqslant p < \infty$ can be obtained by noting that the set of infinite sequences having all but a finite number of components equal to 0 and remaining non-zero components in $\mathbb{Q}$ is countable and dense in $\ell^p(\mathbb{R})$.

On the other hand, let $S \subseteq \mathbf{Seq}_\infty(\mathbb{R})$ be the set of infinite sequences whose components equal either 0 or 1. This set is clearly uncountable. If $\mathbf{x}, \mathbf{y} \in S$, it is clear that $d_\infty(\mathbf{x}, \mathbf{y}) = 1$ if $\mathbf{x} \neq \mathbf{y}$.

Suppose that T is a dense subset of $\ell^\infty(\mathbb{R})$. For every $\mathbf{x} \in S$ there exists $\tilde{\mathbf{x}} \in T$ such that $\|\mathbf{x} - \tilde{\mathbf{x}}\|_\infty < \frac{1}{3}$. Therefore, $\mathbf{x} \neq \mathbf{y}$ implies $\tilde{\mathbf{x}} \neq \tilde{\mathbf{y}}$, so the mapping $f : S \longrightarrow T$ is injective. This implies that T is uncountable, so $\ell^\infty(\mathbb{R})$ is not separable. $\square$

Theorem 9.4. *Let $\{B[x_n, r_n] \mid n \in \mathbb{N}\}$ be a sequence of closed spheres in a Banach space S such that $B[x_n, r_n] \supseteq B[x_{n+1}, r_{n+1}]$ for $n \in \mathbb{N}$. If $\lim_{n \to \infty} r_n = 0$, then there exists $z \in S$ such that $\bigcap_{n \in \mathbb{N}} B[x_n, r_n] = \{z\}$.*

Proof.   Note that if $m > n$ we have $x_m \in B[x_n, r_n]$, so $\|x_m - x_n\| \leqslant r_n$. Therefore, (x_n) is a Cauchy sequence and, since S is a Banach space, there exists $z \in S$ such that $\lim_{n \to \infty} x_n = z$. Since $x_m \in B[x_n, r_n]$ for $m \geqslant n$ and $B[x_n, r_n]$ is a closed set it follows that $z \in B[x_n, r_n]$, so $z \in \bigcap_{n \in \mathbb{N}} B[x_n, r_n]$.

Conversely, if $y \in \bigcap_{n \in \mathbb{N}} B[x_n, r_n]$ we have $\|z - y\| \leqslant \|z - x_n\| + \|z_n - y\| \leqslant 2r_n$ for $n \in \mathbb{N}$ which implies $\|z - y\| = 0$, hence $y = z$. $\square$

Lemma 9.1. *Let $h : S \longrightarrow T$ be a bounded linear operator where $(S, \| \cdot \|)$ and $(T, \| \cdot \|)$ are real normed linear spaces. Then, for any $x \in S$ and $r > 0$ we have*

$$\sup_{x' \in B[x,r]} \|h(x')\| \geqslant \|h\| r.$$

Proof. Observe that $x' \in B[x,r]$ if and only if $\|x' - x\| \leqslant r$ which is equivalent to $x' - x \in B[0_S, r]$ and $x - x' \in B(0_S, r)$.

For $z = x' - x$ or $z = x - x'$ we have $\|z\| \leqslant r$ and

$$\max\{\|h(x+z)\|, \|h(x-z)\|\} \geqslant \frac{1}{2} \left(\|h(x+z)\| + \|h(x-z)\| \right)$$
$$\geqslant \|h(z)\|,$$

by the triangle inequality. By taking the supremum over $z \in B[0_S, r]$ we obtain the desired inequality. $\qquad \square$

Recall that we introduced the notion of precompact set in a metric space in Definition 5.21.

Theorem 9.5. *Let L be a Banach space. A subset U of L is relatively compact if and only if it is precompact.*

Proof. Suppose that U is relatively compact, and for some positive r there is no finite r-net. For $x_1 \in U$ there exists x_2 such that $\|x_1 - x_2\| \geqslant r$ because, otherwise $\{x_1\}$ would be an r-net. There is $x_3 \in U$ with $\|x_1 - x_3\| \geqslant r$ and $\|x_2 - x_3\| \geqslant r$ because, otherwise, $\{x_1, x_2\}$ would be an r-net, etc. Thus, we obtain a sequence (x_n) with $\|x_p - x_q\| \geqslant r$ for all distinct p, q. It is immediate that (x_n) contains no convergent subsequence, which contradicts the relative compactness of U. This implies that there exists a finite r-net for U.

Conversely, suppose now that there exists a finite r-net for U for every positive r. Let $\{a_1^n, a_2^n, \ldots, a_{p_n}^n\}$ be an $\frac{1}{n}$-net.

Let (u_m) be an arbitrary sequence in U. Since $U \subseteq \bigcup_{k=1}^{p_1} B(a_k, 1)$, at least one of the spheres $B(a_k, 1)$ contains an infinite subsequence of (u_m). Let (u_m^1) be an infinite subsequence contained in a sphere $B(a_k, 1)$.

At least one of the spheres $B\left(a_k, \frac{1}{2}\right)$ contains an infinite subsequence of (u_m^1). Let (u_m^2) be an infinite subsequence of (u_m^1) contained in one of the spheres $B\left(a_k, \frac{1}{2}\right)$.

This process produces an infinite sequence of sequences (u_m^q) where (u_m^{q+1}) is a subsequence of (u_m^q) contained in a sphere $B(a_i, \frac{1}{q+1})$.

Consider the diagonal sequence (u_m^m). For every positive r let $h_r = \lceil \frac{1}{r} \rceil$ the terms beyond the term of rank h_r are located inside a sphere of radius $\frac{1}{r}$, hence $\|u_m^m - u_l^l\| < \frac{1}{r}$. We have extracted a Cauchy sequence that must converge since S is a Banach space. $\qquad\square$

This theorem offers an alternative proof of compactness for subsets of Banach spaces because it suffices to show the existence of an r-net for such sets.

In Banach spaces the parallelogram equality (see Theorem 2.27) is a characteristic property of norms generated by the inner products, as we show next.

Theorem 9.6. *Let $(L, \|\cdot\|)$ be a Banach space. The norm $\|\cdot\|$ is induced by an inner product if and only if*

$$\|x\|^2 + \|y\|^2 = \frac{1}{2}\left(\|x+y\|^2 + \|x-y\|^2\right)$$

for $x, y \in L$.

Proof. The necessity of the condition was already shown in Theorem 2.27.

To prove that this inequality is sufficient suppose initially that L is a $\mathbb{C}$-normed linear space. We will show that the mapping $(\cdot, \cdot) : L \longrightarrow \mathbb{C}$ as

$$(x,y) = \frac{1}{4}\left(\|x+y\|^2 - \|x-y\|^2 + i\|x+iy\|^2 - i\|x-iy\|^2\right)$$

for $x, y \in L$ is an inner product.

It is immediate that $(y, x) = \overline{(x, y)}$ for $x, y \in L$, so condition (i) of Definition 2.20 is satisfied.

Note that the real part of (x, y) is

$$\Re(x,y) = \frac{1}{4}\left(\|x+y\|^2 - \|x-y\|^2\right).$$

Therefore,

$$i\Re(ix,y) = \frac{i}{4}(\|ix+y\|^2 + \|ix-y\|^2)$$
$$= \frac{1}{4}(\|x-iy\|^2 - \|x+y\|^2).$$

Therefore, we have

$$(x,y) = \Re(x,y) - i\Re(ix,y). \qquad (9.2)$$

This allows us to write

$$\Re(x+z,y) + \Re(x-z,y)$$

$$= \frac{1}{4}(\|x+z+y\|^2 - \|x+z-y\|^2 + \|x-z+y\|^2 - \|x-z-y\|^2)$$

$$= \frac{1}{4}(\|x+z+y\|^2 - \|x+z-y\|^2 + \|x-z+y\|^2 - \|x-z-y\|^2)$$

$$= \Re(x+z,y) + \Re(x-z,y) = \Re(2x,y).$$

Replacing x by $\frac{1}{2}(x+z)$ and z by $\frac{1}{2}(x-z)$ yields

$$\Re(x,y) + \Re(z,y) = \Re(x+z,y).$$

Further, by substituting ix for x and iz by z, we have

$$\Re(ix,y) + \Re(iz,y) = \Re(i(x+z),y),$$

which, in turn yields $(x,y) + (z,y) = (x+z,y)$ taking into account equality (9.2).

It is easy to see that for each rational number q we have $(qx,y) = q(x,y)$. Since the inner product is continuous, it follows that $(ax,y) = a(x,y)$. Also, it is easy to verify that $(ix,y) = i(x,y)$, so the third condition of Definition 2.20 is satisfied.

A direct application of the definition implies $(x,x) = \|x\|^2$, so the last two condition of Definition 2.20 are also satisfied.

We leave to the reader the simpler case of real Banach spaces. $\qquad\square$

9.3 Linear Operators on Banach Spaces

Theorem 9.7. (The Banach-Steinhaus or the Uniform Boundedness Theorem) *Let $\mathcal{F}$ be a family of bounded linear operators from a Banach space S to a normed linear space T. If $\mathcal{F}$ is pointwise bounded (that is, $\sup_{h \in \mathcal{F}} \|h(x)\| < \infty$ for all $x \in S$), then $\mathcal{F}$ is norm-bounded, that is, $\sup_{h \in \mathcal{F}} \|h\| < \infty$.*

Proof. Suppose that $\sup_{h \in \mathcal{F}} \|h\| = \infty$ and let (h_n) be a sequence of operators in $\mathcal{F}$ such that $\|h_n\| \geqslant 4^n$.

Let $x_0 = 0_S$ and define inductively x_n using Lemma 9.1 by choosing $x_n \in B[x_{n-1}, 3^{-n}]$. Then, by Lemma 9.1,

$$\|h_n(x_n)\| \geqslant \|h_n\| \cdot 3^{-n} \geqslant \frac{2}{3}\|h_n\| \cdot 3^n.$$

We claim that (x_n) is a Cauchy sequence. Indeed, since

$$\|x_n - x_p\| \leqslant \sum_{k=p}^{n-1} \|x_{k+1} - x_k\|$$

$$\leqslant \sum_{k=p}^{n-1} 3^{-(k+1)} = \frac{3}{2}(3^{-(p+1)} - 3^{-(n+1)})$$

it suffices to take $n \geq p > \log_3 \frac{1}{2\epsilon}$ to obtain $\|x_n - x_p\| < \epsilon$. Therefore, (x_n) is convergent to some $x \in S$. It is easy to see that $\|x - x_n\| \leqslant \frac{1}{2} 3^{-n}$, so

$$\|h_n(x)\| \geqslant \frac{1}{6} 3^{-n} \|h_n\| \geqslant \frac{1}{6} \left(\frac{4}{3}\right)^n$$

which implies $\lim_{n\to\infty} \|h_n(x)\| = \infty$. □

The notion of open function was introduced in Definition 4.42.

Theorem 9.8. (Open Mapping Theorem) *Let S and T be Banach spaces. If $h : S \longrightarrow T$ is a surjective bounded linear operator, then h is an open function.*

Proof. Define the sequence of sets (T_n) by $T_n = n\mathbf{K}(h(B(0,1)))$ for $n \in \mathbb{N}$. All sets T_n are closed and the surjectivity of h implies $T = \bigcup_{n\in\mathbb{N}} T_n$. There exists T_n such $\mathbf{I}(T_n)$ is non-empty by Corollary 5.9.

The homogeneity of linear operator h implies that $\mathbf{K}(B(0_S, 1))$ has a non-empty interior, that is, there exists $y_0 \in T$ and $\delta > 0$ such that $B(y_0, 4\delta) \subseteq \mathbf{K}(h(B(0_S, 1)))$. By symmetry, $-y_0 \in \mathbf{K}(h(B(0_S, 1)))$.

Note that if $z \in B(0_T, 2\delta)$, then $u = 2z + y_0$ belongs to $B(0_T, 4\delta)$ because $\|u - y_0\| \leqslant 2\|z\| < 4\delta$. Since z is the midpoint of the segment $[y_0, u]$ and $\mathbf{K}(h(B(0_S, 1)))$ is convex (by Theorem 6.37), it follows that $B(0_T, 2\delta) \subseteq \mathbf{K}(h(B(0_S, 1)))$.

We have $B(0_T, 2\delta r) \subseteq \mathbf{K}(h(B(0_S, r)))$ for every $r > 0$.

To prove that for an open set U in S the set $h(U)$ is open in T it suffices to prove that $B(0_T, \delta) \subseteq h(B(0_S, 1))$, or equivalently, that the equation $h(x) = y$ has a solution x in $B(0_S, 1)$ when $y \in B(0_T, \delta)$.

Let $y \in B(0_T, \delta)$. There exists x_1 such that $\|x\|_S < \frac{1}{2}$ and $\|h(x_1) - y\|_T < \frac{\delta}{2}$. Similarly, there exists x_2 such that $\|x_2\| < \frac{1}{2^2}$ and $\|y - h(x_1) - h(x_2)\| < \frac{\delta}{2^2}$, etc. In general, there exists x_n such that $\|x\| < \frac{1}{2^n}$ and $\|y - \sum_{k=1}^{n} h(x_k)\| < \frac{\delta}{2^k}$. Therefore, the series $\sum x_n$ is absolutely convergent in S and $\left\|\sum x_n\right\| < 1$, hence it converges to some x with $\|x\| < 1$ and $\|y - h(x)\| = 0$. □

Corollary 9.1. *Let S and T be Banach spaces. If $h : S \longrightarrow T$ is a continuous linear bijection, then h has a continuous linear inverse h^{-1}.*

Proof. The linearity of $g = h^{-1}$ is immediate. By the Open Mapping Theorem, $h(U)$ is an open set in T and $U = g(h(U))$ means that $g^{-1}(U) = h(U)$, which means that g is continuous. $\qquad\square$

If S and T be Banach spaces their product $S \times T$ is equipped with the norm defined by $\|(x, y)\| = \|x\| + \|y\|$.

The set of continuous operators between the Banach spaces S and T, $h : S \longrightarrow T$ is denoted by $\mathfrak{B}(S, T)$.

Theorem 9.9. (Closed Graph Theorem) *Let S and T be real Banach spaces. For a linear operator $h : S \longrightarrow T$ we have $h \in \mathfrak{B}(S, T)$ if and only if its graph*

$$\gamma h = \{(x, y) \in S \times T \mid y = h(x)\}$$

is a closed set in $S \times T$.

Proof. If $h \in \mathfrak{B}(S, T)$, it is immediate that γh is closed.

Conversely, suppose that the set γh is closed. Then γh is a Banach space with the norm inherited from $S \times T$, the mapping $f : S \times T \longrightarrow S$ defined by $f(x, h(x)) = x$ is a continuous linear bijective operator. Therefore, by Corollary 9.1, the mapping $f^{-1} : S \longrightarrow S \times T$ defined by $f^{-1}(x) = (x, h(x))$ is continuous, which implies the continuity of h because $h = pf^{-1}$, where $p : S \longrightarrow T \longrightarrow T$ is the projection $p(u, v) = v$ for $(u, v) \in S \times T$ (which is continuous by Theorem 4.99). $\qquad\square$

The next two lemmas establish preliminary facts needed in the proof of a very important result known as Lyusternik's Theorem. We follow the outline of the proof presented in [133, 85].

Lemma 9.2. *Let X and Y be real Banach spaces, $f : X \longrightarrow Y$ be a mapping, $Z = f^{-1}(0_Y)$, and $x_0 \in Z$. If f is Fréchet differentiable in a neighborhood V of x_0, (Df) is continuous at x_0 and $(Df)(x_0)$ is surjective, then*

$$\{x \in S \mid (Df)(x_0)(x) = 0_Y\} \subseteq T(Z, x_0),$$

where $T(Z, x_0)$ is the contingent cone of Z at x_0.

Proof. Since the linear mapping $(Df)(x_0)$ is continuous and surjective, by the Open Mapping Theorem (Theorem 9.8), the mapping $(Df)(\mathbf{x_0})$ is open. Thus, the image of the open ball $B(0_X, 1)$ is open, hence there exists some r such that $B(0_Y, r) \subseteq (Df)(x_0)(B(0_X, 1))$. The continuity of $(Df)(x_0)$ implies that there exists $\rho_0 = \sup\{r \mid r > 0, B(0_Y, \rho_0) \subseteq (Df)(x_0)(B(0_X, 1))\}$.

Let $\epsilon \in (0, \rho_0/2)$. Since (Df) is continuous at x_0 there is $\delta > 0$ such that $\tilde{x} \in B(x_0, 2\delta)$ implies $\|(Df)(\tilde{x}) - (Df)(x_0)\| \leqslant \epsilon$.

Let $u, v \in B(x_0, 2\delta)$. By Theorem 6.51 there exists a continuous linear functional $\ell : Y \longrightarrow \mathbb{R}$ such that $\|\ell\| = 1$ and

$$\ell(f(u) - f(v) - (Df)(x_0)(u - v)) = \|f(u) - f(v) - (Df)(x_0)(u - v)\|.$$

Let $\phi : [0, 1] \longrightarrow \mathbb{R}$ be the differentiable function defined as

$$\phi(t) = \ell((Df)((1 - t)u + tv)(u - v))$$

for $t \in [0, 1]$. We have $\phi'(t) = \phi(t)$ and by the Mean Value Theorem there is a $\overline{t} \in (0, 1)$ such that $\phi(1) - \phi(0) = \phi'(\overline{t})$. Thus, we can write:

$$
\begin{aligned}
&\|f(u) - f(v) - (Df)(x_0)(u - v)\| \\
&= \ell(\|f(u) - f(v) - (Df)(x_0)(u - v)\|) \\
&= \phi(1) - \phi(0) = \phi'(t) \\
&= \ell((Df)((1 - \overline{t})v + \overline{t}u))(u - v) - (Df)(x_0)(u - v)) \\
&\leqslant \|(Df)((1 - \overline{t})v + \overline{t}u)) - (Df)(x_0)\|\|u - v\| \\
&\leqslant \epsilon\|u - v\|,
\end{aligned}
$$

which yields

$$\|f(u) - f(v) - (Df)(x_0)(u - v\| \leqslant \epsilon\|u - v\|,$$

for $v, u \in B(x_0, 2\delta)$.

Since $\frac{\epsilon}{\rho_0} < \frac{1}{2}$ there exists $a > 1$ such that $a(\frac{1}{2} + \frac{\epsilon}{\rho_0})$.

Let $x \in X$ such that $(Df)(x_0)(x) = 0_Y$. If $x_0 = 0_X$ we have immediately

$$\{x \in S \mid (Df)(0_X)(x) = 0_Y\} \subseteq T(Z, 0_X).$$

Assume that $x_0 \neq 0_X$ and let $\lambda \in (0, \frac{\delta}{\|x\|})$. Define the sequences $(r_n)_{n \geqslant 1}$ and $(u_n)_{n \geqslant 1}$ as $r_1 = 0_X$, $(Df)(x_0)(u_n) = h(x_0 + \lambda x + r_n)$ and $r_{n+1} = r_n - u_n$ for $n \geqslant 1$.

The sequences (r_n) and (u_n) are well-defined since $(Df)(x_0)$ is surjective, and therefore, for a given r_n there exists u_n such that $(Df)(x_0)(u_n) = h(x_0 + \lambda x + r_n)$.

Since $B(0_Y, r) \subseteq (Df)(x_0)(B(0_X, 1))\}$ for $r = \frac{\rho_0}{a}$, it follows that

$$\|u_n\| \leqslant \frac{a}{\rho_0} \|h(x_0 + \lambda x + r_n)\|.$$

Denote

$$d(\lambda) = \|f(x_0 + \lambda x)\| \text{ and } q = \frac{\epsilon a}{\rho_0}.$$

Since $\|\lambda x\| \leqslant \delta$ we have

$$d(\lambda) = \|f(x_0 + \lambda x) - f(x_0) - (Df)(x_0)(\lambda x)\| \leqslant \epsilon \|\lambda x\| \leqslant \epsilon \delta.$$

Since $a > 1$ we have $q \leqslant 1 - \frac{a}{2} < \frac{1}{2}$.

We prove by induction on $n \geqslant 1$ that

$$\|r_n\| \leqslant \frac{a}{\rho_0} d(\lambda) \frac{1-q^n}{1-q},$$
$$\|f(x_0 + \lambda x + r_n)\| \leqslant d(\lambda) q^{n-1},$$
$$\|u_n\| \leqslant \frac{a}{rho_0} d(\lambda) q^{n-1}.$$

The base step, $n = 1$ is immediate because $\|r_1\| = 0$, $\|f(x_0 + \lambda r + r_1)\| = d(\lambda)$ and

$$\|u_1\| \leqslant \frac{a}{\rho_0} \|f(x_0 + \lambda x + r_1)\| = \frac{a}{\rho_0} d(\lambda).$$

For the induction step assume that the above inequalities are satisfied for n. Then, we obtain

$$\|r_{n+1}\| = \|r_n - x_n\| \leqslant \|r_n\| + \|u_n\|$$
$$\leqslant \frac{a}{\rho_0} d(\lambda) \left(\frac{1 - q^{n-1}}{1 - q} + q_{n-1} \right)$$
$$= \frac{a}{\rho_0} \frac{1 - q^n}{1 - q},$$

which proves the first inequality.

Note that

$$\|\lambda x + r_n\| \leqslant \|\lambda x\| + \|r_n\|$$
$$\leqslant \delta + \frac{a}{\rho_0} d(\lambda) \frac{1 - q^{n-1}}{1 - q}$$
$$\leqslant \delta + \frac{a \epsilon \delta}{\rho_0} \frac{1 - q^{n-1}}{1 - q}$$
$$\leqslant \delta \left(1 + \frac{q}{1 - q} (1 - q^{n-1}) \right) < 2\delta,$$

because we have $\frac{q}{1-q} < 1$ and $1 - q^{n-1} < 1$. Therefore,

$$\|\lambda x + r_n - u_n\| \leqslant \|\lambda x\| + \|r_{n+1}\|$$
$$\leqslant \delta + \frac{a}{\rho_0} d(\lambda) \frac{1 - q^n}{1 - q}$$
$$\leqslant \delta \left(1 + \frac{q}{1-q}(1 - q^n)\right) < 2\delta.$$

This allows us to conclude that

$$\|f(x_0 + \lambda x + r_{n+1})\| = \|f(x_0 + \lambda x + r_n - u_n)\|$$
$$= \| - (Df)(x_0)(-u_n) - f(x_0 + \lambda x + r_n) + f(x_0 + \lambda x + r_n - u_n)\|$$
$$\leqslant \epsilon\| - u_n\| \leqslant \epsilon \frac{a}{\rho_0} d(\lambda) q^{n-1} = d(\lambda) q^n.$$

The last inequality implies

$$\|u_{n+1}\| \leqslant \frac{a}{\rho_0} \|f(x_0 + \lambda x + r_{n+1})\| \leqslant \delta q^n,$$

which completes the inductive proof of the inequalities.

From these inequalities we infer

$$\|u_n\| \leqslant \frac{a}{\rho_0} d(\lambda) q^{n-1} \leqslant \frac{a\epsilon\delta}{\rho_0} q^{n-1} = \delta q^n$$

for $n \geqslant 1$. Since $q < \frac{1}{2}$, it follows that $\lim_{n\to\infty} u_n = 0_X$. This allows us to write

$$\|r_{n+k} - r_n\| = \|r_n - u_{n-k+1} - u_{n+k-2} - \cdots - u_n - r_n\|$$
$$\leqslant \|u_n\| + \|u_{n+1}\| + \cdots + \|u_{n+k-1}\|$$
$$\leqslant \frac{a}{\rho_0} d(\lambda)(q^{n-1} + q^n + \cdots + q^{n+k-2})$$
$$= \frac{a}{\rho_0} d(\lambda) q^{n-1}(1 + q + \cdots + q^{k-1})$$
$$= \frac{a}{\rho_0} d(\lambda) q^{n-1} \frac{1 - q^k}{1 - q} < \frac{ad(\lambda)}{\rho_0(1 - q)} d^{n-1},$$

for all $n, k \geqslant 1$, hence (r_n) is a Cauchy sequence. The completeness of X means that there exists $r(\lambda) \in X$ such that $\lim_{n\to\infty} r_n = r(\lambda)$. Applying the limit to equality $(Df)(x_0)(u_n) = h(x_0 + \lambda x + r_n)$ yields

$$f(x_0 + \lambda x + r(\lambda)) = 0.$$

Since

$$\frac{r(\lambda)}{\lambda} \leqslant \frac{a}{\lambda\rho_0} d(\lambda) \frac{1}{1-q}$$
$$= \frac{a}{\rho_0(1-q)} \frac{\|f(x_0 + \lambda x) - f(x_0) - \lambda(Df)(x_0)(x)\|}{q},$$

we have $\lim_{\lambda\downarrow 0} \frac{r(\lambda)}{\lambda} = 0$.

The final phase of the proof aims to show that x belongs to the contingency cone $T(Z, x_0)$, where $Z = f^{-1}(0_Y)$.

Consider the sequence $(\lambda_n)_{n \geqslant 1}$ in the interval $(0, \frac{\delta}{\|x\|})$ such that $\lim_{n \to \infty} \lambda_n = 0$. Define the sequences $(\mu_n)_{n \geqslant 1}$ and $(x_n)_{\geqslant 1}$ such that

$$\mu_n = \frac{1}{\lambda_n} > 0 \text{ and } x_n = x_0 + \lambda_n + r(\lambda_n) \text{ for } n \geqslant 1.$$

Since $f(x_0 + \lambda x + r(\lambda)) = 0$, we have $x_n \in Z$ for $n \geqslant 1$. Moreover, we have

$$\lim_{n \to \infty} x_n = \lim_{n \to \infty} (x_0 + \lambda_n x + r(\lambda_n))$$
$$= x_0 + \lim_{n \to \infty} (\lambda_n x + r(\lambda_n)) = x_0,$$

and we may conclude that

$$\lim_{n \to infty} \mu_n (x_n - x_0) = \lim_{n \to \infty} \frac{1}{\lambda_n} (\lambda_n x + r(\lambda_n))$$
$$= x + \lim_{n \to \infty} \frac{r(\lambda_n)}{\lambda_n} = x,$$

hence $x \in T(Z, x_0)$. $\qquad\square$

Lemma 9.3. *Let X and Y be real Banach spaces, $f : X \longrightarrow Y$ be a mapping that is Fréchet differentiable at x_0, where $x_0 \in Z = f^{-1}(0_Y)$. We have*

$$T(Z, x_0) \subseteq \{x \in S \mid (Df)(x_0)(x) = 0_Y\},$$

where $T(Z, x_0)$ is the contingent cone of Z at x_0.

Proof. Let $y \in T(Z, x_0) - \{0_X\}$. By the definition of the contingent cone, there is a sequence $(x_n)_{n \geqslant 1}$ of elements of Z and a sequence of positive real numbers $(\lambda_n)_{n \geqslant 1}$ with $x_0 = \lim_{n \to \infty} x_n$ and $y = \lim_{n \to \infty}$ such that $y_n = \lambda_n (x_n - x_0)$ for $n \geqslant 1$. By the definition of Fréchet derivative we have

$$(Df)(x_0)(y)$$
$$= (Df)(x_0) \left(\lim_{n \to \infty} \lambda_n (x_n - x_0) \right)$$
$$= \lim_{n \to \infty} \lambda_n \lim_{n \to \infty} (Df)(x_0) \left(\lim_{n \to \infty} (x_n - x_0) \right)$$
$$= - \lim_{n \to \infty} \lambda_n \left(h(x_n) - h(x_0) - h'(x_0)(x_n - x_0) \right)$$
$$= - \lim_{n \to \infty} \|y_n\| \frac{h(x_n) - h(x_0) - h'(x_0)(x_n - x_0)}{\|x_n - x_0\|} = 0_Y. \qquad\square$$

Theorem 9.10. (Lyusternik'S Theorem) *Let X and Y be real Banach spaces, $f : X \longrightarrow Y$ be a mapping, $Z = f^{-1}(0_Y)$, and $x_0 \in Z$. If f is Fréchet differentiable in a neighborhood V of x_0, (Df) is continuous at x_0 and $(Df)(x_0)$ is surjective, then*

$$\{x \in S \mid (Df)(x_0)(x) = 0_Y\} = T(Z, x_0),$$

where $T(Z, x_0)$ is the contingent cone of Z at x_0.

Proof.   The hypothesis of this theorem (which is identical to the hypothesis of Lemma 9.2) implies the hypothesis of Lemma 9.3. Therefore, by the previous two lemmas we have $\{x \in S \mid (Df)(x_0)(x) = 0_Y\} = T(Z, x_0)$. $\square$

9.4   Compact Operators

Definition 9.2. Let $(S, \|\cdot\|)$ and $(T, \|\cdot\|)$ be two Banach spaces. A linear operator $h : S \longrightarrow T$ is *compact* if for every bounded subset U of S the closure set $\mathbf{K}(\{h(x) \mid x \in U\})$ is compact.

In other words, h is a compact linear operator if the image $\{h(x) \mid x \in U\}$ of every bounded subset U of S under h is relatively compact.

The definition of compact linear operators is equivalent to the requirement that for every bounded sequence (x_n) in S, the sequence $(h(x_n))$ in T has a convergent subsequence.

Suppose that h is a compact linear operator and let (x_n) be a sequence in the bounded set U. Then, $\{x_n \mid n \in \mathbb{N}\}$ is a bounded set, hence $\{h(x_n) \mid n \in \mathbb{N}\}$ is relatively compact, which means that $(h(x_n))$ contains a convergent subsequence.

Conversely, let U be a bounded subset of S and assume that the set $h(U)$ is relatively compact. Let (y_n) be a sequence in $\mathbf{K}(h(U))$. Then, the sequence (y_n) is also bounded and for each y_n there exists $x_n \in U$ such that $\|y_n - h(x_n)\| \leqslant \frac{1}{n}$, which implies that the sequence $(h(x_n))$ is also bounded. By the assumption made above, there exists a convergent subsequence $(h(x_{n_k}))$ and $\lim_{k\to\infty} y_{n_k} = \lim_{k\to\infty} h(x_{n_k})$. This shows that the arbitrary sequence (y_n) contains a convergent subsequence, so $h(U)$ is indeed relatively compact.

Theorem 9.11. *Each compact operator between Banach spaces is bounded.*

Proof.   Let $h : S \longrightarrow T$ be a compact linear operator between the Banach spaces S and T. Suppose that h is unbounded. Then, there exists a sequence (x_n) in S such that $x_n \neq 0_L$ and $\|h(x_n)\| \geqslant n\|x_n\|$ for $n \in \mathbb{N}$. Note that the sequence (z_n) in S defined as $z_n = \frac{1}{\|x_n\|}x_n$ is bounded because $\|z_n\| =$ for $n \in \mathbb{N}$. Since $h(z_n) \geqslant n$ for $n \in \mathbb{N}$ it is clear that $h(z_n)$ contains no convergent subsequence. $\qquad\square$

Corollary 9.2. *Every compact operator between Banach spaces is continuous.*

Proof. This follows from Theorems 9.11 and 6.25. $\qquad\square$

The set of compact operators between the Banach spaces $(S, \|\cdot\|)$ and $(T, \|\cdot\|)$ is denoted by $COMP(S,T)$.

Theorem 9.12. *The set $COMP(S,T)$ is a closed subspace of the linear space $\mathfrak{L}(S,T)$.*

Proof. Let (h_n) be a sequence of compact operators such that $\lim_{n\to\infty} = h$ in $\mathfrak{L}(S,T)$ (in norm, of course). We prove that h is a compact operator by showing that for every bounded sequence (x_m) in S, $h(x_m)$ contains a convergent subsequence.

Consider a bounded sequence (x_n), that is, $\|x_n\| \leqslant M$ for $n \in \mathbb{N}$ and $M \geqslant 0$.

Since h_0 is compact there is a subsequence (x_{0n}) of (x_n) such that the sequence $(h_0(x_{0n}))$ converges. Since h_1 is compact, there is a subsequence (x_{1n}) of (x_{0n}) such that sequence $(h_1(x_{1n}))$ converges.

Continuing in this manner, we obtain subsequences (x_{jn}) of (x_n) such that $(h_j(x_{jn})$ is a convergent sequence in T for each $j \in \mathbb{N}$ and that (x_{jn}) is a subsequence of (x_{in}) for $0 \leqslant i \leqslant j-1$. The "diagonal subsequence" (x_{nn}) is such that $h(x_{nn})$ converges.

Since $\lim_{j\to\infty} h_j = h$, for every positive ϵ there is $p \in \mathbb{N}$ such that $\|h - h_p\| \leqslant \frac{\epsilon}{3M}$.

Note that $(h_p(x_{nn}))$ is a Cauchy sequence as a subsequence of the convergent sequence $(h_p(x_{pn}))$. Hence, there exists $n_0 > p$ such that $m, n \geqslant n_0$ imply $\|h_p(x_{nn}) - h_p(x_{mm})\| < \frac{\epsilon}{3}$.

For $m, n \geqslant n_0$ we have
$$\|h(x_{nn}) - h(x_{mm})\|$$
$$= \|h(x_{nn}) - h_p(x_{nn}) + h_p(x_{nn}) - h_p(x_{mm}) + h_p(x_{mm}) - h(x_{mm})\|$$
$$\leqslant \|(h - h_p)(x_{nn})\| + \|(h_p(x_{nn}) - h_p(x_{mm})\| + \|(h_p - h)(x_{mm})\|$$
$$\leqslant \|h - h_p\|\|x_{nn}\| + \frac{\epsilon}{3} + \|h_p - h\|\|x_{mm}\|$$
$$\leqslant \frac{\epsilon}{3M} \cdot M + \frac{\epsilon}{3} + \frac{\epsilon}{3M} \cdot M = \epsilon.$$

Thus, $(h(x_{nn}))$ is a Cauchy sequence and therefore, it is convergent by the completeness of T. Since (x_{nn}) is a subsequence of the original sequence, it follows that h is a compact operator. $\qquad\square$

Theorem 9.13. *Let h be a compact operator on a Banach space L and let g be a bounded operator on the same space. Then, both hg and gh are compact operators.*

Proof. Since h is compact for every bounded sequence (x_n) in L there exists a subsequence (x_{n_i}) such that $(h(x_{n_i}))$ is a Cauchy sequence. Since g is bounded we have

$$\|g(h(x_{n_i})) - g(h(x_{n_j}))\| \leqslant \|g\| \, \|h(x_{n_i}) - h(x_{n_j})\|.$$

Therefore, $(g(h(x_{n_i})))$ is also a Cauchy sequence, hence gh is compact.

Since (x_n) is bounded and g is bounded, the sequence $(g(x_n))$ is also bounded. The compactness of h implies the existence of a subsequence $(h(g(x_{n_i})))$ that is Cauchy sequence, hence hg is also compact. $\qquad\square$

9.5 Duals of Normed Linear Spaces

Definition 9.3. Let L be a real normed linear space. The *normed dual* of L is the set of all bounded linear functionals defined on L.

The normed dual space of L is denoted by L^*. If $\phi \in L^*$ its norm is $\|\phi\| = \sup\{|\phi(x)| \mid \|x\| = 1\}$.

As we observed in Corollary 6.8, a functional $\phi : L \longrightarrow \mathbb{R}$ is continuous if and only if it is bounded.

Theorem 9.14. *Let L be a normed linear space and let $\phi : L \longrightarrow \mathbb{R}$ be a linear functional. Then ϕ is continuous if and only if the $\mathsf{Null}(\phi)$ is a closed subspace of S.*

Proof. The continuity of ϕ implies immediately that $\mathsf{Null}(\phi) = \phi^{-1}(\{0\})$ is a closed subspace of L.

Conversely, suppose that $\mathsf{Null}(\phi)$ is a closed subspace of L and that ϕ is not continuous. By Theorem 6.25, ϕ is not bounded. This implies the existence of a sequence (x_n) in L such that $\|x_n\| \leqslant 1$ and $\lim_{n \to \infty} \phi(x_n) = \infty$.

Let $z \in S$ such that $z \notin \mathsf{Null}(\phi)$. We have $\phi(z) \neq 0$. If $y_n = z - \frac{\phi(z)}{\phi(x_n)} x_n$, then $\phi(y_n) = 0$ because ϕ is linear. Thus, $y_n \in \mathsf{Null}(\phi)$ for $n \in \mathbb{N}$.

Furthermore, $\lim_{n\to\infty} y_n = z$ and this leads to a contradiction because $\lim_{n\to\infty} y_n \in \mathsf{Null}(\phi)$ because $\mathsf{Null}(\phi)$ is a closed subspace of L. $\qquad\square$

Theorem 9.15. *The normed dual L^* of a real normed linear space L is a Banach space.*

Proof. We need to show only that L^* is complete. Let (ϕ_n) be a Cauchy sequence in L^*. For $x \in L$ the sequence $(\phi_n(x))$ is a Cauchy sequence in $\mathbb{R}$ because

$$|\phi_n(x) - \phi_m(x)| = |(\phi_n - \phi_m)x| \leqslant \|\phi_n - \phi_m\| \, \|x\|.$$

Therefore, the limit $\lim_{n\to\infty} \phi_n(x)$ exists and depends on x. This introduces a functional $\psi : L \longrightarrow \mathbb{R}$ defined by $\psi(x) = \lim_{n\to\infty} \phi_n(x)$. Note that ψ is linear because

$$
\begin{aligned}
\psi(ax + by) &= \lim_{n\to\infty} \phi_n(ax + by) \\
&= \lim_{n\to\infty} \left(a\phi_n(x) + b\phi_n(y)\right) \\
&\quad \text{(because each } \phi_n \text{ is a linear functional)} \\
&= a \lim_{n\to\infty} \phi_n(x) + b \lim_{n\to\infty} \phi_n(y) \\
&= a\psi(x) + b\psi(y).
\end{aligned}
$$

Since (ϕ_n) is a Cauchy sequence, for every $\epsilon > 0$ there exists n_ϵ such that $m, n \geqslant n_\epsilon$ implies $\|\phi_n - \phi_m\| \leqslant \epsilon$, which, in turn, implies

$$|\phi_n(x) - \phi_m(x)| \leqslant \epsilon \|x\|$$

for $n, m \geqslant n_\epsilon$ and $x \in L$. Since $\lim_{n\to\infty} \phi_n(x) = \psi(x)$ it follows that

$$|\psi(x) - \phi_m(x)| \leqslant \epsilon \|x\| \tag{9.3}$$

when $m \geqslant n_\epsilon$. This allows us to write

$$
\begin{aligned}
|\psi(x)| = |\psi(x) - \phi_m(x) + \phi_m(x)| &\leqslant |\psi(x) - \phi_m(x)| + |\phi_m(x)| \\
&\leqslant (\epsilon + \|\phi_m\|)\|x\|,
\end{aligned}
$$

so ψ is bounded and, therefore, $\psi \in L^*$. Moreover, from inequality (9.3) we obtain $\|\psi - \phi_m\| < \epsilon$ when $m > n_\epsilon$, so $\lim_{m\to\infty} \phi_m = \psi$. $\qquad\square$

Let $(S, \mathcal{E}, m)$ be a measure space. Next, we examine the duals for the Banach spaces $L^p(S, \mathcal{E}, m)$.

Any function $f \in \mathcal{L}^q(S, \mathcal{E}, m)$, where $\frac{1}{p} + \frac{1}{q} = 1$ and $1 \leqslant p \leqslant \infty$, generates a linear functional ϕ_f on $\mathcal{L}^p(S, \mathcal{E}, m)$ defined by

$$\phi_f(u) = \int_S uf \, dm.$$

By Hölder's inequality we have:

$$|\phi_f(u)| = \left| \int_S fu \, dm \right| \leqslant \|f\|_q \|u\|_q.$$

Therefore, $\|\phi_f\| \leqslant \|f\|_q$. Consequently, the mapping $I_p : \mathcal{L}_q(S, \mathcal{E}, m) \longrightarrow \mathcal{L}_p(S, \mathcal{E}, m)^*$ defined by $I_p(f) = \phi_f$ is an injective linear operator with $\|I_p\| \leqslant 1$.

Theorem 9.16. *Let $(S, \mathcal{E}, m)$ be a σ-finite measure space. For $1 \leqslant p < \infty$ the map I_p is a linear bijective isometry between $\mathcal{L}^q(S, \mathcal{E}, m)$ and the dual of $\mathcal{L}^p(S, \mathcal{E}, m)$. That is, for any $\phi \in (\mathcal{L}^p(S, \mathcal{E}, m))^*$ there exists $f \in \mathcal{L}^q(S, \mathcal{E}, m)$, such that $\phi = \phi_f$, $\phi_f(u) = \int_S uf \, dm$ for every $u \in \mathcal{L}^p(S, \mathcal{E}, m)$ and $\|\phi\| = \|f\|_q$.*

The Riesz representation theorem does not hold for $p = \infty$.

We have the following equalities:

$$(I_p(f), u) = \int_S uf \, dm \text{ for } f \in \mathcal{L}^q(S, \mathcal{E}, m), u \in \mathcal{L}^p(S, \mathcal{E}, m),$$

$$(\phi, u) = \int_S uI_p^{-1}(\phi) \, dm \text{ for } \phi \in (\mathcal{L}^p(S, \mathcal{E}, m))^*, u \in \mathcal{L}^p(S, \mathcal{E}, m).$$

Let $L = (L, \|\cdot\|)$ an arbitrary $\mathbb{F}$-normed space. For a fixed $x \in L$ consider the map $F_x : L^* \longrightarrow \mathbb{F}$ such that $F_x(\phi) = \phi(x)$. Clearly $F_x \in (L^*)^*$. Moreover, by the dual expression of the norm

$$\|F_x\|_{X^{**}} = \sup\{F_x(\phi) \mid \|\phi\|_* = 1\}$$
$$= \sup\{F_x(\phi) \mid \|\phi\|_* = 1\} = \|x\|.$$

Hence, the mapping $k : L \longrightarrow L^{**}$ defined by $k(x) = F_x$ is a linear isometry, $\|k(x)\|_{**} = \|x\|$. Thus we obtain a canonical isometric embedding of L into L^{**}.

A Banach space X is called *reflexive* if the canonical isometry k is an onto mapping (and hence k is a linear bijective isometry between L and L^{**}). In general, $k(L) \subseteq L^{**}$ is a proper algebraic subspace of L^{**}. Indeed, L^{**} is complete as a dual of a normed space. Thus, if $k(L) = L^{**}$, it follows that L is complete.

However, the completeness is not sufficient for reflexivity. For many Banach spaces arising in the applications the inclusion $k(L) \subset L^{**}$ is strict.

Theorem 9.17. *For $p \geqslant 1$, the dual space $(\ell^p(\mathbb{R}))^*$ is isometric to the space $\ell^q(\mathbb{R})$, where $\frac{1}{p} + \frac{1}{q} = 1$.*

Proof. We present here the argument for $1 \leqslant p < \infty$; the arguments for $p = \infty$ and $q = 1$ are similar.

Define the mapping $\Phi : \ell^q \longrightarrow (\ell^p)^*(\mathbb{R})$ as $\Phi(\mathbf{y})(\mathbf{x}) = \sum_{n=0}^{infty} y_n x_n$. It is immediate that Φ is linear. This mapping is well-defined because

$$\sum_{i=0}^{m} |x_i y_i| \leqslant \left(\sum_{i=0}^{m} |x_i|^p \right)^{\frac{1}{p}} \left(\sum_{i=0}^{m} |y_i|^q \right)^{\frac{1}{q}},$$

by Hölder's inequality.

Since $|\Phi(\mathbf{y})(\mathbf{x})| \leqslant \|\mathbf{y}\|_q \|\mathbf{x}\|_p$, it follows that

$$\|\Phi(\mathbf{y})\|_{(\ell^p)^*} \leqslant \|\mathbf{y}\|_q, \tag{9.4}$$

so Φ is a bounded linear operator between $\ell^q(\mathbb{R})$ and $(\ell^p(\mathbb{R}))^*$.

To prove that Φ is surjective, let $f \in (\ell^p(\mathbb{R}))^*$. If $\mathbf{e}_i$ is the sequence in $\ell^p(\mathbb{R})$ whose components equal 0, with the exception of the ith component that equals 1, where $i \in \mathbb{N}$, define $\mathbf{y}$ as $y_i = f(\mathbf{e}_i)$.

Let $\mathbf{x}^m$ be the sequence given by

$$(\mathbf{x}^m)_k = \begin{cases} |y_k|^{q-1} & \text{if } k \leqslant m, \\ 0 & \text{if } k > m. \end{cases}$$

We have

$$\|\mathbf{x}^m\|_p = \left(\sum_{i=0}^{m} |y_k|^{p(q-1)} \right)^{\frac{1}{p}} = \left(\sum_{i=0}^{m} |y_k|^q \right)^{\frac{1}{p}},$$

and

$$f(\mathbf{x}^m) = \sum_{k=0}^{m} (\mathbf{x}^m)_k f(\mathbf{e}_k) = \sum_{k=0}^{m} (\mathbf{x}^m)_k y_k = \sum_{k=0}^{m} y_k^q.$$

Consequently,

$$\sum_{k=0}^{m} |y_k|^q = f(\mathbf{x}^m) \leqslant \|f\|_{(\ell^p(\mathbb{R}))^*} \|\mathbf{x}^m\|_p = \|f\|_{(\ell^p(\mathbb{R}))^*} \left(\sum_{k=0}^{m} |y_k|^q \right)^{\frac{1}{p}},$$

which implies $\left(\sum_{k=0}^{m} |y_k|^q \right)^{\frac{1}{q}} \leqslant \|f\|_{(\ell^p(\mathbb{R}))^*}$ for every m. Therefore, $\|\mathbf{y}\|_q \leqslant \|f\|_{(\ell^p(\mathbb{R}))^*}$, or

$$\|\mathbf{y}\|_q \leqslant \|\Phi(\mathbf{y})\|_{(\ell^p(\mathbb{R}))^*}. \tag{9.5}$$

The continuity of f implies that for every $\mathbf{x} \in \ell^p(\mathbb{R})$ we have

$$f(\mathbf{x}) = f \left(\lim_{m \to \infty} \sum_{k=0}^{m} x_k \mathbf{e}_k \right) = \sum_{m=0}^{\infty} x_m f(\mathbf{e}_k) = \sum_{m=0}^{\infty} x_m y_m = \Phi(\mathbf{y})(\mathbf{x}).$$

This shows that Φ is surjective.

By inequalities (9.4) and (9.5) we have $\|\mathbf{y}\|_q = \|\Phi(\mathbf{y})\|_{(\ell^p(\mathbb{R}))^*}$, so Φ is an isometry. $\qquad\square$

Corollary 9.3. *For $p \geqslant 1$ the spaces $\ell^p(\mathbb{R})$ are Banach spaces.*

Proof. This statement is an immediate consequences of Theorems 9.15 and 9.17. $\square$

In the special case $p = 2$, the spaces $\ell^2(\mathbb{R})$ and $(\ell^2(\mathbb{R}))^*$ are isometric; thus, $\ell^2(\mathbb{R})$ is isomorphic with its dual.

9.6   Spectra of Linear Operators on Banach Spaces

The notions of eigenvalue, eigenvector, and resolvent of a linear operators were introduced in Section 2.3.

Definition 9.4. The complex numbers λ for which the resolvent $\mathsf{R}_{h,\lambda}$ is defined on the whole space L and it is continuous are known as *regular values* for h.

The *spectrum* of h is the set of complex numbers $\sigma(h)$ that consists of those complex numbers that are not regular values for h.

Three subsets of $\sigma(h)$ are distinguished:

(i) the *point spectrum* of h, $\sigma_p(h)$ that consists of those numbers λ such that $\mathsf{R}_{h,\lambda}$ does not exists;

(ii) the *continuous spectrum* of h, $\sigma_c(h)$ that consists of those numbers λ such that $\mathsf{R}_{h,\lambda}$ exists, $\mathrm{Dom}(\mathsf{R}_{h,\lambda}) \subset L$ and $\mathbf{K}(\mathrm{Dom}(\mathsf{R}_{h,\lambda})) = L$;

(iii) the *residual spectrum* of h, $\sigma_r(h)$ that consists of those numbers λ such that $\mathsf{R}_{h,\lambda}$ exists and $\mathbf{K}(\mathrm{Dom}(\mathsf{R}_{h,\lambda})) \subset L$.

Example 9.6. Let $h : C[a,b] \longrightarrow C[a,b]$ be the operator defined by $h(\phi) = \psi$, where $\psi(t) = t\phi(t)$. If λ were an eigenvalue of h we would have $h(\phi)(t) = \lambda\phi(t) = t\phi(t)$ for $t \in [a,b]$, which is impossible. Thus, h has no eigenvalues. However, the residual spectrum consists of all numbers $\lambda \in [a,b]$. Indeed, note that if $h(\phi) - \lambda\phi = \psi$, we have $(t - \lambda)\phi(t) = \psi(t)$ if $\psi \in C[a,b]$ is a function such that $\psi(t) = (t - \lambda)\eta(t)$ for some $\eta \in C[a,b]$. This shows that $(\mathsf{R}_{h,\lambda})^{-1}(\psi)$ is defined if ψ has the form $\psi(t) = (t - \lambda)\eta(t)$ for some $\eta \in C[a,b]$, so $\mathbf{K}(\mathrm{Dom}(\mathsf{R}_{h,\lambda})) \subset C[a,b]$.

Example 9.7. Consider the linear operator $\mathsf{s} : \ell^2(\mathbb{R}) \longrightarrow \ell^2(\mathbb{R})$ defined by:

$$\mathsf{s}(x_0, x_1, x_2, \ldots) = (0, x_0, x_1, x_2, \ldots)$$

for $(x_0, x_1, x_2, \ldots) \in \ell^2(\mathbb{R})$. Note that $\|\mathsf{s}(\mathbf{x})\| = \|\mathbf{x}\|$, so s is an isometry and, therefore a bounded operator. Suppose that λ is an eigenvalue of s.

Then, there exists $\mathbf{x} \in \ell^2(\mathbb{R}) - \{\mathbf{0}\}$ such that $\mathbf{s}(\mathbf{x}) = \lambda\mathbf{x}$, which means that

$$0 = \lambda x_0, x_0 = \lambda x_1, \ldots, x_n = \lambda x_{n+1}, \ldots.$$

Thus, either $\lambda = 0$, which yields the contradiction $\mathbf{x} = \mathbf{0}$, or $\lambda \neq 0$, which implies the same conclusion. Thus, $\mathbf{s}$ has no eigenvalue.

Theorem 9.18. *Let L be a Banach space and let h be a bounded linear operator on L. If $x_1, \ldots, x_n$ are n eigenvectors associated to the distinct eigenvalues $\lambda_1, \ldots, \lambda_n$, respectively, then the set $\{x_1, \ldots, x_n\}$ is linearly independent.*

Proof. The proof is by induction on n.

If $n = 1$ the set $\{x_1\}$ is linearly independent because $x_1 \neq 0_L$.

For the induction step assume that $\{x_1, \ldots, x_{j-1}\}$ is linearly independent, where $j \geqslant 2$. If $x_j = a_1 x_1 + \cdots + a_{j-1} x_{j-1}$, then by the linearity of h we have

$$\lambda_j x_j = a_1 \lambda_1 x_1 + \cdots + \lambda_{j-1} a_{j-1} x_{j-1},$$

which implies

$$a_1(\lambda_1 - \lambda_j)x_1 + \cdots + a_{j-1}(\lambda_{j-1} - \lambda_j)x_{j-1} = 0.$$

This contradicts the linear independence of $x_1, \ldots, x_{j-1}$ because the eigenvalues are supposed to be distinct. Therefore, $\{x_1, \ldots, x_{j-1}, x_j\}$ is linearly independent. $\quad\square$

Theorem 9.19. *Let $h : L \longrightarrow L$ a continuous linear operator on a Banach space L and let λ be an eigenvalue of h. The subspace generated by the set of eigenvectors that correspond to λ is a closed subspace L_λ of L.*

Proof. If $x, y \in L_\lambda$, then

$$h(ax + by) = ah(x) + bh(y) = a\lambda x + b\lambda y = \lambda(ax + by),$$

so $ax + by \in L_\lambda$, which shows that L_λ is a subspace.

If (x_n) is a sequence in L_λ such that $\lim_{n\to\infty} x_n = x$, then

$$h(x) = h(\lim_{n\to\infty} x_n) = \lim_{n\to\infty} h(x_n)$$
$$\text{(because } h \text{ is continuous)}$$
$$= \lim_{n\to\infty} \lambda x_n = \lambda \lim_{n\to\infty} x_n = \lambda x,$$

which implies $x \in L_\lambda$. $\quad\square$

Theorem 9.20. *Let $h \in \mathfrak{L}(L, K)$ be a surjective linear operator between the Banach spaces L and K. If there exists an inverse bounded linear operator $h^{-1} : K \longrightarrow L$, then for any bounded linear operator $g : L \longrightarrow K$ such that $\|g\| < \frac{1}{\|h^{-1}\|}$, the operator $h+g$ has the bounded inverse $(h+g)^{-1} \in \mathfrak{L}(K, L)$ and*

$$\|(h + g)^{-1}\| \leqslant \frac{1}{\frac{1}{\|h^{-1}\|} - \|g\|}.$$

Proof. Since h has the inverse operator h^{-1} the equality $(h + g)x = y$ implies $h(x) = y - g(x)$, hence $x = h^{-1}(y - g(x))$. Define the operator $k_y(x) = h^{-1}(y - g(x))$.

We have

$$k_y(x_1) - k_y(x_2) = h^{-1}(y - g(x_1)) - h^{-1}(y - g(x_2))$$
$$= h^{-1}g(x_2 - x_1),$$

which implies

$$\|k_y(x_1) - k_y(x_2)\| \leqslant \|h^{-1}\|\|g\|\|x_2 - x_1\|$$
$$\leqslant a\|x_2 - x_1\|,$$

where $\|h^{-1}\|\|g\| < a < 1$. Thus, k_y is a contraction, which implies that the equation $(h + g)x = y$ has a unique solution for every $y \in K$.

Since $x = h^{-1}(h(x))$ for every $x \in L$, we have $\|x\| \leqslant \|h^{-1}\| \, \|h(x)\|$ which yields $\|h(x)\| \geqslant \frac{1}{\|h^{-1}\|}\|x\|$. Therefore,

$$\|y\| = \|(h + g)(x)\| \geqslant \|h(x)\| - \|g(x)\|$$
$$\geqslant \frac{1}{\|h^{-1}\|}\|x\| - \|g\|\|x\|$$
$$= \left(\frac{1}{\|h^{-1}\|} - \|g\| \right) \|x\|.$$

Consequently,

$$\|(h + g)^{-1}y\| \leqslant \left(\frac{1}{\|h^{-1}\|} - \|g\| \right)^{-1} \|y\|$$

for every $y \in K$. Thus, $(h + g)^{-1}$ is bounded and

$$\|(h + g)^{-1}\| \leqslant \frac{1}{\frac{1}{\|h^{-1}\|} - \|g\|}. \qquad \square$$

Theorem 9.21. *Let $h : L \longrightarrow L$ be a linear operator such that $\|h\| < 1$. Then, the linear operator $1_L - h$ is invertible and*

$$(1_L - h)^{-1} = \sum_{k=0}^{\infty} h^k.$$

Proof. Note that $(1_L - h)(1_L + h + h^2 + \cdots + h^n) = 1_L - h^{n+1}$. We have $\lim_{n \to \infty} \|h^{n+1}\| = 0$ because $\|h^{n+1}\| \leqslant (\|h\|)^{n+1}$ and $\|h\| < 1$, hence $\lim_{n \to \infty}(1_L - h^{n+1}) = 1_L$. Thus,

$$(1_L - h) \lim_{n \to \infty} (1_L + h + h^2 + \cdots + h^n) = 1_L,$$

which proves the equality. $\qquad\square$

Theorem 9.22. *If h is a bounded linear operator in $\mathfrak{L}(L)$, then $\lambda \in \sigma(h)$ implies $\lambda \leqslant \|h\|$. Furthermore, the spectrum of h is a closed set.*

Proof. The operator $h_1 = -\lambda 1_L$ is surjective for any $\lambda \in \mathbb{C}$. Thus, $h_1^{-1} = -\frac{1}{a}1$ and $\|h_1^{-1}\| = \frac{1}{|a|}$. If $\|h\| < |a|$, by Theorem 9.20 applied to the operators h_1 and h, the operator $h_1 + h$ has a bounded inverse and

$$\|(h_1 + h)^{-1}\| \leqslant \frac{1}{\frac{1}{\|h_1^{-1}\|} - \|h\|},$$

which amounts to

$$\|(h - \lambda 1_L)^{-1}\| \leqslant \frac{1}{\lambda - \|h\|}.$$

In turn, this means that $h(x) - \lambda x = y$ has the unique solution, so a is a regular value for h. Thus, for any $\lambda \in \sigma(h)$ we have $\lambda \leqslant \|h\|$.

Suppose now that λ_0 is a regular value for h, that is, $\mathsf{R}_{h,\lambda_0} = (h - \lambda 1_L)^{-1}$ is continuous on L. Let λ be a complex number such that $|\lambda - \lambda_0| < \frac{1}{\|\mathsf{R}_{h,\lambda_0}\|}$.

By applying Theorem 9.20 to the operators $g_1 = h - \lambda_0 1_L$ and $g_2 = (\lambda_0 - \lambda)1_L$, taking into account that $g_1^{-1} = \mathsf{R}_{h,\lambda_0}$ and $\|g_2\| = |\lambda_0 - \lambda|$, we infer that the operator $g_1 + g_2 = h - \lambda 1_L$ has an inverse on L when $|\lambda - \lambda_0| < \frac{1}{\|\mathsf{R}_{h,\lambda_0}\|}$. Therefore, the set of regular values is an open set in $\mathbb{C}$ which implies that its complement, the spectrum of h is a closed set. $\qquad\square$

Exercises and Supplements

(1) Let ϕ be the functional defined on the Banach space $(C[0,1], \|\cdot\|_\infty)$ defined by $\phi(f) = f(0)$. Prove that ϕ is bounded and compute $\|\phi\|$.

(2) Let $(S, \|\cdot\|_1)$ and $(S, \|\cdot\|_2)$ be two Banach spaces defined over the same set S. If $\|x\|_1 \leqslant \|x\|_2$ for all $x \in S$, prove that there exists a positive number c such that $\|x\|_2 \leqslant c\|x\|_1$.

(3) Let $(S, \|\cdot\|_S)$ and $(T, \|\cdot\|_T)$ be two normed spaces. Prove that if $f : S \longrightarrow T$ is a homeomorphism between these spaces, then $(S, \|\cdot\|_S)$ is a Banach space if and only if $(T, \|\cdot\|_T)$ is a Banach space.

(4) Let L be a Banach space and let h be an invertible linear operator on L. Prove that a linear operator g on L such that $\|h - g\| < \frac{1}{\|h\|}$, then g is also invertible.

Solution: Observe that $\|1_L - h^{-1}g\| = \|h^{-1}(h-g)\| \leqslant \|h\|^{-1}\|h-g\| < 1$. Since g can be written as

$$g = h(1_L - (1_L - h^{-1}g)),$$

and the operator $1_L - (1_L - h^{-1}g)$ is invertible by Theorem 9.21, it follows that g is also invertible.

(5) Prove that the set of invertible linear operators defined on a Banach space is open in the topological space of linear operators.

(6) Let L be a normed linear space and T a Banach space. If M is a dense linear subspace of L and $h : M \longrightarrow T$ is a bounded linear map, then there is a unique bounded linear map $\tilde{h} : L \longrightarrow T$ such that $\tilde{h}(x) = h(x)$ for all $x \in M$. Furthermore, $\|\tilde{h}\| = \|h\|$.

Solution: Since M is a dense linear subspace of L for every $x \in L$ there exists a sequence (x_n) of elements of M such that $\lim_{n\to\infty} x_n = x$. Since h is a bounded operator, the sequence $(h(x_n))$ is a Cauchy sequence, and therefore, it is convergent in T. Thus, we can define $\tilde{h}(x) = \lim_{n\to\infty} h(x_n)$.

The function $\tilde{h}$ is well-defined for, if (z_n) is another sequence of elements of M such that $\lim_{n\to\infty} z_n = x$, we have $\|x_n - z_n\| \leqslant \|x_n - x\| + \|x - Z_n\|$, hence $\lim_{n\to\infty} \|x_n - z_n\| = 0$. Since $\|h(x_n) - h(z_n)\| = \|h(x_n - z_n)\| \leqslant \|h\|\|x_n - z_n\|$, it follows that $\lim_{n\to\infty} h(x_n) = \lim_{n\to\infty} h(z_n)$.

The operator $\tilde{h}$ is an extension of h, because if $x \in M$, by using the constant sequence with $x_n = x$ for all n to define $\tilde{h}$ we obtain $\tilde{h}(x) = h(x)$ for $x \in M$. The linearity of $\tilde{h}$ follows from the linearity of h. The boundedness of $\tilde{h}$ follows from the fact that $\|\tilde{h}(x)\| = \lim_{n\to\infty} \|h(x_n)\| \leqslant \lim_{n\to\infty} \|h\|\|x_n\| = \|h\|\|x\|$. Also, we have $\|\tilde{h}\| \leqslant \|h\|$. Since $\tilde{h}(x) = h(x)$ for $x \in M$, it follows that $\|\tilde{h}\| = \|h\|$.

The operator $\tilde{h}$ is the unique bounded linear operator from L to K that coincides with h on M. Suppose that g is another such operator, and let $x \in L$. Let (x_n) be a sequence in M that converges to x. Then, using the continuity of g, the fact that g is an extension of h, and the definition of $\tilde{h}$ we obtain

$$g(x) = \lim_{n\to\infty} g(x_n) = \lim_{n\to\infty} h(x_n) = \tilde{h}(x).$$

(7) Let $B[\mathbf{0}, 1]$ be the open ball centered in $(0, \ldots, 0, \ldots)$ in $\ell^1(\mathbb{R})$. Prove that there exist infinitely many pairwise disjoint balls of a given radius r included in $B[\mathbf{0}, a]$ and that $B[\mathbf{0}, 1]$ is not compact.

(8) Let $(S, \mathcal{O}_d)$ be a metric space and let U be a subspace of S such that $\mathbf{K}(U) = S$. If $h : U \longrightarrow T$ is a bounded linear operator into a Banach space T prove that h has a unique extension to a linear operator $h : S \longrightarrow T$.

It is natural to extend the Riemann integral (discussed in Section 8.5) from real-valued functions to functions ranging over Banach spaces. Let $(T, \| \cdot \|)$ be a Banach space and let $f : [a, b] \longrightarrow T$ be a real-argument function. Then, the notion of Riemann sum introduced in equality (8.14) extends immediately to this more general case, as

$$\sigma(f, \Delta, \Xi) = \sum_{i=1}^{n} f(\xi_i)(a_i - a_{i-1}),$$

where $\Delta = \{a_0, a_1, \ldots, a_n\} \in \mathsf{SUBD}[a, b]$ and $\Xi = \{\xi_1, \ldots, \xi_n\}$ be a set of numbers such that $\xi_i \in [a_{i-1}, a_i]$ for $1 \leqslant i \leqslant n$. Then, the Riemann integral is defined as $\lim_{\nu(\Delta) \to 0} \sigma(f, \Delta, Xi)$ for any choice of Ξ.

It can be shown that if f is a continuous on $[a, b]$ is uniformly continuous and, therefore, integrable.

(9) If X, Y are Banach spaces and $h : X \longrightarrow Y$, then $\int_a^b h(f(t)) \, dt = h(\int_a^b f(t) \, dt)$.

(10) Let $\phi : [a, b] \longrightarrow \mathbb{R}$ be a real-valued integrable function. If $h : [a, b] \longrightarrow X$ is defined by $h(t) = \phi(t)\mathbf{x}_0$, then prove that $\int_a^b h(t) \, dt = (\int_a^b \phi(t) \, dt)\mathbf{x}_0$.

(11) Let $h : [a, b] \longrightarrow X$. Prove that $\| \int_a^b h(t) \, dt \| \leqslant \int_a^b \|f(t)\| \, dt$.

(12) Let X and Y be two Banach spaces and let $h : X \longrightarrow Y$ be a surjective linear continuous function. Prove that there exists a positive number t such that $tB[0_Y, r] \subseteq \mathbf{K}(h(B[0_X, 1]))$.

Solution: Since h is surjective we have:

$$Y = h(X) = h\left(\bigcup_{n=1}^{\infty} nB[0_X, 1] \right) = \bigcup_{n=1}^{\infty} h(nB[0_X, 1]) = \bigcup_{n=1}^{\infty} n \, h(B[0_X, 1]).$$

By Corollary 5.9 there exists a set $n \, h(B[0_X, 1])$ that contains an open set. Therefore, $\mathbf{K}(h(B[0_X, 1])$ contains an open set $y + tB[0_Y, 1]$. Since $B[0_X, 1] = -B[0_X, 1]$ we also have $-y + tB[0_Y, 1] \subseteq \mathbf{K}(h(B[0_X, 1]))$. If $z \in Y$ such that $\|z\| \leqslant r$, then there exist sequences (u_n) and (v_n) in $B[0_X, 1]$ such that $\lim_{n \to \infty} h(u_n) = y + z$ and $\lim_{n \to \infty} h(v_n) = -y + z$, hence $z = \lim_{n \to \infty} h\left(\frac{u_n + v_n}{2} \right) \in \mathbf{K}(h(B[0_X, 1]))$, which implies the existence of $t > 0$ such that $tB[0_Y, r] \subseteq \mathbf{K}(h(B[0_X, 1]))$.

(13) This result contained here is known as Graves' Theorem [65].

Let X and Y be two Banach spaces, $f : B[0_X, r] \longrightarrow Y$ be a function such that $f(0_X) = 0_Y$, and let $g : X \longrightarrow Y$ be a surjective continuous linear mapping such that $tB[0_Y, 1] \subseteq g(B[0_X, 1])$ for some $t > 0$. Suppose that $f - g$ is a Lipschitz function on $B[0_X, r]$ such that

$$\|(f - g)(x_1) - (f - g)(x_2)\| \leqslant c\|x_1 - x_2\|,$$

for all $x_1, x_2 \in B[0_X, r]$, where $0 \leqslant c < t$.
Prove that if $\|y\| \leqslant (t - c)r$, then

$$(t - c)rB[0_Y, 1] \subseteq f\left(rB[0_x, r]\right), \qquad (9.6)$$

that is the equation $y = f(x)$ has a solution $x \in B[0_X, r]$.

Solution: Let $a = t - c$ and let $y \in B[0_Y, ar]$. Consider the sequence (x_n), where $x_0 = 0_X$ and let x_1 is such that $\|x_1\| \leqslant \frac{1}{t}\|y\| \leqslant \frac{ar}{t} < r$. Suppose that we have generated $x_0, x_1, \ldots, x_k$. Then x_{k+1} is defined by

$$g(x_{k+1} - x_k) = (g - f)(x_k) - (g - f)x_{k-1}$$

for $k \geqslant 1$. Since $f - g$ is a Lipschitz function, we have $g(x_{k+1} - x_k) \leqslant c\|x_{k+1} - x_k\|$. Taking into account that $tB[0_Y, 1] \subseteq g(B[0_X, 1])$, x_{k+1} is chosen such that $t\|x_{k+1} - x_k\| \leqslant c\|x_k - x_{k-1}\|$, hence $\|x_{k+1} - x_k\| \leqslant \frac{c}{t}\|x_k - x_{k-1}\|$, which implies

$$\|x_n - x_{n-1}\| \leqslant \left(\frac{c}{t}\right)^{n-1}\|x_1\|.$$

Since $\frac{c}{t} < 1$, (x_n) is a Cauchy sequence. There exists $x \in X$ such that $\lim_{n \to \infty} x_n = x$ because X is a Banach space.

Note that

$$\|x_n\| \leqslant \sum_{k=1}^{n} \|x_k - x_{k-1}\| \leqslant \sum_{k=1}^{n} \left(\frac{c}{t}\right)^{k-1}\|x_1\| \leqslant \frac{\|x_1\|}{1 - \frac{c}{\tau}} \leqslant \frac{dr}{r - c} = r,$$

hence $x_{k+1} \in B[0_X, r]$. Thus, we have $x \in B[0_X, r]$.

(14) Let T be a Banach space and let $f : (a, b) \longrightarrow T$ be a function differentiable on (a, b). Prove that

$$\|f(y) - f(x)\| \leqslant |y - x| \cdot \sup\{(Df)((1 - t)x + ty) \mid t \in [0, 1]\}$$

for $x, y \in I$.

Solution: Let μ be a number such that $\sup\{(Df)((1 - t)x + ty) \mid t \in [0, 1]\} < \mu$ and let

$$K_\mu = \{t \in [0, 1] \mid \|f((1 - t)x + ty) - f(x)\| \leqslant \mu t|y - x|\}.$$

The set K_μ is closed and $0 \in K_\mu$. Let s be the largest element of K_μ. Clearly, $s \leqslant 1$.

Suppose $s < 1$ and let $t \in (s, 1)$. If $t - s$ is sufficiently small we have

$$\|f((1-t)x+ty) - f(x)\|$$
$$\leqslant \|f((1-t)x+ty) - f((1-s)x+sy))\| + \|f((1-s)x+sy)) - f(x)\|$$
$$\leqslant \|(Df)((1-s)x+sy))(t-s)(y-x) + o(|t-s|\,|y-x|)\| + \mu s|y-x|$$
$$\leqslant \mu(t-s)|y-x| + \mu s|y-x| = \mu t|y-x|,$$

hence $t \in K_\mu$, which contradicts the definition of s. Therefore, we must have $s = 1$, which concludes the argument.

(15) Let S, T be Banach spaces, U be an open set in S, and let $f : U \longrightarrow T$. If $x, y \in U$ such that $[x, y] \subseteq U$ and h is a linear mapping, prove that

$$\|f(y) - f(x) - h(\mathbf{y}) - h(\mathbf{x})\| \leqslant \|y - x\| \cdot \sup_{t \in [0,1]} \|(Df)((1-t)x+ty) - h\|.$$

Solution: The function $g(t) = f((1-t)x+ty) - th(y-x)$ is differentiable and $(Dg)(t) = ((Df)((1-t)x+ty) - h)(y-x)$. By Supplement 14 we have $\|g(1) - g(0)\| \leqslant \sup\{\|(Dg)(t)\| \mid t \in [0,1]\}$, hence

$$\|f(y) - f(x) - h(\mathbf{y}) - h(\mathbf{x})\|$$
$$\leqslant \sup_{t \in [0,1]} \|(Df)((1-t)x+ty))(y-x) - h(y-x)\|$$
$$\leqslant \|y-x\| \sup\{\|(Df)((1-t)x+ty) - h\| \mid t \in [0,1]\}.$$

(16) Let (p_n) be a sequence of projections on a Banach space L such that $\lim_{n\to\infty} p_n(y) = y$ for each $y \in L$. Suppose that for each $n \in \mathbb{N}$ there exists x_n such that $p_n(h(x_n) - a) = 0$. Prove that if $\lim_{n\to\infty} x_n = x$, then $h(x) = a$.

Solution: By the continuity of the norm, $\lim_{n\to\infty} p_n(y) = y$ implies $\lim_{n\to\infty} \|p_n(y)\| = \|y\|$, hence $\sup\{p_n(y) \mid n \in \mathbb{N}\}$ is finite.

By the Uniform Boundedness Theorem (Theorem 9.7) $\sup\{\|p_n\| \mid n \in \mathbb{N}\}$ is finite. Since h is continuous, we have $\lim_{n\to\infty} h_n(x) = h(x)$. Therefore, $\lim_{n\to\infty} p_n(h(x_n) - h(x)) = 0$. The definition of (x_n) implies $p_n(h(x_n)) = p_n(a)$, hence $\lim_{n\to\infty} p_n(a) - p_n(h(x)) = 0$. Therefore, $a = h(x)$.

Bibliographical Comments

References on Banach spaces include [22, 7, 40, 8, 101, 26] . The proof of the Uniform Boundedness Theorem (Theorem 9.7) was obtained in [123].

An useful source on infinite-dimensional spaces is the monograph [54].

Chapter 10

Differentiability of Functions Defined on Normed Spaces

10.1 Introduction

In this chapter we present a generalization of the idea of differentiability of classical analysis. Two variants of differentiability, the stronger Fréchet differentiability of functions between normed spaces and the weaker Gâteaux differentiability are discussed.

10.2 The Fréchet and Gâteaux Differentiation

Definition 10.1. Let $(S, \| \cdot \|)$ and $(T, \| \cdot \|)$ be two normed spaces and let X be an open set in $(S, \| \cdot \|)$.

A function $f : X \longrightarrow T$ is *Fréchet differentiable* at x_0, where $x_0 \in X$, if there exists a linear operator $(D_x f)(x_0) : X \longrightarrow T$ such that

$$\lim_{h \to 0} \frac{\|f(x_0 + h) - f(x_0) - (D_x f)(x_0)(h)\|}{\|h\|} = 0.$$

The linear operator $(D_x f)(x_0) : X \longrightarrow T$ is referred to the *Fréchet derivative* at x_0.

Suppose that $X = S$ in Definition 10.1. Note that:

(i) $(D_x f)(x_0)(h)$ is an element of T;

(ii) $(D_x f)(x_0)$ is a linear operator defined on S and ranging into T;

(iii) $(D_x f)$ is a mapping defined on S with values in the space of linear operators between S and T.

The function $\delta f : X \times S \longrightarrow T$ defined by $\delta f(x_0; h) = (D_x f)(x_0)(h)$ is the *Fréchet differential* of f at x_0. Note that the differential is linear in its second argument h. To emphasize the distinct roles played by x_0 and h the arguments of the differential are separated by a semicolon.

If $(D_x f)(x_0)$ is continuous on X, where $X \subseteq S$, we say that f is *continuously differentiable* on X.

Example 10.1. A constant function $k : S \longrightarrow T$ is Fréchet differentiable at every point x_0 of S and $(D_x f)(x_0) = 0$.

Example 10.2. If $f : S \longrightarrow T$ is a continuous linear mapping then $f(x_0 + h) - f(x_0) = f(h)$ for $x_0 \in S$, so $(D_x f)(x_0) = f$.

For instance, consider the linear operator $f : C[a, b] \longrightarrow C[a, b]$ defined as

$$(fu)(x) = \int_a^b K(x, s)u(s) \, ds.$$

Its Fréchet derivative is $(D_x f)(u) = f(u)$ because

$$(f(u + h))(x) - (f(u))(x) = \int_a^b K(x, s)(u(s) + h(s)) \, ds - \int_a^b K(x, s)u(s) \, ds$$

$$= \int_a^b K(x, s)h(s) \, ds.$$

Example 10.3. Let $f : \mathbb{R}^n \longrightarrow \mathbb{R}$ be the function $f(\mathbf{x}) = \mathbf{x}'\mathbf{a}$ for $\mathbf{x}, \mathbf{a} \in \mathbb{R}^n$.

We have $f(\mathbf{x}_0 + \mathbf{h}) - f(\mathbf{x}_0) = (\mathbf{x}_0 + \mathbf{h})'\mathbf{a} - \mathbf{x}_0'\mathbf{a} = \mathbf{h}'\mathbf{a} = \mathbf{a}'\mathbf{h}$. The function is Fréchet differentiable because

$$\lim_{\mathbf{h} \to 0} \frac{\|f(\mathbf{x}_0 + \mathbf{h}) - f(\mathbf{x}_0) - (D_\mathbf{x} f)(\mathbf{x}_0)(\mathbf{h})\|}{\|\mathbf{h}\|}$$

$$= \lim_{\mathbf{h} \to 0} \frac{\|\mathbf{a}'\mathbf{h} - (D_\mathbf{x} f)(\mathbf{x}_0)(\mathbf{h})\|}{\|\mathbf{h}\|} = 0$$

is satisfied by $(D_\mathbf{x})(\mathbf{x}_0)(\mathbf{h}) = \mathbf{a}'\mathbf{h}$, so $D_\mathbf{x}(\mathbf{x}_0)$ is the inner product $(\mathbf{a}, \cdot)$ for every $\mathbf{x}_0$.

Next we introduce the *Landau notations* o and O (known as "small o" and "big O", respectively).

Let $f, g : \mathbb{R} \longrightarrow \mathbb{R}$ be two functions. We write $f = O(g)$ if there exists a positive real number M and a number x_0 such that $x \geqslant x_0$ implies $|f(x)| \leqslant M|g(x)|$.

Also, we write $f = o(g)$ if there exists a number x_0 such that for every $\epsilon > 0$ we have $|f(x)| \leqslant \epsilon|g(x)|$ if $x \geqslant x_0$. If $x \geqslant x_0$ implies $g(x) \neq 0$, this amounts to $\lim_{x \to \infty} \frac{f(x)}{g(x)} = 0$.

We denote by o (with or without subscripts) a function $o : S \longrightarrow \mathbb{R}$ that has the property:

$$\lim_{h \to 0} \frac{o(h)}{\|h\|} = 0.$$

These notations allow us to say that f is Fréchet differentiable at x_0 if and only if there exists a linear transformation $(D_x f)(x_0)$ in $\mathsf{Hom}(S,T)$ such that
$$\|f(x_0 + h) - f(x_0) - \delta f(x_0; h)\| = o(h),$$
or
$$\|f(x_0 + h) - f(x_0) - (D_x f)(x_0)(h)\| = o(h).$$
The Fréchet derivative $(D_x f)(x_0)$ will be simply denoted by $(Df)(x_0)$ when x is clear from the context.

Theorem 10.1. *Let $(S, \|\cdot\|)$ and $(T, \|\cdot\|)$ be two normed spaces and let X be an open subset of S. If a function $f : X \longrightarrow T$ has a Fréchet differential, where $X \subseteq S$, then this differential is unique.*

Proof. Suppose that both $\delta f(x_0; h)$ and $\delta_1 f(x_0, h)$ are differentials of f at x_0. We have
$$\|\delta f(x_0; h) - \delta_1 f(x_0; h)\| \leqslant \|f(x_0 + h) - f(x_0) - \delta f(x_0; h)\|$$
$$+ \|f(x_0 + h) - f(x_0) - \delta_1 f(x_0; h)\|$$
$$= o(h). \qquad \square$$

Since $\delta f(x_0; h) - \delta_1 f(x_0; h)$ is bounded and linear in h it follows that $\delta f(x_0; h) = \delta_1 f(x_0; h)$.

Theorem 10.2. *Let $(S, \|\cdot\|)$ and $(T, \|\cdot\|)$ be two normed spaces. If $f : S \longrightarrow T$ is a Fréchet differentiable function in $x_0 \in S$, then f is continuous in x_0.*

Proof. Since f is Fréchet differentiable in x_0,
$$\lim_{h \to 0} \frac{\|f(x_0 + h) - f(x_0) - (Df)(x_0)(h)\|}{\|h\|} = 0.$$
Let ϵ_1 be a positive number. There exists a positive number $\delta(x_0)$ such that if $\|h\| < \delta(x_0)$ we have
$$\|f(x_0 + h) - f(x_0) - (Df)(x_0)(h)\| < \epsilon_1 \|h\|.$$
If $\|h\| < \delta(x_0)$ we can write
$$\|f(x_0 + h) - f(x_0)\|$$
$$\leqslant \|f(x_0 + h) - f(x_0) - (Df)(x_0)h\| + \|(Df)(x_0)h\|$$
$$\leqslant \|f(x_0 + h) - f(x_0) - (Df)(x_0)h\| + \|(Df)(x_0)\|\|h\|$$
$$\leqslant (\epsilon_1 + \|(Df)(x_0)\|)\|h\|.$$
If we choose h such that $(\epsilon_1 + \|(Df)(x_0)\|)\|h\| < \epsilon$, that is, if
$$\|h\| < \min\left\{ \frac{\epsilon}{\epsilon_1 + \|(Df)(x_0)\|}, \delta \right\},$$
it follows that $\|f(x_0 + h) - f(x_0)\| < \epsilon$, so f is continuous in x_0. $\qquad \square$

A weaker form of differentiability is given next.

Definition 10.2. Let $(S, \|\cdot\|)$ and $(T, \|\cdot\|)$ be normed $\mathbb{F}$-linear spaces, X be an open set in $(S, \|\cdot\|)$ and let $f : X \longrightarrow T$ be a function.

The function f is *Gâteaux differentiable* in x_0 (where $x_0 \in X$) if there exists a linear operator $(D_x f)(x_0) : S \longrightarrow T$ such that

$$(D_x f)(x_0)(u) = \lim_{t \to 0} \frac{f(x_0 + tu) - f(x_0)}{t}$$

for every u such that $x_0 + tu \in X$. The linear operator $(D_x f)(x_0)$ is the *Gâteaux derivative* of f in x_0.

The *Gâteaux differential* of f at x_0 is the linear operator $\delta f(x_0; h)$ given by

$$\delta f(x_0; u) = \lim_{t \to 0} \frac{f(x_0 + tu) - f(x_0)}{t}.$$

The Gâteaux differential is denoted by the same $\delta f(x_0; h)$ as the Fréchet differential. Similarly, the Gâteaux derivative is denoted by $(D_x f)(x_0)$, as we denoted the Fréchet derivative and the subscript x will be omitted when possible. The specific differential (or derivative) we are referring to will result from the context.

The function $f : S \longrightarrow T$ is Gâteaux differentiable in x_0 if for every $\epsilon > 0$ there exists $\delta(x_0, u) > 0$, which depends on x_0 and u such that $t < \delta(x_0, u)$ implies

$$\left\| \frac{f(x_0 + tu) - f(x_0)}{t} - (D_x f)(x_0)(u) \right\| < \epsilon.$$

The function $f : S \longrightarrow T$ is Fréchet differentiable in x_0 if for every $\epsilon > 0$ there exists $\delta(x_0) > 0$, which does not depend on u such that $t < \delta(x_0)$ implies $\| \frac{f(x_0+tu)-f(x_0)}{t} - (D_x f)(x_0)(u) \| < \epsilon$. In this sense, Fréchet differentiability implies that the convergence of $\frac{f(x_0+tu)-f(x_0)}{t}$ to $(D_x f)(x_0)(u)$ is uniform relative to u.

Indeed, if $h \in S$ we can write $h = \|h\| u_h$, where $\|u_h\| = 1$. Thus, if $h \to 0$, we have $\|h\| \to 0$. Since f is Gâteaux uniformly differentiable at x_0, for every $\epsilon > 0$ there is $\delta(x_0)$ such that if $\|h\| < \delta(x_0)$ then

$$\frac{\|f(x_0 + h) - f(x_0) - (D_x f)(x_0)(h)\|}{\|h\|}$$

$$= \frac{\|f(x_0 + h) - f(x_0) - \|h\|(D_x f)(x_0)(u_h)\|}{\|h\|}$$

$$= \left\| \frac{f(x_0 + h) - f(x_0)}{\|h\|} - (D_x f)(x_0)(u_h) \right\| < \epsilon$$

which shows that f is Fréchet differentiable at x_0.

Example 10.4. Let $\mathbf{a}$ be a vector in $\mathbb{R}^n$. Define $f : \mathbb{R}^n \longrightarrow \mathbb{R}$ as $f(\mathbf{x}) = \mathbf{x}'\mathbf{a}$. We have:

$$
\begin{aligned}
(D_x f)(\mathbf{x}_0)(\mathbf{u}) &= \lim_{t \to 0} \frac{f(\mathbf{x}_0 + t\mathbf{u}) - f(\mathbf{x}_0)}{t} \\
&= \lim_{t \to 0} \frac{(\mathbf{x}_0 + t\mathbf{u})'\mathbf{a} - \mathbf{x}_0'\mathbf{a}}{t} \\
&= \lim_{t \to 0} \frac{t\mathbf{u}'\mathbf{a}}{t} = \mathbf{u}'\mathbf{a}.
\end{aligned}
$$

Example 10.5. Let $A \in \mathbb{R}^{n \times n}$ be a matrix and let $f : \mathbb{R}^n \longrightarrow \mathbb{R}$ be the functional $f(\mathbf{x}) = \mathbf{x}'A\mathbf{x}$. We have $(Df)(\mathbf{x}_0) = \mathbf{x}_0'(A + A')$.

By applying the definition of Gâteaux differential we have

$$
\begin{aligned}
(Df)(\mathbf{x}_0)(\mathbf{u}) &= \lim_{t \to 0} \frac{f(\mathbf{x}_0 + t\mathbf{u}) - f(\mathbf{x}_0)}{t} \\
&= \lim_{t \to 0} \frac{(\mathbf{x}_0' + t\mathbf{u}')A(\mathbf{x}_0 + t\mathbf{u}) - \mathbf{x}_0'A\mathbf{x}_0}{t} \\
&= \lim_{t \to 0} \frac{t\mathbf{u}'A\mathbf{x}_0 + t\mathbf{x}_0'A\mathbf{u} + t^2\mathbf{u}'A\mathbf{u}}{t} \\
&= \mathbf{u}'A\mathbf{x}_0 + \mathbf{x}_0'A\mathbf{u} = \mathbf{x}_0'A'\mathbf{u} + \mathbf{x}_0'A\mathbf{u} \\
&= \mathbf{x}_0'(A + A')\mathbf{u},
\end{aligned}
$$

which yields

$$
(Df)(\mathbf{x}_0) = \mathbf{x}_0'(A + A').
$$

If $A \in \mathbb{R}^{n \times n}$ is a symmetric matrix and $f : \mathbb{R}^n \longrightarrow \mathbb{R}$ is the functional $f(\mathbf{x}) = \mathbf{x}'A\mathbf{x}$, then $(Df)(\mathbf{x}_0) = 2\mathbf{x}_0'A$.

Example 10.6. Let $(S, \|\cdot\|)$ be a normed space. The norm $\|\cdot\| : S \longrightarrow \mathbb{R}_{\geqslant 0}$ is not Gâteaux differentiable in 0_S.

Indeed, suppose that $\|\cdot\|$ were differentiable in 0_S, which would mean that the limit:

$$
\lim_{t \to 0} \frac{\|t u\|}{t} = \lim_{t \to 0} \frac{|t|}{t} \|u\|
$$

exists for every $u \in S$, which is contradictory.

However, the square of the norm, $\|\cdot\|^2$ is differentiable in 0_S because

$$
\lim_{t \to 0} \frac{\|t u\|^2}{t} = \lim_{t \to 0} t \|u\| = 0.
$$

Example 10.7. Consider the norm $\|\cdot\|_1$ on $\mathbb{R}^n$ given by

$$\|\mathbf{x}\|_1 = |x_1| + \cdots + |x_n|$$

for $\mathbf{x} \in \mathbb{R}^n$. This norm is not Gâteaux differentiable in any point $\mathbf{x}_0$ located on an axis. Indeed, let $\mathbf{x}_0 = a\mathbf{e}_i$ be a point on the ith axis. The limit

$$\lim_{t \to 0} \frac{\|\mathbf{x}_0 + t\mathbf{u}\|_1 - \|\mathbf{x}_0\|_1}{t}$$

$$= \lim_{t \to 0} \frac{\|a\mathbf{e}_i + t\mathbf{u}\|_1 - \|a\mathbf{e}_i\|_1}{t}$$

$$= \lim_{t \to 0} \frac{|t||u_1| + \cdots + |t||u_{i-1}| + (|t||u_i| - |a|) + |t||u_{i+1}| + \cdots + |t||u_n|}{t}$$

does not exists, so the norm $\|\cdot\|_1$ is not differentiable in any of these points.

Definition 10.3. Let $f : S \longrightarrow T$ be a function between the normed spaces $(S, \|\cdot\|)$ and $(T, \|\cdot\|)$ and let $h \in S - \{0_S\}$.

The *directional derivative at x_0 in the direction h* is the function $\frac{\partial f}{\partial h}(x_0)$ given by

$$\frac{\partial f}{\partial h}(x_0) = \lim_{t \downarrow 0} \frac{f(x_0 + th) - f(x_0)}{t}.$$

Thus, f is Gâteaux differentiable at x_0 if its directional derivative exists in every direction.

Let $f : \mathbb{R}^n \longrightarrow \mathbb{R}$ be a function differentiable at $\mathbf{x}_0 \in \mathbb{R}^n$. If $\{\mathbf{e}_1, \ldots, \mathbf{e}_n\}$ is the standard basis for $\mathbb{R}^n$, then $(Df)(\mathbf{x}_0)(\mathbf{e}_i)$ is known as the *partial derivative* of f with respect to x_i and is denoted by $\frac{\partial f}{\partial x_i}(\mathbf{x}_0)$.

Theorem 10.3. *Let $(S, \|\cdot\|)$ and $(T, \|\cdot\|)$ be two normed $\mathbb{F}$-linear spaces, X be an open set in $(S, \|\cdot\|)$ and let $f : X \longrightarrow T$ be a function.*

If f is Fréchet differentiable in $x_0 \in X$, then it is also Gâteaux differentiable in x_0 and the two differentials are the same.

Proof. Let f be Fréchet differentiable in x_0, that is, $\|f(x_0 + h) - f(x_0) - \delta f(x_0; h)\| = o(h)$, where $\delta f(x_0, h)$ is the Fréchet differential.

For the Gâteaux differential $\delta'(x_0; h)$ of f in x_0 we have

$$\|\delta' f(x_0; h) - \delta f(x_0; h)\|$$

$$= \left\| \lim_{t \to 0} \frac{f(x_0 + tu) - f(x_0)}{t} - \delta f(x_0; h) \right\|$$

$$= \lim_{t \to 0} \left\| \frac{f(x_0 + tu) - f(x_0) - \delta f(x_0; th)}{th} \right\| \|h\|,$$

and $\lim_{t \to 0} \left\| \frac{f(x_0 + tu) - f(x_0) - \delta f(x_0; th)}{th} \right\| = 0$ because $\lim_{t \to 0} \|th\| = 0$. Thus, $\delta' f(x_0; h) = \delta f(x_0; h)$. $\qquad \square$

Theorem 10.4. *Let $(S, \|\cdot\|)$ and $(T, \|\cdot\|)$ be two normed $\mathbb{F}$-linear spaces, X be an open set in $(S, \|\cdot\|)$ and let $f : X \longrightarrow T$ be a function.*

If f is Gâteaux differentiable on X, then

$$\|f(u) - f(v)\| \leqslant \|u - v\| \sup\{f'(au + (1 - a)v) \mid a \in [0, 1]\}.$$

Proof. Let $w \in X$ such that $\|w\| = 1$ and $\|f(u) - f(v)\| = (w, f(u) - f(v))$. Define the real-valued function g as $g(t) = (w, f(u + t(v - u)))$ for $t \in [0, 1]$. We have the inequality

$$\|f(u) - f(v)\| = (w, f(v) - f(u)) = |g(1) - g(0)| \leqslant \sup\{|g'(t)| \mid t \in [0, 1]\}.$$

Since

$$\begin{aligned}
g'(t) &= \left(w, \frac{df(u + t(v - u))}{dt}\right) \\
&= \left(w, \lim_{r \to 0} \frac{f(u + (t + r)(v - u)) - f(u + t(v - u))}{r}\right) \\
&= (w, f'_{u+t(v-u)}(v - u)),
\end{aligned}$$

we have $|g'(t)| \leqslant \|f'_{u+t(v-u)}(v - u)\|$, hence

$$\begin{aligned}
|g'(t)| &\leqslant \|f'_{u+t(v-u)}(v - u)\| \\
&\leqslant \|f'_{u+t(v-u)}\|\|v - u\|. \qquad \square
\end{aligned}$$

Theorem 10.5. *Let $(S, \|\cdot\|), (T, \|\cdot\|)$ be normed $\mathbb{F}$-linear spaces, X be an open set in $(S, \|\cdot\|)$ and let $f : X \longrightarrow T$ be a function.*

If f is Gâteaux differentiable at $x_0 \in X$ and the Gâteaux derivative is continuous in x_0, then f is Fréchet differentiable in x_0.

Proof. For $v \in S$ define the function $g_v : [0, 1] \longrightarrow T$ be the function defined as $g_v(t) = f(x_0 + tv) - f(x_0) - t(Df)(x_0)v$; we have $g(0) = 0$. From the continuity of the Gâteaux derivative it follows that

$$\begin{aligned}
\|g_v(1) - g_v(0)\| &= f(x_0 + v) - f(x_0) - f'(x_0)v \\
&\leqslant \|v\| \sup\{(Df)(x_0 + tv) - (Df)(x_0)\} = o(\|v\|).
\end{aligned}$$

Thus, $g_v = 0$. $\qquad \square$

Example 10.8. A *homogeneous polynomial u of degree k* has the property

$$u(tx_1, \ldots, tx_n) = t^k u(x_1, \ldots, x_n)$$

for $t, x_1, \ldots, x_n \in \mathbb{R}$.

Let $p(x_1, x_2)$ and $q(x_1, x_2)$ be two homogeneous polynomials of degrees r and s, respectively, where $r > s + 1$, and let $f : \mathbb{R}^2 \longrightarrow \mathbb{R}$ be the function defined by

$$f(x_1, x_2) = \begin{cases} \dfrac{p(x_1, x_2)}{q(x_1, x_2)} & \text{if } \mathbf{x} \neq \mathbf{0}_2, \\ 0 & \text{otherwise,} \end{cases}$$

where $\mathbf{x} \neq \mathbf{0}_2$ implies $q(\mathbf{x}) \neq 0$.

We claim that f is Gâteaux differentiable but not Fréchet differentiable. Indeed,

$$\lim_{t \to 0} \frac{f(tu_1, tu_2)}{t} = \lim_{t \to 0} t^{r-s-1} f(u_1, u_2) = 0,$$

and the constant function 0 is linear in $\mathbf{u}$.

Fréchet differentiability in $\mathbf{0}_2$ requires the existence of a linear operator $g : \mathbb{R}^n \longrightarrow \mathbb{R}$ such that

$$\lim_{\mathbf{h} \to \mathbf{0}_2} \frac{\|f(\mathbf{h}) - f(\mathbf{x}_0) - g(\mathbf{h})\|}{\|\mathbf{h}\|} = \lim_{\mathbf{h} \to \mathbf{0}_2} \frac{\|f(\mathbf{h}) - g(\mathbf{h})\|}{\|\mathbf{h}\|} = 0,$$

which is impossible because $f(\mathbf{h})$ grows faster than a linear function in $\mathbf{h}$ assuming that $r > s + 1$. Thus, f is not differentiable Fréchet.

Theorem 10.6. (The Chain Rule) *Let S, T, U be three normed spaces, X be an open subset of S and Y an open subset of T.*

If $f : X \longrightarrow T$ is a function Fréchet differentiable at $x_0 \in X$ and $g : Y \longrightarrow U$ is a Fréchet function differentiable at $y_0 = f(x_0) \in Y$, then gf is Fréchet differentiable at x_0 and

$$D_x(gf)(x_0) = (D_y g)(f(x_0))(D_x f)(x_0).$$

Proof. Since $f(x_0 + h) - f(x_0) - (D_x f)(x_0)(h) = o_1(h)$ and $g(y_0 + k) - g(y_0) - (D_y g)(y_0)(k) = o_2(k)$, we have

$g(f(x_0 + p)) - g(f(x_0))$

$= g\left(f(x_0) + (D_x f)(x_0)(p) + o_1(p)\right) - g(f(x_0))$

$= (D_y g)(y_0)\left((D_x f)(x_0)(p) + o_1(p)\right) + o_2((D_x f)(x_0)(p) + o_1(p))$

$= (D_y g)(y_0)((D_x f)(x_0)(p)) + (D_y g)(y_0)(o_1(p)) + o_2((D_x f)(x_0)(p) + o_1(p)).$

Observe that

$$\lim_{h \to 0} \frac{(D_y g)(y_0)(o_1(p)) + o_2((D_x f)(x_0)(p) + o_1(p))}{\|p\|} = 0,$$

because $\|(D_y g)(y_0)(o_1(p))\| \leqslant \|(D_y g)(y_0)\| \|o_1(p)\|$, and

$$\|o_2((D_x f)(x_0)(p) + o_1(p))\| \leqslant \|o_2((D_x f)(x_0)(p))\| + \|o_2(o_1(p))\|$$

which shows that $D_x(gf)(x_0) = (D_y g)(f(x_0))(D_x f)(x_0)$. $\qquad\square$

Note that in the Chain Rule, $(D_y g)(f(x_0))(D_x f)(x_0)$ is the composition of the operators $(D_y g)(f(x_0))$ and $(D_x f)(x_0)$, which results in the operator $(D_x(gf))(f(x_0))$.

Next we introduce the notation "∇f" (read "*nabla f*"). Let $f : X \longrightarrow \mathbb{R}$, where $X \subseteq \mathbb{R}^n$, and let $\mathbf{z} \in X$. The *gradient* of f in $\mathbf{z}$ is the vector

$$(\nabla f)(\mathbf{z}) = \begin{pmatrix} \dfrac{\partial f}{\partial x_1}(\mathbf{z}) \\ \vdots \\ \dfrac{\partial f}{\partial x_n}(\mathbf{z}) \end{pmatrix} \in \mathbb{R}^n.$$

Example 10.9. Let $\mathbf{b}_j \in \mathbb{R}^n$ and $c_j \in \mathbb{R}$ for $1 \leqslant j \leqslant n$, and let $f : \mathbb{R}^n \longrightarrow \mathbb{R}$ be the function

$$f(\mathbf{x}) = \sum_{j=1}^{n} (\mathbf{b}'_j \mathbf{x} - c_j)^2.$$

We have $\frac{\partial f}{\partial x_i}(\mathbf{x}) = \sum_{j=1}^{n} 2 b_{ij}(\mathbf{b}'_j \mathbf{x} - c_j)$, where $\mathbf{b}_j = \begin{pmatrix} b_{1j} \cdots b_{nj} \end{pmatrix}$ for $1 \leqslant j \leqslant n$. Thus, we obtain:

$$(\nabla f)(\mathbf{x}) = 2 \begin{pmatrix} \sum\limits_{j=1}^{n} 2 b_{1j}(\mathbf{b}'_j \mathbf{x} - c_j) \\ \vdots \\ \sum\limits_{j=1}^{n} 2 b_{nj}(\mathbf{b}'_j \mathbf{x} - c_j) \end{pmatrix} = 2(B'\mathbf{x} - \mathbf{c}')B = 2B'\mathbf{x}B - 2\mathbf{c}'B,$$

where $B = (\mathbf{b}_1 \cdots \mathbf{b}_n) \in \mathbb{R}^{n \times n}$.

Theorem 10.7. (The Mean Value Theorem) *Let $f : X \longrightarrow \mathbb{R}$ be a real-valued function, where X is an open subset of $\mathbb{R}^n$ that contains $[\boldsymbol{a}, \boldsymbol{b}]$. If f is continuous on $[\boldsymbol{a}, \boldsymbol{b}]$ and is Gâteaux differentiable on $(\boldsymbol{a}, \boldsymbol{b})$, then there exists $\boldsymbol{c} \in (\boldsymbol{a}, \boldsymbol{b})$ such that*

$$f(\boldsymbol{b}) - f(\boldsymbol{a}) = (\nabla f)(\boldsymbol{c})'(\boldsymbol{b} - \boldsymbol{a}).$$

Proof. For the real-valued function g defined by $g(t) = f(\mathbf{a} + t(\mathbf{b} - \mathbf{a}))$ we have $g(0) = f(\mathbf{a})$ and $g(1) = f(\mathbf{b})$. By the Mean Value Theorem of calculus, there exists $\theta \in (0, 1)$ such that $g(1) - g(0) = g'(\theta)$. By the Chain Rule, $g'(t) = (\nabla f)(\mathbf{a} + t(\mathbf{b} - \mathbf{a}))'(\mathbf{b} - \mathbf{a})$, so

$$f(\mathbf{b}) - f(\mathbf{a}) = (\nabla f)(\mathbf{a} + \theta(\mathbf{b} - \mathbf{a}))'(\mathbf{b} - \mathbf{a}),$$

which shows that the statement holds for $\mathbf{c} = \mathbf{a} + \theta(\mathbf{b} - \mathbf{a})$. $\qquad \square$

A equivalent form of Mean Value Theorem can be obtained by defining $\mathbf{h} = \mathbf{b} - \mathbf{a}$ and observing that $\mathbf{c} \in (\mathbf{a}, \mathbf{b})$ if and only if $\mathbf{c} = \mathbf{a} + \theta \mathbf{h}$, where $\theta \in (0, 1)$. The Mean Value Theorem amounts to stating the existence of $\theta \in (0, 1)$ such that $f(\mathbf{a} + \mathbf{h}) = f(\mathbf{a}) + (\nabla f)(\mathbf{a} + \theta \mathbf{h})'\mathbf{h}$, when $[\mathbf{a}, \mathbf{a} + \mathbf{h}] \subseteq X$.

If we compute explicitly the derivative of the function g introduced in the proof of Theorem 10.7 we have:

$$g'(t) = \frac{\partial f}{\partial x_1}(\mathbf{a} + t(\mathbf{b} - \mathbf{a}))(b_1 - a_1) + \cdots + \frac{\partial f}{\partial x_n}(\mathbf{a} + t(\mathbf{b} - \mathbf{a}))(b_n - a_n)$$

$$= \begin{pmatrix} \frac{\partial f}{\partial x_1}(\mathbf{a} + t(\mathbf{b} - \mathbf{a})) \\ \vdots \\ \frac{\partial f}{\partial x_n}(\mathbf{a} + t(\mathbf{b} - \mathbf{a})) \end{pmatrix}' (\mathbf{b} - \mathbf{a}).$$

For functions of the form $\mathbf{f} : \mathbb{R}^n \longrightarrow \mathbb{R}^m$ the Gâteaux differential at $\mathbf{x}_0$ has a simple form. Since $(D f)(\mathbf{x}_0)$ is a linear transformation there exists a matrix $A \in \mathbb{R}^{m \times n}$ such that

$$\lim_{t \to 0} \frac{\mathbf{f}(\mathbf{x}_0 + t\mathbf{u}) - \mathbf{f}(\mathbf{x}_0)}{t} = A\mathbf{u}$$

for every $\mathbf{u} \in \mathbb{R}^n$. In other words, A is the matrix of the linear transformation $(D\mathbf{f})(\mathbf{x}_0) : \mathbb{R}^n \longrightarrow \mathbb{R}^m$.

If $\mathbf{a}_i$ is the ith row of A, where $1 \leqslant i \leqslant m$, the previous equality can be written componentwise as

$$\lim_{t \to 0} \frac{f_i(\mathbf{x}_0 + t\mathbf{u}) - f_i(\mathbf{x}_0)}{t} = \mathbf{a}_i\mathbf{u}$$

for $1 \leqslant i \leqslant m$. Thus, we have $\mathbf{a}_i = (\nabla f_i)(\mathbf{x}_0)'$ for $1 \leqslant i \leqslant m$ and the matrix A introduced above is

$$A = \begin{pmatrix} (\nabla f_1)(\mathbf{x}_0)' \\ \vdots \\ (\nabla f_m)(\mathbf{x}_0)' \end{pmatrix} = \begin{pmatrix} \frac{\partial f_1}{\partial x_1}(\mathbf{x}_0) & \cdots & \frac{\partial f_1}{\partial x_n}(\mathbf{x}_0) \\ \vdots & \cdots & \vdots \\ \frac{\partial f_i}{\partial x_1}(\mathbf{x}_0) & \cdots & \frac{\partial f_i}{\partial x_n}(\mathbf{x}_0) \\ \vdots & \cdots & \vdots \\ \frac{\partial f_m}{\partial x_1}(\mathbf{x}_0) & \cdots & \frac{\partial f_m}{\partial x_n}(\mathbf{x}_0) \end{pmatrix}$$

The matrix $A \in \mathbb{R}^{m \times n}$ is referred to as the *Jacobian of* $\mathbf{f} : \mathbb{R}^n \longrightarrow \mathbb{R}^m$ at $\mathbf{x}_0$. As before, if $\mathbf{x}$ is understood from context we may omit occasionally the subscript $\mathbf{x}$ and write A simply as $(D\mathbf{f})(\mathbf{x}_0)$. The rows of Jacobian of $\mathbf{f}$ at $\mathbf{x}_0$ consist of the transposed gradients of its component functions $f_1, \ldots, f_m$ at $\mathbf{x}_0$.

Of course, if $f : \mathbb{R}^n \longrightarrow \mathbb{R}$ we have

$$(D f)(\mathbf{x}_0)(\mathbf{u}) = (\nabla f)(\mathbf{x}_0)'\mathbf{u}$$

for $\mathbf{u} \in \mathbb{R}^n$.

Definition 10.4. The *Jacobian determinant of* $\mathbf{f}$ *at* $\mathbf{x}_0$ is the number $(J\mathbf{f})(\mathbf{x}_0) = \det((D\mathbf{f})(\mathbf{x}_0))$.

Example 10.10. Let $\mathbf{f} : \mathbb{R}^2 \longrightarrow \mathbb{R}^3$ and $\mathbf{g} : \mathbb{R}^4 \longrightarrow \mathbb{R}^3$ be the functions defined by

$$\mathbf{f}(\mathbf{x}) = \begin{pmatrix} x_1 + x_2 \\ x_1^2 - x_2^2 \\ x_1 - x_2 \end{pmatrix} \text{ and } \mathbf{g}(\mathbf{y}) = \begin{pmatrix} y_1 + y_2 \\ y_2 + y_3 \\ y_1 + y_3 \\ y_1^2 \end{pmatrix}$$

for $\mathbf{x} \in \mathbb{R}^2$ and $\mathbf{y} \in \mathbb{R}^3$.

We have

$$(D\mathbf{f})(\mathbf{x}) = \begin{pmatrix} 1 & 1 \\ 2x_1 & -2x_2 \\ 1 & -1 \end{pmatrix} \text{ and } (D\mathbf{g})(\mathbf{y}) = \begin{pmatrix} 1 & 1 & 0 \\ 0 & 1 & 1 \\ 1 & 0 & 1 \\ 2y_1 & 0 & 0 \end{pmatrix}.$$

If $\mathbf{x}_0 = \begin{pmatrix} a \\ b \end{pmatrix}$, then

$$\mathbf{f}(\mathbf{x}_0) = \begin{pmatrix} a + b \\ a^2 - b^2 \\ a - b \end{pmatrix}.$$

By applying the Chain Rule we can write:

$$D(\mathbf{gf})(\mathbf{x}_0) = (D\mathbf{g})(\mathbf{f}(\mathbf{x}_0))(D\mathbf{f})(\mathbf{x}_0)$$

$$= \begin{pmatrix} 1 & 1 & 0 \\ 0 & 1 & 1 \\ 1 & 0 & 1 \\ 2(a + b) & 0 & 0 \end{pmatrix} \begin{pmatrix} 1 & 1 \\ 2a & -2b \\ 1 & -1 \end{pmatrix}$$

$$= \begin{pmatrix} 1 + 2a & 1 - 2b \\ 2a + 1 & -2b - 1 \\ 2 & 0 \\ 2(a + b) & 2(a + b) \end{pmatrix}.$$

Alternatively, the derivative of $\mathbf{gf}$ can be computed by composing first the functions $\mathbf{f}$ and $\mathbf{g}$. This yields

$$\mathbf{gf}(\mathbf{x}) = \begin{pmatrix} x_1 + x_2 + x_1^2 - x_2^2 \\ x_1^2 - x_2^2 + x_1 - x_2 \\ 2x_1 \\ (x_1 + x_2)^2 \end{pmatrix}.$$

This implies

$$(D\mathbf{gf})(\mathbf{x}) = \begin{pmatrix} 1 + 2x_1 & 1 - 2x_2 \\ 2x_1 + 1 & -2x_2 - 1 \\ 2 & 0 \\ 2(x_1 + x_2) & 2(x_1 + x_2) \end{pmatrix}.$$

Substituting a for x_1 and b for x_2 we retrieve the first expression.

Example 10.11. Let

$$\mathbf{h} : \mathbb{R}_{\geqslant 0} \times [0, \pi] \times [0, 2\pi) \longrightarrow \mathbb{R}^3$$

be the function that maps spherical coordinates into Cartesian coordinates. Its components are:

$$h_1(r, \theta, \phi) = r \sin\theta \cos\phi,$$
$$h_2(r, \theta, \phi) = r \sin\theta \sin\phi,$$
$$h_3(r, \theta, \phi) = r \cos\theta.$$

The Jacobian matrix in (r, θ, ϕ) is:

$$(D\mathbf{h})(r, \theta, \phi) = \begin{pmatrix} \sin\theta\cos\phi & r\cos\theta\cos\phi & -r\sin\theta\sin\phi \\ \sin\theta\sin\phi & r\cos\theta\sin\phi & r\sin\theta\cos\phi \\ \cos\theta & -r\sin\theta & 0 \end{pmatrix}.$$

Therefore, $J(\mathbf{h})(r, \theta, \phi) = r^2 \sin\theta$.

Similarly, the function $\mathbf{g} : \mathbb{R}^2 \longrightarrow \mathbb{R}^2$ that maps polar coordinates into Cartesian coordinates, given by

$$g_1(r, \phi) = r \cos\phi,$$
$$g_2(r, \phi) = r \sin\phi$$

has the Jacobian matrix

$$(D\mathbf{g})(r, \phi) = \begin{pmatrix} \cos\phi & -r\sin\phi, \\ \sin\phi & r\cos\phi \end{pmatrix}.$$

Thus, $J(\mathbf{g})(r, \phi) = r$.

Example 10.12. Let $\mathbf{f} : \mathbb{R}^3 \longrightarrow \mathbb{R}^2$ be the function defined by:

$$\mathbf{f}(\mathbf{x}) = \begin{pmatrix} x_1^2 + x_2^2 + x_3^2 \\ e^{x_1} + e^{x_2} + e^{x_3} \end{pmatrix}$$

for $\mathbf{x} = \begin{pmatrix} x_1 \\ x_2 \\ x_3 \end{pmatrix}$. The Jacobian of $\mathbf{f}$ at $\mathbf{x}$ is the matrix

$$(J\mathbf{f})(\mathbf{x}) = \begin{pmatrix} 2x_1 & 2x_2 & 2x_3 \\ e^{x_1} & e^{x_2} & e^{x_3} \end{pmatrix} \in \mathbb{R}^{2 \times 3}.$$

Lemma 10.1. *Let $a, b \in \mathbb{R}$ and let $f : [a, b] \longrightarrow T$ be a continuous function of a real argument, where $(T, \| \cdot \|)$ is a normed space. If $(Df)(x)$ exists for $x \in (a, b)$ and $\|(Df)(x)\| \leqslant m$, then $\|f(b) - f(a)\| \leqslant m(b - a)$.*

Proof. Let $(\alpha, \beta) \subseteq (a, b)$. Since f is continuous, to prove the statement it suffices to show that $\|f(\beta) - f(\alpha)\| \leqslant (m + \epsilon)(b - a)$ for every $\epsilon > 0$.

Let U_ϵ be the closed subset of $\mathbb{R}$:

$$U_\epsilon = \{x \in [\alpha, \beta] \mid \|f(x) - f(\alpha)\| \leqslant (m + \epsilon)(b - a)\}.$$

Let $x_0 = \sup U_\epsilon$. Since U_ϵ is compact, we have $x_0 \in U_\epsilon$, so $x_0 \leqslant \beta$. We show that $x_0 = \beta$ by proving that $x_0 < \beta$ leads to a contradiction.

Suppose that $x_0 < \beta$. Since f is differentiable at x_0, there exists δ such that $0 < \delta < \beta - x_0$ such that $|h| < \delta$ implies

$$\|f(x_0 + h) - f(x_0) - (Df)(x_0)h\| < \epsilon|h|.$$

For $h = \frac{\delta}{2}$ and $u = x_0 + \frac{\delta}{2}$ we have $u = x_0 + h$ and

$$\|f(u) - f(x_0) - (Df)(x_0)(u - x_0)\| < \epsilon|u - x_0|.$$

Therefore,

$$\begin{aligned}
\|f(u) - f(x_0)\| &= \|f(u) - f(x_0) - (Df)(x_0)(u - x_0)\| + \|(Df)(x_0)(u - x_0)\| \\
&< \epsilon|u - x_0| + \|(Df)(x_0)(u - x_0)\| \\
&\leqslant (m + \epsilon)(u - x_0).
\end{aligned}$$

Since $x_0 \in U_\epsilon$, we have $\|f(x_0) - f(\alpha)\| \leqslant (m + \epsilon)(x_0 - \alpha)$, hence

$$\begin{aligned}
\|f(u) - f(\alpha)\| &\leqslant \|f(u) - f(x_0)\| + \|f(x_0) - f(\alpha)\| \\
&\leqslant (m + \epsilon)(u - \alpha),
\end{aligned}$$

which shows that $u \in U_\epsilon$. This contradicts the fact that $u > x_0$. Thus, $x_0 = \beta \in U_\epsilon$ and

$$\|f(\beta) - f(\alpha)\| \leqslant (m + \epsilon)(b - a).$$

The result follows by continuity. $\qquad \square$

Theorem 10.8. (Mean Value Theorem for Functions between Normed Spaces) *Let $(S, \| \cdot \|)$ and $(T, \| \cdot \|)$ be two normed spaces, X be an open subset of S, and let $f : X \longrightarrow T$.*

If $[a, b] \subseteq X$ and $(Df)(x)$ exists in each point x of S, then

$$\|f(b) - f(a)\| \leqslant \|b - a\| \sup\{\|(Df)(x)\| \mid x \in [a, b]\}.$$

Proof. Define the function $p : [0,1] \longrightarrow X$ as $p(t) = at + b(1-t)$. It is clear that $p'(t) = a - b$, so the derivative of p regarded as a function (by the remark following Definition 10.1) maps t into $(a-b)t$.

Consider the function $g : [0,1] \longrightarrow T$ given by $g = fp$. We have $g(1) = f(b)$ and $g(0) = f(a)$. By the chain rule we have $g'(t) = (Df)(at + b(1-t))(a-b)$, which allows us to write:

$$\|f(b) - f(a)\| = \|g(1) - g(0)\|$$
$$\leqslant \sup\{\|g'(t)\| \mid t \in [0,1]\}$$
$$\text{(by Lemma 10.1)}$$
$$\leqslant \|b - a\| \sup\{\|(Df)(x)\| \mid x \in [a,b]\}. \qquad \square$$

Corollary 10.1. *Let $(S, \|\cdot\|)$ and $(T, \|\cdot\|)$ be two normed spaces, X be an open connected subset of S and let $f : X \longrightarrow T$ be a differentiable function on X. If $(D_x f)(x) = 0_T$ for $x \in X$, then f is a constant function on X.*

Proof. The function f is continuous on X because is differentiable on this set. Let $x_0 \in X$, and let W be the set

$$W = \{x \in X \mid f(x) = f(x_0)\}.$$

By Theorem 4.4, W is a closed set in the subspace X.

Since X is an open set in S, there is an open sphere $B(x,r)$ included in X. Let $y \in B(x,r)$. Since $[x,y] \in B(x_0,r)$, by Theorem 10.8, we have

$$\|f(x) - f(y)\| \leqslant \|x - y\| \sup\{\|(Df)(z)\| \mid z \in [x,y]\} = 0,$$

which implies $f(x) = f(y) = f(x_0)$. Thus, $y \in W$, which implies $B(x_0,r) \subseteq W$. This means that W is also an open set. Since $W \subseteq X$, this leads to a contradiction, because, by Theorem 4.91, a connected set may not contain a clopen set. Thus, $X = W$, and f is constant on X. $\qquad \square$

Theorem 10.9. *Let $f : \mathbb{R}^n \longrightarrow \mathbb{R}$ be a continuously differentiable function in an open convex subset U of $\mathbb{R}^n$. For any $\boldsymbol{x} \in U$ and direction $\boldsymbol{h}$ the directional derivative $\frac{\partial f}{\partial h}(\boldsymbol{x})$ exists and equals $(\nabla f)(\boldsymbol{x})' \boldsymbol{h}$. Furthermore, for any $\boldsymbol{x}, \boldsymbol{x} + \boldsymbol{h} \in U$ we have*

$$f(\boldsymbol{x} + \boldsymbol{h}) = f(\boldsymbol{x}) + \int_0^1 (\nabla f)(\boldsymbol{x} + t\boldsymbol{h})' \boldsymbol{h} \, dt.$$

There exists $\boldsymbol{z} \in (\boldsymbol{x}, \boldsymbol{x} + \boldsymbol{h})$ such that $f(\boldsymbol{x} + \boldsymbol{h}) = f(\boldsymbol{x}) + ((\nabla f)(\boldsymbol{z}))' \boldsymbol{h}$.

Proof. Let $g : \mathbb{R} \longrightarrow \mathbb{R}$ be the function defined as $g(t) = f(\mathbf{x} + t\mathbf{h})$. By the Chain Rule, for $a \in [0, 1]$ we have:

$$\frac{dg}{dt} = ((\nabla f)(x + a\mathbf{h}))'\mathbf{h},$$

which implies $\frac{\partial g}{\partial \mathbf{h}} = (\nabla f)(x)'\mathbf{h}$ by taking $a = 0$. Therefore, $g(1) = g(0) + \int_0^1 g'(t)\, dt$, which amounts to $f(\mathbf{x} + \mathbf{h}) = f(\mathbf{x}) + \int_0^1 ((\nabla f)(\mathbf{x} + t\mathbf{h}))'\mathbf{h}\, dt$.

By the Mean Value Theorem, there exists $\xi \in (0, 1)$ such that $g(1) = g(0) + g'(\xi)$. By the definition of g this implies

$$f(\mathbf{x} + \mathbf{h}) = f(\mathbf{x}) + ((\nabla f)(\mathbf{x} + \xi\mathbf{h}))'\mathbf{h},$$

which proves the second part. □

Corollary 10.2. *Let $\boldsymbol{f} : \mathbb{R}^n \longrightarrow \mathbb{R}^m$ be a function that is continuously differentiable in the open convex subset U of $\mathbb{R}^n$. For $\boldsymbol{x}, \boldsymbol{x} + \boldsymbol{h} \in U$ we have*

$$\boldsymbol{f}(\boldsymbol{x} + \boldsymbol{h}) - \boldsymbol{f}(\boldsymbol{x}) = \int_0^1 (D\boldsymbol{f})(\boldsymbol{x} + t\boldsymbol{h})\boldsymbol{h}\, dt.$$

Proof. This follows by an applying Theorem 10.9 to the components of $\mathbf{f}$. □

If there exists $c > 0$ such that $d'(f(x), f(y)) \leqslant cd(x, y)$ for all $x, y \in S$, then we say that f is a *Lipschitz function*. Furthermore, if this inequality is satisfied for a number $c < 1$, then f is a *contraction* with the *contraction constant c*.

Lemma 10.2. *Let X be a Banach space and let $B[x_0, r]$ be a closed sphere in X. If $B[x_0, r] \subseteq V$, where V is open set in X, and $F : V \longrightarrow B[x_0, r]$ is a function that is differentiable on $B[x_0, r]$ such that $\sup\{\|(DF)(x)\| \mid x \in B[x_0, r]\} < 1$, then F has a unique fixed point in $B[x_0, r]$.*

Proof. Let $c = \sup\{\|(D_x F)(x)\| \mid x \in B[x_0, r]\} < 1$. By Theorem 10.8, if $a, b \in B[x_0, r]$ we have

$$\|f(b) - f(a)\| \leqslant c\|b - a\|.$$

By Theorem 5.48 there exists a unique fixed point in $B[x_0, r]$. □

Let X, Y be two Banach spaces. It is easy to verify that $X \times Y$ is a Banach space relative to the norm defined by $\|(x, y)\| = \|x\| + \|y\|$ for $(x, y) \in X \times Y$.

Let X, Y, Z be three Banach spaces and let $F : X \times Y \longrightarrow Z$ be a function. Denote by $D_x F(x_0, y_0)$ and by $D_y F(x_0, y_0)$ the linear operators in $\mathsf{Hom}(X, Z)$ and $\mathsf{Hom}(Y, Z)$, respectively, defined by

$$F(x_0 + h, y_0) - F(x_0, y_0) - D_x F(x_0, y_0)h = o_1(h),$$
$$F(x_0, y_0 + k) - F(x_0, y_0) - D_y F(x_0, y_0)k = o_2(k)$$

if they exist. The operators $D_x F(x_0, y_0)$ and $D_y F(x_0, y_0)$ are the *partial derivatives* of F relative to X and Y, respectively.

Theorem 10.10. (The Implicit Function Theorem) *Let X, Y, Z be three Banach spaces, W be an open subset in $X \times Y$, and let $F : W \longrightarrow Z$. Suppose that $(x_0, y_0) \in W$ and the following conditions are satisfied:*
  (i) *F is continuous at (x_0, y_0),*
  (ii) *$F(x_0, y_0) = 0$,*
  (iii) *$D_y F$ exists in W,*
  (iv) *$D_y F$ is continuous at (x_0, y_0), and*
  (v) *$D_y F(x_0, y_0)$ is invertible.*
  There exists a neighborhood V of x_0 and a unique function $f : V \longrightarrow Y$ such that $F(x, f(x)) = 0$, $f(x_0) = y_0$, f is continuous at x_0.

Proof. The conditions imposed in the function F are satisfied in (x_0, y_0), if and only if the same conditions are satisfied in $(0, 0)$ by the function $H : W_0 \longrightarrow Z$ defined by $H(x, y) = F(x - x_0, y - y_0)$. Therefore, without loss of generality we may assume that $(x_0, y_0) = (0, 0)$.

There exists a positive number δ_0 such that

$$\{(x, y) \mid \|x\| \leqslant \delta_0, \|y\| \leqslant \delta_0\} \subseteq W.$$

Observe that $D_y F(0, 0) \in \mathsf{Hom}(Y, Z)$ and $(D_y F)^{-1}(0, 0) \in \mathsf{Hom}(Z, Y)$ by (v).

For x, y such that $\|x\| \leqslant \delta_0$ and $\|y\| \leqslant \delta_0$ define $G_x(y) = y - (D_y F)^{-1}(0, 0)F(x, y)$.

For the derivative of $G_x(y)$ relative to y we have

$$D_y(G_x(y)) = I - (D_y F)^{-1}(0, 0) \, D_y F(x, y)$$
$$= (D_y F)^{-1}(0, 0)((D_y F)(0, 0) - D_y F(x, y)).$$

Since $D_y F$ is continuous at $(0, 0)$, by (iv) there exists a positive δ_1 such that $\|x\| \leqslant \delta_1$ and $\|y\| \leqslant \delta_1$ implies $\|G_x(y)\| \leqslant \frac{1}{2}$.

We have

$$D_y(G_x)(0) = -(D_y F)^{-1}(0, 0)F(x, 0) = -(D_y F)^{-1}(0, 0)(F(x, 0) - F(0, 0)).$$

If $\delta = \min\{\delta_0, \delta_1\}$ and ϵ is a positive number such that $\epsilon < \delta$, by the continuity of F at $(0,0)$, there exists $\delta_\epsilon < \delta$ such that $\|x\| \leqslant \delta_\epsilon$ implies $\|G_x(0)\| < \frac{\epsilon}{2}$.

If $\|x\| \leqslant \delta_\epsilon$ and $\|y\| \leqslant \epsilon$, then

$$\|G_x(y)\| \leqslant \|G_x(0)\| + \|G_x(y) - G_x(0)\|$$
$$\leqslant \frac{\epsilon}{2} + \sup\{\|D_y(G_x)(\lambda y)\|\|y\| \mid \lambda \in [0,1]\}$$
$$\leqslant \frac{\epsilon}{2} + \frac{\epsilon}{2} = \epsilon.$$

Thus, for $\|x\| \leqslant \delta_\epsilon$ G_x is a transformation of the closed sphere $B[0, \epsilon]$ and $\|G_x(y)\| < 1$. By Lemma 10.2, G_x has a unique fixed point y in $B[0, \epsilon]$. Since y depends on x, we can define the function $f : B[0, \epsilon] \longrightarrow Y$ as $y = f(x)$ such that $F(x, f(x)) = 0$.

Since $F(0,0) = 0$, it follows that $G_0(0) = 0$. We have $0 = f(0)$ by the uniqueness of y.

For each $\epsilon \in (0, \delta)$ there exists a δ_ϵ such that $\|x\| \leqslant \delta_\epsilon$ implies $\|G_x(0)\| \leqslant \frac{\epsilon}{2}$. Thus, $\|x\| \leqslant \delta_\epsilon$ implies $\|f(x)\| \leqslant \epsilon$, which shows that f is continuous.

Suppose that $\tilde{f}$ is another function defined on a neighborhood of 0 such that $\tilde{f}$ is continuous at 0, $\tilde{f}(0) = 0$ and $F(x, \tilde{f}(x)) = 0$. If $0 < \epsilon < \delta$, there exists a positive number θ such that $\theta < \delta_\epsilon$, and $\|x\| \leqslant \theta$ implies $\|\tilde{f}(x)\| \leqslant \epsilon$, so $\tilde{f}(x) \in B[0, \epsilon]$. From the uniqueness of the fixed point for G_x it follows that $f(x) = \tilde{f}(x)$ when $\|x\| \leqslant \theta$. $\qquad \square$

Another variant of the Implicit Function Theorem presented in [41] is obtained by replacing condition (i) of Theorem 10.10 with the continuous differentiability.

Theorem 10.11. *Let X, Y, Z be three Banach spaces, W be an open subset in $X \times Y$, and let $F : W \longrightarrow Z$. Suppose that $(x_0, y_0) \in W$ and the following conditions are satisfied:*

(i) *F is continuously differentiable in W,*

(ii) *$F(x_0, y_0) = 0$,*

(iii) *$D_y F$ exists in W,*

(iv) *$D_y F(x_0, y_0)$ is invertible.*

Then, there exists a neighborhood V of x_0 such that f is unique and

$$(Df)(x) = -(D_y F(x, f(x)))^{-1} D_x F(x, f(x)).$$

Proof. The existence of a neighborhood V of x_0 and a unique function $f : V \longrightarrow Y$ such that $F(x, f(x)) = 0$, $f(x_0) = y_0$, f is continuous at x_0

follows from Theorem 10.10. Differentiating the equality $F(x, f(x)) = 0$ and applying the chain rule yields

$$(D_x F)(x, f(x))(D_x f)(x) + (D_y F)(x, f(x)) = 0,$$

which implies $(D_x f)(x) = -(D_y F(x, f(x)))^{-1}(D_x F)(x, f(x))$. $\square$

Example 10.13. Let us consider a special case of the implicit function theorem that is important for many applications. Suppose that $X = \mathbb{R}^n$ and $Y = Z = \mathbb{R}$ in Theorem 10.11, W is an open subset in $\mathbb{R}^n \times \mathbb{R}$, and $F : W \longrightarrow \mathbb{R}$ is a function that satisfies the conditions of this theorem in $(\mathbf{x}_0, y_0) \in \mathbb{R}^n \times \mathbb{R}$. In other words, F is continuously differentiable in W, $F(\mathbf{x}_0, y_0) = 0$, and $\frac{\partial F}{\partial y}(\mathbf{x}_0, y_0) \neq 0$.

By Theorem 10.11, there exists a neighborhood V of $\mathbf{x}_0$ and a unique function $f : V \longrightarrow Y$ such that $F(\mathbf{x}, f(\mathbf{x})) = 0$, $f(\mathbf{x}_0) = y_0$, f is continuous at $\mathbf{x}_0$ and

$$(Df)(\mathbf{x}_0) = -\frac{1}{\frac{\partial F}{\partial z}(\mathbf{x}, g(\mathbf{x}))}(D_x F)(\mathbf{x}, g(\mathbf{x})).$$

Theorem 10.12. *Let X, Y be two Banach spaces, U be an open set in X, and let $f : U \longrightarrow Y$ be a continuously differentiable function on U. If $x_0 \in U$ and $\epsilon > 0$, then there exists $\delta > 0$ such that if $x_1, x_2 \in B(x_0, \delta)$, then*

$$\|f(x_2) - f(x_1) - f'(x_0)(x_2 - x_1)\| \leqslant \epsilon \|x_2 - x_1\|.$$

Proof. Since the mapping $\phi : X \longrightarrow \mathsf{Hom}(X, Y)$ given by $\phi(x) = (Df)(x)$ is continuous, for $\epsilon > 0$ there exists $\delta_1 > 0$ such that $\|x - x_0\| < \delta_1$ implies $\|(Df)(x) - (Df)(x_0)\| < \epsilon$. Since U is an open set and $x_0 \in U$, there exists $\delta_2 > 0$ such that $B(x_0, \delta_2) \subseteq U$. Let $\delta = \min \delta_1, \delta_2$.

Let $g : U \longrightarrow Y$ be the function given by $g(x) = f(x) - (Df)(x_0)x$ for $x \in U$. Since $(Dg)(x) = (Df)(x) - (Df)(x_0)$, by Theorem 10.8 we have:

$$\|g(x_2) - g(x_1)\| \leqslant \|x_2 - x_1\| \sup\{\|(Df)(x) - (Df)(x_0)\| \mid x \in [x_1, x_2]\},$$

that is

$$\|f(x_2) - f(x_1) - (Df)(x_0)(x_2 - x_1)\| \leqslant \epsilon \|x_2 - x_1\|.$$ $\square$

Theorem 10.13. *Let X, Y be two Banach spaces, U be an open set in X, and let $f : U \longrightarrow Y$ be a continuously differentiable function on U. If $x_0 \in U$ and $(Df)(x_0)$ has a right inverse in $\mathsf{Hom}(X, Y)$, then $f(U)$ is a neighborhood of $y_0 = f(x_0)$.*

Proof.　Since $(Df)(x_0)$ has a right inverse, there exists $\ell \in \mathsf{Hom}(Y, X)$ such that $(Df)(x_0)\ell = 1_Y$. Let $c = \|\ell\|$.

By Theorem 10.12, taking $\epsilon = \frac{1}{2c}$ there exists $\delta > 0$ such that $B(x_0, \delta) \subseteq U$ and $u, v \in B(x_0, \delta)$ imply

$$\|f(u) - f(v) - (Df)(x_0)(u - v)\| \leqslant \frac{1}{2c}\|u - v\|.$$

We prove that $f(U)$ is a neighborhood of $y_0 = f(x_0)$ by showing that $f(U)$ includes the open sphere $B\left(y_0, \frac{\delta}{2c}\right)$, that is, by showing that for $y \in B\left(y_0, \frac{\delta}{2c}\right)$ there exists $x \in U$ such that $y = f(x)$.

Define inductively a sequence (x_n) as follows. The initial member is $x_0 \in U$, $x_1 = x_0 + \ell(y - y_0)$ and

$$x_{n+1} = x_n - \ell\left(f(x_n) - f(x_{n-1}) - (Df)(x_0)(x_n - x_{n-1})\right)$$

for $n \leqslant 1$.

We prove by induction on n that $\|x_n - x_{n-1}\| \leqslant \frac{\delta}{2^n}$ and $x_n \in B(x_0, \delta)$ for $n \geqslant 1$.

For the base case, $n = 1$, we have:

$$\|x_1 - x_0\| = \|\ell(y - y_0)\| \leqslant c\|y - y_0\| \leqslant c\frac{\delta}{2c} = \frac{\delta}{2}.$$

Suppose that the above claims hold for n. We have:

$$
\begin{aligned}
\|x_{n+1} - x_n\| &= \|\ell\left(f(x_n) - f(x_{n-1}) - (Df)(x_0)(x_n - x_{n-1})\right)\| \\
&\leqslant c\|f(x_n) - f(x_{n-1}) - (Df)(x_0)(x_n - x_{n-1})\| \\
&\leqslant c \cdot \frac{1}{2c}\|x_n - x_{n-1}\| \leqslant \frac{\delta}{2^{n+1}}
\end{aligned}
$$

(by the inductive hypothesis).

Also, we have:

$$
\begin{aligned}
\|x_{n+1} - x_0\| &\leqslant \|x_{n+1} - x_n\| + \|x_n - x_{n-1}\| + \cdots + \|x_0 - x_1\| \\
&\leqslant \delta\left(\frac{1}{2^{n+1}} + \frac{1}{2^n} + \cdots + \frac{1}{2}\right) \leqslant \delta,
\end{aligned}
$$

so $x_{n+1} \in B(x_0, \delta)$.

Moreover, (x_n) is a Cauchy sequence because for $m, n \in \mathbb{N}$

$$
\begin{aligned}
\|x_n - x_m\| &\leqslant \|x_n - x_{n-1}\| + \cdots + \|x_{m+1} - x_m\| \\
&\leqslant \frac{\delta}{2^{n+1}} + \frac{\delta}{2^n} + \cdots \leqslant \frac{\delta}{2^n}.
\end{aligned}
$$

Since X is complete, there exists $x = \lim_{n \to \infty} x_n$.

Since $x_n \in B(x_0, \delta)$, it follows that $\|x - x_0\| \leqslant \delta$ and $x \in U$.

By the definition of x_{n+1},

$$x_{n+1} = x_n - \ell \left(f(x_n) - f(x_{n-1}) - (Df)(x_0)(x_n - x_{n-1}) \right)$$

we have

$$(Df)(x_0)(x_{n+1} - x_n)$$
$$= -(Df)(x_0)\ell(f(x_n) - f(x_{n-1}) - (Df)(x_0)(x_n - x_{n-1})$$
$$= (Df)(x_0)(x_n - x_{n-1}) - (f(x_n) - f(x_{n-1}).$$

By a repeated application of this equality for $n, n-1, \ldots, 1$ we have:

$$(Df)(x_0)(x_{n+1} - x_n) = (Df)(x_0)(x_n - x_{n-1}) - (f(x_n) - f(x_{n-1}))$$
$$(Df)(x_0)(x_n - x_{n-1}) = (Df)(x_0)(x_{n-1} - x_{n-2}) - (f(x_{n-1}) - f(x_{n-2}))$$
$$\vdots$$
$$(Df)(x_0)(x_2 - x_1) = (Df)(x_0)(x_1 - x_0) - (f(x_1) - f(x_0)),$$

hence

$$(Df)(x_0)(x_{n+1} - x_n) = (Df)(x_0)(x_1 - x_0) - (f(x_n) - f(x_0))$$
$$= (Df)(x_0)(x_1 - x_0) - (f(x_n) - y).$$

Recall that $f(x_0) = y_0$ and $x_1 = x_0 + \ell(y - y_0)$. Thus, we have

$$(Df)(x_0)(x_{n+1} - x_n) = (Df)(x_0)\ell(y - y_0) - (f(x_n) - y_0) = y - f(x_n).$$

Taking $n \to \infty$ in the above equality we have $y = f(x) \in f(U)$. $\square$

Theorem 10.14. *Let X be a Banach space, U be an open set in X, and let $\boldsymbol{f} : U \longrightarrow \mathbb{R}^n$ be a vector-valued continuously differentiable function on U. If $x \in U$ and $(D\boldsymbol{f})(x)$ is a surjective mapping in $\mathsf{Hom}(X, \mathbb{R}^n)$, then then $\boldsymbol{f}(U)$ is a neighborhood of $y_0 = \boldsymbol{f}(x_0)$.*

Proof. Since $(D\boldsymbol{f})(x)$ is a surjective mapping there exist $u_1, \ldots, u_n \in U$ such that $(D\boldsymbol{f})(x)u_i = \mathbf{e}_i$ for $1 \leqslant i \leqslant n$, where $\{\mathbf{e}_1, \ldots, \mathbf{e}_n\}$ is the standard basis of $\mathbb{R}^n$. Define the linear mapping $\ell : \mathbb{R}^n \longrightarrow X$ by $\ell(\mathbf{e}_i) = u_i$ for $\leqslant i \leqslant n$. We have $(D\boldsymbol{f})(x)\ell(\mathbf{e}_i) = \mathbf{e}_i$ for $1 \leqslant i \leqslant n$, so $(D\boldsymbol{f})(x)\ell = 1_Y$, so $(D\boldsymbol{f})(x)$ has a right inverse. The statement then follows from Theorem 10.13. $\square$

Corollary 10.3. *Let X be a Banach space, U be an open set in X, and let $f : U \longrightarrow Y$, be a vector-valued continuously differentiable function on U, where Y is a finitely dimensional Banach space.*

If $x \in U$ and $(Df)(x)$ is a surjective mapping in $\mathsf{Hom}(X, Y)$, then $f(U)$ is a neighborhood of $y_0 = f(x_0)$.

Proof.   This statement is a direct consequence of Theorem 10.14 because a finitely dimensional Banach space is homeomorphic to a space $\mathbb{R}^n$.   □

We discuss now differentiability of functions whose sets of values are subsets of sets of the form $\mathbb{R}^m$. Such functions will be denoted by bold letters. If $\mathbf{f} : X \longrightarrow \mathbb{R}^m$, where $X \subseteq \mathbb{R}^n$, the components of $\mathbf{f}$ will be denoted by $f_1, \ldots, f_m$.

Definition 10.5. Let $\mathbf{f} : X \longrightarrow \mathbb{R}^m$, where $X \subseteq \mathbb{R}^n$ is an open set and $\mathbf{x}_0 \in X$. If the limit

$$\lim_{t \downarrow 0} \frac{\mathbf{f}(\mathbf{x}_0 + t\mathbf{u}) - \mathbf{f}(\mathbf{x}_0)}{t}$$

exists, then we refer to it as the *directional derivative of $\mathbf{f}$ in $\mathbf{x}_0$ with respect to $\mathbf{u}$* and we denote this limit as $\frac{\partial \mathbf{f}}{\partial \mathbf{u}}(\mathbf{x}_0)$.

If $\mathbf{f}$ is Gâteaux differentiable in $\mathbf{x}_0$, then the directional derivative of $\mathbf{f}$ exists with respect to every direction $\mathbf{u}$ and we have

$$\frac{\partial \mathbf{f}}{\partial \mathbf{u}}(\mathbf{x}_0) = (D\mathbf{f})(\mathbf{x}_0)(\mathbf{u}).$$

The partial derivative of $\mathbf{f} : X \longrightarrow \mathbb{R}^m$ relative to x_i is $(D\mathbf{f})(\mathbf{x}_0)(\mathbf{e}_i)$.

Unlike the case of single-argument functions, where the existence of a derivative at a point $\mathbf{x}_0$ implies the continuity in $\mathbf{x}_0$, the existence of partial derivatives of a multi-argument function does not imply its continuity.

Example 10.14. Let $f : \mathbb{R}^2 \longrightarrow \mathbb{R}$ be the function defined by

$$f(\mathbf{x}) = \begin{cases} \cos \dfrac{\pi}{2} \dfrac{x_1^2 - x_2^2}{x_1^2 + x_2^2} & \text{if } \mathbf{x} \neq \mathbf{0}_2, \\ 0 & \text{if } \mathbf{x} = \mathbf{0}_2. \end{cases}$$

Note that $\lim_{n \to \infty} f\left(\frac{1}{n}, \frac{1}{n}\right) = 1$, while $f(\mathbf{0}_2) = 0$, so f is not continuous in $\mathbf{0}_2$. However, partial derivatives do exist in $\mathbf{0}_2$ because

$$\frac{\partial f}{\partial x_1}(\mathbf{0}_2) = \lim_{x_1 \to 0} \frac{f(x_1, 0)}{x_1} = 0 \text{ and } \frac{\partial f}{\partial x_2}(\mathbf{0}_2) = \lim_{x_2 \to 0} \frac{f(0, x_2)}{x_2} = 0.$$

If $\frac{\partial \mathbf{f}}{\partial \mathbf{u}}$ exists relative to every direction $\mathbf{u}$, then $\frac{\partial \mathbf{f}}{\partial x_i}$ exists for every i, $1 \leqslant i \leqslant n$. The converse is not true, as the next example shows.

Example 10.15. Consider the function $f : \mathbb{R}^n \longrightarrow \mathbb{R}$ defined by

$$f(\mathbf{x}) = \begin{cases} a & \text{if } \mathbf{x} = a\mathbf{e}_i \text{ for some } i, \\ 1 & \text{otherwise.} \end{cases}$$

We have
$$\frac{\partial f}{\partial x_i}(\mathbf{0}) = \lim_{t \to 0} \frac{f(t\mathbf{e}_i) - f(\mathbf{0})}{t} = 1$$
for $1 \leqslant i \leqslant n$. However, if $\mathbf{u} \notin \{\mathbf{e}_1, \dots, \mathbf{e}_n\}$, then
$$\frac{f(t\mathbf{u}) - f(\mathbf{0})}{t} = \frac{1}{t}$$
and $\lim_{t \to 0} \frac{1}{t}$ does not exist, which shows that $\frac{\partial f}{\partial \mathbf{u}}(\mathbf{0})$ does not exists if $\mathbf{u} \notin \{\mathbf{e}_1, \dots, \mathbf{e}_n\}$.

Theorem 10.15. *Let $f : \mathbb{R}^n \longrightarrow \mathbb{R}$ be a functional that has continuous partial derivatives in $\boldsymbol{x}_0$ with respect to each variable x_i. Then f is Fréchet differentiable in x_0 and its Fréchet differential is given by*
$$\delta f(\boldsymbol{x}_0; \boldsymbol{h}) = \sum_{i=1}^n \left(\frac{\partial f}{\partial x_i} \right)(\boldsymbol{x}_0) h_i.$$

Proof. Since the partial derivatives of f are continuous, there exists a sphere $B(x_0, \epsilon)$ such that
$$\left| \frac{\partial f}{\partial x_i}(\mathbf{x}_0) - \frac{\partial f}{\partial x_i}(\mathbf{y}) \right| < \frac{\epsilon}{n}$$
for all $y \in B(x_0, \epsilon)$. Let $\mathbf{h} = \sum_{i=1}^n h_i \mathbf{e}_i$ and let $\mathbf{r}_0, \mathbf{r}_1, \dots, \mathbf{r}_n$ be a sequence of vectors defined by $\mathbf{r}_0 = \mathbf{0}_n$, and $\mathbf{r}_k = \sum_{i=1}^k h_i \mathbf{e}_i$. Clearly, $\|\mathbf{r}_k\| \leqslant \|\mathbf{h}\|$ for $0 \leqslant k \leqslant n$, and $x_0 + r_k = x_0 + r_{k-1} + h_k \mathbf{e}_k$.

Observe that by the mean value theorem for functions of one argument we have
$$f(\mathbf{x}_0 + \mathbf{r}_k) - f(\mathbf{x}_0 + \mathbf{r}_{k-1}) = \frac{\partial f}{\partial x_k}(x_0 + r_{k-1} + \alpha_k \mathbf{e}_k) h_k$$
for some $\alpha_k \in [0, h_k]$. We have $\mathbf{x}_0 + \mathbf{r}_{k-1} + \alpha_k \mathbf{e}_k \in S(\mathbf{x}_0, \delta)$ if $\|\mathbf{h}\| < \delta$. This implies
$$\left| f(x_0 + \mathbf{r}_k) - f(\mathbf{x}_0 + \mathbf{r}_{k-1}) - \frac{\partial f}{\partial x_k}(\mathbf{x}_0) h_k \right| < \frac{\epsilon}{n} \|\mathbf{h}\|.$$
Therefore,
$$\left| f(\mathbf{x}_0 + \mathbf{h}) - f(\mathbf{x}_0) - \sum_{i=1}^n \frac{\partial f}{\partial x_i}(\mathbf{x}_0) h_i \right|$$
$$= \left| \sum_{k=1}^n \left(f(\mathbf{x}_0 + \mathbf{r}_k) - f(\mathbf{x}_0 + \mathbf{r}_{k-1}) - \frac{\partial f}{\partial x_k}(\mathbf{x}_0) h_k \right) \right|$$
$$\leqslant \sum_{k=1}^n \left| f(\mathbf{x}_0 + \mathbf{r}_k) - f(\mathbf{x}_0 + \mathbf{r}_{k-1}) - \frac{\partial f}{\partial x_k}(\mathbf{x}_0) h_k \right| < \epsilon \|\mathbf{h}\|,$$
which concludes the argument. $\square$

Starting with a vector $\mathbf{h} \in \mathbb{R}^n$ and the symbolic vector ∇ we consider a symbolic "scalar product" $\mathbf{h}'\nabla$ defined by

$$\mathbf{h}'\nabla = h_1 \frac{\partial}{\partial x_1} + \cdots + h_n \frac{\partial}{\partial x_n},$$

which is a differential operator that can be applied to a functional $f : \mathbb{R}^n \longrightarrow \mathbb{R}$. The formula in Theorem 10.15 can now be written in a condensed form as

$$\delta f(\mathbf{x}_0; \mathbf{h}) = ((\mathbf{h}'\nabla)f)(\mathbf{x}_0).$$

Let $\mathbf{f} : \mathbb{R}^n \longrightarrow \mathbb{R}^m$ be a vector-valued function that is differentiable at $\mathbf{x}_0$ and let $\mathbf{r}_{\mathbf{x}_0} : \mathbb{R}^n \longrightarrow \mathbb{R}^m$ be the function defined by:

$$\mathbf{r}_{\mathbf{x}_0}(\mathbf{u}) = \mathbf{f}(\mathbf{x}_0 + \mathbf{u}) - \mathbf{f}(\mathbf{x}_0) - (D\mathbf{f})(\mathbf{x}_0)\mathbf{u}.$$

Then, we have

$$\lim_{\mathbf{u} \to \mathbf{0}_n} \frac{\|\mathbf{r}_{\mathbf{x}_0}(\mathbf{u})\|}{\|\mathbf{u}\|} = 0.$$

We have seen that for a function $\mathbf{f} : \mathbb{R}^n \longrightarrow \mathbb{R}^m$ that is Gâteaux differentiable at $\mathbf{x}_0$, the vector $(D_{\mathbf{x}}\mathbf{f})(\mathbf{x}_0)(\mathbf{u})$ is the product of the Jacobian matrix of $\mathbf{f}$ computed at $\mathbf{x}_0$ and $\mathbf{u}$. We will consider first two simple examples.

Example 10.16. Let $\mathbf{h} : \mathbb{R}^n \longrightarrow \mathbb{R}^m$ be the linear operator defined by $\mathbf{h}(\mathbf{x}) = A\mathbf{x}$, where $A \in \mathbb{R}^{m \times n}$. By the definition of the Gâteaux derivative of $\mathbf{h}$ we can write

$$
\begin{aligned}
(D\mathbf{h})(\mathbf{x}_0)(u) &= \lim_{t \to 0} \frac{\mathbf{h}(\mathbf{x}_0 + t\mathbf{u}) - \mathbf{h}(\mathbf{x}_0)}{t} \\
&= \lim_{t \to 0} \frac{A(\mathbf{x}_0 + t\mathbf{u}) - A\mathbf{x}_0}{t} \\
&= \lim_{t \to 0} \frac{tA\mathbf{u}}{t} = A\mathbf{u},
\end{aligned}
$$

hence $(D\mathbf{h})(\mathbf{x}_0) = A$ for every $\mathbf{x}_0 \in \mathbb{R}^n$.

Suppose now that, as before, $\mathbf{h}(\mathbf{x}) = A\mathbf{x}$, and $\mathbf{x} = \mathbf{g}(\mathbf{z})$, where $\mathbf{g} : \mathbb{R}^n \longrightarrow \mathbb{R}^p$ is a Gâteaux differentiable function. An application of the chain rule yields the formula

$$(D_{\mathbf{z}}\mathbf{h})(\mathbf{z}_0) = A(D_{\mathbf{z}}\mathbf{g})(\mathbf{z}_0).$$

Example 10.17. Let $f : \mathbb{R}^m \times \mathbb{R}^n \longrightarrow \mathbb{R}$ be the functional defined by $f(\mathbf{x}, \mathbf{y}) = \mathbf{y}'A\mathbf{x}$, where $\mathbf{y} \in \mathbb{R}^m$, $A \in \mathbb{R}^{m \times n}$, and $\mathbf{x} \in \mathbb{R}^n$. We have:

$$(D_{\mathbf{x}}f)(\mathbf{x}_0, \mathbf{y}_0) = \mathbf{y}_0'A \text{ and } (D_{\mathbf{y}}f)(\mathbf{x}_0, \mathbf{y}_0) = \mathbf{x}_0'A'.$$

By the definition of the Gâteaux differential, $(D_{\mathbf{x}}f)(\mathbf{x}_0, \mathbf{y}_0)$ is given by

$$
\begin{aligned}
(D_{\mathbf{x}}f)(\mathbf{x}_0, \mathbf{y}_0) &= \lim_{t \to 0} \frac{f(\mathbf{x}_0 + t\mathbf{u}, \mathbf{y}_0) - f(\mathbf{x}_0, \mathbf{y}_0)}{t} \\
&= \lim_{t \to 0} \frac{\mathbf{y}_0' A(\mathbf{x}_0 + t\mathbf{u}) - \mathbf{y}_0' A \mathbf{x}_0}{t} \\
&= \lim_{t \to 0} \frac{t\mathbf{y}_0' A\mathbf{u}}{t} \\
&= \mathbf{y}_0' A\mathbf{u}
\end{aligned}
$$

for $\mathbf{u} \in \mathbb{R}^n$. Therefore, since the limit of the fraction when $t \to 0$ is 0, we have $(D_{\mathbf{x}}f)(\mathbf{x}_0) = \mathbf{y}_0' A$.

Similarly, the fraction that enters in the definition of $(D_{\mathbf{x}}f)(\mathbf{x}_0, \mathbf{y}_0)$ is

$$
\begin{aligned}
(D_{\mathbf{y}}f)(\mathbf{x}_0, \mathbf{y}_0)(\mathbf{v}) &= \lim_{t \to 0} \frac{f(\mathbf{x}_0, \mathbf{y}_0 + t\mathbf{v}) - f(\mathbf{x}_0, \mathbf{y}_0)}{t} \\
&= \lim_{t \to 0} \frac{(\mathbf{y}_0' + t\mathbf{v}') A \mathbf{x}_0 - \mathbf{y}_0' A \mathbf{x}_0}{t} \\
&= \lim_{t \to 0} \frac{t\mathbf{v}' A \mathbf{x}_0}{t} = \mathbf{v}' A \mathbf{x}_0.
\end{aligned}
$$

Since $\mathbf{v}' A \mathbf{x}_0$ is a scalar, it is equal to its own transpose, that is $\mathbf{v}' A \mathbf{x}_0 = \mathbf{x}_0' A' \mathbf{v}$ and we have:

$$
(D_{\mathbf{y}}f)(\mathbf{x}_0, \mathbf{y}_0) = \mathbf{x}_0' A'.
$$

Theorem 10.16. *Let $\mathbf{h} : \mathbb{R}^n \longrightarrow \mathbb{R}^m$ and $\mathbf{g} : \mathbb{R}^n \longrightarrow \mathbb{R}^m$ be two differentiable operators in $\mathbf{z}_0 \in \mathbb{R}^n$. We have*

$$
D_z(\mathbf{g}(\mathbf{z})'\mathbf{h}(\mathbf{z}))(\mathbf{z}_0) = \mathbf{h}(\mathbf{z}_0)'(D_z\mathbf{g})(\mathbf{z}_0) + \mathbf{g}(\mathbf{z}_0)'(D_z\mathbf{h})(\mathbf{z}_0).
$$

Proof. Let $k : \mathbb{R}^n \longrightarrow \mathbb{R}$ be defined as $k(\mathbf{z}) = \mathbf{g}'(\mathbf{z})\mathbf{f}(\mathbf{z})$. We have

$$
k(\mathbf{z}) = \sum_{i=1}^{m} g_i(\mathbf{z}) f_i(\mathbf{z})
$$

for $\mathbf{z} \in \mathbb{R}^n$. Then,

$$
\frac{\partial k}{\partial z_j}(\mathbf{z}_0) = \sum_{i=1}^{m} \frac{\partial g_i}{\partial z_j}(\mathbf{z}_0) f_i(\mathbf{z}_0) + \sum_{i=1}^{m} g_i(\mathbf{z}_0) \frac{\partial f_i}{\partial z_j}(\mathbf{z}_0)
$$

for $1 \leqslant j \leqslant n$. This is equivalent to the desired equality. $\qquad \square$

Corollary 10.4. *For $\mathbf{h} : \mathbb{R}^n \longrightarrow \mathbb{R}^m$ be a differentiable operator and let $f : \mathbb{R}^n \longrightarrow \mathbb{R}$ be given by $f(\mathbf{z}) = \mathbf{h}(\mathbf{z})'\mathbf{h}(\mathbf{z})$. We have*

$$
(Df)(\mathbf{z}_0) = 2((D\mathbf{h})(\mathbf{z}_0))'((D\mathbf{h})(\mathbf{z}_0)).
$$

Proof. This follows immediately from Theorem 10.16. $\qquad \square$

Theorem 10.17. *Let $A \in \mathbb{R}^{m \times p}$ and let $\boldsymbol{h} : \mathbb{R}^n \longrightarrow \mathbb{R}^m$ and $\boldsymbol{g} : \mathbb{R}^n \longrightarrow \mathbb{R}^p$ be two functions that are differentiable at $\boldsymbol{z}_0 \in \mathbb{R}^n$. Define the functional $f : \mathbb{R}^n \longrightarrow \mathbb{R}$ as $f(\boldsymbol{z}) = \boldsymbol{h}(\boldsymbol{z})'A\boldsymbol{g}(\boldsymbol{z})$. We have:*

$$(Df)(\boldsymbol{z}_0) = \boldsymbol{g}(\boldsymbol{z}_0)'A'(D\boldsymbol{h})(\boldsymbol{z}_0) + \boldsymbol{h}(\boldsymbol{z}_0)'A(D\boldsymbol{g})(\boldsymbol{z}_0).$$

Proof. Let $\boldsymbol{l} : \mathbb{R}^n \longrightarrow \mathbb{R}^p$ be defined by $\boldsymbol{l}(\boldsymbol{z}) = A'\boldsymbol{h}(\boldsymbol{z})$. We have $f(\boldsymbol{z}) = \boldsymbol{l}(\boldsymbol{z})'\boldsymbol{g}(\boldsymbol{z})$. By Theorem 10.16 we have:

$$D_{\boldsymbol{z}}(\boldsymbol{l}(\boldsymbol{z})'\boldsymbol{g}(\boldsymbol{z}))(\boldsymbol{z}_0) = \boldsymbol{h}(\boldsymbol{z}_0)'(D_{\boldsymbol{z}}\boldsymbol{l})(\boldsymbol{z}_0) + \boldsymbol{l}(\boldsymbol{z}_0)'(D_{\boldsymbol{z}}\boldsymbol{g})(\boldsymbol{z}_0).$$

By Theorem 10.16 we have:

$$(D_{\boldsymbol{z}}\boldsymbol{l})(\boldsymbol{z}_0) = A'(D_{\boldsymbol{z}}\boldsymbol{h})(\boldsymbol{z}_0),$$

which implies

$$D_{\boldsymbol{z}}(\boldsymbol{l}(\boldsymbol{z})'\boldsymbol{g}(\boldsymbol{z}))(\boldsymbol{z}_0) = \boldsymbol{h}(\boldsymbol{z}_0)'A'(D_{\boldsymbol{z}}\boldsymbol{h})(\boldsymbol{z}_0) + A'\boldsymbol{h}(\boldsymbol{z})(D_{\boldsymbol{z}}\boldsymbol{g})(\boldsymbol{z}_0). \qquad \square$$

10.3 Taylor's Formula

Let X be an open subset of $\mathbb{R}^n$. The function $f : X \longrightarrow \mathbb{R}$ belongs to the class $C^k(X)$ if it has continuous partial derivatives of order up to and including k.

Under certain conditions of differentiability of a function $f : X \longrightarrow \mathbb{R}$, Taylor's formula shows the existence of a polynomial that provides an approximation of f.

If X is an interval in $\mathbb{R}$, $x_0 \in X$, and $f : X \longrightarrow \mathbb{R}$ belongs to $C^k(X)$ define the *Taylor polynomial of degree k* $T_k(x)$ as

$$T_k(x) = f(x_0) + \frac{x - x_0}{1!}f'(x_0) + \cdots + \frac{(x - x_0)^k}{k!}f^{(n)}(x_0).$$

The function $R_k : X \longrightarrow \mathbb{R}$ defined as $R_k(x) = f(x) - T_k(x)$ is the *remainder of order k for f*.

The derivatives of $T_k(x)$ are given by

$$T_k'(x) = f'(x_0) + \frac{x - x_0}{1!}f''(x_0) + \cdots + \frac{(x - x_0)^{k-1}}{(k-1)!}f^{(k)}(x_0)$$

$$T_k''(x) = f''(x_0) + \frac{x - x_0}{1!}f'''(x_0) + \cdots + \frac{(x - x_0)^{k-1}}{(k-1)!}f^{(k)}(x_0)$$

$$\vdots$$

$$T_k^{k-1}(x) = f^{(k-1)}(x_0) + \frac{x - x_0}{1!}f^{(k)}(x_0)$$

$$T_k^k(x) = f^{(k)}(x_0).$$

Therefore,

$$T_k(x_0) = f(x_0), T_k'(x_0) = f'(x_0), \ldots, T_k^{(k)}(x_0) = f^{(k-1)}(x_0), T_k^{(k+1)}(x_0) = 0.$$

The definition of R_k implies that this function also belongs to $C^k(X)$ and

$$R_k(x_0) = R_k'(x_0) = \cdots = R_k^{(k-1)}(x_0) = R_k^k(x_0) = 0.$$

Since R_k is continuous on X we have $\lim_{x \to x_0} R_k(x) = R_k(x_0) = 0$. Moreover, the following statement holds.

The next lemma establishes *Taylor's formula* in equality (10.3).

Lemma 10.3. *Let X be an open interval of $\mathbb{R}^n$ and let $f : X \longrightarrow \mathbb{R}$ be a function in $C^k(X)$. We have*

$$f(x) = f(x_0) + \frac{x - x_0}{1!} f'(x_0)$$
$$+ \frac{(x - x_0)^2}{2!} f''(x_0) + \cdots + \frac{(x - x_0)^k}{k!} f^{(k)}(x_0) + R_k(x) \quad (10.1)$$

for every $x \in X$ and $\lim_{x \to x_0} \frac{R_k(x)}{(x - x_0)^k} = 0$.

Proof. Let $g : X \longrightarrow \mathbb{R}$ be defined as $g(x) = (x - x_0)^k$. Note that

$$g(x_0) = g'(x_0) = \cdots = g^{(k-1)}(x_0) = 0 \text{ and } g^{(k)}(x_0) = k!.$$

For $x \in X$, an application of Cauchy's Theorem from elementary calculus to the functions R_n and g yields the existence of c_1 between x_0 and x such that

$$\frac{R_k(x) - R_k(x_0)}{g(x) - g(x_0)} = \frac{R_k(x)}{g(x)} = \frac{R_k'(c_1)}{g'(c_1)}.$$

Since $R_k'(x_0) = g'(x_0) = 0$, applying again Cauchy's Theorem we obtain the existence of c_2 between x_0 and c_1 such that $\frac{R_k'(c_1)}{g'(c_1)} = \frac{R_k''(c_2)}{g''(c_2)}$. Thus,

$$\frac{R_k(x) - R_k(x_0)}{g(x) - g(x_0)} = \frac{R_k''(c_2)}{g''(c_2)}.$$

Continuing this process, we obtain the existence of a point ξ in between x_0 and x, but distinct from both such that

$$\frac{R_k(x) - R_k(x_0)}{g(x) - g(x_0)} = \frac{R_k^{(k-1)}(\xi)}{g^{(k-1)}(\xi)} = \frac{R_k^{(k-1)}(\xi) - R_k^{(k-1)}(x_0)}{g^{(k-1)}(\xi) - g^{(k-1)}(x_0)}$$
$$= \frac{\frac{R_k^{(k-1)}(\xi) - R_k^{(k-1)}(x_0)}{\xi - x_0}}{\frac{g^{(k-1)}(\xi) - g^{(k-1)}(x_0)}{\xi - x_0}}.$$

Let $(x_m)_{m \geqslant 1}$ be an arbitrary sequence in X such that $\lim_{m \to \infty} x_m = x_0$. For each x_m in this sequence denote by ξ_m the point located between x_0 and

x_m constructed as previously shown. Clearly, $\xi_m \neq x_0$ and $\lim_{m \to \infty} \xi_m = x_0$. Therefore, we have

$$\lim_{m \to \infty} \frac{R_k^{(k-1)}(\xi_m) - R_k^{(k-1)}(x_0)}{\xi_m - x_0} = R_k^{(k)}(x_0) = 0,$$

$$\lim_{m \to \infty} \frac{g^{(k-1)}(\xi_m) - g^{(k-1)}(x_0)}{\xi_m - x_0} = g^{(k)}(x_0) = k!,$$

which implies $\lim_{x \to x_0} \frac{R_k(x)}{(x-x_0)^k} = 0$. $\qquad\square$

Theorem 10.18. *If X is an interval in $\mathbb{R}$, $x_0 \in X$, and $f : X \longrightarrow \mathbb{R}$ belongs to $C^k(X)$, there exists a function $\rho : X \longrightarrow \mathbb{R}$ such that*

$$f(x) = f(x_0) + \frac{x - x_0}{1!} f'(x_0) + \frac{(x - x_0)^2}{2!} f''(x_0)$$

$$+ \cdots + \frac{(x - x_0)^k}{k!} f^{(k)}(x_0) + \frac{(x - x_0)^k}{k!} \rho(x_0)$$

for every $x \in X$ and $\lim_{x \to x_0} \rho(x) = 0$.

Proof. By applying Lemma 10.3 we can define

$$\rho(x) = \begin{cases} \dfrac{R_k(x)}{(x - x_0)^k} k! & \text{if } x \neq x_0, \\ 0 & \text{if } x = x_0. \end{cases}$$

Thus, by replacing $R_k(x)$ in equality (10.1) to obtain the desired result. $\square$

If we assume that $f \in C^{(k+1)}(X)$ we can give other forms of the remainder in Taylor's formula.

Let $\phi : X \longrightarrow \mathbb{R}$ be a function given by

$$\phi(t) = f(t) + \frac{x - t}{1!} f'(t) + \cdots + \frac{(x - t)^k}{k!} f^{(k)}(t) + (x - t)^p Q,$$

where $Q \in \mathbb{R}$. Since $f \in C^{(k+1)}(X)$ the function ϕ has a derivative in each point of X. We have $\phi(x) = f(x)$ and $\phi(x_0) = f(x_0) + \frac{x-x_0}{1!} f'(x_0) + \cdots + \frac{(x-x_0)^k}{k!} f^{(k)}(x_0) + (x - x_0)^p Q$ If we choose Q be such that $\phi(x_0) = \phi(x)$, then we can apply Rolle's theorem to ϕ on the interval determined by x_0 and x. There exists c such that $\phi'(\xi) = 0$, which amounts to

$$\frac{(x - \xi)^k}{k!} f^{(k+1)}(\xi) - p(x - \xi)^{p+1} Q = 0,$$

hence $K = \frac{(x-\xi)^{k-p+1}}{pk!} f^{(k+1)}(\xi)$. This allows to write

$$R_k(x) = \frac{(x - x_0)^p (x - \xi)^{k-p+1}}{pk!} f^{(k+1)}(\xi).$$

For $p = 1$ we have the *Cauchy remainder*,

$$R_k(x) = \frac{(x - x_0)(x - \xi)^k}{pk!} f^{(k+1)}(\xi),$$

while for $p = k + 1$ we obtain the *Lagrange*[1] *remainder*:

$$R_k(x) = \frac{(x - x_0)^{k+1}}{(k + 1)!} f^{(k+1)}(\xi).$$

Corollary 10.5. *Let X be an interval of $\mathbb{R}$ and let $f : X \longrightarrow \mathbb{R}$ be a function such that $f \in C^{(k+1)}(X)$. For the Lagrange remainder of the Taylor formula*

$$f(x) = f(x_0) + \frac{x - x_0}{1!} f'(x_0) + \frac{(x - x_0)^2}{2!} f''(x_0) + \cdots + \frac{(x - x_0)^k}{k!} f^{(k)}(x_0)$$
$$+ \frac{(x - x_0)^{k+1}}{(k + 1)!} f^{(k+1)}(\xi)$$

we have $R_k(x) = O((x - x_k)^{k+1})$.

Proof. This statement follows immediately from the previous discussion. $\square$

To extend Taylor's formula to functions defined on $\mathbb{R}^n$ we need to use symbolic powers of the operator $\mathbf{h}'\nabla$ that act as operators on real-valued functions of n variables. These powers are defined inductively by $(\mathbf{h}'\nabla)^0 f = f$, and

$$(\mathbf{h}'\nabla)^{k+1} f = (\mathbf{h}'\nabla)((\mathbf{h}'\nabla)^k f)$$

for $k \in \mathbb{N}$.

Example 10.18. For

$$\nabla = \begin{pmatrix} \frac{\partial}{\partial x_1} \\ \frac{\partial}{\partial x_2} \end{pmatrix}$$

and $\mathbf{h} = \begin{pmatrix} h_1 \\ h_2 \end{pmatrix}$ we have

$$\mathbf{h}'\nabla = h_1 \frac{\partial}{\partial x_1} + h_2 \frac{\partial}{\partial x_2}$$

---

[1] Joseph Louis Lagrange, a French-Italian mathematician was born at Turin on January 25, 1736, and died at Paris on April 10, 1813. He made major contributions to mathematics and is the creator of analytical mechanics and of the calculus of variations. In 1795 Lagrange was appointed to a mathematical chair at the École normale and was a professor at the École polytechnique in starting in 1797.

and $(\mathbf{h}'\nabla)f = h_1\frac{\partial f}{\partial x_1} + h_2\frac{\partial f}{\partial x_2}$. Note that

$$(\mathbf{h}'\nabla)^2 f = (\mathbf{h}'\nabla)\left(h_1\frac{\partial f}{\partial x_1} + h_2\frac{\partial f}{\partial x_2} \right)$$

$$= h_1\frac{\partial}{\partial x_1}\left(h_1\frac{\partial f}{\partial x_1} + h_2\frac{\partial f}{\partial x_2} \right) + h_2\frac{\partial}{\partial x_2}\left(h_1\frac{\partial f}{\partial x_1} + h_2\frac{\partial f}{\partial x_2} \right)$$

$$= h_1^2\frac{\partial^2 f}{\partial x_1^2} + 2h_1h_2\frac{\partial^2 f}{\partial x_1\,\partial x_2} + h_2^2\frac{\partial^2 f}{\partial x_2^2}.$$

The mth iteration of the operator $\mathbf{h}'\nabla$ can be computed using the multinomial formula

$$(\mathbf{h}'\nabla)^m = \sum \left\{ \binom{m}{p_1\ p_2\ \cdots\ p_k} h_1^{p_1} h_2^{p_2} \cdots h_k^{p_k} \frac{\partial^m}{\partial x_1^{p_1} x_2^{p_2} \partial \cdots x_k^{p_k}} \right.$$

$$\left. \Big|\, p_1, p_2, \ldots, p_k \in \mathbb{N}, \sum_{i=1}^{k} p_i = m \right\}.$$

Theorem 10.19. (Taylor's Formula) *Let $f : B(\boldsymbol{x}, r) \longrightarrow \mathbb{R}$ be a function that belongs to the class $C^n(B(\boldsymbol{x}, r))$, where $B(\boldsymbol{x}, r) \subseteq \mathbb{R}^k$. If $\mathbf{h} \in \mathbb{R}^k$ is such that $\|\mathbf{h}\| < r$ then there exists $\theta \in (0, 1)$ such that:*

$$f(\boldsymbol{x} + \boldsymbol{h}) = \sum_{m=0}^{n-1} \frac{1}{m!}((\mathbf{h}'\nabla)^m f)(\boldsymbol{x}) + \frac{1}{n!}((\mathbf{h}'\nabla)^n f)(\boldsymbol{x} + \theta\boldsymbol{h}). \quad (10.2)$$

Proof. Define the function $g : (0, 1) \longrightarrow \mathbb{R}$ by $g(a) = f(\mathbf{x} + a\mathbf{h})$. Since $f \in C^n(B(\mathbf{x}, r))$ it follows that g belongs to the class $C^n([0, 1])$. Thus, by the standard Taylor formula for g there exists $\theta \in (0, 1)$ such that

$$g(1) = \sum_{m=0}^{n-1} \frac{1}{m!}g^{(m)}(0) + \frac{1}{n!}g^{(n)}(\theta). \quad (10.3)$$

Note that differentiating the function $g(a) = f(\mathbf{x} + a\mathbf{h})$ with respect to a is the same thing as applying the differential operator $\mathbf{h}'\nabla$ to f. Indeed, we have

$$g'(a) = (f(x_1 + ah_1, \ldots, x_n + ah_n))'$$

$$= h_1\frac{\partial f}{\partial x_1}(\mathbf{x} + a\mathbf{h}) + \cdots + h_n\frac{\partial f}{\partial x_n}(\mathbf{x} + a\mathbf{h})$$

$$= ((\mathbf{h}'\nabla)f)(\mathbf{x} + a\mathbf{h}).$$

It follows immediately that

$$g^{(m)}(a) = ((\mathbf{h}'\nabla)^m f)(\mathbf{x} + a\mathbf{h})$$

for $m \in \mathbb{N}$, so by equality (10.3) there exists $\theta \in (0, 1)$ such that

$$f(\mathbf{x} + \mathbf{h}) = \sum_{m=0}^{n-1} \frac{1}{m!}((\mathbf{h}'\nabla)^m f)(\mathbf{x}) + \frac{1}{n!}((\mathbf{h}'\nabla)^n f)(\mathbf{x} + \theta\mathbf{h}). \qquad \square$$

The equality proven in Theorem 10.19 can be written as:

$$f(\mathbf{x} + \mathbf{h}) = \sum_{m=0}^{n} \frac{1}{m!}((\mathbf{h}'\nabla)^m f)(\mathbf{x})$$

$$+ \frac{1}{n!}(((\mathbf{h}'\nabla)^n f)(\mathbf{x} + \theta\mathbf{h}) - ((\mathbf{h}'\nabla)^n f)(\mathbf{x}))$$

$$= \sum_{m=0}^{n} \frac{1}{m!}((\mathbf{h}'\nabla)^m f)(\mathbf{x}) + R_n(\mathbf{x}, \mathbf{h}),$$

where $R_n(\mathbf{x}, \mathbf{h})$, the *remainder of order* n is defined by

$$R_n(\mathbf{x}, \mathbf{h}) = \frac{1}{n!}(((\mathbf{h}'\nabla)^n f)(\mathbf{x} + \theta\mathbf{h}) - ((\mathbf{h}'\nabla)^n f)(\mathbf{x})).$$

Let $f \in C^n(B(\mathbf{x}, r))$. We show that the remainder R_n can be written as

$$R_n(\mathbf{x}, \mathbf{h}) = \frac{1}{n!}\|\mathbf{h}\|^n \omega(\mathbf{x}, \mathbf{h}),$$

where $\lim_{\mathbf{h} \to \mathbf{0}_k} \omega(\mathbf{x}, \mathbf{h}) = 0$.

The coefficient of $h_{i_1}^{p_1} \cdots h_{i_k}^{p_k}$ in $(\mathbf{h}'\nabla)^n$ is

$$\frac{n!}{p_1! \cdots p_k!} \frac{\partial^n}{\partial x_1^{p_1} \cdots \partial x_k^{p_k}}.$$

Since the partial derivatives are continuous, it follows that

$$\lim_{\mathbf{h} \to \mathbf{0}} \frac{\partial^n}{\partial x_1^{p_1} \cdots \partial x_k^{p_k}} f(\mathbf{x} + \theta\mathbf{h}) = \frac{\partial^n}{\partial x_1^{p_1} \cdots \partial x_k^{p_k}} f(\mathbf{x}).$$

Define

$$\omega_{p_1 \cdots p_k}(\mathbf{x}, \mathbf{h})$$

$$= \frac{n!}{p_1! \cdots p_k!} \left(\frac{\partial^n}{\partial x_1^{p_1} \cdots \partial x_k^{p_k}} f(\mathbf{x} + \theta\mathbf{h}) - \frac{\partial^n}{\partial x_1^{p_1} \cdots \partial x_k^{p_k}} f(\mathbf{x}) \right),$$

where $\lim_{\mathbf{h} \to \mathbf{0}} \omega_{p_1 \cdots p_k} f(\mathbf{x}, \mathbf{h}) = 0$. Also, let

$$\omega(\mathbf{x}, \mathbf{h}) = \frac{1}{\|\mathbf{h}\|^n} \sum_{(p_1, \ldots, p_k)} \omega_{p_1, \ldots, p_k}(\mathbf{x}, \mathbf{h}) h_1^{p_1} \cdots h_k^{p_k}.$$

These notations allow us to write:

$$R_n(\mathbf{x}, \mathbf{h}) = \frac{1}{n!}(((\mathbf{h}'\nabla)^n f)(\mathbf{x} + \theta\mathbf{h}) - ((\mathbf{h}'\nabla)^n f)(\mathbf{x}))$$

$$= \frac{1}{n!} \sum_{(p_1,\ldots,p_k)} h_1^{p_1} \cdots h_k^{p_k} \omega_{p_1 \cdots p_k}(\mathbf{x}, \mathbf{h})$$

$$= \frac{\|\mathbf{h}\|^n}{n!} \omega(\mathbf{x}, \mathbf{h}).$$

Example 10.19. For the real-valued function $f \in C^2(B(\mathbf{x}, r))$, Theorem 10.19 implies the existence of $\theta \in (0, 1)$ such that

$$f(\mathbf{x} + \mathbf{h}) = f(\mathbf{x}) + ((\mathbf{h}'\nabla)f)(\mathbf{x}) + ((\mathbf{h}'\nabla)^2 f)(\mathbf{x}) + \frac{\|\mathbf{h}\|^2}{2}\omega(\mathbf{x}, \mathbf{h}),$$

where $\lim_{\mathbf{h} \to \mathbf{0}_k} \omega(\mathbf{x}, \mathbf{h}) = 0$.

The matrix-valued function $H_f : \mathbb{R}^k \longrightarrow \mathbb{R}^{k \times k}$ defined by

$$H_f(\mathbf{x}) = \left(\frac{\partial^2 f}{\partial x_{i_1} \partial x_{i_2}} \right)$$

is the *Hessian*[2] *matrix* of f.

Example 10.20. Let $f : \mathbb{R}^2 \longrightarrow \mathbb{R}$ be the function defined by

$$f(\mathbf{x}) = \frac{1}{x_1^2 + x_2^2 - 1}.$$

The Taylor formula for $n = 2$ and $\mathbf{x} = \mathbf{0}_2$ is

$$f(\mathbf{h}) = f(\mathbf{0}_2) + ((\mathbf{h}'\nabla)f)(\mathbf{0}_2) + \frac{1}{2}((\mathbf{h}'\nabla)^2 f)(\theta\mathbf{h}).$$

The partial derivatives of f are:

$$\frac{\partial f}{\partial x_1} = -\frac{2x_1}{(x_1^2 + x_2^2 - 1)^2} \quad \text{and} \quad \frac{\partial f}{\partial x_2} = -\frac{2x_2}{(x_1^2 + x_2^2 - 1)^2}.$$

The second order derivatives are

$$\frac{\partial^2 f}{\partial x_1^2} = \frac{2(3x_1^2 - x_2^2 + 1)}{(x_1^2 + x_2^2 - 1)^3}$$

$$\frac{\partial^2 f}{\partial x_1 \partial x_2} = \frac{\partial^2 f}{\partial x_2 \partial x_1} = \frac{8x_1 x_2}{(x_1^2 + x_2^2 - 1)^3}$$

$$\frac{\partial^2 f}{\partial x_2^2} = \frac{2(3x_2^2 - x_1^2 + 1)}{(x_1^2 + x_2^2 - 1)^3}.$$

---

[2]Ludwig Hesse was born on April 22nd 1811 in Königsberg, Prussia (today Kaliningrad), and died on August 4th 1876 in Munich. He worked mainly on algebraic invariants, and geometry, and taught in several unversities in Königsberg, Halle, Heidelberg and Munich. The Hessian matrix is named after him.

Taking into account that $f(\mathbf{0}_2) = -1$, the Taylor formula can be written:

$$f(\mathbf{h}) = -1 + \left(h_1^2 \frac{\partial^2 f}{\partial x_1^2} + 2h_1 h_2 \frac{\partial^2 f}{\partial x_1 \, \partial x_2} + h_2^2 \frac{\partial^2 f}{\partial x_2^2} \right) \begin{pmatrix} \theta_1 h_1 \\ \theta_2 h_1 \end{pmatrix}$$

$$= -1 + h_1^2 \frac{2(3\theta^2 h_1^2 - \theta^2 h_2^2 + 1)}{(\theta^2 h_1^2 + \theta^2 h_2^2 - 1)^3}$$

$$+ 2h_1 h_2 \frac{8\theta^2 h_1 h_2}{(\theta^2 h_1^2 + \theta h_2^2 - 1)^3} + h_2^2 \frac{2(3\theta^2 h_2^2 - \theta^2 h_1^2 + 1)}{(\theta^2 h_1^2 + \theta^2 h_2^2 - 1)^3}.$$

Definition 10.6. Let $f : U \longrightarrow \mathbb{R}$, where $U \subseteq \mathbb{R}^k$. A point $\mathbf{x}_0 \in U$ is a *local minimum* for f if there exists $V \in neigh_{\mathbf{x}_0}(\mathcal{O})$ such that $f(\mathbf{x}) \geqslant f(\mathbf{x}_0)$ for every $\mathbf{x} \in V$.

A point $\mathbf{x}_0 \in U$ is a *local maximum* for f if there exists $V \in neigh_{\mathbf{x}_0}(\mathcal{O})$ such that $f(\mathbf{x}) \leqslant f(\mathbf{x}_0)$ for every $\mathbf{x} \in V$.

A point is a *local extremum* for f if it either a local minimum or a local maximum for f.

Theorem 10.20. *Let* $f : U \longrightarrow \mathbb{R}$, *where* $U \subseteq \mathbb{R}^k$ *is an open set and* $f \in C^1(U)$. *If* $\mathbf{x}_0 \in U$ *is a local extremum, then* $(Df)(\mathbf{x}_0) = \mathbf{0}_k$.

Proof. Suppose that $\mathbf{x}_0$ is a local maximum for f. Then, for any $\mathbf{h} \in \mathbb{R}^k$, the function $g : \mathbb{R} \longrightarrow \mathbb{R}$ defined by $g(t) = f(\mathbf{x}_0 + t\mathbf{h})$ has a local minimum at $t = 0$. Thus, $g'(0) = 0$. By the Chain Rule, $g'(0) = (Df)(\mathbf{x}_0)'\mathbf{h}$ for every $\mathbf{h}$, hence $(Df)(\mathbf{x}_0) = \mathbf{0}_k$. The argument for the case is a local minimum is similar. $\square$

In other words, if $\mathbf{x}_0$ is a local extremum of f, we have $(\nabla f)(\mathbf{x}_0) = \mathbf{0}_k$.

Definition 10.7. Let $f : B(\mathbf{x}, r) \longrightarrow \mathbb{R}$ be a function that belongs to the class $C^n(B(\mathbf{x}, r))$, where $B(\mathbf{x}, r) \subseteq \mathbb{R}^k$ and $n \geqslant 1$. A point $\mathbf{x}_0$ is a *critical point*, or a *stationary point* if $(D_{\mathbf{x}}f)(\mathbf{x}_0) = \mathbf{0}_k$.

The converse of Theorem 10.20 is false, that is, we may have $(Df)(\mathbf{x}_0) = \mathbf{0}_k$ without $\mathbf{x}_0$ being an extreme point. If $\mathbf{x}_0$ is a critical point of f but not a local extremum we say that $\mathbf{x}_0$ is a *saddle point* for f.

Example 10.21. Consider the function $f : \mathbb{R}^2 \longrightarrow \mathbb{R}$ defined by $f(\mathbf{x}) = x_1^2 - 2x_1 x_2 + x_2^2$. We have

$$(\nabla f)(\mathbf{x}) = \begin{pmatrix} 2(x_1 - x_2) \\ 2(x_2 - x_1) \end{pmatrix} = 2(x_1 - x_2) \begin{pmatrix} 1 \\ -1 \end{pmatrix}.$$

The critical points are located on the first bisecting line $x_1 - x_2 = 0$ and they are clearly local minima for f.

Example 10.22. Let $f : \mathbb{R}^2 \longrightarrow \mathbb{R}$ be defined by $f(\mathbf{x}) = x_1^2 - x_2^2 + 2x_1 x_2$. We have

$$(\nabla f)(\mathbf{x}) = \begin{pmatrix} 2(x_1 + x_2) \\ 2(x_1 - x_2) \end{pmatrix}.$$

This function has a unique critical point, namely $\mathbf{0}_2$, which is a saddle point because $f(\mathbf{0}_2) = 0$ and the function takes both positive and negative values in a neighborhood of $\mathbf{0}_2$.

Next we discuss a sufficient condition for the existence of a local extremum for a function using the Hessian matrix.

Theorem 10.21. *Let U be an open subset of $\mathbb{R}^k$, $f : U \longrightarrow \mathbb{R}$ be a function in $C^2(U)$. Then f is convex on U if and only if the Hessian matrix $H_f(\mathbf{x})$ is positive on U; if $H_f(\mathbf{x})$ is negative on U, then f is concave on U.*

Proof. By Theorem 12.19, f is convex if and only if the function $\phi_{\mathbf{x},\mathbf{h}} : \mathbb{R} \longrightarrow \mathbb{R}$ given by $\phi_{\mathbf{x},\mathbf{h}}(t) = f(\mathbf{x} + t\mathbf{h})$ is convex, which happens only if $\phi''_{\mathbf{x},\mathbf{h}}(t) \geqslant 0$. Note that by the Chain Rule we have

$$\phi'_{\mathbf{x},\mathbf{h}}(t) = \sum_{i=1}^{n} \frac{\partial f}{\partial x_i}(\mathbf{x} + t\mathbf{h})h_i,$$

$$\phi''_{\mathbf{x},\mathbf{h}}(t) = \left(\sum_{i=1}^{n} \frac{\partial f}{\partial x_i}(\mathbf{x} + t\mathbf{h})h_i \right)$$

$$= \sum_{j=1}^{n} \sum_{i=1}^{n} \frac{\partial^2 f}{\partial x_i \, \partial x_j}(\mathbf{x} + t\mathbf{h})h_j h_i$$

$$= \sum_{j=1}^{n} \sum_{i=1}^{n} h_j \frac{\partial^2 f}{\partial x_i \, \partial x_j}(\mathbf{x} + t\mathbf{h})h_i$$

$$= \mathbf{h}' H_f(\mathbf{x} + t\mathbf{h})\mathbf{h}.$$

If $H_f(\mathbf{x} + t\mathbf{h})$ is positive, then every $\phi''_{\mathbf{x},\mathbf{h}}(t) \geqslant 0$, hence every $\phi''_{\mathbf{x},\mathbf{h}}(t)$ is convex, which means that f is convex.

Conversely, suppose that f is convex on U. Let $\mathbf{x} \in U$ and let $\mathbf{h}$ be an arbitrary vector. Since U is open, there exists $t_0 > 0$ such that $\mathbf{x} + t_0 \mathbf{h} \in U$. Since f is convex, $\phi_{\mathbf{x},t_0\mathbf{h}}$ is convex and $\phi''_{\mathbf{x},t_0\mathbf{h}}(0) \geqslant 0$. Therefore,

$$0 \leqslant \phi''_{\mathbf{x},t_0\mathbf{h}}(0) = t_0^2 \mathbf{h}' H_f(\mathbf{x})\mathbf{h},$$

hence $\mathbf{h}' H_f(\mathbf{x})\mathbf{h} \geqslant 0$. Therefore, $H_f(\mathbf{x})$ is positive.

The argument for concave functions is similar. $\qquad\square$

Theorem 10.22. *Let U be an open subset of $\mathbb{R}^k$, $f : U \longrightarrow \mathbb{R}$ be a function in $C^2(U)$, and let $\boldsymbol{x}_0$ be a critical point of f. If the Hessian $H_f(\boldsymbol{x}_0)$ is positive definite, then $\boldsymbol{x}_0$ is a local minimum of f. If $H_f(\boldsymbol{x}_0)$ is negative definite, then $\boldsymbol{x}_0$ is a local maximum of f.*

Proof. This follows immediately from Theorem 10.21. $\square$

10.4 The Inverse Function Theorem in $\mathbb{R}^n$

The inverse function theorem for functions of the form $\mathbf{f} : U \longrightarrow \mathbb{R}^n$, where U is an open subset of $\mathbb{R}^n$, has a local character; in other words, it states that under certain conditions, a function can be inverted in the neighborhood of a point $\mathbf{x}_0 \in U$.

Example 10.23. Let $\mathbf{f} : \mathbb{R}^2 \longrightarrow \mathbb{R}^2$ be the function defined by

$$\mathbf{f}(\mathbf{x}) = \begin{pmatrix} e^{x_1} \cos x_2 \\ e^{x_1} \sin x_2 \end{pmatrix}.$$

Since $\mathbf{f}$ is a periodic function in its second argument, it is clear that $\mathbf{f}$ is not injective. However, as we shall see we can invert $\mathbf{f}$ in the neighborhood of a point $\mathbf{x}_0$.

Lemma 10.4. *Let $\boldsymbol{f} : \mathbb{R}^n \longrightarrow \mathbb{R}^n$ be a continuously differentiable function on $B(\boldsymbol{x}_0, r)$ such that $(D\boldsymbol{f})(\boldsymbol{x})$ is invertible when $\boldsymbol{x} \in B(\boldsymbol{x}_0, r)$. There exists s such that $0 < s \leqslant r$ such that $\boldsymbol{f}$ is injective in $B(\boldsymbol{x}_0, s)$.*

Proof. Let $\gamma_{\mathbf{y}} : B(\mathbf{x}_0, r) \longrightarrow \mathbb{R}^n$ be the function defined by

$$\gamma_{\mathbf{y}}(\mathbf{x}) = \mathbf{x} + ((D\mathbf{f})(\mathbf{x}_0))^{-1}(\mathbf{y} - \mathbf{f}(\mathbf{x})).$$

Note that $g_{\mathbf{y}}(\mathbf{x}) = \mathbf{x}$ is equivalent to $\mathbf{y} = \mathbf{f}(\mathbf{x})$. Also,

$$(D\gamma_{\mathbf{y}})(\mathbf{x}) = I_n - ((D\mathbf{f})(\mathbf{x}_0))^{-1}(D\mathbf{f})(\mathbf{x}) = ((D\mathbf{f})(\mathbf{x}_0))^{-1}((D\mathbf{f})(\mathbf{x}_0) - (D\mathbf{f})(\mathbf{x})).$$

Since $(D\mathbf{f})(\mathbf{x})$ is continuous at $\mathbf{x}_0$, there exists a positive number s such that if $\mathbf{x} \in B(\mathbf{x}_0, s)$, $(D\mathbf{f})(\mathbf{x})$ is invertible and

$$\|(D\gamma_{\mathbf{y}})(\mathbf{x})\| \leqslant \|((D\mathbf{f})(\mathbf{x}_0))^{-1}\| \cdot \|(D\mathbf{f})(\mathbf{x}_0) - (D\mathbf{f})(\mathbf{x})\| \leqslant \frac{1}{2}.$$

Therefore, for $\mathbf{x}_1, \mathbf{x}_2 \in B(\mathbf{x}_0, s)$ we have

$$\|\gamma_{\mathbf{y}}(\mathbf{x}_1) - \gamma_{\mathbf{y}}(\mathbf{x}_2)\| \leqslant \|\mathbf{x}_1 - \mathbf{x}_2\|, \tag{10.4}$$

for any $\mathbf{y} \in \mathbb{R}^n$. This implies that the equation $\gamma_{\mathbf{y}}(\mathbf{x}) = \mathbf{x}$ has at most one solution in $B(\mathbf{x}_0, s)$, so $\mathbf{f}$ is injective in $B(\mathbf{x}_0, s)$. $\square$

The next lemma incorporates the results and notations of Lemma 10.4.

Lemma 10.5. *Let $\boldsymbol{f} \colon \mathbb{R}^n \longrightarrow \mathbb{R}^n$ be a continuously differentiable function on $B(\boldsymbol{x}_0, r)$ such that $(D\boldsymbol{f})(\boldsymbol{x})$ is invertible when $\boldsymbol{x} \in B(\boldsymbol{x}_0, r)$. The set $\boldsymbol{f}(B(\boldsymbol{x}_0, s))$ is open, where $B(\boldsymbol{x}_0, s)$ is an open sphere centered in $\boldsymbol{x}_0$ such that $\boldsymbol{f}$ is injective in $B(\boldsymbol{x}_0, s)$.*

Proof. Let $V = \mathbf{f}(B(\mathbf{x}_0, s))$ and let $\mathbf{y}_1 \in V$. There exists $\mathbf{x}_1 \in B(\mathbf{x}_0, s)$ such that $\mathbf{y}_1 = \mathbf{f}(\mathbf{x}_1)$. Choose t such that the spherical surface $S(\mathbf{x}_1, t)$ is contained in $B(\mathbf{x}_0, s)$ and let $\ell \colon S(\mathbf{x}_1, t) \longrightarrow \mathbb{R}$ given by $\ell(\mathbf{x}) = \|\mathbf{f}(\mathbf{x}) - \mathbf{y}_1\|$. The injectivity of $\mathbf{f}$ established in Lemma 10.4 implies that $\ell(\mathbf{x})$ is never 0 on $S(\mathbf{x}_1, t)$. Since ℓ is continuous, the minimum value m on $S(\mathbf{x}_1, t)$ is positive. Then, for $\|\mathbf{y} - \mathbf{y}_1\| < \frac{m}{3}$, we have

$$\|\mathbf{f}(\mathbf{x}) - \mathbf{y}\| \geqslant \|\mathbf{f}(\mathbf{x}) - \mathbf{y}_1\| - \|\mathbf{y} - \mathbf{y}_1\| \geqslant \frac{2}{3}m.$$

Define the function $h \colon B[\mathbf{x}_1, t] \longrightarrow \mathbb{R}$ as $h(\mathbf{x}) = \|\mathbf{f}(\mathbf{x}) - \mathbf{y}\|^2$. Since $h(\mathbf{x}_1) = \|\mathbf{y} - \mathbf{y}_1\|^2 < \frac{m^2}{9}$ and $h(\mathbf{x}) \geqslant \frac{4}{9}m^2$ on the boundary $S(\mathbf{x}_1, t)$ of the closed sphere $B[\mathbf{x}_1, t]$. Therefore, h must assume its minimum value on the closed sphere at an interior point $\mathbf{z}$, where $\nabla h = 0$. This implies

$$0 = \frac{\partial h}{\partial x_j}(\mathbf{z}) = 2 \sum_{k=1}^{n} \frac{\partial f_k}{\partial x_j}(f_k(\mathbf{z}) - y_k)$$

for $1 \leqslant j \leqslant n$, hence $(D\mathbf{f})(\mathbf{z})'(\mathbf{f}(\mathbf{z}) - \mathbf{y}) = 0$. If $\mathbf{f}(\mathbf{z}) \neq \mathbf{y}$, this implies that $(D\mathbf{f})(\mathbf{z})'$ is not invertible, so $(D\mathbf{f})(\mathbf{z})$ is not invertible. Therefore, $\mathbf{f}(\mathbf{z}) = \mathbf{y}$. Thus, $B(\mathbf{y}_1, m/3) \subseteq V$, which means that V is open. $\qquad \square$

Theorem 10.23. (The Inverse Function Theorem) *Let $\boldsymbol{f} \colon \mathbb{R}^n \longrightarrow \mathbb{R}^n$ be a continuously differentiable function on $B(\boldsymbol{x}_0, r)$ such that $(D\boldsymbol{f})(\boldsymbol{x})$ is invertible when $\boldsymbol{x} \in B(\boldsymbol{x}_0, r)$. If V is the open set whose existence is established by Lemma 10.5, taking into account that $\boldsymbol{f}$ is injective on $B(\boldsymbol{x}_0, s)$, and that $V = \boldsymbol{f}(B(\boldsymbol{x}_0, s))$, there exists a local inverse $\boldsymbol{g} \colon V \longrightarrow \mathbb{R}^n$ at $\boldsymbol{y}_0 = \boldsymbol{f}(\boldsymbol{x}_0)$ such that $\boldsymbol{g}$ is continuously differentiable at $\boldsymbol{y}$, where $\boldsymbol{g}(\boldsymbol{y}) \in B(\boldsymbol{x}_0, s)$, and $\boldsymbol{f}(\boldsymbol{g}(\boldsymbol{y})) = \boldsymbol{y}$. Then, $\boldsymbol{g}$ is continuously differentiable at $\boldsymbol{y}_0$.*

Proof. We begin by proving that $\mathbf{g}$ is differentiable at any point in $\mathbf{y} \in V$. Let $\mathbf{y} \in V$ such that $\mathbf{y} + \mathbf{k} \in V$, where $\|\mathbf{k}\|$ is sufficiently small. There is a unique $\mathbf{x}$ and a unique $\mathbf{h}$ such that $\mathbf{x} \in B(\mathbf{x}_0, s)$, $\mathbf{x} + \mathbf{h} \in B(\mathbf{x}_0, s)$, $\mathbf{f}(\mathbf{x}) = \mathbf{y}$, and $\mathbf{f}(\mathbf{x} + \mathbf{h}) = \mathbf{y} + \mathbf{k}$.

Let $\mathbf{H} = ((D\mathbf{f})(\mathbf{g}(\mathbf{y})))^{-1}$. This inverse exists because $\mathbf{g}(\mathbf{y}) = \mathbf{x} \in B(\mathbf{x}_0, s)$. We have

$$\mathbf{g}(\mathbf{y} + \mathbf{k}) - \mathbf{g}(\mathbf{y}) - H\mathbf{k} = \mathbf{x} + \mathbf{h} - \mathbf{x} - H(\mathbf{f}(\mathbf{x} + \mathbf{h}) - \mathbf{f}(\mathbf{x}))$$
$$= -H(\mathbf{f}(\mathbf{x} + \mathbf{h}) - \mathbf{f}(\mathbf{x}) - (D\mathbf{f})(\mathbf{x})\mathbf{h}).$$

Since $\mathbf{f}$ is differentiable at $\mathbf{x}$, we have

$$\|\mathbf{g}(\mathbf{y} + \mathbf{k}) - g(\mathbf{y}) - H\mathbf{k}\| \leqslant o(\mathbf{h})\|\mathbf{h}\|.$$

By the definition of $\gamma_{\mathbf{y}}$ we have

$$\gamma_{\mathbf{y}}(\mathbf{x} + \mathbf{h}) - \gamma_{\mathbf{y}}(\mathbf{x}) = h - ((D\mathbf{f})(\mathbf{x}_0))^{-1}\mathbf{k}.$$

Taking into account equality (10.4), we have $\|\mathbf{h} - ((D\mathbf{f})(\mathbf{x}_0))^{-1}\mathbf{k}\| \leqslant \frac{1}{2}\mathbf{h}$. By the triangular inequality,

$$\frac{1}{2}\|\mathbf{k}\| \leqslant \|((D\mathbf{f})(\mathbf{x}_0))^{-1}\mathbf{k}\|,$$

hence $\mathbf{h} \leqslant 2\|((D\mathbf{f})(\mathbf{x}_0))^{-1}\| \cdot \|\mathbf{k}\|$. Thus, $\|\mathbf{h}\| \leqslant c\|\mathbf{k}\|$, for some constant c, which shows that $\mathbf{g}$ is differentiable at all point in V and, therefore, is continuous in V. Moreover, $(D\mathbf{g})(\mathbf{y}) = ((D\mathbf{f})(\mathbf{g}(\mathbf{y})))^{-1}$, hence $\mathbf{g}$ is continuously differentiable. $\qquad\square$

Note that the Jacobian matrix of $\mathbf{g}$ at $\mathbf{y}_0 = \mathbf{f}(\mathbf{x}_0)$ is

$$(D\mathbf{g})(\mathbf{y}_0) = ((D\mathbf{f})(\mathbf{f}^{-1}(\mathbf{y}_0))^{-1}.$$

Example 10.24. The Jacobian determinant of the function $\mathbf{f}$ introduced in Example 10.23 is

$$\det((D\mathbf{f})(\mathbf{x})) = \begin{vmatrix} e^{x_1}\cos x_2 & -e^{x_1}\sin x_2 \\ e^{x_1}\sin x_2 & e^{x_1}\cos x_2 \end{vmatrix} = e^{2x_1} \neq 0,$$

so $\mathbf{f}$ has an inverse in a neighborhood of any point of $\mathbb{R}^2$.

Lemma 10.6. *Let U be an open set in $\mathbb{R}^n$ and let $\boldsymbol{h}$ be a continuously differentiable function. If K is a closed interval included in U, $\left|\frac{\partial f_i}{\partial x_j}(\boldsymbol{u}) - \frac{\partial f_i}{\partial x_j}(\boldsymbol{v})\right| \leqslant a$ for $\boldsymbol{u}, \boldsymbol{v} \in K$ and $1 \leqslant i, j \leqslant n$, then*

$$\|\boldsymbol{h}(\boldsymbol{u}) - \boldsymbol{h}(\boldsymbol{v}) - (D\boldsymbol{h})(\boldsymbol{u} - \boldsymbol{v})\| \leqslant an^2\|\boldsymbol{u} - \boldsymbol{v}\|.$$

Proof. Define a sequence of vectors $\mathbf{z}^{(0)}, \ldots, \mathbf{z}^{(k)}$ in $\mathbb{R}^k$ such that $\mathbf{z}^{(j)}$ coincides with $\mathbf{u}$ on its first j components and with $\mathbf{v}$ on the last $k - j$ components. Thus, $\mathbf{z}^{(0)} = \mathbf{v}$ and $\mathbf{z}^{(k)} = \mathbf{u}$, and $\|\mathbf{z}^{(j)} - \mathbf{z}^{(j-1)}\| = |v_j - u_j|$. By the Mean Value Theorem, there exists $\mathbf{w}^{(ij)}$ in $[\mathbf{z}^{(j-1)}, \mathbf{z}^{(j)}]$ such that

$$f_i(\mathbf{z}^{(j)}) - f_i(\mathbf{z}^{(j-1)}) = \frac{\partial f_i}{\partial x_j}(\mathbf{w}^{(ij)})(\mathbf{z}^{(j)} - \mathbf{z}^{(j-1)})_j.$$

Since $(D\mathbf{h})(\mathbf{z}^{(j)} - \mathbf{z}^{(j-1)}))_i = \sum_\ell \frac{\partial f_i}{\partial x_\ell}(\mathbf{z}^{(j)} - \mathbf{z}^{(j-1)})_\ell = \frac{\partial f_i}{\partial x_j}(\mathbf{z}^{(j)} - \mathbf{z}^{(j-1)})_j,$
it follows that

$$\|\mathbf{h}(\mathbf{u}) - \mathbf{h}(\mathbf{v}) - (D\mathbf{h})(\mathbf{u} - \mathbf{v})\|$$
$$= \sum_{ij} |f_i(\mathbf{z}^{(j)}) - f_i(\mathbf{z}^{(j-1)}) - ((D\mathbf{h})(\mathbf{z}^{(j)} - \mathbf{z}^{(j-1)}))_i|$$
$$= \sum_{ij} \left| \frac{\partial f_i}{\partial x_j}(\mathbf{w}^{(ij)}) - \frac{\partial f_i}{\partial x_j}(\mathbf{x}) \right| \cdot |(\mathbf{z}^{(j)} - \mathbf{z}^{(j-1)})_j|$$
$$\leqslant \sum_{ij} a|u_j - v_j| \leqslant an^2 \|\mathbf{u} - \mathbf{v}\|.$$
$$\qquad\qquad\qquad\qquad\qquad\qquad\qquad\qquad\qquad\qquad\qquad \square$$

Lemma 10.7. *Let $G = (a_1, b_1] \times (a_n, b_n]$ be an open-closed interval in $\mathbb{R}^n$, $\mathbf{h}: G \longrightarrow \mathbb{R}^n$ be an injective, continuously differentiable Borel measurable function and let $V = \mathbf{h}(G)$. We have:*

$$m_L(\mathbf{h}(G)) = \int_{\mathbf{h}(G)} dm_L = \int_G |J(\mathbf{h})| \, dm_L.$$

Proof. Partition G into finitely many open-closed sub-intervals G_i such that $diam(G_i) < \delta$. For $\epsilon > 0$ choose δ such that for all $\mathbf{u}, \mathbf{v} \in \mathbf{K}(G)$, $\|\mathbf{u} - \mathbf{v}\| < \epsilon$ implies $\|J(\mathbf{h})(\mathbf{u}) - J(\mathbf{h})(\mathbf{v})\| < \epsilon$.

Since $diam(G_i) < \delta$, for $\mathbf{x}_i \in G_i$ we have:

$$\sum_i |J(\mathbf{h})(\mathbf{x}_i)| m_L(G_i) \leqslant \int_G |J(\mathbf{h})(\mathbf{x})| \, dm + \epsilon m_L(G).$$

If $G_i = (a_1^i, b_1^i] \times \cdots \times (a_n^i, b_n^i]$, define

$$G_i^\epsilon = \left(a_1^i - \frac{\epsilon}{2}, b_1^i + \frac{\epsilon}{2} \right] \times \cdots \times \left(a_n^i - \frac{\epsilon}{2}, b_n^i + \frac{\epsilon}{2} \right].$$

For $\mathbf{x} \in G$ define the affine transformation $\phi_\mathbf{x}$ as

$$\phi_\mathbf{x}(\mathbf{z}) = (D\mathbf{h})(\mathbf{z} - \mathbf{x}) + \mathbf{f}(\mathbf{x}),$$

which approximates $\mathbf{f}(\mathbf{z})$ when $\mathbf{z}$ is close to $\mathbf{x}$.

The set $\mathbf{K}(G) \times \{\mathbf{z} \in \mathbb{R}^n \mid \|\mathbf{z}\| = 1\}$ is a compact subset of $\mathbb{R}^n \times \mathbb{R}^n$. Therefore, for some c we have $\|(D\mathbf{h})^{-1}\mathbf{z}\| \leqslant c\|\mathbf{z}\|$ for $\mathbf{x} \in G$ and $\mathbf{z} \in \mathbb{R}^n$. Since the partial derivatives $\frac{\partial h}{\partial x_i}$ are uniformly continuous on $\mathbf{K}(G)$, we can choose δ such that $\|\mathbf{z} - \mathbf{x}\| < \delta$ implies $\left| \frac{\partial f_i}{\partial x_j}(\mathbf{z}) - \frac{\partial f_i}{\partial x_j}(\mathbf{x}) \right| \leqslant \frac{\epsilon}{an^2}$. By Lemma 10.6, $\left| \frac{\partial f_i}{\partial x_j}(\mathbf{z}) - \frac{\partial f_i}{\partial x_j}(\mathbf{x}) \right| \leqslant \frac{\epsilon\delta}{a}$. Since $diam(G_i) < \delta$, it follows that for $\delta < 1$ we have

$$\|\mathbf{h}(\mathbf{z}) - \phi_{\mathbf{x}_i}(\mathbf{z})\| < \frac{\epsilon}{a}$$

for $\mathbf{z} \in Q_i$. Note that $\mathbf{z} \in Q_i$ implies

$$
\begin{aligned}
\|\phi_{\mathbf{x}_i}^{-1}(\mathbf{h}(\mathbf{z})) - \mathbf{z}\| &= \|\phi_{\mathbf{x}_i}^{-1}(\mathbf{h}(\mathbf{z})) - \phi_{\mathbf{x}_i}^{-1}\phi_{\mathbf{x}_i}^{-1}\phi_{\mathbf{x}_i}(\mathbf{z})\| \\
&= \|((D\mathbf{h})(\mathbf{x}_i))^{-1}(\mathbf{h}(\mathbf{z}) - \phi_{\mathbf{x}_i}(\mathbf{z}))\| \\
&\leqslant a\|\mathbf{h}(\mathbf{z}) - \phi_{\mathbf{x}_i}(\mathbf{z})\| < \epsilon.
\end{aligned}
$$

Therefore, $\phi_{\mathbf{x}_i}^{-1}(\mathbf{h}(\mathbf{z})) \in G_i^\epsilon$. This is equivalent to $\mathbf{h}(\mathbf{z}) \in \phi_{\mathbf{x}_i}(G_i^\epsilon)$, so $\mathbf{h}(G_i) \subseteq \phi_{\mathbf{x}_i}(G_i^\epsilon)$.

By Theorem 7.54, $m_L(\phi_{\mathbf{x}_i}(G_i^\epsilon)) = |J(\mathbf{h})(\mathbf{x}_i)|m_L(G_i^\epsilon)$. Thus, we have for every $\epsilon > 0$:

$$
\begin{aligned}
m_L(\mathbf{h}(G)) &= \sum_i m_L(\mathbf{h}(G_i)) \leqslant \sum_i m_L(\phi_{\mathbf{x}_i}(G_i^\epsilon)) \\
&= \sum_i |J(\mathbf{h})(\mathbf{x}_i)|m_L(G_i^\epsilon) = (1+\epsilon)^n \sum_i |J(\mathbf{h})(\mathbf{x}_i)|m_L(G_i).
\end{aligned}
$$

This implies $m_L(\mathbf{h}(G)) \leqslant \int_G |J(\mathbf{h})(\mathbf{x})|\, dm$ $\qquad\square$

Theorem 10.24. *Let U be an open set in $\mathbb{R}^n$, $\mathbf{h}: U \longrightarrow \mathbb{R}^n$ be an injective, continuously differentiable Borel measurable function and let $V = \mathbf{h}(U)$. If $J(\mathbf{h}) = \det((D\mathbf{h})(\mathbf{x})) \neq 0$ for every $\mathbf{x} \in U$, then for a non-negative measurable function $\mathbf{f}: \mathbb{R}^n \longrightarrow \mathbb{R}^n$ we have:*

$$
\int_{\mathbf{h}(U)} \mathbf{f}\, dm_L = \int_U \mathbf{f}\mathbf{h}J(\mathbf{h})\, dm_L.
$$

Proof. By Lemma 10.7, the equality of the theorem is valid for open-closed intervals, $\mathbf{f} = 1_G$, and injective, continuously differentiable Borel measurable functions $\mathbf{h}$, where $V = \mathbf{h}(G)$.

Let $\mathcal{E}_U = U \cap \mathbb{B}(\mathbb{R}^n)$ and let $\mathcal{S}$ be the semi-ring of open-closed intervals included in U. Then, Theorem 7.9 implies that $\mathbf{K}_{\sigma\text{-alg}}(\mathcal{S}) = \mathcal{E}_U$. Therefore, U is a countable union of open-closed intervals and that the measure $\int_G |J(\mathbf{h})|\, dm_L$ is finite for $G \in \mathcal{S}$ (because $\sup_G |J| < \infty$). Thus, $\int_U |J(\mathbf{h})|\, dm_L \geqslant \int_{\mathbf{h}(U)} dm_L$. This implies, by linearity and monotone convergence:

$$
\int_{\mathbf{h}(U)} \mathbf{f}\, dm_L \leqslant \int_U \mathbf{f}\mathbf{h}J(\mathbf{h})\, dm_L. \tag{10.5}
$$

By the inverse function theorem, the mapping $\mathbf{h}$ is locally invertible and and a similar equality can be inferred for the mapping $\mathbf{h}^{-1}$, that is, for $V = \mathbf{h}(U)$ we have:

$$
\int_{\mathbf{h}^{-1}(V)} \mathbf{g}\, dm_L \leqslant \int_V \mathbf{g}\mathbf{h}^{-1}J(\mathbf{h}^{-1})\, dm_L,
$$

for any measurable non-negative measurable function $\mathbf{g} : \mathbb{R}^n \longrightarrow \mathbb{R}^n$. By substituting $\mathbf{f}(\mathbf{h}(\mathbf{x}))|J(\mathbf{h})(\mathbf{x})|$ for $\mathbf{g}$ in the last equality we have

$$\int_U \mathbf{fh}|J(\mathbf{h})| \, dm_L \leqslant \int_{\mathbf{h}(U)} \mathbf{fhh}^{-1} J(\mathbf{h}) J(\mathbf{h}^{-1}) \, dm_L,$$

we obtain:

$$\int_U \mathbf{fh}|J(\mathbf{h})| \, dm_L \leqslant \int_{\mathbf{h}(U)} \mathbf{f} \, dm_L. \tag{10.6}$$

Inequalities (10.5) and (10.6) yield the equality of the theorem. □

Example 10.25. Let $U = (0, \infty) \times (0, \pi) \times (0, 2\pi)$ be an open set and let $\mathbf{h} : U \longrightarrow \mathbb{R}^3$ be the function defined by

$$h_1(r, \theta, \phi) = r \sin \theta \cos \phi,$$
$$h_2(r, \theta, \phi) = r \sin \theta \sin \phi,$$
$$h_3(r, \theta, \phi) = r \cos \theta.$$

As we saw in Example 10.11 $J(\mathbf{h})(r, \theta, \phi) = r^2 \sin \theta$. Therefore, the formula for integrating in spheric coordinates is

$$\int_U \mathbf{f}(r \sin \theta \cos \phi, r \sin \theta \sin \phi, r \cos \theta) r^2 \sin \theta \, dm_L = \int_{\mathbb{R}^3} \mathbf{f}(x_1, x_2, x_3) \, dm_L.$$

Similarly, the formula for integration in polar coordinates is:

$$\int_U \mathbf{f}(r \cos \phi, r \sin \phi) r \, dm_L = \int_{\mathbb{R}^2} \mathbf{f}(x_1, x_2) \, dm_L,$$

where $U = (0, \infty) \times (0, 2\pi)$.

Let now $V = B(\mathbf{0}_2, a)$ be the two-dimensional open sphere of radius a. To compute $\int_{B(\mathbf{0}_2, r)} dm_L = \int_0^a \int_0^{2\pi} r \, dr \, d\theta$. we apply Fubini's Theorem and we have:

$$\int_0^a r \, dr \int_0^{2\pi} d\theta = \frac{1}{2} \frac{a^2}{2} \cdot 2\pi = \pi a^2.$$

10.5   Normal and Tangent Subspaces for Surfaces in $\mathbb{R}^n$

Let X be an open subset of $\mathbb{R}^n$ and let $h : X \longrightarrow \mathbb{R}$ be a function that is differentiable on X. The set $S_h = \{\mathbf{x} \in \mathbb{R}^n \mid h(\mathbf{x}) = 0\}$ is a *smooth surface* in $\mathbb{R}^n$.

The curve in $\mathbb{R}^n$ determined by a function $\mathbf{g} : [a, b] \longrightarrow \mathbb{R}^n$ is set $C_{\mathbf{g}} = \{\mathbf{x} \in \mathbb{R}^n \mid \mathbf{x} = g(t) \text{ for } t \in [a, b]\}$. The curve $C_{\mathbf{g}}$ is smooth is $\mathbf{g}$

is differentiable on $[a, b]$. $C_{\mathbf{g}}$ is *located on the surface* S_h if $h(\mathbf{g}(t)) = 0$ for $t \in [a, b]$.

Let $C_{\mathbf{g}}$ be a curve located on the surface S_h. Both the curve and the surface are assumed smooth. Differentiating the equality $h(\mathbf{g}(t)) = 0$ using the Chain Rule we obtain

$$(Dh)(\mathbf{g}(t))\frac{d\mathbf{g}}{dt}(t) = 0.$$

If $\mathbf{x}_0 = \mathbf{g}(t_0)$, where $t_0 \in [a, b]$, then $\frac{d\mathbf{g}}{dt}(t_0)$ is the tangent vector to the curve $C_{\mathbf{g}}$ in $\mathbf{x}_0 = \mathbf{g}(t_0)$. Thus,

$$(\nabla h)(\mathbf{x}_0)'\frac{d\mathbf{g}}{dt}(t_0) = 0,$$

which shows that any vector tangent in $\mathbf{x}_0$ to a curve $C_{\mathbf{g}}$ passing through $\mathbf{x}_0$ is orthogonal on $(\nabla h)(\mathbf{x}_0)$. Thus, it is natural to define the *tangent hyperplane to S_h in $\boldsymbol{x}_0$* by the equation

$$(\nabla h)(\mathbf{x}_0)'(\mathbf{x} - \mathbf{x}_0) = 0.$$

The vector $(\nabla h)(\mathbf{x}_0)$ is the *normal* to S_h in $\mathbf{x}_0$.

This example can be generalized by considering surfaces in $\mathbb{R}^n$ determined by differentiable functions of the form $\mathbf{h} : \mathbb{R}^n \longrightarrow \mathbb{R}^m$. The surface determined by $\mathbf{h}$ is the set $S_{\mathbf{h}} = \{\mathbf{x} \in \mathbb{R}^n \mid \mathbf{h}(\mathbf{x}) = \mathbf{0}_m\}$; again, we refer to $S_{\mathbf{h}}$ as the *smooth surface defined by $\mathbf{h}$*. Note that $S_{\mathbf{h}}$ is the intersection $\bigcap_{i=1}^{m} S_{h_i}$.

Definition 10.8. If $\mathbf{h} : X \longrightarrow \mathbb{R}^m$, $\mathbf{h} \in C^1(X)$ and $m \leqslant n$, then $\mathbf{x}_0$ is a *regular point* of $\mathbf{h}$ if the Jacobian matrix $(D\mathbf{h})(\mathbf{x}_0) \in \mathbb{R}^{m \times n}$ has rank m. In other words, $\mathbf{x}_0$ is a regular point of $\mathbf{h}$ if the vectors $(\nabla h_1)(\mathbf{x}_0), \ldots, (\nabla h_m)(\mathbf{x}_0)$ are linear independent.

A *critical point* of $\mathbf{h}$ is a point $\mathbf{x}_0 \in X$ such that $(D\mathbf{h})(\mathbf{x}_0)$ is the zero operator, that is, $\delta f(\mathbf{x}_0; \mathbf{h}) = 0$ for every $\mathbf{h} \in X$.

A curve $C_{\mathbf{g}}$ is located on the surface $S_{\mathbf{h}}$ if and only if it is located on every surface S_{h_i}. Therefore, a tangent $\frac{d\mathbf{g}}{dt}(t_0)$ to the curve $C_{\mathbf{g}}$ in a regular point $\mathbf{x}_0 \in S_{\mathbf{h}}$ must be orthogonal on every vector $(\nabla h_i)(\mathbf{x}_0)$. The subspace $N_{\mathbf{x}_0}$ generated by the vectors

$$(\nabla h_1)(\mathbf{x}_0), \ldots, (\nabla h_m)(\mathbf{x}_0)$$

is the *normal subspace* to $S_{\mathbf{b}}$ in $\mathbf{x}_0$; the orthogonal subspace $T_{\mathbf{x}_0} = (N_{\mathbf{x}_0})^{\perp}$ is the *tangent subspace* to $S_{\mathbf{h}}$ in $\mathbf{x}_0$. Equivalently, the tangent subspace of $S_{\mathbf{h}}$ at $\mathbf{x}_0$ is the null space $T(\mathbf{x}_0)$ of the linear transformation $(D\mathbf{h})(\mathbf{x}_0)$.

Definition 10.9. The *tangent r-plane of M* at $\mathbf{x}_0$ is $\{\mathbf{x}_0 + \mathbf{t} \mid \mathbf{t} \in T(\mathbf{x}_0)\} = \mathbf{t}_{\mathbf{x}_0}(T(\mathbf{x}_0))$.

Example 10.26. The spherical surface $S(\mathbf{0}_n, 1)$ in $\mathbb{R}^n$ is defined by a function $h : \mathbb{R}^n \longrightarrow \mathbb{R}$ given by $h(\mathbf{x}) = \sum_{i=1}^n x_i^2 - 1$. We have:

$$(Dh)(\mathbf{x}_0)(\mathbf{k}) = 2\mathbf{x}_0'\mathbf{k},$$

so $rank((Df)(\mathbf{x}_0)) = 1$ for every $\mathbf{x}_0 \in S(\mathbf{0}_n, 1)$. A normal vector to $S(\mathbf{0}_m, 1)$ in $\mathbf{x}_0$ is $2\mathbf{x}_0$.

Example 10.27. Let M be the subset of $\mathbb{R}^3$:

$$M = S(\mathbf{0}_3, 1) \cap \{\mathbf{x} \in \mathbb{R}^3 \mid x_1 + x_2 + x_3 = 0\}.$$

Define the function $\mathbf{h} : \mathbb{R}^3 \longrightarrow \mathbb{R}^2$ as

$$h_1(\mathbf{x}) = x_1^2 + x_2^2 + x_3^2 - 1,$$
$$h_2(\mathbf{x}) = x_1 + x_2 + x_3$$

for $\mathbf{x} \in \mathbb{R}^3$. Its Jacobian matrix is

$$(D\mathbf{h})(\mathbf{x}) = \begin{pmatrix} 2x_1 & 2x_2 & 2x_3 \\ 1 & 1 & 1 \end{pmatrix}.$$

For any $\mathbf{x} \in M$ we have $rank((D\mathbf{h})(\mathbf{x})) = 2$ and $M = \{\mathbf{x} \in \mathbb{R}^3 \mid \mathbf{h}(\mathbf{x}) = \mathbf{0}_2\}$. This time the normal subspace $N_{\mathbf{x}_0}$ is generated by the vectors $2\mathbf{x}_0$ and $\mathbf{1}_3$.

Example 10.28. Let $M = \{\mathbf{x} \in \mathbb{R}^2 \mid x_1 x_2 = 1,$ or $x_1 = 0$ and $x_2 \neq 0$, or $x_2 = 0$ and $x_1 \neq 0\}$. There are three cases to consider.

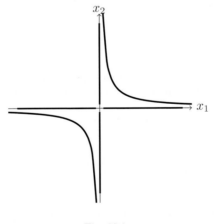

Fig. 10.1

(i) If $x_1 x_2 = 1$, define $h(\mathbf{x}) = x_1 x_2 - 1$; we have $(Dh)(\mathbf{x}) = (x_2, x_1)$ so in this case, $rank((Dh)(\mathbf{x})) = 1$.

(ii) If $x_1 = 0$ and $x_2 \neq 0$, let $h_1(\mathbf{x}) = x_1$, which implies $(Dh_1)(\mathbf{x}) = (1, 0)$, hence $rank((Dh_1)(\mathbf{x})) = 1$.

(iii) Finally, if $x_2 = 0$ and $x_1 \neq 0$, let $h_2(\mathbf{x}) = x_2$, so $(Dh_2)(\mathbf{x}) = (1, 0)$, hence $rank((Dh)(\mathbf{x})) = 1$.

Thus, in each case the normal subspace is unidimensional is an unidimensional manifold.

Exercises and Supplements

(1) Let $f : \mathbb{R}^n \longrightarrow \mathbb{R}$ be a functions such that $|f(x)| \leqslant \|\mathbf{x}\|^{1+a}$, where $a > 0$. Prove that f is Fréchet differentiable in $\mathbf{0}_n$.

(2) Let $f : \mathbb{R} \longrightarrow \mathbb{R}^2$ be the function given by $f(x) = \binom{x}{x^2}$. Is f Fréchet differentiable?

(3) Let $f : \mathbb{R}^2 \longrightarrow \mathbb{R}$ be defined by $f(\mathbf{x}) = x_1 + x_2$ for $\mathbf{x} \in \mathbb{R}^2$. Prove that the Gâteaux derivative of f is

$$(Df)(\mathbf{x}_0)(\mathbf{h}) = f(\mathbf{h})$$

for $\mathbf{h} \in \mathbb{R}^2$.

(4) Let $f : \mathbb{R}^2 \longrightarrow \mathbb{R}$ be defined by

$$f(\mathbf{x}) = \begin{cases} 1 & \text{if } x_1 + x_2 = 0 \text{ and } \mathbf{x} \neq \mathbf{0}_2, \\ 0 & \text{otherwise.} \end{cases}$$

Prove that the partial derivatives $\frac{\partial f}{\partial x_1}(\mathbf{0}_2)$ and $\frac{\partial f}{\partial x_2}(\mathbf{0}_2)$ exists. Find a direction $\mathbf{h}$ such that the directional derivative relative to $\mathbf{u}$ does not exist in $\mathbf{0}_2$.

Solution: We have $\frac{f(\mathbf{0}_2 + t\mathbf{h}) - f(\mathbf{0}_2)}{t} = \frac{f(t\mathbf{h})}{t}$. The definition of f implies

$$f(t\mathbf{h}) = \begin{cases} 1 & \text{if } t(h_1 + h_2) = 0 \text{ and } t\mathbf{h} \neq 0, \\ 0 & \text{otherwise.} \end{cases}$$

If $\mathbf{h}$ is a direction such that $h_1 + h_2 = 0$, the directional derivative with respect to $\mathbf{h}$ in $\mathbf{0}_2$ does not exist. This also imply that $\frac{\partial f}{\partial \mathbf{e}_1}(\mathbf{0}_2) = \frac{\partial f}{\partial x_1}(\mathbf{0}_2)$ and $\frac{\partial f}{\partial \mathbf{e}_1}(\mathbf{0}_2) = \frac{\partial f}{\partial x_1}(\mathbf{0}_2)$ exist.

(5) Let $f : \mathbb{R}^2 \longrightarrow \mathbb{R}$ be defined by

$$f(\mathbf{x}) = \begin{cases} x_1 & \text{if } x_1 = x_2, \\ 0 & \text{otherwise.} \end{cases}$$

Prove that this function has directional derivatives in all directions in $\mathbf{0}_2$ but is not Gâteaux differentiable at $\mathbf{0}_2$.

Solution: We have

$$\frac{f(t\mathbf{h})}{t} = \begin{cases} h_1 & \text{if } h_1 = h_2, \\ 0 & \text{otherwise.} \end{cases}$$

It is clear that $\lim_{t \downarrow 0} \frac{f(t\mathbf{h})}{t}$ exists for ever direction $\mathbf{h}$, so this function has directional derivatives in all directions. However, $(Df)(\mathbf{0})_2(\mathbf{h})$ fails to be a linear operator on $\mathbb{R}^2$, so f is not Gâteaux differentiable in $\mathbf{0}_2$.

(6) Let $f : \mathbb{R}^2 \longrightarrow \mathbb{R}$ be defined by $f(\mathbf{x}) = x_1 x_2$ for $\mathbf{x} \in \mathbb{R}^2$. Prove that the Gâteaux derivative of f is

$$(Df)(\mathbf{x}_0)(\mathbf{h}) = h_1 x_{02} + h_2 x_{01}$$

for $\mathbf{h} \in \mathbb{R}^2$.

Solution: We have:

$$\lim_{t \to 0} \frac{f(\mathbf{x}_0 + t\mathbf{h}) - f(\mathbf{x}_0)}{t}$$
$$= \lim_{t \to 0} \frac{(x_{01} + th_1)(x_{02} + th_2) - x_{01} - x_{02}}{t}$$
$$= h_1 x_{02} + h_2 x_{01}.$$

(7) Let $f : \mathbb{R}^2 \longrightarrow \mathbb{R}$ be given by

$$f(\mathbf{x}) = \begin{cases} x_1 & \text{if } x_2 = x_1^2, \\ 0 & \text{otherwise.} \end{cases}$$

Prove that f is Gâteaux differentiable at $\mathbf{0}_2$.

(8) Let $(S, \|\cdot\|)$ be a normed $\mathbb{F}$-linear space, T be an $\mathbb{F}$-linear space, X be an open set in $(S, \|\cdot\|)$ and let $f : X \longrightarrow T$ be a function that is Gâteaux differentiable in x_0. Prove that $(D_x f)(x_0)(-u) = -(D_x f)(x_0)(u)$ for every $u \in S$.

Solution: Since f is differentiable at x_0 we have

$$(D_x f)(x_0)(-u) = \lim_{t \to 0} \frac{f(x_0 - tu) - f(x_0)}{t}$$

$$= -\lim_{t \to 0} \frac{f(x_0 + (-t)u) - f(x_0)}{-t}$$

$$= -(D_x f)(x_0)(u)$$

for every $u \in S$.

(9) Prove that the function $f : \mathbb{R}^2 \longrightarrow \mathbb{R}$ given by

$$f(\mathbf{x}) = \begin{cases} \dfrac{x_1^2}{x_1^2 + x_2^2} & \text{if } \mathbf{x} \neq \mathbf{0}_2 \\ 0 & \text{if } \mathbf{x} = \mathbf{0}_2 \end{cases}$$

for $\mathbf{x} \in \mathbb{R}^2$ is differentiable everywhere except in $\mathbf{0}_2$.

(10) Let $\mathbf{f} : \mathbb{R}^n \longrightarrow \mathbb{R}^m$ be a Gâteaux differentiable function and let $(D\mathbf{f})(\mathbf{x}) \in \mathbb{R}^{m \times n}$ be its Jacobian matrix. It is clear that $rank((D\mathbf{f})(\mathbf{x})) \leqslant \min\{m, n\}$. Prove that the set

$$T = \{\mathbf{x} \in \mathbb{R}^n \mid rank((D\mathbf{f})(\mathbf{x})) = \min\{m, n\}\}$$

is an open subset of $\mathbb{R}^m$.

Solution: We will show that the set $\mathbb{R}^m - T$ is closed. Suppose that $m < n$. We have $\mathbf{z} \in \mathbb{R}^n - T$ if and only $rank((D\mathbf{f})(\mathbf{z})) < m$, that is, if every determinant of order m extracted from $(D\mathbf{f})(\mathbf{x})$ is 0. Since determinants are continuous functions of their entries, if follows that for a sequence $(\mathbf{x}_n)$ in $\mathbb{R}^n - T$ such that $\lim_{n \to \infty} \mathbf{x}_n = \mathbf{x}$, every determinant of order m extracted from a matrix $(D\mathbf{f})(\mathbf{x}_n)$ is 0, which means that every such determinant from $(D\mathbf{f})(\mathbf{x})$ is 0. Therefore, $rank((D\mathbf{f})(\mathbf{x})) < m$, hence $\mathbf{x} \in \mathbb{R}^m - T$. Thus, $\mathbb{R}^m - T$ is closed, so T is open.

(11) Let $R = \prod_{i=1}^n [a_i, b_i]$ be a rectangle in $\mathbb{R}^n$ and let $\mathbf{f} : R \longrightarrow \mathbb{R}^n$ be a continuously differentiable function on R such that $|\frac{\partial f_i}{\partial x_j}(\mathbf{x})| \leqslant K$ for all $\mathbf{x} \in \mathbf{I}(R)$. Prove that $\|\mathbf{f}(\mathbf{u}) - \mathbf{f}(\mathbf{v})\| \leqslant \|\mathbf{x} - \mathbf{y}\| n^2 K$.

Solution: By the Mean Value Theorem (Theorem 10.8) we have:

$$\|\mathbf{f}(\mathbf{u}) - \mathbf{f}(\mathbf{v})\| \leqslant \|\mathbf{u} - \mathbf{v}\| \sup\{\|(D\mathbf{f})(\mathbf{x})\| \mid \mathbf{x} \in [\mathbf{u}, \mathbf{v}]\}.$$

Note that $\|(D\mathbf{f})(\mathbf{x})\| \leqslant n^2 K$, which gives the desired inequality.

(12) Let D be an open interval of $\mathbb{R}$ and let $f : D \longrightarrow \mathbb{R}$ be a differentiable function such that f' is a Lipschitz function with constant c on D. Prove that for any $x, y \in D$ we have:

(a) $|f(y) - f(x) - f'(x)(y - x)| \leqslant \frac{c(y-x)^2}{2}$;

(b) $\left|\frac{f(x+h) - f(x)}{h} - f'(x)\right| \leqslant \frac{ch}{2}$.

Solution: Since $f(y) - f(x) = \int_x^y f'(z)\,dz$, we have:

$$f(y) - f(x) - f'(x)(y - x) = \int_x^y (f'(z) - f'(x))\,dz$$

$$= \int_0^1 [f'(x + t(y - x)) - f'(x)](y - x)\,dt$$

(using the change of variables

$$z = x + t(y - x)$$

$$= (y - x)\int_0^1 [f'(x + t(y - x)) - f'(x)]\,dt.$$

Therefore,

$$|f(y) - f(x) - f'(x)(y - x)| \leqslant |y - x|\left|\int_0^1 [f'(x + t(y - x)) - f'(x)]\,dt\right|$$

$$\leqslant c(y - x)^2 \int_0^1 t\,dt = \frac{c(y - x)^2}{2}.$$

The second inequality is an immediate consequence of the first.

(13) Let $\mathbf{f} : \mathbb{R}^n \longrightarrow \mathbb{R}^m$ be a continuously differentiable function on an open subset D of $\mathbb{R}^n$, $\mathbf{x} \in D$, and let $(D\mathbf{f})(\mathbf{x})$ be Lipschitz function with constant c. Then, for $\mathbf{x}, \mathbf{y} \in S$ we have

$$\|\mathbf{f}(\mathbf{y}) - \mathbf{f}(\mathbf{x}) - (D\mathbf{f})(\mathbf{x})(\mathbf{y} - \mathbf{x})\| \leqslant \frac{c\|\mathbf{y} - \mathbf{x}\|^2}{2}.$$

Solution: By Corollary 10.2 we have

$$\mathbf{f}(\mathbf{x} + \mathbf{h}) - \mathbf{f}(\mathbf{x}) - (D\mathbf{f})(\mathbf{x})\mathbf{h}$$

$$= \left(\int_0^1 (D\mathbf{f})(\mathbf{x} + t\mathbf{h})\mathbf{h}\,dt\right) - (D\mathbf{f})(\mathbf{x})\mathbf{h}$$

$$= \int_0^1 ((D\mathbf{f})(\mathbf{x} + t\mathbf{h}) - (D\mathbf{f})(\mathbf{x}))\mathbf{h}\,dt.$$

Since $(D\mathbf{f})(\mathbf{x})$ be Lipschitz function with constant c, we obtain

$$\|\mathbf{f}(\mathbf{x} + \mathbf{h}) - \mathbf{f}(\mathbf{x}) - (D\mathbf{f})(\mathbf{x})\mathbf{h}\| \leqslant \int_0^1 \|(D\mathbf{f})(\mathbf{x} + t\mathbf{h}) - (D\mathbf{f})(\mathbf{x})\|\|\mathbf{h}\|\,dt$$

$$\leqslant \int_0^1 c\|t\mathbf{h}\|\|\mathbf{h}\|\,dt = \frac{c}{2}\|\mathbf{h}\|^2.$$

(14) Let $f : \mathbb{R}^n \longrightarrow \mathbb{R}$ be a differentiable function in $C^1(\mathbb{R})$ and let $\mathbf{x}_0 \in \mathbb{R}^n$ such that $f(\mathbf{x}_0) = 0$. Prove that the function g defined as $g(\mathbf{x}) = f(\mathbf{x})\,|f(\mathbf{x})|$ is differentiable in $\mathbf{x}_0$.

Solution: Since $f \in C^1(\mathbb{R})$ we have

$$f(\mathbf{x}_0 + t\mathbf{h}) = f(\mathbf{x}_0) + t(\mathbf{h}'\nabla)(f)(\mathbf{x}_0 + \theta\mathbf{h}))$$
$$= t(\mathbf{h}'\nabla)(f)(\mathbf{x}_0 + \theta\mathbf{h})).$$

Therefore,

$$(Dg)(\mathbf{x}_0)(\mathbf{h}) = \lim_{t \to 0} \frac{g(\mathbf{x}_0 + t\mathbf{h}) - g(\mathbf{x}_0)}{t} = \lim_{t \to 0} \frac{f(\mathbf{x}_0 + t\mathbf{h}) \, |f(\mathbf{x}_0 + t\mathbf{h})|}{t}$$
$$= \lim_{t \to 0} \frac{f(\mathbf{x}_0 + t\mathbf{h}) \, |f(\mathbf{x}_0 + t\mathbf{h})|}{t}$$
$$= \lim_{t \to 0} |t|(\mathbf{h}'\nabla)(f)(\mathbf{x}_0 + \theta\mathbf{h}))(\mathbf{h}'\nabla)(f)(\mathbf{x}_0 + \theta\mathbf{h})) = 0,$$

which shows that g is differentiable in $\mathbf{x}_0$.

(15) Let $c : \mathbb{R}^n \longrightarrow \mathbb{R}$ be a function in $C^1(\mathbb{R})$, $c^+(\mathbf{x}) = \max\{0, c(\mathbf{x})\}$ and let $\ell : \mathbb{R}^n \longrightarrow \mathbb{R}$ be the function defined by $\ell(\mathbf{x}) = (c^+(\mathbf{x}))^2$ for $\mathbf{x} \in \mathbb{R}^n$. Prove that

    (a) the partial derivatives of ℓ are given by

$$\frac{\partial \ell}{\partial x_j} = 2\max\{0, c(\mathbf{x})\}\frac{\partial c}{\partial x_j}(\mathbf{x});$$

    (b) ℓ is Gâteaux differentiable in $\mathbf{x}_0$, where $c(\mathbf{x}_0) = 0$.

    Solution: Note that $c^+(\mathbf{x}) = \frac{1}{2}(c(\mathbf{x}) + |c(\mathbf{x})|)$ for $\mathbf{x} \in \mathbb{R}^n$. We have:

$$\ell(\mathbf{x}) = \left(\frac{c(\mathbf{x}) + |c(\mathbf{x})|}{2}\right)^2$$
$$= \frac{1}{2}c^2(\mathbf{x}) + \frac{1}{2}c(\mathbf{x})|c(\mathbf{x})|).$$

The first term is clearly differentiable; the second is also differentiable by Supplement 14.

(16) The result contained by this supplement is known as Danskin's Theorem [39].

Let $(S, \mathcal{O})$ be a topological space and let $f : X \times Y \longrightarrow \mathbb{R}$ be a function, where X is an open set in $\mathbb{R}^n$ and Y is a compact subset of S. Define the function $\phi : X \longrightarrow \mathbb{R}$ as $\phi(\mathbf{x}) = \max\{f(\mathbf{x}, y) \mid y \in Y\}$ and let $Y(\mathbf{x}) = \{y \in Y \mid \phi(\mathbf{x}) = f(\mathbf{x}, y)\}$ be the set of maximizers.

Prove that the function $\phi : X \longrightarrow \mathbb{R}$ is continuous and has directional derivatives in every direction $\mathbf{h}$ such that

$$\frac{\partial \phi}{\partial \mathbf{h}} = \max\{((D_\mathbf{x}f)(\mathbf{x}, y), \mathbf{h}) \mid y \in Y(\mathbf{x})\}.$$

Solution: Let $(\mathbf{x}_k)$ be a sequence in $\mathbb{R}^n$ such that $\lim_{k \to \infty} \mathbf{x}_k = \mathbf{x}_0$. Let $y_k \in Y$ such that $\phi(\mathbf{x}_k) = f(\mathbf{x}_k, \mathbf{y}_k)$. Since Y is compact, one can assume that $\lim_{k \to \infty} y_k = y_0$. The definition of ϕ implies $\phi(\mathbf{x}_k) = f(\mathbf{x}_k, y_k) \geqslant f(\mathbf{x}_k, y)$. Therefore, for any $y \in Y$ we have:

$$\lim_{k \to \infty} \phi(\mathbf{x}_k) = \lim_{k \to \infty} f(\mathbf{x}_k, y_k) = f(\mathbf{x}_0, y_0) \geqslant \lim_{k \to \infty} f(\mathbf{x}_k, y) = f(\mathbf{x}_0, y)$$

for all $y \in Y$. The inequality $f(\mathbf{x}_0, y_0) \geqslant f(\mathbf{x}_0, y)$ implies $\phi(\mathbf{x}_0) = f(\mathbf{x}_0, y_0) = \lim_{k \to \infty} \phi(\mathbf{x}_k)$, hence ϕ is continuous.

Let $\mathbf{h}$ be a direction and let $(\mathbf{x}_k)$ be a sequence defined as $\mathbf{x}_k = \mathbf{x}_0 + t_k \mathbf{h}$ such that $t_k > 0$ and $\lim_{k \to \infty} \mathbf{x}_k = \mathbf{x}_0$.

If $y \in Y(\mathbf{x}_0)$ and $y_k \in Y(\mathbf{x}_k)$ for $k \geqslant 1$ we can write

$$
\begin{aligned}
\frac{\phi(\mathbf{x}_k) - \phi(\mathbf{x}_0)}{t_k} &= \frac{f(\mathbf{x}_k, y_k) - f(\mathbf{x}_0, y)}{t_k} \\
&= \frac{f(\mathbf{x}_k, y_k) - f(\mathbf{x}_k, y)}{t_k} + \frac{f(\mathbf{x}_k, y) - f(\mathbf{x}_0, y)}{t_k} \\
&\geqslant \frac{f(\mathbf{x}_k, y) - f(\mathbf{x}_0, y)}{t_k} \\
&\qquad \text{(because } f(\mathbf{x}_k, y_k) \geqslant f(\mathbf{x}_k, y)) \\
&= ((\nabla f)(\mathbf{x}_0 + \theta_k \mathbf{h}, y), \mathbf{h}) \text{ for some } \theta_k \in (0,1) \\
&\qquad \text{(by the Mean Value Theorem).}
\end{aligned}
$$

Therefore,

$$\liminf_{k \to \infty} \frac{\phi(\mathbf{x}_k) - \phi(\mathbf{x}_0)}{t_k} \geqslant ((\nabla_{\mathbf{x}} f)(\mathbf{x}_0, y), \mathbf{h})$$

for all $y \in Y(\mathbf{x}_0)$, which implies

$$\liminf_{k \to \infty} \frac{\phi(\mathbf{x}_k) - \phi(\mathbf{x}_0)}{t_k} \geqslant \max\{((\nabla_{\mathbf{x}} f)(\mathbf{x}_0, y), \mathbf{h}) \mid y \in Y(\mathbf{x}_0)\}.$$

If $\phi(\mathbf{x}_k) = f(\mathbf{x}_k, y_k)$ and $\lim_{k \to \infty} y_k = y_0$ we have

$$
\begin{aligned}
\frac{\phi(\mathbf{x}_k) - \phi(\mathbf{x}_0)}{t_k} &= \frac{f(\mathbf{x}_k, y_k) - f(\mathbf{x}_0, y_0)}{t_k} \\
&= \frac{f(\mathbf{x}_k, y_k) - f(\mathbf{x}_0, y_k)}{t_k} + \frac{f(\mathbf{x}_0, y_k) - f(\mathbf{x}_0, y_0)}{t_k} \\
&\leqslant \frac{f(\mathbf{x}_k, y_k) - f(\mathbf{x}_0, y_k)}{t_k} \\
&\qquad \text{(because } f(\mathbf{x}_0, y_0) \geqslant f(\mathbf{x}_0, y_k)) \\
&= ((\nabla f)(\mathbf{x}_0 + \theta_k' \mathbf{h}, y_k), \mathbf{h}) \text{ for some } \theta_k' \in (0,1) \\
&\qquad \text{(by the Mean Value Theorem).}
\end{aligned}
$$

Consequently,

$$\limsup_{k \to \infty} \frac{\phi(\mathbf{x}_k) - \phi(\mathbf{x}_0)}{t_k} \leqslant \max\{((\nabla_{\mathbf{x}} f)(\mathbf{x}_0, y), \mathbf{h}) \mid y \in Y(\mathbf{x}_0)\},$$

which allows to conclude that

$$\frac{\partial \phi}{\partial \mathbf{h}} = \max\{((D_{\mathbf{x}} f)(\mathbf{x}, y), \mathbf{h}) \mid y \in Y(\mathbf{x})\}.$$

(17) Let $(S, \mathcal{O}_d)$ be a metric space. For $\alpha > 0$ define "$\preceq_\alpha$" on $S \times \mathbb{R}$ as

$$(x_1, a_1) \preceq_\alpha (x_2, a_2) \text{ if } (a_2 - a_1) + \alpha d(x_1, x_2) \leqslant 0.$$

The relation $\preceq_\alpha$ is a partial order on $S \times \mathbb{R}$.

Solution: This relation is clearly reflexive.

If $(x_1, a_1) \preceq_\alpha (x_2, a_2)$ and $(x_2, a_2) \preceq_\alpha (x_1, a_1)$, then $(a_2 - a_1) + \alpha d(x_1, x_2) \leqslant 0$ and $(a_1 - a_2) + \alpha d(x_1, x_2) \leqslant 0$, so

$$\alpha d(x_1, x_2) \leqslant a_1 - a_2 \text{ and } \alpha d(x_1, x_2) \leqslant a_2 - a_1.$$

Suppose that $a_1 \neq a_2$. Then at least of the numbers $a_1 - a_2, a_2 - a_1$ is negative and this leads to a contradiction because $\alpha d(x_1, x_2)$ is non-negative. Thus, $a_1 = a_2$, which implies $d(x_1, x_2) \leqslant 0$, so $x_1 = x_2$, so $\preceq_\alpha$ is antisymmetric.

If $(x_1, a_1) \preceq_\alpha (x_2, a_2)$ and $(x_2, a_2) \preceq_\alpha (x_3, a_3)$, then $(a_2 - a_1) + \alpha d(x_1, x_2) \leqslant 0$ and $(a_3 - a_2) + \alpha d(x_2, x_3) \leqslant 0$, which implies

$$(a_3 - a_1) + \alpha(d(x_1, x_2) + d(x_2, x_3)) \leqslant 0.$$

By applying the triangular inequality we have $(a_3 - a_1) + \alpha d(x_1, x_3) \leqslant 0$, so $\preceq_\alpha$ is a partial order.

(18) Let V be a Banach space and let $f : V \longrightarrow \mathbb{R} \cup \{\infty\}$. Let $S_\epsilon f(v)$ be the set of continuous linear functionals that ϵ-support f at v. Prove that
   (a) $S_\epsilon f(v) = \emptyset$ if $v \notin \text{Dom}(f)$;
   (b) $S_\epsilon f(v)$ is a convex subset of V^*;
   (c) $S_\epsilon f(v) + S_\theta f(v) \subseteq S_{\epsilon+\theta}(f + g)(v)$;
   (d) if $\theta \geqslant \epsilon$, then $S_\epsilon f(v) \subseteq S_\theta f(v)$;
   (e) if $v^* \in \bigcap_{\epsilon > 0} S_\epsilon f(v) \cap \left(-\bigcap_{\epsilon > 0} S_\epsilon(-f)(v)\right)$, then f is Fréchet differentiable and $(Df)(v) = v^*$;
   (f) if $S_\epsilon f(v) \neq \emptyset$, then f is lower semicontinuous at v.

Solution: Suppose that $S_\epsilon f(v) \neq \emptyset$ and let $v^* \in V$ be a continuous linear functional such that there exists $\eta > 0$ such that

$$\|w - v\| \leqslant \eta \text{ implies } f(w) \geqslant f(v) + v * (w - v) - \epsilon\|w - v\|.$$

We have $\{x \in S \mid f(x) > v\}$.

Let X, Y be two Banach spaces, $[x_0, x_0 + d]$ be an interval in X, and let h be a mapping defined on $[x_0, x_0 + k]$ and ranging over the set of operators defined on X with values in Y.

Define $\int_{x_0}^{x_0+k} h(x)\, dx$ as

$$\int_{x_0}^{x_0+k} h(x)\, dx = \int_0^1 h(x_0 + tk)(k)\, dt = \lim_{\nu(\Delta) \to 0} \sum_{p=0}^{n-1} h(x_0 + \xi_p k)(k)(t_{p+1} - t_p),$$

where $\Delta = \{t_0, \ldots, t_n\} \in \mathsf{SUBD}[0, 1]$ and $\xi_p \in [t_p, t_{p+1}]$ for $0 \leqslant p \leqslant n - 1$. Note that this definition makes sense as we noted in the Supplements of Chapter 9, because $h(x_0 + tk)(k)$ is a function defined on $[0, 1]$ ranging in the Banach space Y.

(19) Let X, Y be two Banach spaces, $[x_0, x_0 + k]$ be an interval in X, and let $f : X \longrightarrow Y$ be a function such that $(Df)(\mathbf{x})$ is continuous in $[x_0, x_0+k]$. Prove that $\int_{x_0}^{x_0+k}(Df)\, dx$ exists and

$$\int_{x_0}^{x_0+k} (Df)(x)\, dx = f(x_0 + k) - f(x_0).$$

Solution: By the definition of Riemann integral we have

$$\int_{x_0}^{x_0+k} (Df)(x)\, dx = \lim_{\nu(\Delta) \to 0} \sum_{p=0}^{n-1} f(x_0 + \xi_p k)(k)(t_{p+1} - t_p)$$

$$= \lim_{\nu(\Delta) \to 0} \sum_{p=0}^{n-1} f'(\overline{x}_p)(t_{p+1} - t_p)k.$$

Note that

$$f(x_0+k) - f(x_0) = \sum_{p=0}^{n-1}(f(x_0+t_{p+1}k) - f(x_0+t_p k)) = \sum_{p=0}^{n-1}(f(x_{p+1}) - f(x_p)).$$

By the Mean Value Theorem (Theorem 10.8) we have

$$\left\| \sum_{p=0}^{n-1}(f(x_{p+1}) - f(x_p)) - (Df)(\overline{x}_p)(t_{p+1} - t_p)k \right\|$$

$$\leqslant \|k\| \sum_{p=0}^{n-1}(t_{k+1} - t_k) \sup_{\theta \in (0,1)} \|f'(x_p + \theta(t_{p+1} - t_p)k) - f'(\overline{x}_p)\|.$$

Since f' is uniformly continuous on $[x_0, x_0+k]$, the desired result follows.

Let $f : [a, b] \longrightarrow T$ be a function of a real argument whose values belong to a Banach space T. The notions of subdivision of $[a, b]$, Darboux sums, and Riemann integral, etc. can be immediately transferred to functions of this form. The function $f : [a, b] \longrightarrow \mathbb{R}$ is Riemann integrable if $\int_{\underline{a}}^b f \, dx = \overline{\int_a^b} f \, dx$. When f Riemann integrable on $[a, b]$, its integral is denoted by $\int_a^b f(t) \, dt$ as usual.

(20) Let T, U be Banach spaces. Prove that if $f : [a, b] \longrightarrow T$ is a Riemann integrable function and $h : T \longrightarrow U$ is a linear operator between Banach spaces, then the function hf is integrable and $\int_a^b uf \, dt = u\left(\int_a^b f \, dt\right)$.

(21) Let $\phi : [a, b] \longrightarrow \mathbb{R}$ be real-valued integrable function, T be a Banach space, and let $\mathbf{x}_0 \in T$. Prove that the function $f : [a, b] \longrightarrow T$ defined by $f(t) = \phi(t)\mathbf{x}_0$ is integrable and $\int_a^b f \, dt = \left(\int_a^b \phi(t); dt\right)\mathbf{x}_0$.

(22) Let $f : [a, b] \longrightarrow T$ be a Riemann integrable function. Prove that the function $\psi : [a, b] \longrightarrow \mathbb{R}$ defined by $\psi(t) = \|f(t)\|$ is integrable and $\left\| \int_a^b f(t) \, dt \right\| \leqslant \int_a^b \psi(t) \, dt$.

(23) Recall that the set of continuous operators between the Banach spaces S, T is denoted by $\mathfrak{B}(S, T)$. Let $[u, v]$ be an interval in S and let $\Phi : [u, v] \longrightarrow \mathfrak{B}(S, T)$. Define

$$\int_u^v \Phi(x) \, dx = \int_0^1 \Phi((1 - t)\mathbf{u} + t\mathbf{u})(\mathbf{v} - \mathbf{v}) \, dt. \tag{10.7}$$

Since Φ is continuous, the integral exists and is an element of T.

Let $X \subseteq S$, and let $P : X \longrightarrow T$ be an operator such that $\Phi(x) = (DP)(x)$ for $x \in [u, v]$. Prove that $\int_u^v \Phi(x) \, dx = P(v) - P(u)$.

Solution: By the defining equality (10.7) we have:

$$\int_u^v \Phi(x) \, dx = \int_0^1 \Phi((1 - t)\mathbf{u} + t\mathbf{u})(\mathbf{v} - \mathbf{u}) \, dt.$$

Let $\Delta = \{t_0, t_1, \ldots, t_n\}$ be a subdivision of the interval $[0, 1]$ such that $0 = t_0 < t_1 < \cdots < t_{n-1} < t_n = 1$. The interval $[u, v]$ in S is subdivided by the points $x_0, x_1, \ldots, X_n$, where $x_k = (1 - t_k)\mathbf{u} + t_k\mathbf{v}$. If $\overline{t_k} \in (t_k, t_{k+1})$ the point $olx_k = (1 - t_k)x_k + t_k\mathbf{x}_{k+1}$ belongs to $[x_k, x_{k+1}]$.

Using notations introduced in Definition 8.8, we have

$$\int_0^1 \Phi((1 - t)\mathbf{u} + t\mathbf{u})(\mathbf{v} - \mathbf{u}) \, dt$$

$$= \lim_{\nu(\Delta) \to 0} \sum_{k=0}^{n-1} \Phi((1 - t_k)\mathbf{u} + t_k\mathbf{v})(t_{k+1} - t_k)(\mathbf{v} - \mathbf{u})$$

$$= \lim_{\nu(\Delta) \to 0} \sum_{k=0}^{n-1} \Phi(\overline{x}_k)(t_{k+1} - t_k)(\mathbf{v} - \mathbf{u}).$$

Since $P(v) - P(u) = \sum_{k=0}^{n-1}(P(x_{k+1}) - P(x_k))$ we have

$$\left\|\sum_{k=0}^{n-1}(P(x_{k+1}) - P(x_k)) - \Phi(\overline{x}_k)(t_{k+1} - t_k)(v - u)\right\|$$

$$\leqslant \|v - u\| \sum_{k=0}^{n-1} sup_{\theta \in (0,1)}\|\Phi(x_k + \theta(x_{k+1} - x_k) - \Phi(\overline{x}_k)\|,$$

by the Mean Value Theorem. Since Φ is uniformly continuous on $[u, v]$ the result follows.

Bibliographical Comments

The monograph [94] is fully dedicated to a study of the history, proofs, and applications of the implicit function theorem.

An up-to-date lucid reference on optimization is [71].

The presentation of the Implicit Function Theorem follows [29]. The extension of Riemann integrals to functions of a real argument that range in a Banach space follows [86] and is contained in Supplements 20–23.

Supplement 18 was obtained in [50].

Chapter 11

Hilbert Spaces

11.1 Introduction

Hilbert spaces are inner product spaces that are complete with respect to the topology induced by the metrics generated by inner products. In other words, Hilbert spaces are special Banach spaces whose norm is generated by an inner product. This concept originated in the work on integral equations and Fourier series of the German mathematician David Hilbert.[1]

The term *Hilbert space* was introduced by John von Neumann[2] in 1929 in order to describe these spaces in an axiomatic way.

11.2 Hilbert Spaces — Examples

Definition 11.1. A *Hilbert space* is a linear space H equipped with an inner product such that H is complete relative to the metric defined by the inner product.

As usual, we denote the inner product of $x, y \in L$ by (x, y).

---

[1] The German mathematician David Hilbert (Jan. 23rd 1862–Feb. 14th 1943) was one of the most influential mathematicians of the last two centuries. His contributions span the foundations of mathematics, axiomatization of geometry and functional analysis. Hilbert taught at the University of Königsberg until 1895 and later at the University of Göttingen.

[2] John von Neumann (born on December 28th, 1903, Budapest, Hungary, died February 8th, 1957, in Washington, D.C., U.S.) was a Hungarian-born American mathematician. Von Neumann was one of worlds foremost mathematicians and made important contributions in set theory, quantum theory, automata theory, economics, and game theory. Von Neumann was one of the inventors of the stored-program digital computer. He was a professor at the Institute of Advanced Studies in Princeton, NJ.

Example 11.1. The real linear space $\mathbb{R}^n$ equipped with the usual inner product defined by

$$(\mathbf{x}, \mathbf{y}) = \sum_{i=1}^{n} x_i y_i$$

for $\mathbf{x} = \begin{pmatrix} x_1 \\ \vdots \\ x_n \end{pmatrix}$ and $\mathbf{y} = \begin{pmatrix} y_1 \\ \vdots \\ y_n \end{pmatrix}$ is a Hilbert space.

The complex linear space $\mathbb{C}^n$ is a Hilbert space for the inner product given by

$$(\mathbf{x}, \mathbf{y}) = \sum_{i=1}^{n} x_i \overline{y_i}$$

for $\mathbf{x} = \begin{pmatrix} x_1 \\ \vdots \\ x_n \end{pmatrix}$ and $\mathbf{y} = \begin{pmatrix} y_1 \\ \vdots \\ y_n \end{pmatrix}$.

Example 11.2. The real Banach space $\ell^2(\mathbb{R})$ introduced in Example 9.5 is a Hilbert space relative to the inner product

$$(\mathbf{x}, \mathbf{y}) = \sum_{i \in \mathbb{N}} x_i y_i$$

for $\mathbf{x}, \mathbf{y} \in \ell^2(\mathbb{R})$.

Its counterpart on the set of complex numbers, $\ell^2(\mathbb{C})$ is equipped with the inner product

$$(\mathbf{x}, \mathbf{y}) = \sum_{i \in \mathbb{N}} x_i \overline{y_i}.$$

Example 11.3. As a consequence of Cauchy-Schwarz inequality, $L^2(S, \mathcal{E}, m)$ is a Hilbert space relative to the inner product defined by $(f, g) = \int_S fg \, dm$.

For the special case of random variables X, Y defined on a probability space $(\Omega, \mathcal{E}, P)$, we have $(X, Y) = \int_\Omega XY \, dP$. Also, $\|X\|_2 = \sqrt{(X, X)} = \sqrt{E(X^2)}$.

Note that for $X \in L^2(\Omega, \mathcal{E}, P)$ we have

$$E(X) = (|X|, 1) \leqslant \sqrt{(X, X)}\sqrt{(1, 1)} = \sqrt{E(X^2)},$$

hence $\|X\|_1 \leqslant \|X\|_2$. Therefore, we have $L^2(\Omega, \mathcal{E}, P) \subseteq L^1(\Omega, \mathcal{E}, P)$. Thus, if $X, Y \in L^2(\Omega, \mathcal{E}, P)$ the variance $var(X) = E((X - E(X))^2)$ and the *covariance* of X and Y defined by

$$cov(X, Y) = E((X - E(X))(Y - E(Y))) = (X, Y) - E(X)E(Y),$$

exist and are finite.

11.3 Classes of Linear Operators in Hilbert Spaces

Theorem 6.25 shows that a linear operator between two normed spaces is continuous if and only if it is bounded.

For Hilbert spaces one can prove an inequality that links the norm of a linear operator to the inner product.

Theorem 11.1. *A linear operator on a Hilbert space* $h : H \longrightarrow H$ *is continuous if and only if there exists a positive number* M *such that* $|(h(x), y)| \leqslant M \|x\| \|y\|$ *for* $x, y \in H$. *Moreover,*

$$\|h\| = \inf\{M > 0 \mid (h(x), y) \leqslant M \|x\| \|y\| \text{ for } x, y \in H\}.$$

Proof. Let $h : H \longrightarrow H$ be a continuous linear operator. By Theorem 6.25 h is bounded and we have $\|h(x)\| \leqslant \|h\| \|x\|$. Therefore, by applying Cauchy-Schwarz inequality we have:

$$|(h(x), y)| \leqslant \|h(x)\| \|y\| \leqslant \|h\| \|x\| \|y\|. \tag{11.1}$$

Conversely, suppose that the inequality of the theorem holds. Taking $y = h(x)$ we obtain

$$\|h(x)\|^2 \leqslant \|h\| \|x\| \|h(x)\|,$$

hence $\|h(x)\| \leqslant \|h\| \|x\|$ when $\|h(x)\| \neq 0$. If $\|h(x)\| = 0$, the inequality obviously holds.

Observe that if $(h(x), y) \leqslant M \|x\| \|y\|$ then $(h(x), y) \leqslant M \|y\|$ when $\|x\| = 1$, so $|h(x)| \leqslant M$ (by taking $y = h(x)$) for $\|x\| = 1$ which implies $\|h\| \leqslant M$. This, in turn yields

$$\|h\| = \inf\{M > 0 \mid (h(x), y) \leqslant M \|x\| \|y\| \text{ for } x, y \in H\}. \qquad \square$$

Theorem 11.2. *Let* $h : H \longrightarrow H$ *be a continuous linear operator defined on a Hilbert space* H. *There exists an operator* h^* *such that*

(i) $(h(x), y) = (x, h^*(y))$ *for every* $x, y \in H$;
(ii) h^* *is linear and continuous;*
(iii) $\|h^*\| = \|h\|$.

Proof. Let $f_y : H \longrightarrow \mathbb{C}$ be linear continuous functional given by $f_y(x) = (h(x), y)$. By Riesz' Theorem there exists a unique $y^* \in H$ such that $f_y(x) = (x, y^*)$ by . Define the operator $h^* : H \longrightarrow H$ as $h^*(y) = y^*$. We have

$$(h(x), y) = (x, h^*(y))$$

for $x, y \in H$.

We claim that the operator h^* is linear and continuous.
Indeed, for every x, y, z we have

$$
\begin{aligned}
(x, h^*(ay + bz)) &= (h(x), ay + bz) = \overline{a}(h(x), y) + \overline{b}(h(x), z) \\
&= \overline{a}(x, h^*(y)) + \overline{b}(x, h^*(z)) \\
&= (x, ah^*(y)) + (x, bh^*(z)) = (x, ah^*(x) + bh^*(y),
\end{aligned}
$$

which implies $h^*(ay + bz) = ah^*(y) + bh^*(z)$. In other words, h^* is a linear operator.

Furthermore, since $|(h(x), y)|^2 \leqslant M\|x\|\|y\|$ it follows that $|x, h^*(y)|^2 \leqslant M\|x\|\|y\|$ for $x, y \in H$, so h^* is continuous and $\|h^*\| = \|h\|$.   □

Definition 11.2. If $h : H \longrightarrow H$ is a linear continuous operator on the Hilbert space H, the h^* is the *adjoint operator* of h.

Example 11.4. Let $h : L^2([a, b]) \longrightarrow L^2([a, b])$ be the operator defined by

$$
h(f)(x) = \int_a^b K(x, y) f(y) \, dy,
$$

where K is a continuous function. Note that

$$
\begin{aligned}
(h(f), g) &= \int_a^b h(f)(x) \, \overline{g(x)} \, dx \\
&= \int_a^b \left(\int_a^b K(x, y) f(y) \, dy \right) \overline{g(x)} \, dx \\
&= \int_a^b \left(\int_a^b \overline{K(y, x) g(x)} \, dx \right) f(y) \, dy
\end{aligned}
$$

(by exchanging the order of integration)

$$
= \int_a^b \left(\int_a^b \overline{K(x, y) g(y)} \, dy \right) f(x) \, dx
$$

(by renaming the variables).

Therefore, the equality $(h(f), g) = (f, h^*(g))$ that defines the adjoint operator is satisfied by the operator h^* if we define

$$
h^*(\overline{g})(x) = \int_a^b \overline{K(x, y) g(y)} \, dy = \int_a^b \overline{K(y, x) g(y)} \, dy
$$

for $x \in [a, b]$. By the uniqueness of the adjoint operator we have:

$$
h^*(f)(x) = \int_a^b \overline{K(x, y)} f(y) \, dy = \int_a^b K(y, x) f(y) \, dy, \tag{11.2}
$$

where we replaced $\bar{g}$ by f. Thus, when $\overline{K(y,x)} = K(x,y)$, h^* coincides with h.

We examine several classes of continuous linear operators that act on Hilbert spaces.

Definition 11.3. A continuous linear operator $h \in \mathfrak{L}(H)$ on a complex Hilbert space H is

  (i) *self-adjoint* if $h^* = h$;
 (ii) *normal* if $hh^* = h^*h$;
(iii) *unitary* if it is surjective and $(h(x), h(y)) = (x, y)$ for every $x, y \in H$;
 (iv) *positive* if $(h(x), x) \geqslant 0$ for every $x \in H$;
  (v) *positive definite* if it is positive and invertible;
 (vi) *idempotent* if $hh = h$;
(vii) *projection* if it is both self-adjoint and idempotent.

11.3.1 *Self-Adjoint Operators*

Let $\mathsf{SA}(H)$ be the set of self-adjoint operators defined on the Hilbert space H.

If $h \in \mathsf{SA}(H)$, where H is a complex Hilbert space then $(h(x), x)$ is a real number for every $x \in H$ because

$$\overline{(h(x), x)} = \overline{(x, h(x))} = (h(x), x).$$

Theorem 11.3. *If h is a self-adjoint linear operator on a Hilbert space H, then $\mathsf{Null}(h)$ and $\mathsf{Img}(h)$ are orthogonal closed subspaces of H.*

Proof. Let $u \in \mathsf{Null}(h)$ and let $v \in \mathsf{Img}(h)$. Then $h(u) = 0_H$ and $v = h(x)$ for some $x \in H$. Since $h \in SA(H)$, we have

$$(u, v) = (u, h(x)) = (h(u), v) = (0_H, v) = 0.$$

so $\mathsf{Null}(h) \perp \mathsf{Img}(h)$. By Theorem 6.19 $\mathsf{Null}(h)$ and $\mathsf{Img}(h)$ are orthogonal closed subspaces of H. $\qquad\square$

Theorem 11.4. *If H is a real Hilbert space, $\mathsf{SA}(H)$ is a closed linear subspace of $\mathfrak{L}(H)$.*

If H is a complex Hilbert space, then $\mathsf{SA}(H)$ is a closed subset of $\mathfrak{L}(H)$ that is closed with respect to addition and with multiplication with real numbers.

Proof. It is immediate that $\mathsf{SA}(H)$ is a subspace of $\mathfrak{L}(H)$. Let (h_n) be a sequence in $\mathsf{SA}(H)$ that converges uniformly to $h \in \mathfrak{L}(H)$. For every $x, y \in H$ we have

$$(h(x), y) = \lim_{n \to \infty} (h_n(x), y) = \lim_{n \to \infty} (x, h_n(y)) = (x, h(y)),$$

which shows that h is self-adjoint. The last part of the theorem is immediate. $\qquad\square$

Lemma 11.1. *Let H be a complex Hilbert space. For every $y, z \in H$ there exists a such that $(e^{ia}y, z)$ is a real non-negative number.*

Proof. The inner product (y, z) which is a complex number can be written in polar form as $(y, z) = |(y, z)|e^{i\alpha}$. Thus, if suffices to take $a = -\alpha$ to write

$$(e^{ia}y, z) = e^{ia}(y, z) = e^{-i\alpha}|(y, z)|e^{i\alpha} = |(y, z)|,$$

which is a real non-negative number. $\qquad\square$

Theorem 11.5. *Let H be a complex Hilbert space and let $h \in \mathsf{SA}(H)$. We have $\|h\| = \sup\{|(h(x), x)| \mid \|x\| = 1\}$.*

Proof. Let $c = \sup\{(h(x), x) \mid \|x\| = 1\}$. By equality (11.1) we have $c \leqslant \|h\|$.

We will show now that $\|h\| \leqslant c$. By the Polarization Identity (see Theorem 2.26) we have:

$$(y, h(x)) = \frac{1}{4}\left((x + y, h(x + y)) - (x - y, h(x - y))\right.$$
$$\left. -i(y + ih(x), h(x + iy)) + i(x - iy, h(x - iy))\right).$$

Since h is a self-adjoint operator the first two terms in the right member are real and the last two terms are imaginary. By Lemma 11.1 there exists $a \in \mathbb{R}$ such that $(e^{ia}y, h(x)) = |(y, h(x))|$ is a real non-negative number.

Replacing y by $e^{ia}y$ in the Polarization Identity mentioned above leads to the disappearance of the imaginary terms and we have

$$(y, h(x)) = \frac{1}{4}\left((x + y, h(x + y)) - (x - y, h(x - y))\right).$$

Thus,

$$|(y, h(x))|^2 = \frac{1}{16}\left|(x + y, h(x + y)) - (x - y, h(x - y))\right|^2$$
$$\leqslant \frac{c^2}{16}\left(\|x + y\|^2 + \|x - y\|^2\right)$$
$$\text{(by the definition of } c\text{)}$$
$$= \frac{c^2}{8}\left(\|x\|^2 + \|y\|^2\right)$$
$$\text{(by the Parallelogram Equality).}$$

For $\|x\| = \|y\| = 1$ we have $|(y, h(x))|^2 \leqslant \frac{c^2}{4}$, so $\|h\| \leqslant \frac{c}{2} < c$. $\qquad\square$

Example 11.5. If h is a linear operator on the Hilbert space H, then h^*h and hh^* are positive operators.

Indeed, by the definition of the adjoint operator we have

$$(h^*h(x), x) = (h(x), h(x)) = \|h(x)\|^2 \geqslant 0.$$

The argument for hh^* is similar.

11.3.2 *Normal and Unitary Operators*

Theorem 11.6. *The set of normal operators is closed in* $\mathfrak{L}(H)$.

Proof. If (h_n) is a sequence of normal operators that converge in norm to an operator h, then (h_n^*) converges to h^*, and, by the continuity of composition we have

$$hh^* = \lim_{n \to \infty} h_n h_n^* = \lim_{n \to \infty} h_n^* h_n = h^*h.$$

$\square$

Unitary operators were defined as surjective continuous linear mappings that preserve the inner product.

Lemma 11.2. *Let* $h : H \longrightarrow H$ *be a surjective function defined on a Hilbert space* $H \neq \{0_H\}$ *that preserves the inner product, i.e.,* $(h(x), h(y)) = (x, y)$ *for every* $x, y \in H$. *Then,* h *is a continuous linear mapping.*

Proof. Let $u, v, x \in H$ and let a, b two scalars. We have

$$(h(au + bv) - ah(u) - bh(v), h(x))$$
$$= (h(au + bv), h(x)) - a(h(u), h(x)) - b(h(v), h(x))$$
$$= (au + bv, x) - a(u, x) - b(u, x) = 0$$

(due to the linearity of the inner product).

Since every $z \in H$ can be written as $z = h(x)$ (because h is surjective), it follows that $h(au + bv) - ah(u) - bh(v) \in H^\perp$, which implies that $h(au + bv) - ah(u) - bh(v) = 0$ for every $u, v \in H$. Thus, h is indeed a linear mapping.

Choosing $x = y \neq 0_H$ in the equality $(h(x), h(y)) = (x, y)$ implies $\|h(x)\| = \|x\|$ for $x \in H - \{0_H\}$, which, in turn, implies that h is a continuous mapping. $\square$

Theorem 11.7. *A surjective mapping* $h : H \longrightarrow H$ *on a Hilbert space* $H \neq 0_H$ *that preserves the inner product is a unitary operator on* H.

Proof. This follows from the previous lemma and its proof. $\square$

Corollary 11.1. *For a unitary operator h on a Hilbert space $H \neq 0_H$ we have $\|h\| = 1$.*

Proof. This follows immediately from the fact that $\|h(x)\| = \|x\|$ for every $x \in H$. $\square$

11.3.3 *Projection Operators*

We shall prove that each projection operator on a Hilbert space corresponds to a closed subspace S.

Theorem 11.8. *Let p be a projection operator on a Hilbert space H. There exists a closed subspace S of H such that $p = p_S$.*

Proof. Let $S_p = \{x \in H \mid p(x) = x\}$. It is clear that S_p is a subspace of H. If (x_n) is a sequence of elements in S_p such that $\lim_{n \to \infty} x_n = x$, then

$$p(x) = p(\lim_{n \to \infty} x_n) = \lim_{n \to \infty} p(x_n) = \lim_{n \to \infty} x_n = x,$$

so $x \in S_p$. Thus, S_p is a closed subspace of H.

If $x \in H$ we can write $x = p(x) + (x - p(x))$, where $p(x) \in S_p$ because $p(p(x)) = p(x)$.

We claim that $x - p(x) \in S_p^{\perp}$. Indeed, if $y \in S_p$ we have

$$(x - p(x), y) = (x - p(x), p(y)) = (p(x - p(x)), y) = (0_H, y) = 0,$$

hence $x - p(x) \in S_p^{\perp}$. We conclude that p is indeed the projection on the closed subspace S_p. In other words, $p = p_{S_p}$ for every projection operator p of H. $\square$

Theorem 11.9. *Let S and T be two closed subspaces of a Hilbert space H. We have $p_S p_T = p_T p_S$ if and only if $p_S p_T$ is a projection.*

Proof. Suppose that $p_S p_T = p_T p_S$. This allows us to write

$$(p_S p_T)^* = p_T^* p_S^* = p_T p_S = p_S p_T,$$

which proves that $p_S p_T$ is self-adjoint. Furthermore,

$$(p_S p_T)^2 = (p_S p_T)(p_S p_T) = p_S (p_T p_S) p_T = (p_S p_S)(p_T p_T) = p_S p_T,$$

which implies that $p_S p_T$ is a projection.

Conversely, suppose that $p_S p_T$ is a projection. Then,

$$p_S p_T = p_S^* p_T^* = (p_T p_S)^* = p_T p_S.$$

$\square$

Theorem 11.10. *Let S and T be two closed subspaces of a Hilbert space H. If $p_S p_T$ is a projection, then $p_S p_T = p_{S \cap T}$.*

Proof. By Theorem 11.9, we have $p_S p_T = p_T p_S$. Therefore, $p_S p_T(H) = p_S(p_T(H)) \subseteq p_S(H) \subseteq S$ and $p_S p_T(H) = p_T p_S(H) = p_T(p_S(H)) \subseteq p_T(H) \subseteq T$, which implies $p_S p_T(H) \subseteq S \cap T$.

Conversely, if $x \in S \cap T$ we have $x = p_T(x) = p_S p_T(x)$, hence $S \cap T \subseteq p_S p_T(H)$. Thus, $p_S p_T(H) = S \cap T$, which concludes the argument. $\square$

Theorem 11.11. *Let S and T be two closed subspaces of a Hilbert space H. We have $S \perp T$ if and only if $p_S + p_T$ is a projection.*

Proof. Suppose that $p_S + p_T$ is a projection. If $x \in S$ we have
$$\|x\|^2 \geqslant \|(p_S + p_T)(x)\|^2 = ((p_S + p_T)(x), (p_S + p_T)(x))$$
$$= ((p_S + p_T)^2(x), x)$$
(because $p_S = p_T$ is self-adjoint)
$$= ((p_S + p_T)(x), x)$$
(because $p_S = p_T$ is idempotent)
$$= (p_S(x), x) + (p_T(x), x) = (x, x) + (p_T(x), x) = \|x\|^2 + (p_T(x), x).$$
This implies $(p_T(x), x) = 0$. For $y \in T$ we can write
$$(x, y) = (x, p_T(y)) = (p_T(x), y) = 0,$$
which shows that $S \perp T$.

Conversely, suppose that $S \perp T$. Since $T \subseteq S^\perp$, it follows that $p_S(T) = \{0_H\}$, hence $p_S(p_T(x)) = 0_H$ for every $x \in H$. Similarly, $p_T(p_S(x)) = 0_H$ for $x \in H$. This allows us to write
$$(p_S + p_T)^2 = p_S^2 + p_S p_T + p_T p_S + p_T^2 = p_S + p_T,$$
$$(p_S + p_T)^* = p_S^* + p_T^* = p_S + p_T,$$
hence $p_S + p_T$ is a self-adjoint and idempotent operator, that is, a projection.
$\square$

The proof of Theorem 11.11 shows that if $p_S + p_T$ is a projection then $p_S p_T = 0$. This suggests the following definition.

Definition 11.4. *The projection operators p, q in the Hilbert space H are orthogonal if $pq = qp = 0$.*

Theorem 11.12. *Let S and T be two closed subspaces of a Hilbert space H. The following statements are equivalent:*
  (i) $S \subseteq T$;
  (ii) $p_T p_S = p_S$;

(iii) $p_S p_T = p_S$;
(iv) $p_T - p_S$ *is a projection operator;*
(v) $((p_T - p_S)(x), x) \geqslant 0$ *for every* $x \in H$;
(vi) $\|p_S(x)\| \leqslant \|p_T(x)\|$ *for every* $x \in H$.

Proof. (i) implies (ii): Since $p_S(x) \in S \subseteq T$, it follows that $p_T(p_S(x)) = p_S(x)$ for all $x \in H$, hence $p_T p_S = p_S$.

(ii) implies (iii): We have: $p_S p_T = p_S^* p_T^* = (p_T p_S)^* = p_S^* = p_S$.

(iii) implies (iv): We need to verify that the operator $p_T - p_S$ is both self-adjoint and idempotent. Assuming (iii) we can write

$$(p_T - p_S)^* = p_T^* - p_S^* = p_T - p_S,$$
$$(p_T - p_S)^2 = p_T^2 - p_T p_S - p_S p_T + p_S^2$$
$$= p_T - (p_S p_T)^* - p_S + p_S = p_T - p_S.$$

(iv) implies (v): Suppose that $p_T - p_S$ is a projection. We have

$$((p_T - p_S)(x), x) = ((p_T - p_S)(x), (p_T - p_S)(x)) = \|(p_T - p_S)(x)\| \geqslant 0.$$

(v) implies (vi): It (v) holds we can write

$$\|p_T(x)\|^2 - \|p_S(x)\|^2 = (p_T(x), x) - (p_S(x), x)$$
$$= ((p_T - p_S)(x), x) \geqslant 0,$$

which yields (vi).

(vi) implies (i): Suppose that $\|p_S(x)\| \leqslant \|p_T(x)\|$ for every $x \in H$. Then, for $x \in S$ we have

$$\|x\| = \|p_S(x)\| \leqslant \|p_T(x)\| \leqslant \|x\|,$$

hence $x \in T$. $\qquad\square$

11.4   Orthonormal Sets in Hilbert Spaces

Definition 11.5. A subset S of a Hilbert space H is *orthogonal* if $x, y \in S$ and $x \neq y$ imply $(x, y) = 0$. S is an *orthonormal* set if it is orthogonal and $\|x\| = 1$ for every $x \in S$.

An orthonormal set S is called a *complete orthonormal* set if no orthonormal subset of H contains S as a proper subset.

Theorem 11.13. *A non-trivial Hilbert space H (that is, a Hilbert space such that $H \neq \{0_H\}$) contains a complete orthonormal set. If S is any orthonormal set in H then there exists a complete orthonormal set that includes S.*

Proof. Every non-trivial Hilbert space contains an orthonormal set. Indeed, if $x \in H - \{0_H\}$, then the set $\{\frac{1}{\|x\|}x\}$ is orthonormal. Consider the collection of orthonormal subsets $\mathcal{S}$ that contain S as a subset. $\mathcal{S}$ is partially ordered by the inclusion relation. If $\mathcal{S}'$ is a totally ordered subcollection of $\mathcal{S}$, then $\bigcup \mathcal{S}'$ is an orthonormal set and an upper bound of $\mathcal{S}'$. By Zorn's Lemma, there exists a maximal element S_0 of $\mathcal{S}$, which is an orthonormal set that contains S. Since S_0 is maximal it must be a complete orthonormal set. $\qquad\square$

Example 11.6. The set

$$\frac{1}{\sqrt{2\pi}}, \frac{1}{\sqrt{\pi}}\sin t, \frac{1}{\sqrt{\pi}}\cos t, \frac{1}{\sqrt{\pi}}\sin 2t, \frac{1}{\sqrt{\pi}}\cos 2t, \ldots$$

is an orthonormal set in the Hilbert space $L^2([-\pi, \pi])$. This fact is a consequence of the elementary equalities:

$$\int_{-pi}^{\pi} \cos mx \cos nx = \begin{cases} 0 & \text{if } m \neq n, \\ \pi & \text{if } m = n \geqslant 1, \\ 2\pi & \text{if } m = n = 0, \end{cases}$$

$$\int_{-pi}^{\pi} \sin mx \sin nx = \begin{cases} 0 & \text{if } m \neq n, \\ \pi & \text{if } m = n, \end{cases}$$

$$\int_{-pi}^{\pi} \cos mx \sin nx = 0 \text{ for } m, n \in \mathbb{N}.$$

Example 11.7. For $H = \ell^2(\mathbb{C})$ define e_n as the sequence

$$e_n = (0, 0, \ldots, 0, 1, 0, \ldots),$$

where 1 is in the nth position. The set $S = \{e_0, e_1, \ldots, e_n, \ldots\}$ is orthonormal because $\|e_n\| = 1$ and $(e_n, e_m) = 0$, when $n \neq m$.

We saw that the inner product is continuous in the topology induced by the norm induced by the inner product (Theorem 2.53).

Theorem 11.14. *If T is a non-empty set in a Hilbert space then $x \in \mathbf{K}(T)$ and $x \perp T$ implies $x = 0_H$.*

Proof. Since $x \in \mathbf{K}(T)$ there exists a sequence (x_n) in T such that $\lim_{n \to \infty} x_n = x$. By the continuity of the inner product, since $(x, x_n) = 0$, it follows that $(x, x) = 0$, so $x = 0_H$. □

Corollary 11.2. *If T is a dense subset in the Hilbert space H and $x \perp T$, then $x = 0_H$.*

Proof. Since $\mathbf{K}(T) = H$, this statement follows immediately from Theorem 11.14. □

Let $X = \{x_1, \ldots, x_n\}$ be a finite orthonormal set in a Hilbert space H and let $x \in H$. To determine the best approximation of x by linear combinations of elements of X we need to evaluate $\left\| x - \sum_{i=1}^n a_i x_i \right\|$:

$$\left\| x - \sum_{i=1}^n a_i x_i \right\|^2$$

$$= \left(x - \sum_{i=1}^n a_i x_i, x - \sum_{j=1}^n a_j x_j \right)$$

$$= (x, x) - \sum_{j=1}^n \overline{a_j}(x, x_j) - \sum_{i=1}^n a_i(x_i, x) + \sum_{i=1}^n \sum_{j=1}^n a_i \overline{a_j}(x_i, x_j)$$

$$= (x, x) - \sum_{i=1}^n |(x, x_i)|^2$$

$$+ \sum_{i=1}^n |(x, x_i)|^2 - \sum_{j=1}^n \overline{a_j}(x, x_j) - \sum_{i=1}^n a_i(x_i, x) + \sum_{i=1}^n \sum_{j=1}^n |a_i|^2 \overline{a_j}(x_i, x_j)$$

$$= (x, x) - \sum_{i=1}^n |(x, x_i)|^2 + \sum_{i=1}^n |a_i - (x, x_i)|^2.$$

These equalities show that the best approximation of x be linear combinations of a finite orthonormal set $X = \{x_1, \ldots, x_n\}$ is obtained when the coefficients a_i are chosen as $a_i = (x, x_i)$ for $1 \leqslant i \leqslant n$. The minimal distance between x and the finite-dimensional subspace $\langle X \rangle$ is $\|x\|^2 - \sum_{i=1}^n |(x, x_i)|^2$.

Lemma 11.3. (Finite Bessel Inequality) *Let X be a finite orthonormal subset of a Hilbert space H, $X = \{x_1, \ldots, x_n\}$. We have:*

$$\sum_{i=1}^n |(x, x_i)|^2 \leqslant \|x\|^2$$

for every $x \in H$.

Proof. If $a_i = (x, x_i)$ for $1 \leqslant i \leqslant n$ the previous equalities imply

$$\left\| x - \sum_{i=1}^{n} a_i x_i \right\|^2 = (x, x) - \sum_{i=1}^{n} |(x, x_i)|^2 \geqslant 0,$$

which yields the inequality of the lemma. $\qquad\square$

Theorem 11.15. *If S is an orthonormal subset of a Hilbert space H and $x \in H$, then the set $S_x = \{s \in S \mid (x, s) \neq 0\}$ is at most countable.*

Proof. Let $S_x^n = \{s \in S_x \mid |(s, x)| \geqslant \frac{1}{n}\}$. It is clear that $S_x = \bigcup_{n \geqslant 1} S_x^n$.

We claim that each set S_x^n is finite. Indeed, if $s_1, \ldots, s_m$ are m distinct elements of S_x^n, by Lemma 11.3 we have

$$\|x\|^2 \geqslant \sum_{i=1}^{m} |(x, s_j)|^2 \geqslant m \cdot \frac{1}{n^2},$$

which implies $m \leqslant n^2 \|x\|^2$. Thus, each set S_x^n is finite. This implies that S_x itself is at most countable. $\qquad\square$

Corollary 11.3. (Bessel's Inequality) *If S is an orthonormal subset of a Hilbert space H and $x \in H$, then*

$$\sum_{s \in S} |(x, s)|^2 \leqslant \|x\|^2$$

for every $x \in H$.

Proof. This more general form of Bessel inequality follows by listing the elements of S_x and applying the finite form of Bessel inequality. $\qquad\square$

Definition 11.6. Let H be a Hilbert space. An *orthonormal basis* is a maximal orthonormal subset of H.

An orthonormal subset B of H is said to be *total* if $x \perp B$ implies $x = 0_H$.

If $\{x_1, \ldots, x_n\}$ is a finite total sequence in H, then H is said to have dimension n. H is *infinite dimensional* if there exists an infinite total orthonormal set in H.

Theorem 11.16. *Let H be a Hilbert space. A subset B of H is an orthonormal basis if and only if it is a total set.*

Proof. Let B be an orthonormal basis and suppose that B is not total. Then, there exists $x_0 \in H$ such that $x_0 \neq 0$ and $(x_0, y) = 0$ for every $y \in B$. This implies that the set $B \cup \{\frac{1}{\|x_0\|} x_0\}$ is orthonormal and strictly includes B, which violates the maximality of B.

Conversely, let B be a total subset and suppose that B is not an orthonormal basis. This may happen only if B is not maximal, which implies the existence of an orthonormal basis B_1 with $B \subset B_1$. Thus, for $x \in B_1 - B$ we would have $x \perp B$ and $\|x\| = 1$ (and therefore, $x \neq 0_H$), which contradicts the totality of B. $\qquad \square$

Theorem 11.17. *Let H be a Hilbert space. A subset $X = \{x_1, x_2, \dots\}$ of H is total if and only if for every $x \in H$ we have the equality $x = \sum \{(x, x_i) x_i \mid x_i \in X\}$.*

Proof. Suppose that X is a total set. Let $y = \sum \{(x, x_i) x_i \mid x_i \in X\}$. For $x_j \in X$ we have:

$$(x - y, x_j) = (x, x_j) - (y, x_j)$$
$$= (x, x_j) - \sum \{(x, x_i)(x_i, x_j) \mid x_i \in X\}$$
$$\text{(by the continuity of the inner product)}$$
$$= (x, x_j) - (x, x_j) = 0,$$

for every $x_j \in X$. Thus, $x - y \perp X$, hence $x = y$.

Conversely, suppose that $x = \sum \{(x, x_i) x_i \mid x_i \in X\}$ for every $x \in H$. If $x \perp X$, $(x, x_j) = 0$ for every $x_j \in X$, hence $x = 0_H$. $\qquad \square$

Definition 11.7. Let H be a Hilbert space and let $X = \{x_1, x_2, \dots\}$ be a total set in H. The *Fourier coefficients* of an element x of H relative to X are the numbers $a_i = (x, x_i)$. The series $\sum_{i \geq 1} a_i x_i$ is the *Fourier series* of x with respect to X.

Theorem 11.18. *Let H be a Hilbert space, $X = \{x_1, x_2, \dots\}$ be a total set in H, and let $\sum_{i \geq 1} a_i x_i$ be the Fourier series of x with respect to X.*

The sequence (s_n) of partial sums of the Fourier series converges to x in H, where $s_n = \sum_{i=1}^{n} a_i x_i$.

Proof. Observe that if $i \leq n$, then $(x - s_n, x_i) = 0$ because $(x, x_i) = (s_n, x_i) = c_i$ for $i \leq n$. Therefore, $(x - s_n, s_n) = 0$, that is, $x - s_n \perp s_n$. Therefore, $\|x\|^2 = \|x - s_n\|^2 + \|s_n\|^2 \geq \|s_n\|^2$.

Since X is total we have $\|s_n\|^2 = (\sum_{i=1}^{n} a_i x_i, \sum_{i=1}^{n} a_i x_i) = \sum_{i=1}^{n} |a_i|^2$, hence $\sum_{i=1}^{n} |a_i|^2 \leq \|f\|^2$, which shows that the series $\sum_{i=1}^{\infty} |a_i|^2$ converges.

Since $\|s_n - s_m\|^2 = \sum_{i=m+1}^n |a_i|^2$, it follows that (s_n) is a Cauchy sequence. The completeness of H means that there exists $y \in H$ such that $\lim_{n \to \infty} s_n = y$. Since $(y, x_i) = \lim_{n \to \infty}(s_n, x_i) = a_i$ for $i \geqslant 1$, it follows that $(x - y, x_i) = 0$, so $y = x$ because X is a total set. $\qquad \square$

Theorem 11.19. *Let H be a Hilbert space and let X be an orthonormal subset in H. For $x \in H$ we have $x = \sum\{(x, x_i)x_i \mid x_i \in X\}$ if and only if $\|x\|^2 = \sum\{|(x, x_i)|^2 \mid x_i \in X\}$.*

Proof. Suppose that $x = \sum\{(x, x_i)x_i \mid x_i \in X\}$. Then,

$$\|x\|^2 = \lim_{n \to \infty} \left\|\sum_{i \leqslant n}(x, x_i)\right\|^2 = \lim_{n \to \infty}\sum_{i \leqslant n}|(x, x_i)|^2 = \sum_{x_i \in X}|(x, x_i)|^2.$$

Conversely, suppose that $\|x\|^2 = \sum\{|(x, x_i)|^2 \mid x_i \in X\}$ for every $x \in H$. It is easy to see that

$$\left\|x - \sum_{i \leqslant n}(x, x_i)x_i\right\|^2 = \|x\|^2 - \sum_{i=1}^n |(x, x_i)|^2.$$

By taking the limit when $n \to \infty$ we obtain $x - \sum\{(x, x_i)x_i \mid x_i \in X\} = 0_H$. $\qquad \square$

Corollary 11.4. *Let H be a Hilbert space and let X be an orthonormal subset in H. The following statements are equivalent:*
  (i) *X is an orthonormal basis;*
  (ii) *X is a total subset;*
  (iii) *$x = \sum\{(x, x_i)x_i \mid x_i \in X\}$ for every $x \in H$;*
  (iv) *$\|x\|^2 = \sum\{|(x, x_i)|^2 x_i \in X\}$;*
  (v) *$K(\langle X \rangle) = H$, that is, the subspace generated by X is dense in H.*

Proof. The equivalence of (i) and (ii) was shown in Theorem 11.16. In Theorem 11.17 we proved that (ii) is equivalent to (iii). Theorem 11.19 states the equivalence of (iii) and (iv).

To complete the argument we prove two more implications.

(iii) implies (v): Suppose that $x = \sum\{(x, x_i)x_i \mid x_i \in X\}$ for every $x \in H$. Then $x = \lim_{k \to \infty}\sum_{i \leqslant k}(x, x_i)x_i$, which proves that $x \in K(\langle X \rangle)$. Thus, $K(\langle X \rangle) = H$.

(v) implies (ii) Suppose that $K(\langle X \rangle) = H$. If $x \perp X$, then x is orthogonal on a set that is dense in H (by hypothesis), so $x = 0_H$ by Corollary 11.2. $\qquad \square$

Example 11.8. Consider the set of complex-valued functions $\{f_k \mid k \in \mathbb{Z}, f_k : [-\pi, \pi] \longrightarrow \mathbb{C}\}$, where $f_k(x) = \frac{1}{\sqrt{2\pi}} e^{ikx}$ for $k \in \mathbb{Z}$ and $x \in [-\pi, \pi]$.

It is immediate that

$$\|f_k\|^2 = \int_{-\pi}^{\pi} |f_k|^2 \, dx = \frac{1}{2\pi} \int_{-\pi}^{\pi} dx = 1,$$

for $k \in \mathbb{Z}$. Furthermore, for $k \neq h$ we have:

$$(f_k, f_h) = \frac{1}{2\pi} \int_{-\pi}^{\pi} f_k(x) \overline{f_h(x)} \, dx$$

$$= \frac{1}{2\pi} \int_{-\pi}^{\pi} e^{i(k-h)x} \, dx = 0,$$

hence $\{f_k \mid k \in \mathbb{Z}\}$ is an orthonormal set in $\mathcal{L}^2([-\pi, \pi])$.

The subalgebra $\mathcal{U}$ of the algebra of complex-valued continuous function on $[-\pi, \pi]$ generated by the functions $\{f_k \mid k \in \mathbb{Z}, f_k : [-\pi, \pi] \longrightarrow \mathbb{C}\}$ contains the constant functions because $1 = \sqrt{2\pi} f_0(x)$ for every $x \in [-\pi, \pi]$.

The conjugate of the function f_k is the function f_{-k}, so $\mathcal{U}$ is closed with respect to conjugation. Furthermore, $\mathcal{U}$ separates points. Indeed, suppose that $x, y \in [-\pi, \pi]$ and that $f_k(x) = f_k(y)$ for every $k \in \mathbb{Z}$. This means that $e^{ikx} = e^{iky}$, or $e^{ik(x-y)} = 1$ for every $k \in \mathbb{Z}$, or that $\cos k(x - y) = 1$ and $\sin k(x - y) = 0$ for every $k \in \mathbb{Z}$, which implies $x = y$. Since this is not the case, $\mathcal{U}$ separates points.

By the Complex Stone-Weierstrass Theorem (Theorem 5.40), it follows that the subspace of $\mathcal{L}^1([-\pi, \pi])$ generated by the functions $\{f_k \mid k \in \mathbb{Z}\}$ is dense in $\mathcal{L}^1([-\pi, \pi])$, which by Corollary 11.4 implies that the set $\{\frac{1}{\sqrt{2\pi}} e^{ikx} \mid k \in \mathbb{Z}\}$ is an orthonormal basis in $C([-\pi, \pi])$.

Since $f_k(x) = \frac{1}{\sqrt{2\pi}}(\cos kx + i \sin kx)$ for $k \in \mathbb{Z}$ and $x \in [-\pi, \pi]$, we have:

$$\frac{1}{\sqrt{\pi}} \cos kz = \sqrt{\frac{1}{2}}(f_k(x) + f_{-k}(x)) \text{ and } \frac{1}{\sqrt{\pi}} \sin kz = \sqrt{\frac{1}{2i}}(f_k(x) - f_{-k}(x)).$$

Therefore, the set

$$\frac{1}{\sqrt{2\pi}}, \frac{1}{\sqrt{\pi}} \sin t, \frac{1}{\sqrt{\pi}} \cos t, \frac{1}{\sqrt{\pi}} \sin 2t, \frac{1}{\sqrt{\pi}} \cos 2t, \dots$$

is also an orthonormal basis in $L^2([-\pi, \pi])$.

Theorem 11.20. *Let H be a Hilbert space and let (x_n) be an orthogonal sequence in H. The series $\sum_n x_n$ converges if and only if the numerical series $\sum_n \|x_n\|^2$ converges. In this case, $\|\sum_n x_n\|^2 = \sum_n \|x_n\|^2$ and the sum $\sum_n x_n$ is independent of the order of the terms.*

Proof. Since the sequence (x_n) consists of pairwise orthogonal elements it is immediate that

$$\|x_{n+1} + x_{n+2} + \cdots + x_m\|^2 \leqslant \|x_{n+1}\|^2 + \|x_{n+2}\|^2 + \cdots + \|x_m\|^2$$

for $m \geqslant n+1$. This shows that the sequences of partial sums of the series $\sum_n x_n$ and $\sum \|x_n\|^2$ are simultaneously Cauchy sequences.

Since $\sum \|x_n\|^2$ has non-negative terms its sum does not depend on the order of the terms.

If the series $\sum_n x_n$ is convergent its sum is independent of the order of the terms.

Suppose that the series $\sum y_n$ is obtained from the series $\sum x_n$ be permuting the order of the terms. Let $y = \sum y_n$. Then,

$$x - y = \sum (x_n - y_n) = \lim_{k \to \infty} \sum_k (x_k - y_k),$$

which shows that $x - y$ belongs to the closure of the subspace generated by the set $\{x_n \mid n \in \mathbb{N}\}$. For x_p in this set, we have

$$(x - y, x_p) = \lim_{n \to \infty} \left(\sum_{k=1}^{n} (x_k - y_k), x_p \right) = \lim_{n \to \infty} \sum_{k=1}^{n} ((x_k, x_p) - (y_k, x_p)) = 0,$$

so $x - y$ is orthogonal on the set $\{x_n \mid n \in \mathbb{N}\}$. Thus, $x = y$. $\qquad\square$

Theorem 11.21. *Let H be a Hilbert space and let $S = \{x_1, x_2, \ldots\}$ be an orthonormal basis in H. For $u, v \in H$ we have*

$$(u, v) = \sum_{n \geqslant 1} (u, x_n)(x_n, v)$$

and

$$\|u\|^2 = \sum_{n \geqslant 1} |(u, x_n)|^2.$$

Proof. We have shown (see Theorem 11.15) that if S is an orthonormal set in H then the sets $S_u = \{s \in S \mid (u, s) \neq 0\}$ and $S_v = \{s \in S \mid (v, s) \neq 0\}$ are at most countable, $u = \lim_{n \to \infty} \sum_{j=1}^{n} (u, x_j) x_j$ and $v = \lim_{n \to \infty} \sum_{k=1}^{n} (u, x_k) x_k$. Since the inner product is continuous, we may further write

$$(x, y) = \lim_{n \to \infty} \left(\sum_{j=1}^{n} (u, x_j)x_j, \sum_{k=1}^{n} (v, x_k)x_k \right)$$

$$= \lim_{n \to \infty} \sum_{j=1}^{n} \sum_{k=1}^{n} (u, x_j)\overline{(v, x_k)}(x_j, x_k)$$

$$= \lim_{n \to \infty} \sum_{j=1}^{n} (u, x_j)\overline{(v, x_j)})$$

$$= \lim_{n \to \infty} \sum_{j=1}^{n} (u, x_j)(x_j.v)) = \sum_{j=1}^{\infty} (u, x_j)(x_j, v)).$$

Taking $u = v$ we obtain the second part of the theorem. $\qquad \square$

Theorem 11.22. *Let H be a Hilbert space. The following statements are equivalent:*

    (i) *H is a separable space;*

    (ii) *there exists an orthonormal basis for H that is countable.*

Proof.   (i) implies (ii): Suppose that H is separable, that is, it contains a countable dense subset. Let X be an orthonormal basis. The separability of H implies the separability of X and since X is the unique dense subset of X, it follows that X must be countable.

    (ii) implies (i): Suppose that $X = \{x_1, x_2, \ldots\}$ is a countable orthonormal basis for H. We deal initially with a real Hilbert space H.

    Let $D_n = \{x \in H \mid x = \sum_{j=1}^{n} q_j x_j, q_j \in \mathbb{Q} \text{ for } 1 \leqslant j \leqslant n\}$ for $n \geqslant 1$. We have $\mathbf{K}(D_n) = \langle x_1, \ldots, x_n \rangle$. Therefore, for $D = \bigcup_{n \geqslant 1} D_n$ we have $\mathbf{K}(D) = H$, so H is separable.

    If H is a complex Hilbert space, define D_n as $D_n = \{x \in H \mid x = \sum_{j=1}^{n} (q_j + ir_j)x_j, q_j \in \mathbb{Q} \text{ for } 1 \leqslant j \leqslant n\}$ for $n \geqslant 1$ and proceed in a similar manner. $\qquad \square$

Theorem 11.23. *Every infinitely dimensional, separable Hilbert space is isometric to ℓ^2.*

Proof.   Since H is infinitely dimensional and separable, it has a countably infinite orthonormal basis $S = \{x_1, \ldots, x_n, \ldots\}$ by Theorem 11.22. Define the linear mapping $f : H \longrightarrow \ell^2$ as

$$f(x) = (x, x_n)_{n \geqslant 1}$$

for $x \in H$. We saw that $(x, y) = (f(x), f(y))$ and $\|x\| = \|h(x)\|_2$. Since $\text{Null}(f) = \{0_H\}$, f is injective.

Let $a = (a_n) \in \ell^2$. Since $a_n x_n$ and $a_m x_m$ are orthogonal and

$$\sum_{n=1}^{\infty} \|a_n x_n\|^2 = \sum_{n=1}^{\infty} |a_n|^2,$$

it follows that the series $\sum_{n=1}^{\infty} a_n x_n$ is convergent. If we define $x = \sum_{n=1}^{\infty} a_n x_n$, then $a = f(x)$, so f is surjective. Since f preserves the norm, it follows that H is isometric with ℓ^2. $\qquad\square$

Let h be a bounded operator on a Hilbert space H and let $\{e_i \mid i \in I\}$ be an orthonormal basis in H. Recall that we proved in Theorem 11.21 that if $x = \sum_{i \in I}(x, e_i)e_i$ and $y = \sum_{j \in I}(y, e_j)e_j$, it follows that

$$(x, y) = \sum_{i \in I}(x, e_i)(e_i, y).$$

Theorem 11.24. *Let $\{e_i \mid i \in I\}$ and $\{f_j \mid j \in J\}$ be two orthonormal bases in a Hilbert space H and let h be a bounded linear operator on H. We have*

$$\sum_{i} \|h(e_i)\|^2 = \sum_{j} \|h(f_j)\|^2 = \sum_{i} \sum_{j} |(h(e_i), f_j)|^2.$$

Proof. We have:

$$\sum_{i} \sum_{j} |(h(e_i), f_j)|^2 = \sum_{i} \sum_{j}(h(e_i), f_j)\overline{(h(e_i), f_j)}$$

$$= \sum_{i}\left(\sum_{j}(h(e_i), f_j)(f_j, h(e_i))\right)$$

$$= \sum_{i}(h(e_i), h(e_i)) = \sum_{i} \|h(e_i)\|^2.$$

In a similar manner it is possible to prove the other equality. $\qquad\square$

Theorem 11.24 shows that the value of $\sum_{i} \|h(e_i)\|^2$ depends only on the operator h and not the orthonormal basis. The number $\sqrt{\sum_{i} \|h(e_i)\|^2}$ is denoted by $\nu_{SC}(h)$.

Note that

$$\nu_{SC}(h)^2 = \sum_{i} \|h(e_i)\|^2 = \sum_{i} \sum_{j} |(e_i, h^*(f_j))|^2$$

$$= \sum_{j} \|h^*(f_j)\|^2 = \nu_{SC}(h^*)^2.$$

Theorem 11.25. *For a linear operator h we have $\|h\| \leqslant \nu_{SC}(h)$. Moreover ν_{SC} is a norm on the linear space of linear operators on H.*

Proof.   Let ϵ be an arbitrary positive number. Since

$$\nu_{SC}(h) = \sum_i \|h(e_i)\|^2,$$

if the basis $\{e_i \mid i \in I\}$ is chosen such that $\|h(e_1)\| \geqslant \|h\| - \epsilon$ (which is possible by the definition of $\|h\|$) we have $\nu_{SC}(h)^2 = \sum_i \|h(e_i)\|^2 \geqslant (\|h\| - \epsilon)^2$. Since this inequality holds for every ϵ we have $\nu_{SC}(h) \geqslant \|h\|$.

Let h, g be two linear operators on H and let $\{e_i \mid i \in I\}$ be an orthonormal basis of H. We have:

$$\nu_{SC}(h + g)^2 = \sum_i \|(h + g)(e_i)\|^2 = \sum_i \|(h(e_i) + g(e_i)\|^2$$

$$= \sum_i \|h(e_i)\|^2 + \sum_i \|g(e_i)\|^2 + 2\sum_i \|h(e_i)\|\|g(e_i)\|$$

$$\leqslant \nu_{SC}(h)^2 + \nu_{SC}(g)^2 + 2\nu_{SC}(h)\nu_{SC}(g)$$

$$= (\nu_{SC}(h) + \nu_{SC}(g))^2,$$

because

$$\sum_i \|h(e_i)\|\|g(e_i)\| \leqslant \sqrt{\sum_i \|h(e_i)\|^2}\sqrt{\sum_i \|g(e_i)\|^2}.$$

Thus, $\nu_{SC}(h + g) \leqslant \nu_{SC}(h) + \nu_{SC}(g)$. The equality $\nu_{SC}(ah) = |a|\nu_{SC}(h)$ for $a \in \mathbb{C}$ is immediate, so ν_{SC} is indeed a norm. $\square$

We refer to ν_{SC} as the *Schmidt norm*.

Theorem 11.26. *Let h be a linear operator on a Hilbert space H. If $\nu_{SC}(h)$ is finite, then the operator h is compact.*

Proof.   Let (e_n) be an orthonormal basis in H. For $n \in \mathbb{N}$ define the operator g_n with a finite-dimensional range as

$$g_n(x) = \sum_{i=0}^{n} (h(x), e_i)e_i,$$

for $x \in H$.

Each of the operators g_n is compact because it has a finite-dimensional range. Since $h(x) = \sum_{i=0}^{\infty}(h(x), e_i)e_i$, it follows that

$$\|h(x) - g_n(x)\|^2 = \left\| \sum_{i=n+1}^{\infty} (h(x), e_i)e_i \right\|^2$$

$$= \sum_{i=n+1}^{\infty} |(h(x), e_i)|^2$$

$$= \sum_{i=n+1}^{\infty} |(x, h^*(e_i))|^2$$

$$\leqslant \|x\|^2 \sum_{i=n+1}^{\infty} \|h^*(e_i)\|^2.$$

If $\nu_{SC}(h)$ is finite, then for any $\epsilon > 0$ and sufficiently large n we have

$$\|h(x) - g_n(x)\| \leqslant \epsilon\|x\|,$$

so $\|h - h_n\| < \epsilon$, so, by Theorem 9.12 h is a compact operator. $\qquad\square$

Definition 11.8. A *Hilbert-Schmidt operator* is a linear operator on a Hilbert space H such that $\nu_{SC}(h)$ is finite.

The set of Hilbert-Schmidt operators on the Hilbert space is denoted by $\mathsf{HS}(H)$.

Example 11.9. Let $\mathcal{L}^2(S, \mathcal{E}, m)$ be a separable space and let $K : S \times S \longrightarrow \mathbb{C}$ be a Hermitian function such that

$$\int_S \int_S |K(x, y)|^2 \, d_x m \, d^y m < \infty.$$

Consider the linear operator $h : \mathcal{L}^2(S, \mathcal{E}, m) \longrightarrow \mathcal{L}^2(S, \mathcal{E}, m)$ defined by

$$(h(f))(x) = \int_S K(x, y) f(y) \, d^y m.$$

We show that h is a Hilbert-Schmidt operator and that every such operator on $\mathcal{L}^2(S, \mathcal{E}, m)$ can be obtained in this manner.

Since $\mathcal{L}^2(S, \mathcal{E}, m)$ is separable, by Theorem 11.22 there exists a countable orthonormal basis $\{e_n \mid n \in \mathbb{N}\}$ in this space. By Fubini-Lebesgue Theorem (Theorem 8.68), for almost every $x \in S$, $K_x(y) = K(x, y)$ defines a function in $\mathcal{L}^2(S, \mathcal{E}, m)$. Hence, for almost every $x \in S$ we have

$$h(e_n)(x) = \int_S K(x, y) e_n(y) \, d^y m = \int_S K_x(y) e_n(y) \, d^y m$$

$$= \int_S \sum_{n \in \mathbb{N}} |(K_x, \overline{e_n})|^2 \, d^y m.$$

By the Dominated Convergence Theorem (Theorem 8.37),

$$\sum_{n \in \mathbb{N}} \|h(e_n)\|^2 = \sum_{n \in \mathbb{N}} \int_S |(K_x, \overline{e_n})|^2 \, d^y m = \int_X \sum_{n \in \mathbb{N}} |(K_x, \overline{e_n})|^2 \, d^y m.$$

Since $\{e_n \mid n \in \mathbb{N}\}$ is an orthonormal basis in H, by Supplement 4, the set $\{\overline{e_n} \mid n \in \mathbb{N}\}$ is also an orthonormal basis in H. Thus,

$$K_x = \sum_{n \in \mathbb{N}} (K_x, \overline{e_n}) \overline{e_n}$$

and

$$\|K_x\|^2 = \sum_{n \in \mathbb{N}} |(K_x, \overline{e_n})|^2.$$

We conclude that

$$\sum_{n \in \mathbb{N}} \|h(e_n)\|^2 = \int_S \|K_x\|^2 \, d^y m = \int_S (K(x, y) \, d^y m) \, d_x m < \infty$$

because $K \in \mathcal{L}^2(S \times T, \mathcal{E} \times \mathcal{E}, m \times m)$. This shows that h is a Hilbert-Schmidt operator.

Conversely, any Hilbert-Schmidt operator on $\mathcal{L}^2(S, \mathcal{E}, m)$ is an operator defined by a Hermitian function $K \in \mathcal{L}^2(S \times S, \mathcal{E} \times \mathcal{E}, m \times m)$. Indeed, suppose that h is a Hilbert-Schmidt operator on $\mathcal{L}^2(S, \mathcal{E}, m)$ and let $\{e_n \mid n \in \mathbb{N}\}$ be an orthonormal basis of $\mathcal{L}^2(X, \mathcal{E}, m)$. If $f \in \mathcal{L}^2(S, \mathcal{E}, m)$ we have

$$h(f)(x) = h \left(\sum_{n \in \mathbb{N}} (f, e_n) e_n \right)(x) = \sum_{n \in \mathbb{N}} \left(\int_S f(y) \overline{e_n(y)} \, d^y m \right) (h(e_n))(x).$$

Since $\sum_{n \in \mathbb{N}} \|h(e_n)\|^2 < \infty$, the series $\sum_{n \in \mathbb{N}} h(e_n)$ converges in $\mathcal{L}^2(S, \mathcal{E}, m)$. By Fubini's Theorem, the function $K : S \times S \longrightarrow \mathbb{C}$ defined by

$$K(x, y) = \sum_{n \in \mathbb{N}} h(e_n)(x) \overline{e_n(y)}$$

belongs to $\mathcal{L}^2(S, \mathcal{E}, m)$. By the dominated convergence theorem

$$(h(f))(x) = \sum_{n \in \mathbb{N}} \left(\int_S f(y) \overline{e_n(x)} \, d^y m \right) (h(e_n))(x)$$

$$= \int_S f(y) \left(\sum_{n \in \mathbb{N}} (h(e_n))(x) e_n(y) \right) d^y m$$

$$= \int_S K(x, y) f(y) \, d^y m.$$

We shall refer to the function K as an *integral kernel*.

Example 11.10. Let $S = [0, \infty)$ and let K be defined by

$$K(x, y) = \begin{cases} 1 & \text{if } 0 \leqslant y \leqslant x, \\ 0 & \text{if } x < y. \end{cases}$$

Define the integral operator v as

$$(vf)(x) = \int_0^1 K(x, y) f(y) \, dy.$$

The operator v is compact because it is a Hilbert-Schmidt operator. We have

$$\int_0^1 K(x, y) f(y) \, dy = \int_0^x f(y) \, dy.$$

Thus, for the function g defined by $g(x) = (vf)(x)$ for $x \in [0, \infty)$ we have $g(0) = 0$ and $g'(x) = f(x)$.

Suppose that $\lambda \neq 0$ is an eigenvalue of v and $(vf)(x) = \lambda f(x)$. Then $f(x) = \lambda f'(x)$ and this implies that $f(x) = ke^{\frac{x}{\lambda}}$ for some $k \in \mathbb{R}$. However, we have

$$\lambda k e^{\frac{x}{\lambda}} - \lambda k = \lambda k e^{\frac{x}{\lambda}},$$

which implies $\lambda k = 0$. Since $\lambda \neq 0$, this implies $k = 0$, so f is the function that is constant 0 on $[0, \infty)$, which contradicts the assumption that λ is an eigenvalue.

For $\lambda = 0$ there are no eigenvectors because $(vf)(x) = 0$ implies $f(x) = 0$ for $x \in [0, \infty]$.

The operator v is known as the *Volterra operator*.

The completeness of Hilbert spaces allows us to prove a stronger form of Theorem 2.53.

Theorem 11.27. *Let H be a Hilbert space. If S is a closed subspace of H and $x \in H$, then there exists a unique $m_0 \in S$ such that $\|x - m_0\| \leqslant \|x - y\|$ for every $y \in S$. Furthermore, m_0 is a unique vector in S that minimizes $\|x - y\|$ if and only if $x - m_0$ is orthogonal on S.*

Proof. In view of Theorem 2.53 we need to establish only the existence of m_0.

If x belongs to S, then $m_0 = x$ and the argument is completed.

Suppose that $x \notin S$ (see Figure 11.1). Let $d = \inf\{\|x - y\| \mid y \in S\}$ and let $z_0, \ldots, z_n, \ldots$ be a sequence of members of S such that $\lim_{n \to \infty} \|x - z_i\| = d$.

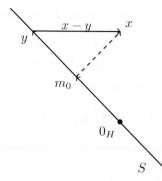

Fig. 11.1   Configuration of elements involved in Theorem 11.27.

By an application of the parallelogram equality (Theorem 2.27) to $x - z_i$ and $z_j - x$ we have:

$$2(\|x - z_i\|^2 + \|z_j - x\|^2) = \|z_j - z_i\|^2 + \|2x - z_i - z_j\|^2,$$

which implies:

$$\|z_j - z_i\|^2 = 2(\|x - z_i\|^2 + \|z_j - x\|^2) - \|2x - z_i - z_j\|^2$$

$$= 2(\|x - z_i\|^2 + \|z_j - x\|^2) - 4\left\|x - \frac{z_i + z_j}{2}\right\|^2.$$

Since S is a subspace of H, we have $\frac{z_i + z_j}{2} \in S$, so $\|x - \frac{z_i + z_j}{2}\| \geqslant d$, which implies

$$\|z_j - z_i\|^2 \leqslant 2(\|x - z_i\|^2 + \|z_j - x\|^2) - 4d^2.$$

By the definition of the sequence (z_i), we conclude that this is a Cauchy sequence and, since S is a closed subspace, there exists $m_0 \in S$ such that $z_i \to m_0$. By the continuity of the norm (see Corollary 6.6) it follows that $\|x - m_0\| = d$.   □

Corollary 11.5. *Let H be a Hilbert space, S be a closed subspace of H, and let $x \in H$. If $V = t_x(S)$, there exists a unique vector x_0 in V of minimum norm and $x_0 \in S^\perp$.*

Proof.   Let $m_0 \in S$ be the element of S whose existence and uniqueness was established in Theorem 11.27 (see Figure 11.2). For $x_0 = x - m_0$ we have $\|x_0\| \leqslant \|x - y\|$ for every $y \in S$ and $x_0 - m_0$ is orthogonal on S, hence $x_0 \in S^\perp$.   □

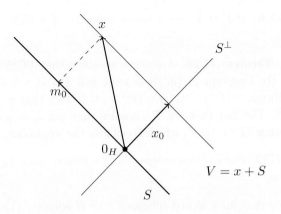

Fig. 11.2   Configuration of elements involved in Corollary 11.5.

Theorem 11.27 shows that $x_0 = x - m_0 \in S^{\perp}$ is of minimal norm among the vectors of the form $x - y$, where $y \in S$. It allows us to introduce an operator p_S on the Hilbert space H defined by $p_S(x) = x_0$, where $x_0 \in S$ is such that $\|x - y\|$ is minimal and $x - p_S(x)$ is orthogonal on S.

Definition 11.9. Let S a closed subspace of a Hilbert space. The *projection* of H on S is the operator p_S.

Recall that for any subset T of a topological inner product space we have shown that $T^{\perp}$ is a closed subspace (see Theorem 6.19). This holds, of course, in a Hilbert space.

Theorem 11.28. *If T is a subset of a Hilbert space, then $(T^{\perp})^{\perp}$ is the smallest closed subspace of H that contains T.*

Proof. We already know that $(T^{\perp})^{\perp}$ is a closed subspace of H that contains T. Suppose that W is a subspace of H that contains T. Then, $(T^{\perp})^{\perp} \subseteq (W^{\perp})^{\perp} = W$, which concludes the proof. □

Theorem 11.29. *Let S be a closed subspace of a Hilbert space H. Then, $H = S \oplus S^{\perp}$.*

Proof. This follows immediately from the equality

$$x = p_S(x) + (x - p_S(x)) \tag{11.3}$$

for $x \in H$ because $p_S(x) \in S$ and $x - p_S(x) \in S^{\perp}$. □

Corollary 11.6. *If T is a closed linear subspace of a Hilbert space, then $T = (T^\perp)^\perp$.*

Proof. By Theorem 11.28, it suffices to show that $(T^\perp)^\perp \subseteq T$. Let $x \in (T^\perp)^\perp$. By Theorem 11.29, there exist $y \in T$ and $z \in T^\perp$ such that $x = y + z$. Since $x \in (T^\perp)^\perp$ and $y \in (T^\perp)^\perp$, it follows that $x - y \in (T^\perp)^\perp$, so $z \in (T^\perp)^\perp$. The fact that $z \in T^\perp$ implies that $z \perp z$, so $z = 0_H$. Thus, $x = y \in T$, hence $(T^\perp)^\perp \subseteq T$, which concludes the argument. $\square$

Theorem 11.30. *For a closed subspace S of a Hilbert space p_S is a bounded linear operator.*

Proof. Note that for a closed subspace S of H equality (11.3) is equivalent to $x = p_S(x) + p_{S^\perp}(x)$. Therefore, for $x, y \in H$ we have

$$x = p_S(x) + p_{S^\perp}(x) \text{ and } y = p_S(y) + p_{S^\perp}(y),$$

which implies

$$x + y = p_S(x) + p_{S^\perp}(x) + p_S(y) + p_{S^\perp}(y)$$
$$= p_S(x) + p_S(y) + p_{S^\perp}(x) + p_{S^\perp}(y).$$

From the uniqueness of the decomposition, it follows that $p_S(x + y) = p_S(x) + p_S(y)$ and $p_{S^\perp}(x + y) = p_{S^\perp}(x) + p_{S^\perp}(y)$.

Similarly, $ax = ap_S(x) + ap_{S^\perp}(x)$, where $ap_S(x) \in S$ and $ap_{S^\perp}(x) \in S^\perp$, which implies $p_S(ax) = ap_S(x)$, showing that p_S is a linear operator.

Since $\|x\|^2 = \|p_S(x)\|^2 + \|p_{S^\perp}(x)\|^2$, it follows that $\|x\| \geqslant \|p_S(x)\|$, so $\|p_S\| \leqslant 1$. On the other hand, if $x \in S$ we have $p_S(x) = x$, hence $\|p_S\| = 1$. $\square$

Theorem 11.31. *For a closed subspace S of a Hilbert space H we have $p_{S^\perp} = 1_H - p_S$ and $S^\perp = \{x \in S \mid p_S(x) = 0_H\}$.*

Proof. Since every $x \in H$ can be written as $x = p_S(x) + p_{S^\perp}(x)$, it follows that $p_{S^\perp}(x) = x - p_S(x)$ for every $x \in H$, that is, $p_{S^\perp} = 1_H - p_S$. Thus, $S^\perp = \{x \in H \mid x = p_{S^\perp}(x)\} = \{x \in H \mid x - p_S(x) = x\} = \{x \in H \mid p_S(x) = 0_H\}$. $\square$

The next statement is a stronger form of a previous theorem for inner product spaces (Theorem 2.44).

Theorem 11.32. *Let H be a Hilbert space, $B = \{b_1, \ldots, b_k\}$ be a linearly independent set in H and let $S = \langle B \rangle$.*

For $\mathbf{c} = \begin{pmatrix} c_1 \\ \vdots \\ c_k \end{pmatrix} \in \mathbb{R}^k$ let $U_{\mathbf{c}} = \{x \in H \mid (x, b_i) = c_i \text{ for } 1 \leqslant i \leqslant k\}.$

The vector x_0 of minimal norm in $U_{\mathbf{c}}$ belongs to the subspace S. Furthermore, if $x_0 = \sum_{i=1}^{k} d_i b_i$, then $G_Y \mathbf{d} = \mathbf{c}$, where $\mathbf{d} = \begin{pmatrix} d_1 \\ \vdots \\ d_k \end{pmatrix}$ and G_B is the Gram matrix of the set B.

Proof. We have shown in Theorem 2.44 that $U_{\mathbf{c}}$ is the translation of $S^{\perp}$ (which is a closed subspace), where $S = \langle b_1, \ldots, b_k \rangle$. Since $S^{\perp}$ is closed, by Corollary 11.5, there exists a unique $x_0 \in (S^{\perp})^{\perp} = S$ such that $\|x_0\|$ is minimal. Since $S = \langle Y \rangle$, $x_0 = \sum_{i=1}^{k} d_i y_i$. The definition of $U_{\mathbf{c}}$ implies the equality $G_B \mathbf{d} = \mathbf{c}$. $\qquad \square$

11.5 The Dual Space of a Hilbert Space

Theorem 11.33. (The Riesz'[3] Representation Theorem) *Let H be a Hilbert space and let $f : H \longrightarrow \mathbb{F}$ be a continuous linear functional. There is a unique $a \in H$ such that $f(x) = (x, a)$ for every $x \in H$. Moreover, $\|f\| = \|a\|$.*

Proof. If f is the zero functional the statement is immediate by taking $a = 0$. So, suppose that f is a non-trivial functional and, therefore, a surjective function.

Since f is continuous, $\mathsf{Null}(f)$ is a closed subspace of H by Theorem 9.14. We have $\mathsf{Null}(f) \subset H$, so $(\mathsf{Null}(f))^{\perp} \neq \{0\}$. There exists $b \in (\mathsf{Null}(f))^{\perp}$ such that $f(b) = 1$. For $x \in H$ we have

$$f(x - f(x)b) = f(x) - f(x)f(b) = 0,$$

so $x - f(x)b \in \mathsf{Null}(f)$. Taking into account that $b \in (\mathsf{Null}(f))^{\perp}$, it follows that

$$0 = (x - f(x)b, b) = (x, b) - f(x)(b, b) = (x, b) - f(x)\|b\|^2,$$

which yields $f(x) = \frac{1}{\|b\|^2}(x, b)$. Taking $a = \frac{b}{\|b\|^2}$ gives the desired representation of f.

---

[3] Frigyes Riesz (Jan. 22, 1880–Feb. 28, 1956) was a Hungarian mathematician and pioneer of functional analysis. Riesz taught mathematics at the University of Cluj from 1911 and later at the University of Budapest.

To prove the uniqueness of a suppose that $(x, a) = (x, b)$ for $x \in H$. Then, $(x, a - b) = 0$, and, by taking $x = a - b$ we have $\|a - b\| = 0$, which yields $a - b = 0$.

By Cauchy-Schwarz Inequality (Theorem 2.23) we have $|f(x)| = |(x, a)| \leqslant \|x\|\|a\|$. Thus, f is bounded and $\|f\| \leqslant \|a\|$. Moreover, we have

$$f\left(\frac{a}{\|a\|}\right) = \left(\frac{a}{\|a\|}, a\right) = \|a\|,$$

so $\|f\| = \|a\|$. $\square$

Corollary 11.7. *Each real Hilbert space is isomorphic with its dual H^*.*

Proof.   This is a direct consequence of Theorem 11.33. $\square$

If T is an orthonormal set in a Hilbert space H, then there exists a basis B for H that contains T.

11.6   Weak Convergence

Convergence of sequences in a Hilbert in the sense of the norm is also known as *strong convergence*. We consider in this section an alternative, weaker form of convergence.

Definition 11.10. A sequence $\mathbf{x}$ in a Hilbert space *converges weakly* if for every $y \in H$ the sequence of scalars $((x_n, y))$ is convergent.

An element x of H is the *weak limit* of a sequence (x_n) if $\lim_{n \to \infty}(x_n, y) = (x, y)$ for every $y \in H$. This is denoted by $x_n \to_w x$.

Example 11.11. Note that if $\lim_{n \to \infty} x_n = x$, them $x_n \to_w x$ due to the continuity of the inner product in Hilbert spaces. The converse implication is false. Indeed, consider an infinite orthonormal basis (e_n) in a Hilbert space H and let $y = \sum_n a_n e_n$. The series $\sum_n |(y, e_n)|^2$ is convergent, hence $\lim_{n \to \infty}(y, e_n) = 0$ for every $y \in H$, so (e_n) is a weakly convergent sequence. However the sequence (e_n) does not converge because $\|e_n\| = 1$ for every $n \in \mathbb{N}$.

Lemma 11.4. *Let (x_n) be a weakly convergent sequence in a Hilbert space H. There exists $\tilde{y} \in H$ and two positive numbers M and r such that for all $n \in \mathbb{N}$ we have $|(x_n, y)| < M$ for all $y \in B(\tilde{y}, r)$.*

Proof. The lemma stipulates that there exists an open sphere $B(\tilde{y}, r)$ such that $|(x_n, y)|$ is bounded when y ranges in this sphere.

Suppose that the statement is false, that is, $|(x_n, y)|$ is unbounded in every sphere. Thus, n_1, y_1 exist such that $|(x_{n_1}, y_1)| > 1$. Since the inner product is continuous we have $(x_{n_1}, y) > 1$ for every $y \in B(y_1, r_1)$ for some $r_1 > 0$. Further, suppose that exists n_2, y_2 such that $y_2 \in B(y_1, r_1)$ and $|(x_{n_2}, y_2)| > 2$. As before, the continuity of the inner product we have $|(x_{n_2}, y)| > 2$ for $y \in B(y_2, r_2)$ such that $B(y_2, r_2) \subseteq B(y_1, r_1)$ and $r_2 < \frac{r_1}{2}$. By continuing this process we construct the sequences (n_p), (y_p), and (r_p) such that

$$|(x_{n_p}, y)| > p \text{ for } y \in B(y_p, r_p), \|y_p - y_{p+1}\| < r_p,$$

and

$$r_p < \frac{1}{2} r_{p-1} < \cdots < \left(\frac{1}{2}\right)^{p-1} r_1.$$

This implies

$$\|y_p - y_{p+q}\| \leqslant \|y_p - y_{p+1}\| + \cdots + \|y_{p+q-1} - y_{p+q}\|$$

$$< r_p \left(1 + \frac{1}{2} + \cdots + \left(\frac{1}{2}\right)^{q-1}\right)$$

$$= 2r_p \left(1 - \frac{1}{2^q}\right) < 2 \left(\frac{1}{2}\right)^{p-1} r_1.$$

Thus, $\lim_{p \to \infty} \|y_p - y_{p+q}\| = 0$, so (y_p) is a Cauchy sequence, which implies the existence of $y = \lim_{n \to \infty} y_n$. Since each sphere $B(y_p, r_p)$ contains almost all members of the sequence (y_n) it must contain y, so $|(x_{n_p}, y)| > p$ for all p. Since (x_{n_p}) converges weakly, the sequence $((x_{n_p}, y))$ is bounded, which contradicts the previous inequality. □

Theorem 11.34. *Every weakly convergent sequence in a Hilbert space is bounded.*

Proof. Let $\mathbf{x}$ be a weakly convergent sequence. Since the sequence $((x_n, y))$ is convergent, it is also bounded. In principle, the bound depends on y. However, we will show that an upper bound can be chosen independent of y.

By Lemma 11.4, since (x_n) be a weakly convergent sequence, there exists $\tilde{y} \in H$ and two numbers M and r such that for all $n \in \mathbb{N}$ we have $|(x_n, y)| < M$ for all $y \in B(\tilde{y}, r)$. For any z with $\|z\| \leqslant 1$, we have $|(x_n, \tilde{y} + rz)| < M$, hence $|(x_n, \tilde{y}) + r(x_n, z)| < M$. This implies

$$r|(x_n, z)| \leqslant |r(x_n, z) + (x_n, \tilde{y})| + |-r(x_n, \tilde{y})| < 2M.$$

Taking $z = \frac{1}{2\|x_n\|} x_n$ we obtain $\|x_n\| < \frac{4M}{r}$. □

Theorem 11.35. *A sequence (x_n) in a Hilbert space may have at most one week limit.*

Proof. Suppose that (x_n) is a sequence in H and we have both $x_n \to_w u$ and $x_n \to_w v$. Then, $\lim_{n\to\infty}(x_n, y) = (u, y)$ and $\lim_{n\to\infty}(x_n, y) = (v, y)$ for each $y \in H$. This implies $(u - v, y) = 0$ for every $y \in H$, so $u - v = 0_H$, which yields $u = v$. $\qquad\square$

Lemma 11.5. *Let (x_n) be a sequence in a Hilbert space such that every subsequence $(x_{n_i})_{i\in\mathbb{N}}$ contains a subsequence $(x_{n_{ij}})_{j\in\mathbb{N}}$ that converges strongly to an element x of H. Then $\lim_{n\to\infty} x_n = x$, that is, (x_n) converges strongly at x.*

Proof. Suppose that the condition of the lemma is satisfied but (x_n) does not converge strongly at x. Then, there exists a positive number ϵ such that for any n_0 there exists $n_1 > n_0$ such that $\|x_{n_1} - x\| \geqslant \epsilon$. Similarly, there exists $n_2 > n_1$ such that $\|x_{n_2} - x\| \geqslant \epsilon$, etc. Thus, we have a subsequence $(x_{n_i})_{i\in\mathbb{N}}$ with $\|x_{n_i} - x\| \geqslant \epsilon$, which cannot converge to x. Therefore, no subsequence of this subsequence may converge to x, which contradicts the hypothesis. Thus, $\lim_{n\to\infty} x_n = x$. $\qquad\square$

Theorem 11.36. *Let C be a compact subset of a Hilbert space H and let (x_n) be a sequence such that $\{x_n \mid n \in \mathbb{N}\} \subseteq C$. If $x_n \to_w x$, then $\lim_{n\to\infty} x_n = x$.*

Proof. By the compactness of C, every subsequence $(x_{n_i})_{i\in\mathbb{N}}$ contains a subsequence $(x_{n_{ij}})_{j\in\mathbb{N}}$ that converges strongly to some $u \in H$. By Lemma 11.5, we have $x_{n_{ij}} \to_w v$ for some $v \in H$. However, we also have $x_{n_{ij}} \to_w u$ as a subsequence of (x_n). By Theorem 11.35 we have $u = v$, which gives the desired conclusion. $\qquad\square$

Theorem 11.37. *Let (x_n) be a sequence in a Hilbert space H. If $x_n \to_w x$ and h is a compact linear operator on H, then $\lim_{n\to\infty} h(x_n) = h(x)$.*

Proof. Since $x_n \to_w x$, the sequence (x_n) is bounded by Theorem 11.34. Therefore, the sequence $(h(x_n))$ is mapped by h into a subset of a compact set (by Definition 9.2).

Note that $(h(x_n), y) = (x_n, h^*(y))$. Since $x_n \to_w x$ we also have $\lim_{n\to\infty}(x_n, h * (y)) = (x, h^*(y)) = (h(x), y)$, so $\lim_{n\to\infty}(h(x_n), y) = (h(x), y)$ for every y. By Theorem 11.36 we have the strong convergence $\lim_{n\to\infty} h(x_n) = h(x)$. $\qquad\square$

11.7 Spectra of Linear Operators on Hilbert Spaces

In this section we focus on spectral properties of Hilbert space operators.

Example 11.12. Take $K(x,y) = \cos(x-y)$ in the operator $h : L^2([0,2\pi]) \longrightarrow L^2([0,2\pi])$ defined in Example 11.4. Seeking an eigenvalue λ and an eigenvector u (that is, a function from $L^2([0,2\pi])$) for this operator amounts to

$$h(f)(x) = \int_a^b \cos(x-y) f(y) \, dy = \lambda f(x)$$

for $x \in [0,2\pi]$. Note that the last equality can be written as

$$\cos x \int_a^b \cos y f(y) \, dy + \sin x \int_a^b \sin y \, dy = \lambda f(x), \tag{11.4}$$

which means that every eigenvector (in this case we use the term *eigenfunction*) has the form $f(x) = a\cos x + b\sin x$ for some $a, b \in \mathbb{R}$. Substituting f in equality (11.4) and taking into account that

$$\int_0^{2\pi} \cos^y \, dy = \int_0^{2\pi} \sin^y \, dy = \pi,$$

and $\int_0^{2\pi} \cos y \sin y dy = 0$, it follows that $\lambda = \pi$. Thus, h has a unique eigenvalue, π, and every eigenfunction has the form $a\cos x + b\sin x$.

The set of eigenfunctions for $\lambda = \pi$ has dimension 2. The invariant subspace that corresponds to $\lambda = 0$ consists of all functions f such that $\int_0^{2\pi} \cos y f(y) \, dy = \int_0^{2\pi} \sin y f(y) \, dy = 0$ and this is an infinitely dimensional subspace of $L^2([0,2\pi])$.

Theorem 11.38. *Let* $h : H \longrightarrow H$ *be a self-adjoint linear operator on a Hilbert space* H. *If* K *is an invariant subspace for* h, *then so is* $K^\perp$.

Proof. Let $x \in K^\perp$ and $y \in K$. We have $h(y) \in K$ because K is an invariant subspace. This implies $(h(x), y) = (x, h(y)) = 0$, so $h(x) \in K^\perp$. Since x is an arbitrary element of K, $K^\perp$ is also an invariant subspace for h. $\square$

Let $h : H \longrightarrow H$ be a self-adjoint operator on the Hilbert space H. Define the numbers m_h and M_h as

$$m_h = \inf\{(h(x), x) \mid x \in B[0_H, 1]\} \text{ and } M_h = \sup\{(h(x), x) \mid x \in B[0_H, 1]\}.$$

It follows immediately that

$$m_h \|x\|^2 \leqslant (h(x), x) \leqslant M_h \|x\|^2$$

for $x \in H$.

Theorem 11.39. *If λ is an eigenvalue of a self-adjoint operator h on H, then λ is a real number and $m_h \leqslant \lambda \leqslant M_h$.*

Proof. Since h is self-adjoint we have $(h(x), x) = (x, h(x))$ for an eigenvector x that corresponds to λ, which amounts to $\lambda(x, x) = \overline{\lambda}(x, x)$. We have $\lambda = \overline{\lambda}$ because $x \neq 0_H$, which means that λ is a real number.

If y is an eigenvector corresponding to λ, then $x = \frac{1}{\|y\|}y$ is an eigenvector corresponding to the same λ and $\|x\| = 1$.

Since $(h(x), x) = (\lambda x, x) = \lambda(x, x) = \lambda$ we obtain $m_h \leqslant \lambda \leqslant M_h$. $\quad\square$

Corollary 11.8. *If λ is an eigenvalue of a self-adjoint linear operator h on H then $|\lambda| \leqslant \|h\|$.*

Proof. By Theorem 11.39, we have $|\lambda| \leqslant \max\{|m_h|, |M_h|\} = \|h\|$. $\quad\square$

Theorem 11.40. *If λ and μ are two distinct eigenvalues of a self-adjoint linear operator h on the Hilbert space H, then $H_\lambda \perp H_\mu$.*

Proof. Let $x \in H_\lambda$ and $y \in H_\mu$. We have $h(x) = \lambda x$ and $h(y) = \mu y$. This implies

$$
\begin{aligned}
\lambda(x, y) = (\lambda x, y) &= (h(x), h) \\
&= (x, h(y)) \\
&\quad \text{(because } h \text{ is self-adjoint)} \\
&= (x, \mu y) = \mu(x, y),
\end{aligned}
$$

which implies $(x, y) = 0$. Thus, $H_\lambda \perp H_\mu$. $\quad\square$

Theorem 11.41. *Any compact self-adjoint operator has at least one eigenvalue.*

Proof. Let h be a compact self-adjoint operator on the Hilbert space H. Since $\|h\| = \sup\{(h(x), x) \mid \|x\| = 1\}$, there exists a sequence (x_n) in H such that $\|x_n\| = 1$ for $n \in \mathbb{N}$, $\lim_{n \to \infty} |(h(x_n), x_n)| = 1$, and all numbers $(h(x_n), x_n)$ are real. Therefore, we may have the following three case:

    (i) the sequence $((h(x_n), x_n))$ converges to $\|h\|$,

    (ii) the sequence $((h(x_n), x_n))$ converges to $-\|h\|$,

    (iii) the sequence $((h(x_n), x_n))$ has two limit points, $\|h\|$ and $-\|h\|$.

The sequence $((h(x_n), x_n)$ may always be assumed to be convergent. This is obvious in the first two cases; in the last case, we can select the subsequence that converges to $\|h\|$ or the subsequence that converges to $-\|h\|$ and we reach the same conclusion.

Let $\lambda = \lim_{n \to \infty}(h(x_n), x_n)$. Since h is compact and the sequence (x_n) is bounded, there exists a subsequence $(h(x_{n_k}))$ that is convergent. Let $z = \lim_{k \to \infty} h(x_{n_k})$.

Since h is self-adjoint, λ is a real number. Define the sequence (y_{n_k}) as $y_{n_k} = h(x_{n_k}) - \lambda x_{n_k}$. We have:

$$\|y_{n_k}\|^2 = \|h(x_{n_k}) - \lambda x_{n_k}\|^2 = \|h(x_{n_k})\|^2 - 2\lambda(h(x_{n_k}), x_{n_k}) + \lambda^2.$$

By the definition of λ we have:

$$\lim_{k \to \infty} \|h(x_{n_k}) - \lambda x_{n_k}\|^2 = \|z\|^2 - \lambda^2. \tag{11.5}$$

We have

$$\|z\| = \lim_{k \to \infty} h(x_{n_j}) \leqslant \|h\| = |\lambda|. \tag{11.6}$$

Equality (11.5) and inequality (11.6) imply $\|z\| = \lambda$ and $\lim_{k \to \infty}(h(x_{n_k}) - \lambda x_{n_k}) = 0$. It follows that the sequence (x_{n_k}) is convergent and

$$x = \lim_{k \to \infty} x_{n_k} = \lim_{k \to \infty} \frac{h(x_{n_k}) - y_{n_k}}{\lambda} = \frac{z}{\lambda}.$$

Since $\lim_{k \to \infty} x_{n_k} = x$, it follows that $\lim_{k \to \infty} h(x_{n_k}) = h(x)$.

Thus, we have $\lim_{k \to \infty} h(x_{n_k}) = z = \lambda x$ and, also, $\lim_{k \to \infty} h(x_{n_k}) = h(x)$. Consequently, $h(x) = \lambda x$, which shows that λ is an eigenvalue of h having $x = \lim_{k \to \infty} x_{n_k}$ as an eigenvector with $\|x\| = 1$. $\qquad \square$

Theorem 11.42. *Let h be compact self-adjoint linear operator on a Hilbert space H. We have* $\max\{|\lambda| \mid \lambda \in \sigma(h)\} = \|h\|$.

Proof. We have shown in Corollary 11.8 that $|\lambda| \leqslant \|h\|$ for every eigenvalue of a self-adjoint operator h on H. The eigenvalue λ whose existence we have shown in Theorem 11.41 satisfies this statement. $\qquad \square$

Now we can formulate a much stronger version of Theorem 11.41.

Theorem 11.43. *The set of eigenvalues of a compact self-adjoint linear operator h on a Hilbert space H is a set of real numbers that is at most countable. If this set is not finite, than the set consists of members of a sequence that converges to 0.*

Proof. Suppose that the set of eigenvalues of h is infinite and does not consist of the members of a sequence that converges to 0. Then, there exists $a \in \mathbb{R}$ such that the set $\{\lambda \in \sigma(h) \mid |\lambda| > a\}$ is infinite. Let (λ_n) be a sequence of distinct eigenvalues that belong to this set and let u_n be an eigenvector of λ_n with $\|u_n\| = 1$. The set $\{u_n \mid n \in \mathbb{N}\}$ is orthonormal (by Theorem 11.40) and we have

$$\|h(u_n) - h(u_m)\|^2 = \|\lambda_n u_n - \lambda_m u_m\|^2 = \lambda_n^2 + \lambda_m^2 \geqslant 2a^2,$$

which implies that $(h(u_n))$ has no Cauchy subsequence, and therefore, no convergent subsequence. This contradicts the compactness of h because the sequence (u_n) is bounded. $\qquad\square$

Lemma 11.6. *Let h be a compact, self-adjoint operator on a Hilbert space H. There exists an orthonormal set of eigenvectors $\{x_1, x_2, \ldots\}$ with the corresponding eigenvalues $\lambda_1, \lambda_2, \ldots$ such that for any $x \in H$ we have*

$$x = \sum_n c_n x_n + y \tag{11.7}$$

for some scalars c_n where $y \in \mathsf{Null}(h)$. If H is infinite-dimensional, then $\lim_{n \to \infty} \lambda_n = 0$.

Proof. Let λ_1 be the eigenvalue of h such that $|\lambda_1| = \|h\|$ and let G_1 be the subspace of H generated by an eigenvector x_1 that corresponds to λ_1 such that $\|x_1\| = 1$.

Define $H_1 = G_1$ and $H_2 = H_1^\perp$. Note that if $y \in H_2$, then $h(y) \in H_2$ because for $x \in H_1$ we have $(h(y), x) = (y, h(x)) = 0$ and, therefore, $h(x) \in H_1^\perp = H_2$. Moreover, the operator h_2 obtained by restricting h to H_2 is self-adjoint, so an application of Theorem 11.41 to h_2 yields the existence of an eigenvalue λ_2 with

$$|\lambda_2| = \sup\{|(h(x), x)| \mid \|x\| = 1, h(x) = \lambda x \text{ and } (x, x_1) = 0\} \leqslant |\lambda_1|,$$

and an unit eigenvector x_2.

The process continues an follows. Suppose that G_{n-1} is the subspace generated by the first $n - 1$ orthonormal eigenvectors $x_1, \ldots, x_{n-1}$. The restriction of h to $G_{n-1}^\perp$ is self-adjoint and we have the eigenvalue λ_n

$$\lambda_n = \sup\{(h(x), x) \mid \|x\| = 1 \text{ and } (x, x_1) = \cdots = (x, x_{n-1}) = 0\}$$

and a corresponding eigenvector x_n with $\|x_n\| = 1$. Note that

$$|\lambda_n| = |\lambda_n| \|x_n\| = \|\lambda_n x_n\| = \|h(x_n)\|.$$

The process ends after n steps if H is n-dimensional, we have a set n orthogonal vectors that form a basis, hence equality (11.7) holds with $y = 0_H$.

If H is infinite-dimensional, the sequence (x_n) converges weakly to 0_H, as we saw in Example 11.11. Since h is compact, by Theorem 11.37 we have $\lim_{n\to\infty} h(x_n) = 0$. Consequently, $\lim_{n\to\infty} |\lambda_n| = \lim_{n\to\infty} \|h(x_n)\| = 0$.

Let T be the subspace of H that consists of all infinite linear combinations of $\{x_1, x_2, \ldots\}$. Every $x \in H$ can be written as $x = \sum_n c_n x_n + y$, where $\sum_n c_n x_n \in T$ and $y \in T^\perp$. The subspace $U = T^\perp$ is contained in every subspace G_n because every element of U is orthogonal to all x_n.

If $y \in U$ let $y_1 = \frac{1}{\|y\|} y$. We have $\|y_1\| = 1$ and $(y, h(y)) = \|y\|^2(y_1, h(y_1))$. Since $y_1 \in U \subseteq G_n$, we have $(y, h(y)) \leqslant \lambda_n \|y\|^2$. Since $\lim_{n\to\infty} \lambda_n = 0$ it follows that $(y, h(y)) = 0$ for all $y \in U$. This implies $h(y) = 0$, so $y \in \mathsf{Null}(h)$. ☐

Theorem 11.44. (The Spectral Theorem for Compact Self-adjoint Operators) *Let h be a compact self-adjoint operator on a Hilbert space H. There exists an orthonormal basis $e_1, \ldots, e_n, \ldots$ in H that consists of eigenvectors of h that correspond to the eigenvalues $\lambda_1, \ldots, \lambda_n, \ldots$, respectively. If H is infinite-dimensional, then $\lim_{n\to\infty} \lambda_n = 0$. Furthermore, if $x = \sum_n c_n e_n$, then $h(x) = \sum_n c_n \lambda_n e_n$.*

Proof. By Lemma 11.6, there exists an orthonormal set of eigenvectors $\{x_1, x_2, \ldots\}$ with the corresponding eigenvalues $\lambda_1, \lambda_2, \ldots$ such that for any $x \in H$ we have $x = \sum_n c_n x_n + y$ for some scalars c_n where $y \in \mathsf{Null}(h)$. Let $y_1, y_2, \ldots$ be an orthonormal basis for $\mathsf{Null}(h)$ that consists of eigenvectors that correspond to the eigenvalue 0 of h. The set $\{x_1, x_2, \ldots, y_1, y_2, \ldots\}$ is an orthonormal basis for H. With the 0 eigenvalue included we still have $\lim_{n\to\infty} \lambda_n = 0$.

Since h is continuous we have

$$h\left(\sum_{n=1}^{\infty} c_n x_n\right) = h\left(\lim_{m\to\infty} \sum_{n=1}^{m} c_n x_n\right) = \lim_{m\to\infty} h\left(\sum_{n=1}^{m} c_n x_n\right)$$

$$= \lim_{m\to\infty} \sum_{n=1}^{m} c_n h(x_n) = \lim_{m\to\infty} \sum_{n=1}^{m} c_n \lambda_n x_n$$

$$= \sum_{n=1}^{\infty} c_n \lambda_n x_n.$$

☐

11.8 Functions of Positive and Negative Type

Definition 11.11. Let S be a non-empty set. A function $K : S \times S \longrightarrow \mathbb{C}$ is of *positive type* if for every $n \geqslant 1$ we have:

$$\sum_{i=1}^{n} \sum_{j=1}^{n} a_i K(x_i, x_j) \overline{a_j} \geqslant 0$$

for every $a_i \in \mathbb{C}$ and $x_i \in S$, where $1 \leqslant i \leqslant n$.

If $K : S \times S \longrightarrow \mathbb{C}$ is of positive type, then specializing the inequality of Definition 11.11 for $n = 1$ we have $aK(x, x)\overline{a} = K(x, x)|a|^2 \geqslant 0$ for every $a \in \mathbb{C}$ and $x \in S$. This implies $K(x, x) \geqslant 0$ for $x \in S$.

Note that $K : S \times S \longrightarrow \mathbb{C}$ is of positive type if for every $n \geqslant 1$ and for every $x_1, \ldots, x_s$ the matrix $A_{n,K}(x_1, \ldots, x_n) = (K(x_i, x_j))$ is positive.

Example 11.13. The function $K : \mathbb{R} \times \mathbb{R} \longrightarrow \mathbb{R}$ given by $K(x, y) = \cos(x - y)$ is of positive type because

$$\sum_{i=1}^{n} \sum_{j=1}^{n} a_i K(x_i, x_j) \overline{a_j} = \sum_{i=1}^{n} \sum_{j=1}^{n} a_i \cos(x_i - x_j) \overline{a_j}$$

$$= \sum_{i=1}^{n} \sum_{j=1}^{n} a_i (\cos x_i \cos x_j + \sin x_i \sin x_j) \overline{a_j}$$

$$= \left| \sum_{i=1}^{n} a_i \cos x_i \right|^2 + \left| \sum_{i=1}^{n} a_i \sin x_i \right|^2.$$

for every $a_i \in \mathbb{C}$ and $x_i \in S$, where $1 \leqslant i \leqslant n$.

Definition 11.12. Let S be a non-empty set. A function $K : S \times S \longrightarrow \mathbb{C}$ is *Hermitian* if $K(x, y) = \overline{K(y, x)}$ for every $x, y \in S$.

The notion of Hermitian function is useful in defining functions of negative type.

Definition 11.13. Let S be a non-empty set. A complex-valued function $K : S \times S \longrightarrow \mathbb{C}$ is of *negative type* if and only if the following conditions are satisfied:

    (i) K is Hermitian, and

    (ii) for every $a_i \in \mathbb{C}$ such that $\sum_{i=1}^{n} a_i = 0$, and $x_i \in S$, where $1 \leqslant i \leqslant n$ we have;

$$\sum_{i=1}^{n} \sum_{j=1}^{n} a_i K(x_i, x_j) \overline{a_j} \leqslant 0.$$

Theorem 11.45. *Let S be a non-empty set and let S_1 be a non-empty subset of S. If $K : S \times S \longrightarrow \mathbb{C}$ is a complex-valued function of positive type (of negative type), then the restriction $K_1 = K \!\restriction_{S_1 \times S_1}$ is of positive type (of negative type).*

Proof.   This is an immediate consequence of Definitions 11.11 and 11.13.

$\square$

Theorem 11.46. *Let H be a Hilbert space, S be a non-empty set and let $f : S \longrightarrow H$ be a function. The function $K : S \times S \longrightarrow \mathbb{C}$ defined by*
$$K(s,t) = (f(s), f(t))$$
is of positive type.

Proof.   We can write
$$\sum_{i=1}^{n} \sum_{j=1}^{n} a_i \overline{a_j} K(t_i, t_j) = \sum_{i=1}^{n} \sum_{j=1}^{n} a_i \overline{a_j} (f(t_i), f(t_j))$$

$$= \left\| \sum_{i=1}^{n} a_i f(a_i) \right\|^2 \geqslant 0,$$

which means that K is of positive type. $\square$

Example 11.14. Let $S = \mathbb{R}^k$ and let $K : \mathbb{R}^k \times \mathbb{R}^k \longrightarrow \mathbb{R}$ be given by $K(\mathbf{x}, \mathbf{y}) = (\mathbf{x}, \mathbf{y})^d$, where $d \in \mathbb{N}$ and $d \geqslant 1$.

To show that K is of positive type we shall prove the existence of a function $\phi : \mathbb{R}^k \longrightarrow \mathbb{R}^m$, where $m = \binom{k+d-1}{d}$ such that $K(\mathbf{x}, \mathbf{y}) = (\phi(x), \phi(y))$.

Note that if
$$\mathbf{x} = \begin{pmatrix} x_1 \\ \vdots \\ x_k \end{pmatrix} \text{ and } \mathbf{y} = \begin{pmatrix} y_1 \\ \vdots \\ y_k \end{pmatrix},$$
then
$$K(\mathbf{x}, \mathbf{y}) = (x_1 y_1 + \cdots + x_k y_k)^d.$$
The expansion of $(x_1 y_1 + \cdots + x_k y_k)^d$ results into a sum of m monomials of the form
$$\binom{d}{n_1 \ \cdots \ n_k} x_1^{n_1} y_1^{n_1} \cdots x_k^{n_k} y_k^{n_k},$$
where $n_1 + \cdots + n_k = d$ and $n_j \geqslant 0$.   The number m of these monomials equals the number of non-negative solutions of the equation

$n_1 + \cdots + n_k = d$. To evaluate this number we start from a sequence of $d+k-1$ binary digits that contains $d = n_1 + \cdots + n_k$ ones and $k-1$ zeroes:

$$\underbrace{11\cdots1}_{n_1}0\underbrace{11\cdots1}_{n_2}0\cdots0\underbrace{11\cdots1}_{n_k}.$$

A solution of $n_1 + \cdots + n_k = d$ and $n_j \geqslant 0$ is given by the lengths of the sequences of ones determined by the positions of the $k-1$ zeroes. Note that the total length of the sequence is $d+k-1$. Since the positioning of the zeroes is defined by a subset containing $k-1$ elements of the set of $d+k-1$ positions it follows that the number of solutions is

$$\binom{d+k-1}{k-1} = \binom{d+k-1}{d}.$$

Thus, ϕ is a sum of $\binom{d+k-1}{d}$ monomials:

$$\phi(\mathbf{x}) = \left(\ldots, \sqrt{\binom{d}{n_1 \ \cdots \ n_k}} x_1^{n_1} \cdots x_k^{n_k}, \ldots \right),$$

and $K(\mathbf{x}, \mathbf{y}) = (\phi(\mathbf{x}), \phi(\mathbf{y}))$ for $\mathbf{x}, \mathbf{y} \in \mathbb{R}^k$.

For $d=2$ we have $\binom{d+k-1}{d} = \binom{3}{2} = 3$ and we can write:

$$
\begin{aligned}
K(\mathbf{x}, \mathbf{y}) &= (x_1 y_1 + x_2 y_2)^2 \\
&= x_1^2 y_1^2 + 2 x_1 y_1 x_2 y_2 + x_2^2 y_2^2 \\
&= \left(\begin{pmatrix} x_1^2 \\ \sqrt{2} x_1 x_2 \\ x_2^2 \end{pmatrix}, \begin{pmatrix} y_1^2 \\ \sqrt{2} y_1 y_2 \\ y_2^2 \end{pmatrix} \right),
\end{aligned}
$$

so

$$\phi(\mathbf{x}) = \begin{pmatrix} x_1^2 \\ \sqrt{2} x_1 x_2 \\ x_2^2 \end{pmatrix}$$

for $\mathbf{x} \in \mathbb{R}^2$.

Example 11.15. Let $K : \mathbb{R}^k \times \mathbb{R}^k \longrightarrow \mathbb{C}$ be the function defined by $K(\mathbf{x}, \mathbf{y}) = ((\mathbf{x}, \mathbf{y}) + a)^d$, where $d \in \mathbb{N}$, $d \geqslant 1$ and $a > 0$. We prove that K is of positive type. We have

$$
\begin{aligned}
K(\mathbf{x}, \mathbf{y}) \\
&= ((\mathbf{x}, \mathbf{y}) + a)^d \\
&= (x_1 y_1 + \cdots + x_n y_n + \sqrt{a}\sqrt{a})^d \\
&= \sum_{n_1 + \cdots + n_k + n_{k+1} = d} \binom{d}{n_1 \ \cdots \ n_k \ n_{k+1}} x_1^{n_1} y_1^{n_1} \cdots x_k^{n_k} y_k^{n_k} a^{\frac{n_{k+1}}{2}} a^{\frac{n_{k+1}}{2}} \\
&= (\phi(\mathbf{x}), \phi(\mathbf{y})),
\end{aligned}
$$

where, this time we have:

$$\phi(\mathbf{x}) = \left(\dots, \sqrt{\binom{d}{n_1 \ \cdots \ n_{k+1}}} x_1^{n_1} \cdots x_k^{n_k} a^{\frac{n_{k+1}}{2}}, \dots \right).$$

For each monomial that is a component of $\phi(x)$ we have $\sum_{j=1}^{k+1} n_j = d$ and $n_j \geqslant 0$ for $1 \leqslant j \leqslant k+1$. Note that the function $\phi(\mathbf{x})$ is a sum of $\binom{d+k}{k}$ monomials whose global degree is less or equal to d.

For instance, in the case of $k = 2$ and $d = 2$ we have:

$$\begin{aligned} K(\mathbf{x}, \mathbf{y}) &= (x_1 y_1 + x_2 y_2 + a)^2 \\ &= x_1^2 y_1^2 + x_2^2 y_2^2 + a^2 + 2x_1 y_1 x_2 y_2 + 2a x_1 y_1 + 2a x_2 y_2 \\ &= (\phi(\mathbf{x}), \phi(\mathbf{y})), \end{aligned}$$

where $\phi : \mathbb{R}^2 \longrightarrow \mathbb{R}^6$ is defined as

$$\phi(\mathbf{x}) = \begin{pmatrix} x_1^2 \\ x_2^2 \\ \sqrt{2} x_1 x_2 \\ \sqrt{2a} x_1 \\ \sqrt{2a} x_2 \\ a \end{pmatrix}.$$

Example 11.16. The *radial basis* function is the function $K : \mathbb{R}^k \times \mathbb{R}^k \longrightarrow \mathbb{C}$ defined by $K(\mathbf{x}, \mathbf{y}) = e^{-\frac{\|\mathbf{x} - \mathbf{y}\|^2}{2\sigma^2}}$. We shall prove that K is of positive type by showing that $K(\mathbf{x}, \mathbf{y}) = (\phi(\mathbf{x}), \phi(\mathbf{y}))$, where $\phi : \mathbb{R}^k \longrightarrow \ell^2(\mathbb{R})$. Note that for this example ϕ ranges over an infinite-dimensional space.

We have

$$\begin{aligned} K(\mathbf{x}, \mathbf{y}) &= e^{-\frac{\|\mathbf{x} - \mathbf{y}\|^2}{2\sigma^2}} \\ &= e^{-\frac{\|\mathbf{x}\|^2 + \|\mathbf{y}\|^2 - 2(\mathbf{x}, \mathbf{y})}{2\sigma^2}} \\ &= e^{-\frac{\|\mathbf{x}\|^2}{2\sigma^2}} \cdot e^{-\frac{\|\mathbf{y}\|^2}{2\sigma^2}} \cdot e^{\frac{(\mathbf{x}, \mathbf{y})}{\sigma^2}}. \end{aligned}$$

Taking into account that

$$e^{\frac{(\mathbf{x}, \mathbf{y})}{\sigma^2}} = \sum_{j=0}^{\infty} \frac{1}{j!} \frac{(\mathbf{x}, \mathbf{y})^j}{\sigma^{2j}},$$

we can write

$$\begin{aligned} e^{\frac{(\mathbf{x}, \mathbf{y})}{\sigma^2}} \cdot e^{-\frac{\|\mathbf{x}\|^2}{2\sigma^2}} \cdot e^{-\frac{\|\mathbf{y}\|^2}{2\sigma^2}} &= \sum_{j=0}^{\infty} \frac{(\mathbf{x}, \mathbf{y})^j}{j! \sigma^{2j}} e^{-\frac{\|\mathbf{x}\|^2}{2\sigma^2}} \cdot e^{-\frac{\|\mathbf{y}\|^2}{2\sigma^2}} \\ &= \sum_{j=0}^{\infty} \left(\frac{e^{-\frac{\|\mathbf{x}\|^2}{2j\sigma^2}}}{\sigma \sqrt[j]{j!}} \frac{e^{-\frac{\|\mathbf{y}\|^2}{2j\sigma^2}}}{\sigma \sqrt[j]{j!}} (\mathbf{x}, \mathbf{y}) \right)^j = (\phi(\mathbf{x}), \phi(\mathbf{y})), \end{aligned}$$

where

$$\phi(\mathbf{x}) = \left(\dots, \frac{e^{-\frac{\|\mathbf{x}\|^2}{2j\sigma^2}}}{\sigma^j \sqrt{j!}^{\frac{1}{j}}} \binom{j}{n_1, \dots, n_k}^{\frac{1}{2}} x_1^{n_1} \cdots x_k^{n_k}, \dots \right).$$

In this formula j varies in $\mathbb{N}$ and $n_1 + \cdots + n_k = j$.

In the next statement we prove that a complex-valued function of positive type is necessarily Hermitian. Note that for functions of negative type this property was included in their definition.

Theorem 11.47. *Let S be a set and let $F : S \times S \longrightarrow \mathbb{C}$ be a complex-valued of positive type function. The following statements hold:*
  (i) *$F(x, y) = \overline{F(y, x)}$ for every $x, y \in S$, that is, F is Hermitian;*
  (ii) *$\overline{F}$ is a positive type function;*
  (iii) *$|F(x, y)|^2 \leqslant F(x, x) F(y, y)$.*

Proof. Take $n = 2$ in the definition of positive type functions. We have

$$a_1 \overline{a_1} F(x_1, x_1) + a_1 \overline{a_2} F(x_1, x_2) + a_2 \overline{a_1} F(x_2, x_1) + a_2 \overline{a_2} F(x_2, x_2) \geqslant 0, \quad (11.8)$$

which amounts to

$$|a_1|^2 F(x_1, x_1) + a_1 \overline{a_2} F(x_1, x_2) + a_2 \overline{a_1} F(x_2, x_1) + |a_2|^2 F(x_2, x_2) \geqslant 0.$$

By taking $a_1 = a_2 = 1$ we obtain

$$p = F(x_1, x_1) + F(x_1, x_2) + F(x_2, x_1) + F(x_2, x_2) \geqslant 0,$$

where p is a positive real number.

Similarly, by taking $a_1 = i$ and $a_2 = 1$ we have

$$q = -F(x_1, x_1) + iF(x_1, x_2) - iF(x_2, x_1) + F(x_2, x_2) \geqslant 0,$$

where q is a positive real number.

Thus, we have

$$F(x_1, x_2) + F(x_2, x_1) = p - F(x_1, x_1) - F(x_2, x_2),$$
$$iF(x_1, x_2) - iF(x_2, x_1) = q + F(x_1, x_1) - F(x_2, x_2).$$

These equalities imply

$$2F(x_1, x_2) = P - iQ$$
$$2F(x_2, x_1) = P + iQ,$$

where $P = p - F(x_1, x_1) - F(x_2, x_2)$ and $Q = q + F(x_1, x_1) - F(x_2, x_2)$, which shows the first statement holds.

The second part of the theorem follows by applying the conjugation in the equality of Definition 11.11.

For the final part, note that if $F(x_1, x_2) = 0$ the desired inequality holds immediately. Therefore, assume that $F(x_1, x_2) \neq 0$ and apply equality (11.8) to $a_1 = a \in \mathbb{R}$ and to $a_2 = F(x_1, x_2)$. We have

$$a^2 F(x_1, x_1) + a\overline{F(x_1, x_2)}F(x_1, x_2)$$
$$+ F(x_1, x_2)aF(x_2, x_1) + F(x_1, x_2)\overline{F(x_1, x_2)}F(x_2, x_2) \geqslant 0,$$

which amounts to

$$a^2 F(x_1, x_1) + 2a|F(x_1, x_2)| + |F(x_1, x_2)|^2 F(x_2, x_2) \geqslant 0.$$

If $F(x_1, x_1)$ this trinomial in a must be non-negative for every a, which implies

$$|F(x_1, x_2)|^4 - |F(x_1, x_2)|^2 F(x_1, x_1)F(x_2, x_2) \leqslant 0.$$

Since $F(x_1, x_2) \neq 0$, the desired inequality follows. $\qquad\square$

Corollary 11.9. *Let S be a set and let $F : S \times S \longrightarrow \mathbb{C}$ be a function. Then F is of positive type if and only if $-F$ is of negative type.*

Proof. If F is of positive type, F is Hermitian by Theorem 11.47, which implies that $-F$ is Hermitian. The second condition of Definition 11.13 for $-F$ follows immediately, so $-F$ is indeed of negative type.

The reverse implication is also immediate. $\qquad\square$

Theorem 11.48. *A real-valued function $G : S \times S \longrightarrow \mathbb{R}$ is a positive type function if it is symmetric and*

$$\sum_{i=1}^{n}\sum_{i=1}^{n} a_i a_j G(x_i, x_j) \geqslant 0 \qquad (11.9)$$

for $a_1, \ldots, a_n \in \mathbb{R}$ and $x_1, \ldots, x_n \in S$.

Proof. The necessity of the conditions of the theorem is clear. To prove that they are sufficient let G a function of positive type such that

$$\sum_{i=1}^{n}\sum_{j=1}^{n} a_i \overline{a_j} G(x_i, x_j) \geqslant 0 \qquad (11.10)$$

for every $a_i \in \mathbb{C}$ and $x_i \in S$, where $1 \leqslant i \leqslant n$.

If $a_i = c_i + id_i$ we have

$$\sum_{i=1}^{n}\sum_{j=1}^{n} (c_i + id_i)(c_j - id_j)G(x_i, x_j) \geqslant 0.$$

Thus, we have:

$$\sum_{i=1}^{n}\sum_{j=1}^{n} a_i \overline{a_j} G(x_i, G_j)$$

$$= \sum_{i=1}^{n}\sum_{j=1}^{n} c_i c_j G(x_i, x_j) + \sum_{i=1}^{n}\sum_{j=1}^{n} d_i d_j G(x_i, x_j)$$

$$+i\left(\sum_{i=1}^{n}\sum_{j=1}^{n} d_i c_j G(x_i, x_j) - \sum_{i=1}^{n}\sum_{j=1}^{n} c_i d_j G(x_i, x_j)\right).$$

Observe that

$$\sum_{i=1}^{n}\sum_{j=1}^{n} d_i c_j G(x_i, x_j) - \sum_{i=1}^{n}\sum_{j=1}^{n} c_i d_j G(x_i, x_j) = 0$$

because G is symmetric. Thus, $\sum_{i=1}^{n}\sum_{j=1}^{n} a_i \overline{a_j} G(x_i, G_j)$ is a non-negative real number, so G is of positive type. $\qquad\square$

Theorem 11.49. *Let S be a non-empty set. If $K_i : S \times S \longrightarrow \mathbb{C}$ for $i = 1, 2$ are functions of positive type, then their pointwise product $K_1 K_2$ defined by $(K_1 K_2)(x, y) = K_1(x, y) K_2(x, y)$ is of positive type.*

Proof. Since K_i is a function of positive type, the matrix

$$A_{n, K_i}(x_1, \ldots, x_n) = (K_i(x_j, x_h))$$

is positive, where $i = 1, 2$. Therefore, these matrices can be factored as

$$A_{n, K_1}(x_1, \ldots, x_n) = P^{\mathsf{H}} P \text{ and } A_{n, K_2}(x_1, \ldots, x_n) = R^{\mathsf{H}} R$$

for $i = 1, 2$. Therefore, we have:

$$\sum_{i=1}^{n}\sum_{j=1}^{n} a_i K_1(x_i, x_j) K_2(x_i, x_j) \overline{a_j}$$

$$= \sum_{i=1}^{n}\sum_{j=1}^{n} a_i K(x_i, x_j) \cdot \left(\sum_{m=1}^{n} \overline{r_{mi}} r_{mj}\right) \overline{a_j}$$

$$= \sum_{m=1}^{n} \left(\sum_{i=1}^{n} a_i \overline{r_{mi}}\right) K(x_i, x_j) \left(\sum_{j=1}^{n} r_{jm} \overline{a_j}\right) \geqslant 0,$$

which shows that $(K_1 K_2)(x, y)$ is a function of positive type. $\qquad\square$

Theorem 11.50. *Let S, T be two non-empty sets and let $K_1 : S \times S \longrightarrow$ $\mathbb{C}$ and $K_2 : T \times T \longrightarrow \mathbb{C}$ be two positive type functions. The function $K_1 \otimes K_2 : (S \times T) \times (S \times T) \longrightarrow \mathbb{C}$ defined by*

$$(K_1 \otimes K_2)((s,t),(s',t')) = K_1(s,s')K_2(t,t')$$

for $(s,t),(s',t') \in S \times T$ is of positive type.

Proof. Note that the functions $\tilde{K}$ and $\hat{K}$ defined on $(S \times T) \times (S \times T)$ by

$$\tilde{K}((s,t),(s',t')) = K_1(s,s'),$$
$$\hat{K}((s,t),(s',t')) = K_2(t,t')$$

for $(s,t),(s',t') \in S \times T$ are of positive type. The statement follows immediately by observing that $K_1 \otimes K_2 = \tilde{K}\hat{K}$ and applying Theorem 11.49.

$\square$

The function $K_1 \otimes K_2$ introduced in Theorem 11.50 is known as the *tensor product* of K_1 and K_2.

For a non-empty set S the set of functions $\mathbb{C}^{S \times S}$ is a linear space if the addition is defined by

$$(F + G)(s_1, s_2) = F(s_1, s_2) + G(s_1, s_2)$$

and the multiplication with scalars is

$$(aF)(s_1, s_2) = aF(s_1, s_2)$$

for $s_1, s_2 \in S$.

Theorem 11.51. *Let S be a non-empty set. The set of functions of positive (negative) type is closed with respect to multiplication with non-negative scalars and with respect to addition; in other words, these sets are convex cones.*

Furthermore, these sets are closed with respect to pointwise convergence.

Proof. We discuss only the case of functions of positive type. It follows immediately from Definition 11.11 that the set of functions of positive type in $\mathbb{C}^{S \times S}$ is closed with respect to multiplication with non-negative scalars and with respect to addition, so this set is indeed a convex cone.

Suppose that (F_p) is a sequence of functions of positive type in $\mathbb{C}^{S \times S}$ that converges pointwise to F that is, $\lim_{n \to \infty} F_p(s,t) = F(s,t)$ for every

$(s, t) \in S \times S$. Then,

$$\sum_{i=1}^{n} \sum_{j=1}^{n} a_i F(x_i, x_j) \overline{a_j}$$

$$= \sum_{i=1}^{n} \sum_{j=1}^{n} a_i \lim_{p \to \infty} F_p(x_i, x_j) \overline{a_j}$$

$$= \lim_{p \to \infty} \sum_{i=1}^{n} \sum_{j=1}^{n} a_i F_p(x_i, x_j) \overline{a_j} \geqslant 0,$$

which shows that F is a function of positive type. $\qquad\square$

Theorem 11.52. *Let S be a non-empty set and let $F : S \times S \longrightarrow \mathbb{C}$ be a Hermitian function. For $x_0 \in S$ define the functions $G_{x_0} : S \times S \longrightarrow \mathbb{C}$ and $g_{x_0} : S \times S \longrightarrow \mathbb{C}$ as*

$$G_{x_0}(x, y) = F(x, x_0) + \overline{F(y, x_0)} - F(x, y) - F(x_0, x_0),$$
$$g_{x_0}(x, y) = F(x, x_0) + \overline{F(y, x_0)} - F(x, y),$$

for $(x, y) \in S \times S$. We have:

  (i) *G_{x_0} is of positive type if and only if F is of negative type;*

  (ii) *if $F(x_0, x_0) \geqslant 0$ then g_{x_0} is of positive type if and only if F is of negative type.*

Proof. Let $a_i \in \mathbb{C}$ where $1 \leqslant i \leqslant n$ such that $\sum_{i=1}^{n} a_i = 0$, and let $x_i \in S$, where $1 \leqslant i \leqslant n$. We have

$$\sum_{i=1}^{n} \sum_{j=1}^{n} a_i G_{x_0}(x_i, x_j) \overline{a_j}$$

$$= \sum_{i=1}^{n} \sum_{j=1}^{n} a_i (F(x_i, x_0) + \overline{F(x_j, x_0)} - F(x_i, x_j) - F(x_0, x_0)) \overline{a_j}.$$

Note that

$$\sum_{i=1}^{n} \sum_{j=1}^{n} a_i F(x_i, x_0) \overline{a_j} = \left(\sum_{i=1}^{n} a_i F(x_i, x_0) \right) \left(\sum_{j=1}^{n} \overline{a_j} \right) = 0,$$

$$\sum_{i=1}^{n} \sum_{j=1}^{n} a_i \overline{F(x_j, x_0)} \overline{a_j} = \left(\sum_{i=1}^{n} a_i \right) \left(\sum_{j=1}^{n} \overline{F(x_j, x_0)} \overline{a_j} \right) = 0,$$

$$\sum_{i=1}^{n} \sum_{j=1}^{n} a_i F(x_0, x_0) \overline{a_j} = F(x_0, y_0) \left(\sum_{i=1}^{n} a_i \right) \left(\sum_{j=1}^{n} \overline{a_j} \right) = 0.$$

Therefore,

$$\sum_{i=1}^{n}\sum_{j=1}^{n} a_i G_{x_0}(x_i, x_j)\overline{a_j} = -\sum_{i=1}^{n}\sum_{j=1}^{n} a_i F(x_i, x_j)\overline{a_j}.$$

The last equality shows that if G_{x_0} is of positive type then F is of negative type.

Let now F be of negative type and $a_i \in \mathbb{C}$ and $x_i \in S$, where $1 \leqslant i \leqslant n$. Define $a_0 = -\sum_{i=1}^{n} a_i$. Since F is of negative type and $\sum_{i=0}^{n} c_i = 0$, we can write:

$$\sum_{i=0}^{n}\sum_{j=0}^{n} a_i F(x_i, x_j)\overline{a_j}$$

$$= \sum_{i=1}^{n}\sum_{j=1}^{n} a_i F(x_i, x_j)\overline{a_j} + \sum_{j=1}^{n} a_0 F(x_0, x_j)\overline{a_j}$$

$$+ \sum_{i=1}^{n} a_i F(x_i, x_j)\overline{a_0} + a_0 F(x_0, x_0)\overline{a_0}$$

$$= \sum_{i=1}^{n}\sum_{j=1}^{n} a_i (F(x_i, x_j) - F(x_i, x_0) - F(x_0, x_j) + F(x_0, x_0))\overline{a_j}$$

$$\text{(by substituting} -\sum_{i=1}^{n} a_i \text{ for } a_0)$$

$$= -\sum_{i=1}^{n}\sum_{j=1}^{n} G_{x_0}(x_i, x_j) \leqslant 0.$$

Consequently, G_{x_0} is of positive type. Since $g_{x_0} = G_{x_0} + F(x_0, x_0)$, it follows that g_{x_0} is also of positive type. $\qquad\square$

A special case of kernels on $\mathbb{R}^n$ is obtained by defining $K : \mathbb{R}^n \times \mathbb{R}^n \longrightarrow \mathbb{R}$ as $K_f(\mathbf{x}, \mathbf{y}) = f(\mathbf{x} - \mathbf{y})$, where $f : \mathbb{R}^n \longrightarrow \mathbb{C}$ is a continuous function on $\mathbb{R}^n$. K is translation invariant and is designated as a *stationary kernel*. If K_f is of positive type we say that f is of *positive type*. In Example 11.13 we have shown that cos is a function of positive type.

Theorem 11.53. *If $f : \mathbb{R}^n \longrightarrow \mathbb{R}$ is of positive type the following properties hold:*

    (i) $f(\mathbf{0}) \geqslant 0$;

    (ii) $f(-\mathbf{x}) = \overline{f(\mathbf{x})}$;

    (iii) $|f(\mathbf{x})| \leqslant f(\mathbf{0})$ *for all* $\mathbf{x} \in \mathbb{R}^n$;

    (iv) $f(\mathbf{0}) = 0$ *if and only if f is the constant function 0.*

Proof. Since f is of positive type, we have

$$\sum_{i=1}^{n}\sum_{j=1}^{n} a_i f(\mathbf{x}_i - \mathbf{x}_j)\overline{a_j} \geqslant 0 \qquad (11.11)$$

for every $a_i \in \mathbb{C}$ and $x_i \in S$, where $1 \leqslant i \leqslant n$.

Part (i): Since $f(\mathbf{0}) = K_f(\mathbf{0}, \mathbf{0}) \geqslant 0$, the desired inequality is immediate.

Part (ii): Note that $f(-\mathbf{x}) = K_f(\mathbf{0}, \mathbf{x}) = \overline{K_f(\mathbf{x}, \mathbf{0})} = \overline{f(\mathbf{x})}$.

Part (iii): Take $n = 2$, $a_1 = |f(\mathbf{x})|$, $a_2 = -f(\mathbf{x})$, $\mathbf{x}_1 = \mathbf{0}$ and $\mathbf{x}_2 = \mathbf{x}$ in inequality (11.11). We have:

$$a_1 f(\mathbf{x}_1 - \mathbf{x}_1)\overline{a_1} + a_1 f(\mathbf{x}_1 - \mathbf{x}_2)\overline{a_2} + a_2 f(\mathbf{x}_2 - \mathbf{x}_1)\overline{a_1} + a_2 f(\mathbf{x}_2 - \mathbf{x}_2)\overline{a_2}$$

$$= |f(\mathbf{x})|^2 f(\mathbf{0}) - |f(\mathbf{x})| f(\mathbf{x}) f(-\mathbf{x}) - \overline{f(\mathbf{x})} f(\mathbf{x})|f(\mathbf{x})| + \overline{f(\mathbf{x})} f(\mathbf{0}) f(\mathbf{x})$$

$$= |f(\mathbf{x})|^2 f(\mathbf{0}) - |f(\mathbf{x})| f(\mathbf{x})\overline{f(\mathbf{x})} - \overline{f(\mathbf{x})} f(\mathbf{x})|f(\mathbf{x})| + \overline{f(\mathbf{x})} f(\mathbf{0}) f(\mathbf{x})$$

(by part (ii))

$$= 2|f(\mathbf{x})|^2 f(\mathbf{0}) - 2|f(\mathbf{x})|^3 \geqslant 0,$$

which amounts to $|f(\mathbf{x})| \leqslant f(\mathbf{0})$ for all $\mathbf{x} \in \mathbb{R}^n$.

Part (iv): If $f(\mathbf{0}) = 0$, from part (iii) it follows that $f(\mathbf{x}) = 0$. The converse implication is immediate. $\qquad\square$

11.9 Reproducing Kernel Hilbert Spaces

Let S be a non-empty set and let $K : S \times S \longrightarrow \mathbb{C}$ be a function. If we fix the second argument of K, the resulting function $K(\cdot, t)$ is defined on S and ranges on $\mathbb{C}$.

If H is a Hilbert space whose elements are complex-valued functions defined on S and $K(\cdot, t) \in H$, it makes sense to consider inner products of the form $(f, K(\cdot, t))$.

Definition 11.14. Let H be a Hilbert space of complex-valued functions defined on a set S.

A *reproducing kernel* is a function $K : S \times S \longrightarrow \mathbb{C}$ such that $K(\cdot, t) \in H$ for every $t \in S$ and $(f, K(\cdot, t)) = f(t)$ for every $t \in S$.

A Hilbert space of complex-valued functions defined on a set S that has a reproducing kernel is called a *reproducing kernel Hilbert space* (RKHS).

Theorem 11.54. *A reproducing kernel K on a Hilbert space of functions of the form $f : S \longrightarrow \mathbb{C}$ is a function of positive type. Furthermore, we have $\|K(\cdot, t)\| = \sqrt{K(t, t)}$ for $t \in S$.*

Proof. Let $f = K(\cdot, s)$. Since K is a reproducing kernel we have $(f, K(\cdot, t)) = f(t)$, that is

$$(K(\cdot, s), K(\cdot, t)) = K(t, s) \tag{11.12}$$

for every $s, t \in S$. By Theorem 11.46, K is a function of positive type.

Choosing $s = t$ in equality (11.12) we obtain

$$(K(\cdot, t), K(\cdot, t)) = K(t, t),$$

which amounts to

$$\|K(\cdot, t)\|^2 = (K(\cdot, t), K(\cdot, t)) = K(t, t). \qquad \square$$

Theorem 11.55. *If a Hilbert space of functions of the form $f : S \longrightarrow \mathbb{C}$ has a reproducing kernel, then this kernel is unique.*

Proof. Suppose that K_1 and K_2 are kernels for H. We have $(f, K_1(\cdot, t)) = (f, K_2(\cdot, t) = f(t)$ for every $t \in S$. Therefore, $(f, K_1(\cdot, t) - K_2(\cdot, t)) = 0$. Taking $f(t) = K_1(\cdot, t) - K_2(\cdot, t)$ implies $\|K_1(\cdot, t) - K_2(\cdot, t)\|^2 = 0$, hence $K_1(\cdot, t) = K_2(\cdot, t)$ for every $t \in S$, that is, $K_1 = K_2$. $\qquad \square$

Example 11.17. We have shown in Example 2.3 that for a finite set S and a linear space L, L^S is a finite-dimensional space of functions. Namely, if $S = \{x_1, \ldots, x_n\}$, a basis of this space consists of functions of the form $e_i \in L^S$ defined as

$$e_i(x) = \begin{cases} 1 & \text{if } x = x_i, \\ 0 & \text{otherwise}, \end{cases}$$

for $1 \leqslant i \leqslant n$. Any function $f \in L^S$ can be written as

$$f = f(x_1)e_1 + \cdots + f(x_n)e_n.$$

If instead of a general linear space, we consider the set $\mathbb{C}^S$, the set $\mathbb{C}^S$ is a finite-dimensional complex Hilbert space, where

$$(f, g) = \sum_{i=1}^{n} f(x_i)\overline{g(x_i)}.$$

Let $K : S \times S \longrightarrow \mathbb{C}$ be the function defined by $K(x_i, x_j) = \delta_{ij}$, where δ_{ij} is Kronecker's symbol given by

$$\delta_{ij} = \begin{cases} 1 & \text{if } i = j, \\ 0 & \text{otherwise} \end{cases}$$

for $1 \leqslant i, j \leqslant n$.

For $x_j \in S$ we have

$$(f, K(\cdot, x_j)) = \sum_{i=1}^{n} f(x_i)\overline{K(x_i, x_j)} = f(x_j),$$

for every $x_j \in S$ which shows that K is indeed a self-reproducing kernel on $\mathbb{C}^S$.

Definition 11.15. For a Hilbert space of complex-valued functions defined on a set S, the *evaluation functional at* x is the functional $\mathsf{e}_x : H \longrightarrow \mathbb{C}$ defined by $\mathsf{e}_x(f) = f(x)$ for every $f \in H$.

Theorem 11.56. *A Hilbert space of complex-valued functions defined on a set S has a reproducing kernel if and only if every evaluation functional e_t for $t \in S$ is continuous.*

Proof. Suppose that H has a reproducing kernel K. We have

$$\mathsf{e}_t(f) = f(t) = (f, K(\cdot, t)).$$

By Cauchy-Schwarz inequality we have

$$|\mathsf{e}_t(f)| = |(f, K(\cdot, t))| \leqslant \|f\| \|K(\cdot, t)\| = \|f\| \sqrt{K(t, t)}$$

Since $\mathsf{e}_t(K(\cdot, t)) = K(t, t)$, we actually have $\|\mathsf{e}_t\| = \sqrt{K(t, t)}$, so e_t is bounded and, therefore, it is continuous.

Conversely, if e_t is continuous, by Riesz' Representation Theorem (Theorem 11.33), there exists a function h_t such that $\mathsf{e}_t(f) = (f, h_t) = f(t)$. Thus, we obtain the reproducing kernel K given by $K(s, t) = h_t(s)$. $\qquad\square$

Corollary 11.10. *In a RKHS H space of complex-valued functions defined on a set S, a sequence (f_n) of functions that converges in norm is also pointwise convergent.*

Proof. If (f_n) converges in norm to f then

$$|f_n(t) - f(t)| = |\mathsf{e}_t(f_n) - \mathsf{e}_t(f)|$$
$$= |\mathsf{e}_t(f_n - f)| \leqslant \|\mathsf{e}_t\| \cdot \|f_n - f\|.$$

Thus, if $\lim_{n \to \infty} \|f_n - f\| = 0$, it follows that $\lim_{n \to \infty} |f_n(t) - f(t)| = 0$ for $t \in S$. $\qquad\square$

Example 11.18. Let S be a finite set and let H be the finite-dimensional complex linear space that consists of complex-valued functions defined on S. Suppose that $B = \{e_1, \ldots, e_n\}$ is a basis in H.

The linear space H is equipped with the inner product defined as follows. If $f, g \in H$ we can write uniquely $f = \sum_{j=1}^{n} a_j e_j$ and $g = \sum_{j=1}^{n} b_j e_j$. Then, an inner product (f, g) can be defined as

$$(f, g) = \sum_{i=1}^{n} a_i \bar{b}_i (e_i, e_j).$$

If G_B is the Gram matrix of B we have $(f, g) = \mathbf{a}' G_B \mathbf{b}$, where $\mathbf{a} = \begin{pmatrix} a_1 \\ \vdots \\ a_n \end{pmatrix}$

and $\mathbf{b} = \begin{pmatrix} b_1 \\ \vdots \\ b_n \end{pmatrix}$. It is clear that H is a Hilbert space.

Assume now that B is an orthonormal basis. For $x, y \in S$ define the *kernel* K as the function $K : S^2 \longrightarrow \mathbb{C}$ given by

$$K(x, y) = \sum_{i=1}^{n} e_i(x) \overline{e_i(y)}$$

for $x, y \in S$. We claim that $(f, K(\cdot, y)) = f$. Indeed, we have

$$K(\cdot, y) = \sum_{i=1}^{n} e_i(\cdot) \overline{e_i(y)},$$

so the coefficients of $K(\cdot, y)$ relative to the basis B are $\overline{e_i(y)}$. Therefore,

$$(f, K(\cdot, y)) = \sum_{i=1}^{n} a_i \overline{\overline{e_i(y)}} = \sum_{i=1}^{n} a_i e_i(y) = f(y).$$

Example 11.19. Let $S = \mathbb{N}$ and let H be the $\ell^2(\mathbb{C})$. Consider the function $K : S^2 \longrightarrow \mathbb{C}$ defined by

$$K(i, j) = \begin{cases} 1 & \text{if } i = j, \\ 0 & \text{otherwise} \end{cases}$$

for $i, j \in \mathbb{N}$. Then, $K(\cdot, t)$ is the sequence $e_t = (0, 0, \ldots, 0, 1, 0, \ldots)$, where the unique 1 that occurs in this sequence is located on position t.

Then, for $f \in \ell^2(\mathbb{C})$ we have

$$(f, K(\cdot, t)) = (f, e_t) = f(t),$$

which shows that K is a reproducing kernel.

Theorem 11.57. *Let H_0 be a Hilbert space of functions of the form $f :$ $S \longrightarrow \mathbb{C}$ having the inner product $(\cdot, \cdot)_{H_0}$. Suppose that the evaluation functionals e_x (for $x \in S$) are continuous on H_0 and any Cauchy sequence (f_n) convergent pointwise to 0_{H_0} also converges in norm to 0_{H_0}.*

If H is the set of complex functions defined on S that are pointwise limits of functions from H_0, an inner product can be defined on H such that the following statements hold:

(i) *If (f_n) and (g_n) are two sequences in H_0 that converge pointwise to $f, g \in H$, respectively, then the sequence $((f_n, g_n)_{H_0})$ is convergent and its limit depends only on f and g.*

(ii) *If $f \in H$ and (f_n) is a sequence in H_0 that converges pointwise to f such that $\lim_{n \to \infty} \|f_n\|_{H_0} = 0$, then $f = 0_H$.*

(iii) *Let $f \in H$ and (f_n) be a Cauchy sequence in H_0 converging pointwise to f. Then (f_n) converges to f in the norm sense in H.*

(iv) *H_0 is dense in H.*

(v) *The evaluation functionals are continuous on H.*

Proof. Part (i): Since (f_n) and (g_n) are Cauchy sequences in H_0 they are bounded. This allows us to write

$$|(f_n, g_n)_{H_0} - (f_m, g_m)_{H_0}|$$
$$= |(f_n - f_m, g_n)_{H_0} + (f_m, g_n - g_m)_{H_0}|$$
$$\leqslant \|f_n - f_m\|_{H_0} \cdot \|g_n\|_{H_0} + \|f_m\|_{H_0} \cdot \|g_n - g_m\|_{H_0}$$

(by Cauchy-Schwarz inequality).

Thus, $((f_n, f_m)_{H_0})$ is a Cauchy sequence of complex numbers and, therefore, it is convergent. If $(\tilde{f}_n)$ and $(\tilde{g}_n)$ are two other Cauchy sequences converging pointwise to f and g, respectively, then

$$|(f_n, g_n)_{H_0} - (\tilde{f}_n, \tilde{g}_n)_{H_0}|$$
$$\leqslant \|f_n - \tilde{f}_n\|_{H_0} \cdot \|g_n\|_{H_0} + \|\tilde{f}_n\| \cdot \|g_n - \tilde{g}_n\|_{H_0}.$$

Since $(f_n - \tilde{f}_n)$ and $(g_n - \tilde{g}_n)$ are Cauchy sequences in H_0 converging pointwise to 0, these sequences converge to 0 in norm. Therefore, $\lim_{n \to \infty} (f_n, g_n)_{H_0} = \lim_{n \to \infty} (\tilde{f}_n, \tilde{g}_n)_{H_0}$.

Part (ii): The pointwise convergence of f_n to f means that for every $x \in S$ we have $f(x) = \lim_{n \to \infty} f_n(x) = \lim_{n \to x} e_x(f_n) = 0$, because of the continuity of the evaluation functionals on H_0. Therefore, $f = 0_H$.

Part (iii): Let f, g be two functions in H that are pointwise limits of the sequences (f_n) and (g_n) in H_0. The inner product on H is

$$(f, g)_H = \lim_{n \to \infty} (f_n, g_n)_{H_0},$$

as it can be easily verified. The topology defined on H_0 by the inner product coincides with the trace topology on H_0 induced by the topology of H.

For $\epsilon > 0$ let $n_\epsilon \in \mathbb{N}$ such that $m, n \geqslant n_\epsilon$ implies $\|f_n - f_m\|_{H_0} < \epsilon$.

For a fixed n, $n > n_\epsilon$. The sequence $(f_m - f_n)_{m \in \mathbb{N}}$ is a Cauchy sequence in H_0 that converges pointwise to $f - f_n$. Therefore,

$$\|f - f_n\|_H = \lim_{m \to \infty} \|f_m - f_n\| \leqslant \epsilon.$$

Thus, (f_n) converges to f in the norm sense.

Part (iv): By hypothesis, for every $f \in H$ there exists a Cauchy sequence (f_n) in H_0 that is convergent to f. By part (iii), f_n converges to f in a norm sense, so H_0 is dense in H.

Part (v): Since the evaluation functionals are linear it is sufficient to show that they are continuous at 0_H.

We start from the fact that each evaluation functional e_x is continuous on H_0. For $\epsilon > 0$ let η such that $f \in H_0$ and $\|f\|_{H_0} < \eta$ implies $|f(x)| < \frac{\epsilon}{2}$. By part (iii), for and function $f \in H$ with $\|f\|_H < \frac{\eta}{2}$ there exists $g \in H_0$ such that $|g(x) - f(x)| < \frac{\epsilon}{2}$ and $\|g - f\|_H < \frac{\eta}{2}$. This implies

$$\|g\|_{H_0} = \|g\|_H \leqslant \|g - f\|_H + \|f\|_H < \eta,$$

hence $|g(x)| < \frac{\epsilon}{2}$ and $|f(x)| < \epsilon$. Thus, e_x is continuous on H. $\qquad\square$

Theorem 11.58. *Let H_0 be a Hilbert space of functions of the form $f : S \longrightarrow \mathbb{C}$ having the inner product $(\cdot, \cdot)_{H_0}$. There exists a Hilbert space H such that the topology induced by $(\cdot, \cdot)_{H_0}$ on H_0 coincides with the trace topology of H on H_0 and H has a reproducing kernel if and only if*

> (i) *the evaluation functionals e_x (for $x \in S$) are continuous on H_0, and*
>
> (ii) *any Cauchy sequence (f_n) convergent pointwise to 0_{H_0} also converges in norm to 0_{H_0}.*

Proof. Suppose that a Hilbert space H exists that satisfies the conditions of the theorem. By Theorem 11.56 the evaluation functionals are continuous on H, and, therefore are continuous on H_0.

If (f_n) is a Cauchy sequence in H_0 that converges pointwise to 0_{H_0}, then (f_n) converges in norm in H to some f because H is complete. We have $f(x) = \mathsf{e}_x(f) = \lim_{n \to \infty} \mathsf{e}_x(f_n) = \lim_{n \to \infty} f_n(x) = 0$, so f is the constant function 0.

Thus, the conditions of the theorem are necessary.

To prove that they are sufficient, define H as the set of complex-valued functions defined on S for which there exists a Cauchy sequence (f_n) in H_0 convergent pointwise to f.

By part (i) of Theorem 11.57, the inner product of H_0 can be extended to H. To prove that H has a reproducing kernel, it is sufficient to prove that H is complete (by Theorem 11.56) because the evaluation functionals are continuous on H according to part (v) of Theorem 11.57.

Let (f_n) be a Cauchy sequence in H and let $x \in S$. If $x \in S$, $(f_n(x))$ is a Cauchy sequence in $\mathbb{C}$ (because every evaluation functional e_x is continuous), so $\lim_{n\to\infty} f_n(x)$ exists. Let $f : S \longrightarrow \mathbb{C}$ be defined as $f(x) = \lim_{n\to\infty} f_n(x)$.

To prove that $f \in H$ let (ϵ_n) be a sequence of positive numbers such that $\lim_{n\to\infty} \epsilon_n = 0$. Since H_0 is dense in H (by part (iv) of Theorem 11.57) it follows that for every $i \in \mathbb{N}$ there exists $g_i \in H_0$ such that $\|f_i - g_i\|_H < \epsilon_i$. We have

$$|g_i(x) - f(x)| \leqslant |g_i(x) - f_i(x)| + |f_i(x) - f(x)|$$
$$\leqslant |e_x(g_i - f_i)| + |f_i(x) - f(x)|.$$

Since the evaluation functionals are continuous on H (by part (v) of Theorem 11.57) it follows that $\lim_{n\to\infty} g_n(x) = f(x)$. This implies

$$\|g_i - g_j\|_{H_0} = \|g_i - g_j\|_H$$
$$\leqslant \|g_i - f_i\|_H + \|f_i - f_j\|_H + \|f_j - g_j\|_H$$
$$\leqslant \epsilon_i + \|f_i - f_j\|_H + \epsilon_j,$$

which shows that (g_n) is a Cauchy sequence in H_0 that tends pointwise to $f \in H$. By part (iii) of Theorem 11.57), (g_n) tends in norm to f. Since $\|f_i - f\|_H \leqslant \|f_i - g_i\|_H + \|g_i - f\|_H$, (f_n) converges to f is norm and H is complete. $\qquad\square$

Example 11.20. The function $K : \mathbb{R}^k \times \mathbb{R}^k \longrightarrow \mathbb{R}$ introduced in Example 11.14 as $K(\mathbf{x}, \mathbf{y}) = (\mathbf{x}, \mathbf{y})^d$, where $d \in \mathbb{N}$ and $d \geqslant 1$ is a reproducing kernel because, as we saw earlier, it is of positive type. This function is known as the *homogeneous polynomial kernel*.

The functions introduced in Examples 11.15, and 11.16 are reproducing kernels named *polynomial non-homogeneous kernel* and *radial basis kernel*, respectively.

Recall that we have shown in Theorem 11.46 that a function $K : S \times S \longrightarrow \mathbb{C}$ defined by $K(s,t) = (f(s), f(t))$, where $f : S \longrightarrow H$ is of positive type, where H is a Hilbert space. Next, we show that if K is of positive type a special Hilbert space exists such that K can be expressed as an inner product on this space. This fact is essential for data kernelization, a process described in Chapter 17, that is essential for support vector machines.

A RKHS of functions is characterized by its kernel; furthermore, K is a reproducing kernel is equivalent to being a positive type function.

Theorem 11.59. (Aronszajn's[4] Theorem) *Let S be a set and let K : $S \times S \longrightarrow \mathbb{C}$ be a positive type function. There exists a unique Hilbert space H of complex-valued functions defined on S having K as a reproducing kernel.*

The subspace H_0 of H spanned by the set of functions $\{K(\cdot, t) \mid t \in S\}$ is dense in H. Furthermore, H consists of those functions defined on E that are pointwise limits of Cauchy sequences in H_0. The inner product of the functions $f = \sum_{i=1}^{n} a_i K(\cdot, x_i)$ and $g = \sum_{j=1}^{m} b_j K(\cdot, y_j)$ in H_0 is $(f, g)_{H_0} = \sum_{i=1}^{n} \sum_{j=1}^{m} a_i \overline{b_j} K(y_j, x_i)$.

Proof. By part (i) of Theorem 11.47 we have:

$$\overline{g(x_i)} = \sum_{j=1}^{m} \overline{b_j K(x_i, y_j)} = \sum_{j=1}^{m} \overline{b_j} K(y_j, x_i),$$

which yields $(f, g)_{H_0} = \sum_{i=1}^{n} a_i \overline{g(x_i)}$. Since $f(y_j) = \sum_{i=1}^{n} a_i K(y_j, x_i)$, we also have $(f, g)_{H_0} = \sum_{i=1}^{n} \overline{b_j} f(y_j)$. Thus, the inner product $(f, g)_{H_0}$ depends on f and g through their values $f(y_j)$ and $g(x_i)$.

K is a reproducing kernel because

$$(f, K(\cdot, x))_{H_0} = \sum_{i=1}^{n} a_i \overline{K(x, x_i)} = \sum_{i=1}^{n} a_i \overline{K(x_i, x)} = f(x).$$

Note that

$$\|K(\cdot, x)\|_{H_0}^2 = (K(\cdot, x), K(\cdot, x)) = K(x, x).$$

Suppose that $\|f\|_{H_0} = 0$. Then, by Cauchy-Schwarz inequality

$$|f(x)| = |(f, K(\cdot, x))_{H_0}| \leqslant \sqrt{(f, f)_{H_0}} \sqrt{K(x, x)} = 0,$$

and f is the constant function 0.

We claim that the Hilbert space H_0 satisfies conditions (i) and (ii) of Theorem 11.58.

---

[4] Nachman Aronszajn was born on July 26th 1907 in Warsaw, Poland and died on February 5th in Corvallis, Oregon. He received his Ph.D. from the University of Warsaw, in 1930, in Poland under Stefan Mazurkiewicz. He also received a Ph.D. from Paris University, in 1935, where he studied with Maurice Fréchet. Aronszajn taught at Oklahoma A&M and the University of Kansas and retired in 1977. His main contributions were in mathematical analysis and logic.

The continuity of the evaluation functionals follows from the fact that for $f, g \in H_0$ and $x \in S$ we have

$$|e_x(f) - e_x(g)| = |(f - g, K(\cdot, x)_{H_0})|$$
$$\leqslant \|f - g\|_{H_0} \sqrt{K(x, x)}.$$

To verify the second condition of Theorem 11.58, let (f_n) be a Cauchy sequence of functions in H_0 convergent pointwise to 0_{H_0}. Since (f_n) is bounded there exists $M > 0$ such that $\|f_n\| < M$ for $n \in \mathbb{N}$. There exists n_ϵ such that $n > n_\epsilon$ implies $\|f_{n_\epsilon} - f_n\|_{H_0} < \frac{\epsilon}{M}$. Since H_0 is spanned by the set of functions $\{K(\cdot, t) \mid t \in S\}$, there exists $k, a_1, \ldots, a_k, x_1, \ldots, x_k$ such that

$$f_{n_\epsilon} = \sum_{i=1}^{k} a_i K(\cdot, x_i).$$

Note that

$$\|f_n\|_{H_0}^2 = (f_n - f_{n_\epsilon} + f_{n_\epsilon}, f_n)_{H_0}$$
$$= (f_n - f_{n_\epsilon}, f_n)_{H_0} + (f_{n_\epsilon}, f_n)_{H_0}.$$

Therefore, $n > n_\epsilon$ implies

$$\|f_n\|_{H_0}^2 < \epsilon + \sum_{i=1}^{k} f_n(x_i).$$

Since $\lim_{n \to \infty} f_n(x_i) = 0$, the sequence (f_n) converges in norm to 0_{H_0}. By Theorem 11.58 there exists a Hilbert space H that has a reproducible kernel such that the topology induced by inner product on H_0 coincides with the trace topology of H on H_0. Namely, H consists of complex-valued functions defined on S that are pointwise limits of Cauchy sequences of functions in H_0. By part (iii) of Theorem 11.57, these functions are also limits in the sense of the norm of H, so H_0 is dense in H. The space H_0 is unique and for every $x \in S$ we have

$$f(x) = \lim_{n \to \infty} f_n(x) = \lim_{n \to \infty} (f_n, K(\cdot, x))_{H_0} = (f, K(\cdot, x))_H,$$

which means that K is a reproducing kernel for H. $\qquad\square$

Definition 11.16. The Hilbert space H of complex-valued functions defined on S having K as a reproducing kernel will be referred as the *Hilbert space associated* to the positive type function K.

Theorem 11.60. (Schoenberg's[5] Theorem) *Let S be a non-empty set and let $K : S \times S \longrightarrow \mathbb{C}$ be a function of negative type. Define the function $F : S \times S \longrightarrow \mathbb{C}$ as*

$$F(x,y) = \frac{1}{2}(K(x,x_0) + \overline{K(y,x_0)} - K(x,y) - K(x_0,x_0)),$$

for a fixed x_0 and let $f_x = F(x, \cdot)$ for $x \in S$.

The following statements hold:

(i) *There exists a Hilbert space $H \subseteq \mathbb{C}^S$ and a function $g : S \longrightarrow \mathbb{C}$ such that:*

$$K(x,y) = \|f_x\|^2 + \|f_y\|^2 - 2(f_x, f_y) + g(x) + \overline{g(y)},$$

(ii) *If there exists $x_0 \in S$ such that $K(x_0,y)$ is a real number and $K(x,x) = 0$ for $x \in S$, then g may be chosen to be 0.*

(iii) *If K is real-valued, then H may be chosen as a real Hilbert space and we have*

$$K(x,y) = \|f_x - f_y\|^2 + g(x) + g(y),$$

where $f : S \longrightarrow \mathbb{R}$ is non-negative when K is.

(iv) *If K is real-valued and $K(x,x) = 0$ for every $x \in S$, then $g = 0$, $\sqrt{K(x,y)}$ is a semimetric on S such that $\Phi : S \longrightarrow H$ defined by $\Phi(x) = f_x$ is an isometry.*
If $K(x,y) = 0$ implies $x = y$, then $\sqrt{K}$ is a metric on S induced by an inner product.

Proof. Part (i): By Theorem 11.52 $F(x,y)$ is a function of positive type. A basis in the RKHS H associated to F consists of functions of the form $F(x_i, \cdot)$. If f, g are two functions in this space

$$f = \sum_i a_i F(x_i, \cdot) \text{ and } g = \sum_j b_j F(y_j, \cdot),$$

their inner product is

$$(f,g) = \sum_i \sum_j a_i \overline{b_j} F(y_j, x_i),$$

and the corresponding norm is

$$\|f\|^2 = \sum_i \sum_j a_i \overline{a_j} F(x_j, x_i).$$

---

[5]Isaac J. Schoenberg (April 21st 1903-February 21st 1990) was an American mathematician of Romanian-Jewish origin. He is the discoverer of splines and has major contributions in the area of positive functions. Schoenberg obtained his Ph.D. at the University of Iasi, Romania in 1926. His american career included positions at Swarthmore College, University of Pennsylvania, and the University of Wisconsin at Madison.

Note that

$$F(x,x) = \frac{1}{2}(K(x,x_0) + \overline{K(x,x_0)} - K(x,x) - K(x_0,x_0))$$

$$= \Re K(x,x_0) - \frac{1}{2}K(x,x) - \frac{1}{2}K(x_0,x_0).$$

Similarly,

$$F(y,y) = \Re K(y,x_0) - \frac{1}{2}K(y,y) - \frac{1}{2}K(x_0,x_0).$$

Also,

$$2\Re F(x,y) = F(x,y) + \overline{F(x,y)}$$

$$= \frac{1}{2}(K(x,x_0) + \overline{K(x_0,y)} - K(x,y) - K(x_0,x_0)$$

$$+ K(x_0,x) + K(y,x_0) - K(y,x) - K(x_0,x_0)).$$

Consequently, we have:

$$F(x,x) + F(y,y) - 2\Re F(x,y)$$

$$= \Re K(x,y) - \frac{1}{2}(K(x,x) + K(y,y)).$$

Let $f_z = F(z,\cdot)$ for $z \in S$. We have

$$(f_x, f_x) = F(x,x), (f_y, f_y) = F(y,y), \text{ and } (f_x, f_y) = F(x,y),$$

which implies

$$\|f_x - f_y\|^2 = (f_x, f_x) + (f_y, f_y) - (f_x, f_y) - (f_y, f_x)$$

$$= F(x,x) + F(y,y) - 2\Re F(x,y)$$

$$= \Re K(x,y) - \frac{1}{2}(K(x,x) + K(y,y)) \qquad (11.13)$$

and

$$\|f_x\|^2 + \|f_y\|^2 - 2(f_x, f_y) = \|f_x - f_y\|^2 - 2i(f_x, f_y)$$
$$= K(x,y) - \tfrac{1}{2}(K(x,x) + K(y,y)) - i\Im(K(x,x_0) + \overline{K(y,x_0)}).$$

By defining $g(x) = \frac{1}{2}K(x,x) + i\Im K(x,x_0)$ we obtain

$$K(x,y) = \|f_x\|^2 + \|f_y\|^2 - 2(f_x, f_y) + g(x) + \overline{g(y)},$$

which concludes the argument for part (i) of the theorem.

Part (ii): Suppose that there exists $x_0 \in S$ such that $K(x_0, y)$ is a real number and $K(x,x) = 0$ for $x \in S$. The previous definition of g, $g(x) = \frac{1}{2}K(x,x) + i\Im K(x,x_0)$ yields to $g(x) = 0$.

Part (iii): If K is a real-valued function, $g(x) = \frac{1}{2}K(x,x)$, $g(y) = \overline{g(y)} = \frac{1}{2}K(y,y)$. Equality 11.13 implies

$$\|f_x - f_y\|^2 = K(x,y) - \frac{1}{2}(K(x,x) + K(y,y)).$$

Therefore,

$$K(x,y) = \|f_x - f_y\|^2 + \frac{1}{2}(K(x,x) + K(y,y))$$
$$= \|f_x - f_y\|^2 + \frac{1}{2}(K(x,x) + K(y,y))$$
$$= \|f_x - f_y\|^2 + g(x) + g(y).$$

The inner product of f_x and f_y is real because $F(x,y)$ is real.

Part (iv): Part (ii) implies that if K is real-valued and $K(x,x) = 0$, then $g = 0$. Then, $\sqrt{K(x,y)} = \|f_x - f_y\|$ is clearly a semimetric on S and Φ is an isometry. The last part of (iv) is immediate. $\qquad\square$

11.10 Positive Operators in Hilbert Spaces

Theorem 11.61. *Let h be a positive operator on $L^2([0,1])$ having the kernel $K(x,y)$. Then, $K(x,x) \geqslant 0$ for $x \in [0,1]$.*

Proof. Suppose that there exists $x_0 \in [0,1]$ such that $K(x_0, x_0) < 0$. Since K is continuous, there exists a neighborhood of (x_0, x_0) such that $K(x,y) < 0$; in other words, there exists $\delta > 0$ such that $K(x,y) < 0$ if $|x - x_0| + |y - y_0| < \delta$.

Let $f_0 : [0,1] \longrightarrow \mathbb{R}$ be defined as:

$$f_0(x) = \begin{cases} 1 & \text{if } |x - x_0| \leqslant \frac{\delta}{2}, \\ 0 & \text{if } |x - x_0| > \frac{\delta}{2}. \end{cases}$$

We have

$$(hf_0, f_0) = \int_0^1 \int_0^1 K(x,y)f_0(y)f_0(x)\, dx\, dy$$
$$= \int_{x_0 - \frac{\delta}{2}}^{x_0 + \frac{\delta}{2}} \int_{x_0 - \frac{\delta}{2}}^{x_0 + \frac{\delta}{2}} K(x,y)\, dx\, dy$$
$$< 0,$$

which contradicts the positivity of h. $\qquad\square$

Theorem 11.62. (Mercer's Theorem) *Let $K : [0,1] \times [0,1] \longrightarrow \mathbb{R}$ be a function continuous in both variables that is the kernel of a positive operator h on $L^2([0,1])$. Suppose that the eigenfunctions of h are $\phi_1, \phi_2, \ldots$ and they correspond to the eigenvalues $\mu_1, \mu_2, \ldots$, respectively. Then, we have*

$$K(x,y) = \sum_{j=1}^{\infty} \mu_j \phi_j(x) \overline{\phi_j(y)},$$

where the series $\sum_{j=1}^{\infty} \mu_j \phi_j(x) \overline{\phi_j(y)}$ converges uniformly and absolutely to $K(x,y)$.

Proof. Since $\int_0^1 K(x,y) \phi_j(y) \, dy = \mu_j \phi_j(x)$ and K is continuous, it follows that each of the eigenfunctions ϕ_j is continuous on $[0,1]$.

Let $K_n : [0,1] \times [0,1] \longrightarrow \mathbb{R}$ be defined as

$$K_n(x,y) = K(x,y) - \sum_{j=1}^{n} \mu_j \phi_j(x) \overline{\phi_j(y)}.$$

K_n is clearly continuous.

Let h_n the linear operator defined by the integral kernel K_n. Since $K_n(x,y) = \sum_{j=n+1}^{\infty} \mu_j \phi_j(x) \overline{\phi_j(y)}$ in the sense of the norm in the Hilbert space, it follows that

$$(h_n(f), f) = \int_0^1 \int_0^1 K_n(x,y) f(x) \overline{f(y)} \, dx \, dy = \sum_{n+1}^{\infty} \mu_i (\phi_i, f)(f, \overline{\phi_j}) \geqslant 0,$$

for every $f \in L^2([0,1])$. By Theorem 11.61, we have $K_n(x,x) \geqslant 0$ for $x \in [0,1]$. This implies that the series $\sum_{n=1}^{\infty} \mu_i \phi_i(x) \overline{\phi_i(x)} \geqslant 0$ and its sum is less than $(h(x), x)$. Let $M = \max\{K(x,x) \mid x \in [0,1]\}$ we have, by Cauchy-Schwartz inequality:

$$\left| \sum_{j=m}^{n} \mu_j \phi_j(x) \overline{\phi_i(y)} \right|^2 \leqslant \sum_{j=m}^{n} |\phi_j(x)|^2 \sum_{j=m}^{n} |\phi_j(y)|^2 \leqslant M \sum_{j=m}^{n} |\phi_j(x)|^2.$$

Therefore, for each x, the series $\sum_{i=1}^{\infty} \mu_i \phi_i(x) \overline{\phi_i(y)}$ converges uniformly in y. Its sum, $\Phi(x,y)$ is therefore, a continuous function in y and for each continuous function f we have

$$\int_0^1 \Phi(x,y) f(y) \, dy = \sum_{i=1}^{\infty} \mu_i \phi_i(x) \int_0^1 \overline{\phi_i(y)} f(y) \, dy.$$

The series $\sum_{i=1}^{\infty} \mu_i \phi_i(x) \int_0^1 \overline{\phi_i(y)} f(y) \, dy$ converges to $(hf)(x)$ and, therefore, we have

$$\int_0^1 (\Phi(x,y) - K(x,y)) f(y) \, dy = 0.$$

Choosing $f(y) = \Phi(x, y) - K(x, y)$ for a fixed value of x implies that $\Phi(x, y) = K(x, y)$ for $y \in [0, 1]$, hence

$$K(x, x) = \Phi(x, x) = \sum_{i=1}^{\infty} \mu_i |\phi_i(x)|^2.$$

Since the terms of this series are positive continuous functions, by Dini's theorem (Theorem 5.37), the series converges uniformly on $[0, 1]$. Applying again Cauchy's inequality, we obtain that the series $\sum_{i=1}^{\infty} \mu_i \phi_i(x) \overline{\phi_i(y)}$ converges uniformly with respect to both variables. $\square$

Example 11.21. Let $K : [0, 1] \times [0, 1] \longrightarrow \mathbb{R}$ be a continuous, Hermitian kernel. The second iteration of K is the kernel $K^{(2)}$ defined by

$$K^{(2)}(x, y) = \int_0^1 K(x, z) K(z, y) \, dz.$$

It is clear that $K^{(2)}$ is continuous and of positive type. If h is the operator defined by K and $h^{(2)}$ is the operator defined by $K^{(2)}$, then

$$
\begin{aligned}
(h^{(2)}(f), f) &= \int_0^1 \int_0^1 K^{(2)}(x, y) f(y) \overline{f(x)} \, dx \, dy \\
&= \int_0^1 \int_0^1 \int_0^1 K(x, z) K(z, y) f(y) \overline{f(x)} \, dx \, dy \\
&= \int_0^1 \left(\int_0^1 K(z, y) f(y) \right) \left(\int_0^1 K(x, z) \overline{f(x)} \right) \\
&= (h(f), h(f)) \geqslant 0.
\end{aligned}
$$

The eigenfunctions of h are also eigenfunctions of $h^{(2)}$; if ϕ_i is an eigenfunction of h that corresponds to an eigenvalue μ_i, the corresponding eigenvalue for $h^{(2)}$ is μ_i^2. The sequence $\mu_1^2, \mu_2^2, \ldots$ contains all non-zero eigenvalues of $h^{(2)}$, with the same multiplicities. Otherwise, if ψ would be an eigenfunction of $h^{(2)}$ corresponding to an eigenvalue $\mu \neq 0$ of $h^{(2)}$ and orthogonal on all ϕ_i we could write

$$\mu \phi = h^{(2)}(\phi) = \sum_{i=1}^{\infty} (h^2 \phi, \phi_i) \phi_i$$

$$= \sum_{i=1}^{\infty} \mu_i^2 (\phi, \phi_i) = 0,$$

leading to a contradiction. By Mercer's Theorem, we would have

$$K^{(2)}(x, y) = \sum_{j=1}^{\infty} \mu_j^2 \phi_j(x) \overline{\phi_j(y)}.$$

Theorem 11.63. *Let h be a compact self-adjoint operator on a Hilbert space defined by the kernel $K(x, y)$ that is continuous on $[0, 1] \times [0, 1]$. If h has a finite number of negative eigenvalues, then*

$$K(x, y) = \sum_{i=1}^{\infty} \mu_i \phi_i(x) \overline{\phi_i(y)},$$

where the series $\sum_{i=1}^{\infty} \mu_i \phi_i(x) \overline{\phi_i(y)}$ converges absolutely and uniformly to $K(x, y)$.

Moreover, we have

$$\int_0^1 K(x, x) \, dx = \sum_{i=1}^{\infty} \mu_i.$$

Proof. Without loss of generality we may assume that the negative eigenvalues are $\mu_1, \ldots, \mu_n$, so that $\mu_{n+1}, \mu_{n+2}, \ldots$ are positive. Then the kernel

$$K_n(x, y) = K(x, y) - \sum_{j=1}^{n} \mu_j \phi_j(x) \overline{\phi_j(y)},$$

has no negative eigenvalues, so the operator h_n is positive. Then, the series $\sum_{j=n+1}^{\infty} \mu_j \phi_j(x) \phi_j(y)$ converges uniformly and absolutely to $K_n(x, y)$, which implies the statement of the theorem.

Since the series $\sum_{i=1}^{\infty} \mu_i \phi_i(x) \overline{\phi_i(y)}$ converges absolutely and uniformly, we have

$$\int_0^1 K(x, x) \, dx = \int_0^1 \left(\sum_{i=1}^{\infty} \mu_i \phi_i(x) \overline{\phi_i(x)} \right) \, dx$$

$$= \sum_{i=1}^{\infty} \mu_i \int_0^1 \phi_i(x) \overline{\phi_i(x)} \, dx$$

$$= \sum_{i=1}^{\infty} \mu_i. \qquad \square$$

Exercises and Supplements

(1) Let G be the set of complex functions defined on $\mathbb{N}$ that take only a finite number of non-zero values. G is a complex linear space with respect to addition and scalar multiplication and $(f, g) = \sum \{ f(n) \overline{g(n)} \mid n \in \mathbb{N} \}$ is an inner product on G. For $a \in (0, 1)$ define the sequence of functions $(f_k)_{k \in \mathbb{N}}$ as

$$f_k(n) = \begin{cases} a^n & \text{if } n \leqslant k, \\ 0 & \text{otherwise} \end{cases}$$

for $n \in \mathbb{N}$. Prove that $(f_k)_{k \in \mathbb{N}}$ is a Cauchy sequence that does not converge to a function in G.

(2) Let $\{H_i \mid i \in I\}$ be a collection of disjoint Hilbert spaces. Denote by $\sum_{i \in I} H_i$ the set of all collections $\{x_i\} = \{x_i \mid x_i \in H_i \text{ for } i \in I\}$. Scalar multiplication, addition and inner product are defined on $\sigma_{i \in I} H_i$ by

$$a\{x_i\} = \{ax_i\}, \{x_i\} + \{y_i\} = \{x_i + y_i\}, (\{x_i\}, \{y_i\}) = \sum_{i \in I} (x_i, y_i).$$

Prove that with the above definitions, $\sum_{i \in I} H_i$ is a Hilbert space. This space is called the *direct sum* of the collection $\{H_i \mid i \in I\}$.

(3) Let $U = \{u_n \mid n \in \mathbb{N}, n \geqslant 1\}$ be an orthonormal set in a Hilbert space H. Prove that:

   (a) $u = \lim_{n \to \infty} \sum_{i=1}^{n} \frac{u_i}{i}$ exists;
   (b) u is not a linear combination of U.

   Hint: Note that

$$\left\| \sum_{i=n}^{m} \frac{u_i}{i} \right\|^2 = \sum_{i=n}^{m} \frac{1}{i^2} < \sum_{i=n}^{\infty} \frac{1}{i^2},$$

   and $\lim_{n \to \infty} \sum_{i=n}^{\infty} \frac{1}{i^2} = 0$.

(4) Prove that if $\{e_n \mid n \in \mathbb{N}\}$ is an orthonormal basis in a $\mathbb{C}$-Hilbert space of functions $H = \mathbb{C}^S$, then $\{\overline{e_n} \mid n \in \mathbb{N}\}$ is also an orthonormal basis in H.

   Solution: It is immediate that the set $\{\overline{e_n} \mid n \in \mathbb{N}\}$ is orthonormal.

   Let $f \in \mathbb{C}^S$. Since $\{e_n \mid n \in \mathbb{N}\}$ is an orthonormal basis we can write $\overline{f} = \sum_{n \in \mathbb{N}} (\overline{f}, e_n) e_n$, which implies $f = \sum_{n \in \mathbb{N}} \overline{(\overline{f}, e_n)} \overline{e_n}$. This shows that $\{\overline{e_n} \mid n \in \mathbb{N}\}$ is also a basis for H, hence, an orthonormal basis for this space.

(5) Let $Q \in \mathbb{R}^{m \times m}$ be a positive definite matrix. Prove that the mapping $(\cdot, \cdot)_Q : \mathbb{R}^m \times \mathbb{R}^m \longrightarrow \mathbb{R}$ defined by $(\mathbf{x}, \mathbf{y}) = \mathbf{x}' Q \mathbf{y}$ for $\mathbf{x}, \mathbf{y} \in \mathbb{R}^m$ is an inner product on $\mathbb{R}^m$.

(6) Let $Q \in \mathbb{R}^{m \times m}$ be a positive definite matrix and let $B = \{\mathbf{b}_1, \dots, \mathbf{b}_n\}$ be a linearly independent set of vectors in $\mathbb{R}^m$. Prove that the vector $\mathbf{x}_0 \in \mathbb{R}^m$ for which $\mathbf{x}' Q \mathbf{x}$ is minimal and the conditions

$$\mathbf{x}' \mathbf{b}_j = \begin{cases} 1 & \text{if } j = i, \\ 0 & \text{otherwise} \end{cases} \tag{11.14}$$

are satisfied for $1 \leqslant j \leqslant n$ is given by $\mathbf{x} = Q^{-1} B (B' Q^{-1} B)^{-1} \mathbf{e}_i$.

   Solution: Note that Q is symmetric because it is a real and positive definite matrix. Let $\| \cdot \|_Q$ be the norm generated by the inner product introduced in Exercise 5. Then $\mathbf{x}'Q\mathbf{x} = \|\mathbf{x}\|_Q^2$. The restrictions (11.14) can be written as

$$
(\mathbf{x}, Q^{-1}\mathbf{b}_i)_Q = \begin{cases} 1 & \text{if } j = i, \\ 0 & \text{otherwise,} \end{cases}
$$

which allows us to express this optimization problem in terms of the inner product mentioned above. Thus, Theorem 11.32 is applicable to the set of vectors $\{Q^{-1}\mathbf{b}_i \mid 1 \leqslant i \leqslant n\}$. Note that the Gram matrix of $\{\mathbf{b}_1, \ldots, \mathbf{b}_n\}$ relative to the inner product $(\cdot, \cdot)_Q$ is $G_{Q^{-1}Y} = Y'Q^{-1}Y$, hence $\mathbf{x}_0 = Q^{-1}B\mathbf{b}$, where $G_{Q^{-1}B}\mathbf{b} = B'Q^{-1}B\mathbf{b} = \mathbf{e}_i$. Thus, $\mathbf{b} = (B'Q^{-1}B)^{-1}\mathbf{e}_i$, hence

$$
\mathbf{x}_0 = Q^{-1}B(B'Q^{-1}B)^{-1}\mathbf{e}_i.
$$

(7) Let $B = \{\mathbf{b}_1, \ldots, \mathbf{b}_n\}$ be a linearly independent set of vectors in $\mathbb{R}^n$ and let $Q \in \mathbb{R}^{m \times m}$ be a positive definite matrix. Show that the matrix $K \in \mathbb{R}^{n \times m}$ that minimizes $trace(KQK')$ subjected to the condition $KB = I_n$ is given by $K' = Q^{-1}B(B'(Q^{-1})'B)^{-1}$.

(8) Let S is a closed subspace of the Hilbert space H and let M be subspace in H such that $M \subseteq S$. Prove that $\mathbf{K}(M) \neq S$ if and only if there exists $x \in S$ that is orthogonal on M.

Solution: Suppose that $\mathbf{K}(M) \neq S$ and let $y \in S - \mathbf{K}(M)$. Then, $x = y - p_{\mathbf{K}(M)}(y) \neq 0_H$ is orthogonal on M. The reverse implication is immediate.

(9) Let (x_n) and (y_m) be two orthonormal sequences in a Hilbert space H such that $x_n \perp y_m$ for $n, m \in \mathbb{N}$ and let (z_n) be a sequence defined by $z_n = x_n \cos \frac{1}{n} + y_n \sin \frac{1}{n}$. Let X and Y be the closed subspaces of H generated by the sets $\{x_n \mid n \in \mathbb{N}\}$ and $\{y_n \mid n \in \mathbb{N}\}$, respectively. Prove that

   (a) (z_n) is an orthonormal sequence and $\lim_{n \to \infty}(x_n, z_n) = 1$;
   (b) the series $\sum_n y_n \sin \frac{1}{n}$ is convergent;
   (c) if Z is the closed subspace generated by $\{z_n \mid n \in \mathbb{N}\}$, then $X \cap Z = \{0_H\}$ and for $x \in X$ and $z \in Z$ the inner product (x, z) is arbitrarily close to 1;
   (d) there exists a vector $y \in \mathbf{K}(X \cup Z) - (X + Z)$.

Solution: The definition of (z_n) implies immediately that if $n \neq p$, then $(z_n, z_p) = 0$. Also, we have

$$
\|z_n\|^2 = (z_n, z_n) = \cos^2 \frac{1}{n} + \sin^2 \frac{1}{n} = 1,
$$

so (z_n) is an orthonormal sequence. The convergence of the series $\sum_n y_n \sin \frac{1}{n}$ follows from Theorem 11.20 because $\sum_n \|y_n \sin \frac{1}{n}\|^2 = \sum_n \sin^2 \frac{1}{n}$.

Let $y = \sum_m y_m \sin \frac{1}{m}$. Note that

$$y_m = \frac{1}{\sin \frac{1}{m}} \left(z_m - x_m \cos \frac{1}{m} \right) \in X + Z$$

for every m, so $y \in \mathbf{K}(X + Z)$. We claim that $y \notin X + Z$. Indeed, if this were the case, say $y = x + z$, where $x \in X$ and $z \in Z$, this would imply

$$\sin \frac{1}{m} = (y, y_m) = (x + z, y_m) = (z, y_m)$$

$$= \left(\sum (z, z_n) z_n, y_m \right) = (z, z_m)(z_m, y_m)$$

$$= (z, z_m) \sin \frac{1}{m}$$

for every m. This would imply $(z, z_m) = 1$ for every m, which contradicts Bessel Inequality (Corollary 11.3).

(10) Let H be a complex Hilbert space and let $B : H \times H \longrightarrow \mathbb{C}$ be a function such that for a fixed y, $B(x, y)$ is a linear function of x, and for a fixed x, $B(x, y)$ is a skew-linear function of y, $|B(x, y)| \leqslant c\|x\|\|y\|$ and $|B(y, y)| \geqslant b\|y\|$ for a positive b for all $y \in H$. Prove that every linear functional $f : H \longrightarrow \mathbb{C}$ such that there exists $c \geqslant 0$ and $|f(x)| \leqslant c\|x\|$ for $x \in H$ has the form $f(x) = B(x, y)$ for a unique y. This statement is known as the *Lax-Milgram theorem*.

Solution: Since $B(x, y)$ is a bounded linear functional of x for a fixed y, by Riesz' Theorem, it can be written as $B(x, y) = (x, z)$ for a unique z determined by y. Then, z depends linearly on y and the set of all such zs is a linear subspace H_1 of H as y varies in H. Since $B(y, y) = (y, z)$, by Cauchy-Schwarz inequality, $b\|y\| \leqslant \|z\|$. If (z_n) is a sequence defined by $B(x, y_n) = (x, z_n)$, then $B(x, y_n - y_m) = (x, z_n - z_m)$, hence $b\|y_n - y_m\| \leqslant \|z_n - z_m\|$. If $\lim_{n \to \infty} z_n = z$, the sequence (y_n) is a Cauchy sequence, hence there exists $y = \lim_{n \to \infty} y_n$. Therefore, $\lim_{n \to \infty} B(x, y_n) = B(x, y)$ and $\lim_{n \to \infty} (x, z_n) = (x, z)$, so z belongs to a closed subspace.

We have $H_1 = H$ since, otherwise, there would be $x_1 \neq 0_H$ such that $x_1 \perp H_1$. This would imply $B(x_1, y) = 0$ for all y. Taking $y = x_1$ gives $B(x_1, x_1) = 0$, hence $\|x_1\| = 0$ contradicting the assumption $x_1 \neq 0_H$.

By Riesz' Theorem all linear functionals can be represented as $f(x) = (x, z)$. Combined with $B(x, y) = (x, z)$, this yields $f(x) = B(x, y)$, so y is uniquely determined.

(11) Consider the sequence $(\mathbf{e}_n)$ in the Hilbert space $\ell^2(\mathbb{R})$, where $\mathbf{e}_n = (0, \ldots, 0, 1, 0, \ldots)$, and 1 occupies the nth place in $\mathbf{e}_n$. Prove that this sequence converges weakly to $0_{\ell^2(\mathbb{R})}$ but not strongly.

(12) Let (x_n) be an orthonormal sequence in a Hilbert space. Prove that (x_n) converges weakly to 0_H but not strongly.

(13) Prove that the linear operator $h : \mathbb{R}^2 \longrightarrow \mathbb{R}^2$ defined on the real Hilbert $\mathbb{R}^2$ space by:

$$h(\mathbf{x}) = \begin{pmatrix} -x_2 \\ x_1 \end{pmatrix}$$

for $\mathbf{x} \in \mathbb{R}^2$ is self-adjoint.

(14) Prove that if H is an infinite-dimensional Hilbert space, then the identity operator 1_H is not compact.

Solution: Let (x_n) be an infinite orthonormal set in H. Since $\|x_n - x_m\|^2 = \sqrt{2}$ for $m, n \in \mathbb{N}$, the sequence $(1_H(x_n))$ contains no Cauchy subsequence, and therefore, it contains no convergent subsequence.

(15) Prove that for a non-zero linear operator h defined on a real Hilbert space H it is possible to have $(h(x), x) = 0$ for some $x \neq 0_H$.

Solution: Let $h : \mathbb{R}^2 \longrightarrow \mathbb{R}^2$ be the linear operator defined by

$$h(\mathbf{x}) = \begin{pmatrix} -x_2 \\ x_1 \end{pmatrix}.$$

Note that

$$(h(\mathbf{x}), \mathbf{x}) = -x_1 x_2 + x_2 x_1 = 0,$$

while $h \neq 0$.

(16) Prove that a linear operator h on a Hilbert space H is normal if and only if $\|h(x)\| = \|h^*(x)\|$ for every $x \in H$.

(17) Prove that a linear operator h on a Hilbert space H is an automorphism of H if and only it is a unitary operator.

(18) Let S, T be two subspaces of a Hilbert space S. Prove that the following conditions are equivalent:

    (a) $S \perp T$;
    (b) $p_S p_T = 0_H$;
    (c) $p_T p_S = 0_H$;
    (d) $p_S(T) = \{0_H\}$;
    (e) $p_T(S) = \{0_H\}$.

(19) Let $h : L^2([0, 1]) \longrightarrow L^2([0, 1])$ be the operator determined by the integral kernel $K(x, y) = a(x)a(y)$, where $a \in L^2([0, 1])$. Prove that $a(x)$ is an eigenfunction of h that corresponds to the eigenvalue $\|a\|^2$ and that $\|h\| = \|a\|^2$.

(20) Let $\Lambda = \{\lambda_n \mid n \in \mathbb{N}\}$ be a countable set of complex numbers. Define the operator $h : \ell^2(\mathbb{C}) \longrightarrow \ell^2(\mathbb{C})$ as

$$h(x_0, x_1, \ldots, x_n, \ldots) = (\lambda_0 x_0, \lambda_1 x_1, \ldots, \lambda_n x_n, \ldots)$$

for $(x_0, x_1, \ldots, x_n, \ldots) \in \ell^2(\mathbb{C})$. Prove that:

(a) h is a linear operator and h^* is given by

$$h^*(x_0, x_1, \ldots, x_n, \ldots) = (\overline{\lambda_0}x_0, \overline{\lambda_1}x_1, \ldots, \overline{\lambda_n}x_n, \ldots);$$

(b) h is a normal operator;

(c) the spectrum of h equals Λ and $e_i = (0, 0, \ldots, 1, \ldots)$ is an eigenvector that corresponds to λ_i.

(21) Let h be a self-adjoint operator on a complex Hilbert space H. Prove that for every $a \in \mathbb{C}$ we have

$$\Im((h - a\mathbf{1}_H)x, x) \geqslant \|x\|\Im(a).$$

Solution: If $x = 0_H$ the inequality obviously holds. Let $x \in H - \{0_H\}$. Since h is self adjoint, $(h(x), x)$ is a real number. We have

$$((h - a\mathbf{1}_H)x, x) = (h(x) - ax, x) = (h(x), x) - a\|x\|^2,$$

which implies

$$|\Im((h - a\mathbf{1}_H)x, x)| = \|x\|^2|\Im(a)|.$$

By Cauchy-Schwarz inequality we have

$$\|x\|\|h - a\mathbf{1}_H\| \geqslant |(h - a\mathbf{1}_H)x, x)|$$
$$\geqslant \Im((h - a\mathbf{1}_H)x, x)) = \|x\|^2|\Im(a)|,$$

which gives the desired inequality because $\|x\| \neq 0$.

(22) Let h and g be two compact and self-adjoint operators on a Hilbert space H that commute, that is, $hg = gh$. Prove that h and g have a common total orthogonal set of eigenvectors.

Solution: Let S be the eigenspace in H that corresponds to an eigenvalue λ of h. for $x \in S$ we have

$$hg(x) = gh(x) = g(\lambda x) = \lambda g(x).$$

Thus, if $g(x) \neq 0_H$, $g(x)$ is an eigenvector of h relative to the eigenvalue λ, which shows that g maps S into S. Since g is a compact, self-adjoint operator on S, S has a basis of eigenvectors of g by the Spectral Theorem. There vectors are also eigenvectors of h because they belong to S. The union of all such bases for each eigenspace of h yields a total orthogonal set of eigenvectors for h, so the set of eigenvectors of h is included in the set of eigenvectors for g. In a similar way we can show the reverse inclusion.

(23) Prove that the function $N : \mathbb{C}^2 \longrightarrow \mathbb{C}$ defined by $N(x, y) = \|x - y\|^2$ for $\mathbf{x}, \mathbf{y} \in \mathbb{C}^n$ is of negative type.

Solution: Note that $N(x, y)$ is real-valued function, so the condition $N(x, y) = \overline{N(y, x)}$ is satisfied. We have

$$
\begin{aligned}
\|x_i - x_j\|^2 &= (x_i, x_i) - (x_i, x_j) - (x_j, x_i) + (x_j, x_j) \\
&= (x_i, x_i) + (x_j, x_j) - 2\Re(x_i, x_j) \\
&= \|x_i\|^2 + \|x_j\|^2 - 2\Re(x_i, x_j)
\end{aligned}
$$

for $1 \leqslant i, j \leqslant n$. Let $a_i \in \mathbb{C}$ and $x_i \in L$ for $1 \leqslant i \leqslant n$, and $a_1 + \cdots + a_n = 0$. We have

$$
\begin{aligned}
&\sum_{i=1}^{n} \sum_{j=1}^{n} a_i N(x_i, x_j) \overline{a_j} \\
&= \sum_{i=1}^{n} \sum_{j=1}^{n} a_i \|x_i\|^2 \overline{a_j} + \sum_{i=1}^{n} \sum_{j=1}^{n} a_i \|x_j\|^2 \overline{a_j} \\
&\quad - 2 \sum_{i=1}^{n} \sum_{j=1}^{n} a_i \Re(x_i, x_j) \overline{a_j} \\
&= \left(\sum_{j=1}^{n} \overline{a_j} \right) \sum_{i=1}^{n} a_i \|x_i\|^2 + \left(\sum_{i=1}^{n} a_i \right) \sum_{j=1}^{n} \|x_j\|^2 \overline{a_j} \\
&\quad - 2 \sum_{i=1}^{n} \sum_{j=1}^{n} a_i \Re(x_i, x_j) \overline{a_j} \\
&= -2 \sum_{i=1}^{n} \sum_{j=1}^{n} a_i \Re(x_i, x_j) \overline{a_j} \\
&= -2 \Re \left(\sum_{i=1}^{n} a_i x_i, \sum_{j=1}^{n} a_j x_j \right) = -2\Re(v, v) \leqslant 0,
\end{aligned}
$$

where $v = \sum_{i=1}^{n} a_i x_i$.

(24) A matrix $A \in \mathbb{R}^{n \times n}$ is *conditionally positive definite* if for all $\mathbf{x} \in \mathbb{R}^n - \{\mathbf{0}_n\}$ such that $\mathbf{1}_n' \mathbf{x} = 0$ we have $\mathbf{x}' A \mathbf{x} > 0$; A is *conditionally positive semi-definite* if under the same assumptions on $\mathbf{x}$ we have $\mathbf{x}' A \mathbf{x} \geqslant 0$.

Prove that A is conditionally positive definite if and only if $A + a\mathbf{1}_n\mathbf{1}_n'$ is positive definite for every $a \in \mathbb{R}$.

Solution: Suppose that the matrix $A + a\mathbf{1}_n\mathbf{1}_n'$ is positive definite for every $a \in \mathbb{R}$. For $\mathbf{x} \in \mathbb{R}^n - \{\mathbf{0}_n\}$ we have

$$
\begin{aligned}
0 &< \mathbf{x}'(A + a\mathbf{1}_n\mathbf{1}_n')\mathbf{x} \\
&= \mathbf{x}' A \mathbf{x} + a(\mathbf{1}_n'\mathbf{x})'(\mathbf{1}_n'\mathbf{x}) = \mathbf{x}' A \mathbf{x},
\end{aligned}
$$

hence A is conditionally positive definite.

Conversely, suppose that A is conditionally positive definite but there is no $a \in \mathbb{R}$ such that $A + a\mathbf{1}_n\mathbf{1}_n'$ is positive definite. Let $(\mathbf{x}_n, a_n)_{n \in \mathbb{N}}$ be a sequence in $\mathbb{R}^{n+1}$ such that $\|\mathbf{x}_n\| = 1$ for $n \in \mathbb{N}$ and $\lim_{n\to\infty} a_n = \infty$ such that $\mathbf{x}_n'(A + a\mathbf{1}_n\mathbf{1}_n')\mathbf{x}_n \leqslant 0$. Since $\{\mathbf{x}_n \mid n \in \mathbb{N}\}$ is a subset of the compact sphere $B[\mathbf{0}_n, 1]$ there exists a subsequence $(\mathbf{x}_{n_i})$ of $(\mathbf{x}_n)$ that is convergent. Suppose that $\lim_{i\to\infty} \mathbf{x}_{n_i} = \mathbf{z}$. Then,

$$\lim_{i\to\infty} \frac{\mathbf{x}_{n_i}'(A + a_i\mathbf{1}_n\mathbf{1}_n')\mathbf{x}_{n_i}}{a_i} = (\mathbf{1}_n'\mathbf{z})^2 \leqslant 0,$$

which implies $\mathbf{1}_n'\mathbf{z} = 0$. Since A is conditionally positive definite, $\mathbf{z}'A\mathbf{z} > 0$, so $\mathbf{x}_{n_i}'(A + a_i\mathbf{1}_n\mathbf{1}_n')\mathbf{x}_{n_i} > 0$ for sufficiently large i, which contradicts the initial supposition.

(25) Let $F : S \times S \longrightarrow \mathbb{C}$ be a function of negative type. Prove that the function $k : S \times S \longrightarrow \mathbb{C}$ given by $k(x, y) = e^{-F(x,y)}$ for $x, y \in S$ is of positive type.

Solution: Let $x_0 \in S$ and let $G_{x_0}(x, y) = F(x, x_0) + \overline{F(y, x_0)} - F(x, y) - F(x_0, x_0)$ be a function of positive type. Since

$$-F(x, y) = G_{x_0}(x, y) - F(x, x_0) - \overline{F(y, x_0)} + F(x_0, x_0),$$

it follows that

$$e^{-F(x,y)} = e^{G_{x_0}(x,y)} e^{-F(x,x_0)} e^{-\overline{F(y,s_0)}} e^{F(x_0,x_0)},$$

which implies that $e^{-F(x,y)}$ is a function of positive type.

(26) Let $\{a_{jk} \mid j, k \geqslant 1\}$ be a set of complex numbers such that $a_{jk} = \overline{a_{kj}}$. There exists a sequence (x_n) in a Hilbert space H such that $a_{jk} = (x_j, x_k)$ if and only if the inequalities $\sum_{j=1}^n \sum_{k=1}^n a_{jk} r_j \overline{r_k} \geqslant 0$ hold for every finite set of complex numbers $\{r_1, \ldots, r_n\}$.

(27) Let $h : X \longrightarrow \mathbb{R}$ be a function with $X \subseteq \mathbb{R}^n$ be a function such that $f(\mathbf{x}) \geqslant 0$ for $\mathbf{x} \in X$ such that $f(\mathbf{0}_n) = 0$. Then, the function $K : \mathbb{R}^n \times \mathbb{R}^n \longrightarrow \mathbb{R}$ defined as

$$K(\mathbf{x}, \mathbf{y}) = \frac{1}{4} \left(f(\mathbf{x} + \mathbf{y}) - f(\mathbf{x} - \mathbf{y}) \right)$$

for $\mathbf{x}, \mathbf{y} \in X$ is of positive type.

(28) Let $H = \mathbb{R}^X$. Prove that H is a Hilbert space of functions if for every $x \in X$ there exists M_x such that $|f(x)| \leqslant M_x \|f\|_H$.

(29) Let $h : H \longrightarrow H$ be a linear operator, where H is a Hilbert space. If there exists $g : H \longrightarrow H$ such that $(h(x), y) = (x, g(y))$ for $x, y \in H$, prove that h is bounded.

Solution: By Theorem 9.9 it suffices to show that the graph $\gamma h = \{(x, y) \in S \times T \mid y = h(x)\}$ is a closed set. Let (x_n) be a sequence in H

such that $\lim_{n\to\infty}(x_n, h(x_n)) = (x, y) \in H \times H$. Note that $(x_n, h(x_n)) \in \gamma h$ for $n \in \mathbb{N}$. For any $z \in H$ we have $(h(x_n), z) = (x_n, g(z))$, which implies $(x, g(z)) = (h(x), z)$ as $n \to \infty$. Since $\lim_{n\to\infty}(h(x_n), z) = (y, z)$, it follows that $(h(x), z) = (y, z)$ for all $z \in H$. This shows that $(x, y) \in \gamma h$, hence h is closed.

(30) Prove that if S is a closed subspace of a Hilbert space and p_S is the corresponding projection operator, then p_S is a self-adjoint operator.

Solution: For every $x, y \in H$ we have

$$(p_S(x), p_{S^\perp}(y)) = (p_{S^\perp}(x), p_S(y)) = 0,$$

which implies

$$(p_S(x), y) = (p_S(x), p_S(y) + p_{S^\perp}(y)) = (p_S(x), p_S(y))$$
$$= (p_S(x) + p_{S^\perp}(x), p_S(y)) = (x, p_S(y)).$$

This means that p_S is a self-adjoint operator.

(31) Let H be a Hilbert space and let $f : H \longrightarrow H$ be a mapping that satisfies the conditions:

   (a) $(f(x) - f(y), x - y) \geqslant a\|x - y\|^2$ for some $a > 0$, and
   (b) $\|f(x) - f(y)\| \leqslant b\|x - y\|$ for some $b > 0$.

Prove that f is a bijection.

Solution: If $f(x) = f(y)$, by (i) we have $x = y$, so f is injective. Let w be an arbitrary element of H. To prove that f is surjective we need to show that there exists x such that $f(x) = w$, which is equivalent to showing that for an arbitrary $\lambda > 0$ there exists x such that $x - \lambda(f(x) - w) = x$. Define the function $g_w : H \longrightarrow H$ as

$$g_w(x) = x - \lambda(f(x) - w).$$

$$
\begin{aligned}
\|g_w(x) - g_w(y)\|^2 &= \|x - \lambda(f(x) - w) - y + \lambda(f(y) - w)\|^2 \\
&= \|x - y - \lambda(f(x) - f(y))\|^2 \\
&= \|x - y\|^2 - 2\lambda(x - y, f(x) - f(y)) \\
&\quad + \lambda^2\|f(x) - f(y)\|^2 \\
&\leqslant \|x - y\|^2 - 2\lambda a\|x - y\|^2 + \lambda^2 b^2\|x - y\|^2 \\
&= \|x - y\|^2(1 - 2\lambda a + \lambda^2 b^2).
\end{aligned}
$$

If $\lambda = \frac{a}{b^2}$ we have $\|g_w(x) - g_w(y)\|^2 \leqslant \|x - y\|^2 \left(1 - \frac{a^2}{b^2}\right)$, which proves that g_w is a contraction. The fixed point of g_w is that x such that $f(x) = w$, so f is surjective, and therefore is a bijection.

(32) Let H be a Hilbert space and let $f : H \longrightarrow H$ be a mapping such that $(f(x) - f(y), x - y) \geqslant a\|x - y\|^2$ for some positive a, and $\|f(x) - f(y)\| \leqslant b\|x - y\|$. Prove that f is a bijection.

Solution: The injectivity of f follows immediately from the first property. Let $w \in H$ and $g_\lambda(x) = x - \lambda(f(x) - w)$ for $\lambda > 0$. We have

$$
\begin{aligned}
\|g_\lambda(u) - g_\lambda(v)\|^2 &= \|u - \lambda(f(u) - w) - v - \lambda(f(v) - w)\|^2 \\
&= \|u - v - \lambda(f(u) - f(v))\|^2 \\
&= \|u - v\|^2 - 2\lambda(f(u) - f(v), u - v) + \lambda^2\|f(u) - f(v)\|^2 \\
&\leqslant \|u - v\|^2 - 2\lambda a\|u - v\|^2 + \lambda^2 b^2\|u - v\|^2 \\
&\qquad \text{(by the conditions satisfied by } f) \\
&= \|u - v\|^2(1 - 2\lambda a + \lambda^2 b^2).
\end{aligned}
$$

If $\lambda = \frac{a}{b^2}$ we have $\|g(u) - g(v)\| \leqslant \sqrt{1 - \frac{a^2}{b^2}}\|u - v\|$, hence g_λ is a contraction. By Banach's Fixed Point Theorem (Theorem 5.48), g_λ has a fixed point, hence $x - \lambda(f(x) - w) = x$, which implies the existence of x such that $f(x) = w$. Thus, f is a bijection.

Bibliographical Comments

A readable and very useful introduction to Hilbert spaces is [68]. The main source for Section 11.9 on Hilbert spaces of functions is the monograph [10].

Two important surveys [125, 81] of kernel-based techniques that are 32 years apart are very valuable for gaining a perspective of the use of kernel-related methods.

Supplement 9 appears in [72]. Supplements 5-7 are discussed in [102].

Chapter 12

Convex Functions

12.1 Introduction

This chapter is a continuation of Chapter 2.7; instead of convex sets we focus now on convex function. The study of convex functions is very significant in optimization algorithms due to the global character of their minima.

We begin with basic properties of convex functions and two other related families (concave and affine functions) and provide several examples of such functions. Then, alternative characterizations of convex and concave functions are discussed using epigraphs and hypographs, respectively.

Methods for constructing new convex functions and several examples of the applications of these methods are presented. This is followed by a discussion of extrema of convex functions and of the connection between differentiability and convexity.

The chapter includes a section focused on two generalization of smaller classes: the class of quasi-convex functions is an extension of the class of convex functions; another class, that of pseudo-convex functions over a convex set generalizes the class of all differentiable convex functions on that set.

Convexity is introduced via inequalities and is, in turn, a strong source of interesting inequalities. Certain of these are included in a dedicated section. The last section presents subgradients of convex functions, a helpful concept in identification of extrema of non-differentiable convex functions.

12.2   Convex Functions — Basics

Definition 12.1. Let S be a non-empty convex subset of a real linear space L.

A function $f : S \longrightarrow \mathbb{R}$ is *convex* if $f((1-t)x+ty) \leqslant (1-t)f(x)+tf(y)$ for every $x, y \in S$ and $t \in [0, 1]$.

If $f((1-t)x+ty) < (1-t)f(x)+tf(y)$ for every $x, y \in S$ and $t \in (0, 1)$ such that $x \neq y$, then f is said to be *strictly convex*.

The function $g : S \longrightarrow \mathbb{R}$ is *(strictly) concave* if $-g$ is (strictly) convex.

The set S will be referred to as the domain of f and will be denoted, as usual by $\mathrm{Dom}(f)$.

Recall that for $u, v \in \mathbb{R} \cup \{\infty\}$, the sum $u + v$ is always defined.

It is useful to extend the notion of convex function by allowing ∞ as a value. Thus, if a function f is defined on a subset S of a linear space L, $f : S \longrightarrow \mathbb{R}$, the *extended-value function* of f is the function $\hat{f} : L \longrightarrow \mathbb{R} \cup \{\infty\}$ defined by

$$\hat{f}(x) = \begin{cases} f(x) & \text{if } x \in S, \\ \infty & \text{otherwise.} \end{cases}$$

If a function $f : S \longrightarrow \mathbb{R}$ is convex, where $S \subseteq L$ is a convex set, then its extended-value function $\hat{f}$ satisfies the inequality that defines convexity $\hat{f}((1-t)x+ty) \leqslant (1-t)\hat{f}(x)+t\hat{f}(y)$ for every $x, y \in L$ and $t \in [0, 1]$, if we adopt the convention that $0 \cdot \infty = 0$.

Definition 12.2. The trivial convex function is the function $f_\infty : S \longrightarrow \mathbb{R} \cup \{\infty\}$ defined by $f(x) = \infty$ for every $x \in S$.

A extended-value convex function $\hat{f} : S \longrightarrow \mathbb{R} \cup \{\infty\}$ is *properly convex* or a *proper function* if $\hat{f} \neq f_\infty$.

The *domain* of a function $f : S \longrightarrow \mathbb{R} \cup \{\infty\}$ is the set $\mathrm{Dom}(f) = \{x \in S \mid f(\mathbf{x}) < \infty\}$.

Example 12.1. Let $f : (0, \infty) \longrightarrow \mathbb{R}$ be defined by $f(x) = x^2$. The definition domain of f is clearly convex and we have:

$$\begin{aligned} f((1-t)x_1 + tx_2) &= ((1-t)x_1 + tx_2)^2 \\ &= (1-t)^2 x_1^2 + t^2 x_2^2 + 2(1-t)tx_1 x_2. \end{aligned}$$

Therefore,

$$f((1-t)x_1 + tx_2) - (1-t)f(x_1) - tf(x_2)$$
$$= (1-t)^2 x_1^2 + t^2 x_2^2 + 2(1-t)tx_1 x_2 - (1-t)x_1^2 - tx_2^2$$
$$= -t(1-t)(x_1 - x_2)^2 \leqslant 0,$$

which implies that f is indeed convex.

Example 12.2. The function $f : \mathbb{R} \longrightarrow \mathbb{R}$ defined by $f(x) = |a - xb|$ is convex because

$$f((1-t)x_1 + tx_2) = |a - ((1-t)x_1 + tx_2)b|$$
$$= |a(1-t) + at - ((1-t)x_1 + tx_2)b|$$
$$= |(1-t)(a - x_1 b) + t(a - x_2 b)|$$
$$\leqslant |(1-t)(a - x_1 b)| + |t(a - x_2 b)|$$
$$= (1-t)f(x_1) + tf(x_2)$$

for $t \in [0, 1]$.

Example 12.3. The function $g : \mathbb{R}^2 \longrightarrow \mathbb{R}$ given by $g(\mathbf{x}) = |a - x_1 x_2|$ is not convex, in general. Consider, for example the special case $g(\mathbf{x}) = |12 - x_1 x_2|$. We have

$$f \begin{pmatrix} 6 \\ 2 \end{pmatrix} = f \begin{pmatrix} 2 \\ 6 \end{pmatrix} = 0.$$

Note that

$$\begin{pmatrix} 4 \\ 4 \end{pmatrix} = \frac{1}{2} \begin{pmatrix} 6 \\ 2 \end{pmatrix} + \frac{1}{2} \begin{pmatrix} 2 \\ 6 \end{pmatrix} \text{ and } f \begin{pmatrix} 4 \\ 4 \end{pmatrix} = 4 > \frac{1}{2} f \begin{pmatrix} 6 \\ 2 \end{pmatrix} + a\frac{1}{2} f \begin{pmatrix} 2 \\ 6 \end{pmatrix}.$$

Example 12.4. Any norm ν on a real linear space L is convex. Indeed, for $t \in [0, 1]$ we have

$$\nu(tx + (1-t)y) \leqslant \nu(tx) + \nu((1-t)y) = t\nu(x) + (1-t)\nu(y)$$

for $x, y \in L$.

It is easy to verify that any linear combination of convex functions with non-negative coefficients defined on a real linear space L (of functions convex at $x_0 \in L$) is a convex function (a function convex at x_0).

Example 12.5. This important example of convex function was given by Kuhn and Tucker [95].

Let $A \in \mathbb{R}^{n \times n}$ be a matrix. If A is a positive matrix then the function $f : \mathbb{R}^n \longrightarrow \mathbb{R}$ defined by $f(\mathbf{x}) = \mathbf{x}' A \mathbf{x}$ for $\mathbf{x} \in \mathbb{R}^n$ is convex on $\mathbb{R}^n$.

Let $t \in [0, 1]$ and let $\mathbf{x}, \mathbf{y} \in \mathbb{R}^n$. By hypothesis we have

$$(t - t^2)(\mathbf{x} - \mathbf{y})' A(\mathbf{x} - \mathbf{y}) \geqslant 0$$

for $\mathbf{x}, \mathbf{y} \in \mathbb{R}^n$ because $t - t^2 \geqslant 0$. Therefore,

$$\begin{aligned}
(1 - t)\mathbf{x}' A\mathbf{x} &+ t\mathbf{y}' A\mathbf{y} \\
&= \mathbf{x}' A\mathbf{x} + t\mathbf{x}' A(\mathbf{y} - \mathbf{x}) + t(\mathbf{y} - \mathbf{x})' A\mathbf{x} + t(\mathbf{y} - \mathbf{x})' A(\mathbf{y} - \mathbf{x}) \\
&\geqslant \mathbf{x}' A\mathbf{x} + t\mathbf{x}' A(\mathbf{y} - \mathbf{x}) + t(\mathbf{y} - \mathbf{x})' A\mathbf{x} + t^2(\mathbf{y} - \mathbf{x})' A(\mathbf{y} - \mathbf{x}) \\
&= (\mathbf{x} + t(\mathbf{y} - \mathbf{x}))' A(\mathbf{x} + t(\mathbf{y} - \mathbf{x}))
\end{aligned}$$

for $t \in [0, 1]$, which proves the convexity of f.

Definition 12.3. Let S be a non-empty convex subset of a real linear space L. A function $f : S \longrightarrow \mathbb{R}$ is *affine* if it is both concave and convex, that is, $f((1 - t)x + ty) = (1 - t)f(x) + tf(y)$ for all $t \in [0, 1]$ and $x, y \in S$.

If $f : L \longrightarrow \mathbb{R}$ is an affine function on L and $f(0_L) = 0$, then taking $x = 0_L$ we have $f(ty) = f((1 - t)0_L + ty) = tf(y)$ for $t \in [0, 1]$. Moreover,

$$f(x + y) = 2f\left(\frac{x + y}{2}\right) = 2f\left(\frac{1}{2}x + \frac{1}{2}y\right) = f(x) + f(y),$$

which shows that f is linear.

If g is an affine function on L, then the function $\ell : L \longrightarrow \mathbb{R}$ defined by $\ell(x) = g(x) - g(0_L)$ is affine and $\ell(0_L) = 0$, which implies that ℓ is linear. This shows that every affine function g on L can be written as $g(x) = g(0_L) + \ell(x)$, where ℓ is a linear function.

The notions of epigraph and hypograph of a function introduced in Definition 4.48 can be used to characterize convex and concave functions.

Theorem 12.1. *Let $f : S \longrightarrow \mathbb{R}$ be a function defined on the convex subset S of a real linear space L. Then, f is convex on S if and only if its epigraph is a convex subset of $S \times \mathbb{R}$; f is concave if and only if its hypograph is a convex subset of $S \times \mathbb{R}$.*

Proof. Let f be a convex function on S. We have $f((1 - t)\mathbf{x} + t\mathbf{y}) \leqslant (1 - t)f(\mathbf{x}) + tf(\mathbf{y})$ for every $\mathbf{x}, \mathbf{y} \in S$ and $t \in [0, 1]$.

If $(\mathbf{x}_1, y_1), (\mathbf{x}_2, y_2) \in \mathsf{epi}(f)$ we have $f(\mathbf{x}_1) \leqslant y_1$ and $f(\mathbf{x}_2) \leqslant y_2$. Therefore,

$$\begin{aligned}
f((1 - t)\mathbf{x}_1 + t\mathbf{x}_2) &\leqslant (1 - t)f(\mathbf{x}_1) + tf(\mathbf{x}_2) \\
&\leqslant (1 - t)y_1 + ty_2,
\end{aligned}$$

so $((1-t)\mathbf{x}_1 + t\mathbf{x}_2, (1-t)y_1 + ty_2) = (1-t)(\mathbf{x}_1, y_1) + t(\mathbf{x}_2, y_2) \in \mathsf{epi}(f)$ for $t \in [0, 1]$. This shows that $\mathsf{epi}(f)$ is convex.

Conversely, suppose that $\mathsf{epi}(f)$ is convex, that is, if $(\mathbf{x}_1, y_1) \in \mathsf{epi}(f)$ and $(\mathbf{x}_2, y_2) \in \mathsf{epi}(f)$, then

$$(1-t)(\mathbf{x}_1, y_1) + t(\mathbf{x}_2, y_2) = ((1-t)\mathbf{x}_1 + t\mathbf{x}_2, (1-t)y_1 + ty_2) \in \mathsf{epi}(f)$$

for $t \in [0, 1]$. By applying the definition of the epigraph we have $f(\mathbf{x}_1) \leqslant y_1$, $f(\mathbf{x}_2) \leqslant y_2$, which implies $f((1-t)\mathbf{x}_1 + t\mathbf{x}_2) \leqslant (1-t)y_1 + ty_2$. Choosing $y_1 = f(\mathbf{x}_1)$ and $y_2 = f(\mathbf{x}_2)$ yields $f((1-t)\mathbf{x}_1 + t\mathbf{x}_2) \leqslant (1-t)f(\mathbf{x}_1) + tf(\mathbf{x}_2)$, which means that f is convex.

The second part of the theorem follows by applying the first part to the function $-f$. $\square$

The notion of level set for a function was introduced in Definition 4.49.

Theorem 12.2. *Let $D \subseteq \mathbb{R}^n$ and let $f : D \longrightarrow \mathbb{R}$ be a function. If f is convex, then every level set $L_{f,a}$ is convex set.*

Proof. Let $\mathbf{x}_1, \mathbf{x}_2 \in L_{f,a}$. We have $f(\mathbf{x}_1) \leq a$ and $f(\mathbf{x}_2) \leq a$ so

$$f((1-t)\mathbf{x}_1 + t\mathbf{x}_2) \leq (1-t)f(\mathbf{x}_1) + tf(\mathbf{x}_2) \leq a,$$

which implies $t\mathbf{x}_1 + (1-t)\mathbf{x}_2 \in L_{f,a}$ for every $t \in [0, 1]$. This shows that $L_{f,a}$ is convex. $\square$

Definition 12.4. A convex function $f : \mathbb{R}^n \longrightarrow \mathbb{R}$ is *closed* if its epigraph is closed.

If f is a closed convex function than all its level sets are closed because $L_{f,a}, a) = \mathsf{epi}(f) \cap (\mathbb{R}^n \times \{a\})$.

Example 12.6. The function $f : \mathbb{R} \longrightarrow \mathbb{R}$ given by $f(x) = |x|$ is convex and closed because $\mathsf{epi}(f) = \{(x, t) \mid -t \leqslant x \leqslant t\}$.

Example 12.7. Let U be a non-empty, bounded, and closed subset of $\mathbb{R}^n$ and let $d(\mathbf{x}, U)$ be the distance between $\mathbf{x} \in \mathbb{R}^n$ and U introduced in Definition 5.12, which in our current framework is:

$$d(\mathbf{x}, U) = \min\{\|\mathbf{x} - \mathbf{u}\| \mid \mathbf{u} \in U\}.$$

If $d(\mathbf{x}, U)$ is a convex function relative to $\mathbf{x}$, then U is a convex set because we can write $U = L_{f,0}$.

It is interesting that the converse is also true. If U is a convex set, them $d(\mathbf{x}, U)$ is a convex function. Indeed, let $\mathbf{x}_1, \mathbf{x}_2 \in \mathbb{R}^n$ and let $\mathbf{y}_1$ be the nearest point in C to $\mathbf{x}_1$, and $\mathbf{y}_2$ be the nearest point in C to $\mathbf{x}_2$. Let $\mathbf{x} = (1-t)\mathbf{x}_1 + t\mathbf{x}_2$ and $\mathbf{y} = (1-t)\mathbf{y}_1 + t\mathbf{y}_2 \in C$, where $t \in [0,1]$. We have $d(\mathbf{x}, U) \leqslant d(\mathbf{x}, \mathbf{y}) = \|\mathbf{x} - \mathbf{y}\|$. Furthermore,

$$\begin{aligned}
\|\mathbf{x} - \mathbf{y}\| &= \|(1-t)\mathbf{x}_1 + t\mathbf{x}_2 - (1-t)\mathbf{y}_1 - t\mathbf{y}_2\| \\
&= \|(1-t)(\mathbf{x}_1 - \mathbf{y}_1) + t(\mathbf{x}_2 - \mathbf{y}_2)\| \\
&\leqslant (1-t)\|\mathbf{x}_1 - \mathbf{y}_1\| + t\|\mathbf{x}_2 - \mathbf{y}_2\| \\
&= (1-t)d(\mathbf{x}_1, U) + td(\mathbf{x}_2, U),
\end{aligned}$$

which shows that $d(\mathbf{x}, U)$ is indeed convex.

Example 12.8. If $f : \mathbb{R} \longrightarrow \mathbb{R}$ is a monotonic (but not necessarily convex) function, then every level set $L_{f,a}$ is convex. Indeed, suppose that $x_1, x_2 \in \mathbb{R}$, $x_1 < x_2$, and $x_1, x_2 \in L_{f,a}$, that is, $f(x_1) \leqslant a$ and $f(x_2) \leqslant a$ and let $x = tx_1 + (1-t)x_2$ for $t \in (0,1)$. Since $x_1 < x < x_2$, we have $f(x_1) < f(x) < f(x_2) \leqslant a$, so $x \in L_{f,a}$. This shows that the convexity of level set does not imply function convexity.

Theorem 12.3. (Almgren's Theorem) *Let C be an open convex set of $\mathbb{R}^n$. If $f : C \longrightarrow \mathbb{R}$ is a convex function on C, then f is continuous on C.*

Proof. We prove that that f is continuous in every $\mathbf{x} \in C$.

Let $d = d_2(\mathbf{x}, \mathbb{R}^n - C)$ be the distance between $\mathbf{x}$ and the closest point in $\mathbb{R}^n - C$. Using notations introduced in Example 3.7 the cube $K(n, \mathbf{x}, \delta)$ is included in C if the length of the diagonal of this cube, $\sqrt{n}\delta$ is less than d.

Let $b = \max\{f(\mathbf{x}) \mid \mathbf{x} \in V_{n,\mathbf{u},\delta}\}$. We have seen (in Example 3.7) that $K_{n,\mathbf{x},\delta} = \mathbf{K}_{\mathrm{conv}}(V_{n,\mathbf{u},\delta})$. Since f is convex, the level set $L_{f,b}$ is convex and, since $V_{n,\mathbf{u},\delta} \subseteq L_{f,b}$, we have $K_{n,\mathbf{x},\delta} \subseteq L_{f,b}$, so $f(\mathbf{w}) \leq b$ for every $\mathbf{w} \in K_{n,\mathbf{x},\delta}$.

We shall prove that f is locally Lipschitz in every $\mathbf{x} \in D$. Let $\mathbf{z} \in B(\mathbf{x}, \delta)$. We claim that

$$|f(\mathbf{x}) - f(\mathbf{z})| \leqslant \frac{b - f(\mathbf{x})}{\delta}\|\mathbf{x} - \mathbf{z}\|.$$

Let $\mathbf{u} = \frac{\delta}{\|\mathbf{x}-\mathbf{z}\|}(\mathbf{x} - \mathbf{z})$. Clearly, $\|\mathbf{u}\| = \delta$ and we have

$$\mathbf{z} = \mathbf{x} + a\mathbf{u} = a(\mathbf{x} + \mathbf{u}) + (1 - a)\mathbf{x},$$

where $a = \frac{\|\mathbf{x}-\mathbf{z}\|}{\delta} \in [0, 1)$. Thus, $\mathbf{z}$ is a convex combination of $\mathbf{x} + \mathbf{u}$ and $\mathbf{x}$. The convexity of f on C implies

$$f(\mathbf{z}) \leqslant af(\mathbf{x} + \mathbf{u}) + (1 - a)f(\mathbf{x}). \tag{12.1}$$

Observe that
$$\frac{1}{1+a}\mathbf{z} + \frac{a}{1+a}(\mathbf{x}-\mathbf{u}) = \frac{1}{1+a}(\mathbf{x}+a\mathbf{u}) + \frac{a}{1+a}(\mathbf{x}-\mathbf{u}) = \mathbf{x},$$

so
$$f(\mathbf{x}) \leqslant \frac{1}{1+a}f(\mathbf{z}) + \frac{a}{1+a}f(\mathbf{x}-\mathbf{u}). \tag{12.2}$$

Inequalities (12.1) and (12.2) imply
$$-a(b-f(\mathbf{x})) \leqslant -a(f(\mathbf{x}-\mathbf{u})-f(\mathbf{x})) \leqslant f(\mathbf{z})-f(\mathbf{x})$$
$$\leqslant a(f(\mathbf{x}+\mathbf{u})-f(\mathbf{x})) \leqslant a(b-f(\mathbf{x})).$$

Therefore,
$$|f(\mathbf{z})-f(\mathbf{x})| \leqslant a(b-f(\mathbf{x})) = (b-f(\mathbf{x}))\frac{\|\mathbf{x}-\mathbf{z}\|}{\delta}$$

because $\|\mathbf{x}-\mathbf{z}\| = a\|\mathbf{u}\| = a\delta$. The last inequality shows that f is locally Lipschitz in $\mathbf{x}$ and, therefore, f is continuous in every $\mathbf{x} \in C$, so it is continuous on C. $\qquad\square$

The defining inequality of convex function can be extended to involve convex combinations of n elements of a linear space, as we show next.

Theorem 12.4. (Jensen's Theorem) *Let S be a convex subset of a real linear space L and let $f : S \longrightarrow \mathbb{R}$ be a convex function. If $t_1, \ldots, t_n \in [0,1]$ are n numbers such that $\sum_{i=1}^{n} t_i = 1$, then*
$$f\left(\sum_{i=1}^{n} t_i x_i\right) \leqslant \sum_{i=1}^{n} t_i f(x_i)$$

for every $x_1, \ldots, x_n \in S$.

Proof. The argument is by induction on n, where $n \geqslant 2$. The basis step, $n = 2$, follows immediately from Definition 12.1.

Suppose that the statement holds for n, and let $u_1, \ldots, u_n, u_{n+1}$ be $n+1$ numbers such that $\sum_{i=1}^{n+1} u_i = 1$. We have
$$f(u_1 x_1 + \cdots + u_{n-1}x_{n-1} + u_n x_n + u_{n+1}x_{n+1})$$
$$= f\left(u_1 x_1 + \cdots + u_{n-1}x_{n-1} + (u_n + u_{n+1})\frac{u_n x_n + u_{n+1}x_{n+1}}{u_n + u_{n+1}}\right).$$

By the inductive hypothesis, we can write
$$f(u_1 x_1 + \cdots + u_{n-1}x_{n-1} + u_n x_n + u_{n+1}x_{n+1})$$
$$\leqslant u_1 f(x_1) + \cdots + u_{n-1}f(x_{n-1}) + (u_n + u_{n+1})f\left(\frac{u_n x_n + u_{n+1}x_{n+1}}{u_n + u_{n+1}}\right).$$

Next, by the convexity of f, we have
$$f\left(\frac{u_n x_n + u_{n+1}x_{n+1}}{u_n + u_{n+1}}\right) \leqslant \frac{u_n}{u_n + u_{n+1}}f(x_n) + \frac{u_{n+1}}{u_n + u_{n+1}}f(x_{n+1}).$$

Combining this inequality with the previous inequality gives the desired conclusion. $\qquad\square$

Of course, if f is a concave function and $t_1, \ldots, t_n \in [0, 1]$ are n numbers such that $\sum_{i=1}^{n} t_i = 1$, then

$$f\left(\sum_{i=1}^{n} t_i x_i\right) \geqslant \sum_{i=1}^{n} t_i f(x_i). \tag{12.3}$$

Example 12.9. We saw that the function $f(x) = \ln x$ is concave. Therefore, if $t_1, \ldots, t_n \in [0, 1]$ are n numbers such that $\sum_{i=1}^{n} t_i = 1$, then

$$\ln\left(\sum_{i=1}^{n} t_i x_i\right) \geqslant \sum_{i=1}^{n} t_i \ln x_i.$$

This inequality can be written as

$$\ln\left(\sum_{i=1}^{n} t_i x_i\right) \geqslant \ln \prod_{i=1}^{n} x_i^{t_i},$$

or equivalently

$$\sum_{i=1}^{n} t_i x_i \geqslant \prod_{i=1}^{n} x_i^{t_i},$$

for $x_1, \ldots, x_n \in (0, \infty)$.

If $t_1 = \cdots = t_n = \frac{1}{n}$, we have the inequality that relates the arithmetic to the geometric average on n positive numbers:

$$\frac{x_1 + \cdots + x_n}{n} \geqslant \left(\prod_{i=1}^{n} x_i\right)^{\frac{1}{n}}. \tag{12.4}$$

Let $\mathbf{w} = (w_1, \ldots, w_n) \in \mathbb{R}^n$ be such that $\sum_{i=1}^{n} w_i = 1$. For $r \neq 0$, the $\boldsymbol{w}$-*weighted mean of order* r of a sequence of n positive numbers $\mathbf{x} = (x_1, \ldots, x_n) \in \mathbb{R}_{>0}^n$ is the number

$$\mu_{\mathbf{w}}^r(\mathbf{x}) = \left(\sum_{i=1}^{n} w_i x_i^r\right)^{\frac{1}{r}}.$$

Of course, $\mu_{\mathbf{w}}^r(\mathbf{x})$ is not defined for $r = 0$; we will give as special definition

$$\mu_{\mathbf{w}}^0(\mathbf{x}) = \lim_{r \to 0} \mu_{\mathbf{w}}^r(\mathbf{x}).$$

We have

$$\lim_{r \to 0} \ln \mu_{\mathbf{w}}^r(\mathbf{x}) = \lim_{r \to 0} \frac{\ln \sum_{i=1}^{n} w_i x_i^r}{r} = \lim_{r \to 0} \frac{\sum_{i=1}^{n} w_i x_i^r \ln x_i}{\sum_{i=1}^{n} w_i x_i^r}$$

$$= \sum_{i=1}^{n} w_i \ln x_i = \ln \prod_{i=1}^{n} x_i^{w_i}.$$

Thus, if we define $\mu_{\mathbf{w}}^0(\mathbf{x}) = \prod_{i=1}^n x_i^{w_i}$, the weighted mean of order r becomes a function continuous everywhere with respect to r.

For $w_1 = \cdots = w_n = \frac{1}{n}$, we have

$$\mu_{\mathbf{w}}^{-1}(\mathbf{x}) = \frac{n x_1 \cdots x_n}{x_2 \cdots x_n + \cdots + x_1 \cdots x_{n-1}}$$

(the harmonic average of $\mathbf{x}$),

$$\mu_{\mathbf{w}}^0(\mathbf{x}) = (x_1 \ldots x_n)^{\frac{1}{n}}$$

(the geometric average of $\mathbf{x}$),

$$\mu_{\mathbf{w}}^1(\mathbf{x}) = \frac{x_1 + \cdots + x_n}{n}$$

(the arithmetic average of $\mathbf{x}$).

Theorem 12.5. *If $p < r$, we have $\mu_w^p(x) \leqslant \mu_w^r(x)$.*

Proof. There are three cases depending on the position of 0 relative to p and r.

In the first case, suppose that $r > p > 0$. The function $f(x) = x^{\frac{r}{p}}$ is convex, so by Jensen's inequality applied to $x_1^p, \ldots, x_n^p$, we have

$$\left(\sum_{i=1}^n w_i x_i^p \right)^{\frac{r}{p}} \leqslant \sum_{i=1}^n w_i x_i^r,$$

which implies

$$\left(\sum_{i=1}^n w_i x_i^p \right)^{\frac{1}{p}} \leqslant \left(\sum_{i=1}^n w_i x_i^r \right)^{\frac{1}{r}},$$

which is the inequality of the theorem.

If $r > 0 > p$, the function $f(x) = x^{\frac{r}{p}}$ is again convex because $f''(x) = \frac{r}{p}(\frac{r}{p} - 1)x^{\frac{r}{p} - 2} \geq 0$. Thus, the same argument works as in the previous case.

Finally, suppose that $0 > r > p$. Since $0 < \frac{r}{p} < 1$, the function $f(x) = x^{\frac{r}{p}}$ is concave. Thus, by Jensen's inequality,

$$\left(\sum_{i=1}^n w_i x_i^p \right)^{\frac{r}{p}} \geq \sum_{i=1}^n w_i x_i^r.$$

Since $\frac{1}{r} < 0$, we obtain again

$$\left(\sum_{i=1}^n w_i x_i^p \right)^{\frac{1}{p}} \leqslant \left(\sum_{i=1}^n w_i x_i^r \right)^{\frac{1}{r}}.$$

$\square$

Example 12.10. Note that the function $f : (0, \infty) \longrightarrow \mathbb{R}$ given by $f(x) = -\log_2 x$ is convex. Therefore, if $p_1, \ldots, p_n$ are n numbers in $[0, 1]$ such that $\sum_{i=1}^{n} p_i = 1$, by Jensen's inequality we have:

$$-\log_2 \left(\sum_{i=1}^{n} p_i x_i \right) \leqslant -\sum_{i=1}^{n} p_i \log_2 x_i.$$

If $x_i = \frac{1}{p_i}$, we obtain

$$-\log_2 n \leqslant -\sum_{i=1}^{n} p_i \log_2 \frac{1}{p_i}.$$

The quantity $H(p_1, \ldots, p_n) = \sum_{i=1}^{n} p_i \log_2 \frac{1}{p_i}$ is *Shannon's entropy* of the probability distribution $(p_1, \ldots, p_n)$ and the previous inequality shows that $H(p_1, \ldots, p_n) \leqslant \log_2 n$. This shows that the maximum Shannon entropy, $\log_2 n$ is obtained when $p_1 = \cdots = p_n = \frac{1}{n}$.

Theorem 12.6. *A set $S \subseteq \mathbb{R}^n$ is convex if and only if its indicator function I_S is convex.*

Proof. If I_S is convex, we have $I_S(t\mathbf{x} + (1 - t)\mathbf{y}) \leqslant tI_S(\mathbf{x}) + (1 - t)I_S(\mathbf{y})$ for every $\mathbf{x}, \mathbf{y} \in S$. Therefore, if $\mathbf{x}, \mathbf{y} \in S$ we have $I_S(\mathbf{x}) = I_S(\mathbf{y}) = 0$, which implies $I_S(t\mathbf{x} + (1 - t)\mathbf{y}) = 0$, so $t\mathbf{x} + (1 - t)\mathbf{y} \in S$. Thus, S is convex.

Conversely, suppose that S is convex. We need to prove that

$$I_S(t\mathbf{x} + (1 - t)\mathbf{y}) \leqslant tI_S(\mathbf{x}) + (1 - t)I_S(\mathbf{y}). \tag{12.5}$$

If at least one of $\mathbf{x}$ or $\mathbf{y}$ does not belong to S, inequality (12.5) is satisfied. The remaining case occurs when we have both $\mathbf{x} \in S$ and $\mathbf{y} \in S$, in which case, $t\mathbf{x} + (1 - t)\mathbf{y} \in S$ and $I_S(\mathbf{x}) = I_S(\mathbf{y}) = I_S(t\mathbf{x} + (1 - t)\mathbf{y}) = 0$, and, again, inequality (12.5) is satisfied. $\square$

Let I be an interval in $\mathbb{R}$. If $f : I \longrightarrow \mathbb{R}$ is a convex function, by Jensen's inequality we have:

$$f\left(\frac{x + y}{2}\right) \leqslant \frac{1}{2}f(x) + \frac{1}{2}f(y)$$

for $x, y \in I$. This property is known as the *mid-point* convexity.

12.3   Constructing Convex Functions

If $f_1, \ldots, f_k$ are k convex functions on a linear space, it is straightforward to verify that any positive combination $a_1 f_1 + \cdots + a_k f_k$ is a convex function.

Theorem 12.7. *If f, g are convex functions defined on a real linear space L, then the function h defined by $h(x) = \max\{f(x), g(x)\}$ for $x \in \mathrm{Dom}(f) \cap \mathrm{Dom}(g)$ is a convex function.*

Proof. Let $t \in [0, 1]$ and let $x_1, x_2 \in \text{Dom}(f) \cap \text{Dom}(g)$. We have

$$
\begin{aligned}
h((1-t)x_1 + tx_2) &= \max\{f((1-t)x_1 + tx_2), g((1-t)x_1 + tx_2)\} \\
&\leqslant \max\{(1-t)f(x_1) + tf(x_2), (1-t)g(x_1) + tg(x_2)\} \\
&\leqslant (1-t)\max\{f(x_1), g(x_1)\} + t\max\{f(x_2), g(x_2)\} \\
&= (1-t)h(x_1) + th(x_2),
\end{aligned}
$$

which implies that h is convex. $\square$

Theorem 12.7 can be extended to the supremum of a family of convex functions.

Theorem 12.8. *Let C be a convex subset of $\mathbb{R}^n$, b be a number in $\mathbb{R}$, and let $\mathcal{F} = \{f_i \mid f_i : C \longrightarrow \mathbb{R}, i \in I\}$ be a family of convex functions such that $f_i(x) \leqslant b$ for every $i \in I$ and $x \in C$. Then, the function $f : C \longrightarrow \mathbb{R}$ defined by*

$$
f(x) = \sup\{f_i(x) \mid i \in I\}
$$

for $x \in C$ is a convex function.

Proof. Since the family of function $\mathcal{F}$ is upper bounded, the definition of f is correct. Let $\mathbf{x}, \mathbf{y} \in C$. We have $(1-t)\mathbf{x} + t\mathbf{y} \in C$ because C is convex.

For every $i \in I$ we have $f_i((1-t)\mathbf{x} + t\mathbf{y}) \leqslant (1-t)f_i(\mathbf{x}) + tf_i(\mathbf{y})$. The definition of f implies $f_i(\mathbf{x}) \leqslant f(\mathbf{x})$ and $f_i(\mathbf{y}) \leqslant f(\mathbf{y})$, so $(1-t)f_i(\mathbf{x}) + tf_i(\mathbf{y}) \leqslant (1-t)f(\mathbf{x}) + tf(\mathbf{y})$ for $i \in I$ and $t \in [0, 1]$.

The definition of f implies $f((1-t)\mathbf{x} + t\mathbf{y}) \leqslant (1-t)f(\mathbf{x}) + tf(\mathbf{y})$ for $\mathbf{x}, \mathbf{y} \in C$ and $t \in [0, 1]$, so f is convex on C. $\square$

Theorem 12.9. *Let $f_i : \mathbb{R}^n \longrightarrow \mathbb{R}$ be proper convex functions for $1 \leqslant i \leqslant m$. Then the function $f : \mathbb{R}^n \longrightarrow \mathbb{R}$ defined as*

$$
f(x) = \inf\left\{ f_1(x_1) + \cdots + f_m(x_m) \mid x_i \in \mathbb{R} \text{ for } 1 \leqslant i \leqslant n, x = \sum_{i=1}^{m} x_i \right\}
$$

is a convex function on $\mathbb{R}^n$.

Proof. Since f_i are convex functions, the sets $\text{epi}(f_i)$ are convex (by Theorem 12.1), and therefore, their Minkowski sum $E = \text{epi}(f_1) + \cdots + \text{epi}(f_m)$ is convex by Theorem 3.12. The set E can be written as

$$
E = \left\{ \begin{pmatrix} \sum_{i=1}^{m} \mathbf{x}_i \\ \sum_{i=1}^{m} y_i \end{pmatrix} \,\middle|\, f(\mathbf{x}_i) \leqslant y_i \text{ for } 1 \leqslant i \leqslant m \right\}.
$$

The value of the function constructed starting from E as shown in Supplement 3 is

$$\inf\left\{y \,\middle|\, y = \sum_{i=1}^{m} y_i, \mathbf{x} = \sum_{i=1}^{m} \mathbf{x}_i, f(\mathbf{x}_i) \leqslant y_i \text{ for } 1 \leqslant i \leqslant m\right\}$$

$$= \inf\left\{\sum_{i=1}^{m} f_i(\mathbf{x}_i) \,\middle|\, \mathbf{x} = \sum_{i=1}^{m} \mathbf{x}_i\right\} = f(\mathbf{x}),$$

hence f is convex. □

Definition 12.5. Let $f : S \longrightarrow \mathbb{R}$ be a convex function and let $g_{\mathbf{x}} : \mathbb{R}^n \longrightarrow \mathbb{R}$ be defined by $g_{\mathbf{x}}(\mathbf{y}) = \mathbf{y}'\mathbf{x} - f(\mathbf{x})$. The *conjugate function* of f is the function $f^* : \mathbb{R}^n \longrightarrow \mathbb{R}$ given by $f^*(\mathbf{y}) = \sup_{\mathbf{x} \in \mathbb{R}^n} g_{\mathbf{x}}(\mathbf{y})$ for $\mathbf{y} \in \mathbb{R}^n$.

Note that for each $\mathbf{x} \in \mathbb{R}^n$ the function $g_{\mathbf{x}} = \mathbf{y}'\mathbf{x} - f(\mathbf{x})$ is a convex function in the $\mathbf{y}$ variable. Therefore, by Theorem 12.8, f^* is a convex function.

Example 12.11. Let $f : \mathbb{R} \longrightarrow \mathbb{R}$ be the function $f(x) = e^x$. We have $g_x(y) = yx - e^x$. Note that:

- if $y < 0$, each such function is unbounded, so $f^*(y) = \infty$;
- if $y = 0$, $f^*(0) = \sup_x e^{-x} = 0$;
- if $y > 0$, g_x reaches its maximum when $x = \ln y$, so $f^*(y) = y \ln y - y$.

Thus, $\mathrm{Dom}(f^*) = \mathbb{R}_{\geqslant 0}$ and $f^*(y) = y \ln y - y$ (with the convention $0\infty = 0$).

Example 12.12. Let a be a positive number and let $f : \mathbb{R} \longrightarrow \mathbb{R}$ be the function $f(x) = \frac{a}{2}x^2$. We have $g_x(y) = yx - \frac{a}{2}x^2$ and

$$\sup_{x \in \mathbb{R}} \left(yx - \frac{a}{2}x^2\right) = \frac{1}{2a}y^2$$

and therefore

$$f^*(y) = \frac{1}{2a}y^2.$$

Example 12.13. Let $f : \mathbb{R}^n \longrightarrow \mathbb{R}$ be $f(\mathbf{x}) = \|\mathbf{x}\|_2$ for $\mathbf{x} \in \mathbb{R}^n$. We have $g_{\mathbf{x}} = \mathbf{y}'\mathbf{x} - \|\mathbf{x}\|_2$.

If $\|\mathbf{y}\|_2 \leqslant 1$, taking into account that $\mathbf{y}'\mathbf{x} \leqslant \|\mathbf{x}\|_2\|\mathbf{y}\|_2$, it follows that $\mathbf{y}'\mathbf{x} \leqslant \|\mathbf{y}\|_2$, so $\mathbf{y}'\mathbf{x} - \|\mathbf{x}\|_2 \leqslant 0$. Therefore, $\mathbf{x} = \mathbf{0}_n$ maximizes $\mathbf{y}'\mathbf{x} - \|\mathbf{x}\|_2$, so $f^*(\mathbf{y}) = 0$.

If $\|\mathbf{y}\|_2 > 1$, there is a $\mathbf{z}$ such that $\|\mathbf{z}\|_2 \leqslant 1$ and $\mathbf{y}'\mathbf{z} > 1$. It suffices to choose $\mathbf{z}$ such that

$$\frac{1}{\|\mathbf{y}\|_2} < \|\mathbf{z}\|_2 \leqslant 1.$$

Choosing $\mathbf{x} = t\mathbf{z}$ and letting $t \to \infty$ we have $\mathbf{y}'\mathbf{x} - \|\mathbf{x}\|_2 = t(\mathbf{y}'\mathbf{z} - \|\mathbf{z}\|_2) \to \infty$. Thus, we have

$$f^*(\mathbf{y}) = \begin{cases} 0 & \text{if } \|\mathbf{y}\|_2 \leqslant 1, \\ \infty & \text{otherwise.} \end{cases}$$

12.4 Extrema of Convex Functions

This section is dedicated to the examination of extrema of functions in the presence of convexity.

Theorem 12.10. *Any local minimum of a convex function $f : \mathbb{R}^n \longrightarrow \mathbb{R}$ is a global minimum.*

Proof. Let $\mathbf{x}_0$ be a global minimum of f and let $\mathbf{x}_1$ be a local minimum. We have $f(\mathbf{x}_0) \leqslant f(\mathbf{x}_1)$. Since $\mathbf{x}_1$ is a local minimum, there exists ϵ such that if $\|\mathbf{x}_1 - \mathbf{x}\| \geqslant \epsilon$, then $f(\mathbf{x}_1) \leqslant f(\mathbf{x})$.

Let $\mathbf{z} = (1 - a)\mathbf{x}_1 + a\mathbf{x}_0$, where $a \in [0, 1]$. We have $\mathbf{x}_1 - \mathbf{z} = a(\mathbf{x}_1 - \mathbf{x}_0)$. By choosing a such that

$$a < \frac{\epsilon}{\|\mathbf{x}_1 - \mathbf{x}_0\|},$$

we have $\|\mathbf{x}_1 - \mathbf{z}\| \leqslant \epsilon$, which implies $\mathbf{z} \in B[\mathbf{x}_1, \epsilon]$, so $f(\mathbf{z}) \geqslant f(\mathbf{x}_1)$ because $\mathbf{x}_1$ is a local minimum. By the convexity of f we have

$$f(\mathbf{z}) = f((1 - a)\mathbf{x}_1 + a\mathbf{x}_0) \leqslant (1 - a)f(\mathbf{x}_1) + af(\mathbf{x}_0) \leqslant f(\mathbf{x}_1),$$

so $f(\mathbf{z}) = f(\mathbf{x}_1)$. This, in turn implies

$$f(\mathbf{x}_1) \leqslant (1 - a)f(\mathbf{x}_1) + af(\mathbf{x}_0),$$

which yields $f(\mathbf{x}_1) \leqslant f(\mathbf{x}_0)$, hence $f(\mathbf{x}_1) = f(\mathbf{x}_0)$. Therefore, the local minimum $\mathbf{x}_1$ is also a global minimum. $\square$

Theorem 12.11. (The Maximum Principle for Convex Functions) *Let f be a convex function defined on a subset of $\mathbb{R}^n$ and let C be a convex set such that $C \subseteq \text{Dom}(f)$. If there exists $\mathbf{z} \in \boldsymbol{RI}(C)$ such that $f(\mathbf{z}) = \sup\{f(\boldsymbol{x}) \mid \boldsymbol{x} \in C\}$, then f is constant on C.*

Proof. Let $\mathbf{x} \in C - \{\mathbf{z}\}$. Since $\mathbf{z} \in \boldsymbol{RI}(C)$, there exists $t > 1$ such that $\mathbf{y} = (1 - t)\mathbf{x} + t\mathbf{z} \in C$. Thus, $\mathbf{z} = \frac{1}{t}\mathbf{y} + \frac{t-1}{t}\mathbf{x}$. Since $t > 1$, this implies $\mathbf{z} \in (\mathbf{x}, \mathbf{y})$, so $\mathbf{z} \in C$. By the convexity of f we have $f(\mathbf{z}) \leqslant \frac{1}{t}f(\mathbf{y}) + \frac{t-1}{t}f(\mathbf{x})$.

From the definition of $\mathbf{z}$ it follows that $f(\mathbf{x}) \leqslant f(\mathbf{z})$ and $f(\mathbf{y}) \leqslant f(\mathbf{z})$. If we would have $f(\mathbf{x}) \neq f(\mathbf{z})$, this would imply $f(\mathbf{z}) > f(\mathbf{x})$. This, in turn, would imply that $f(\mathbf{y})$ is finite and this would yield $f(\mathbf{z}) < (1-t)f(\mathbf{z}) + tf(\mathbf{z}) = f(\mathbf{z})$, which is a contradiction. Thus, $f(\mathbf{x}) = f(\mathbf{z})$ for $\mathbf{x} \in C$, which means that f is constant on C. $\qquad\square$

12.5   Differentiability and Convexity

Theorem 12.12. *Let (a,b) be an open interval of $\mathbb{R}$ and let $f : (a,b) \longrightarrow \mathbb{R}$ be a differentiable function on (a,b). Then, f is convex on (a,b) if and only if $f(y) \geqslant f(x) + f'(x)(y-x)$ for every $x, y \in (a,b)$.*

Proof.   Suppose that f is convex on (a,b). Then, for $x, y \in (a,b)$ we have
$$f((1-t)x + ty) \leqslant (1-t)f(x) + tf(y)$$
for $t \in [0,1]$. Therefore, for $t < 1$ we have
$$f(y) \geqslant f(x) + \frac{f(x + t(y-x)) - f(x)}{t(y-x)}(y-x).$$
When $t \to 0$ we obtain $f(y) \geqslant f(x) + f'(x)(y-x)$.

Conversely, suppose that $f(y) \geqslant f(x) + f'(x)(y-x)$ for every $x, y \in (a,b)$ and let $z = (1-t)x + ty$. We have
$$f(x) \geqslant f(z) + f'(z)(x-z),$$
$$f(y) \geqslant f(z) + f'(z)(y-z).$$
By multiplying the first inequality by $1-t$ and the second by t we obtain
$$(1-t)f(x) + tf(y) \geqslant f(z),$$
which shows that f is convex. $\qquad\square$

Theorem 12.12 can be extended to functions of n arguments.

Theorem 12.13. *Let S be a convex subset of $\mathbb{R}^n$ and let $f : S \longrightarrow \mathbb{R}$ be a Gâteaux differentiable function on S. Then, f is convex on S if and only if $f(\boldsymbol{y}) \geqslant f(\boldsymbol{x}) + (\nabla f)(\boldsymbol{x})'(\boldsymbol{y} - \boldsymbol{x})$ for every $\boldsymbol{x}, \boldsymbol{y} \in S$.*

Proof.   Let $g : \mathbb{R} \longrightarrow \mathbb{R}$ be the one-argument function defined by
$$g(t) = f(t\mathbf{y} + (1-t)\mathbf{x}).$$
We have $g'(t) = (\nabla f)((t\mathbf{y} + (1-t)\mathbf{x})(\mathbf{y} - \mathbf{x})$. If f is convex, then g is convex and we have $g(1) \geqslant g(0) + g'(0)$, which implies
$$f(\mathbf{y}) \geqslant f(\mathbf{x}) + (\nabla f)(\mathbf{x})(\mathbf{y} - \mathbf{x}).$$
Conversely, suppose that for the inequality $f(\mathbf{y}) \geqslant f(\mathbf{x}) + (\nabla f)(\mathbf{x})'(\mathbf{y} - \mathbf{x})$ holds for every $\mathbf{x}, \mathbf{y} \in S$. Since $(1-t)\mathbf{x} + t\mathbf{y} \in S$ and $(1-r)\mathbf{x} + r\mathbf{y} \in S$ (by the convexity of S), then

$$f((1-t)\mathbf{x}+t\mathbf{y}) \geqslant f((1-r)\mathbf{x}+r\mathbf{y}) + (\nabla f)((1-r)\mathbf{x}+r\mathbf{y})'(\mathbf{y}-\mathbf{x})(t-r),$$

so $g(t) \geqslant g(r) + g'(r)(t-r)$. Therefore g is convex by Theorem 12.12. The convexity of f follows immediately. $\qquad \square$

Corollary 12.1. *Let S be an convex subset of $\mathbb{R}^n$ and let $f : S \longrightarrow \mathbb{R}$ be a Gâteaux differentiable function on S. If $(\nabla f)(\mathbf{x}_0)'(\mathbf{x} - \mathbf{x}_0) \geqslant 0$ for every $\mathbf{x} \in S$, then $\mathbf{x}_0$ is a minimizer for f in S.*

Proof. This statement follows immediately from the inequality of Theorem 12.13. $\qquad \square$

Theorem 12.14. *Let $S \subseteq \mathbb{R}^n$ be a convex set such that $\mathbf{I}(S) \neq \emptyset$ and let $f : S \longrightarrow \mathbb{R}$ be a convex function. If $\mathbf{x} \in S$ and the partial derivatives $\frac{\partial f}{\partial}(x_i)$ exist for $1 \leqslant i \leqslant n$, then f is Fréchet differentiable at $\mathbf{x}$.*

Proof. Define the function $g_{\mathbf{x}}$ as $g_{\mathbf{x}}(\mathbf{h}) = f(\mathbf{x} + \mathbf{h}) - f(\mathbf{x}) - (\nabla f)(\mathbf{x})'\mathbf{h}$. Note that $g_{\mathbf{x}}(\mathbf{0}_n) = 0$.

The function g is clearly convex and $(\nabla g)(\mathbf{0}_n) = \mathbf{0}_n$. Since g is convex, we have

$$0 = 2g(0) \leqslant g(-\mathbf{h}) + g(\mathbf{h}). \tag{12.6}$$

We have:

$$g(\mathbf{h}) = g\left(\frac{1}{n}\sum_{i=1}^{n} nh_i\mathbf{e}_i\right)$$

(by Jensen's inequality)

$$\leqslant \sum \left\{h_i \frac{nh_i\mathbf{e}_i}{nh_i} \,\middle|\, h_i \neq 0\right\}$$

(by Cauchy-Schwarz Inequality)

$$\leqslant \|\mathbf{h}\| \cdot \sum \left\{\left\|\frac{nh_i\mathbf{e}_i}{nh_i}\right\| \,\middle|\, h_i \neq 0\right\}$$

(because $\|\mathbf{u}\| \leqslant \|u\|_1 = \sum_{i=1}^{n}|u_i|$).

Inequality (12.6) together with the last inequality allows us to write:

$$-\sum\left\{\left|\frac{g(-nh_i\mathbf{e}_i)}{nh_i}\right| \,\middle|\, h_i \neq 0\right\} \leqslant \frac{-g(-\mathbf{h})}{\|\mathbf{h}\|} \leqslant \frac{g(\mathbf{h})}{\|\mathbf{h}\|} \leqslant \sum\left\{\left|\frac{g(nh_i\mathbf{e}_i)}{nh_i}\right| \,\middle|\, h_i \neq 0\right\}.$$

The terms inside the above sums converge to $\mathsf{pf}g_{x_i}(\mathbf{0}_n)$ when $h_i \to 0$. Thus, $g(\mathbf{h}) = o(\mathbf{b})$, hence f is Fréchet differentiable at $\mathbf{x}$. $\qquad \square$

Corollary 12.2. *Let $S \subseteq \mathbb{R}^n$ be a convex set such that $I(S) \neq \emptyset$ and let $f : S \longrightarrow \mathbb{R}$ be a convex function. If f is Gâteaux differentiable at $x \in S$, then f is Fréchet differentiable at x.*

Proof.   This follows from Theorem 12.14.   □

Thus, for convex function, Gâteaux differentiability coincides with Fréchet differentiability.

Example 12.14. Let $S = \mathbf{K}_{\mathrm{conv}}\{\mathbf{a}_1, \ldots, \mathbf{a}_m\} \subseteq \mathbb{R}^n$ and let $f : S \longrightarrow \mathbb{R}$ be the linear function defined by $f(\mathbf{x}) = \mathbf{c}'\mathbf{x}$. We have $(\nabla f)(\mathbf{x}) = \mathbf{c}$.

By Corollary 12.1, if

$$\mathbf{c}'(\mathbf{x} - \mathbf{x}_0) \geqslant 0 \tag{12.7}$$

for every $\mathbf{x} \in S$, then $\mathbf{x}_0$ is a minimizer for f. Note that $\mathbf{x} \in S$ if and only if $\mathbf{x} = \sum_{i=1}^m b_i \mathbf{a}_i$, where $b_i \geqslant 0$ for $1 \leqslant i \leqslant m$ and $\sum_{i=1}^m b_i = 1$. Inequality (12.7) can now be written as

$$\mathbf{c}' \left(\sum_{i=1}^m b_i \mathbf{a}_i - \mathbf{x}_0 \right) = \mathbf{c}' \sum_{i=1}^m b_i (\mathbf{a}_i - \mathbf{x}_0) \geqslant 0$$

for $b_i \geqslant 0$, $1 \leqslant i \leqslant m$, and $\sum_{i=1}^m b_i = 1$. When $\mathbf{x}_0 = \mathbf{a}_i$ and

$$b_j = \begin{cases} 1 & \text{if } j = i, \\ 0 & \text{otherwise} \end{cases}$$

this condition is satisfied. Thus, there exists a point $\mathbf{a}_i$ that is a minimizer for f on S.

Theorem 12.15. *Let $f : \mathbb{R}^n \longrightarrow \mathbb{R}$ be a convex, differentiable function. Any critical point $\mathbf{x}_0$ of f is a global minimum for f.*

Proof.   Let $\mathbf{x}_0$ be a critical point for f. Suppose that $\mathbf{x}_0$ is not a global minimum for f. Then, there exists $\mathbf{z}$ such that $f(\mathbf{z}) < f(\mathbf{x}_0)$. Since f is *differentiable* in $\mathbf{x}_0$, we have

$$\begin{aligned}
(\nabla f)'_{\mathbf{x}_0}(\mathbf{z} - \mathbf{x}_0) &= \frac{d}{dt} f(\mathbf{x}_0 + t(\mathbf{z} - \mathbf{x}_0))_{t=0} \\
&= \lim_{t \to 0} \frac{f(\mathbf{x}_0 + t(\mathbf{z} - \mathbf{x}_0)) - f(\mathbf{x}_0)}{t} \\
&= \lim_{t \to 0} \frac{f(t\mathbf{z} + (1-t)\mathbf{x}_0))) - f(\mathbf{x}_0)}{t} \\
&\leqslant \frac{tf(\mathbf{z}) + (1-t)f(\mathbf{x}_0) - f(\mathbf{x}_0)}{t} \\
&= \frac{t(f(\mathbf{z}) - tf(\mathbf{x}_0))}{t} < 0,
\end{aligned}$$

which implies $(\nabla f)_{\mathbf{x}_0} \neq \mathbf{0}_n$, thus contradicting the fact that $\mathbf{x}_0$ is a critical point. □

For functions that are twice continuously differentiable on a convex subset S of $\mathbb{R}^n$ with a non-empty interior we have the following statement:

Theorem 12.16. *Let S be a convex subset of $\mathbb{R}^n$ with a non-empty interior. If $f : S \longrightarrow \mathbb{R}$ is a function in $C^2(S)$, then, f is convex on S if and only if the Hessian matrix $H_f(\boldsymbol{x})$ is positive for every $\boldsymbol{x} \in S$.*

Proof. Suppose that the Hessian matrix $H_f(\mathbf{x})$ is positive for every $\mathbf{x} \in S$. By Taylor's theorem,

$$f(\mathbf{x}) - f(\mathbf{x}_0) = (\nabla f)_{\mathbf{x}_0}(\mathbf{x} - \mathbf{x}_0) + \frac{1}{2}(\mathbf{x} - \mathbf{x}_0)' H_f(\mathbf{x}_0 + t(\mathbf{x} - \mathbf{x}_0))(\mathbf{x} - \mathbf{x}_0)$$

for some $t \in [0, 1]$. The positivity of H_f means that $\frac{1}{2}(\mathbf{x} - \mathbf{x}_0)' H_f(\mathbf{x}_0 + t(\mathbf{x} - \mathbf{x}_0))(\mathbf{x} - \mathbf{x}_0) \geqslant 0$, so $f(\mathbf{x}) \geqslant f(\mathbf{x}_0) + (\nabla f)_{\mathbf{x}_0}(\mathbf{x} - \mathbf{x}_0)$, which implies the convexity of f by Theorem 12.13.

Suppose now that $H_f(\mathbf{x}_0)$ is not positive at some $\mathbf{x}_0 \in S$. We may assume that $\mathbf{x}_0$ is an interior point of S since H_f is continuous. There exists $\mathbf{x} \in S$ such that $(\mathbf{x} - \mathbf{x}_0)' H_f(\mathbf{x}_0)(\mathbf{x} - \mathbf{x}_0) < 0$. Applying again the continuity of the Hessian matrix, $\mathbf{x}$ may be selected such that $(\mathbf{x} - \mathbf{x}_0)' H_f(\mathbf{x}_0 + t(\mathbf{x} - \mathbf{x}_0))(\mathbf{x} - \mathbf{x}_0) < 0$, which means that $f(\mathbf{x}) < f(\mathbf{x}_0) + f(\mathbf{x}_0) + (\nabla f)_{\mathbf{x}_0}(\mathbf{x} - \mathbf{x}_0)$, thus contradicting the convexity of f. □

Corollary 12.3. *Let $f : (a, b) \longrightarrow \mathbb{R}$ be a function such that its second derivative f'' exists on (a, b). Then, f is convex if and only if $f''(t) \geqslant 0$ for $t \in (a, b)$.*

Proof. This is an immediate consequence of Theorem 12.16 for the case $n = 1$. □

For an one-argument function $f : [u, v] \longrightarrow \mathbb{R}$ f is convex if its graph is located below the chord determined by the endpoints of the interval (see Figure 12.1).

Lemma 12.1. *Let $f : [a, b] \longrightarrow \mathbb{R}$ be a convex function. If $x \in (a, b)$, then*

$$\frac{f(x) - f(a)}{x - a} \leqslant \frac{f(b) - f(a)}{b - a} \leqslant \frac{f(b) - f(x)}{b - x}.$$

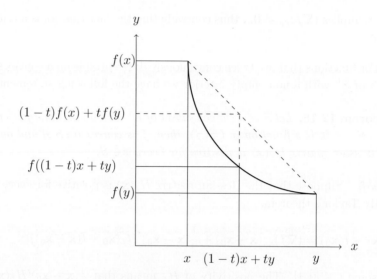

Fig. 12.1   Convex function on the interval $[u, v]$ of $\mathbb{R}$.

Proof.   It is easy to see that x can be regarded as either of the following convex combinations:

$$x = \left(1 - \frac{x - a}{b - a}\right) a + \frac{x - a}{b - a} b,$$

$$= \frac{b - x}{b - a} a + \left(1 - \frac{b - x}{b - a}\right) b.$$

The existence of the first convex combination implies

$$f(x) = f\left(1 - \frac{x - a}{b - a}\right) a + \frac{x - a}{b - a} b,$$

$$\leqslant \left(1 - \frac{x - a}{b - a}\right) f(a) + \frac{x - a}{b - a} f(b),$$

which is equivalent to

$$f(x) \leqslant \frac{b - x}{b - a} f(a) + \frac{x - a}{b - a} f(b).$$

This, in turn gives the first inequality of the lemma. The second one can be obtained similarly starting from the second convex combination. $\square$

Lemma 12.2. *Let $f : I \longrightarrow \mathbb{R}$ be a function, where I is an open interval. The following statements are equivalent for $a < b < c$, where $a, b, c \in I$:*

(i) $(c - a)f(b) \leqslant (b - a)f(c) + (c - b)f(a)$;

(ii) $\frac{f(b)-f(a)}{b-a} \leqslant \frac{f(c)-f(a)}{c-a}$;

(iii) $\frac{f(c)-f(a)}{c-a} \leqslant \frac{f(c)-f(b)}{c-b}$.

Proof. (i) is equivalent to (ii): Suppose that (i) holds. Then we have

$$(c - a)f(b) - (c - a)f(a) \leqslant (b - a)f(c) + (c - b)f(a) - (c - a)f(a),$$

which is equivalent to

$$(c - a)(f(b) - f(a)) \leqslant (b - a)(f(c) - f(a)). \tag{12.8}$$

By dividing both sides by $(b - a)(c - a) > 0$ we obtain inequality (ii).

Conversely, note that (ii) implies inequality (12.8). By adding $(c-a)f(a)$ to both sides of this inequality we obtain (i).

In a similar manner it is possible to prove the equivalence between (i) and (iii). $\square$

Theorem 12.17. *Let I be an open interval and let $f : I \longrightarrow \mathbb{R}$ is a function. Each of the conditions of Lemma 12.2 for $a < b < c$ in I is equivalent to the convexity of f.*

Proof. Let $f : I \longrightarrow \mathbb{R}$ be a convex function and let $a, b, c \in I$ be such that $a < b < c$. Define $t = \frac{c-b}{c-a}$. Clearly $0 < t < 1$ and by the convexity property,

$$f(b) = f(at + (1 - t)c) \leqslant tf(a) + (1 - t)f(c)$$
$$= \frac{c - b}{c - a}f(a) + \frac{b - a}{c - a}f(c),$$

which yields the first inequality of Lemma 12.2.

Conversely, suppose that the first inequality of Lemma 12.2 is satisfied. Choose $a = x$, $c = y$ and $b = tx + (1 - t)y$ for $t \in (0, 1)$. We have $(c - a)f(b) = (y - x)f(tx + (1 - t)y)$ and $(b - a)f(c) + (c - b)f(a) = (1 - t)(y - x)f(y) + t(y - x)f(x)$ Taking into account that $y > x$, we obtain the inequality $f(tx + (1 - t)y) \leqslant tf(x) + (1 - t)f(y)$, which means that f is convex. $\square$

Theorem 12.18. *Let I be an open interval and let $f : \mathbb{R} \longrightarrow \mathbb{R}$ is a convex function. The function $g(x, h)$ defined for $x \in I$ and $h \in \mathbb{R} - \{0\}$ as*

$$g(x, h) = \frac{f(x + h) - f(x)}{h}$$

is increasing with respect to each of its arguments.

Proof. We need to examine three cases: $0 < h_1 < h_2$, $h_1 < h_2 < 0$, and $h_1 < 0 < h_2$.

In the first case choose $a = x$, $b = x + h_1$ and $c = x + h_2$ in the second inequality of Lemma 12.2, where all three numbers x, $x + h_1$ and $x + h_2$ belong to I. We obtain $\frac{f(x+h_1)-f(x)}{h_1} \leqslant \frac{f(x+h_2)-f(x)}{h_2}$, which shows that $g(x, h_1) \leqslant g(x, h_2)$.

If $h_1 < h_2 < 0$, choose $a = x + h_1$, $b = x + h_2$ and $c = x$ in the last inequality of Lemma 12.2. This yields: $\frac{f(x)-f(x+h_1)}{-h_1} \leqslant \frac{f(x)-f(x+h_2)}{-h_2}$, that is $g(x, h_1) \leqslant g(x, h_2)$.

In the last case, $h_1 < 0 < h_2$, begin by noting that the last two inequalities of Lemma 12.2 imply

$$\frac{f(b) - f(a)}{b - a} \leqslant \frac{f(c) - f(b)}{c - b}.$$

By taking $a = x + h_1$, $b = x$, and $c = x + h_2$ in this inequality we obtain

$$\frac{f(x) - f(x + h_1)}{-h_1} \leqslant \frac{f(x + h_2) - f(x)}{h_2},$$

which is equivalent to $g(x, h_1) \leqslant g(x, h_2)$. This g is increasing with respect to its second argument.

To prove the monotonicity in the first argument let x_1, x_2 be in I such that $x_1 < x_2$ and let h be a number such that both $x_1 + h$ and $x_2 + h$ belong to I. Since g is monotonic in its second argument we have

$$g(x_1, h) = \frac{f(x_1 + h) - f(x_1)}{h} \leqslant \frac{f(x_2 + h) - f(x_1)}{h + (x_2 - x_1)}$$

and

$$\begin{aligned}
&\frac{f(x_2 + h) - f(x_1)}{h + (x_2 - x_1)} \\
&= \frac{f(x_1) - f(x_2 + h)}{-h - (x_2 - x_1)} \\
&= \frac{f((x_2 + h) - h - (x_2 - x_1)) - f(x_2 + h)}{-h - (x_2 - x_1)} \\
&\leqslant \frac{f((x_2 + h) - h) - f(x_2 + h)}{-h} = \frac{f(x_2 + h) - f(x_2)}{h},
\end{aligned}$$

which proves the monotonicity in its first argument. $\qquad\square$

The functions listed in the Table 12.1, defined on the set $\mathbb{R}_{\geqslant 0}$, provide examples of convex (or concave) functions.

The next theorem allows us to reduce convexity of functions of n arguments to convexity of one-argument functions.

Theorem 12.19. *Let $f : \mathbb{R}^n \longrightarrow \mathbb{R} \cup \{\infty\}$ be a function. The function f is convex (concave) if and only if the function $\phi_{x,h} : \mathbb{R} \longrightarrow \mathbb{R} \cup \{\infty\}$ given by $\phi_{x,h}(t) = f(x + th)$ is a convex (concave) function for every x and h in $\mathbb{R}^n$.*

Proof. Suppose that f is convex. We have

$$
\begin{aligned}
\phi_{\mathbf{x},\mathbf{h}}(ta + (1-t)b) &= f(\mathbf{x} + (ta + (1-t)b)\mathbf{h}) \\
&= f(t(\mathbf{x} + a\mathbf{h}) + (1-t)(\mathbf{x} + b\mathbf{h})) \\
&\leqslant t f(\mathbf{x} + a\mathbf{h}) + (1-t)f(\mathbf{x} + b\mathbf{h}) \\
&= t\phi_{\mathbf{x},\mathbf{h}}(a) + (1-t)\phi_{\mathbf{x},\mathbf{h}}(b),
\end{aligned}
$$

which shows that $\phi_{\mathbf{x},\mathbf{h}}$ is indeed convex. The converse implication follows in a similar manner.

The argument for concave functions is also similar. $\qquad\square$

Since each set of the form $L_{\mathbf{x},\mathbf{h}} = \{\mathbf{x} + t\mathbf{h} \mid t \in \mathbb{R}\}$ is a line in $\mathbb{R}^n$ if $\mathbf{h} \neq \mathbf{0}$ and $\phi_{\mathbf{x},\mathbf{h}}$ is the restriction of f to $L_{\mathbf{x},\mathbf{h}}$, it follows that $f : \mathbb{R}^n \longrightarrow \mathbb{R} \cup \{\infty\}$ is convex if and only if its restriction to any line $L_{\mathbf{x},\mathbf{h}}$ is an one-argument convex function or is ∞.

Theorem 12.20. *Let I be an interval, $I \subseteq \mathbb{R}$. A function $f : I \longrightarrow \mathbb{R}$ is convex if and only if for all $x, y, z \in I$ such that $x < y < z$ we have*

$$
\begin{vmatrix}
1 & x & f(x) \\
1 & y & f(y) \\
1 & z & f(z)
\end{vmatrix} \geqslant 0.
$$

Proof. Since $x < y < z$ there exists $t \in (0,1)$ such that $y = tx + (1-t)z$. This allows us to write

Function	Second Derivative	Convexity Property
x^r for $r > 0$	$r(r-1)x^{r-2}$	concave for $r < 1$ convex for $r \geqslant 1$
$\ln x$	$-\dfrac{1}{x^2}$	concave
$x \ln x$	$\dfrac{1}{x}$	convex
e^x	e^x	convex

$$\begin{vmatrix} 1 & x & f(x) \\ 1 & y & f(y) \\ 1 & z & f(z) \end{vmatrix} = \begin{vmatrix} 1 & x & f(x) \\ 1 & tx + (1-t)z & f(y) \\ 1 & z & f(z) \end{vmatrix}$$

$$= \begin{vmatrix} 1 & x & f(x) \\ 0 & 0 & f(y) - tf(x) - (1-t)f(z) \\ 1 & z & f(z) \end{vmatrix}$$

$$= -(f(y) - tf(x) - (1-t)f(z))(z - x).$$

Therefore, the condition of the theorem is satisfied if and only if $f(y) \leqslant tf(x) + (1-t)f(z)$, that is, if and only if f is convex on I. $\qquad \square$

Corollary 12.4. *Let I be an interval, $I \subseteq \mathbb{R}$. A function $f : I \longrightarrow \mathbb{R}$ is strictly convex if and only if for all $x, y, z \in I$ such that $x < y < z$ we have*

$$\begin{vmatrix} 1 & x & f(x) \\ 1 & y & f(y) \\ 1 & z & f(z) \end{vmatrix} > 0.$$

Proof. The proof can be obtained from the proof of Theorem 12.20. $\qquad \square$

Theorem 12.21. *Let $f : [a, b] \longrightarrow \mathbb{R}$ be a convex function. The function f is continuous at every $x_0 \in (a, b)$.*

Proof. Let $g : (a - x_0, b - x_0) \longrightarrow \mathbb{R}$ be defined as $g(x) = f(x + x_0) - f(x_0)$. It is clear that g is convex on $(a - x_0, b - x_0)$, $0 \in (a - x_0, b - x_0)$, and $g(0) = 0$; also, g is continuous in 0 if and only if f is continuous at x_0.

For $x \in (a - x_0, b - x_0)$ let

$$s(x) = \begin{cases} 1 & \text{if } x \leqslant 0, \\ -1 & \text{if } x < 0. \end{cases}$$

If $|x| < \delta$, then the convexity of g implies

$$g(x) = g\left(\frac{|x|}{\delta} s(x)\delta + \left(1 - \frac{|x|}{\delta} \right) 0 \right)$$

$$\leqslant \frac{|x|}{\delta} g(s(x)\delta) + \left(1 - \frac{|x|}{\delta} \right) g(0)$$

$$= \frac{|x|}{\delta} g(s(x)\delta).$$

Therefore, $g(x) \leqslant \frac{1}{\delta} \max\{g(-\delta), g(\delta)\}|x|$. The convexity of g implies that $-g(-x) \leqslant g(x)$ by Supplement 17, so $|g(x)| \leqslant \frac{1}{\delta} \max\{g(-\delta), g(\delta)\}|x|$.

If $\lim_{n \to snn} x_n = 0$, where (x_n) is a sequence in $(a - x_0, b - x_0)$, then $\lim_{n \to \infty} g(x_n) = 0 = g(0)$, so g is continuous in 0. This implies that f is continuous in x_0. $\qquad \square$

Let $f : I \longrightarrow \mathbb{R}$ be a convex function where I is an interval of $\mathbb{R}$ and let $a \in I$. The function f is *left-differentiable* if the limit

$$f'(a-) = \lim_{x \to a, x < a} \frac{f(x) - f(a)}{x - a}$$

exists. In this case, the value of the limit is known as *left derivative* of f in a.

Similarly, f is *right-differentiable* if the limit

$$f'(a+) = \lim_{x \to a, x > a} \frac{f(x) - f(a)}{x - a}$$

exists. In this case, the value of the limit is known as the *right derivative of f in a*.

Example 12.15. Let $f : \mathbb{R} \longrightarrow \mathbb{R}$ be the function defined by $f(x) = |x|$. We have:

$$f'(0-) = \lim_{x \to 0, x < 0} \frac{|x|}{x} = -1$$

and

$$f'(0+) = \lim_{x \to 0, x > 0} \frac{|x|}{x} = 1.$$

Note that if both $f'(a-)$ and $f'(a+)$ exist and are finite, then f is continuous in a.

Theorem 12.22. Let $f : (a, b) \longrightarrow \mathbb{R}$ be convex function on $[a, b]$. If $x, y \in (a, b)$ and $x < y$, then

$$f'(x-) \leqslant f'(x+) \leqslant f'(y-) \leqslant f'(y+).$$

Proof. If $a < x < b$, by Lemma 12.1 we have

$$\frac{f(x) - f(a)}{x - a} \leqslant \frac{f(b) - f(a)}{b - a} \leqslant \frac{f(b) - f(x)}{b - x}.$$

Since $\lim_{a \to x, a < x} \frac{f(x) - f(a)}{x - a} \leqslant \lim_{b \to x, b > x} \frac{f(b) - f(x)}{b - x}$, it follows that $f'(x-) \leqslant f'(x^+)$; similarly, $f'(y-) \leqslant f'(y+)$.

Let $t \in (x, y)$. By the same lemma we have:

$$\frac{f(t) - f(x)}{t - x} \leqslant \frac{f(y) - f(x)}{y - x} \leqslant \frac{f(y) - f(t)}{y - t}.$$

The first inequality implies

$$f'(x+) = \lim_{t \to x, t > x} \frac{f(t) - f(x)}{t - x} \leqslant \frac{f(y) - f(x)}{y - x},$$

while the second yields

$$\frac{f(y) - f(x)}{y - x} \leqslant \lim_{t \to y, t < y} \frac{f(y) - f(t)}{y - t} = f'(y-),$$

so $f'(x+) \leqslant f'(y-)$. $\qquad \square$

12.6 Quasi-Convex and Pseudo-Convex Functions

Quasi-convex functions introduced next generalize convex function.

Definition 12.6. Let D be a non-empty convex subset of $\mathbb{R}^n$ and let $f : D \longrightarrow \mathbb{R}^n$. We say that f is *quasi-convex* on D if

$$f((1-t)\mathbf{x} + t\mathbf{y}) \leqslant \max\{f(\mathbf{x}), f(\mathbf{y})\}$$

for every $\mathbf{x}, \mathbf{y} \in D$ and $t \in [0, 1]$.

The function f is *strictly quasi-convex* if for each $\mathbf{x}, \mathbf{y} \in D$ such that $f(\mathbf{x}) \neq f(\mathbf{y})$ we have the strict inequality

$$f((1-t)\mathbf{x} + t\mathbf{y}) < \max\{f(\mathbf{x}), f(\mathbf{y})\}$$

for $t \in (0, 1)$.

Clearly, every convex function is quasi-convex.

In a similar manner it is possible to define quasi-concave functions.

Definition 12.7. Let D be a non-empty convex subset of $\mathbb{R}^n$ and let $f : D \longrightarrow \mathbb{R}^n$. We say that f is *quasi-concave* on D if

$$f((1-t)\mathbf{x} + t\mathbf{y}) \geqslant \min\{f(\mathbf{x}), f(\mathbf{y})\}$$

for every $\mathbf{x}, \mathbf{y} \in D$ and $t \in (0, 1)$.

The function f is *strictly quasi-concave* if for each $\mathbf{x}, \mathbf{y} \in D$ such that $f(\mathbf{x}) \neq f(\mathbf{y})$ we have the strict inequality

$$f(t\mathbf{x} + (1-t)\mathbf{y}) > \min\{f(\mathbf{x}), f(\mathbf{y})\}$$

for $t \in (0, 1)$.

The notions introduced in Definition 12.6 can be localized to a point as follows:

Definition 12.8. Let D be a non-empty convex subset of $\mathbb{R}^n$ and let $f : D \longrightarrow \mathbb{R}^n$. We say that f is *quasi-convex* at $\mathbf{x} \in D$ if

$$f(t\mathbf{x} + (1-t)\mathbf{y}) \leqslant \max\{f(\mathbf{x}), f(\mathbf{y})\}$$

for every $\mathbf{y} \in D$ and $t \in (0, 1)$.

The function f is *strictly quasi-convex* at $\mathbf{x} \in D$ if for each $\mathbf{y} \in D$ such that $f(\mathbf{x}) \neq f(\mathbf{y})$ we have the strict inequality

$$f(t\mathbf{x} + (1-t)\mathbf{y}) < \max\{f(\mathbf{x}), f(\mathbf{y})\}$$

for $t \in (0, 1)$.

The local form of quasi-concavity can be obtained by replacing max by min and by reversing the inequalities of Definition 12.8.

We saw (in Theorem 12.1) that convexity of functions is equivalent to convexity of their epigraph. The next theorem provides a characterization of quasi-convex functions in terms of their level sets.

Theorem 12.23. *Let D be a non-empty convex subset of $\mathbb{R}^n$ and let $f : D \longrightarrow \mathbb{R}^n$ be a function. The function f is quasi-convex if and only if each level set $L_{f,a} = \{\boldsymbol{x} \in \mathbb{R}^n \mid f(\boldsymbol{x}) \leqslant a\}$ is a convex set.*

Proof. Suppose that f is quasi-convex and $\mathbf{x}, \mathbf{y} \in L_{f,a}$. Since $f(\mathbf{x}) = f(\mathbf{y}) = a$ it follows that for $\mathbf{z} = t\mathbf{x} + (1-t)\mathbf{y}$ we have $\mathbf{z} \in D$ (because D is convex) and $f(\mathbf{z}) \leq a$ due to the quasi-convexity of f. Thus, $\mathbf{z} \in L_{f,a}$, so $L_{f,a}$ is convex for all a.

Conversely, suppose that all level sets are convex. If $\mathbf{x}, \mathbf{y} \in L_{f,a}$ we have $\mathbf{x}, \mathbf{y} \in L_{f,a}$ for $a = \max\{f(\mathbf{x}), f(\mathbf{y})\}$. Since $L_{f,a}$ is convex, $t\mathbf{x} + (1-t)\mathbf{y} \in L(f,a)$, which means that $f(t\mathbf{x} + (1-t)\mathbf{y}) \in L_{f,a}$. Thus, $f(t\mathbf{x} + (1-t)\mathbf{y}) \leq a = \max\{f(\mathbf{x}), f(\mathbf{y})\}$, which means that f is indeed quasi-convex. $\square$

Example 12.16. The function $f : \mathbb{R}_{>0} \longrightarrow \mathbb{R}$ defined by $f(x) = \ln x$ is concave because $f''(x) < 0$ for $x > 0$. However, f is also quasi-convex. Indeed, let $x, y > 0$ and let $t \in (0,1)$. If $x < y$, then $f(x) < f(y)$ and the defining inequality of quasi-convexity amounts to

$$\ln(tx + (1-t)y) \leqslant \ln y$$

holds because $tx + (1-t)y \leqslant y$ for $t \in (0,1)$.

Example 12.17. The function $f : \mathbb{R} \longrightarrow \mathbb{R}$ defined by $f(x) = \lfloor x \rfloor$ is quasi-convex. Indeed, if $x \leqslant y$ we have $f(x) \leqslant f(y)$, because

$$\lfloor tx + (1-t)y \rfloor \leqslant \lfloor y \rfloor$$

for $t \in (0,1)$.

Theorem 12.24. *Let D be a non-empty open and convex subset of $\mathbb{R}^n$ and let $f : D \longrightarrow \mathbb{R}^n$ be a function differentiable on D. The following assertions are equivalent:*

    (i) *f is quasi-convex on D;*
    (ii) *if $\boldsymbol{x}, \boldsymbol{y} \in D$, $f(\boldsymbol{x}) \leq f(\boldsymbol{y})$ implies $(\nabla f)(\boldsymbol{y})'(\boldsymbol{x} - \boldsymbol{y}) \leq 0$;*
    (iii) *if $\boldsymbol{x}, \boldsymbol{y} \in D$, $(\nabla f)(\boldsymbol{y})'(\boldsymbol{x} - \boldsymbol{y}) > 0$ implies $f(\boldsymbol{x}) > f(\boldsymbol{y})$.*

Proof. We begin by proving that (i) is equivalent to (ii). Let f be quasi-convex and let $\mathbf{x}, \mathbf{y} \in D$ be such that $f(\mathbf{x}) \leq f(\mathbf{y})$. Since f is differentiable at $\mathbf{y}$ we have

$$f(t\mathbf{x} + (1 - t)\mathbf{y}) = f(\mathbf{y}) + t(\nabla f)(\mathbf{y})'(\mathbf{x} - \mathbf{y}) + t\|\mathbf{x} - \mathbf{y}\|_2 \alpha(t\mathbf{x} + (1 - t)\mathbf{y}),$$

where $\alpha : D \longrightarrow \mathbb{R}$ is a continuous function in $\mathbf{y}$ such $\alpha(\mathbf{y}) = \mathbf{0}_m$. The quasi-convexity of f implies $f(t\mathbf{x} + (1 - t)\mathbf{y}) \leq f(\mathbf{y})$, and therefore,

$$(\nabla f)(\mathbf{y})'(\mathbf{x} - \mathbf{y}) + \|\mathbf{x} - \mathbf{y}\|_2 \alpha(t\mathbf{x} + (1 - t)\mathbf{y}) \leq 0.$$

The continuity of α implies, in turn,

$$\lim_{t \to 0} (\nabla f)(\mathbf{y})'(\mathbf{x} - \mathbf{y}) + \|\mathbf{x} - \mathbf{y}\|_2 \alpha(t\mathbf{x} + (1 - t)\mathbf{y})$$
$$= (\nabla f)(\mathbf{y})'(\mathbf{x} - \mathbf{y}) + \|\mathbf{x} - \mathbf{y}\|_2 < \alpha(\mathbf{y}) \leq 0,$$

which allows us to conclude that $(\nabla f)(\mathbf{y})'(\mathbf{x} - \mathbf{y}) \leq 0$.

Conversely, suppose that (ii) holds. To show that f is quasi-convex it suffices to prove that if $f(\mathbf{x}) \leq f(\mathbf{y})$, then $f(t\mathbf{x} + (1 - t)\mathbf{y}) \leq f(\mathbf{y})$ for $t \in (0, 1)$.

Let $f(\mathbf{x}) \leq f(\mathbf{y})$. By (ii) we have $(\nabla f)(\mathbf{y})'(\mathbf{x} - \mathbf{y}) \leq 0$.

Suppose that f were not quasi-convex. This would imply the existence of $\mathbf{z} \in D$ such that $\mathbf{z} = t\mathbf{x} + (1 - t)\mathbf{y}$ for $t \in (0, 1)$ and $f(\mathbf{z}) > f(\mathbf{y})$. The continuity of f implies that there exists $r \in (0, 1)$ such that $f(s\mathbf{z} + (1 - s)\mathbf{y}) > f(\mathbf{y})$ for every $s \in [r, 1]$ and $f(\mathbf{z}) > f(r\mathbf{z} + (1 - r)\mathbf{y})$. By the Mean Value Theorem, there exists $\mathbf{w} = t\mathbf{z} + (1 - t)\mathbf{y}$ such that

$$f(\mathbf{z}) - f(r\mathbf{z} + (1 - r)\mathbf{y}) = (1 - r)(\nabla f)(\mathbf{w})'(\mathbf{z} - \mathbf{y}),$$

where $t \in (r, 1)$. It is clear that $f(\mathbf{w}) \geq f(\mathbf{y})$. We also have $(\nabla f)(\mathbf{w})'(\mathbf{z} - \mathbf{y}) > 0$. Since $f(\mathbf{w}) > f(\mathbf{y}) \geq f(\mathbf{x})$ and $\mathbf{w}$ is a convex combination of $\mathbf{x}$ and $\mathbf{y}$, $\mathbf{w} = s\mathbf{x} + (1 - s)\mathbf{y}$, where $s \in (0, 1)$. Since $(\nabla f)(\mathbf{w})'(\mathbf{x} - \mathbf{w}) \leq 0$, we have $0 \geq (\nabla f)(\mathbf{w})'(\mathbf{x} - \mathbf{w}) = (1 - s)(\nabla f)(\mathbf{w})'(\mathbf{x} - \mathbf{w})$, which contradicts (ii). Thus, f is quasi-convex.

The equivalence between (ii) and (iii) is straightforward.   □

Theorem 12.25. *Let D be a non-empty compact polytope in $\mathbb{R}^n$ and let $f : D \longrightarrow \mathbb{R}$ be a quasi-convex and continuous function on D. There exists an extreme point $\boldsymbol{x} \in \mathsf{extr}(D)$ such that $f(\boldsymbol{x})$ is a maximum on D.*

Proof. Since D is compact and f is continuous on D, then there exists $\mathbf{x}^* \in D$ such that $f(\mathbf{x}^*)$ is the maximum of f on D.

If $\mathbf{x} \in \mathsf{extr}(D)$ and $f(\mathbf{x}) = f(\mathbf{x}^*)$, the result follows.

Otherwise, let $\mathbf{x}_1, \ldots, \mathbf{x}_k$ be extreme points of D such that $f(\mathbf{x}) > f(\mathbf{x}_i)$ for $1 \leq i \leq k$. By Krein and Milman's Theorem (Theorem 6.69) $\mathbf{x}$ is a convex combination of $\mathbf{x}_1, \ldots, \mathbf{x}_k$, $\mathbf{x} = \sum_{i=1}^{k} a_i \mathbf{x}_i$, where $a_i \in [0,1]$ for $1 \leq i \leq k$ and $\sum_{i=1}^{k} a_i = 1$. By the assumption made above we have $f(\mathbf{x}) > f(\mathbf{x}_i)$ for $1 \leq i \leq k$, so

$$f(\mathbf{x}) > \max\{f(\mathbf{x}_i) \mid 1 \leq i \leq k\}. \tag{12.9}$$

Therefore, $\mathbf{x}_i \in L(f, a)$, where $a = \max\{f(\mathbf{x}_i) \mid 1 \leq i \leq k\}$. Since f is quasi-convex, $L(f, a)$ is convex, which implies $\mathbf{x} \in L(f, a)$. This contradicts inequality (12.9). $\qquad\square$

Another type of convexity-related property that is introduced for differentiable functions was introduced by O. L. Mangasarian in [104].

Definition 12.9. Let D be a non-empty convex subset of $\mathbb{R}^n$ and let $f : D \longrightarrow \mathbb{R}^n$ be a differentiable function. We say that f is *pseudo-convex* if $(\nabla f)(\mathbf{y})'(\mathbf{x} - \mathbf{y}) \geqslant 0$ implies $f(\mathbf{x}) \geqslant f(\mathbf{y})$ for every $\mathbf{x} \in D$.

The function f is *strictly pseudo-convex* at $\mathbf{y}$ if for each $\mathbf{x} \in D$ such that $\mathbf{x} \neq \mathbf{y}$ and $(\nabla f)(\mathbf{y})'(\mathbf{x} - \mathbf{y}) \geqslant 0$ we have $f(\mathbf{x}) > f(\mathbf{y})$.

The function f is pseudo-convex (strictly pseudo-convex) on D if it is pseudo-convex (strictly pseudo-convex) at every $\mathbf{y} \in D$.

Example 12.18. Let $f : \mathbb{R} \longrightarrow \mathbb{R}$ be the function defined by $f(t) = te^t$. Since $f'(t) = (1 + t)e^t$ for $t \in \mathbb{R}$ and $f''(t) = (2 + t)e^t$, the function f is not convex (it is concave for $t < 2$, 2 is an inflexion point, and it is convex for $t > 2$). Also, f has a minimum for $t = -1$ equal to $f(-1) = -\frac{1}{e}$.

We claim that this function is pseudo-convex at each $y \in \mathbb{R}$. Indeed

$$f'(y)(x - y) = (1 + y)e^y(x - y) \geqslant 0.$$

If this inequality is satisfied the following cases may occur:

    (i) $y = -1$;
    (ii) $x \geqslant y > -1$;
    (iii) $x \leqslant y < -1$.

In the first case, $y = -1$ we have $f(x) > f(-1)$ because the function has a minimum in -1. In the second case, $f(x) \geqslant f(y)$ because f is increasing on the set $(-1, \infty)$. Finally, in the third case we have again $f(x) \geqslant f(y)$ because f is decreasing on $(-\infty, -1)$.

Thus, f is pseudo-convex in each $\mathbf{y}$.

The class of all pseudo-convex functions over a convex set D includes the class of all differentiable convex functions on D and is included in the class of all differentiable quasi-convex functions on D. An interesting property of pseudo-convex functions is that a local condition, such as the vanishing of the gradient, is a global optimality condition.

Theorem 12.26. *Let D be a non-empty convex subset of $\mathbb{R}^n$ and let $f : D \longrightarrow \mathbb{R}$ be a differentiable function at $\boldsymbol{y} \in D$. If $\boldsymbol{y}$ is an extreme point of f, then $(\nabla f)(\boldsymbol{y}) = 0$. Furthermore, if f is pseudo-convex at $\boldsymbol{y}$, then $(\nabla f)(\boldsymbol{y}) = \boldsymbol{0}_n$ implies that $\boldsymbol{y}$ is a minimum point for f.*

Proof. Let us assume initially that f is just differentiable. Suppose $f(\mathbf{y}) = \min\{f(\mathbf{x}) \mid \mathbf{x} \in D\}$. Since D is convex we have $(1-t)\mathbf{y} + t\mathbf{x} \in D$ for $t \in (0,1)$, so the differentiability of f implies that

$$f((1-t)\mathbf{y} + t\mathbf{x}) - f(\mathbf{y}) = t(\nabla f)(\mathbf{y})'(\mathbf{x} - \mathbf{y}) + t\|\mathbf{x} - \mathbf{y}\|_2 \gamma(t(\mathbf{x} - \mathbf{y})),$$

where γ is a continuous function in $\mathbf{0}_n$ such $\gamma(\mathbf{0}) = 0$. Since $f((1-t)\mathbf{y} + t\mathbf{x}) - f(\mathbf{y}) \geq 0$ we have

$$(\nabla f)(\mathbf{y})'(\mathbf{x} - \mathbf{y}) + \|\mathbf{x} - \mathbf{y}\|_2 \gamma(t(\mathbf{x} - \mathbf{y})) \geq 0.$$

When t tends to 0 the last inequality implies $(\nabla f)(\mathbf{y})'(\mathbf{x} - \mathbf{y}) \geq 0$.

Similarly, it is possible to show that if $\mathbf{y}$ is such that $f(\mathbf{y}) = \max\{f(\mathbf{x}) \mid \mathbf{x} \in D\}$, then $(\nabla f)(\mathbf{y})'(\mathbf{x} - \mathbf{y}) \leq 0$.

Suppose now that $f : D \longrightarrow \mathbb{R}$ is pseudo-convex at $\mathbf{y}$. If $(\nabla f)(\mathbf{y})'(\mathbf{x} - \mathbf{y}) \geq 0$ for every $\mathbf{x} \in D$, it follows that $f(\mathbf{x}) \geq f(\mathbf{y})$, so $f(\mathbf{y}) = \min\{f(\mathbf{x}) \mid \mathbf{x} \in D\}$. Similarly, $(\nabla f)(\mathbf{y})'(\mathbf{x} - \mathbf{y}) \leq 0$ for every $\mathbf{x} \in D$, implies $f(\mathbf{y}) = \max\{f(\mathbf{x}) \mid \mathbf{x} \in D\}$.

If f is differentiable in $\mathbf{y}$ and $f(\mathbf{y}) = \min\{f(\mathbf{x}) \mid \mathbf{x} \in D\}$, then, by the previous argument, $(\nabla f)(\mathbf{y})'(\mathbf{x} - \mathbf{y}) \geq 0$ for every $\mathbf{x} \in D$. Since D is open, $\mathbf{y} - r(\nabla f)(\mathbf{y}) \in D$ for some positive r. By substituting $\mathbf{y} - r(\nabla f)(\mathbf{y})$ for $\mathbf{x}$ we obtain $-r(\nabla f)(\mathbf{y})'(\nabla f)(\mathbf{y}) \geq 0$ which implies $(\nabla f)(\mathbf{y}) = \mathbf{0}$. The conclusion for max is obtained similarly.

Let now f be pseudo-convex. Since $(\nabla f)(\mathbf{y})'(\mathbf{x} - \mathbf{y}) = 0$ we have $f(\mathbf{x}) \geq f(\mathbf{y})$, for every $\mathbf{x} \in D$, so $f(\mathbf{y}) = \min\{f(\mathbf{x}) \mid \mathbf{x} \in D\}$. $\square$

Theorem 12.27. *Let D be a non-empty convex subset of $\mathbb{R}^n$ and let $f : D \longrightarrow \mathbb{R}$ be a differentiable pseudo-convex function. Then f is strictly quasi-convex on D.*

Proof. Suppose that f is not strictly quasi-convex. This means that there exist $\mathbf{x}, \mathbf{y} \in D$ such that $f(\mathbf{x}) \neq f(\mathbf{y})$ and

$$f(t\mathbf{x} + (1-t)\mathbf{y}) \geq \max\{f(\mathbf{x}), f(\mathbf{y})\}$$

for $t \in (0,1)$.

Suppose that $f(\mathbf{y}) < f(\mathbf{x})$. Then, if $\mathbf{z} = t\mathbf{x} + (1-t)\mathbf{y}$ we have $f(\mathbf{z}) \geq f(\mathbf{x}) > f(\mathbf{y})$. Therefore, there exists $\mathbf{u}$ such that $\mathbf{u}$ has the form $\mathbf{u} = s\mathbf{x} + (1-s)\mathbf{y}$ for some $s \in (0,1)$ such that $f(\mathbf{u})$ is the maximum of $\{f(\mathbf{z}) \mid \mathbf{z} = t\mathbf{x} + (1-t)\mathbf{y}, t \in (0,1)\}$. Thus, $(\nabla f)(\mathbf{u})(\mathbf{x}-\mathbf{u}) \leq 0$ and $(\nabla f)(\mathbf{u})(\mathbf{y}-\mathbf{u}) \leq 0$ by the proof of Theorem 12.26, which imply $(1-s)(\nabla f)(\mathbf{u})(\mathbf{x}-\mathbf{y}) \leq 0$ and $-s(\nabla f)(\mathbf{u})(\mathbf{x}-\mathbf{y}) \leq 0$, respectively. Therefore, $(\nabla f)(\mathbf{u})(\mathbf{x}-bf\mathbf{y}) = 0$ and $(\nabla f)(\mathbf{u})(\mathbf{y}-bf\mathbf{u}) = 0$. Since f is pseudo-convex and $(\nabla f)(\mathbf{u})(\mathbf{y}-bf\mathbf{u}) = 0$, we have $f(\mathbf{y}) \geq f(\mathbf{u})$, so $f(\mathbf{x}) > f(\mathbf{u})$. This contradicts the choice we made for $\mathbf{u}$. Therefore, f is strictly quasi-convex on D. $\qquad\square$

12.7 Convexity and Inequalities

Theorem 12.28. (Fan-Glicksburg-Hoffman's Theorem) *Let C be a convex subset of $\mathbb{R}^n$, $\boldsymbol{f} : C \longrightarrow \mathbb{R}^m$ be a convex function, and let $\boldsymbol{h} : \mathbb{R}^n \longrightarrow \mathbb{R}^k$ be a linear function. If there exists no $\boldsymbol{x} \in C$ such that*

$$\boldsymbol{f}(\boldsymbol{x}) < \mathbf{0}_m \ \text{and} \ \boldsymbol{h}(\boldsymbol{x}) = \mathbf{0}_k,$$

then there exist $\boldsymbol{p} \in \mathbb{R}^m$ and $\boldsymbol{q} \in \mathbb{R}^k$ such that $\boldsymbol{p}'\boldsymbol{f}(\boldsymbol{x}) + \boldsymbol{q}'\boldsymbol{h}(\boldsymbol{x}) \geqslant 0$ for every $\boldsymbol{x} \in C$, $\boldsymbol{p} \geq \mathbf{0}_m$, and

$$\begin{pmatrix} \boldsymbol{p} \\ \boldsymbol{q} \end{pmatrix} \neq \mathbf{0}_{m+k}.$$

Proof. Let

$$L_\mathbf{x} = \left\{ \begin{pmatrix} \mathbf{y} \\ \mathbf{z} \end{pmatrix} \in \mathbb{R}^{m+k} \,\middle|\, \mathbf{y} > \mathbf{f}(\mathbf{x}), \mathbf{z} = \mathbf{h}(\mathbf{x}) \right\}$$

and let $L = \bigcup \{L_\mathbf{x} \mid \mathbf{x} \in D\}$.

The assumptions made on $\mathbf{f}$ and $\mathbf{h}$ imply that $\mathbf{0}_{m+k} \notin L_\mathbf{x}$ for any $\mathbf{x} \in C$ and, therefore, $\mathbf{0}_{m+k} \notin L$.

The set L is convex. Indeed, if

$$\begin{pmatrix} \mathbf{y}_1 \\ \mathbf{z}_1 \end{pmatrix} \ \text{and} \ \begin{pmatrix} \mathbf{y}_2 \\ \mathbf{z}_2 \end{pmatrix}$$

belong to L, then $\mathbf{y}_1 > \mathbf{f}(\mathbf{x}_1), \mathbf{z}_1 = \mathbf{h}(\mathbf{x}_1)$ and $\mathbf{y}_2 > \mathbf{f}(\mathbf{x}_2), \mathbf{z}_2 = \mathbf{h}(\mathbf{x}_2)$, so

$$(1-a)\mathbf{y}_1 + a\mathbf{y}_2 > (1-a)\mathbf{f}(\mathbf{x}_1) + a\mathbf{f}(\mathbf{x}_2) \geqslant \mathbf{f}((1-a)\mathbf{x}_1 + a\mathbf{x}_2)$$

because $\mathbf{f}$ is convex on D, and

$$(1-a)\mathbf{z}_1 + a\mathbf{z}_2 = (1-a)\mathbf{h}(\mathbf{x}_1) + a\mathbf{h}(\mathbf{x}_2) = \mathbf{h}((1-a)\mathbf{x}_1 + a\mathbf{x}_2)$$

because the linearity of $\mathbf{h}$. Thus,

$$(1-a)\begin{pmatrix}\mathbf{y}_1\\\mathbf{z}_1\end{pmatrix} + a\begin{pmatrix}\mathbf{y}_2\\\mathbf{z}_2\end{pmatrix} \in L.$$

By Theorem 6.56 the sets L and $\{\mathbf{0}_{m+k}\}$ are linearly separable, so there exists

$$\begin{pmatrix}\mathbf{p}\\\mathbf{q}\end{pmatrix} \in \mathbb{R}^{m+k} - \{\mathbf{0}_{m+k}\}$$

such that $\mathbf{p}'\mathbf{u} + \mathbf{q}'\mathbf{v} \geq 0$ for every $\begin{pmatrix}\mathbf{u}\\\mathbf{v}\end{pmatrix} \in L$. Since this holds for arbitrary $\mathbf{u}$, we have $\mathbf{p} \geq \mathbf{0}_m$.

Let a be a positive number. If $\mathbf{u} = \mathbf{f}(\mathbf{x}) + a\mathbf{1}_m \in \mathbb{R}^m$ and $\mathbf{v} = \mathbf{h}(\mathbf{x}) \in \mathbb{R}^k$ we have

$$\begin{pmatrix}\mathbf{u}\\\mathbf{v}\end{pmatrix} \in L_{\mathbf{x}} \subseteq L,$$

and

$$\mathbf{p}'\mathbf{u} + \mathbf{q}'\mathbf{v} = \mathbf{p}'(\mathbf{f}(\mathbf{x}) + a\mathbf{1}_m) + \mathbf{q}'\mathbf{h}(\mathbf{x}) = \mathbf{p}'\mathbf{f}(\mathbf{x}) + a\mathbf{p}'\mathbf{1}_m + \mathbf{q}'\mathbf{h}(\mathbf{x}) \geq 0$$

for $\mathbf{x} \in C$.

Suppose that $\inf\{\mathbf{p}'\mathbf{f}(\mathbf{x}) + \mathbf{q}'\mathbf{h}(\mathbf{x}) \mid \mathbf{x} \in C\}$ is a negative number $-d$ (where $d > 0$). By choosing a such that $a\mathbf{p}'\mathbf{1}_m < d$, this would imply $\inf\{\mathbf{p}'\mathbf{f}(\mathbf{x}) + \mathbf{q}'\mathbf{h}(\mathbf{x}) \mid \mathbf{x} \in C\} = -d < -a\mathbf{p}\mathbf{1}_m$, contradicting the fact that $\mathbf{p}'\mathbf{f}(\mathbf{x}) + a\mathbf{p}'\mathbf{1}_m + \mathbf{q}'\mathbf{h}(\mathbf{x}) \geq 0$ for $\mathbf{x} \in C$. Thus, $\inf_{\mathbf{x} \in C}\{\mathbf{p}'f(\mathbf{x}) + \mathbf{q}'h(\mathbf{x})\} \geqslant 0$. $\square$

The next statement is a stronger form of Theorem 12.28.

Theorem 12.29. *Let* $\boldsymbol{f} : \mathbb{R}^n \longrightarrow \mathbb{R}^m$ *be a convex function, and let* $\boldsymbol{h} :$ $\mathbb{R}^n \longrightarrow \mathbb{R}^k$ *be a linear function given by* $\boldsymbol{h}(\boldsymbol{x}) = B\boldsymbol{x} - \boldsymbol{d}$ *for* $\boldsymbol{x} \in \mathbb{R}^n$, *where* $B \in \mathbb{R}^{k\times n}$ *is a matrix with* $\operatorname{rank}(B) = k$. *Then, exactly one of the following situations occur:*

(i) *there exists* $\boldsymbol{x} \in \mathbb{R}^n$ *such that* $\boldsymbol{f}(\boldsymbol{x}) < \boldsymbol{0}_m$ *and* $\boldsymbol{h}(\boldsymbol{x}) = B\boldsymbol{x} - \boldsymbol{d} = \boldsymbol{0}_k$;

(ii) *there exist* $\boldsymbol{p} \in \mathbb{R}^m$ *and* $\boldsymbol{q} \in \mathbb{R}^k$ *such that* $\boldsymbol{p} \geq \boldsymbol{0}_m$,

$$\begin{pmatrix}\boldsymbol{p}\\\boldsymbol{q}\end{pmatrix} \neq \boldsymbol{0}_{m+k}$$

and $\boldsymbol{p}'f(\boldsymbol{x}) + \boldsymbol{q}'(B\boldsymbol{x} - \boldsymbol{d}) \geq 0$ *for every* $\boldsymbol{x} \in \mathbb{R}^n$.

Proof. If the first situation does not occur, then by Theorem 12.28, there exist $\mathbf{p} \in \mathbb{R}^m$ and $\mathbf{q} \in \mathbb{R}^k$ such that $\mathbf{p} \geq \mathbf{0}_m$,

$$\begin{pmatrix} \mathbf{p} \\ \mathbf{q} \end{pmatrix} \neq \mathbf{0}_{m+k},$$

and $\mathbf{p}' f(\mathbf{x}) + \mathbf{q}' h(\mathbf{x}) \geq 0$ for every $\mathbf{x} \in C$. If $\mathbf{p} \geq \mathbf{0}_m$ the second situation takes place. So, suppose that $\mathbf{p} = \mathbf{0}_m$. This implies

$$\mathbf{q}'(B\mathbf{x} - \mathbf{d}) = (B'\mathbf{q})'\mathbf{x} - \mathbf{q}'\mathbf{d} \geq 0 \tag{12.10}$$

for $\mathbf{x} \in \mathbb{R}^n$. We will show that $\mathbf{q}'B = \mathbf{0}'_n$. Suppose that $\mathbf{q}'B \neq \mathbf{0}'_n$. This allows us to choose $\mathbf{x}$ as

$$\mathbf{x} = \begin{cases} -\mathbf{q}'B & \text{if } \mathbf{q}'\mathbf{d} \geq 0, \\ \dfrac{2(\mathbf{q}'\mathbf{d})\mathbf{q}'B}{(\mathbf{q}'B)(\mathbf{q}'B)'} & \text{if } \mathbf{q}'\mathbf{d} < 0. \end{cases}$$

With this choice we have $\mathbf{q}'(B\mathbf{x} - \mathbf{d}) < 0$, which contradicts inequality (12.10). Thus, $\mathbf{q}'B = \mathbf{0}'$, which contradicts the linear independence of the rows of B, a consequence of the fact that $rank(B) = k$. Therefore, we cannot have $\mathbf{p} = \mathbf{0}_m$, so the second situation occurs.

Conversely, suppose that the first situation occurs, so there exists $\mathbf{x}_0 \in \mathbb{R}^n$ such that $f(\mathbf{x}_0) < \mathbf{0}_m$ and $h(\mathbf{x}_0) = B\mathbf{x}_0 - \mathbf{d} = \mathbf{0}_k$. Then, for $\mathbf{p} \geq \mathbf{0}_m$ we have

$$\mathbf{p}'f(\mathbf{x}_0) + \mathbf{q}'(B\mathbf{x}_0 - \mathbf{d}) = \mathbf{p}'f(\mathbf{x}_0) < 0,$$

so the second situation cannot take place. □

Corollary 12.5. *Let C be a convex set, $C \subseteq \mathbb{R}^n$, $f_i : C \longrightarrow \mathbb{R}^{m_i}$ for $1 \leq i \leq 3$ be three convex functions, and let $h : \mathbb{R}^n \longrightarrow \mathbb{R}^k$, where h is a linear function. If the system*

$$f_1(x) < \mathbf{0}_{m_1}, f_2(x) \leqslant \mathbf{0}_{m_2}, f_3(x) \leq \mathbf{0}_{m_3}, h(x) = \mathbf{0}_k$$

has no solution $x \in C$, then there exist $p_1 \in \mathbb{R}^{m_1}$, $p_2 \in \mathbb{R}^{m_2}$, $p_3 \in \mathbb{R}^{m_3}$, and $q \in \mathbb{R}^k$ such that $p_1 \geq \mathbf{0}_{m_1}$, $p_2 \geq \mathbf{0}_{m_2}$, $p_3 \geq \mathbf{0}_{m_3}$,

$$\begin{pmatrix} p_1 \\ p_2 \\ p_3 \\ q \end{pmatrix} \neq \mathbf{0}_{m_1+m_2+m_3+k},$$

and

$$p_1'f_1(x) + p_2'f_2(x) + p_3'f_3(x) + q'h(x) \geq 0$$

for all $x \in C$.

Proof. Suppose that the first system has no solution in C. In this case, neither does the system

$$\mathbf{f}_1(\mathbf{x}) < \mathbf{0}_{m_1}, \mathbf{f}_2(\mathbf{x}) < \mathbf{0}_{m_2}, \mathbf{f}_3(\mathbf{x}) < \mathbf{0}_{m_3}, \mathbf{h}(\mathbf{x}) = \mathbf{0}_k.$$

By Fan-Glicksburg-Hoffman's Theorem if there is no $\mathbf{x} \in C$ such that $\mathbf{f}(\mathbf{x}) < \mathbf{0}_{m_1+m_2+m_3}$ and $\mathbf{h}(\mathbf{x}) = \mathbf{0}_k$, where $\mathbf{f} : \mathbb{R}^n \longrightarrow \mathbb{R}^{m_1+m_2+m_3}$ is defined by

$$\mathbf{f}(\mathbf{x}) = \begin{pmatrix} \mathbf{f}_1(\mathbf{x}) \\ \mathbf{f}_2(\mathbf{x}) \\ \mathbf{f}_3(\mathbf{x}) \end{pmatrix},$$

for $\mathbf{x} \in C$, it follows that there exists $\mathbf{p} \in \mathbb{R}^{m_1+m_2+m_3}$ and $\mathbf{q} \in \mathbb{R}^k$ such that $\mathbf{p} \geq \mathbf{0}_{m_1+m_2+m_3}$,

$$\mathbf{p} = \begin{pmatrix} \mathbf{p}_1 \\ \mathbf{p}_2 \\ \mathbf{p}_3 \end{pmatrix},$$

$$\begin{pmatrix} \mathbf{p}_1 \\ \mathbf{p}_2 \\ \mathbf{p}_3 \\ \mathbf{q} \end{pmatrix} \neq \mathbf{0}_{m_1+m_2+m_3+k}$$

and

$$\mathbf{p}'\mathbf{f}(\mathbf{x}) + \mathbf{q}'\mathbf{h}(\mathbf{x}) = \mathbf{p}_1'\mathbf{f}_1(\mathbf{x}) + \mathbf{p}_2'\mathbf{f}_2(\mathbf{x}) + \mathbf{p}_3'\mathbf{f}_3(\mathbf{x}) + \mathbf{q}'\mathbf{h}(\mathbf{x}) \geq 0$$

for all $\mathbf{x} \in C$. $\qquad\qquad\square$

Corollary 12.6. *Let C be a convex subset of $\mathbb{R}^n$ and $\boldsymbol{f} : C \longrightarrow \mathbb{R}^m$. Exactly one of the following situations occur:*

    (i) *there exists $\boldsymbol{x} \in C$ such that $\boldsymbol{f}(\boldsymbol{x}) < \mathbf{0}_m$;*

    (ii) *there exists $\boldsymbol{p} \in \mathbb{R}^m$ such that $\boldsymbol{p} \geq \mathbf{0}_m$ and $\boldsymbol{p}' f(\boldsymbol{x}) \geq 0$ for all $\boldsymbol{x} \in C$.*

Proof. Suppose that there exists $\mathbf{x} \in C$ such that $\mathbf{f}(\mathbf{x}) < 0$, so for every $\mathbf{p} \geq \mathbf{0}_m$ we have $\mathbf{p}' f(\mathbf{x}) < 0$. Thus, the second alternative fails.

Assume now that the first alternative fails, that is, $\mathbf{f}(\mathbf{x}) \geq \mathbf{0}_m$ for $\mathbf{x} \in C$. By taking $\mathbf{h}$ to be the linear function $\mathbf{h}(\mathbf{x}) = \mathbf{0}_k$ for $\mathbf{x} \in \mathbb{R}^n$ in Theorem 12.28 we obtain the existence of $\mathbf{p} \in \mathbb{R}^m$ such that $\mathbf{p}'\mathbf{f}(\mathbf{x}) + \mathbf{q}'\mathbf{h}(\mathbf{x}) \geq 0$ for every $\mathbf{x} \in C$. $\qquad\qquad\square$

Corollary 12.6 is a generalization of Gordan's Alternative Theorem (Theorem 6.62). Indeed, take $\mathbf{f}$ to be the function $\mathbf{f}(\mathbf{x}) = -A\mathbf{x}$ for $\mathbf{x} \in \mathbb{R}^n$. Then, Corollary 12.6 implies that exactly one of the following situations occur:

(i) there exists $\mathbf{x} \in \mathbb{R}^n$ such that $A\mathbf{x} > \mathbf{0}_m$;

(ii) there exists $\mathbf{p} \geq \mathbf{0}_m$ such that $\mathbf{p}'A\mathbf{x} \leq 0$ for all $\mathbf{x} \in \mathbb{R}^n$.

The first of the above alternatives is exactly the first alternative of Gordan's Alternative Theorem and we can prove that the second alternative is equivalent to the second alternative of Gordan's Alternative Theorem.

Suppose that the second alternative [ii] holds. Choosing $\mathbf{x} = \mathbf{e}_i$ it follows that $\mathbf{p}'\mathbf{a}_i \leq 0$ for every column $\mathbf{a}_i$ of A; choosing $\mathbf{x} = -\mathbf{e}_i$ implies $\mathbf{p}'\mathbf{a}_i \geq 0$, so $\mathbf{p}\mathbf{a}_i = 0$ for every column $\mathbf{a}_i$ of A. Therefore, $\mathbf{p}'A = \mathbf{0}_n'$. This is equivalent to $A'\mathbf{p} = \mathbf{0}_n$, which is exactly the second alternative of Gordan's Alternative Theorem (with $\mathbf{p}$ playing the role of $\mathbf{y}$).

Conversely, if the second Gordan's alternative holds, the first Gordan's alternative fails, so $A\mathbf{x} \leq \mathbf{0}$ for every $\mathbf{x} \in \mathbb{R}^n$. Thus, if $\mathbf{p} \geq \mathbf{0}_m$, we have $\mathbf{p}'A\mathbf{x} \leq 0$ for all $\mathbf{x} \in \mathbb{R}^n$, which is exactly the alternative [ii].

The next result was obtained in [17].

Theorem 12.30. (Bohnenblust-Karlin-Shapley Theorem) *Let C be a compact subset in $\mathbb{R}^n$ and let $\mathcal{F} = \{f_i : C \longrightarrow \mathbb{R} \mid i \in I\}$ be a collection of convex, lower semicontinuous functions on C.*

If $\bigcap_{i \in I}\{\boldsymbol{x} \in C \mid f_i(\boldsymbol{x}) \leq 0\} = \emptyset$, then for any finite subcollection $\{f_{i_1}, \ldots, f_{i_m}\} \subseteq \mathcal{F}$ there exists $\boldsymbol{p} \in \mathbb{R}^m$, $\boldsymbol{p} \geq \mathbf{0}_m$, and $\sum_{r=1}^m p_i = 1$ such that

$$\sum_{r=1}^m p_r f_{i_r}(\boldsymbol{x}) > 0.$$

Proof. We claim that $\bigcap_{\epsilon > 0} \bigcap_{i \in I}\{\mathbf{x} \in C \mid f_i(\mathbf{x}) \leq \epsilon\} = \emptyset$. Indeed, suppose that $\mathbf{x} \in \bigcap_{\epsilon > 0} \bigcap_{i \in I}\{\mathbf{x} \in C \mid f_i(\mathbf{x}) \leq \epsilon\}$. Then, $f_i(\mathbf{x}) \leqslant 0$ for every $i \in I$, and this contradicts the hypothesis.

Note that the sets $K(i, \epsilon) = \{\mathbf{x} \in C \mid f_i(\mathbf{x}) \leq \epsilon\}$ are closed sets because C is compact and f_i are semicontinuous functions. Therefore, $\bigcap_{\epsilon > 0} \bigcap_{i \in I} K(i, \epsilon) = \emptyset$. By the finite intersection property, there is a finite set $\{i_1, \ldots, i_m\} \subseteq I$ and a finite set of numbers $\{\epsilon_1, \ldots, \epsilon_m\}$ such that $\bigcap_{j=1}^m K(f_{i_j}, \epsilon_j) = \emptyset$. This is equivalent to saying that the system $f_{i_j}(\mathbf{x}) - \epsilon_j < 0$ for $1 \leq j \leq m$ has no solution. Let $f : C \longrightarrow \mathbb{R}^m$ be the function defined by

$$f(\mathbf{x}) = \begin{pmatrix} f_{i_1}(\mathbf{x}) - \epsilon_1 \\ \vdots \\ f_{i_m}(\mathbf{x}) - \epsilon_m \end{pmatrix},$$

for $\mathbf{x} \in C$. Then, there exists no $\mathbf{x} \in C$ such that $f(\mathbf{x}) < \mathbf{0}_m$, so, by Corollary 12.6, there exists $\mathbf{p} \in \mathbb{R}^m$ such that $\mathbf{p} \geq \mathbf{0}_m$ and $\mathbf{p}'f(\mathbf{x}) \geq$

$\sum_{j=1}^{m} p_j \epsilon_j > 0$ for all $\mathbf{x} \in C$. Since

$$\mathbf{p}'f(\mathbf{x}) = \sum_{r=1}^{m} p_r f_{i_r}(\mathbf{x}),$$

we have reached the desired conclusion. □

12.8   Subgradients

Definition 12.10. Let $f : \mathbb{R}^n \longrightarrow \mathbb{R} \cup \{\infty\}$. The function f is:

(i) *sublinear* if

$$f(a\mathbf{x} + b\mathbf{y}) \leqslant af(\mathbf{x}) + bf(\mathbf{y}) \qquad (12.11)$$

for every $a, b \in \mathbb{R}_{\geqslant 0}$ and $\mathbf{x}, \mathbf{y} \in \mathbb{R}^n$;

(ii) *subadditive* if $f(\mathbf{x} + \mathbf{y}) \leqslant f(\mathbf{x}) + f(\mathbf{y})$ for $\mathbf{x}, \mathbf{y} \in \mathbb{R}^n$;

(iii) *positively homogeneous* if $f(a\mathbf{x}) = af(\mathbf{x})$ for $a > 0$.

Theorem 12.31. *A function* $f : \mathbb{R}^n \longrightarrow \mathbb{R} \cup \{\infty\}$ *is sublinear if and only if it is positively homogeneous and subadditive.*

Proof.   Let $f : \mathbb{R}^n \longrightarrow \mathbb{R} \cup \{\infty\}$ be a sublinear function. The subadditivity of f follows from inequality (12.11) by taking $a = b = 1$. The positive homogeneity follows from the same by taking $a = 1$ and $b = 0$.

Conversely, suppose that f is both subadditive and positively homogeneous and let $a, b \in \mathbb{R}_{\geqslant 0}$. We can write

$$f(a\mathbf{x} + b\mathbf{y}) \leqslant f(a\mathbf{x}) + f(b\mathbf{y})$$

$$\text{(by subadditivity)}$$

$$= af(\mathbf{x}) + bf(\mathbf{y})$$

$$\text{(by positive homogeneity).} \qquad □$$

Corollary 12.7. *A function* $f : \mathbb{R}^n \longrightarrow \mathbb{R} \cup \{\infty\}$ *is linear if and only if it is sublinear and* $f(-\boldsymbol{x}) = -f(\boldsymbol{x})$ *for* $\boldsymbol{x} \in \mathbb{R}^n$.

Proof.   Suppose that f is sublinear and $f(-\mathbf{x}) = -f(\mathbf{x})$ for $\mathbf{x} \in \mathbb{R}^n$. Let $a > 0$. We have $f((-a)\mathbf{x}) = f(-a\mathbf{x}) = -f(a\mathbf{x}) = -af(\mathbf{x})$, so f is actually homogeneous. Furthermore, by subadditivity, we have $f(-\mathbf{x}-\mathbf{y}) \leqslant f(-\mathbf{x}) + f(-\mathbf{y})$, which implies $-f(\mathbf{x}+\mathbf{y}) \leqslant -f(\mathbf{x}) - f(\mathbf{y})$ (by homogeneity), hence $f(\mathbf{x}+\mathbf{y}) \geqslant f(\mathbf{x}) + f(\mathbf{y})$. Thus, f is additive and homogeneous, hence linear.

The reverse implication is immediate. □

Theorem 12.32. *Let* $f : \mathbb{R}^n \longrightarrow \mathbb{R} \cup \{\infty\}$ *be a convex function. For every* $\boldsymbol{x}_0 \in \mathrm{Dom}(f)$ *the directional derivative* $\frac{\partial f}{\partial \boldsymbol{u}}(\boldsymbol{x}_0)$ *is defined and is sublinear.*

Proof. Let $g(\mathbf{x}, \mathbf{u}, a) = \frac{f(\mathbf{x}+a\mathbf{u})-f(\mathbf{x})}{a}$. By Supplement 11, $0 < a_1 \leqslant a_2$ imply

$$g(\mathbf{x}_0, \mathbf{u}, -a_2) \leqslant g(\mathbf{x}_0, \mathbf{u}, -a_1) \leqslant g(\mathbf{x}_0, \mathbf{u}, a_1) \leqslant g(\mathbf{x}_0, \mathbf{u}, a_2).$$

Since $\mathbf{x}_0 \in \mathrm{Dom}(f)$, both $g(\mathbf{x}_0, \mathbf{u}, -a_2)$ and $g(\mathbf{x}_0, \mathbf{u}, a_2)$ are finite. Since $\frac{\partial f}{\partial u}(\mathbf{x}_0) = \lim_{a_2 \downarrow 0} g(\mathbf{x}_0, \mathbf{u}, a_2)$, it follows that the directional derivative is everywhere finite. Supplement 12 implies

$$g(\mathbf{x}_0, \mathbf{u}_1 + \mathbf{u}_2, a) \leqslant g(\mathbf{x}_0, \mathbf{u}_1, 2a) + g(\mathbf{x}_0, \mathbf{u}_2, 2a).$$

Taking $a \to 0$ shows that $\frac{\partial f}{\partial \mathbf{u}}(\mathbf{x}_0)$ is subadditive. The positive homogeneity is immediate, hence $\frac{\partial f}{\partial \mathbf{u}}(\mathbf{x}_0)$ is sublinear. $\qquad\square$

Definition 12.11. Let $f : S \longrightarrow \mathbb{R} \cup \{\infty\}$ be a non-trivial convex function, where $S \subseteq \mathbb{R}^n$. A *subgradient* of f at $\mathbf{x}_0$ is a vector $\mathbf{s} \in \mathbb{R}^n$ such that

$$f(\mathbf{x}) - f(\mathbf{x}_0) \geqslant \mathbf{s}'(\mathbf{x} - \mathbf{x}_0)$$

for every $\mathbf{x} \in \mathbb{R}^n$.

If $f : S \longrightarrow \mathbb{R}$ be a non-trivial concave function, where $S \subseteq \mathbb{R}^n$, then $\mathbf{s} \in \mathbb{R}^n$ is a *subgradient* of f in $\mathbf{x}_0$ if

$$f(\mathbf{x}) - f(\mathbf{x}_0) \leqslant \mathbf{s}'(\mathbf{x} - \mathbf{x}_0)$$

for every $\mathbf{x} \in \mathbb{R}^n$.

Theorem 12.33. *Let* $f : \mathbb{R}^n \longrightarrow \mathbb{R} \cup \{\infty\}$ *be a convex function and let* $\boldsymbol{x}_0 \in \boldsymbol{I}(\mathrm{Dom}(f))$. *There exists a subgradient of* f *at* $\boldsymbol{x}_0$.

Proof. Note that if $\mathbf{x}_0 \in \boldsymbol{I}(\mathrm{Dom}(f))$ the point $\begin{pmatrix} \mathbf{x}_0 \\ f(\mathbf{x}_0) \end{pmatrix}$ belongs to $\partial(\mathrm{epi}(f))$. Since $\mathrm{epi}(f)$ is a convex set, by Theorem 6.49 there exists a supporting hyperplane H of $\mathrm{epi}(f)$ in $\mathbb{R}^{n+1}$ at $\begin{pmatrix} \mathbf{x}_0 \\ f(\mathbf{x}_0) \end{pmatrix}$, that is, there exist $\mathbf{a} \in \mathbb{R}^n$ and $b \in \mathbb{R}$ such that

$$(\mathbf{a}'\, b)\left(\begin{pmatrix} \mathbf{x} \\ y \end{pmatrix} - \begin{pmatrix} \mathbf{x}_0 \\ f(\mathbf{x}_0) \end{pmatrix} \right) \geqslant 0,$$

or

$$\mathbf{a}'(\mathbf{x} - \mathbf{x}_0) + b(y - f(\mathbf{x}_0)) \geqslant 0 \tag{12.12}$$

for all $\begin{pmatrix} \mathbf{x} \\ y \end{pmatrix} \in \mathrm{epi}(f)$.

Since $(\mathbf{x}_0, y) \in \mathsf{epi}(f)$ if $y > f(\mathbf{x}_0)$, by substituting $\mathbf{x}_0$ for $\mathbf{x}$ in inequality (12.12) it follows that $b \geqslant 0$.

We claim that $b > 0$, that is, H is not a vertical hyperplane. Indeed, since $\mathbf{x}_0 \in \mathbf{I}(\mathrm{Dom}(f))$, there exists $\epsilon > 0$ such that $\|\mathbf{x} - \mathbf{x}_0\| < \epsilon$ implies $\mathbf{x} \in \mathbf{I}(\mathrm{Dom}(f))$. If $\mathbf{a} \neq \mathbf{0}_n$, $\mathbf{a}'(\mathbf{x} - \mathbf{x}_0)$ can be made negative for a suitable choice of $\mathbf{x}$ (according to Theorem 2.12), which implies $b > 0$ in order for $\mathbf{a}'(\mathbf{x} - \mathbf{x}_0) + b(y - f(\mathbf{x}_0)) \geqslant 0$ to hold. In this case, we must have $b > 0$ because we cannot have both $\mathbf{a} = \mathbf{0}$ and $b = 0$. Therefore, $b > 0$.

Since $b > 0$ we have

$$\frac{1}{b}\mathbf{a}'(\mathbf{x} - \mathbf{x}_0) + y - f(\mathbf{x}_0) \geqslant 0.$$

Substituting $y = f(\mathbf{x})$, it follows that $\frac{1}{b}\mathbf{a}'$ is a subgradient of f at $\mathbf{x}_0$. $\qquad \square$

Note that if $\mathbf{x}_0 \notin \mathrm{Dom}(f)$, that is, if $f(\mathbf{x}_0) = \infty$ then there is no subgradient at $\mathbf{x}_0$. Indeed, if $\mathbf{s}$ would be such a subgradient, the inequality $f(\mathbf{x}) \geqslant f(\mathbf{x}_0) + \mathbf{s}'(\mathbf{x} - \mathbf{x}_0)$ would imply $f(\mathbf{x}) = \infty$ for every $\mathbf{x} \in \mathbb{R}^n$, hence f would be the trivial function f_∞, which is excluded from the definition of the subgradient.

Definition 12.12. The *sign function* is the function $sign : \mathbb{R} \longrightarrow \{-1, 0, 1\}$ given by:

$$sign(x) = \begin{cases} 1 & \text{if } x > 0, \\ 0 & \text{if } x = 0, \\ -1 & \text{if } x < 0. \end{cases}$$

This function can be extended to $\mathbb{R}^n$, as $sign : \mathbb{R}^n \longrightarrow \{-1, 0, 1\}^n$, where

$$sign(\mathbf{x}) = \begin{pmatrix} sign(x_1) \\ \vdots \\ sign(x_n) \end{pmatrix}.$$

Example 12.19. Let $f : \mathbb{R} \longrightarrow \mathbb{R}$ be the absolute value function, $f(x) = |x|$. For $x_0 \neq 0$ there exists a unique subgradient, -1 for $x_0 < 0$ and 1 for $x_0 > 0$.

Indeed, suppose that $x_0 > 0$ and let $x = x_0 + h$. We have $|x_0 + h| - x_0 \geqslant sh$ for every h. For $h > 0$ we have $h \geqslant sh$, so $s \leqslant 1$. For $h < 0$ and $x_0 + h > 0$ (which is possible since $x_0 > 0$) we have $h \geqslant sh$, which yields $s \geqslant 1$. Thus $s = 1$. A similar argument shows that if $x_0 < 0$, then $s = -1$.

If $x_0 = 0$, then any $s \in [-1, 1]$ is a subgradient because, in this case we have $|x| \geqslant sx$ for every $s \in [-1, 1]$. We conclude that the subdifferential of f is

$$\text{subd}(f)(x) = \begin{cases} sign(x) & \text{if } x \neq 0, \\ [-1, 1] & \text{if } x = 0. \end{cases}$$

Theorem 12.34. *The set of subgradients of a convex function at a given point is convex.*

Proof. Let $\mathbf{s}_1, \mathbf{s}_2$ be subgradients of a convex function $f : S \longrightarrow \mathbb{R}$ at $\mathbf{x}_0$, that is,

$$f(\mathbf{x}) \geqslant f(\mathbf{x}_0) + \mathbf{s}_1'(\mathbf{x} - \mathbf{x}_0),$$
$$f(\mathbf{x}) \geqslant f(\mathbf{x}_0) + \mathbf{s}_2'(\mathbf{x} - \mathbf{x}_0)$$

for every $\mathbf{x} \in \mathbb{R}^n$. Therefore, for $t \in [0, 1]$ we have

$$f(\mathbf{x}) \geqslant f(\mathbf{x}_0) + ((1 - t)\mathbf{s}_1 + t\mathbf{s}_2)(\mathbf{x} - \mathbf{x}_0),$$

which shows that $(1 - t)\mathbf{s}_1 + t\mathbf{s}_2$ is also a subgradient of f at $\mathbf{x}_0$. □

The same convexity property holds for the set of subgradients of a concave function.

Definition 12.13. Let S be a subset of $\mathbb{R}^n$. The *subdifferential of a function* $f : S \longrightarrow \mathbb{R}$ *at* $\mathbf{x}_0$ is the set of all subgradients at $\mathbf{x}_0$ denoted by $\text{subd}(f)(\mathbf{x}_0)$,

$$\text{subd}(f)(\mathbf{x}_0) = \{\mathbf{s} \mid \mathbf{s}'(\mathbf{x} - \mathbf{x}_0) \leqslant f(\mathbf{x}) - f(\mathbf{x}_0) \text{ for all } \mathbf{x} \in \mathbb{R}^n\}.$$

If $\text{subd}(f)(\mathbf{x}_0) \neq \emptyset$, we say that f is *subdifferentiable* at $\mathbf{x}_0$.

Theorem 12.35. *Let* $f : \mathbb{R}^n \longrightarrow \mathbb{R} \cup \{\infty\}$ *be a convex function, and let* $x_0 \in \text{Dom}(f)$. *The subdifferential* $\text{subd}(f)(x_0)$ *is a convex, compact, and closed set.*

Proof. Let $D_{\mathbf{x}, \mathbf{x}_0} = \{\mathbf{s} \in \mathbb{R}^n \mid \mathbf{s}'(\mathbf{x} - \mathbf{x}_0) \leqslant f(\mathbf{x}) - f(\mathbf{x}_0)\}$. Each set $D_{\mathbf{x}, \mathbf{x}_0}$ is a closed half-space that is convex. Since $\text{subd}(f)(\mathbf{x}_0) = \bigcap_{\mathbf{x} \in \mathbb{R}^n} D_{\mathbf{x}, \mathbf{x}_0}$, it follows that $\text{subd}(f)(\mathbf{x}_0)$ is closed and convex.

In the proof of Almgren's Theorem (Theorem 12.3), we have shown that f is locally Lipschitz in $\mathbf{x}_0$, hence $|f(\mathbf{x}) - f(\mathbf{x}_0)| \leqslant c\|\mathbf{x} - \mathbf{x}_0\|$ for some constant c and for every $\mathbf{x} \in B(\mathbf{x}_0, r)$. Therefore, if $\mathbf{s} \in \text{subd}(f)(\mathbf{x}_0)$, we have

$$\mathbf{s}'(\mathbf{x} - \mathbf{x}_0) \leqslant f(\mathbf{x}) - f(\mathbf{x}_0) \leqslant c\|\mathbf{x} - \mathbf{x}_0\|.$$

Choosing $\mathbf{x} - \mathbf{x}_0 = a\mathbf{s}$ for a sufficiently small and positive a, we have $\|\mathbf{s}\| \leqslant c$, so $\mathsf{subd}(f)(\mathbf{x}_0)$ is a bounded set. Since $\mathsf{subd}(f)(\mathbf{x}_0)$ is closed and bounded, it follows by Heine-Borel Theorem (Theorem 5.44) that $\mathsf{subd}(f)(\mathbf{x}_0)$ is compact. □

Let $\mathbf{x}_0, \mathbf{x}$ and let $\mathbf{x} - \mathbf{x}_0 = t\mathbf{u}$. A vector $\mathbf{s}$ is a subgradient of a function $f : \mathbb{R}^n \longrightarrow \mathbb{R} \cup \{\infty\}$ at $\mathbf{x}_0$ if and only if $f(\mathbf{x}_0 + t\mathbf{u}) - f(\mathbf{x}_0) \geqslant t\mathbf{s}'\mathbf{u}$, which is equivalent to

$$\mathbf{s}'\mathbf{u} \leqslant \frac{\partial f}{\partial \mathbf{u}}(\mathbf{x}_0). \tag{12.13}$$

If $f : \mathbb{R}^n \longrightarrow \mathbb{R}$, then it is straightforward to verify that $\mathsf{subd}(af)(\mathbf{x}) = a\mathsf{subd}(f)(\mathbf{x})$ for every positive a.

Theorem 12.36. (Moreau-Rockafellar Theorem) *Let $f, g : \mathbb{R}^n \longrightarrow \mathbb{R}$ be convex functions. We have*

$$\mathsf{subd}(f)(\boldsymbol{x}_0) + \mathsf{subd}(g)(\boldsymbol{x}_0) \subseteq \mathsf{subd}(f+g)(\boldsymbol{x}_0).$$

Furthermore, if $\boldsymbol{I}(\mathrm{Dom}(f)) \cap \mathrm{Dom}(g) \neq \emptyset$ then we have the equality:

$$\mathsf{subd}(f)(\boldsymbol{x}_0) + \mathsf{subd}(g)(\boldsymbol{x}_0) = \mathsf{subd}(f+g)(\boldsymbol{x}_0)$$

for $\boldsymbol{x} \in \mathbb{R}^n$.

Proof. Suppose that $\mathbf{u} \in \mathsf{subd}(f)(\mathbf{x}_0)$ and $\mathbf{v} \in \mathsf{subd}(g)(\mathbf{x}_0)$ and let $\mathbf{w} = \mathbf{u} + \mathbf{v}$. Then for all $\mathbf{x} \in \mathbb{R}^n$ we have

$$f(\mathbf{x}) \geqslant f(\mathbf{x}_0) + \mathbf{u}'(\mathbf{x} - \mathbf{x}_0) \text{ and } g(\mathbf{x}) \geqslant g(\mathbf{x}_0) + \mathbf{v}'(\mathbf{x} - \mathbf{x}_0).$$

This implies

$$f(x) + g(x) \geqslant f(\mathbf{x}_0) + g(\mathbf{x}_0) + (\mathbf{u} + \mathbf{v})'(\mathbf{x} - \mathbf{x}_0),$$

hence $\mathbf{u} + \mathbf{v} \in \mathsf{subd}(f+g)(\mathbf{x}_0)$, which completes the argument for the first part.

Let $\mathbf{s} \in \mathsf{subd}(f+g)(\mathbf{x}_0)$. Note that $f(\mathbf{x}_0) = \infty$ or $g(\mathbf{x}_0) = \infty$ imply $(f+g)(\mathbf{x}_0) = \infty$, which is not the case because of the existence of $\mathbf{s}$. Thus, we may assume that $f(\mathbf{x}_0)$ and $g(\mathbf{x}_0)$ belong to $\mathbb{R}$.

Define the subsets $U_{\mathbf{s}}, V$ of $\mathbb{R}^n \times \mathbb{R}$ as

$$U_{\mathbf{s}} = \{(\mathbf{x} - \mathbf{x}_0, y) \in \mathbb{R}^n \times \mathbb{R} \mid y > f(\mathbf{x}) - f(\mathbf{x}_0) - \mathbf{s}'(\mathbf{x} - \mathbf{x}_0)\},$$
$$V = \{(\mathbf{x} - \mathbf{x}_0, y) \in \mathbb{R}^n \times \mathbb{R} \mid -y \leqslant g(\mathbf{x}) - g(\mathbf{x}_0)\}.$$

The sets $U_{\mathbf{s}}$ and V are disjoint. Indeed, suppose that $(\mathbf{x}_0, y) \in U_{\mathbf{s}} \cap V$. This would imply $y > f(\mathbf{x}) - f(\mathbf{x}_0) - \mathbf{s}'(\mathbf{x} - \mathbf{x}_0)$ and $-y \leqslant g(\mathbf{x}) - g(\mathbf{x}_0)\}$, or $y \geqslant g(\mathbf{x}_0) - g(\mathbf{x})$, hence

$$f(\mathbf{x}) - f(\mathbf{x}_0) - \mathbf{s}'(\mathbf{x} - \mathbf{x}_0) < g(\mathbf{x}_0) - g(\mathbf{x}).$$

The last inequality is equivalent to

$$(f + g)(\mathbf{x}) - (f + g)(\mathbf{x}_0) < \mathbf{s}'(\mathbf{x} - \mathbf{x}_0),$$

which contradicts the fact that $\mathbf{s} \in \mathsf{subd}(f + g)(\mathbf{x}_0)$.

Since the sets $U_{\mathbf{s}}$ and V are convex and disjoint, they can be separated and there exists $(\mathbf{s}_0, a) \in \mathbb{R}^{n+1} - \{\mathbf{0}_{n+1}\}$ and $b \in \mathbb{R}$ such that

$$y > f(\mathbf{x}) - f(\mathbf{x}_0) - \mathbf{s}'(\mathbf{x} - \mathbf{x}_0) \text{ implies } \mathbf{s}_0'(\mathbf{x} - \mathbf{x}_0) + ay \leqslant b, \quad (12.14)$$

$$-y \leqslant g(\mathbf{x}) - g(\mathbf{x}_0) \text{ implies } \mathbf{s}_0'(\mathbf{x} - \mathbf{x}_0) + ay \geqslant b. \quad (12.15)$$

Since $\mathbf{0}_{n+1} \in V$, $b \leqslant 0$. Also, since $(\mathbf{0}_n, \epsilon) \in U_{\mathbf{s}}$ for every $\epsilon > 0$, we have $a\epsilon \leqslant b$, hence $a \leqslant 0$. If $\epsilon \to 0$, we obtain $b \geqslant 0$, hence $b = 0$.

Note that we cannot have $a = 0$. Indeed, if $a = 0$, then the implication (12.14) would mean that

$$y > f(\mathbf{x}) - f(\mathbf{x}_0) - \mathbf{s}'(\mathbf{x} - \mathbf{x}_0) \text{ implies } \mathbf{s}_0'(\mathbf{x} - \mathbf{x}_0) \leqslant 0,$$

hence $\mathbf{s}_0'(\mathbf{x} - \mathbf{x}_0) \leqslant 0$ for $x \in \mathsf{Dom}(f)$ because when $f(\mathbf{x}) < \infty$ there exists a sufficiently large y such that $y > f(\mathbf{x}) - f(\mathbf{x}_0) - \mathbf{s}'(\mathbf{x} - \mathbf{x}_0)$.

The second implication yields $\mathbf{s}_0'(\mathbf{x} - \mathbf{x}_0) \geqslant 0$ for $x \in \mathsf{Dom}(g)$.

If $\tilde{\mathbf{x}} \in \mathbf{I}(\mathsf{Dom}(f)) \cap \mathsf{Dom}(g)$ we have $\mathbf{s}_0'(\tilde{\mathbf{x}} - \mathbf{x}_0) = 0$. Since $\tilde{\mathbf{x}} \in \tilde{\mathbf{x}} \in \mathbf{I}(\mathsf{Dom}(f))$, there exists $\delta > 0$ such that $\tilde{\mathbf{x}} \in B(\tilde{x}, \delta) \subseteq \mathsf{Dom}(f)$, hence $\mathbf{s}_0'\mathbf{u} = \mathbf{s}_0'(\tilde{\mathbf{x}} + \mathbf{u} - \mathbf{x}_0) \leqslant 0$ for all $\mathbf{u} \in B(\mathbf{x}_0, \delta)$. Choosing $\mathbf{u} = \frac{\delta}{2}\mathbf{s}$ this would imply $\mathbf{s}_0' = \mathbf{0}$, contradicting the fact that $(\mathbf{s}_0, a) \in \mathbb{R}^{n+1} - \{\mathbf{0}_{n+1}\}$. Hence $a < 0$.

For $\mathbf{s}_1 = -\frac{1}{a}\mathbf{s}_0$ the previous implications become

$$y > f(\mathbf{x}) - f(\mathbf{x}_0) - \mathbf{s}'(\mathbf{x} - \mathbf{x}_0) \text{ implies } \mathbf{s}_1'(\mathbf{x} - \mathbf{x}_0) \leqslant y, \quad (12.16)$$

$$-y \leqslant g(\mathbf{x}) - g(\mathbf{x}_0) \text{ implies } \mathbf{s}_1'(\mathbf{x} - \mathbf{x}_0) \geqslant y. \quad (12.17)$$

By taking $y = g(\mathbf{x}_0) - g(\mathbf{x})$ in the last inequality we have $-\mathbf{s}_1 \in \mathsf{subd}(g)(\mathbf{x}_0)$.

By taking $y = f(\mathbf{x}) - f(\mathbf{x}_0) - \mathbf{s}'(\mathbf{x} - \mathbf{x}_0) + \epsilon$ in inequality (12.16) we have $\mathbf{s} + \mathbf{s}_1 \in \mathsf{subd}(f)(\mathbf{x}_0)$. Since

$$\mathbf{s} = (\mathbf{s} + \mathbf{s}_1) - \mathbf{s}_1 \in \mathsf{subd}(f)(\mathbf{x}_0) + \mathsf{subd}(g)(\mathbf{x}_0),$$

this concludes the proof. $\qquad\square$

Theorem 12.37. *Let $f : S \longrightarrow \mathbb{R} \cup \{\infty\}$ be a proper convex function. A point $\mathbf{x}_0$ is a global minimizer for f if and only if $\mathbf{0}_n \in \mathsf{subd}(f)(\mathbf{x}_0)$.*

Proof. If $\mathbf{x}_0 \in \mathbb{R}^n$ is a global minimizer of f, that is, $f(\mathbf{x}_0) \leqslant f(\mathbf{x})$ for every $\mathbf{x} \in \mathbb{R}^n$.

If $\mathbf{0}_n \in \mathsf{subd}(f)(\mathbf{x}_0)$, then $f(\mathbf{x}) - f(\mathbf{x}_0) \geqslant \mathbf{0}_n'(\mathbf{x} - \mathbf{x}_0) = 0$, hence $f(\mathbf{x}_0) \leqslant f(\mathbf{x})$ and $\mathbf{x}_0$ is a global minimizer.

Conversely, suppose that $\mathbf{x}_0$ is a global minimizer. The inequality $f(\mathbf{x}) - f(\mathbf{x}_0) \geqslant \mathbf{s}'(\mathbf{x} - \mathbf{x}_0)$ is satisfied for $\mathbf{0}_n$, so $\mathbf{0}_n \in \mathsf{subd}(f)(\mathbf{x}_0)$. $\qquad\square$

A more general statement is given next.

Theorem 12.38. *Let C be a non-empty convex subset of $\mathbb{R}^n$ and let $f : \mathbb{R}^n \longrightarrow \mathbb{R}$ be a convex function. The vector $\boldsymbol{x}_0$ is a minimizer of f restricted to C if and only if there exists $\boldsymbol{s} \in \mathsf{subd}(f)(\boldsymbol{x}_0)$ such that $\boldsymbol{s}'(\boldsymbol{x} - \boldsymbol{x}_0) \geqslant 0$ for every $\boldsymbol{x} \in C$.*

Proof. The condition is obviously sufficient.

Consider the convex function $g = f + I_C$, where I_C is the indicator function of C. If $\mathbf{x}_0 \in C$ is a minimizer for f, it follows that $\mathbf{x}_0$ is a minimizer for g because $I_C(\mathbf{x}_0) = 0$, hence $\mathbf{0}_n \in \mathsf{subd}(f + I_C)(\mathbf{x}_0)$. Observe that

$$\mathbf{I}(\mathrm{Dom}(f)) \cap \mathrm{Dom}(I_C) = \mathbb{R}^n \cap C = C,$$

hence by Moreau-Rockafellar Theorem (Theorem 12.36), we have $\mathsf{subd}(f + I_C)(\mathbf{x}_0) = \mathsf{subd}(f)(\mathbf{x}_0)\mathsf{subd}(I_C)(\mathbf{x}_0)$. Thus, we must have $\mathbf{0}_n = \mathbf{s} + \mathbf{z}$, where $\mathbf{s} \in \mathsf{subd}(f)(\mathbf{x}_0)$ and $\mathbf{z} \in \mathsf{subd}(I_C)(\mathbf{x}_0)$. Since $\mathbf{z} = -\mathbf{s}$, we have $I_C(\mathbf{x}) - I_C(\mathbf{x}_0) = 0 \geqslant -\mathbf{s}'(\mathbf{x} - \mathbf{x}_0)$, which amounts to $\mathbf{s}'(\mathbf{x} - \mathbf{x}_0) \geqslant 0$ for every $\mathbf{x} \in C$. $\qquad\square$

Lemma 12.3. *Let $S \subseteq \mathbb{R}^n$ and let $f : S \longrightarrow \mathbb{R} \cup \{\infty\}$ be a proper and convex function. If $\boldsymbol{x}_0 \in \mathrm{Dom}(f)$, then for each $\boldsymbol{u} \in S$ and $\boldsymbol{s} \in \mathsf{subd}(f)(\boldsymbol{x}_0)$ we have:*

$$\boldsymbol{s}'\boldsymbol{u} \leqslant \frac{\partial f}{\partial \boldsymbol{u}}(\boldsymbol{x}_0).$$

Proof. For $\mathbf{s} \in \mathsf{subd}(f)(\mathbf{x}_0)$ we have $\mathbf{s}'(\mathbf{x} - \mathbf{x}_0) \leqslant f(\mathbf{x}) - f(\mathbf{x}_0)$ for all $\mathbf{x} \in \mathbb{R}^n$. Let $\mathbf{x} = \mathbf{x}_0 + t\mathbf{u}$ with $t > 0$. The previous inequality amounts to

$$t\mathbf{s}'\mathbf{u} \leqslant f(\mathbf{x}_0 + t\mathbf{u}) - f(\mathbf{x}_0),$$

hence $\mathbf{s}'\mathbf{u} \leqslant \frac{f(\mathbf{x}_0 + t\mathbf{u}) - f(\mathbf{x}_0)}{t}$ for every $t > 0$. Therefore,

$$\mathbf{s}'\mathbf{u} \leqslant \lim_{t \downarrow 0} \frac{f(\mathbf{x}_0 + t\mathbf{u}) - f(\mathbf{x}_0)}{t} = \frac{\partial f}{\partial \mathbf{u}}(\mathbf{x}_0). \qquad\square$$

The following result obtained in [19] is also known as the MAX Theorem.

Theorem 12.39. (Borwein's Theorem) *Let $S \subseteq \mathbb{R}^n$ and let $f : S \longrightarrow \mathbb{R} \cup \{\infty\}$ be a proper and convex function. If $\boldsymbol{x}_0 \in \mathrm{Dom}(f)$, then for each $\boldsymbol{u} \in S$ we have:*

$$\frac{\partial f}{\partial \boldsymbol{u}}(\boldsymbol{x}_0) = \max\{\boldsymbol{s}'\boldsymbol{u} \mid \boldsymbol{s} \in \mathsf{subd}(f)(\boldsymbol{x}_0)\}.$$

Proof. Lemma 12.3 shows that $\frac{\partial f}{\partial \mathbf{u}}(\mathbf{x}_0)$ is an upper bound of the set $\{\mathbf{s}'\mathbf{u} \mid \mathbf{s} \in \mathrm{subd}(f)(\mathbf{x}_0)\}$. To prove the theorem, it suffices to show that there exists a subgradient $\mathbf{s}_*$ such that $\mathbf{s}'_*\mathbf{u} = \frac{\partial f}{\partial \mathbf{u}}(\mathbf{x}_0)$.

Let $\{\mathbf{b}_1, \ldots, \mathbf{b}_n\}$ be a base for $\mathbb{R}^n$, where $\mathbf{b}_1 = \mathbf{h}$. Define the sequence of functions $p_0, p_1, \ldots, p_n$ as

$$p_0(\mathbf{u}) = \frac{\partial f}{\partial \mathbf{u}}(\mathbf{x}_0), p_k(\mathbf{u}) = \frac{\partial p_{k-1}}{\partial \mathbf{u}}(\mathbf{b}_k)$$

for $1 \leqslant k \leqslant n$. Each of the function $p_0, \ldots, p_n$ is sublinear and finite.

By Supplement 11 we have:

$$\frac{p_{k-1}(\mathbf{x}_0 + r\mathbf{u}) - p_{k-1}(\mathbf{x}_0)}{r} \geqslant \lim_{t \downarrow 0} \frac{p_{k-1}(\mathbf{x}_0 + t\mathbf{u}) - p_{k-1}(\mathbf{x}_0)}{t} = \frac{\partial p_{k-1}}{\partial \mathbf{u}}(x_0)$$

for $r \geqslant 0$. Taking $r = 1$ this implies:

$$p_k(\mathbf{u}) = \frac{\partial p_{k-1}}{\partial \mathbf{u}}(\mathbf{b}_k) \leqslant p_{k-1}(\mathbf{x}_0 + \mathbf{u}) - p_{k-1}(\mathbf{x}_0)$$
$$= \leqslant p_{k-1}(\mathbf{u}).$$

Thus, for $\mathbf{x} \in S$ and $1 \leqslant k \leqslant n$ we have

$$p_n(\mathbf{u}) \leqslant \cdots \leqslant p_k(\mathbf{u}) \leqslant p_{k-1}(\mathbf{u}) \leqslant \cdots \leqslant p_0(\mathbf{u}).$$

The definition of p_k implies that for $1 \leqslant k \leqslant m \leqslant n$ we have

$$0 \leqslant p_m(\mathbf{b}_k) + p_m(-\mathbf{b}_k) \leqslant p_k(\mathbf{b}_k) + p_k(-\mathbf{b}_k)$$
$$= p_{k-1}(\mathbf{b}_k) - p_{k-1}(\mathbf{b}_k) = 0.$$

This shows that $p_m(-\mathbf{b}_k) = -p_m(\mathbf{b}_k)$ for $1 \leqslant k \leqslant m \leqslant n$, which implies that the sublinear function p_m is actually linear on $\langle \mathbf{b}_1, \ldots, \mathbf{b}_m \rangle$. In particular, p_n is be linear on $\langle \mathbf{b}_1, \ldots, \mathbf{b}_n \rangle = \mathbb{R}^n$.

Set $\mathbf{s}_* = p_n(\mathbf{u})$. We have $\mathbf{s}'_*(\mathbf{x} - \mathbf{x}_0) \leqslant p_0(\mathbf{x} - \mathbf{x}_0) \leqslant f(\mathbf{x}) - f(\mathbf{x}_0)$ for $\mathbf{x} \in S$, hence $\mathbf{s}_* \in \mathrm{subd}(f)(\mathbf{x}_0)$. Finally, we have

$$-\mathbf{s}'_*\mathbf{u} = \mathbf{s}'_*(-\mathbf{b}_1) \leqslant p_1(-\mathbf{b}_1) = -p_0(\mathbf{b}_1) = -p_0(\mathbf{u}).$$

This implies $\mathbf{s}'_*\mathbf{u} = \frac{\partial f}{\partial \mathbf{u}}(\mathbf{x}_0)$, as needed. □

Theorem 12.40. *Let S be a convex subset of $\mathbb{R}^n$ with a non-empty interior and let $\boldsymbol{x}_0 \in \boldsymbol{I}(S)$. If $f : S \longrightarrow \mathbb{R}$ is convex and differentiable in $\boldsymbol{x}_0$, then its gradient at $\boldsymbol{x}_0$ is its only subgradient at $\boldsymbol{x}_0$.*

Proof. By Theorem 12.16 the Hessian matrix $H_f(\mathbf{x})$ is positive for every $\mathbf{x} \in S$. Therefore we have:

$$f(\mathbf{x}) - f(\mathbf{x}_0) \geqslant ((\mathbf{x} - \mathbf{x}_0)'(\nabla f)(\mathbf{x}_0) = ((\nabla f)(\mathbf{x}_0))'(\mathbf{x} - \mathbf{x}_0),$$

hence $(\nabla f)(\mathbf{x}_0)$ is a subgradient of f.

Suppose that $\mathbf{s}$ belongs to $\mathsf{subd}(f)(\mathbf{x}_0)$, that is, $f(\mathbf{x}) - f(\mathbf{x}_0) \geqslant \mathbf{s}'(\mathbf{x} - \mathbf{x}_0)$. If $\mathbf{x} = \mathbf{x}_0 + t\mathbf{z}$ for $t > 0$, we have $f(\mathbf{x}_0 + t\mathbf{z}) - f(\mathbf{x}_0) \geqslant t\mathbf{s}'\mathbf{z}$, hence

$$\frac{f(\mathbf{x}_0 + t\mathbf{z}) - f(\mathbf{x}_0)}{t} \geqslant \mathbf{s}'\mathbf{z}.$$

Since $\lim_{t \to 0} \frac{f(\mathbf{x}_0 + t\mathbf{z}) - f(\mathbf{x}_0)}{t} = (\nabla f)(\mathbf{x}_0)'\mathbf{z}$, it follows that $((\nabla f)(\mathbf{x}_0) - \mathbf{s})'\mathbf{z} \geqslant 0$. Choosing $\mathbf{z} = -((\nabla f)(\mathbf{x}_0) - \mathbf{s})$, it follows that $\mathbf{s} = (\nabla f)(\mathbf{x}_0)$, so $(\nabla f)(\mathbf{x}_0)$ is the unique subgradient of f at $\mathbf{x}_0$. $\square$

Example 12.20. Let $f : \mathbb{R}^n \longrightarrow \mathbb{R}$ be defined by $f(\mathbf{x}) = \|\mathbf{x}\|_2$ for $\mathbf{x} \in \mathbb{R}^n$. The function f is not differentiable in $\mathbf{0}_n$ because

$$\lim_{t \to 0} \frac{\|t\mathbf{u}\|}{t} = \begin{cases} \|\mathbf{u}\| & \text{if } t > 0, \\ -\|\mathbf{u}\| & \text{if } t < 0 \end{cases}$$

depends on $\mathbf{u}$ and on the sign of t. However, f is subdifferentiable in $\mathbf{0}_n$. Indeed, a subgradient of f at $\mathbf{0}_n$ is a vector $\mathbf{s}$ such that $\|\mathbf{x}\|_2 \geqslant \mathbf{s}'\mathbf{x}$ for every $\mathbf{x} \in \mathbb{R}^n$. By taking $\mathbf{x} = \mathbf{s}$, the previous inequality amounts to $\|\mathbf{s}\|_2 \leqslant 1$. Thus, the subdifferential of f at $\mathbf{0}_n$ is $B[\mathbf{0}_n, 1]$.

Theorem 12.41. *Let $f_i : \mathbb{R}^n \longrightarrow \mathbb{R}$ be n convex functions for $1 \leqslant i \leqslant m$ and let $f : \mathbb{R}^n \longrightarrow \mathbb{R}$ be their pointwise maximum, that is $f(\boldsymbol{x}) = \max\{f_i(\boldsymbol{x}) \mid 1 \leqslant i \leqslant m\}$.*

Define $I(\boldsymbol{x}_0)$ as the subset of $\{1, \ldots, m\}$ that contains the indices of the functions f_i that are "active" at $\boldsymbol{x}_0$, that is, $I(\boldsymbol{x}_0) = \{i \mid 1 \leqslant i \leqslant m \text{ and } f_i(\boldsymbol{x}_0) = f(\boldsymbol{x}_0)\}$. If the functions f_i are subdifferentiable, then

$$\boldsymbol{K}_{\mathrm{conv}} \left(\bigcup_{i \in I(\boldsymbol{x}_0)} \mathsf{subd}(f_i)(\boldsymbol{x}_0) \right) \subseteq \mathsf{subd}(f)(\boldsymbol{x}_0).$$

Proof.   Let i be any index in $I(\mathbf{x}_0)$ and let $\mathbf{s} \in \mathsf{subd}(f_i)(\mathbf{x}_0)$. Since

$$f(\mathbf{x}) \geqslant f_i(\mathbf{x}) \geqslant f_i(\mathbf{x}_0) + \mathbf{s}'(\mathbf{x} - \mathbf{x}_0) = f(\mathbf{x}_0) + \mathbf{s}'(\mathbf{x} - \mathbf{x}_0),$$

it follows that $\mathbf{s} \in \mathsf{subd}(f)(\mathbf{x}_0)$, so $\bigcup_{i \in I(\mathbf{x}_0)} \mathsf{subd}(f_i)(\mathbf{x}_0) \mathsf{subd}(f)(\mathbf{x}_0)$. Since $\mathsf{subd}(f)(\mathbf{x}_0)$ is convex, it follows that

$$\boldsymbol{K}_{\mathrm{conv}} \left(\bigcup_{i \in I(\boldsymbol{x}_0)} \mathsf{subd}(f_i)(\mathbf{x}_0) \right) \subseteq \mathsf{subd}(f)(\mathbf{x}_0). \qquad \square$$

Under certain conditions the inclusion of Theorem 12.41 can be replaced by equality.

Theorem 12.42. *Let $f_i : \mathbb{R}^n \longrightarrow \mathbb{R}$ be m convex functions for $1 \leqslant i \leqslant m$, let $f : \mathbb{R}^n \longrightarrow \mathbb{R}$ be given by $f(\boldsymbol{x}) = \max\{f_i(\boldsymbol{x}) \mid 1 \leqslant i \leqslant m\}$, and let $\boldsymbol{x}_0 \in \bigcap_{i=1}^{m} \boldsymbol{I}(\mathrm{Dom}\, f_i)$.*
With the same definition of $I(\boldsymbol{x}_0)$ as in Theorem 12.41 we have:

$$\boldsymbol{K}_{\mathrm{conv}}\left(\bigcup_{i \in I(\boldsymbol{x}_0)} subd(f_i)(\boldsymbol{x}_0) \right) = subd(f)(\boldsymbol{x}_0).$$

Proof. We need to prove only the inclusion

$$\mathsf{subd}(f)(\mathbf{x}_0) \subseteq \boldsymbol{K}_{\mathrm{conv}}\left(\bigcup_{i \in I(\mathbf{x}_0)} \mathsf{subd}(f_i)(\mathbf{x}_0) \right),$$

because the reverse inclusion was already shown in Theorem 12.41.

Let $\mathbf{s}_0$ be an arbitrary vector in $\mathsf{subd}(f)(\mathbf{x}_0)$ and assume that $\mathbf{s}_0 \notin \boldsymbol{K}_{\mathrm{conv}}(\bigcup_{i \in I(\mathbf{x}_0)} \mathsf{subd}(f_i)(\mathbf{x}_0))$. Recall that by Theorem 12.35 every subdifferential $\mathsf{subd}(f_i)(\mathbf{x}_0)$ is convex, closed and compact, which implies that $\boldsymbol{K}_{\mathrm{conv}}(\bigcup_{i \in I(\mathbf{x}_0)} \mathsf{subd}(f_i)(\mathbf{x}_0))$ is a compact set.

By Theorem 6.55 there exists $\mathbf{w} \in \mathbb{R}^n - \{\mathbf{0}_n\}$ and $a \in R$ such that $\mathbf{w}'\mathbf{s} > a \geqslant \mathbf{w}'\mathbf{x}$ for $\mathbf{x} \in \boldsymbol{K}_{\mathrm{conv}}(\bigcup_{i \in I(\mathbf{x}_0)} \mathsf{subd}(f_i)(\mathbf{x}_0))$.

Observe that

$$\frac{\partial f}{\partial \mathbf{w}}(\mathbf{x}_0) = \lim_{t \downarrow 0} \max_{i \in I(\mathbf{x}_0)} \frac{f_i(\mathbf{x}_0 + t\mathbf{w}) - f_i(\mathbf{x}_0)}{t}$$

$$= \max_{i \in I(\mathbf{x}_0)} \lim_{t \downarrow 0} \frac{f_i(\mathbf{x}_0 + t\mathbf{w}) - f_i(\mathbf{x}_0)}{t}$$

$$= \max_{i \in I(\mathbf{x}_0)} \frac{\partial f_i}{\partial \mathbf{w}},$$

which implies $\mathbf{s}'\mathbf{w} > \mathsf{pf} f\mathbf{w}$.

Since $\mathbf{s} \in \mathsf{subd}(f)(\mathbf{x}_0)$ we have $f(\mathbf{x}_0 + t\mathbf{w}) - f(\mathbf{x}_0) \geqslant t\mathbf{s}'\mathbf{w}$ for every $t > 0$, hence $\frac{\partial f}{\partial \mathbf{w}} \geqslant \mathbf{s}'\mathbf{w}$, which contradicts the previous inequality. Therefore, $\mathbf{s}_0 \in \boldsymbol{K}_{\mathrm{conv}}(\bigcup_{i \in I(\mathbf{x}_0)} \mathsf{subd}(f_i)(\mathbf{x}_0))$. $\square$

Example 12.21. This example extends Example 12.19. Let $f : \mathbb{R}^n \longrightarrow \mathbb{R}$ be the 1-norm, $f(\mathbf{x}) = \|\mathbf{x}\|_1 = \sum_{j=1}^{n} |x_j|$, which is a convex but not differentiable function.

Note that there are 2^n vectors in $\mathbb{R}^n$ such that $a_i \in \{-1, 1\}$. For the linear function $g_{\mathbf{a}} : \mathbb{R}^n \longrightarrow \mathbb{R}$ defined as $g_{\mathbf{a}}(\mathbf{x}) = \mathbf{a}'\mathbf{x}$ we have $(\nabla g)(\mathbf{x}) = \mathbf{a}$. The function f is the maximum of these 2^n linear functions namely, $\|\mathbf{x}\|_1 = \max\{\mathbf{a}'\mathbf{x} \mid \mathbf{a} \in \{-1, 1\}\}$. For $\mathbf{x}_0 \in \mathbb{R}^n$ the set of indices of active functions is corresponds to those $\mathbf{a}$ such that $\mathbf{a}'\mathbf{x} = \|\mathbf{x}\|_1$, which implies $a_i = 1$ if $x_i > 0$ and $a_i = -1$ if $x_i < 0$. If $x_i = 0$, then both $a_i = 1$ or $a_i = -1$ are valid. The subdifferential is the convex hull of the vectors that can be produced in this way. For $\mathbf{x} \in \mathbb{R}^n$ and $1 \leqslant k \leqslant n$ define the sets $T_k(\mathbf{x})$ as

$$T_k(\mathbf{x}) = \begin{cases} [-1, 1] & \text{if } x_k = 0, \\ \{1\} & \text{if } x_k = 1, \\ \{-1\} & \text{if } x_k = -1 \end{cases}$$

for $1 \leqslant k \leqslant n$. Then, the subdifferential of $\|\mathbf{x}\|_1$ at $\mathbf{x}$ equals $\prod_{k=1}^n T_k(\mathbf{x})$.

Example 12.22. The function $f : \mathbb{R} \longrightarrow \mathbb{R}$ defined as

$$f(x) = \begin{cases} 1 & \text{if } x = 0, \\ 0 & \text{if } x \neq 0 \end{cases}$$

has an empty subdifferential at $x_0 = 0$. Indeed, if s were a subgradient of f at $x_0 = 0$ we would have $f(x) - f(0) = 1 > sx$ for every $x \neq 0$.which is impossible. Thus, f is not subdifferentiable at $x_0 = 0$.

Theorem 12.43. *Let $S \subseteq \mathbb{R}^n$ be a convex set and let $f : S \longrightarrow \mathbb{R}$ be a convex function. If $\mathbf{x}_0 \in \mathbf{I}(S)$, then there exists $\mathbf{s} \in \mathbb{R}^n$ such that $f(\mathbf{x}) - f(\mathbf{x}_0) \geqslant \mathbf{s}'(\mathbf{x} - \mathbf{x}_0)$ for $\mathbf{x} \in S$.*

If f is strictly convex and $\mathbf{x} \in \mathbf{I}(S)$, then there exists $\mathbf{s} \in \mathbb{R}^n$ such that the strict inequality $f(\mathbf{x}) - f(\mathbf{x}_0) > \mathbf{s}'(\mathbf{x} - \mathbf{x}_0)$ holds for $\mathbf{x} \in S$.

Proof. By Theorem 12.1, the epigraph of f, is a convex set. Note that $\binom{\mathbf{x}_0}{f(\mathbf{x}_0)} \in \partial(\mathsf{epi}(f))$ because a sphere $B\left(\binom{\mathbf{x}_0}{f(\mathbf{x}_0)}, \epsilon\right)$ contains both points from $\mathbf{K}(\mathsf{epi}(f))$ and from $\mathbf{K}(R^n - \mathsf{epi}(f))$. Therefore, by Theorem 6.56, there exists a vector $\mathbf{w} = \binom{\mathbf{u}}{v} \in \mathbb{R}^{n+1} - \mathbf{0}_{n+1}$ such that

$$(\mathbf{u}' \ v)\left(\binom{\mathbf{x}}{y} - \binom{\mathbf{x}_0}{f(\mathbf{x}_0)}\right) \leqslant 0,$$

which is equivalent to

$$\mathbf{u}'(\mathbf{x} - \mathbf{x}_0) + v(y - f(\mathbf{x}_0)) \leqslant 0$$

for $\binom{\mathbf{x}}{y} \in \mathsf{epi}(f)$.

We claim that $v \leqslant 0$. Indeed, if v were positive we would have $\mathbf{u}'(\mathbf{x} - \mathbf{x}_0) + v(y - f(\mathbf{x}_0)) > 0$ by choosing y sufficiently large.

The assumption $v = 0$ also leads to a contradiction because this would imply $\mathbf{u}'(\mathbf{x} - \mathbf{x}_0) \leqslant 0$ for $\mathbf{x} \in S$. Since $\mathbf{x}_0 \in I(S)$, there exists $a > 0$ such that $\mathbf{x} = \mathbf{x}_0 + a\mathbf{u} \in S$, which implies $a\mathbf{u}'\mathbf{u} \leqslant 0$. Therefore, $\mathbf{u} = \mathbf{0}$, hence $\mathbf{w} = \mathbf{0}_{n+1}$, thus contradicting the initial assumption involving $\mathbf{w}$. Consequently, $v < 0$, and we obtain

$$\frac{1}{v}\mathbf{u}'(\mathbf{x} - \mathbf{x}_0) + y - f(\mathbf{x}_0) \geqslant 0$$

for $\begin{pmatrix} \mathbf{x} \\ y \end{pmatrix} \in \operatorname{epi}(f)$. Choosing $y = f(\mathbf{x})$ we have

$$\frac{1}{v}\mathbf{u}'(\mathbf{x} - \mathbf{x}_0) + f(x) - f(\mathbf{x}_0) \geqslant 0,$$

which is desired inequality with $\mathbf{s} = \frac{1}{v}\mathbf{u}$.

For the second part of the theorem, since every strictly convex function is convex, if $\mathbf{x}_0 \in \mathbf{I}(S)$ there exists $\mathbf{s} \in \mathbb{R}^n$ such that $f(\mathbf{x}) \geqslant f(\mathbf{x}_0) + \mathbf{s}'(\mathbf{x} - \mathbf{x}_0)$ for $\mathbf{x} \in S$. Suppose that there exists $\mathbf{x}_1 \neq \mathbf{x}_0$ such that $f(\mathbf{x}) = f(\mathbf{x}_1) + \mathbf{s}'(\mathbf{x} - \mathbf{x}_1)$ for $\mathbf{x} \in S$. The strict convexity of f implies that for $t \in (0, 1)$ we have

$$f(t\mathbf{x}_0 + (1 - t)\mathbf{x}_1) < tf(\mathbf{x}_0) + (1 - t)f(\mathbf{x}_1)$$
$$= tf(\mathbf{x}_0) + (1 - t)(f(\mathbf{x}) - \mathbf{s}'(\mathbf{x} - \mathbf{x}_1)).$$

By the first part of the theorem, for $\mathbf{x} = t\mathbf{x}_0 + (1 - t)\mathbf{x}_1$ we have

$$f(t\mathbf{x}_0 + (1 - t)\mathbf{x}_1) \geqslant f(\mathbf{x}_0) + (1 - t)\mathbf{s}'(\mathbf{x}_1 - \mathbf{x}_0)$$
$$= tf(\mathbf{x}_0) + (1 - t)(f(\mathbf{x}_0) - \mathbf{s}'(\mathbf{x} - \mathbf{x}_1)),$$

contradicting the previous inequality. □

Theorem 12.43 shows that there exists at least one subgradient of a convex function defined on a convex set S at each point $\mathbf{x} \in \mathbf{I}(S)$.

Theorem 12.44. *Let S be a non-empty and convex subset of $\mathbb{R}^n$ and let $f : S \longrightarrow \mathbb{R}$ be a function. If a subgradient of f exists for every $\boldsymbol{x}_0 \in \boldsymbol{I}(S)$, then f is convex on $\boldsymbol{I}(S)$.*

Proof. Let $\mathbf{u}, \mathbf{v} \in \mathbf{I}(S)$. By Theorem 6.37 the set $\mathbf{I}(S)$ is convex, so $t\mathbf{u} + (1-t)\mathbf{v} \in \mathbf{I}(S)$. If $\mathbf{s}$ is a subgradient at $t\mathbf{u} + (1-t)\mathbf{v}$, then we have

$$f(\mathbf{u}) \geqslant f(t\mathbf{u} + (1-t)\mathbf{v}) + \mathbf{s}'(\mathbf{u} - t\mathbf{u} - (1-t)\mathbf{v})$$
$$= f(t\mathbf{u} + (1-t)\mathbf{v}) + (1-t)\mathbf{s}'(\mathbf{u} - \mathbf{v})$$

and

$$f(\mathbf{v}) \geqslant f(t\mathbf{u} + (1-t)\mathbf{v}) + \mathbf{s}'(\mathbf{v} - t\mathbf{u} - (1-t)\mathbf{v})$$
$$= f(t\mathbf{u} + (1-t)\mathbf{v}) + t\mathbf{s}'(\mathbf{v} - \mathbf{u}).$$

These inequalities imply

$$tf(\mathbf{u}) + (1-t)f(\mathbf{v}) \geqslant f(t\mathbf{u} + (1-t)\mathbf{v}),$$

which shows that f is convex on $\mathbf{I}(S)$. $\square$

The existence of the subgradients of a function $f : S \longrightarrow \mathbb{R}$ in every point of $\mathbf{I}(S)$ does not imply the convexity of f on the entire set S; note that Theorem 12.44 guarantees convexity only on $\mathbf{I}(S)$! This point is illustrated by the next example.

Example 12.23. Let $f : [0, 1]^2 \longrightarrow \mathbb{R}$ be the function given by

$$f(\mathbf{x}) = \begin{cases} 1 & \text{if } x_2 = 0, \\ 0 & \text{if } 0 < x_2 \leqslant 1, \end{cases}$$

where $\mathbf{x} = \begin{pmatrix} x_1 \\ x_2 \end{pmatrix}$. The interior of the definition domain S is the set $[0, 1] \times (0, 1]$, and for any $\mathbf{x}_0 \in \mathbf{I}(S)$ we have $f(\mathbf{x}) \geqslant f(\mathbf{x}_0) + \mathbf{0}_2'(\mathbf{x} - \mathbf{x}_0)$, which means that $\mathbf{0}_2$ is a subgradient for $\mathbf{x}_0$. The function f is convex on $\mathbf{I}(S)$ by Theorem 12.43; however, f is not convex on S itself. Indeed, take $\mathbf{u} = \begin{pmatrix} 0.5 \\ 0 \end{pmatrix}$ and $\mathbf{v} = \begin{pmatrix} 0 \\ 0.5 \end{pmatrix}$. We have $f(\mathbf{u}) = 1$ and $f(\mathbf{v}) = 0$ and

$$f(t\mathbf{u} + (1-t)\mathbf{v}) = f\left(\begin{pmatrix} 0.5t \\ 0.5(1-t) \end{pmatrix}\right) = \begin{cases} 1 & \text{if } t = 0, \\ 0 & \text{if } 0 < t \leqslant 1, \end{cases}$$

so the convexity inequality is violated when $t = 0$. Therefore f, is not convex on the entire set S.

The next theorem shows that convex functions are pointwise suprema of sets of affine functions.

Theorem 12.45. *Let $f : \mathbb{R}^n \longrightarrow \mathbb{R}$ be a convex function (so, $\mathrm{Dom}(f) = \mathbb{R}$). We have*

$$f(\boldsymbol{x}) = \sup\{g(\boldsymbol{x}) \mid g \text{ affine and } g(\boldsymbol{z}) \leqslant f(\boldsymbol{z}) \text{ for all } \boldsymbol{z} \in \mathbb{R}^n\}.$$

Proof. It is immediate that

$$f(\mathbf{x}) \geqslant \sup\{g(\mathbf{x}) \mid g \text{ affine and } g(\mathbf{z}) \leqslant f(\mathbf{z}) \text{ for all } \mathbf{z} \in \mathbb{R}^n\}.$$

Since $\mathsf{epi}(f)$ is a convex set, there exists a supporting hyperplane of $\mathsf{epi}(f)$ at $(\mathbf{x}, f(\mathbf{x}))$, $\mathbf{a}'(\mathbf{x} - \mathbf{z}) + b(f(\mathbf{x}) - t) \leqslant 0$ for some $\binom{\mathbf{a}}{b} \neq \mathbf{0}_{n+1}$. If $(\mathbf{z}, t) \in \mathsf{epi}(f)$ we have $t = f(\mathbf{z}) + s$ for some $s \geqslant 0$. Therefore,

$$\mathbf{a}'(\mathbf{x} - \mathbf{z}) + b(f(\mathbf{x}) - f(\mathbf{z}) - s) \leqslant 0 \tag{12.18}$$

for all $\mathbf{z} \in \mathbb{R}^n$ and all $s \geqslant 0$.

If $b = 0$ inequality 12.18 yields $\mathbf{a}'(\mathbf{x} - \mathbf{z}) \leqslant 0$ for all $\mathbf{z} \in \mathbb{R}^n$, which implies $\mathbf{a} = \mathbf{0}_n$ and contradicts $\binom{\mathbf{a}}{b} \neq \mathbf{0}_{n+1}$. This means that $b > 0$. Inequality 12.18 for $s = 0$ amounts to $g(\mathbf{z}) = f(\mathbf{x}) + \frac{1}{b}\mathbf{a}'(\mathbf{x} - \mathbf{z}) \leqslant f(\mathbf{z})$ for all $\mathbf{z} \in \mathbb{R}^n$. Note that g is an affine function and $g(\mathbf{x}) = f(\mathbf{x})$. $\qquad\square$

Theorem 12.46. (Conditional Jensen Inequality) *Let $f : \mathbb{R} \longrightarrow \mathbb{R}$ be a convex function, $(\Omega, \mathcal{E}, P)$ be a probability space, and let X be a random variable such that fX is an integrable random variable. We have:*

$$E(fX|\mathcal{G}) \geqslant f(E(X|\mathcal{G})).$$

Proof. By Theorem 12.45 a convex function $f : \mathbb{R} \longrightarrow \mathbb{R}$ is the pointwise supremum of a sequence of affine functions (f_n), where $f_n(x) = a_n x + b_n$ for $n \in \mathbb{N}$. We have $f(X(\omega)) \geqslant a_n X(\omega) + b_n$ for $\omega \in \Omega$. This implies

$$E(fX|\mathcal{G})(\omega) \geqslant E((aX_n + b_n)|\mathcal{G})(\omega) = a_n E(X|\mathcal{G})(\omega) + b_n$$

for all $\omega \in \Omega$ with the possible exception of some ω that belong to an event null A_n. Since $A = \bigcup_{n \in \mathbb{N}} A_n$ is also null, we have $E(fX|\mathcal{G})(\omega) \geqslant E((aX_n + b_n)|\mathcal{G})(\omega) = a_n E(X|\mathcal{G})(\omega) + b_n$ a.e. Therefore,

$$E(fX|\mathcal{G})(\omega) \geqslant \sup E((aX_n + b_n)|\mathcal{G})(\omega) = f(E(X|\mathcal{G})(\omega)). \qquad\square$$

Exercises and Supplements

Convex Functions — Basics

(1) Let I be an interval in $\mathbb{R}$. Prove that a function $f : I \to \mathbb{R}$ is convex if and only if for every distinct numbers $a, b, c \in I$ we have:

$$\frac{1}{(c-b)(c-a)}f(c) + \frac{1}{(b-a)(b-c)}f(b)\frac{1}{(a-b)(a-a)}f(a) \geqslant 0.$$

(2) Prove that the hinge function $h : \mathbb{R} \longrightarrow \mathbb{R}$ defined as $h(x) = \max\{0, 1 - x\}$ for $x \in \mathbb{R}$ is convex.

(3) Let $C \subseteq \mathbb{R}^{n+1}$ be a convex set. For $\mathbf{x} \in \mathbb{R}^n$ define

$$A_{\mathbf{x}} = \left\{ y \,\middle|\, \begin{pmatrix} \mathbf{x} \\ y \end{pmatrix} \in C \right\}$$

and $f : \mathbb{R}^n \longrightarrow \mathbb{R}$ as $f(\mathbf{x}) = \inf A_{\mathbf{x}}$. Prove that f is a convex function.

Solution: Let $\mathbf{u}, \mathbf{v} \in \mathbb{R}^n$. Suppose initially that $A_{\mathbf{u}} \neq \emptyset$ and $A_{\mathbf{v}} \neq \emptyset$. We need to prove that for $t \in [0, 1]$,

$$\inf A_{(1-t)\mathbf{u}+t\mathbf{v}} \leqslant (1 - t) \inf A_{\mathbf{u}} + t \inf A_{\mathbf{v}}.$$

It is immediate that $y_1 \in A_{\mathbf{u}}$ and $y_2 \in A_{\mathbf{v}}$, then $(1 - t)y_1 + ty_2 \in A_{(1-t)\mathbf{u}+t\mathbf{v}}$ because C is convex.

Let $y_{\mathbf{u}} = \inf A_{\mathbf{u}}$ and $y_{\mathbf{v}} = \inf A_{\mathbf{v}}$. For every $y_1 \in A\mathbf{u}$ we have $y_{\mathbf{u}} \leqslant y_1$; similarly, for every $y_2 \in A_{\mathbf{v}}$ we have $y_{\mathbf{v}} \leqslant y_2$. This implies

$$(1 - t)y_{\mathbf{u}} + ty_{\mathbf{v}} \leqslant (1 - t)y_1 + ty_2$$

for $t \in [0, 1]$. Thus, $\inf A_{(1-t)\mathbf{u}+t\mathbf{v}} \leqslant (1 - t)y_{\mathbf{u}} + ty_{\mathbf{v}}$.

Note that if any of the sets $A_{\mathbf{u}}, A_{\mathbf{v}}$ is empty, the convexity follows immediately from the observation that $\inf \emptyset = \infty$.

(4) Let C be a subset of $\mathbb{R}^n$. Prove that its indicator function I_C is convex if and only if C is a convex set.

(5) Let $f : (\mathbb{R}_{\geqslant 0})^2 \longrightarrow \mathbb{R}$ be the function defined by $f(\mathbf{x}) = \min\{x_1, x_2\}$. Prove that f is concave.

(6) Let ν be a norm on a linear space. Prove, by applying the definition of convex functions that the function ν^2 is convex.

(7) Prove that a subset C of $\mathbb{R}^n$ is convex if and only if its indicator function I_C is a convex function.

Solution: Suppose that C is a convex set but I_C is not a convex function. Then, there exists $a \in [0, 1]$ and $\mathbf{x}, \mathbf{y}$ such that $I_C((1 - a)\mathbf{x} + a\mathbf{y}) \not\leqslant (1 - a)I_C(\mathbf{x}) + aI_C(\mathbf{y})$. This is possible only if $I_C((1 - a)\mathbf{x} + a\mathbf{y}) = \infty$ and $I_C(\mathbf{x}) = I_C(\mathbf{y}) = 0$, which amounts to $\mathbf{x}, \mathbf{y} \in C$ and $(1 - a)\mathbf{x} + a\mathbf{y} \notin C$, which contradicts the convexity of C. Thus, if C is convex, I_C is a convex function.

Conversely, suppose that $I_C : \mathbb{R}^n \longrightarrow \hat{\mathbb{R}}_{\geqslant 0}$ is a convex function and let $\mathbf{x}, \mathbf{y} \in C$. We have $I_C(\mathbf{x}) = I_C(\mathbf{y}) = 0$. Since $I_C((1 - a)\mathbf{x} + a\mathbf{y}) \not\leqslant (1 - a)I_C(\mathbf{x}) + aI_C(\mathbf{y})$, it follows that $I_C((1 - a)\mathbf{x} + a\mathbf{y}) = 0$, so $(1 - a)\mathbf{x} + a\mathbf{y} \in C$.

(8) Let $f_i : \mathbb{R}^n \longrightarrow \mathbb{R}$ be convex functions for $1 \leqslant i \leqslant m$. If $a_1, \ldots, a_m$ are m non-negative numbers, prove that the function $f : \mathbb{R}^n \longrightarrow \mathbb{R}$ defined as $f(\mathbf{x}) = \sum_{i=1}^{m} f_i(\mathbf{x})$ for $\mathbf{x} \in \mathbb{R}^n$ is convex.

(9) Let L be a real linear space and let $f : L \longrightarrow \mathbb{R}_{\geqslant 0}$ be a function such that $f(ax) = af(x)$ for every $x \in L$ and every $a \geqslant 0$ (which means that f is a homogeneous function). Prove that the following statements are equivalent:

   (a) f is convex;
   (b) the set $C = \{x \in L \mid f(x) \leqslant 1\}$ is convex;
   (c) $f(x + y) \leqslant f(x) + f(y)$ for $x, y \in L$.

   Solution: (a) implies **(b)**: Suppose that f is convex and let $x, y \in C$. If $t \in [0, 1]$ we have $f((1 - t)x + ty) \leqslant (1 - t)f(x) + tf(y) \leqslant 1$, hence $(1 - t)x + ty \in C$, which shows that C is convex.

   (b) implies **(c)**: Suppose that C is a convex set.

If we have both $f(x) > 0$ and $f(y) > 0$ we conclude that $\frac{1}{f(x)}x \in C$ and $\frac{1}{f(y)}y \in C$. Since C is convex, taking $t = \frac{f(y)}{f(x)+f(y)}$ we have

$$(1 - t)\frac{1}{f(x)}x + t\frac{1}{f(y)}y = \frac{1}{f(x) + f(y)}(x + y) \in C,$$

so $f(x + y) \leqslant f(x) + f(y)$.

Consider the case when $f(x) = 0$ and $f(y) = 1$. We have $ax \in C$ and $y \in C$. If $t = \frac{a}{a+1} \in [0, 1]$, we have $(1 - t)ax + ty = \frac{a}{a+1}(x + y) \in C$, hence $f(x + y) \leqslant \frac{a+1}{a}$ for $a > 0$. Taking $a \to \infty$ we have $f(x + y) \leqslant 1$, so $x + y \in C$. If $f(y) > 0$ but $f(y) \neq 1$, apply the previous argument to $\frac{1}{f(y)}x$ and to $\frac{1}{f(y)}y$. The case when $f(x) > 0$ and $f(y) = 0$ is similar.

If $f(x) = f(y) = 0$, then $ax, ay \in C$ for any $a > 0$, so $\frac{a}{2}x + \frac{a}{2}y \in C$, which implies $f(x + y) \leqslant \frac{2}{a}$ for every $a > 0$. This, in turn, implies $f(x + y) = 0$ and, therefore, $f(x + y) \leqslant f(x) + f(y)$.

   (c) implies **(a)**: Suppose that for the homogeneous function f we have the subadditive property $f(x + y) \leqslant f(x) + f(y)$ for $x, y \in L$. For $t \in [0, 1]$ we have

$$f((1 - t)x + ty) \leqslant f((1 - t)x) + f(ty)$$
$$= (1 - t)f(x) + tf(y),$$

which shows that f is convex.

(10) Let $f : S \to \mathbb{R}$ be a function, where S is a convex and open subset of $\mathbb{R}^n$ and $f(\mathbf{x}) > 0$ for $\mathbf{x} \in S$. Prove that if $g : \mathbb{R}_{>0} \longrightarrow \mathbb{R}$ is strictly increasing and concave, and gf is convex, then f is a convex function.

   Solution: The convexity of gf means that

$$gf((1 - t)\mathbf{x} + t\mathbf{y}) \leqslant (1 - t)\, gf(\mathbf{x}) + t\, gf(\mathbf{y})$$

for $\mathbf{x}, \mathbf{y} \in S$.

Since g is concave, we have $g((1-t)u + tv) \geqslant (1-t)g(u) + tg(v)$ for $t \in [0,1]$. Substituting $f(x)$ for u and $f(y)$ for v we obtain

$$g((1-t)f(x) + tf(y)) \geqslant (1-t)g(f(x)) + tg(f(y))$$

for $t \in [0,1]$. The above inequalities imply

$$g((1-t)f(x) + tf(y)) \geqslant gf((1-t)\mathbf{x} + t\mathbf{y}).$$

Finally, since g is strictly increasing we have

$$(1-t)f(x) + tf(y) \geqslant f((1-t)\mathbf{x} + t\mathbf{y})$$

for $t \in [0,1]$, so f is convex.

(11) Let $f : \mathbb{R}^n \longrightarrow \hat{\mathbb{R}}$ be a convex function and let $\mathbf{x}$ be such that $f(\mathbf{x})$ is finite. Prove that $\lambda_1 \geqslant \lambda_2 > 0$ implies

$$\frac{f(\mathbf{x} + \lambda_1 \mathbf{y}) - f(\mathbf{x})}{\lambda_1} \geqslant \frac{f(\mathbf{x} + \lambda_2 \mathbf{y}) - f(\mathbf{x})}{\lambda_2}.$$

Solution: Let $t = \frac{\lambda_2}{\lambda_1} \in (0,1]$, $\mathbf{u} = \mathbf{x} + \lambda_1 \mathbf{y}$ and $\mathbf{v} = \mathbf{x}$. Note that

$$t\mathbf{u} + (1-t)\mathbf{v} = \frac{\lambda_2}{\lambda_1}(\mathbf{x} + \lambda_1 \mathbf{y}) + \left(1 - \frac{\lambda_2}{\lambda_1}\right)\mathbf{x} = \mathbf{x} + \lambda_2 \mathbf{y}.$$

Since f is convex, we have

$$f(t\mathbf{u} + (1-t)\mathbf{v}) \leqslant tf(\mathbf{u}) + (1-t)f(\mathbf{v}).$$

Substituting $t, \mathbf{u}, \mathbf{v}$ in this inequality yields

$$f(\mathbf{x} + \lambda_2 \mathbf{y}) \leqslant \frac{\lambda_2}{\lambda_1}f(\mathbf{x} + \lambda_1 \mathbf{y}) + \left(1 - \frac{\lambda_2}{\lambda_1}\right)f(\mathbf{x}),$$

which is equivalent with the desired inequality.

(12) Let $f : \mathbb{R}^n \longrightarrow \hat{\mathbb{R}}$ be a convex function and let $\mathbf{x}$ be such that $f(\mathbf{x})$ is finite. Prove that if $t \geqslant 0$, then

$$\frac{f(\mathbf{x} + \lambda(\mathbf{y}_1 + \mathbf{y}_2)) - f(\mathbf{x})}{\lambda} \geqslant \frac{f(\mathbf{x} + 2\lambda\mathbf{y}_1) - f(\mathbf{x})}{2\lambda} + \frac{f(\mathbf{x} + 2\lambda\mathbf{y}_1) - f(\mathbf{x})}{2\lambda}.$$

Hint: This follows immediately from the convexity of f.

(13) Prove that if $f : \mathbb{R}^p \longrightarrow \mathbb{R}$ is a convex function, $A \in \mathbb{R}^{p \times n}$ and $\mathbf{b} \in \mathbb{R}^p$, then the function $g : \mathbb{R}^n \longrightarrow \mathbb{R}$ defined by $g(\mathbf{x}) = f(A\mathbf{x} + \mathbf{b})$ for $\mathbf{x} \in \mathbb{R}^n$ is convex.

(14) Let $f : \mathbb{R}^m \times \mathbb{R}^n \longrightarrow \hat{\mathbb{R}}$ be a convex function in the aggregate argument $\mathbf{z} = (\mathbf{x}, \mathbf{y})$, where $\mathbf{x} \in \mathbb{R}^m$ and $\mathbf{y} \in \mathbb{R}^n$, and let $g : \mathbb{R}^m \longrightarrow \hat{\mathbb{R}}$ be defined as $g(\mathbf{x}) = \inf_{\mathbf{y}} f(\mathbf{x}, \mathbf{y})$. Prove that if $g(\mathbf{x}) > -\infty$ for $\mathbf{x} \in \mathbb{R}^m$, then g is a convex function.

Solution: Let $\mathbf{x}_1, \mathbf{x}_2 \in \mathrm{Dom}(g)$ and let $\mathbf{x} = (1 - t)\mathbf{x}_1 + t\mathbf{x}_2$, where $t \in [0, 1]$. For $\epsilon > 0$, there exist $\mathbf{y}_1, \mathbf{y}_2$ such that $g(\mathbf{x}_1) + \epsilon > f(\mathbf{x}_1, \mathbf{y}_1)$ and $g(\mathbf{x}_2) + \epsilon > f(\mathbf{x}_2, \mathbf{y}_2)$ by the definition of the infimum. Therefore, if $t \in [0, 1]$ we have

$$
\begin{aligned}
(1 - t)g(\mathbf{x}_1) + tg(\mathbf{x}_2) + \epsilon &= (1 - t)(g(\mathbf{x}_1) + \epsilon) + t(g(\mathbf{x}_2) + \epsilon) \\
&\geqslant (1 - t)f(\mathbf{x}_1, \mathbf{y}_1) + tf(\mathbf{x}_2, \mathbf{y}_2) \\
&\geqslant f((1 - t)(\mathbf{x}_1, \mathbf{y}_1) + t(\mathbf{x}_2, \mathbf{y}_2)) \\
&= f(\mathbf{x}, (1 - t)\mathbf{y}_1 + t\mathbf{y}_2) \geqslant g(\mathbf{x}),
\end{aligned}
$$

which proves that g is convex.

(15) Let $f : \mathbb{R}^n \longrightarrow \mathbb{R}$ be a convex function. Define $g : \mathbb{R}_{>0} \times \mathbb{R}^n \longrightarrow \mathbb{R}$ as $g(t, \mathbf{x}) = tf\left(\frac{1}{t}\mathbf{x}\right)$ for $t > 0$ and $\mathbf{x} \in \mathbb{R}^n$. Prove that g is convex.

(16) We observed that the convexity of a function $f : I \longrightarrow \mathbb{R}$ (where I is an interval of $\mathbb{R}$) implies mid-point convexity. Prove that if $f : [a, b] \longrightarrow \mathbb{R}$ is a continuous function that is mid-point convex on $[a, b]$ implies that f is convex on $[a, b]$.

Solution: Suppose that f is a continuous mid-point convex function that is not convex on $[a, b]$. Then, there exist $c, d \in [a, b]$ and $t \in (0, 1)$ such that

$$
f(tc + (1 - t)d) > tf(c) + (1 - t)f(d).
$$

Define the function $g : [c, d] \longrightarrow \mathbb{R}$ as $g(x) = f(x) - f(c) - \frac{f(d) - f(c)}{d - c}(x - c)$ for $x \in [c, d]$. Note that

$$
\begin{aligned}
g(tc + (1 - t)d) &= f(tc + (1 - t)d) - f(c) - \frac{f(d) - f(c)}{d - c}(1 - t)(d - c) \\
&= f(tc + (1 - t)d) - f(c) - (1 - t)(f(d) - f(c)) \\
&= f(tc + (1 - t)d) - f(c) - (1 - t)(f(d) - f(c)) \\
&= f(tc + (1 - t)d) - (tf(c) + (1 - t)f(d)) \geqslant 0,
\end{aligned}
$$

and $g(c) = g(d) = 0$. Moreover, g itself satisfies the inequality

$$
g\left(\frac{x + y}{2}\right) \leqslant \frac{g(x) + g(y)}{2} \tag{12.19}
$$

for $x, y \in [c, d]$. The function g is continuous on $[c, d]$ because of the continuity of f.

Let $M = \sup\{g(x) \mid x \in [c, d]\}$, and let $x_0 = \inf\{x \in [c, d] \mid g(x) = M\}$. The continuity of g implies that $g(x_0) = M > 0$, so $x_0 \in (c, d)$.

By the definition of x_0, for every $h > 0$ such that $x - h \in (c, d)$ and $x_0 + h \in (c, d)$ we have $g(x_0 - h) < g(x_0)$ and $g(x_0 + h) \leqslant g(x_0)$, so $g(x_0) > \frac{g(x_0-h)+g(x_0+h)}{2}$, which contradicts inequality (12.19).

(17) Let $g : \mathbb{R}^n \longrightarrow \mathbb{R}$ be a convex function such that $g(\mathbf{0}_n) = 0$. Prove that $-g(\mathbf{x}) \leqslant g(\mathbf{x})$ for $\mathbf{x} \in \mathbb{R}^n$.

Solution: Note that if $\mathbf{x} \neq \mathbf{0}_n$, $\mathbf{0}_n \in [-\mathbf{x}, \mathbf{x}]$. Since g is mid-point convex, we have

$$0 = g(\mathbf{0}_n) = g\left(\frac{-\mathbf{x}+\mathbf{x}}{2}\right) \leqslant \frac{1}{2}g(-\mathbf{x}) + \frac{1}{2}g(\mathbf{x}),$$

which implies the desired inequality.

(18)   (a) Prove that the function $f_\beta : \mathbb{R}_{\geqslant 0} \longrightarrow \mathbb{R}$ defined by

$$f_\beta(x) = \frac{x - x^\beta}{1 - 2^{1-\beta}}$$

is concave for every $\beta \in [0, 1) \cup (1, \infty)$. Furthermore, show that f_β is subadditive, that, is $f_\beta(x + y) \leqslant f_\beta(x) + f_\beta(y)$ for $x, y \in \mathbb{R}$.

(b) Let $H_\beta : S_n \longrightarrow \mathbb{R}$ be defined as

$$H_\beta(\mathbf{p}) = \frac{1}{1 - 2^{1-\beta}}\left(1 - \sum_{i=1}^{n} p_i^\beta\right),$$

for $\mathbf{p} \in S_n$, where S_n is the probability simplex in $\mathbb{R}^n$. H_β is known as the β-*entropy* of $\mathbf{p}$. Prove that:

i. $H_\beta(\mathbf{p}) = \sum_{i=1}^{n} f_\beta(p_i)$;

ii. H_β is a concave function on the probability simplex S_n;

iii. for every $\mathbf{p} \in S_n$ we have $H_\beta(\mathbf{p}) \leqslant \frac{1-n^{1-\beta}}{1-2^{1-\beta}}$ and the maximum value of $H_\beta(\mathbf{p})$ is obtained when $p_1 = \cdots = p_n = \frac{1}{n}$;

iv. we have $\lim_{\beta \to 1} H_\beta(\mathbf{p}) = H(\mathbf{p})$, where $H(\mathbf{p})$ is the Shannon entropy of $\mathbf{p}$.

For $\beta = 2$, we have

$$H_2(\mathbf{p}) = 2(1 - \|p\|^2).$$

This quantity is known as the *Gini index*.

Solution: The concavity of f_β implies

$$f_\beta\left(\sum_{i=1}^{n} p_i x_i\right) \geqslant \sum_{i=1}^{n} p_i f_\beta(x_i)$$

for $\mathbf{p} \in S_n$. Taking $x_i = \frac{1}{p_i}$ yields

$$f_\beta(n) \geqslant \sum_{i=1}^{n} p_i \frac{1 - \frac{1}{p_i^{1-\beta}}}{1 - 2^{1-\beta}} = \frac{1}{1 - 2^{1-\beta}} \sum_{i=1}^{n} (p_i - p_i^\beta)$$

$$= \frac{1}{1 - 2^{1-\beta}} \left(1 - \sum_{i=1}^{n} p_i^\beta \right) = H_\beta(\mathbf{p}).$$

Therefore $H_\beta(\mathbf{p}) \leqslant \frac{1 - n^{1-\beta}}{1 - 2^{1-\beta}}$.

(19) Prove that the Shannon entropy $H : S_n \longrightarrow \mathbb{R}$ is a concave function on the probability simplex S_n.

(20) Let $\mathbf{p}, \mathbf{q} \in S_n$, where S_n is the probability simplex in $\mathbb{R}^n$. Prove that the number $H(\mathbf{p} \parallel \mathbf{q})$ defined as

$$H(\mathbf{p} \parallel \mathbf{q}) = \sum_{i=1}^{n} p_i \log_2 \frac{p_i}{q_i}$$

is non-negative; furthermore, $H(\mathbf{p} \parallel \mathbf{q}) = 0$ if and only if $\mathbf{p} = \mathbf{q}$. The number is known as the *Kullback-Leibler relative entropy* of $\mathbf{p}$ and $\mathbf{q}$.

(21) Let $\beta \geqslant 1$.
   (a) Prove that the function $\phi_\beta : [0, 1] \longrightarrow \mathbb{R}$ defined by $\phi_\beta(x) = 1 - x^\beta - (1 - x)^\beta$ is concave on $[0, 1]$.
   (b) Let $w_1, \ldots, w_n$ be n positive numbers such that $\sum_{i=1}^{n} w_i = 1$. Prove that for $a_1, \ldots, a_n \in [0, 1]$ we have

$$1 - \left(\sum_{i=1}^{n} w_i a_i \right)^\beta - \left(\sum_{i=1}^{n} w_i (1 - a_i) \right)^\beta \geqslant \sum_{i=1}^{n} w_i^\beta (1 - a_i^\beta - (1 - a_i)^\beta).$$

Solution: By Jensen's inequality we have $\phi_\beta \left(\sum_{i=1}^{n} w_i a_i \right) \geqslant \sum_{i=1}^{n} w_i \phi_\beta(a_i)$, which amounts to

$$1 - \left(\sum_{i=1}^{n} w_i a_i \right)^\beta - \left(1 - \sum_{i=1}^{n} w_i a_i \right)^\beta$$

$$\geqslant \sum_{i=1}^{n} w_i (1 - a_i^\beta - (1 - a_i)^\beta)$$

(by Jensen's inequality)

$$\geqslant \sum_{i=1}^{n} w_i^\beta (1 - a_i^\beta - (1 - a_i)^\beta)$$

(because $w_i \in [0, 1]$ for $1 \leqslant i \leqslant n$).

(22) Infer Cauchy's inequality in $\mathbb{R}^n$ by applying Jensen's inequality to the convex function $f(x) = x^2$ defined on $\mathbb{R}$.

(23) Let $A \in \mathbb{R}^{n \times n}$, $\mathbf{c} \in \mathbb{R}^n$, and $d \in \mathbb{R}$. Prove that the quadratic function $f : \mathbb{R}^n \longrightarrow \mathbb{R}$ defined by $f(\mathbf{x}) = \mathbf{x}'A\mathbf{x} + \mathbf{c}'\mathbf{x} + d$ is

   (a) convex if and only if A is positive;
   (b) strictly convex if and only if A is positive definite.

   Solution: For $t \in (0, 1)$ we have

$$(1 - t)f(\mathbf{x}) + tf(\mathbf{y}) - f((1 - t)\mathbf{x} + t\mathbf{y})$$
$$= (1 - t)(\mathbf{x}'A\mathbf{x} + \mathbf{c}'\mathbf{x} + d) + t(\mathbf{y}'A\mathbf{y} + \mathbf{c}'\mathbf{y} + d)$$
$$- ((1 - t)\mathbf{x}' + t\mathbf{y}')A((1 - t)\mathbf{x} + t\mathbf{y}) - \mathbf{c}'((1 - t)\mathbf{x} + t\mathbf{y}) - d$$
$$= t(1 - t)(\mathbf{x} - \mathbf{y})'A(\mathbf{x} - \mathbf{y}),$$

which implies immediately both statements.

Quasi-Convex and Pseudo-Convex Functions

(24) Prove that the function $f : \mathbb{R} \longrightarrow \mathbb{R}$ defined by $f(x) = \sqrt{|x|}$ is quasi-convex but not convex.

(25) Prove that every increasing function $f : \mathbb{R} \longrightarrow \mathbb{R}$ is quasi-convex.

(26) Let $f, g : \mathbb{R}^2 \longrightarrow \mathbb{R}$ be the functions defined by $f(\mathbf{x}) = x_1^2 - x_2^2$ and $g(\mathbf{x}) = x_1^2 - x_2$, respectively. Prove that f is not quasi-convex and that $g : \mathbb{R}^2 \longrightarrow \mathbb{R}$ given by is quasi-convex.

(27) Prove that the function $f : \mathbb{R} \longrightarrow \mathbb{R}$ defined by $f(x) = \min\{|x|, 2\}$ is quasi-convex but not convex.

(28) Let $f, g : \mathbb{R}^n \longrightarrow \mathbb{R}_{\geqslant 0}$ be two quasi-convex non-negative functions. Prove that the function $h : \mathbb{R}^n \longrightarrow \mathbb{R}$ defined by $h(\mathbf{x}) = f(\mathbf{x})g(\mathbf{x})$ for $\mathbf{x} \in \mathbb{R}^n$ is quasi-convex.

(29) The definition of strict quasi-convexity may suggest that every strictly quasi-convex function is quasi-convex. This is not the case as observed in [87]. Prove that for $C = [-1, 1]$ and $f : C \longrightarrow \mathbb{R}$ defined as

$$f(x) = \begin{cases} 1 & \text{if } x = 0, \\ 0 & \text{if } x \in [-1, 1] - \{0\}, \end{cases}$$

f is strictly quasi-convex but it is not quasi-convex.

   Hint: Note that the level set $\{x \in [-1, 1] \mid f(x) \leqslant 0\}$ is not convex, so f is not a quasi-convex function.

(30) Let S be a non-empty convex subset of $\mathbb{R}^n$, $g : S \longrightarrow \mathbb{R}$ be a non-negative convex function on S, and let $g : S \longrightarrow \mathbb{R}$ be a concave, positive function

on S. Prove that the function $f : S \longrightarrow \mathbb{R}$ defined by $f(\mathbf{x}) = \frac{g(\mathbf{x})}{h(\mathbf{x})}$ is quasi-convex on S.

Solution: By Theorem 12.23 it suffices to show that each level set

$$L_{f,a} = \{\mathbf{x} \in \mathbb{R}^n \mid f(\mathbf{x}) \leqslant a\} = \{\mathbf{x} \in \mathbb{R} \mid g(\mathbf{x}) \leqslant ah(\mathbf{x})\}$$

is convex. Suppose that $\mathbf{x}_1, \mathbf{x}_2 \in L_{f,a}$. For $t \in [0, 1]$ we have

$$
\begin{aligned}
f((1-t)\mathbf{x}_1 + t\mathbf{x}_2) &= \frac{g((1-t)\mathbf{x}_1 + t\mathbf{x}_2)}{h((1-t)\mathbf{x}_1 + t\mathbf{x}_2)} \\
&\leqslant \frac{(1-t)g(\mathbf{x}_1) + tg(\mathbf{x}_2)}{(1-t)h(\mathbf{x}_1) + t\mathbf{x}_2} \\
&\qquad \text{(because } g \text{ is convex and } h \text{ is concave on } S) \\
&\leqslant a \\
&\qquad \text{(because } g(\mathbf{x}_1) \leqslant ah(\mathbf{x}_1) \text{ and } g(\mathbf{x}_2) \leqslant ah(\mathbf{x}_2)).
\end{aligned}
$$

Thus, $(1-t)\mathbf{x}_1 + a\mathbf{x}_2 \in L_{f,a}$, so f is indeed quasi-convex.

(31) Let S be a convex subset of $\mathbb{R}^n$. Prove that a function $f : S \longrightarrow \mathbb{R}$ is quasi-convex on S if for every $a \in \mathbb{R}$ the set $f^{-1}(-\infty, a]$ is convex.

Solution: Let $\mathbf{x}_1, \mathbf{x}_2 \in S$. To prove that $f((1 - t)\mathbf{x}_1 + t\mathbf{x}_2) \leqslant \max\{f(\mathbf{x}_1), \mathbf{x}_2)\}$ assume that $f(\mathbf{x}_1) \leqslant f(\mathbf{x}_2)$. This implies $\mathbf{x}_1 \in f^{-1}(-\infty, f(\mathbf{x}_2)]$. It is clear that $\mathbf{x}_2 \in f^{-1}(-\infty, f(\mathbf{x}_2)]$, so by the convexity of $f^{-1}(-\infty, f(\mathbf{x}_2)]$ we have $(1 - t)\mathbf{x}_1 + t\mathbf{x}_2 \leqslant f^{-1}(-\infty, f(\mathbf{x}_2)]$. Therefore, $f((1 - t)\mathbf{x}_1 + t\mathbf{x}_2) \leqslant f(\mathbf{x}_2) = \max\{f(\mathbf{x}_1), f(\mathbf{x}_2)\}$, so f is quasi-convex. The case when $f(\mathbf{x}_2) \leqslant f(\mathbf{x}_1)$ is similar.

Convexity and Inequalities

(32) Let C be a convex set in a real linear space and let $f_1, \ldots, f_m$ be m real-valued convex functions defined on C.

Prove that exactly one the following alternatives:

> the system $f_i(x) < 0$
> for $1 \leqslant i \leqslant m$ is consistent,

or

> there exist m numbers $\lambda_1, \ldots, \lambda_m$
> not all 0 such that
> $\sum_{i=1}^{m} \lambda_i f_i(x) \geqslant 0$
> for all $x \in C$

holds.

Solution: It is immediate that the alternatives above are mutually exclusive.

Assume that the first system is inconsistent. For $x \in C$ let U_x be the open set

$$U_x = \{\boldsymbol{\xi} \in \mathbb{R}^m \mid \xi_i > f_i(x) \text{ for } 1 \leqslant i \leqslant m\},$$

and let $U = \bigcup \{U_x \mid x \in C\}$. The convexity of f_i implies that U is convex.

Since the first system is inconsistent, $\mathbf{0}_m \notin U$. By a separation result (Theorem 6.55) there exist m numbers $\lambda_1, \ldots, \lambda_m$ not all 0 such that $\sum_{i=1}^m \lambda_i \xi_i > 0$ for all $\boldsymbol{\xi} \in U$. This implies the second alternative. Additionally, $\lambda_i \geqslant 0$ for $1 \leqslant i \leqslant m$. Indeed, for any $\boldsymbol{\xi} \in U$ and for $\eta > 0$ we have $(\xi_1, \ldots, \xi_i + \eta, \ldots, \xi_m) \in U$. If $\lambda_i < 0$, then by taking η sufficiently large we would have $\lambda_1 \xi_i + \cdots + \lambda_i(\xi_i + \eta) + \cdots + \lambda_m \xi_m < 0$.

(33) Let C be a convex set in a real linear space and let $f_1, \ldots, f_m$ be m real-valued convex functions defined on C such that the system

the system $f_i(x) < 0$
    for $1 \leqslant i \leqslant m$

is consistent and let g be a concave function. Prove that:

(a) for every solution x of the system we have $g(x) \leqslant 0$ if and only if there exist m non-negative numbers $\lambda_1, \ldots, \lambda_m$ such that $g(x) \leqslant \sum_{i=1}^m \lambda_i f_i(x)$;

(b) $\gamma = \sup\{g(x) \mid x \text{ is a solution of the system }\}$ is finite if and only if there exists m non-negative numbers $\lambda_1, \ldots, \lambda_m$ such that $g(x) - \sum_{i=1}^m \lambda_i f_i(x)$ is bounded above on C. When this is the case we have:

$$\gamma = \min_{\lambda_i \geqslant 0} \sup_{x \in C} \left(g(x) - \sum_{i=1}^m \lambda_i f_i(x) \right).$$

Solution: Suppose that for every solution x of the system we have $g(x) \leqslant 0$. Therefore, the system

$f_i(x) < 0$ for $1 \leqslant i \leqslant m$,
$-g(x) < 0$

is inconsistent. By Supplement 32 we obtain the existence of the numbers $\lambda_1, \ldots, \lambda_m$ such that $g(x) \leqslant \sum_{i=1}^m \lambda_i f_i(x)$; the inverse implication is immediate.

For the second part note that γ is finite only if every solution of the system satisfies the inequality $g(x) - \beta \leqslant 0$. The first part implies the existence of m non-negative numbers $\lambda_1, \ldots, \lambda_m$ such that $g(x) - \beta \leqslant \sum_{i=1}^m \lambda_i f_i(x)$, which means that $g(x) - \sum_{i=1}^m \lambda_i f_i(x)$ is bounded above on C.

Assume now that $\gamma = \sup\{g(x) \mid x \text{ is a solution of the system }\}$ is finite. Then every solution of the system satisfies $g(x) - \gamma \leqslant 0$. By the first part, there are m non-negative numbers such that $g(x) - \sum_{i=1}^m \rho_i f_i(x) \leqslant \gamma$ for all $x \in C$. By the definition of γ, for every $\epsilon > 0$

there is a solution $x_\epsilon \in C$ such that $g(x_\epsilon) > \gamma - \epsilon$. If $\lambda_i \geqslant 0$ and

$$\alpha = \sup\left\{ g(x) - \sum_{i=1}^{m} \lambda_i f_i(x) \,\middle|\, x \in C \right\},$$

then $\gamma - \epsilon < g(x_\epsilon) \leqslant \alpha + \sum_{i=1}^{m} \lambda_i f_i(x_\epsilon) \leqslant \alpha$ for every $\epsilon > 0$. Therefore, $\gamma \leqslant \alpha$.

Let C be a convex set in a real linear space and let $f_1, \ldots, f_m$ be m real-valued functions defined on C. The system of inequalities $f_i(x) < 0$ for $1 \leqslant i \leqslant m$ is consistent of there exists $x \in C$ that satisfies all m inequalities; otherwise, the system is *inconsistent*. Recall that a system is minimally inconsistent if it is inconsistent and every one of its proper subsystems in consistent.

The set of convex functions $f_1, \ldots, f_m$ defined on C are *linearly independent* if there is no linear combination $f = \sum_{i=1}^{m} \lambda_i f_i$ with real coefficients $\lambda_1, \ldots, \lambda_m$ not all 0 such that $f(x) \geqslant 0$ for $x \in C$.

(34) Prove that the set of m convex functions $\{f_i : [0, 1] \longrightarrow \mathbb{R} \mid 1 \leqslant i \leqslant m\}$, where $f_i(x) = x^i - \frac{1}{i+1}$ are linearly independent for every m.

Solution: Suppose that the set of functions $\{f_1, \ldots, f_m\}$ are not linearly independent, so there exist $\lambda_1, \ldots, \lambda_m$ not all 0 such that $\sum_{i=1}^{m} \lambda_i f_i(x) \geqslant 0$. Since

$$\int_0^1 \left[\sum_{i=1}^{m} \lambda_i \left(x^i - \frac{1}{i+1} \right) \right] dx = 0,$$

the polynomial $\sum_{i=1}^{m} \lambda_i(x^i - \frac{1}{i+1})$ must vanish identically and therefore, all we have $\lambda_i = 0$ for $1 \leqslant i \leqslant m$.

(35) Let C be a convex set in a real linear space and let $f_1, \ldots, f_m$ be real-valued convex functions defined on C. For a function $g : C \longrightarrow \mathbb{R}$ an inequality $g(x) \leqslant 0$ is a consequence of the system $f_i(x) < 0$ for $1 \leqslant i \leqslant m$ if every solution of the system satisfies the inequality.

Prove that if g is a concave function and $g(x) \leqslant 0$ is a consequence of the system and it is not a consequence of any subsystem of the system, then $f_1, \ldots, f_m$ are linearly independent.

Solution: By the first part of Supplement 33, there exist m non-negative numbers $\lambda_1, \ldots, \lambda_m$ such that $g(x) \leqslant \sum_{i=1}^{m} \lambda_i f_i(x)$. Since $g(x) \leqslant 0$ is not a consequence of any subsystem of the system $f_i(x) < 0$, it follows that $\lambda_i > 0$ for $1 \leqslant i \leqslant m$.

Suppose that there exist m real numbers $\mu_1, \ldots, \mu_m$ not all 0 such that $\sum_{i=1}^{m} \mu_i f_i(x) \geqslant 0$ for all $x \in C$. Since the system $f_i(x) < 0$ is consistent, there exists x_0 such that $f_i(x_0) < 0$ for $1 \leqslant i \leqslant m$, which implies that at least one of the numbers μ_i is negative. Define

$$I = \{i \mid 1 \leqslant i \leqslant m \text{ and } \mu_i < 0\}$$

and

$$\nu = \max\left\{\frac{\lambda_i}{\mu_i} \,\middle|\, i \in I \text{ and } \frac{\lambda_i}{\mu_i} < 0\right\}.$$

If $\eta_i = \lambda_i - \nu\mu_i$ for $1 \leqslant i \leqslant m$ we have

$$g(\mathbf{x}) \leqslant \sum_{i=1}^{m} \lambda_i f_i(x)$$

$$\leqslant \sum_{i=1}^{m} \lambda_i f_i(x) - \nu \sum_{i=1}^{m} \mu_i f_i(x)$$

$$= \sum_{i=1}^{m} \eta_i f_i(x)$$

for all $x \in C$. Since each η_i is non-negative and at least one of them is 0, $g(x) \leqslant 0$ would be a consequence of a proper subsystem, which implies that $f_1, \ldots, f_m$ are linearly independent.

(36) Let C be a convex set in a real linear space and let $f_1, \ldots, f_m$ be real-valued convex functions defined on C. Prove that the system $f_i(x) < 0$ for $1 \leqslant i \leqslant m$ is minimally inconsistent, if and only if the following conditions are satisfied:

(a) there exist m positive numbers $\lambda_1, \ldots, \lambda_m$ such that $\sum_{i=1}^{m} \lambda_i f_i(x) \geqslant 0$;

(b) any $m - 1$ of the functions $f_1, \ldots, f_m$ are linearly independent.

Solution: Assume that the system $f_i(x) < 0$ for $1 \leqslant i \leqslant m$ is inconsistent. By Supplement 32 there exist $\lambda_1, \ldots, \lambda_m$ not all 0 such that $\sum_{i=1}^{m} \lambda_i f_i(x) \geqslant 0$ for all $x \in C$.

Furthermore, since $f_i(x) < 0$ for $1 \leqslant i \leqslant m$ is minimally inconsistent, every solution of the system $f_i(x) < 0$ for $1 \leqslant i \leqslant m - 1$ satisfies the inequality $f_m(x) \geqslant 0$, or, equivalently, $-f_m(x) \leqslant 0$. Therefore, by Supplement 35, $f_1, \ldots, f_{m-1}$ are linearly independent, which proves that the second condition is satisfied.

Conversely, by Supplement 32, the second condition implies that every proper subsystem is consistent, while the first condition implies that the whole system $f_i(x) < 0$ for $1 \leqslant i \leqslant m$ is inconsistent.

Let S be an interval of $\mathbb{R}$ and let $(x_1, \ldots, x_n), (y_1, \ldots, y_n)$ be two sequences of numbers from S such that $x_1 \geqslant x_2 \geqslant \cdots \geqslant x_n$, $y_1 \geqslant y_2 \geqslant \cdots \geqslant y_n$, $\sum_{i=1}^{k} x_i \geqslant \sum_{i=1}^{k} y_i$ for $1 \leqslant k < n$ and $\sum_{i=1}^{n} x_i = \sum_{i=1}^{n} y_i$. When these conditions are satisfied we say that $(x_1, \ldots, x_n)$ majorizes $(y_1, \ldots, y_n)$ and we write $(x_1, \ldots, x_n) \succeq (y_1, \ldots, y_n)$.

(37) Let S be an interval of $\mathbb{R}$, $x_1, \ldots, x_n, y_1, \ldots, y_n \in S$ and let $f : S \longrightarrow \mathbb{R}$ be a convex function. Prove the *HLPK inequality*[1] which states that if $(x_1, \ldots, x_n) \succeq (y_1, \ldots, y_n)$, then

$$\sum_{i=1}^{n} f(x_i) \geqslant \sum_{i=1}^{n} f(y_i).$$

Solution: The proof is by induction on $n \geqslant 2$. For the base step, $n = 2$, we have $x_1 \geqslant x_2$, $y_1 \geqslant y_2$, $x_1 \geqslant y_1$, and $x_1 + x_2 \geqslant y_1 + y_2$, which imply $x_1 \geqslant y_1 \geqslant y_2 \geqslant x_2$. Therefore, there exists $p \in [0, 1]$ such that $y_1 = px_1 + (1 - p)x_2$. Since

$$y_2 = x_1 + x_2 - y_1 = x_1 + x_2 - px_1 - (1 - p)x_2,$$

it follows that $y_2 = (1 - p)x_1 + px_2$, so $f(y_1) \leqslant pf(x_1) + (1 - p)f(x_2)$ and $f(y_1) \leqslant (1 - p)f(x_1) + pf(x_2)$ because f is convex. By adding these inequalities we obtain Karamata's inequality for $n = 2$.

Suppose that the inequality holds for sequences of length n and let $(x_1, \ldots, x_{n+1})$, $(y_1, \ldots, y_{n+1})$ be two sequences that satisfy the previous conditions. Then, $x_1 + \cdots + x_n \geqslant y_1 + \cdots + y_n$, so there exists a non-negative number z such that

$$x_1 + \cdots + x_n = y_1 + \cdots + (y_n + z).$$

Taking into account that

$$x_1 + \cdots + x_n + x_{n+1} = y_1 + \cdots + y_n + y_{n+1},$$

it follows that $z + x_{n+1} = y_{n+1}$.

By the inductive hypothesis

$$f(x_1) + \cdots + f(x_n) \geqslant f(y_1) + \cdots + f(y_n + z),$$

so

$$f(x_1) + \cdots + f(x_n) + f(x_{n+1}) \geqslant f(y_1) + \cdots + f(y_n + z) + f(x_{n+1}).$$

The needed equality will be proven if we can show that

$$f(y_n + z) + f(x_{n+1}) \geqslant f(y_n) + f(y_{n+1}). \tag{12.20}$$

Since $y_n + z \geqslant y_n \geqslant y_{n+1} \geqslant x_{n+1}$ and $y_n + z + x_{n+1} = y_n + y_{n+1}$, by using again the base case, we obtain inequality (12.20).

---

[1]HLPK is an acronym of the authors G. H. Hardy, J. E. Littlewook, G. Polya [73] and J. Karamata [88] who discovered independently this inequality.

(38) A reciprocal result of HLPK inequality introduced in Supplement 37 holds as well. Namely, prove that if $n \geq 2$, and the sequences $x_1 \geqslant \cdots \geqslant x_n$ and $y_1 \geqslant \cdots \geqslant y_n$ from an interval S satisfy the inequality $\sum_{i=1}^{n} f(x_i) \geqslant \sum_{i=1}^{n} f(y_i)$ for every convex function, then $\sum_{i=1}^{k} x_i \geqslant \sum_{i=1}^{k} y_i$ for $1 \leqslant k \leqslant n-1$ and $\sum_{i=1}^{n} x_i \geqslant \sum_{i=1}^{n} y_i$.

Solution: The choice $f(x) = x$ for $x \in S$ yields the inequality $x_1 + \cdots + x_n \geqslant y_1 + \cdots + y_n$; the choice $f(x) = -x$ yields $-x_1 - \cdots - x_n \geqslant -y_1 - \cdots - y_n$, so $x_1 + \cdots + x_n = y_1 + \cdots + y_n$. Let now $f_k : S \longrightarrow \mathbb{R}$ be the convex function given by

$$f_k(x) = \begin{cases} 0 & \text{if } x < x_k, \\ x - x_k & \text{if } x \geq x_k. \end{cases}$$

Using f_k we obtain the inequality

$$\begin{aligned} x_1 + \cdots + x_k - kx_k &= h(x_1) + \cdots + h(x_n) \\ &\geqslant h(y_1) + \cdots + h(y_n) \geqslant h(y_1) + \cdots + h(y_k) \\ &\geqslant y_1 + \cdots + y_k - kx_k, \end{aligned}$$

which implies $x_1 + \cdots + x_k \geqslant y_1 + \cdots + y_k$.

(39) Let $f : \mathbb{R} \longrightarrow \mathbb{R}$ be a convex, increasing function.

(a) Prove that for any two sequences $(x_1, \ldots, x_n)$ and $(y_1, \ldots, y_n)$ of real numbers such that $y_1 \geqslant \cdots \geqslant y_n$ and $x_1 + \cdots + x_k \geqslant y_1 + \cdots + y_k$ for $1 \leqslant k \leqslant n$ we have

$$f(x_1) + \cdots + f(x_n) \geqslant f(y_1) + \cdots + f(y_n).$$

(b) Prove that for any two sequences of positive real numbers $(a_1, \ldots, a_n)$ and $(b_1, \ldots, b_n)$ such that $a_1 \geqslant \cdots \geqslant a_n$ and $b_1 \geqslant \cdots \geqslant b_n$,

$$a_1 \cdots a_k \geqslant b_1 \cdots b_k$$

for $1 \leqslant k \leqslant n$, we have

$$f(a_1) + \cdots + f(a_n) \geqslant f(b_1) + \cdots + f(b_n).$$

Solution: This statement can be obtained from the HLPK inequality as follows. Let $c = x_1 + \cdots + x_n - (y_1 + \cdots + y_n)$. Clearly, we have $c \geq 0$. Let y_{n+1} be a number such that $y_n \geqslant y_{n+1}$ and consider the sequences $(x_1, \ldots, x_n, y_{n+1} - c)$ and $(y_1, \ldots, y_n, y_{n+1})$.

The HLPK inequality is applicable to these sequences and it yields

$$f(x_1) + \cdots + f(x_n) + f(y_{n+1} - c) \geq f(y_1) + \cdots + f(y_n) + f(y_{n+1}).$$

Since f is an increasing function we have

$$f(x_1) + \cdots + f(x_n) + f(y_{n+1}) \geq f(y_1) + \cdots + f(y_n) + f(y_{n+1}),$$

which amounts to the equality to be proven.

To prove the second part apply the first part to the numbers $x_i = \log a_i$ and $b_i = \log b_i$.

Differentiability and Convexity

(40) Let $f : \mathbb{R}^n \longrightarrow \mathbb{R} \cup \{\infty\}$ be a convex function and let $\mathbf{x}_0 \in \mathrm{Dom}(f)$. Prove that the function $g_{\mathbf{u}} : \mathbb{R}_{>0} \longrightarrow \mathbb{R}$ defined as

$$g_{\mathbf{u}}(t) = \frac{f(\mathbf{x}_0 + t\mathbf{u}) - f(\mathbf{x}_0)}{t}$$

is non-decreasing. Conclude that for a point $\mathbf{x}_0$ in the domain of a convex function f the directional derivative $\frac{\partial f}{\partial \mathbf{u}}(\mathbf{x}_0)$ exists.

Hint: Substitute in the defining inequality of convexity $f((1-a)\mathbf{y} + a\mathbf{z}) \leqslant (1-a)f(\mathbf{y}) + af(z)$, $a = 1 - \frac{t_1}{t_2}$, $\mathbf{y} = \mathbf{x}_0 + t_2\mathbf{u}$, and $\mathbf{z} = \mathbf{x}_0$ to obtain the desired inequality.

(41) Let $f : \mathbb{R}^n \longrightarrow \mathbb{R}$ be a convex function. Prove that

(a) the function $g : \mathbb{R}^{n+1} \longrightarrow \mathbb{R}$ defined by

$$g(x_1, \ldots, x_n, x_{n+1}) = f(x_1, \ldots, x_n) - x_{n+1}$$

for $(x_1, \ldots, x_n, x_{n+1}) \in \mathbb{R}^{n+1}$ is convex;

(b) the function $h : \mathbb{R}^{n+1} \longrightarrow \mathbb{R}$ defined by

$$h(x_1, \ldots, x_n, x_{n+1}) = f(x_1, \ldots, x_n) - x_{n+1}^2$$

for $(x_1, \ldots, x_n, x_{n+1}) \in \mathbb{R}^{n+1}$ is not convex.

(42) Prove that every monotonic function $f : \mathbb{R} \longrightarrow \mathbb{R}$ is both quasi-convex and quasi-concave.

(43) Let $F : \mathbb{R}^{m \times p} \times \mathbb{R}^{p \times n} \longrightarrow \mathbb{R}$ be the function defined by $F(U, V) = \|A - UV\|_F$ for $U \in \mathbb{R}^{m \times p}$ and $V \in \mathbb{R}^{p \times n}$. Prove that both $F_U : \mathbb{R}^{p \times n} \longrightarrow \mathbb{R}$ and $F_V : \mathbb{R}^{m \times p} \longrightarrow \mathbb{R}$ given by $F_U(V) = F(U, V)$ for $V \in \mathbb{R}^{p \times n}$ and $F_V : \mathbb{R}^{m \times p} \longrightarrow \mathbb{R}$ given by $F_V(U) = F(U, V)$ are convex function, while F itself is not convex.

(44) Let C be a subset of $\mathbb{R}^n$ and let $f : C \longrightarrow \mathbb{R}$ be a function. Prove that f is convex if and only if for every $\mathbf{x}, \mathbf{y} \in C$ the function $g_{\mathbf{x},\mathbf{y}} : [0, 1] \longrightarrow \mathbb{R}$ defined by $g_{\mathbf{x},\mathbf{y}}(a) = f(a\mathbf{x} + (1-a)\mathbf{y})$ is convex.

(45) Let $f : \mathbb{R}^n \longrightarrow \mathbb{R}$ be an arbitrary function. Its *Fenchel conjugate* is the function $g : \mathbb{R}^n \longrightarrow \mathbb{R}$ defined by $g(\mathbf{z}) = \sup\{\mathbf{z}'\mathbf{x} - f(\mathbf{x}) \mid \mathbf{x} \in \mathbb{R}^n\}$ for $\mathbf{z} \in \mathbb{R}^n$. Prove that g is a convex function.

 Solution: It suffices to show that $\text{epi}(g)$ is a convex set. So let $(\mathbf{z}_1, y_1), (\mathbf{z}_2, y_2) \in \text{epi}(g)$, that is, $g(\mathbf{z}_1) \leqslant y_1$ and $g(\mathbf{z}_2) \leqslant y_2$. By the definition of g we have $\mathbf{z}_1'\mathbf{x} - f(\mathbf{x}) \leqslant y_1$ and $\mathbf{z}_2'\mathbf{x} - f(\mathbf{x}) \leqslant y_2$ for every $\mathbf{x} \in \mathbb{R}^n$. If a_1, a_2 are two non-negative numbers such that $a_1 + a_2 = 1$ we need to show that $a_1(\mathbf{z}_1, y_1) + a_2(\mathbf{z}_2, y_2) = (a_1\mathbf{z}_1 + a_2\mathbf{z}_2, a_1 y_1 + a_2 y_2) \in \text{epi}(g)$, which follows from

$$(a_1\mathbf{z}_1 + a_2\mathbf{z}_2)'\mathbf{x} - f(\mathbf{x}) = a_1(\mathbf{z}_1'\mathbf{x} - f(\mathbf{x})) + a_2(\mathbf{z}_2'\mathbf{x} - f(\mathbf{x})) \leqslant a_1 y_1 + a_2 y_2.$$

Thus, $g(a_1\mathbf{z}_1 + a_2\mathbf{z}_2) \leqslant a_1 y_1 + a_2 y_2$, which proves that g is indeed convex. Note that this property of g holds regardless of the convexity of f.

(46) Denote by f^* the Fenchel conjugate of f. Prove that:
 (a) if $f \leqslant g$, then $f^* \geqslant g^*$;
 (b) $f^{**} \leqslant f$;
 (c) $f^{***} = f$,
where $f^{**} = (f^*)^*$ and $f^{***} = ((f^*)^*)^*$.

(47) Prove that $f(\mathbf{x}) + f^*(\mathbf{y}) \geqslant \mathbf{y}'\mathbf{x}$ for every $\mathbf{x} \in \mathbb{R}^n$, where the equality $f(\mathbf{x}) + f^*(\mathbf{y}) = \mathbf{y}'\mathbf{x}$ occurs if and only if $\mathbf{y} \in \text{subd}(f)(\mathbf{x})$.

(48) Prove that every conjugate function f^* is lower semicontinuous.

 Solution: This follows from Theorem 4.108 because f^* is the supremum of a collection of continuous functions.

(49) Let $A \in \mathbb{R}^{p \times q}$ be a matrix. Prove that if ν is a norm on $\mathbb{R}^{p \times q}$ and $f_A : \mathbb{R}^{p \times k} \times \mathbb{R}^{k \times q} \longrightarrow \mathbb{R}_{\geqslant 0}$ is the function defined by $f_A(X, Y) = \|A - XY\|_F^2$ for $X \in \mathbb{R}^{p \times k}$ and $Y \in \mathbb{R}^{k \times q}$, then f_A is not a convex function.

 Solution: It suffices to consider the case $p = k = 1$. In this case, the convexity of f_a amounts to

$$|a - [tx + (1-t)u][ty + (1-t)v]|^2 \leq t|a - xy|^2 + (1-t)|a - uv|^2$$

for $(x, y), (u, v) \in \mathbb{R}^2$ and $t \in [0, 1]$. Choosing $u = -x$ and $v = -y|$ and $t = 0.5$, the convexity condition implies

$$|a|^2 \leq |a - xy|^2.$$

This inequality is clearly violated if, for example, $xy = \frac{a}{2}$ and $a > 1$.

(50) Let $f : \mathbb{R}^n \longrightarrow \mathbb{R}$. The perspective of f is the function $g : \mathbb{R}^n \times \mathbb{R}_{>0} \longrightarrow \mathbb{R}$ defined by

$$g(\mathbf{x}, u) = uf\left(\frac{1}{u}\mathbf{x}\right)$$

for $\mathbf{x} \in \mathbb{R}^n$ and $u > 0$. Prove that if f is a convex function, then g is also convex.

Solution: Let $(\mathbf{x}, t), (\mathbf{y}, s) \in \mathbb{R}^n \times \mathbb{R}_{>0}$. For $t \in [0, 1]$ we have

$$
\begin{aligned}
g(t&(\mathbf{x}, u) + (1 - t)(\mathbf{y}, v)) \\
&= g(t\mathbf{x} + (1 - t)\mathbf{y}, tu + (1 - t)v) \\
&= (tu + (1 - t)v)f\left(\frac{1}{tu + (1 - t)v}(t\mathbf{x} + (1 - t)\mathbf{y})\right) \\
&= (tu + (1 - t)v)f\left(\frac{tu}{tu + (1 - t)v}\frac{1}{u}\mathbf{x} + \frac{(1 - t)v}{tu + (1 - t)v}\frac{1}{v}\mathbf{y}\right) \\
&\leq tuf\left(\frac{1}{u}\mathbf{x}\right) + (1 - t)vf\left(\frac{1}{v}\mathbf{y}\right) \\
&\quad \text{(because } f \text{ is convex)} \\
&= tg(\mathbf{x}, u) + (1 - t)g(\mathbf{y}, v),
\end{aligned}
$$

which shows that g is convex.

(51) Let $f : \mathbb{R} \longrightarrow \mathbb{R}$ be the function $f(x) = x^3$. Verify that f is strictly quasi-convex but not pseudo-convex on $\mathbb{R}$.

(52) Let $f : \mathbb{R} \longrightarrow \mathbb{R}$ be a function and let $F : \mathbb{R}^n \longrightarrow \mathbb{R}$ be the function defined by $F(\mathbf{x}) = f(x_1) + \cdots + f(x_n)$ for $\mathbf{x} \in \mathbb{R}^n$. Prove that

    (a) F is a convex function if and only if f is a convex function;

    (b) if f has a minimal point x_0, then $(x_0, \ldots, x_0)$ is a minimal point for F.

Solution: Suppose that f is convex, that is, $f(ar + (1 - a)s) \leq af(r) + (1 - a)f(s)$ for $a \in [0, 1]$. Then, we can write

$$
\begin{aligned}
F(a\mathbf{x} + (1 - a)\mathbf{y}) &= f(ax_1 + (1 - a)y_1) + \cdots + f(ax_n + (1 - a)y_n) \\
&\leq af(x_1) + (1 - a)f(y_1) + \cdots af(x_n) + (1 - a)f(y_n) \\
&= aF(\mathbf{x}) + (1 - a)F(\mathbf{y}),
\end{aligned}
$$

for $\mathbf{x}, \mathbf{y} \in \mathbb{R}^n$ which shows that F is indeed convex.

Conversely, suppose that F is convex. Note that, by the definition of F we have $f(x) = \frac{1}{n}F(x\mathbf{1})$. Thus,

$$
\begin{aligned}
f(ar + (1 - a)s) &= \frac{1}{n}F((ar + (1 - a)s)\mathbf{1}) \\
&= \frac{1}{n}F(a(r\mathbf{1}) + (1 - a)(s\mathbf{1})) \\
&\leq \frac{1}{n}aF(r\mathbf{1}) + (1 - a)F(s\mathbf{1}) \\
&= af(r) + (1 - a)f(s),
\end{aligned}
$$

which proves the convexity of f.

Since the function f is convex, its minimal point, if it exists is unique and is characterized by $f'(x_0) = 0$. Note that if F has a minimal point, since $\frac{\partial F}{\partial x_i} = f'(x_i)$ for $1 \leq i \leq n$, we have the minimal point $(x_0, \ldots, x_0)$ for F.

(53) Let $f : S \longrightarrow \mathbb{R}$ and $g : T \longrightarrow \mathbb{R}$ be two convex functions, where $S, T \subseteq \mathbb{R}^n$, and let $a, b \in \mathbb{R}_{\geq 0}$. Prove that $af + bg$ is a convex function.

(54) Let $F : S \longrightarrow \mathbb{R}^m$ be a function, where S is a non-empty convex subset of $\mathbb{R}^n$. Prove that if each component f_i of F is a convex function on S and $g : \mathbb{R}^m \longrightarrow \mathbb{R}$ is a monotonic function, then the function gF defined by $gF(\mathbf{x}) = g(F(\mathbf{x}))$ for $\mathbf{x} \in S$ is convex.

(55) Let $f : S \longrightarrow \mathbb{R}$ be a convex function, where S is a convex subset of $\mathbb{R}^n$. Define the function $g : \mathbb{R}_{>0} \times S \longrightarrow \mathbb{R}$ by $g(t, \mathbf{x}) = tf\left(\frac{x}{t}\right)$. Prove that g is a convex function.

(56) Let $f : \mathbb{R} \geqslant 0 \longrightarrow \mathbb{R}$ be a convex function. Prove that if $f(0) = 0$ and f is monotonic and convex, then f is subadditive.

Solution: By applying the convexity of f to the interval $[0, x + y]$ with $a = \frac{x}{x+y}$, we have

$$f(a \cdot 0 + (1 - a)(x + y)) \leqslant af(0) + (1 - a)f(x + y),$$

we have $f(y) \leqslant \frac{y}{x+y} f(x + y)$. Similarly, we can show that $f(x) \leqslant \frac{x}{x+y} f(x + y)$. By adding the last two inequalities, we obtain the subadditivity of f.

(57) Let S be a convex subset of $\mathbb{R}^n$ and let I be an open interval of $\mathbb{R}$. If $f : S \longrightarrow \mathbb{R}$ and $g : I \longrightarrow \mathbb{R}$ are convex functions such that $g(I) \subseteq S$ and g is non-decreasing, prove that gf is a convex function on S.

(58) Let $S \subseteq \mathbb{R}^n$ be a convex set, $S \neq \emptyset$. Define the *support function of S*, $h_S : \mathbb{R}^n \longrightarrow \mathbb{R}$ by $h_S(\mathbf{x}) = \sup\{\mathbf{s}'\mathbf{x} \mid \mathbf{s} \in S\}$. Prove that $\mathrm{Dom}(h_S)$ is a cone in $\mathbb{R}^n$, h_S is a convex function and $h_S(a\mathbf{x}) = ah_S(\mathbf{x})$ for $a \geqslant 0$.

(59) Give an example of a non-convex function whose level sets are convex.

(60) Let $U \in \mathbb{R}^{n \times k}$ be a matrix such that $U'U = I_k$, where $k \leq n$. Prove that for every $\mathbf{x} \in \mathbb{R}^n$ we have

$$\|\mathbf{x}\|_2 \geq \|U'\mathbf{x}\|_2.$$

Solution: It is immediate that the columns $\mathbf{u}_1, \ldots, \mathbf{u}_k$ of matrix U form an orthonormal set. Let $\{\mathbf{u}_1, \ldots, \mathbf{u}_k, \mathbf{u}_{k+1}, \ldots, \mathbf{u}_n\}$ be the completion of this set to an orthonormal set of $\mathbb{R}^n$. If $\mathbf{x} = \sum_{i=1}^n a_i \mathbf{u}_i$, then $\|\mathbf{x}\|_2^2 = \sum_{i=1}^n a_i^2$.

On the other hand,

$$U'\mathbf{x} = \begin{pmatrix} \mathbf{u}'_1 \\ \vdots \\ \mathbf{u}'_k \end{pmatrix} \mathbf{x} = \begin{pmatrix} \mathbf{u}'_1\mathbf{x} \\ \vdots \\ \mathbf{u}'_k\mathbf{x} \end{pmatrix} = \begin{pmatrix} a_1 \\ \vdots \\ a_k \end{pmatrix},$$

because of the orthonormality of the set $\{\mathbf{u}_1, \ldots, \mathbf{u}_k\}$, so

$$\|Y'\mathbf{x}\|_2^2 = \sum_{i=1}^{k} a_i^2 \le \sum_{i=1}^{n} a_i^2 = \|\mathbf{x}\|_2^2.$$

(61) Let $Y \in \mathbb{R}^{n \times k}$ be a matrix such that $Y'Y = I_k$, where $k \le n$. Prove that the matrix $I_n - YY'$ is positive.

Solution: Let $\mathbf{x} \in \mathbb{R}^n$. We have

$$\mathbf{x}'(I_n - YY')\mathbf{x} = \mathbf{x}'\mathbf{x} - (\mathbf{Y}'\mathbf{x})'(\mathbf{Y}'\mathbf{x}) = \|\mathbf{x}\|_2^2 - \|Y'\mathbf{x}\|_2^2.$$

The desired inequality follows immediately from Supplement 60.

(62) Let $f : S \longrightarrow \mathbb{R}$, where $S \subseteq \mathbb{R}^{n \times n}$ is the set of symmetric real matrices and $f(A)$ is the largest eigenvalue of A. Prove that f is a convex function.

(63) If $A \in \mathbb{C}^{m \times n}$, prove that the matrices $A^{\mathsf{H}}A \in \mathbb{C}^{n \times n}$ and $AA^{\mathsf{H}} \in \mathbb{C}^{m \times m}$ are positive. Furthermore, if $rank(A) = n$, then both $A^{\mathsf{H}}A$ and AA^{H} are positive definite.

Solution: For $\mathbf{x} \in \mathbb{C}^n$ we have:

$$\mathbf{x}^{\mathsf{H}}(A^{\mathsf{H}}A)\mathbf{x} = (\mathbf{x}^{\mathsf{H}}A^{\mathsf{H}})(A\mathbf{x}) = (A\mathbf{x})^{\mathsf{H}}(A\mathbf{x}) = \|A\mathbf{x}\|_2^2 \ge 0.$$

The argument for AA^{H} is similar.

If $rank(A) = n$, then the matrix $A^{\mathsf{H}}A$ is positive definite because $\mathbf{x}^{\mathsf{H}}(A^{\mathsf{H}}A)\mathbf{x} = 0$ implies $A\mathbf{x} = \mathbf{0}$, which, in turn, implies $\mathbf{x} = \mathbf{0}$.

(64) Let $\mathcal{M}_1 = \{YY' \mid Y \in \mathbb{R}^{n \times k} \text{ and } Y'Y = I_k\}$ and

$$\mathcal{M}_2 = \{W \in \mathbb{R}^{n \times n} \mid W = W', trace(W) = k \text{ and } \\ W \text{ and } I_n - W \text{ are positive}\}.$$

Prove that

(a) we have $\mathcal{M}_2 = \mathbf{K}_{\text{conv}}(\mathcal{M}_1)$;
(b) $\mathcal{M}_1$ is the set of extreme points of the polytope $\mathcal{M}_2$.

Solution: Every convex combination of elements of $\mathcal{M}_1$ lies in $\mathcal{M}_2$. Indeed, let $Z = a_1 Y_1 Y_1' + \cdots + a_p Y_p Y_p'$ be a convex combination of $\mathcal{M}_1$.

It is immediate that Z is a symmetric matrix. Furthermore, we have

$$trace(Z) = \sum_{h=1}^{p} a_h \, trace(Y_h Y_h') = \sum_{h=1}^{p} a_h \, trace(Y_h' Y_h) = \sum_{h=1}^{p} a_h \, trace(I_k) = k.$$

because $\sum_{h=1}^{p} a_h = 1$. The positive semi-definiteness of YY' follows from Supplement 63, while the positive semi-definiteness of $I_n - YY'$ follows from Supplement 61. Thus, $\mathbf{K}_{\text{conv}}(\mathcal{M}_1) \subseteq \mathcal{M}_2$.

Conversely, let $W \in \mathcal{M}_2$. By the spectral theorem for Hermitian matrices applied to real symmetric matrices, W can be written as $W = U'DU$, where U is an unitary matrix. Clearly, all eigenvalues of W belong to the interval $[0, 1]$.

If the columns of the matrix U' are $\mathbf{u}_1, \ldots, \mathbf{u}_n$ and the eigenvalues of W are $a_1, \ldots, a_n$, then

$$W = (\mathbf{u}_1 \;\; \cdots \;\; \mathbf{u}_n) \begin{pmatrix} a_1 & 0 & \cdots & 0 \\ 0 & a_2 & \cdots & 0 \\ \vdots & \vdots & \cdots & \vdots \end{pmatrix} \begin{pmatrix} \mathbf{u}_1' \\ \vdots \\ \mathbf{u}_n' \end{pmatrix},$$

which allows us to write $W = a_1 \mathbf{u}_1 \mathbf{u}_1' + \cdots + a_r \mathbf{u}_r \mathbf{u}_r'$, where W has rank r, $a_1, \ldots, a_r$ are the non-zero eigenvalues of W, and $\sum_{i=1}^{r} a_i = trace(W) = k$. Note that the rank of W is at least k because its eigenvalues reside in the interval $[0, 1]$ and their sum is k.

If the rank of W equals k, then $W = \mathbf{u}_1 \mathbf{u}_1' + \cdots + \mathbf{u}_k \mathbf{u}_k'$ because all eigenvalues equal 1. This allows us to write $W = ZZ'$, where $Z \in \mathbb{R}^{n \times k}$ is the matrix $Z = (\mathbf{u}_1 \;\; \cdots \;\; \mathbf{u}_k)$. Since $Z'Z = I_k$ it follows that in this case $W \in \mathcal{M}_1$. In other words, $\mathcal{M}_1$ is exactly the subset of $\mathcal{M}_2$ that consists of rank k matrices.

If $rank(W) = r > k$ we have $W = a_1 \mathbf{u}_1 \mathbf{u}_1' + \cdots + a_r \mathbf{u}_r \mathbf{u}_r'$. Starting from the r matrices $\mathbf{u}_i \mathbf{u}_i'$ we can form $\binom{r}{k}$ matrices of rank k of the form $\sum_{i \in I} \mathbf{u}_i \mathbf{u}_i'$ by considering all subsets I of $\{1, \ldots, r\}$ that contain k elements. We have $W = \sum_{j=1}^{r} a_j \mathbf{u}_j \mathbf{u}_j' = \sum_{I, |I|=k} \alpha_I \sum_{i \in I} \mathbf{u}_i \mathbf{u}_i'$. If we match the coefficients of $\mathbf{u}_i \mathbf{u}_i'$ we have $a_i = \sum_{I, i \in I, |I|=k} \alpha_I$. If we add these equalities we obtain

$$k = \sum_{i=1}^{r} \sum_{I, i \in I, |I|=k} \alpha_I.$$

We choose α_I to depend on the cardinality of I and take into account that each α_I occurs k times in the previous sum. This implies $\sum_{I, i \in I, |I|=k} \alpha_I = 1$, so each W is a convex combination of matrices of rank k, so $\mathbf{K}_{\text{conv}}(\mathcal{M}_1) = \mathcal{M}_2$. No matrix of rank greater than k can be an extreme point. Since every convex and compact set has extreme elements, only matrices of rank k can play this role. Since the definition of $\mathcal{M}_2$ makes no distinction between the k-rank matrices, it follows that the set of extreme elements coincides with $\mathcal{M}_1$.

(65) A *perspective function* is a function $g : \mathbb{R}^n \times \mathbb{R}_{>0} \longrightarrow \mathbb{R}^n$ given by $g\begin{pmatrix} \mathbf{x} \\ t \end{pmatrix} = \frac{1}{t}\mathbf{x}$. Prove that if $C \subseteq \mathbb{R}^{n+1}$ is a convex set, then $g(C)$ is a convex subset of $\mathbb{R}^n$. Also, if $D \subseteq \mathbb{R}^n$ is a convex set, then $g^{-1}(D)$ is a convex set in $\mathbb{R}^{n+1}$.

Solution: Let $\mathbf{y}_1, \mathbf{y}_2 \in g(C)$. We have $\mathbf{y}_i = \frac{1}{t_i}\mathbf{x}_i$ for $i = 1, 2$, where $\begin{pmatrix} \mathbf{x}_1 \\ t_1 \end{pmatrix}, \begin{pmatrix} \mathbf{x}_2 \\ t_2 \end{pmatrix} \in C$. A convex combination $(1-a)\mathbf{y}_1 + a\mathbf{y}_2$, where $a \in [0, 1]$ can be written as

$$(1-a)\mathbf{y}_1 + a\mathbf{y}_2 = \frac{1-a}{t_1}\mathbf{x}_1 + \frac{a}{t_2}\mathbf{x}_2$$
$$= \frac{1}{b}((1-c)\mathbf{x}_1 + c\mathbf{x}_2)),$$

where $c = \frac{at_1}{at_1 + (1-a)t_2} \in [0, 1]$ and $b = \frac{1-a}{t_1} + \frac{a}{t_2} > 0$. Thus, $(1-a)\mathbf{y}_1 + a\mathbf{x}_2 \in g(C)$, so $g(C)$ is convex.

For the second part of the statement let D be a convex subset of $\mathbb{R}^n$ and let $\begin{pmatrix} \mathbf{x}_1 \\ t_1 \end{pmatrix}, \begin{pmatrix} \mathbf{x}_2 \\ t_2 \end{pmatrix} \in g^{-1}(D)$, that is, $\frac{1}{t_1}\mathbf{x}_1, \frac{1}{t_2}\mathbf{x}_2 \in D$. Observe that we can write

$$g\left((1-a)\begin{pmatrix} \mathbf{x}_1 \\ t_1 \end{pmatrix} + a\begin{pmatrix} \mathbf{x}_2 \\ t_2 \end{pmatrix}\right) = \frac{(1-a)\mathbf{x}_1 + a\mathbf{x}_2}{(1-a)t_1 + at_2} = \frac{1-p}{t_1}\mathbf{x}_1 + \frac{p}{t_2}\mathbf{x}_2 \in D,$$

where $p = \frac{at_2}{(1-a)t_1 + at_2} \in [0, 1]$. Therefore,

$$(1-a)\begin{pmatrix} \mathbf{x}_1 \\ t_1 \end{pmatrix} + a\begin{pmatrix} \mathbf{x}_2 \\ t_2 \end{pmatrix} \in g^{-1}(D),$$

so $g^{-1}(D)$ is a convex set.

Subgradients

(66) Let $f : \mathbb{R}^n \longrightarrow \mathbb{R} \cup \{\infty\}$ be a convex function and let $\mathbf{x}_0 \in \mathrm{Dom}(f)$. Prove that $\mathbf{s}$ is a subgradient of f at $\mathbf{x}_0$ if and only if $\frac{\partial f}{\partial \mathbf{u}}(\mathbf{x}_0) \geqslant \mathbf{s}'\mathbf{u}$ for every direction $\mathbf{u}$.

Solution: If $\mathbf{s}$ is a subgradient of f at $\mathbf{x}_0$ we have $f(\mathbf{x}) \geqslant f(\mathbf{x}_0) + \mathbf{s}'(\mathbf{x} - \mathbf{x}_0)$. For $\mathbf{u} = \frac{1}{t}(\mathbf{x} - \mathbf{x}_0)$ this inequality amounts to $\frac{f(\mathbf{x}_0 + t\mathbf{u}) - f(\mathbf{x}_0)}{t} \geqslant \mathbf{s}'\mathbf{h}$, which, by Supplement 40 implies $\frac{\partial f}{\partial \mathbf{u}}(\mathbf{x}_0) \geqslant \mathbf{s}'\mathbf{u}$.

Conversely, if $\frac{\partial f}{\partial \mathbf{u}}(\mathbf{x}_0) \geqslant \mathbf{s}'\mathbf{u}$ we have $\lim_{t \to 0} \frac{f(\mathbf{x}_0 + t\mathbf{u}) - f(\mathbf{x}_0)}{t} \geqslant \mathbf{s}'\mathbf{u}$. By the same Supplement 40, we have $\frac{f(\mathbf{x}_0 + t\mathbf{u}) - f(\mathbf{x}_0)}{t} \geqslant \mathbf{s}'\mathbf{u}$, so $\mathbf{s}$ is a subgradient of f at $\mathbf{x}_0$.

(67) Prove that the hinge function $h : \mathbb{R} \longrightarrow \mathbb{R}$ introduced in Exercise 2 is not differentiable in $x = 1$ and compute $\mathsf{subd}(h)(1)$.

Solution: If s is a subgradient of h at 1 we have $\max\{0, 1 - x\} \geqslant s(x - 1)$ for every $x \in \mathbb{R}$. For $x < 1$, this amounts to $1 - x \geqslant s(x - 1)$, or $s \geqslant -1$. For $x \geqslant 1$, we have $0 \geqslant s(x - 1)$, which is equivalent to $s \leqslant 0$. Thus, $\mathsf{subd}(h)(1) = [-1, 0]$.

(68) Let U be an open and convex subset of $\mathbb{R}^n$ and let $f : U \longrightarrow \mathbb{R}$ be a convex function. Prove that f is a Lipschitz function with constant c if and only if for all $\mathbf{u} \in U$ and $\mathbf{v} \in \mathsf{subd}(f)(\mathbf{u})$ we have $\|\mathbf{v}\| \leqslant c$.

Solution: Suppose that for all $\mathbf{u} \in U$ and $\mathbf{v} \in \mathsf{subd}(f)(\mathbf{u})$ we have $\|\mathbf{v}\| \leqslant c$. Since $\mathbf{v} \in \mathsf{subd}(f)(\mathbf{u})$ it follows that $f(\mathbf{u}) - f(\mathbf{v}) \leqslant \mathbf{v}'(\mathbf{u} - \mathbf{v}) \leqslant \|\mathbf{v}\|\|\mathbf{u} - \mathbf{v}\| \leqslant c\|\mathbf{u} - \mathbf{v}\|$.

Conversely, suppose that f is Lipschitz with the constant c. Let $\mathbf{u} \in U$ and let $\mathbf{v} \in \mathsf{subd}(f)(\mathbf{u})$. Since U is an open set, there exists $\epsilon > 0$ such that $S(\mathbf{u}, \frac{\epsilon}{\|\mathbf{v}\|}\mathbf{v}) \subseteq U$.

Let $\mathbf{z} \in S(\mathbf{u}, \frac{\epsilon}{\|\mathbf{v}\|}\mathbf{v})$. We have $(\mathbf{z} - \mathbf{u})'\mathbf{v} = \epsilon\|\mathbf{v}\|$ and $\|\mathbf{z} - \mathbf{u}\| = \epsilon$. Since $\mathbf{v}$ is a subgradient, $f(\mathbf{z}) - f(\mathbf{u}) \geqslant \mathbf{v}'(\mathbf{z} - \mathbf{u}) = \epsilon\|\mathbf{v}\|$. Since f is Lipschitz, $c\epsilon = c\|\mathbf{z} - \mathbf{u}\| \geqslant f(\mathbf{z}) - f(\mathbf{u})$, so $\|\mathbf{v}\| \leqslant c$.

(69) Let $\mathbf{w} \in \mathbb{R}^n, y \in \mathbb{R}$ and let $f_{\mathbf{w}} : \mathbb{R}^n \longrightarrow \mathbb{R}$ be defined by $f_{\mathbf{w},y}(\mathbf{x}) = h(y\mathbf{w}'\mathbf{x})$ for $\mathbf{x} \in \mathbb{R}^n$, where h is the hinge function. Prove that $f_{\mathbf{w},y}$ is a Lipschitz function.

A convex function $f : \mathbb{R}^n \longrightarrow \mathbb{R}$ is *a-strongly convex* if there exists $a > 0$ such that $f(\mathbf{x}) - \frac{a}{2}\|\mathbf{x}\|_2^2$ is convex. The number a is the *modulus of strong convexity* of f.

A function f is *strongly convex* if it is a-strongly convex for some positive number a.

(70) Prove that the convex function $f : \mathbb{R}^n \longrightarrow \mathbb{R}$ is a-strongly convex if and only if

$$f((1 - t)\mathbf{x} + t\mathbf{y}) \leqslant (1 - t)f(\mathbf{x}) + tf(\mathbf{y}) - \frac{a}{2}(1 - t)t\|\mathbf{y} - \mathbf{x}\|_2^2.$$

for $\mathbf{x}, \mathbf{y} \in \mathbb{R}^n$ and $t \in [0, 1]$. Conclude that every strongly convex function is strictly convex.

(71) Prove that the function $f : \mathbb{R} \longrightarrow \mathbb{R}$ defined by $f(x) = x^4$ is strictly convex but not strongly convex.

(72) Prove that if $f : \mathbb{R}^n \longrightarrow \mathbb{R}$ is a-strongly convex $g : \mathbb{R}^n \longrightarrow \mathbb{R}$ is convex, then $f + g$ is a-strongly convex.

(73) Let $\mathbf{u}$ be a minimizer of an a-strongly convex function $f : \mathbb{R}^n \longrightarrow \mathbb{R}$. Prove that:

    (a) $f(\mathbf{x}) - f(\mathbf{u}) \geqslant \frac{a}{2}\|\mathbf{x} - \mathbf{u}\|^2$ for every $\mathbf{x} \in \mathbb{R}^n$;

    (b) the minimizer $\mathbf{u}$ is unique.

Bibliographical Comments

Convex function play an essential role in optimization theory and have a multitude of applications in various areas of mathematics. Fundamental references that focus on convex functions are [111, 99, 120]. Other useful readings are [107, 97, 18]. An application-focused approach is provided in [23]. Convex polytopes and related topics are studied in [69, 115]. Properties of quasi-convex functions are surveyed in [66].

Supplement 9 appears in [120]. Supplements 32-36 are results of Ky Fan, Glicksberg and Hoffman [55].

The treatment of subgradients was inspired by [19, 20].

PART V

Applications

Chapter 13

Optimization

13.1 Introduction

Optimization techniques play an important role in machine learning because of their wide applicability in such areas as clustering, regression, classification, and especially support vector machines. We aim to present in this chapter and subsequent chapter the state of the interaction between optimization and machine learning in a way that is accessible to researchers in machine learning.

Regularized optimization is presented in subsequent application chapters. After discussing fundamental issues such as local extrema, ascent and descent directions, general optimization problems, optimization with and without differentiability is studied. Weak and strong duality are presented in view of their application in the study of support vector machines.

13.2 Local Extrema, Ascent and Descent Directions

Definition 13.1. Let X be a open subset in $\mathbb{R}^n$ and let $f : X \longrightarrow \mathbb{R}$ be a functional.

The point $\mathbf{x}_0 \in X$ is a *local minimum* for f if there exists $\delta > 0$ such that $B(\mathbf{x}_0, \delta) \subseteq X$ and $f(\mathbf{x}_0) \leqslant f(\mathbf{x})$ for every $\mathbf{x} \in B(\mathbf{x}_0, \delta)$.

The point $\mathbf{x}_0$ is a *strict local minimum* if $f(\mathbf{x}_0) < f(\mathbf{x})$ for every $x \in B(\mathbf{x}_0, \delta) - \{\mathbf{x}_0\}$.

The notions of local maximum and strict local maximum are defined similarly. Namely, $\mathbf{x}_0 \in X$ is a *local maximum* for f if there exists $\delta > 0$ such that $B(\mathbf{x}_0, \delta) \subseteq X$ and $f(\mathbf{x}_0) \geqslant f(\mathbf{x})$ for every $\mathbf{x} \in B(\mathbf{x}_0, \delta)$. The point $\mathbf{x}_0$ is a *strict local maximum* if $f(\mathbf{x}_0) > f(\mathbf{x})$ for every $\mathbf{x} \in B(\mathbf{x}_0, \delta) - \{\mathbf{x}_0\}$.

A *local extremum* of a functional $f : X \longrightarrow \mathbb{R}$ is a local maximum or a local minimum of f.

Theorem 13.1. *Let X be a open subset in $\mathbb{R}^n$ and let $f : X \longrightarrow \mathbb{R}$ be a functional that has a Gâteaux derivative on X. Every local extremum point of f is a critical point of f.*

Proof. Define the function $g : \mathbb{R} \longrightarrow \mathbb{R}$ as $g(a) = f(\mathbf{x}_0 + a\mathbf{h})$. Since $\mathbf{x}_0$ is a local extremum the function g is differentiable and has a minimum in $a = 0$. Therefore, $g'(0) = 0$ and

$$g'(0) = \lim_{r \to 0} \frac{g(r) - g(0)}{r} = \lim_{r \to 0} \frac{f(\mathbf{x}_0 + r\mathbf{h}) - f(\mathbf{x}_0)}{r}$$
$$= ((Df)(\mathbf{x}_0))'\mathbf{h} = \delta f(\mathbf{x}_0; \mathbf{h}) = 0,$$

for every $\mathbf{h} \in X$. $\qquad\square$

Definition 13.2. Let U be a open subset in $\mathbb{R}^n$. If $\mathbf{x}_0 \in U$, then $\mathbf{d}$ is a *feasible direction at $\mathbf{x}_0$ for U* if
(i) $\mathbf{d} \neq \mathbf{0}_n$, and
(ii) there exists $a > 0$ such that $\mathbf{x}_0 + t\mathbf{d} \in U$ for every $t \in [0, a]$.
The set of feasible directions at $\mathbf{x}_0$ is denoted by $\mathsf{FD}(U, \mathbf{x}_0)$.

If $\mathbf{x}_0 \in \mathbf{I}(U)$, then there exists an open sphere $B(\mathbf{x}_0, r)$ included in U, so every direction $\mathbf{d}$ is feasible.

Definition 13.3. Let U be a open subset in $\mathbb{R}^n$ and let $f : U \longrightarrow \mathbb{R}$ be a functional.
If $\mathbf{x}_0 \in \mathbf{K}(U)$ then $\mathbf{d} \in S$ is a *descent direction* for f at $\mathbf{x}_0$ if there exists $\delta > 0$ such that $f(\mathbf{x}_0 + a\mathbf{d}) < f(\mathbf{x}_0)$ for $0 < a < \delta$.
The vector $\mathbf{d}$ is an *ascent direction* of f at $\mathbf{x}_0$ if there exists $\delta > 0$ such that $f(\mathbf{x}_0 + a\mathbf{d}) > f(\mathbf{x}_0)$ for $0 < a < \delta$.
The set of ascent directions of f at $\mathbf{x}_0$ is denoted by $\mathsf{AD}(f, \mathbf{x}_0)$; the set of descent directions of f at $\mathbf{x}_0$ is denoted by $\mathsf{DD}(f, \mathbf{x}_0)$.

Note that for descent or ascent directions at $\mathbf{x}_0$ the number δ depends on the direction $\mathbf{d}$.

Theorem 13.2. *Let U be a open subset in $\mathbb{R}^n$ and let $f : U \longrightarrow \mathbb{R}$ be a differentiable functional U. Let $\boldsymbol{d}$ be a feasible direction at $\boldsymbol{x}_0$ for U.*
If $((\nabla f)(\boldsymbol{x}_0))'\boldsymbol{d} < 0$, then $\boldsymbol{d} \in \mathsf{DD}(f, \boldsymbol{x}_0)$; if $((\nabla f)(\boldsymbol{x}_0))'\boldsymbol{d} > 0$, then $\boldsymbol{d} \in \mathsf{AD}(f, \boldsymbol{x}_0)$.

Proof.   We give the argument for the case when $((\nabla f)(\mathbf{x}_0))'d < 0$. Since f is differentiable at $\mathbf{x}_0$ we have

$$f(\mathbf{x}_0 + ad) - f(\mathbf{x}_0) - a((\nabla f)(\mathbf{x}_0))'(\mathbf{d}) = o(\mathbf{d}).$$

Therefore, $f(\mathbf{x}_0 + ad) - f(\mathbf{x}_0) = a((\nabla f)(x_0))'\mathbf{d} + o(\mathbf{d})$.

Since $\lim_{\mathbf{d} \to \mathbf{0}} o(d) = 0$, for a sufficiently small a we have $f(\mathbf{x}_0 + ad) - f(\mathbf{x}_0) < 0$, so $\mathbf{d}$ is indeed a descent direction at $\mathbf{x}_0$. $\qquad\square$

Theorem 13.3. *Let U be a open subset of $\mathbb{R}^n$ and let $f : U \longrightarrow \mathbb{R}$ be a functional in $C^1(U)$. If $\boldsymbol{x}_0$ is a local minimum (maximum) of f, then every feasible direction at $\boldsymbol{x}_0$ is an ascent (descent) direction, that is, $\mathsf{FD}(f, \boldsymbol{x}_0) \subseteq \mathsf{AD}(f, \boldsymbol{x}_0)$ (and, $\mathsf{FD}(f, \boldsymbol{x}_0) \subseteq \mathsf{DD}(f, \boldsymbol{x}_0)$, respectively).*

Proof.   Suppose that $\mathbf{x}_0$ is a local minimum of f and that $\mathbf{d}$ is a feasible direction at $\mathbf{x}_0$, that is, $\mathbf{x}_0 + td \in U$ for $t \in [0, a]$ (for some $a > 0$).

Let $g : [0, a] \longrightarrow \mathbb{R}$ be the function defined by $g(t) = f(\mathbf{x}_0 + td)$. Clearly, g has a local minimum at $t = 0$, so $g'(0) \geqslant 0$. Since $\frac{d}{dt} g(0) = (\nabla f)(\mathbf{x}_0)'\mathbf{d} \geqslant 0$, it follows that $\mathbf{d}$ is an ascent direction. $\qquad\square$

Theorem 13.3 means that if $\mathbf{x}_0$ is a local minimum for f, then

$$\mathsf{FD}(f, \mathbf{x}_0) \cap \mathsf{DD}(f, \mathbf{x}_0) = \emptyset. \tag{13.1}$$

Theorem 13.4. *Let $f : B(\boldsymbol{x}_0, r) \longrightarrow \mathbb{R}$ be a function that belongs to the class $C^2(B(\boldsymbol{x}_0, r))$, where $B(\boldsymbol{x}_0, r) \subseteq \mathbb{R}^k$ and $\boldsymbol{x}_0$ is a critical point for f. If the Hessian matrix $H_f(\boldsymbol{x}_0)$ is positive semidefinite, then $\boldsymbol{x}_0$ is a local minimum for f; if $H_f(\boldsymbol{x}_0)$ is negative semidefinite, then $\boldsymbol{x}_0$ is a local maximum for f.*

Proof.   The Taylor formula implies

$$f(\mathbf{x}) = f(\mathbf{x}_0) + ((\mathbf{h}'\nabla)f)(\mathbf{x}_0) + \mathbf{h}'H_f(\mathbf{x}_0 + \theta\mathbf{h})\mathbf{h},$$

where $\mathbf{h} = \mathbf{x} - \mathbf{x}_0$ is such that $\|\mathbf{h}\| \leqslant r$. Since $\mathbf{x}_0$ is a critical point, it follows that

$$f(\mathbf{x}) = f(\mathbf{x}_0) + \mathbf{h}'H_f(\mathbf{x}_0 + \theta\mathbf{h})\mathbf{h}.$$

Therefore, if $H_f(\mathbf{x}_0)$ is positive semidefinite we have $\mathbf{h}'H_f(\mathbf{x}_0)\mathbf{h} \geqslant 0$ for $\mathbf{h} \in \mathbb{R}^k$. Since the second derivatives of f are continuous, if θ is sufficiently small, $H_f(\mathbf{x}_0 + \theta\mathbf{h})$ is also positive semidefinite, hence $f(\mathbf{x}) \geqslant f(\mathbf{x}_0)$, which means that $\mathbf{x}_0$ is a local minimum; if $H_f(\mathbf{x}_0)$ is negative semidefinite, it follows that $f(\mathbf{x}) \leqslant f(\mathbf{x}_0)$ so $\mathbf{x}_0$ is a local maximum for f. $\qquad\square$

Example 13.1. Let $f : \mathbb{R}^2 \longrightarrow \mathbb{R}$ be a function in $C^2(B(\mathbf{x}_0, r))$. The Hessian matrix in $\mathbf{x}_0$ is

$$H_f(\mathbf{x}_0) = \begin{pmatrix} \dfrac{\partial^2 f}{\partial x_1{}^2} & \dfrac{\partial^2 f}{\partial x_1 \, \partial x_2} \\ \dfrac{\partial^2 f}{\partial x_2 \, \partial x_1} & \dfrac{\partial^2 f}{\partial x_2{}^2} \end{pmatrix}(\mathbf{x}_0).$$

Let $a_{11} = \frac{\partial^2 f}{\partial x_1{}^2}(\mathbf{x}_0)$, $a_{12} = \frac{\partial^2 f}{\partial x_1 \, \partial x_2}(\mathbf{x}_0)$, and $a_{22} = \frac{\partial^2 f}{\partial x_2{}^2}(\mathbf{x}_0)$. Note that

$$\mathbf{h}' H_f(\mathbf{x}_0)\mathbf{h} = a_{11}h_1^2 + 2a_{12}h_1 h_2 + a_{22}h_2^2$$
$$= h_2^2 \left(a_{11}\xi^2 + 2a_{12}\xi + a_{22} \right),$$

where $\xi = \frac{h_1}{h_2}$. For a critical point $\mathbf{x}_0$ we have:

- (i) $\mathbf{h}' H_f(\mathbf{x}_0)\mathbf{h} \geqslant 0$ for every $\mathbf{h}$ if $a_{11} > 0$ and $a_{12}^2 - a_{11}a_{22} < 0$; in this case, $H_f(\mathbf{x}_0)$ is positive semidefinite and $\mathbf{x}_0$ is a local minimum;
- (ii) $\mathbf{h}' H_f(\mathbf{x}_0)\mathbf{h} \leqslant 0$ for every $\mathbf{h}$ if $a_{11} < 0$ and $a_{12}^2 - a_{11}a_{22} < 0$; in this case, $H_f(\mathbf{x}_0)$ is negative semidefinite and $\mathbf{x}_0$ is a local maximum;
- (iii) if $a_{12}^2 - a_{11}a_{22} \geqslant 0$; in this case, $H_f(\mathbf{x}_0)$ is neither positive nor negative definite, so $\mathbf{x}_0$ is a saddle point.

Note that in the first two previous cases we have $a_{12}^2 < a_{11}a_{22}$, so a_{11} and a_{22} have the same sign.

Example 13.2. Let $\mathbf{a}_1, \ldots, \mathbf{a}_m$ be m points in $\mathbb{R}^n$. The function $f(\mathbf{x}) = \sum_{i=1}^m \|\mathbf{x} - \mathbf{a}_i\|^2$ gives the sum of squares of the distances between $\mathbf{x}$ and the points $\mathbf{a}_1, \ldots, \mathbf{a}_m$. We will prove that this sum has a global minimum obtained when $\mathbf{x}$ is the barycenter of the set $\{\mathbf{a}_1, \ldots, \mathbf{a}_m\}$.

We have

$$f(\mathbf{x}) = m\|\mathbf{x}\|^2 - 2\sum_{i=1}^m \mathbf{a}_i'\mathbf{x} + \sum_{i=1}^m \|\mathbf{a}_i\|^2$$
$$= m(x_1^2 + \cdots + x_n^2) - 2\sum_{j=1}^n \sum_{i=1}^m a_{ij}x_j + \sum_{i=1}^m \|\mathbf{a}_i\|^2,$$

which implies

$$\frac{\partial f}{\partial x_j} = 2mx_j - 2\sum_{i=1}^m a_{ij}$$

for $1 \leqslant j \leqslant n$. Thus, there exists only one critical point given by

$$x_j = \frac{1}{m}\sum_{i=1}^m a_{ij}$$

for $1 \leqslant j \leqslant n$. The Hessian matrix $H_f = 2mI_n$ is obviously positive definite, so the critical point is a local minimum and, in view of convexity of f, the global minimum. This point is the barycenter of the set $\{\mathbf{a}_1, \ldots, \mathbf{a}_m\}$.

Example 13.3. Let $f : \mathbb{R}^n \longrightarrow \mathbb{R}$ be a linear functional defined as $f(\mathbf{x}) = \mathbf{a}'\mathbf{x} + b$ whose values $y_1, \ldots, y_m$ are obtained by performing a series of experiments starting with the values $\mathbf{x}_1, \ldots, \mathbf{x}_m \in \mathbb{R}^n$ of the input parameters of the experiments. The goal of the experiments is to determine $\mathbf{a} \in \mathbb{R}^n$ and $b \in \mathbb{R}$. Noise and experimental errors affect the values of the results of the experiment such that the system in $\mathbf{a}$ and b:

$$\mathbf{a}'\mathbf{x}_k + b = y_k$$

for $1 \leqslant k \leqslant m$ is not compatible in general. The next best thing to solving this system is to determine $\mathbf{a}$ and b such that the square error

$$r(a_1, \ldots, a_n, b) = \sum_{k=1}^{m} (\mathbf{a}'\mathbf{x}_k + b - y_k)^2$$

is minimal.

If $X = (\mathbf{1}_n \ \mathbf{x}_1 \cdots \mathbf{x}_m) \in \mathbb{R}^{n \times (1+m)}$ and $\mathbf{y} = \begin{pmatrix} y_1 \\ \vdots \\ y_m \end{pmatrix}$, then r can be written as:

$$r(\mathbf{c}) = \|\mathbf{y} - X\mathbf{c}\|^2,$$

where $\mathbf{c} = \begin{pmatrix} b \\ \mathbf{a} \end{pmatrix}$. Observe that

$$r(\mathbf{c}) = (\mathbf{y} - X\mathbf{c})'(\mathbf{y} - X\mathbf{c})$$
$$= \mathbf{y}'\mathbf{y} - \mathbf{y}'X\mathbf{c} - \mathbf{c}'X'\mathbf{y} + \mathbf{c}'X'X\mathbf{c},$$

where $\mathbf{c}'X'\mathbf{y} = \mathbf{y}'X\mathbf{c}$ is a scalar (and, therefore, equals its transpose). Thus,

$$r(\mathbf{c}) = \mathbf{y}'\mathbf{y} - 2\mathbf{y}'X\mathbf{c} + \mathbf{c}'X'X\mathbf{c}.$$

The necessary conditions for the minimum yield $(D_\mathbf{c} r)(\mathbf{c}_0) = \mathbf{0}$, which amount to

$$-X'\mathbf{y} + (X'X)\mathbf{c} = \mathbf{0}.$$

If $rank(X'X) = n$, the matrix $X'X$ is invertible and $\mathbf{c} = (X'X)^{-1}X'\mathbf{y}$.

Example 13.4. Let $f : \mathbb{R}^2 \longrightarrow \mathbb{R}$ be the function defined by $f(\mathbf{x}) = \sin(x_1 x_2)$. We have

$$\frac{\partial f}{\partial x_1} = x_2 \cos(x_1 x_2) \text{ and } \frac{\partial f}{\partial x_2} = x_1 \cos(x_1 x_2),$$

which yield

$$\frac{\partial^2 f}{\partial x_1{}^2} = x_2^2 \cos(x_1 x_2),$$

$$\frac{\partial^2 f}{\partial x_1 \, \partial x_2} = \cos(x_1 x_2) - x_1 x_2 \sin(x_1 x_2), \frac{\partial^2 f}{\partial x_2{}^2} = x_1^2 \cos x_1 x_2.$$

The set of critical points of f are given by $x_1 x_2 = \pi(k \pm \frac{\pi}{2})$ for $k \in Z$.

Let $f : \mathbb{R}^n \longrightarrow \mathbb{R}$ be a function having the critical point $\mathbf{x}_0$. To determine whether $\mathbf{x}_0$ is an extremum for f whenever $H_f(\mathbf{x}_0) = 0$ we need to examine the first non-zero term of the Taylor formula:

$$f(\mathbf{x}_0 + a\mathbf{d}) = f(x_0) + \frac{a^n}{n!}((\mathbf{d}'\nabla)^n f)(\mathbf{x}_0 + a\theta\mathbf{d}),$$

where we assume that $\frac{1}{k!}((\mathbf{d}'\nabla)^m f)(\mathbf{x}_0) = 0$ for $1 \leqslant k \leqslant n - 1$. If $\mathbf{x}_0$ is a minimum, n must be an even number and we need to have $((\mathbf{d}'\nabla)^n f)(\mathbf{x}_0 + a\theta\mathbf{d}) > 0$. Similarly, if $\mathbf{x}_0$ is a maximum, n must be even, and $((\mathbf{d}'\nabla)^n f)(\mathbf{x}_0 + a\theta\mathbf{d}) < 0$.

Example 13.5. It is interesting to note that the conditions mentioned above for having an extremum in $\mathbf{x}_0$ for a function $f : \mathbb{R}^n \longrightarrow \mathbb{R}$ are only necessary but not sufficient. An interesting, classic example in this sense was given by A. Gennochi and G. Peano in [64]. The reader should also consult [9] and [52].

Let $f : \mathbb{R}^2 \longrightarrow \mathbb{R}$ be the function

$$\begin{aligned} f(\mathbf{x}) &= (x_2^2 - 2px_1)(x_2^2 - 2qx_1) \\ &= 4pqx_1^2 - 2(p + q)x_1 x_2^2 + x_2^4, \end{aligned}$$

where $p > q > 0$.

The partial derivatives are:

$$\frac{\partial f}{\partial x_1} = -2(p + q)x_2^2 + 8pqx_1, \frac{\partial f}{\partial x_2} = 4x_2^3 - 4(p + q)x_1 x_2,$$

$$\frac{\partial^2 f}{\partial x_1{}^2} = 8pq, \frac{\partial^2 f}{\partial x_1 \, \partial x_2} = -4(p + q)x_2, \frac{\partial^2 f}{\partial x_2{}^2} = 12x_2^2 - 4(p + q)x_1$$

$$\frac{\partial^3 f}{\partial x_1{}^3} = 0, \frac{\partial^3 f}{\partial x_1{}^2 \, \partial x_2} = 0, \frac{\partial^3 f}{\partial x_1 \, \partial x_2{}^2} = -4(p + q), \frac{\partial^3 f}{\partial x_2{}^3} = 24x_2.$$

Finally, $\frac{\partial^4 f}{\partial x_2{}^4} = 24$, and all other partial derivatives are 0. The terms that occur in Taylor formula at $\mathbf{x}_0 = \mathbf{0}_2$ are:

$$f(\mathbf{0}_2) = 0,$$

$$(\mathbf{h}'\nabla)f(\mathbf{0}_2) = \mathbf{0}_2,$$

$$(\mathbf{h}'\nabla)^2 f(\mathbf{0}_2) = \left(h_1\frac{\partial}{\partial x_1} + h_2\frac{\partial}{\partial x_2}\right)^2 f(\mathbf{x}_0)$$

$$= \left(h_1^2\frac{\partial^2 f}{\partial x_1{}^2} + 2h_1 h_2\frac{\partial^2 f}{\partial x_1\,\partial x_2} + h_2^2\frac{\partial^2 f}{\partial x_2{}^2}\right)(\mathbf{0}_2)$$

$$= 4pqh_1^2,$$

$$(\mathbf{h}'\nabla)^3 f(\mathbf{0}_2) = \left(h_1\frac{\partial}{\partial x_1} + h_2\frac{\partial}{\partial x_2}\right)^3 f(\mathbf{x}_0)$$

$$= \left((h_1^3\frac{\partial^3 f}{\partial x_1{}^3} + 3h_1^2 h_2\frac{\partial^3 f}{\partial x_1{}^2\,\partial x_2}\right.$$

$$\left. + 3h_1 h_2^2\frac{\partial^3 f}{\partial x_1\,\partial x_2{}^2} + h_2^3\frac{\partial^3 f}{\partial x_2{}^3}\right)(\mathbf{0}_2)$$

$$= -2(p+q)h_1 h_2^2,$$

$$(\mathbf{h}'\nabla)^4 f(\mathbf{0}_2) = h_2^4,$$

and the Taylor expansion is

$$f(\mathbf{h}) = 4pqh_1^2 - 2(p+q)h_1 h_2^2 + h_2^4.$$

Note that $f(\mathbf{h})$ considered as a trinomial of degree 2 in h_1 has the roots $\frac{h_2^2}{2p}$ and $\frac{h_2^2}{2q}$, where $0 < \frac{h_2^2}{2p} < \frac{h_2^2}{2q}$. If

$$\frac{h_2^2}{2p} < h_1 < \frac{h_2^2}{2q}$$

$f(\mathbf{h}) < 0$. If $h_1 < \frac{h_2^2}{2p}$ or if $h_1 > \frac{h_2^2}{2q}$ then $f(\mathbf{h}) > 0$. Thus, $0 = f(\mathbf{0}_2)$ is neither a maximum nor a minimum for f.

Note that each of the terms in the Taylor expansion of a function $f : \mathbb{R}^n \longrightarrow \mathbb{R}$, $\frac{1}{m!}((\mathbf{h}'\nabla)^m f)(\mathbf{x})$ is a homogeneous function of degree m in $h_1, \ldots, h_n$. We will refer to such function as forms of degree of degree m. A form is *definite* if it vanishes only when all variables vanishes simultaneously. It is *indefinite* if it may assume negative and positive values. Thus, a form of odd degree which does not vanish identically is always indefinite. A form may be neither definite nor indefinite. For example, the form $(\mathbf{h}'\nabla)^2 f(\mathbf{0}_2) = 4pqh_1^2$ that occurs in Example 13.5 is indefinite: it is always positive when it is not 0 and it vanishes when $\mathbf{h} \in V$. The criterion formulated in [64] is the following: If for $\mathbf{x} = \mathbf{x}_0$ all partial derivatives of order n or less vanish, and in the Taylor's expression for $f(\mathbf{x}_0 + \mathbf{h})$ and if the term that is a homogeneous n degree form in $\mathbf{h}$ is an indefinite form then $f(\mathbf{x}_0)$ is neither a minimum or a maximum. If however, this form is definite and positive, then $f(\mathbf{x}_0)$ is a minimum; if it is definite and negative, then $f(\mathbf{x}_0)$ is a maximum.

13.3 General Optimization Problems

Let $f : \mathbb{R}^n \longrightarrow \mathbb{R}$, $\mathbf{c} : \mathbb{R}^n \longrightarrow \mathbb{R}^m$, and $\mathbf{d} : \mathbb{R}^n \longrightarrow \mathbb{R}^p$ be three functions defined on $\mathbb{R}^n$. A general formulation of a *constrained optimization problem* is

$$\text{minimize } f(\mathbf{x}), \text{ where } \mathbf{x} \in \mathbb{R}^n,$$
$$\text{subject to } \mathbf{c}(\mathbf{x}) \leqslant \mathbf{0}_m, \text{ where } \mathbf{c} : \mathbb{R}^n \longrightarrow \mathbb{R}^m,$$
$$\text{and } \mathbf{d}(\mathbf{x}) = \mathbf{0}_p, \text{ where } \mathbf{d} : \mathbb{R}^n \longrightarrow \mathbb{R}^p.$$

Here $\mathbf{c}$ specifies *inequality constraints* placed on $\mathbf{x}$, while $\mathbf{d}$ defines *equality constraints*.

The *feasible region* of the constrained optimization problem is the set

$$R_{\mathbf{c},\mathbf{d}} = \{\mathbf{x} \in \mathbb{R}^n \mid \mathbf{c}(\mathbf{x}) \leqslant \mathbf{0}_m \text{ and } \mathbf{d}(\mathbf{x}) = \mathbf{0}_p\}.$$

If the feasible region $R_{\mathbf{c},\mathbf{d}}$ is non-empty and bounded, then, under certain conditions a solution exists. If $R_{\mathbf{c},\mathbf{d}} = \emptyset$ we say that the constraints are *inconsistent*.

Note that equality constraints can be replaced in a constrained optimization problem by inequality constraints. Indeed, a constraint of the form $\mathbf{d}(\mathbf{x}) = \mathbf{0}_p$ can be replaced by a pair of constraints $\mathbf{d}(\mathbf{x}) \leqslant \mathbf{0}_p$ and $-\mathbf{d}(\mathbf{x}) \leqslant \mathbf{0}_p$. Note that this transformation is inapplicable if we assume that all equality constraints must be convex (or concave) because this transformation may introduce constraints that violate convexity (or concavity, respectively). On the other hand, if $\mathbf{d}$ is an affine function, replacing $\mathbf{d}(\mathbf{x}) = \mathbf{0}_p$ by both $\mathbf{d}(\mathbf{x}) \leqslant \mathbf{0}_p$ and $-\mathbf{d}(\mathbf{x}) \leqslant \mathbf{0}_p$ results in two affine restrictions that are both convex and concave functions.

If only inequality constraints are present (as specified by the function $\mathbf{c}$) the feasible region is:

$$R_{\mathbf{c}} = \{\mathbf{x} \in \mathbb{R}^n \mid \mathbf{c}(\mathbf{x}) \leqslant \mathbf{0}_m\}.$$

Let $\mathbf{x} \in R_{\mathbf{c}}$. The *set of active constraints* at $\mathbf{x}$ is

$$\text{ACT}(R_{\mathbf{c}}, \mathbf{c}, \mathbf{x}) = \{i \in \{1, \ldots, m\} \mid c_i(\mathbf{x}) = 0\}.$$

If $i \in \text{ACT}(R_{\mathbf{c}}, \mathbf{c}, \mathbf{x})$, we say that c_i is an *active constraint* or that c_i is *tight* on $\mathbf{x} \in S$; otherwise, that is, if $c_i(\mathbf{x}) < 0$, c_i is an *inactive* constraint on $\mathbf{x}$.

13.4 Optimization without Differentiability

Recall that $R_{\mathbf{c}}$ is the feasible region determined by the constraint $\mathbf{c}(\mathbf{x}) \leqslant \mathbf{0}_m$:

$$R_{\mathbf{c}} = \{\mathbf{x} \in \mathbb{R}^n \mid \mathbf{c}(\mathbf{x}) \leqslant \mathbf{0}_m\}.$$

Definition 13.4. Let $f : \mathbb{R}^n \longrightarrow \mathbb{R}$ and $\mathbf{c} : \mathbb{R}^n \longrightarrow \mathbb{R}^m$ be two functions. The minimization problem $\mathsf{MP}(f, \mathbf{c})$ is

minimize $f(\mathbf{x})$, where $\mathbf{x} \in \mathbb{R}^n$,

subject to $\mathbf{x} \in R_{\mathbf{c}}$.

If $\mathbf{x}_0$ exists in $R_{\mathbf{c}}$ that $f(\mathbf{x}_0) = \min\{f(\mathbf{x}) \mid \mathbf{x} \in R_{\mathbf{c}}\}$ we refer to $\mathbf{x}_0$ as a solution of $\mathsf{MP}(f, \mathbf{c})$.

Theorem 13.5. *Consider the minimization problem* $\mathsf{MP}(f, \mathbf{c})$. *If* f *is a convex function and the set of feasible solution* $R_{\mathbf{c}}$ *is convex then the set of solutions of* $\mathsf{MP}(f, \mathbf{c})$ *is convex.*

Proof. Suppose that $\mathbf{u}, \mathbf{v} \in R$ are two solutions of $\mathsf{MP}(f, \mathbf{c})$. Then,

$$f(\mathbf{u}) = f(\mathbf{v}) = \min\{f(\mathbf{x}) \mid \mathbf{c}(\mathbf{x}) \leqslant \mathbf{0}_m\}.$$

Since $R_{\mathbf{c}}$ is convex, $(1 - t)\mathbf{u} + t\mathbf{v} \in R_{\mathbf{c}}$ for $t \in [0, 1]$. By the convexity of f we have

$$f((1 - t)\mathbf{u} + t\mathbf{v}) \leqslant (1 - t)f(\mathbf{u}) + tf(\mathbf{v})$$
$$= \min\{f(\mathbf{x}) \mid \mathbf{c}(\mathbf{x}) \leqslant \mathbf{0}_m\},$$

so $(1 - t)\mathbf{u} + t\mathbf{v}$ is also a solution of the problem. □

Corollary 13.1. *If* f *is a strictly convex function at* $\mathbf{x}_0$, *where* $\mathbf{x}_0$ *is a solution of* $\mathsf{MP}(f, \mathbf{c})$ *and* $R_{\mathbf{c}}$ *is convex, then* $\mathbf{x}_0$ *is the unique solution of* $\mathsf{MP}(f, \mathbf{c})$.

Proof. Suppose that $\mathbf{x}_1$ is another solution of $\mathsf{MP}(f, \mathbf{c})$. Then, $f(\mathbf{x}_0) = f(\mathbf{x}_1) = m$ by Theorem 13.5. Since $R_{\mathbf{c}}$ is convex, $(1 - t)\mathbf{x}_0 + t\mathbf{x}_1 \in R_{\mathbf{c}}$ for $t \in (0, 1)$ and the strict convexity of f at $\mathbf{x}_0$ implies

$$f((1 - t)\mathbf{x}_0 + t\mathbf{x}_1) < (1 - t)f(\mathbf{x}_0) + tf(\mathbf{x}_1) = f(\mathbf{x}_0),$$

contradicting the minimality of $f(\mathbf{x}_0)$. □

Definition 13.5. Let $f : \mathbb{R}^n \longrightarrow \mathbb{R}$ and $\mathbf{c} : \mathbb{R}^n \longrightarrow \mathbb{R}^m$ be two functions. The local minimization problem $\mathsf{LMP}(f, \mathbf{c})$ consists of finding $\mathbf{x}_0 \in R_{\mathbf{c}}$ such that there exists a positive number δ such that $\mathbf{x} \in B(\mathbf{x}_0, \delta) \cap R_{\mathbf{c}}$ implies $f(\mathbf{x}_0) \leqslant f(\mathbf{x})$.

Theorem 13.6. *If x_0 is a solution of the minimization problem $\mathsf{MP}(f, c)$, then x_0 is a solution of $\mathsf{LMP}(f, c)$; if R_c is convex and f is locally convex at x_0, then a solution of $\mathsf{LMP}(f, c)$ is a solution of $\mathsf{MP}(f, c)$.*

Proof. The first part of the theorem is immediate.

Suppose now that $\mathbf{x}_0$ is a solution of $\mathsf{LMP}(f, c)$, where R_c is convex and f is locally convex at $\mathbf{x}_0$. There exists a positive δ such that $\mathbf{x} \in B(\mathbf{x}_0, \delta) \cap R_c$ implies $f(\mathbf{x}_0) \leqslant f(\mathbf{x})$.

Let $\mathbf{y} \in R_c$. Since R_c is convex, $(1 - t)\mathbf{x}_0 + t\mathbf{y} \in R_c$ for $t \in (0, 1]$. If $t < \frac{\delta}{\|\mathbf{y}-\mathbf{x}_0\|}$ we have

$$\|(\mathbf{x}_0 + t(\mathbf{y} - \mathbf{x}_0)) - \mathbf{x}_0\| = t\|\mathbf{y} - \mathbf{x}_0\| < \delta,$$

so $\mathbf{x}_0 + t(\mathbf{y} - \mathbf{x}_0) \in B(\mathbf{x}_0) \cap R_c$. Consequently, $f(\mathbf{x}_0) \leqslant f(\mathbf{x}_0 + t(\mathbf{y} - \mathbf{x}_0))$, as $\mathbf{x}_0$ is a solution of $\mathsf{LMP}(f, c)$, hence

$$f(\mathbf{x}_0) \leqslant (1 - t)f(\mathbf{x}_0) + tf(\mathbf{y}),$$

because of the convexity of f at $\mathbf{x}_0$. The last inequality implies $f(\mathbf{x}_0) \leqslant f(\mathbf{y})$, so $\mathbf{x}_0$ is a solution of $\mathsf{MP}(f, c)$. $\qquad\square$

Definition 13.6. Let $f : \mathbb{R}^n \longrightarrow \mathbb{R}$ and $c : \mathbb{R}^n \longrightarrow \mathbb{R}^m$ be two functions.

The *Fritz John Lagrangian function* of the minimization problem $\mathsf{MP}(f, c)$ is the function $L : R_c \times \mathbb{R}_{\geqslant 0} \times \mathbb{R}^m_{\geqslant 0} \longrightarrow \mathbb{R}$ defined as

$$L(\mathbf{x}, r, \mathbf{r}) = rf(\mathbf{x}) + \mathbf{r}'c(\mathbf{x}).$$

A *Fritz John saddle point* of L is a triplet $(\mathbf{x}_0, r_0, \mathbf{r}_0) \in R_c \times \mathbb{R}_{\geqslant 0} \times \mathbb{R}^m_{\geqslant 0}$ such that

$$L(\mathbf{x}_0, r_0, \mathbf{r}) \leqslant L(\mathbf{x}_0, r_0, \mathbf{r}_0) \leqslant L(\mathbf{x}, r_0, \mathbf{r}_0)$$

for $r \in \mathbb{R}_{\geqslant 0}$, $\mathbf{r} \in (\mathbb{R}_{\geqslant 0})^m$ and $\mathbf{x} \in R_c$.

Note that $(\mathbf{x}_0, r_0, \mathbf{r}_0)$ is a saddle point for the Fritz John Lagrangean if and only if

$$r_0 f(\mathbf{x}_0) + \mathbf{r}'c(\mathbf{x}_0) \leqslant r_0 f(\mathbf{x}_0) + \mathbf{r}'_0 c(\mathbf{x}_0) \leqslant r_0 f(\mathbf{x}) + \mathbf{r}'_0 c(\mathbf{x}). \qquad (13.2)$$

Definition 13.7. The *Kuhn-Tucker Lagrangian function* of the minimization problem $\mathsf{MP}(f, c)$ is the function $K : \mathbb{R}^n \times \mathbb{R}^m_{\geqslant 0} \longrightarrow \mathbb{R}$ defined as

$$K(\mathbf{x}, \mathbf{r}) = f(\mathbf{x}) + \mathbf{r}'c(\mathbf{x}).$$

A *Kuhn-Tucker saddle point* of K is a pair $(\mathbf{x}_0, \mathbf{r}_0) \in R_c \times \mathbb{R}^m_{\geqslant 0}$ such that

$$K(\mathbf{x}_0, \mathbf{r}) \leqslant K(\mathbf{x}_0, \mathbf{r}_0) \leqslant K(\mathbf{x}, \mathbf{r}_0)$$

for $\mathbf{r} \in (\mathbb{R}_{\geqslant 0})^m$ and $\mathbf{x} \in R_c$.

Theorem 13.7. *If x_0 is a solution of the optimization problem*
  minimize $f(x)$, where $x \in \mathbb{R}^n$,
    subject to $c(x) \leqslant 0_m$,
where f and c are convex functions, there exist $r_0 \geqslant 0$ and $r_0 \geqslant 0_m$ such that the triplet (x_0, r_0, r_0) is a Fritz John saddle point,

Proof. Since $\mathbf{x}_0$ is a solution of the optimization problem of the theorem the inequality system $f(\mathbf{x}) - f(\mathbf{x}_0) < 0, \mathbf{c}(\mathbf{x}) \geqslant 0$ has no solution. By Corollary 12.5, there exist $r_0 \in \mathbb{R}$ and $\mathbf{r}_0 \in \mathbb{R}^m$ such that

$$\binom{r_0}{\mathbf{r}_0} \geqslant 0_{1+m},$$

and

$$r_0(f(\mathbf{x}) - f(\mathbf{x}_0)) + \mathbf{r}_0'\mathbf{c}(\mathbf{x}) \geqslant 0. \tag{13.3}$$

For $\mathbf{x} = \mathbf{x}_0$ we obtain $\mathbf{r}_0'\mathbf{c}(\mathbf{x}_0) \geqslant 0$. Since $\mathbf{r}_0 \geqslant 0_m$ and $\mathbf{c}(\mathbf{x}_0) \leqslant 0_m$ we also have $\mathbf{r}_0'\mathbf{c}(\mathbf{x}_0) \leqslant 0$, hence $\mathbf{r}_0'\mathbf{c}(\mathbf{x}_0) = 0$. Therefore, inequality (13.3) amounts to

$$r_0 f(\mathbf{x}_0) + \mathbf{r}_0'\mathbf{c}(\mathbf{x}_0) \leqslant r_0 f(\mathbf{x}) + \mathbf{r}_0'\mathbf{c}(\mathbf{x}),$$

which is the second of inequalities (13.2).

Since $\mathbf{c}(\mathbf{x}_0) \leqslant 0_m$, $\mathbf{r}'\mathbf{c}(\mathbf{x}_0) \leqslant 0$ for all $\mathbf{r} \geqslant 0_m$. Taking into account that $\mathbf{r}_0'\mathbf{c}(\mathbf{x}_0) = 0$ we obtain

$$r_0 f(\mathbf{x}_0) + \mathbf{r}'\mathbf{c}(\mathbf{x}_0) \leqslant r_0 f(\mathbf{x}_0) + \mathbf{r}_0'\mathbf{c}(\mathbf{x}_0),$$

which is the first of Inequalities (13.2), so $(\mathbf{x}_0, r_0, \mathbf{r}_0)$ is a Fritz John saddle point. $\square$

Theorem 13.8. *If (x_0, r_0) is a saddle point of the Kuhn-Tucker Lagrangian K of $MP(f, c)$, then x_0 is a solution of $MP(f, c)$.*

Proof. Let $(\mathbf{x}_0, \mathbf{r}_0)$ be a saddle point of the Kuhn-Tucker Lagrangian K of $MP(f, \mathbf{c})$. We have

$$f(\mathbf{x}_0) + \mathbf{r}'\mathbf{c}(\mathbf{x}_0) \leqslant f(\mathbf{x}_0) + \mathbf{r}_0'\mathbf{c}(\mathbf{x}_0) \leqslant f(\mathbf{x}) + \mathbf{r}_0'\mathbf{c}(\mathbf{x})$$

for $\mathbf{r} \in (\mathbb{R}_{\geqslant 0})^m$ and $\mathbf{x} \in R_{\mathbf{c}}$.

The first inequality yields

$$(\mathbf{r} - \mathbf{r}_0)'\mathbf{c}(\mathbf{x}_0) \leqslant 0, \tag{13.4}$$

while the second inequality implies

$$f(\mathbf{x}_0) \leqslant f(\mathbf{x}) + \mathbf{r}_0'(\mathbf{c}(\mathbf{x}) - \mathbf{c}(\mathbf{x}_0)) \tag{13.5}$$

for $\mathbf{r} \in (\mathbb{R}_{\geqslant 0})^m$ and $\mathbf{x} \in R_{\mathbf{c}}$.

Since $\mathbf{r}_0 \in \mathbb{R}_{\geqslant 0}^m$ it follows that $\mathbf{r} = \mathbf{r}_0 + \mathbf{e}_j \in \mathbb{R}_{\geqslant 0}^n$ for every j, $1 \leqslant j \leqslant m$. Substituting these values of $\mathbf{r}$ in Inequality (13.4) implies $\mathbf{e}_j' \mathbf{c}(\mathbf{x}_0) \leqslant 0$ for $1 \leqslant j \leqslant m$, so $\mathbf{c}(\mathbf{x}_0) \leqslant \mathbf{0}_m$, so $\mathbf{x}_0 \in R_{\mathbf{c}}$.

Since $\mathbf{r}_0 \geqslant \mathbf{0}_m$ and $\mathbf{c}(\mathbf{x}_0) \leqslant \mathbf{0}_m$ it follows that $\mathbf{r}_0' \mathbf{c}(\mathbf{x}_0) \leqslant 0$. Taking $\mathbf{r} = \mathbf{0}_m$ in inequality (13.4) implies $\mathbf{r}_0' \mathbf{c}(\mathbf{x}_0) \geqslant 0$, so $\mathbf{r}_0' \mathbf{c}(\mathbf{x}_0) = 0$.

Thus, inequality (13.5) becomes

$$f(\mathbf{x}_0) \leqslant f(\mathbf{x}) + \mathbf{r}_0' \mathbf{c}(\mathbf{x}) \leqslant f(\mathbf{x})$$

because $\mathbf{r}_0 \geqslant \mathbf{0}_m$ and $\mathbf{c}(\mathbf{x}) \leqslant \mathbf{0}_m$, which implies that $\mathbf{x}_0$ is a solution of $\mathsf{MP}(f, \mathbf{c})$. $\qquad\square$

Corollary 13.2. *If* $(\boldsymbol{x}_0, r_0, \boldsymbol{r}_0)$ *is a saddle point of the Fritz John Lagrangian* L *of* $\mathsf{MP}(f, \boldsymbol{c})$ *such that* $r_0 > 0$, *then* $\boldsymbol{x}_0$ *is a solution of* $\mathsf{MP}(f, \boldsymbol{c})$.

Proof. Note that if $(\mathbf{x}_0, r_0, \mathbf{r}_0)$ is a saddle point of the Fritz John's Lagrangian, then

$$r_0 f(\mathbf{x}_0) + \mathbf{r}' \mathbf{c}(\mathbf{x}_0) \leqslant r_0 f(\mathbf{x}_0) + \mathbf{r}_0' \mathbf{c}(\mathbf{x}_0) \leqslant r_0 f(\mathbf{x}) + \mathbf{r}_0' \mathbf{c}(\mathbf{x}_0).$$

Since $r_0 > 0$ these in equalities amount to

$$f(\mathbf{x}_0) + \frac{1}{r_0} \mathbf{r}' \mathbf{c}(\mathbf{x}_0) \leqslant f(\mathbf{x}_0) + \frac{1}{r_0} \mathbf{r}_0' \mathbf{c}(\mathbf{x}_0) \leqslant f(\mathbf{x}) + \frac{1}{r_0} \mathbf{r}_0' \mathbf{c}(\mathbf{x}_0),$$

which means that the pair $(\mathbf{x}_0, \mathbf{r}_0)$ is a saddle point of the Kuhn-Tucker Lagrangian function $K(\mathbf{x}, \frac{1}{r_0}\mathbf{r})$. By Theorem 13.8, $(\mathbf{x}_0, \mathbf{r}_0)$ is a solution of $\mathsf{MP}(f, \mathbf{c})$. $\qquad\square$

If $r_0 = 0$, Corollary 13.2 is inapplicable. This situation can be avoided if the constraint function $\mathbf{c}$ satisfies a certain condition (generally referred to as a *constraint qualification.*

Definition 13.8. Let C be a convex subset of $\mathbb{R}^m$ such that $R_{\mathbf{c}} = \{\mathbf{x} \in C \mid \mathbf{c}(\mathbf{x}) \leqslant \mathbf{0}_m\}$ is a convex subset of $\mathbb{R}^n$. The convex function $\mathbf{c} : \mathbb{R}^n \longrightarrow \mathbb{R}^m$ satisfies *Karlin constraint qualification* if there exists no $\mathbf{p} \in \mathbb{R}^m$, $\mathbf{p} \geqslant \mathbf{0}_m$ such that $\mathbf{p}' \mathbf{c}(\mathbf{x}) \geqslant 0$ for all $\mathbf{x} \in R_{\mathbf{c}}$.

Theorem 13.9. *If* $\boldsymbol{x}_0$ *is a solution of the optimization problem*
$$\text{minimize } f(\boldsymbol{x}), \text{ where } \boldsymbol{x} \in \mathbb{R}^n,$$
$$\text{subject to } \boldsymbol{c}(\boldsymbol{x}) \leqslant \boldsymbol{0}_m,$$
where f *and* $\boldsymbol{c}$ *are convex functions and* $\boldsymbol{c}$ *satisfies Karlin constraint qualification, then* $\boldsymbol{x}_0$ *and some* $\boldsymbol{r} \in \mathbb{R}^m$ *with* $\boldsymbol{r} \geqslant \boldsymbol{0}_m$ *are a solution of the Kuhn-Tucker saddle problem (introduced in Definition 13.6) and* $\boldsymbol{r}' \boldsymbol{c}(\boldsymbol{x}_0) = 0$.

Proof. By Theorem 13.7, there exist $r_0 \geqslant 0$ and $\mathbf{r}_0 \geqslant \mathbf{0}_m$ such that the triplet $(\mathbf{x}_0, r_0, \mathbf{r}_0)$ is a Fritz John saddle point and $\mathbf{r}_0' \mathbf{c}(\mathbf{x}_0) = 0$, as we have shown in the proof of the mentioned theorem. If $r_0 > 0$, the argument is completed. If $r_0 = 0$ we have $\mathbf{r}_0 \geqslant 0$ and the second Inequality (13.2) implies $0 \leqslant \mathbf{r}_0' \mathbf{c}(\mathbf{x})$. This contradicts Karlin's constraint qualification. $\square$

13.5 Optimization with Differentiability

Theorem 13.10. *Let* $f : \mathbb{R}^n \longrightarrow \mathbb{R}$ *be a function that is differentiable in* $\mathbf{x}_0$. *If there exists* $\mathbf{r} \in \mathbb{R}^n$ *such that* $(\nabla f)(\mathbf{x}_0)' \mathbf{r} < 0$, *then there exists* $\epsilon > 0$ *such that*

$$f(\mathbf{x}_0 + a\mathbf{r}) < f(\mathbf{x}_0)$$

for $a \in (0, \epsilon)$.

Proof. Since f is differentiable in $\mathbf{x}$, we have

$$f(\mathbf{x}_0 + a\mathbf{r}) = f(\mathbf{x}_0) + a(\nabla f)(\mathbf{x}_0)' \mathbf{r} + a\|\mathbf{r}\|_2 \alpha(\mathbf{x}_0 + a\mathbf{r}),$$

where $\alpha : D \longrightarrow \mathbb{R}$ is a continuous function in $\mathbf{x}_0$ such $\alpha(\mathbf{x}_0) = 0$.

The inequality $(\nabla f)(\mathbf{x}_0)' \mathbf{r} < 0$ implies

$$f(\mathbf{x}_0 + a\mathbf{r}) < f(\mathbf{x}_0) + a\|\mathbf{r}\|_2 \alpha(\mathbf{x}_0 + a\mathbf{r}).$$

Since $\lim_{a \to 0} \alpha(\mathbf{x}_0 + a\mathbf{r}) = 0$, it follows that there exists $\epsilon > 0$ such that $f(\mathbf{x}_0 + a\mathbf{r}) < f(\mathbf{x}_0)$ when $a \in (0, \epsilon)$. $\square$

Recall that the set of descent directions of a functional $f : X \longrightarrow \mathbb{R}$ at $\mathbf{x}_0$ that is differentiable was denoted in Chapter 10 by

$$\mathrm{DD}(f, \mathbf{x}_0) = \{\mathbf{r} \in \mathbb{R}^n \mid (\nabla f)(\mathbf{x}_0)' \mathbf{r} < 0\}.$$

Theorem 13.11. *Let* S *be a subset of* $\mathbb{R}^n$ *and let* $f : S \longrightarrow \mathbb{R}$ *be a function differentiable on the set* S. *If* $\mathbf{x}_0 \in S$ *is a local minimum of* f, *then* $\mathrm{DD}(f, \mathbf{x}_0) \cap \mathrm{FD}(S, \mathbf{x}_0) = \emptyset$, *where* $\mathrm{DD}(f, \mathbf{x}_0) = \{\mathbf{r} \in \mathbb{R}^n \mid (\nabla f)(\mathbf{x}_0)' \mathbf{r} < 0\}$.

Proof. Suppose that $\mathrm{DD}(f, \mathbf{x}_0) \cap \mathrm{FD}(S, \mathbf{x}_0) \neq \emptyset$ and let $\mathbf{r} \in \mathrm{DD}(f, \mathbf{x}_0) \cap \mathrm{FD}(S, \mathbf{x}_0)$. By Theorem 13.10, there exists ϵ such that $f(\mathbf{x}_0 + a\mathbf{r}) < f(\mathbf{x}_0)$ for $a \in (0, \epsilon)$. Since $\mathbf{r}$ is a feasible direction of S in $\mathbf{x}_0$ there exists $\epsilon' > 0$ such that $\mathbf{x}_0 + a\mathbf{r} \in S$ for $a \in (0, \epsilon')$. Thus, by taking $\mu = \min\{\epsilon, \epsilon'\}$ we have both $f(\mathbf{x}_0 + a\mathbf{r}) < f(\mathbf{x}_0)$ and $\mathbf{x}_0 + a\mathbf{r} \in S$ for $a \in (0, \mu)$, which contradicts the fact that $\mathbf{x}_0$ is a local minimum of f. $\square$

Theorem 13.12. *Let U be an open, nonempty subset of $\mathbb{R}^n$, $f : U \longrightarrow \mathbb{R}$ and let $\boldsymbol{c} : \mathbb{R}^n \longrightarrow \mathbb{R}$ be a constraint function for the following optimization problem:*

$$\text{minimize } f(\boldsymbol{x}), \text{ where } \boldsymbol{x} \in U,$$
$$\text{subject to } \boldsymbol{c}(\boldsymbol{x}) \leqslant \boldsymbol{0}_m.$$

Suppose that:

(i) *f is a differentiable at $\boldsymbol{x}_0$;*

(ii) *for $i \in \text{ACT}(U, \boldsymbol{c}, \boldsymbol{x}_0)$, c_i is differentiable at $\boldsymbol{x}_0$;*

(iii) *c_i is continuous at $\boldsymbol{x}_0$ for $i \notin \text{ACT}(U, \boldsymbol{c}, \boldsymbol{x}_0)$.*

Let

$$G_0(\boldsymbol{c}, \boldsymbol{x}_0) = \{\boldsymbol{r} \in \mathbb{R}^n \mid (\nabla c_i)(\boldsymbol{x}_0)'\boldsymbol{r} < 0 \text{ for } i \in \text{ACT}(U, \boldsymbol{c}, \boldsymbol{x}_0)\}.$$

If $\boldsymbol{x}_0$ is a local optimal solution, then the sets $DD(f, \boldsymbol{x}_0)$ and $G_0(\boldsymbol{c}, \boldsymbol{x}_0)$ are disjoint.

Proof. We claim that $G_0(\boldsymbol{c}, \boldsymbol{x}_0) \subseteq \text{FD}(U, \boldsymbol{x}_0)$, where $\text{FD}(U, \boldsymbol{x}_0)$ is the set of feasible directions at $\boldsymbol{x}_0$. Indeed, let $\boldsymbol{r} \in G_0(\boldsymbol{c}, \boldsymbol{x}_0)$. Since U is an open set and $\boldsymbol{x}_0 \in U$, there exists $\epsilon > 0$ such that $\boldsymbol{x}_0 + t\boldsymbol{r} \in U$ for $0 < t < \epsilon$.

By the definition of $\text{ACT}(U, \boldsymbol{c}, \boldsymbol{x}_0)$, if $i \notin \text{ACT}(U, \boldsymbol{c}, \boldsymbol{x}_0)$ we have $c_i(\boldsymbol{x}_0) < 0$. Since c_i is continuous at $\boldsymbol{x}_0$ for $i \notin \text{ACT}(U, \boldsymbol{c}, \boldsymbol{x}_0)$, it follows that there exists an ϵ_1 such that $c_i(\boldsymbol{x}_0 + t\boldsymbol{r}) < 0$ for $0 < t < \epsilon_1$.

By the definition of $G_0(\boldsymbol{c}, \boldsymbol{x}_0)$, $(\nabla c_i)(\boldsymbol{x}_0)'\boldsymbol{r} < 0$ for each $i \in \text{ACT}(U, \boldsymbol{c}, \boldsymbol{x}_0)$. Therefore, by Theorem 13.2, $\boldsymbol{r}$ is a descent direction for c_i in $\boldsymbol{x}_0$, that is, there is $\epsilon_2 > 0$ such that $c_i(\boldsymbol{x}_0 + t\boldsymbol{r}) < c_i(\boldsymbol{x}_0) = 0$ for $0 < t < \epsilon_2$. Thus, if $\epsilon = \min\{\epsilon_0, \epsilon_1, \epsilon_2\}$ and $0 < t < \epsilon$, we have

(i) $\boldsymbol{x}_0 + t\boldsymbol{r} \in U$;

(ii) $c_i(\boldsymbol{x}_0 + t\boldsymbol{r}) < 0$ for $1 \leqslant i \leqslant m$.

Therefore, $\boldsymbol{x}_0 + t\boldsymbol{r}$ is feasible for each t such that $0 < t < \epsilon$, which implies that $\boldsymbol{r} \in \text{FD}(U, \boldsymbol{x}_0)$, so $G_0(\boldsymbol{c}, \boldsymbol{x}_0) \subseteq \text{FD}(U, \boldsymbol{x}_0)$.

Since $\boldsymbol{x}_0$ is a local minimum for f in U, by Equality (13.1) we have $DD(f, \boldsymbol{x}_0) \cap \text{FD}(U, \boldsymbol{x}_0) = \emptyset$, which implies the desired conclusion. $\square$

We present necessary conditions for optimality that assume differentiability but not convexity of the functions involved.

Theorem 13.13. (Fritz John's Necessary Conditions Theorem) *Let S be a non-empty open subset of $\mathbb{R}^n$, and let $f : \mathbb{R}^n \longrightarrow \mathbb{R}$ and $\boldsymbol{c} : \mathbb{R}^n \longrightarrow \mathbb{R}^m$. Let $\boldsymbol{x}_0$ be a local minimum in S of f subjected to the restriction $\boldsymbol{c}(\boldsymbol{x}_0) \leqslant \boldsymbol{0}_m$.*

If f is differentiable in $\boldsymbol{x}_0$, the component functions c_i are differentiable in $\boldsymbol{x}_0$ for $i \in \text{ACT}(S, \boldsymbol{c}, \boldsymbol{x}_0)$, and c_i are continuous in $\boldsymbol{x}_0$ for $i \notin \text{ACT}(S, \boldsymbol{c}, \boldsymbol{x}_0)$,

*then there is a non-negative number u_0 and the non-negative numbers u_i
for $i \in \text{ACT}(S, \mathbf{c}, \mathbf{x}_0)$ such that*

    (i) $u_0(\nabla f)(\mathbf{x}_0) + \sum\{u_i(\nabla c_i)(\mathbf{x}_0) \mid i \in \text{ACT}(S, \mathbf{c}, \mathbf{x}_0)\} = \mathbf{0}_n;$

    (ii) *at least one of the members of $\{u_0\} \cup \{u_i \mid i \in \text{ACT}(S, \mathbf{c}, \mathbf{x}_0)\}$ is
       positive.*

*If, in addition, for $i \notin \text{ACT}(S, \mathbf{c}, \mathbf{x}_0)$, the functions c_i are differentiable in
$\mathbf{x}_0$, then the previous condition can be written as*

    (i) $u_0(\nabla f)(\mathbf{x}_0) + \sum_{i=1}^{m} u_i(\nabla c_i)(\mathbf{x}_0) = \mathbf{0}_n;$

    (ii) $u_i c_i(\mathbf{x}_0) = 0$ *for* $1 \leqslant i \leqslant m;$

   (iii) $\begin{pmatrix} u_0 \\ \mathbf{u} \end{pmatrix} \geq \begin{pmatrix} 0 \\ \mathbf{0}_m \end{pmatrix}.$

Proof.   By Theorem 13.12 there is no $\mathbf{r}$ such that

$$(\nabla f)(\mathbf{x}_0)'\mathbf{r} < 0 \text{ and } (\nabla c_i)(\mathbf{x}_0)'\mathbf{r} < 0 \text{ for } i \in \text{ACT}(S, \mathbf{c}, \mathbf{x}_0). \tag{13.6}$$

Consider the matrix

$$A(\mathbf{x}_0) = \begin{pmatrix} (\nabla f)(\mathbf{x}_0)' \\ (\nabla c_{i_1})(\mathbf{x}_0)' \\ \vdots \\ (\nabla c_{i_k})(\mathbf{x}_0)' \end{pmatrix},$$

where $\text{ACT}(S, \mathbf{c}, \mathbf{x}_0) = \{i_0, i_1, \dots, i_k\}$.

The conditions (13.6) can be restated by saying that there is no $\mathbf{r} \in \mathbb{R}^{k+1}$
such that $A(\mathbf{x}_0)\mathbf{r} < \mathbf{0}_m$. By Gordan's Alternative Theorem (Theorem 6.62)
there is a non-zero vector $\mathbf{u}$ such that $\mathbf{u} \geqslant \mathbf{0}$ such that $A(\mathbf{x}_0)'\mathbf{u} = \mathbf{0}$. Using
the components $u_0, u_1, \dots, u_k$ of $\mathbf{u}$ we obtain

$$u_0(\nabla f)(\mathbf{x}_0) + \sum\{u_i(\nabla c_i)(\mathbf{x}_0) \mid i \in \text{ACT}(S, \mathbf{c}, \mathbf{x}_0)\} = \mathbf{0}_n.$$

By taking $u_i = 0$ for $i \notin \text{ACT}(S, \mathbf{c}, \mathbf{x}_0)$, the conditions follow. $\qquad\square$

    The numbers u_0 and u_i whose existence is established by Fritz John's
Theorem are known as *Lagrange multipliers*.

    The equality $\mathbf{u}'\mathbf{c}(\mathbf{x}_0) = 0$ is known as the *complementary slack condi-
tion*. In view of the non-negativity of the numbers u_i, it expresses succinctly
two facts:

    (i) if $c_i(\mathbf{x}_0) = 0$, that is, if $i \in \text{ACT}(S, \mathbf{c}, \mathbf{x}_0)$ (which means that c_i is an
       active constraint for $\mathbf{x}_0$) *it allows* u_i to be positive, and

    (ii) if $c_i(\mathbf{x}_0) < 0$, that is, if $i \notin \text{ACT}(S, \mathbf{c}, \mathbf{x}_0)$ (which means that c_i is
       not an active constraint for $\mathbf{x}_0$) *it requires* u_i to equal 0.

Example 13.6. Let $f : \mathbb{R}^2 \longrightarrow \mathbb{R}$ be the function defined by

$$f(\mathbf{x}) = x_1 x_2$$

for $\mathbf{x} \in \mathbb{R}^2$. Consider the minimization problem for f where the feasible region is the area in the first quadrant defined by the inequality

$$x_1 + x_2 \geqslant 2.$$

The feasible region is determined by the inequalities:

$$-x_1 \leqslant 0, -x_2 \leqslant 0, \text{ and } 2 - x_1 - x_2 \leqslant 0,$$

which means that the function $\mathbf{c} = \begin{pmatrix} c_1 \\ c_2 \\ c_3 \end{pmatrix}$ can be written as

$$c_1(\mathbf{x}) = -x_1,$$
$$c_2(\mathbf{x}) = -x_2,$$
$$c_3(\mathbf{x}) = 2 - x_1 - x_2.$$

The gradient of he functions involved are

$$(\nabla f)(\mathbf{x}) = \begin{pmatrix} x_2 \\ x_1 \end{pmatrix}, \ (\nabla c_1)(\mathbf{x}) = \begin{pmatrix} -1 \\ 0 \end{pmatrix},$$

$$(\nabla c_2)(\mathbf{x}) = \begin{pmatrix} 0 \\ -1 \end{pmatrix}, \ (\nabla c_3)(\mathbf{x}) = \begin{pmatrix} -1 \\ -1 \end{pmatrix}.$$

Note that $\mathbf{x}_0 = \begin{pmatrix} 1 \\ 1 \end{pmatrix}$ is a minimum for the function f. Only c_3 is an active constraint at $\mathbf{x}_0$. Fritz John's theorem implies the existence of $u_0 \geqslant 0$ and $u_1 > 0$ such that

$$u_0(\nabla f)(\mathbf{x}_0) + u_3(\nabla c_3)(\mathbf{x}_0) = \mathbf{0}_2,$$

which amounts to

$$u_0 \begin{pmatrix} x_1 \\ x_2 \end{pmatrix} + u_3 \begin{pmatrix} -1 \\ -1 \end{pmatrix} = \mathbf{0}_2.$$

Thus, the conditions of Fritz John's theorem are satisfied in $\mathbf{x}_0 = \begin{pmatrix} 1 \\ 1 \end{pmatrix}$ by taking the Lagrange multipliers as $u_0 > 0$, $u_1 = u_2 = 0$ and $u_3 = u_0$.

In the previous example the Lagrange multiplier u_0, the coefficient of $(\nabla f)(\mathbf{x}_0)$ is positive. This is important because, if $u_0 = 0$, the Fritz John's conditions make no use of the properties of $(\nabla f)(\mathbf{x}_0)$, which prevents us from finding an optimal point. The next example due to Kuhn and Tucker shows that this is possible.

Example 13.7. Let k be a positive natural number and let us maximize x_1 subjected to the restrictions $x_2 \leqslant (a - x_1)^{2k+1}$ and $x_2 \geqslant 0$.

In standard form, this amount to minimizing the function $f(\mathbf{x}) = -x_1$, subjected to the restrictions

$$c_1(\mathbf{x}) = x_2 - (1 - x_1)^{2k+1} \leqslant 0,$$

$$c_2(\mathbf{x}) = -x_2 \leqslant 0.$$

The gradients of the functions involved are:

$$(\nabla f)_{\mathbf{x}} = \begin{pmatrix} -1 \\ 0 \end{pmatrix}, (\nabla c_1)_{\mathbf{x}} = \begin{pmatrix} (2k+1)(1-x_1)^{2k} \\ 1 \end{pmatrix}, (\nabla c_2)_{\mathbf{x}} = \begin{pmatrix} 0 \\ -1 \end{pmatrix}.$$

Let us examine the point $\mathbf{x}_0 = \begin{pmatrix} 1 \\ 0 \end{pmatrix}$. Note that we have both $c_1(\mathbf{x}_0) = 0$ and $c_2(\mathbf{x}_0) = 0$, so both restrictions c_1, c_2 are active on $\mathbf{x}_0$. Since

$$(\nabla f)(\mathbf{x}_0) = \begin{pmatrix} -1 \\ 0 \end{pmatrix},$$

$$(\nabla c_1)(\mathbf{x}_0) = \begin{pmatrix} 0 \\ 1 \end{pmatrix},$$

$$(\nabla c_2)(\mathbf{x}_0) = \begin{pmatrix} 0 \\ -1 \end{pmatrix},$$

we have

$$u_0 \begin{pmatrix} -1 \\ 0 \end{pmatrix} + u_1 \begin{pmatrix} 0 \\ 1 \end{pmatrix} + u_2 \begin{pmatrix} 0 \\ -1 \end{pmatrix} = \begin{pmatrix} 0 \\ 0 \end{pmatrix},$$

which amounts to $-u_0 = 0$ and $u_1 - u_2 = 0$.

When equality constraints are added into the mix, Fritz John's Theorem 13.13 can be extended using Lyusternik's Theorem (Theorem 9.10).

Definition 13.9. Let $f : \mathbb{R}^n \longrightarrow \mathbb{R}$, $\mathbf{c} : \mathbb{R}^n \longrightarrow \mathbb{R}^m$ and $\mathbf{d} : \mathbb{R}^n \longrightarrow \mathbb{R}^p$ be three functions. The minimization problem with equalities $\mathsf{MPEQ}(f, \mathbf{c}, \mathbf{d})$ is

minimize $f(\mathbf{x})$, where $\mathbf{x} \in \mathbb{R}^n$,
subject to $\mathbf{x} \in R_{\mathbf{c},\mathbf{d}}$,

where the feasible region $R_{\mathbf{c},\mathbf{d}}$ is defined as

$$R_{\mathbf{c},\mathbf{d}} = \{\mathbf{x} \in \mathbb{R}^n \mid \mathbf{c}(\mathbf{x}) \leqslant \mathbf{0}_m \text{ and } \mathbf{d}(\mathbf{x}) = \mathbf{0}_p\}.$$

If $\mathbf{x}_0$ exists in $R_{\mathbf{c},\mathbf{d}}$ that $f(\mathbf{x}_0) = \min\{f(\mathbf{x}) \mid \mathbf{x} \in R_{\mathbf{c},\mathbf{d}}\}$ we refer to $\mathbf{x}_0$ as a solution of $\mathsf{MPEQ}(f, \mathbf{c}, \mathbf{d})$.

Let $\mathbf{x} \in R_{\mathbf{c},\mathbf{d}}$. The *set of active constraints* at $\mathbf{x}$ is

$$\mathsf{ACT}(R_{\mathbf{c}}, \mathbf{c}, \mathbf{d}, \mathbf{x}) = \{i \in \{1, \ldots, m\} \mid c_i(\mathbf{x}) = 0\}.$$

If $i \in \mathsf{ACT}(R_{\mathbf{c}}, \mathbf{c}, \mathbf{d}, \mathbf{x})$, we say that c_i is an *active constraint* or that c_i is *tight* on $\mathbf{x} \in S$; otherwise, that is, if $c_i(\mathbf{x}) < 0$, c_i is an *inactive* constraint on $\mathbf{x}$.

Theorem 13.14. (Fritz John's Necessary Conditions Theorem with Equality Constraints) *If $\mathbf{x}_0$ is a local minimizer of $\mathsf{MPEQ}(f, \mathbf{c}, \mathbf{d})$ there exist $r_0 \geqslant 0$, $\mathbf{r} \geqslant \mathbf{0}_m$ and $\mathbf{q} \in \mathbf{0}_p$ such that not all numbers $r_0, r_1, \ldots, r_m, q_1, \ldots, q_p$ are 0 and*

$$r_0(\nabla f)(\mathbf{x}_0) + \sum_{i=1}^{m} r_i(\nabla c_i)(\mathbf{x}_0) + \sum_{j=1}^{p} q_j(\nabla d_j)(\mathbf{x}_0) = 0, \tag{13.7}$$

$$r_i \geqslant 0, \mathbf{c}(\mathbf{x}_0) \leqslant \mathbf{0}_m, r_i c_i(\mathbf{x}_0) = 0 \text{ for } 1 \leqslant i \leqslant p. \tag{13.8}$$

Proof.   As before, we refer to Equalities (13.8) as *complementary conditions*. They allow us to reformulate Condition (13.7) of the theorem as

$$r_0(\nabla f)(\mathbf{x}_0) + \sum \{(\nabla c_i)(\mathbf{x}_0) \mid i \in \mathsf{ACT}(R_{\mathbf{c}}, \mathbf{c}, \mathbf{d}, \mathbf{x})\} + \sum_{j=1}^{p} q_j(\nabla d_j)(\mathbf{x}_0) = 0.$$

Note that if the set $\{(\nabla d_j)(\mathbf{x}_0) \mid 1 \leqslant j \leqslant p\}$ is linearly dependent there exist $q_1, \ldots, q_p$ not all zero such that $\sum_{j=1}^{p} q_j(\nabla d_j)(\mathbf{x}_0) = 0$ and the condition of the theorem can be satisfied by taking $r_0 = r_1 = \cdots = r_m = 0$.

Assume that $\{\nabla d_j)(\mathbf{x}_0) \mid 1 \leqslant j \leqslant p\}$ is linearly independent. We will show that that there is no $\mathbf{v}$ such that $\mathbf{v}'(\nabla f)(\mathbf{x}_0) < 0$, $\mathbf{v}'(\nabla c_i) < 0$ for $i \in \mathsf{ACT}(R_{\mathbf{c}}, \mathbf{c}, \mathbf{d}, \mathbf{x})$ and $\mathbf{v}'(\nabla d_j)(\mathbf{x}_0) = 0$ for $1 \leqslant j \leqslant p$. In other words, we claim that the system

$$\begin{aligned} &\mathbf{v}'(\nabla f)(\mathbf{x}_0) < 0, \mathbf{v}'(\nabla c_i) < 0 \text{ for } i \in \mathsf{ACT}(R_{\mathbf{c}}, \mathbf{c}, \mathbf{d}, \mathbf{x}) \\ &\text{and } \mathbf{v}'(\nabla d_j)(\mathbf{x}_0) = 0 \text{ for } 1 \leqslant j \leqslant p \end{aligned} \tag{13.9}$$

is inconsistent.

Indeed, suppose that there exists $\mathbf{v}$ satisfying these conditions and $\|\mathbf{v}\| = 1$. Since $\{(\nabla d_j)(\mathbf{x}_0) \mid 1 \leqslant j \leqslant p\}$ is linearly independent, it follows from Lyusternik's Theorem there exists a sequence $(x_n)_{n \geqslant 1}$ such that $\lim_{n\to\infty} x_n = x_0$ such that has the tangent direction $\mathbf{v}$ such that $d_j(x_n) = 0$ for $1 \leqslant j \leqslant p$. We have:

$$f(\mathbf{x}_n) = f(\mathbf{x}_0) + \left(\left((\nabla f)(\mathbf{x}_0), \frac{\mathbf{x}_n - \mathbf{x}_0}{\|\mathbf{x}_n - \mathbf{x}_0\|} \right) + \frac{o(\mathbf{x}_n - \mathbf{x}_0)}{\|\mathbf{x}_n - \mathbf{x}_0\|} \right) \|\mathbf{x}_n - \mathbf{x}_0\|,$$

where

$$\lim_{n\to\infty} \frac{\mathbf{x}_n - \mathbf{x}_0}{\|\mathbf{x}_n - \mathbf{x}_0\|} = \mathbf{v} \text{ and } \lim_{n\to\infty} \frac{o(\mathbf{x}_n - \mathbf{x}_0)}{\|\mathbf{x}_n - \mathbf{x}_0\|} = 0.$$

Therefore, for sufficiently large n we have:

$$\left((\nabla f)(\mathbf{x}_0), \frac{\mathbf{x}_n - \mathbf{x}_0}{\|\mathbf{x}_n - \mathbf{x}_0\|} \right) + \frac{o(\mathbf{x}_n - \mathbf{x}_0)}{\|\mathbf{x}_n - \mathbf{x}_0\|} < 0$$

and therefore $f(x_n) < f(x_0)$.

Similarly, if c_i is an active constraint at $\mathbf{x}_0$, then $c_i(\mathbf{x}_n) < c_i(\mathbf{x}_0) = 0$ for sufficiently large n. Thus, $(\mathbf{x}_i)$ is a feasible sequence such that $f(\mathbf{x}_n) < f(\mathbf{x}_0)$ for sufficiently large n. This contradicts the fact that $\mathbf{x}_0$ is a local minimizer for f and proves that System (13.8) is inconsistent.

The statement of the theorem follows immediately by an application of Motzkin's Transposition Theorem (Theorem 6.63). □

The next theorem provides necessary conditions for optimality that include the linear independence of the gradients of the components of the constraints $(\nabla c_i)(\mathbf{x}_0)$ for $i \in \text{ACT}(S, \mathbf{c}, \mathbf{x}_0)\}$ and ensure that the coefficient of the gradient of the objective function $(\nabla f)(\mathbf{x}_0)$ is not null. These conditions are known as the *Karush-Kuhn-Tucker conditions* or the *KKT conditions*.

Theorem 13.15. (Karush-Kuhn-Tucker Theorem) *Let S be a non-empty open subset of $\mathbb{R}^n$ and let $f : \mathbb{R}^n \longrightarrow \mathbb{R}$ and $\mathbf{c} : \mathbb{R}^n \longrightarrow \mathbb{R}^m$. Let $\boldsymbol{x}_0$ be a local minimum in S of f subjected to the restriction $\mathbf{c}(\boldsymbol{x}_0) \leqslant \boldsymbol{0}_m$.*

Suppose that f is differentiable in $\boldsymbol{x}_0$, c_i are differentiable in $\boldsymbol{x}_0$ for $i \in \text{ACT}(S, \mathbf{c}, \boldsymbol{x}_0)$, and c_i are continuous in $\boldsymbol{x}_0$ for $i \notin \text{ACT}(S, \mathbf{c}, \boldsymbol{x}_0)$.

If $\{(\nabla c_i)(\boldsymbol{x}_0) \mid i \in \text{ACT}(S, \mathbf{c}, \boldsymbol{x}_0)\}$ is a linearly independent set, then there exist non-negative numbers w_i for $i \in \text{ACT}(S, \mathbf{c}, \boldsymbol{x}_0)$ such that

$$(\nabla f)(\boldsymbol{x}_0) + \sum \{w_i(\nabla c_i)(\boldsymbol{x}_0) \mid i \in \text{ACT}(S, \mathbf{c}, \boldsymbol{x}_0)\} = \boldsymbol{0}_n.$$

Furthermore, if the functions c_i are differentiable in $\boldsymbol{x}_0$ for $i \notin \text{ACT}(S, \mathbf{c}, \boldsymbol{x}_0)$, then the previous condition can be written as:

(i) $(\nabla f)(\boldsymbol{x}_0) + \sum_{i=1}^m w_i(\nabla c_i)(\boldsymbol{x}_0) = \boldsymbol{0}_n$;

(ii) $\boldsymbol{w}' \mathbf{c}(\boldsymbol{x}_0) = 0$;

(iii) $\boldsymbol{w} \geqslant \boldsymbol{O}_m$, *where* $\boldsymbol{w} = \begin{pmatrix} w_1 \\ \vdots \\ w_m \end{pmatrix}$.

Proof. By Fritz John's Theorem there exist u_0 and the non-negative numbers u_i for $i \in \text{ACT}(S, \mathbf{c}, \mathbf{x}_0)$ such that

(i) at least one of the members of $\{u_0\} \cup \{u_i \mid i \in \text{ACT}(S, \mathbf{c}, \mathbf{x}_0)\}$ is positive;

(ii) $u_0 (\nabla f)(\mathbf{x}_0) + \sum \{u_i (\nabla c_i)(\mathbf{x}_0) \mid i \in \text{ACT}(S, g, \mathbf{x}_0)\} = \boldsymbol{O}_n$.

Note that $u_0 > 0$ because the gradients $(\nabla c_i)(\mathbf{x}_0)$ are linearly independent. Then, by defining $w_i = \frac{u_i}{u_0}$ for $i \in \text{ACT}(S, g, \mathbf{x}_0)$, the statement of the theorem follows. $\qquad\square$

If an optimization problem contains both inequality constraints and equality constraints, a similar necessary condition involving Lagrange multipliers can be proven. We include here an argument presented in [106].

Lemma 13.1. *Let S be a subset of $\mathbb{R}^n$ such that $f : S \longrightarrow \mathbb{R}$, $\boldsymbol{h} : S \longrightarrow \mathbb{R}^k$ and $\boldsymbol{c} : S \longrightarrow \mathbb{R}^s$ be three functions that are continuous and have continuous partial derivatives relative to all their arguments on S. Suppose that $\boldsymbol{O}_n \in \boldsymbol{I}(S)$ be an interior point of S that satisfies the conditions $c_1(\boldsymbol{O}_n) = \cdots = c_z(\boldsymbol{O}_n) = 0$ and $c_r(\boldsymbol{O}_n) < 0$ for $z + 1 \leqslant r \leqslant s$.*

Let $\epsilon_1 > 0$ be such that $B[\boldsymbol{O}_n, \epsilon_1] \subseteq S$ and $c_r(\boldsymbol{x}) < 0$ for $z + 1 \leqslant r \leqslant s$ and $\boldsymbol{x} \in B[\boldsymbol{O}_n, \epsilon_1]$. For each $\epsilon \in (0, \epsilon_1)$ there corresponds an N such that

$$f(\boldsymbol{x}) + \|\boldsymbol{x}\|^2 + N \left(\sum_{i=1}^{k} h_i(\boldsymbol{x})^2 + \sum_{r=1}^{z} (c_r^+(\boldsymbol{x}))^2 \right) > 0$$

for all $\boldsymbol{x}$ such that $\|\boldsymbol{x}\| = \epsilon$.

Proof. Suppose that the statement is false. Then, there exists a sequence (N_m) such that $\lim_{m \to \infty} N_m = \infty$ and a sequence $(\mathbf{x}_m)$ such that $\|\mathbf{x}_m\| = \epsilon$ such that for all m,

$$f(\mathbf{x}_m) + \|\mathbf{x}_m\|^2 \leqslant -N_m \left(\sum_{i=1}^{k} h_i(\mathbf{x}_m)^2 + \sum_{r=1}^{z} (c_r^+(\mathbf{x}_m))^2 \right). \qquad (13.10)$$

A subsequence of $(\mathbf{x}_m)$ converges to a point $\mathbf{x}_*$; without loss of generality we suppose that this sequence is the entire sequence. Then, we have $\|\mathbf{x}_*\| = \lim_{m \to \infty} \|\mathbf{x}_m\| = \epsilon$ and $\lim_{m \to \infty} f(\mathbf{x}_m) = f(\mathbf{x}_*)$. Therefore, letting $m \to \infty$ we obtain

$$\sum_{i=1}^{k} h_i(\mathbf{x}_*)^2 + \sum_{r=1}^{z} (c_r^+(\mathbf{x}_*))^2 = 0.$$

Therefore, $h_i(\mathbf{x}_*) = 0$ for $1 \leqslant i \leqslant k$ and $c_r(\mathbf{x}_*) \leqslant 0$ for $1 \leqslant r \leqslant s$, so $\lim_{m \to \infty} f(\mathbf{x}_m) = f(\mathbf{x}_*) \geqslant f(\mathbf{0}_n) = 0$. Inequality (13.10) implies $f(\mathbf{x}_m) \leqslant -\epsilon^2$, hence we obtain a contradiction. Thus, the inequality of the lemma is valid. □

Lemma 13.2. *Using the same notations as in Lemma 13.1, for each $\epsilon \in (0, \epsilon_1]$ there exists $\overline{\boldsymbol{x}}$ and a unit vector $\boldsymbol{u}' = (\lambda_0, \lambda_1, \ldots, \lambda_k, \mu_1, \ldots, \mu_z)$, where $\lambda_0, \mu_1, \ldots, \mu_z$ are non-negative numbers such that $\|\overline{\boldsymbol{x}}\| < \epsilon$ and*

$$\lambda_0 \left(\frac{\partial f}{\partial x_j}(\overline{\boldsymbol{x}}) + 2(\overline{\boldsymbol{x}})_j \right) + \sum_{i=1}^{k} \lambda_j \frac{\partial h}{\partial x_j}(\overline{\boldsymbol{x}}) + \sum_{r=1}^{z} \mu_r c_r(\overline{\boldsymbol{x}}) = 0$$

for $1 \leqslant j \leqslant n$.

Proof. Let N be the number whose existence was established in Lemma 13.1. Define the function $F : S \longrightarrow \mathbb{R}$ as

$$F(\mathbf{x}) = f(\mathbf{x}) + \|\mathbf{x}\|^2 + N \left(\sum_{i=1}^{k} h_i(\mathbf{x})^2 + \sum_{r=1}^{z} (c_r^+(\mathbf{x}))^2 \right).$$

There exists a point $\overline{\mathbf{x}} \in B[\mathbf{0}_n, \epsilon]$ at which F assumes its least value; then $F(\overline{\mathbf{x}}) \leqslant F(\mathbf{0}_n) = 0$. By Lemma 13.1 we cannot have $\|\overline{\mathbf{x}}\| = \epsilon$, hence $\overline{\mathbf{x}}$ is interior to $B[\mathbf{0}_n, \epsilon]$, and all first order partial derivatives vanish at $\overline{\mathbf{x}}$. The derivatives of $(c_r^+(\mathbf{x}))^2$ are $2c_r^+ \frac{\partial c_r}{\partial x_j}(\mathbf{x})$ by Supplement 15. Thus,

$$\frac{\partial f}{\partial x_j}(\overline{\mathbf{x}}) + 2\overline{\mathbf{x}}_j + 2Nh_i(\overline{\mathbf{x}}) \frac{\partial h_i}{\partial x_j}(\overline{\mathbf{x}}) + \sum_{r=1}^{z} 2Nc_r^+(\overline{\mathbf{x}}) \frac{\partial c_r}{\partial x_j}(\overline{\mathbf{x}}) = 0.$$

By defining

$$L = \left(1 + \sum_{i=1}^{k} (2Nh_i(\overline{\mathbf{x}}))^2 + \sum_{r=1}^{z} (2Nc_r^+(\overline{\mathbf{x}}))^2 \right)^{\frac{1}{2}},$$

$$\lambda_0 = \frac{1}{L},$$

$$\lambda_i = 2Nh_i(\overline{\mathbf{x}})/L \text{ for } 1 \leqslant i \leqslant k,$$

$$\mu_r = 2Nc_r^+(\overline{\mathbf{x}})/L, \text{ for } 1 \leqslant r \leqslant z,$$

$$\mu_r = 0, \text{ for } z+1 \leqslant r \leqslant s$$

we obtain a unit vector $(\lambda_0, \lambda_1, \ldots, \lambda_k, \mu_1, \ldots, \mu_s)$, where λ_0 and the μ_r are non-negative. This implies the equality of the lemma. □

Theorem 13.16. *Let $f : S \longrightarrow \mathbb{R}$, $\boldsymbol{h} : S \longrightarrow \mathbb{R}^k$ and $\boldsymbol{c} : S \longrightarrow \mathbb{R}^s$ be three functions that are continuous and have continuous partial derivatives relative to all their arguments on a subset S of $\mathbb{R}^n$. Let $\boldsymbol{x}_0 \in \boldsymbol{I}(S)$ be an interior point of S that satisfies the conditions*

$$c(\boldsymbol{x}) \leqslant \boldsymbol{0}_s \text{ and } h(\boldsymbol{x}) = \boldsymbol{0}_k, \tag{13.11}$$

and $f(\boldsymbol{x}_0) \leqslant f(x)$ for all $\boldsymbol{x} \in S$ that satisfy Conditions 13.11. Then, there are numbers $\lambda_0, \lambda_1, \ldots, \lambda_k, \mu_0, \ldots, \mu_s$ not all 0 such that

$$\lambda_0 \frac{\partial f}{\partial x_j}(\boldsymbol{x}_0) + \sum_{i=1}^{k} \lambda_i \frac{\partial h_i}{\partial x_j}(\boldsymbol{x}_0) + \sum_{r=1}^{s} \mu_r \frac{\partial c_r}{\partial x_j}(\boldsymbol{x}_0) = 0$$

for $1 \leqslant j \leqslant n$.

Moreover, we have

(i) *$\lambda_0 \geqslant 0$ and $\mu_r \geqslant 0$ for $1 \leqslant r \leqslant s$;*

(ii) *for each r such that $c_r(\boldsymbol{x}_0), 0$ we have $\mu_r = 0$;*

(iii) *if the gradients at $\boldsymbol{x}_0$ of the h_i and those c_r for which $c_r(\boldsymbol{x}_0) = 0$ are linearly independent, it is possible to choose $\lambda_0 = 1$.*

Proof. Let $(\epsilon_n)_{n \geqslant 1}$ be a sequence of positive numbers such that $\lim_{n \to \infty} \epsilon_n = 0$. For $m \geqslant 1$ choose $\overline{\mathbf{x}}_m$ with $\|\overline{\mathbf{x}}_m\| < \epsilon_m$ and a unit vector $\mathbf{u}'_m = (\lambda_{0,m}, \lambda_{1,m}, \ldots, \lambda_{k,m}, \ldots, \mu_{z,m}, 0, \ldots, 0)$ such that the equality of Lemma 13.16

$$\lambda_{0,m} \left(\frac{\partial f}{\partial x_j}(\overline{\mathbf{x}}_m) + 2(\overline{\mathbf{x}})_j \right) + \sum_{i=1}^{k} \lambda_{j,m} \frac{\partial h}{\partial x_j}(\overline{\mathbf{x}}_m) + \sum_{r=1}^{z} \mu_{r,m} c_r(\overline{\mathbf{x}}_m) = 0$$

holds for $m \geqslant 1$ and $1 \leqslant j \leqslant n$.

Choose a subsequence of $(\mathbf{u}_m)$ that converges to a limit $(\lambda_0, \lambda_1, \ldots, \lambda_k, \mu_1, \ldots, \mu_s)$. Since $\lim_{m \to \infty} \overline{\mathbf{x}}_m = \mathbf{x}_0$, Lemma 13.16 implies

$$\lambda_0 \frac{\partial f}{\partial x_j}(\mathbf{x}_0) + \sum_{i=1}^{k} \lambda_i \frac{\partial h_i}{\partial x_j}(\mathbf{x}_0) + \sum_{r=1}^{s} \mu_r \frac{\partial c_r}{\partial x_j}(\mathbf{x}_0) = 0$$

for $1 \leqslant j \leqslant n$.

If the constraint conditions hold we cannot have $\lambda_0 = 0$ because this would contradict the linear independence of the gradients at $\mathbf{x}_0$ of the h_i and those c_r for which $c_r(\mathbf{x}_0) = 0$. So, $\lambda_0 > 0$ and the multipliers $(1, \frac{\lambda_1}{\lambda_0}, \ldots, \frac{\lambda_k}{\lambda_0}, \frac{\mu_1}{\lambda_0}, \ldots, \frac{\mu_s}{\lambda_0})$ satisfy the conditions of the theorem. $\qquad \square$

Example 13.8. Let $A \in \mathbb{R}^{n \times n}$ be a symmetric matrix and let $f : \mathbb{R}^n \longrightarrow \mathbb{R}$ be the function defined by $f(\mathbf{x}) = \mathbf{x}'A\mathbf{x}$. We seek to minimize f subjected to the restriction $\|\mathbf{x}\| = 1$, or equivalently, $h(\mathbf{x}) = \|\mathbf{x}\|^2 - 1 = 0$. Since $(\nabla f) = 2A\mathbf{x}$ and $(\nabla h)(\mathbf{x}) = 2\mathbf{x}$, there exists λ such that $2A\mathbf{x}_0 = 2\lambda\mathbf{x}_0$ for any extremum of f subjected to $\|\mathbf{x}_0\| = 1$. Thus, $\mathbf{x}_0$ must be a unit eigenvector of A and λ must be an eigenvalue of the same matrix.

Example 13.9. Let us consider a variant of the optimization problem discussed in Example 13.2. As before, we start with m points in $\mathbb{R}^n$, $\mathbf{a}_1, \ldots, \mathbf{a}_m$. This time we seek to minimize $f(\mathbf{x}) = \sum_{i=1}^m \|\mathbf{x} - \mathbf{a}_i\|^2$ subjected to the restriction $\|\mathbf{x} - \mathbf{b}\| = r$, where $\mathbf{b} \in \mathbb{R}^n$ and $r \geqslant 0$. Equivalently, this restriction is equivalent to $\|\mathbf{x} - \mathbf{b}\|^2 = r^2$.

We saw that

$$\frac{\partial f}{\partial x_j} = 2mx_j - 2\sum_{i=1}^m a_{ij}$$

for $1 \leqslant j \leqslant n$, so

$$(\nabla f)(\mathbf{x}_0) = 2m\mathbf{x} - 2A\mathbf{1}_m,$$

where $A = (\mathbf{a}_1, \ldots, \mathbf{a}_m) \in \mathbb{R}^{n \times m}$. For $h(\mathbf{x}) = \|\mathbf{x} - \mathbf{b}\|^2 - r^2$ we have $\frac{\partial h}{\partial x_j} = 2(x_j - b_j)$ for $1 \leqslant j \leqslant n$, so $(\nabla h)(\mathbf{x}_0) = 2(\mathbf{x} - \mathbf{b})$. There exists λ such that

$$2m\mathbf{x}_0 - 2A\mathbf{1}_m = 2\lambda(\mathbf{x}_0 - \mathbf{b}),$$

hence $\mathbf{x}_0$ satisfies the equality

$$\mathbf{x}_0 = \frac{1}{m - \lambda}(A\mathbf{1}_m - \lambda\mathbf{b}).$$

Since $\mathbf{x}_0$ must be located on the sphere $S(\mathbf{b}, r)$ it follows that we must have

$$\lambda = m - \frac{1}{r}\|A\mathbf{1}_m - m\mathbf{b}\|,$$

which means that the extremum is reached when

$$\mathbf{x}_0 = r\frac{A\mathbf{1}_m - m\mathbf{b}}{\|A\mathbf{1}_m - m\mathbf{b}\|}.$$

If $\mathbf{c}$ is the barycenter of the set $\{\mathbf{a}_1, \ldots, \mathbf{m}\}$, $\mathbf{c} = \frac{1}{m}A\mathbf{1}_m$, the extremum can be written as

$$\mathbf{x}_0 = r\frac{\mathbf{c} - \mathbf{b}}{\|\mathbf{c} - \mathbf{b}\|}.$$

If the matrix $(D\mathbf{h})(\mathbf{x})$ is not of full rank, that is, if $rank((D\mathbf{h})(\mathbf{x})) < m$, the gradients $(\nabla h_1)(\mathbf{x}), \ldots (\nabla h_m)(\mathbf{x})$ may not be linearly independent and Lagrange multipliers may not exist.

Example 13.10. Let $f : \mathbb{R}^2 \longrightarrow \mathbb{R}$ be given by $f(\mathbf{x}) = x_1$ and let $\mathbf{h} : \mathbb{R}^2 \longrightarrow \mathbb{R}_2$ be given by

$$h_1(\mathbf{x}) = x_1^2 + x_2^2 - 1,$$
$$h_2(\mathbf{x}) = \frac{5}{4} - x_1^2 - x_2.$$

Note that the feasible region consists of two points:

$$\mathbf{x}_1 = \begin{pmatrix} \frac{\sqrt{3}}{2} \\ \frac{1}{2} \end{pmatrix} \text{ and } \mathbf{x}_1 = \begin{pmatrix} -\frac{\sqrt{3}}{2} \\ \frac{1}{2} \end{pmatrix}.$$

Since

$$(\nabla h_1)(\mathbf{x}) = \begin{pmatrix} 2x_1 \\ 2x_2 \end{pmatrix} \text{ and } (\nabla h_2)(\mathbf{x}) = \begin{pmatrix} -2x_1 \\ -1 \end{pmatrix},$$

we have

$$(\nabla h_1)(\mathbf{x}_1) = \begin{pmatrix} \sqrt{3} \\ 1 \end{pmatrix} \text{ and } (\nabla h_2)(\mathbf{x}_1) = \begin{pmatrix} -\sqrt{3} \\ -1 \end{pmatrix} = -(\nabla h_1)(\mathbf{x}_1),$$

so the vectors $(\nabla h_1)(\mathbf{x}_1)$ and $(\nabla h_2)(\mathbf{x}_1)$ are not linearly independent and x_1 is not a regular point of $\mathbf{h}$. The same conclusion can be reached for $\mathbf{x}_2$. Both $\mathbf{x}_1$ and $\mathbf{x}_2$ are minima of f. However, $(\nabla f)(\mathbf{x}_1) = (\nabla f)(\mathbf{x}_2) = \begin{pmatrix} 0 \\ 1 \end{pmatrix}$ is not a linear combination of $(\nabla h_1(\mathbf{x})$ and $(\nabla h_2)(\mathbf{x})$ for $\mathbf{x} \in \{\mathbf{x}_1, \mathbf{x}_2\}$.

Supplementary convexity assumptions allow the formulation of sufficient conditions for optimality.

Theorem 13.17. (Karush-Kuhn-Tucker Sufficient Conditions) *Let S be an open non-empty subset of $\mathbb{R}^n$, $f : S \longrightarrow \mathbb{R}$ and let $\mathbf{c} : \mathbb{R}^n \longrightarrow \mathbb{R}^m$ be a function. Consider the minimization of f subjected to the restriction $\mathbf{c}(\mathbf{x}) \leqslant \mathbf{0}_m$ and let $\mathtt{ACT}(S, \mathbf{c}, \mathbf{x}) = \{i \in \{1, \ldots, m\} \mid c_i(\mathbf{x}) = 0\}$.*

If $\mathbf{x}_0$ is a feasible solution, f is pseudo-convex at $\mathbf{x}_0$, c_i is quasi-convex and differentiable at $\mathbf{x}_0$ for $1 \leqslant i \leqslant m$, and there exist non-negative numbers u_i for $i \in \mathtt{ACT}(S, \mathbf{c}, \mathbf{x}_0)$ such that

$$(\nabla f)(\mathbf{x}_0) + \sum \{u_i(\nabla c_i)(\mathbf{x}_0) \mid i \in \mathtt{ACT}(S, \mathbf{c}, \mathbf{x}_0)\} = \mathbf{0}_n,$$

then $\mathbf{x}_0$ is global optimum for f subjected to $\mathbf{c}(\mathbf{x}_0) < \mathbf{0}_m$.

Proof. If $\mathbf{x}$ is a feasible solution for this optimization problem we have $c_i(\mathbf{x}) \leqslant c_i(\mathbf{x}_0)$ for $i \in \text{ACT}(S, \mathbf{c}, \mathbf{x}_0)$ because $c_i(\mathbf{x}) \leqslant 0$ and $c_i(\mathbf{x}_0) = 0$.

Since c_i is quasi-convex at $\mathbf{x}_0$ we have $c_i(t\mathbf{x} + (1 - t)\mathbf{x}_0) \leqslant \max\{c_i(\mathbf{x}), c_i(\mathbf{x}_0)\} = c_i(\mathbf{x}_0)$ for $t \in (0, 1)$. Equivalently, we have $c_i(\mathbf{x}_0 + t(\mathbf{x} - \mathbf{x}_0)) - c_i(\mathbf{x}_0) \leqslant 0$ for each $t \in (0, 1)$. Since c_i is differentiable at $\mathbf{x}_0$, there exists a function α that is continuous at $\mathbf{0}$ such that $\alpha(\mathbf{0}_n) = 0$ and

$$c_i(\mathbf{x}_0 + t(\mathbf{x} - \mathbf{x}_0)) - c_i(\mathbf{x}_0) = t(\nabla c_i)(\mathbf{x}_0)'(\mathbf{x} - \mathbf{x}_0) + t\|\mathbf{x} - \mathbf{x}_0\|\alpha(\mathbf{x}_0 + t(\mathbf{x} - \mathbf{x}_0)),$$

for $t \in (0, 1)$. Therefore $(\nabla c_i)(\mathbf{x}_0)'(\mathbf{x} - \mathbf{x}_0) \leqslant 0$. This implies $\sum\{u_i(\nabla c_i)(\mathbf{x}_0)'(\mathbf{x} - \mathbf{x}_0) \mid i \in \text{ACT}(S, \mathbf{c}, \mathbf{x}_0)\} \leqslant 0$, which implies $(\nabla f)(\mathbf{x}_0)'(\mathbf{x} - \mathbf{x}_0) \geqslant 0$. The pseudo-convexity of f implies $f(\mathbf{x}) \geqslant f(\mathbf{x}_0)$, so $\mathbf{x}_0$ is a global minimum for f. $\qquad\square$

Of course, if both f and $\mathbf{c}$ are convex and satisfy the conditions of Theorem 13.17 that do not involve convexity, the theorem is valid and we obtain the existence of the numbers u_i.

13.6 Duality

Consider the following optimization problem for an object function $f : \mathbb{R}^n \longrightarrow \mathbb{R}$, a subset $C \subseteq \mathbb{R}^n$, and the constraint functions $\mathbf{c} : \mathbb{R}^n \longrightarrow \mathbb{R}^m$ and $\mathbf{d} : \mathbb{R}^n \longrightarrow \mathbb{R}^p$:

     minimize $f(\mathbf{x})$, where $\mathbf{x} \in C$,
         subject to $\mathbf{c}(\mathbf{x}) \leqslant \mathbf{0}_m$
         and $\mathbf{d}(\mathbf{x}) = \mathbf{0}_p$.

We refer to this optimization problem as the *primal problem*.

Definition 13.10. The *Lagrangian* associated to the primal problem is the function $L : \mathbb{R}^n \times \mathbb{R}^m \times \mathbb{R}^p \longrightarrow \mathbb{R}$ given by:

$$L(\mathbf{x}, \mathbf{u}, \mathbf{v}) = f(\mathbf{x}) + \mathbf{u}'\mathbf{c}(\mathbf{x}) + \mathbf{v}'\mathbf{d}(\mathbf{x})$$

for $\mathbf{x} \in \mathbb{R}^n$, $\mathbf{u} \in \mathbb{R}^m$, and $\mathbf{v} \in \mathbb{R}^p$.

The component u_i of $\mathbf{u}$ is the *Lagrangian multiplier* corresponding to the constraint $c_i(\mathbf{x}) \leqslant 0$; the component v_j of $\mathbf{v}$ is the *Lagrangian multiplier* corresponding to the constraint $d_j(\mathbf{x}) = 0$.

The *dual optimization problem* starts with the *Lagrange dual function* $g : \mathbb{R}^m \times \mathbb{R}^p \longrightarrow \mathbb{R}$ defined by

$$g(\mathbf{u}, \mathbf{v}) = \inf_{\mathbf{x} \in C} L(\mathbf{x}, \mathbf{u}, \mathbf{v}) \qquad (13.12)$$

and consists of

$$\text{maximize } g(\mathbf{u}, \mathbf{v}), \text{ where } \mathbf{u} \in \mathbb{R}^m \text{ and } \mathbf{v} \in \mathbb{R}^p,$$
$$\text{subject to } \mathbf{u} \geqslant \mathbf{0}_m.$$

Theorem 13.18. *For every primal problem the Lagrange dual function* $g : \mathbb{R}^m \times \mathbb{R}^p \longrightarrow \mathbb{R}$ *defined by Equality (13.12) is concave over* $\mathbb{R}^m \times \mathbb{R}^p$.

Proof. For $\mathbf{u}_1, \mathbf{u}_2 \in \mathbb{R}^m$ and $\mathbf{v}_1, \mathbf{v}_2 \in \mathbb{R}^p$ we have:
$$g(t\mathbf{u}_1 + (1-t)\mathbf{u}_2, t\mathbf{v}_1 + (1-t)\mathbf{v}_2)$$
$$= \inf\{f(\mathbf{x}) + (t\mathbf{u}'_1 + (1-t)\mathbf{u}'_2)\mathbf{c}(\mathbf{x}) + (t\mathbf{v}'_1 + (1-t)\mathbf{v}'_2)\mathbf{d}(\mathbf{x}) \mid \mathbf{x} \in S\}$$
$$= \inf\{t(f(\mathbf{x}) + \mathbf{u}'_1\mathbf{c} + \mathbf{v}'_1\mathbf{d}) + (1-t)(f(\mathbf{x}) + \mathbf{u}'_2\mathbf{c}(\mathbf{x}) + \mathbf{v}'_2\mathbf{d}(\mathbf{x})) \mid \mathbf{x} \in S\}$$
$$\geqslant t\inf\{f(\mathbf{x}) + \mathbf{u}'_1\mathbf{c} + \mathbf{v}'_1\mathbf{d} \mid \mathbf{x} \in S\}$$
$$+(1-t)\inf\{f(\mathbf{x}) + \mathbf{u}'_2\mathbf{c}(\mathbf{x}) + \mathbf{v}'_2\mathbf{d}(\mathbf{x}) \mid \mathbf{x} \in S\}$$

(by Supplement 24 of Chapter 1)
$$= tg(\mathbf{u}_1, \mathbf{v}_1) + (1-t)g(\mathbf{u}_2, \mathbf{v}_2),$$
which shows that g is concave. $\qquad\square$

The concavity of g is significant because a local optimum of g is a global optimum regardless of convexity properties of $f, \mathbf{c}$ or $\mathbf{d}$. Although the dual function g is not given explicitly, the restrictions of the dual have a simpler form and this may be an advantage in specific cases.

The dual function produces lower bounds for the optimal value of the primal problem, as we show in the next statement.

Theorem 13.19. (The Weak Duality Theorem) *Suppose that* x_* *is an optimum of* f *and* $f_* = f(x_*)$, $(\mathbf{u}_*, \mathbf{v}_*)$ *is an optimum for* g, *and* $g_* = g(\mathbf{u}_*, \mathbf{v}_*)$. *We have* $g_* \leqslant f_*$.

Proof. Since $\mathbf{c}(\mathbf{x}_*) \leqslant \mathbf{0}_m$ and $\mathbf{d}(\mathbf{x}_*) = \mathbf{0}_p$ it follows that
$$L(\mathbf{x}_*, \mathbf{u}, \mathbf{v}) = f(\mathbf{x}_*) + \mathbf{u}'\mathbf{c}(\mathbf{x}_*) + \mathbf{v}'\mathbf{d}(\mathbf{x}_*) \leqslant f_*.$$
Therefore, $g(\mathbf{u}, \mathbf{v}) = \inf_{\mathbf{x} \in C} L(\mathbf{x}, \mathbf{u}, \mathbf{v}) \leqslant f_*$ for all $\mathbf{u}$ and $\mathbf{v}$.

Since g_* is the optimal value of g, the last inequality implies $g_* \leqslant f_*$. $\square$

The inequality of Theorem 13.19 holds when f_* and g_* are finite or infinite. The difference $f_* - g_*$ is the *duality gap* of the primal problem.

Strong duality holds when the duality gap is 0.

Note that for the Lagrangian function of the primal problem we can write
$$\sup_{\mathbf{u} \geqslant \mathbf{0}_m, \mathbf{v}} L(\mathbf{x}, \mathbf{u}, \mathbf{v}) = \sup_{\mathbf{u} \geqslant \mathbf{0}_m, \mathbf{v}} f(\mathbf{x}) + \mathbf{u}'\mathbf{c}(\mathbf{x}) + \mathbf{v}'\mathbf{d}(\mathbf{x})$$
$$= \begin{cases} f(\mathbf{x}) & \text{if } \mathbf{c}(\mathbf{x}) \leqslant \mathbf{0}_m, \\ \infty & \text{otherwise,} \end{cases}$$

which implies $f_* = \inf_{\mathbf{x}\in\mathbb{R}^n} \sup_{\mathbf{u}\geqslant\mathbf{0}_m,\mathbf{v}} L(\mathbf{x},\mathbf{u},\mathbf{v})$. By the definition of g_* we also have

$$g_* = \sup_{\mathbf{u}\geqslant\mathbf{0}_m,\mathbf{v}} \inf_{\mathbf{x}\in\mathbb{R}^n} L(\mathbf{x},\mathbf{u},\mathbf{v}).$$

Thus, the weak duality amounts to the inequality

$$\sup_{\mathbf{u}\geqslant\mathbf{0}_m,\mathbf{v}} \inf_{\mathbf{x}\in\mathbb{R}^n} L(\mathbf{x},\mathbf{u},\mathbf{v}) \leqslant \inf_{\mathbf{x}\in\mathbb{R}^n} \sup_{\mathbf{u}\geqslant\mathbf{0}_m,\mathbf{v}} L(\mathbf{x},\mathbf{u},\mathbf{v}),$$

and the strong duality is equivalent to the equality

$$\sup_{\mathbf{u}\geqslant\mathbf{0}_m,\mathbf{v}} \inf_{\mathbf{x}\in\mathbb{R}^n} L(\mathbf{x},\mathbf{u},\mathbf{v}) = \inf_{\mathbf{x}\in\mathbb{R}^n} \sup_{\mathbf{u}\geqslant\mathbf{0}_m,\mathbf{v}} L(\mathbf{x},\mathbf{u},\mathbf{v}).$$

Example 13.11. Let $f : \mathbb{R}^n \longrightarrow \mathbb{R}$ be the linear function $f(\mathbf{x}) = \mathbf{a}'\mathbf{x}$, $A \in \mathbb{R}^{p\times n}$, and $\mathbf{b} \in \mathbb{R}^p$. Consider the primal problem:

minimize $\mathbf{a}'\mathbf{x}$, where $\mathbf{x} \in \mathbb{R}^n$,
    subject to $\mathbf{x} \geqslant \mathbf{0}_n$ and
    $A\mathbf{x} - \mathbf{b} = \mathbf{0}_p$.

The constraint functions are $\mathbf{c}(\mathbf{x}) = -\mathbf{x}$ and $\mathbf{d}(\mathbf{x}) = A\mathbf{x} - \mathbf{b}$ and the Lagrangian L is

$$\begin{aligned} L(\mathbf{x},\mathbf{u},\mathbf{v}) &= \mathbf{a}'\mathbf{x} - \mathbf{u}'\mathbf{x} + \mathbf{v}'(A\mathbf{x} - \mathbf{b}) \\ &= -\mathbf{v}'\mathbf{b} + (\mathbf{a}' - \mathbf{u}' + \mathbf{v}'A)\mathbf{x}. \end{aligned}$$

This yields the dual function

$$g(\mathbf{u},\mathbf{v}) = -\mathbf{v}'\mathbf{b} + \inf_{\mathbf{x}\in\mathbb{R}^n} (\mathbf{a}' - \mathbf{u}' + \mathbf{v}'A)\mathbf{x}.$$

Unless $\mathbf{a}' - \mathbf{u}' + \mathbf{v}'A = \mathbf{0}'_n$ we have $g(\mathbf{u},\mathbf{v}) = -\infty$. Therefore, we have

$$g(\mathbf{u},\mathbf{v}) = \begin{cases} -\mathbf{v}'\mathbf{b} & \text{if } \mathbf{a} - \mathbf{u} + A'\mathbf{v} = \mathbf{0}_n, \\ -\infty & \text{otherwise.} \end{cases}$$

Thus, the dual problem is

maximize $g(\mathbf{u},\mathbf{v})$,
    subject to $\mathbf{u} \geqslant \mathbf{0}_m$.

An equivalent of the dual problem is

maximize $-\mathbf{v}'\mathbf{b}$,
    subject to $\mathbf{a} - \mathbf{u} + A'\mathbf{v} = \mathbf{0}_n$
    and $\mathbf{u} \geqslant \mathbf{0}_m$.

In turn, this problem is equivalent to:

maximize $-\mathbf{v}'\mathbf{b}$,

subject to $\mathbf{a} + A'\mathbf{v} \geqslant \mathbf{0}_n$.

Example 13.12. Let us consider a variant of the primal problem discussed in Example13.11. The objective function is again $f(\mathbf{x}) = \mathbf{a}'\mathbf{x}$. However, now we have only the inequality constraints $\mathbf{c}(\mathbf{x}) \leqslant \mathbf{0}_m$, where $\mathbf{c}(\mathbf{x}) = A\mathbf{x} - \mathbf{b}$, $A \in \mathbb{R}^{m \times n}$ and $\mathbf{b} \in \mathbb{R}^m$. Thus, the primal problem can be stated as

minimize $\mathbf{a}'\mathbf{x}$, where $\mathbf{x} \in \mathbb{R}^n$,

subject to $A\mathbf{x} \leqslant \mathbf{b}$.

The Lagrangian L is

$$L(\mathbf{x}, \mathbf{u}) = \mathbf{a}'\mathbf{x} + \mathbf{u}'(A\mathbf{x} - \mathbf{b}) = -\mathbf{u}'\mathbf{b} + (\mathbf{a}' + \mathbf{u}'A)\mathbf{x},$$

which yields the dual function:

$$g(\mathbf{u}) = \begin{cases} -\mathbf{u}'\mathbf{b} & \text{if } \mathbf{a}' + \mathbf{u}'A = \mathbf{0}_m, \\ -\infty & \text{otherwise,} \end{cases}$$

and the dual problem is

maximize $-\mathbf{b}'\mathbf{u}$ subject to $\mathbf{a}' + \mathbf{u}'A = \mathbf{0}_m$

and $\mathbf{u} \geqslant \mathbf{0}$.

Example 13.13. The following optimization problem

minimize $\frac{1}{2}\mathbf{x}'Q\mathbf{x} - \mathbf{r}'\mathbf{x}$,

where $\mathbf{x} \in \mathbb{R}^n$,

subject to $A\mathbf{x} \geqslant \mathbf{b}$,

where $Q \in \mathbb{R}^{n \times n}$ is a positive definite matrix, $\mathbf{r} \in \mathbb{R}^n$, $A \in \mathbb{R}^{p \times n}$, and $\mathbf{b} \in \mathbb{R}^p$ is known as a *quadratic optimization problem*.

The Lagrangian L is

$$L(\mathbf{x}, \mathbf{u}) = \frac{1}{2}\mathbf{x}'Q\mathbf{x} - \mathbf{r}'\mathbf{x} + \mathbf{u}'(A\mathbf{x} - \mathbf{b}) = \frac{1}{2}\mathbf{x}'Q\mathbf{x} + (\mathbf{u}'A - \mathbf{r}')\mathbf{x} - \mathbf{u}'\mathbf{b}$$

and the dual function is $g(\mathbf{u}) = \inf_{\mathbf{x} \in \mathbb{R}^n} L(\mathbf{x}, \mathbf{u})$ subject to $\mathbf{u} \geq \mathbf{0}_m$. Since $\mathbf{x}$ is unconstrained in the definition of g, the minimum is attained when we have the equalities

$$\frac{\partial}{\partial x_i}\left(\frac{1}{2}\mathbf{x}'Q\mathbf{x} + (\mathbf{u}'A - \mathbf{r}')\mathbf{x} - \mathbf{u}'\mathbf{b}\right) = 0$$

for $1 \leqslant i \leqslant n$, which amount to $\mathbf{x} = Q^{-1}(\mathbf{r} - A\mathbf{u})$. Thus, the dual optimization function is: $g(\mathbf{u}) = -\frac{1}{2}\mathbf{u}'P\mathbf{u} - \mathbf{u}'\mathbf{d} - \frac{1}{2}\mathbf{r}'Q\mathbf{r}$ subject to $\mathbf{u} \geqslant \mathbf{0}_p$, where $P = AQ^{-1}A'$, $\mathbf{d} = \mathbf{b} - AQ^{-1}\mathbf{r}$. This shows that the dual problem of this quadratic optimization problem is itself a quadratic optimization problem.

Example 13.14. Let $\mathbf{a}_1, \ldots, \mathbf{a}_m \in \mathbb{R}^n$. We seek to determine a closed sphere $B[\mathbf{x}, r]$ of minimal radius that includes all points $\mathbf{a}_i$ for $1 \leqslant i \leqslant m$. This is the *minimum bounding sphere* problem, formulated by J. J. Sylvester in [127]. This problem amounts to solving the following primal optimization problem:

minimize r, where $r \geq 0$,

subject to $\|\mathbf{x} - \mathbf{a}_i\| \leqslant r$ for $1 \leqslant i \leqslant m$.

An equivalent formulation requires minimizing r^2 and stating the restrictions as $\|\mathbf{x} - \mathbf{a}_i\|^2 - r^2 \leqslant 0$ for $1 \leqslant i \leqslant m$. The Lagrangian of this problem is:

$$L(r, \mathbf{x}, \mathbf{u}) = r^2 + \sum_{i=1}^{m} u_i(\|\mathbf{x} - \mathbf{a}_i\|^2 - r^2)$$

$$= r^2 \left(1 - \sum_{i=1}^{m} u_i\right) + \sum_{i=1}^{m} u_i \|\mathbf{x} - \mathbf{a}_i^2\|$$

and the dual function is:

$$g(\mathbf{u}) = \inf_{r \in \mathbb{R}_{\geqslant 0}, \mathbf{x} \in \mathbb{R}^n} L(r, \mathbf{x}, \mathbf{u})$$

$$= \inf_{r \in \mathbb{R}_{\geqslant 0}, \mathbf{x} \in \mathbb{R}^n} r^2 \left(1 - \sum_{i=1}^{m} u_i\right) + \sum_{i=1}^{m} u_i \|\mathbf{x} - \mathbf{a}_i|^2 \|.$$

This leads to the following conditions:

$$\frac{\partial L(r, \mathbf{x}, \mathbf{u})}{\partial r} = 2r \left(1 - \sum_{i=1}^{m} u_i\right) = 0$$

$$\frac{\partial L(r, \mathbf{x}, \mathbf{u})}{\partial x_p} = 2 \sum_{i=1}^{m} u_i(\mathbf{x} - \mathbf{a}_i)_p = 0 \text{ for } 1 \leqslant p \leqslant n.$$

The first equality yields $\sum_{i=1}^{m} u_i = 1$. Therefore, from the second equality we obtain $\mathbf{x} = \sum_{i=1}^{m} u_i \mathbf{a}_i$. This shows that for $\mathbf{x}$ is a convex combination of $\mathbf{a}_1, \ldots, \mathbf{a}_m$. The dual function is

$$g(\mathbf{u}) = \sum_{i=1}^{m} u_i \left(\sum_{h=1}^{m} u_h \mathbf{a}_h - \mathbf{a}_i\right) = 0$$

because $\sum_{i=1}^{m} u_i = 1$.

Note that the restriction functions $g_i(\mathbf{x}, r) = \|\mathbf{x} - \mathbf{a}_i\|^2 - r^2 \leqslant 0$ are not convex.

Example 13.15. Consider the primal problem

$$\text{minimize } x_1^2 + x_2^2, \text{ where } x_1, x_2 \in \mathbb{R},$$
$$\text{subject to } x_1 - 1 \geqslant 0.$$

It is clear that the minimum of $f(\mathbf{x})$ is obtained for $x_1 = 1$ and $x_2 = 0$ and this minimum is 1. The Lagrangian is

$$L(\mathbf{u}) = x_1^2 + x_2^2 + u_1(x_1 - 1)$$

and the dual function is

$$g(\mathbf{u}) = \inf_{\mathbf{x}}\{x_1^2 + x_2^2 + u_1(x_1 - 1) \mid \mathbf{x} \in \mathbb{R}^2\} = -\frac{u_1^2}{4}.$$

Then $\sup\{g(u_1) \mid u_1 \geq 0\} = 0$ and a gap exists between the minimal value of the primal function and the maximal value of the dual function.

Example 13.16. Let $a, b > 0$, $p, q < 0$ and let $r > 0$. Consider the following primal problem:

$$\text{minimize } f(\mathbf{x}) = ax_1^2 + bx_2^2$$
$$\text{subject to } px_1 + qx_2 + r \leqslant 0 \text{ and } x_1 \geqslant 0, x_2 \geqslant 0.$$

The set C is $\{\mathbf{x} \in \mathbb{R}^2 \mid x_1 \geqslant 0, x_2 \geqslant 0\}$. The constraint function is $c(\mathbf{x}) = px_1 + qx_2 + r \leqslant 0$ and the Lagrangian of the primal problem is

$$L(\mathbf{x}, u) = ax_1^2 + bx_2^2 + u(px_1 + qx_2 + r),$$

where u is a Lagrangian multiplier. Thus, the dual problem objective function is

$$
\begin{aligned}
g(u) &= \inf_{\mathbf{x} \in C} L(\mathbf{x}, u) \\
&= \inf_{\mathbf{x} \in C} ax_1^2 + bx_2^2 + u(px_1 + qx_2 + r) \\
&= \inf_{\mathbf{x} \in C}\{ax_1^2 + upx_1 \mid x_1 \geqslant 0\} \\
&\quad + \inf_{\mathbf{x} \in C}\{bx_2^2 + uqx_2 \mid x_2 \geqslant 0\} + ur.
\end{aligned}
$$

The infima are achieved when $x_1 = -\frac{up}{2a}$ and $x_2 = -\frac{uq}{2b}$ if $u \geqslant 0$ and at $\mathbf{x} = \mathbf{0}_2$ if $u < 0$. Thus,

$$
g(u) = \begin{cases}
-\left(\frac{p^2}{4a} + \frac{q^2}{4b}\right)u^2 + ru & \text{if } u \geq 0, \\
ru & \text{if } u < 0,
\end{cases}
$$

which is a concave function.

The maximum of $g(u)$ is achieved when $u = \frac{2r}{\frac{p^2}{a} + \frac{q^2}{b}}$ and equals

$$\frac{r^2}{\left(\frac{p^2}{a} + \frac{q^2}{b}\right)}.$$

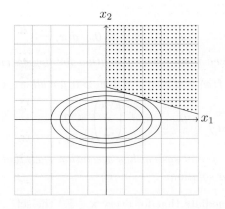

Fig. 13.1   Family of Concentric Ellipses; the ellipse that "touches" the line $px_1 + qx_2 + r = 0$ gives the optimum value for f. The dotted area is the feasible region.

Note that if $\mathbf{x}$ is located on an ellipse $ax_1^2 + bx_2^2 - k = 0$, then $f(\mathbf{x}) = k$ (see Figure 13.1). Thus, the minimum of f is achieved when k is chosen such that the ellipse is tangent to the line $px_1 + qx_2 + r = 0$. In other words, we seek to determine k such that the tangent of the ellipse at $\mathbf{x}_0 = \begin{pmatrix} x_{01} \\ x_{02} \end{pmatrix}$ located on the ellipse coincides with the line given by $px_1 + qx_2 + r = 0$.

The equation of the tangent is

$$ax_1 x_{01} + bx_2 x_{02} - k = 0.$$

Therefore, we need to have:

$$\frac{ax_{01}}{p} = \frac{bx_{02}}{q} = \frac{-k}{r},$$

hence $x_{01} = -\frac{kp}{ar}$ and $x_{02} = -\frac{kq}{br}$. Substituting back these coordinates in the equation of the ellipse yields $k_1 = 0$ and $k_2 = \frac{r^2}{\frac{p^2}{a} + \frac{q^2}{b}}$. In this case no duality gap exists.

13.7   Strong Duality

The following alternative theorem is an useful preliminary result.

Theorem 13.20. *Let C be a convex subset of $\mathbb{R}^n$, $f : \mathbb{R}^n \longrightarrow \mathbb{R}$ and $\mathbf{c} : \mathbb{R}^n \longrightarrow \mathbb{R}^m$ be convex functions, and let $\mathbf{d} : \mathbb{R}^n \longrightarrow \mathbb{R}^p$ be given by $\mathbf{d}(\boldsymbol{x}) = A\boldsymbol{x} - \boldsymbol{b}$, where $A \in \mathbb{R}^{p \times n}$ and $b \in \mathbb{R}^p$.*

If the system

$$f(\boldsymbol{x}) < 0, \boldsymbol{c}(\boldsymbol{x}) \leqslant \boldsymbol{0}_m, \boldsymbol{d}(\boldsymbol{x}) = 0$$

has no solution, then there exists a solution for the system

$$u_0 f(\boldsymbol{x}) + \boldsymbol{u}' \boldsymbol{c}(\boldsymbol{x}) + \boldsymbol{v}' \boldsymbol{d}(\boldsymbol{x}) \geqslant 0 \text{ for all } \boldsymbol{x} \in C,$$

$$\begin{pmatrix} u_0 \\ \boldsymbol{u} \end{pmatrix} \geqslant \boldsymbol{0}_{m+1} \text{ and } \begin{pmatrix} u_0 \\ \boldsymbol{u} \\ \boldsymbol{v} \end{pmatrix} \neq \boldsymbol{0}_{1+m+k}.$$

Conversely, if the second system has a solution such that $u_0 > 0$, then the first system has no solution.

Proof. It is immediate that for every $\mathbf{x} \in \mathbb{R}^n$ the set

$$U_{\mathbf{x}} = \left\{ \begin{pmatrix} p \\ \mathbf{q} \\ \mathbf{r} \end{pmatrix} \middle| p > f(\mathbf{x}), \mathbf{q} \geqslant \mathbf{c}(\mathbf{x}), \mathbf{r} = \mathbf{d}(\mathbf{x}) \right\}$$

is a convex subset of $\mathbb{R}^{1+m+p}$. Note that if $U_{\mathbf{x}} \neq \emptyset$ then p and $\mathbf{q}$ can be arbitrarily large.

Since the first system has no solution, the vector $\begin{pmatrix} 0 \\ \boldsymbol{0}_m \\ \boldsymbol{0}_p \end{pmatrix}$ does not belong

to $U_{\mathbf{x}}$. By Corollary 6.18 there exists $\mathbf{w} = \begin{pmatrix} u_0 \\ \boldsymbol{u} \\ \boldsymbol{v} \end{pmatrix} \in \mathbb{R}^{1+m+p}$, $\mathbf{w} \neq \boldsymbol{0}_{1+m+p}$,

such that $\mathbf{w}'\mathbf{x} \geqslant 0$ for $\mathbf{x} \in \mathbf{K}(U_{\mathbf{x}})$, that is,

$$u_0 p + \boldsymbol{u}' \mathbf{q} + \boldsymbol{v}' \mathbf{r} \geqslant 0$$

for each $\begin{pmatrix} p \\ \mathbf{q} \\ \mathbf{r} \end{pmatrix} \in \mathbf{K}(U_{\mathbf{x}})$.

Since p and $\mathbf{q}$ can be arbitrarily large, the above inequality holds only if $u_0 > 0$ and $\mathbf{u} \geqslant \boldsymbol{0}_m$. From

$$\begin{pmatrix} f(\mathbf{x}) \\ \mathbf{c}(\mathbf{x}) \\ \mathbf{d}(\mathbf{x}) \end{pmatrix} \in \mathbf{K}(U_{\mathbf{x}}),$$

it follows that

$$u_0 f(\mathbf{x}) + \boldsymbol{u}' \mathbf{c}(\mathbf{x}) + \boldsymbol{v}' \mathbf{d}(\mathbf{x}) \geqslant 0.$$

Thus, the second system has a solution.

Conversely, suppose that the second system has a solution $\begin{pmatrix} u_0 \\ \mathbf{u} \\ \mathbf{v} \end{pmatrix}$ such that $u_0 > 0$, $\mathbf{u} \geqslant \mathbf{0}_m$ and

$$u_0 f(\mathbf{x}) + \mathbf{u}' \mathbf{c}(\mathbf{x}) + \mathbf{v}' \mathbf{d}(\mathbf{x}) \geqslant 0$$

for $\mathbf{x} \in C$. For $\mathbf{x} \in C$ such that $\mathbf{c}(\mathbf{x}) \leqslant \mathbf{0}_m$ and $\mathbf{d}(\mathbf{x}) = \mathbf{0}_p$ we obtain $u_0 f(\mathbf{x}) \geqslant 0$ because $\mathbf{u} \geqslant \mathbf{0}_m$. Since $u_0 > 0$, we have $f(\mathbf{x}) \geqslant 0$, so the first system has no solution. $\qquad\square$

The next result offers sufficient conditions for eliminating the duality gap.

Theorem 13.21. (Strong Duality Theorem) *Let C be a non-empty convex subset of $\mathbb{R}^n$, $f : \mathbb{R}^n \longrightarrow \mathbb{R}$ and $\mathbf{c} : \mathbb{R}^n \longrightarrow \mathbb{R}^m$ be convex functions, and let $\boldsymbol{d} : \mathbb{R}^n \longrightarrow \mathbb{R}^p$ be given by $d(\boldsymbol{x}) = A\boldsymbol{x} - \boldsymbol{b}$, where $A \in \mathbb{R}^{p \times n}$ and $b \in \mathbb{R}^p$.*

Consider the primal problem
$$\text{minimize } f(\boldsymbol{x}), \text{ where } \boldsymbol{x} \in C,$$
$$\text{subject to } \boldsymbol{c}(\boldsymbol{x}) \leqslant \boldsymbol{0}_m$$
$$\text{and } \boldsymbol{d}(\boldsymbol{x}) = \boldsymbol{0}_p,$$

and its dual
$$\text{maximize } g(\boldsymbol{u}, \boldsymbol{v}), \text{ where } \boldsymbol{u} \in \mathbb{R}^m \text{ and } \boldsymbol{v} \in \mathbb{R}^p,$$
$$\text{subject to } \boldsymbol{u} \geqslant \boldsymbol{0}_m,$$

where

$$g(\boldsymbol{u}, \boldsymbol{v}) = \inf\{f(\boldsymbol{x}) + \boldsymbol{u}' \boldsymbol{c}(\boldsymbol{x}) + \boldsymbol{v}' \boldsymbol{d}(\boldsymbol{x}) \mid \boldsymbol{x} \in \mathbb{R}^n\}.$$

Additionally, we assume that

(i) *there exists $\boldsymbol{z} \in C$ such that $\boldsymbol{c}(\boldsymbol{z}) < \boldsymbol{0}_m$ and $\boldsymbol{d}(\boldsymbol{z}) = \boldsymbol{0}_p$;*
(ii) *$\boldsymbol{0}_p \in \boldsymbol{I}(\boldsymbol{d}(C))$.*

We have the strong duality:

$$\sup\{g(\boldsymbol{u}, \boldsymbol{v}) \mid \boldsymbol{u} \geqslant \boldsymbol{0}_m\} = \inf\{f(\boldsymbol{x}) \mid \boldsymbol{x} \in C, \boldsymbol{c}(\boldsymbol{x}) \leqslant \boldsymbol{0}_m, \boldsymbol{d}(\boldsymbol{x}) = \boldsymbol{0}_p\}. \tag{13.13}$$

If

$$\inf\{f(\boldsymbol{x}) \mid \boldsymbol{x} \in C, \boldsymbol{c}(\boldsymbol{x}) \leqslant \boldsymbol{0}_m, \boldsymbol{d}(\boldsymbol{x}) = \boldsymbol{0}_p\}$$

is finite, then there exist $\boldsymbol{u}_*, \boldsymbol{v}_*$ with $\boldsymbol{u}_* \geqslant \boldsymbol{0}_m$ such that $g(\boldsymbol{u}_*, \boldsymbol{v}_*) = \sup\{g(\boldsymbol{u}, \boldsymbol{v}) \mid \boldsymbol{u} \geqslant \boldsymbol{0}_m\}$.

If the infimum of f is achieved at $\boldsymbol{x}_0$, that is,

$$f(\boldsymbol{x}_0) = \inf\{f(\boldsymbol{x}) \mid \boldsymbol{x} \in C, \boldsymbol{c}(\boldsymbol{x}) \leqslant \boldsymbol{0}_m, \boldsymbol{d}(\boldsymbol{x}) = \boldsymbol{0}_p\},$$

then $\boldsymbol{u}_*' c(\boldsymbol{x}_0) = 0$.

Proof. Define

$$\alpha = \inf\{f(\mathbf{x}) \mid \mathbf{c}(\mathbf{x}) \leqslant \mathbf{0}_m, \mathbf{d}(\mathbf{x}) = \mathbf{0}_p\}.$$

If $\alpha = -\infty$, then $\sup\{g(\mathbf{u}, \mathbf{v}) \mid \mathbf{u} \geqslant \mathbf{0}_m\} = -\infty$, and Equality (13.13) holds. If α is finite, the system

$$\begin{aligned} f(\mathbf{x}) - \alpha &< 0, \\ \mathbf{c}(\mathbf{x}) &\leqslant \mathbf{0}_m, \\ \mathbf{d}(\mathbf{x}) &= \mathbf{0}_p \end{aligned}$$

has no solution in C. By Theorem 13.20 there exist $u_0 \geqslant 0$, $\mathbf{u} \geqslant \mathbf{0}_m$ and $\mathbf{v} \in \mathbb{R}^p$ such that $u_0(f(\mathbf{x}) - \alpha) + \mathbf{u}'\mathbf{c}(\mathbf{x}) + \mathbf{v}'\mathbf{d}(\mathbf{x}) \geqslant 0$ for $\mathbf{x} \in C$.

Suppose that $u_0 = 0$. By the hypothesis of the theorem there exists $\mathbf{z} \in \mathbb{R}^n$ such that $\mathbf{c}(\mathbf{z}) < \mathbf{0}_m$ and $\mathbf{d}(\mathbf{z}) = \mathbf{0}_k$, which implies $\mathbf{u}'\mathbf{c}(\mathbf{z}) \geqslant 0$. Since $\mathbf{u} \geqslant \mathbf{0}_m$ and $\mathbf{c}(\mathbf{z}) < \mathbf{0}_m$, this is possible only if $\mathbf{u} = \mathbf{0}_m$, so $\mathbf{v}'\mathbf{d}(\mathbf{z}) \geqslant 0$.

Since $\mathbf{0}_p \in \mathbf{I}(\mathbf{d}(C))$, it follows that there exists $\epsilon > 0$ such that $B(\mathbf{0}_p, \epsilon) \subseteq \mathbf{d}(C)$. Note that if $0 < \alpha < \epsilon$, then $-\alpha\frac{\mathbf{v}}{\|\mathbf{v}\|} \in B(\mathbf{0}_p, \epsilon)$, and therefore there exists $\mathbf{x}_0 \in C$ such that $-\alpha\frac{\mathbf{v}}{\|\mathbf{v}\|} = \mathbf{d}(\mathbf{x}_0)$, which means that $\mathbf{v} = -\frac{1}{\alpha}\|\mathbf{v}\|\mathbf{d}(\mathbf{x}_0)$. Consequently, we have

$$0 \leqslant \mathbf{v}'\mathbf{d}(\mathbf{x}_0) = -\alpha\frac{1}{\|\mathbf{v}\|}\mathbf{v}'\mathbf{v} = -\alpha\|\mathbf{v}\|,$$

and this implies $\mathbf{v} = \mathbf{0}_n$. Thus, $u_0 = 0$ implies $\mathbf{u} = \mathbf{0}_n$ and $\mathbf{v} = \mathbf{0}_n$, which is impossible. Therefore, we have $u_0 > 0$.

Since $u_0 > 0$, we have $f(\mathbf{x}) - \alpha + \mathbf{u}'_*\mathbf{c}(\mathbf{x}) + \mathbf{v}'_*\mathbf{d}(\mathbf{x}) \geqslant 0$ for $\mathbf{x} \in C$, where $\mathbf{u}_* = \frac{1}{u_0}\mathbf{u}$ and $\mathbf{v}_* = \frac{1}{u_0}\mathbf{v}$. This implies $g(\mathbf{u}_*, \mathbf{v}_*) \geqslant \alpha$, so $g(\mathbf{u}_*, \mathbf{v}_*) = \alpha$, by the Weak Duality Theorem.

Suppose that $\mathbf{x}_0$ is an optimal solution to the primal problem. Then, $f(\mathbf{x}_0) = \alpha$, $\mathbf{c}(\mathbf{x}_0) \leqslant \mathbf{0}_m$ and $\mathbf{d}(\mathbf{x}_0) = \mathbf{0}_p$. Since $f(\mathbf{x}_0) - \alpha + \mathbf{u}'_*\mathbf{c}(\mathbf{x}_0) + \mathbf{v}'_*\mathbf{d}(\mathbf{x}_0) \geqslant 0$, it follows that $\mathbf{u}'_*\mathbf{x}_0 \geqslant 0$. Since $\mathbf{u}_* \geqslant \mathbf{0}_m$ and $\mathbf{c}(\mathbf{x}_0) \leqslant \mathbf{0}_m$, we obtain $\mathbf{u}'_*\mathbf{c}(\mathbf{x}_0) = 0$. $\square$

The existence of $\mathbf{z} \in C$ such that $\mathbf{c}(\mathbf{z}) < 0$ and $\mathbf{d}(\mathbf{z}) = \mathbf{0}_k$ together with the condition $\mathbf{0}_p \in \mathbf{I}(\mathbf{d}(C))$ are known as the *constraint qualification conditions* for the strong duality theorem.

Definition 13.11. A *saddle point* for the Lagrangian $L(\mathbf{x}, \mathbf{u}, \mathbf{v})$ is a vector

$$\begin{pmatrix} \mathbf{x}_0 \\ \mathbf{u}_* \\ \mathbf{v}_* \end{pmatrix} \in \mathbb{R}^{n+m+p} \text{ such that }$$

$$L(\mathbf{x}_0, \mathbf{u}, \mathbf{v}) \leqslant L(\mathbf{x}_0, \mathbf{u}_*, \mathbf{v}_*) \leqslant L(\mathbf{x}, \mathbf{u}_*, \mathbf{v}_*),$$

for every $\mathbf{x}, \mathbf{u}$ and $\mathbf{v}$.

The existence of a saddle point of the Lagrangian suffices to ensure that the primal problem and dual problem satisfy strong duality.

Theorem 13.22. *Let C be a non-empty subset of $\mathbb{R}^n$, $f : \mathbb{R}^n \longrightarrow \mathbb{R}$, $g : \mathbb{R}^n \longrightarrow \mathbb{R}^m$, and $d : \mathbb{R}^n \longrightarrow \mathbb{R}^p$, and let $L(\boldsymbol{x}, \boldsymbol{u}, \boldsymbol{v}) = f(\boldsymbol{x}) + \boldsymbol{u}' \boldsymbol{c}(\boldsymbol{x}) + \boldsymbol{v}' \boldsymbol{d}(\boldsymbol{x})$ be the Lagrangian function.*

If L has a saddle point $\begin{pmatrix} \boldsymbol{x}_0 \\ \boldsymbol{u}_* \\ \boldsymbol{v}_* \end{pmatrix} \in \mathbb{R}^{n+m+p}$ with $\boldsymbol{u}_* \geqslant \boldsymbol{0}_m$, then $\boldsymbol{x}_0$ is a solution for the primal problem and (u_*, v_*) is a solution for the dual problem.

Proof. Suppose that the vectors $\mathbf{x}_0$ and $\mathbf{u}_*, \mathbf{v}_*$ form a saddle point. The inequalities

$$f(x_*) + \mathbf{u}\mathbf{c}(\mathbf{x}_0) + \mathbf{v}'\mathbf{d}(\mathbf{x}_0) = L(\mathbf{x}_0, \mathbf{u}, \mathbf{v}) \leqslant L(\mathbf{x}_0, \mathbf{u}_*, \mathbf{v}_*)$$

which hold for all $\mathbf{u} \geqslant \boldsymbol{0}_m$ and $\mathbf{v} \in \mathbb{R}^p$ imply $g(\mathbf{x}_0) \leqslant \boldsymbol{0}_m$ and $\mathbf{d}(\mathbf{x}_0) = \boldsymbol{0}_p$. Therefore, $\mathbf{x}_0$ is a feasible solution of the primal problem.

Taking $\mathbf{u} = \boldsymbol{0}_m$, it follows that $\mathbf{u}'_*\mathbf{x}(\mathbf{x}_0) = 0$. Since $\mathbf{u}_* \geqslant \boldsymbol{0}_m$ and $\mathbf{c}(\mathbf{x}_0) \leqslant \boldsymbol{0}_m$, we have $\mathbf{u}'_*\mathbf{c}(\mathbf{x}_0) = 0$ and the definition of the saddle point implies

$$f(\mathbf{x}_0) = f(\mathbf{x}_0) + \mathbf{u}'_*\mathbf{c}(\mathbf{x}_0) + \mathbf{v}'_*\mathbf{d}(\mathbf{x}_0) = L(\mathbf{x}_0, \mathbf{u}_*, \mathbf{v}_*)$$
$$\leqslant L(\mathbf{x}, \mathbf{u}_*, \mathbf{v}_*) = f(\mathbf{x}) + \mathbf{u}'_*\mathbf{c}(\mathbf{x}) + \mathbf{v}'_*\mathbf{d}(\mathbf{x})$$

for each $\mathbf{x} \in C$. This implies $f(\mathbf{x}_0) \leqslant g(\mathbf{u}_*, \mathbf{v}_*)$. This implies that $\mathbf{x}_0$ and $(\mathbf{u}_*, \mathbf{v}_*)$ are solutions to the primal and dual problems, respectively, and that the duality gap is 0. $\square$

The existence of a saddle point follows from convexity assumptions and from constraint qualification conditions.

Theorem 13.23. *If C is a convex set, f and $\boldsymbol{c}$ are convex functions, $\boldsymbol{d}(\boldsymbol{x}) = A\boldsymbol{x} - \boldsymbol{b}$ and the constraint qualification conditions are satisfied, then there exists a saddle point $\begin{pmatrix} \boldsymbol{x}_0 \\ \boldsymbol{u}_* \\ \boldsymbol{v}_* \end{pmatrix} \in \mathbb{R}^{n+m+p}$, where $\boldsymbol{u}_* \geqslant \boldsymbol{0}_m$.*

Proof. By the Strong Duality Theorem (Theorem 13.21), there exists a solution $\mathbf{x}_0$ of the primal problem such that $f(\mathbf{x}_0) = g(\mathbf{u}_*, \mathbf{v}_*)$, where $\mathbf{u}_* \geqslant \boldsymbol{0}_m$ and $\mathbf{u}'_*\mathbf{c}(\mathbf{x}_0) = 0$. Thus, we have

$$f(\mathbf{x}_0) = g(\mathbf{u}_*, \mathbf{v}_*) \leqslant f(\mathbf{x}) + \mathbf{u}'_*\mathbf{c}(\mathbf{x}) + \mathbf{v}'_*\mathbf{d}(\mathbf{x}) = L(\mathbf{x}, \mathbf{u}_*, \mathbf{v}_*)$$

for $\mathbf{x} \in C$.

Since $\mathbf{u}'_* \mathbf{c}(\mathbf{x}_0) = \mathbf{v}'_* \mathbf{d}(\mathbf{x}_0) = 0$, we also have

$$L(\mathbf{x}_0, \mathbf{u}_*, \mathbf{v}_*) = f(\mathbf{x}_0) + \mathbf{u}'_* \mathbf{c}(\mathbf{x}_0) + \mathbf{v}'_* \mathbf{d}(\mathbf{x}_0) \leqslant L(\mathbf{x}, \mathbf{u}_*, \mathbf{v}_*)$$

for $\mathbf{x} \in C$. The inequality

$$L(\mathbf{x}_0, \mathbf{u}, \mathbf{v}) \leqslant L(\mathbf{x}, \mathbf{u}_*, \mathbf{v}_*),$$

follows from $\mathbf{x}_0 \mathbf{c}(\mathbf{x}_0) = 0$, $\mathbf{d}(\mathbf{x}_0) = \mathbf{0}_p$, $\mathbf{c}(\mathbf{x}_0) \leqslant \mathbf{0}_p$ and $\mathbf{u} \geq \mathbf{0}_m$. Therefore $\mathbf{x}_0, \mathbf{u}_*$ and $\mathbf{v}_*$ are the components of a saddle point for L. $\square$

Exercises and Supplements

(1) Solve the following optimization problem in $\mathbb{R}^2$:

$$\text{minimize } x_1 + x_2,$$
$$\text{subject to } x_1 x_2 \geqslant 10, \ x_1 x_2 - 5(x_1 + x_2) + 25 \leqslant 0,$$
$$x_1 \geqslant 0, \ x_1 \geqslant 0, \ x_2 \geqslant 0.$$

(2) Let C be a convex subset of $\mathbb{R}^m$ such that $R_{\mathbf{c}} = \{\mathbf{x} \in C \mid \mathbf{c}(\mathbf{x}) \leqslant \mathbf{0}_m\}$ is a convex subset of $\mathbb{R}^n$. Prove that Karlin's constraint qualification is equivalent to requiring the existence of $\mathbf{x} \in C$ such that $\mathbf{c}(\mathbf{x}) < \mathbf{0}_m$. This is the *Slater constraint qualification*.

   Hint: Apply Theorem 12.28.

(3) Using Lagrange multipliers retrieve the formula for the distance of a point $\mathbf{x}_0$ to a hyperplane $\mathbf{w}'\mathbf{x} - a$ in $\mathbb{R}^n$.

(4) Let $f : \mathbb{R}^n_{\geqslant 0} \times \mathbb{R}^m_{\geqslant 0} \longrightarrow \mathbb{R}$ be a function that is differentiable. Prove that if $(\mathbf{x}_0, \mathbf{r}_0)$ is a Kuhn-Tucker saddle point of f, that is, if

$$f(\mathbf{x}_0, \mathbf{r}) \leqslant f(\mathbf{x}_0, \mathbf{r}_0) \leqslant f(\mathbf{x}, \mathbf{r}_0),$$

for $\mathbf{x} \in \mathbb{R}^n_{\geqslant 0}$ and $\mathbf{r} \in \mathbb{R}^m_{\geqslant 0}$ then

$$(\nabla_{\mathbf{x}} f)(\mathbf{x}_0, \mathbf{r}_0) \leqslant \mathbf{0}_n, (\nabla_{\mathbf{x}} f)(\mathbf{x}_0, \mathbf{r}_0)'\mathbf{x}_0 = 0, \mathbf{x}_0 \geqslant \mathbf{0}_n,$$
$$(\nabla_{\mathbf{r}} f)(\mathbf{x}_0, \mathbf{r}_0) \geqslant \mathbf{0}_m, (\nabla_{\mathbf{r}} f)(\mathbf{x}_0, \mathbf{r}_0)'\mathbf{r}_0 = 0, \mathbf{r}_0 \geqslant \mathbf{0}_m.$$

   Solution: Note that $f(\mathbf{x}, \mathbf{r}_0)$ has a minimum in $\mathbf{x}_0$ and $f(\mathbf{x}_0, \mathbf{r})$ has a maximum in $\mathbf{r}_0$. Therefore, the components of $(\nabla_{\mathbf{x}} f)(\mathbf{x}_0, \mathbf{r}_0)$ and $(\nabla_{\mathbf{r}} f)(\mathbf{x}_0, \mathbf{r}_0)$ must vanish except possibly when the corresponding components of $\mathbf{x}_0$ and $\mathbf{r}_0$ vanish, in which case they must be non-positive and non-negative respectively.

(5) Let $f : \mathbb{R}_{\geq 0}^n \times \mathbb{R}_{\geq 0}^m \longrightarrow \mathbb{R}$ be a function that is differentiable. Prove that if $(\mathbf{x}_0, \mathbf{r}_0)$ is such that

$$(\nabla_{\mathbf{x}} f)(\mathbf{x}_0, \mathbf{r}_0) \leqslant \mathbf{0}_n, (\nabla_{\mathbf{x}} f)(\mathbf{x}_0, \mathbf{r}_0)' \mathbf{x}_0 = 0, \mathbf{x}_0 \geqslant \mathbf{0}_n,$$
$$(\nabla_{\mathbf{r}} f)(\mathbf{x}_0, \mathbf{r}_0) \geqslant \mathbf{0}_m, (\nabla_{\mathbf{x}} f)(\mathbf{x}_0, \mathbf{r}_0)' \mathbf{r}_0 = 0, \mathbf{u}_0 \geqslant \mathbf{0}_m,$$
$$f(\mathbf{x}, \mathbf{r}_0) \text{ is a concave function,}$$
$$f(\mathbf{x}_0, \mathbf{r}) \text{ is a convex function,}$$

then $(\mathbf{x}_0, \mathbf{r}_0)$ is a Kuhn-Tucker saddle point of f.

Solution: Note that the convexity of $f(\mathbf{x}_0, \mathbf{r})$ and the concavity of $f(\mathbf{x}, \mathbf{r}_0)$ imply

$$f(\mathbf{x}, \mathbf{r}_0) \leqslant f(\mathbf{x}_0, \mathbf{r}_0) + (\nabla_{\mathbf{x}} f)(\mathbf{x}_0, \mathbf{r}_0)'(\mathbf{x} - \mathbf{x}_0),$$
$$f(\mathbf{x}_0, \mathbf{r}) \geqslant f(\mathbf{x}_0, \mathbf{r}_0) + (\nabla_{\mathbf{u}} f)(\mathbf{x}_0, \mathbf{r}_0)'(\mathbf{u} - \mathbf{u}_0).$$

Applying the above conditions we obtain:

$$\begin{aligned}
f(\mathbf{x}, \mathbf{r}_0) &\leqslant f(\mathbf{x}_0, \mathbf{r}_0) + (\nabla_{\mathbf{x}} f)(\mathbf{x}_0, \mathbf{r}_0)'(\mathbf{x} - \mathbf{x}_0) \\
&\leqslant f(\mathbf{x}_0, \mathbf{r}_0) \\
&\leqslant f(\mathbf{x}_0, \mathbf{r}_0) + (\nabla_{\mathbf{u}} f)(\mathbf{x}_0, \mathbf{r}_0)'(\mathbf{u} - \mathbf{u}_0) \\
&\leqslant f(\mathbf{x}_0, \mathbf{r}),
\end{aligned}$$

for $\mathbf{x} \in \mathbb{R}_{\geq 0}^n$ and $\mathbf{r} \in \mathbb{R}_{\geq 0}^m$. Thus, $(\mathbf{x}_0, \mathbf{r}_0)$ is a saddle point for f.

(6) Prove that the minimum bounding sphere problem discussed in Example 13.14 can be transformed into a quadratic programming problem, that is, into an optimization problem with a quadratic objective function subjected to linear restrictions.

Solution: Starting from the problem

minimize r^2
$$\text{subject to } \|\mathbf{x} - \mathbf{a}_i\|^2 - r^2 \leqslant 0$$
$$\text{for } 1 \leqslant i \leqslant m,$$

let $\rho = \frac{1}{2}(\|\mathbf{x}\|^2 - r^2)$. Note that the following conditions are equivalent:

(a) $\|\mathbf{x} - \mathbf{a}_i\|^2 \leqslant r^2$;
(b) $\|\mathbf{x}\|^2 - 2\mathbf{a}_i'\mathbf{x} + \|\mathbf{a}_i\|^2 \leqslant r^2$;
(c) $-2\mathbf{a}_i'\mathbf{x} \leqslant r^2 - \|\mathbf{x}\|^2 - \|\mathbf{a}_i\|^2$;
(d) $2\mathbf{a}_i'\mathbf{x} \geqslant -r^2 + \|\mathbf{x}\|^2 + \|\mathbf{a}_i\|^2$;
(e) $\mathbf{a}_i'\mathbf{x} \geqslant \frac{1}{2}\rho + \frac{1}{2}\|\mathbf{a}_i\|^2$.

Thus, the original problem is equivalent to

minimize $\frac{1}{2}\|\mathbf{x}\|^2 - \rho$
$$\text{subject to } \mathbf{a}_i'\mathbf{x} \geqslant \frac{1}{2}\rho + \frac{1}{2}\|\mathbf{a}_i\|^2$$
$$\text{for } 1 \leqslant i \leqslant m,$$

which is a quadratic programming problem.

(7) Let $f : \mathbb{R}^n \longrightarrow \mathbb{R}$ be a convex function with a Lipschitz continuous derivative such that $\|(\nabla f)(\mathbf{x}) - (\nabla f)(\mathbf{y})\| \leqslant \ell \|\mathbf{x} - \mathbf{y}\|$ for $\mathbf{x}, \mathbf{y} \in \mathbb{R}^n$. Prove that

$$f(y) \leqslant f(\mathbf{x}) + ((\nabla f)(\mathbf{x}), \mathbf{y} - \mathbf{x}) + \frac{\ell}{2} \|\mathbf{y} - \mathbf{x}\|^2.$$

Solution: Define the function $g : \mathbb{R} \longrightarrow \mathbb{R}$ as $g(t) = f(\mathbf{x} + t(\mathbf{y} - \mathbf{x}))$. We have:

$$g(1) - g(0) = \int_0^1 g'(t) \, dt = g'(0) + \int_0^1 (g'(t) - g'(0)) \, dt.$$

Since $g(1) = f(\mathbf{y})$, $g(0) = f(\mathbf{x})$ and $g'(t) = ((\nabla f)(\mathbf{x} + t(\mathbf{y} - \mathbf{x})), \mathbf{y} - \mathbf{x})$, we have

$$f(\mathbf{y}) - f(\mathbf{x}) - ((\nabla f)(\mathbf{x}), \mathbf{y} - bfx)$$
$$= \int_0^1 ((\nabla f)(\mathbf{x} + t(\mathbf{y} - \mathbf{x})) - (\nabla f)(\mathbf{x})), \mathbf{y} - \mathbf{x}) \, dt$$
$$\leqslant \|\mathbf{y} - \mathbf{x}\| \int_0^1 \|(\nabla f)(\mathbf{x} + t(\mathbf{y} - \mathbf{x})) - (\nabla f)(\mathbf{x})\| \, dt$$
$$\leqslant \ell \|\mathbf{y} - \mathbf{x}\|^2 \int_0^1 t \, dt = \frac{\ell}{2} \|\mathbf{y} - \mathbf{x}\|^2.$$

(8) Let C be a convex subset of $\mathbb{R}^n$ and let $f : C \longrightarrow \mathbb{R}$ be a differentiable convex function. Prove that the following conditions are equivalent:

(a) $\|(\nabla f)(\mathbf{x}) - (\nabla f)(\mathbf{y})\| \leqslant \ell \|\mathbf{x} - \mathbf{y}\|$ for $\mathbf{x}, \mathbf{y} \in C$;
(b) $\frac{1}{2\ell} \|(\nabla f)(\mathbf{x}) - (\nabla f)(\mathbf{y})\|^2 \leqslant f(\mathbf{y}) - f(\mathbf{x}) - ((\nabla f)(\mathbf{x}), \mathbf{y} - \mathbf{x})$
$\leqslant \frac{\ell}{2} \|\mathbf{y} - \mathbf{x}\|^2$ for $\mathbf{x}, \mathbf{y} \in C$;
(c) $\frac{1}{\ell} \|(\nabla f)(\mathbf{x}) - (\nabla f)(\mathbf{y})\|^2 \leqslant ((\nabla f)(\mathbf{y}) - (\nabla f)(\mathbf{x}), \mathbf{y} - \mathbf{x})$
$\leqslant \ell \|\mathbf{y} - \mathbf{x}\|^2$ for $\mathbf{x}, \mathbf{y} \in C$.

Solution: (a) implies (b): Suppose that (a) holds. The second inequality of (b) follows from Supplement 7. Let $h(\mathbf{x}, \mathbf{y}) = f(\mathbf{y}) - ((nabla f)(\mathbf{x}), \mathbf{y})$. We have $(\nabla_{\mathbf{y}} h)(\mathbf{x}, \mathbf{y}) = (\nabla f)(\mathbf{y}) - (\nabla f)(\mathbf{x})$. Since $(\nabla_{\mathbf{y}} h)(\mathbf{x}, \mathbf{x}) = 0$, $\mathbf{x}$ is a global minimizer of $h(\mathbf{x}, \mathbf{x})$ and we have

$$h(\mathbf{x}, \mathbf{x}) \leqslant h\left(\mathbf{x}, \mathbf{y} - \frac{1}{\ell} (\nabla_{\mathbf{y}} h(\mathbf{x}, \mathbf{y})\right) \leqslant h(\mathbf{x}, \mathbf{y}) - \frac{1}{2\ell} \|(\nabla_{\mathbf{y}} h(\mathbf{x}, \mathbf{y})\|^2,$$

by Supplement 7.

(b) implies (c): Suppose that (b) holds, that is,

$$\frac{1}{2\ell} \|(\nabla f)(\mathbf{x}) - (\nabla f)(\mathbf{y})\|^2 \leqslant f(\mathbf{y}) - f(\mathbf{x}) - ((\nabla f)(\mathbf{x}), \mathbf{y} - \mathbf{x}) \leqslant \frac{\ell}{2} \|\mathbf{y} - \mathbf{x}\|^2.$$

Similar inequalities can be obtained by swapping $\mathbf{x}$ and $\mathbf{y}$:

$$\frac{1}{2\ell}\|(\nabla f)(\mathbf{y}) - (\nabla f)(\mathbf{x})\|^2 \leqslant f(\mathbf{x}) - f(\mathbf{y}) - ((\nabla f)(\mathbf{y}), \mathbf{x} - \mathbf{y}) \leqslant \frac{\ell}{2}\|\mathbf{x} - \mathbf{y}\|^2.$$

Adding these inequalities yields Inequalities (c).

(c) implies (a): this implication is immediate.

The next supplement is concerned with a generalization of the classical variational principle that stipulates that if $f : U \longrightarrow \mathbb{R}$ is a differentiable function, where U is an open subset of $\mathbb{R}^n$ and $\mathbf{x}_0 \in U$ is a point where f attains its minimum, than $f'(\mathbf{x}_0) = 0$. When f has a finite lower bound that it does not necessarily attain, then, under certain conditions, for every $\epsilon > 0$ there exists an approximate solution $\mathbf{x}_0$ such that $\inf f \leqslant f(\mathbf{x}_0) \leqslant \inf f + \epsilon$. This result, included in Supplement 9, is known as Ekeland's variational principle [48, 49] and is presented in the version of Hiriart-Urruty [79].

(9) Let $f : \mathbb{R}^n \longrightarrow (-\infty, \infty]$ be a lower semicontinuous function, not identically ∞, bounded from below. Then, for every point $\mathbf{x}_\epsilon$ such that $\inf f \leqslant f(\mathbf{x}_\epsilon) \leqslant \inf f + \epsilon$ and for every $\lambda > 0$, there exists some point $\mathbf{z}_\epsilon$ such that

   (a) $f(\mathbf{z}_\epsilon) \leqslant f(\mathbf{x}_\epsilon)$;
   (b) $\|\mathbf{z}_\epsilon - \mathbf{x}_\epsilon\| \leqslant \lambda$;
   (c) for every $\mathbf{x} \in \mathbb{R}^n$, $f(\mathbf{z}_\epsilon) \leqslant f(\mathbf{x}) + \frac{\epsilon}{\lambda}\|\mathbf{x} - \mathbf{z}_\epsilon\|$.

   Solution: Consider the perturbed function $g : \mathbb{R}^n \longrightarrow \mathbb{R}$ given by $g(\mathbf{x}) = f(\mathbf{x}) + \frac{\epsilon}{\lambda}\|\mathbf{x} - \mathbf{x}_\epsilon\|$. Since f is lower semicontinuous and bounded from below, g is lower semicontinuous and $\lim_{\|\mathbf{x}\| \to \infty} g(\mathbf{x}) = \infty$. Therefore, by Theorem 4.109, there exists $\mathbf{z}_\epsilon$ minimizing g on $\mathbb{R}^n$ such that for all $\mathbf{x} \in \mathbb{R}^n$ we have:

$$f(\mathbf{z}_\epsilon) + \frac{\epsilon}{\lambda}\|\mathbf{z}_\epsilon - \mathbf{x}_\epsilon\| \leqslant f(\mathbf{x}) + \frac{\epsilon}{\lambda}\|\mathbf{x} - \mathbf{x}_\epsilon\|. \tag{13.14}$$

Choosing $\mathbf{x} = \mathbf{x}_\epsilon$ we obtain $f(\mathbf{z}_\epsilon) + \frac{\epsilon}{\lambda}\|\mathbf{z}_\epsilon - \mathbf{x}_\epsilon\| \leqslant f(\mathbf{x}_\epsilon)$, hence $f(\mathbf{z}_\epsilon) \leqslant f(\mathbf{x}_\epsilon)$.

Since $f(\mathbf{x}_\epsilon) \leqslant \inf f + \epsilon$, it follows that

$$f(\mathbf{z}_\epsilon) + \frac{\epsilon}{\lambda}\|\mathbf{z}_\epsilon - \mathbf{x}_\epsilon\| \leqslant f(\mathbf{x}_\epsilon) \leqslant \inf f + \epsilon,$$

hence

$$\frac{\epsilon}{\lambda}\|\mathbf{z}_\epsilon - \mathbf{x}_\epsilon\| \leqslant f(\mathbf{x}_\epsilon) \leqslant \inf f - f(\mathbf{z}_\epsilon) + \epsilon \leqslant \epsilon,$$

which implies $\|\mathbf{z}_\epsilon - \mathbf{x}_\epsilon\| \leqslant \lambda$.

Inequality (13.14) implies

$$f(\mathbf{z}_\epsilon) \leqslant f(x) + \frac{\epsilon}{\lambda}(\|\mathbf{x} - \mathbf{x}_\epsilon\| - \|\mathbf{z}_\epsilon - \mathbf{x}_\epsilon\|)$$
$$\leqslant f(\mathbf{x}) + \frac{\epsilon}{\lambda}(\|\mathbf{x} - \mathbf{z}_\epsilon\|)$$

for all $\mathbf{x}$, which is the desired inequality.

Thus, the closer to $\mathbf{x}_\epsilon$ we need $\mathbf{z}_\epsilon$ to be, the larger the perturbation of f that must be accepted.

(10) Let $f : \mathbb{R}^n \longrightarrow \mathbb{R}$ be a Gâteaux differentiable function, that is lower semicontinuous, and bounded from below. Let ϵ be a positive number and let $\mathbf{x}_\epsilon \in \mathbb{R}^m$ be a point such that $\inf f \leqslant f(\mathbf{x}_\epsilon) \leqslant \inf f + \epsilon$. Prove that:

(a) there exists $\mathbf{z}_\epsilon \in \mathbb{R}^m$ such that $f(\mathbf{z}_\epsilon) \leqslant f(\mathbf{x}_\epsilon)$, $\|\mathbf{x}_\epsilon - \mathbf{z}_\epsilon\| \leqslant 1$, and $\|(\nabla f)(\mathbf{z}_\epsilon)\| \leqslant \epsilon$;

(b) there exists a sequence $(\mathbf{x}_k)$ such that $\lim_{k\to\infty} \mathbf{x}_k = \inf f$ and $\lim_{k\to\infty}(\nabla f)(\mathbf{x}_k) = \mathbf{0}_n$.

Solution: By Ekeland's variational principle (Supplement 9), for $\lambda = 1$ there exists $\mathbf{z}_\epsilon$ such that

(a) $f(\mathbf{z}_\epsilon) \leqslant f(\mathbf{x}_\epsilon)$;

(b) $\|\mathbf{z}_\epsilon - \mathbf{x}_\epsilon\| \leqslant 1$;

(c) for every $\mathbf{x} \in \mathbb{R}^n$, $f(\mathbf{z}_\epsilon) \leqslant f(\mathbf{x}) + \epsilon\|\mathbf{x} - \mathbf{z}_\epsilon\|$.

Choose $\mathbf{x} = \mathbf{z}_\epsilon + t\mathbf{d}$, where $\|\mathbf{d}\| = 1$. Then, $f(\mathbf{z}_\epsilon) \leqslant f(\mathbf{z}_\epsilon + t\mathbf{d}) + t\epsilon$, or

$$f(\mathbf{z}_\epsilon + t\mathbf{d}) - f(\mathbf{z}_\epsilon) \geqslant -t\epsilon.$$

Since f is Gâteaux differentiable,

$$f(\mathbf{z}_\epsilon + t\mathbf{d}) - f(\mathbf{z}_\epsilon) = t(\nabla f)(\mathbf{z}_\epsilon'\mathbf{d} + o(t) \geqslant -t\epsilon.$$

Thus, as t tends to 0, $(\nabla f)(\mathbf{z}_\epsilon'\mathbf{d} \geqslant -\epsilon$ for all $\mathbf{d}$ with $\|\mathbf{d}\| = 1$. Therefore, $\|(\nabla f)(\mathbf{z}_\epsilon)\| \leqslant \epsilon$, which concludes the argument for the first part.

Let $\mathbf{y}_k$ be a point such that $f(\mathbf{y}_k) \leqslant \inf f + \frac{1}{k}$. There exists $\mathbf{x}_k$ such that $f(\mathbf{x}_k) \leqslant f(\mathbf{y}_k) \leqslant \inf f + \frac{1}{k}$ and $\|(\nabla f)(\mathbf{x}_k)\| \leqslant \frac{1}{k}$, hence $(\mathbf{x}_k)$ satisfies the conditions of the second part.

(11) Prove that the probability distribution $\mathbf{p} = \begin{pmatrix} p_1 \\ \vdots \\ p_n \end{pmatrix}$ that maximizes the

entropy $H(\mathbf{p}) = -\sum_{j=1}^{n} p_j \log p_j$ subjected to the constraints

$$p_j > 0 \text{ for } 1 \leqslant j \leqslant n,$$

$$\sum_{j=1}^{n} p_j = 1,$$

$$\sum_{j=1}^{n} x_j p_j = m$$

is $p_j = \frac{1}{\Phi(\beta)} e^{-\lambda x_j}$ for $1 \leqslant j \leqslant n$, where $\Phi(\lambda) = \sum_{j=1}^{n} e^{-\lambda x_j}$ and λ is the unique solution of the equation $\frac{d \log \Phi(\lambda)}{d\lambda} = -m$. This is the *Gibbs distribution*.

Solution: The function $H(\mathbf{p})$ is concave and continuous on the subset of $\mathbb{R}^n$ defined by the above constraints. Therefore, there is a unique global maximum point for $H(\mathbf{p})$ in this subset.

The Lagrange function

$$L = H(\mathbf{p}) - \theta \left(\sum_{j=1}^{n} p_j - 1 \right) - \lambda \left(\sum_{j=1}^{n} x_j p_j - m \right),$$

where θ, λ are the Lagrange multipliers yields the conditions

$$\frac{\partial L}{\partial p_j} = - \log p_j - 1 - \theta - \lambda x_j = 0$$

for $1 \leqslant j \leqslant n$. The solution of the system

$$\frac{\partial L}{\partial p_j} = - \log p_j - 1 - \theta - \lambda x_j = 0 \text{ for } 1 \leqslant j \leqslant n,$$
$$\sum_{j=1}^{n} p_j = 1,$$
$$\sum_{j=1}^{n} x_j p_j = m.$$

The first n equalities mean that $p_j = A e^{-\lambda x_j}$, where $A = e^{-1-\theta}$. By the second equality, $A \sum_{k=1}^{n} e^{-\lambda x_k} = 1$, hence $A = \frac{1}{\sum_{k=1}^{n} e^{-\lambda x_k}}$, which yields $p_j = \frac{e^{-\lambda x_j}}{\sum_{k=1}^{n} e^{-\lambda x_k}}$. The parameter λ is the solution of the equation

$$\sum_{j=1}^{n} x_j \frac{e^{-\lambda x_j}}{\sum_{k=1}^{n} e^{-\lambda x_k}} = m.$$

If $\Phi(\lambda) = \sum_{j=1}^{n} e^{-\lambda x_j}$ we have

$$\frac{d \log \Phi(\lambda)}{d\lambda} = - \frac{1}{\sum_{j=1}^{n} e^{-\lambda x_j}} \sum_{j=1}^{n} x_j e^{-\lambda x_j} = - \sum_{j=1}^{n} p_j x_j = -m,$$

which, in principle, allows the determination of λ because Φ is a strictly decreasing function.

(12) Let $\{\mathbf{a}_1, \ldots, \mathbf{a}_m\}$ be m vectors in $\mathbb{R}^n$ and let $f : \mathbb{R}^n \longrightarrow \mathbb{R}$ be the function defined by $f(\mathbf{x}) = \ln \sum_{i=1}^m e^{\mathbf{a}_i' \mathbf{x}}$ for $\mathbf{x} \in \mathbb{R}^n$. Prove that if f is bounded from below then there exists $\mathbf{y} \in \mathbb{R}^m$, $\mathbf{y} \geq \mathbf{0}_m$ such that $\sum_{j=1}^m y_j \mathbf{a}_j = \mathbf{0}_n$.

Solution:

Suppose that f is unbounded below. Then $\sum_{i=1}^m e^{\mathbf{a}_i' \mathbf{x}}$ must be arbitrarily close to 0, which is possible only if there is $\mathbf{x} \in \mathbb{R}^n$ such that $\mathbf{a}_i' \mathbf{x} < 0$ for $1 \leqslant i \leqslant m$. Thus, if there is no $\mathbf{x} \in \mathbb{R}^n$ such that $\mathbf{a}_i' \mathbf{x} < 0$ for $1 \leqslant i \leqslant m$ it follows that f is bounded below. Let $A \in \mathbb{R}^{m \times n}$ be the matrix

$$A = \begin{pmatrix} \mathbf{a}_1' \\ \vdots \\ \mathbf{a}_m' \end{pmatrix}.$$

The previous condition means that the system $A\mathbf{x} < \mathbf{0}_m$ has no solution. By Gordan's Alternative Theorem (Theorem 6.62) there exists $\mathbf{y} \in \mathbb{R}^m$ such that $\mathbf{y} \geq \mathbf{0}_m$ and $A'\mathbf{y} = \sum_{j=1}^m y_j \mathbf{a}_j = \mathbf{0}_m$.

(13) Let $A \in \mathbb{R}^{n \times n}$ be a symmetric positive definite matrix having positive eigenvalues $\lambda_1 \geqslant \lambda_2 \geqslant \cdots \geqslant \lambda_n > 0$. Prove that

$$\max\{(A\mathbf{x}, \mathbf{x}) \cdot (A^{-1}\mathbf{x}, \mathbf{x})\} \leqslant \frac{(\lambda_1 + \lambda_n)^2}{4\lambda_1 \lambda_n}.$$

This is *Kantorovich's inequality.*.

Solution: The inequality can be shown starting from an optimization problem:

maximize $(A\mathbf{x}, \mathbf{x}) \cdot (A^{-1}\mathbf{x}, \mathbf{x})$
subject to $\|\mathbf{x}\|^2 = 1$.

Consider the spectral decomposition of A, $A = U'DU$, where U is an unitary matrix and D is a diagonal matrix whose diagonal entries are $\lambda_1, \ldots, \lambda_n$. Since $U^{-1} = U'$ we have $A^{-1} = U^{-1}D^{-1}(U')^{-1} = U'D^{-1}U$.

Let $\mathbf{v} = U\mathbf{x}$. We have:

$$(A\mathbf{x}, \mathbf{x}) = (U'DU\mathbf{x}, \mathbf{x}) = (D\mathbf{v}, \mathbf{v}) = \sum_{j=1}^n \lambda_j v_j^2,$$

$$(A^{-1}\mathbf{x}, \mathbf{x}) = (U'D^{-1}U\mathbf{x}, \mathbf{x}) = (D^{-1}\mathbf{v}, \mathbf{v}) = \sum_{j=1}^n \lambda_j^{-1} v_j^2$$

and $\|v\| = \|x\|$ This, allows us to rewrite the optimization problem as

maximize $\left(\sum_{j=1}^n \lambda_j v_j^2\right) \cdot \left(\sum_{j=1}^n \lambda_j^{-1} v_j^2\right)$
subject to $\|\mathbf{v}\|^2 = 1$.

because multiplication by unitary matrices preserves the Euclidean norms of vectors; in other words, we have $\|\mathbf{v}\| = \|U\mathbf{x}\| = \|\mathbf{x}\|$ for every $\mathbf{x} \in \mathbb{R}^n$.

By substituting v_i^2 by y_i we obtain yet one more form of the optimization problem:

$$\text{maximize } \left(\sum_{j=1}^n \lambda_j y_j\right) \cdot \left(\sum_{j=1}^n \lambda_j^{-1} y_j\right)$$
$$\text{subject to } \sum_{j=1}^n y_j = 1, \ y_j \geqslant 0 \text{ for } 1 \leqslant j \leqslant n.$$

The equivalent minimization problem is

$$\text{minimize } -\left(\sum_{j=1}^n \lambda_j y_j\right) \cdot \left(\sum_{j=1}^n \lambda_j^{-1} y_j\right)$$
$$\text{subject to } \sum_{j=1}^n y_j = 1, \ y_j \geqslant 0 \text{ for } 1 \leqslant j \leqslant n.$$

The Lagrangean of this problem is

$$L(\mathbf{y}, \lambda, \mu) = -\left(\sum_{j=1}^n \lambda_j y_j\right) \cdot \left(\sum_{j=1}^n \lambda_j^{-1} y_j\right) + \lambda \left(\sum_{j=1}^n y_j - 1\right) - \sum_{j=1}^n \mu_j y_j.$$

The KKT conditions are:

$$\frac{\partial L}{\partial y_i} = -\lambda_i \left(\sum_{j=1}^n \lambda_j^{-1} y_j\right) - \lambda_i^{-1} \left(\sum_{j=1}^n \lambda_j y_j\right) + \lambda - \mu_i = 0,$$

$$\sum_{j=1}^n y_j = 1, y_j \geqslant 0, \lambda \geqslant 0, \sum_{j=1}^n \mu_j y_j = 0.$$

The first condition implies:

$$-\lambda_i \left(\sum_{j=1}^n \lambda_j^{-1} y_j y_i\right) - \lambda_i^{-1} \left(\sum_{j=1}^n \lambda_j y_j y_i\right) + \lambda y_i - \mu_i y_i = 0.$$

Adding these equalities for $1 \leqslant i \leqslant n$ results in

$$-\left(\sum_{j=1}^n \lambda_j^{-1} y_j\right)\left(\sum_{i=1}^n \lambda_i y_i\right) - \left(\sum_{j=1}^n \lambda_j y_j\right)\left(\sum_{i=1}^n \lambda_i^{-1} y_i\right) + \lambda \sum_{i=1}^n y_i - \sum_{i=1}^n \mu_i y_i = 0,$$

or

$$\lambda = 2\left(\sum_{j=1}^n \lambda_j^{-1} y_j\right)\left(\sum_{j=1}^n \lambda_j y_j\right).$$

Let $I = \{i \mid 1 \leqslant i \leqslant n \text{ and } y_i > 0\}$. If $i \in I$ we have $\mu_i = 0$, Consequently, for $i \in I$ we have

$$\frac{\lambda_i}{\sum_{j=1}^n \lambda_j y_j} + \frac{\lambda_i^{-1}}{\sum_{j=1}^n \lambda_j^{-1} y_j} = 2.$$

Therefore, for $i, j \in J$ we have

$$\frac{\lambda_i}{\sum_{k=1}^{n} \lambda_k y_k} + \frac{\lambda_i^{-1}}{\sum_{j=1}^{n} \lambda_k^{-1} y_k} = \frac{\lambda_j}{\sum_{k=1}^{n} \lambda_k y_k} + \frac{\lambda_j^{-1}}{\sum_{j=1}^{n} \lambda_k^{-1} y_k},$$

which can be written as

$$\lambda_i \lambda_j = \frac{\sum_{k=1}^{n} \lambda_k y_k}{\sum_{k=1}^{n} \lambda_k^{-1} y_k}$$

for $i, j \in I$ and $\lambda_i \neq \lambda_j$. If we set $A = \sum_{k=1}^{n} \lambda_k y_k$ and $B = \sum_{k=1}^{n} \lambda_k^{-1} y_k$ we have

$$\frac{\lambda_i}{A} + \frac{\lambda_i^{-1}}{B} = 2,$$
$$\frac{A}{B} = \lambda_i \lambda_j,$$

which implies

$$A = \frac{2\lambda_i^2 \lambda_j^2}{\lambda_i + \lambda_j}, B = \frac{2\lambda_i \lambda_j}{\lambda_i + \lambda_j}.$$

Substituting in the first equation yields

$$\frac{\lambda_i + \lambda_j}{2\lambda_i \lambda_j^2} + \frac{\lambda_i + \lambda_j}{2\lambda_i^2 \lambda_j} = 2,$$

or

$$\sum_{k=1}^{n} \lambda_k y_k = \frac{\lambda_i + \lambda_j}{2}.$$

Similarly,

$$\sum_{k=1}^{n} \lambda_k y_k = \frac{\lambda_i + \lambda_j}{2\lambda_i \lambda_j}.$$

The objective function value is

$$\left(\sum_{k=1}^{n} \lambda_k y_k \right) \cdot \left(\sum_{k=1}^{n} \lambda_k^{-1} y_k \right) = \frac{\lambda_i + \lambda_j}{4\lambda_i \lambda_j} = \frac{1}{4} \left(t + \frac{1}{t} \right)^2.$$

The largest value of $\left(t + \frac{1}{t} \right)^2$ is achieved when $t = \frac{\lambda_n}{\lambda_1}$.

(14) Consider the optimization problem

$$\text{minimize } f(\mathbf{x})$$
$$\text{subject to } c_i(\mathbf{x}) \leqslant 0 \text{ for } 1 \leqslant i \leqslant r,$$
$$\text{and } d_j(\mathbf{x}) = 0 \text{ for } 1 \leqslant j \leqslant m,$$

Define $c_i^+(\mathbf{x}) = \max\{0, c_i(\mathbf{x})\}$. Let $k \in \mathbb{N}$ be a parameter and let $F_k : \mathbb{R}^n \longrightarrow \mathbb{R}$ be defined as

$$F_k(\mathbf{x}) = f(\mathbf{x}) + \frac{k}{2}\sum_{i=1}^{r}(c_i^+(\mathbf{x}))^2 + \frac{k}{2}\sum_{j=1}^{m}(d_j(\mathbf{x}))^2 + \frac{1}{2}\|\mathbf{x} - \mathbf{x}_*\|,$$

where $\mathbf{x}_*$ is a local solution of the optimization problem. In other words, there exists $B[\mathbf{x}_*, \epsilon]$ such that $f(\mathbf{x}) \geqslant f(\mathbf{x}_*)$ for every $\mathbf{x} \in B[\mathbf{x}_*, \epsilon]$ that satisfies the constraints. Show that if $\mathbf{x}_k$ is a global minimizer for F_k over $B[\mathbf{x}_*, \epsilon]$, then $\lim_{k \to \infty} \mathbf{x}_k = \mathbf{x}_*$.

Solution: It is immediate that $F_k(\mathbf{x}_*) = f(\mathbf{x}_*)$ because $c_i(\mathbf{x}) \leqslant 0$, hence $c_i^+(\mathbf{x}) = 0$. Therefore,

$$f(\mathbf{x}_k) \leqslant f(\mathbf{x}_k) + \frac{k}{2}\sum_{i=1}^{r}(c_i^+(\mathbf{x}_k))^2 + \frac{k}{2}\sum_{j=1}^{m}(d_j(\mathbf{x}_k))^2 + \frac{1}{2}\|\mathbf{x}_k - \mathbf{x}_*\|$$
$$= F(\mathbf{x}_k) \leqslant F(\mathbf{x}_*) = f(x_*).$$

This inequality implies $\lim_{k \to \infty} c_i^+(\mathbf{x}_k) = 0$ and $\lim_{k \to \infty} d_j(\mathbf{x}_k) = 0$. If $\overline{\mathbf{x}}$ is a limit point of $(\mathbf{x}_k)$ in $B[\mathbf{x}_*, \epsilon]$, we have $c_i^+(\overline{\mathbf{x}}) = 0$, which implies $c_i(\overline{\mathbf{x}}) \leqslant 0$, and $d_j(\overline{\mathbf{x}}) = 0$, which means that $\overline{\mathbf{x}}$ is a feasible point of the initial problem. Passing to limits we have

$$f(\overline{\mathbf{x}}) \leqslant f(\overline{\mathbf{x}}) + \frac{1}{2}\|\overline{\mathbf{x}} - \mathbf{x}_*\|^2 \leqslant f(\mathbf{x}_*).$$

Since $f(\mathbf{x}_*) \leqslant f(\mathbf{x})$ for all feasible $\mathbf{x} \in B[\mathbf{x}_*, \epsilon]$, we also have $f(\mathbf{x}_*) \leqslant f(\overline{\mathbf{x}})$. Therefore, $\|\overline{\mathbf{x}} - \mathbf{x}_*\| = 0$, hence $\overline{\mathbf{x}} = \mathbf{x}_*$.

Bibliographical Comments

One of the best sources for optimization theory is by-now classic book of O. L. Mangasarian [105] that presents a rich collection of results in a terse form but very readable form. A comprehensive series of references is [13, 12, 14, 9].

In [122] a generalization of the Kuhn-Tucker saddle-point equivalence theorem is presented.

The presentation of the stochastic gradient is based on [118] and [117].

Chapter 14

Iterative Algorithms

14.1 Introduction

One of the very important task of numerical methods is to solve equations of the form $f(x) = 0$, where $f : U \longrightarrow \mathbb{R}$ is a function defined on an open subset U of $\mathbb{R}$ that may have various continuity or differentiability properties. The general approach presented here makes use of sequences $(x_n) \in \mathbf{Seq}(U)$ that converge to a solution x_* of the equation $f(x) = 0$ and such sequences are constructed iteratively. This means that the current term x_n of an approximating sequence depends on a number of predecessors in the sequence, that is, it has the form $x_n = \phi(x_{n_m}, x_{n_{m-1}}, \ldots, x_{n-1})$.

Let (x_n) be sequence such that $\lim_{n \to \infty} x_n = x_*$. If there exists a constant $c \in [0, 1)$ and a number $n_0 \in \mathbb{N}$ such that for $n \geqslant n_0$ we have $|x_{n+1} - x_*| \leqslant c\, |x_n - x_*|$ we say that the sequence (x_n) *converges linearly* to x_*.

If there exists a sequence (c_n) such that $\lim_{n \to \infty} c_n = 0$, and a number $n_0 \in \mathbb{N}$ such that for $n \geqslant n_0$ we have $|x_{n+1} - x_*| \leqslant c_n\, |x_n - x_*|$, we say that the sequence (x_n) converges superlinearly to x_*.

If there exist $p > 1$, $c \geqslant 0$ and $n_0 \in \mathbb{N}$ such that for $n \geqslant n_0$, $|x_{n+1} - x_*| \leqslant c|x_n - x_*|^p$, we say that the sequence (x_n) converges to x_* with order at least p. If $p = 2$ the convergence is said to be *quadratic*.

14.2 Newton's Method

Let U be an open subset of $\mathbb{R}$ and let $f : U \longrightarrow \mathbb{R}$ be a differentiable function on U. We seek to find solutions of the equation $f(x) = 0$ using a process known as Newton's method.

Any $x_* \in U$ that is a solution of the equation $f(\mathbf{x}) = 0$ is a *root* of f.

We can approximate f by the tangent in x_k, namely,

$$y = f(x_k) + f'(x_k)(x - x_k).$$

Then, the next member x_{k+1} of the sequence is the intersection of this line with the x-axis, defined by

$$0 = f(x_k) + f'(x_k)(x_{k+1} - x_k),$$

that is,

$$x_{k+1} = x_k - \frac{f(x_k)}{f'(x_k)} \tag{14.1}$$

for $k \in \mathbb{N}$. In other words, the successive members of the sequence (x_k) are obtained as $x_{k+1} = h(x_k)$, where $h(x) = x - \frac{f(x)}{f'(x)}$ for $x \in U$, as shown in Figure 14.1. Thus, if the sequence (x_n) is convergent and $\lim_{n \to \infty} x_n = x_*$ we have $x_* = x_* - \frac{f(x_*)}{f'(x_*)}$, that is, $f(x_*) = 0$.

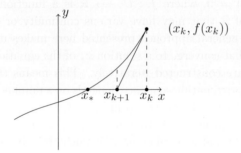

Fig. 14.1   Newton one-dimensional method.

If f has a second derivative, we have

$$h'(x) = 1 - \frac{f'(x)^2 - f(x)f''(x)}{f'(x)^2} = \frac{f(x)f''(x)}{f'(x)^2}.$$

Thus, if $f(x_*) = 0$, then $h(x_*) = 0$ and $h'(x_*) = 0$. By Taylor's formula we have

$$h(x) = h(x_*) + h'(x_*)(x - x_*) + \frac{1}{2}h''(z)(x - x_*)^2$$

$$= x_* + \frac{1}{2}h''(z)(x - x_*)^2,$$

where $z \in (x_*, x)$. Therefore, $x_{k+1} = h(x_k) = x_* + \frac{1}{2}h''(z)(x_k - x_*)^2$, which means that

$$x_{k+1} - x_* = \frac{1}{2}h''(z)(x_k - x_*)^2,$$

which shows that Newton's method is quadratically convergent, under the assumption that $f'(x_*) \neq 0$.

A generalization of Newton's method involves solving equations of the form $\mathbf{f}(\mathbf{x}) = \mathbf{0}_n$, where $\mathbf{f} : U \longrightarrow \mathbb{R}^n$ and U is an open set of $\mathbb{R}^n$. Now Newton's method consists in computing a sequence $(\mathbf{x}_n)$ defined by

$$\mathbf{x}_{k+1} = \mathbf{x}_k - ((D\mathbf{f})(\mathbf{x}_k))^{-1}\mathbf{f}(\mathbf{x}_k)$$

for $k \in \mathbb{N}$ such that the members of the sequence $(\mathbf{x}_k)$ are successive approximations of the root. Thus, Jacobian matrix $(D\mathbf{f})(\mathbf{x}_k)$ must be invertible at each step $\mathbf{x}_k$ of the sequence.

Theorem 14.1. *Let U be an open subset of $\mathbb{R}^n$, and let $\boldsymbol{f} : U \longrightarrow \mathbb{R}^n$ be a continuously differentiable function on U. If $\boldsymbol{f}(\boldsymbol{x}_*) = \boldsymbol{0}_n$ and $(D\boldsymbol{f})(\boldsymbol{x}_*)$ is invertible, then*

$$\boldsymbol{f}(\boldsymbol{x}) = \int_0^1 (D\boldsymbol{f})(\boldsymbol{x}_* + t(\boldsymbol{x} - \boldsymbol{x}_*))(\boldsymbol{x} - \boldsymbol{x}_*)\, dt.$$

Proof. Let α_i be the function $\alpha_i(t) = f_i(\mathbf{x}_* + t(\mathbf{x} - \mathbf{x}_*))$; we have $\alpha_i'(t) = ((\nabla f_i)\mathbf{x}_* + t(\mathbf{x} - \mathbf{x}_*), \mathbf{x} - \mathbf{x}_*)$. Since $\alpha_i(1) - \alpha_i(0) = \int_0^1 \alpha_i'(t)\, dt$, $\alpha_i(1) = f_i(\mathbf{x})$ and $\alpha_i(0) = f_i(\mathbf{x}_*) = 0$, we have:

$$f_i(\mathbf{x}) = \int_0^1 ((\nabla f_i)(\mathbf{x}_* + t(\mathbf{x} - \mathbf{x}_*), \mathbf{x} - \mathbf{x}_*)\, dt$$

for $1 \leqslant i \leqslant n$. The aggregate of these equality for $1 \leqslant i \leqslant n$ yields the equality of the theorem. $\qquad\square$

Theorem 14.2. *Let U be an open subset of $\mathbb{R}^n$, and let $\boldsymbol{f} : U \longrightarrow \mathbb{R}^n$ be a continuously differentiable function on U. If*

(i) $\boldsymbol{f}(\boldsymbol{x}_*) = \boldsymbol{0}_n$;

(ii) $(D\boldsymbol{f})(\boldsymbol{x}_*)$ *is invertible, and*

(iii) *there exists a number M such that $\|(D\boldsymbol{f})(\boldsymbol{x})^{-1}\| \leqslant M$ when $\boldsymbol{x} \in U$,*

then there exists an open sphere $B(\boldsymbol{x}_*, \delta)$ such that $\boldsymbol{x}_0 \in B(\boldsymbol{x}_*, \delta)$ implies that the members of the sequence $(\boldsymbol{x}_n)$ defined by $\boldsymbol{x}_{k+1} = \boldsymbol{x}_k - ((D\boldsymbol{f})(\boldsymbol{x}_k))^{-1}\boldsymbol{f}(\boldsymbol{x}_k)$ belong to $B(\boldsymbol{x}_*, \delta)$ and

$$\lim_{k \to \infty} \frac{\|\boldsymbol{x}_{k+1} - \boldsymbol{x}_*\|}{\|\boldsymbol{x}_k - \boldsymbol{x}_*\|} = 0.$$

If $(D\boldsymbol{f})(\boldsymbol{x})$ is Lipshitzian in U, that is, $\|(D\boldsymbol{f})(\boldsymbol{y}) - (D\boldsymbol{f})(\boldsymbol{x})\| \leqslant L\|\boldsymbol{y} - \boldsymbol{x}\|$ for $\boldsymbol{x}, \boldsymbol{y} \in U$, then there exists $K \in \mathbb{N}$ such that

$$\|\boldsymbol{x}_{k+1} - \boldsymbol{x}_*\| \leqslant K\|\boldsymbol{x}_k - \boldsymbol{x}_*\|^2.$$

Proof.　We have

$$
\begin{aligned}
&\mathbf{x}_{k+1} - \mathbf{x}_* \\
&= \mathbf{x}_k - \mathbf{x}_* - ((D\mathbf{f})(\mathbf{x}_k))^{-1} f(\mathbf{x}_k) \\
&= (D\mathbf{f})(\mathbf{x}_k))^{-1}((D\mathbf{f})(\mathbf{x}_k)(\mathbf{x}_k - \mathbf{x}_*) - f(\mathbf{x}_k)) \\
&= (D\mathbf{f})(\mathbf{x}_k))^{-1} \\
&\quad \times \left((D\mathbf{f})(\mathbf{x}_k)(\mathbf{x}_k - \mathbf{x}_*) - \int_0^1 (D\mathbf{f})(\mathbf{x}_* + t(\mathbf{x}_k - \mathbf{x}_*))(\mathbf{x}_k - \mathbf{x}_*)\, dt \right) \\
&= (D\mathbf{f})(\mathbf{x}_k))^{-1} \int_0^1 [(D\mathbf{f})(\mathbf{x}_k) - (D\mathbf{f})(\mathbf{x}_* + t(\mathbf{x}_k - \mathbf{x}_*))](\mathbf{x}_k - \mathbf{x}_*)\, dt.
\end{aligned}
$$

This implies:

$$
\begin{aligned}
\|\mathbf{x}_{k+1} - \mathbf{x}_*\| &\leqslant \|(D\mathbf{f})(\mathbf{x}_k)^{-1}\| \cdot \|\mathbf{x}_k - \mathbf{x}_*\| \\
&\quad \cdot \int_0^1 \|(D\mathbf{f})(\mathbf{x}_k) - (D\mathbf{f})(\mathbf{x}_* + t(\mathbf{x}_k - \mathbf{x}_*))\|\, dt.
\end{aligned}
$$

Since $\|(Df)(\mathbf{x})^{-1}\| \leqslant M$ when $\mathbf{x} \in U$ by choosing δ sufficiently small such that $\|(Df)(\mathbf{x}_k) - (Df)(\mathbf{x}_* + t(\mathbf{x}_k - \mathbf{x}_*))\| < \frac{1}{2M}$, it follows that

$$
\|\mathbf{x}_{k+1} - \mathbf{x}_*\| \leqslant \frac{1}{2}\|\mathbf{x}_k - \mathbf{x}_*\|.
$$

This proves that all members of the sequence $\mathbf{x}_k$ are located in $B(\mathbf{x}_*, \delta)$. Furthermore, since

$$
\frac{\|\mathbf{x}_{k+1} - \mathbf{x}_*\|}{\|\mathbf{x}_k - \mathbf{x}_*\|} \leqslant M \int_0^1 \|(Df)(\mathbf{x}_k) - (Df)(\mathbf{x}_* + t(\mathbf{x}_k - \mathbf{x}_*))\|\, dt,
$$

it follows that

$$
\lim_{k \to \infty} \frac{\|\mathbf{x}_{k+1} - \mathbf{x}_*\|}{\|\mathbf{x}_k - \mathbf{x}_*\|} = 0.
$$

If Df is Lipschitz function, then

$$
\begin{aligned}
\frac{\|\mathbf{x}_{k+1} - \mathbf{x}_*\|}{\|\mathbf{x}_k - \mathbf{x}_*\|} &\leqslant M \int_0^1 L\|\mathbf{x}_k - (\mathbf{x}_* + t(\mathbf{x}_k - \mathbf{x}_*))\|\, dt \\
&= ML\|\mathbf{x}_k - \mathbf{x}_*\| \int_0^1 (1 - t)\, dt = \frac{ML}{2}\|\mathbf{x}_k - \mathbf{x}_*\|,
\end{aligned}
$$

which establishes that $\|\mathbf{x}_{k+1} - \mathbf{x}_*\| \leqslant \frac{ML}{2}\|\mathbf{x}_k - \mathbf{x}_*\|^2$. Thus, the convergence of $(\mathbf{x}_k)$ to $\mathbf{x}_*$ is quadratic. $\qquad\square$

14.3   The Secant Method

When the function f is given in tabular form instead on an analytical expression, the derivative (or the Jacobian) used by Newton's method cannot be used and the approximating sequence (x_k) must be constructed by using only the values of f. Also, even when the function is analytically specified computing the inverse of the Jacobian $((D\mathbf{f})(\mathbf{x}_k))^{-1}$ at every step can be computationally very expensive.

The idea of the secant method is to approximate the derivative of f (when $n = 1$) or the inverse of the Jacobian (when $n > 1$) with expressions that are easier to computed. As we did in the previous section we present the secant method starting with $n = 1$.

The secant method (see Figure 14.2) requires two initial estimates of x_* that bracket the root. If we obtained two such estimates x_k and x_{k+1}, then the line that passes through the points $(x_k, f(x_k))$ and $(x_{k+1}, f(x_{k+1}))$, referred to as a *secant line* has the slope $a_k = \frac{f(x_{k+1}) - f(x_k)}{x_{k+1} - x_k}$ and the equation

$$y = f(x_k) + \frac{f(x_{k+1}) - f(x_k)}{x_{k+1} - x_k}(x - x_k).$$

The next approximant x_{k+2} of x_* is the intersection of the secant line with the x-axis and is given by

$$x_{k+2} = \frac{f(x_{k+1})x_k - f(x_k)x_{k+1}}{f(x_{k+1}) - f(x_k)}.$$

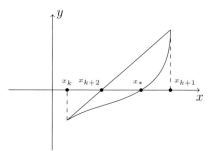

Fig. 14.2   Secant one-dimensional method.

Let e_k be the error at the k iteration, that is, $e_k = x_k - x_*$. The last equality can be written as

$$e_{k+2} + x_* = \frac{f(x_{k+1})(e_k + x_*) - f(x_k)(e_{k+1} + x_*)}{f(x_{k+1}) - f(x_k)},$$

or

$$e_{k+2} = \frac{f(x_{k+1})e_k - f(x_k)(e_{k+1})}{f(x_{k+1}) - f(x_k)}.$$

By Taylor's Formula and Corollary 10.5 we can write:

$$f(x_k) = f(x_*) + e_k f'(x_*) + \frac{e_k^2}{2} f''(x_*) + O(e_k^3),$$

$$f(x_{k+1}) = f(x_*) + e_{k+1} f'(x_*) + \frac{e_{k+1}^2}{2} f''(x_*) + O(e_{k+1}^3).$$

Taking into account that $f(x_*) = 0$ we have:

$$f(x_k) = e_k f'(x_*) + \frac{e_k^2}{2} f''(x_*) + O(e_k^3),$$

$$f(x_{k+1}) = e_{k+1} f'(x_*) + \frac{e_{k+1}^2}{2} f''(x_*) + O(e_{k+1}^3).$$

This allows us to further write:

$$f(x_{k+1})e_k - f(x_k)(e_{k+1})$$

$$= e_k e_{k+1} f'(x_*) + e_k \frac{e_{k+1}^2}{2} f''(x_*) + e_k O(e_{k+1}^3)$$

$$- e_k e_{k+1} f'(x_*) - e_{k+1} \frac{e_k^2}{2} f''(x_*) - e_{k+1} O(e_k^3),$$

$$= e_k e_{k+1} \left(\frac{e_{k+1} - e_k}{2} f''(x_*) + O(e_{k+1}^2) - O(e_k^2) \right),$$

and

$$f(x_{k+1}) - f(x_k) = (e_{k+1} - e_k)f'(x_*) + \frac{e_{k+1}^2 - e_k^2}{2} f''(x_*)$$

$$+ O(e_{k+1}^3) - O(e_k^3).$$

Thus, e_{k+2} can be written as

$$e_{k+2} = \frac{f(x_{k+1})e_k - f(x_k)(e_{k+1})}{f(x_{k+1}) - f(x_k)}$$

$$= \frac{e_k e_{k+1} \left(\frac{e_{k+1} - e_k}{2} f''(x_*) + O(e_{k+1}^2) - O(e_k^2) \right)}{(e_{k+1} - e_k)f'(x_*) + \frac{e_{k+1}^2 - e_k^2}{2} f''(x_*) + O(e_{k+1}^3) - O(e_k^3)}$$

$$= e_k e_{k+1} \frac{\frac{f''(x_*)}{2} + \frac{O(e_{k+1}^2) - O(e_k^2)}{e_{k+1} - e_k}}{f'(x_*) + \frac{e_{k+1} + e_k}{2} f''(x_*) + \frac{O(e_{k+1}^3) - O(e_k^3)}{e_{k+1} - e_k}}$$

$$= e_k e_{k+1} \frac{f''(x_*)}{2f'(x_*)} \frac{1 + \frac{2}{f''(x_*)} \frac{O(e_{k+1}^2) - O(e_k^2)}{e_{k+1} - e_k}}{1 + \frac{e_{k+1} + e_k}{2f'(x_*)} f''(x_*) + \frac{O(e_{k+1}^3) - O(e_k^3)}{e_{k+1} - e_k}}.$$

Thus, the variation of the errors is approximately described by the equality

$$e_{k+2} = e_k e_{k+1} \frac{f''(x_*)}{2f'(x_*)}.$$

Let $F = \frac{f''(x_*)}{2f'(x_*)}$. We seek a solution of this recurrence of the form $e_{k+1} = e_k^a F^b$, with $a > 0$. This implies

$$e_{k+2} = e_{k+1}^a F^b = e_k^{a^2} F^{ab+b},$$

hence

$$e_k^{a^2} F^{ab+b} = e_k^{a+1} F^{b+1},$$

which can be satisfied if $a^2 = a + 1$, and $ab + b = b + 1$. This implies $b = \frac{1}{a}$ and $a = \frac{1+\sqrt{5}}{2} \approx 1.62$. Thus, the secant method converges somewhat slower than the Newton's method.

The secant method was extended by C. G. Broyden [24] who proposed a technique that avoids the repeated computation of the inverse of the Jacobian matrix that is required by Newton's method.

14.4   Newton's Method in Banach Spaces

In a more general setting Newton's method is an algorithm for solving equations of the form $f(x) = 0$, where $f : S \longrightarrow Y$ is a differentiable function between an open subset S of a Banach space X and a Banach space Y.

Definition 14.1. Let $f : B(\mathbf{x}_0, r) \longrightarrow X$ be a function defined on the open sphere $B(x_0, R) \subseteq X$, where X is a Banach space, and let $\phi : [t_0, t'] \longrightarrow \mathbb{R}$, where $t' = t_0 + r < t_0 + R$. The function ϕ majorized f if
  (i) $\|f(\mathbf{x}_0) - x_0\| \leq \phi(t_0) - t_0$;
  (ii) $\|(Df)(\mathbf{x})\| \leqslant \phi'(t)$ when $\|x - x_0\| \leqslant t - t_0$.

Theorem 14.3. (Kantorovich's Theorem) *Let $f : B[x_0, r] \longrightarrow X$ be a function defined on the closed sphere $B[x_0, r] \subseteq X$, where X is a Banach space, and let $\phi : [t_0, t'] \longrightarrow \mathbb{R}$, where $t' = t_0 + r < t_0 + R$. Assume that f has a continuous derivative in $B[x_0, r]$ and ϕ is differentiable in $[t_0, t']$.*

If ϕ majorizes f and $t = \phi(t)$ has a root $\bar{t}$ in $[t_0, t']$, then the equation $x = f(x)$ has a root x_*, and the sequence of successive approximations $x_{n+1} = f(x_n)$ for $n \geqslant 0$ converges to x_*. Furthermore, we have $\|x_* - x_0\| \leqslant t_* - t_0$, where t_* is the smallest root of $t = f(t)$ in $[t_0, t']$.

Proof.   The sequence (t_n) defined by $t_{n+1} = \phi(t_n)$ is convergent. Note that $\phi'(t) \geqslant 0$ when $t \in [t_0, t']$, so ϕ is increasing in that interval. It follows that t_n is well-defined and $t_n \leqslant \bar{t}$, as it can immediately be shown by induction on n. Also, the sequence (t_n) is monotone. Indeed, we have $t_0 \leqslant t_1$ and $t_n \leqslant t_{n+1}$ implies $t_{n+1} = \phi(t_n) \leqslant \phi(t_{n+1}) = t_{n+2}$. Thus, we may conclude that $t_* = \lim_{n \to \infty} t_n$ exists. Since ϕ is continuous, it follows that $t_* = \phi(t_*)$, so t_* is a root of ϕ; moreover, it is the smallest root in $[t_0, t']$.

One could prove by strong induction on n that

$$\|x_n - x_{n-1}\| \leqslant t_n - t_{n-1} \tag{14.2}$$

for $n \geqslant 1$. The condition (i) of the theorem amounts to $\|x_1 - x_0\| \leqslant t_1 - t_0$, so $x_1 \in B[x_0, r]$.

Suppose that we have shown that $\|x_{k+1} - x_k\| \leqslant t_{k+1} - t_k$ for $0 \leqslant k \leqslant n - 1$. Then,

$$x_{n+1} - x_n = f(x_n) - f(x_{n-1}) = \int_{[x_{n-1}, x_n]} (Df)(x)\, dx.$$

Let $x = x_{n-1} + \tau(x_n - x_{n-1}) \in [x_{n-1}, x_n]$ and $t = t_{n-1} + \tau(t_n - t_{n-1})$, where $\tau \in [0, 1]$. Since $\|x_{n+1} - x_n\| \leqslant t_{n+1} - t_n$, we have

$$\|x - x_0\| \leqslant \tau\|x_n - x_{n-1}\| + \|x_{n-1} - x_{n-2}\| + \cdots + \|x_1 - x_0\|$$
$$\leqslant \tau(t_n - t_{n-1}) + (t_{n-1} - t_{n-2}) + \cdots + (t_1 - t_0) = t - t_0,$$

hence $\|(Df)(x)\| \leqslant \phi'(t)$ because ϕ majorizes f.

Therefore,

$$\|x_{n+1} - x_n\| = \left\| \int_{x_{n-1}}^{x_n} (Df)(x)\, dx \right\|$$
$$\leqslant \int_{t_{n-1}}^{t_n} \phi'(t)\, dt = \phi(t_n) - \phi(t_{n-1}) = t_{n+1} - t_n,$$

which completes the proof of inequality (14.2).

Note that $x_{n+1} \in B[x_0, r]$ because

$$\|x_{n+1} - x_0\| \leqslant \|x_{n+1} - x_n\| + \|x_n - x_{n-1}\| + \cdot + \|x_1 - x_0\|$$
$$\leqslant (t_{n+1} - t_n) + (t_n - t_{n-1}) + \cdots + (t_1 - t_0)$$
$$= t_{n-1} - t_0 \leqslant t' - t_0 = r.$$

Inequality (14.2) implies

$$\|x_{n+p} - x_n\| \leqslant \|x_{n+p} - x_{n+p-1}\| + \cdots + \|x_{n+1} - x_n\|$$
$$\leqslant (t_{n+p} - t_{n+p-1}) + \cdots + (t_{n+1} - t_n) = t_{n+p} - t_n,$$

hence (x_n) is a Cauchy sequence. Therefore (x_n) has a limit x_*. The continuity of f and the equality $x_{n+1} = f(x_n)$ imply $x_* = f(x_*)$.

Since $\|x_{n+p} - x_n\| \leqslant t_{n+p} - t_n$, by taking $p \to \infty$ we obtain $\|x_* - x_n\| \leqslant t_* - t_n$, which gives a bound on the convergence of (x_n) to x_*. $\qquad \square$

Corollary 14.1. *Under the same notations and assumptions as in Theorem 14.3, if $\phi(t') \leqslant t'$, and the equation $t = \phi(t)$ has a unique solution in the interval $[t_0, t']$, then $x = f(x)$ has a unique root in $B[x_0, r]$ and the sequence of successive approximations starting from an arbitrary $\overline{x}_0 \in B[x_0, r]$ converges to a root of f.*

Proof. Consider the sequence (t_n) defined as $t_0 = t'$ and $t_{n+1} = \phi(t_n)$. The sequence (t_n) is monotonically decreasing and bounded below by t_* and has a limit $\tilde{t}$. Since $t = \phi(t)$ has a unique solution, $\lim_{n \to \infty} t_n = t_*$.

The sequence of successive approximations starting with $\overline{x}_0$ is defined by $\overline{x}_{n+1} = f(\overline{x}_n)$ for $n \geqslant 0$.

Next we prove by strong induction on n that $\overline{x}_n \in B[x_0, r]$.

Note that

$$\overline{x}_1 - x_1 = f(\overline{x}_0) - f(x_0) = \int_{x_0}^{\overline{x}_0} (Df)(x)\, dx.$$

Therefore,

$$\|\overline{x}_1 - x_1\| \leqslant \int_{t_0}^{\overline{t}_0} \phi'(t)\, dt = \phi(\overline{t}_0) - \phi(t_0) = \overline{t}_1 - t_1,$$

which implies

$$\|\overline{x}_1 - x_0\| \leqslant \|\overline{x}_1 - x_1\| + \|x_1 - x_0\| \leqslant (\overline{t}_1 - t_1) + (t_1 - t_0) = \overline{t}_1 - t_0 \leqslant r,$$

hence $\overline{x}_1 \in B[x_0, r]$.

Suppose that we have $\overline{x}_k \in B[x_0, r]$ and $\|\overline{x}_k - x_k\| \leqslant \overline{t}_k - t_k$ for $1 \leqslant k \leqslant n$. Then,

$$\overline{x}_{n+1} - x_{n+1} = f(\overline{x}_n) - f(x_n) = \int_{x_n}^{\overline{x}_n} (Df)(x)\, dx.$$

Suppose that $x \in [x_n, \overline{x}_n]$ and $t \in [t_n, \overline{t}_n]$ are points in similar positions, that is

$$x = (1 - \theta)\mathbf{x}_n + \theta\overline{x}_n \text{ and } t = (1 - \theta)\mathbf{t}_n + \theta\overline{t}_n$$

for some $\theta \in [0, 1]$. We have:

$$\begin{aligned}
\|x - x_0\| &= \|(1 - \theta)\mathbf{x}_n + \theta\overline{x}_n - x_0\| = \|\theta(\overline{x}_n - x_n) + x_n - x_0\| \\
&\leqslant \theta\|\overline{x}_n - x_n\| + \|x_n - x_{n-1}\| + \cdots + \|x_1 - x_0\| \\
&\leqslant \theta(\overline{t}_n - t_n) + (t_n - t_{n-1}) + \cdots + (t_1 - t_0) \\
&= \theta(\overline{t}_n - t_n) + (t_n - t_0) = (1 - \theta)t_n + \theta\overline{t}_n - t_0 = t - t_0.
\end{aligned}$$

Therefore, for points x and t as above we have $\|(Df)(\mathbf{x})\| \leqslant \phi'(t)$. Consequently,

$$\|\bar{x}_{n+1} - x_{n+1}\| \leqslant \int_{t_n}^{\bar{t}_n} \phi'(t)\, dt = \phi(\bar{t}_n) - \phi(t_n) = \bar{t}_{n+1} - t_{n+1},$$

which implies

$$\|\bar{x}_{n+1} - x_0\| \leqslant \|\bar{x}_{n+1} - x_{n+1}\| + \|x_{n+1} - x_0\|$$
$$\leqslant \bar{t}_{n+1} - t_{n+1} + t_{n+1} - t_0 = \bar{t}_{n+1} - t_0 \leqslant r,$$

hence $\bar{x}_{n+1} \in B[x_0, r]$, which completes the induction argument.

Since $\lim_{n\to\infty} t_n = \lim_{n\to\infty} \bar{t}_n = t_*$, it follows that if $\lim_{n\to\infty} x_n = x_*$, then $\lim_{n\to\infty} \bar{x}_n = x_*$. Thus, regardless of the initial approximation (x_0 or $\bar{x}_0$) the sequence of approximants converges to the same limit. The uniqueness of the limit follows immediately. □

14.5   Conjugate Gradient Method

Let $A \in \mathbb{R}^{n\times n}$ be a symmetric and positive definite matrix. Define the function $(\cdot, \cdot)_A : \mathbb{R}^n \longrightarrow \mathbb{R}^n \longrightarrow \mathbb{R}$ as $(\mathbf{x}, \mathbf{y})_A = (A\mathbf{x}, \mathbf{y})$. It is easy to verify that $(\cdot, \cdot)_A$ is an inner product on $\mathbb{R}^n$ (see Exercise 3).

The *norm generated by the inner product* $(\cdot, \cdot)_A$ is $\|\mathbf{x}\|_A = \sqrt{(A\mathbf{x}, \mathbf{x})}$.

The vectors $\mathbf{u}, \mathbf{v} \in \mathbb{R}^n - \{\mathbf{0}_n\}$ are *A-conjugate* if they are orthogonal with respect to the $(\cdot, \cdot)_A$ inner product, that is, if $(\mathbf{u}, \mathbf{v})_A = 0$. A set of vectors $\{\mathbf{x}_1, \dots, \mathbf{x}_k\}$ is said to be *A-conjugate* if they are pairwise *A*-conjugate.

Consider now the function $f : \mathbb{R}^n \longrightarrow \mathbb{R}$ defined by $f(\mathbf{x}) = \frac{1}{2}(A\mathbf{x}, \mathbf{x}) - (\mathbf{b}, \mathbf{x}) + a$. Note that $(\nabla f)(\mathbf{x}) = A\mathbf{x} - \mathbf{b}$. Thus, $\mathbf{x}$ is a solution of the system $A\mathbf{x} - \mathbf{b} = \mathbf{0}_n$ if and only if $(\nabla f)(\mathbf{x}) = \mathbf{0}_n$. Thus, minimizing the quadratic function f defined above is equivalent to solving the linear system $A\mathbf{x} = \mathbf{b}$.

For $\mathbf{x} \in \mathbb{R}^n$, $\mathbf{r}(\mathbf{x}) = A\mathbf{x} - \mathbf{b}$ is the *residual* in $\mathbf{x}$.

Theorem 14.4. *Let $A \in \mathbb{R}^{n\times n}$ be a symmetric and positive definite matrix. A set of A-conjugate vectors is linearly independent.*

Proof.   Let $\{\mathbf{d}_1, \dots, \mathbf{d}_k\}$ be an *A*-conjugate set in $\mathbb{R}^n$ and assume that $a_1\mathbf{d}_1 + \cdots + a_k\mathbf{d}_k = \mathbf{0}_n$. Then,

$$\left(\sum_{i=1}^k a_i\mathbf{d}_i, A\mathbf{d}_j \right) = \sum_{i=1}^k a_i(\mathbf{d}_i, A\mathbf{d}_j)$$
$$= a_j(\mathbf{d}_j, A\mathbf{d}_j) = 0.$$

Since $(\mathbf{d}_j, A\mathbf{d}_j) \neq 0$ due to the fact that A is positive definite, we have $a_j = 0$ for $1 \leqslant j \leqslant k$, hence X is linearly independent. □

Theorem 14.5. *Let $A \in \mathbb{R}^{n \times n}$ be a symmetric and positive definite matrix and let $D = \{\boldsymbol{d}_1, \ldots, \boldsymbol{d}_k\}$ be an A-conjugate set in $\mathbb{R}^n$. If M is an affine subspace $M = \boldsymbol{d}_0 + \langle D \rangle$, then the minimum of the quadratic function*

$$f(\boldsymbol{x}) = \frac{1}{2}(A\boldsymbol{x}, \boldsymbol{x}) - (\boldsymbol{b}, \boldsymbol{x}) + a$$

on M is achieved in $\boldsymbol{x}_* = \boldsymbol{x}_0 - \sum_{j=1}^{k} \frac{(r(\boldsymbol{x}_0), \boldsymbol{d}_j)}{(A\boldsymbol{d}_j, \boldsymbol{d}_j)} \boldsymbol{d}_j$.

Proof. Let $\mathbf{x} = \mathbf{x}_0 + \sum_{j=1}^{k} a_j \mathbf{d}_j \in M$. For $f(\mathbf{x}) = \frac{1}{2}(A\mathbf{x}, \mathbf{x}) - (\mathbf{b}, \mathbf{x}) + a$ we have

$$f(\mathbf{x}) - f(\mathbf{x}_0) = \frac{1}{2}(A\mathbf{x}, \mathbf{x}) - (\mathbf{b}, \mathbf{x}) + a - \left(\frac{1}{2}(A\mathbf{x}, \mathbf{x}) - (\mathbf{b}, \mathbf{x}) + a \right)$$

$$= \frac{1}{2}((A\mathbf{x}, \mathbf{x}) - (A\mathbf{x}_0, \mathbf{x}_0)) - (\mathbf{b}, \mathbf{x} - \mathbf{x}_0).$$

Since D is an A-conjugate set we can write:

$$(A\mathbf{x}, \mathbf{x}) = \left(A\mathbf{x}_0 + \sum_{j=1}^{k} a_j A\mathbf{d}_j, \mathbf{x}_0 + \sum_{j=1}^{k} a_j \mathbf{d}_j \right)$$

$$= (A\mathbf{x}_0, \mathbf{x}_0) + \left(A\mathbf{x}_0, \sum_{j=1}^{k} a_j \mathbf{d}_j \right)$$

$$+ \left(\sum_{j=1}^{k} a_j A\mathbf{d}_j, \mathbf{x}_0 \right) + \left(\sum_{j=1}^{k} a_j A\mathbf{d}_j, \sum_{j=1}^{k} a_j \mathbf{d}_j \right)$$

$$= (A\mathbf{x}_0, \mathbf{x}_0) + \sum_{j=1}^{k} a_j (A\mathbf{x}_0, \mathbf{d}_j)$$

$$+ \sum_{j=1}^{k} a_j (A\mathbf{d}_j, \mathbf{x}_0) + \sum_{j=1}^{k} \sum_{\ell=1}^{k} a_j a_\ell (A\mathbf{d}_j, \mathbf{d}_\ell)$$

$$= (A\mathbf{x}_0, \mathbf{x}_0) + \sum_{j=1}^{k} a_j (A\mathbf{x}_0, \mathbf{d}_j)$$

$$+ \sum_{j=1}^{k} a_j (A\mathbf{d}_j, \mathbf{x}_0) + \sum_{j=1}^{k} \sum_{\ell=1}^{k} a_j^2 (A\mathbf{d}_j, \mathbf{d}_j),$$

(because the vectors $\mathbf{d}_j$ are A-conjugate)

$$= (A\mathbf{x}_0, \mathbf{x}_0) + 2 \sum_{j=1}^{k} a_j (A\mathbf{x}_0, \mathbf{d}_j) + \sum_{j=1}^{k} a_j^2 (A\mathbf{d}_j, \mathbf{d}_j)$$

(because A is a symmetric matrix).

Consequently,

$$
f(\mathbf{x}) - f(\mathbf{x}_0) = \frac{1}{2}\left(2\sum_{j=1}^{k} a_j(A\mathbf{x}_0,\mathbf{d}_j) + \sum_{j=1}^{k} a_j^2(A\mathbf{d}_j,\mathbf{d}_j)\right) - (\mathbf{b}, \mathbf{x} - \mathbf{x}_0)
$$

$$
= \frac{1}{2}\sum_{j=1}^{k} a_j^2(A\mathbf{d}_j,\mathbf{d}_j) + \sum_{j=1}^{k} a_j(A\mathbf{x}_0,\mathbf{d}_j) - \left(\mathbf{b},\sum_{j=1}^{k} a_j\mathbf{d}_j\right)
$$

$$
= \sum_{j=1}^{k} \left(\frac{1}{2}a_j^2(A\mathbf{d}_j,\mathbf{d}_j) + a_j(A\mathbf{x}_0 - \mathbf{b},\mathbf{d}_j)\right).
$$

The minimizer of f can be obtained by minimizing each term $\frac{1}{2}a_j^2(A\mathbf{d}_j,\mathbf{d}_j) + a_j(A\mathbf{x}_0 - \mathbf{b},\mathbf{d}_j)$ separately, which can be achieved by taking

$$
a_j = -\frac{(A\mathbf{x}_0 - \mathbf{b},\mathbf{d}_j)}{(A\mathbf{d}_j,\mathbf{d}_j)} = -\frac{(\mathbf{r}(\mathbf{x}_0),\mathbf{d}_j)}{(A\mathbf{d}_j,\mathbf{d}_j)}
$$

for $1 \leqslant j \leqslant k$. □

Let $\{\mathbf{r}_0,\mathbf{r}_1,\ldots,\mathbf{r}_k\}$ be a linearly independent set in $\mathbb{R}^n$. Using the Gram-Schmidt algorithm described in Section 2.5 we can construct a set of A-conjugate vectors $\mathbf{d}_0,\mathbf{d}_1,\ldots,\mathbf{d}_k$ such that $\mathbf{d}_0 = \mathbf{r}_0$ and $\langle \mathbf{r}_0,\ldots,\mathbf{r}_j\rangle = \langle \mathbf{d}_0,\ldots,\mathbf{d}_j\rangle$ for $0 \leqslant k \leqslant k$.

Definition 14.2. Let $D = \{\mathbf{d}_0,\ldots,\mathbf{d}_{n-1}\}$ be an A-conjugate set in $\mathbb{R}^n$. The sequence $(\mathbf{x}_0,\mathbf{x}_1,\ldots,\mathbf{x}_n)$ *generated by* D *and* $\boldsymbol{x}_0$ *using the conjugate-direction method* is given by

$$
\mathbf{x}_{k+1} = \mathbf{x}_k - \frac{(\mathbf{r}_k,\mathbf{d}_k)}{(A\mathbf{d}_k,\mathbf{d}_k)}\mathbf{d}_k,
$$

where $\mathbf{r}_k = \mathbf{r}(\mathbf{x}_k)$ is the residual in $\mathbf{x}_k$ for $0 \leqslant k \leqslant n - 1$.

Thus, an A-conjugate set of directions in $\mathbb{R}^n$ and a vector $\mathbf{x}_0$ determine a sequence of coefficients (a_k), where $a_k = -\frac{(\mathbf{r}_{k-1},\mathbf{d}_k)}{(A\mathbf{d}_k,\mathbf{d}_k)}$ for $1 \leqslant k \leqslant n$.

Theorem 14.6. *The vector* $\boldsymbol{x}_{k+1}$ *is the minimizer of the function* f *defined by* $f(\boldsymbol{x}) = \frac{1}{2}(A\boldsymbol{x},\boldsymbol{x}) - (\boldsymbol{b},\boldsymbol{x}) + a$ *along the uni-dimensional affine subspace* $L_k = \{\boldsymbol{x}_k + t\boldsymbol{d}_k \mid t \in \mathbb{R}\}$.

Proof. Consider the function $\phi : \mathbb{R} \longrightarrow \mathbb{R}$ defined by $\phi(t) = f(\mathbf{x}_k + t\mathbf{d}_k)$.

By the definition of f we have

$$f(\mathbf{x}_k + t\mathbf{d}_k) = \frac{1}{2}(A(\mathbf{x}_k + t\mathbf{d}_k), \mathbf{x}_k + t\mathbf{d}_k) - (\mathbf{b}, \mathbf{x}_k + t\mathbf{d}_k) + a$$

$$= \frac{1}{2}(A\mathbf{x}_k + tA\mathbf{d}_k, \mathbf{x}_k + t\mathbf{d}_k)) - (\mathbf{b}, \mathbf{x}_k + t\mathbf{d}_k) + a$$

$$= \frac{1}{2}(A\mathbf{x}_k, \mathbf{x}_k) + \frac{1}{2}t(A\mathbf{x}_k, \mathbf{d}_k)) + \frac{1}{2}t(A\mathbf{d}_k, \mathbf{x}_k) + \frac{1}{2}t^2(A\mathbf{d}_k, \mathbf{d}_k))$$
$$- (\mathbf{b}, \mathbf{x}_k) - t(\mathbf{b}, \mathbf{d}_k) + a$$

$$= \frac{1}{2}(A\mathbf{x}_k, \mathbf{x}_k) - (\mathbf{b}, \mathbf{x}_k) + a + t((A\mathbf{x}_k, \mathbf{d}_k) - t(\mathbf{b}, \mathbf{d}_k))$$
$$+ \frac{1}{2}t^2(A\mathbf{d}_k, \mathbf{d}_k))$$

$$= f(\mathbf{x}_k) + t(\mathbf{r}(\mathbf{x}_k), \mathbf{d}_k) + \frac{1}{2}t^2(A\mathbf{d}_k, \mathbf{d}_k)).$$

The minimizer is obtained for $t = -\frac{(\mathbf{r}(\mathbf{x}_k), \mathbf{d}_k)}{(A\mathbf{d}_k, \mathbf{d}_k)}$, that is, for

$$\mathbf{x}_k - \frac{(\mathbf{r}(\mathbf{x}_k), \mathbf{d}_k)}{(A\mathbf{d}_k, \mathbf{d}_k)}\mathbf{d}_k,$$

which is $\mathbf{x}_{k+1}$. $\qquad\square$

Theorem 14.7. *Let $D = \{\mathbf{d}_0, \ldots, \mathbf{d}_{n-1}\}$ be A-conjugate directions in $\mathbb{R}^n$ and let $(\mathbf{x}_0, \mathbf{x}_1, \ldots, \mathbf{x}_{n-1})$ be the sequence generated from D and $\mathbf{x}_0$ using the conjugate-direction method (as in Definition 14.2).*

The vector $\mathbf{x}_k$ is the global minimizer of the function $f : \mathbb{R}^n \longrightarrow \mathbb{R}$ defined by $f(\mathbf{x}) = \frac{1}{2}(A\mathbf{x}, \mathbf{x}) - (\mathbf{b}, \mathbf{x}) + a$ on the affine subspace $M_k = \mathbf{x}_0 + \langle\{\mathbf{d}_0, \ldots, \mathbf{d}_{k-1}\}\rangle$ for $1 \leqslant k \leqslant n$. The residual $\mathbf{r}(\mathbf{x}_k)$ is orthogonal on $\mathbf{d}_1, \ldots, \mathbf{d}_k$.

Proof. Let $\bar{\mathbf{x}} = \mathbf{x}_0 + c_1\mathbf{d}_1 + \cdots + c_{k-1}\mathbf{d}_{k-1}$ be the minimizer of f on M_k. By Theorem 14.5, we have $c_j = -\frac{(\mathbf{r}(\mathbf{x}_0), \mathbf{d}_j)}{(A\mathbf{d}_j, \mathbf{d}_j)}$ for $0 \leqslant j \leqslant k - 1$.

If $\mathbf{x} \in M_i$ we have $\mathbf{x} = \mathbf{x}_0 + k_0\mathbf{d}_0 + \cdots + k_{i-1}\mathbf{d}_{i-1}$, hence

$$\mathbf{r}(\mathbf{x}_i) = A\mathbf{x}_0 + k_0A\mathbf{d}_0 + \cdots + k_{i-1}A\mathbf{d}_{i-1} - \mathbf{b} = \mathbf{r}(\mathbf{x}_0) + k_0A\mathbf{d}_0 + \cdots + k_{i-1}A\mathbf{d}_{i-1},$$

and $(\mathbf{r}(\mathbf{x}), \mathbf{d}_i) = (\mathbf{r}(\mathbf{x}_0), \mathbf{d}_i) + k_0A(\mathbf{d}_1, \mathbf{d}_i) + \cdots + k_iA(\mathbf{d}_{i-1}, \mathbf{d}_i) = (\mathbf{r}(\mathbf{x}_0), \mathbf{d}_i)$.

This shows that $(\mathbf{r}(\mathbf{x}), \mathbf{d}_i) = (\mathbf{r}(\mathbf{x}_0), \mathbf{d}_i)$ for all $\mathbf{x} \in M_i$. Therefore, the coefficients c_i coincide with the coefficients of Definition 14.2 and this proves the first part of the statement.

For the second part, define the function $h : \mathbb{R}^k \longrightarrow \mathbb{R}$ as

$$h(c_0, \ldots, c_{k-1}) = f(\mathbf{x}_0 + c_0\mathbf{d}_0 + \ldots + c_{k-1}\mathbf{d}_{k-1}). \quad \text{Then, } \mathbf{c} = \begin{pmatrix} c_1 \\ \vdots \\ c_{k-1} \end{pmatrix}$$

minimizes h, hence $(\nabla h)(\mathbf{c}) = \mathbf{0}_k$. Note that $\frac{\partial h}{\partial c_j} = (\mathbf{r}(\mathbf{x}_k), \mathbf{d}_j) = 0$, which implies the second part of the theorem. $\qquad \square$

Corollary 14.2. *The solution of the equation $A\boldsymbol{x} = \boldsymbol{b}$ can be found in at most n steps by computing the A-conjugate directions.*

Proof. This is an immediate from Theorem 14.7. $\qquad \square$

The A-conjugate directions $\mathbf{d}_1, \ldots, \mathbf{d}_k$ can constructed starting from the negative residuals $-\mathbf{r}(\mathbf{x}_0), \ldots - \mathbf{r}(\mathbf{x}_{k-1})$ by applying the Gram-Schmidt algorithm discussed in Section 2.5. A less complex alternative is offered by the conjugate gradient (CG) method introduced in [78]. The central idea is contained by the next statement.

Theorem 14.8. *Let $\boldsymbol{x}_0 \in \mathbb{R}^n$ such that $\boldsymbol{d}_0 = -\boldsymbol{r}(\boldsymbol{x}_0) \neq \boldsymbol{0}_n$. If $\boldsymbol{r}_k = \boldsymbol{r}(\boldsymbol{x}_k)$, where $(\boldsymbol{d}_1, \ldots, \boldsymbol{d}_k)$ and $(\boldsymbol{x}_1, \ldots, \boldsymbol{x}_k)$ are defined by*

$$\boldsymbol{d}_k = -\boldsymbol{r}_k + \sum_{j=0}^{k-1} \frac{(A\boldsymbol{r}_k, \boldsymbol{d}_j)}{(A\boldsymbol{d}_j, \boldsymbol{d}_j)} \boldsymbol{d}_j,$$

$$c_k = \frac{\|\boldsymbol{r}_k\|}{(A\boldsymbol{d}_k, \boldsymbol{d}_k)},$$

$$\boldsymbol{x}_{k+1} = \boldsymbol{x}_k + c_k \boldsymbol{d}_k.$$

The vectors $\{\boldsymbol{r}_0, \ldots, \boldsymbol{r}_k\}$ are pairwise orthogonal and

$$\boldsymbol{d}_k = -\boldsymbol{r}_k + \frac{\|\boldsymbol{r}_k\|}{\|\boldsymbol{r}_{k-1}\|^2} \boldsymbol{d}_{k-1}.$$

Proof. The first equality of the theorem shows that the vectors $\mathbf{d}_i$ are generated from $\mathbf{r}_i$ using the Gram-Schmidt algorithm, hence $\langle \mathbf{d}_0, \ldots, \mathbf{d}_{k-1} \rangle = \langle \mathbf{r}_0, \ldots, \mathbf{r}_{k-1} \rangle$. Since $\mathbf{r}_k$ is orthogonal on $\mathbf{d}_1, \ldots, \mathbf{d}_{k-1}$ by Theorem 14.7, it follows that $\mathbf{r}$ is orthogonal on $\mathbf{r}_0, \ldots, \mathbf{r}_{k-1}$, which proves the first part.

Note that the equality $\mathbf{x}_{k+1} = \mathbf{x}_k + c_k \mathbf{d}_k$ implies $c_k \neq 0$ because, otherwise, we would have $\mathbf{x}_{k+1} = \mathbf{x}_k$ which would contradict $\mathbf{r}_{k+1} \perp \mathbf{r}_k$. Also,

$$A\mathbf{d}_j = \frac{1}{c_j} A(\mathbf{x}_{j+1} - A\mathbf{x}_j) = \frac{\mathbf{r}_{j+1} - \mathbf{r}_j}{c_j}.$$

For $j < k - 1$ this implies

$$\left(A\mathbf{r}_k, \mathbf{d}_j \right) = (\mathbf{r}_k, A\mathbf{d}_j) = \left(\mathbf{r}_k, \frac{\mathbf{r}_{j+1} - \mathbf{r}_j}{c_j} \right) = 0$$

and $(A\mathbf{r}_k, d_{k-1}) = \frac{\|\mathbf{r}_k\|^2}{c_{k-1}}$. The previous expression for $\mathbf{d}_k$, can now be considerably simplified as

$$\mathbf{d}_k = -\mathbf{r}_k + \sum_{j=0}^{k-1} \frac{(A\mathbf{r}_k, \mathbf{d}_j)}{(A\mathbf{d}_j, \mathbf{d}_j)} \mathbf{d}_j$$

$$= -\mathbf{r}_k + \frac{(A\mathbf{r}_k, \mathbf{d}_{k-1})}{(A\mathbf{d}_{k-1})} \mathbf{d}_{k-1}$$

$$= -\mathbf{r}_k + \frac{\|\mathbf{r}_k\|^2}{(A\mathbf{d}_{k-1}, \mathbf{d}_{k-1})c_{k-1}} \mathbf{d}_{k-1}$$

$$= -\mathbf{r}_k + \frac{\|\mathbf{r}_k\|^2}{(A\mathbf{d}_{k-1}, \mathbf{d}_{k-1})c_{k-1}} \mathbf{d}_{k-1}$$

$$= -\mathbf{r}_k + \frac{\|\mathbf{r}_k\|^2}{\|\mathbf{r}_{k-1}\|^2 c_{k-1}} \mathbf{d}_{k-1}$$

taking into account that $c_{k-1} = \frac{\|\mathbf{r}_{k-1}\|}{(A\mathbf{d}_{k-1}, \mathbf{d}_{k-1})}$. $\qquad\square$

Definition 14.3. Let $A \in \mathbb{R}^{n \times n}$ be a matrix and let $\mathbf{d} \in \mathbb{R}^n$. The *Krylov subspace of A of order k in the direction $\mathbf{d}$* is the subspace

$$\mathcal{K}_r(A, \mathbf{d}) = \langle \mathbf{d}, A\mathbf{d}, \dots, A^{k-1}\mathbf{d} \rangle.$$

14.6 Gradient Descent Algorithm

The *gradient-descent* algorithm aims to minimize the value of a convex differentiable function $f : U \longrightarrow \mathbb{R}$, where $U \subseteq \mathbb{R}^n$ by constructing a sequence of points $(\mathbf{x}_k)$ using the gradient of the function.

Algorithm 14.6.1: Gradient Descent Algorithm

Input : a Frèchet differentiable function $f : U \longrightarrow \mathbb{R}$, where $U \subseteq \mathbb{R}^n$, a positive constant η

Output: an approximation $\mathbf{x}_m$ of a minimizer $\mathbf{x}_*$ of f

1 **begin**
2   initialize $\mathbf{x}_0$;
3   **for** $k \leftarrow 1$ **to** m **do**
4   set $\mathbf{x}_{k+1} = \mathbf{x}_k - \eta(\nabla f)(\mathbf{x}_k)$;
5   **end**
6   **return** x_m;
7 **end**

The idea of this method is that each point $\mathbf{x}_{k+1}$ in this sequence is obtained from its predecessor $\mathbf{x}_k$ by a move in a descent direction, that is, by a move that belongs to $\mathrm{DD}(f, \mathbf{x}_k)$. We prove that under certain conditions the sequence $(\mathbf{x}_k)$ converges to a minimizer of f.

Theorem 14.9. *Let $f : \mathbb{R}^n \longrightarrow \mathbb{R}$ be a convex differentiable function with a Lipschitz continuous derivative, that is,*

$$\|(\nabla f)(\boldsymbol{y}) - (\nabla f)(\boldsymbol{x})\| \leqslant \frac{1}{\eta}\|\boldsymbol{y} - \boldsymbol{x}\|$$

for some $\eta > 0$ and $\boldsymbol{x}, \boldsymbol{y} \in \mathbb{R}^n$. Suppose that $\boldsymbol{x}_*$ is a minimizer of f and consider the sequence $(\boldsymbol{x}_k)$ defined by

$$\boldsymbol{x}_{k+1} = \boldsymbol{x}_k - \eta(\nabla f)(\boldsymbol{x}_k) \tag{14.3}$$

for $k \in \mathbb{N}$, where $\boldsymbol{x}_0$ is given.

We have $\lim_{k \to \infty} \boldsymbol{x}_k = \boldsymbol{x}_*$, the sequence of numbers $(\|\boldsymbol{x}_k - \boldsymbol{x}_*\|)$ is strictly decreasing and converges to 0 and

$$f(\boldsymbol{x}_k) - f(\boldsymbol{x}_*) \leqslant \frac{5}{2\eta \sum_{j=0}^{k-1} \|\boldsymbol{x}_j - \boldsymbol{x}_*\|^{-2}}.$$

Proof. By Supplement 7 we have:

$$f(\mathbf{x}_{k+1}) - f(\mathbf{x}_k)$$
$$\leqslant ((\nabla f)(\mathbf{x}_k), \mathbf{x}_{k+1} - \mathbf{x}_k) + \frac{1}{2\eta}\|\mathbf{x}_{k+1} - \mathbf{x}_k\|^2$$
$$= -\eta\|(\nabla f)(\mathbf{x}_k)\|^2 + \frac{\eta}{2}\|(\nabla f)(\mathbf{x}_k)\|^2$$
$$= -\frac{\eta}{2}\|(\nabla f)(\mathbf{x}_k)\|^2 = -\frac{1}{2\eta}\|\mathbf{x}_{k+1} - \mathbf{x}_k\|^2.$$

Since f is convex, by Theorem 12.13, we have $f(\mathbf{x}_*) \geqslant f(\mathbf{x}_k) + (\nabla f)(\mathbf{x}_k)'(\mathbf{x}_* - \mathbf{x}_k)$ for $k \in \mathbb{N}$. By defining $w_k = f(\mathbf{x}_k) - f(\mathbf{x}_*)$ for $k \in \mathbb{N}$ we have

$$w_k \leqslant (\nabla f)(\mathbf{x}_k)'(\mathbf{x}_k - \mathbf{x}_*) \leqslant \frac{1}{\eta}\|\mathbf{x}_k - \mathbf{x}_{k+1}\|\|\mathbf{x}_k - \mathbf{x}_*\|.$$

Therefore,

$$f(\mathbf{x}_k) - f(\mathbf{x}_{k+1}) = w_k - w_{k+1} \geqslant \frac{1}{2\eta}\|\mathbf{x}_k - \mathbf{x}_{k+1}\|^2$$
$$\geqslant \frac{1}{2\eta}\left(\frac{\eta w_k}{\|\mathbf{x}_k - \mathbf{x}_*\|}\right)^2 = \frac{\eta w_k^2}{2\|\mathbf{x}_k - \mathbf{x}_*\|^2}$$
$$\geqslant \frac{\eta w_{k+1}^2}{\|\mathbf{x}_k - \mathbf{x}_*\|^2}.$$

Note that the inequality shown above,

$$w_k - w_{k+1} \geqslant \frac{\eta w_{k+1}^2}{\|\mathbf{x}_k - \mathbf{x}_*\|^2}$$

can be written as

$$w_k^{-1} \leqslant w_{k+1}^{-1} \left(1 + \frac{\eta w_{k+1}}{2\|\mathbf{x}_k - \mathbf{x}_*\|^2} \right)^{-1}. \tag{14.4}$$

By Supplement 7 we have $w_k = f(\mathbf{x}_k) - f(\mathbf{x}_*) \leqslant \frac{1}{2\eta}\|\mathbf{x}_k - \mathbf{x}_*\|^2$. Therefore, $w_{k+1} \leqslant w_k \leqslant \frac{1}{2\eta}\|\mathbf{x}_k - \mathbf{x}_*\|^2$. This implies $\frac{\eta w_{k+1}}{2\|\mathbf{x}_k - \mathbf{x}_*\|^2} \leqslant \frac{1}{4}$.

It is immediate that $t \in [0, 1/4]$ implies

$$\frac{1}{1+t} \leqslant 1 - \frac{4t}{5}.$$

Thus,

$$w_k^{-1} \leqslant w_{k+1}^{-1} - \frac{2\eta}{5\|\mathbf{x}_k - \mathbf{x}_*\|^2}.$$

Taking into account the first k of the above inequalities we have

$$w_0^{-1} \leqslant w_k^{-1} - \frac{2\eta}{5\sum_{j=0}^{k-1}\|\mathbf{x}_j - \mathbf{x}_*\|^{-2}},$$

which produces the desired inequality. $\qquad\square$

Corollary 14.3. *For the approximating sequence* $(\boldsymbol{x}_k)$ *of the minimizer* $\boldsymbol{x}_*$ *defined in Theorem 14.9 we have* $f(\boldsymbol{x}_k) - f(\boldsymbol{x}_*) = o(1/k)$.

Proof. Observe that

$$\begin{aligned}
\|\mathbf{x}_{k+1} - \mathbf{x}_*\|^2 &= \left\| \mathbf{x}_k - \mathbf{x}_* - \eta(\nabla f)(\mathbf{x}_k) \right\|^2 \\
&= \|\mathbf{x}_k - \mathbf{x}_*\|^2 + \eta^2\|(\nabla f)(\mathbf{x}_k)\|^2 \\
&\quad - 2\eta\langle \mathbf{x}_k - \mathbf{x}_*, (\nabla f)(\mathbf{x}_k) - (\nabla f)(\mathbf{x}_*)\rangle \\
&\leqslant \|\mathbf{x}_k - \mathbf{x}_*\|^2 + \eta^2\|(\nabla f)(\mathbf{x}_k)\|^2 - 2\eta^2\|(\nabla f)(\mathbf{x}_k)\|^2 \\
&< \|\mathbf{x}_k - \mathbf{x}_*\|^2.
\end{aligned}$$

This implies that $(\|\mathbf{x}_k - \mathbf{x}_*\|)$ is a strictly decreasing sequence. Therefore, the sequence $(\mathbf{x}_k)$ is bounded and, consequently, it contains a subsequence $(\mathbf{x}_{k_n})$ that converges to a point $\tilde{\mathbf{x}}$. Since $f(x_{k+1}) - f(x_k) \leqslant -\frac{1}{2\eta}\|\mathbf{x}_k - \mathbf{x}_{k+1}\|^2$, it follows that $(\nabla f)(\tilde{\mathbf{x}}) = 0$, so $\tilde{\mathbf{x}}$ is a minimizer of f.

Since the sequence $(\|\mathbf{x}_k - \tilde{\mathbf{x}}\|)$ is decreasing, $(\mathbf{x}_k)$ converges to $\tilde{\mathbf{x}}$.

Define $a_k = \|\mathbf{x}_k - \mathbf{x}_*\|^{-2}$ for $k \in \mathbb{N}$, where $\mathbf{x}_*$ is the point $\tilde{\mathbf{x}}$ such that $\lim_{k\to\infty}\|\mathbf{x}_k - \mathbf{x}_*\| = 0$. The sequence (a_k) is an increasing sequence and $\lim_{k\to\infty} a_k = \infty$.

Define $\tilde{a}_k = \frac{\sum_{j=0}^{k-1} a_j}{k}$ for $k \in \mathbb{N}$. This definition implies $k(\tilde{a}_k - \tilde{a}_{k+1}) = \tilde{a}_{k+1} - a_k$. Since (a_k) is an increasing sequence, it follows that

$$(k+1)\tilde{a}_{k+1} \leqslant \sum_{j=0}^{k} a_j \leqslant (k+1)a_k,$$

hence $\tilde{a}_{k+1} \leqslant a_k$. This implies $\tilde{a}_k \leqslant \tilde{a}_{k+1}$ for $k \in \mathbb{N}$, hence (a_k) is a increasing sequence. Let M be a positive number. There exists $N \in \mathbb{N}$ such that $k \geqslant N$ implies $a_k \geqslant M$. We have

$$\tilde{a}_{2N} = \frac{1}{2N} \sum_{j=0}^{2N-1} a_j \geqslant \frac{1}{2N} \sum_{j=N}^{2N-1} a_j \geqslant \frac{M}{2}.$$

Thus, $\lim_{k \to \infty} \tilde{a}_k = \infty$.

By Theorem 14.9 we have

$$k(f(\mathbf{x}_k) - f(\mathbf{x}_*)) \leqslant \frac{5k}{2\eta \sum_{j=0}^{k-1} \|\mathbf{x}_j - \mathbf{x}_*\|^{-2}} \leqslant \frac{5}{2\eta} \left(\frac{1}{k} \sum_{j=0}^{k-1} a_j \right)^{-1}.$$

Therefore, $f(\mathbf{x}_k) - f(\mathbf{x}_*) = o(1/k)$. $\qquad\square$

Example 14.1. Let $f : \mathbb{R} \longrightarrow \mathbb{R}$ be the function given by $f(x) = x^3 - 3x^2 + 6$. It is immediate to establish analytically that the function has a minimum in $x_* = 2$ and that $f(2) = 2$.

We have

$$\|(\nabla f)(\mathbf{y}) - (\nabla f)(\mathbf{x})\| = |f'(y) - f'(x)|$$
$$= |3y^2 - 6y - 3x^2 + 6x| = 3|y - x| \cdot |x + y - 2|$$
$$\leqslant 9 \cdot |y - x|,$$

when $|x + y - 2| \leqslant 3$. The minimal point $(2, 2)$ is included in the stripe defined by $|x + y - 2| \leqslant 3$ and we can take $\eta = 1/9$.

14.7 Stochastic Gradient Descent

The *stochastic gradient descent* (SGD) differs from the gradient descent in that the descent direction is replaced by a random vector whose expected value is a descent direction; another approach, applicable to a convex function that is not necessarily differentiable is to construct a sequence of approximations of a minimizer of a function using randomly chosen subgradients of the objective function at the current approximation.

Algorithm 14.7.1: Stochastic Gradient Descent Algorithm

    Input : a convex function $f : \mathbb{R}^n \longrightarrow \mathbb{R}$, a scalar η, the number of iterations m, $m \geqslant 1$
    Output: an approximation $\tilde{\mathbf{x}}$ of the minimizer $\mathbf{x}_*$ of f

1 **begin**
2   initialize $\mathbf{x}_1 = \mathbf{0}_n$;
3   **for** $i \leftarrow 1$ **to** m **do**
4   choose $\mathbf{v}_i$ at random such that $E(\mathbf{v}_i|\mathbf{x}_i) \in \mathsf{subd}(f)(\mathbf{x}_i)$;
5   set $\mathbf{x}_{i+1} = \mathbf{x}_i - \eta\mathbf{v}_i$;
6   **end**
7   **return** $\tilde{\boldsymbol{x}} = \frac{1}{m}\sum_{i=1}^{m}\boldsymbol{x}_i$;
8 **end**

In the recurrence

$$x_{k+1} = \mathbf{x}_k - \eta\mathbf{v}_k, \tag{14.5}$$

$\mathbf{v}_k$ is a random vector whose conditional expectation $E(\mathbf{v}_k|\mathbf{x}_k)$ is a subgradient of f at $\mathbf{x}_k$. The output of the algorithm is the vector

$$\tilde{\mathbf{x}} = \frac{1}{m}\sum_{k=1}^{m}\mathbf{x}_k,$$

when the algorithm is run for m steps. Note that $\mathbf{x}_i$ is a random variable whose values are determined by the values of the random vectors $\mathbf{v}_1, \ldots, \mathbf{v}_{i-1}$.

Theorem 14.10. *Let $f : \mathbb{R}^n \longrightarrow \mathbb{R}$ be a convex function and let $\boldsymbol{x}_*$ a point where f has a minimum. Assume that:*

   (i) *the algorithm constructs the sequence $\boldsymbol{x}_1, \ldots, \boldsymbol{x}_m$;*
   (ii) *a minimum of f is sought in the sphere $B[\mathbf{0}_n, b]$;*
   (iii) *we have $P(\boldsymbol{x}_k \in B(\mathbf{0}_n, r)) = 1$ for $1 \leqslant k \leqslant m$.*
If $\eta = \frac{b}{r\sqrt{m}}$, then $E(f(\tilde{\boldsymbol{x}})) - f(\boldsymbol{x}_*) \leqslant \frac{br}{\sqrt{m}}$.

Proof. We have

$$f(\tilde{\mathbf{x}}) - f(\mathbf{x}_*) = f\left(\frac{1}{m}\sum_{k=1}^{m}\mathbf{x}_k\right) - f(\mathbf{x}_*) \leqslant \left(\frac{1}{m}\sum_{k=1}^{m}f(\mathbf{x}_k)\right) - f(\mathbf{x}_*)$$

(by Jensen's Inequality, because f is convex)

$$= \frac{1}{m}\sum_{k=1}^{m}(f(\mathbf{x}_k) - f(\mathbf{x}_*)).$$

By taking the expectation on $\mathbf{Seq}_m(\mathbb{R}^n)$ we have

$$E_{\mathbf{v}_{1:m}}(f(\tilde{\mathbf{x}}) - f(\mathbf{x}_*)) \leqslant E_{\mathbf{v}_{1:m}}\left(\frac{1}{m}\sum_{k=1}^{m}(f(\mathbf{x}_k) - f(\mathbf{x}_*))\right).$$

Inequality (14.8) of Supplement 8 is applicable to every sequence of vectors $(\mathbf{v}_1, \ldots, \mathbf{v}_m)$. Therefore, by inequality (14.7) we have:

$$E_{\mathbf{v}_{1:m}}\left(\sum_{i=1}^{m}(\mathbf{x}_i - \mathbf{x}_*, \mathbf{v}_i)\right) \leqslant \frac{br}{\sqrt{m}}.$$

Next, we prove that

$$E_{\mathbf{v}_{1:m}}\left(\frac{1}{m}\sum_{i=1}^{m}(f(\mathbf{x}_i) - f(\mathbf{x}_*))\right) \leqslant E_{\mathbf{v}_{1:m}}\left(\frac{1}{m}\sum_{i=1}^{m}(\mathbf{x}_i - \mathbf{x}_*, \mathbf{v}_i)\right). \quad (14.6)$$

The linearity of the expectation implies

$$E_{\mathbf{v}_{1:m}}\left(\frac{1}{m}\sum_{i=1}^{m}(\mathbf{x}_i - \mathbf{x}_*, \mathbf{v}_i)\right) = \frac{1}{m}\sum_{i=1}^{m}E_{\mathbf{v}_{1:m}}(\mathbf{x}_i - \mathbf{x}_*, \mathbf{v}_i).$$

By the Tower Property of Conditional Expectations (Theorem 8.109) we have $E(g(X)) = E(E(g(X)|Y))$ for the random variables X and Y and the measurable function g. Choosing $X = \mathbf{v}_{1:t}$, $Y = \mathbf{v}_{1:t-1}$, and $g(\mathbf{v}_{1:t}) = (\mathbf{x}_t - \mathbf{x}_*, \mathbf{v}_i)_{1:t}$ we have:

$$E_{\mathbf{v}_{1:t}}((\mathbf{x}_t - \mathbf{x}_*, \mathbf{v}_i)_{1:t}) = E_{\mathbf{v}_{1:t-1}}(E_{\mathbf{v}_{1:t}}((\mathbf{x}_t - \mathbf{x}_*, \mathbf{v}_i)_{1:t}|\mathbf{v}_{1:t-1})).$$

Since the value of $\mathbf{x}_t$ is determined by $\mathbf{v}_{1:t-1}$, we have

$$E_{\mathbf{v}_{1:t-1}}(E_{\mathbf{v}_{1:t}}((\mathbf{x}_t - \mathbf{x}_*, \mathbf{v}_i)_{1:t}|\mathbf{v}_{1:t-1})) = E_{\mathbf{v}_{1:t-1}}(\mathbf{x}_t - \mathbf{x}_*, E_{\mathbf{v}_t}(\mathbf{v}_t|\mathbf{v}_{1:t-1})).$$

By the definition of the sequence $(\mathbf{v}_t)$, $E_{\mathbf{v}_t}(\mathbf{v}_t|\mathbf{x}_t) \in \mathsf{subd}(f)(\mathbf{x}_t)$. Therefore,

$$E_{\mathbf{v}_{1:t}}(\mathbf{x}_t - \mathbf{x}_*, E(\mathbf{v}_t|\mathbf{v}_{1:t-1})) \geqslant E_{\mathbf{v}_{1:t-1}}(f(\mathbf{x}_t) - f(\mathbf{x}_*)) = E_{\mathbf{v}_{1:t}}(f(\mathbf{x}_t) - f(\mathbf{x}_*)),$$

which yields inequality (14.6) after summing over t, dividing by m and using the linearity of expectation.   □

Exercises and Supplements

(1) Let $f : \mathbb{R} \longrightarrow \mathbb{R}$ be defined as $f(x) = \tanh(x)$. It is clear that f has the unique root $x_0 = 0$. Prove that
   (a) the sequence constructed by Newton's method (equality (14.1)) is
   $$x_{k+1} = x_k - \tfrac{1}{2}\sinh(2x_k) \text{ for } k \in \mathbb{N};$$
   (b) the signs of the members of the sequence (x_k) alternate;

(c) for the sequence $(|x_k|)$ we have $|x_{k+1}| = h(|x_k|)$, where $h(x) = \frac{1}{2}\sinh(2x) - x$;

(d) the equation $h(x) = x$ has the non-negative solutions $x_0 = 0$ and $\tilde{x}_0 > 1$; the sequence of approximants (x_k) where $x_0 = 0$ converges to the solution 0; the sequence $(\tilde{x}_k)$ that starts with $\tilde{x}_0$ diverges, and thus, the method fails.

(2) Let $f : \mathbb{R} \longrightarrow \mathbb{R}$ be defined by $f(x) = \arctan x$. Clearly, the equation $f(x) = 0$ has the solution $x = 0$. If (x_k) is the sequence constructed by Newton's method, $x_{k+1} = x_k - (1 + x_k^2)\arctan x_k$ starting with the initial value x_0, prove that if $\arctan |x_0| \geqslant \frac{2|x_0|}{1+x_0^2}$, then the sequence $(|x_k|)$ diverges to ∞.

(3) Prove that if $A \in \mathbb{R}^{n \times n}$ is a symmetric and positive matrix, then $\wp : \mathbb{R}^n \times \mathbb{R}^n \longrightarrow \mathbb{R}$ given by $\wp(\mathbf{x}, \mathbf{y}) = (A\mathbf{x}, \mathbf{y})$ is an inner product on $\mathbb{R}^n$.

(4) Let $A \in \mathbb{R}^{n \times n}$. The matrix is *diagonally dominant* if $|a_{ii}| > \sum\{|a_{ij}| \mid 1 \leqslant j \leqslant n, j \neq i\}$ for every i, $1 \leqslant i \leqslant n$. Prove that the matrix A is invertible.

Solution: We shall prove that if A is diagonally dominant then 0 is not an eigenvalue of A. Suppose that 0 is an eigenvalue of A, that is, $A\mathbf{x} = \mathbf{0}_n$. Let p be such that $|x_p| = \max\{|x_i| \mid 1 \leqslant i \leqslant n\}$, hence $\sum_{j=1, j\neq p}^n a_{pj}x_j = -a_{pp}x_p$. This implies

$$|a_{pp}|\,|x_p| \leqslant \sum_{j=1, j\neq p}^n |a_{pj}|\,|x_j| \leqslant |x_p| \sum_{j=1, j\neq p}^n |a_{pj}|,$$

which contradicts the fact that A is diagonally dominant.

(5) This supplement introduces *Jacobi's method* for solving the equation $A\mathbf{x} = \mathbf{b}$, where $A \in \mathbb{R}^{n \times n}$ and $\mathbf{b} \in \mathbb{R}^n$.

Let D be the diagonal matrix

$$D = \begin{pmatrix} a_{11} & 0 & \cdots & 0 \\ 0 & a_{22} & \cdots & 0 \\ \vdots & \vdots & \cdots & \vdots \\ 0 & \cdots & 0 & a_{nn} \end{pmatrix},$$

and let $E = A - D$. Suppose that $a_{ii} \neq 0$ for $1 \leqslant i \leqslant n$. Consider the iterative construction of the sequence $(\mathbf{x}_n)$ given by

$$\mathbf{x}_{i+1} = \mathbf{x}_i + D^{-1}(\mathbf{b} - A\mathbf{x}_i)$$

for $i \geqslant 0$, where $\mathbf{x}_0$ is an arbitrary initial vector. Prove that if A is a diagonally dominant matrix then $\lim_{k\to\infty} \mathbf{x}_k = \mathbf{x}_*$, where $\mathbf{x}_*$ is the solution of $A\mathbf{x} = \mathbf{b}$.

Solution: Let $\mathbf{x}_*$ be the solution of $A\mathbf{x} = \mathbf{b}$. We have $\mathbf{x}_{i+1} - \mathbf{x}_* = (\mathbf{x}_i - \mathbf{x}_*)(I_n - D^{-1}A)$ for $i \geqslant 0$. This implies $\mathbf{x}_k - \mathbf{x}_* = (\mathbf{x}_0 - \mathbf{x}_*)(I_n - D^{-1}A)^k$. Next we use the norm $\|\mathbf{x}\|_\infty = \max\{|x_i| \mid 1 \leqslant i \leqslant n\}$ and the corresponding matrix norm $\|P\|_\infty = \max_{1 \leqslant i \leqslant n} \sum_{j=1}^n |p_{ij}|$. Since

$$\|\mathbf{x}_k - \mathbf{x}_*\|_\infty \leqslant \|\mathbf{x}_0 - \mathbf{x}_*\|_\infty \|I_n - D^{-1}A\|_\infty^k,$$

it suffices to show that $\|I_n - D^{-1}A\|_\infty < 1$ to obtain the convergence of the Jacobi method. This is indeed the case because

$$\|I_n - D^{-1}A\|_\infty = \max_{1 \leqslant j \leqslant n} \sum \left\{ \frac{|a_{ji}|}{|a_{jj}|} \,\middle|\, 1 \leqslant i \leqslant n, i \neq j \right\} < 1$$

because A is diagonally dominant.

(6) Let $f : [a,b] \longrightarrow \mathbb{R}$ be a monotonic and continuous function on $[a,b]$ such that $f(a)f(b) < 0$. Thus, f has a unique root $x_* \in [a,b]$. Consider a sequence of intervals $([a_n, b_n])_{n \geqslant 1}$ constructed inductively as follows. The initial interval is $[a_1, b_1] = [a,b]$. Assume that we constructed the interval $[a_n, b_n]$ such that $f(a_n)f(b_n) < 0$. Let $c_n = \frac{a_n + b_n}{2}$. If $f(c_n) = 0$, then stop. Otherwise, $f(c_n)$ has either the sign of $f(a_n)$ or the sign of $f(b_n)$. In the first case, let $a_{n+1} = c_n$ and $b_{n+1} = b_n$; in the second case let $a_{n+1} = a_n$ and $b_{n+1} = c_n$. Prove that $|c_n - x_*| \leqslant \left(\frac{1}{2}\right)^n (b-a)$ for $n \geqslant 1$. This is the *bisection method* for finding the root x_*.

(7) Show that the function $f(x) = x^3 + x - 1$ has a root in the interval $(0,1)$. Determine the number of steps in the bisection method to approximate this root to at least within 10^{-5}.

(8) Let $(\mathbf{v}_1, \ldots, \mathbf{v}_m)$ be sequence of vectors in $\mathbb{R}^n$. Define the sequence $(\mathbf{x}_1, \ldots, \mathbf{x}_m, \mathbf{x}_{m+1})$ by $\mathbf{x}_1 = \mathbf{0}_n$ and $\mathbf{x}_{i+1} = \mathbf{x}_i - \eta \mathbf{v}_i$ for $1 \leqslant i \leqslant m$.

Prove that:

(a) for any $\mathbf{z} \in \mathbb{R}^n$ we have:

$$\sum_{i=1}^m (\mathbf{x}_i - \mathbf{z}, \mathbf{v}_i) \leqslant \frac{1}{2\eta} \|\mathbf{z}\|^2 + \frac{\eta}{2} \sum_{i=1}^m \|\mathbf{v}_i\|^2; \qquad (14.7)$$

(b) if $\|\mathbf{v}_i\| \leqslant r$, $\|\mathbf{z}\| \leqslant b$, and $\eta = \frac{b}{r\sqrt{m}}$ then

$$\frac{1}{m} \sum_{i=1}^m (\mathbf{x}_i - \mathbf{z}, \mathbf{v}_i) \leqslant \frac{br}{\sqrt{m}}. \qquad (14.8)$$

Solution: The definition of the sequence $(\mathbf{x}_i)$ allows us to write

$$(\mathbf{x}_i - \mathbf{z}, \mathbf{v}_i) = \frac{1}{\eta}(\mathbf{x}_i - \mathbf{z}, \eta\mathbf{v}_i)$$

$$= \frac{1}{2\eta}(\|\mathbf{x}_i - \mathbf{z}\|^2 + \eta^2\|\mathbf{v}_i\|^2 - \|\mathbf{x}_i - \mathbf{z} - \eta\mathbf{v}_i\|^2)$$

$$= \frac{\eta}{2}\|\mathbf{v}_i\|^2 + \frac{1}{2\eta}(\|\mathbf{x}_i - \mathbf{z}\|^2 - \|\mathbf{x}_{i+1} - \mathbf{z}\|^2)$$

for $1 \leqslant i \leqslant m - 1$. Therefore,

$$\sum_{i=1}^{m}(\mathbf{x}_i - \mathbf{z}, \mathbf{v}_i)$$

$$= \frac{1}{2\eta}\sum_{i=1}^{m}\left(\|\mathbf{x}_i - \mathbf{z}\|^2 - \|\mathbf{x}_{i+1} - \mathbf{z}\|^2\right) + \frac{\eta}{2}\sum_{i=1}^{m}\|\mathbf{v}_i\|^2$$

$$= \frac{1}{2\eta}\left(\|\mathbf{x}_1 - \mathbf{z}\|^2 - \|\mathbf{x}_{m+1} - \mathbf{z}\|^2\right) + \frac{\eta}{2}\sum_{i=1}^{m}\|\mathbf{v}_i\|^2$$

$$\leqslant \frac{1}{2\eta}\|\mathbf{x}_1 - \mathbf{z}\|^2 + \frac{\eta}{2}\sum_{i=1}^{m}\|\mathbf{v}_i\|^2 = \frac{1}{2\eta}\|\mathbf{z}\|^2 + \frac{\eta}{2}\sum_{i=1}^{m}\|\mathbf{v}_i\|^2,$$

which proves inequality (14.7).

Taking into account the assumptions made in the second part we have

$$\frac{1}{m}\sum_{i=1}^{m}(\mathbf{x}_i - \mathbf{z}, \mathbf{v}_i) \leqslant \frac{1}{2m\eta}\|\mathbf{z}\|^2 + \frac{\eta}{2m}\sum_{i=1}^{m}\|\mathbf{v}_i\|^2$$

$$= \frac{1}{2m}\frac{r\sqrt{m}}{b}\|\mathbf{z}\|^2 + \frac{b}{2mr\sqrt{m}}\sum_{i=1}^{m}\|\mathbf{v}_i\|^2 \leqslant \frac{br}{\sqrt{m}},$$

which shows inequality (14.8).

(9) Theorem 9.2 suggests an iterative method for solving equations of the form $h(x) = a$ in a Banach space L, when h is bounded linear operator on L.

Suppose that g is linear operator on L such that $\|1_L - hg\| < 1$. Define a sequence (x_n) of elements of L by

$$x_0 = g(a) \text{ and } x_{n+1} = x_n + g(a - h(x_n)) \text{ for } n \geqslant 0.$$

Prove that (x_n) is convergent to a solution of the equation $h(x) = a$.

Solution: It is clear that $x_* = g(hg)^{-1}(a)$ is a solution of equation $h(x) = 1$. Note that by Theorem 9.2, hg is invertible and $(hg)^{-1} =$

$\sum_{k=0}^{\infty}(1_L - hg)^k$. This allows to write the solution x_* as

$$x_* = g(hg)^{-1}(a) = g\sum_{k=0}^{\infty}(1_L - hg)^k(a) = \sum_{k=0}^{\infty}g(1_L - hg)^k(a).$$

We prove by induction on n that $y_n = x_n$, where $y_n = gs_n(a)$ and $s_n = \sum_0^n(1_n - hg)^k$.

For $n = 0$ we have $y_0 = g(a) = x_0$. For the inductive step assume that $y_n = x_n$. Then,

$$\begin{aligned}
x_{n+1} &= x_n + g(a - h(x_n)) = x_n + g(a) - g(h(x_n))) \\
&= y_n + g(a) - g(h(x_n))) \\
&\quad \text{(by inductive hypothesis)} \\
&= gs_n(a) + g(a) - gh(gs_n(a)) \\
&\quad \text{(by inductive hypothesis)} \\
&= g(s_n + 1_L - hgs_n)(a) = g((1_L - hg)s_n + 1_L)(a) \\
&= gs_{n+1}(a) = y_{n+1}.
\end{aligned}$$

(10) Let H be a real Hilbert space and let h be a linear positive self-adjoint operator on H. Prove that y is a solution of the equation $h(y) = b$ if and only of it is a global minimum of the functional $f : H \longrightarrow \mathbb{R}$ defined as $f(x) = (h(x) - 2b, x)$.

Solution: Let $x \in H$ and let $v \in H - \{0_H\}$. We have

$$\begin{aligned}
f(x + tv) &= (h(x + tv) - 2b, x + tv) \\
&= (h(x) + th(v) - 2b, x + tv) \\
&= t^2(h(v), v) + 2t(h(x) - b, v) + f(x).
\end{aligned}$$

The minimum of $f(x + tv)$ as a function of t occurs when t equals $t_* = -\frac{(b - h(x), v)}{(h(v), v)}$. In this case we have:

$$f(x + t_* v) = f(x) - \frac{(b - h(x), v)^2}{(h(v), v)}.$$

If $h(y) = b$, $f(y + t_* v) = f(y)$, hence no decrease of f is possible regardless of the direction v. Thus, y is a minimum of f. Conversely, if y is a global minimum of f we have $f(y) \leqslant f(y + tv)$ for every $t \in \mathbb{R}$ and $v \in H$, and this implies $-\frac{(b - h(x), v)^2}{(h(v), v)} \geqslant 0$ for every $v \in H - \{0_h\}$. This, in turn means that $h(x) = b$.

(11) Let $F : \mathbb{R}^n \longrightarrow \mathbb{R}^n$ be the affine mapping defined as $F(\mathbf{x}) = A\mathbf{x} + \mathbf{b}$, where $A \in \mathbb{R}^{n \times n}$ and $\mathbf{b} \in \mathbb{R}^n$, and let $B \in \mathbb{R}^{n \times n}$. Suppose that $\mathbf{x}, \mathbf{y} \in$

$\mathbb{R}^n$, $\mathbf{x} \neq \mathbf{y}$ and let

$$\mathbf{p} = \mathbf{x} - \mathbf{y}, \text{ and } \mathbf{q} = F(\mathbf{x}) - F(\mathbf{y}) = A\mathbf{p}.$$

Prove that the matrix $\tilde{B}$ given by

$$\tilde{B} = B + \frac{1}{\mathbf{p'p}}(\mathbf{q} - B\mathbf{p})\mathbf{p'}$$

satisfies $\|\tilde{B} - A\| \leqslant \|B - A\|$ and $\tilde{B}\mathbf{p} = A\mathbf{p} = \mathbf{q}$.

Solution: Note that $(\mathbf{q} - B\mathbf{p})\mathbf{p'} = (A\mathbf{p} - B\mathbf{p})\mathbf{p'} = (A - B)\mathbf{pp'}$. Therefore, the definition of $\tilde{B}$ implies

$$(\tilde{B} - A)\mathbf{p} = \left(B + \frac{1}{\mathbf{p'p}}(\mathbf{q} - B\mathbf{p})\mathbf{p'} - A \right)\mathbf{p} = \mathbf{0}_n.$$

Each vector $\mathbf{u} \in \mathbb{R}^n$ with $\|\mathbf{u}\| = 1$ can be written as $\mathbf{u} = a\mathbf{p} + \mathbf{v}$ such that $\mathbf{v'p} = 0$, $\|\mathbf{v}\| \leqslant 1$ and $a \in rr$. For $\mathbf{u}$ with $\|\mathbf{u}\| = 1$ we have

$$\|(\tilde{B} - A)\mathbf{u}\| = \|(\tilde{B} - A)\mathbf{v}\|$$
$$= \|(B - A)\mathbf{v}\| \leqslant \|B - A\|\|\mathbf{v}\| \leqslant \|B - A\|,$$

hence

$$\|\tilde{B} - A\| = \sup\{\|(\tilde{B} - A)\mathbf{u}\| \mid \|\mathbf{u}\| = 1\} \leqslant \|B - A\|.$$

Newton's method for solving $f(\mathbf{x}) = \mathbf{0}_n$ for a function $f : \mathbb{R}^n \longrightarrow \mathbb{R}^n$ may be quite expensive because of the need to compute the Jacobian $(Df)(\mathbf{x}_k)$ and its inverse at each iteration.

Supplement 11 shows that the Jacobian $(DF)(\mathbf{x}) = A$ of F is approximated by $\tilde{B}$ at least as well as it is approximated by B, and that both $\tilde{B}$ and A both map $\mathbf{p}$ to the same vector $\mathbf{q}$. Since a differentiable function $f : \mathbb{R}^n \longrightarrow \mathbb{R}^n$ has a first-order approximation in the neighborhood of one of its zeros $\tilde{\mathbf{x}}$ by an affine function, this suggests the following iterative process

$$\mathbf{d}_k = B_k^{-1} f(\mathbf{x}_k),$$
$$\mathbf{x}_{k+1} = \mathbf{x}_k - \lambda_k \mathbf{d}_k,$$
$$\mathbf{p}_k = \mathbf{x}_{k+1} - \mathbf{x}_k,$$
$$\mathbf{q}_k = f(\mathbf{x}_{k+1}) - f(\mathbf{x}_k).$$
$$B_{k+1} = B_k + \frac{1}{\mathbf{p}_k'\mathbf{p}_k}(\mathbf{q}_k - B_k\mathbf{p}_k)\mathbf{p}_k'.$$

This new iterative process was proposed by Broyden [24, 126].

(12) Let p be a polynomial of degree n, $n \geqslant 2$ with real coefficients and real roots, having the largest root ξ_1. Prove that Newton's method starting with a value $x_0 > \xi_1$ produces a strictly decreasing sequence (x_k) that converges to ξ_1.

Solution: Let $p(x) = a_0 x^n + \cdots + a_{n-1} x + a_n$. Without loss of generality we may assume that $p(x_0) > 0$. Therefore, if $x > \xi_1$ we have $p(x) > 0$. This implies $a_0 > 0$. By Rolle's Theorem the derivative $p'(x)$ has $n - 1$ real roots $\alpha_1, \ldots, \alpha_{n-1}$ such that

$$\xi_1 \geqslant \alpha_1 \geqslant \xi_2 \geqslant \alpha_2 \geqslant \cdots \geqslant \alpha_{n-1} \geqslant \xi_n.$$

Since p' is of degree $n - 1$, $\alpha_1, \ldots, \alpha_{n-1}$ are all its roots and $p'(x) > 0$ for $x > \alpha_1$ because $a_0 > 0$. Applying Rolle's theorem again we obtain

$$p''(x) > 0 \text{ and } p'''(x) \geqslant 0 \tag{14.9}$$

for $x \geqslant \alpha_1$. Thus, both p and p' are convex functions for $x \geqslant \alpha_1$.

Note that $x_k > \xi_1$ implies

$$x_{k+1} = x_k - \frac{p(x_k)}{p'(x_k)} < x_k$$

because $p'(x_k) > 0$ and $p(x_k) > 0$.

Since $x_k > \xi_1 \geqslant \alpha_1$, by Taylor's theorem we have

$$0 = p(\xi_1) = p(x_k) + (\xi_1 - x_k)p'(x_k) + \frac{(\xi_1 - x_k)^2}{2}p''(\delta), \xi_1 < \delta < x_k,$$
$$> p(x_k) + (\xi_1 - x_k)p'(x_k).$$

By the definition of x_{k+1} we have $p(x_k) = p'(x_k)(x_k - x_{k+1})$. Thus,

$$0 > p'(x_k)(x_k - x_{k+1} + \xi_1 - x_k) = p'(x_k)(\xi_1 - x_{k+1}),$$

hence $x_{k+1} > \xi_1$ follows because $p'(x_k) > 0$.

(13) exer:jan0518e Let $p = a_0 x^n + \cdots + a_{n-1}x + a_n$ be a polynomial with real coefficients, where $a_0 \neq 0$. If p has a complex root $a + ib$, then p has also the root $a - ib$ and p is divisible by $(x - a)^2 + b^2 = x^2 - rx - q$, where $r = 2a$ and $q = -(a^2 + b^2)$. We can write

$$p(x) = p_1(x)(x^2 - rx - s) + A(r, s)x + B(r, s),$$

where $p_1(x) = b_0 x^{n-2} + \cdots + b_{n-2}$, and seek r, q such that $A(r, s) = 0$ and $B(r, s) = 0$ in order to determine $x^2 - rx - s$ and the pair of conjugate complex roots of this trinomial. Note that q is of degree $n - 2$.

This process known as *Bairstow method* entails applying Newton's method for solving the system $A(r, s) = 0, B(r, s) = 0$. Once r and

s are determined, the pair of conjugate roots mentioned above can be determined immediately.

Newton's method applied to $A(r,s) = 0, B(r,s) = 0$ leads to the computation of the sequence of vectors $\begin{pmatrix} r_i \\ s_i \end{pmatrix}$ defined by

$$\begin{pmatrix} r_{i+1} \\ s_{i+1} \end{pmatrix} = \begin{pmatrix} r_i \\ s_i \end{pmatrix} - \begin{pmatrix} \dfrac{\partial A}{\partial r} & \dfrac{\partial A}{\partial s} \\ \dfrac{\partial B}{\partial r} & \dfrac{\partial B}{\partial s} \end{pmatrix}^{-1} \begin{pmatrix} A \\ B \end{pmatrix}.$$

By dividing p_1 by $x^2 - rx - s$ we have

$$p_1(x) = p_2(x)(x^2 - rx - s) + A_1 x + B_1.$$

Prove that:

(a) the partial derivatives that enter Newton's scheme are given by:

$$\frac{\partial A}{\partial s} = A_1, \frac{\partial B}{\partial s} = B_1,$$

$$\frac{\partial A}{\partial r} = rA_1 + B_1, \frac{\partial B}{\partial r} = sA_1;$$

(b) the coefficients of p_1 are:

$$b_0 = a_0, b_1 = b_0 r + a_1,$$
$$b_i = b_{i-2}s + b_{i-1}r + a_i \text{ for } 2 \leqslant i \leqslant n-2,$$
$$A = b_{n-3}s + b_{n-2}r + a_{n-1},$$
$$B = b_{n-2}s + a_n.$$

(14) *Regula falsi* is an interpolation method that can be used to solve equations of the form $f(x) = 0$ for a continuous function f. It consists of an iterative process that constructs a sequence of pairs (a_i, x_i) such that $f(a_i)f(x_i) < 0$. Thus, each interval $[x_i, a_i]$ contains a zero of f.

Let $p(x) = f(x_i) + (x - x_i)\frac{f(x_i)-f(a_i)}{x_i-a_i}$, and let $\mu_i = \frac{a_i f(x_i)-x_i f(a_i)}{f(x_i)-f(a_i)}$ be the zero of $p(x)$. Note that μ_i is well-defined because $f(x_i)f(a_i) < 0$ implies $f(x_i) \neq f(a_i)$.

IF $f(\mu_i) = 0$ the algorithm stops; otherwise, define $x_{i+1} = \mu_i$ and

$$a_{i+1} = \begin{cases} a_i & \text{if } f(\mu_i)f(x_i) > 0, \\ x_i & \text{if } f(\mu_i)f(x_i) < 0. \end{cases}$$

Suppose that $f''(x)$ exists, $x_i < a_i$, $f(x_i) < 0 < f(a_i)$, and $f''(x) \geqslant 0$ for $x \in [x_i, a_i]$. Prove that the sequence (x_i) converges linearly to a zero of f.

Bibliographical Comments

Newton's algorithm and many of its variants is discussed in [86], and in [126] from a numerical perspective. The treatment of conjugate-direction methods follows [71]. The method of conjugate gradients was introduced in [78].

Two important and readable sources for iterative algorithms are [29, 71]. An encyclopedic source for numerical algorithms is [126].

Chapter 15

Neural Networks

15.1 Introduction

In this chapter we discuss application of mathematical analysis techniques in the study of neural networks (NN).

Neural networks are aggregates of computational devices referred to as *neurons* that model loosely the working of biological components of nervous systems (also named neurons).

The use of NNs, as a part of the more general paradigm of *neural computing* has broad applications in pattern recognition and in various types of data analysis. After discussing the neuron as the main component of a NN, we focus on a common architectures of NN. Properties of NN as universal approximators are treated in Section 15.4. Finally in Supplements where we present in detail the rich collection of results contained in [83, 82, 60, 62].

15.2 Neurons

The time in an NN is discrete, which means that it varies in the set $\mathbb{N}$. The current time is $t \in \mathbb{N}$, the next time is $t + 1$ and the preceding one is $t - 1$.

Informally, a neural network is a directed graph whose set of nodes N consists of *neurons*; edges of this graph represent the information flows between neurons. As we shall see, there are several types of neural networks depending on the structure of the underlying graph.

A neuron is defined by a *threshold value* θ, an *activation function* $\sigma :$ $\mathbb{R} \longrightarrow \mathbb{R}$ and a *vector of weights* $\mathbf{w} \in \mathbb{R}^n$. When an input vector $\mathbf{x} \in \mathbb{R}^n$ is fed into the n inputs of the neuron, the processing unit computes $y = \sigma(\mathbf{w}'\mathbf{x} + \theta)$. The value of y is taken as the unit output.

Definition 15.1. A *sigmoidal function* or a *squashing function* is a non-decreasing function $\sigma : \mathbb{R} \longrightarrow \mathbb{R}$ such that $\lim_{x \to \infty} \sigma(x) = 1$ and $\lim_{x \to -\infty} \sigma(x) = 0$.

In general, activation functions are sigmoidal functions. By Theorem 4.62, the set of their discontinuity points of the first kind is at most countable, and therefore, they are measurable functions by Corollary 7.7. The monotonicity may be dropped if measurability is required explicitly.

Example 15.1. Several of the most common sigmoidal activation functions are listed next:

(i) The *Heaviside function* is the function f defined by:

$$f(x) = \begin{cases} 1 & \text{if } x \geqslant 0, \\ 0 & \text{if } x < 0. \end{cases}$$

This function is discontinuous at $x = 0$.

(ii) The *Fermi logistic function* is defined as

$$f_T(x) = \frac{1}{1 - e^{-\frac{x}{T}}},$$

where $T > 0$ is a parameter, is continuous everywhere and ranges in the open interval $(0, 1)$.

(iii) The *logistic function* is given by $L(x) = \frac{e^x}{1 + e^x}$.

(iv) The *ramp function* is given by

$$f(x) = \begin{cases} 0 & \text{if } x < 0, \\ x & \text{if } 0 \leqslant x \leqslant 1, \\ 1 & \text{if } x > 1. \end{cases}$$

(v) The *cosine squasher* of Gallant and White [62] is the function csq given by:

$$\text{csq}(x) = \begin{cases} 0 & \text{if } x \in \left(-\infty, -\frac{\pi}{2}\right], \\ \dfrac{\cos\left(x + \dfrac{3\pi}{2}\right) + 1}{2} & \text{if } x \in \left(-\frac{\pi}{2}, \frac{\pi}{2}\right), \\ 1 & \text{if } x \in \left[\frac{\pi}{2}, \infty\right) \end{cases}$$

$$= \begin{cases} 0 & \text{if } x \in \left(-\infty, -\frac{\pi}{2}\right], \\ \dfrac{1 + \sin x}{2} & \text{if } x \in \left(-\frac{\pi}{2}, \frac{\pi}{2}\right), \\ 1 & \text{if } x \in \left[\frac{\pi}{2}, \infty\right). \end{cases}$$

15.3 Neural Networks

Definition 15.2. A *neural network* (NN) is a triplet $\mathcal{N} = (N, E, w)$, where $\mathcal{G} = (N, E)$ is a graph (as above) and $w : E \longrightarrow \mathbb{R}$ is a function that specifies the weight $w(i, j)$ of an edge (i, j) between the neurons i and j. We denote by $w_{ij} = w(i, j)$ the weight of the connection between the neurons i and j.

A simple NN consists of a layer of n input units and a layer of m processing units (see Figure 15.1).

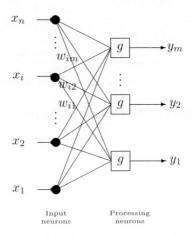

Fig. 15.1   Simple neural network with n input neurons and m processing neurons.

A neural network can be extended to include an output unit that sums the outputs of the processing units (see Figure 15.2).

The network can be trained to approximate a class of functions $\mathcal{F}$ of the form $f : \mathbb{R}^n \longrightarrow \mathbb{R}^m$. When the network is supplied with new examples $(\mathbf{x}, f(\mathbf{x}))$, where $\mathbf{x} \in \mathbb{R}^n$ an algorithm is applied to modify the weights w_{ij} and the thresholds θ_j such that the difference between $f(\mathbf{x})$ and the network output $\mathbf{y} = \begin{pmatrix} y_1 \\ \vdots \\ y_m \end{pmatrix}$ is minimized.

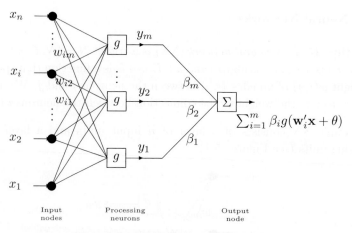

Fig. 15.2   Single output neural network.

15.4   Neural Networks as Universal Approximators

Let $I_n = [0, 1]^n$ be the n-dimensional cube. The set of finite signed regular Borel measures on I_n is denoted by $M(I_n)$. In [37] it is shown that sums of sigmoidal functions of the form $\sum_{i=1}^{N} \alpha_j \sigma(\mathbf{w}_j' \mathbf{x} + \theta_j)$ are dense in the space $C(I_n)$ of real-valued continuous on I_n equipped with the metric d_{sup} for any sigmoidal function σ.

Definition 15.3. Let m be a finite signed regular Borel measure on I_n. A function $\sigma \in C(I_n)$ is *discriminatory* relative to m if

$$\int_{I_n} \sigma(\mathbf{w}'\mathbf{x} + \theta) \, dm = 0$$

for all $\mathbf{w} \in I_n$ and $\theta \in \mathbb{R}$ imply $m = 0$.

Theorem 15.1. *Let σ be a continuous discriminatory function. Then the set of finite sums of the form $g(x) = \sum_{i=1}^{N} \alpha_j \sigma(\mathbf{w}_j' \mathbf{x} + \theta_j)$ is dense in $C(I_n)$.*

Proof.   The statement amounts to the fact that for every $f \in C(I_n)$ and $\epsilon > 0$, there exists a sum $g(x)$ of the above form such that $|g(x) - f(x)| < \epsilon$ for $x \in I_n$.

Let S be the subset of $C(I_n)$ that consist of functions the form $g(x) = \sum_{i=1}^{N} \alpha_j \sigma(\mathbf{w}_j' \mathbf{x} + \theta_j)$. It is clear that S is a linear subspace of $C(I_n)$.

Suppose that the topological closure $R = \mathbf{K}(S)$ of S is strictly included in $C(I_n)$, that is, S is not dense in $C(I_n)$. Then R is a closed proper subspace of $C(I_n)$. By the Hahn-Banach theorem, there is a non-zero bounded linear functional ℓ on $C(_n)$ such that $\ell(R) = 0$ (hence $\ell(S) = 0$).

By the Riesz-Kakutani Theorem (Theorem 8.69), ℓ is of the form $\ell(h) = \int_{I_n} h(x)\, dm$ for some measure $m \in M(I_n)$ for all $h \in C(I_n)$. In particular, since $\sigma(\mathbf{w}'\mathbf{x} + \theta) \in R$ for all $\mathbf{w}$ and θ, we must have $\int_{I_n} \sigma(\mathbf{w}'\mathbf{x} + \theta)\, dm = 0$ for all $\mathbf{w}$ and θ.

Since σ is discriminatory, $m = 0$, which contradicts the fact that ℓ is not zero. Hence $R = C(I_n)$ and therefore S must be dense in $C(I_n)$. $\quad\square$

Theorem 15.2. *Any bounded and measurable sigmoidal function σ is discriminatory.*

Proof. Let $\sigma \in C(I_n)$ be a function such that $\int_{I_n} \sigma(\mathbf{w}'\mathbf{x} + \theta)\, dm = 0$ for all $\mathbf{w} \in I_n$ and $\theta \in \mathbb{R}$. Note that for the function σ_λ defined by

$$\sigma_{\lambda,\phi}(\mathbf{x}) = \sigma(\lambda(\mathbf{w}'\mathbf{x} + \theta) + \phi)$$

for $\mathbf{x} \in I_n$ enjoys the same property, namely $\int_{I_n} \sigma_{\lambda,\phi}(\mathbf{w}'\mathbf{x} + \theta)\, dm = 0$ for all $\mathbf{w} \in I_n$ and $\theta \in \mathbb{R}$. In other words, σ is discriminatory if and only if each function $\sigma_{\lambda,\phi}$ is discriminatory.

If $\mathbf{w}'\mathbf{x} + \theta = 0$ we have $\sigma(\lambda(\mathbf{w}'\mathbf{x} + \theta) + \phi) = \sigma(\phi)$. Furthermore,

$$\lim_{\lambda \to \infty} \sigma(\lambda(\mathbf{w}'\mathbf{x} + \theta) + \phi) = \begin{cases} 1 & \text{if } \mathbf{w}'\mathbf{x} + \theta > 0, \\ 0 & \text{if } \mathbf{w}'\mathbf{x} + \theta < 0, \end{cases}$$

and $\sigma(\lambda(\mathbf{w}'\mathbf{x} + \theta) + \phi) = \sigma(\phi)$ if $\mathbf{w}'\mathbf{x} + \theta = 0$.

The family of functions $\{\sigma_{\lambda,\phi} \mid \lambda \in \mathbb{R}_{\geqslant 0}\}$ converges pointwise to and is dominated by the integrable function $\gamma : I_n \longrightarrow \mathbb{R}$ defined by

$$\gamma(x) = \begin{cases} 1 & \text{if } \mathbf{w}'\mathbf{x} + \theta > 0, \\ 0 & \text{if } \mathbf{w}'\mathbf{x} + \theta < 0, \\ \sigma(\phi) & \text{if } \mathbf{w}'\mathbf{x} + \theta = 0. \end{cases}$$

Let $H_{\mathbf{w},-\theta}$ be a hyperplane and let $H^{>0}_{\mathbf{w},-\theta}$ be the corresponding half-space. By the Dominated Convergence Theorem (Theorem 8.37) $\lim_{\lambda \to \infty} \int_{I_n} \sigma_\lambda\, dm = \int_{I_n} \gamma\, dm$.

Note that

$$0 = \int_{I_n} \sigma_\lambda\, dm = \int_{H^{>0}_{\mathbf{w},-\theta}} \sigma_\lambda\, dm + \int_{H_{\mathbf{w},-\theta}} \sigma_\lambda\, dm + \int_{H^{<0}_{\mathbf{w},-\theta}} \sigma_\lambda\, dm$$

$$= \int_{H^{>0}_{\mathbf{w},-\theta}} 1\, dm + \int_{H_{\mathbf{w},-\theta}} \sigma(\phi)\, dm$$

$$= m(H^{>0}_{\mathbf{w},-\theta}) + \sigma(\phi)m(H_{\mathbf{w},-\theta}).$$

For a fixed $\mathbf{y} \in \mathbb{R}^n$ let $J_{\mathbf{y}}$ be a compact interval that contains the set $\{\mathbf{y}'\mathbf{x} \mid \mathbf{x} \in I_n\}$. Define the linear functional F as

$$F(h) = \int_{I_n} h(\mathbf{y}'\mathbf{x}) dm_{\mathbf{x}}.$$

Since μ is a finite signed measure, F is a bounded functional on $L^\infty(J)$. Taking $h = 1_{[\theta,\infty)}$ we have

$$F(h) = \int_{I_n} h(\mathbf{y}'\mathbf{x}) dm_{\mathbf{x}} = m(H_{\mathbf{w},\theta}) + \sigma()m() = 0.$$

Similarly, $F(h) = 0$ if $h = 1_{(\theta,\infty)}$. By linearity, $F(h) = 0$ for the indicator function of any interval and, therefore for any simple function. Since simple functions are dense in $L^\infty(J)$, if follows that $F = 0$.

In particular, the bounded measurable functions $s(\mathbf{u}) = \sin(\mathbf{m}'\mathbf{u})$ and $c(\mathbf{u}) = \cos(\mathbf{m}'\mathbf{u})$ yield

$$\hat{m} = \int_{I_n} (\cos \mathbf{m}'\mathbf{x} + i \sin \mathbf{m}'\mathbf{x}) \, dm = \int_{I_n} e^{i(\mathbf{m},\mathbf{x})} \, dm = 0,$$

hence $m = 0$ because its Fourier transform is 0. Thus, σ is discriminatory. $\square$

Networks with one internal layer and arbitrary continuous sigmoidal functions can approximate continuous functions with any precision, provided that no constraints are imposed on the number of nodes or the magnitude of the weights.

Corollary 15.1. *Let σ be any continuous sigmoidal function. Then finite sums of the form $g(x) = \sum_{i=1}^{N} \alpha_j \sigma(\mathbf{w}'_j \mathbf{x} + \theta_j)$ are dense in $C(I_n)$. In other words, for any $f \in C(I_n)$ and $\epsilon > 0$ there exists a function g as above such that $\|g(x) - f(x)\| < \epsilon$ for $x \in I_n$.*

Proof.   This statement follows from the fact that continuous sigmoidal functions are discriminatory. $\square$

Let $\pi = \{P_1, \dots, P_k\}$ be a partition of I_n, where P_i is m_L-measurable subsets of I_n for $1 \leqslant i \leqslant k$. Define the *decision function* $f_\pi : I_n \longrightarrow \{1, \dots, k\}$ as $f(x) = j$ if $x \in P_j$.

Theorem 15.3. *Let σ be a continuous sigmoidal function and let f_π be the decision function of the finite measurable partition π of I_n. For any $\epsilon > 0$ there is a finite sum of the form $g(x) = \sum_{i=1}^{N} \alpha_j \sigma(\mathbf{w}'_j \mathbf{x} + \theta_j)$ and a set $D \subseteq I_n$ so that $m_L(D) \geqslant 1 - \epsilon$ and $|g(x) - f(x)| < \epsilon$ for $x \in D$.*

Proof. By Lusin's Theorem (Supplement 49 of Chapter 8) there is a continuous function h and a set D with $m(D) \geqslant 1 - \epsilon$ so that $h(x) = f(x)$ for $x \in D$. Since h is continuous, by Corollary 15.1 there is a sum of the form $g(x) = \sum_{i=1}^{N} \alpha_j \sigma(\mathbf{w}'_j \mathbf{x} + \theta_j)$ that satisfies $|g(x) - h(x)| < \epsilon$ for all $x \in I_n$. Then, for $x \in D$ we have $|g(x) - f(x)| = |g(x) - h(x)| < \epsilon$. $\qquad \square$

15.5 Weight Adjustment by Back Propagation

We consider now a neural network architecture involving three layers of vertices: input nodes, inner layer neurons, and output layer neurons. The task of the network is to learn an approximation of a bounded function $\mathbf{f} : A \longrightarrow \mathbb{R}^h$, where A is a compact subset of $\mathbb{R}^n$. The training set is $((\mathbf{x}_1, \mathbf{t}_1), \ldots, (\mathbf{x}_m, \mathbf{t}_m)) \in \mathbf{Seq}(\mathbb{R}^n \times \mathbb{R}^h)$, where $\mathbf{x}_1, \ldots, \mathbf{x}_m$ are m input vectors that are randomly selected from A, and $\mathbf{t}_1, \ldots, \mathbf{t}_m$ are the expected output vectors, respectively, where $\mathbf{t}_i = \mathbf{f}(\mathbf{x}_i)$ for $1 \leqslant i \leqslant m$.

The back propagation process consists of two phases: in the first phase (the forward pass) vectors $\mathbf{x}_j$ are supplied to the input units and the output $\mathbf{y}_j$ is collected from the output units. Then the correct output $\mathbf{t}_j$ is compared to $\mathbf{y}_j$ and a second backward sweep of the network involving weight adjustments begins.

The activation functions of the internal nodes and of the output nodes are assumed to be the logistic functions $L : \mathbb{R} \longrightarrow \mathbb{R}$ having the form $L(x) = \frac{e^x}{1+e^x}$. Note that

$$L'(x) = \frac{e^x}{(1 + e^x)^2} = L(x)(1 - L(x)) \tag{15.1}$$

for $x \in \mathbb{R}$.

The weights w_{ij} of the edges of a neural network are adjusted through a sequential process. Suppose that the training sample of a neural network is the sequence $((\mathbf{x}_1, \mathbf{t}_1), \ldots, (\mathbf{x}_m, \mathbf{t}_m)) \in \mathbf{Seq}(\mathbb{R}^n \times \mathbb{R}^h)$, where $\mathbf{x}_1, \ldots, \mathbf{x}_m$ are the input vectors and $\mathbf{t}_1, \ldots, \mathbf{t}_m$ are the expected output vectors, respectively. In general, the network will produce the outputs $\mathbf{y}_1, \ldots, \mathbf{y}_m$ instead of $\mathbf{t}_1, \ldots, \mathbf{t}_m$, which will trigger an incremental readjustment process of the weights of the network w_{ij}.

When the expected output is $\mathbf{t}$ and the network produces the answer $\mathbf{y}$, the error of the network is the function $R : \mathbb{R}^{n \times k} \times \mathbb{R}^{k \times h} \longrightarrow \mathbb{R}$ defined as $R(V; W) = \frac{1}{2}\|\mathbf{t} - \mathbf{y}\|^2$, where $V = (v_{\ell i}) \in \mathbb{R}^{n \times k}$ is the matrix of weights of edges between input units and neurons in the hidden layer, and $W = (w_{ij})$,

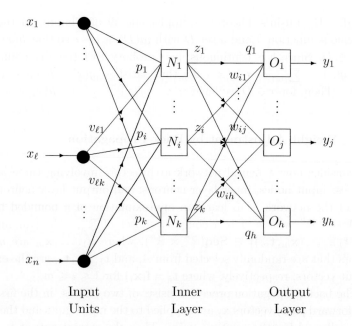

Fig. 15.3　Neural networks with inner and output neurons.

w_{ij} is the matrix of weights of the edges between the hidden and the output neurons (see Figure 15.3).

The jth component of the input vector $\mathbf{x}_i$ is denoted by x_{ij}.

The set of indices of output neurons connected to the neuron N_i from the hidden layer is denoted by $D(i)$.

The input of an inner layer neuron N_i is $p_i = \sum_{\ell=1}^{n} x_\ell v_{\ell i}$ for $1 \leqslant i \leqslant k$; the input of an output layer neuron O_j is $q_j = \sum_{i=1}^{k} w_{ij} z_i$ for $1 \leqslant j \leqslant h$, where z_i is the output of the hidden layer neuron N_i.

Finding a minimum of $R(V;W)$ using a gradient descent algorithm (actually a stochastic gradient descent) requires the computation of $\nabla R(V;W)$, that is, of the partial derivatives $\frac{\partial R(V;W)}{\partial v_{\ell i}}$ and $\frac{\partial R(V;W)}{\partial w_{ij}}$.

$R(V;W)$ depends on $v_{\ell i}$ via p_i; therefore,

$$\frac{\partial R(V;W)}{\partial v_{\ell i}} = \frac{\partial R(V;W)}{\partial p_i} \frac{\partial p_i}{\partial v_{\ell i}} = \frac{\partial R(V;W)}{\partial p_i} x_\ell.$$

Similarly, $R(V;W)$ depends on w_{ij} via q_j, the input of the output neuron O_j.

Thus, we have:

$$\frac{\partial R(V;W)}{\partial w_{ij}} = \frac{\partial R(V;W)}{\partial q_j}\frac{\partial q_j}{\partial w_{ij}} = \frac{\partial R(V;W)}{\partial q_j}z_i.$$

To compute the error gradient component $\frac{\partial R(V;W)}{\partial w_{ij}}$ for an output neuron observe that $R(V;W)$ depends on q_j via y_j, the output of O_j. Thus,

$$\frac{\partial R(V;W)}{\partial q_j} = \frac{\partial R(V;W)}{\partial y_j}\frac{\partial y_j}{\partial q_j}.$$

Since $R(V;W) = \frac{1}{2}\|\mathbf{t} - \mathbf{y}\|^2 = \frac{1}{2}\sum_{j=1}^{h}(t_j - y_j)^2$, we have:

$$\frac{\partial R(V;W)}{\partial y_j} = -(t_j - y_j).$$

Since $y_j = L(q_j)$,

$$\frac{\partial y_j}{\partial q_j} = L(q_j)(1 - L(q_j)),$$

which allows us to write

$$\frac{\partial R(V;W)}{\partial q_j} = -(t_j - y_j)L(q_j)(1 - L(q_j)),$$

hence

$$\frac{\partial R(V;W)}{\partial w_{ij}} = -(t_j - y_j)L(q_j)(1 - L(q_j))z_i.$$

To compute the error gradient component $\frac{\partial R(V;W)}{\partial v_{\ell i}}$ for an inner layer neuron note that $v_{\ell i}$ influences the error through the output neurons in D_i located downstream from N_i. Therefore, we have:

$$\frac{\partial R(V;W)}{\partial p_i} = \sum_{j\in D(i)}\frac{\partial R(V;W)}{\partial q_j}\frac{\partial q_j}{\partial p_i}$$

$$= \sum_{j\in D(i)}\frac{\partial R(V;W)}{\partial q_j}\frac{\partial q_j}{\partial z_i}\frac{\partial z_i}{\partial p_i}$$

$$= -z_i(1 - z_i)\sum_{j\in D(i)}(t_j - y_j)L(q_j)(1 - L(q_j))w_{ij},$$

because $\frac{\partial q_j}{\partial z_i} = w_{ij}$ and $\frac{\partial z_i}{\partial p_i} = z_i(1 - z_i)$.

Weights of the network are adjusted using the gradient descent rule $v_{\ell i} := v_{\ell i} - \eta\frac{\partial R(V;W)}{\partial v_{\ell i}}$ and $w_{ij} := w_{ij} - \eta\frac{\partial R(V;W)}{\partial w_{ij}}$, where η is a small positive constant called the *learning rate*.

Exercises and Supplements

Several notations for classes of functions are needed to present some of the rich collection of approximation results given in [82].

- the set of affine functions $h : \mathbb{R}^r \longrightarrow \mathbb{R}$ of the form $h(\mathbf{x}) = \mathbf{a}'\mathbf{x} + b$, where $\mathbf{a}' \in \mathbb{R}^r\}$ is denoted by $\mathbb{A}^r$;

- for a Borel measurable function $g : \mathbb{R}^r \longrightarrow \mathbb{R}$ the class of function $\Sigma^r(g)$ consists of functions of the form $f : \mathbb{R}^r \longrightarrow \mathbb{R}$ given by:

$$f(\mathbf{x}) = \sum_{j=1}^{q} \beta_j g(h_j(\mathbf{x})),$$

where $\beta_j \in \mathbb{R}$ and $h_j \in \mathbb{A}^r$ for $1 \leqslant j \leqslant q$; networks that implement these functions consist of a single layer of neurons having activation function g;

- the class $\Sigma\Pi^r(g)$ consists of functions $f : \mathbb{R}^r \longrightarrow \mathbb{R}$ of the form

$$f(\mathbf{x}) = \sum_{j=1}^{q} \beta_i \prod_{k=1}^{\ell_j} g(h_{jk}(\mathbf{x})),$$

where $h_j \in \mathbb{A}^r$ for $1 \leqslant j \leqslant q$ and $1 \leqslant k \leqslant \ell_j$;

- the set of continuous functions of the form $f : \mathbb{R}^r \longrightarrow \mathbb{R}$ is denoted by C^r;

- the set of Borel measurable functions from $\mathbb{R}^r$ to $\mathbb{R}$ is denoted by M^r.

Also, by Theorem 7.13, we have $C^r \subseteq \mathbb{B}(\mathbb{R}^r)$.

(1) For every Borel measurable function g we have:

$$\Sigma^r(g) \subseteq \mathbb{B}(\mathbb{R}^r) \text{ and } \Sigma\Pi^r(g) \subseteq \mathbb{B}(\mathbb{R}^r).$$

(2) Let M be a positive integer. Prove that for the cosine squasher csq we have:

$$\sum_{m=-M}^{M} 2 \left[\text{csq}\left(-t + \frac{\pi}{2} - 2\pi m\right) + \text{csq}\left(t - \frac{3\pi}{2} + 2\pi m\right) - 1 \right]$$

$$= \begin{cases} 0 & \text{if } -\infty < t < -2\pi M, \\ \cos t - 1 & \text{if } -2\pi M \leqslant t \leqslant 2\pi(M+1), \\ 0 & \text{if } 2\pi(M+1) < t < \infty. \end{cases}$$

Solution: The definition of csq allows us to write

$$\operatorname{csq}\left(t - \frac{3\pi}{2} + 2\pi m\right) = \begin{cases} 0 & \text{if } t \leqslant \pi - 2\pi m, \\ \frac{\cos t + 1}{2} & \text{if } \pi - 2\pi m < t < 2\pi - 2\pi m, \\ 1 & \text{if } t \geqslant 2\pi - 2\pi m, \end{cases}$$

and

$$\operatorname{csq}\left(-t + \frac{\pi}{2} - 2\pi m\right) = \begin{cases} 0 & \text{if } t \geqslant \pi - 2\pi m, \\ \frac{\cos t + 1}{2} & \text{if } -2\pi m < t < \pi - 2\pi m, \\ 1 & \text{if } t \leqslant -2\pi m. \end{cases}$$

Substituting these expressions in the left member of the equality of the supplement yields the right member.

Let K be a compact subset of $\mathbb{R}^r$. Define the semi-metric d_K on C^r as

$$d_K(f, g) = \sup_{x \in K} |f(x) - g(x)|.$$

A sequence of functions (f_n) in C^r *converges to a function f uniformly on compact sets* if for all compact subsets K of $\mathbb{R}^n$ we have $\lim_{n \to \infty} d_K(f_n, f) = 0$.

A set S of continuous functions of the form $f : \mathbb{R}^r \longrightarrow \mathbb{R}$ is *uniformly dense on compact sets* in C^r if for every $\epsilon > 0$, compact set K, and for every $g \in C^r$, there is $f \in S$ such that $d_K(f, g) < \epsilon$.

(3) If $g : \mathbb{R} \longrightarrow \mathbb{R}$ is a continuous non-constant function, prove that $\Sigma\Pi^r(g)$ is uniformly dense on compact sets in C^r. This means that $\Sigma\Pi$ NNs are capable of approximating arbitrarily close any real-valued continuous function over a compact set.

    Solution: Let K be an arbitrary compact set in $\mathbb{R}^r$. It is immediate that for any g, $\Sigma\Pi^r(g)$ is an algebra of functions defined on K. If $\mathbf{x}, \mathbf{y} \in K$ and $\mathbf{x} \neq \mathbf{y}$, there exists an affine function $h \in \mathbb{A}^r$ such that $g(h(\mathbf{x})) \neq g(h(\mathbf{y}))$. Indeed, since g is not a constant function there exist $a, b \in \mathbb{R}$ such that $a \neq b$ and $g(a) \neq g(b)$. Let h be such that $h(\mathbf{x}) = a$ and $h(\mathbf{y}) = b$. Then, $g(h(\mathbf{x})) \neq g(h(\mathbf{y}))$, so $\Sigma\Pi^r(g)$ separates points. Therefore, $\Sigma\Pi^r(g)$ is separating on K.

    Let $b \in \mathbb{R}$ be such that $g(b) \neq 0$ and define h as $h(\mathbf{x}) = \mathbf{0}_r'\mathbf{x} + b$. For all $\mathbf{x} \in K$, $g(h(\mathbf{x})) = g(b)$, so $\Sigma\Pi^r(g)$ contains the constant functions. The Stone-Weierstrass Theorem (Theorem 5.40) implies that $\Sigma\Pi^r(g)$ is uniformly dense on compact sets in C^r.

(4) Let d be the semi-metric introduced in Exercise 18 of Chapter 7 on $\mathbb{B}(\mathbb{R}^r)$, the set of Borel measurable functions of r arguments.

Prove that the following statements that concern a sequence (f_n) of functions in $\mathbb{B}(\mathbb{R}^r)$ and a function $f :\in \mathbb{B}(\mathbb{R}^r)$ are equivalent:

(a) $\lim_{n \to \infty} d(f_n, f) = 0$;
(b) for every $\epsilon > 0$, $\lim_{n \to \infty} m_L(\{\mathbf{x} \mid |f_n(\mathbf{x}) - f(\mathbf{x})| > \epsilon\}) = 0$;
(c) $\lim_{n \to \infty} \int_{\mathbb{R}^r} \min\{|f_n(\mathbf{x}) - f(\mathbf{x})|, 1\} \, dm_L = 0$.

Solution: The equivalence of the first two parts is immediate.

Define the subsets A_n, B_n of $\mathbb{R}^r$ as:

$$A_n = \{\mathbf{x} \in \mathbb{R}^r \mid |f_n(\mathbf{x}) - f(\mathbf{x})| \leqslant 1\} \text{ and}$$
$$B_n = \{\mathbf{x} \in \mathbb{R}^r \mid |f_n(\mathbf{x}) - f(\mathbf{x})| > 1\}.$$

Clearly, A_n and B_n partition $\mathbb{R}^r$ and we have:

$$\int_{\mathbb{R}^r} \min\{|f_n(\mathbf{x}) - f(\mathbf{x})|, 1\} \, dm_L$$
$$= \int_{A_n} \min\{|f_n(\mathbf{x}) - f(\mathbf{x})|, 1\} \, dm_L + \int_{B_n} \min\{|f_n(\mathbf{x}) - f(\mathbf{x})|, 1\} \, dm_L$$
$$= \int_{A_n} |f_n(\mathbf{x}) - f(\mathbf{x})| \, dm_L + \int_{B_n} 1 \, dm_L.$$

Suppose that the second statement holds. Then, for sufficiently large n we have

$$\int_{A_n} |f_n(\mathbf{x}) - f(\mathbf{x})| \, dm_L < \frac{\epsilon}{2},$$

and

$$\int_{B_n} 1 \, dm_L < \frac{\epsilon}{2},$$

hence

$$\int_{\mathbb{R}^r} \min\{|f_n(\mathbf{x}) - f(\mathbf{x})|, 1\} \, dm_L < \epsilon$$

when n is sufficiently large, and this implies the third statement.

The third statement implies the second by Markov's inequality.

Recall that the semimetric $\eth$ on M^r was introduced in Supplement 18 of Chapter 7. It will play an important role in the current collection of supplements.

(5) If (f_n) is a sequence of functions in M^r that converges uniformly on compacta to a function f, prove that $\lim_{n \to \infty} \eth(f_n, f) = 0$.

Solution: Let ϵ be a positive number. By Supplement 4, it suffices to find $n_0 \in \mathbb{N}$ such that for all $n \geqslant n_0$, we have $\int \min\{f_n(x) - f(x), 1\} \, dm < \epsilon$. Without loss of generality we can assume that $m(\mathbb{R}^r) = 1$. By Theorem 7.61 m is a regular measure. There exists a compact subset K

of $\mathbb{R}^r$ with $m(K) > 1 - \epsilon/2$. Choose n_0 such that for $n \geqslant n_0$ we have $\sup_{x \in K} |f_n(x) - f(x)| < \epsilon/2$. Now,

$$\int_{\mathbb{R}^r - K} \min\{f_n(x) - f(x), 1\} \, dm + \int_K \min\{f_n(x) - f(x), 1\} \, dm < \epsilon$$

for $n \geqslant n_0$.

(6) Prove that for every continuous non-constant function g, every r, and every measure space $(\mathbb{R}^r, \mathbb{B}(\mathbb{R}^r), m)$ with $m(\mathbb{R}^r) < \infty$, $\Sigma\Pi^r(g)$ is $\eth$-dense in M^r, where $\eth$ is the semimetric introduced in Exercise 18 of Chapter 7.

Solution: Since g is a continuous non-constant function, by Supplement 3, $\Sigma\Pi^r(g)$ is $\eth$-dense on compact sets in C^r. On other hand, since C^r is $\eth$-dense in M^r, it follows that $\Sigma\Pi^r(g)$ is $\eth$-dense in M^r.

(7) Prove that for every continuous squashing function f, every squashing function ψ, and every $\epsilon > 0$ there is a function $g_\epsilon \in \Sigma^1(\psi)$ such that $\sup_{\lambda \in \mathbb{R}} |f(\lambda) - g_\epsilon(\lambda)| < \epsilon$.

Solution: Let $\epsilon \in (0, 1)$. We seek a finite set $\{\beta_1, \ldots, \beta_{q-1}\}$ such that

$$\sup_{\lambda \in \mathbb{R}} \left| f(\lambda) - \sum_{j=1}^{q-1} \beta_j \psi(h_j(\lambda)) \right| < \epsilon,$$

where $\beta_j \in \mathbb{R}$ and $h_j \in \mathbb{A}^r$ for $1 \leqslant j \leqslant q - 1$. Let q be such that $q > 2/\epsilon$. For $j \in \{1, \ldots, q - 1\}$ let $\beta_j = \frac{1}{q}$. Since ψ is a squashing function there exists M such that:

$$\psi(-M) < \frac{\epsilon}{2q} \text{ and } \psi(M) > 1 - \frac{\epsilon}{2q}.$$

Since f is a continuous squashing function there exist $r_1, \ldots, r_q$ defined by:

$$r_j = \sup \left\{ \lambda \middle| f(\lambda) = \frac{j}{q} \right\} \text{ for } 1 \leqslant j \leqslant q - 1,$$

$$r_q = \sup \left\{ \lambda \middle| f(\lambda) = 1 - \frac{1}{2q} \right\}.$$

For any $r < s$ let $h_{r,s}$ be the unique affine function that satisfies the equalities $h_{r,s}(r) = M$ and $h_{r,s}(s) = -M$. The desired function is given by

$$g_\epsilon(\lambda) = \sum_{j=1}^{q-1} \beta_j (h_{r_j \, r_{j+1}}(\lambda)).$$

It is easy to verify that on each interval $(-\infty, r_1], (r_1, r_2], \ldots, (r_{q-1}, r_q], (r_q, \infty)$ we have: $|f(\lambda) - g_\epsilon(\lambda)| < \epsilon$.

(8) Prove that for every squashing function ψ, every $r \in \mathbb{N}$, and every measure space $(\mathbb{R}^r, \mathbb{B}(\mathbb{R}^r), m)$, where m is a finite measure, the set $\Sigma\Pi^r(\psi)$ is uniformly dense on compacta in C^r and d-dense in the set of Borel functions M^r.

Solution: We begin by showing that every function of the form $\Pi_{k=1}^{\ell} g h_k$ can be uniformly approximated by members of $\Sigma\Pi^r(\psi)$. Let $\epsilon > 0$. Since multiplication is continuous and $(0,1)^{\ell}$, there is $\delta > 0$ such that $|a_k - b_k| < \delta$ for $0 \leqslant a_k, b_k \leqslant 1$ and $1 \leqslant k \leqslant \ell$ imply

$$\left| \prod_{k=1}^{\ell} a_k - \prod_{k=1}^{\ell} b_k \right| < \epsilon.$$

By Supplement 7, there is a function $g_\epsilon \in \Sigma^1(\psi)$ such that $\sup_{\lambda \in \mathbb{R}} |f(\lambda) - g_\epsilon| < \epsilon$.

(9) Prove that for every squashing function ψ, every positive ϵ, and every $M > 0$ there is a function $\kappa_{M,\epsilon} \in \Sigma^1(\psi)$ such that

$$\sup_{x \in [-M,M]} |\kappa_{M,\epsilon}(x) - \cos x| < \epsilon.$$

Solution: If $\psi = $ csq the result follows from Supplement 2. For an arbitrary squashing function the result follows from Supplement 7.

(10) Let $g : \mathbb{R}^r \longrightarrow \mathbb{R}$ be the function defined as $g(\mathbf{x}) = \sum_{j=1}^{q} \beta_j \cos(h_j(\mathbf{x}))$, where $h_j \in \mathbb{A}^r$. Prove that for an arbitrary squashing function ψ, an compact $K \subseteq \mathbb{R}^r$, and $\epsilon > 0$ there exists $f \in \Sigma^r(\psi)$ such that $\sup_{x \in K} |g(x) - f(x)| < \epsilon$.

Solution: Since K is compact and h_j are continuous, there exists $M > 0$ such that $h_j(K) \subseteq [-M, M]$ for $1 \leqslant j \leqslant q$. Define $q' = q \sum_{j=1}^{q} \sum_{j=1}^{q} |\beta_j|$. By Supplement 9 for all $x \in K$ we have $|\sum_{j=1}^{q} \kappa_{M,\epsilon/q'}(h_j(x)) - g(x)| < \epsilon$ for all $x \in K$. This implies $f = \sum_{j=1}^{q} \kappa_{M,\epsilon/q'}(h_j) \in \Sigma^r(\Psi)$ because $\kappa_{M,\epsilon/q'} \in \Sigma^1(\psi)$.

(11) Prove that for every squashing function ψ, the set $\Sigma^r(\psi)$ is uniformly dense on compact sets in C^r.

Solution: By Supplement 3 the trigonometric polynomials of the form $\sum_{j=1}^{q} \beta_j \Pi_{k=1}^{\ell_j} \cos h_{jk}$, where $q \geqslant 1$, $\ell_j \in \mathbb{N}$ and $h_{jk} \in \mathbb{A}^r$ are uniformly dense on compacta in C^r. Since $\cos a \cos b = \frac{1}{2}(\cos(a+b) + \cos(a-b))$, each of the previous trigonometric polynomials is a sum of the form $\sum_{i=1}^{m} a_i \cos h_i$, where $h_i \in \mathbb{A}^r$. The result follows by an application of Supplement 10.

Next, we show that standard NNs with a single hidden layer can approximate any continuous function uniformly on any compact set, and any measurable function in the sense of the $\eth$ semimetric, regardless of ψ, the dimension r and the measure that generates $\eth$.

(12) Prove that for every squashing function ψ, $r \geqslant 1$, and every finite measure space $(\mathbb{R}^r, \mathbb{B}(\mathbb{R}^r), m)$ the set $\sigma^r(\psi)$ is uniformly dense on compacta in C^r.

   Solution: By Supplement 11, $\Sigma^r(\psi)$ is uniformly dense on compact sets in C^r. Therefore, by Supplement 5, $\Sigma^r(\psi)$ is ∂-dense in C^r.

(13) Let $\mathcal{N}$ be a neural net that contains three layers of neurons: two input neurons, two inner layer neurons and two output neurons (as shown in Figure 15.3. The activation function is the logistic function L. Suppose that the initial values of the matrices V and W are

$$V = \begin{pmatrix} 1 & 1 \\ 1 & 1 \end{pmatrix} \text{ and } W = \begin{pmatrix} 1 & 1 \\ 1 & 1 \end{pmatrix}$$

and that the network is intended to learn the function $f : \{0,1\}^2 \longrightarrow \{-1,1\}$ given by

$$\mathbf{f}(0,1) = \mathbf{f}(1,0) = (1,-1), \mathbf{f}(0,0) = \mathbf{f}(1,1) = (-1,1).$$

Apply the back propagation algorithm to determine the appropriate weights of the network capable of approximating $\mathbf{f}$.

(14) Prove that $(\tanh(x))' = 1 - \tanh^2(x)$; reformulate the back propagation algorithm by replacing the sigmoidal activation function of the neurons by the hyperbolic tangent.

Bibliographical Comments

The cosine squasher was introduced by A. R. Galant and H. White in [62] where the equality of Supplement 2 is stated.

In [83] it was shown that standard NN with one hidden layer using arbitrary squashing functions are capable of approximating and Borel measurable function with a any degree of accuracy by using an adequate number of hidden units. The approach in [83, 82, 6] is based on the application of Stone-Weierstrass theorem and provide a distinct approach to the uniform approximation results obtained in [37, 38], which make use of the Hahn-Banach Theorem. See also [100]. Useful sources for approximation results for neural networks are [134] and [44]. The references [76] and [77] provide broad perspectives on neural computing.

Chapter 16

Regression

16.1 Introduction

The term regression covers a series of techniques that explain the relationships between a variable that represents the results of an experiment and the independent variables that represent input parameters of the experiment. These techniques have been long explored by statisticians and machine learning researchers. The ideas and algorithms they developed are useful in forecasting and classification.

We use regression to illustrate two of the most popular regularization techniques ($\|\cdot\|_2$ and $\|\cdot\|_1$ regularization) which involve modifying the objective function of certain optimization problems in order to obtain solutions with certain desirable properties.

16.2 Linear Regression

Suppose that the results of a series of m experiments are the components of a vector $\mathbf{y} \in \mathbb{R}^m$. For the ith experiment, the values of the n input variables $x_1, \ldots, x_n$ are placed in the ith row of a matrix $B \in \mathbb{R}^{m \times n}$ known as the *design matrix*, and we assume that the outcome of the ith experiment y_i is a linear function of the values $b_{i1}, \ldots, b_{in}$ of $x_1, \ldots, x_n$, that is

$$y_i = b_{i1} r_1 + \cdots + b_{in} r_n.$$

The variables $x_1, \ldots, x_n$ are referred to as the *regressors*. Note that the values assumed by the variable x_j in the series of m experiments, $b_{1j}, \ldots,$ b_{mj} have been placed in the jth column $\mathbf{b}^j$ of the matrix B.

Linear regression assumes the existence of a linear relationship between the outcome of an experiment and values of variables that are measured during the experiment.

In general there are more experiments than variables, that is, we have $n < m$. In matrix form we have $\mathbf{y} = B\mathbf{r}$, where $B \in \mathbb{R}^{m \times n}$ and $\mathbf{r} \in \mathbb{R}^n$. The problem is to determine $\mathbf{r}$, when B and $\mathbf{y}$ are known. Since $n < m$, this linear system is inconsistent, but is possible to obtain an approximative solution by determining $\mathbf{r}$ such that $\|B\mathbf{r} - \mathbf{y}\|$ is minimal. This amounts to approximating $\mathbf{y}$ by a vector in the subspace $\mathsf{Ran}(B)$ generated by the columns of the matrix B.

The columns $\mathbf{b}^1, \ldots, \mathbf{b}^n$ of the matrix B are referred to as the *regressors*; the linear combination $r_1 \mathbf{b}^1 + \cdots + r_n \mathbf{b}^n$ is the *regression of $\mathbf{y}$ onto the regressors* $\mathbf{b}^1, \ldots, \mathbf{b}^n$.

A variant of the previous model is to assume that $\mathbf{y}$ is affinely dependent on $\mathbf{b}^1, \ldots, \mathbf{b}^q$, that is,

$$\mathbf{y} = r_0 + r_1 \mathbf{b}^1 + \cdots + r_n \mathbf{b}^n,$$

and we seek to determine the coefficients $r_0, r_1, \ldots, r_n$. The term r_0 is the *bias* of the model. The dependency of $\mathbf{y}$ on $\mathbf{b}^1, \ldots, \mathbf{b}^n$ can be homogenized by introducing a dummy vector $\mathbf{b}^0$ having all components equal to 1, which gives

$$\mathbf{y} = r_0 \mathbf{b}^0 + r_1 \mathbf{b}^1 + \cdots + r_n \mathbf{b}^n,$$

as the defining assumption of the model.

If the linear system $B\mathbf{r} = \mathbf{y}$ has no solution $\mathbf{r}$, the "next best thing" is to find a vector $\mathbf{r}_* \in \mathbb{R}^n$ such that

$$\|B\mathbf{r}_* - \mathbf{y}\|_2 \leqslant \|B\mathbf{w} - \mathbf{y}\|_2$$

for every $\mathbf{w} \in \mathbb{R}^n$. This approach is known as *the least square method*. We refer to the triple $(B, \mathbf{r}, \mathbf{y})$ as an *instance of the least square problem*.

Note that $B\mathbf{r} \in \mathsf{Ran}(B)$ for any $\mathbf{r} \in \mathbb{R}^n$. Thus, solving this problem amounts to finding a vector $B\mathbf{r}$ in the subspace $\mathsf{Ran}(B)$ such that $B\mathbf{r}$ is as close to $\mathbf{y}$ as possible.

Let $B \in \mathbb{R}^{m \times n}$ be a full-rank matrix such that $m > n$, so $rank(B) = n$. In this case, the symmetric square matrix $B'B \in \mathbb{R}^{n \times n}$ has the same rank n as the matrix B, and $B'B$ is an invertible matrix. Therefore, the system

$$(B'B)\mathbf{r} = B'\mathbf{y} \tag{16.1}$$

has a unique solution $\mathbf{r} = (B'B)^{-1}B'\mathbf{y}$. Moreover, $B'B$ is positive definite because $\mathbf{r}'B'B\mathbf{r} = (B\mathbf{r})'B\mathbf{r} = \|B\mathbf{r}\|_2^2 > 0$ for $\mathbf{r} \neq \mathbf{0}_n$.

Theorem 16.1. *Let $B \in \mathbb{R}^{m \times n}$ be a full-rank matrix such that $m > n$ and let $\mathbf{y} \in \mathbb{R}^m$. The unique solution $\mathbf{r} = (B'B)^{-1}B'\mathbf{y}$ of the system $(B'B)\mathbf{r} = B'\mathbf{y}$ equals the projection of the vector $\mathbf{y}$ on the subspace $\mathsf{Ran}(B)$.*

Proof. The n columns of the matrix $B = (\mathbf{b}^1 \; \cdots \; \mathbf{b}^n)$ constitute a basis of the subspace $\mathsf{Ran}(B)$. Therefore, we seek the projection $\mathbf{c}$ of $\mathbf{y}$ on $\mathsf{Ran}(B)$ as a linear combination of the columns of B, $\mathbf{c} = B\mathbf{r}$, which allows us to reduce this problem to a minimization of the function

$$
\begin{aligned}
f(\mathbf{r}) &= \|B\mathbf{r} - \mathbf{y}\|_2^2 \\
&= (B\mathbf{r} - \mathbf{y})'(B\mathbf{r} - \mathbf{y}) = (\mathbf{r}'B' - \mathbf{y}')(B\mathbf{r} - \mathbf{y}) \\
&= \mathbf{r}'B'B\mathbf{r} - \mathbf{y}'B\mathbf{r} - \mathbf{r}'B'\mathbf{y} + \mathbf{y}'\mathbf{y} \\
&= \mathbf{r}'B'B\mathbf{r} - 2\mathbf{y}'B\mathbf{r} + \mathbf{y}'\mathbf{y}.
\end{aligned}
\tag{16.2}
$$

The necessary condition for the minimum is

$$
(\nabla f)(\mathbf{r}) = 2B'B\mathbf{r} - 2B'\mathbf{y} = 0,
$$

which implies $B'B\mathbf{r} = B'\mathbf{y}$. $\qquad\square$

The linear system $(B'B)\mathbf{r} = B'\mathbf{y}$ is known as the *system of normal equations* of B and $\mathbf{y}$. The solution of this system, $\mathbf{r} = (B'B)^{-1}B'\mathbf{y}$ is known as the *linear estimator*.

Suppose now that $B \in \mathbb{R}^{m \times n}$ has rank k, where $k < \min\{m, n\}$, and $U \in \mathbb{R}^{m \times m}$, $V \in \mathbb{R}^{n \times n}$ are orthonormal matrices such that B can be factored as $B = UMV'$, where

$$
M = \begin{pmatrix} R & O_{k,n-k} \\ O_{m-k,k} & O_{m-k,n-k} \end{pmatrix} \in \mathbb{R}^{m \times n},
$$

$R \in \mathbb{R}^{k \times k}$ and $rank(R) = k$.

For $\mathbf{y} \in \mathbb{R}^m$ define $\mathbf{c} = U'\mathbf{y} \in \mathbb{R}^m$ and let $\mathbf{c} = \begin{pmatrix} \mathbf{c}_1 \\ \mathbf{c}_2 \end{pmatrix}$, where $\mathbf{c}_1 \in \mathbb{R}^k$ and $\mathbf{c}_2 \in \mathbb{R}^{m-k}$. Since $rank(R) = k$, the linear system $R\mathbf{z} = \mathbf{c}_1$ has a unique solution $\mathbf{z}_1$.

Theorem 16.2. *All vectors $\mathbf{r}$ that minimize $\|B\mathbf{r} - \mathbf{y}\|_2$ have the form*

$$
\mathbf{r} = V\begin{pmatrix} \mathbf{z} \\ \mathbf{w} \end{pmatrix},
$$

for an arbitrary $\mathbf{w}$.

Proof. We have

$$
\begin{aligned}
\|B\mathbf{r} - \mathbf{y}\|_2^2 &= \|UMV'\mathbf{r} - UU'\mathbf{y}\|_2^2 \\
&= \|U(MV'\mathbf{r} - U'\mathbf{y})\|_2^2 = \|MV'\mathbf{r} - U'\mathbf{y}\|_2^2 \\
&\qquad \text{(because multiplication by an orthonormal matrix} \\
&\qquad \text{is norm-preserving)} \\
&= \|MV'\mathbf{r} - \mathbf{c}\|_2^2 = \|M\mathbf{y} - \mathbf{c}\|_2^2 \\
&= \|R\mathbf{z} - \mathbf{c}_1\|_2^2 + \|\mathbf{c}_2\|_2^2,
\end{aligned}
$$

where $\mathbf{z}$ consists of the first r components of $\mathbf{y}$. This shows that the minimal value of $\|B\mathbf{r} - \mathbf{y}\|_2^2$ is achieved by the solution of the system $R\mathbf{z} = \mathbf{c}_1$ and is equal to $\|\mathbf{c}_2\|_2^2$. Therefore, the vectors $\mathbf{r}$ that minimize $\|B\mathbf{r} - \mathbf{y}\|_2^2$ have the form $\begin{pmatrix} \mathbf{z} \\ \mathbf{w} \end{pmatrix}$ for an arbitrary $\mathbf{w} \in \mathbb{R}^{n-r}$. $\qquad\square$

Instead of the Euclidean norm we can use the $\|\cdot\|_\infty$. Note that we have $t = \|B\mathbf{r} - \mathbf{y}\|_\infty$ if and only if $-t\mathbf{1} \leqslant B\mathbf{r} - \mathbf{y} \leqslant t\mathbf{1}$, so finding $\mathbf{r}$ that minimizes $\|\cdot\|_\infty$ amounts to solving a linear programming problem: minimize t subjected to the restrictions $-t\mathbf{1} \leqslant B\mathbf{r} - \mathbf{y} \leqslant t\mathbf{1}$.

16.3 A Statistical Model of Linear Regression

We discuss now a statistical model of the problem stated in Section 16.2. We assume that the results of the experiments are described by an m-dimensional random vector $\mathbf{y}$ that is affected by errors. These errors are represented by an m-dimensional *error random vector* $\boldsymbol{\epsilon}$:

$$\mathbf{y} = B\mathbf{r} + \boldsymbol{\epsilon}.$$

We also assume that the random vector $\boldsymbol{\epsilon}$ is centered, that is, $E(\boldsymbol{\epsilon}) = \mathbf{0}_m$. Its covariance matrix $cov(\boldsymbol{\epsilon}) \in \mathbb{R}^{m \times m}$ is positive definite.

We seek an linear estimate of the constant vector $\mathbf{r}$ as the random vector $\hat{\mathbf{r}} = K\mathbf{y}$, where $K \in \mathbb{R}^{n \times m}$. We aim to minimize the expectation $E(\|\hat{\mathbf{r}} - \mathbf{r}\|^2)$ of the Euclidean norm of *error random vector* $\hat{\mathbf{r}} - \mathbf{r}$ by an appropriate choice of the matrix K. Note that we have:

$$E(\hat{\mathbf{r}}) = E(K\mathbf{y}) = E(K(B\mathbf{r} + \boldsymbol{\epsilon})) = KB\mathbf{r}.$$

If $KB = I_n$, then $E(\hat{\mathbf{r}}) = \mathbf{r}$, and the random vector $\hat{\mathbf{r}}$ is an *unbiased estimator* of $\mathbf{r}$.

Assuming that $KB = I_n$ we have:

$$\begin{aligned}
E(\|\hat{\mathbf{r}} - \mathbf{r}\|^2) &= E(\|K\mathbf{y} - \mathbf{r}\|^2) \\
&= E(\|K(B\mathbf{r} + \boldsymbol{\epsilon}) - \mathbf{r}\|^2) \\
&= E(\|K\boldsymbol{\epsilon}\|^2),
\end{aligned}$$

so in this case the expected norm of the error is independent of $\mathbf{r}$.

Note that for $\mathbf{v} \in \mathbb{R}^m$ we have $\|\mathbf{v}\|^2 = \mathbf{v}'\mathbf{v} = trace(\mathbf{v}\mathbf{v}')$. This allows us to write

$$E(\|\hat{\mathbf{r}} - \mathbf{r}\|^2) = E(trace(K\boldsymbol{\epsilon}'\boldsymbol{\epsilon}K')) = trace(K\,cov(\boldsymbol{\epsilon})K').$$

Conversely, if we require that a random vector of the form $\hat{\mathbf{r}} = K\mathbf{y}$ is an unbiased estimator of $\mathbf{r}$, that is, $E(\hat{\mathbf{r}}) = \mathbf{r}$, it follows that $KB = I_n$.

Lemma 16.1. *Let $Q \in \mathbb{R}^{m \times m}$ be a positive definite matrix and let $B \in \mathbb{R}^{m \times n}$ be a full-rank matrix such that $m > n$, so $\text{rank}(B) = n$.*

The optimization problem that seeks a matrix $K \in \mathbb{R}^{n \times m}$ that minimizes $\text{trace}(KQK')$ subjected to the constraint $KB = I_n$ has as a solution the matrix K given by $K = Q^{-1}B(B'Q^{-1}B)^{-1}$.

Proof. Let $\mathbf{k}^1, \ldots, \mathbf{k}^m$ be the columns of matrix K. We have

$$\text{trace}(KQK') = \sum_{j=1}^{m} \mathbf{k}^i Q(\mathbf{k}^i)'.$$

Since Q is positive definite, we have $\mathbf{k}^i Q(\mathbf{k}^i)' \geqslant 0$ for $1 \leqslant i \leqslant m$, so the previous problem amounts to m optimization problems:

   minimize $(\mathbf{k}^i)'Q\mathbf{k}^i$,
      subject to $(\mathbf{k}^i)'\mathbf{b}^j = \delta_{ij}$,

where

$$\delta_{ij} = \begin{cases} 1 & \text{if } i = j, \\ 0 & \text{if } i \neq j. \end{cases}$$

In terms of the inner product defined by the matrix Q an equivalent formulation is

   minimize $\|\mathbf{k}^i\|_Q$,
      subject to $(\mathbf{k}^i, Q^{-1}\mathbf{b}^j)_Q = \delta_{ij}$ for $1 \leqslant j \leqslant n$,

because

$$(\mathbf{k}^i)'\mathbf{b}^j = \mathbf{k}^i Q(Q^{-1}\mathbf{b}^j) = (\mathbf{k}^i, Q^{-1}\mathbf{b}^j)_Q.$$

By Supplement 6 of Chapter 11, the solution of this optimization problem is $\mathbf{k}^i = Q^{-1}B(B'Q^{-1}B)^{-1}\mathbf{e}_i$. Therefore, $K = Q^{-1}B(B'Q^{-1}B)^{-1}$. $\qquad\square$

Theorem 16.3. (Gauss-Markov Theorem) *Suppose that $\mathbf{y} = B\mathbf{r} + \boldsymbol{\epsilon}$, where $\mathbf{y}$ and $\boldsymbol{\epsilon}$ are random vectors such that $E(\boldsymbol{\epsilon}) = \mathbf{0}_m$ and $Q = E(\boldsymbol{\epsilon}'\boldsymbol{\epsilon})$ is a positive definite matrix.*

The linear minimum-variance unbiased estimate of $\mathbf{r}$ is $\hat{\mathbf{r}} = (B'Q^{-1}B)^{-1}B'Q^{-1}\mathbf{y}$ and the error covariance is $E((\hat{\mathbf{r}} - \mathbf{r})(\hat{\mathbf{r}} - \mathbf{r})') = (B'Q^{-1}B)^{-1}$.

Proof. By Lemma 16.1, the minimum-variance estimate $\hat{\mathbf{r}} = K\mathbf{y}$ is given by $\hat{\mathbf{r}} = (B'Q^{-1}B)^{-1}B'Q^{-1}\mathbf{y}$.

For the error covariance matrix we have:

$$E((\hat{\mathbf{r}} - \mathbf{r})(\hat{\mathbf{r}} - \mathbf{r})') = E((K\mathbf{y} - \mathbf{r})(K\mathbf{y} - \mathbf{r})')$$
$$= E(K\epsilon\epsilon'K') = KQK'$$
$$= Q^{-1}B(B'Q^{-1}B)^{-1}QQ^{-1}B(B'Q^{-1}B)^{-1}$$
$$= (B'Q^{-1}B)^{-1}.$$

$\square$

Corollary 16.1. *If the covariance matrix $Q = E(\epsilon'\epsilon)$ equals I_m, then the minimum-variance estimate $\hat{\mathbf{r}}$ equals the least-square estimate $(B'B)^{-1}B'\mathbf{y}$.*

Proof. This fact follows directly from Theorem 16.3. $\square$

16.4 Logistic Regression

Despite its name *logistic regression* is essentially a classification technique. The term "regression" is justified by the use of a probabilistic approach involving the linear model defined for linear regression. The typical problem involves classifying objects into two classes, designated as C_1 and C_{-1}.

Let $\mathbf{s}$ be a data sample of size m, that consists of the pairs of values of a random vector $\mathbf{X}$ ranging over $\mathbb{R}^n$ and a random variable Y ranging over $\{-1, 1\}$, namely

$$\mathbf{s} = ((\mathbf{x}_1, y_1), \dots, (\mathbf{x}_m, y_m)),$$

where $\mathbf{x}_1, \dots, \mathbf{x}_m$ belong to $\mathbb{R}^n$ and $y_i \in \{-1, 1\}$ for $1 \leqslant i \leqslant m$.

In logistic regression we assume that the logarithmic ratio $\ln \frac{P(Y=1|\mathbf{X}=\mathbf{x})}{P(Y=-1|\mathbf{X}=\mathbf{x})}$ is an affine function $r_0 + r_1 x_1 + \dots + r_n x_n$. If a dummy component x_0 that is set to 1 is added, as we did for linear regression, then the above assumption can be written as

$$\ln \frac{P(Y = 1|\mathbf{X} = \mathbf{x})}{P(Y = -1|\mathbf{X} = \mathbf{x})} = \mathbf{r}'\mathbf{x}, \tag{16.3}$$

where $\mathbf{r}, \mathbf{x} \in \mathbb{R}^{n+1}$.

Let $\ell : (0, 1) \longrightarrow \mathbb{R}$ be the *logit function* defined as

$$\ell(p) = \ln \frac{p}{1 - p}$$

for $p \in (0, 1)$ and let $f : \mathbb{R} \longrightarrow (0, 1)$ be the logistic function $L(x) = \frac{e^x}{1+e^x}$ defined in Example 15.1. Note that $L(x) + L(-x) = 1$ for $x \in \mathbb{R}$ and the fact that L and ℓ are inverse functions.

Equality (16.3) can be written as

$$P(Y = 1|X = \mathbf{x}) = \frac{e^{\mathbf{r}'\mathbf{x}}}{1 + e^{\mathbf{r}'\mathbf{x}}} = L(\mathbf{r}'\mathbf{x})$$

and

$$P(Y = -1|X = \mathbf{x}) = \frac{1}{1 + e^{\mathbf{r}'\mathbf{x}}} = 1 - L(\mathbf{r}'\mathbf{x}) = L(-\mathbf{r}'\mathbf{x}).$$

Both cases are captured by the equality

$$P(Y = y|X = \mathbf{x}) = L(y\mathbf{r}'\mathbf{x}).$$

Equivalently, we have $\ell(P(Y = y|X = \mathbf{x})) = y\mathbf{r}'\mathbf{x}$.

The object $\mathbf{x}$ is placed in the class C_y where $y \in \{-1, 1\}$), where y is the values that maximizes $f(y\mathbf{r}'\mathbf{x})$.

Since the example of $\mathbf{s}$ are independently generated the probability of obtaining the class y_i for each of the examples $\mathbf{x}_i$ is defined by the *likelihood function* $\prod_{i=1}^{m} P(Y = y_i|X = \mathbf{x}_i)$. To simplify notations we denote this function of y_i and $\mathbf{x}_i$ as $\prod_{i=1}^{m} P(y_i|\mathbf{x}_i)$. Maximizing this function is equivalent to minimizing

$$\Lambda(\mathbf{r}) = -\frac{1}{m} \ln \left(\prod_{i=1}^{m} P(y_i|\mathbf{x}_i) \right) = -\frac{1}{m} \sum_{i=1}^{m} \ln P(y_i|\mathbf{x}_i)$$

$$= -\frac{1}{m} \sum_{i=1}^{m} \ln L(y_i\mathbf{r}\mathbf{x}_i) = \frac{1}{m} \sum_{i=1}^{m} \ln \frac{1}{L(y_i\mathbf{r}\mathbf{x}_i)} = \frac{1}{m} \sum_{i=1}^{m} \ln(1 + e^{-y_i\mathbf{r}\mathbf{x}_i}),$$

with respect to $\mathbf{r}$. Note that small values of this expression can be obtained when $y_i\mathbf{r}'\mathbf{x}_i$ is large, that is, when $\mathbf{r}'\mathbf{x}_i$ has the same sign as y_i.

The decision boundary that separates the classes C_1 and C_{-1} is given by the hyperplane $\mathbf{x} - y\mathbf{r} = 0$ in $\mathbb{R}^{n+1}$. Note that the distance of an example $(\mathbf{x}_i, y_i)$ to this hyperplane is $\frac{|\mathbf{x}_i - y_i\mathbf{r}|}{\|(1, \mathbf{r})\|}$.

To minimize $\Lambda(\mathbf{r})$ we need to impose the conditions $\frac{\partial \Lambda}{\partial r_j} = 0$ for $1 \leqslant j \leqslant n + 1$, which amount to

$$\sum_{i=1}^{m} L'(y_i\mathbf{r}\mathbf{x}_i) \frac{\partial(y_i\mathbf{r}\mathbf{x}_i)}{\partial r_j} = 0,$$

or

$$\sum_{i=1}^{m} L(y_i\mathbf{r}\mathbf{x}_i)(1 - L(y_i\mathbf{r}\mathbf{x}_i))y_j x_{ji} = 0,$$

by equality (15.1) of Chapter 15, for $1 \leqslant j \leqslant n + 1$. This is a non-linear system in $\mathbf{r}$ which can be solved by approximation methods.

16.5 Ridge Regression

When the number n of input variables is large, the assumption previously made concerning the linear independence of the columns $\mathbf{b}^1, \ldots, \mathbf{b}^n$ of the design matrix B may not hold and the rank of B may be smaller than n. In such a case, previous models are not applicable. The linear dependencies that may exist between the columns of B (reflecting linear dependencies among experiment variables) invalidate the assumptions previously made. These dependencies are known as *colinearities* among variables.

The solution proposed in [80] is to replace $B'B$ in the least-square estimate $\hat{\mathbf{r}} = (B'B)^{-1}B'\mathbf{y}$ by $B'B + \lambda I_n$ and to define the *ridge regression estimate* as $\mathbf{r}(\lambda) = (B'B + \lambda I_n)^{-1}B'\mathbf{y}$. The term *ridge regression* is justified by the fact that the main diagonal in the correlation matrix may be thought of as a ridge.

We retrieve the ridge regression estimate as a solution of a regularized optimization problem, that is, as an optimization problem where the objective function is modified by adding a term that has an effect the shrinking of regression coefficients.

Instead of minimizing the function $f(\mathbf{r}) = \|B\mathbf{r} - \mathbf{y}\|_2$ we use the objective function $g(\mathbf{r}, \lambda) = \|B\mathbf{r} - \mathbf{y}\|_2^2 + \lambda \|\mathbf{r}\|_2^2$. This approach is known as *Tikhonov regularization method* and g is known as the *ridge loss function*. A necessary condition of optimality is $(\nabla g)_{\mathbf{r}} = \mathbf{0}_n$. This yields:

$$\begin{aligned}(\nabla g)_{\mathbf{r}} &= 2B'B\mathbf{r} - 2B'\mathbf{y} + 2\lambda\mathbf{r} \\ &= 2(B'B\mathbf{r} - B'\mathbf{y} + \lambda\mathbf{r}) \\ &= 2[(B'B + \lambda I_n)\mathbf{r} - B'\mathbf{y}] = \mathbf{0}_n,\end{aligned}$$

which yields the previous estimate of $\mathbf{r}$. The ridge estimator is therefore a stationary point of g. The Hessian of g is the matrix $H_g(\mathbf{x}) = \left(\frac{\partial^2 f}{\partial r_j\, \partial r_k}\right)$, and it is easy to see that

$$H_g(\mathbf{x}) = 2(B'B + \lambda I_n).$$

This implies that H_g is positive definite, hence the stationary point is a minimum.

Note that the ridge loss function is convex, as a sum of two convex functions. Therefore, the stationary point mentioned above is a global minimum.

16.6 Lasso Regression and Regularization

In regression problems it is often the case that the number of observations is too small, or the problem dimension too high which makes the data sparse. Without prior knowledge about data, it is difficult to estimate a model or make predictions. When a problem solution is known to be sparse, sparsity-inducing penalties improve both the quality of the prediction and its interpretability. In particular, the $\| \cdot \|_1$ is used for that purpose in the *Lasso regression* introduced in [131].

In this section we use the *sign* and its extension to $\mathbb{R}^n$ as introduced in Definition 12.12.

Let $\mathbf{u} \in \mathbb{R}^n$ and let J be a subset of $\{1, \ldots, n\}$, $J = \{j_1, \ldots, j_m\}$. The projection of $\mathbf{u}$ on the subspace generated by the set $\{\mathbf{e}_{j_1}, \ldots, \mathbf{e}_{j_m}\}$ is denoted by $\mathbf{u}_J = \begin{pmatrix} u_{j_1} \\ \vdots \\ u_{j_m} \end{pmatrix}$.

Theorem 16.4. *Let* $\mathbf{y} \in \mathbb{R}^m$ *and let* $B = (\mathbf{b}^1, \ldots, \mathbf{b}^n) \in \mathbb{R}^{m \times n}$. *Consider the following optimization problem*

minimize for $\mathbf{r} \in \mathbb{R}^n$

$$\frac{1}{2} \| B\mathbf{r} - \mathbf{y} \|_2^2 + \lambda \| \mathbf{r} \|_1,$$

where $\lambda > 0$.

A vector $\mathbf{r}_* \in \mathbb{R}^n$ *is a solution if and only if for all* j, $1 \leqslant j \leqslant n$ *we have* $(\mathbf{b}^j)'(B\mathbf{r}_* - \mathbf{y}) + \lambda \, sign((\mathbf{r}_*)_j) = 0$ *if* $(\mathbf{r}_*)_j \neq 0$, *and* $|(\mathbf{b}^j)'(B\mathbf{r}_* - \mathbf{y})| \leqslant \lambda$, *otherwise.*

Let

$$J = \{ j \mid 1 \leqslant j \leqslant n, |(\mathbf{b}^j)'(B\mathbf{r}_* - \mathbf{y})| = \lambda \}.$$

If the matrix $B_J = (\mathbf{b}^j)_{j \in J}$ *is of full rank, the solution is unique and we have:*

$$(\mathbf{r}^*)_J = (B_J' B_J)^{-1} ((B_J' \mathbf{y} - \lambda \boldsymbol{\eta}_J),$$

where $\boldsymbol{\eta} = sign(B'(\mathbf{y} - B\mathbf{r}^*)) \in \{-1, 0, 1\}^n$.

Proof. Since $\| \cdot \|_1$ is not differentiable, we need to apply the subgradient optimality condition contained in Theorem 12.37, that requires

$$\mathbf{0}_n \in \text{subd} \left(\frac{1}{2} \| B\mathbf{r} - \mathbf{y} \|_2^2 + \lambda \| \mathbf{r} \|_1 \right) (\mathbf{r}_*).$$

Since $\frac{1}{2}\|Br - \mathbf{y}\|_2^2$ is differentiable, its subdifferential consists of its gradient $B'Br - B'\mathbf{y}$. As we saw in Example 12.21, the subgradients in $\mathsf{subd}(\|\cdot\|_1)(\mathbf{r})$ are the vectors $\mathbf{p}$ in $\mathbb{R}^n$ such that for $j \in \{1, \ldots, n\}$ we have $p_j = sign(r_j)$ if $(\mathbf{r}_*)_j \neq 0$, and $|p_j| \leqslant 1$, otherwise. Thus, the optimality condition can be written as:

$$\mathbf{0}_n \in \{B'Br - B'\mathbf{y} + \lambda \mathbf{p} \mid \mathbf{p} \in \mathsf{subd}(\|\cdot\|_1)(\mathbf{r})\}.$$

This condition amounts to

$$(\mathbf{b}^j)'(Br_* - \mathbf{y}) + \lambda \, sign((\mathbf{r}_*)_j) = 0 \qquad (16.4)$$

if $(\mathbf{r}_*)_j \neq 0$, and

$$|(\mathbf{b}^j)'(Br_* - \mathbf{y})| \leqslant \lambda, \qquad (16.5)$$

if $(\mathbf{r}_*)_j = 0$.

Let J be the set of column indices of the matrix B that correspond to equalities in Conditions 16.4 and 16.5:

$$J = \{j \mid (\mathbf{b}^j)'(Br_* - \mathbf{y})| = \lambda\} = \{j_1, \ldots, j_q\}.$$

Equalities (16.4) define a linear system that can be written as:

$$(B_J)'(B_J r_* - \mathbf{y}) + \lambda \, sign((\mathbf{r}_*)_J) = \mathbf{0}_q,$$

or

$$(B_J)'B_J r_* = (B_J)'\mathbf{y} - \lambda \, sign((\mathbf{r}_*)_J),$$

similar to the system 16.1. If $B_J \in \mathbb{R}^{m \times q}$ is a full rank matrix, this system has a unique solution

$$r_* = ((B_J)'B_J)^{-1}((B_J)'\mathbf{y} - \lambda \, sign((\mathbf{r}_*)_J))$$
$$= ((B_J)'B_J)^{-1}((B_J)'\mathbf{y} - \lambda \, \boldsymbol{\eta}_J),$$

where

$$\boldsymbol{\eta} = sign(B_J)'(\mathbf{y} - Br_*) \in \{-1, 0, 1\}^p.$$

To show the uniqueness of the solution let $\mathbf{s}$ be another solution and let $\theta \in (0, 1)$. By convexity, $r_\theta = (1 - \theta)r_* + \theta\mathbf{s}$ is also a solution. If $j \notin J$ we have

$$(\mathbf{b}^j)'(Br_\theta - \mathbf{y})| \leqslant (1 - \theta)(\mathbf{b}^j)'(Br_* - \mathbf{y}) + \theta(\mathbf{b}^j)'(Bs - \mathbf{y}) < \lambda.$$

Let $\bar{J}$ be the complement of the set J, that is, $\bar{J} = \{j \mid 1 \leqslant j \leqslant n\} - J$. Taking into account Conditions 16.4 and 16.5, it follows that $(\mathbf{r}_\theta)_{\bar{J}} = (\mathbf{r}_*)_{\bar{J}} = \mathbf{0}_{n-q}$ and the vector $\mathbf{r}_\theta$ is also a solution of the reduced problem

minimize for $\tilde{\mathbf{r}} \in \mathbb{R}^{|J|}$

$$\frac{1}{2}\|B_J\tilde{\mathbf{r}} - \mathbf{y}\|_2^2 + \lambda\|\tilde{\mathbf{r}}\|_1,$$

where $\lambda > 0$.

When B_J is of full rank, the matrix $(B_J)'B_J$ is positive definite and the reduced problem admits a unique solution $\mathbf{r}_\theta = (\mathbf{r}_*)_J$. Then $\mathbf{r}_* = \mathbf{r}_\theta = \mathbf{s}$. $\qquad\square$

The optimal solution of the Lasso regression problem is dependent on the parameter λ. Therefore, it is interesting to examine the geometric properties of the *regularization path* $\{\mathbf{r}_*(\lambda) \mid \lambda > 0\}$. The Lasso regression has the *parsimony property* [45]: for any give λ value only a subset of the variables have non-zero values of their respective coefficients r_j ($1 \leqslant j \leqslant n$).

The set $\{\boldsymbol{\eta}_*(\lambda) \mid \boldsymbol{\eta}_*(\lambda) = sign(\mathbf{r}_*(0)), \lambda > 0\}$ is the *set of sparsity patterns*.

Theorem 16.5. *Assume that for any $\lambda > 0$ and solution of the Lasso regression problem, the matrix X_J is of full rank. Then, the regularization path $\{\mathbf{r}_*(\lambda) \mid \lambda > 0\}$ is well-defined, unique and continuous piecewise linear.*

Proof. The existence and uniqueness of the regularization path was shown in Theorem 16.4.

Let λ_1 and λ_2 be such that $\lambda_1 < \lambda_2$ but $\boldsymbol{\eta}_*(\lambda_1) = \boldsymbol{\eta}_*(\lambda_2)$. If $\theta \in [0, 1]$, and $\lambda = (1 - \theta)\lambda_1 + \theta\lambda_2$, then the solution $\mathbf{r}_*(\theta) = (1 - \theta)\mathbf{r}_*(\lambda_1) + \theta\mathbf{r}_*(\lambda_2)$ satisfies the optimality conditions of Theorem 16.4.

This shows that whenever two solutions $\mathbf{r}_*(\lambda_1)$ and $\mathbf{r}_*(\lambda_2)$ have the same sign vector for $\lambda_1 \neq \lambda_2$, the regularization path between λ_1 and λ_2 is a line segment. Note that the number of linear segments of the regularization path is no larger than 3^n, the number of possible sparsity patterns. Therefore, the regularization path is piecewise linear and contains a finite number of segments.

Since the function $h : \mathbb{R}_{>0} \longrightarrow \mathbf{r}^n$ defined by $h(\lambda) = \mathbf{r}_*(\lambda)$ is piecewise continuous and has left and right limits for every positive λm and these limits also satisfy the optimality conditions and are equal to $\mathbf{r}_*(\lambda)$, it follows that h is continuous. $\qquad\square$

Exercises and Supplements

(1) Let $\{\mathbf{b}^j \mid 1 \leqslant j \leqslant m\}$ be a set of points in $\mathbb{R}^n$ such that $\sum_{i=1}^m \mathbf{b}^j = \mathbf{0}_n$. Determine a hyperplane H defined by $\mathbf{r}'\mathbf{x} = 0$ that passes through $\mathbf{0}_n$ such that the sum of the square distances from the points $\mathbf{x}_i$ to H is minimal and prove that in this case $\mathbf{r}$ is an eigenvector of the square matrix $B'B \in \mathbb{R}^{n \times n}$, where $B = (\mathbf{b}^1 \ \cdots \ \mathbf{b}^m)$

Solution: Without loss of generality assume that the hyperplane H is defined by the equation $\mathbf{r}'\mathbf{x} = 0$, where $\|\mathbf{r}\| = 1$. The distance from $\mathbf{b}^j$ to H is $d_j = \mathbf{r}'\mathbf{b}^j$. Therefore, we need to minimize $L(\mathbf{r}) = \sum_{j=1}^m (\mathbf{r}'\mathbf{b}^j)^2 = \sum_{j=1}^m \left(\sum_{i=1}^n r_i b_i^j\right)^2$, where $\mathbf{b}^j = \begin{pmatrix} b_1^j \\ \vdots \\ b_n^j \end{pmatrix}$ for $1 \leqslant j \leqslant m$.

Thus, we have a constrained minimization problem

$$\text{minimize } L(\mathbf{r}) = \sum_{j=1}^m \left(\sum_{i=1}^n r_i b_i^j\right)^2,$$
$$\text{subject to } \sum_{i=1}^n r_i^2 - 1 = 0.$$

The necessary extremum condition yields

$$(\nabla L)(\mathbf{r}) = \lambda \nabla \left(\sum_{i=1}^n r_i^2 - 1\right).$$

Since $\frac{\partial L}{\partial r_k} = 2 \sum_{j=1}^m \left(\sum_{i=1}^n r_i b_i^j\right) b_j^k$, we have

$$2 \sum_{j=1}^m \left(\sum_{i=1}^n r_i b_i^j\right) b_j^k = \lambda \cdot 2 r_k.$$

If $B = (\mathbf{b}^1, \ldots, \mathbf{b}^n) \in \mathbb{R}^{m \times n}$, we have $\mathbf{b}_j^i = b_{ji}$ and the previous equality can be written as $\sum_{j=1}^m \sum_{i=1}^n r_i b_{ji} b^{jk} = \lambda r_k$ for $1 \leqslant j \leqslant m$ and $1 \leqslant i \leqslant n$ which amounts to $(B'B)\mathbf{r} = \lambda \mathbf{r}$, which shows that $\mathbf{r}$ is an eigenvector of $B'B$.

Data fitting is a generalization of linear regression that seeks to determine a function $f_{\mathbf{a}} : \mathbb{R}^n \longrightarrow \mathbb{R}$ that belongs to a prescribed class of functions parametrized by $\mathbf{a} \in \mathbb{R}^n$ such that $f_{\mathbf{a}}$ will best fit the data set. This means that for a data set $D = \{(\mathbf{x}_i, y_i) \mid 1 \leqslant i \leqslant m\} \subseteq \mathbb{R}^n$ we seek $\mathbf{a}$ such that $g(\mathbf{a}) = \sum_{i=1}^m \|y_i - f_{\mathbf{a}}(x_i)\|^2$ is minimized.

(2) Let $D = \{(x_i, y_i) \mid 1 \leqslant i \leqslant m\}$ be a data set in $\mathbb{R}^2$. Determine a polynomial p of degree n $p_{\mathbf{a}}(x) = a_1 x^{n-1} + \cdots + a_{n-1} x + a_n$ that will fit D. In other words, determine the vector $\mathbf{a} \in \mathbb{R}^n$ such that $\|X\mathbf{a} - \mathbf{y}\|^2$ is

minimal, where

$$\mathbf{a} = \begin{pmatrix} a_1 \\ a_2 \\ \vdots \\ a_n \end{pmatrix}$$

and

$$X = \begin{pmatrix} x_1^{n-1} & x_1^{n-2} & \cdots & x_1 & 1 \\ x_2^{n-1} & x_2^{n-2} & \cdots & x_2 & 1 \\ \vdots & \vdots & \vdots & \vdots & \\ x_m^{n-1} & x_m^{n-2} & \cdots & x_m & 1 \end{pmatrix}, \mathbf{y} = \begin{pmatrix} y_1 \\ y_2 \\ \vdots \\ y_n \end{pmatrix}.$$

(3) Let $\mathbf{b} \in \mathbb{R}^m - \{\mathbf{0}_m\}$ and $\mathbf{y} \in \mathbb{R}^m$. Prove that $\|\mathbf{b}r - \mathbf{y}\|$ is minimal when $r = \frac{(\mathbf{y}, \mathbf{b})}{\|\mathbf{b}\|^2}$.

(4) Let $B = (\mathbf{b}^1, \dots, \mathbf{b}^n) \in \mathbb{R}^{m \times n}$ be a matrix having orthogonal columns (in other words, $i \neq j$ implies $(\mathbf{b}^i, \mathbf{b}^j) = 0$) such that $m > n$. Prove that

 (a) matrix B has full rank, that is, $rank(B) = n$;

 (b) if $\mathbf{r}$ is the solution of the optimization problem that consists in minimizing the function $f(\mathbf{r}) = \|B\mathbf{r} - \mathbf{y}\|^2$, then $r_j = \frac{(\mathbf{y}, \mathbf{b}^j)}{\|\mathbf{b}^j\|^2}$ for $1 \leqslant j \leqslant n$. In other words, the components of the solution of linear regression do not influence each other.

(5) By applying Gram-Schmidt orthogonalization algorithm to the set of columns $\mathbf{b}^1, \dots, \mathbf{b}^n$ that represent the values of the regressors and taking into account Exercise 4 formulate an algorithm for the linear regression.

(6) Let $B \in \mathbb{R}^{m \times n}$ be a matrix of full rank, where $m > n$, and let $C = B(B'B)^{-1}B' \in \mathbb{R}^{m \times m}$. As the regressor vector $\mathbf{r}$ is computed, the vector $\hat{\mathbf{y}} = C\mathbf{y} = B(B'B)^{-1}B'\mathbf{y} = B\mathbf{r}$ is the expectation of the output vector conditioned on the regression model.

Prove that C is a symmetric and idempotent, $trace(C) = n$, $rank(C) = n$, and $c_{ii} \in [0, 1]$; also, prove that the matrix $I_m - C$ is symmetric and idempotent.

Let $B = (\mathbf{b}^1 \quad \cdots \quad \mathbf{b}^n) \in \mathbb{R}^{m \times n}$ be a matrix that contains input data of m experiments. The rows of this matrix are denoted by $\mathbf{u}_1, \dots, \mathbf{u}_m$, where $\mathbf{u}_i \in \mathbb{R}^n$ contains the input values of the variable for the ith experiment. The *average* of B is the vector $\tilde{\mathbf{u}} = \frac{1}{m} sum_{i=1}^m \mathbf{u}_i$. The matrix is *centered* if $\tilde{\mathbf{u}} = \mathbf{0}'_n$. Note that $\tilde{u} = \frac{1}{m}\mathbf{1}'_m B$. Note that the matrix

$$\hat{B} = \left(I_m - \frac{1}{m}\mathbf{1}_m\mathbf{1}'_m \right) B$$

because

$$\frac{1}{m}\mathbf{1}_m'\hat{B} = \frac{1}{m}\mathbf{1}_m'\left(I_m - \frac{1}{m}\mathbf{1}_m\mathbf{1}_m'\right)B$$

$$= \frac{1}{m}\left(\mathbf{1}_m' - \frac{1}{m}\mathbf{1}_m'\mathbf{1}_m\mathbf{1}_m'\right)B$$

$$= \frac{1}{m}\left(\mathbf{1}_m' - \mathbf{1}_m'\right)B = 0.$$

The matrix $H_m = I_m - \frac{1}{m}\mathbf{1}_m\mathbf{1}_m' \in \mathbb{R}^{m\times m}$ is the *centering matrix*.

If the measurement scales of the variables $x_1, \ldots, x_n$ involved in the series are very different due to different measurement units, some variables may influence inappropriately the certain regression processes. The *standard deviation* of a vector $\mathbf{b} \in \mathbb{R}^m$ is $s(\mathbf{b}) = \sqrt{\frac{1}{m-1}\sum_{b_i-\tilde{b}}}$, where $\tilde{b} = \frac{1}{m}\sum_{i=1}^{m} b_i$. To scale a matrix we need to replace each column $\mathbf{b}^j$ by $\frac{1}{s(\mathbf{b}^j)}\mathbf{b}^j$.

(7) Prove that the centering matrix H_n is symmetric and idempotent.

(8) Let $B \in \mathbb{R}^{m\times n}$ and $\mathbf{y} \in \mathbb{R}^m$ the data used in linear regression. Suppose that B is centered and define the matrix $\hat{B} = \begin{pmatrix} B \\ \sqrt{\lambda}I_n \end{pmatrix} \in \mathbb{R}^{(m+n)\times n}$ and $\hat{\mathbf{y}} = \begin{pmatrix} \mathbf{y} \\ \mathbf{0}_n \end{pmatrix} \in \mathbb{R}^{m+n}$. Prove that the ordinary regression applied to this data amounts to ridge regression.

Solution: Starting from the objective function of the ordinary linear regression (as shown in equality (16.2), the objective function of the new optimization problem is

$$f(\mathbf{r}) = \|\hat{B}\mathbf{r} - \hat{\mathbf{y}}\|_2$$

$$= \mathbf{r}'(B'|\sqrt{\lambda}I_n)\begin{pmatrix} B \\ \sqrt{\lambda}I_n \end{pmatrix}\mathbf{r} - 2(\mathbf{y}'|\mathbf{0}_n')\begin{pmatrix} B \\ \sqrt{\lambda}I_n \end{pmatrix}\mathbf{r} + (\mathbf{y}'|\mathbf{0}_n')\begin{pmatrix} \mathbf{y} \\ \mathbf{0}_n \end{pmatrix}$$

$$= \mathbf{r}'B'B\mathbf{r} - 2\mathbf{y}'B\mathbf{r} + \mathbf{y}'\mathbf{y} + \lambda\mathbf{r}'\mathbf{r},$$

which is precisely the objective function of the ridge regression.

(9) Prove that if the set of columns of the matrix B is orthonormal, $\mathbf{r}_*$ is the optimal estimation of $\mathbf{r}$ for the ridge regression and $\tilde{\mathbf{r}}$ is the optimal estimation of $\mathbf{r}$ for the least square regression, then

$$\frac{\mathbf{r}_*}{\tilde{\mathbf{r}}_*} = \frac{1}{1+\lambda}.$$

(10) Let $\mathbf{s} = ((\mathbf{x}_1, y_1), \ldots, (\mathbf{x}_m, y_m))$ be a sample and let $F : \mathbb{R}^n \longrightarrow \mathbb{R}$ be the function defined by

$$F(\mathbf{r}) = \frac{1}{m} \sum_{i=1}^{m} \ln \frac{1}{1 + e^{-y_i \mathbf{r} \mathbf{x}_i}}$$

that evaluates the error of the logistic regression algorithm. Prove that

$$(\nabla F)(\mathbf{r}) = -\frac{1}{m} \sum_{i=1}^{m} \frac{y_i \mathbf{x}_i}{1 + e^{y_i \mathbf{r}' \mathbf{x}_i}} = \frac{1}{m} \sum_{i=1}^{m} -y_i \mathbf{x}_i L(-y_i \mathbf{r}' \mathbf{x}_i),$$

where L is the logistic function.

(11) Develop a gradient descent algorithm to approximate a minimum for the error function F introduced in Exercise 10.

(12) The logistic regression can be extended to the classification into k classes $C_1, \ldots, C_k$ by extending equality (16.3) as

$$\ln \frac{P(Y = 1 | \mathbf{X} = \mathbf{x})}{P(Y = k | \mathbf{X} = \mathbf{x})} = \mathbf{r}_1' \mathbf{x}$$

$$\ln \frac{P(Y = 2 | \mathbf{X} = \mathbf{x})}{P(Y = k | \mathbf{X} = \mathbf{x})} = \mathbf{r}_2' \mathbf{x}$$

$$\vdots$$

$$\ln \frac{P(Y = k - 1 | \mathbf{X} = \mathbf{x})}{P(Y = k | \mathbf{X} = \mathbf{x})} = \mathbf{r}_2' \mathbf{x}.$$

Prove that $\sum_{i=1}^{k} P(Y = i | \mathbf{X} = \mathbf{x}) = 1$.

(13) Suppose that for the sparsity pattern $\boldsymbol{\eta}_*(\lambda_1)$ we have $\boldsymbol{\eta}_*(\lambda_1) \neq \mathbf{0}_n$ for some $\lambda_1 > 0$. Prove that for all $\lambda_2 > 0$ such that $\lambda_1 \neq \lambda_2$ we have $\boldsymbol{\eta}_*(\lambda_2) \neq -\boldsymbol{\eta}_*(\lambda_1)$.

Solution: Suppose that for $\lambda_2 > 0$ such that $\lambda_1 \neq \lambda_2$ we would have $\boldsymbol{\eta}_*(\lambda_2) \neq -\boldsymbol{\eta}_*(\lambda_1)$.

Let $J' = \{j \mid 1 \leqslant j \leqslant n, (\boldsymbol{\eta}_*(\lambda_1))_j \neq 0\}$. Note that the matrix $B_{J'}$ is of full rank. Therefore, the reduced problem

minimize for $\tilde{\mathbf{r}} \in \mathbb{R}^{|J|}$

$$\frac{1}{2} \| B_J \tilde{\mathbf{r}} - \mathbf{y} \|_2^2 + \lambda \| \tilde{\mathbf{r}} \|_1,$$

where $\lambda \geqslant 0$.

involves a strictly convex function, hence the solution is well-defined. Observe that $\tilde{r}_*(\lambda_1) = (\mathbf{r}_*(\lambda_1))_{J'}$ and $\tilde{r}_*(\lambda_2) = (\mathbf{r}_*(\lambda_2))_{J'}$.

Theorem 16.4 implies that

$$\tilde{\mathbf{r}}_*(0) = (B'_{J'} B_{J'})^{-1} B'_{J'} \mathbf{y} = \frac{\lambda_2}{\lambda_1 + \lambda_2} \tilde{\mathbf{r}}_*(\lambda_1) + \frac{\lambda_1}{\lambda_1 + \lambda_2} \tilde{\mathbf{r}}_*(\lambda_2).$$

Since the signs of $\tilde{\mathbf{r}}_*(\lambda_1)$ and $\tilde{\mathbf{r}}_*(\lambda_2)$ are opposite and non-zero, we have $\|\tilde{\mathbf{r}}_*(0)\|_1 < \|\tilde{\mathbf{r}}_*(\lambda_1)\|_1$. It is easy to see that the function that maps λ to $\|\tilde{\mathbf{r}}_*(\lambda)\|$ is non-increasing, we have a contradiction.

(14) By using Supplement 13 prove that the number of linear segments on the regularization path is less than $\frac{3^n+1}{2}$.

Bibliographical Comments

The main sources for the lasso regression are [131, 136, 74, 75]; our presentation follows [103].

Supplement 8 originates in [75] and is inspired by [1], where the idea of adding artificial data that satisfies model constraints was developed.

Chapter 17

Support Vector Machines

17.1 Introduction

Support vector machines (SVMs) were introduced in statistical learning theory by V. N. Vapnik[1] and his collaborators in a series of publications [21, 34].

One of the earliest success stories of SVMs was the handwritten digit recognition. The results obtained with SVMs show superior classification performance comparable with the best classifiers developed in machine learning. Although intended initially for classifying data where classes are linearly separable, using techniques from functional analysis, SVMs manage to successfully classify data where classes are separated by non-linear boundaries.

17.2 Linearly Separable Data Sets

In Chapter 1 we saw that the distance between a point $\mathbf{x}_0 \in \mathbb{R}^n$ and a hyperplane $H_{\mathbf{w},a}$ defined by the equation $\mathbf{w}'\mathbf{x} = a$ is given by equality (2.14):

$$d(H_{\mathbf{w},a}, \mathbf{x}_0) = \frac{|\mathbf{w}'\mathbf{x}_0 - a|}{\|\mathbf{w}\|}.$$

---

[1]V. N. Vapnik was born on December 6, 1936. He is the co-inventor of support vector machines and the creator of the Vapnik-Chervonenkis dimension theory. V. N. Vapnik received his Ph.D. in statistics at the Institute of Control Sciences, Moscow in 1964 and moved to USA at the end of 1990. He is a Professor of Computer Science at the University of London since 1995, as well as a Professor of Computer Science at Columbia University.

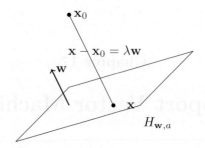

Fig. 17.1   The distance between $\mathbf{x}_0$ and the hyperplane $H_{\mathbf{w},a}$.

A *data sample* of size m is a sequence
$$\mathbf{s} = ((\mathbf{x}_1, y_1), \ldots, (\mathbf{x}_m, y_m)),$$
where $\mathbf{x}_1, \ldots, \mathbf{x}_m$ belong to $\mathbb{R}^n$ and $y_i \in \{-1, 1\}$ for $1 \leqslant i \leqslant m$. The *positive examples* of $\mathbf{s}$ are those pairs $(\mathbf{x}_i, y_i)$ such that $y_i = 1$; the remaining pairs are the *negative examples*.

The task of a linear classifier is to construct a hyperplane $H_{\mathbf{w},a}$ starting from the sample $\mathbf{s}$ such that for each positive example $(\mathbf{x}_i, 1)$ we have $\mathbf{x}_i \in H_{\mathbf{w},a}^{>0}$ and for each negative example we have $\mathbf{x}_i \in H_{\mathbf{w},a}^{<0}$. Initially, we assume that such a hyperplane exists, that is, the sample $\mathbf{s}$ is *linearly separable* (see Figure 17.2).

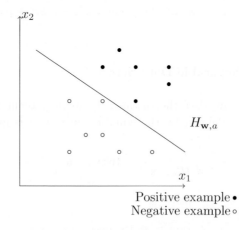

Fig. 17.2   Linear separability of the sample $\mathbf{s}$.

If $\mathbf{s}$ is a linearly separable sample there are, in general, infinitely many hyperplanes that can do the separation.

Definition 17.1. A hyperplane $H_{\mathbf{w},a}$ that does not pass through a point of the sample $\mathbf{s}$ is in *canonical form relative to $\mathbf{s}$* if

$$\min_{(\mathbf{x},y)\in S} |\mathbf{w}'\mathbf{x} - a| = 1.$$

Note that we may always assume that the separating hyperplane is in canonical form relative by $\mathbf{s}$ by rescaling the coefficients of the equation that define the hyperplane (a and the components of $\mathbf{w}$).

If the hyperplane $\mathbf{w}'\mathbf{x} = a$ is in canonical form relative to the sample $\mathbf{s}$, then the distance to the hyperplane of the closest points in $\mathbf{s}$ (the *margin of the hyperplane*) is the same, namely,

$$\rho = \min_{(\mathbf{x},y)\in\mathbf{s}} \frac{|\mathbf{w}'\mathbf{x} - a|}{\|\mathbf{w}\|} = \frac{1}{\|\mathbf{w}\|}.$$

Vectors that are closest to the separating hyperplane are referred to as *support vectors*.

For a canonical separating hyperplane we have

$$|\mathbf{w}'\mathbf{x} - a| \geqslant 1$$

for any pair $(\mathbf{x}, y)$ of the sample, and

$$|\mathbf{w}'\mathbf{x} - a| = 1$$

for every support vector. The pair $(\mathbf{x}_i, y_i)$ is classified correctly if y_i has the same sign as $\mathbf{w}'\mathbf{x}_i - a$, that is, $y_i(\mathbf{w}'\mathbf{x}_i - a) \geqslant 1$.

Example 17.1. Let $x_1 + 2x_2 - x_3 = -5$ be the equation defining a hyperplane $H_{\mathbf{w},a}$ in $\mathbb{R}^3$ and let $\mathbf{s}$ consist of the pairs

$$(\mathbf{x}_1, y_1) = \left(\begin{pmatrix} 1 \\ 0 \\ 2 \end{pmatrix}, 1 \right), (\mathbf{x}_2, y_2) = \left(\begin{pmatrix} -2 \\ 0 \\ 5 \end{pmatrix}, -1 \right),$$

$$(\mathbf{x}_3, y_3) = \left(\begin{pmatrix} -1 \\ 3 \\ 2 \end{pmatrix}, 1 \right), (\mathbf{x}_4, y_4) = \left(\begin{pmatrix} -1 \\ 4 \\ 1 \end{pmatrix}, -1 \right).$$

For $\mathbf{w} = \begin{pmatrix} 1 \\ 2 \\ -1 \end{pmatrix}$ we have $\|\mathbf{w}\| = \sqrt{5}$.

The sample $\mathbf{s}$ is linearly separable by $H_{\mathbf{w},a}$ because

$$\mathbf{w}'\mathbf{x}_1 - a = 4, \mathbf{w}'\mathbf{x}_2 - a = -2, \mathbf{w}'\mathbf{x}_3 - a = 8, \mathbf{w}'\mathbf{x}_2 - a = -3$$

and the distances to $H_{\mathbf{w},a}$ of $\mathbf{x}_i$ are $\frac{4}{\sqrt{5}}, \frac{2}{\sqrt{5}}, \frac{8}{\sqrt{5}}$, and $\frac{3}{\sqrt{5}}$, respectively, making $\mathbf{x}_2$ the support vector.

The hyperplane $H_{\mathbf{w},a}$ is not in canonical form relative to $\mathbf{s}$. This form can be obtained by dividing its coefficients by $2 = \min_{1 \leqslant i \leqslant 4} |\mathbf{w}'\mathbf{x}_i - a|$. Thus, the canonical form of the hyperplane is

$$\frac{1}{2}x_1 + x_2 - \frac{1}{2}x_3 = -\frac{5}{2}.$$

The margin of the hyperplane is $\rho = \frac{1}{\sqrt{5}}$.

Maximizing the margin is equivalent to minimizing $\|\mathbf{w}\|$ or, equivalently, to minimizing $\frac{1}{2}\|\mathbf{w}\|^2$. Thus, if $\mathbf{s}$ is separable, the SVM problem is equivalent to the following convex optimization problem relative to $\mathbf{w}$ and a:

minimize $\frac{1}{2}\|\mathbf{w}\|^2$

subject to $y_i(\mathbf{w}'\mathbf{x}_i - a) \geqslant 1$ for $1 \leqslant i \leqslant m$.

Note that the new objective function,

$$\frac{1}{2}\|\mathbf{w}\|^2 = \frac{1}{2}(w_1^2 + \cdots + w_n^2)$$

is differentiable; furthermore, we have $\nabla\left(\frac{1}{2}\|\mathbf{w}\|^2\right) = \mathbf{w}$ and the Hessian of this function is

$$H_{\frac{1}{2}\|\mathbf{w}\|^2} = \mathbf{I}_n,$$

which shows that $\frac{1}{2}\|\mathbf{w}\|^2$ is a convex function of $\mathbf{w}$.

The Lagrangian of the primal optimization problem

minimize $\frac{1}{2}\|\mathbf{w}\|^2$

subject to $y_i(\mathbf{w}'\mathbf{x}_i - a) \geqslant 1$ for $1 \leqslant i \leqslant m$.

is

$$L(\mathbf{w}, a, \mathbf{u}) = \frac{1}{2}\|\mathbf{w}\|^2 - \sum_{i=1}^{m} u_i\left(y_i(\mathbf{w}'\mathbf{x}_i - a) - 1\right),$$

where u_i are the Lagrange multipliers for $1 \leqslant i \leqslant m$.

To compute the dual objective function g we impose the Karush-Kuhn-Tucker optimality conditions on the Lagrangian L:

$$\frac{\partial L}{\partial w_j} = w_j - \sum_{i=1}^{m} u_i y_i (\mathbf{x}_i)_j = 0$$

$$\frac{\partial L}{\partial a} = \sum_{i=1}^{m} u_i y_i = 0,$$

$$u_i(y_i(\mathbf{w}'\mathbf{x}_i + b) - 1) = 0 \text{ for all } i,$$

which imply

$$\mathbf{w} = \sum_{i=1}^{m} u_i y_i \mathbf{x}_i = 0,$$

$$\sum_{i=1}^{m} u_i y_i = 0,$$

$$u_i = 0 \text{ or } y_i(\mathbf{w}'\mathbf{x}_i - a) = 1 \text{ for } 1 \leqslant i \leqslant m.$$

This shows that the weight vector is a linear combination of the training vectors $\mathbf{x}_1, \ldots, \mathbf{x}_m$, where $\mathbf{x}_i$ effectively occurs in this linear combination only if $u_i \neq 0$ (support vectors).

Since $u_i = 0$ or $y_i(\mathbf{w}'\mathbf{x}_i - a) = 1$ for all i, if $u_i \neq 0$, then $y_i(\mathbf{w}'\mathbf{x}_i - a) = 1$ for the support vectors; thus, all these vectors lie on the marginal hyperplanes $\mathbf{w}'\mathbf{x} - a = 1$ or $\mathbf{w}'\mathbf{x} - a = -1$. If non-support vector are removed the solution remains the same; however, while the solution of the problem remains the same different choices may be possible for the support vectors.

The dual problem can now be stated as follows:

maximize $g(\mathbf{u}) = \sum_{i=1}^{m} u_i - \frac{1}{2} \sum_{i=1}^{m} \sum_{j=1}^{m} u_i u_j y_i y_j \mathbf{x}_i' \mathbf{x}_j$

subject to $u_i \geqslant 0$ for $1 \leqslant i \leqslant m$ and $\sum_{i=1}^{m} u_i y_i = 0$.

The dual objective function $g(\mathbf{u})$ depends on the vector of Lagrange multipliers $\mathbf{u} = \begin{pmatrix} u_1 \\ \vdots \\ u_m \end{pmatrix}$. Constraints are affine, so the strong duality holds; therefore, the primal and the dual problems are equivalent.

The solution $\mathbf{u}$ of the dual problem can be used directly to determine the classifying function returned by the SVM as:

$$h(\mathbf{x}) = sign(\mathbf{w}'\mathbf{x} - a) = sign\left(\sum_{i=1}^{m} u_i y_i(\mathbf{x}_i'\mathbf{x}) - a\right).$$

Since support vectors lie on the marginal hyperplanes, for every support vector $\mathbf{x}_i$ we have $\mathbf{w}'\mathbf{x}_i - a = y_i$, so

$$a = \sum_{j=1}^{m} u_j y_j(\mathbf{x}_j'\mathbf{x}) - y_i.$$

Example 17.2. Let $\mathbf{s}$ be a sample in $\mathbb{R}^3 \times \{-1, 1\}$ that consist of the pairs $(\mathbf{x}_j, y_j)$ for $1 \leqslant j \leqslant 4$:

$$((0, 1, 0), 1), ((0, 1, 1), -1), ((1, 1, 0), 1), ((1, 1, 1), -1),$$

respectively. The primal problem is:

$$\text{minimize } \tfrac{1}{2}\|\mathbf{w}\|^2$$
$$\text{subject to}$$
$$1(w_2 - a) \geqslant 1,$$
$$-1(w_2 + w_3 - a) \geqslant 1,$$
$$1(w_1 + w_2 - a) \geqslant 1,$$
$$-1(w_1 + w_2 + w_3 - a) \geqslant 1.$$

Note that the vectors $\mathbf{x}_i$ of the sample are pairwise orthogonal. Therefore, the dual problem is:

$$\text{maximize } g(\mathbf{u}) = \sum_{i=1}^{4} u_i$$
$$- \tfrac{1}{2}\left(u_1^2 + 4u_2^2 + 4u_3^2 + 9u_4^2\right)$$
$$\text{subject to } u_i \geqslant 0 \text{ for } 1 \leqslant i \leqslant 4 \text{ and}$$
$$u_1 - u_2 + u_3 - u_4 = 0.$$

17.3 Soft Support Vector Machines

If data is not separable the conditions $y_i(\mathbf{w}'\mathbf{x}_i - a) \geqslant 1$ cannot all hold (for $1 \leqslant i \leqslant m$). Instead, we impose a relaxed version of the constraints, namely

$$y_i(\mathbf{w}'\mathbf{x}_i - a) \geqslant 1 - \xi_i,$$

where ξ_i are non-negative new variables known as *slack variables*. Slack variables ξ_i measure the extent of the violations of the constraints $y_i(\mathbf{w}'\mathbf{x}_i - a) \geqslant 1$. This version of the SVM is known as the *soft SVM*.

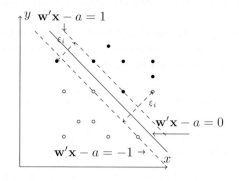

Fig. 17.3   Objects misclassified and slack variables.

A vector $\mathbf{x}_i$ is an *outlier* if $\mathbf{x}_i$ is not positioned correctly on the side of the appropriate hyperplane. A vector $\mathbf{x}_i$ with $0 < y_i(\mathbf{w}'\mathbf{x}_i - a) < 1$ is still an outlier even if it is correctly classified by the hyperplane $\mathbf{w}'\mathbf{x} - a = 0$ but is misplaced relative to the shifted separating hyperplane.

If we omit the outliers the data is correctly separated by the hyperplane $\mathbf{w}'\mathbf{x} - a = 0$ with a *soft margin* $\rho = \frac{1}{\|\mathbf{w}\|}$.

The total slack due to outliers is $\sum_{i=1}^{m} \xi_i$. We seek a hyperplane with a large margin (even though this may lead to more outliers).

The optimization problem for the non-separable data relative to $\mathbf{w}, a$ and ξ_i (for $1 \leqslant i \leqslant m$) is:

$$\text{minimize } \tfrac{1}{2}\|\mathbf{w}\|^2 + C\sum_{i=1}^{m} \xi_i$$
$$\text{subject to } y_i(\mathbf{w}'\mathbf{x}_i - a) \geqslant 1 - \xi_i \text{ and } \xi_i \geqslant 0 \text{ for } 1 \leqslant i \leqslant m,$$

where the parameter C controls the tradeoff between the two terms and is determined in the process of cross-validation.

This is a convex optimization problem with affine constraints. As in the separable case, constraints are affine and thus, qualified, the objective function and the affine constraints are convex and differentiable, so the KKT conditions apply.

If $u_i \geqslant 0$ are the Lagrange multipliers associated with m constraints and $v_i \geqslant 0$ are Lagrange multipliers associated with the non-negativity constraints of the slack variables for $1 \leqslant i \leqslant m$, then the Lagrangian is defined as:

$$L(\mathbf{w}, a, \xi_1, \ldots, \xi_m, \mathbf{u}, \mathbf{v}) = \frac{1}{2}\|\mathbf{w}\|^2 + C\sum_{i=1}^{m} \xi_i$$
$$- \sum_{i=1}^{m} u_i[y_i(\mathbf{w}'\mathbf{x}_i - a) - 1 + \xi_i]$$
$$- \sum_{i=1}^{n} v_i\xi_i,$$

where $\mathbf{v}$ is the vector whose components are v_i. The KKT conditions are listed in the table below:

KKT Condition	Consequence
$\nabla_{\mathbf{w}}L = \mathbf{w} - \sum_{i=1}^{m} u_iy_i\mathbf{x}_i = 0$	$\mathbf{w} = \sum_{i=1}^{m} u_iy_i\mathbf{x}_i$
$\nabla_a L = \sum_{i=1}^{m} u_iy_i = 0$	$\sum_{i=1}^{m} u_iy_i = 0$
$\nabla_{\xi_i} L = C - u_i - v_i = 0$ for $1 \leqslant i \leqslant m$	$u_i + v_i = C$ for $1 \leqslant i \leqslant m$
$u_i[y_i(\mathbf{w}'\mathbf{x}_i - a) - 1 + \xi_i] = 0$ for $1 \leqslant i \leqslant m$	$u_i = 0$ or $y_i(\mathbf{w}'\mathbf{x}_i - a) = 1 - \xi_i$ for $1 \leqslant i \leqslant m$
$v_i\xi_i = 0$ for $1 \leqslant i \leqslant m$	$v_i = 0$ or $\xi_i = 0$ for $1 \leqslant i \leqslant m$

These conditions have several consequences:

- $\mathbf{w}$ is a linear combination of the training vectors $\mathbf{x}_1, \ldots, \mathbf{x}_m$, where $\mathbf{x}_i$ appears in the combination only if $u_i \neq 0$;
- if $u_i \neq 0$, then $y_i(\mathbf{w}'\mathbf{x}_i - a) = 1 - \xi_i$;

- if $\xi_i = 0$, then $y_i(\mathbf{w}'\mathbf{x}_i - a) = 1$ and $\mathbf{x}_i$ lies on marginal hyperplane as in the separable case; otherwise, $\mathbf{x}_i$ is an outlier;
- if $\mathbf{x}_i$ is an outlier, $v_i = 0$ and $u_i = C$ or $\mathbf{x}_i$ is located on the marginal hyperplane;
- $\mathbf{w}$ is unique; the support vectors are not.

The objective function of the dual problem is obtained by substituting $\mathbf{w}$ and incorporating the consequences of the KKT conditions:

$$
\begin{aligned}
g(\mathbf{u}, \mathbf{v}) \\
&= \frac{1}{2}\|\mathbf{w}\|^2 + C\sum_{i=1}^{m}\xi_i - \sum_{i=1}^{m}u_i\xi_i - \sum_{i=1}^{m}v_i\xi_i \\
&\quad - \sum_{i=1}^{m}u_i[y_i(\mathbf{w}'\mathbf{x}_i - a) - 1] \\
&= \frac{1}{2}\|\mathbf{w}\|^2 + \sum_{i=1}^{m}(C - u_i - v_i)\xi_i - \sum_{i=1}^{m}u_i[y_i(\mathbf{w}'\mathbf{x}_i - a) - 1] \\
&= \frac{1}{2}\left\|\sum_{i=1}^{m}u_iy_i\mathbf{x}_i\right\|^2 - \sum_{i=1}^{m}\sum_{j=1}^{m}u_iu_jy_iy_j\mathbf{x}_i'\mathbf{x}_j \\
&\quad + \sum_{i=1}^{m}u_iy_ia + \sum_{i=1}^{m}u_i \\
&= \sum_{i=1}^{m}u_i - \frac{1}{2}\sum_{i=1}^{m}\sum_{j=1}^{m}u_iu_jy_iy_j\mathbf{x}_i'\mathbf{x}_j.
\end{aligned}
$$

Note that g depends only on $\mathbf{u}$ and we have:

$$
g(\mathbf{u}) = \sum_{i=1}^{m}u_i - \frac{1}{2}\sum_{i=1}^{m}\sum_{j=1}^{m}u_iu_jy_iy_j\mathbf{x}_i'\mathbf{x}_j.
$$

has exactly the same form as in the separable case. Also, observe that $0 \leqslant u_i \leqslant C$ for $1 \leqslant i \leqslant m$ because both u_i and v_i are non-negative and $u_i + v_i = C$.

The dual optimization problem for the non-separable case becomes:

maximize $\sum_{i=1}^{m}u_i - \frac{1}{2}u_iu_jy_iy_j\mathbf{x}_i'\mathbf{x}_j$
subject to $0 \leqslant u_i \leqslant C$ and $\sum_{i=1}^{m}u_iy_i = 0$
for $1 \leqslant i \leqslant m$.

The objective function is concave and differentiable and the solution can be used to determine the separating hyperplane. As in the separable case, the hyperplane depends only on the inner products between the vectors and not directly on the vectors themselves.

17.4 Non-linear Support Vector Machines

One of the reasons for the success of support vector machines is the possibility of constructing classifiers for data where the separation cannot be achieved by hyperplanes. The general idea is to map data in the input spaces using a non-linear map $\phi : \mathbb{R}^n \longrightarrow H$ into a Hilbert spaces H.

Definition 17.2. If $K : S \times S \longrightarrow \mathbb{R}$ is a kernel such that there exists a Hilbert space H and a function $\phi : S \longrightarrow H$ such that $K(x, y) = (\phi(x), \phi(y))$ for $x, y \in S$, then ϕ is a feature map and H is a *feature space* of K.

If $\mathbf{x} \in \mathbb{R}^n$ is a datum having the image $\phi(\mathbf{x}) \in H$, we shall seek a hyperplane in the Hilbert space H that achieves the linear separation of the images of the classes in the data space. This is possible because the objective function of the dual problem of SVM:

$$g(\mathbf{u}) = \sum_{i=1}^{m} u_i - \frac{1}{2} \sum_{i=1}^{m} \sum_{j=1}^{m} u_i u_j y_i y_j \mathbf{x}_i' \mathbf{x}_j$$

depends just on the inner products $\mathbf{x}_i' \mathbf{x}_j$ of the vectors from $\mathbb{R}^n$, in other words, on the entries of the Gram matrix of the set of vectors $\{\mathbf{x}_1, \ldots, \mathbf{x}_m\}$. If a transformation $\phi : \mathbb{R}^n \longrightarrow H$ is applied the input vectors $\mathbf{x}_1, \ldots, \mathbf{x}_m$, these vectors are transformed into members of the space Hilbert H, $\phi(\mathbf{x}_1), \ldots, \phi(\mathbf{x}_m)$. To construct an SVM in H we need to maximize an objective function of the form

$$g(\mathbf{u}) = \sum_{i=1}^{m} u_i - \frac{1}{2} \sum_{i=1}^{m} \sum_{j=1}^{m} u_i u_j y_i y_j (\phi(\mathbf{x}_i), \phi(\mathbf{x}_j)),$$

which depends on the values of the inner products $(\phi(\mathbf{x}_i), \phi(\mathbf{x}_j))$ in H. In certain situations, a function $K : \mathbb{R}^n \times \mathbb{R}^n \longrightarrow \mathbb{R}$ exists such that $K(\mathbf{x}_i, \mathbf{x}_j) = (\phi(\mathbf{x}_i), \phi(\mathbf{x}_j))$ for $1 \leqslant i, j \leqslant m$. As we have shown in Theorem 11.46, K is a symmetric function of positive type. Several such functions K, referred previously as kernels were considered in Examples 11.14, 11.15, and 11.16. When a suitable kernel exists it is not necessary to compute effectively the transformation ϕ of various data points; instead, the computation of $(\phi(\mathbf{x}_i), \phi(\mathbf{x}_j))$ is replaced by the computation of $K(\mathbf{x}_i, \mathbf{x}_j)$ on the original $\mathbb{R}^n$ space. The process is known as the *kernelization* of support vector machines.

Example 17.3. In Example 11.15 we have shown that for the non-homogeneous polynomial kernel $K(\mathbf{x}, \mathbf{y}) = (\mathbf{x}'\mathbf{y} + 1)^2$ we have $K(\mathbf{x}, \mathbf{y}) =$

$(\phi(\mathbf{x}), \phi(\mathbf{y}))$, where

$$\phi \begin{pmatrix} x_1 \\ x_2 \end{pmatrix} = \begin{pmatrix} x_1^2 \\ x_2^2 \\ \sqrt{2}x_1 x_2 \\ \sqrt{2}x_1 \\ \sqrt{2}x_2 \\ 1 \end{pmatrix}.$$

Data shown in the left part of Figure 17.4 is not linearly separable. The images of the points in the left-half of Figure 17.4 under ϕ are:

$$\Phi \begin{pmatrix} 1 \\ 1 \end{pmatrix} = \begin{pmatrix} 1 \\ 1 \\ \sqrt{2} \\ \sqrt{2} \\ \sqrt{2} \\ 1 \end{pmatrix}, \Phi \begin{pmatrix} -1 \\ -1 \end{pmatrix} = \begin{pmatrix} 1 \\ 1 \\ \sqrt{2} \\ -\sqrt{2} \\ -\sqrt{2} \\ 1 \end{pmatrix},$$

and

$$\Phi \begin{pmatrix} -1 \\ 1 \end{pmatrix} = \begin{pmatrix} 1 \\ 1 \\ -\sqrt{2} \\ -\sqrt{2} \\ \sqrt{2} \\ 1 \end{pmatrix}, \Phi \begin{pmatrix} 1 \\ -1 \end{pmatrix} = \begin{pmatrix} 1 \\ 1 \\ -\sqrt{2} \\ \sqrt{2} \\ -\sqrt{2} \\ 1 \end{pmatrix}.$$

However, the data obtained by mapping the $\mathbb{R}^2$ points in $\mathbb{R}^6$ is linearly separable. In the right part of Figure 17.4 we show the third and fourth components of the images under ϕ.

For this set of points differences occur in the third, fourth, and fifth features.

Theorem 17.1. *Let $f : \mathbb{R}^m \longrightarrow \mathbb{R}$ be a function, $R : \mathbb{R}_{\geqslant 0} \longrightarrow \mathbb{R}$ be a monotonic, non-decreasing function, and let $\phi : \mathbb{R}^n \longrightarrow H$, where H is a real Hilbert space. There exists $\mathbf{a} \in \mathbb{R}^m$ such that $\mathbf{w} = \sum_{i=1}^m a_i \phi(x_i) \in H$ is a minimizer of the function $F : H \longrightarrow \mathbb{R}$ given by:*

$$F(\mathbf{w}) = f((\mathbf{w}, \phi(\mathbf{x}_1)), \ldots, (\mathbf{w}, \phi(\mathbf{x}_m)) + R(\|\mathbf{w}\|).$$

Proof. Let $\mathbf{w}_* \in H$ be a minimizer of F. We have

$$\mathbf{w}_* = \sum_{i=1}^m a_i \phi(\mathbf{x}_i) + \mathbf{u},$$

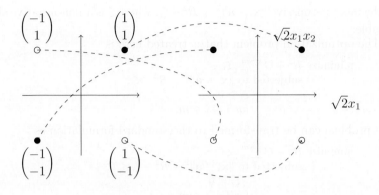

Fig. 17.4 Transforming a non-linearly separable data into a linearly separable one.

where $\mathbf{u}$ is orthogonal on each $\phi(\mathbf{x}_i)$ for $1 \leqslant i \leqslant m$. If $\mathbf{w} = \mathbf{w}_* - \mathbf{u} = \sum_{i=1}^m a_i \phi(\mathbf{x}_i)$ we have $\|\mathbf{w}_*\|^2 = \|\mathbf{w}\|^2 + \|\mathbf{u}\|^2$, hence $\|\mathbf{w}\| \leqslant \|\mathbf{w}_*\|$. Since R is non-decreasing, $R(\|\mathbf{w}\|) \leqslant R(\|\mathbf{w}_*\|)$.

Taking into account that

$$(\mathbf{w}, \phi(\mathbf{x}_i)) = (\mathbf{w}_* - \mathbf{u}, \phi(\mathbf{x}_i)) = (\mathbf{w}_*, \phi(\mathbf{x}_i)),$$

hence

$$f((\mathbf{w}, \phi(\mathbf{x}_1)), \ldots, (\mathbf{w}, \phi(\mathbf{x}_m))) = f((\mathbf{w}_*, \phi(\mathbf{x}_1)), \ldots, (\mathbf{w}_*, \phi(\mathbf{x}_m))),$$

hence $F(\mathbf{w}) \leqslant F(\mathbf{w}_*)$. Thus, $\mathbf{w}$ is also an optimal solution (a minimizer). The conclusion follows since $\mathbf{w} = \sum_{i=1}^m a_i \phi(\mathbf{x}_i)$. $\qquad\square$

Data description (also called an *one-class classification*) aims to give a description of a set of objects. The description should apply to the class of objects represented by the training set and reject all other objects in the training space. Thus, data description can be used to identify outlier objects and is especially useful when nothing is known about the distribution of outliers.

The support vector data description (SVDD) is a technique for data description developed in [128, 129] which is inspired by ideas developed in support vector machines. The goal is to identify a sphere with minimal radius containing all objects of the class.

Let $\{\mathbf{x}_i \mid 1 \leqslant i \leqslant m\} \subseteq \mathbb{R}^n$ be a set of m vectors in $\mathbb{R}^n$. As in Example 13.14, we seek to determine a sphere $B[\mathbf{a}, R]$ having a minimal radius R that contains these m vectors albeit with some extra flexibility. The flexibility refers to the replacement of the inequality $\|\mathbf{x}_i - \mathbf{a}\|^2 \leqslant R^2$

by the more permissive $\|\mathbf{x}_i - \mathbf{a}\|^2 \leqslant R^2 + \xi$, where ξ is a non-negative slack variable.

The optimization problem that is treated here is

$$\begin{aligned}
\text{minimize } & R^2 + C \textstyle\sum_{i=1}^{m} \xi_i \\
\text{subjected to } & \|\mathbf{x}_i - \mathbf{a}\|^2 \leqslant R^2 + \xi_i, \\
& \xi_i \geqslant 0 \\
& \text{for } 1 \leqslant i \leqslant m.
\end{aligned}$$

This problem can be transformed to the standard formulation as

$$\begin{aligned}
\text{minimize } & R^2 + C \textstyle\sum_{i=1}^{m} \xi_i \\
\text{subjected to } & \|\mathbf{x}_i - \mathbf{a}\|^2 - R^2 - \xi_i \leqslant 0, \\
& -\xi_i \leqslant 0 \\
& \text{for } 1 \leqslant i \leqslant m.
\end{aligned}$$

Here C is a constant. This relaxed formulation is helpful in handling outliers in training sets whose distance to the center of the sphere should not be strictly smaller than R by penalizing distances greater than R. We refer to this problem as usual, as the primal optimization problem.

As observed in [28], the restrictions as formulated above are not convex due to the presence of the term $-R^2$ which prevents the application of the Strong Duality Theorem (Theorem 13.20). To obtain convexity we replace R^2 by r and add the constraint $-r \leqslant 0$ (equivalent to $r \geqslant 0$) resulting in the following minimization problem:

$$\begin{aligned}
\text{minimize } & r + C \textstyle\sum_{i=1}^{m} \xi_i \\
\text{subjected to } & \|\mathbf{x}_i - \mathbf{a}\|^2 - r - \xi_i \leqslant 0 \\
& -\xi_i \leqslant 0, \\
& -r \leqslant 0, \\
& \text{for } 1 \leqslant i \leqslant m.
\end{aligned}$$

The Lagrangian of the primal optimization problem is

$$
L(r, \mathbf{a}, \boldsymbol{\xi}, \mathbf{u}, \mathbf{v}, \gamma)
$$
$$
= r + C \sum_{i=1}^{m} \xi_i
$$
$$
+ \sum_{i=1}^{m} u_i \left[(\|\mathbf{x}_i\|^2 - 2\mathbf{a}'\mathbf{x}_i + \|a\|^2) - r - \xi_i \right] - \sum_{i=1}^{m} v_i \xi_i - \gamma r
$$
$$
= r + C \sum_{i=1}^{m} \xi_i
$$
$$
+ \sum_{i=1}^{m} u_i \left[\left(\|\mathbf{x}_i\|^2 - 2\sum_{j=1}^{n} u_j x_{ij} + \sum_{j=1}^{n} u_i^2 \right) - r - \xi_i \right] - \sum_{i=1}^{m} v_i \xi_i - \gamma r,
$$

where $\boldsymbol{\xi}$ is the vector of slack variables, $\mathbf{u}$ and $\mathbf{v}$ are the Lagrange multiplier vectors having $u_1, \ldots, u_m$, and $v_1, \ldots, v_m$ as components, respectively, and γ is the Lagrange multiplier for the restriction $-r \leqslant 0$.

To compute the dual objective function we need to impose the Karush-Kuhn-Tucker optimality conditions on the Lagrangian function:

$$\frac{\partial L}{\partial r} = 0, \frac{\partial L}{\partial u_i} = 0, \frac{\partial L}{\partial \xi_i} = 0,$$

for $1 \leqslant i \leqslant m$, which amount to

$$\frac{\partial L}{\partial r} = 0 : 1 - \sum_{i=1}^{m} u_i - \gamma = 0,$$

$$\frac{\partial L}{\partial u_j} = 0 : -2 \sum_{i=1}^{m} u_i (x_{ij} - u_j),$$

$$\frac{\partial L}{\partial \xi_j} = 0 : C - u_j - v_j = 0,$$

for $1 \leqslant j \leqslant n$. These equalities yield

$$\sum_{i=1}^{m} u_i = 1 - \gamma, \tag{17.1}$$

$$u_j = \frac{1}{1-\gamma} \sum_{i=1}^{m} u_i x_{ij}, \tag{17.2}$$

$$u_j = C - v_j, \tag{17.3}$$

for $1 \leqslant j \leqslant m$, respectively. We have used the notation $x_{ij} = (\mathbf{x}_i)_j$.

Taking into account that $\sum_{i=1}^{m} \frac{u_i}{1-\gamma} = 1$, equality (17.2) implies $\mathbf{a} = \sum_{i=1}^{m} \frac{u_i}{1-\gamma} \mathbf{x}_i$, which shows that the center of the enclosing sphere $\mathbf{a}$ must be a convex combination of the points of the training set $\mathbf{x}_1, \ldots, \mathbf{x}_m$. Furthermore, we have

$$\|\mathbf{a}\|^2 = (\mathbf{a}, \mathbf{a}) = \frac{1}{(1-\gamma)^2} \sum_{i=1}^{m} \sum_{k=1}^{m} u_i u_k (\mathbf{x}_i, \mathbf{x}_k). \tag{17.4}$$

The remaining KKT conditions amount to

$$u_i [(\|\mathbf{x}_i\|^2 - 2 \sum_{j=1}^{n} u_j x_{ij} + \sum_{j=1}^{n} u_i^2) - r - \xi_i] = 0,$$

$$v_i \xi_i = 0,$$

$$\gamma r = 0.$$

Since we assume $r > 0$, this implies $\gamma = 0$. In turn, this implies

$$\sum_{i=1}^{m} u_i = 1, \tag{17.5}$$

$$u_j = \sum_{i=1}^{m} u_i x_{ij}, \text{ for } 1 \leqslant j \leqslant n, \tag{17.6}$$

$$u_j = C - v_j. \tag{17.7}$$

Using equality (17.5) in equality (17.6) implies that $\mathbf{a}$ is a convex combination of $\mathbf{x}_1, \ldots, \mathbf{x}_m$. Using equalities (17.5)-(17.7) the dual objective function is

$$g(\mathbf{u}, \mathbf{v}, \gamma)$$

$$= r + C \sum_{i=1}^{m} \xi_i + \sum_{i=1}^{m} u_i(\|\mathbf{x}_i - \mathbf{a}\|^2 - r - \xi_i) - \sum_{i=1}^{m} v_i \xi_i - \gamma r$$

$$= r + C \sum_{i=1}^{m} \xi_i + \sum_{i=1}^{m} u_i \|\mathbf{x}_i - \mathbf{a}\|^2 - r \sum_{i=1}^{m} u_i - \sum_{i=1}^{m} u_i \xi_i - \sum_{i=1}^{m} v_i \xi_i - \gamma r$$

$$= r + C \sum_{i=1}^{m} \xi_i + \sum_{i=1}^{m} u_i \|\mathbf{x}_i - \mathbf{a}\|^2 - r \sum_{i=1}^{m} u_i - \sum_{i=1}^{m} u_i \xi_i - \sum_{i=1}^{m} (C - u_i) \xi_i - \gamma r$$

(because $v_i = C - u_i$)

$$= \sum_{i=1}^{m} u_i \|\mathbf{x}_i - \mathbf{a}\|^2 + r - r \sum u_i - r\gamma$$

Taking into account the KKT conditions (which imply, as we saw $\gamma = 0$ and $\sum_{i=1}^{m} u_i = 1$) the objective function of the dual problem is:

$$g(\mathbf{u}, \mathbf{v}, \gamma) = \inf_{r, \mathbf{a}, \boldsymbol{\xi}} L(r, \mathbf{a}, \boldsymbol{\xi}, \mathbf{u}, \mathbf{v}, \gamma)$$

$$= \sum_{i=1}^{m} u_i \|\mathbf{x}_i - \mathbf{a}\|^2 = \sum_{i=1}^{m} u_i (\mathbf{x}_i - \mathbf{a})'(\mathbf{x}_i - \mathbf{a})$$

$$= \sum_{i=1}^{m} u_i \mathbf{x}_i' \mathbf{x}_i - 2 \sum_{i=1}^{m} u_i \mathbf{x}_i' \mathbf{a} + \mathbf{a}' \mathbf{a} \sum_{i=1}^{m} u_i$$

$$= \sum_{i=1}^{m} u_i \mathbf{x}_i' \mathbf{x}_i - \sum_{i=1}^{m} \sum_{k=1}^{m} u_i u_k (\mathbf{x}_i, \mathbf{x}_k).$$

17.5 Perceptrons

For support vector machines the training set part of the data set to be classified is presented to the algorithm, the classification function is inferred, and then the algorithm is tested on the test set part of the data set. The perceptron constructs the classification function contemporaneously with the analysis of the training set; this exemplifies the paradigm of *on-line learning*.

The terminology is the same as the one used for support vector machines.

A training set is a sequence of pairs $S = ((\mathbf{x}_1, y_1), \ldots, (\mathbf{x}_\ell, y_\ell))$, where $(\mathbf{x}_i, y_i) \in \mathbb{R}^n \times \{-1, 1\}$ for $1 \leqslant i \leqslant n$. If $y = 1$, $\mathbf{x}$ is a positive example; if $y = -1$, $\mathbf{x}$ is a negative example. The sequence S is *linearly separable* if there exists a hyperplane $\mathbf{w}'_* \mathbf{x} + b_* = 0$ such that $\mathbf{w}'_* \mathbf{x}_i + b_* \geqslant 0$ if $y_i = 1$ and $\mathbf{w}'_* \mathbf{x}_i + b_* < 0$ if $y_i = -1$. Both cases are captured by the inequality $\gamma_i = y_i(\mathbf{w}'_* \mathbf{x}_i + b_*) \geqslant 0$. The number γ_i is the *functional margin* of $(\mathbf{x}_i, y_i)$. If $\gamma_i > 0$ then $(\mathbf{x}_i, y_i)$ is classified correctly; otherwise, it is incorrectly classified and we say that a mistake occurred. Without loss of generality we may assume that $\|\mathbf{w}_*\| = 1$; if this is not the case, the coefficients of the hyperplane $\mathbf{w}'_* \mathbf{x} + b_* = 0$ may be rescaled. Also, we may assume that there exists $\gamma > 0$ such that

$$y_i(\mathbf{w}'_* \mathbf{x}_i + b_*) \geqslant \gamma. \tag{17.8}$$

The algorithm builds a sequence of weight vectors $(\mathbf{w}_k)$ and a sequence of bias values (b_k).

Upon examining the first $m - 1$ training examples

$$(\mathbf{x}_1, y_1), \ldots, (\mathbf{x}_{m-1}, y_{m-1})$$

and making the predictions $y_1, \ldots, y_{m-1}$ (some of which may be erroneous, in which cases modification are applied to parameters maintained by the algorithm), the algorithm is presented with the input x_m. Asumming that at that moment the parameters of the algorithm are $\mathbf{w}_k$ and b_k, an error is committed if $y_i(\mathbf{w}'_k \mathbf{x}_m + b_k) < 0$. In this case, a correction of the parameters of the algorithm is applied; otherwise, the algorithm continues by analyzing the next example. The processing of the sequence of pairs $((\mathbf{x}_1, y_1), \ldots, (\mathbf{x}_\ell, y_\ell))$ is referred to as an *epoch* of the algorithm.

Let R be the minimum radius of a closed ball centered in $\mathbf{0}$, that contains all points $\mathbf{x}_i$, that is $R = \max\{\|\mathbf{x}_i\| \mid 1 \leqslant i \leqslant \ell\}$ and let η be a parameter called the *learning rate*.

If a correction is applied, the new weight vector will be

$$\mathbf{w}_{k+1} = \mathbf{w}_k + \eta y_i \mathbf{x}_i,$$

while the new bias value will be $b_{k+1} = b_k + \eta y_i R^2$. In other words, the correction of the weight vector is $\Delta \mathbf{w}_k = \mathbf{w}_{k+1} - \mathbf{w}_k = \eta y_i \mathbf{x}_i$ and the correction of the bias is $\Delta b_k = \eta y_i R^2$.

Algorithm 17.5.1: Learning Algorithm for Perceptron

Data: labelled training sequence S of length ℓ and learning rate η
Result: weight vector $\mathbf{w}$ and parameter b

1   initialize $\mathbf{w}_0 = \mathbf{0}$, $b_0 = 0$, $k = 0$;
2   $R = \max\{\|\mathbf{x}_i\| \mid 1 \leqslant i \leqslant \ell\}$;
3   **repeat**
4   **for** $i = 1$ *to* ℓ **do**
5   **if** $y_i(\mathbf{w}_k'\mathbf{x}_i + b_k) < 0$ **then**
6             $\mathbf{w}_{k+1} \leftarrow \mathbf{w}_k + \eta y_i \mathbf{x}_i$;
7             $b_{k+1} \leftarrow b_k + \eta y_i R^2$;
8             $k \leftarrow k + 1$;
9   **end**
10   **end**
11 **until** *no mistakes are made in the for loop*;
12 return k, $\mathbf{w}_* = \mathbf{w}_k$ and $b_* = b_k$ where k is the number of mistakes;

Note that, in principle, the algorithm may go through the sequence S cyclically, until no mistakes are made. If S is not linearly separable the algorithm will cycle indefinitely.

Theorem 17.2. *Let $S = ((\boldsymbol{x}_1, y_1), \dots, (\boldsymbol{x}_\ell, y_\ell))$ be a training sequence that is linearly separable by the hyperplane $\boldsymbol{w}_*'\boldsymbol{x} + b_* = 0$, and let $R = \max\{\|\boldsymbol{x}_i\| \mid 1 \leqslant i \leqslant \ell\}$. The number of mistakes made by the algorithm is at most*

$$\left(\frac{2R}{\gamma}\right)^2.$$

Proof. As we noted before, we may assume that $\|\mathbf{w}_*\| = 1$ Let k be the update counter and let $\mathbf{w}_k$ be the weight vector when the algorithm makes error k on example $\mathbf{x}_i$. Then, $\mathbf{w}_{k+1} = \mathbf{w}_k + \eta y_i \mathbf{x}_i$ and $b_{k+1} = b_k + \eta y_i R$. Let $\tilde{\mathbf{w}}_k = \begin{pmatrix} \mathbf{w}_k \\ \frac{b_k}{R} \end{pmatrix}$, and $\tilde{\mathbf{w}}_* = \begin{pmatrix} \mathbf{w}_* \\ \frac{b_*}{R} \end{pmatrix}$, and $\tilde{\mathbf{x}}_i = \begin{pmatrix} \mathbf{x}_i \\ R \end{pmatrix}$.

Note that

$$\tilde{\mathbf{w}}_{k+1} = \begin{pmatrix} \mathbf{w}_{k+1} \\ \dfrac{b_{k+1}}{R} \end{pmatrix} = \begin{pmatrix} \mathbf{w}_k + \eta y_i \mathbf{x}_i \\ \dfrac{b_k + \eta y_i R^2}{R} \end{pmatrix} = \begin{pmatrix} \mathbf{w}_k \\ \dfrac{b_k}{R} \end{pmatrix} + \eta y_i \tilde{\mathbf{x}}_i = \tilde{\mathbf{w}}_k + \eta y_i \tilde{\mathbf{x}}_i.$$

Since $y_i \tilde{\mathbf{w}}_*' \tilde{\mathbf{x}}_i = y_i(\mathbf{w}_*' \mathbf{x}_i + b_*) \geqslant \gamma$, it follows that

$$\tilde{\mathbf{w}}_* \tilde{\mathbf{w}}_{k+1} = \tilde{\mathbf{w}}_* \tilde{\mathbf{w}}_k + \eta y_i \tilde{\mathbf{w}}_*' \mathbf{w}_k \geqslant \tilde{\mathbf{w}}_* \tilde{\mathbf{w}}_k + \eta \gamma.$$

By repeated application of the above equality we obtain $\tilde{\mathbf{w}}_* \mathbf{w}_k \geqslant k \eta \gamma$.

If the kth error occurs on input $\mathbf{x}_i$ we have $\tilde{\mathbf{w}}_{k+1} = \tilde{\mathbf{w}}_k + \eta y_i \tilde{\mathbf{x}}_i$. This implies

$$\begin{aligned}
\|\tilde{\mathbf{w}}_{k+1}\|^2 &= \tilde{\mathbf{w}}_{k+1}' \tilde{\mathbf{w}}_{k+1} = (\tilde{\mathbf{w}}_k' + \eta y_i \tilde{\mathbf{x}}_i')(\tilde{\mathbf{w}}_k + \eta y_i \tilde{\mathbf{x}}_i) \\
&= \|\tilde{\mathbf{w}}_k\|^2 + 2\eta y_i \tilde{\mathbf{w}}_k' \tilde{\mathbf{x}}_i + \eta^2 \|\tilde{\mathbf{x}}_i\|^2 \\
&\quad \text{(because } y_i \tilde{\mathbf{w}}_k' \mathbf{x}_i < 0 \text{ when an error occurs and } y_i^2 = 1) \\
&\leqslant \|\tilde{\mathbf{w}}_k\|^2 + \eta^2 \|\tilde{\mathbf{x}}_i\|^2 \\
&\leqslant \|\tilde{\mathbf{w}}_k\|^2 + \eta^2(\|\mathbf{x}_i\|^2 + R^2) \\
&\leqslant \|\tilde{\mathbf{w}}_k\|^2 + 2\eta^2 R^2.
\end{aligned}$$

This implies $\|\tilde{\mathbf{w}}_k\|^2 \leqslant 2k\eta^2 R^2$, hence $\|\tilde{\mathbf{w}}_k\| \leqslant \eta R \sqrt{2k}$. By combining the equalities

$$\tilde{\mathbf{w}}_* \mathbf{w}_k \geqslant k\eta\gamma \text{ and } \|\tilde{\mathbf{w}}_k\| \leqslant \eta R \sqrt{2k}$$

we obtain

$$\|\tilde{\mathbf{w}}_*\| \eta R \sqrt{2k} \geqslant \|\tilde{\mathbf{w}}_*\| \cdot \|\tilde{\mathbf{w}}_k\| \geqslant \tilde{\mathbf{w}}_*' \tilde{\mathbf{w}}_k \geqslant k\eta\gamma,$$

which imply

$$k \leqslant 2\left(\frac{R^2}{\gamma}\right) \|\tilde{\mathbf{w}}_*\|^2 \leqslant \left(\frac{2R}{\gamma}\right)^2$$

because $b_* \leqslant R$, hence $\|\tilde{\mathbf{w}}_*\|^2 \leqslant \|\mathbf{w}_*\|^2 + 1 = 2$. $\qquad\square$

Exercises and Supplements

Linearly Separable Data Sets

Let $B_n = \{0, 1\}^n$ and let $K \subseteq B_n$. The *sequence of Chow parameters* of K is $\mathsf{chow}(K) = (c_1, \ldots, c_n, c_K) \in \mathbb{N}^n$ defined as $c_K = |K|$ and $c_i = |\{\mathbf{x} \in K \mid x_i = 1\}|$. For example, for $n = 4$ and $K = \{(0, 1, 1, 1), (0, 0, 1, 1), (0, 0, 0, 1)\}$ we have $\mathsf{chow}(K) = (0, 1, 2, 3, 3)$.

Two subsets K, G of B_n are *equipollent* if they have the same Chow parameters.

The subsets K and $B_n - K$ are *linearly separable* if there exists a pair $(\mathbf{w}, t) \in \mathbb{R}^n \times \mathbb{R}$ such that

$$K = \{\mathbf{x} \in B_n \mid \mathbf{w}'\mathbf{x} \geqslant t\} \text{ and } B_n - K = \{\mathbf{x} \in B_n \mid \mathbf{w}'\mathbf{x} < t\}.$$

We say that K is *linearly separable* if K and $B_n - K$ are linearly separable. The vector $(\mathbf{w}, t)$ is the *separating weight* for K.

(1) Let $K \subseteq B_n$. Prove that $\mathsf{chow}(K) = (\sum_{\mathbf{x} \in K} \mathbf{x}, |K|)$.

(2) A *diagonal of* B_n is a pair $(\mathbf{u}, \mathbf{v}) \in B_n^2$ such that $\mathbf{u} = \mathbf{1}_n - \mathbf{v}$. Prove that if K is a linearly separable subset of B_n that contains a diagonal of B_n, then it contains a point of every other diagonal of B_n.

Solution: Since K is linearly separable, there exist $\mathbf{w}, \mathbf{t}$ such that $K = \{\mathbf{x} \in B_n \mid \mathbf{w}'\mathbf{x} \geqslant t\}$. If the diagonal $(\mathbf{u}, \mathbf{v})$ is contained in K we have both $\mathbf{w}'\mathbf{u} \geqslant t$ and $\mathbf{w}'\mathbf{v} = \mathbf{w}'\mathbf{1}_n - \mathbf{w}'\mathbf{u} \geqslant t$, hence $\mathbf{u}'(\mathbf{u} + \mathbf{v}) = \mathbf{w}'\mathbf{1}_n \geqslant 2t$. Let $(\mathbf{y}, \mathbf{z})$ be another diagonal and suppose that neither $\mathbf{y}$ nor $\mathbf{z}$ belong to K. Then, $\mathbf{w}'\mathbf{y} < t$ and $\mathbf{w}'\mathbf{z} = \mathbf{w}'(\mathbf{1}_n - \mathbf{y}) < t$, which implies $\mathbf{w}'\mathbf{1}_n < 2t$, thereby contradicting the previous inequality. Therefore, at least one of $\mathbf{y}, \mathbf{z}$ must belong to K.

(3) Let $K = \{\mathbf{v}_1, \ldots, \mathbf{v}_m\}$ be a subset of B_n and let $B_n - K = \{\mathbf{v}_{m+1}, \ldots, \mathbf{v}_{2^n}\}$. Prove that if K is linearly separable then for any non-negative numbers a_i where $1 \leqslant i \leqslant 2^n$ the equalities $\sum_{i=1}^m a_i = \sum_{i=m+1}^{2^n} a_i$ and $\sum_{i=1}^m a_i \mathbf{v}_i = \sum_{i=m+1}^{2^n} a_i \mathbf{v}_i$ imply $a_i = 0$ for $1 \leqslant i \leqslant 2^n$.

Solution: Suppose that K is linearly separable. There exists $\mathbf{w}$ and t such that $\mathbf{w}'\mathbf{v}_i \geqslant t$ for $1 \leqslant i \leqslant m$ and $\mathbf{w}'\mathbf{v}_i < t$ for $m + 1 \leqslant i \leqslant 2^n$, hence

$$\mathbf{w}' \sum_{i=1}^m a_i \mathbf{v}_i = \sum_{i=1}^m a_i \mathbf{w}'\mathbf{v}_i \geqslant t \sum_{i=1}^m a_i, \text{ and}$$

$$\mathbf{w}' \sum_{i=m+1}^{2^n} a_i \mathbf{v}_i = \sum_{i=m+1}^{2^n} a_i \mathbf{w}'\mathbf{v}_i < t \sum_{i=m+1}^{2^n} a_i.$$

Suppose that $\sum_{i=1}^m a_i = \sum_{i=m+1}^{2^n} a_i > 0$. Then, we have both

$$t > \frac{\mathbf{w}' \sum_{i=m+1}^{2^n} a_i \mathbf{v}_i}{\sum_{i=m+1}^{2^n} a_i} = \frac{\mathbf{w}' \sum_{i=1}^m a_i \mathbf{v}_i}{\sum_{i=1}^m a_i} \geqslant t,$$

which is contradictory. Therefore, $\sum_{i=1}^m a_i = \sum_{i=m+1}^{2^n} a_i = 0$ and this implies $a_i = 0$ for $1 \leqslant i \leqslant 2^n$ because the numbers a_i are non-negative.

A subset K of B_n is *k-summable* for $k \geqslant 2$ if there exists j such that $2 \leqslant j \leqslant k$ such that there exist j points $\mathbf{u}_1, \ldots, \mathbf{u}_j$ in K (not necessarily distinct) and j points $\mathbf{v}_1, \ldots, \mathbf{v}_j$ in $B_n - K$ (not necessarily distinct) such that $\sum_{i=1}^j \mathbf{u}_i = \sum_{i=1}^j \mathbf{v}_i$. K is *summable* if it is k-summable for some $k \geqslant 2$.

If K is not k-summable, then K is said to be k-*assumable*. K is said to be *summable* if it is k-summable for some $k \geqslant 2$; otherwise K is said to be *assumable*.

(4) Let K be a linearly separable subset of B_n by the separating weight $(\mathbf{w}_t)$. Suppose that $\mathsf{chow}(K) = (c_1, \ldots, c_n, c_K)$. Prove that

    (a) if $c_i < \frac{c_K}{2}$, then $w_i < 0$;

    (b) if $c_i > \frac{c_K}{2}$, then $w_i > 0$;

    (c) if $c_i = \frac{c_K}{2}$, then $(x_1, \ldots, x_{i-1}, 0, x_{i+1}, \ldots, x_n) \in K$ if and only if $(x_1, \ldots, x_{i-1}, 1, x_{i+1}, \ldots, x_n) \in K$;

    (d) if $c_i > c_j$ then $w_i > w_j$;

    (e) if $c_i = c_j$, then there exists a separating weight $(\mathbf{w}, t)$ such that $w_i = w_j$.

(5) If K is a separable subset of B_n, $c_i < \frac{c_K}{2}$ for $1 \leqslant i \leqslant n$, $\mathbf{v} \in K$ and $\mathbf{u} \leqslant \mathbf{v}$, prove that $\mathbf{u} \in K$.

(6) Prove that if a set K, $K \subseteq B_n$ is linearly separable, then it is assumable.

    Solution: Suppose that $(\mathbf{w}, t)$ is a separating weight for K and there exist k elements, $\mathbf{v}_1, \ldots, \mathbf{v}_k$ in K and $\mathbf{u}_1, \ldots, \mathbf{u}_k \in B_n - K$. Then, $\mathbf{w}'\mathbf{u}_i < t$ and $t \geqslant \mathbf{w}'\mathbf{v}$, hence $\sum_{i=1}^k u_i < \sum_{i=1}^k v_i$ which means that K is assumable.

(7) Prove that if K is not linearly separable, then K is summable.

    Solution: Suppose that K is not linearly separable, where $K = \{\mathbf{u}_1, \ldots, \mathbf{u}_m\}$ and $B_n - K = \{\mathbf{u}_{m+1}, \ldots, \mathbf{u}_{2^n}\}$. By standard separation results the convex sets $\mathbf{K}_{\text{conv}}(K) \cap \mathbf{K}_{\text{conv}}(B_n - K) \neq \emptyset$ have a non-empty intersection.

Therefore, the following system

$$\sum_{i=1}^m a_i \mathbf{u}_i = \sum_{j=m+1}^{2^n} a_j \mathbf{u}_j,$$
$$\sum_{i=1}^m a_i = \sum_{j=m+1}^{2^n} a_j = 1,$$
$$a_i \geqslant 0, b_j \geqslant 0 \text{ for } 1 \leqslant i \leqslant m \text{ and } m+1 \leqslant j \leqslant 2^n$$

has a feasible solution with rational values because the system has rational coefficients. Thus, for some positive integer p all components of the vector $(pa_1, \ldots, pa_{2^n})$ are non-negative integers and

$$\sum_{i=1}^m (pa_i) \mathbf{u}_i = \sum_{j=m+1}^{2^n} (pa_j) \mathbf{u}_j,$$
$$\sum_{i=1}^m (pa_i) = \sum_{j=m+1}^{2^n} (pa_j) = p,$$

hence K is summable (by considering pa_i copies of $\mathbf{u}_i$ and pa_j copies of $\mathbf{u}_j$).

(8) Prove that for two equipollent subsets K, G of B_n, either both are linearly separable and $K = G$, or neither is linearly separable; in other words, prove that there is at most one linearly separable set for any set of Chow parameters.

Solution: Let K, G be equipollent sets in B_n. If $K \subseteq G$ or $G \subseteq K$, then $c_K = c_G$ imply $K = G$. If $K \not\subseteq G$ and $G \not\subseteq K$ and $|K| = |G|$, then

$$|K \cap (B_n - G)| = |K| - |K \cap G| = |G| - |G \cap K| = |(B_n - K) \cap G|.$$

Also,

$$\sum_{\mathbf{x} \in K \cap B_n - G} \mathbf{x} = \sum_{\mathbf{x} \in K} \mathbf{x} - \sum_{\mathbf{x} \in K \cap G} \mathbf{x} = c_K - \sum_{\mathbf{x} \in K \cap G} \mathbf{x}$$

$$= c_G - \sum_{\mathbf{x} \in K \cap G} \mathbf{x} = \sum_{\mathbf{x} \in G} - \sum_{\mathbf{x} \in K \cap G} \mathbf{x}$$

$$= \sum_{\mathbf{x} \in (B_n - K) \cap G} \mathbf{x}.$$

Therefore, K and G are $|K \cap (B_n - G)|$-summable, hence they are not linearly separable.

(9) Prove that if two equipollent subsets of B_n are distinct, then neither is linearly separable.

(10) The optimization problem of the separable data case that seeks to determine a separating hyperplane in $\mathbb{R}^n$ can be transformed into an equivalent optimization problem in $\mathbb{R}^{n+1}$ that seeks to identify a separating subspace. Given a data set $\mathbf{s} = ((\mathbf{x}_1, y_1), \ldots, (\mathbf{x}_m, y_m))$ prove that there exists $\mathbf{r} \in \mathbb{R}^n$ such that $\mathbf{s}$ is separable by a hyperplane if and only if the set $\tilde{\mathbf{s}} = ((\mathbf{x}_1 + \mathbf{r}, y_1), \ldots, (\mathbf{x}_m + \mathbf{r}, y_m))$ is separable be a subspace M of $\mathbb{R}^n$.

(11) Apply the Karush-Kuhn-Tucker Theorem (Theorem 13.15) to the optimization problem in the case of a separable data set. Prove that a constraint $\mathbf{c}_i(\mathbf{w}, a) = y_i(\mathbf{w}'\mathbf{x}_i - a)$ is active if and only if $\mathbf{x}_i$ is a support vector, and show that the optimal value of $\mathbf{w}$ is a linear combination of support vectors.

SVM — The Non-separable Case

(12) Consider the data set D in $\mathbb{R}^2$ shown in Figure 17.5, where C is a circle centered in $(6, 4)$ having radius 3. Define a transformation $\phi : \mathbb{R}^2 \longrightarrow \mathbb{R}^2$ such that $\phi(D)$ is linearly separable.

(13) The hinge function h was defined in Exercise 2 of Chapter 12 as $h(x) = \max\{0, 1 - x\}$. Let $L_h : \mathbb{R}^n \times \mathbb{R} \longrightarrow \mathbb{R}$ be the function given

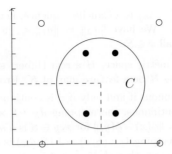

Fig. 17.5   Non-linearly separable data.

by $L_h(\mathbf{w}, a) = \sum_{i=1}^{m} h(y_i(\mathbf{w}'\mathbf{x}_i - a))$. Prove that the optimization problem for the soft SVM non-separable case is equivalent to minimizing the function

$$f(\mathbf{w}, a) = \frac{1}{2}\|\mathbf{w}\|^2 + CL_h(\mathbf{w}, a).$$

Solution: The defining condition for the slack variables in the soft SVM case is $\xi_i \geqslant 1 - y_i(\mathbf{w}'\mathbf{x}_i - a)$. Since these variables are non-negative, the smallest value of these variables are $h(1 - y_i(\mathbf{w}'\mathbf{x}_i - a))$. Thus, the total slack is at least $L_h(\mathbf{w}, a)$. This equivalent form of the optimization problem for soft SVMs has the advantage to be a regularized form.

Non-linear Support Vector Machines

(14) Let S be a non-empty set, H_1, H_2 be Hilbert spaces, and $K : S \times S \longrightarrow \mathbb{R}$ be a kernel. Suppose that $\phi_1 : S \longrightarrow H_1$ and $\phi_2 : S \longrightarrow H_2$ are both feature maps K. Prove that for all $w_1 \in H_1$ there exists $w_2 \in H_2$ with $\|w_2\| \leqslant \|w_1\|$ and $(w_1, \phi_1(x)) = (w_2, \phi_2(x))$ for all $x \in S$.

Solution: Let $U_1 = \mathbf{K}(\langle\phi_1(S)\rangle)$ and let $U_1^\perp$ be its orthogonal complement in H_1. If $w_1 \in H_1$ we have $w_1 = u_1 + u_1^\perp$ with $u_1 \in U_1$ and $u_1^\perp \in U_1^\perp$. Given $x \in S$ we have $(u_1^\perp, \phi_1(x)) = 0$ and, therefore, $(w_1, \phi_1(x)) = (u_1, \phi_1(x))$ for all $x \in S$. The definition of U_1 implies the existence of a sequence (z_n) in $\langle\phi_1(S)\rangle$ such that $z_n = \sum_{m=1}^{m_n} a_{nm}\phi_1(x_{nm})$ and $u_1 = \sum_{n=1}^{\infty} z_n$. Then, for $\tilde{z}_n = \sum_{m=1}^{m_n} a_{nm}\phi_2(x_{nm})$ and $\ell_2 \geqslant \ell_1 \geqslant 1$ we have

$$\left\| \sum_{n=\ell_1}^{\ell_2} z_n \right\|^2 = \sum_{n=\ell_1}^{\ell_2} \sum_{m=1}^{m_n} \sum_{i=\ell_1}^{\ell_2} \sum_{j=1}^{m_i} a_{mn} a_{ji}(\phi_1(x_{mn}), \phi_1(x_{ji}))$$

$$= \sum_{n=\ell_1}^{\ell_2} \sum_{m=1}^{m_n} \sum_{i=\ell_1}^{\ell_2} \sum_{j=1}^{m_i} a_{mn} a_{ji}(\phi_2(x_{mn}), \phi_2(x_{ji})) = \left\| \sum_{n=\ell_1}^{\ell_2} \tilde{z}_n \right\|^2.$$

Therefore, $\left(\sum_{n=1}^{m} \tilde{z}_n\right)$ is a Cauchy sequence, hence it converges to $w_2 = \sum_{n=1}^{\infty} \tilde{z}_n \in H_2$. We have $\|w_2\| = \|u_1\| \leqslant \|w_1\|$; also, $(w_1, \phi_1(x)) = (w_2, \phi_2(x))$ for all $x \in S$.

(15) Let (S, d) be a metric space, H a real Hilbert space, $K : S \times S \longrightarrow H$ and let $\phi : S \longrightarrow H$ be a feature map of K. Prove that:

(a) K is continuous if and only if ϕ is continuous;

(b) if K is continuous, the mapping $d_K : S \times S \longrightarrow \mathbb{R}_{\geqslant 0}$ defined by $d_K(x, y) = \|\phi(x) - \phi(y)\|$ for $x, y \in S$ is a semimetric on S and the identity mapping $1_S : (S, d) \longrightarrow (S, d_K)$ is continuous;

(c) if ϕ is injective, then d_K is a metric.

Solution: Since

$$
\begin{aligned}
d_K(x, y)^2 &= (\phi(x) - \phi(y), \phi(x) - \phi(y)) \\
&= (\phi(x), \phi(x)) - 2(\phi(x), \phi(y)) + (\phi(y), \phi(y)) \\
&= K(x, x) - 2K(x, y) + K(y, y),
\end{aligned}
$$

it follows that d_K is continuous. This implies that $\{y \in S \mid d_K(x, y) < \epsilon\}$ is open and therefore 1_S is continuous. Furthermore, $\phi : (S, d_K) \longrightarrow H$ is continuous, hence ϕ regarded as a mapping from (S, d) to H is also continuous.

Conversely, assume that ϕ is continuous. Since

$$
\begin{aligned}
|K(x, y) - K(x', y')| &\leqslant |(\phi(x), \phi(y) - \phi(y'))| + |(\phi(x) - \phi(x'), \phi(y'))| \\
&\leqslant \|\phi(x)\| \cdot \|\phi(y) - \phi(y')\| + \|\phi(y')\| \|\phi(x) - \phi(y)\|,
\end{aligned}
$$

it follows that K is also continuous.

Perceptrons

(16) There are 16 functions of the form $f : \{0, 1\}^2 \longrightarrow \{0, 1\}$. For each such function consider the sequence $S_f = ((\mathbf{x}_1, y_1), \ldots, (\mathbf{x}_4, y_4))$, where $\mathbf{x}_i \in \{0, 1\}^2$ and

$$
y_i = \begin{cases} -1 & \text{if } f(\mathbf{x}_i) = 0, \\ 1 & \text{if } f(\mathbf{x}_i) = 1 \end{cases}
$$

for $1 \leqslant i \leqslant 4$.

(a) For how many of these functions is S_f linearly separable?

(b) Note that for $f : \{0, 1\}^2 \longrightarrow \{0, 1\}$ defined by $f(\mathbf{x}) = \min\{x_1, x_2\}$ is linearly separable. For $\eta = 0.1$ and $\eta = 0.8$ draw the sequence of weights of the perceptron during the learning process.

(17) Provide a robust implementation of the perceptron algorithm that will cycle through a prescribed number of iterations (and, thus, will cope with the case when data is not linearly separable).

Bibliographical Comments

Support vector data description was introduced in [128, 129]. See also [28, 91] for related results.

The perceptron algorithm is due to F. Rosenblatt [112]. There are several variants of this algorithm in the literature [108, 59, 36].

Chow parameters were introduced in [31, 30]. Exercises 1-9 contain results of from [51, 84]. See also [70]. A comprehensive reference for applications of Boolean concepts is [35].

There is a large body of reference works on support vector machines. We suggest [36, 124] as main references for the study of these algorithms, and [119] and [96] for kernelization techniques, as well as the excellent tutorial [25].

Bibliography

[1] Abu-Mostafa, Y. S. (1995). Hints, *Neural Computation* **7**, 4, pp. 639–671.

[2] Aliprantis, C. D. and Border, K. C. (2006). *Infinite Dimensional Analysis*, 3rd edn. (Springer, Berlin).

[3] Ash, R. B. (1972). *Real Analysis and Probability* (Academic Press, New York).

[4] Axler, S. J. (1995). Down with determinants! *American Mathematical Monthly* **102**, pp. 139–154.

[5] Axler, S. J. (2015). *Linear Algebra Done Right*, 3rd edn. (Springer, Heidelberg).

[6] Baldi, P. and Hornik, K. (1995). Learning in linear neural networks: a survey, *IEEE Transactions on Neural Networks* **6**, 4, pp. 837–858.

[7] Banach, S. (1963). *Théorie des opérations linéaires*, 2nd edn. (Chelsea Pub. Co., New York).

[8] Barbu, V. and Precupanu, T. (2012). *Convexity and Optimization in Banach Spaces*, 4th edn. (Springer, Dordrecht).

[9] Bazaraa, M. S., Sherali, H. D. and Shetty, C. M. (2006). *Nonlinear Programming — Theory and Algorithms*, 3rd edn. (Wiley-Interscience, Hoboken, NJ).

[10] Berlinet, A. and Thomas-Agnan, C. (2004). *Reproducing Kernel Hilbert Spaces in Probability and Statistics* (Kluwer Academic Publishers, Boston).

[11] Berry, A. C. (1931). A metric for the space of measurable functions, *Proceedings of the National Academy of Sciences* **17**, pp. 456–459.

[12] Bertsekas, D. M. (1982). *Constrained Optimization and Lagrange Multiplier Methods* (Academic Press, New York).

[13] Bertsekas, D. M. (1999). *Nonlinear Programming*, 2nd edn. (Athena Scientific, Belmont, MA).

[14] Bertsekas, D. M. (2015). *Convex Optimization Algorithms* (Athena Scientific, Belmont, MA).

[15] Bertsekas, D. P., Nedić, A. and Ozdaglar, A. E. (2003). *Convex Analysis and Optimization* (Athena Scientific, Cambridge, MA).

[16] Billingsley, P. (2012). *Probability and Measure*, anniversary edn. (Wiley, Hoboken, NJ).

[17] Bohnenblust, H. F., Karlin, S. and Shapley, L. S. (1950). Solution of discrete, two-person games, in *Contribution to the Theory of Games, Vol. 1*, Annals of Mathematics Studies, Vol. 24, pp. 51–72.

[18] Borvinok, A. (2002). *A Course in Convexity* (American Mathematical Society, Providence, RI).

[19] Borwein, J. M. (1982). A note on the existence of subgradients, *Mathematical Programming* **24**, pp. 225–228.

[20] Borwein, J. M. and Lewis, A. S. (2006). *Convex Analysis and Nonlinear Optimization*, 2nd edn. (Springer, Canadian Mathematical Society).

[21] Boser, B. E., Guyon, I. and Vapnik, V. (1992). A training algorithm for optimal margin classifiers, in *Proceedings of the Fifth Annual ACM Conference on Computational Learning Theory, COLT 1992*, Pittsburgh, PA, USA, July 27-29, 1992, pp. 144–152.

[22] Bourbaki, N. (1987). *Topological Vector Spaces* (Springer, Berlin).

[23] Boyd, S. and Vandenberghe, L. (2004). *Convex Optimization* (Cambridge University Press, Cambridge, UK).

[24] Broyden, C. G. (1965). A class of methods for solving nonlinear simultaneous equations, *Mathematics of Computation* **19**, pp. 577–593.

[25] Burges, C. J. C. (1998). A tutorial on support vector machines for pattern recognition, *Data Mining and Knowledge Discovery* **2**, 2, pp. 121–167.

[26] Carothers, N. (2005). *A Short Course on Banach Space Theory* (Cambridge University, Cambridge, UK).

[27] Carver, W. B. (1922). Systems of linear inequalities, *Annals of Mathematics* **23**, pp. 212–220.

[28] Chen, G., Zhang, X., Wang, Z. J. and Li, F. (2015). Robust support vector data description for outlier detection with noise or uncertain data, *Knowledge-Based Systems* **90**, pp. 129–137.

[29] Cheney, W. (2001). *Analysis for Applied Mathematics* (Springer, New York).

[30] Chow, C. K. (1961). Boolean functions realizable with single threshold functions, *Proceedings of IRE* **49**, pp. 370–371.

[31] Chow, C. K. (1961). On the characterization of threshold functions, in *Proceedings of the Second Annual Symposium on Switching Theory and Logical Design*, pp. 34–38.

[32] Cohn, D. J. (1997). *Measure Theory* (Birkhäuser, Boston).

[33] Cohn, P. M. (1981). *Universal Algebra* (D. Reidel, Dordrecht).

[34] Cortes, C. and Vapnik, V. (1995). Support-vector networks, *Machine Learning* **20**, 3, pp. 273–297.

[35] Crama, Y. and Hammer, P. L. (2011). *Boolean Functions — Theory, Algorithms and Applications* (Cambridge University Press, Cambridge, UK).

[36] Cristianini, N. and Shawe-Taylor, J. (2000). *Support Vector Machines* (Cambridge, Cambridge, UK).

[37] Cybenko, G. (1989). Approximation by superposition of sigmoidal functions, *Mathematics of Control, Signals, and Systems* **2**, pp. 303–314.

[38] Cybenko, G. (1992). Correction: Approximation by superposition of sigmoidal functions, *Mathematics of Control, Signals, and Systems* **5**, p. 445.

[39] Danskin, J. M. (1966). The theory of max-min, with applications, *SIAM Journal on Applied Mathematics* **14**, 4, pp. 641–664.

[40] Diestel, J. (1975). *Geometry of Banach Spaces: Selected Topics* (Springer Verlag, New York).

[41] Dieudonné, J. (1969). *Foundations of Modern Analysis* (Academic Press, New York).

[42] Dixmier, J. (1984). *General Topology* (Springer-Verlag, New York).

[43] Edgar, G. (1990). *Measure, Topology, and Fractal Geometry* (Springer-Verlag, New York).

[44] Taylor, J. G. (1993). *Mathematical Approaches to Neural Networks* (North-Holland, Amsterdam).

[45] Efron, B., Hastie, T., Johnstone, I. and Tibshirani, R. (2004). Least angle regression, *Annals of Statistics* **32**, pp. 407–499.

[46] Eidelheit, M. (1936). Zur Theorie der konvexen Mengen in linear und normierten Räumen, *Studia Mathematica* **6**, pp. 104–111.

[47] Eisenberg, M. (1974). *Topology* (Holt, Rinehart and Winston, Inc., New York).

[48] Ekeland, I. (1974). On the variational principle, *Journal of Mathematical Analysis and Applications* **47**, pp. 324–353.

[49] Ekeland, I. (1979). Nonconvex minimization problems, *Bulletin of American Mathematical Society* **3**, pp. 443–474.

[50] Ekeland, I. and Lebourg, G. (1976). Generic fréchet-differentiability and perturbed optimization problems in banach spaces, *Transactions of the American Mathematical Society* **224**, pp. 193–216.

[51] Elgot, C. C. (1961). Truth functions realizable by single threshold engine, in *Proceedings of IEEE Symposium on Switching Theory and Logical Design*, pp. 225–245.

[52] Emch, A. (1922). A model for the Peano surface, *The American Mathematical Monthly* **29**, pp. 388–391.

[53] Engelking, R. and Siekluchi, K. (1992). *Topology — A Geometric Approach* (Heldermann Verlag, Berlin).

[54] Fabian, M., Habala, P., Hàjek, P., Santalucia, V. M., Pelant, J. and Zizler, V. (2001). *Functional Analysis and Infinite-Dimensional Geometry* (Springer, NY).

[55] Fan, K., Glicksberg, I. and Hoffman, A. J. (1957). Systems of inequalities involving convex functions, *Proceedings of the American Mathematical Society* **8**, pp. 617–622.

[56] Fejer, P. A. and Simovici, D. A. (1991). *Mathematical Foundations of Computer Science*, Vol. 1 (Springer-Verlag, New York).

[57] Folland, G. B. (1999). *Real Analysis — Modern Techniques and Their Applications*, 2nd edn. (Wiley Interscience, New York).

[58] Fréchet, M. (1906). Sur quelques points du calcul fonctionnel, *Rendiconti del Circolo Matematico di Palermo* **22**, pp. 1–47.

[59] Freund, Y. and Shapire, R. E. (1999). Large margin classification using the perceptron algorithm, *Machine Learning* **37**, pp. 277–296.

[60] Funahashi, S. (1989). On the approximate realization of continuous mapping by neural networks, *Neural Networks* **2**, pp. 183–192.

[61] Furstenberg, H. (1955). On the infinitude of primes, *American Mathematical Monthly* **62**, p. 353.

[62] Gallant, A. R. and White, H. (1988). There exists a neural network that does not make avoidable mistakes, in *Proceedings of IEEE Second International Conference on Neural Networks* (University of California Press, San Diego, CA), pp. 657–664.

[63] Garling, D. J. H. (2014). *A Course in Mathematical Analysis — Volume III: Complex Analysis, Measure and Integration* (Cambridge University, Cambridge, UK).

[64] Genocchi, A. and Peano, G. (1884). *Calcolo differenziale e principii di calcolo integrale* (Fratelli Bocca, Roma, Italy).

[65] Graves, L. M. (1950). Some mapping theorems, *Duke Mathematical Journal* **17**, pp. 111–114.

[66] Greenberg, H. J. and Pierskalla, W. P. (1971). A review of quasi-convex functions, *Operations Research* **19**, pp. 1553–1570.

[67] Greub, W. (1981). *Linear Algebra*, 4th edn. (Springer-Verlag, New York).

[68] Griffel, D. H. (2002). *Applied Functional Analysis* (Dover Publications, Mineola, NY).

[69] Grünbaum, B. (1967). *Convex Polytopes* (Wiley-Interscience, London).

[70] Gruzling, N. (2006). *Linear separability of the vertices of an n-dimensional hypercube*, Master's thesis, University of Northern British Columbia.

[71] Güler, O. (2010). *Foundations of Optimization* (Springer, New York).

[72] Halmos, P. R. (1951). *Introduction to Hilbert Spaces and the Theory of Spectral Multiplicity* (Chelsea Publishing Company, New York).

[73] Hardy, G. H., Littlewood, J. E. and Polya, G. (1929). Some simple inequalities satisfied by convex functions, *Messenger Mathematics* **58**, pp. 145–152.

[74] Hastie, T., Rosset, S., Tibshirani, R. and Zhu, J. (2004). The entire regularization path for the support vector machine, in *Advances in Neural Information Processing Systems 17 [Neural Information Processing Systems, NIPS 2004, December 13-18, 2004, Vancouver, British Columbia, Canada]*, pp. 561–568.

[75] Hastie, T., Tibshirani, R. and Friedman, J. H. (2003). Note on "comparison of model selection for regression" by vladimir cherkassky and yunqian ma, *Neural Computation* **15**, 7, pp. 1477–1480.

[76] Haykin, S. (2008). *Neural Networks and Learning Machines*, 3rd edn. (Prentice-Hall, New York).

[77] Hecht-Nielsen, R. (1991). *Neurocomputing* (Addison-Wesley, Reading, MA).

[78] Hestenes, M. E. and Stiefel, E. (1952). Methods of conjugate gradients for solving linear systems, *Journal of Research of the National Bureau of Standards* **49**, pp. 409–436.

[79] Hiriart-Urruty, J. B. (1983). A short proof of the variational principle for approximate solution of a minimization problem, *American Mathematical Monthly* **90**, pp. 206–207.

[80] Hoerl, A. E. and Kennard, R. W. (1970). Ridge regression: Biased estimation for nonorthogonal problems, *Technometrics* **12**, pp. 55–67.

[81] Hoffman, T., Schölkopf, B. and Smola, A. J. (2008). Kernel methods in machine learning, *Annals of Statistics* **36**, pp. 1171–1220.

[82] Hornik, K. (1991). Approximation capabilities of multilayer feedforward networks, *Neural Networks* **4**, pp. 251–257.

[83] Hornik, K., Stinchcombe, M. B. and White, H. (1989). Multilayer feedforward networks are universal approximators, *Neural Networks* **2**, 5, pp. 359–366.

[84] Hu, S. T. (1965). *Threshold Logic* (University of California Press, Berkeley).

[85] Jahn, J. (2007). *Introduction to the Theory of Nonlinear Optimization*, 3rd edn. (Springer, Berlin).

[86] Kantorovich, L. V. and Akilov, G. P. (1982). *Functional Analysis*, 2nd edn. (Pergamon Press, Oxford, England).

[87] Karamardian, S. (1967). Strictly quasi-convex (concave) functions and duality in mathematical programming, *J. of Mathematical Analysis and Applications* **20**, pp. 344–358.

[88] Karamata, J. (1932). Sur une inégalité relative aux fonctions convexes, *Publications Mathématiques de l'Université de Belgrade* **1**, pp. 145–148.

[89] Kelley, J. L. (1955). *General Topology* (Van Nostrand, Princeton, NJ).

[90] Kelley, J. L. and Namioka, I. (1963). *Linear Topological Spaces* (Van Nostrand, Princeton).

[91] Kim, S., Choi, Y. and Lee, M. (2015). Deep learning with support vector data description, *Neurocomputing* **165**, pp. 111–117.

[92] Korn, F., Pagel, B.-U. and Faloutsos, C. (2001). On the "dimensionality curse" and the "self similarity blessing", *IEEE Transactions on Knowledge and Data Engineering* **13**, pp. 96–111.

[93] Kostrikin, A. I. and Manin, Y. I. (1989). *Linear Algebra and Geometry (Algebra, Logic and Applications)* (Gordon and Breach Science Publishers, New York).

[94] Kranz, S. G. and Parks, H. P. (2003). *The Implicit Function Theorem — History, Theory, and Applications* (Birkhäuser, Boston).

[95] Kuhn, H. W. and Tucker, A. W. (1950). Nonlinear programming, in *Proceedings of the Second Berkeley Symposium on Mathematical Statistics and Probability* (University of California Press), pp. 481–492.

[96] Kung, S. Y. (2014). *Kernel Methods and Machine Learning* (Cambridge University Press, Cambridge, UK).

[97] Lauritzen, N. (2013). *Undergraduate Convexity* (World Scientific, New Jersey).

[98] Lax, P. D. (2007). *Linear Algebra and Its Applications* (Wiley-International, Hoboken, NJ).

[99] Lay, S. R. (1982). *Convex Sets and Their Applications* (Wiley, New York).

[100] Leshno, M., Lin, V. Y., Pinkus, A. and Schocken, S. (1993). Multi-layer feedforward networks with a nonpolynomial activation function can approximate any function, *Neural Networks* **6**, 6, pp. 861–867.

[101] Lindenstrauss, J. and Tzafriri, L. (1973). *Classical Banach Spaces* (Springer Verlag, New York).

[102] Luenberger, D. G. (1969). *Optimization by Vector Space Methods* (Wiley, New York).

[103] Mairal, J. and Yu, B. (2012). Complexity analysis of the lasso regularization path, in *Proceedings of the 29th International Conference on Machine Learning, ICML 2012*, Edinburgh, Scotland, UK, June 26–July 1, 2012.

[104] Mangasarian, O. L. (1965). Pseudo-convex functions, *SIAM Journal on Control* **3**, pp. 281–290.

[105] Mangasarian, O. L. (1969). *Nonlinear Programming* (McGraw-Hill, New York).

[106] McShane, E. T. (1973). The Lagrange multiplier rule, *The American Mathematical Monthly* **80**, pp. 922–925.

[107] Niculescu, C. and Persson, L. E. (2006). *Convex Functions and Their Applications — A Contemporary Approach* (Springer, New York).

[108] Novikoff, A. B. J. (1962). On convergence proofs on perceptrons, in *Proceedings of the Symposium on Mathematical Theory of Automata* (Polytechnic Institute of Brooklyn, Brooklyn, NY), pp. 615–622.

[109] Pagel, B.-U., Korn, F. and Faloutsos, C. (2000). Deflating the dimensionality curse using multiple fractal dimensions, in *International Conference on Data Engineering*, pp. 589–598.

[110] Pervin, W. J. (1964). *Foundations of General Topology* (Academic Press, New York).

[111] Rockafellar, R. T. (1970). *Convex Analysis* (Princeton University Press, Princeton, NJ).

[112] Rosenblatt, F. (1958). The perceptron: A probabilistic model for information storage and organization in the brain, *Psychological Review* **65**, pp. 386–407.

[113] Royden, H. L. (1988). *Real Analysis*, 3rd edn. (Prentice-Hall, Englewood Cliffs, NJ).

[114] Rudin, W. (1986). *Real and Complex Analysis*, 3rd edn. (McGraw-Hill, New York).

[115] Schneider, R. (1993). *Convex Bodies: The Brun-Minkowski Theory* (Cambridge University Press, Cambridge, UK).

[116] Shafarevich, I. R. and Remizov, A. O. (2013). *Linear Algebra and Geometry* (Springer, Heidelberg).

[117] Shalev-Shwartz, S. and Ben-David, S. (2016). *Understanding Machine Learning — From Theory to Practice* (Cambridge University Press, Cambridge, UK).

[118] Shalev-Shwartz, S., Singer, Y. and Srebro, N. (2007). Pegasos: Primal Estimated sub-GrAdient solver for SVM, in *Machine Learning, Proceedings of the Twenty-Fourth International Conference (ICML 2007)*, Corvallis, Oregon, USA, June 20-24, 2007, pp. 807–814.

[119] Shawe-Taylor, J. and Cristianini, N. (2004). *Kernel Methods for Pattern Analysis* (Cambridge, Cambridge, UK).

[120] Simon, B. (2011). *Convexity: An Analytic Viewpoint* (Cambridge University Press, Cambridge, UK).

[121] Simovici, D. A. (2012). *Linear Algebra Tools for Data Mining* (World Scientific, New Jersey).

[122] Slater, M. (1950). Lagrange multipliers revisited, *Cowles Foundation for Research in Economics at Yale University*, Discussion Paper Mathematics 403, pp. 1–13.

[123] Sokal, A. D. (2011). A really simple elementary proof of the uniform boundedness theorem, *American Mathematical Monthly* **118**, pp. 450–452.

[124] Steinwart, I. and Christman, A. (2008). *Support Vector Machines* (Springer, New York).

[125] Stewart, J. (1976). Positive definite functions and generalizations, an historical survey, *Rocky Mountain Journal of Mathematics* **6**, pp. 409–484.

[126] Stoer, J. and Bulirsh, R. (2010). *Introduction to Numerical Analysis*, 3rd edn. (Springer, New York).

[127] Sylvester, J. J. (1857). A question in the geometry of situation, *Quarterly Journal in Pure and Applied Mathematics* **1**, p. 19.

[128] Tax, D. M. J. and Duin, R. P. W. (1999). Support vector domain description, *Pattern Recognition Letters* **20**, 11-13, pp. 1191–1199.

[129] Tax, D. M. J. and Duin, R. P. W. (2004). Support vector data description, *Machine Learning* **54**, 1, pp. 45–66.

[130] Taylor, M. E. (2006). *Measure Theory and Integration* (American Mathematical Society, Providence, RI).

[131] Tibshirani, R. (1996). Regression shrinkage and selection via the lasso, *Journal of the Royal Statistical Society. Series B (Methodological)* **58**, 1, pp. 267–288.

[132] Trefethen, L. N. and III, D. B. (1997). *Numerical Linear Algebra* (SIAM, Philadelphia).

[133] Werner, J. (1984). *Optimization — Theory and Applications* (Vieweg, Braunschweig).

[134] White, H., Gallant, A. R., Hornik, K., Stinchcombe, M. and Woolridge, J. (1992). *Artificial Neural Networks — Approximation and Learning Theory* (Blackwell, Oxford, UK).

[135] Willard, S. (2004). *General Topology* (Dover, Mineola, New York).

[136] Zhu, J., Rosset, S., Hastie, T. and Tibshirani, R. (2003). 1-Norm support vector machines, in *Advances in Neural Information Processing Systems 16 [Neural Information Processing Systems, NIPS 2003, December 8-13, 2003, Vancouver and Whistler, British Columbia, Canada]*, pp. 49–56.

Index